Praise for *Advanced Programming in the UNIX® Environment, Second Edition*

"Stephen Rago's update is a long overdue benefit to the community of professionals using the versatile family of UNIX and UNIX-like operating environments. It removes obsolescence and includes newer developments. It also thoroughly updates the context of all topics, examples, and applications to recent releases of popular implementations of UNIX and UNIX-like environments. And yet, it does all this while retaining the style and taste of the original classic."

—Mukesh Kacker, cofounder and former CTO of Pronto Networks, Inc.

"One of the essential classics of UNIX programming."

—Eric S. Raymond, author of *The Art of UNIX Programming*

"This is the definitive reference book for any serious or professional UNIX systems programmer. Rago has updated and extended the classic Stevens text while keeping true to the original. The APIs are illuminated by clear examples of their use. He also mentions many of the pitfalls to look out for when programming across different UNIX system implementations and points out how to avoid these pitfalls using relevant standards such as POSIX 1003.1, 2004 edition and the Single UNIX Specification, Version 3."

—Andrew Josey, Director, Certification, The Open Group, and
Chair of the POSIX 1003.1 Working Group

"*Advanced Programming in the UNIX® Environment, Second Edition,* is an essential reference for anyone writing programs for a UNIX system. It's the first book I turn to when I want to understand or re-learn any of the various system interfaces. Stephen Rago has successfully revised this book to incorporate newer operating systems such as GNU/Linux and Apple's OS X while keeping true to the first edition in terms of both readability and usefulness. It will always have a place right next to my computer."

—Dr. Benjamin Kuperman, Swarthmore College

Praise for the First Edition

Advanced Programming
in the UNIX® Environment
Second Edition

Addison-Wesley Professional Computing Series

Brian W. Kernighan, Consulting Editor

Matthew H. Austern, *Generic Programming and the STL: Using and Extending the C++ Standard Template Library*

David R. Butenhof, *Programming with POSIX® Threads*

Brent Callaghan, *NFS Illustrated*

Tom Cargill, *C++ Programming Style*

William R. Cheswick/Steven M. Bellovin/Aviel D. Rubin, *Firewalls and Internet Security, Second Edition: Repelling the Wily Hacker*

David A. Curry, *UNIX® System Security: A Guide for Users and System Administrators*

Stephen C. Dewhurst, *C++ Gotchas: Avoiding Common Problems in Coding and Design*

Dan Farmer/Wietse Venema, *Forensic Discovery*

Erich Gamma/Richard Helm/Ralph Johnson/John Vlissides, *Design Patterns: Elements of Reusable Object-Oriented Software*

Erich Gamma/Richard Helm/Ralph Johnson/John Vlissides, *Design Patterns CD: Elements of Reusable Object-Oriented Software*

Peter Haggar, *Practical Java™ Programming Language Guide*

David R. Hanson, *C Interfaces and Implementations: Techniques for Creating Reusable Software*

Mark Harrison/Michael McLennan, *Effective Tcl/Tk Programming: Writing Better Programs with Tcl and Tk*

Michi Henning/Steve Vinoski, *Advanced CORBA® Programming with C++*

Brian W. Kernighan/Rob Pike, *The Practice of Programming*

S. Keshav, *An Engineering Approach to Computer Networking: ATM Networks, the Internet, and the Telephone Network*

John Lakos, *Large-Scale C++ Software Design*

Scott Meyers, *Effective C++ CD: 85 Specific Ways to Improve Your Programs and Designs*

Scott Meyers, *Effective C++, Third Edition: 55 Specific Ways to Improve Your Programs and Designs*

Scott Meyers, *More Effective C++: 35 New Ways to Improve Your Programs and Designs*

Scott Meyers, *Effective STL: 50 Specific Ways to Improve Your Use of the Standard Template Library*

Robert B. Murray, *C++ Strategies and Tactics*

David R. Musser/Gillmer J. Derge/Atul Saini, *STL Tutorial and Reference Guide, Second Edition: C++ Programming with the Standard Template Library*

John K. Ousterhout, *Tcl and the Tk Toolkit*

Craig Partridge, *Gigabit Networking*

Radia Perlman, *Interconnections, Second Edition: Bridges, Routers, Switches, and Internetworking Protocols*

Stephen A. Rago, *UNIX® System V Network Programming*

Eric S. Raymond, *The Art of UNIX Programming*

Marc J. Rochkind, *Advanced UNIX Programming, Second Edition*

Curt Schimmel, *UNIX® Systems for Modern Architectures: Symmetric Multiprocessing and Caching for Kernel Programmers*

W. Richard Stevens, *TCP/IP Illustrated, Volume 1: The Protocols*

W. Richard Stevens, *TCP/IP Illustrated, Volume 3: TCP for Transactions, HTTP, NNTP, and the UNIX® Domain Protocols*

W. Richard Stevens/Bill Fenner/Andrew M. Rudoff, *UNIX Network Programming Volume 1, Third Edition: The Sockets Networking API*

W. Richard Stevens/Stephen A. Rago, *Advanced Programming in the UNIX® Environment, Second Edition*

W. Richard Stevens/Gary R. Wright, *TCP/IP Illustrated Volumes 1-3 Boxed Set*

John Viega/Gary McGraw, *Building Secure Software: How to Avoid Security Problems the Right Way*

Gary R. Wright/W. Richard Stevens, *TCP/IP Illustrated, Volume 2: The Implementation*

Ruixi Yuan/W. Timothy Strayer, *Virtual Private Networks: Technologies and Solutions*

Visit www.awprofessional.com/series/professionalcomputing for more information about these titles.

Advanced Programming in the UNIX® Environment
Second Edition

W. Richard Stevens
Stephen A. Rago

⋏⋎Addison-Wesley

Upper Saddle River, NJ • Boston • Indianapolis • San Francisco
New York • Toronto • Montreal • London • Munich • Paris • Madrid
Capetown • Sydney • Tokyo • Singapore • Mexico City

1284618

NOV 2 3 2010

Many of the designations used by manufacturers and sellers to distinguish their products are claimed as trademarks. Where those designations appear in this book, and the publisher was aware of a trademark claim, the designations have been printed with initial capital letters or in all capitals.

The authors and publisher have taken care in the preparation of this book, but make no expressed or implied warranty of any kind and assume no responsibility for errors or omissions. No liability is assumed for incidental or consequential damages in connection with or arising out of the use of the information or programs contained herein.

The publisher offers excellent discounts on this book when ordered in quantity for bulk purchases or special sales, which may include electronic versions and/or custom covers and content particular to your business, training goals, marketing focus, and branding interests. For more information, please contact:

U.S. Corporate and Government Sales
(800) 382-3419
corpsales@pearsontechgroup.com

For sales outside the U.S., please contact:

International Sales
international@pearsoned.com

Visit us on the Web: www.informit.com/aw

The Library of Congress has cataloged the hardcover edition as follows:

Stevens, W. Richard.
  Advanced programming in the Unix environment / W. Richard Stevens, Stephen A. Rago.—2nd ed.
      p. cm.
  Includes bibliographical references and index.
  ISBN 0-201-43307-9 (hardcover : alk. paper)
  1. Operating systems (Computers) 2. UNIX (Computer file) I. Rago, Stephen A. II. Title.

  QA76.76.O63S754 2005
  005.4'32—dc22

                                                        2005007943

ISBN-13: 978-0-321-52594-9
ISBN-10:   0-321-52594-9
Text printed in the United States on recycled paper at Courier Stoughton in Stoughton, Massachusetts.
Third printing, December 2009

To Jeanne

Contents

Foreword   **xix**

Preface   **xxi**

Preface to the First Edition   **xxv**

Chapter 1.   UNIX System Overview   **1**

    1.1   Introduction   1
    1.2   UNIX Architecture   1
    1.3   Logging In   2
    1.4   Files and Directories   4
    1.5   Input and Output   8
    1.6   Programs and Processes   10
    1.7   Error Handling   14
    1.8   User Identification   16
    1.9   Signals   18
    1.10   Time Values   20
    1.11   System Calls and Library Functions   21
    1.12   Summary   23

Chapter 2.   UNIX Standardization and Implementations   **25**

    2.1   Introduction   25
    2.2   UNIX Standardization   25
    2.2.1   ISO C   25

2.2.2   IEEE POSIX   26
2.2.3   The Single UNIX Specification   29
2.2.4   FIPS   33
2.3   UNIX System Implementations   33
2.3.1   UNIX System V Release 4   33
2.3.2   4.4BSD   34
2.3.3   FreeBSD   35
2.3.4   Linux   35
2.3.5   Mac OS X   35
2.3.6   Solaris   35
2.3.7   Other UNIX Systems   36
2.4   Relationship of Standards and Implementations   36
2.5   Limits   36
2.5.1   ISO C Limits   38
2.5.2   POSIX Limits   38
2.5.3   XSI Limits   40
2.5.4   `sysconf`, `pathconf`, and `fpathconf` Functions   41
2.5.5   Indeterminate Runtime Limits   48
2.6   Options   52
2.7   Feature Test Macros   55
2.8   Primitive System Data Types   56
2.9   Conflicts Between Standards   56
2.10   Summary   58

Chapter 3.   File I/O   59

3.1   Introduction   59
3.2   File Descriptors   59
3.3   `open` Function   60
3.4   `creat` Function   62
3.5   `close` Function   63
3.6   `lseek` Function   63
3.7   `read` Function   67
3.8   `write` Function   68
3.9   I/O Efficiency   68
3.10   File Sharing   70
3.11   Atomic Operations   74
3.12   `dup` and `dup2` Functions   76
3.13   `sync`, `fsync`, and `fdatasync` Functions   77
3.14   `fcntl` Function   78
3.15   `ioctl` Function   83
3.16   `/dev/fd`   84
3.17   Summary   85

Chapter 4.   **Files and Directories**   **87**

4.1   Introduction   87
4.2   `stat`, `fstat`, and `lstat` Functions   87
4.3   File Types   88
4.4   Set-User-ID and Set-Group-ID   91
4.5   File Access Permissions   92
4.6   Ownership of New Files and Directories   95
4.7   `access` Function   95
4.8   `umask` Function   97
4.9   `chmod` and `fchmod` Functions   99
4.10   Sticky Bit   101
4.11   `chown`, `fchown`, and `lchown` Functions   102
4.12   File Size   103
4.13   File Truncation   105
4.14   File Systems   105
4.15   `link`, `unlink`, `remove`, and `rename` Functions   108
4.16   Symbolic Links   112
4.17   `symlink` and `readlink` Functions   115
4.18   File Times   115
4.19   `utime` Function   116
4.20   `mkdir` and `rmdir` Functions   119
4.21   Reading Directories   120
4.22   `chdir`, `fchdir`, and `getcwd` Functions   125
4.23   Device Special Files   127
4.24   Summary of File Access Permission Bits   130
4.25   Summary   130

Chapter 5.   **Standard I/O Library**   **133**

5.1   Introduction   133
5.2   Streams and `FILE` Objects   133
5.3   Standard Input, Standard Output, and Standard Error   135
5.4   Buffering   135
5.5   Opening a Stream   138
5.6   Reading and Writing a Stream   140
5.7   Line-at-a-Time I/O   142
5.8   Standard I/O Efficiency   143
5.9   Binary I/O   145
5.10   Positioning a Stream   147
5.11   Formatted I/O   149
5.12   Implementation Details   153
5.13   Temporary Files   155

5.14   Alternatives to Standard I/O   159
5.15   Summary   159

Chapter 6.   System Data Files and Information   161

6.1   Introduction   161
6.2   Password File   161
6.3   Shadow Passwords   165
6.4   Group File   166
6.5   Supplementary Group IDs   167
6.6   Implementation Differences   169
6.7   Other Data Files   169
6.8   Login Accounting   170
6.9   System Identification   171
6.10   Time and Date Routines   173
6.11   Summary   177

Chapter 7.   Process Environment   179

7.1   Introduction   179
7.2   main Function   179
7.3   Process Termination   180
7.4   Command-Line Arguments   185
7.5   Environment List   185
7.6   Memory Layout of a C Program   186
7.7   Shared Libraries   188
7.8   Memory Allocation   189
7.9   Environment Variables   192
7.10   setjmp and longjmp Functions   195
7.11   getrlimit and setrlimit Functions   202
7.12   Summary   206

Chapter 8.   Process Control   209

8.1   Introduction   209
8.2   Process Identifiers   209
8.3   fork Function   211
8.4   vfork Function   216
8.5   exit Functions   218
8.6   wait and waitpid Functions   220
8.7   waitid Function   226
8.8   wait3 and wait4 Functions   227
8.9   Race Conditions   227
8.10   exec Functions   231

8.11   Changing User IDs and Group IDs   237
8.12   Interpreter Files   242
8.13   `system` Function   246
8.14   Process Accounting   250
8.15   User Identification   256
8.16   Process Times   257
8.17   Summary   259

Chapter 9.   Process Relationships   **261**

9.1   Introduction   261
9.2   Terminal Logins   261
9.3   Network Logins   266
9.4   Process Groups   269
9.5   Sessions   270
9.6   Controlling Terminal   272
9.7   `tcgetpgrp`, `tcsetpgrp`, and `tcgetsid` Functions   273
9.8   Job Control   274
9.9   Shell Execution of Programs   278
9.10   Orphaned Process Groups   282
9.11   FreeBSD Implementation   285
9.12   Summary   287

Chapter 10.   Signals   **289**

10.1   Introduction   289
10.2   Signal Concepts   289
10.3   `signal` Function   298
10.4   Unreliable Signals   301
10.5   Interrupted System Calls   303
10.6   Reentrant Functions   305
10.7   `SIGCLD` Semantics   308
10.8   Reliable-Signal Terminology and Semantics   310
10.9   `kill` and `raise` Functions   311
10.10   `alarm` and `pause` Functions   313
10.11   Signal Sets   318
10.12   `sigprocmask` Function   320
10.13   `sigpending` Function   322
10.14   `sigaction` Function   324
10.15   `sigsetjmp` and `siglongjmp` Functions   329
10.16   `sigsuspend` Function   333
10.17   `abort` Function   340
10.18   `system` Function   342

10.19   sleep Function   347
10.20   Job-Control Signals   349
10.21   Additional Features   352
10.22   Summary   353

Chapter 11.   Threads   **355**

11.1   Introduction   355
11.2   Thread Concepts   355
11.3   Thread Identification   356
11.4   Thread Creation   357
11.5   Thread Termination   360
11.6   Thread Synchronization   368
11.7   Summary   385

Chapter 12.   Thread Control   **387**

12.1   Introduction   387
12.2   Thread Limits   387
12.3   Thread Attributes   388
12.4   Synchronization Attributes   393
12.5   Reentrancy   401
12.6   Thread-Specific Data   406
12.7   Cancel Options   410
12.8   Threads and Signals   413
12.9   Threads and fork   416
12.10   Threads and I/O   420
12.11   Summary   420

Chapter 13.   Daemon Processes   **423**

13.1   Introduction   423
13.2   Daemon Characteristics   423
13.3   Coding Rules   425
13.4   Error Logging   428
13.5   Single-Instance Daemons   432
13.6   Daemon Conventions   434
13.7   Client–Server Model   439
13.8   Summary   439

Chapter 14.   Advanced I/O   **441**

14.1   Introduction   441
14.2   Nonblocking I/O   441
14.3   Record Locking   444

14.4   STREAMS   460
14.5   I/O Multiplexing   472
14.5.1   `select` and `pselect` Functions   474
14.5.2   `poll` Function   479
14.6   Asynchronous I/O   481
14.6.1   System V Asynchronous I/O   481
14.6.2   BSD Asynchronous I/O   482
14.7   `readv` and `writev` Functions   483
14.8   `readn` and `writen` Functions   485
14.9   Memory-Mapped I/O   487
14.10   Summary   492

Chapter 15.   Interprocess Communication   **495**

15.1   Introduction   495
15.2   Pipes   496
15.3   `popen` and `pclose` Functions   503
15.4   Coprocesses   510
15.5   FIFOs   514
15.6   XSI IPC   518
15.6.1   Identifiers and Keys   518
15.6.2   Permission Structure   520
15.6.3   Configuration Limits   521
15.6.4   Advantages and Disadvantages   521
15.7   Message Queues   522
15.8   Semaphores   527
15.9   Shared Memory   533
15.10   Client–Server Properties   541
15.11   Summary   543

Chapter 16.   Network IPC: Sockets   **545**

16.1   Introduction   545
16.2   Socket Descriptors   546
16.3   Addressing   549
16.3.1   Byte Ordering   549
16.3.2   Address Formats   551
16.3.3   Address Lookup   553
16.3.4   Associating Addresses with Sockets   560
16.4   Connection Establishment   561
16.5   Data Transfer   565
16.6   Socket Options   579
16.7   Out-of-Band Data   581

16.8   Nonblocking and Asynchronous I/O   582
16.9   Summary   583

Chapter 17.   Advanced IPC   **585**

17.1   Introduction   585
17.2   STREAMS-Based Pipes   585
17.2.1   Naming STREAMS Pipes   589
17.2.2   Unique Connections   590
17.3   UNIX Domain Sockets   594
17.3.1   Naming UNIX Domain Sockets   595
17.3.2   Unique Connections   597
17.4   Passing File Descriptors   601
17.4.1   Passing File Descriptors over STREAMS-Based Pipes   604
17.4.2   Passing File Descriptors over UNIX Domain Sockets   606
17.5   An Open Server, Version 1   615
17.6   An Open Server, Version 2   620
17.7   Summary   629

Chapter 18.   Terminal I/O   **631**

18.1   Introduction   631
18.2   Overview   631
18.3   Special Input Characters   638
18.4   Getting and Setting Terminal Attributes   643
18.5   Terminal Option Flags   643
18.6   stty Command   651
18.7   Baud Rate Functions   652
18.8   Line Control Functions   653
18.9   Terminal Identification   654
18.10   Canonical Mode   660
18.11   Noncanonical Mode   663
18.12   Terminal Window Size   670
18.13   termcap, terminfo, and curses   672
18.14   Summary   673

Chapter 19.   Pseudo Terminals   **675**

19.1   Introduction   675
19.2   Overview   675
19.3   Opening Pseudo-Terminal Devices   681
19.3.1   STREAMS-Based Pseudo Terminals   683
19.3.2   BSD-Based Pseudo Terminals   686
19.3.3   Linux-Based Pseudo Terminals   689

19.4   `pty_fork` Function   691
19.5   `pty` Program   694
19.6   Using the `pty` Program   698
19.7   Advanced Features   705
19.8   Summary   706

Chapter 20.   A Database Library   **709**

20.1   Introduction   709
20.2   History   709
20.3   The Library   710
20.4   Implementation Overview   712
20.5   Centralized or Decentralized?   716
20.6   Concurrency   718
20.7   Building the Library   719
20.8   Source Code   719
20.9   Performance   747
20.10   Summary   752

Chapter 21.   Communicating with a Network Printer   **753**

21.1   Introduction   753
21.2   The Internet Printing Protocol   753
21.3   The Hypertext Transfer Protocol   756
21.4   Printer Spooling   757
21.5   Source Code   758
21.6   Summary   805

Appendix A.   Function Prototypes   **807**

Appendix B.   Miscellaneous Source Code   **843**

B.1   Our Header File   843
B.2   Standard Error Routines   846

Appendix C.   Solutions to Selected Exercises   **853**

Bibliography   **885**

Index   **891**

Foreword

At some point during nearly every interview I give, as well as in question periods after talks, I get asked some variant of the same question: "Did you expect Unix to last for so long?" And of course the answer is always the same: No, we didn't quite anticipate what has happened. Even the observation that the system, in some form, has been around for well more than half the lifetime of the commercial computing industry is now dated.

The course of developments has been turbulent and complicated. Computer technology has changed greatly since the early 1970s, most notably in universal networking, ubiquitous graphics, and readily available personal computing, but the system has somehow managed to accommodate all of these phenomena. The commercial environment, although today dominated on the desktop by Microsoft and Intel, has in some ways moved from single-supplier to multiple sources and, in recent years, to increasing reliance on public standards and on freely available source.

Fortunately, Unix, considered as a phenomenon and not just a brand, has been able to move with and even lead this wave. AT&T in the 1970s and 1980s was protective of the actual Unix source code, but encouraged standardization efforts based on the system's interfaces and languages. For example, the SVID—the System V Interface Definition—was published by AT&T, and it became the basis for the POSIX work and its follow-ons. As it happened, Unix was able to adapt rather gracefully to a networked environment and, perhaps less elegantly, but still adequately, to a graphical one. And as it also happened, the basic Unix kernel interface and many of its characteristic user-level tools were incorporated into the technological foundations of the open-source movement.

It is important that papers and writings about the Unix system were always encouraged, even while the software of the system itself was proprietary, for example Maurice Bach's book, *The Design of the Unix Operating System*. In fact, I would claim that a central reason for the system's longevity has been that it has attracted remarkably talented writers to explain its beauties and mysteries. Brian Kernighan is one of these; Rich Stevens is certainly another. The first edition of this book, along with his series of books about networking, are rightfully regarded as remarkably well-crafted works of exposition, and became hugely popular.

However, the first edition of this book was published before Linux and the several open-source renditions of the Unix interface that stemmed from the Berkeley CSRG became widespread, and also at a time when many people's networking consisted of a serial modem. Steve Rago has carefully updated this book to account for the technology changes, as well as developments in various ISO and IEEE standards since its first publication. Thus his examples are fresh, and freshly tested.

It's a most worthy second edition of a classic.

Murray Hill, New Jersey   Dennis Ritchie
March 2005

Preface

Introduction

Rich Stevens and I first met through an e-mail exchange when I reported a typographical error in his first book, *UNIX Network Programming*. He used to kid me about being the person to send him his first errata notice for the book. Until his death in 1999, we exchanged e-mail irregularly, usually when one of us had a question we thought the other might be able to answer. We met for dinner at USENIX conferences and when Rich was teaching in the area.

Rich Stevens was a friend who always conducted himself as a gentleman. When I wrote *UNIX System V Network Programming* in 1993, I intended it to be a System V version of Rich's *UNIX Network Programming*. As was his nature, Rich gladly reviewed chapters for me, and treated me not as a competitor, but as a colleague. We often talked about collaborating on a STREAMS version of his *TCP/IP Illustrated* book. Had events been different, we might have actually done it, but since Rich is no longer with us, revising *Advanced Programming in the UNIX Environment* is the closest I'll ever get to writing a book with him.

When the editors at Addison-Wesley told me that they wanted to update Rich's book, I thought that there wouldn't be too much to change. Even after 13 years, Rich's work still holds up well. But the UNIX industry is vastly different today from what it was when the book was first published.

- The System V variants are slowly being replaced by Linux. The major system vendors that ship their hardware with their own versions of the UNIX System have either made Linux ports available or announced support for Linux. Solaris is perhaps the last descendant of UNIX System V Release 4 with any appreciable market share.

- After 4.4BSD was released, the Computing Science Research Group (CSRG) from the University of California at Berkeley decided to put an end to its development of the UNIX operating system, but several different groups of volunteers still maintain publicly available versions.

- The introduction of Linux, supported by thousands of volunteers, has made it possible for anyone with a computer to run an operating system similar to the UNIX System, with freely available source code for the newest hardware devices. The success of Linux is something of a curiosity, given that several free BSD alternatives are readily available.

- Continuing its trend as an innovative company, Apple Computer abandoned its old Mac operating system and replaced it with one based on Mach and FreeBSD.

Thus, I've tried to update the information presented in this book to reflect these four platforms.

After Rich wrote *Advanced Programming in the UNIX Environment* in 1992, I got rid of most of my UNIX programmer's manuals. To this day, the two books I keep closest to my desk are a dictionary and a copy of *Advanced Programming in the UNIX Environment*. I hope you find this revision equally useful.

Changes from the First Edition

Rich's work holds up well. I've tried not to change his original vision for this book, but a lot has happened in 13 years. This is especially true with the standards that affect the UNIX programming interface.

Throughout the book, I've updated interfaces that have changed from the ongoing efforts in standards organizations. This is most noticeable in Chapter 2, since its primary topic is standards. The 2001 version of the POSIX.1 standard, which we use in this revision, is much more comprehensive than the 1990 version on which the first edition of this book was based. The 1990 ISO C standard was updated in 1999, and some changes affect the interfaces in the POSIX.1 standard.

A lot more interfaces are now covered by the POSIX.1 specification. The base specifications of the Single UNIX Specification (published by The Open Group, formerly X/Open) have been merged with POSIX.1. POSIX.1 now includes several 1003.1 standards and draft standards that were formerly published separately.

Accordingly, I've added chapters to cover some new topics. Threads and multithreaded programming are important concepts because they present a cleaner way for programmers to deal with concurrency and asynchrony.

The socket interface is now part of POSIX.1. It provides a single interface to interprocess communication (IPC), regardless of the location of the process, and is a natural extension of the IPC chapters.

I've omitted most of the real-time interfaces that appear in POSIX.1. These are best treated in a text devoted to real-time programming. One such book appears in the bibliography.

I've updated the case studies in the last chapters to cover more relevant real-world examples. For example, few systems these days are connected to a PostScript printer via a serial or parallel port. Most PostScript printers today are accessed via a network, so I've changed the case study that deals with PostScript printer communication to take this into account.

The chapter on modem communication is less relevant these days. So that the original material is not lost, however, it is available on the book's Web site in two formats: PostScript (http://www.apuebook.com/lostchapter/modem.ps) and PDF (http://www.apuebook.com/lostchapter/modem.pdf).

The source code for the examples shown in this book is also available at www.apuebook.com. Most of the examples have been run on four platforms:

1. FreeBSD 5.2.1, a derivative of the 4.4BSD release from the Computer Systems Research Group at the University of California at Berkeley, running on an Intel Pentium processor

2. Linux 2.4.22 (the Mandrake 9.2 distribution), a free UNIX-like operating system, running on Intel Pentium processors

3. Solaris 9, a derivative of System V Release 4 from Sun Microsystems, running on a 64-bit UltraSPARC IIi processor

4. Darwin 7.4.0, an operating environment based on FreeBSD and Mach, supported by Apple Mac OS X, version 10.3, on a PowerPC processor

Acknowledgments

Rich Stevens wrote the first edition of this book on his own, and it became an instant classic.

I couldn't have updated this book without the support of my family. They put up with piles of papers scattered about the house (well, more so than usual), my monopolizing most of the computers in the house, and lots of hours with my face buried behind a computer terminal. My wife, Jeanne, even helped out by installing Linux for me on one of the test machines.

The technical reviewers suggested many improvements and helped make sure that the content was accurate. Many thanks to David Bausum, David Boreham, Keith Bostic, Mark Ellis, Phil Howard, Andrew Josey, Mukesh Kacker, Brian Kernighan, Bengt Kleberg, Ben Kuperman, Eric Raymond, and Andy Rudoff.

I'd also like to thank Andy Rudoff for answering questions about Solaris and Dennis Ritchie for digging up old papers and answering history questions. Once again, the staff at Addison-Wesley was great to work with. Thanks to Tyrrell Albaugh, Mary Franz, John Fuller, Karen Gettman, Jessica Goldstein, Noreen Regina, and John Wait. My thanks to Evelyn Pyle for the fine job of copyediting.

As Rich did, I also welcome electronic mail from any readers with comments, suggestions, or bug fixes.

Warren, New Jersey   Stephen A. Rago
April 2005   sar@apuebook.com

Preface to the First Edition

Introduction

This book describes the programming interface to the Unix system—the system call interface and many of the functions provided in the standard C library. It is intended for anyone writing programs that run under Unix.

Like most operating systems, Unix provides numerous services to the programs that are running—open a file, read a file, start a new program, allocate a region of memory, get the current time-of-day, and so on. This has been termed the *system call interface*. Additionally, the standard C library provides numerous functions that are used by almost every C program (format a variable's value for output, compare two strings, etc.).

The system call interface and the library routines have traditionally been described in Sections 2 and 3 of the *Unix Programmer's Manual*. This book is not a duplication of these sections. Examples and rationale are missing from the *Unix Programmer's Manual*, and that's what this book provides.

Unix Standards

The proliferation of different versions of Unix during the 1980s has been tempered by the various international standards that were started during the late 1980s. These include the ANSI standard for the C programming language, the IEEE POSIX family (still being developed), and the X/Open portability guide.

This book also describes these standards. But instead of just describing the standards by themselves, we describe them in relation to popular implementations of the standards—System V Release 4 and the forthcoming 4.4BSD. This provides a real-world description, which is often lacking from the standard itself and from books that describe only the standard.

Organization of the Book

This book is divided into six parts:

1. An overview and introduction to basic Unix programming concepts and terminology (Chapter 1), with a discussion of the various Unix standardization efforts and different Unix implementations (Chapter 2).

2. I/O—unbuffered I/O (Chapter 3), properties of files and directories (Chapter 4), the standard I/O library (Chapter 5), and the standard system data files (Chapter 6).

3. Processes—the environment of a Unix process (Chapter 7), process control (Chapter 8), the relationships between different processes (Chapter 9), and signals (Chapter 10).

4. More I/O—terminal I/O (Chapter 11), advanced I/O (Chapter 12), and daemon processes (Chapter 13).

5. IPC—Interprocess communication (Chapters 14 and 15).

6. Examples—a database library (Chapter 16), communicating with a PostScript printer (Chapter 17), a modem dialing program (Chapter 18), and using pseudo terminals (Chapter 19).

A reading familiarity with C would be beneficial as would some experience using Unix. No prior programming experience with Unix is assumed. This text is intended for programmers familiar with Unix and programmers familiar with some other operating system who wish to learn the details of the services provided by most Unix systems.

Examples in the Text

This book contains many examples—approximately 10,000 lines of source code. All the examples are in the C programming language. Furthermore, these examples are in ANSI C. You should have a copy of the *Unix Programmer's Manual* for your system handy while reading this book, since reference is made to it for some of the more esoteric and implementation-dependent features.

Almost every function and system call is demonstrated with a small, complete program. This lets us see the arguments and return values and is often easier to comprehend than the use of the function in a much larger program. But since some of the small programs are contrived examples, a few bigger examples are also included (Chapters 16, 17, 18, and 19). These larger examples demonstrate the programming techniques in larger, real-world examples.

All the examples have been included in the text directly from their source files. A machine-readable copy of all the examples is available via anonymous FTP from the Internet host `ftp.uu.net` in the file `published/books/stevens.advprog.tar.Z`. Obtaining the source code allows you to modify the programs from this text and experiment with them on your system.

Systems Used to Test the Examples

Unfortunately all operating systems are moving targets. Unix is no exception. The following diagram shows the recent evolution of the various versions of System V and 4.xBSD.

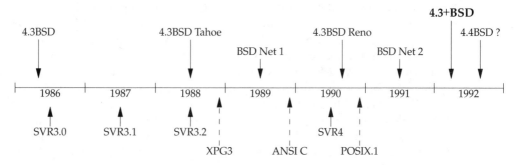

4.xBSD are the various systems from the Computer Systems Research Group at the University of California at Berkeley. This group also distributes the BSD Net 1 and BSD Net 2 releases—publicly available source code from the 4.xBSD systems. SVRx refers to System V Release x from AT&T. XPG3 is the X/Open Portability Guide, Issue 3, and ANSI C is the ANSI standard for the C programming language. POSIX.1 is the IEEE and ISO standard for the interface to a Unix-like system. We'll have more to say about these different standards and the various versions of Unix in Sections 2.2 and 2.3.

> **In this text we use the term *4.3+BSD* to refer to the Unix system from Berkeley that is somewhere between the BSD Net 2 release and 4.4BSD.**
>
> At the time of this writing, 4.4BSD was not released, so the system could not be called 4.4BSD. Nevertheless a simple name was needed to refer to this system and *4.3+BSD* is used throughout the text.

Most of the examples in this text have been run on four different versions of Unix:

1. Unix System V/386 Release 4.0 Version 2.0 ("vanilla SVR4") from U.H. Corp. (UHC), on an Intel 80386 processor.

2. 4.3+BSD at the Computer Systems Research Group, Computer Science Division, University of California at Berkeley, on a Hewlett Packard workstation.

3. BSD/386 (a derivative of the BSD Net 2 release) from Berkeley Software Design, Inc., on an Intel 80386 processor. This system is almost identical to what we call 4.3+BSD.

4. SunOS 4.1.1 and 4.1.2 (systems with a strong Berkeley heritage but many System V features) from Sun Microsystems, on a SPARCstation SLC.

Numerous timing tests are provided in the text and the systems used for the test are identified.

Acknowledgments

Once again I am indebted to my family for their love, support, and many lost weekends over the past year and a half. Writing a book is, in many ways, a family affair. Thank you Sally, Bill, Ellen, and David.

I am especially grateful to Brian Kernighan for his help in the book. His numerous thorough reviews of the entire manuscript and his gentle prodding for better prose hopefully show in the final result. Steve Rago was also a great resource, both in reviewing the entire manuscript and answering many questions about the details and history of System V. My thanks to the other technical reviewers used by Addison-Wesley, who provided valuable comments on various portions of the manuscript: Maury Bach, Mark Ellis, Jeff Gitlin, Peter Honeyman, John Linderman, Doug McIlroy, Evi Nemeth, Craig Partridge, Dave Presotto, Gary Wilson, and Gary Wright.

Keith Bostic and Kirk McKusick at the U.C. Berkeley CSRG provided an account that was used to test the examples on the latest BSD system. (Many thanks to Peter Salus too.) Sam Nataros and Joachim Sacksen at UHC provided the copy of SVR4 used to test the examples. Trent Hein helped obtain the alpha and beta copies of BSD/386.

Other friends have helped in many small, but significant ways over the past few years: Paul Lucchina, Joe Godsil, Jim Hogue, Ed Tankus, and Gary Wright. My editor at Addison-Wesley, John Wait, has been a great friend through it all. He never complained when the due date slipped and the page count kept increasing. A special thanks to the National Optical Astronomy Observatories (NOAO), especially Sidney Wolff, Richard Wolff, and Steve Grandi, for providing computer time.

Real Unix books are written using troff and this book follows that time-honored tradition. Camera-ready copy of the book was produced by the author using the groff package written by James Clark. Many thanks to James Clark for providing this excellent system and for his rapid response to bug fixes. Perhaps someday I will really understand troff footer traps.

I welcome electronic mail from any readers with comments, suggestions, or bug fixes.

Tucson, Arizona   W. Richard Stevens
April 1992   rstevens@kohala.com
                                            http://www.kohala.com/~rstevens

1

UNIX System Overview

1.1   Introduction

All operating systems provide services for programs they run. Typical services include executing a new program, opening a file, reading a file, allocating a region of memory, getting the current time of day, and so on. The focus of this text is to describe the services provided by various versions of the UNIX operating system.

Describing the UNIX System in a strictly linear fashion, without any forward references to terms that haven't been described yet, is nearly impossible (and would probably be boring). This chapter provides a whirlwind tour of the UNIX System from a programmer's perspective. We'll give some brief descriptions and examples of terms and concepts that appear throughout the text. We describe these features in much more detail in later chapters. This chapter also provides an introduction and overview of the services provided by the UNIX System, for programmers new to this environment.

1.2   UNIX Architecture

In a strict sense, an operating system can be defined as the software that controls the hardware resources of the computer and provides an environment under which programs can run. Generally, we call this software the *kernel*, since it is relatively small and resides at the core of the environment. Figure 1.1 shows a diagram of the UNIX System architecture.

The interface to the kernel is a layer of software called the *system calls* (the shaded portion in Figure 1.1). Libraries of common functions are built on top of the system call

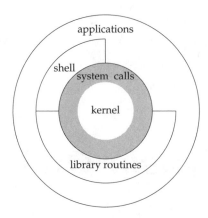

Figure 1.1 Architecture of the UNIX operating system

interface, but applications are free to use both. (We talk more about system calls and library functions in Section 1.11.) The shell is a special application that provides an interface for running other applications.

In a broad sense, an operating system is the kernel and all the other software that makes a computer useful and gives the computer its personality. This other software includes system utilities, applications, shells, libraries of common functions, and so on.

For example, Linux is the kernel used by the GNU operating system. Some people refer to this as the GNU/Linux operating system, but it is more commonly referred to as simply Linux. Although this usage may not be correct in a strict sense, it is understandable, given the dual meaning of the phrase *operating system*. (It also has the advantage of being more succinct.)

1.3   Logging In

Login Name

When we log in to a UNIX system, we enter our login name, followed by our password. The system then looks up our login name in its password file, usually the file /etc/passwd. If we look at our entry in the password file we see that it's composed of seven colon-separated fields: the login name, encrypted password, numeric user ID (205), numeric group ID (105), a comment field, home directory (/home/sar), and shell program (/bin/ksh).

```
sar:x:205:105:Stephen Rago:/home/sar:/bin/ksh
```

All contemporary systems have moved the encrypted password to a different file. In Chapter 6, we'll look at these files and some functions to access them.

Shells

Once we log in, some system information messages are typically displayed, and then we can type commands to the shell program. (Some systems start a window management program when you log in, but you generally end up with a shell running in one of the windows.) A *shell* is a command-line interpreter that reads user input and executes commands. The user input to a shell is normally from the terminal (an interactive shell) or sometimes from a file (called a *shell script*). The common shells in use are summarized in Figure 1.2.

Name	Path	FreeBSD 5.2.1	Linux 2.4.22	Mac OS X 10.3	Solaris 9
Bourne shell	`/bin/sh`	•	link to bash	link to bash	•
Bourne-again shell	`/bin/bash`	optional	•	•	•
C shell	`/bin/csh`	link to `tcsh`	link to `tcsh`	link to `tcsh`	•
Korn shell	`/bin/ksh`				•
TENEX C shell	`/bin/tcsh`	•	•	•	•

Figure 1.2 Common shells used on UNIX systems

The system knows which shell to execute for us from the final field in our entry in the password file.

The Bourne shell, developed by Steve Bourne at Bell Labs, has been in use since Version 7 and is provided with almost every UNIX system in existence. The control-flow constructs of the Bourne shell are reminiscent of Algol 68.

The C shell, developed by Bill Joy at Berkeley, is provided with all the BSD releases. Additionally, the C shell was provided by AT&T with System V/386 Release 3.2 and is also in System V Release 4 (SVR4). (We'll have more to say about these different versions of the UNIX System in the next chapter.) The C shell was built on the 6th Edition shell, not the Bourne shell. Its control flow looks more like the C language, and it supports additional features that weren't provided by the Bourne shell: job control, a history mechanism, and command line editing.

The Korn shell is considered a successor to the Bourne shell and was first provided with SVR4. The Korn shell, developed by David Korn at Bell Labs, runs on most UNIX systems, but before SVR4 was usually an extra-cost add-on, so it is not as widespread as the other two shells. It is upward compatible with the Bourne shell and includes those features that made the C shell popular: job control, command line editing, and so on.

The Bourne-again shell is the GNU shell provided with all Linux systems. It was designed to be POSIX-conformant, while still remaining compatible with the Bourne shell. It supports features from both the C shell and the Korn shell.

The TENEX C shell is an enhanced version of the C shell. It borrows several features, such as command completion, from the TENEX operating system (developed in 1972 at Bolt Beranek and Newman). The TENEX C shell adds many features to the C shell and is often used as a replacement for the C shell.

> Linux uses the Bourne-again shell for its default shell. In fact, `/bin/sh` is a link to `/bin/bash`. The default user shell in FreeBSD and Mac OS X is the TENEX C shell, but they use the Bourne shell for their administrative shell scripts because the C shell's programming

language is notoriously difficult to use. Solaris, having its heritage in both BSD and System V, provides all the shells shown in Figure 1.2. Free ports of most of the shells are available on the Internet.

Throughout the text, we will use parenthetical notes such as this to describe historical notes and to compare different implementations of the UNIX System. Often the reason for a particular implementation technique becomes clear when the historical reasons are described.

Throughout this text, we'll show interactive shell examples to execute a program that we've developed. These examples use features common to the Bourne shell, the Korn shell, and the Bourne-again shell.

1.4   Files and Directories

File System

The UNIX file system is a hierarchical arrangement of directories and files. Everything starts in the directory called *root* whose name is the single character /.

A *directory* is a file that contains directory entries. Logically, we can think of each directory entry as containing a filename along with a structure of information describing the attributes of the file. The attributes of a file are such things as type of file—regular file, directory—the size of the file, the owner of the file, permissions for the file—whether other users may access this file—and when the file was last modified. The stat and fstat functions return a structure of information containing all the attributes of a file. In Chapter 4, we'll examine all the attributes of a file in great detail.

We make a distinction between the logical view of a directory entry and the way it is actually stored on disk. Most implementations of UNIX file systems don't store attributes in the directory entries themselves, because of the difficulty of keeping them in synch when a file has multiple hard links. This will become clear when we discuss hard links in Chapter 4.

Filename

The names in a directory are called *filenames*. The only two characters that cannot appear in a filename are the slash character (/) and the null character. The slash separates the filenames that form a pathname (described next) and the null character terminates a pathname. Nevertheless, it's good practice to restrict the characters in a filename to a subset of the normal printing characters. (We restrict the characters because if we use some of the shell's special characters in the filename, we have to use the shell's quoting mechanism to reference the filename, and this can get complicated.)

Two filenames are automatically created whenever a new directory is created: . (called *dot*) and . . (called *dot-dot*). Dot refers to the current directory, and dot-dot refers to the parent directory. In the root directory, dot-dot is the same as dot.

The Research UNIX System and some older UNIX System V file systems restricted a filename to 14 characters. BSD versions extended this limit to 255 characters. Today, almost all commercial UNIX file systems support at least 255-character filenames.

Pathname

A sequence of one or more filenames, separated by slashes and optionally starting with a slash, forms a *pathname*. A pathname that begins with a slash is called an *absolute pathname*; otherwise, it's called a *relative pathname*. Relative pathnames refer to files relative to the current directory. The name for the root of the file system (/) is a special-case absolute pathname that has no filename component.

Example

Listing the names of all the files in a directory is not difficult. Figure 1.3 shows a bare-bones implementation of the ls(1) command.

```
#include "apue.h"
#include <dirent.h>

int
main(int argc, char *argv[])
{
    DIR             *dp;
    struct dirent   *dirp;

    if (argc != 2)
        err_quit("usage: ls directory_name");

    if ((dp = opendir(argv[1])) == NULL)
        err_sys("can't open %s", argv[1]);
    while ((dirp = readdir(dp)) != NULL)
        printf("%s\n", dirp->d_name);

    closedir(dp);
    exit(0);
}
```

Figure 1.3 List all the files in a directory

The notation ls(1) is the normal way to reference a particular entry in the UNIX system manuals. It refers to the entry for ls in Section 1. The sections are normally numbered 1 through 8, and all the entries within each section are arranged alphabetically. Throughout this text, we assume that you have a copy of the manuals for your UNIX system.

> Historically, UNIX systems lumped all eight sections together into what was called the *UNIX Programmer's Manual*. As the page count increased, the trend changed to distributing the sections among separate manuals: one for users, one for programmers, and one for system administrators, for example.

> Some UNIX systems further divide the manual pages within a given section, using an uppercase letter. For example, all the standard input/output (I/O) functions in AT&T [1990e] are indicated as being in Section 3S, as in fopen(3S). Other systems have replaced the numeric sections with alphabetic ones, such as C for commands.

Today, most manuals are distributed in electronic form. If your manuals are online, the way to see the manual pages for the ls command would be something like

```
man 1 ls
```

or

```
man -s1 ls
```

Figure 1.3 is a program that just prints the name of every file in a directory, and nothing else. If the source file is named myls.c, we compile it into the default a.out executable file by

```
cc myls.c
```

> Historically, cc(1) is the C compiler. On systems with the GNU C compilation system, the C compiler is gcc(1). Here, cc is often linked to gcc.

Some sample output is

```
$ ./a.out /dev
.
..
console
tty
mem
kmem
null
mouse
stdin
stdout
stderr
zero
```
                              many more lines that aren't shown
```
cdrom
$ ./a.out /var/spool/cron
can't open /var/spool/cron: Permission denied
$ ./a.out /dev/tty
can't open /dev/tty: Not a directory
```

Throughout this text, we'll show commands that we run and the resulting output in this fashion: Characters that we type are shown in **this font**, whereas output from programs is shown like this. If we need to add comments to this output, we'll show the comments in *italics*. The dollar sign that precedes our input is the prompt that is printed by the shell. We'll always show the shell prompt as a dollar sign.

Note that the directory listing is not in alphabetical order. The ls command sorts the names before printing them.

There are many details to consider in this 20-line program.

- First, we include a header of our own: apue.h. We include this header in almost every program in this text. This header includes some standard system headers and defines numerous constants and function prototypes that we use throughout the examples in the text. A listing of this header is in Appendix B.

- The declaration of the `main` function uses the style supported by the ISO C standard. (We'll have more to say about the ISO C standard in the next chapter.)

- We take an argument from the command line, `argv[1]`, as the name of the directory to list. In Chapter 7, we'll look at how the `main` function is called and how the command-line arguments and environment variables are accessible to the program.

- Because the actual format of directory entries varies from one UNIX system to another, we use the functions `opendir`, `readdir`, and `closedir` to manipulate the directory.

- The `opendir` function returns a pointer to a `DIR` structure, and we pass this pointer to the `readdir` function. We don't care what's in the `DIR` structure. We then call `readdir` in a loop, to read each directory entry. The `readdir` function returns a pointer to a `dirent` structure or, when it's finished with the directory, a null pointer. All we examine in the `dirent` structure is the name of each directory entry (`d_name`). Using this name, we could then call the `stat` function (Section 4.2) to determine all the attributes of the file.

- We call two functions of our own to handle the errors: `err_sys` and `err_quit`. We can see from the preceding output that the `err_sys` function prints an informative message describing what type of error was encountered ("Permission denied" or "Not a directory"). These two error functions are shown and described in Appendix B. We also talk more about error handling in Section 1.7.

- When the program is done, it calls the function `exit` with an argument of 0. The function `exit` terminates a program. By convention, an argument of 0 means OK, and an argument between 1 and 255 means that an error occurred. In Section 8.5, we show how any program, such as a shell or a program that we write, can obtain the `exit` status of a program that it executes.   □

Working Directory

Every process has a *working directory*, sometimes called the *current working directory*. This is the directory from which all relative pathnames are interpreted. A process can change its working directory with the `chdir` function.

For example, the relative pathname `doc/memo/joe` refers to the file or directory `joe`, in the directory `memo`, in the directory `doc`, which must be a directory within the working directory. From looking just at this pathname, we know that both `doc` and `memo` have to be directories, but we can't tell whether `joe` is a file or a directory. The pathname `/usr/lib/lint` is an absolute pathname that refers to the file or directory `lint` in the directory `lib`, in the directory `usr`, which is in the root directory.

Home Directory

When we log in, the working directory is set to our *home directory*. Our home directory is obtained from our entry in the password file (Section 1.3).

1.5   Input and Output

File Descriptors

File descriptors are normally small non-negative integers that the kernel uses to identify the files being accessed by a particular process. Whenever it opens an existing file or creates a new file, the kernel returns a file descriptor that we use when we want to read or write the file.

Standard Input, Standard Output, and Standard Error

By convention, all shells open three descriptors whenever a new program is run: standard input, standard output, and standard error. If nothing special is done, as in the simple command

```
ls
```

then all three are connected to the terminal. Most shells provide a way to redirect any or all of these three descriptors to any file. For example,

```
ls > file.list
```

executes the `ls` command with its standard output redirected to the file named `file.list`.

Unbuffered I/O

Unbuffered I/O is provided by the functions `open`, `read`, `write`, `lseek`, and `close`. These functions all work with file descriptors.

Example

If we're willing to read from the standard input and write to the standard output, then the program in Figure 1.4 copies any regular file on a UNIX system.

```
#include "apue.h"

#define BUFFSIZE    4096

int
main(void)
{
    int     n;
    char    buf[BUFFSIZE];

    while ((n = read(STDIN_FILENO, buf, BUFFSIZE)) > 0)
        if (write(STDOUT_FILENO, buf, n) != n)
            err_sys("write error");
```

```
        if (n < 0)
            err_sys("read error");

        exit(0);
    }
```

Figure 1.4 Copy standard input to standard output

The `<unistd.h>` header, included by `apue.h`, and the two constants `STDIN_FILENO` and `STDOUT_FILENO` are part of the POSIX standard (about which we'll have a lot more to say in the next chapter). In this header are function prototypes for many of the UNIX system services, such as the `read` and `write` functions that we call.

The constants `STDIN_FILENO` and `STDOUT_FILENO` are defined in `<unistd.h>` and specify the file descriptors for standard input and standard output. These values are typically 0 and 1, respectively, but we'll use the new names for portability.

In Section 3.9, we'll examine the `BUFFSIZE` constant in detail, seeing how various values affect the efficiency of the program. Regardless of the value of this constant, however, this program still copies any regular file.

The `read` function returns the number of bytes that are read, and this value is used as the number of bytes to write. When the end of the input file is encountered, `read` returns 0 and the program stops. If a read error occurs, `read` returns –1. Most of the system functions return –1 when an error occurs.

If we compile the program into the standard name (`a.out`) and execute it as

```
./a.out > data
```

standard input is the terminal, standard output is redirected to the file `data`, and standard error is also the terminal. If this output file doesn't exist, the shell creates it by default. The program copies lines that we type to the standard output until we type the end-of-file character (usually Control-D).

If we run

```
./a.out < infile > outfile
```

then the file named `infile` will be copied to the file named `outfile`.   □

In Chapter 3, we describe the unbuffered I/O functions in more detail.

Standard I/O

The standard I/O functions provide a buffered interface to the unbuffered I/O functions. Using standard I/O prevents us from having to worry about choosing optimal buffer sizes, such as the `BUFFSIZE` constant in Figure 1.4. Another advantage of using the standard I/O functions is that they simplify dealing with lines of input (a common occurrence in UNIX applications). The `fgets` function, for example, reads an entire line. The `read` function, on the other hand, reads a specified number of bytes. As we shall see in Section 5.4, the standard I/O library provides functions that let us control the style of buffering used by the library.

The most common standard I/O function is printf. In programs that call printf, we'll always include <stdio.h>—normally by including apue.h—as this header contains the function prototypes for all the standard I/O functions.

Example

The program in Figure 1.5, which we'll examine in more detail in Section 5.8, is like the previous program that called read and write. This program copies standard input to standard output and can copy any regular file.

```
#include "apue.h"

int
main(void)
{
    int     c;

    while ((c = getc(stdin)) != EOF)
        if (putc(c, stdout) == EOF)
            err_sys("output error");

    if (ferror(stdin))
        err_sys("input error");

    exit(0);
}
```

Figure 1.5 Copy standard input to standard output, using standard I/O

The function getc reads one character at a time, and this character is written by putc. After the last byte of input has been read, getc returns the constant EOF (defined in <stdio.h>). The standard I/O constants stdin and stdout are also defined in the <stdio.h> header and refer to the standard input and standard output.   □

1.6   Programs and Processes

Program

A *program* is an executable file residing on disk in a directory. A program is read into memory and is executed by the kernel as a result of one of the six exec functions. We'll cover these functions in Section 8.10.

Processes and Process ID

An executing instance of a program is called a *process*, a term used on almost every page of this text. Some operating systems use the term *task* to refer to a program that is being executed.

The UNIX System guarantees that every process has a unique numeric identifier called the *process ID*. The process ID is always a non-negative integer.

Example

The program in Figure 1.6 prints its process ID.

```
#include "apue.h"

int
main(void)
{
    printf("hello world from process ID %d\n", getpid());
    exit(0);
}
```

Figure 1.6 Print the process ID

If we compile this program into the file a.out and execute it, we have

```
$ ./a.out
hello world from process ID 851
$ ./a.out
hello world from process ID 854
```

When this program runs, it calls the function getpid to obtain its process ID.   □

Process Control

There are three primary functions for process control: fork, exec, and waitpid. (The exec function has six variants, but we often refer to them collectively as simply the exec function.)

Example

The process control features of the UNIX System are demonstrated using a simple program (Figure 1.7) that reads commands from standard input and executes the commands. This is a bare-bones implementation of a shell-like program. There are several features to consider in this 30-line program.

- We use the standard I/O function fgets to read one line at a time from the standard input. When we type the end-of-file character (which is often Control-D) as the first character of a line, fgets returns a null pointer, the loop stops, and the process terminates. In Chapter 18, we describe all the special terminal characters—end of file, backspace one character, erase entire line, and so on—and how to change them.

- Because each line returned by fgets is terminated with a newline character, followed by a null byte, we use the standard C function strlen to calculate the length of the string, and then replace the newline with a null byte. We do this because the execlp function wants a null-terminated argument, not a newline-terminated argument.

```
#include "apue.h"
#include <sys/wait.h>

int
main(void)
{
    char    buf[MAXLINE];    /* from apue.h */
    pid_t   pid;
    int     status;

    printf("%% ");   /* print prompt (printf requires %% to print %) */
    while (fgets(buf, MAXLINE, stdin) != NULL) {
        if (buf[strlen(buf) - 1] == '\n')
            buf[strlen(buf) - 1] = 0; /* replace newline with null */

        if ((pid = fork()) < 0) {
            err_sys("fork error");
        } else if (pid == 0) {        /* child */
            execlp(buf, buf, (char *)0);
            err_ret("couldn't execute: %s", buf);
            exit(127);
        }

        /* parent */
        if ((pid = waitpid(pid, &status, 0)) < 0)
            err_sys("waitpid error");
        printf("%% ");
    }
    exit(0);
}
```

Figure 1.7 Read commands from standard input and execute them

- We call `fork` to create a new process, which is a copy of the caller. We say that the caller is the parent and that the newly created process is the child. Then `fork` returns the non-negative process ID of the new child process to the parent, and returns 0 to the child. Because `fork` creates a new process, we say that it is called once—by the parent—but returns twice—in the parent and in the child.

- In the child, we call `execlp` to execute the command that was read from the standard input. This replaces the child process with the new program file. The combination of a `fork`, followed by an `exec`, is what some operating systems call spawning a new process. In the UNIX System, the two parts are separated into individual functions. We'll have a lot more to say about these functions in Chapter 8.

- Because the child calls `execlp` to execute the new program file, the parent wants to wait for the child to terminate. This is done by calling `waitpid`, specifying which process we want to wait for: the `pid` argument, which is the process ID of the child. The `waitpid` function also returns the termination status of the child—the `status` variable—but in this simple program, we don't do anything with this value. We could examine it to determine exactly how the child terminated.

- The most fundamental limitation of this program is that we can't pass arguments to the command that we execute. We can't, for example, specify the name of a directory to list. We can execute `ls` only on the working directory. To allow arguments would require that we parse the input line, separating the arguments by some convention, probably spaces or tabs, and then pass each argument as a separate argument to the `execlp` function. Nevertheless, this program is still a useful demonstration of the process control functions of the UNIX System.

If we run this program, we get the following results. Note that our program has a different prompt—the percent sign—to distinguish it from the shell's prompt.

```
$ ./a.out
% date
Sun Aug  1 03:04:47 EDT 2004            programmers work late
% who
sar       :0        Jul 26 22:54
sar       pts/0     Jul 26 22:54  (:0)
sar       pts/1     Jul 26 22:54  (:0)
sar       pts/2     Jul 26 22:54  (:0)
% pwd
/home/sar/bk/apue/2e
% ls
Makefile
a.out
shell1.c
% ^D                                    type the end-of-file character
$                                       the regular shell prompt
```
                                                                              □

The notation `^D` is used to indicate a control character. Control characters are special characters formed by holding down the control key—often labeled `Control` or `Ctrl`—on your keyboard and then pressing another key at the same time. Control-D, or `^D`, is the default end-of-file character. We'll see many more control characters when we discuss terminal I/O in Chapter 18.

Threads and Thread IDs

Usually, a process has only one thread of control—one set of machine instructions executing at a time. Some problems are easier to solve when more than one thread of control can operate on different parts of the problem. Additionally, multiple threads of control can exploit the parallelism possible on multiprocessor systems.

All the threads within a process share the same address space, file descriptors, stacks, and process-related attributes. Each thread executes on its own stack, although any thread can access the stacks of other threads in the same process. Because they can access the same memory, the threads need to synchronize access to shared data among themselves to avoid inconsistencies.

As with processes, threads are identified by IDs. Thread IDs, however, are local to a process. A thread ID from one process has no meaning in another process. We use thread IDs to refer to specific threads as we manipulate the threads within a process.

Functions to control threads parallel those used to control processes. Because threads were added to the UNIX System long after the process model was established, however, the thread model and the process model have some complicated interactions, as we shall see in Chapter 12.

1.7   Error Handling

When an error occurs in one of the UNIX System functions, a negative value is often returned, and the integer errno is usually set to a value that gives additional information. For example, the open function returns either a non-negative file descriptor if all is OK or –1 if an error occurs. An error from open has about 15 possible errno values, such as file doesn't exist, permission problem, and so on. Some functions use a convention other than returning a negative value. For example, most functions that return a pointer to an object return a null pointer to indicate an error.

The file <errno.h> defines the symbol errno and constants for each value that errno can assume. Each of these constants begins with the character E. Also, the first page of Section 2 of the UNIX system manuals, named intro(2), usually lists all these error constants. For example, if errno is equal to the constant EACCES, this indicates a permission problem, such as insufficient permission to open the requested file.

> On Linux, the error constants are listed in the errno(3) manual page.

POSIX and ISO C define errno as a symbol expanding into a modifiable lvalue of type integer. This can be either an integer that contains the error number or a function that returns a pointer to the error number. The historical definition is

```
extern int errno;
```

But in an environment that supports threads, the process address space is shared among multiple threads, and each thread needs its own local copy of errno to prevent one thread from interfering with another. Linux, for example, supports multithreaded access to errno by defining it as

```
extern int *__errno_location(void);
#define errno (*__errno_location())
```

There are two rules to be aware of with respect to errno. First, its value is never cleared by a routine if an error does not occur. Therefore, we should examine its value only when the return value from a function indicates that an error occurred. Second, the value of errno is never set to 0 by any of the functions, and none of the constants defined in <errno.h> has a value of 0.

Two functions are defined by the C standard to help with printing error messages.

```
#include <string.h>

char *strerror(int errnum);
```
Returns: pointer to message string

This function maps *errnum*, which is typically the errno value, into an error message string and returns a pointer to the string.

The perror function produces an error message on the standard error, based on the current value of errno, and returns.

```
#include <stdio.h>

void perror(const char *msg);
```

It outputs the string pointed to by *msg*, followed by a colon and a space, followed by the error message corresponding to the value of errno, followed by a newline.

Example

Figure 1.8 shows the use of these two error functions.

```
#include "apue.h"
#include <errno.h>

int
main(int argc, char *argv[])
{
    fprintf(stderr, "EACCES: %s\n", strerror(EACCES));
    errno = ENOENT;
    perror(argv[0]);
    exit(0);
}
```

Figure 1.8 Demonstrate strerror and perror

If this program is compiled into the file a.out, we have

```
$ ./a.out
EACCES: Permission denied
./a.out: No such file or directory
```

Note that we pass the name of the program—argv[0], whose value is ./a.out—as the argument to perror. This is a standard convention in the UNIX System. By doing this, if the program is executed as part of a pipeline, as in

```
prog1 < inputfile | prog2 | prog3 > outputfile
```

we are able to tell which of the three programs generated a particular error message. □

Instead of calling either `strerror` or `perror` directly, all the examples in this text use the error functions shown in Appendix B. The error functions in this appendix let us use the variable argument list facility of ISO C to handle error conditions with a single C statement.

Error Recovery

The errors defined in `<errno.h>` can be divided into two categories: fatal and nonfatal. A fatal error has no recovery action. The best we can do is print an error message on the user's screen or write an error message into a log file, and then exit. Nonfatal errors, on the other hand, can sometimes be dealt with more robustly. Most nonfatal errors are temporary in nature, such as with a resource shortage, and might not occur when there is less activity on the system.

Resource-related nonfatal errors include `EAGAIN`, `ENFILE`, `ENOBUFS`, `ENOLCK`, `ENOSPC`, `ENOSR`, `EWOULDBLOCK`, and sometimes `ENOMEM`. `EBUSY` can be treated as a nonfatal error when it indicates that a shared resource is in use. Sometimes, `EINTR` can be treated as a nonfatal error when it interrupts a slow system call (more on this in Section 10.5).

The typical recovery action for a resource-related nonfatal error is to delay a little and try again later. This technique can be applied in other circumstances. For example, if an error indicates that a network connection is no longer functioning, it might be possible for the application to delay a short time and then reestablish the connection. Some applications use an exponential backoff algorithm, waiting a longer period of time each iteration.

Ultimately, it is up to the application developer to determine which errors are recoverable. If a reasonable strategy can be used to recover from an error, we can improve the robustness of our application by avoiding an abnormal exit.

1.8   User Identification

User ID

The *user ID* from our entry in the password file is a numeric value that identifies us to the system. This user ID is assigned by the system administrator when our login name is assigned, and we cannot change it. The user ID is normally assigned to be unique for every user. We'll see how the kernel uses the user ID to check whether we have the appropriate permissions to perform certain operations.

We call the user whose user ID is 0 either *root* or the *superuser*. The entry in the password file normally has a login name of `root`, and we refer to the special privileges of this user as superuser privileges. As we'll see in Chapter 4, if a process has superuser privileges, most file permission checks are bypassed. Some operating system functions are restricted to the superuser. The superuser has free rein over the system.

> Client versions of Mac OS X ship with the superuser account disabled; server versions ship with the account already enabled. Instructions are available on Apple's Web site describing how to enable it. See `http://docs.info.apple.com/article.html?artnum=106290`.

Group ID

Our entry in the password file also specifies our numeric *group ID*. This too is assigned by the system administrator when our login name is assigned. Typically, the password file contains multiple entries that specify the same group ID. Groups are normally used to collect users together into projects or departments. This allows the sharing of resources, such as files, among members of the same group. We'll see in Section 4.5 that we can set the permissions on a file so that all members of a group can access the file, whereas others outside the group cannot.

There is also a group file that maps group names into numeric group IDs. The group file is usually /etc/group.

The use of numeric user IDs and numeric group IDs for permissions is historical. With every file on disk, the file system stores both the user ID and the group ID of a file's owner. Storing both of these values requires only four bytes, assuming that each is stored as a two-byte integer. If the full ASCII login name and group name were used instead, additional disk space would be required. In addition, comparing strings during permission checks is more expensive than comparing integers.

Users, however, work better with names than with numbers, so the password file maintains the mapping between login names and user IDs, and the group file provides the mapping between group names and group IDs. The ls -l command, for example, prints the login name of the owner of a file, using the password file to map the numeric user ID into the corresponding login name.

> Early UNIX systems used 16-bit integers to represent user and group IDs. Contemporary UNIX systems use 32-bit integers.

Example

The program in Figure 1.9 prints the user ID and the group ID.

```
#include "apue.h"

int
main(void)
{
    printf("uid = %d, gid = %d\n", getuid(), getgid());
    exit(0);
}
```

Figure 1.9 Print user ID and group ID

We call the functions getuid and getgid to return the user ID and the group ID. Running the program yields

```
$ ./a.out
uid = 205, gid = 105
```

Supplementary Group IDs

In addition to the group ID specified in the password file for a login name, most versions of the UNIX System allow a user to belong to additional groups. This started with 4.2BSD, which allowed a user to belong to up to 16 additional groups. These *supplementary group IDs* are obtained at login time by reading the file /etc/group and finding the first 16 entries that list the user as a member. As we shall see in the next chapter, POSIX requires that a system support at least eight supplementary groups per process, but most systems support at least 16.

1.9   Signals

Signals are a technique used to notify a process that some condition has occurred. For example, if a process divides by zero, the signal whose name is SIGFPE (floating-point exception) is sent to the process. The process has three choices for dealing with the signal.

1. Ignore the signal. This option isn't recommended for signals that denote a hardware exception, such as dividing by zero or referencing memory outside the address space of the process, as the results are undefined.

2. Let the default action occur. For a divide-by-zero condition, the default is to terminate the process.

3. Provide a function that is called when the signal occurs (this is called "catching" the signal). By providing a function of our own, we'll know when the signal occurs and we can handle it as we wish.

Many conditions generate signals. Two terminal keys, called the *interrupt key*— often the DELETE key or Control-C—and the *quit key*—often Control-backslash—are used to interrupt the currently running process. Another way to generate a signal is by calling the kill function. We can call this function from a process to send a signal to another process. Naturally, there are limitations: we have to be the owner of the other process (or the superuser) to be able to send it a signal.

Example

Recall the bare-bones shell example (Figure 1.7). If we invoke this program and press the interrupt key, the process terminates because the default action for this signal, named SIGINT, is to terminate the process. The process hasn't told the kernel to do anything other than the default with this signal, so the process terminates.

To catch this signal, the program needs to call the signal function, specifying the name of the function to call when the SIGINT signal is generated. The function is named sig_int; when it's called, it just prints a message and a new prompt. Adding

11 lines to the program in Figure 1.7 gives us the version in Figure 1.10. (The 11 new lines are indicated with a plus sign at the beginning of the line.)

```
  #include "apue.h"
  #include <sys/wait.h>

+ static void sig_int(int);        /* our signal-catching function */
+
  int
  main(void)
  {
      char    buf[MAXLINE];     /* from apue.h */
      pid_t   pid;
      int     status;

+     if (signal(SIGINT, sig_int) == SIG_ERR)
+         err_sys("signal error");
+
      printf("%% ");  /* print prompt (printf requires %% to print %) */
      while (fgets(buf, MAXLINE, stdin) != NULL) {
          if (buf[strlen(buf) - 1] == '\n')
              buf[strlen(buf) - 1] = 0; /* replace newline with null */

          if ((pid = fork()) < 0) {
              err_sys("fork error");
          } else if (pid == 0) {       /* child */
              execlp(buf, buf, (char *)0);
              err_ret("couldn't execute: %s", buf);
              exit(127);
          }

          /* parent */
          if ((pid = waitpid(pid, &status, 0)) < 0)
              err_sys("waitpid error");
          printf("%% ");
      }
      exit(0);
  }
+
+ void
+ sig_int(int signo)
+ {
+     printf("interrupt\n%% ");
+ }
```

Figure 1.10 Read commands from standard input and execute them

In Chapter 10, we'll take a long look at signals, as most nontrivial applications deal with them.   □

1.10   Time Values

Historically, UNIX systems have maintained two different time values:

1. Calendar time. This value counts the number of seconds since the Epoch: 00:00:00 January 1, 1970, Coordinated Universal Time (UTC). (Older manuals refer to UTC as Greenwich Mean Time.) These time values are used to record the time when a file was last modified, for example.

    The primitive system data type `time_t` holds these time values.

2. Process time. This is also called CPU time and measures the central processor resources used by a process. Process time is measured in clock ticks, which have historically been 50, 60, or 100 ticks per second.

    The primitive system data type `clock_t` holds these time values. (We'll show how to obtain the number of clock ticks per second with the `sysconf` function in Section 2.5.4.)

When we measure the execution time of a process, as in Section 3.9, we'll see that the UNIX System maintains three values for a process:

* Clock time
* User CPU time
* System CPU time

The clock time, sometimes called *wall clock time*, is the amount of time the process takes to run, and its value depends on the number of other processes being run on the system. Whenever we report the clock time, the measurements are made with no other activities on the system.

The user CPU time is the CPU time attributed to user instructions. The system CPU time is the CPU time attributed to the kernel when it executes on behalf of the process. For example, whenever a process executes a system service, such as `read` or `write`, the time spent within the kernel performing that system service is charged to the process. The sum of user CPU time and system CPU time is often called the *CPU time*.

It is easy to measure the clock time, user time, and system time of any process: simply execute the `time(1)` command, with the argument to the `time` command being the command we want to measure. For example:

```
$ cd /usr/include
$ time -p grep _POSIX_SOURCE */*.h > /dev/null

real    0m0.81s
user    0m0.11s
sys     0m0.07s
```

The output format from the `time` command depends on the shell being used, because some shells don't run `/usr/bin/time`, but instead have a separate built-in function to measure the time it takes commands to run.

In Section 8.16, we'll see how to obtain these three times from a running process. The general topic of times and dates is covered in Section 6.10.

1.11 System Calls and Library Functions

All operating systems provide service points through which programs request services from the kernel. All implementations of the UNIX System provide a well-defined, limited number of entry points directly into the kernel called *system calls* (recall Figure 1.1). Version 7 of the Research UNIX System provided about 50 system calls, 4.4BSD provided about 110, and SVR4 had around 120. Linux has anywhere between 240 and 260 system calls, depending on the version. FreeBSD has around 320.

The system call interface has always been documented in Section 2 of the *UNIX Programmer's Manual*. Its definition is in the C language, regardless of the actual implementation technique used on any given system to invoke a system call. This differs from many older operating systems, which traditionally defined the kernel entry points in the assembler language of the machine.

The technique used on UNIX systems is for each system call to have a function of the same name in the standard C library. The user process calls this function, using the standard C calling sequence. This function then invokes the appropriate kernel service, using whatever technique is required on the system. For example, the function may put one or more of the C arguments into general registers and then execute some machine instruction that generates a software interrupt in the kernel. For our purposes, we can consider the system calls as being C functions.

Section 3 of the *UNIX Programmer's Manual* defines the general-purpose functions available to programmers. These functions aren't entry points into the kernel, although they may invoke one or more of the kernel's system calls. For example, the `printf` function may use the `write` system call to output a string, but the `strcpy` (copy a string) and `atoi` (convert ASCII to integer) functions don't involve the kernel at all.

From an implementor's point of view, the distinction between a system call and a library function is fundamental. But from a user's perspective, the difference is not as critical. From our perspective in this text, both system calls and library functions appear as normal C functions. Both exist to provide services for application programs. We should realize, however, that we can replace the library functions, if desired, whereas the system calls usually cannot be replaced.

Consider the memory allocation function `malloc` as an example. There are many ways to do memory allocation and its associated garbage collection (best fit, first fit, and so on). No single technique is optimal for all programs. The UNIX system call that handles memory allocation, sbrk(2), is not a general-purpose memory manager. It increases or decreases the address space of the process by a specified number of bytes. How that space is managed is up to the process. The memory allocation function, malloc(3), implements one particular type of allocation. If we don't like its operation, we can define our own `malloc` function, which will probably use the `sbrk` system call. In fact, numerous software packages implement their own memory allocation algorithms with the `sbrk` system call. Figure 1.11 shows the relationship between the application, the `malloc` function, and the `sbrk` system call.

Here we have a clean separation of duties: the system call in the kernel allocates an additional chunk of space on behalf of the process. The `malloc` library function manages this space from user level.

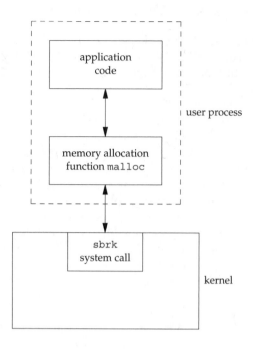

Figure 1.11 Separation of `malloc` function and `sbrk` system call

    Another example to illustrate the difference between a system call and a library
function is the interface the UNIX System provides to determine the current time and
date. Some operating systems provide one system call to return the time and another to
return the date. Any special handling, such as the switch to or from daylight saving
time, is handled by the kernel or requires human intervention. The UNIX System, on
the other hand, provides a single system call that returns the number of seconds since
the Epoch: midnight, January 1, 1970, Coordinated Universal Time. Any interpretation
of this value, such as converting it to a human-readable time and date using the local
time zone, is left to the user process. The standard C library provides routines to handle
most cases. These library routines handle such details as the various algorithms for
daylight saving time.
    An application can call either a system call or a library routine. Also realize that
many library routines invoke a system call. This is shown in Figure 1.12.
    Another difference between system calls and library functions is that system calls
usually provide a minimal interface, whereas library functions often provide more
elaborate functionality. We've seen this already in the difference between the `sbrk`
system call and the `malloc` library function. We'll see this difference later, when we
compare the unbuffered I/O functions (Chapter 3) and the standard I/O functions
(Chapter 5).
    The process control system calls (`fork`, `exec`, and `wait`) are usually invoked by the
user's application code directly. (Recall the bare-bones shell in Figure 1.7.) But some

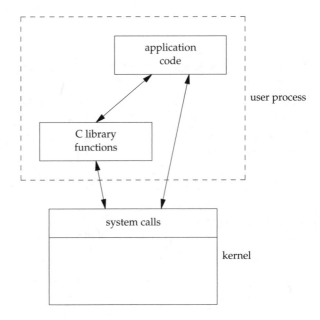

Figure 1.12   Difference between C library functions and system calls

library routines exist to simplify certain common cases: the `system` and `popen` library routines, for example. In Section 8.13, we'll show an implementation of the `system` function that invokes the basic process control system calls. We'll enhance this example in Section 10.18 to handle signals correctly.

To define the interface to the UNIX System that most programmers use, we have to describe both the system calls and some of the library functions. If we described only the `sbrk` system call, for example, we would skip the more programmer-friendly `malloc` library function that many applications use. In this text, we'll use the term *function* to refer to both system calls and library functions, except when the distinction is necessary.

1.12   Summary

This chapter has been a short tour of the UNIX System. We've described some of the fundamental terms that we'll encounter over and over again. We've seen numerous small examples of UNIX programs to give us a feel for what the remainder of the text talks about.

The next chapter is about standardization of the UNIX System and the effect of work in this area on current systems. Standards, particularly the ISO C standard and the POSIX.1 standard, will affect the rest of the text.

Exercises

1.1 Verify on your system that the directories dot and dot-dot are not the same, except in the root directory.

1.2 In the output from the program in Figure 1.6, what happened to the processes with process IDs 852 and 853?

1.3 In Section 1.7, the argument to perror is defined with the ISO C attribute const, whereas the integer argument to strerror isn't defined with this attribute. Why?

1.4 In the error-logging function log_doit in Appendix B, why is the value of errno saved when the function is called?

1.5 If the calendar time is stored as a signed 32-bit integer, in what year will it overflow? What ways can be used to extend the overflow point? Are they compatible with existing applications?

1.6 If the process time is stored as a signed 32-bit integer, and if the system counts 100 ticks per second, after how many days will the value overflow?

2

UNIX Standardization and

Implementations

2.1   Introduction

Much work has gone into standardizing the UNIX programming environment and the C programming language. Although applications have always been quite portable across different versions of the UNIX operating system, the proliferation of versions and differences during the 1980s led many large users, such as the U.S. government, to call for standardization.

In this chapter we first look at the various standardization efforts that have been under way over the past two decades. We then discuss the effects of these UNIX programming standards on the operating system implementations that are described in this book. An important part of all the standardization efforts is the specification of various limits that each implementation must define, so we look at these limits and the various ways to determine their values.

2.2   UNIX Standardization

2.2.1 ISO C

In late 1989, ANSI Standard X3.159–1989 for the C programming language was approved. This standard has also been adopted as international standard ISO/IEC 9899:1990. ANSI is the American National Standards Institute, the U.S. member in the International Organization for Standardization (ISO). IEC stands for the International Electrotechnical Commission.

The C standard is now maintained and developed by the ISO/IEC international standardization working group for the C programming language, known as ISO/IEC JTC1/SC22/WG14, or WG14 for short. The intent of the ISO C standard is to provide portability of conforming C programs to a wide variety of operating systems, not only the UNIX System. This standard defines not only the syntax and semantics of the programming language but also a standard library [Chapter 7 of ISO 1999; Plauger 1992; Appendix B of Kernighan and Ritchie 1988]. This library is important because all contemporary UNIX systems, such as the ones described in this book, provide the library routines that are specified in the C standard.

In 1999, the ISO C standard was updated and approved as ISO/IEC 9899:1999, largely to improve support for applications that perform numerical processing. The changes don't affect the POSIX standards described in this book, except for the addition of the `restrict` keyword to some of the function prototypes. This keyword is used to tell the compiler which pointer references can be optimized, by indicating that the object to which the pointer refers is accessed in the function only via that pointer.

As with most standards, there is a delay between the standard's approval and the modification of software to conform to it. As each vendor's compilation systems evolve, they add more support for the latest version of the ISO C standard.

> A summary of the current level of conformance of gcc to the 1999 version of the ISO C standard is available at http://www.gnu.org/software/gcc/c99status.html.

The ISO C library can be divided into 24 areas, based on the headers defined by the standard. Figure 2.1 lists the headers defined by the C standard. The POSIX.1 standard includes these headers, as well as others. We also list which of these headers are supported by the four implementations (FreeBSD 5.2.1, Linux 2.4.22, Mac OS X 10.3, and Solaris 9) that are described later in this chapter.

> The ISO C headers depend on which version of the C compiler is used with the operating system. When considering Figure 2.1, note that FreeBSD 5.2.1 ships with version 3.3.3 of gcc, Solaris 9 ships with both version 2.95.3 and version 3.2 of gcc, Mandrake 9.2 (Linux 2.4.22) ships with version 3.3.1 of gcc, and Mac OS X 10.3 ships with version 3.3 of gcc. Mac OS X also includes older versions of gcc.

2.2.2 IEEE POSIX

POSIX is a family of standards developed by the IEEE (Institute of Electrical and Electronics Engineers). POSIX stands for Portable Operating System Interface. It originally referred only to the IEEE Standard 1003.1–1988—the operating system interface—but was later extended to include many of the standards and draft standards with the 1003 designation, including the shell and utilities (1003.2).

Of specific interest to this book is the 1003.1 operating system interface standard, whose goal is to promote the portability of applications among various UNIX System environments. This standard defines the services that must be provided by an operating system if it is to be "POSIX compliant," and has been adopted by most computer vendors. Although the 1003.1 standard is based on the UNIX operating

Header	FreeBSD 5.2.1	Linux 2.4.22	Mac OS X 10.3	Solaris 9	Description
`<assert.h>`	•	•	•	•	verify program assertion
`<complex.h>`	•	•	•		complex arithmetic support
`<ctype.h>`	•	•	•	•	character types
`<errno.h>`	•	•	•	•	error codes (Section 1.7)
`<fenv.h>`		•	•		floating-point environment
`<float.h>`	•	•	•	•	floating-point constants
`<inttypes.h>`	•	•	•	•	integer type format conversion
`<iso646.h>`	•	•	•	•	alternate relational operator macros
`<limits.h>`	•	•	•	•	implementation constants (Section 2.5)
`<locale.h>`	•	•	•	•	locale categories
`<math.h>`	•	•	•	•	mathematical constants
`<setjmp.h>`	•	•	•	•	nonlocal goto (Section 7.10)
`<signal.h>`	•	•	•	•	signals (Chapter 10)
`<stdarg.h>`	•	•	•	•	variable argument lists
`<stdbool.h>`	•	•	•	•	boolean type and values
`<stddef.h>`	•	•	•	•	standard definitions
`<stdint.h>`	•	•	•		integer types
`<stdio.h>`	•	•	•	•	standard I/O library (Chapter 5)
`<stdlib.h>`	•	•	•	•	utility functions
`<string.h>`	•	•	•	•	string operations
`<tgmath.h>`		•			type-generic math macros
`<time.h>`	•	•	•	•	time and date (Section 6.10)
`<wchar.h>`	•	•	•	•	extended multibyte and wide character support
`<wctype.h>`	•	•	•	•	wide character classification and mapping support

Figure 2.1 Headers defined by the ISO C standard

system, the standard is not restricted to UNIX and UNIX-like systems. Indeed, some vendors supplying proprietary operating systems claim that these systems have been made POSIX compliant, while still leaving all their proprietary features in place.

Because the 1003.1 standard specifies an *interface* and not an *implementation*, no distinction is made between system calls and library functions. All the routines in the standard are called *functions*.

Standards are continually evolving, and the 1003.1 standard is no exception. The 1988 version of this standard, IEEE Standard 1003.1–1988, was modified and submitted to the International Organization for Standardization. No new interfaces or features were added, but the text was revised. The resulting document was published as IEEE Std 1003.1–1990 [IEEE 1990]. This is also the international standard ISO/IEC 9945–1:1990. This standard is commonly referred to as *POSIX.1*, which we'll use in this text.

The IEEE 1003.1 working group continued to make changes to the standard. In 1993, a revised version of the IEEE 1003.1 standard was published. It included 1003.1-1990 standard and the 1003.1b-1993 real-time extensions standard. In 1996, the standard was again updated as international standard ISO/IEC 9945–1:1996. It included interfaces for multithreaded programming, called *pthreads* for POSIX threads. More real-time interfaces were added in 1999 with the publication of IEEE Standard

1003.1d-1999. A year later, IEEE Standard 1003.1j-2000 was published, including even more real-time interfaces, and IEEE Standard 1003.1q-2000 was published, adding event-tracing extensions to the standard.

The 2001 version of 1003.1 departed from the prior versions in that it combined several 1003.1 amendments, the 1003.2 standard, and portions of the Single UNIX Specification (SUS), Version 2 (more on this later). The resulting standard, IEEE Standard 1003.1-2001, includes the following other standards:

- ISO/IEC 9945-1 (IEEE Standard 1003.1-1996), which includes
  - IEEE Standard 1003.1-1990
  - IEEE Standard 1003.1b-1993 (real-time extensions)
  - IEEE Standard 1003.1c-1995 (pthreads)
  - IEEE Standard 1003.1i-1995 (real-time technical corrigenda)
- IEEE P1003.1a draft standard (system interface revision)
- IEEE Standard 1003.1d-1999 (advanced real-time extensions)
- IEEE Standard 1003.1j-2000 (more advanced real-time extensions)
- IEEE Standard 1003.1q-2000 (tracing)
- IEEE Standard 1003.2d-1994 (batch extensions)
- IEEE P1003.2b draft standard (additional utilities)
- Parts of IEEE Standard 1003.1g-2000 (protocol-independent interfaces)
- ISO/IEC 9945-2 (IEEE Standard 1003.2-1993)
- The Base Specifications of the Single UNIX Specification, version 2, which include
  - System Interface Definitions, Issue 5
  - Commands and Utilities, Issue 5
  - System Interfaces and Headers, Issue 5
- Open Group Technical Standard, Networking Services, Issue 5.2
- ISO/IEC 9899:1999, Programming Languages - C

Figure 2.2, Figure 2.3, and Figure 2.4 summarize the required and optional headers as specified by POSIX.1. Because POSIX.1 includes the ISO C standard library functions, it also requires the headers listed in Figure 2.1. All four figures summarize which headers are included in the implementations discussed in this book.

In this text we describe the 2001 version of POSIX.1, which includes the functions specified in the ISO C standard. Its interfaces are divided into required ones and optional ones. The optional interfaces are further divided into 50 sections, based on functionality. The sections containing nonobsolete programming interfaces are summarized in Figure 2.5 with their respective option codes. Option codes are two- to three-character abbreviations that help identify the interfaces that belong to each functional area. The option codes highlight text on manual pages where interfaces depend on the support of a particular option. Many of the options deal with real-time extensions.

POSIX.1 does not include the notion of a superuser. Instead, certain operations require "appropriate privileges," although POSIX.1 leaves the definition of this term up to the implementation. UNIX systems that conform to the Department of Defense security guidelines have many levels of security. In this text, however, we use the traditional terminology and refer to operations that require superuser privilege.

Header	FreeBSD 5.2.1	Linux 2.4.22	Mac OS X 10.3	Solaris 9	Description
`<dirent.h>`	•	•	•	•	directory entries (Section 4.21)
`<fcntl.h>`	•	•	•	•	file control (Section 3.14)
`<fnmatch.h>`	•	•	•	•	filename-matching types
`<glob.h>`	•	•	•	•	pathname pattern-matching types
`<grp.h>`	•	•	•	•	group file (Section 6.4)
`<netdb.h>`	•	•	•	•	network database operations
`<pwd.h>`	•	•	•	•	password file (Section 6.2)
`<regex.h>`	•	•	•	•	regular expressions
`<tar.h>`	•	•	•	•	`tar` archive values
`<termios.h>`	•	•	•	•	terminal I/O (Chapter 18)
`<unistd.h>`	•	•	•	•	symbolic constants
`<utime.h>`	•	•	•	•	file times (Section 4.19)
`<wordexp.h>`	•	•		•	word-expansion types
`<arpa/inet.h>`	•	•	•	•	Internet definitions (Chapter 16)
`<net/if.h>`	•	•	•	•	socket local interfaces (Chapter 16)
`<netinet/in.h>`	•	•	•	•	Internet address family (Section 16.3)
`<netinet/tcp.h>`	•	•	•	•	Transmission Control Protocol definitions
`<sys/mman.h>`	•	•	•	•	memory management declarations
`<sys/select.h>`	•	•	•	•	`select` function (Section 14.5.1)
`<sys/socket.h>`	•	•	•	•	sockets interface (Chapter 16)
`<sys/stat.h>`	•	•	•	•	file status (Chapter 4)
`<sys/times.h>`	•	•	•	•	process times (Section 8.16)
`<sys/types.h>`	•	•	•	•	primitive system data types (Section 2.8)
`<sys/un.h>`	•	•	•	•	UNIX domain socket definitions (Section 17.3)
`<sys/utsname.h>`	•	•	•	•	system name (Section 6.9)
`<sys/wait.h>`	•	•	•	•	process control (Section 8.6)

Figure 2.2 Required headers defined by the POSIX standard

After almost twenty years of work, the standards are mature and stable. The POSIX.1 standard is maintained by an open working group known as the Austin Group (`http://www.opengroup.org/austin`). To ensure that they are still relevant, the standards need to be either updated or reaffirmed every so often.

2.2.3 The Single UNIX Specification

The Single UNIX Specification, a superset of the POSIX.1 standard, specifies additional interfaces that extend the functionality provided by the basic POSIX.1 specification. The complete set of system interfaces is called the *X/Open System Interface* (XSI). The `_XOPEN_UNIX` symbolic constant identifies interfaces that are part of the XSI extensions to the base POSIX.1 interfaces.

The XSI also defines which optional portions of POSIX.1 must be supported for an implementation to be deemed *XSI conforming*. These include file synchronization, memory-mapped files, memory protection, and thread interfaces, and are marked in Figure 2.5 as "SUS mandatory." Only XSI-conforming implementations can be called UNIX systems.

The Open Group owns the UNIX trademark and uses the Single UNIX Specification to define the interfaces an implementation must support to call itself a UNIX system. Implementations must file conformance statements, pass test suites that verify conformance, and license the right to use the UNIX trademark.

Header	FreeBSD 5.2.1	Linux 2.4.22	Mac OS X 10.3	Solaris 9	Description
`<cpio.h>`	•	•		•	cpio archive values
`<dlfcn.h>`	•	•	•	•	dynamic linking
`<fmtmsg.h>`	•	•		•	message display structures
`<ftw.h>`		•		•	file tree walking (Section 4.21)
`<iconv.h>`		•	•	•	codeset conversion utility
`<langinfo.h>`	•	•	•	•	language information constants
`<libgen.h>`	•	•	•	•	definitions for pattern-matching function
`<monetary.h>`	•	•	•	•	monetary types
`<ndbm.h>`	•		•	•	database operations
`<nl_types.h>`	•	•	•	•	message catalogs
`<poll.h>`	•	•	•	•	poll function (Section 14.5.2)
`<search.h>`	•	•	•	•	search tables
`<strings.h>`	•	•	•	•	string operations
`<syslog.h>`	•	•	•	•	system error logging (Section 13.4)
`<ucontext.h>`	•	•	•	•	user context
`<ulimit.h>`	•	•	•	•	user limits
`<utmpx.h>`		•		•	user accounting database
`<sys/ipc.h>`	•	•	•	•	IPC (Section 15.6)
`<sys/msg.h>`	•	•		•	message queues (Section 15.7)
`<sys/resource.h>`	•	•	•	•	resource operations (Section 7.11)
`<sys/sem.h>`	•	•	•	•	semaphores (Section 15.8)
`<sys/shm.h>`	•	•	•	•	shared memory (Section 15.9)
`<sys/statvfs.h>`	•	•		•	file system information
`<sys/time.h>`	•	•	•	•	time types
`<sys/timeb.h>`	•	•	•	•	additional date and time definitions
`<sys/uio.h>`	•	•	•	•	vector I/O operations (Section 14.7)

Figure 2.3 XSI extension headers defined by the POSIX standard

Header	FreeBSD 5.2.1	Linux 2.4.22	Mac OS X 10.3	Solaris 9	Description
`<aio.h>`	•	•	•	•	asynchronous I/O
`<mqueue.h>`	•				message queues
`<pthread.h>`	•	•	•	•	threads (Chapters 11 and 12)
`<sched.h>`	•	•	•	•	execution scheduling
`<semaphore.h>`	•	•	•	•	semaphores
`<spawn.h>`		•			real-time spawn interface
`<stropts.h>`		•		•	XSI STREAMS interface (Section 14.4)
`<trace.h>`					event tracing

Figure 2.4 Optional headers defined by the POSIX standard

Code	SUS mandatory	Symbolic constant	Description
ADV		_POSIX_ADVISORY_INFO	advisory information (real-time)
AIO		_POSIX_ASYNCHRONOUS_IO	asynchronous input and output (real-time)
BAR		_POSIX_BARRIERS	barriers (real-time)
CPT		_POSIX_CPUTIME	process CPU time clocks (real-time)
CS		_POSIX_CLOCK_SELECTION	clock selection (real-time)
CX	•		extension to ISO C standard
FSC	•	_POSIX_FSYNC	file synchronization
IP6		_POSIX_IPV6	IPv6 interfaces
MF	•	_POSIX_MAPPED_FILES	memory-mapped files
ML		_POSIX_MEMLOCK	process memory locking (real-time)
MLR		_POSIX_MEMLOCK_RANGE	memory range locking (real-time)
MON		_POSIX_MONOTONIC_CLOCK	monotonic clock (real-time)
MPR	•	_POSIX_MEMORY_PROTECTION	memory protection
MSG		_POSIX_MESSAGE_PASSING	message passing (real-time)
MX			IEC 60559 floating-point option
PIO		_POSIX_PRIORITIZED_IO	prioritized input and output
PS		_POSIX_PRIORITIZED_SCHEDULING	process scheduling (real-time)
RS		_POSIX_RAW_SOCKETS	raw sockets
RTS		_POSIX_REALTIME_SIGNALS	real-time signals extension
SEM		_POSIX_SEMAPHORES	semaphores (real-time)
SHM		_POSIX_SHARED_MEMORY_OBJECTS	shared memory objects (real-time)
SIO		_POSIX_SYNCHRONIZED_IO	synchronized input and output (real-time)
SPI		_POSIX_SPIN_LOCKS	spin locks (real-time)
SPN		_POSIX_SPAWN	spawn (real-time)
SS		_POSIX_SPORADIC_SERVER	process sporadic server (real-time)
TCT		_POSIX_THREAD_CPUTIME	thread CPU time clocks (real-time)
TEF		_POSIX_TRACE_EVENT_FILTER	trace event filter
THR	•	_POSIX_THREADS	threads
TMO		_POSIX_TIMEOUTS	timeouts (real-time)
TMR		_POSIX_TIMERS	timers (real-time)
TPI		_POSIX_THREAD_PRIO_INHERIT	thread priority inheritance (real-time)
TPP		_POSIX_THREAD_PRIO_PROTECT	thread priority protection (real-time)
TPS		_POSIX_THREAD_PRIORITY_SCHEDULING	thread execution scheduling (real-time)
TRC		_POSIX_TRACE	trace
TRI		_POSIX_TRACE_INHERIT	trace inherit
TRL		_POSIX_TRACE_LOG	trace log
TSA	•	_POSIX_THREAD_ATTR_STACKADDR	thread stack address attribute
TSF	•	_POSIX_THREAD_SAFE_FUNCTIONS	thread-safe functions
TSH	•	_POSIX_THREAD_PROCESS_SHARED	thread process-shared synchronization
TSP		_POSIX_THREAD_SPORADIC_SERVER	thread sporadic server (real-time)
TSS	•	_POSIX_THREAD_ATTR_STACKSIZE	thread stack address size
TYM		_POSIX_TYPED_MEMORY_OBJECTS	typed memory objects (real-time)
XSI	•	_XOPEN_UNIX	X/Open extended interfaces
XSR		_XOPEN_STREAMS	XSI STREAMS

Figure 2.5 POSIX.1 optional interface groups and codes

Some of the additional interfaces defined in the XSI are required, whereas others are optional. The interfaces are divided into *option groups* based on common functionality, as follows:

- Encryption: denoted by the `_XOPEN_CRYPT` symbolic constant

- Real-time: denoted by the `_XOPEN_REALTIME` symbolic constant

- Advanced real-time

- Real-time threads: denoted by the `_XOPEN_REALTIME_THREADS` symbolic constant

- Advanced real-time threads

- Tracing

- XSI STREAMS: denoted by the `_XOPEN_STREAMS` symbolic constant

- Legacy: denoted by the `_XOPEN_LEGACY` symbolic constant

The Single UNIX Specification (SUS) is a publication of The Open Group, which was formed in 1996 as a merger of X/Open and the Open Software Foundation (OSF), both industry consortia. X/Open used to publish the *X/Open Portability Guide*, which adopted specific standards and filled in the gaps where functionality was missing. The goal of these guides was to improve application portability past what was possible by merely conforming to published standards.

The first version of the Single UNIX Specification was published by X/Open in 1994. It was also known as "Spec 1170," because it contained roughly 1,170 interfaces. It grew out of the Common Open Software Environment (COSE) initiative, whose goal was to further improve application portability across all implementations of the UNIX operating system. The COSE group—Sun, IBM, HP, Novell/USL, and OSF—went further than endorsing standards. In addition, they investigated interfaces used by common commercial applications. The resulting 1,170 interfaces were selected from these applications, and also included the X/Open Common Application Environment (CAE), Issue 4 (known as "XPG4" as a historical reference to its predecessor, the X/Open Portability Guide), the System V Interface Definition (SVID), Edition 3, Level 1 interfaces, and the OSF Application Environment Specification (AES) Full Use interfaces.

The second version of the Single UNIX Specification was published by The Open Group in 1997. The new version added support for threads, real-time interfaces, 64-bit processing, large files, and enhanced multibyte character processing.

The third version of the Single UNIX Specification (SUSv3, for short) was published by The Open Group in 2001. The Base Specifications of SUSv3 are the same as the IEEE Standard 1003.1-2001 and are divided into four sections: Base Definitions, System Interfaces, Shell and Utilities, and Rationale. SUSv3 also includes X/Open Curses Issue 4, Version 2, but this specification is not part of POSIX.1.

In 2002, ISO approved this version as International Standard ISO/IEC 9945:2002. The Open Group updated the 1003.1 standard again in 2003 to include technical corrections, and ISO approved this as International Standard ISO/IEC 9945:2003. In April 2004, The Open Group published the Single UNIX Specification, Version 3, 2004 Edition. It included more technical corrections edited in with the main text of the standard.

2.2.4 FIPS

FIPS stands for Federal Information Processing Standard. It was published by the U.S. government, which used it for the procurement of computer systems. FIPS 151−1 (April 1989) was based on the IEEE Std. 1003.1−1988 and a draft of the ANSI C standard. This was followed by FIPS 151−2 (May 1993), which was based on the IEEE Standard 1003.1−1990. FIPS 151−2 required some features that POSIX.1 listed as optional. All these options have been included as mandatory in POSIX.1-2001.

The effect of the POSIX.1 FIPS was to require any vendor that wished to sell POSIX.1-compliant computer systems to the U.S. government to support some of the optional features of POSIX.1. The POSIX.1 FIPS has since been withdrawn, so we won't consider it further in this text.

2.3   UNIX System Implementations

The previous section described ISO C, IEEE POSIX, and the Single UNIX Specification; three standards created by independent organizations. Standards, however, are interface specifications. How do these standards relate to the real world? These standards are taken by vendors and turned into actual implementations. In this book, we are interested in both these standards and their implementation.

Section 1.1 of McKusick et al. [1996] gives a detailed history (and a nice picture) of the UNIX System family tree. Everything starts from the Sixth Edition (1976) and Seventh Edition (1979) of the UNIX Time-Sharing System on the PDP-11 (usually called Version 6 and Version 7). These were the first releases widely distributed outside of Bell Laboratories. Three branches of the tree evolved.

1. One at AT&T that led to System III and System V, the so-called commercial versions of the UNIX System.

2. One at the University of California at Berkeley that led to the 4.xBSD implementations.

3. The research version of the UNIX System, developed at the Computing Science Research Center of AT&T Bell Laboratories, that led to the UNIX Time-Sharing System 8th Edition, 9th Edition, and ended with the 10th Edition in 1990.

2.3.1   UNIX System V Release 4

UNIX System V Release 4 (SVR4) was a product of AT&T's UNIX System Laboratories (USL, formerly AT&T's UNIX Software Operation). SVR4 merged functionality from AT&T UNIX System V Release 3.2 (SVR3.2), the SunOS operating system from Sun Microsystems, the 4.3BSD release from the University of California, and the Xenix system from Microsoft into one coherent operating system. (Xenix was originally developed from Version 7, with many features later taken from System V.) The SVR4 source code was released in late 1989, with the first end-user copies becoming available during 1990. SVR4 conformed to both the POSIX 1003.1 standard and the X/Open Portability Guide, Issue 3 (XPG3).

AT&T also published the System V Interface Definition (SVID) [AT&T 1989]. Issue 3 of the SVID specified the functionality that an operating system must offer to qualify as a conforming implementation of UNIX System V Release 4. As with POSIX.1, the SVID specified an interface, not an implementation. No distinction was made in the SVID between system calls and library functions. The reference manual for an actual implementation of SVR4 must be consulted to see this distinction [AT&T 1990e].

2.3.2   4.4BSD

The Berkeley Software Distribution (BSD) releases were produced and distributed by the Computer Systems Research Group (CSRG) at the University of California at Berkeley; 4.2BSD was released in 1983 and 4.3BSD in 1986. Both of these releases ran on the VAX minicomputer. The next release, 4.3BSD Tahoe in 1988, also ran on a particular minicomputer called the Tahoe. (The book by Leffler et al. [1989] describes the 4.3BSD Tahoe release.) This was followed in 1990 with the 4.3BSD Reno release; 4.3BSD Reno supported many of the POSIX.1 features.

The original BSD systems contained proprietary AT&T source code and were covered by AT&T licenses. To obtain the source code to the BSD system you had to have a UNIX source license from AT&T. This changed as more and more of the AT&T source code was replaced over the years with non-AT&T source code and as many of the new features added to the Berkeley system were derived from non-AT&T sources.

In 1989, Berkeley identified much of the non-AT&T source code in the 4.3BSD Tahoe release and made it publicly available as the BSD Networking Software, Release 1.0. This was followed in 1991 with Release 2.0 of the BSD Networking Software, which was derived from the 4.3BSD Reno release. The intent was that most, if not all, of the 4.4BSD system would be free of any AT&T license restrictions, thus making the source code available to all.

4.4BSD-Lite was intended to be the final release from the CSRG. Its introduction was delayed, however, because of legal battles with USL. Once the legal differences were resolved, 4.4BSD-Lite was released in 1994, fully unencumbered, so no UNIX source license was needed to receive it. The CSRG followed this with a bug-fix release in 1995. This release, 4.4BSD-Lite, release 2, was the final version of BSD from the CSRG. (This version of BSD is described in the book by McKusick et al. [1996].)

The UNIX system development done at Berkeley started with PDP-11s, then moved to the VAX minicomputer, and then to other so-called workstations. During the early 1990s, support was provided to Berkeley for the popular 80386-based personal computers, leading to what is called 386BSD. This was done by Bill Jolitz and was documented in a series of monthly articles in *Dr. Dobb's Journal* throughout 1991. Much of this code appears in the BSD Networking Software, Release 2.0.

2.3.3 FreeBSD

FreeBSD is based on the 4.4BSD-Lite operating system. The FreeBSD project was formed to carry on the BSD line after the Computing Science Research Group at the University of California at Berkeley decided to end its work on the BSD versions of the UNIX operating system, and the 386BSD project seemed to be neglected for too long.

All software produced by the FreeBSD project is freely available in both binary and source forms. The FreeBSD 5.2.1 operating system was one of the four used to test the examples in this book.

> Several other BSD-based free operating systems are available. The NetBSD project (http://www.netbsd.org) is similar to the FreeBSD project, with an emphasis on portability between hardware platforms. The OpenBSD project (http://www.openbsd.org) is similar to FreeBSD but with an emphasis on security.

2.3.4 Linux

Linux is an operating system that provides a rich UNIX programming environment, and is freely available under the GNU Public License. The popularity of Linux is somewhat of a phenomenon in the computer industry. Linux is distinguished by often being the first operating system to support new hardware.

Linux was created in 1991 by Linus Torvalds as a replacement for MINIX. A grass-roots effort then sprang up, whereby many developers across the world volunteered their time to use and enhance it.

The Mandrake 9.2 distribution of Linux was one of the operating systems used to test the examples in this book. That distribution uses the 2.4.22 version of the Linux operating system kernel.

2.3.5 Mac OS X

Mac OS X is based on entirely different technology than prior versions. The core operating system is called "Darwin," and is based on a combination of the Mach kernel (Accetta et al. [1986]) and the FreeBSD operating system. Darwin is managed as an open source project, similar to FreeBSD and Linux.

Mac OS X version 10.3 (Darwin 7.4.0) was used as one of the operating systems to test the examples in this book.

2.3.6 Solaris

Solaris is the version of the UNIX System developed by Sun Microsystems. It is based on System V Release 4, with more than ten years of enhancements from the engineers at Sun Microsystems. It is the only commercially successful SVR4 descendant, and is formally certified to be a UNIX system. (For more information on UNIX certification, see http://www.opengroup.org/certification/idx/unix.html.)

The Solaris 9 UNIX system was one of the operating systems used to test the examples in this book.

2.3.7 Other UNIX Systems

Other versions of the UNIX system that have been certified in the past include

- AIX, IBM's version of the UNIX System
- HP-UX, Hewlett-Packard's version of the UNIX System
- IRIX, the UNIX System version shipped by Silicon Graphics
- UnixWare, the UNIX System descended from SVR4 and currently sold by SCO

2.4 Relationship of Standards and Implementations

The standards that we've mentioned define a subset of any actual system. The focus of this book is on four real systems: FreeBSD 5.2.1, Linux 2.4.22, Mac OS X 10.3, and Solaris 9. Although only Solaris can call itself a UNIX system, all four provide a UNIX programming environment. Because all four are POSIX compliant to varying degrees, we will also concentrate on the features that are required by the POSIX.1 standard, noting any differences between POSIX and the actual implementations of these four systems. Those features and routines that are specific to only a particular implementation are clearly marked. As SUSv3 is a superset of POSIX.1, we'll also note any features that are part of SUSv3 but not part of POSIX.1.

Be aware that the implementations provide backward compatibility for features in earlier releases, such as SVR3.2 and 4.3BSD. For example, Solaris supports both the POSIX.1 specification for nonblocking I/O (O_NONBLOCK) and the traditional System V method (O_NDELAY). In this text, we'll use only the POSIX.1 feature, although we'll mention the nonstandard feature that it replaces. Similarly, both SVR3.2 and 4.3BSD provided reliable signals in a way that differs from the POSIX.1 standard. In Chapter 10 we describe only the POSIX.1 signal mechanism.

2.5 Limits

The implementations define many magic numbers and constants. Many of these have been hard coded into programs or were determined using ad hoc techniques. With the various standardization efforts that we've described, more portable methods are now provided to determine these magic numbers and implementation-defined limits, greatly aiding the portability of our software.

Two types of limits are needed:

1. Compile-time limits (e.g., what's the largest value of a short integer?)
2. Runtime limits (e.g., how many characters in a filename?)

Compile-time limits can be defined in headers that any program can include at compile time. But runtime limits require the process to call a function to obtain the value of the limit.

Additionally, some limits can be fixed on a given implementation—and could therefore be defined statically in a header—yet vary on another implementation and would require a runtime function call. An example of this type of limit is the maximum number of characters in a filename. Before SVR4, System V historically allowed only 14 characters in a filename, whereas BSD-derived systems increased this number to 255. Most UNIX System implementations these days support multiple file system types, and each type has its own limit. This is the case of a runtime limit that depends on where in the file system the file in question is located. A filename in the root file system, for example, could have a 14-character limit, whereas a filename in another file system could have a 255-character limit.

To solve these problems, three types of limits are provided:

1. Compile-time limits (headers)

2. Runtime limits that are not associated with a file or directory (the `sysconf` function)

3. Runtime limits that are associated with a file or a directory (the `pathconf` and `fpathconf` functions)

To further confuse things, if a particular runtime limit does not vary on a given system, it can be defined statically in a header. If it is not defined in a header, however, the application must call one of the three `conf` functions (which we describe shortly) to determine its value at runtime.

Name	Description	Minimum acceptable value	Typical value
CHAR_BIT	bits in a `char`	8	8
CHAR_MAX	max value of `char`	(see later)	127
CHAR_MIN	min value of `char`	(see later)	−128
SCHAR_MAX	max value of `signed char`	127	127
SCHAR_MIN	min value of `signed char`	−127	−128
UCHAR_MAX	max value of `unsigned char`	255	255
INT_MAX	max value of `int`	32,767	2,147,483,647
INT_MIN	min value of `int`	−32,767	−2,147,483,648
UINT_MAX	max value of `unsigned int`	65,535	4,294,967,295
SHRT_MIN	min value of `short`	−32,767	−32,768
SHRT_MAX	max value of `short`	32,767	32,767
USHRT_MAX	max value of `unsigned short`	65,535	65,535
LONG_MAX	max value of `long`	2,147,483,647	2,147,483,647
LONG_MIN	min value of `long`	−2,147,483,647	−2,147,483,648
ULONG_MAX	max value of `unsigned long`	4,294,967,295	4,294,967,295
LLONG_MAX	max value of `long long`	9,223,372,036,854,775,807	9,223,372,036,854,775,807
LLONG_MIN	min value of `long long`	−9,223,372,036,854,775,807	−9,223,372,036,854,775,808
ULLONG_MAX	max value of `unsigned long long`	18,446,744,073,709,551,615	18,446,744,073,709,551,615
MB_LEN_MAX	max number of bytes in a multibyte character constant	1	16

Figure 2.6 Sizes of integral values from `<limits.h>`

2.5.1 ISO C Limits

All the limits defined by ISO C are compile-time limits. Figure 2.6 shows the limits from the C standard that are defined in the file <limits.h>. These constants are always defined in the header and don't change in a given system. The third column shows the minimum acceptable values from the ISO C standard. This allows for a system with 16-bit integers using one's-complement arithmetic. The fourth column shows the values from a Linux system with 32-bit integers using two's-complement arithmetic. Note that none of the unsigned data types has a minimum value, as this value must be 0 for an unsigned data type. On a 64-bit system, the values for long integer maximums match the maximum values for long long integers.

One difference that we will encounter is whether a system provides signed or unsigned character values. From the fourth column in Figure 2.6, we see that this particular system uses signed characters. We see that CHAR_MIN equals SCHAR_MIN and that CHAR_MAX equals SCHAR_MAX. If the system uses unsigned characters, we would have CHAR_MIN equal to 0 and CHAR_MAX equal to UCHAR_MAX.

The floating-point data types in the header <float.h> have a similar set of definitions. Anyone doing serious floating-point work should examine this file.

Another ISO C constant that we'll encounter is FOPEN_MAX, the minimum number of standard I/O streams that the implementation guarantees can be open at once. This value is in the <stdio.h> header, and its minimum value is 8. The POSIX.1 value STREAM_MAX, if defined, must have the same value as FOPEN_MAX.

ISO C also defines the constant TMP_MAX in <stdio.h>. It is the maximum number of unique filenames generated by the tmpnam function. We'll have more to say about this constant in Section 5.13.

In Figure 2.7, we show the values of FOPEN_MAX and TMP_MAX on the four platforms we discuss in this book.

> ISO C also defines the constant FILENAME_MAX, but we avoid using it, because some operating system implementations historically have defined it to be too small to be of use.

Limit	FreeBSD 5.2.1	Linux 2.4.22	Mac OS X 10.3	Solaris 9
FOPEN_MAX	20	16	20	20
TMP_MAX	308,915,776	238,328	308,915,776	17,576

Figure 2.7 ISO limits on various platforms

2.5.2 POSIX Limits

POSIX.1 defines numerous constants that deal with implementation limits of the operating system. Unfortunately, this is one of the more confusing aspects of POSIX.1. Although POSIX.1 defines numerous limits and constants, we'll only concern ourselves with the ones that affect the base POSIX.1 interfaces. These limits and constants are divided into the following five categories:

1. Invariant minimum values: the 19 constants in Figure 2.8

2. Invariant value: SSIZE_MAX

3. Runtime increasable values: CHARCLASS_NAME_MAX, COLL_WEIGHTS_MAX, LINE_MAX, NGROUPS_MAX, and RE_DUP_MAX

4. Runtime invariant values, possibly indeterminate: ARG_MAX, CHILD_MAX, HOST_NAME_MAX, LOGIN_NAME_MAX, OPEN_MAX, PAGESIZE, RE_DUP_MAX, STREAM_MAX, SYMLOOP_MAX, TTY_NAME_MAX, and TZNAME_MAX

5. Pathname variable values, possibly indeterminate: FILESIZEBITS, LINK_MAX, MAX_CANON, MAX_INPUT, NAME_MAX, PATH_MAX, PIPE_BUF, and SYMLINK_MAX

Of these 44 limits and constants, some may be defined in <limits.h>, and others may or may not be defined, depending on certain conditions. We describe the limits and constants that may or may not be defined in Section 2.5.4, when we describe the sysconf, pathconf, and fpathconf functions. The 19 invariant minimum values are shown in Figure 2.8.

Name	Description: minimum acceptable value for	Value
_POSIX_ARG_MAX	length of arguments to exec functions	4,096
_POSIX_CHILD_MAX	number of child processes per real user ID	25
_POSIX_HOST_NAME_MAX	maximum length of a host name as returned by gethostname	255
_POSIX_LINK_MAX	number of links to a file	8
_POSIX_LOGIN_NAME_MAX	maximum length of a login name	9
_POSIX_MAX_CANON	number of bytes on a terminal's canonical input queue	255
_POSIX_MAX_INPUT	space available on a terminal's input queue	255
_POSIX_NAME_MAX	number of bytes in a filename, not including the terminating null	14
_POSIX_NGROUPS_MAX	number of simultaneous supplementary group IDs per process	8
_POSIX_OPEN_MAX	number of open files per process	20
_POSIX_PATH_MAX	number of bytes in a pathname, including the terminating null	256
_POSIX_PIPE_BUF	number of bytes that can be written atomically to a pipe	512
_POSIX_RE_DUP_MAX	number of repeated occurrences of a basic regular expression permitted by the regexec and regcomp functions when using the interval notation \{m,n\}	255
_POSIX_SSIZE_MAX	value that can be stored in ssize_t object	32,767
_POSIX_STREAM_MAX	number of standard I/O streams a process can have open at once	8
_POSIX_SYMLINK_MAX	number of bytes in a symbolic link	255
_POSIX_SYMLOOP_MAX	number of symbolic links that can be traversed during pathname resolution	8
_POSIX_TTY_NAME_MAX	length of a terminal device name, including the terminating null	9
_POSIX_TZNAME_MAX	number of bytes for the name of a time zone	6

Figure 2.8 POSIX.1 invariant minimum values from <limits.h>

These values are invariant; they do not change from one system to another. They specify the most restrictive values for these features. A conforming POSIX.1 implementation must provide values that are at least this large. This is why they are called minimums, although their names all contain MAX. Also, to ensure portability, a strictly-conforming application must not require a larger value. We describe what each of these constants refers to as we proceed through the text.

> A strictly-conforming POSIX application is different from an application that is merely POSIX conforming. A POSIX-conforming application uses only interfaces defined in IEEE Standard 1003.1-2001. A strictly-conforming application is a POSIX-conforming application that does not rely on any undefined behavior, does not use any obsolescent interfaces, and does not require values of constants larger than the minimums shown in Figure 2.8.

Unfortunately, some of these invariant minimum values are too small to be of practical use. For example, most UNIX systems today provide far more than 20 open files per process. Also, the minimum limit of 255 for _POSIX_PATH_MAX is too small. Pathnames can exceed this limit. This means that we can't use the two constants _POSIX_OPEN_MAX and _POSIX_PATH_MAX as array sizes at compile time.

Each of the 19 invariant minimum values in Figure 2.8 has an associated implementation value whose name is formed by removing the _POSIX_ prefix from the name in Figure 2.8. The names without the leading _POSIX_ were intended to be the actual values that a given implementation supports. (These 19 implementation values are items 2–5 from our list earlier in this section: the invariant value, the runtime increasable value, the runtime invariant values, and the pathname variable values.) The problem is that not all of the 19 implementation values are guaranteed to be defined in the <limits.h> header.

For example, a particular value may not be included in the header if its actual value for a given process depends on the amount of memory on the system. If the values are not defined in the header, we can't use them as array bounds at compile time. So, POSIX.1 decided to provide three runtime functions for us to call—sysconf, pathconf, and fpathconf—to determine the actual implementation value at runtime. There is still a problem, however, because some of the values are defined by POSIX.1 as being possibly "indeterminate" (logically infinite). This means that the value has no practical upper bound. On Linux, for example, the number of iovec structures you can use with readv or writev is limited only by the amount of memory on the system. Thus, IOV_MAX is considered indeterminate on Linux. We'll return to this problem of indeterminate runtime limits in Section 2.5.5.

2.5.3 XSI Limits

The XSI also defines constants that deal with implementation limits. They include:

1. Invariant minimum values: the ten constants in Figure 2.9

2. Numerical limits: LONG_BIT and WORD_BIT

3. Runtime invariant values, possibly indeterminate: ATEXIT_MAX, IOV_MAX, and PAGE_SIZE

The invariant minimum values are listed in Figure 2.9. Many of these values deal with message catalogs. The last two illustrate the situation in which the POSIX.1 minimums were too small—presumably to allow for embedded POSIX.1 implementations—so the

Single UNIX Specification added symbols with larger minimum values for XSI-conforming systems.

Name	Description	Minimum acceptable value	Typical value
NL_ARGMAX	maximum value of digit in calls to printf and scanf	9	9
NL_LANGMAX	maximum number of bytes in LANG environment variable	14	14
NL_MSGMAX	maximum message number	32,767	32,767
NL_NMAX	maximum number of bytes in N-to-1 mapping characters	(none specified)	1
NL_SETMAX	maximum set number	255	255
NL_TEXTMAX	maximum number of bytes in a message string	_POSIX2_LINE_MAX	2,048
NZERO	default process priority	20	20
_XOPEN_IOV_MAX	maximum number of iovec structures that can be used with readv or writev	16	16
_XOPEN_NAME_MAX	number of bytes in a filename	255	255
_XOPEN_PATH_MAX	number of bytes in a pathname	1,024	1,024

Figure 2.9 XSI invariant minimum values from <limits.h>

2.5.4 `sysconf`, `pathconf`, and `fpathconf` Functions

We've listed various minimum values that an implementation must support, but how do we find out the limits that a particular system actually supports? As we mentioned earlier, some of these limits might be available at compile time; others must be determined at runtime. We've also mentioned that some don't change in a given system, whereas others can change because they are associated with a file or directory. The runtime limits are obtained by calling one of the following three functions.

```
#include <unistd.h>

long sysconf(int name);

long pathconf(const char *pathname, int name);

long fpathconf(int filedes, int name);
```
                    All three return: corresponding value if OK, −1 on error (see later)

The difference between the last two functions is that one takes a pathname as its argument and the other takes a file descriptor argument.

Figure 2.10 lists the *name* arguments that sysconf uses to identify system limits. Constants beginning with _SC_ are used as arguments to sysconf to identify the runtime limit. Figure 2.11 lists the *name* arguments that are used by pathconf and fpathconf to identify system limits. Constants beginning with _PC_ are used as arguments to pathconf and fpathconf to identify the runtime limit.

Name of limit	Description	*name* argument
ARG_MAX	maximum length, in bytes, of arguments to the exec functions	_SC_ARG_MAX
ATEXIT_MAX	maximum number of functions that can be registered with the atexit function	_SC_ATEXIT_MAX
CHILD_MAX	maximum number of processes per real user ID	_SC_CHILD_MAX
clock ticks/second	number of clock ticks per second	_SC_CLK_TCK
COLL_WEIGHTS_MAX	maximum number of weights that can be assigned to an entry of the LC_COLLATE order keyword in the locale definition file	_SC_COLL_WEIGHTS_MAX
HOST_NAME_MAX	maximum length of a host name as returned by gethostname	_SC_HOST_NAME_MAX
IOV_MAX	maximum number of iovec structures that can be used with readv or writev	_SC_IOV_MAX
LINE_MAX	maximum length of a utility's input line	_SC_LINE_MAX
LOGIN_NAME_MAX	maximum length of a login name	_SC_LOGIN_NAME_MAX
NGROUPS_MAX	maximum number of simultaneous supplementary process group IDs per process	_SC_NGROUPS_MAX
OPEN_MAX	maximum number of open files per process	_SC_OPEN_MAX
PAGESIZE	system memory page size, in bytes	_SC_PAGESIZE
PAGE_SIZE	system memory page size, in bytes	_SC_PAGE_SIZE
RE_DUP_MAX	number of repeated occurrences of a basic regular expression permitted by the regexec and regcomp functions when using the interval notation \{m,n\}	_SC_RE_DUP_MAX
STREAM_MAX	maximum number of standard I/O streams per process at any given time; if defined, it must have the same value as FOPEN_MAX	_SC_STREAM_MAX
SYMLOOP_MAX	number of symbolic links that can be traversed during pathname resolution	_SC_SYMLOOP_MAX
TTY_NAME_MAX	length of a terminal device name, including the terminating null	_SC_TTY_NAME_MAX
TZNAME_MAX	maximum number of bytes for the name of a time zone	_SC_TZNAME_MAX

Figure 2.10 Limits and *name* arguments to sysconf

We need to look in more detail at the different return values from these three functions.

1. All three functions return −1 and set errno to EINVAL if the *name* isn't one of the appropriate constants. The third column in Figures 2.10 and 2.11 lists the limit constants we'll deal with throughout the rest of this book.

2. Some *name*s can return either the value of the variable (a return value ≥ 0) or an indication that the value is indeterminate. An indeterminate value is indicated by returning −1 and not changing the value of errno.

3. The value returned for _SC_CLK_TCK is the number of clock ticks per second, for use with the return values from the times function (Section 8.16).

Name of limit	Description	*name* argument
FILESIZEBITS	minimum number of bits needed to represent, as a signed integer value, the maximum size of a regular file allowed in the specified directory	_PC_FILESIZEBITS
LINK_MAX	maximum value of a file's link count	_PC_LINK_MAX
MAX_CANON	maximum number of bytes on a terminal's canonical input queue	_PC_MAX_CANON
MAX_INPUT	number of bytes for which space is available on terminal's input queue	_PC_MAX_INPUT
NAME_MAX	maximum number of bytes in a filename (does not include a null at end)	_PC_NAME_MAX
PATH_MAX	maximum number of bytes in a relative pathname, including the terminating null	_PC_PATH_MAX
PIPE_BUF	maximum number of bytes that can be written atomically to a pipe	_PC_PIPE_BUF
SYMLINK_MAX	number of bytes in a symbolic link	_PC_SYMLINK_MAX

Figure 2.11 Limits and *name* arguments to pathconf and fpathconf

There are some restrictions for the *pathname* argument to pathconf and the *filedes* argument to fpathconf. If any of these restrictions isn't met, the results are undefined.

1. The referenced file for _PC_MAX_CANON and _PC_MAX_INPUT must be a terminal file.

2. The referenced file for _PC_LINK_MAX can be either a file or a directory. If the referenced file is a directory, the return value applies to the directory itself, not to the filename entries within the directory.

3. The referenced file for _PC_FILESIZEBITS and _PC_NAME_MAX must be a directory. The return value applies to filenames within the directory.

4. The referenced file for _PC_PATH_MAX must be a directory. The value returned is the maximum length of a relative pathname when the specified directory is the working directory. (Unfortunately, this isn't the real maximum length of an absolute pathname, which is what we want to know. We'll return to this problem in Section 2.5.5.)

5. The referenced file for _PC_PIPE_BUF must be a pipe, FIFO, or directory. In the first two cases (pipe or FIFO) the return value is the limit for the referenced pipe or FIFO. For the other case (a directory) the return value is the limit for any FIFO created in that directory.

6. The referenced file for _PC_SYMLINK_MAX must be a directory. The value returned is the maximum length of the string that a symbolic link in that directory can contain.

Example

The awk(1) program shown in Figure 2.12 builds a C program that prints the value of
each pathconf and sysconf symbol.

```
BEGIN   {
    printf("#include \"apue.h\"\n")
    printf("#include <errno.h>\n")
    printf("#include <limits.h>\n")
    printf("\n")
    printf("static void pr_sysconf(char *, int);\n")
    printf("static void pr_pathconf(char *, char *, int);\n")
    printf("\n")
    printf("int\n")
    printf("main(int argc, char *argv[])\n")
    printf("{\n")
    printf("\tif (argc != 2)\n")
    printf("\t\terr_quit(\"usage: a.out <dirname>\");\n\n")
    FS="\t+"
    while (getline <"sysconf.sym" > 0) {
        printf("#ifdef %s\n", $1)
        printf("\tprintf(\"%s defined to be %%d\\n\", %s+0);\n", $1, $1)
        printf("#else\n")
        printf("\tprintf(\"no symbol for %s\\n\");\n", $1)
        printf("#endif\n")
        printf("#ifdef %s\n", $2)
        printf("\tpr_sysconf(\"%s =\", %s);\n", $1, $2)
        printf("#else\n")
        printf("\tprintf(\"no symbol for %s\\n\");\n", $2)
        printf("#endif\n")
    }
    close("sysconf.sym")
    while (getline <"pathconf.sym" > 0) {
        printf("#ifdef %s\n", $1)
        printf("\tprintf(\"%s defined to be %%d\\n\", %s+0);\n", $1, $1)
        printf("#else\n")
        printf("\tprintf(\"no symbol for %s\\n\");\n", $1)
        printf("#endif\n")
        printf("#ifdef %s\n", $2)
        printf("\tpr_pathconf(\"%s =\", argv[1], %s);\n", $1, $2)
        printf("#else\n")
        printf("\tprintf(\"no symbol for %s\\n\");\n", $2)
        printf("#endif\n")
    }
    close("pathconf.sym")
    exit
}
END {
    printf("\texit(0);\n")
    printf("}\n\n")
    printf("static void\n")
```

```
        printf("pr_sysconf(char *mesg, int name)\n")
        printf("{\n")
        printf("\tlong  val;\n\n")
        printf("\tfputs(mesg, stdout);\n")
        printf("\terrno = 0;\n")
        printf("\tif ((val = sysconf(name)) < 0) {\n")
        printf("\t\tif (errno != 0) {\n")
        printf("\t\t\tif (errno == EINVAL)\n")
        printf("\t\t\t\tfputs(\" (not supported)\\n\", stdout);\n")
        printf("\t\t\telse\n")
        printf("\t\t\t\terr_sys(\"sysconf error\");\n")
        printf("\t\t} else {\n")
        printf("\t\t\tfputs(\" (no limit)\\n\", stdout);\n")
        printf("\t\t}\n")
        printf("\t} else {\n")
        printf("\t\tprintf(\" %%ld\\n\", val);\n")
        printf("\t}\n")
        printf("}\n\n")
        printf("static void\n")
        printf("pr_pathconf(char *mesg, char *path, int name)\n")
        printf("{\n")
        printf("\tlong  val;\n")
        printf("\n")
        printf("\tfputs(mesg, stdout);\n")
        printf("\terrno = 0;\n")
        printf("\tif ((val = pathconf(path, name)) < 0) {\n")
        printf("\t\tif (errno != 0) {\n")
        printf("\t\t\tif (errno == EINVAL)\n")
        printf("\t\t\t\tfputs(\" (not supported)\\n\", stdout);\n")
        printf("\t\t\telse\n")
        printf("\t\t\t\terr_sys(\"pathconf error, path = %%s\", path);\n")
        printf("\t\t} else {\n")
        printf("\t\t\tfputs(\" (no limit)\\n\", stdout);\n")
        printf("\t\t}\n")
        printf("\t} else {\n")
        printf("\t\tprintf(\" %%ld\\n\", val);\n")
        printf("\t}\n")
        printf("}\n")
}
```

Figure 2.12 Build C program to print all supported configuration limits

The awk program reads two input files—pathconf.sym and sysconf.sym—that contain lists of the limit name and symbol, separated by tabs. All symbols are not defined on every platform, so the awk program surrounds each call to pathconf and sysconf with the necessary #ifdef statements.

For example, the awk program transforms a line in the input file that looks like

```
NAME_MAX        _PC_NAME_MAX
```

into the following C code:

```
          #ifdef NAME_MAX
              printf("NAME_MAX is defined to be %d\n", NAME_MAX+0);
          #else
              printf("no symbol for NAME_MAX\n");
          #endif
          #ifdef _PC_NAME_MAX
              pr_pathconf("NAME_MAX =", argv[1], _PC_NAME_MAX);
          #else
              printf("no symbol for _PC_NAME_MAX\n");
          #endif
```

The program in Figure 2.13, generated by the awk program, prints all these limits, handling the case in which a limit is not defined.

```
#include "apue.h"
#include <errno.h>
#include <limits.h>

static void pr_sysconf(char *, int);
static void pr_pathconf(char *, char *, int);

int
main(int argc, char *argv[])
{
    if (argc != 2)
        err_quit("usage: a.out <dirname>");

#ifdef ARG_MAX
    printf("ARG_MAX defined to be %d\n", ARG_MAX+0);
#else
    printf("no symbol for ARG_MAX\n");
#endif
#ifdef _SC_ARG_MAX
    pr_sysconf("ARG_MAX =", _SC_ARG_MAX);
#else
    printf("no symbol for _SC_ARG_MAX\n");
#endif

/* similar processing for all the rest of the sysconf symbols... */

#ifdef MAX_CANON
    printf("MAX_CANON defined to be %d\n", MAX_CANON+0);
#else
    printf("no symbol for MAX_CANON\n");
#endif
#ifdef _PC_MAX_CANON
    pr_pathconf("MAX_CANON =", argv[1], _PC_MAX_CANON);
#else
    printf("no symbol for _PC_MAX_CANON\n");
#endif

/* similar processing for all the rest of the pathconf symbols... */

    exit(0);
}
```

```
static void
pr_sysconf(char *mesg, int name)
{
    long    val;

    fputs(mesg, stdout);
    errno = 0;
    if ((val = sysconf(name)) < 0) {
        if (errno != 0) {
            if (errno == EINVAL)
                fputs(" (not supported)\n", stdout);
            else
                err_sys("sysconf error");
        } else {
            fputs(" (no limit)\n", stdout);
        }
    } else {
        printf(" %ld\n", val);
    }
}

static void
pr_pathconf(char *mesg, char *path, int name)
{
    long    val;

    fputs(mesg, stdout);
    errno = 0;
    if ((val = pathconf(path, name)) < 0) {
        if (errno != 0) {
            if (errno == EINVAL)
                fputs(" (not supported)\n", stdout);
            else
                err_sys("pathconf error, path = %s", path);
        } else {
            fputs(" (no limit)\n", stdout);
        }
    } else {
        printf(" %ld\n", val);
    }
}
```

Figure 2.13 Print all possible `sysconf` and `pathconf` values

Figure 2.14 summarizes results from Figure 2.13 for the four systems we discuss in this book. The entry "no symbol" means that the system doesn't provide a corresponding _SC or _PC symbol to query the value of the constant. Thus, the limit is undefined in this case. In contrast, the entry "unsupported" means that the symbol is defined by the system but unrecognized by the `sysconf` or `pathconf` functions. The entry "no limit" means that the system defines no limit for the constant, but this doesn't mean that the limit is infinite.

Limit	FreeBSD 5.2.1	Linux 2.4.22	Mac OS X 10.3	Solaris 9 UFS file system	Solaris 9 PCFS file system
ARG_MAX	65,536	131,072	262,144	1,048,320	1,048,320
ATEXIT_MAX	32	2,147,483,647	no symbol	no limit	no limit
CHARCLASS_NAME_MAX	no symbol	2,048	no symbol	14	14
CHILD_MAX	867	999	100	7,877	7,877
clock ticks/second	128	100	100	100	100
COLL_WEIGHTS_MAX	0	255	2	10	10
FILESIZEBITS	unsupported	64	no symbol	41	unsupported
HOST_NAME_MAX	255	unsupported	no symbol	no symbol	no symbol
IOV_MAX	1,024	no limit	no symbol	16	16
LINE_MAX	2,048	2,048	2,048	2,048	2,048
LINK_MAX	32,767	32,000	32,767	32,767	1
LOGIN_NAME_MAX	17	256	no symbol	9	9
MAX_CANON	255	255	255	256	256
MAX_INPUT	255	255	255	512	512
NAME_MAX	255	255	765	255	8
NGROUPS_MAX	16	32	16	16	16
OPEN_MAX	1,735	1,024	256	256	256
PAGESIZE	4,096	4,096	4,096	8,192	8,192
PAGE_SIZE	4,096	4,096	no symbol	8,192	8,192
PATH_MAX	1,024	4,096	1,024	1,024	1,024
PIPE_BUF	512	4,096	512	5,120	5,120
RE_DUP_MAX	255	32,767	255	255	255
STREAM_MAX	1,735	16	20	256	256
SYMLINK_MAX	unsupported	no limit	no symbol	no symbol	no symbol
SYMLOOP_MAX	32	no limit	no symbol	no symbol	no symbol
TTY_NAME_MAX	255	32	no symbol	128	128
TZNAME_MAX	255	6	255	no limit	no limit

Figure 2.14 Examples of configuration limits

We'll see in Section 4.14 that UFS is the SVR4 implementation of the Berkeley fast file system. PCFS is the MS-DOS FAT file system implementation for Solaris.   □

2.5.5 Indeterminate Runtime Limits

We mentioned that some of the limits can be indeterminate. The problem we encounter is that if these limits aren't defined in the `<limits.h>` header, we can't use them at compile time. But they might not be defined at runtime if their value is indeterminate! Let's look at two specific cases: allocating storage for a pathname and determining the number of file descriptors.

Pathnames

Many programs need to allocate storage for a pathname. Typically, the storage has been allocated at compile time, and various magic numbers—few of which are the correct value—have been used by different programs as the array size: 256, 512, 1024, or the standard I/O constant BUFSIZ. The 4.3BSD constant MAXPATHLEN in the header <sys/param.h> is the correct value, but many 4.3BSD applications didn't use it.

POSIX.1 tries to help with the PATH_MAX value, but if this value is indeterminate, we're still out of luck. Figure 2.15 shows a function that we'll use throughout this text to allocate storage dynamically for a pathname.

If the constant PATH_MAX is defined in <limits.h>, then we're all set. If it's not, we need to call pathconf. The value returned by pathconf is the maximum size of a relative pathname when the first argument is the working directory, so we specify the root as the first argument and add 1 to the result. If pathconf indicates that PATH_MAX is indeterminate, we have to punt and just guess a value.

Standards prior to SUSv3 were unclear as to whether or not PATH_MAX included a null byte at the end of the pathname. If the operating system implementation conforms to one of these prior versions, we need to add 1 to the amount of memory we allocate for a pathname, just to be on the safe side.

The correct way to handle the case of an indeterminate result depends on how the allocated space is being used. If we were allocating space for a call to getcwd, for example—to return the absolute pathname of the current working directory; see Section 4.22—and if the allocated space is too small, an error is returned and errno is set to ERANGE. We could then increase the allocated space by calling realloc (see Section 7.8 and Exercise 4.16) and try again. We could keep doing this until the call to getcwd succeeded.

```
#include "apue.h"
#include <errno.h>
#include <limits.h>

#ifdef   PATH_MAX
static int  pathmax = PATH_MAX;
#else
static int  pathmax = 0;
#endif

#define SUSV3    200112L

static long posix_version = 0;

/* If PATH_MAX is indeterminate, no guarantee this is adequate */
#define PATH_MAX_GUESS  1024

char *
path_alloc(int *sizep) /* also return allocated size, if nonnull */
{
    char    *ptr;
    int size;

    if (posix_version == 0)
        posix_version = sysconf(_SC_VERSION);

    if (pathmax == 0) {      /* first time through */
        errno = 0;
```

```
        if ((pathmax = pathconf("/", _PC_PATH_MAX)) < 0) {
            if (errno == 0)
                pathmax = PATH_MAX_GUESS;    /* it's indeterminate */
            else
                err_sys("pathconf error for _PC_PATH_MAX");
        } else {
            pathmax++;         /* add one since it's relative to root */
        }
    }
    if (posix_version < SUSV3)
        size = pathmax + 1;
    else
        size = pathmax;

    if ((ptr = malloc(size)) == NULL)
        err_sys("malloc error for pathname");

    if (sizep != NULL)
        *sizep = size;
    return(ptr);
}
```

Figure 2.15 Dynamically allocate space for a pathname

Maximum Number of Open Files

A common sequence of code in a daemon process—a process that runs in the background, not connected to a terminal—is one that closes all open files. Some programs have the following code sequence, assuming the constant NOFILE was defined in the <sys/param.h> header:

```
#include  <sys/param.h>

for (i = 0; i < NOFILE; i++)
    close(i);
```

Other programs use the constant _NFILE that some versions of <stdio.h> provide as the upper limit. Some hard code the upper limit as 20.

We would hope to use the POSIX.1 value OPEN_MAX to determine this value portably, but if the value is indeterminate, we still have a problem. If we wrote the following and if OPEN_MAX was indeterminate, the loop would never execute, since sysconf would return –1:

```
#include  <unistd.h>

for (i = 0; i < sysconf(_SC_OPEN_MAX); i++)
    close(i);
```

Our best option in this case is just to close all descriptors up to some arbitrary limit, say 256. As with our pathname example, this is not guaranteed to work for all cases, but it's the best we can do. We show this technique in Figure 2.16.

```
#include "apue.h"
#include <errno.h>
#include <limits.h>

#ifdef  OPEN_MAX
static long openmax = OPEN_MAX;
#else
static long openmax = 0;
#endif

/*
 * If OPEN_MAX is indeterminate, we're not
 * guaranteed that this is adequate.
 */
#define OPEN_MAX_GUESS   256

long
open_max(void)
{
    if (openmax == 0) {       /* first time through */
        errno = 0;
        if ((openmax = sysconf(_SC_OPEN_MAX)) < 0) {
            if (errno == 0)
                openmax = OPEN_MAX_GUESS;   /* it's indeterminate */
            else
                err_sys("sysconf error for _SC_OPEN_MAX");
        }
    }

    return(openmax);
}
```

Figure 2.16 Determine the number of file descriptors

We might be tempted to call `close` until we get an error return, but the error return from `close` (`EBADF`) doesn't distinguish between an invalid descriptor and a descriptor that wasn't open. If we tried this technique and descriptor 9 was not open but descriptor 10 was, we would stop on 9 and never close 10. The `dup` function (Section 3.12) does return a specific error when `OPEN_MAX` is exceeded, but duplicating a descriptor a couple of hundred times is an extreme way to determine this value.

Some implementations will return `LONG_MAX` for limits values that are effectively unlimited. Such is the case with the Linux limit for `ATEXIT_MAX` (see Figure 2.14). This isn't a good idea, because it can cause programs to behave badly.

For example, we can use the `ulimit` command built into the Bourne-again shell to change the maximum number of files our processes can have open at one time. This generally requires special (superuser) privileges if the limit is to be effectively unlimited. But once set to infinite, `sysconf` will report `LONG_MAX` as the limit for

OPEN_MAX. A program that relies on this value as the upper bound of file descriptors to close as shown in Figure 2.16 will waste a lot of time trying to close 2,147,483,647 file descriptors, most of which aren't even in use.

Systems that support the XSI extensions in the Single UNIX Specification will provide the getrlimit(2) function (Section 7.11). It can be used to return the maximum number of descriptors that a process can have open. With it, we can detect that there is no configured upper bound to the number of open files our processes can open, so we can avoid this problem.

> The OPEN_MAX value is called runtime invariant by POSIX, meaning that its value should not change during the lifetime of a process. But on systems that support the XSI extensions, we can call the setrlimit(2) function (Section 7.11) to change this value for a running process. (This value can also be changed from the C shell with the limit command, and from the Bourne, Bourne-again, and Korn shells with the ulimit command.) If our system supports this functionality, we could change the function in Figure 2.16 to call sysconf every time it is called, not only the first time.

2.6 Options

We saw the list of POSIX.1 options in Figure 2.5 and discussed XSI option groups in Section 2.2.3. If we are to write portable applications that depend on any of these optionally-supported features, we need a portable way to determine whether an implementation supports a given option.

Just as with limits (Section 2.5), the Single UNIX Specification defines three ways to do this.

1. Compile-time options are defined in <unistd.h>.

2. Runtime options that are not associated with a file or a directory are identified with the sysconf function.

3. Runtime options that are associated with a file or a directory are discovered by calling either the pathconf or the fpathconf function.

The options include the symbols listed in the third column of Figure 2.5, as well as the symbols listed in Figures 2.17 and 2.18. If the symbolic constant is not defined, we must use sysconf, pathconf, or fpathconf to determine whether the option is supported. In this case, the *name* argument to the function is formed by replacing the _POSIX at the beginning of the symbol with _SC or _PC. For constants that begin with _XOPEN, the *name* argument is formed by prepending the string with _SC or _PC. For example, if the constant _POSIX_THREADS is undefined, we can call sysconf with the *name* argument set to _SC_THREADS to determine whether the platform supports the POSIX threads option. If the constant _XOPEN_UNIX is undefined, we can call sysconf with the *name* argument set to _SC_XOPEN_UNIX to determine whether the platform supports the XSI extensions.

If the symbolic constant is defined by the platform, we have three possibilities.

1. If the symbolic constant is defined to have the value −1, then the corresponding option is unsupported by the platform.

2. If the symbolic constant is defined to be greater than zero, then the corresponding option is supported.

3. If the symbolic constant is defined to be equal to zero, then we must call `sysconf`, `pathconf`, or `fpathconf` to determine whether the option is supported.

Figure 2.17 summarizes the options and their symbolic constants that can be used with `sysconf`, in addition to those listed in Figure 2.5.

Name of option	Description	*name* argument
`_POSIX_JOB_CONTROL`	indicates whether the implementation supports job control	`_SC_JOB_CONTROL`
`_POSIX_READER_WRITER_LOCKS`	indicates whether the implementation supports reader–writer locks	`_SC_READER_WRITER_LOCKS`
`_POSIX_SAVED_IDS`	indicates whether the implementation supports the saved set-user-ID and the saved set-group-ID	`_SC_SAVED_IDS`
`_POSIX_SHELL`	indicates whether the implementation supports the POSIX shell	`_SC_SHELL`
`_POSIX_VERSION`	indicates the POSIX.1 version	`_SC_VERSION`
`_XOPEN_CRYPT`	indicates whether the implementation supports the XSI encryption option group	`_SC_XOPEN_CRYPT`
`_XOPEN_LEGACY`	indicates whether the implementation supports the XSI legacy option group	`_SC_XOPEN_LEGACY`
`_XOPEN_REALTIME`	indicates whether the implementation supports the XSI real-time option group	`_SC_XOPEN_REALTIME`
`_XOPEN_REALTIME_THREADS`	indicates whether the implementation supports the XSI real-time threads option group	`_SC_XOPEN_REALTIME_THREADS`
`_XOPEN_VERSION`	indicates the XSI version	`_SC_XOPEN_VERSION`

Figure 2.17 Options and *name* arguments to `sysconf`

The symbolic constants used with `pathconf` and `fpathconf` are summarized in Figure 2.18. As with the system limits, there are several points to note regarding how options are treated by `sysconf`, `pathconf`, and `fpathconf`.

1. The value returned for `_SC_VERSION` indicates the four-digit year and two-digit month of the standard. This value can be 198808L, 199009L, 199506L, or some other value for a later version of the standard. The value associated with Version 3 of the Single UNIX Specification is 200112L.

Name of option	Description	*name* argument
`_POSIX_CHOWN_RESTRICTED`	indicates whether use of chown is restricted	`_PC_CHOWN_RESTRICTED`
`_POSIX_NO_TRUNC`	indicates whether pathnames longer than NAME_MAX generate an error	`_PC_NO_TRUNC`
`_POSIX_VDISABLE`	if defined, terminal special characters can be disabled with this value	`_PC_VDISABLE`
`_POSIX_ASYNC_IO`	indicates whether asynchronous I/O can be used with the associated file	`_PC_ASYNC_IO`
`_POSIX_PRIO_IO`	indicates whether prioritized I/O can be used with the associated file	`_PC_PRIO_IO`
`_POSIX_SYNC_IO`	indicates whether synchronized I/O can be used with the associated file	`_PC_SYNC_IO`

Figure 2.18 Options and *name* arguments to `pathconf` and `fpathconf`

2. The value returned for `_SC_XOPEN_VERSION` indicates the version of the XSI that the system complies with. The value associated with Version 3 of the Single UNIX Specification is 600.

3. The values `_SC_JOB_CONTROL`, `_SC_SAVED_IDS`, and `_PC_VDISABLE` no longer represent optional features. As of Version 3 of the Single UNIX Specification, these features are now required, although these symbols are retained for backward compatibility.

4. `_PC_CHOWN_RESTRICTED` and `_PC_NO_TRUNC` return −1 without changing `errno` if the feature is not supported for the specified *pathname* or *filedes*.

5. The referenced file for `_PC_CHOWN_RESTRICTED` must be either a file or a directory. If it is a directory, the return value indicates whether this option applies to files within that directory.

6. The referenced file for `_PC_NO_TRUNC` must be a directory. The return value applies to filenames within the directory.

7. The referenced file for `_PC_VDISABLE` must be a terminal file.

In Figure 2.19 we show several configuration options and their corresponding values on the four sample systems we discuss in this text. Note that several of the systems haven't yet caught up to the latest version of the Single UNIX Specification. For example, Mac OS X 10.3 supports POSIX threads but defines `_POSIX_THREADS` as

```
#define _POSIX_THREADS
```

without specifying a value. To conform to Version 3 of the Single UNIX Specification, the symbol, if defined, should be set to −1, 0, or 200112.

An entry is marked as "undefined" if the feature is not defined, i.e., the system doesn't define the symbolic constant or its corresponding `_PC` or `_SC` name. In contrast, the "defined" entry means that the symbolic constant is defined, but no value is specified, as in the preceding `_POSIX_THREADS` example. An entry is "unsupported" if the system defines the symbolic constant, but it has a value of −1, or it has a value of 0 but the corresponding `sysconf` or `pathconf` call returned −1.

Limit	FreeBSD 5.2.1	Linux 2.4.22	Mac OS X 10.3	Solaris 9	
				UFS file system	PCFS file system
`_POSIX_CHOWN_RESTRICTED`	1	1	1	1	1
`_POSIX_JOB_CONTROL`	1	1	1	1	1
`_POSIX_NO_TRUNC`	1	1	1	1	unsupported
`_POSIX_SAVED_IDS`	unsupported	1	unsupported	1	1
`_POSIX_THREADS`	200112	200112	defined	1	1
`_POSIX_VDISABLE`	255	0	255	0	0
`_POSIX_VERSION`	200112	200112	198808	199506	199506
`_XOPEN_UNIX`	unsupported	1	undefined	1	1
`_XOPEN_VERSION`	unsupported	500	undefined	3	3

Figure 2.19 Examples of configuration options

Note that `pathconf` returns a value of −1 for `_PC_NO_TRUNC` when used with a file from a PCFS file system on Solaris. The PCFS file system supports the DOS format (for floppy disks), and DOS filenames are silently truncated to the 8.3 format limit that the DOS file system requires.

2.7   Feature Test Macros

The headers define numerous POSIX.1 and XSI symbols, as we've described. But most implementations can add their own definitions to these headers, in addition to the POSIX.1 and XSI definitions. If we want to compile a program so that it depends only on the POSIX definitions and doesn't use any implementation-defined limits, we need to define the constant `_POSIX_C_SOURCE`. All the POSIX.1 headers use this constant to exclude any implementation-defined definitions when `_POSIX_C_SOURCE` is defined.

> Previous versions of the POSIX.1 standard defined the `_POSIX_SOURCE` constant. This has been superseded by the `_POSIX_C_SOURCE` constant in the 2001 version of POSIX.1.

The constants `_POSIX_C_SOURCE` and `_XOPEN_SOURCE` are called *feature test macros*. All feature test macros begin with an underscore. When used, they are typically defined in the `cc` command, as in

```
cc -D_POSIX_C_SOURCE=200112 file.c
```

This causes the feature test macro to be defined before any header files are included by the C program. If we want to use only the POSIX.1 definitions, we can also set the first line of a source file to

```
#define _POSIX_C_SOURCE  200112
```

To make the functionality of Version 3 of the Single UNIX Specification available to applications, we need to define the constant `_XOPEN_SOURCE` to be 600. This has the same effect as defining `_POSIX_C_SOURCE` to be 200112L as far as POSIX.1 functionality is concerned.

The Single UNIX Specification defines the `c99` utility as the interface to the C compilation environment. With it we can compile a file as follows:

```
c99 -D_XOPEN_SOURCE=600 file.c -o file
```

To enable the 1999 ISO C extensions in the `gcc` C compiler, we use the `-std=c99` option, as in

```
gcc -D_XOPEN_SOURCE=600 -std=c99 file.c -o file
```

Another feature test macro is `__STDC__`, which is automatically defined by the C compiler if the compiler conforms to the ISO C standard. This allows us to write C programs that compile under both ISO C compilers and non-ISO C compilers. For example, to take advantage of the ISO C prototype feature, if supported, a header could contain

```
#ifdef __STDC__
void    *myfunc(const char *, int);
#else
void    *myfunc();
#endif
```

Although most C compilers these days support the ISO C standard, this use of the `__STDC__` feature test macro can still be found in many header files.

2.8   Primitive System Data Types

Historically, certain C data types have been associated with certain UNIX system variables. For example, the major and minor device numbers have historically been stored in a 16-bit short integer, with 8 bits for the major device number and 8 bits for the minor device number. But many larger systems need more than 256 values for these device numbers, so a different technique is needed. (Indeed, Solaris uses 32 bits for the device number: 14 bits for the major and 18 bits for the minor.)

The header `<sys/types.h>` defines some implementation-dependent data types, called the *primitive system data types*. More of these data types are defined in other headers also. These data types are defined in the headers with the C `typedef` facility. Most end in `_t`. Figure 2.20 lists many of the primitive system data types that we'll encounter in this text.

By defining these data types this way, we do not build into our programs implementation details that can change from one system to another. We describe what each of these data types is used for when we encounter them later in the text.

2.9   Conflicts Between Standards

All in all, these various standards fit together nicely. Our main concern is any differences between the ISO C standard and POSIX.1, since SUSv3 is a superset of POSIX.1. There are some differences.

Type	Description
caddr_t	core address (Section 14.9)
clock_t	counter of clock ticks (process time) (Section 1.10)
comp_t	compressed clock ticks (Section 8.14)
dev_t	device numbers (major and minor) (Section 4.23)
fd_set	file descriptor sets (Section 14.5.1)
fpos_t	file position (Section 5.10)
gid_t	numeric group IDs
ino_t	i-node numbers (Section 4.14)
mode_t	file type, file creation mode (Section 4.5)
nlink_t	link counts for directory entries (Section 4.14)
off_t	file sizes and offsets (signed) (lseek, Section 3.6)
pid_t	process IDs and process group IDs (signed) (Sections 8.2 and 9.4)
ptrdiff_t	result of subtracting two pointers (signed)
rlim_t	resource limits (Section 7.11)
sig_atomic_t	data type that can be accessed atomically (Section 10.15)
sigset_t	signal set (Section 10.11)
size_t	sizes of objects (such as strings) (unsigned) (Section 3.7)
ssize_t	functions that return a count of bytes (signed) (read, write, Section 3.7)
time_t	counter of seconds of calendar time (Section 1.10)
uid_t	numeric user IDs
wchar_t	can represent all distinct character codes

Figure 2.20 Some common primitive system data types

ISO C defines the function clock to return the amount of CPU time used by a process. The value returned is a clock_t value. To convert this value to seconds, we divide it by CLOCKS_PER_SEC, which is defined in the <time.h> header. POSIX.1 defines the function times that returns both the CPU time (for the caller and all its terminated children) and the clock time. All these time values are clock_t values. The sysconf function is used to obtain the number of clock ticks per second for use with the return values from the times function. What we have is the same term, clock ticks per second, defined differently by ISO C and POSIX.1. Both standards also use the same data type (clock_t) to hold these different values. The difference can be seen in Solaris, where clock returns microseconds (hence CLOCKS_PER_SEC is 1 million), whereas sysyconf returns the value 100 for clock ticks per second.

Another area of potential conflict is when the ISO C standard specifies a function, but doesn't specify it as strongly as POSIX.1 does. This is the case for functions that require a different implementation in a POSIX environment (with multiple processes) than in an ISO C environment (where very little can be assumed about the host operating system). Nevertheless, many POSIX-compliant systems implement the ISO C function, for compatibility. The signal function is an example. If we unknowingly use the signal function provided by Solaris (hoping to write portable code that can be run in ISO C environments and under older UNIX systems), it'll provide semantics different from the POSIX.1 sigaction function. We'll have more to say about the signal function in Chapter 10.

2.10   Summary

Much has happened over the past two decades with the standardization of the UNIX programming environment. We've described the dominant standards—ISO C, POSIX, and the Single UNIX Specification—and their effect on the four implementations that we'll examine in this text: FreeBSD, Linux, Mac OS X, and Solaris. These standards try to define certain parameters that can change with each implementation, but we've seen that these limits are imperfect. We'll encounter many of these limits and magic constants as we proceed through the text.

The bibliography specifies how one can obtain copies of the standards that we've discussed.

Exercises

2.1   We mentioned in Section 2.8 that some of the primitive system data types are defined in more than one header. For example, on FreeBSD 5.2.1, `size_t` is defined in 26 different headers. Because all 26 headers could be included in a program and because ISO C does not allow multiple `typedefs` for the same name, how must the headers be written?

2.2   Examine your system's headers and list the actual data types used to implement the primitive system data types.

2.3   Update the program in Figure 2.16 to avoid the needless processing that occurs when `sysconf` returns `LONG_MAX` as the limit for `OPEN_MAX`.

3

File I/O

3.1 Introduction

We'll start our discussion of the UNIX System by describing the functions available for file I/O—open a file, read a file, write a file, and so on. Most file I/O on a UNIX system can be performed using only five functions: open, read, write, lseek, and close. We then examine the effect of various buffer sizes on the read and write functions.

The functions described in this chapter are often referred to as *unbuffered I/O*, in contrast to the standard I/O routines, which we describe in Chapter 5. The term *unbuffered* means that each read or write invokes a system call in the kernel. These unbuffered I/O functions are not part of ISO C, but are part of POSIX.1 and the Single UNIX Specification.

Whenever we describe the sharing of resources among multiple processes, the concept of an atomic operation becomes important. We examine this concept with regard to file I/O and the arguments to the open function. This leads to a discussion of how files are shared among multiple processes and the kernel data structures involved. After describing these features, we describe the dup, fcntl, sync, fsync, and ioctl functions.

3.2 File Descriptors

To the kernel, all open files are referred to by file descriptors. A file descriptor is a non-negative integer. When we open an existing file or create a new file, the kernel returns a file descriptor to the process. When we want to read or write a file, we identify the file with the file descriptor that was returned by open or creat as an argument to either read or write.

By convention, UNIX System shells associate file descriptor 0 with the standard input of a process, file descriptor 1 with the standard output, and file descriptor 2 with the standard error. This convention is used by the shells and many applications; it is not a feature of the UNIX kernel. Nevertheless, many applications would break if these associations weren't followed.

The magic numbers 0, 1, and 2 should be replaced in POSIX-compliant applications with the symbolic constants STDIN_FILENO, STDOUT_FILENO, and STDERR_FILENO. These constants are defined in the <unistd.h> header.

File descriptors range from 0 through OPEN_MAX. (Recall Figure 2.10.) Early historical implementations of the UNIX System had an upper limit of 19, allowing a maximum of 20 open files per process, but many systems increased this limit to 63.

> With FreeBSD 5.2.1, Mac OS X 10.3, and Solaris 9, the limit is essentially infinite, bounded by the amount of memory on the system, the size of an integer, and any hard and soft limits configured by the system administrator. Linux 2.4.22 places a hard limit of 1,048,576 on the number of file descriptors per process.

3.3   open **Function**

A file is opened or created by calling the open function.

```
#include <fcntl.h>

int open(const char *pathname, int oflag, ... /* mode_t mode */ );
```
                                                    Returns: file descriptor if OK, −1 on error

We show the third argument as . . ., which is the ISO C way to specify that the number and types of the remaining arguments may vary. For this function, the third argument is used only when a new file is being created, as we describe later. We show this argument as a comment in the prototype.

The *pathname* is the name of the file to open or create. This function has a multitude of options, which are specified by the *oflag* argument. This argument is formed by ORing together one or more of the following constants from the <fcntl.h> header:

O_RDONLY   Open for reading only.

O_WRONLY   Open for writing only.

O_RDWR   Open for reading and writing.

> Most implementations define O_RDONLY as 0, O_WRONLY as 1, and O_RDWR as 2, for compatibility with older programs.

One and only one of these three constants must be specified. The following constants are optional:

O_APPEND   Append to the end of file on each write. We describe this option in detail in Section 3.11.

O_CREAT   Create the file if it doesn't exist. This option requires a third argument to the open function, the *mode*, which specifies the access permission bits of the new file. (When we describe a file's access permission bits in Section 4.5, we'll see how to specify the *mode* and how it can be modified by the umask value of a process.)

O_EXCL   Generate an error if O_CREAT is also specified and the file already exists. This test for whether the file already exists and the creation of the file if it doesn't exist is an atomic operation. We describe atomic operations in more detail in Section 3.11.

O_TRUNC   If the file exists and if it is successfully opened for either write-only or read–write, truncate its length to 0.

O_NOCTTY   If the *pathname* refers to a terminal device, do not allocate the device as the controlling terminal for this process. We talk about controlling terminals in Section 9.6.

O_NONBLOCK   If the *pathname* refers to a FIFO, a block special file, or a character special file, this option sets the nonblocking mode for both the opening of the file and subsequent I/O. We describe this mode in Section 14.2.

> In earlier releases of System V, the O_NDELAY (no delay) flag was introduced. This option is similar to the O_NONBLOCK (nonblocking) option, but an ambiguity was introduced in the return value from a read operation. The no-delay option causes a read to return 0 if there is no data to be read from a pipe, FIFO, or device, but this conflicts with a return value of 0, indicating an end of file. SVR4-based systems still support the no-delay option, with the old semantics, but new applications should use the nonblocking option instead.

The following three flags are also optional. They are part of the synchronized input and output option of the Single UNIX Specification (and thus POSIX.1):

O_DSYNC   Have each write wait for physical I/O to complete, but don't wait for file attributes to be updated if they don't affect the ability to read the data just written.

O_RSYNC   Have each read operation on the file descriptor wait until any pending writes for the same portion of the file are complete.

O_SYNC   Have each write wait for physical I/O to complete, including I/O necessary to update file attributes modified as a result of the write. We use this option in Section 3.14.

> The O_DSYNC and O_SYNC flags are similar, but subtly different. The O_DSYNC flag affects a file's attributes only when they need to be updated to reflect a change in the file's data (for example, update the file's size to reflect more data). With the O_SYNC flag, data and attributes are always updated synchronously. When overwriting an existing part of a file opened with the O_DSYNC flag, the file times wouldn't be updated synchronously. In contrast, if we had opened the file with the O_SYNC flag, every write to the file would update the file's times before the write returns, regardless of whether we were writing over existing bytes or appending to the file.

Solaris 9 supports all three flags. FreeBSD 5.2.1 and Mac OS X 10.3 have a separate flag (O_FSYNC) that does the same thing as O_SYNC. Because the two flags are equivalent, FreeBSD 5.2.1 defines them to have the same value (but curiously, Mac OS X 10.3 doesn't define O_SYNC). FreeBSD 5.2.1 and Mac OS X 10.3 don't support the O_DSYNC or O_RSYNC flags. Linux 2.4.22 treats both flags the same as O_SYNC.

The file descriptor returned by open is guaranteed to be the lowest-numbered unused descriptor. This fact is used by some applications to open a new file on standard input, standard output, or standard error. For example, an application might close standard output—normally, file descriptor 1—and then open another file, knowing that it will be opened on file descriptor 1. We'll see a better way to guarantee that a file is open on a given descriptor in Section 3.12 with the dup2 function.

Filename and Pathname Truncation

What happens if NAME_MAX is 14 and we try to create a new file in the current directory with a filename containing 15 characters? Traditionally, early releases of System V, such as SVR2, allowed this to happen, silently truncating the filename beyond the 14th character. BSD-derived systems returned an error status, with errno set to ENAMETOOLONG. Silently truncating the filename presents a problem that affects more than simply the creation of new files. If NAME_MAX is 14 and a file exists whose name is exactly 14 characters, any function that accepts a *pathname* argument, such as open or stat, has no way to determine what the original name of the file was, as the original name might have been truncated.

With POSIX.1, the constant _POSIX_NO_TRUNC determines whether long filenames and long pathnames are truncated or whether an error is returned. As we saw in Chapter 2, this value can vary based on the type of the file system.

> Whether or not an error is returned is largely historical. For example, SVR4-based systems do not generate an error for the traditional System V file system, S5. For the BSD-style file system (known as UFS), however, SVR4-based systems do generate an error.
>
> As another example, see Figure 2.19. Solaris will return an error for UFS, but not for PCFS, the DOS-compatible file system, as DOS silently truncates filenames that don't fit in an 8.3 format.
>
> BSD-derived systems and Linux always return an error.

If _POSIX_NO_TRUNC is in effect, errno is set to ENAMETOOLONG, and an error status is returned if the entire pathname exceeds PATH_MAX or any filename component of the pathname exceeds NAME_MAX.

3.4   creat Function

A new file can also be created by calling the creat function.

```
#include <fcntl.h>

int creat(const char *pathname, mode_t mode);
```

                          Returns: file descriptor opened for write-only if OK, −1 on error

Note that this function is equivalent to

open (*pathname*, O_WRONLY | O_CREAT | O_TRUNC, *mode*);

> Historically, in early versions of the UNIX System, the second argument to open could be only
> 0, 1, or 2. There was no way to open a file that didn't already exist. Therefore, a separate
> system call, creat, was needed to create new files. With the O_CREAT and O_TRUNC options
> now provided by open, a separate creat function is no longer needed.

We'll show how to specify *mode* in Section 4.5 when we describe a file's access permissions in detail.

One deficiency with creat is that the file is opened only for writing. Before the new version of open was provided, if we were creating a temporary file that we wanted to write and then read back, we had to call creat, close, and then open. A better way is to use the open function, as in

open (*pathname*, O_RDWR | O_CREAT | O_TRUNC, *mode*);

3.5   close **Function**

An open file is closed by calling the close function.

```
#include <unistd.h>

int close(int filedes);
```
                                                            Returns: 0 if OK, −1 on error

Closing a file also releases any record locks that the process may have on the file. We'll discuss this in Section 14.3.

When a process terminates, all of its open files are closed automatically by the kernel. Many programs take advantage of this fact and don't explicitly close open files. See the program in Figure 1.4, for example.

3.6   lseek **Function**

Every open file has an associated "current file offset," normally a non-negative integer that measures the number of bytes from the beginning of the file. (We describe some exceptions to the "non-negative" qualifier later in this section.) Read and write operations normally start at the current file offset and cause the offset to be incremented by the number of bytes read or written. By default, this offset is initialized to 0 when a file is opened, unless the O_APPEND option is specified.

An open file's offset can be set explicitly by calling lseek.

```
#include <unistd.h>

off_t lseek(int filedes, off_t offset, int whence);
```
                                                Returns: new file offset if OK, −1 on error

The interpretation of the *offset* depends on the value of the *whence* argument.

- If *whence* is SEEK_SET, the file's offset is set to *offset* bytes from the beginning of the file.

- If *whence* is SEEK_CUR, the file's offset is set to its current value plus the *offset*. The *offset* can be positive or negative.

- If *whence* is SEEK_END, the file's offset is set to the size of the file plus the *offset*. The *offset* can be positive or negative.

Because a successful call to lseek returns the new file offset, we can seek zero bytes from the current position to determine the current offset:

```
off_t    currpos;

currpos = lseek(fd, 0, SEEK_CUR);
```

This technique can also be used to determine if a file is capable of seeking. If the file descriptor refers to a pipe, FIFO, or socket, lseek sets errno to ESPIPE and returns −1.

> The three symbolic constants—SEEK_SET, SEEK_CUR, and SEEK_END—were introduced with System V. Prior to this, *whence* was specified as 0 (absolute), 1 (relative to current offset), or 2 (relative to end of file). Much software still exists with these numbers hard coded.
>
> The character l in the name lseek means "long integer." Before the introduction of the off_t data type, the *offset* argument and the return value were long integers. lseek was introduced with Version 7 when long integers were added to C. (Similar functionality was provided in Version 6 by the functions seek and tell.)

Example

The program in Figure 3.1 tests its standard input to see whether it is capable of seeking.

```
#include "apue.h"

int
main(void)
{
    if (lseek(STDIN_FILENO, 0, SEEK_CUR) == -1)
        printf("cannot seek\n");
    else
        printf("seek OK\n");
    exit(0);
}
```

Figure 3.1 Test whether standard input is capable of seeking

If we invoke this program interactively, we get

```
$ ./a.out < /etc/motd
seek OK
$ cat < /etc/motd | ./a.out
cannot seek
$ ./a.out < /var/spool/cron/FIFO
cannot seek
```

Normally, a file's current offset must be a non-negative integer. It is possible, however, that certain devices could allow negative offsets. But for regular files, the offset must be non-negative. Because negative offsets are possible, we should be careful to compare the return value from lseek as being equal to or not equal to −1 and not test if it's less than 0.

> The /dev/kmem device on FreeBSD for the Intel x86 processor supports negative offsets.
>
> Because the offset (off_t) is a signed data type (Figure 2.20), we lose a factor of 2 in the maximum file size. If off_t is a 32-bit integer, the maximum file size is $2^{31}-1$ bytes.

lseek only records the current file offset within the kernel—it does not cause any I/O to take place. This offset is then used by the next read or write operation.

The file's offset can be greater than the file's current size, in which case the next write to the file will extend the file. This is referred to as creating a hole in a file and is allowed. Any bytes in a file that have not been written are read back as 0.

A hole in a file isn't required to have storage backing it on disk. Depending on the file system implementation, when you write after seeking past the end of the file, new disk blocks might be allocated to store the data, but there is no need to allocate disk blocks for the data between the old end of file and the location where you start writing.

Example

The program shown in Figure 3.2 creates a file with a hole in it.

```
#include "apue.h"
#include <fcntl.h>

char    buf1[] = "abcdefghij";
char    buf2[] = "ABCDEFGHIJ";

int
main(void)
{
    int     fd;

    if ((fd = creat("file.hole", FILE_MODE)) < 0)
        err_sys("creat error");

    if (write(fd, buf1, 10) != 10)
        err_sys("buf1 write error");
    /* offset now = 10 */

    if (lseek(fd, 16384, SEEK_SET) == -1)
        err_sys("lseek error");
    /* offset now = 16384 */

    if (write(fd, buf2, 10) != 10)
        err_sys("buf2 write error");
    /* offset now = 16394 */

    exit(0);
}
```

Figure 3.2 Create a file with a hole in it

Running this program gives us

```
$ ./a.out
$ ls -l file.hole                           check its size
-rw-r--r--  1 sar          16394 Nov 25 01:01 file.hole
$ od -c file.hole                           let's look at the actual contents
0000000   a   b   c   d   e   f   g   h   i   j  \0  \0  \0  \0  \0  \0
0000020  \0  \0  \0  \0  \0  \0  \0  \0  \0  \0  \0  \0  \0  \0  \0  \0
*
0040000   A   B   C   D   E   F   G   H   I   J
0040012
```

We use the od(1) command to look at the contents of the file. The -c flag tells it to print
the contents as characters. We can see that the unwritten bytes in the middle are read
back as zero. The seven-digit number at the beginning of each line is the byte offset in
octal.

To prove that there is really a hole in the file, let's compare the file we've just created
with a file of the same size, but without holes:

```
$ ls -ls file.hole file.nohole      compare sizes
  8 -rw-r--r--  1 sar          16394 Nov 25 01:01 file.hole
 20 -rw-r--r--  1 sar          16394 Nov 25 01:03 file.nohole
```

Although both files are the same size, the file without holes consumes 20 disk blocks,
whereas the file with holes consumes only 8 blocks.

In this example, we call the write function (Section 3.8). We'll have more to say
about files with holes in Section 4.12.   □

Because the offset address that lseek uses is represented by an off_t,
implementations are allowed to support whatever size is appropriate on their particular
platform. Most platforms today provide two sets of interfaces to manipulate file offsets:
one set that uses 32-bit file offsets and another set that uses 64-bit file offsets.

The Single UNIX Specification provides a way for applications to determine which
environments are supported through the sysconf function (Section 2.5.4). Figure 3.3
summarizes the sysconf constants that are defined.

Name of option	Description	*name* argument
_POSIX_V6_ILP32_OFF32	int, long, pointer, and off_t types are 32 bits.	_SC_V6_ILP32_OFF32
_POSIX_V6_ILP32_OFFBIG	int, long, and pointer types are 32 bits; off_t types are at least 64 bits.	_SC_V6_ILP32_OFFBIG
_POSIX_V6_LP64_OFF64	int types are 32 bits; long, pointer, and off_t types are 64 bits.	_SC_V6_LP64_OFF64
_POSIX_V6_LP64_OFFBIG	int types are 32 bits; long, pointer, and off_t types are at least 64 bits.	_SC_V6_LP64_OFFBIG

Figure 3.3 Data size options and *name* arguments to sysconf

The c99 compiler requires that we use the getconf(1) command to map the desired data size model to the flags necessary to compile and link our programs. Different flags and libraries might be needed, depending on the environments supported by each platform.

> Unfortunately, this is one area in which implementations haven't caught up to the standards. Confusing things further is the name changes that were made between Version 2 and Version 3 of the Single UNIX Specification.
>
> To get around this, applications can set the _FILE_OFFSET_BITS constant to 64 to enable 64-bit offsets. Doing so changes the definition of off_t to be a 64-bit signed integer. Setting _FILE_OFFSET_BITS to 32 enables 32-bit file offsets. Be aware, however, that although all four platforms discussed in this text support both 32-bit and 64-bit file offsets by setting the _FILE_OFFSET_BITS constant to the desired value, this is not guaranteed to be portable.

Note that even though you might enable 64-bit file offsets, your ability to create a file larger than 2 GB ($2^{31}-1$ bytes) depends on the underlying file system type.

3.7   read **Function**

Data is read from an open file with the read function.

```
#include <unistd.h>

ssize_t read(int filedes, void *buf, size_t nbytes);
```
                                Returns: number of bytes read, 0 if end of file, −1 on error

If the read is successful, the number of bytes read is returned. If the end of file is encountered, 0 is returned.

There are several cases in which the number of bytes actually read is less than the amount requested:

- When reading from a regular file, if the end of file is reached before the requested number of bytes has been read. For example, if 30 bytes remain until the end of file and we try to read 100 bytes, read returns 30. The next time we call read, it will return 0 (end of file).

- When reading from a terminal device. Normally, up to one line is read at a time. (We'll see how to change this in Chapter 18.)

- When reading from a network. Buffering within the network may cause less than the requested amount to be returned.

- When reading from a pipe or FIFO. If the pipe contains fewer bytes than requested, read will return only what is available.

- When reading from a record-oriented device. Some record-oriented devices, such as magnetic tape, can return up to a single record at a time.

- When interrupted by a signal and a partial amount of data has already been read. We discuss this further in Section 10.5.

The read operation starts at the file's current offset. Before a successful return, the offset is incremented by the number of bytes actually read.

POSIX.1 changed the prototype for this function in several ways. The classic definition is

```
int read(int filedes, char *buf, unsigned nbytes);
```

- First, the second argument was changed from a char * to a void * to be consistent with ISO C: the type void * is used for generic pointers.

- Next, the return value must be a signed integer (ssize_t) to return a positive byte count, 0 (for end of file), or −1 (for an error).

- Finally, the third argument historically has been an unsigned integer, to allow a 16-bit implementation to read or write up to 65,534 bytes at a time. With the 1990 POSIX.1 standard, the primitive system data type ssize_t was introduced to provide the signed return value, and the unsigned size_t was used for the third argument. (Recall the SSIZE_MAX constant from Section 2.5.2.)

3.8   write **Function**

Data is written to an open file with the write function.

```
#include <unistd.h>

ssize_t write(int filedes, const void *buf, size_t nbytes);
```
                              Returns: number of bytes written if OK, −1 on error

The return value is usually equal to the *nbytes* argument; otherwise, an error has occurred. A common cause for a write error is either filling up a disk or exceeding the file size limit for a given process (Section 7.11 and Exercise 10.11).

For a regular file, the write starts at the file's current offset. If the O_APPEND option was specified when the file was opened, the file's offset is set to the current end of file before each write operation. After a successful write, the file's offset is incremented by the number of bytes actually written.

3.9   I/O Efficiency

The program in Figure 3.4 copies a file, using only the read and write functions. The following caveats apply to this program.

- It reads from standard input and writes to standard output, assuming that these have been set up by the shell before this program is executed. Indeed, all normal UNIX system shells provide a way to open a file for reading on standard input and to create (or rewrite) a file on standard output. This prevents the program from having to open the input and output files.

```
#include "apue.h"

#define BUFFSIZE    4096

int
main(void)
{
    int     n;
    char    buf[BUFFSIZE];

    while ((n = read(STDIN_FILENO, buf, BUFFSIZE)) > 0)
        if (write(STDOUT_FILENO, buf, n) != n)
            err_sys("write error");

    if (n < 0)
        err_sys("read error");

    exit(0);
}
```

Figure 3.4 Copy standard input to standard output

- Many applications assume that standard input is file descriptor 0 and that standard output is file descriptor 1. In this example, we use the two defined names, STDIN_FILENO and STDOUT_FILENO, from <unistd.h>.

- The program doesn't close the input file or output file. Instead, the program uses the feature of the UNIX kernel that closes all open file descriptors in a process when that process terminates.

- This example works for both text files and binary files, since there is no difference between the two to the UNIX kernel.

One question we haven't answered, however, is how we chose the BUFFSIZE value. Before answering that, let's run the program using different values for BUFFSIZE. Figure 3.5 shows the results for reading a 103,316,352-byte file, using 20 different buffer sizes.

The file was read using the program shown in Figure 3.4, with standard output redirected to /dev/null. The file system used for this test was the Linux ext2 file system with 4,096-byte blocks. (The st_blksize value, which we describe in Section 4.12, is 4,096.) This accounts for the minimum in the system time occurring at a BUFFSIZE of 4,096. Increasing the buffer size beyond this has little positive effect.

Most file systems support some kind of read-ahead to improve performance. When sequential reads are detected, the system tries to read in more data than an application requests, assuming that the application will read it shortly. From the last few entries in Figure 3.5, it appears that read-ahead in ext2 stops having an effect after 128 KB.

We'll return to this timing example later in the text. In Section 3.14, we show the effect of synchronous writes; in Section 5.8, we compare these unbuffered I/O times with the standard I/O library.

BUFFSIZE	User CPU (seconds)	System CPU (seconds)	Clock time (seconds)	#loops
1	124.89	161.65	288.64	103,316,352
2	63.10	80.96	145.81	51,658,176
4	31.84	40.00	72.75	25,829,088
8	15.17	21.01	36.85	12,914,544
16	7.86	10.27	18.76	6,457,272
32	4.13	5.01	9.76	3,228,636
64	2.11	2.48	6.76	1,614,318
128	1.01	1.27	6.82	807,159
256	0.56	0.62	6.80	403,579
512	0.27	0.41	7.03	201,789
1,024	0.17	0.23	7.84	100,894
2,048	0.05	0.19	6.82	50,447
4,096	0.03	0.16	6.86	25,223
8,192	0.01	0.18	6.67	12,611
16,384	0.02	0.18	6.87	6,305
32,768	0.00	0.16	6.70	3,152
65,536	0.02	0.19	6.92	1,576
131,072	0.00	0.16	6.84	788
262,144	0.01	0.25	7.30	394
524,288	0.00	0.22	7.35	198

Figure 3.5 Timing results for reading with different buffer sizes on Linux

Beware when trying to measure the performance of programs that read and write files. The operating system will try to cache the file in core, so if you measure the performance of the program repeatedly, the successive timings will likely be better than the first. This is because the first run will cause the file to be entered into the system's cache, and successive runs will access the file from the system's cache instead of from the disk. (The term *incore* means *in main memory*. Back in the day, a computer's main memory was built out of ferrite core. This is where the phrase "core dump" comes from: the main memory image of a program stored in a file on disk for diagnosis.)

In the tests reported in Figure 3.5, each run with a different buffer size was made using a different copy of the file so that the current run didn't find the data in the cache from the previous run. The files are large enough that they all don't remain in the cache (the test system was configured with 512 MB of RAM).

3.10 File Sharing

The UNIX System supports the sharing of open files among different processes. Before describing the dup function, we need to describe this sharing. To do this, we'll examine the data structures used by the kernel for all I/O.

The following description is conceptual. It may or may not match a particular implementation. Refer to Bach [1986] for a discussion of these structures in System V. McKusick et al. [1996] describes these structures in 4.4BSD. McKusick and Neville-Neil [2005] cover FreeBSD 5.2. For a similar discussion of Solaris, see Mauro and McDougall [2001].

The kernel uses three data structures to represent an open file, and the relationships among them determine the effect one process has on another with regard to file sharing.

1. Every process has an entry in the process table. Within each process table entry is a table of open file descriptors, which we can think of as a vector, with one entry per descriptor. Associated with each file descriptor are

    (a) The file descriptor flags (close-on-exec; refer to Figure 3.6 and Section 3.14)

    (b) A pointer to a file table entry

2. The kernel maintains a file table for all open files. Each file table entry contains

    (a) The file status flags for the file, such as read, write, append, sync, and nonblocking; more on these in Section 3.14

    (b) The current file offset

    (c) A pointer to the v-node table entry for the file

3. Each open file (or device) has a v-node structure that contains information about the type of file and pointers to functions that operate on the file. For most files, the v-node also contains the i-node for the file. This information is read from disk when the file is opened, so that all the pertinent information about the file is readily available. For example, the i-node contains the owner of the file, the size of the file, pointers to where the actual data blocks for the file are located on disk, and so on. (We talk more about i-nodes in Section 4.14 when we describe the typical UNIX file system in more detail.)

> Linux has no v-node. Instead, a generic i-node structure is used. Although the implementations differ, the v-node is conceptually the same as a generic i-node. Both point to an i-node structure specific to the file system.

We're ignoring some implementation details that don't affect our discussion. For example, the table of open file descriptors can be stored in the user area instead of the process table. These tables can be implemented in numerous ways—they need not be arrays; they could be implemented as linked lists of structures, for example. These implementation details don't affect our discussion of file sharing.

Figure 3.6 shows a pictorial arrangement of these three tables for a single process that has two different files open: one file is open on standard input (file descriptor 0), and the other is open on standard output (file descriptor 1). The arrangement of these three tables has existed since the early versions of the UNIX System [Thompson 1978], and this arrangement is critical to the way files are shared among processes. We'll return to this figure in later chapters, when we describe additional ways that files are shared.

> The v-node was invented to provide support for multiple file system types on a single computer system. This work was done independently by Peter Weinberger (Bell Laboratories) and Bill Joy (Sun Microsystems). Sun called this the Virtual File System and called the file system–independent portion of the i-node the v-node [Kleiman 1986]. The v-node propagated through various vendor implementations as support for Sun's Network File System (NFS) was

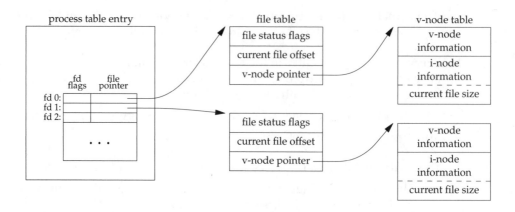

Figure 3.6 Kernel data structures for open files

added. The first release from Berkeley to provide v-nodes was the 4.3BSD Reno release, when NFS was added.

In SVR4, the v-node replaced the file system–independent i-node of SVR3. Solaris is derived from SVR4 and thus uses v-nodes.

Instead of splitting the data structures into a v-node and an i-node, Linux uses a file system–independent i-node and a file system–dependent i-node.

If two independent processes have the same file open, we could have the arrangement shown in Figure 3.7. We assume here that the first process has the file open on descriptor 3 and that the second process has that same file open on descriptor 4. Each process that opens the file gets its own file table entry, but only a single v-node table entry is required for a given file. One reason each process gets its own file table entry is so that each process has its own current offset for the file.

Given these data structures, we now need to be more specific about what happens with certain operations that we've already described.

- After each `write` is complete, the current file offset in the file table entry is incremented by the number of bytes written. If this causes the current file offset to exceed the current file size, the current file size in the i-node table entry is set to the current file offset (for example, the file is extended).

- If a file is opened with the `O_APPEND` flag, a corresponding flag is set in the file status flags of the file table entry. Each time a `write` is performed for a file with this append flag set, the current file offset in the file table entry is first set to the current file size from the i-node table entry. This forces every `write` to be appended to the current end of file.

- If a file is positioned to its current end of file using `lseek`, all that happens is the current file offset in the file table entry is set to the current file size from the i-node table entry. (Note that this is not the same as if the file was opened with the `O_APPEND` flag, as we will see in Section 3.11.)

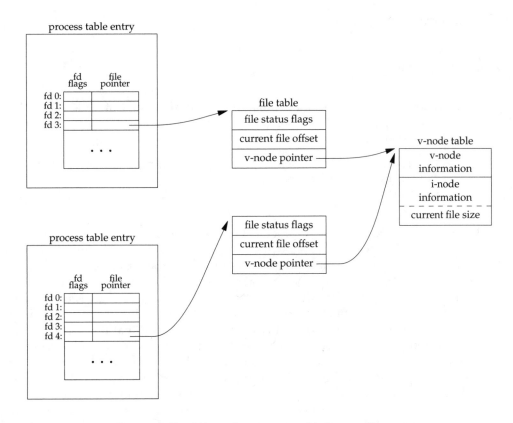

Figure 3.7 Two independent processes with the same file open

- The lseek function modifies only the current file offset in the file table entry. No I/O takes place.

It is possible for more than one file descriptor entry to point to the same file table entry, as we'll see when we discuss the dup function in Section 3.12. This also happens after a fork when the parent and the child share the same file table entry for each open descriptor (Section 8.3).

Note the difference in scope between the file descriptor flags and the file status flags. The former apply only to a single descriptor in a single process, whereas the latter apply to all descriptors in any process that point to the given file table entry. When we describe the fcntl function in Section 3.14, we'll see how to fetch and modify both the file descriptor flags and the file status flags.

Everything that we've described so far in this section works fine for multiple processes that are reading the same file. Each process has its own file table entry with its own current file offset. Unexpected results can arise, however, when multiple processes write to the same file. To see how to avoid some surprises, we need to understand the concept of atomic operations.

3.11 Atomic Operations

Appending to a File

Consider a single process that wants to append to the end of a file. Older versions of the UNIX System didn't support the O_APPEND option to open, so the program was coded as follows:

```
if (lseek(fd, 0L, 2) < 0)            /* position to EOF */
    err_sys("lseek error");
if (write(fd, buf, 100) != 100)     /* and write */
    err_sys("write error");
```

This works fine for a single process, but problems arise if multiple processes use this technique to append to the same file. (This scenario can arise if multiple instances of the same program are appending messages to a log file, for example.)

Assume that two independent processes, A and B, are appending to the same file. Each has opened the file but *without* the O_APPEND flag. This gives us the same picture as Figure 3.7. Each process has its own file table entry, but they share a single v-node table entry. Assume that process A does the lseek and that this sets the current offset for the file for process A to byte offset 1,500 (the current end of file). Then the kernel switches processes, and B continues running. Process B then does the lseek, which sets the current offset for the file for process B to byte offset 1,500 also (the current end of file). Then B calls write, which increments B's current file offset for the file to 1,600. Because the file's size has been extended, the kernel also updates the current file size in the v-node to 1,600. Then the kernel switches processes and A resumes. When A calls write, the data is written starting at the current file offset for A, which is byte offset 1,500. This overwrites the data that B wrote to the file.

The problem here is that our logical operation of "position to the end of file and write" requires two separate function calls (as we've shown it). The solution is to have the positioning to the current end of file and the write be an atomic operation with regard to other processes. Any operation that requires more than one function call cannot be atomic, as there is always the possibility that the kernel can temporarily suspend the process between the two function calls (as we assumed previously).

The UNIX System provides an atomic way to do this operation if we set the O_APPEND flag when a file is opened. As we described in the previous section, this causes the kernel to position the file to its current end of file before each write. We no longer have to call lseek before each write.

pread and pwrite Functions

The Single UNIX Specification includes XSI extensions that allow applications to seek and perform I/O atomically. These extensions are pread and pwrite.

```
#include <unistd.h>

ssize_t pread(int filedes, void *buf, size_t nbytes, off_t offset);
```
>   Returns: number of bytes read, 0 if end of file, −1 on error

```
ssize_t pwrite(int filedes, const void *buf, size_t nbytes, off_t offset);
```
>   Returns: number of bytes written if OK, −1 on error

Calling `pread` is equivalent to calling `lseek` followed by a call to `read`, with the following exceptions.

- There is no way to interrupt the two operations using `pread`.
- The current file offset is not updated.

Calling `pwrite` is equivalent to calling `lseek` followed by a call to `write`, with similar exceptions.

Creating a File

We saw another example of an atomic operation when we described the `O_CREAT` and `O_EXCL` options for the `open` function. When both of these options are specified, the open will fail if the file already exists. We also said that the check for the existence of the file and the creation of the file was performed as an atomic operation. If we didn't have this atomic operation, we might try

```
if ((fd = open(pathname, O_WRONLY)) < 0) {
    if (errno == ENOENT) {
        if ((fd = creat(pathname, mode)) < 0)
            err_sys("creat error");
    } else {
        err_sys("open error");
    }
}
```

The problem occurs if the file is created by another process between the `open` and the `creat`. If the file is created by another process between these two function calls, and if that other process writes something to the file, that data is erased when this `creat` is executed. Combining the test for existence and the creation into a single atomic operation avoids this problem.

In general, the term *atomic operation* refers to an operation that might be composed of multiple steps. If the operation is performed atomically, either all the steps are performed, or none are performed. It must not be possible for a subset of the steps to be performed. We'll return to the topic of atomic operations when we describe the `link` function (Section 4.15) and record locking (Section 14.3).

3.12   `dup` and `dup2` Functions

An existing file descriptor is duplicated by either of the following functions.

```
#include <unistd.h>

int dup(int filedes);

int dup2(int filedes, int filedes2);
```
Both return: new file descriptor if OK, −1 on error

The new file descriptor returned by `dup` is guaranteed to be the lowest-numbered available file descriptor. With `dup2`, we specify the value of the new descriptor with the *filedes2* argument. If *filedes2* is already open, it is first closed. If *filedes* equals *filedes2*, then `dup2` returns *filedes2* without closing it.

The new file descriptor that is returned as the value of the functions shares the same file table entry as the *filedes* argument. We show this in Figure 3.8.

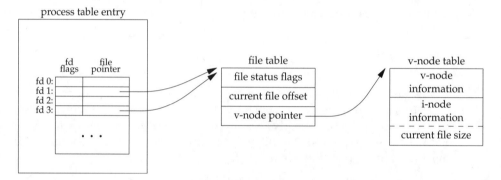

Figure 3.8   Kernel data structures after dup(1)

In this figure, we're assuming that when it's started, the process executes

```
newfd = dup(1);
```

We assume that the next available descriptor is 3 (which it probably is, since 0, 1, and 2 are opened by the shell). Because both descriptors point to the same file table entry, they share the same file status flags—read, write, append, and so on—and the same current file offset.

Each descriptor has its own set of file descriptor flags. As we describe in the next section, the close-on-exec file descriptor flag for the new descriptor is always cleared by the `dup` functions.

Another way to duplicate a descriptor is with the `fcntl` function, which we describe in Section 3.14. Indeed, the call

```
dup(filedes);
```

is equivalent to

```
fcntl(filedes, F_DUPFD, 0);
```

Similarly, the call

```
dup2(filedes, filedes2);
```

is equivalent to

```
close(filedes2);
fcntl(filedes, F_DUPFD, filedes2);
```

In this last case, the dup2 is not exactly the same as a close followed by an fcntl. The differences are as follows.

1. dup2 is an atomic operation, whereas the alternate form involves two function calls. It is possible in the latter case to have a signal catcher called between the close and the fcntl that could modify the file descriptors. (We describe signals in Chapter 10.)

2. There are some errno differences between dup2 and fcntl.

> The dup2 system call originated with Version 7 and propagated through the BSD releases. The fcntl method for duplicating file descriptors appeared with System III and continued with System V. SVR3.2 picked up the dup2 function, and 4.2BSD picked up the fcntl function and the F_DUPFD functionality. POSIX.1 requires both dup2 and the F_DUPFD feature of fcntl.

3.13   sync, fsync, **and** fdatasync **Functions**

Traditional implementations of the UNIX System have a buffer cache or page cache in the kernel through which most disk I/O passes. When we write data to a file, the data is normally copied by the kernel into one of its buffers and queued for writing to disk at some later time. This is called *delayed write*. (Chapter 3 of Bach [1986] discusses this buffer cache in detail.)

The kernel eventually writes all the delayed-write blocks to disk, normally when it needs to reuse the buffer for some other disk block. To ensure consistency of the file system on disk with the contents of the buffer cache, the sync, fsync, and fdatasync functions are provided.

```
#include <unistd.h>

int fsync(int filedes);

int fdatasync(int filedes);
```
                                                  Returns: 0 if OK, −1 on error
```
void sync(void);
```

The sync function simply queues all the modified block buffers for writing and returns; it does not wait for the disk writes to take place.

The function sync is normally called periodically (usually every 30 seconds) from a system daemon, often called update. This guarantees regular flushing of the kernel's block buffers. The command sync(1) also calls the sync function.

The function fsync refers only to a single file, specified by the file descriptor *filedes*, and waits for the disk writes to complete before returning. The intended use of fsync is for an application, such as a database, that needs to be sure that the modified blocks have been written to the disk.

The fdatasync function is similar to fsync, but it affects only the data portions of a file. With fsync, the file's attributes are also updated synchronously.

> All four of the platforms described in this book support sync and fsync. However, FreeBSD
> 5.2.1 and Mac OS X 10.3 do not support fdatasync.

3.14   fcntl **Function**

The fcntl function can change the properties of a file that is already open.

```
#include <fcntl.h>

int fcntl(int filedes, int cmd, ... /* int arg */ );
```
                                    Returns: depends on *cmd* if OK (see following), −1 on error

In the examples in this section, the third argument is always an integer, corresponding to the comment in the function prototype just shown. But when we describe record locking in Section 14.3, the third argument becomes a pointer to a structure.

The fcntl function is used for five different purposes.

1.   Duplicate an existing descriptor (*cmd* = F_DUPFD)
2.   Get/set file descriptor flags (*cmd* = F_GETFD or F_SETFD)
3.   Get/set file status flags (*cmd* = F_GETFL or F_SETFL)
4.   Get/set asynchronous I/O ownership (*cmd* = F_GETOWN or F_SETOWN)
5.   Get/set record locks (*cmd* = F_GETLK, F_SETLK, or F_SETLKW)

We'll now describe the first seven of these ten *cmd* values. (We'll wait until Section 14.3 to describe the last three, which deal with record locking.) Refer to Figure 3.6, since we'll be referring to both the file descriptor flags associated with each file descriptor in the process table entry and the file status flags associated with each file table entry.

F_DUPFD   Duplicate the file descriptor *filedes*. The new file descriptor is returned as the value of the function. It is the lowest-numbered descriptor that is not already open, that is greater than or equal to the third argument (taken as an integer). The new descriptor shares the same file table entry as *filedes*. (Refer to Figure 3.8.) But the new descriptor has its own set of file descriptor flags, and its FD_CLOEXEC file descriptor flag is cleared. (This means that the descriptor is left open across an exec, which we discuss in Chapter 8.)

F_GETFD   Return the file descriptor flags for *filedes* as the value of the function. Currently, only one file descriptor flag is defined: the FD_CLOEXEC flag.

F_SETFD   Set the file descriptor flags for *filedes*. The new flag value is set from the third argument (taken as an integer).

> Be aware that some existing programs that deal with the file descriptor flags don't use the constant FD_CLOEXEC. Instead, the programs set the flag to either 0 (don't close-on-exec, the default) or 1 (do close-on-exec).

F_GETFL   Return the file status flags for *filedes* as the value of the function. We described the file status flags when we described the open function. They are listed in Figure 3.9.

File status flag	Description
O_RDONLY	open for reading only
O_WRONLY	open for writing only
O_RDWR	open for reading and writing
O_APPEND	append on each write
O_NONBLOCK	nonblocking mode
O_SYNC	wait for writes to complete (data and attributes)
O_DSYNC	wait for writes to complete (data only)
O_RSYNC	synchronize reads and writes
O_FSYNC	wait for writes to complete (FreeBSD and Mac OS X only)
O_ASYNC	asynchronous I/O (FreeBSD and Mac OS X only)

Figure 3.9 File status flags for fcntl

Unfortunately, the three access-mode flags—O_RDONLY, O_WRONLY, and O_RDWR—are not separate bits that can be tested. (As we mentioned earlier, these three often have the values 0, 1, and 2, respectively, for historical reasons. Also, these three values are mutually exclusive; a file can have only one of the three enabled.) Therefore, we must first use the O_ACCMODE mask to obtain the access-mode bits and then compare the result against any of the three values.

F_SETFL   Set the file status flags to the value of the third argument (taken as an integer). The only flags that can be changed are O_APPEND, O_NONBLOCK, O_SYNC, O_DSYNC, O_RSYNC, O_FSYNC, and O_ASYNC.

F_GETOWN   Get the process ID or process group ID currently receiving the SIGIO and SIGURG signals. We describe these asynchronous I/O signals in Section 14.6.2.

F_SETOWN   Set the process ID or process group ID to receive the SIGIO and SIGURG signals. A positive *arg* specifies a process ID. A negative *arg* implies a process group ID equal to the absolute value of *arg*.

The return value from fcntl depends on the command. All commands return −1 on an error or some other value if OK. The following four commands have special return values: F_DUPFD, F_GETFD, F_GETFL, and F_GETOWN. The first returns the new file descriptor, the next two return the corresponding flags, and the final one returns a positive process ID or a negative process group ID.

Example

The program in Figure 3.10 takes a single command-line argument that specifies a file descriptor and prints a description of selected file flags for that descriptor.

```
#include "apue.h"
#include <fcntl.h>

int
main(int argc, char *argv[])
{
    int     val;

    if (argc != 2)
        err_quit("usage: a.out <descriptor#>");

    if ((val = fcntl(atoi(argv[1]), F_GETFL, 0)) < 0)
        err_sys("fcntl error for fd %d", atoi(argv[1]));

    switch (val & O_ACCMODE) {
    case O_RDONLY:
        printf("read only");
        break;

    case O_WRONLY:
        printf("write only");
        break;

    case O_RDWR:
        printf("read write");
        break;

    default:
        err_dump("unknown access mode");
    }

    if (val & O_APPEND)
        printf(", append");
    if (val & O_NONBLOCK)
        printf(", nonblocking");
#if defined(O_SYNC)
    if (val & O_SYNC)
        printf(", synchronous writes");
#endif
#if !defined(_POSIX_C_SOURCE) && defined(O_FSYNC)
    if (val & O_FSYNC)
        printf(", synchronous writes");
#endif
    putchar('\n');
    exit(0);
}
```

Figure 3.10 Print file flags for specified descriptor

Note that we use the feature test macro _POSIX_C_SOURCE and conditionally compile the file access flags that are not part of POSIX.1. The following script shows the operation of the program, when invoked from bash (the Bourne-again shell). Results vary, depending on which shell you use.

```
$ ./a.out 0 < /dev/tty
read only
$ ./a.out 1 > temp.foo
$ cat temp.foo
write only
$ ./a.out 2 2>>temp.foo
write only, append
$ ./a.out 5 5<>temp.foo
read write
```

The clause 5<>temp.foo opens the file temp.foo for reading and writing on file descriptor 5.   □

Example

When we modify either the file descriptor flags or the file status flags, we must be careful to fetch the existing flag value, modify it as desired, and then set the new flag value. We can't simply do an F_SETFD or an F_SETFL, as this could turn off flag bits that were previously set.

Figure 3.11 shows a function that sets one or more of the file status flags for a descriptor.

```
#include "apue.h"
#include <fcntl.h>

void
set_fl(int fd, int flags) /* flags are file status flags to turn on */
{
    int     val;

    if ((val = fcntl(fd, F_GETFL, 0)) < 0)
        err_sys("fcntl F_GETFL error");

    val |= flags;          /* turn on flags */

    if (fcntl(fd, F_SETFL, val) < 0)
        err_sys("fcntl F_SETFL error");
}
```

Figure 3.11 Turn on one or more of the file status flags for a descriptor

If we change the middle statement to

```
    val &= ~flags;       /* turn flags off */
```

we have a function named clr_fl, which we'll use in some later examples. This statement logically ANDs the one's complement of flags with the current val.

If we call `set_fl` from Figure 3.4 by adding the line

```
set_fl(STDOUT_FILENO, O_SYNC);
```

at the beginning of the program, we'll turn on the synchronous-write flag. This causes each `write` to wait for the data to be written to disk before returning. Normally in the UNIX System, a `write` only queues the data for writing; the actual disk write operation can take place sometime later. A database system is a likely candidate for using `O_SYNC`, so that it knows on return from a `write` that the data is actually on the disk, in case of an abnormal system failure.

We expect the `O_SYNC` flag to increase the clock time when the program runs. To test this, we can run the program in Figure 3.4, copying 98.5 MB of data from one file on disk to another and compare this with a version that does the same thing with the `O_SYNC` flag set. The results from a Linux system using the `ext2` file system are shown in Figure 3.12.

Operation	User CPU (seconds)	System CPU (seconds)	Clock time (seconds)
read time from Figure 3.5 for BUFFSIZE = 4,096	0.03	0.16	6.86
normal write to disk file	0.02	0.30	6.87
write to disk file with O_SYNC set	0.03	0.30	6.83
write to disk followed by fdatasync	0.03	0.42	18.28
write to disk followed by fsync	0.03	0.37	17.95
write to disk with O_SYNC set followed by fsync	0.05	0.44	17.95

Figure 3.12 Linux `ext2` timing results using various synchronization mechanisms

The six rows in Figure 3.12 were all measured with a BUFFSIZE of 4,096. The results in Figure 3.5 were measured reading a disk file and writing to /dev/null, so there was no disk output. The second row in Figure 3.12 corresponds to reading a disk file and writing to another disk file. This is why the first and second rows in Figure 3.12 are different. The system time increases when we write to a disk file, because the kernel now copies the data from our process and queues the data for writing by the disk driver. We expect the clock time to increase also when we write to a disk file, but it doesn't increase significantly for this test, which indicates that our writes go to the system cache, and we don't measure the cost to actually write the data to disk.

When we enable synchronous writes, the system time and the clock time should increase significantly. As the third row shows, the time for writing synchronously is about the same as when we used delayed writes. This implies that the Linux `ext2` file system isn't honoring the `O_SYNC` flag. This suspicion is supported by the sixth line, which shows that the time to do synchronous writes followed by a call to `fsync` is just as large as calling `fsync` after writing the file without synchronous writes (line 5). After writing a file synchronously, we expect that a call to `fsync` will have no effect.

Figure 3.13 shows timing results for the same tests on Mac OS X 10.3. Note that the times match our expectations: synchronous writes are far more expensive than delayed writes, and using `fsync` with synchronous writes makes no measurable difference. Note also that adding a call to `fsync` at the end of the delayed writes makes no measurable difference. It is likely that the operating system flushed previously written data to disk as we were writing new data to the file, so by the time that we called fsync, very little work was left to be done.

Operation	User CPU (seconds)	System CPU (seconds)	Clock time (seconds)
write to /dev/null	0.06	0.79	4.33
normal write to disk file	0.05	3.56	14.40
write to disk file with O_FSYNC set	0.13	9.53	22.48
write to disk followed by fsync	0.11	3.31	14.12
write to disk with O_FSYNC set followed by fsync	0.17	9.14	22.12

Figure 3.13 Mac OS X timing results using various synchronization mechanisms

Compare fsync and fdatasync, which update a file's contents when we say so, with the O_SYNC flag, which updates a file's contents every time we write to the file. □

With this example, we see the need for fcntl. Our program operates on a descriptor (standard output), never knowing the name of the file that was opened by the shell on that descriptor. We can't set the O_SYNC flag when the file is opened, since the shell opened the file. With fcntl, we can modify the properties of a descriptor, knowing only the descriptor for the open file. We'll see another need for fcntl when we describe nonblocking pipes (Section 15.2), since all we have with a pipe is a descriptor.

3.15 ioctl **Function**

The ioctl function has always been the catchall for I/O operations. Anything that couldn't be expressed using one of the other functions in this chapter usually ended up being specified with an ioctl. Terminal I/O was the biggest user of this function. (When we get to Chapter 18, we'll see that POSIX.1 has replaced the terminal I/O operations with separate functions.)

```
#include <unistd.h>      /* System V */
#include <sys/ioctl.h>   /* BSD and Linux */
#include <stropts.h>     /* XSI STREAMS */

int ioctl(int filedes, int request, ...);
```

Returns: −1 on error, something else if OK

The ioctl function is included in the Single UNIX Specification only as an extension for dealing with STREAMS devices [Rago 1993]. UNIX System implementations, however, use it for many miscellaneous device operations. Some implementations have even extended it for use with regular files.

The prototype that we show corresponds to POSIX.1. FreeBSD 5.2.1 and Mac OS X 10.3 declare the second argument as an `unsigned long`. This detail doesn't matter, since the second argument is always a `#defined` name from a header.

For the ISO C prototype, an ellipsis is used for the remaining arguments. Normally, however, there is only one more argument, and it's usually a pointer to a variable or a structure.

In this prototype, we show only the headers required for the function itself. Normally, additional device-specific headers are required. For example, the `ioctl` commands for terminal I/O, beyond the basic operations specified by POSIX.1, all require the `<termios.h>` header.

Each device driver can define its own set of `ioctl` commands. The system, however, provides generic `ioctl` commands for different classes of devices. Examples of some of the categories for these generic `ioctl` commands supported in FreeBSD are summarized in Figure 3.14.

Category	Constant names	Header	Number of ioctls
disk labels	DIOxxx	`<sys/disklabel.h>`	6
file I/O	FIOxxx	`<sys/filio.h>`	9
mag tape I/O	MTIOxxx	`<sys/mtio.h>`	11
socket I/O	SIOxxx	`<sys/sockio.h>`	60
terminal I/O	TIOxxx	`<sys/ttycom.h>`	44

Figure 3.14 Common FreeBSD `ioctl` operations

The mag tape operations allow us to write end-of-file marks on a tape, rewind a tape, space forward over a specified number of files or records, and the like. None of these operations is easily expressed in terms of the other functions in the chapter (`read`, `write`, `lseek`, and so on), so the easiest way to handle these devices has always been to access their operations using `ioctl`.

We use the `ioctl` function in Section 14.4 when we describe the STREAMS system, in Section 18.12 to fetch and set the size of a terminal's window, and in Section 19.7 when we access the advanced features of pseudo terminals.

3.16 /dev/fd

Newer systems provide a directory named `/dev/fd` whose entries are files named 0, 1, 2, and so on. Opening the file `/dev/fd/`n is equivalent to duplicating descriptor n, assuming that descriptor n is open.

> The /dev/fd feature was developed by Tom Duff and appeared in the 8th Edition of the Research UNIX System. It is supported by all of the systems described in this book: FreeBSD 5.2.1, Linux 2.4.22, Mac OS X 10.3, and Solaris 9. It is not part of POSIX.1.

In the function call

```
fd = open("/dev/fd/0", mode);
```

most systems ignore the specified mode, whereas others require that it be a subset of the mode used when the referenced file (standard input, in this case) was originally opened. Because the previous open is equivalent to

```
fd = dup(0);
```

the descriptors 0 and fd share the same file table entry (Figure 3.8). For example, if descriptor 0 was opened read-only, we can only read on fd. Even if the system ignores the open mode, and the call

```
fd = open("/dev/fd/0", O_RDWR);
```

succeeds, we still can't write to fd.

We can also call creat with a /dev/fd pathname argument, as well as specifying O_CREAT in a call to open. This allows a program that calls creat to still work if the pathname argument is /dev/fd/1, for example.

Some systems provide the pathnames /dev/stdin, /dev/stdout, and /dev/stderr. These pathnames are equivalent to /dev/fd/0, /dev/fd/1, and /dev/fd/2.

The main use of the /dev/fd files is from the shell. It allows programs that use pathname arguments to handle standard input and standard output in the same manner as other pathnames. For example, the cat(1) program specifically looks for an input filename of - and uses this to mean standard input. The command

```
filter file2 | cat file1 - file3 | lpr
```

is an example. First, cat reads file1, next its standard input (the output of the filter program on file2), then file3. If /dev/fd is supported, the special handling of - can be removed from cat, and we can enter

```
filter file2 | cat file1 /dev/fd/0 file3 | lpr
```

The special meaning of - as a command-line argument to refer to the standard input or standard output is a kludge that has crept into many programs. There are also problems if we specify - as the first file, as it looks like the start of another command-line option. Using /dev/fd is a step toward uniformity and cleanliness.

3.17 Summary

This chapter has described the basic I/O functions provided by the UNIX System. These are often called the unbuffered I/O functions because each read or write invokes a system call into the kernel. Using only read and write, we looked at the effect of various I/O sizes on the amount of time required to read a file. We also looked at several ways to flush written data to disk and their effect on application performance.

Atomic operations were introduced when multiple processes append to the same file and when multiple processes create the same file. We also looked at the data structures used by the kernel to share information about open files. We'll return to these data structures later in the text.

We also described the `ioctl` and `fcntl` functions. We return to both of these functions in Chapter 14, where we'll use `ioctl` with the STREAMS I/O system, and `fcntl` for record locking.

Exercises

3.1 When reading or writing a disk file, are the functions described in this chapter really unbuffered? Explain.

3.2 Write your own `dup2` function that performs the same service as the `dup2` function described in Section 3.12, without calling the `fcntl` function. Be sure to handle errors correctly.

3.3 Assume that a process executes the following three function calls:

```
fd1 = open(pathname, oflags);
fd2 = dup(fd1);
fd3 = open(pathname, oflags);
```

Draw the resulting picture, similar to Figure 3.8. Which descriptors are affected by an `fcntl` on `fd1` with a command of `F_SETFD`? Which descriptors are affected by an `fcntl` on `fd1` with a command of `F_SETFL`?

3.4 The following sequence of code has been observed in various programs:

```
dup2(fd, 0);
dup2(fd, 1);
dup2(fd, 2);
if (fd > 2)
        close(fd);
```

To see why the `if` test is needed, assume that `fd` is 1 and draw a picture of what happens to the three descriptor entries and the corresponding file table entry with each call to `dup2`. Then assume that `fd` is 3 and draw the same picture.

3.5 The Bourne shell, Bourne-again shell, and Korn shell notation

   digit1 >&*digit2*

says to redirect descriptor *digit1* to the same file as descriptor *digit2*. What is the difference between the two commands

```
./a.out > outfile 2>&1
```

```
./a.out 2>&1 > outfile
```

(Hint: the shells process their command lines from left to right.)

3.6 If you open a file for read–write with the append flag, can you still `read` from anywhere in the file using `lseek`? Can you use `lseek` to replace existing data in the file? Write a program to verify this.

4

Files and Directories

4.1 Introduction

In the previous chapter we covered the basic functions that perform I/O. The discussion centered around I/O for regular files—opening a file, and reading or writing a file. We'll now look at additional features of the file system and the properties of a file. We'll start with the stat functions and go through each member of the stat structure, looking at all the attributes of a file. In this process, we'll also describe each of the functions that modify these attributes: change the owner, change the permissions, and so on. We'll also look in more detail at the structure of a UNIX file system and symbolic links. We finish this chapter with the functions that operate on directories, and we develop a function that descends through a directory hierarchy.

4.2 stat, fstat, and lstat Functions

The discussion in this chapter centers around the three stat functions and the information they return.

```
#include <sys/stat.h>

int stat(const char *restrict pathname, struct stat *restrict buf);

int fstat(int filedes, struct stat *buf);

int lstat(const char *restrict pathname, struct stat *restrict buf);
```
                                        All three return: 0 if OK, –1 on error

Given a *pathname*, the stat function returns a structure of information about the named file. The fstat function obtains information about the file that is already open on the descriptor *filedes*. The lstat function is similar to stat, but when the named file is a symbolic link, lstat returns information about the symbolic link, not the file referenced by the symbolic link. (We'll need lstat in Section 4.21 when we walk down a directory hierarchy. We describe symbolic links in more detail in Section 4.16.)

The second argument is a pointer to a structure that we must supply. The function fills in the structure pointed to by *buf*. The definition of the structure can differ among implementations, but it could look like

```
struct stat {
    mode_t    st_mode;    /* file type & mode (permissions) */
    ino_t     st_ino;     /* i-node number (serial number) */
    dev_t     st_dev;     /* device number (file system) */
    dev_t     st_rdev;    /* device number for special files */
    nlink_t   st_nlink;   /* number of links */
    uid_t     st_uid;     /* user ID of owner */
    gid_t     st_gid;     /* group ID of owner */
    off_t     st_size;    /* size in bytes, for regular files */
    time_t    st_atime;   /* time of last access */
    time_t    st_mtime;   /* time of last modification */
    time_t    st_ctime;   /* time of last file status change */
    blksize_t st_blksize; /* best I/O block size */
    blkcnt_t  st_blocks;  /* number of disk blocks allocated */
};
```

> The st_rdev, st_blksize, and st_blocks fields are not required by POSIX.1. They are defined as XSI extensions in the Single UNIX Specification.

Note that each member is specified by a primitive system data type (see Section 2.8). We'll go through each member of this structure to examine the attributes of a file.

The biggest user of the stat functions is probably the ls -l command, to learn all the information about a file.

4.3   File Types

We've talked about two different types of files so far: regular files and directories. Most files on a UNIX system are either regular files or directories, but there are additional types of files. The types are:

1. Regular file. The most common type of file, which contains data of some form. There is no distinction to the UNIX kernel whether this data is text or binary. Any interpretation of the contents of a regular file is left to the application processing the file.

    > One notable exception to this is with binary executable files. To execute a program, the kernel must understand its format. All binary executable files conform to a format that allows the kernel to identify where to load a program's text and data.

2. Directory file. A file that contains the names of other files and pointers to information on these files. Any process that has read permission for a directory file can read the contents of the directory, but only the kernel can write directly

to a directory file. Processes must use the functions described in this chapter to make changes to a directory.

3. Block special file. A type of file providing buffered I/O access in fixed-size units to devices such as disk drives.

4. Character special file. A type of file providing unbuffered I/O access in variable-sized units to devices. All devices on a system are either block special files or character special files.

5. FIFO. A type of file used for communication between processes. It's sometimes called a named pipe. We describe FIFOs in Section 15.5.

6. Socket. A type of file used for network communication between processes. A socket can also be used for non-network communication between processes on a single host. We use sockets for interprocess communication in Chapter 16.

7. Symbolic link. A type of file that points to another file. We talk more about symbolic links in Section 4.16.

The type of a file is encoded in the `st_mode` member of the `stat` structure. We can determine the file type with the macros shown in Figure 4.1. The argument to each of these macros is the `st_mode` member from the `stat` structure.

Macro	Type of file
`S_ISREG()`	regular file
`S_ISDIR()`	directory file
`S_ISCHR()`	character special file
`S_ISBLK()`	block special file
`S_ISFIFO()`	pipe or FIFO
`S_ISLNK()`	symbolic link
`S_ISSOCK()`	socket

Figure 4.1 File type macros in `<sys/stat.h>`

POSIX.1 allows implementations to represent interprocess communication (IPC) objects, such as message queues and semaphores, as files. The macros shown in Figure 4.2 allow us to determine the type of IPC object from the `stat` structure. Instead of taking the `st_mode` member as an argument, these macros differ from those in Figure 4.1 in that their argument is a pointer to the `stat` structure.

Macro	Type of object
`S_TYPEISMQ()`	message queue
`S_TYPEISSEM()`	semaphore
`S_TYPEISSHM()`	shared memory object

Figure 4.2 IPC type macros in `<sys/stat.h>`

Message queues, semaphores, and shared memory objects are discussed in Chapter 15. However, none of the various implementations of the UNIX System discussed in this book represent these objects as files.

Example

The program in Figure 4.3 prints the type of file for each command-line argument.

```
#include "apue.h"

int
main(int argc, char *argv[])
{
    int         i;
    struct stat buf;
    char        *ptr;

    for (i = 1; i < argc; i++) {
        printf("%s: ", argv[i]);
        if (lstat(argv[i], &buf) < 0) {
            err_ret("lstat error");
            continue;
        }
        if (S_ISREG(buf.st_mode))
            ptr = "regular";
        else if (S_ISDIR(buf.st_mode))
            ptr = "directory";
        else if (S_ISCHR(buf.st_mode))
            ptr = "character special";
        else if (S_ISBLK(buf.st_mode))
            ptr = "block special";
        else if (S_ISFIFO(buf.st_mode))
            ptr = "fifo";
        else if (S_ISLNK(buf.st_mode))
            ptr = "symbolic link";
        else if (S_ISSOCK(buf.st_mode))
            ptr = "socket";
        else
            ptr = "** unknown mode **";
        printf("%s\n", ptr);
    }
    exit(0);
}
```

Figure 4.3   Print type of file for each command-line argument

Sample output from Figure 4.3 is

```
$ ./a.out /etc/passwd /etc /dev/initctl /dev/log /dev/tty \
> /dev/scsi/host0/bus0/target0/lun0/cd /dev/cdrom
/etc/passwd: regular
/etc: directory
/dev/initctl: fifo
/dev/log: socket
/dev/tty: character special
/dev/scsi/host0/bus0/target0/lun0/cd: block special
/dev/cdrom: symbolic link
```

(Here, we have explicitly entered a backslash at the end of the first command line, telling the shell that we want to continue entering the command on another line. The shell then prompts us with its secondary prompt, >, on the next line.) We have specifically used the lstat function instead of the stat function to detect symbolic links. If we used the stat function, we would never see symbolic links.

To compile this program on a Linux system, we must define _GNU_SOURCE to include the definition of the S_ISSOCK macro.   □

Historically, early versions of the UNIX System didn't provide the S_ISxxx macros. Instead, we had to logically AND the st_mode value with the mask S_IFMT and then compare the result with the constants whose names are S_IFxxx. Most systems define this mask and the related constants in the file <sys/stat.h>. If we examine this file, we'll find the S_ISDIR macro defined something like

```
#define  S_ISDIR(mode)  (((mode) & S_IFMT) == S_IFDIR)
```

We've said that regular files are predominant, but it is interesting to see what percentage of the files on a given system are of each file type. Figure 4.4 shows the counts and percentages for a Linux system that is used as a single-user workstation. This data was obtained from the program that we show in Section 4.21.

File type	Count	Percentage
regular file	226,856	88.22 %
directory	23,017	8.95
symbolic link	6,442	2.51
character special	447	0.17
block special	312	0.12
socket	69	0.03
FIFO	1	0.00

Figure 4.4 Counts and percentages of different file types

4.4 Set-User-ID and Set-Group-ID

Every process has six or more IDs associated with it. These are shown in Figure 4.5.

real user ID real group ID	who we really are
effective user ID effective group ID supplementary group IDs	used for file access permission checks
saved set-user-ID saved set-group-ID	saved by exec functions

Figure 4.5 User IDs and group IDs associated with each process

- The real user ID and real group ID identify who we really are. These two fields are taken from our entry in the password file when we log in. Normally, these values don't change during a login session, although there are ways for a superuser process to change them, which we describe in Section 8.11.

- The effective user ID, effective group ID, and supplementary group IDs determine our file access permissions, as we describe in the next section. (We defined supplementary group IDs in Section 1.8.)

- The saved set-user-ID and saved set-group-ID contain copies of the effective user ID and the effective group ID when a program is executed. We describe the function of these two saved values when we describe the setuid function in Section 8.11.

> The saved IDs are required with the 2001 version of POSIX.1. They used to be optional in older versions of POSIX. An application can test for the constant _POSIX_SAVED_IDS at compile time or can call sysconf with the _SC_SAVED_IDS argument at runtime, to see whether the implementation supports this feature.

Normally, the effective user ID equals the real user ID, and the effective group ID equals the real group ID.

Every file has an owner and a group owner. The owner is specified by the st_uid member of the stat structure; the group owner, by the st_gid member.

When we execute a program file, the effective user ID of the process is usually the real user ID, and the effective group ID is usually the real group ID. But the capability exists to set a special flag in the file's mode word (st_mode) that says "when this file is executed, set the effective user ID of the process to be the owner of the file (st_uid)." Similarly, another bit can be set in the file's mode word that causes the effective group ID to be the group owner of the file (st_gid). These two bits in the file's mode word are called the *set-user-ID* bit and the *set-group-ID* bit.

For example, if the owner of the file is the superuser and if the file's set-user-ID bit is set, then while that program file is running as a process, it has superuser privileges. This happens regardless of the real user ID of the process that executes the file. As an example, the UNIX System program that allows anyone to change his or her password, passwd(1), is a set-user-ID program. This is required so that the program can write the new password to the password file, typically either /etc/passwd or /etc/shadow, files that should be writable only by the superuser. Because a process that is running set-user-ID to some other user usually assumes extra permissions, it must be written carefully. We'll discuss these types of programs in more detail in Chapter 8.

Returning to the stat function, the set-user-ID bit and the set-group-ID bit are contained in the file's st_mode value. These two bits can be tested against the constants S_ISUID and S_ISGID.

4.5   File Access Permissions

The st_mode value also encodes the access permission bits for the file. When we say *file*, we mean any of the file types that we described earlier. All the file types—directories, character special files, and so on—have permissions. Many people think only of regular files as having access permissions.

There are nine permission bits for each file, divided into three categories. These are shown in Figure 4.6.

st_mode mask	Meaning
S_IRUSR	user-read
S_IWUSR	user-write
S_IXUSR	user-execute
S_IRGRP	group-read
S_IWGRP	group-write
S_IXGRP	group-execute
S_IROTH	other-read
S_IWOTH	other-write
S_IXOTH	other-execute

Figure 4.6 The nine file access permission bits, from `<sys/stat.h>`

The term *user* in the first three rows in Figure 4.6 refers to the owner of the file. The chmod(1) command, which is typically used to modify these nine permission bits, allows us to specify u for user (owner), g for group, and o for other. Some books refer to these three as owner, group, and world; this is confusing, as the chmod command uses o to mean other, not owner. We'll use the terms *user*, *group*, and *other*, to be consistent with the chmod command.

The three categories in Figure 4.6—read, write, and execute—are used in various ways by different functions. We'll summarize them here, and return to them when we describe the actual functions.

- The first rule is that *whenever* we want to open any type of file by name, we must have execute permission in each directory mentioned in the name, including the current directory, if it is implied. This is why the execute permission bit for a directory is often called the search bit.

  For example, to open the file /usr/include/stdio.h, we need execute permission in the directory /, execute permission in the directory /usr, and execute permission in the directory /usr/include. We then need appropriate permission for the file itself, depending on how we're trying to open it: read-only, read–write, and so on.

  If the current directory is /usr/include, then we need execute permission in the current directory to open the file stdio.h. This is an example of the current directory being implied, not specifically mentioned. It is identical to our opening the file ./stdio.h.

  Note that read permission for a directory and execute permission for a directory mean different things. Read permission lets us read the directory, obtaining a list of all the filenames in the directory. Execute permission lets us pass through the directory when it is a component of a pathname that we are trying to access. (We need to search the directory to look for a specific filename.)

  Another example of an implicit directory reference is if the PATH environment variable, described in Section 8.10, specifies a directory that does not have execute permission enabled. In this case, the shell will never find executable files in that directory.

- The read permission for a file determines whether we can open an existing file for reading: the O_RDONLY and O_RDWR flags for the open function.

- The write permission for a file determines whether we can open an existing file for writing: the O_WRONLY and O_RDWR flags for the open function.

- We must have write permission for a file to specify the O_TRUNC flag in the open function.

- We cannot create a new file in a directory unless we have write permission and execute permission in the directory.

- To delete an existing file, we need write permission and execute permission in the directory containing the file. We do not need read permission or write permission for the file itself.

- Execute permission for a file must be on if we want to execute the file using any of the six exec functions (Section 8.10). The file also has to be a regular file.

The file access tests that the kernel performs each time a process opens, creates, or deletes a file depend on the owners of the file (st_uid and st_gid), the effective IDs of the process (effective user ID and effective group ID), and the supplementary group IDs of the process, if supported. The two owner IDs are properties of the file, whereas the two effective IDs and the supplementary group IDs are properties of the process. The tests performed by the kernel are as follows.

1. If the effective user ID of the process is 0 (the superuser), access is allowed. This gives the superuser free rein throughout the entire file system.

2. If the effective user ID of the process equals the owner ID of the file (i.e., the process owns the file), access is allowed if the appropriate user access permission bit is set. Otherwise, permission is denied. By *appropriate access permission bit*, we mean that if the process is opening the file for reading, the user-read bit must be on. If the process is opening the file for writing, the user-write bit must be on. If the process is executing the file, the user-execute bit must be on.

3. If the effective group ID of the process or one of the supplementary group IDs of the process equals the group ID of the file, access is allowed if the appropriate group access permission bit is set. Otherwise, permission is denied.

4. If the appropriate other access permission bit is set, access is allowed. Otherwise, permission is denied.

These four steps are tried in sequence. Note that if the process owns the file (step 2), access is granted or denied based only on the user access permissions; the group permissions are never looked at. Similarly, if the process does not own the file, but belongs to an appropriate group, access is granted or denied based only on the group access permissions; the other permissions are not looked at.

4.6   Ownership of New Files and Directories

When we described the creation of a new file in Chapter 3, using either open or creat, we never said what values were assigned to the user ID and group ID of the new file. We'll see how to create a new directory in Section 4.20 when we describe the mkdir function. The rules for the ownership of a new directory are identical to the rules in this section for the ownership of a new file.

The user ID of a new file is set to the effective user ID of the process. POSIX.1 allows an implementation to choose one of the following options to determine the group ID of a new file.

1. The group ID of a new file can be the effective group ID of the process.

2. The group ID of a new file can be the group ID of the directory in which the file is being created.

> FreeBSD 5.2.1 and Mac OS X 10.3 always uses the group ID of the directory as the group ID of the new file.
>
> The Linux ext2 and ext3 file systems allow the choice between these two POSIX.1 options to be made on a file system basis, using a special flag to the mount(1) command. On Linux 2.4.22 (with the proper mount option) and Solaris 9, the group ID of a new file depends on whether the set-group-ID bit is set for the directory in which the file is being created. If this bit is set for the directory, the group ID of the new file is set to the group ID of the directory; otherwise, the group ID of the new file is set to the effective group ID of the process.

Using the second option—inheriting the group ID of the directory—assures us that all files and directories created in that directory will have the group ID belonging to the directory. This group ownership of files and directories will then propagate down the hierarchy from that point. This is used, for example, in the /var/spool/mail directory on Linux.

> As we mentioned, this option for group ownership is the default for FreeBSD 5.2.1 and Mac OS X 10.3, but an option for Linux and Solaris. Under Linux 2.4.22 and Solaris 9, we have to enable the set-group-ID bit, and the mkdir function has to propagate a directory's set-group-ID bit automatically for this to work. (This is described in Section 4.20.)

4.7   access Function

As we described earlier, when we open a file, the kernel performs its access tests based on the effective user and group IDs. There are times when a process wants to test accessibility based on the real user and group IDs. This is useful when a process is running as someone else, using either the set-user-ID or the set-group-ID feature. Even though a process might be set-user-ID to root, it could still want to verify that the real user can access a given file. The access function bases its tests on the real user and group IDs. (Replace *effective* with *real* in the four steps at the end of Section 4.5.)

```
#include <unistd.h>

int access(const char *pathname, int mode);
```
                                                        Returns: 0 if OK, −1 on error

The *mode* is the bitwise OR of any of the constants shown in Figure 4.7.

mode	Description
R_OK	test for read permission
W_OK	test for write permission
X_OK	test for execute permission
F_OK	test for existence of file

Figure 4.7 The *mode* constants for access function, from `<unistd.h>`

Example

Figure 4.8 shows the use of the `access` function.

```c
#include "apue.h"
#include <fcntl.h>

int
main(int argc, char *argv[])
{
    if (argc != 2)
        err_quit("usage: a.out <pathname>");
    if (access(argv[1], R_OK) < 0)
        err_ret("access error for %s", argv[1]);
    else
        printf("read access OK\n");
    if (open(argv[1], O_RDONLY) < 0)
        err_ret("open error for %s", argv[1]);
    else
        printf("open for reading OK\n");
    exit(0);
}
```

Figure 4.8 Example of access function

Here is a sample session with this program:

```
$ ls -l a.out
-rwxrwxr-x  1 sar           15945 Nov 30 12:10 a.out
$ ./a.out a.out
read access OK
open for reading OK
$ ls -l /etc/shadow
-r--------  1 root           1315 Jul 17  2002 /etc/shadow
$ ./a.out /etc/shadow
access error for /etc/shadow: Permission denied
open error for /etc/shadow: Permission denied
$ su                                    become superuser
Password:                               enter superuser password
# chown root a.out                      change file's user ID to root
# chmod u+s a.out                       and turn on set-user-ID bit
# ls -l a.out                           check owner and SUID bit
-rwsrwxr-x  1 root           15945 Nov 30 12:10 a.out
```

```
    # exit                                    go back to normal user
    $ ./a.out /etc/shadow
    access error for /etc/shadow: Permission denied
    open for reading OK
```

In this example, the set-user-ID program can determine that the real user cannot
normally read the file, even though the open function will succeed.   □

> In the preceding example and in Chapter 8, we'll sometimes switch to become the superuser,
> to demonstrate how something works. If you're on a multiuser system and do not have
> superuser permission, you won't be able to duplicate these examples completely.

4.8   umask Function

Now that we've described the nine permission bits associated with every file, we can
describe the file mode creation mask that is associated with every process.

The umask function sets the file mode creation mask for the process and returns the
previous value. (This is one of the few functions that doesn't have an error return.)

```
#include <sys/stat.h>

mode_t umask(mode_t cmask);
```
                                       Returns: previous file mode creation mask

The *cmask* argument is formed as the bitwise OR of any of the nine constants from
Figure 4.6: S_IRUSR, S_IWUSR, and so on.

The file mode creation mask is used whenever the process creates a new file or a
new directory. (Recall from Sections 3.3 and 3.4 our description of the open and creat
functions. Both accept a *mode* argument that specifies the new file's access permission
bits.) We describe how to create a new directory in Section 4.20. Any bits that are *on* in
the file mode creation mask are turned *off* in the file's *mode*.

Example

The program in Figure 4.9 creates two files, one with a umask of 0 and one with a
umask that disables all the group and other permission bits.

```
#include "apue.h"
#include <fcntl.h>

#define RWRWRW (S_IRUSR|S_IWUSR|S_IRGRP|S_IWGRP|S_IROTH|S_IWOTH)

int
main(void)
{
    umask(0);
    if (creat("foo", RWRWRW) < 0)
        err_sys("creat error for foo");
    umask(S_IRGRP | S_IWGRP | S_IROTH | S_IWOTH);
    if (creat("bar", RWRWRW) < 0)
```

```
                err_sys("creat error for bar");
            exit(0);
    }
```

Figure 4.9 Example of umask function

If we run this program, we can see how the permission bits have been set.

```
$ umask                         first print the current file mode creation mask
002
$ ./a.out
$ ls -l foo bar
-rw-------  1 sar              0 Dec  7 21:20 bar
-rw-rw-rw-  1 sar              0 Dec  7 21:20 foo
$ umask                         see if the file mode creation mask changed
002
```

□

Most users of UNIX systems never deal with their umask value. It is usually set once, on login, by the shell's start-up file, and never changed. Nevertheless, when writing programs that create new files, if we want to ensure that specific access permission bits are enabled, we must modify the umask value while the process is running. For example, if we want to ensure that anyone can read a file, we should set the umask to 0. Otherwise, the umask value that is in effect when our process is running can cause permission bits to be turned off.

In the preceding example, we use the shell's umask command to print the file mode creation mask before we run the program and after. This shows us that changing the file mode creation mask of a process doesn't affect the mask of its parent (often a shell). All of the shells have a built-in umask command that we can use to set or print the current file mode creation mask.

Users can set the umask value to control the default permissions on the files they create. The value is expressed in octal, with one bit representing one permission to be masked off, as shown in Figure 4.10. Permissions can be denied by setting the corresponding bits. Some common umask values are 002 to prevent others from writing your files, 022 to prevent group members and others from writing your files, and 027 to prevent group members from writing your files and others from reading, writing, or executing your files.

Mask bit	Meaning
0400	user-read
0200	user-write
0100	user-execute
0040	group-read
0020	group-write
0010	group-execute
0004	other-read
0002	other-write
0001	other-execute

Figure 4.10 The umask file access permission bits

The Single UNIX Specification requires that the shell support a symbolic form of the umask command. Unlike the octal format, the symbolic format specifies which permissions are to be allowed (i.e., clear in the file creation mask) instead of which ones are to be denied (i.e., set in the file creation mask). Compare both forms of the command, shown below.

```
$ umask                         first print the current file mode creation mask
002
$ umask -S                      print the symbolic form
u=rwx,g=rwx,o=rx
$ umask 027                     change the file mode creation mask
$ umask -S                      print the symbolic form
u=rwx,g=rx,o=
```

4.9 chmod and fchmod Functions

These two functions allow us to change the file access permissions for an existing file.

```
#include <sys/stat.h>

int chmod(const char *pathname, mode_t mode);

int fchmod(int filedes, mode_t mode);
```
                                                    Both return: 0 if OK, −1 on error

The chmod function operates on the specified file, whereas the fchmod function operates on a file that has already been opened.

To change the permission bits of a file, the effective user ID of the process must be equal to the owner ID of the file, or the process must have superuser permissions.

The *mode* is specified as the bitwise OR of the constants shown in Figure 4.11.

mode	Description
S_ISUID	set-user-ID on execution
S_ISGID	set-group-ID on execution
S_ISVTX	saved-text (sticky bit)
S_IRWXU	read, write, and execute by user (owner)
S_IRUSR	read by user (owner)
S_IWUSR	write by user (owner)
S_IXUSR	execute by user (owner)
S_IRWXG	read, write, and execute by group
S_IRGRP	read by group
S_IWGRP	write by group
S_IXGRP	execute by group
S_IRWXO	read, write, and execute by other (world)
S_IROTH	read by other (world)
S_IWOTH	write by other (world)
S_IXOTH	execute by other (world)

Figure 4.11 The *mode* constants for chmod functions, from <sys/stat.h>

Note that nine of the entries in Figure 4.11 are the nine file access permission bits from Figure 4.6. We've added the two set-ID constants (S_ISUID and S_ISGID), the saved-text constant (S_ISVTX), and the three combined constants (S_IRWXU, S_IRWXG, and S_IRWXO).

> The saved-text bit (S_ISVTX) is not part of POSIX.1. It is defined as an XSI extension in the Single UNIX Specification. We describe its purpose in the next section.

Example

Recall the final state of the files foo and bar when we ran the program in Figure 4.9 to demonstrate the umask function:

```
$ ls -l foo bar
-rw-------  1 sar           0 Dec  7 21:20 bar
-rw-rw-rw-  1 sar           0 Dec  7 21:20 foo
```

The program shown in Figure 4.12 modifies the mode of these two files.

```
#include "apue.h"

int
main(void)
{
    struct stat     statbuf;

    /* turn on set-group-ID and turn off group-execute */
    if (stat("foo", &statbuf) < 0)
        err_sys("stat error for foo");
    if (chmod("foo", (statbuf.st_mode & ~S_IXGRP) | S_ISGID) < 0)
        err_sys("chmod error for foo");

    /* set absolute mode to "rw-r--r--" */
    if (chmod("bar", S_IRUSR | S_IWUSR | S_IRGRP | S_IROTH) < 0)
        err_sys("chmod error for bar");

    exit(0);
}
```

Figure 4.12 Example of chmod function

After running the program in Figure 4.12, we see that the final state of the two files is

```
$ ls -l foo bar
-rw-r--r--  1 sar           0 Dec  7 21:20 bar
-rw-rwSrw-  1 sar           0 Dec  7 21:20 foo
```

In this example, we have set the permissions of the file bar to an absolute value, regardless of the current permission bits. For the file foo, we set the permissions relative to their current state. To do this, we first call stat to obtain the current permissions and then modify them. We have explicitly turned on the set-group-ID bit and turned off the group-execute bit. Note that the ls command lists the group-execute permission as S to signify that the set-group-ID bit is set without the group-execute bit being set.

> On Solaris, the `ls` command displays an `l` instead of an `s` to indicate that mandatory file and record locking has been enabled for this file. This applies only to regular files, but we'll discuss this more in Section 14.3.

Finally, note that the time and date listed by the `ls` command did not change after we ran the program in Figure 4.12. We'll see in Section 4.18 that the `chmod` function updates only the time that the i-node was last changed. By default, the `ls -l` lists the time when the contents of the file were last modified.   □

The `chmod` functions automatically clear two of the permission bits under the following conditions:

- On systems, such as Solaris, that place special meaning on the sticky bit when used with regular files, if we try to set the sticky bit (`S_ISVTX`) on a regular file and do not have superuser privileges, the sticky bit in the *mode* is automatically turned off. (We describe the sticky bit in the next section.) This means that only the superuser can set the sticky bit of a regular file. The reason is to prevent malicious users from setting the sticky bit and adversely affecting system performance.

  > On FreeBSD 5.2.1, Mac OS X 10.3, and Solaris 9, only the superuser can set the sticky bit on a regular file. Linux 2.4.22 places no such restriction on the setting of the sticky bit, because the bit has no meaning when applied to regular files on Linux. Although the bit also has no meaning when applied to regular files on FreeBSD and Mac OS X, these systems prevent everyone but the superuser from setting it on a regular file.

- It is possible that the group ID of a newly created file is a group that the calling process does not belong to. Recall from Section 4.6 that it's possible for the group ID of the new file to be the group ID of the parent directory. Specifically, if the group ID of the new file does not equal either the effective group ID of the process or one of the process's supplementary group IDs and if the process does not have superuser privileges, then the set-group-ID bit is automatically turned off. This prevents a user from creating a set-group-ID file owned by a group that the user doesn't belong to.

  > FreeBSD 5.2.1, Linux 2.4.22, Mac OS X 10.3, and Solaris 9 add another security feature to try to prevent misuse of some of the protection bits. If a process that does not have superuser privileges writes to a file, the set-user-ID and set-group-ID bits are automatically turned off. If malicious users find a set-group-ID or a set-user-ID file they can write to, even though they can modify the file, they lose the special privileges of the file.

4.10 Sticky Bit

The `S_ISVTX` bit has an interesting history. On versions of the UNIX System that predated demand paging, this bit was known as the *sticky bit*. If it was set for an executable program file, then the first time the program was executed, a copy of the program's text was saved in the swap area when the process terminated. (The text portion of a program is the machine instructions.) This caused the program to load into memory more quickly the next time it was executed, because the swap area was handled as a contiguous file, compared to the possibly random location of data blocks in a normal UNIX file system. The sticky bit was often set for common application programs, such as the text editor and the passes of the C compiler. Naturally, there was a limit to the number of sticky files that could be contained in the swap area before running out of swap space, but it was a useful technique. The name *sticky* came about because the text portion of the file stuck around in the swap area until the system was rebooted. Later versions of the UNIX System referred to this as the *saved-text* bit; hence, the constant S_ISVTX. With today's newer UNIX systems, most of which have a virtual memory system and a faster file system, the need for this technique has disappeared.

On contemporary systems, the use of the sticky bit has been extended. The Single UNIX Specification allows the sticky bit to be set for a directory. If the bit is set for a directory, a file in the directory can be removed or renamed only if the user has write permission for the directory and one of the following:

- Owns the file
- Owns the directory
- Is the superuser

The directories /tmp and /var/spool/uucppublic are typical candidates for the sticky bit—they are directories in which any user can typically create files. The permissions for these two directories are often read, write, and execute for everyone (user, group, and other). But users should not be able to delete or rename files owned by others.

> The saved-text bit is not part of POSIX.1. It is an XSI extension to the basic POSIX.1 functionality defined in the Single UNIX Specification, and is supported by FreeBSD 5.2.1, Linux 2.4.22, Mac OS X 10.3, and Solaris 9.
>
> Solaris 9 places special meaning on the sticky bit if it is set on a regular file. In this case, if none of the execute bits is set, the operating system will not cache the contents of the file.

4.11 chown, fchown, and lchown Functions

The chown functions allow us to change the user ID of a file and the group ID of a file.

```
#include <unistd.h>

int chown(const char *pathname, uid_t owner, gid_t group);

int fchown(int filedes, uid_t owner, gid_t group);

int lchown(const char *pathname, uid_t owner, gid_t group);
                                        All three return: 0 if OK, −1 on error
```

These three functions operate similarly unless the referenced file is a symbolic link. In that case, lchown changes the owners of the symbolic link itself, not the file pointed to by the symbolic link.

> The lchown function is an XSI extension to the POSIX.1 functionality defined in the Single UNIX Specification. As such, all UNIX System implementations are expected to provide it.

If either of the arguments *owner* or *group* is −1, the corresponding ID is left unchanged.

Historically, BSD-based systems have enforced the restriction that only the superuser can change the ownership of a file. This is to prevent users from giving away their files to others, thereby defeating any disk space quota restrictions. System V, however, has allowed any user to change the ownership of any files they own.

> POSIX.1 allows either form of operation, depending on the value of `_POSIX_CHOWN_RESTRICTED`.
>
> With Solaris 9, this functionality is a configuration option, whose default value is to enforce the restriction. FreeBSD 5.2.1, Linux 2.4.22, and Mac OS X 10.3 always enforce the `chown` restriction.

Recall from Section 2.6 that the `_POSIX_CHOWN_RESTRICTED` constant can optionally be defined in the header `<unistd.h>`, and can always be queried using either the `pathconf` function or the `fpathconf` function. Also recall that this option can depend on the referenced file; it can be enabled or disabled on a per file system basis. We'll use the phrase, if `_POSIX_CHOWN_RESTRICTED` is in effect, to mean if it applies to the particular file that we're talking about, regardless of whether this actual constant is defined in the header.

If `_POSIX_CHOWN_RESTRICTED` is in effect for the specified file, then

1. Only a superuser process can change the user ID of the file.

2. A nonsuperuser process can change the group ID of the file if the process owns the file (the effective user ID equals the user ID of the file), *owner* is specified as −1 or equals the user ID of the file, and *group* equals either the effective group ID of the process or one of the process's supplementary group IDs.

This means that when `_POSIX_CHOWN_RESTRICTED` is in effect, you can't change the user ID of other users' files. You can change the group ID of files that you own, but only to groups that you belong to.

If these functions are called by a process other than a superuser process, on successful return, both the set-user-ID and the set-group-ID bits are cleared.

4.12 File Size

The `st_size` member of the `stat` structure contains the size of the file in bytes. This field is meaningful only for regular files, directories, and symbolic links.

> Solaris also defines the file size for a pipe as the number of bytes that are available for reading from the pipe. We'll discuss pipes in Section 15.2.

For a regular file, a file size of 0 is allowed. We'll get an end-of-file indication on the first read of the file.

For a directory, the file size is usually a multiple of a number, such as 16 or 512. We talk about reading directories in Section 4.21.

For a symbolic link, the file size is the number of bytes in the filename. For example, in the following case, the file size of 7 is the length of the pathname `usr/lib`:

```
lrwxrwxrwx  1 root            7 Sep 25 07:14 lib -> usr/lib
```

(Note that symbolic links do not contain the normal C null byte at the end of the name, as the length is always specified by `st_size`.)

Most contemporary UNIX systems provide the fields st_blksize and st_blocks. The first is the preferred block size for I/O for the file, and the latter is the actual number of 512-byte blocks that are allocated. Recall from Section 3.9 that we encountered the minimum amount of time required to read a file when we used st_blksize for the read operations. The standard I/O library, which we describe in Chapter 5, also tries to read or write st_blksize bytes at a time, for efficiency.

> Be aware that different versions of the UNIX System use units other than 512-byte blocks for st_blocks. Using this value is nonportable.

Holes in a File

In Section 3.6, we mentioned that a regular file can contain "holes." We showed an example of this in Figure 3.2. Holes are created by seeking past the current end of file and writing some data. As an example, consider the following:

```
$ ls -l core
-rw-r--r--  1 sar    8483248 Nov 18 12:18 core
$ du -s core
272     core
```

The size of the file core is just over 8 MB, yet the du command reports that the amount of disk space used by the file is 272 512-byte blocks (139,264 bytes). (The du command on many BSD-derived systems reports the number of 1,024-byte blocks; Solaris reports the number of 512-byte blocks.) Obviously, this file has many holes.

As we mentioned in Section 3.6, the read function returns data bytes of 0 for any byte positions that have not been written. If we execute the following, we can see that the normal I/O operations read up through the size of the file:

```
$ wc -c core
 8483248 core
```

> The wc(1) command with the -c option counts the number of characters (bytes) in the file.

If we make a copy of this file, using a utility such as cat(1), all these holes are written out as actual data bytes of 0:

```
$ cat core > core.copy
$ ls -l core*
-rw-r--r--  1 sar    8483248 Nov 18 12:18 core
-rw-rw-r--  1 sar    8483248 Nov 18 12:27 core.copy
$ du -s core*
272     core
16592   core.copy
```

Here, the actual number of bytes used by the new file is 8,495,104 (512 × 16,592). The difference between this size and the size reported by ls is caused by the number of blocks used by the file system to hold pointers to the actual data blocks.

Interested readers should refer to Section 4.2 of Bach [1986], Sections 7.2 and 7.3 of McKusick et al. [1996] (or Sections 8.2 and 8.3 in McKusick and Neville-Neil [2005]), and

Section 14.2 of Mauro and McDougall [2001] for additional details on the physical layout of files.

4.13   File Truncation

There are times when we would like to truncate a file by chopping off data at the end of the file. Emptying a file, which we can do with the O_TRUNC flag to open, is a special case of truncation.

```
#include <unistd.h>

int truncate(const char *pathname, off_t length);

int ftruncate(int filedes, off_t length);
```

Both return: 0 if OK, −1 on error

These two functions truncate an existing file to *length* bytes. If the previous size of the file was greater than *length*, the data beyond *length* is no longer accessible. If the previous size was less than *length*, the effect is system dependent, but XSI-conforming systems will increase the file size. If the implementation does extend a file, data between the old end of file and the new end of file will read as 0 (i.e., a hole is probably created in the file).

> The ftruncate function is part of POSIX.1. The truncate function is an XSI extension to the POSIX.1 functionality defined in the Single UNIX Specification.
>
> BSD releases prior to 4.4BSD could only make a file smaller with truncate.
>
> Solaris also includes an extension to fcntl (F_FREESP) that allows us to free any part of a file, not just a chunk at the end of the file.

We use ftruncate in the program shown in Figure 13.6 when we need to empty a file after obtaining a lock on the file.

4.14   File Systems

To appreciate the concept of links to a file, we need a conceptual understanding of the structure of the UNIX file system. Understanding the difference between an i-node and a directory entry that points to an i-node is also useful.

Various implementations of the UNIX file system are in use today. Solaris, for example, supports several different types of disk file systems: the traditional BSD-derived UNIX file system (called UFS), a file system (called PCFS) to read and write DOS-formatted diskettes, and a file system (called HSFS) to read CD file systems. We saw one difference between file system types in Figure 2.19. UFS is based on the Berkeley fast file system, which we describe in this section.

We can think of a disk drive being divided into one or more partitions. Each partition can contain a file system, as shown in Figure 4.13.

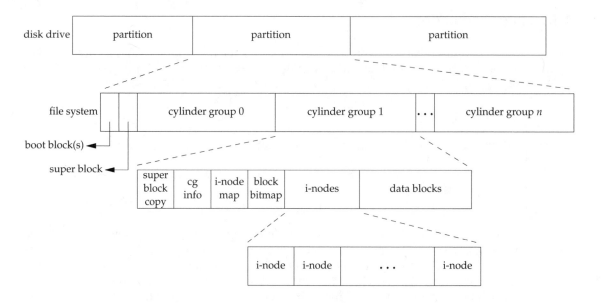

Figure 4.13 Disk drive, partitions, and a file system

The i-nodes are fixed-length entries that contain most of the information about a file.

If we examine the i-node and data block portion of a cylinder group in more detail, we could have what is shown in Figure 4.14.

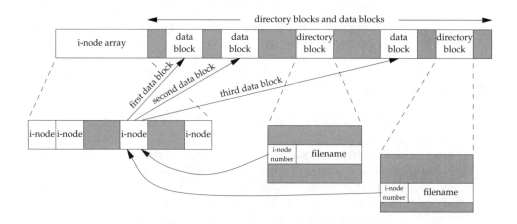

Figure 4.14 Cylinder group's i-nodes and data blocks in more detail

Note the following points from Figure 4.14.

- We show two directory entries that point to the same i-node entry. Every i-node has a link count that contains the number of directory entries that point to the i-node. Only when the link count goes to 0 can the file be deleted (i.e., can the data blocks associated with the file be released). This is why the operation of "unlinking a file" does not always mean "deleting the blocks associated with the file." This is why the function that removes a directory entry is called unlink, not delete. In the stat structure, the link count is contained in the st_nlink member. Its primitive system data type is nlink_t. These types of links are called hard links. Recall from Section 2.5.2 that the POSIX.1 constant LINK_MAX specifies the maximum value for a file's link count.

- The other type of link is called a *symbolic link*. With a symbolic link, the actual contents of the file—the data blocks—store the name of the file that the symbolic link points to. In the following example, the filename in the directory entry is the three-character string lib and the 7 bytes of data in the file are usr/lib:

```
lrwxrwxrwx  1 root      7 Sep 25 07:14 lib -> usr/lib
```

The file type in the i-node would be S_IFLNK so that the system knows that this is a symbolic link.

- The i-node contains all the information about the file: the file type, the file's access permission bits, the size of the file, pointers to the file's data blocks, and so on. Most of the information in the stat structure is obtained from the i-node. Only two items of interest are stored in the directory entry: the filename and the i-node number; the other items—the length of the filename and the length of the directory record—are not of interest to this discussion. The data type for the i-node number is ino_t.

- Because the i-node number in the directory entry points to an i-node in the same file system, we cannot have a directory entry point to an i-node in a different file system. This is why the ln(1) command (make a new directory entry that points to an existing file) can't cross file systems. We describe the link function in the next section.

- When renaming a file without changing file systems, the actual contents of the file need not be moved—all that needs to be done is to add a new directory entry that points to the existing i-node, and then unlink the old directory entry. The link count will remain the same. For example, to rename the file /usr/lib/foo to /usr/foo, the contents of the file foo need not be moved if the directories /usr/lib and /usr are on the same file system. This is how the mv(1) command usually operates.

We've talked about the concept of a link count for a regular file, but what about the link count field for a directory? Assume that we make a new directory in the working directory, as in

```
$ mkdir testdir
```

Figure 4.15 shows the result. Note that in this figure, we explicitly show the entries for dot and dot-dot.

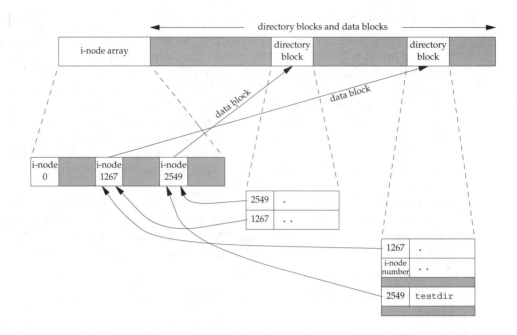

Figure 4.15 Sample cylinder group after creating the directory `testdir`

The i-node whose number is 2549 has a type field of "directory" and a link count equal to 2. Any leaf directory (a directory that does not contain any other directories) always has a link count of 2. The value of 2 is from the directory entry that names the directory (`testdir`) and from the entry for dot in that directory. The i-node whose number is 1267 has a type field of "directory" and a link count that is greater than or equal to 3. The reason we know that the link count is greater than or equal to 3 is that minimally, it is pointed to from the directory entry that names it (which we don't show in Figure 4.15), from dot, and from dot-dot in the `testdir` directory. Note that every subdirectory in a parent directory causes the parent directory's link count to be increased by 1.

This format is similar to the classic format of the UNIX file system, which is described in detail in Chapter 4 of Bach [1986]. Refer to Chapter 7 of McKusick et al. [1996] or Chapter 8 of McKusick and Neville-Neil [2005] for additional information on the changes made with the Berkeley fast file system. See Chapter 14 of Mauro and McDougall [2001] for details on UFS, the Solaris version of the Berkeley fast file system.

4.15 `link`, `unlink`, `remove`, and `rename` Functions

As we saw in the previous section, any file can have multiple directory entries pointing to its i-node. The way we create a link to an existing file is with the `link` function.

```
#include <unistd.h>

int link(const char *existingpath, const char *newpath);
```

Returns: 0 if OK, −1 on error

This function creates a new directory entry, *newpath*, that references the existing file *existingpath*. If the *newpath* already exists, an error is returned. Only the last component of the *newpath* is created. The rest of the path must already exist.

The creation of the new directory entry and the increment of the link count must be an atomic operation. (Recall the discussion of atomic operations in Section 3.11.)

Most implementations require that both pathnames be on the same file system, although POSIX.1 allows an implementation to support linking across file systems. If an implementation supports the creation of hard links to directories, it is restricted to only the superuser. The reason is that doing this can cause loops in the file system, which most utilities that process the file system aren't capable of handling. (We show an example of a loop introduced by a symbolic link in Section 4.16.) Many file system implementations disallow hard links to directories for this reason.

To remove an existing directory entry, we call the unlink function.

```
#include <unistd.h>

int unlink(const char *pathname);
```

Returns: 0 if OK, −1 on error

This function removes the directory entry and decrements the link count of the file referenced by *pathname*. If there are other links to the file, the data in the file is still accessible through the other links. The file is not changed if an error occurs.

We've mentioned before that to unlink a file, we must have write permission and execute permission in the directory containing the directory entry, as it is the directory entry that we will be removing. Also, we mentioned in Section 4.10 that if the sticky bit is set in this directory we must have write permission for the directory and one of the following:

- Own the file
- Own the directory
- Have superuser privileges

Only when the link count reaches 0 can the contents of the file be deleted. One other condition prevents the contents of a file from being deleted: as long as some process has the file open, its contents will not be deleted. When a file is closed, the kernel first checks the count of the number of processes that have the file open. If this count has reached 0, the kernel then checks the link count; if it is 0, the file's contents are deleted.

Example

The program shown in Figure 4.16 opens a file and then unlinks it. The program then goes to sleep for 15 seconds before terminating.

```
#include "apue.h"
#include <fcntl.h>

int
main(void)
{
    if (open("tempfile", O_RDWR) < 0)
        err_sys("open error");
    if (unlink("tempfile") < 0)
        err_sys("unlink error");
    printf("file unlinked\n");
    sleep(15);
    printf("done\n");
    exit(0);
}
```

Figure 4.16 Open a file and then `unlink` it

Running this program gives us

```
$ ls -l tempfile                    look at how big the file is
-rw-r-----  1 sar      413265408 Jan 21 07:14 tempfile
$ df /home                          check how much free space is available
Filesystem     1K-blocks      Used  Available  Use%  Mounted on
/dev/hda4       11021440   1956332    9065108   18%  /home
$ ./a.out &                         run the program in Figure 4.16 in the background
1364                                the shell prints its process ID
$ file unlinked                     the file is unlinked
ls -l tempfile                      see if the filename is still there
ls: tempfile: No such file or directory      the directory entry is gone
$ df /home                          see if the space is available yet
Filesystem     1K-blocks      Used  Available  Use%  Mounted on
/dev/hda4       11021440   1956332    9065108   18%  /home
$ done                              the program is done, all open files are closed
df /home                            now the disk space should be available
Filesystem     1K-blocks      Used  Available  Use%  Mounted on
/dev/hda4       11021440   1552352    9469088   15%  /home
                                    now the 394.1 MB of disk space are available
```

This property of `unlink` is often used by a program to ensure that a temporary file it creates won't be left around in case the program crashes. The process creates a file using either `open` or `creat` and then immediately calls `unlink`. The file is not deleted, however, because it is still open. Only when the process either closes the file or terminates, which causes the kernel to close all its open files, is the file deleted.

If *pathname* is a symbolic link, `unlink` removes the symbolic link, not the file referenced by the link. There is no function to remove the file referenced by a symbolic link given the name of the link.

The superuser can call `unlink` with *pathname* specifying a directory, but the function `rmdir` should be used instead to unlink a directory. We describe the `rmdir` function in Section 4.20.

We can also unlink a file or a directory with the `remove` function. For a file, `remove` is identical to `unlink`. For a directory, `remove` is identical to `rmdir`.

```
#include <stdio.h>

int remove(const char *pathname);
```
Returns: 0 if OK, −1 on error

> ISO C specifies the `remove` function to delete a file. The name was changed from the historical
> UNIX name of `unlink` because most non-UNIX systems that implement the C standard didn't
> support the concept of links to a file at the time.

A file or a directory is renamed with the `rename` function.

```
#include <stdio.h>

int rename(const char *oldname, const char *newname);
```
Returns: 0 if OK, −1 on error

> This function is defined by ISO C for files. (The C standard doesn't deal with directories.)
> POSIX.1 expanded the definition to include directories and symbolic links.

There are several conditions to describe, depending on whether *oldname* refers to a file, a directory, or a symbolic link. We must also describe what happens if *newname* already exists.

1. If *oldname* specifies a file that is not a directory, then we are renaming a file or a symbolic link. In this case, if *newname* exists, it cannot refer to a directory. If *newname* exists and is not a directory, it is removed, and *oldname* is renamed to *newname*. We must have write permission for the directory containing *oldname* and for the directory containing *newname*, since we are changing both directories.

2. If *oldname* specifies a directory, then we are renaming a directory. If *newname* exists, it must refer to a directory, and that directory must be empty. (When we say that a directory is empty, we mean that the only entries in the directory are dot and dot-dot.) If *newname* exists and is an empty directory, it is removed, and *oldname* is renamed to *newname*. Additionally, when we're renaming a directory, *newname* cannot contain a path prefix that names *oldname*. For example, we can't rename `/usr/foo` to `/usr/foo/testdir`, since the old name (`/usr/foo`) is a path prefix of the new name and cannot be removed.

3. If either *oldname* or *newname* refers to a symbolic link, then the link itself is processed, not the file to which it resolves.

4. As a special case, if the *oldname* and *newname* refer to the same file, the function returns successfully without changing anything.

If *newname* already exists, we need permissions as if we were deleting it. Also, because we're removing the directory entry for *oldname* and possibly creating a directory entry for *newname*, we need write permission and execute permission in the directory containing *oldname* and in the directory containing *newname*.

4.16   Symbolic Links

A symbolic link is an indirect pointer to a file, unlike the hard links from the previous section, which pointed directly to the i-node of the file. Symbolic links were introduced to get around the limitations of hard links.

- Hard links normally require that the link and the file reside in the same file system

- Only the superuser can create a hard link to a directory

There are no file system limitations on a symbolic link and what it points to, and anyone can create a symbolic link to a directory. Symbolic links are typically used to move a file or an entire directory hierarchy to another location on a system.

> Symbolic links were introduced with 4.2BSD and subsequently supported by SVR4.

When using functions that refer to a file by name, we always need to know whether the function follows a symbolic link. If the function follows a symbolic link, a pathname argument to the function refers to the file pointed to by the symbolic link. Otherwise, a pathname argument refers to the link itself, not the file pointed to by the link. Figure 4.17 summarizes whether the functions described in this chapter follow a symbolic link. The functions mkdir, mkfifo, mknod, and rmdir are not in this figure, as they return an error when the pathname is a symbolic link. Also, the functions that take a file descriptor argument, such as fstat and fchmod, are not listed, as the handling of a symbolic link is done by the function that returns the file descriptor (usually open). Whether or not chown follows a symbolic link depends on the implementation.

> In older versions of Linux (those before version 2.1.81), chown didn't follow symbolic links. From version 2.1.81 onward, chown follows symbolic links. With FreeBSD 5.2.1 and Mac OS X 10.3, chown follows symbolic links. (Prior to 4.4BSD, chown didn't follow symbolic links, but this was changed in 4.4BSD.) In Solaris 9, chown also follows symbolic links. All of these platforms provide implementations of lchown to change the ownership of symbolic links themselves.

One exception to Figure 4.17 is when the open function is called with both O_CREAT and O_EXCL set. In this case, if the pathname refers to a symbolic link, open will fail with errno set to EEXIST. This behavior is intended to close a security hole so that privileged processes can't be fooled into writing to the wrong files.

Function	Does not follow symbolic link	Follows symbolic link
`access`		•
`chdir`		•
`chmod`		•
`chown`	•	•
`creat`		•
`exec`		•
`lchown`	•	
`link`		•
`lstat`	•	
`open`		•
`opendir`		•
`pathconf`		•
`readlink`	•	
`remove`	•	
`rename`	•	
`stat`		•
`truncate`		•
`unlink`	•	

Figure 4.17   Treatment of symbolic links by various functions

Example

It is possible to introduce loops into the file system by using symbolic links. Most functions that look up a pathname return an `errno` of `ELOOP` when this occurs. Consider the following commands:

```
$ mkdir foo                        make a new directory
$ touch foo/a                      create a 0-length file
$ ln -s ../foo foo/testdir         create a symbolic link
$ ls -l foo
total 0
-rw-r-----   1 sar          0 Jan 22 00:16 a
lrwxrwxrwx   1 sar          6 Jan 22 00:16 testdir -> ../foo
```

This creates a directory `foo` that contains the file a and a symbolic link that points to `foo`. We show this arrangement in Figure 4.18, drawing a directory as a circle and a file as a square. If we write a simple program that uses the standard function `ftw`(3) on Solaris to descend through a file hierarchy, printing each pathname encountered, the output is

```
foo
foo/a
foo/testdir
foo/testdir/a
foo/testdir/testdir
foo/testdir/testdir/a
foo/testdir/testdir/testdir
foo/testdir/testdir/testdir/a
     (many more lines until we encounter an ELOOP error)
```

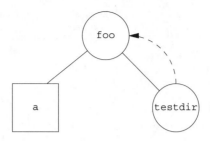

Figure 4.18 Symbolic link `testdir` that creates a loop

In Section 4.21, we provide our own version of the `ftw` function that uses `lstat` instead of `stat`, to prevent it from following symbolic links.

> Note that on Linux, the `ftw` function uses `lstat`, so it doesn't display this behavior.

A loop of this form is easy to remove. We are able to `unlink` the file `foo/testdir`, as `unlink` does not follow a symbolic link. But if we create a hard link that forms a loop of this type, its removal is much more difficult. This is why the `link` function will not form a hard link to a directory unless the process has superuser privileges.

> Indeed, Rich Stevens did this on his own system as an experiment while writing the original version of this section. The file system got corrupted and the normal `fsck`(1) utility couldn't fix things. The deprecated tools `clri`(8) and `dcheck`(8) were needed to repair the file system.

> The need for hard links to directories has long since passed. With symbolic links and the `mkdir` function, there is no longer any need for users to create hard links to directories.

When we open a file, if the pathname passed to `open` specifies a symbolic link, `open` follows the link to the specified file. If the file pointed to by the symbolic link doesn't exist, `open` returns an error saying that it can't open the file. This can confuse users who aren't familiar with symbolic links. For example,

```
$ ln -s /no/such/file myfile          create a symbolic link
$ ls myfile
myfile                                 ls says it's there
$ cat myfile                           so we try to look at it
cat: myfile: No such file or directory
$ ls -l myfile                         try -l option
lrwxrwxrwx  1 sar        13 Jan 22 00:26 myfile -> /no/such/file
```

The file `myfile` does exist, yet `cat` says there is no such file, because `myfile` is a symbolic link and the file pointed to by the symbolic link doesn't exist. The `-l` option to `ls` gives us two hints: the first character is an `l`, which means a symbolic link, and the sequence `->` also indicates a symbolic link. The `ls` command has another option (`-F`) that appends an at-sign to filenames that are symbolic links, which can help spot symbolic links in a directory listing without the `-l` option.   □

4.17 `symlink` and `readlink` Functions

A symbolic link is created with the `symlink` function.

```
#include <unistd.h>

int symlink(const char *actualpath, const char *sympath);
```
Returns: 0 if OK, –1 on error

A new directory entry, *sympath*, is created that points to *actualpath*. It is not required that *actualpath* exist when the symbolic link is created. (We saw this in the example at the end of the previous section.) Also, *actualpath* and *sympath* need not reside in the same file system.

Because the `open` function follows a symbolic link, we need a way to open the link itself and read the name in the link. The `readlink` function does this.

```
#include <unistd.h>

ssize_t readlink(const char* restrict pathname, char *restrict buf,
                 size_t bufsize);
```
Returns: number of bytes read if OK, –1 on error

This function combines the actions of `open`, `read`, and `close`. If the function is successful, it returns the number of bytes placed into *buf*. The contents of the symbolic link that are returned in *buf* are not null terminated.

4.18 File Times

Three time fields are maintained for each file. Their purpose is summarized in Figure 4.19.

Field	Description	Example	`ls(1)` option
`st_atime`	last-access time of file data	`read`	`-u`
`st_mtime`	last-modification time of file data	`write`	default
`st_ctime`	last-change time of i-node status	`chmod`, `chown`	`-c`

Figure 4.19 The three time values associated with each file

Note the difference between the modification time (`st_mtime`) and the changed-status time (`st_ctime`). The modification time is when the contents of the file were last modified. The changed-status time is when the i-node of the file was last modified. In this chapter, we've described many operations that affect the i-node without changing the actual contents of the file: changing the file access permissions, changing the user

ID, changing the number of links, and so on. Because all the information in the i-node is stored separately from the actual contents of the file, we need the changed-status time, in addition to the modification time.

Note that the system does not maintain the last-access time for an i-node. This is why the functions access and stat, for example, don't change any of the three times.

The access time is often used by system administrators to delete files that have not been accessed for a certain amount of time. The classic example is the removal of files named a.out or core that haven't been accessed in the past week. The find(1) command is often used for this type of operation.

The modification time and the changed-status time can be used to archive only those files that have had their contents modified or their i-node modified.

The ls command displays or sorts only on one of the three time values. By default, when invoked with either the -l or the -t option, it uses the modification time of a file. The -u option causes it to use the access time, and the -c option causes it to use the changed-status time.

Figure 4.20 summarizes the effects of the various functions that we've described on these three times. Recall from Section 4.14 that a directory is simply a file containing directory entries: filenames and associated i-node numbers. Adding, deleting, or modifying these directory entries can affect the three times associated with that directory. This is why Figure 4.20 contains one column for the three times associated with the file or directory and another column for the three times associated with the parent directory of the referenced file or directory. For example, creating a new file affects the directory that contains the new file, and it affects the i-node for the new file. Reading or writing a file, however, affects only the i-node of the file and has no effect on the directory. (The mkdir and rmdir functions are covered in Section 4.20. The utime function is covered in the next section. The six exec functions are described in Section 8.10. We describe the mkfifo and pipe functions in Chapter 15.)

4.19 `utime` Function

The access time and the modification time of a file can be changed with the utime function.

```
#include <utime.h>

int utime(const char *pathname, const struct utimbuf *times);
```

                                                         Returns: 0 if OK, –1 on error

The structure used by this function is

```
struct utimbuf {
  time_t  actime;   /* access time */
  time_t  modtime;  /* modification time */
}
```

Function	Referenced file or directory			Parent directory of referenced file or directory			Section	Note
	a	m	c	a	m	c		
chmod, fchmod			•				4.9	
chown, fchown			•				4.11	
creat	•	•	•	•		•	3.4	O_CREAT new file
creat		•	•				3.4	O_TRUNC existing file
exec	•						8.10	
lchown			•				4.11	
link			•		•	•	4.15	parent of second argument
mkdir	•	•	•		•	•	4.20	
mkfifo	•	•	•		•	•	15.5	
open	•	•	•		•	•	3.3	O_CREAT new file
open		•	•				3.3	O_TRUNC existing file
pipe	•	•	•				15.2	
read	•						3.7	
remove			•		•	•	4.15	remove file = unlink
remove					•	•	4.15	remove directory = rmdir
rename			•		•	•	4.15	for both arguments
rmdir					•	•	4.20	
truncate, ftruncate		•	•				4.13	
unlink			•		•	•	4.15	
utime	•	•	•				4.19	
write		•	•				3.8	

Figure 4.20 Effect of various functions on the access, modification, and changed-status times

The two time values in the structure are calendar times, which count seconds since the Epoch, as described in Section 1.10.

The operation of this function, and the privileges required to execute it, depend on whether the *times* argument is NULL.

- If *times* is a null pointer, the access time and the modification time are both set to the current time. To do this, either the effective user ID of the process must equal the owner ID of the file, or the process must have write permission for the file.

- If *times* is a non-null pointer, the access time and the modification time are set to the values in the structure pointed to by *times*. For this case, the effective user ID of the process must equal the owner ID of the file, or the process must be a superuser process. Merely having write permission for the file is not adequate.

Note that we are unable to specify a value for the changed-status time, st_ctime—the time the i-node was last changed—as this field is automatically updated when the utime function is called.

On some versions of the UNIX System, the touch(1) command uses this function. Also, the standard archive programs, tar(1) and cpio(1), optionally call utime to set the times for a file to the time values saved when the file was archived.

Example

The program shown in Figure 4.21 truncates files to zero length using the O_TRUNC option of the open function, but does not change their access time or modification time. To do this, the program first obtains the times with the stat function, truncates the file, and then resets the times with the utime function.

```c
#include "apue.h"
#include <fcntl.h>
#include <utime.h>

int
main(int argc, char *argv[])
{
    int             i, fd;
    struct stat     statbuf;
    struct utimbuf  timebuf;

    for (i = 1; i < argc; i++) {
        if (stat(argv[i], &statbuf) < 0) {  /* fetch current times */
            err_ret("%s: stat error", argv[i]);
            continue;
        }
        if ((fd = open(argv[i], O_RDWR | O_TRUNC)) < 0) { /* truncate */
            err_ret("%s: open error", argv[i]);
            continue;
        }
        close(fd);
        timebuf.actime  = statbuf.st_atime;
        timebuf.modtime = statbuf.st_mtime;
        if (utime(argv[i], &timebuf) < 0) {      /* reset times */
            err_ret("%s: utime error", argv[i]);
            continue;
        }
    }
    exit(0);
}
```

Figure 4.21 Example of utime function

We can demonstrate the program in Figure 4.21 with the following script:

```
$ ls -l changemod times            look at sizes and last-modification times
-rwxrwxr-x  1 sar    15019 Nov 18 18:53 changemod
-rwxrwxr-x  1 sar    16172 Nov 19 20:05 times
$ ls -lu changemod times           look at last-access times
-rwxrwxr-x  1 sar    15019 Nov 18 18:53 changemod
-rwxrwxr-x  1 sar    16172 Nov 19 20:05 times
$ date                             print today's date
Thu Jan 22 06:55:17 EST 2004
$ ./a.out changemod times          run the program in Figure 4.21
$ ls -l changemod times            and check the results
```

```
-rwxrwxr-x  1 sar          0 Nov 18 18:53 changemod
-rwxrwxr-x  1 sar          0 Nov 19 20:05 times
$ ls -lu changemod times              check the last-access times also
-rwxrwxr-x  1 sar          0 Nov 18 18:53 changemod
-rwxrwxr-x  1 sar          0 Nov 19 20:05 times
$ ls -lc changemod times              and the changed-status times
-rwxrwxr-x  1 sar          0 Jan 22 06:55 changemod
-rwxrwxr-x  1 sar          0 Jan 22 06:55 times
```

As we expect, the last-modification times and the last-access times are not changed. The changed-status times, however, are changed to the time that the program was run.   □

4.20 mkdir and rmdir Functions

Directories are created with the mkdir function and deleted with the rmdir function.

```
#include <sys/stat.h>

int mkdir(const char *pathname, mode_t mode);
```

                                                       Returns: 0 if OK, −1 on error

---

This function creates a new, empty directory. The entries for dot and dot-dot are automatically created. The specified file access permissions, *mode*, are modified by the file mode creation mask of the process.

A common mistake is to specify the same *mode* as for a file: read and write permissions only. But for a directory, we normally want at least one of the execute bits enabled, to allow access to filenames within the directory. (See Exercise 4.16.)

The user ID and group ID of the new directory are established according to the rules we described in Section 4.6.

> Solaris 9 and Linux 2.4.22 also have the new directory inherit the set-group-ID bit from the parent directory. This is so that files created in the new directory will inherit the group ID of that directory. With Linux, the file system implementation determines whether this is supported. For example, the ext2 and ext3 file systems allow this behavior to be controlled by an option to the mount(1) command. With the Linux implementation of the UFS file system, however, the behavior is not selectable; it inherits the set-group-ID bit to mimic the historical BSD implementation, where the group ID of a directory is inherited from the parent directory.

> BSD-based implementations don't propagate the set-group-ID bit; they simply inherit the group ID as a matter of policy. Because FreeBSD 5.2.1 and Mac OS X 10.3 are based on 4.4BSD, they do not require this inheriting of the set-group-ID bit. On these platforms, newly created files and directories always inherit the group ID of the parent directory, regardless of the set-group-ID bit.

> Earlier versions of the UNIX System did not have the mkdir function. It was introduced with 4.2BSD and SVR3. In the earlier versions, a process had to call the mknod function to create a new directory. But use of the mknod function was restricted to superuser processes. To circumvent this, the normal command that created a directory, mkdir(1), had to be owned by root with the set-user-ID bit on. To create a directory from a process, the mkdir(1) command had to be invoked with the system(3) function.

An empty directory is deleted with the `rmdir` function. Recall that an empty directory is one that contains entries only for dot and dot-dot.

```
#include <unistd.h>

int rmdir(const char *pathname);
```
                                                        Returns: 0 if OK, –1 on error

If the link count of the directory becomes 0 with this call, and if no other process has the directory open, then the space occupied by the directory is freed. If one or more processes have the directory open when the link count reaches 0, the last link is removed and the dot and dot-dot entries are removed before this function returns. Additionally, no new files can be created in the directory. The directory is not freed, however, until the last process closes it. (Even though some other process has the directory open, it can't be doing much in the directory, as the directory had to be empty for the `rmdir` function to succeed.)

4.21 Reading Directories

Directories can be read by anyone who has access permission to read the directory. But only the kernel can write to a directory, to preserve file system sanity. Recall from Section 4.5 that the write permission bits and execute permission bits for a directory determine if we can create new files in the directory and remove files from the directory—they don't specify if we can write to the directory itself.

The actual format of a directory depends on the UNIX System implementation and the design of the file system. Earlier systems, such as Version 7, had a simple structure: each directory entry was 16 bytes, with 14 bytes for the filename and 2 bytes for the i-node number. When longer filenames were added to 4.2BSD, each entry became variable length, which means that any program that reads a directory is now system dependent. To simplify this, a set of directory routines were developed and are part of POSIX.1. Many implementations prevent applications from using the `read` function to access the contents of directories, thereby further isolating applications from the implementation-specific details of directory formats.

```
#include <dirent.h>

DIR *opendir(const char *pathname);
```
                                            Returns: pointer if OK, NULL on error
```
struct dirent *readdir(DIR *dp);
```
                                Returns: pointer if OK, NULL at end of directory or error
```
void rewinddir(DIR *dp);

int closedir(DIR *dp);
```
                                                        Returns: 0 if OK, –1 on error
```
long telldir(DIR *dp);
```
                                    Returns: current location in directory associated with *dp*
```
void seekdir(DIR *dp, long loc);
```

The `telldir` and `seekdir` functions are not part of the base POSIX.1 standard. They are XSI extensions in the Single UNIX Specifications, so all conforming UNIX System implementations are expected to provide them.

Recall our use of several of these functions in the program shown in Figure 1.3, our bare-bones implementation of the `ls` command.

The `dirent` structure defined in the file `<dirent.h>` is implementation dependent. Implementations define the structure to contain at least the following two members:

```
struct dirent {
  ino_t  d_ino;                    /* i-node number */
  char   d_name[NAME_MAX + 1];     /* null-terminated filename */
}
```

> The d_ino entry is not defined by POSIX.1, since it's an implementation feature, but it is defined in the XSI extension to POSIX.1. POSIX.1 defines only the d_name entry in this structure.

Note that `NAME_MAX` is not a defined constant with Solaris—its value depends on the file system in which the directory resides, and its value is usually obtained from the `fpathconf` function. A common value for `NAME_MAX` is 255. (Recall Figure 2.14.) Since the filename is null terminated, however, it doesn't matter how the array d_name is defined in the header, because the array size doesn't indicate the length of the filename.

The `DIR` structure is an internal structure used by these six functions to maintain information about the directory being read. The purpose of the `DIR` structure is similar to that of the `FILE` structure maintained by the standard I/O library, which we describe in Chapter 5.

The pointer to a `DIR` structure that is returned by `opendir` is then used with the other five functions. The `opendir` function initializes things so that the first `readdir` reads the first entry in the directory. The ordering of entries within the directory is implementation dependent and is usually not alphabetical.

Example

We'll use these directory routines to write a program that traverses a file hierarchy. The goal is to produce the count of the various types of files that we show in Figure 4.4. The program shown in Figure 4.22 takes a single argument—the starting pathname—and recursively descends the hierarchy from that point. Solaris provides a function, `ftw(3)`, that performs the actual traversal of the hierarchy, calling a user-defined function for each file. The problem with this function is that it calls the `stat` function for each file, which causes the program to follow symbolic links. For example, if we start at the root and have a symbolic link named `/lib` that points to `/usr/lib`, all the files in the directory `/usr/lib` are counted twice. To correct this, Solaris provides an additional function, `nftw(3)`, with an option that stops it from following symbolic links. Although we could use `nftw`, we'll write our own simple file walker to show the use of the directory routines.

In the Single UNIX Specification, both `ftw` and `nftw` are included in the XSI extensions to the base POSIX.1 specification. Implementations are included in Solaris 9 and Linux 2.4.22. BSD-based systems have a different function, `fts(3)`, that provides similar functionality. It is available in FreeBSD 5.2.1, Mac OS X 10.3, and Linux 2.4.22.

```c
#include "apue.h"
#include <dirent.h>
#include <limits.h>

/* function type that is called for each filename */
typedef int Myfunc(const char *, const struct stat *, int);

static Myfunc    myfunc;
static int       myftw(char *, Myfunc *);
static int       dopath(Myfunc *);

static long nreg, ndir, nblk, nchr, nfifo, nslink, nsock, ntot;

int
main(int argc, char *argv[])
{
    int     ret;

    if (argc != 2)
        err_quit("usage:  ftw  <starting-pathname>");

    ret = myftw(argv[1], myfunc);       /* does it all */

    ntot = nreg + ndir + nblk + nchr + nfifo + nslink + nsock;
    if (ntot == 0)
        ntot = 1;          /* avoid divide by 0; print 0 for all counts */
    printf("regular files  = %7ld, %5.2f %%\n", nreg,
        nreg*100.0/ntot);
    printf("directories    = %7ld, %5.2f %%\n", ndir,
        ndir*100.0/ntot);
    printf("block special  = %7ld, %5.2f %%\n", nblk,
        nblk*100.0/ntot);
    printf("char special   = %7ld, %5.2f %%\n", nchr,
        nchr*100.0/ntot);
    printf("FIFOs          = %7ld, %5.2f %%\n", nfifo,
        nfifo*100.0/ntot);
    printf("symbolic links = %7ld, %5.2f %%\n", nslink,
        nslink*100.0/ntot);
    printf("sockets        = %7ld, %5.2f %%\n", nsock,
        nsock*100.0/ntot);

    exit(ret);
}

/*
 * Descend through the hierarchy, starting at "pathname".
 * The caller's func() is called for every file.
 */
#define FTW_F    1        /* file other than directory */
```

```
#define FTW_D    2       /* directory */
#define FTW_DNR  3       /* directory that can't be read */
#define FTW_NS   4       /* file that we can't stat */

static char *fullpath;      /* contains full pathname for every file */

static int                  /* we return whatever func() returns */
myftw(char *pathname, Myfunc *func)
{
    int len;
    fullpath = path_alloc(&len);     /* malloc's for PATH_MAX+1 bytes */
                                     /* (Figure 2.15) */
    strncpy(fullpath, pathname, len);   /* protect against */
    fullpath[len-1] = 0;                /* buffer overrun */

    return(dopath(func));
}

/*
 * Descend through the hierarchy, starting at "fullpath".
 * If "fullpath" is anything other than a directory, we lstat() it,
 * call func(), and return.  For a directory, we call ourself
 * recursively for each name in the directory.
 */
static int                  /* we return whatever func() returns */
dopath(Myfunc* func)
{
    struct stat     statbuf;
    struct dirent   *dirp;
    DIR             *dp;
    int             ret;
    char            *ptr;

    if (lstat(fullpath, &statbuf) < 0)   /* stat error */
        return(func(fullpath, &statbuf, FTW_NS));
    if (S_ISDIR(statbuf.st_mode) == 0)   /* not a directory */
        return(func(fullpath, &statbuf, FTW_F));

    /*
     * It's a directory.  First call func() for the directory,
     * then process each filename in the directory.
     */
    if ((ret = func(fullpath, &statbuf, FTW_D)) != 0)
        return(ret);

    ptr = fullpath + strlen(fullpath);  /* point to end of fullpath */
    *ptr++ = '/';
    *ptr = 0;

    if ((dp = opendir(fullpath)) == NULL)   /* can't read directory */
        return(func(fullpath, &statbuf, FTW_DNR));

    while ((dirp = readdir(dp)) != NULL) {
        if (strcmp(dirp->d_name, ".") == 0  ||
```

```
                strcmp(dirp->d_name, "..") == 0)
                    continue;          /* ignore dot and dot-dot */

            strcpy(ptr, dirp->d_name);  /* append name after slash */

            if ((ret = dopath(func)) != 0)          /* recursive */
                break;  /* time to leave */
        }
        ptr[-1] = 0;    /* erase everything from slash onwards */

        if (closedir(dp) < 0)
            err_ret("can't close directory %s", fullpath);

        return(ret);
}

static int
myfunc(const char *pathname, const struct stat *statptr, int type)
{
        switch (type) {
        case FTW_F:
            switch (statptr->st_mode & S_IFMT) {
            case S_IFREG:    nreg++;       break;
            case S_IFBLK:    nblk++;       break;
            case S_IFCHR:    nchr++;       break;
            case S_IFIFO:    nfifo++;      break;
            case S_IFLNK:    nslink++;     break;
            case S_IFSOCK:   nsock++;      break;
            case S_IFDIR:
                err_dump("for S_IFDIR for %s", pathname);
                        /* directories should have type = FTW_D */
            }
            break;

        case FTW_D:
            ndir++;
            break;

        case FTW_DNR:
            err_ret("can't read directory %s", pathname);
            break;

        case FTW_NS:
            err_ret("stat error for %s", pathname);
            break;

        default:
            err_dump("unknown type %d for pathname %s", type, pathname);
        }

        return(0);
}
```

Figure 4.22 Recursively descend a directory hierarchy, counting file types

We have provided more generality in this program than needed. This was done to illustrate the ftw function. For example, the function myfunc always returns 0, even though the function that calls it is prepared to handle a nonzero return.   □

For additional information on descending through a file system and the use of this technique in many standard UNIX System commands—find, ls, tar, and so on—refer to Fowler, Korn, and Vo [1989].

4.22 `chdir`, `fchdir`, and `getcwd` Functions

Every process has a current working directory. This directory is where the search for all relative pathnames starts (all pathnames that do not begin with a slash). When a user logs in to a UNIX system, the current working directory normally starts at the directory specified by the sixth field in the /etc/passwd file—the user's home directory. The current working directory is an attribute of a process; the home directory is an attribute of a login name.

We can change the current working directory of the calling process by calling the chdir or fchdir functions.

```
#include <unistd.h>

int chdir(const char *pathname);

int fchdir(int filedes);
```
                                                        Both return: 0 if OK, −1 on error

We can specify the new current working directory either as a *pathname* or through an open file descriptor.

> The fchdir function is not part of the base POSIX.1 specification. It is an XSI extension in the Single UNIX Specification. All four platforms discussed in this book support fchdir.

Example

Because it is an attribute of a process, the current working directory cannot affect processes that invoke the process that executes the chdir. (We describe the relationship between processes in more detail in Chapter 8.) This means that the program in Figure 4.23 doesn't do what we might expect.

```
#include "apue.h"

int
main(void)
{
    if (chdir("/tmp") < 0)
        err_sys("chdir failed");
    printf("chdir to /tmp succeeded\n");
    exit(0);
}
```

Figure 4.23 Example of chdir function

If we compile it and call the executable `mycd`, we get the following:

```
$ pwd
/usr/lib
$ mycd
chdir to /tmp succeeded
$ pwd
/usr/lib
```

The current working directory for the shell that executed the `mycd` program didn't change. This is a side effect of the way that the shell executes programs. Each program is run in a separate process, so the current working directory of the shell is unaffected by the call to `chdir` in the program. For this reason, the `chdir` function has to be called directly from the shell, so the `cd` command is built into the shells.   □

Because the kernel must maintain knowledge of the current working directory, we should be able to fetch its current value. Unfortunately, the kernel doesn't maintain the full pathname of the directory. Instead, the kernel keeps information about the directory, such as a pointer to the directory's v-node.

> The Linux kernel can determine the full pathname. Its components are distributed throughout the mount table and the dcache table, and are reassembled, for example, when you read the `/proc/self/cwd` symbolic link.

What we need is a function that starts at the current working directory (dot) and works its way up the directory hierarchy, using dot-dot to move up one level. At each directory, the function reads the directory entries until it finds the name that corresponds to the i-node of the directory that it just came from. Repeating this procedure until the root is encountered yields the entire absolute pathname of the current working directory. Fortunately, a function already exists that does this for us.

```
#include <unistd.h>

char *getcwd(char *buf, size_t size);
```
                                                              Returns: *buf* if OK, NULL on error

We must pass to this function the address of a buffer, *buf*, and its *size* (in bytes). The buffer must be large enough to accommodate the absolute pathname plus a terminating null byte, or an error is returned. (Recall the discussion of allocating space for a maximum-sized pathname in Section 2.5.5.)

> Some older implementations of `getcwd` allow the first argument *buf* to be NULL. In this case, the function calls `malloc` to allocate *size* number of bytes dynamically. This is not part of POSIX.1 or the Single UNIX Specification and should be avoided.

Example

The program in Figure 4.24 changes to a specific directory and then calls `getcwd` to print the working directory. If we run the program, we get

```
$ ./a.out
cwd = /var/spool/uucppublic
$ ls -l /usr/spool
lrwxrwxrwx  1 root  12 Jan 31 07:57 /usr/spool -> ../var/spool
```

```
#include "apue.h"

int
main(void)
{
    char    *ptr;
    int      size;

    if (chdir("/usr/spool/uucppublic") < 0)
        err_sys("chdir failed");

    ptr = path_alloc(&size);       /* our own function */
    if (getcwd(ptr, size) == NULL)
        err_sys("getcwd failed");

    printf("cwd = %s\n", ptr);
    exit(0);
}
```

Figure 4.24 Example of getcwd function

Note that chdir follows the symbolic link—as we expect it to, from Figure 4.17—but when it goes up the directory tree, getcwd has no idea when it hits the /var/spool directory that it is pointed to by the symbolic link /usr/spool. This is a characteristic of symbolic links.   □

The getcwd function is useful when we have an application that needs to return to the location in the file system where it started out. We can save the starting location by calling getcwd before we change our working directory. After we complete our processing, we can pass the pathname obtained from getcwd to chdir to return to our starting location in the file system.

The fchdir function provides us with an easy way to accomplish this task. Instead of calling getcwd, we can open the current directory and save the file descriptor before we change to a different location in the file system. When we want to return to where we started, we can simply pass the file descriptor to fchdir.

4.23 Device Special Files

The two fields st_dev and st_rdev are often confused. We'll need to use these fields in Section 18.9 when we write the ttyname function. The rules are simple.

- Every file system is known by its major and minor device numbers, which are encoded in the primitive system data type dev_t. The major number identifies the device driver and sometimes encodes which peripheral board to communicate with; the minor number identifies the specific subdevice. Recall from Figure 4.13 that a disk drive often contains several file systems. Each file system on the same disk drive would usually have the same major number, but a different minor number.

- We can usually access the major and minor device numbers through two macros defined by most implementations: `major` and `minor`. This means that we don't care how the two numbers are stored in a `dev_t` object.

> Early systems stored the device number in a 16-bit integer, with 8 bits for the major number and 8 bits for the minor number. FreeBSD 5.2.1 and Mac OS X 10.3 use a 32-bit integer, with 8 bits for the major number and 24 bits for the minor number. On 32-bit systems, Solaris 9 uses a 32-bit integer for `dev_t`, with 14 bits designated as the major number and 18 bits designated as the minor number. On 64-bit systems, Solaris 9 represents `dev_t` as a 64-bit integer, with 32 bits for each number. On Linux 2.4.22, although `dev_t` is a 64-bit integer, currently the major and minor numbers are each only 8 bits.

> POSIX.1 states that the `dev_t` type exists, but doesn't define what it contains or how to get at its contents. The macros `major` and `minor` are defined by most implementations. Which header they are defined in depends on the system. They can be found in `<sys/types.h>` on BSD-based systems. Solaris defines them in `<sys/mkdev.h>`. Linux defines these macros in `<sys/sysmacros.h>`, which is included by `<sys/types.h>`.

- The `st_dev` value for every filename on a system is the device number of the file system containing that filename and its corresponding i-node.

- Only character special files and block special files have an `st_rdev` value. This value contains the device number for the actual device.

Example

The program in Figure 4.25 prints the device number for each command-line argument. Additionally, if the argument refers to a character special file or a block special file, the `st_rdev` value for the special file is also printed.

```
#include "apue.h"
#ifdef SOLARIS
#include <sys/mkdev.h>
#endif

int
main(int argc, char *argv[])
{
    int            i;
    struct stat buf;

    for (i = 1; i < argc; i++) {
        printf("%s: ", argv[i]);
        if (stat(argv[i], &buf) < 0) {
            err_ret("stat error");
            continue;
        }

        printf("dev = %d/%d", major(buf.st_dev),  minor(buf.st_dev));
```

```
        if (S_ISCHR(buf.st_mode) || S_ISBLK(buf.st_mode)) {
            printf(" (%s) rdev = %d/%d",
                    (S_ISCHR(buf.st_mode)) ? "character" : "block",
                    major(buf.st_rdev), minor(buf.st_rdev));
        }
        printf("\n");
    }

    exit(0);
}
```

Figure 4.25 Print st_dev and st_rdev values

Running this program gives us the following output:

```
$ ./a.out / /home/sar /dev/tty[01]
/: dev = 3/3
/home/sar: dev = 3/4
/dev/tty0: dev = 0/7 (character) rdev = 4/0
/dev/tty1: dev = 0/7 (character) rdev = 4/1
$ mount                                which directories are mounted on which devices?
/dev/hda3 on / type ext2 (rw,noatime)
/dev/hda4 on /home type ext2 (rw,noatime)
$ ls -lL /dev/tty[01] /dev/hda[34]
brw-------  1 root         3,   3 Dec 31  1969 /dev/hda3
brw-------  1 root         3,   4 Dec 31  1969 /dev/hda4
crw-------  1 root         4,   0 Dec 31  1969 /dev/tty0
crw-------  1 root         4,   1 Jan 18 15:36 /dev/tty1
```

The first two arguments to the program are directories (/ and /home/sar), and the next two are the device names /dev/tty[01]. (We use the shell's regular expression language to shorten the amount of typing we need to do. The shell will expand the string /dev/tty[01] to /dev/tty0 /dev/tty1.)

We expect the devices to be character special files. The output from the program shows that the root directory has a different device number than does the /home/sar directory. This indicates that they are on different file systems. Running the mount(1) command verifies this.

We then use ls to look at the two disk devices reported by mount and the two terminal devices. The two disk devices are block special files, and the two terminal devices are character special files. (Normally, the only types of devices that are block special files are those that can contain random-access file systems: disk drives, floppy disk drives, and CD-ROMs, for example. Some older versions of the UNIX System supported magnetic tapes for file systems, but this was never widely used.)

Note that the filenames and i-nodes for the two terminal devices (st_dev) are on device 0/7—the devfs pseudo file system, which implements the /dev—but that their actual device numbers are 4/0 and 4/1.   □

4.24 Summary of File Access Permission Bits

We've covered all the file access permission bits, some of which serve multiple purposes. Figure 4.26 summarizes all these permission bits and their interpretation when applied to a regular file and a directory.

Constant	Description	Effect on regular file	Effect on directory
S_ISUID	set-user-ID	set effective user ID on execution	(not used)
S_ISGID	set-group-ID	if group-execute set then set effective group ID on execution; otherwise enable mandatory record locking (if supported)	set group ID of new files created in directory to group ID of directory
S_ISVTX	sticky bit	control caching of file contents (if supported)	restrict removal and renaming of files in directory
S_IRUSR	user-read	user permission to read file	user permission to read directory entries
S_IWUSR	user-write	user permission to write file	user permission to remove and create files in directory
S_IXUSR	user-execute	user permission to execute file	user permission to search for given pathname in directory
S_IRGRP	group-read	group permission to read file	group permission to read directory entries
S_IWGRP	group-write	group permission to write file	group permission to remove and create files in directory
S_IXGRP	group-execute	group permission to execute file	group permission to search for given pathname in directory
S_IROTH	other-read	other permission to read file	other permission to read directory entries
S_IWOTH	other-write	other permission to write file	other permission to remove and create files in directory
S_IXOTH	other-execute	other permission to execute file	other permission to search for given pathname in directory

Figure 4.26 Summary of file access permission bits

The final nine constants can also be grouped into threes, since

```
S_IRWXU = S_IRUSR | S_IWUSR | S_IXUSR
S_IRWXG = S_IRGRP | S_IWGRP | S_IXGRP
S_IRWXO = S_IROTH | S_IWOTH | S_IXOTH
```

4.25 Summary

This chapter has centered around the stat function. We've gone through each member in the stat structure in detail. This in turn led us to examine all the attributes of UNIX files. A thorough understanding of all the properties of a file and all the functions that operate on files is essential to UNIX programming.

Exercises

4.1 Modify the program in Figure 4.3 to use `stat` instead of `lstat`. What changes if one of the command-line arguments is a symbolic link?

4.2 What happens if the file mode creation mask is set to 777 (octal)? Verify the results using your shell's `umask` command.

4.3 Verify that turning off user-read permission for a file that you own denies your access to the file.

4.4 Run the program in Figure 4.9 *after* creating the files `foo` and `bar`. What happens?

4.5 In Section 4.12, we said that a file size of 0 is valid for a regular file. We also said that the `st_size` field is defined for directories and symbolic links. Should we ever see a file size of 0 for a directory or a symbolic link?

4.6 Write a utility like cp(1) that copies a file containing holes, without writing the bytes of 0 to the output file.

4.7 Note in output from the `ls` command in Section 4.12 that the files `core` and `core.copy` have different access permissions. If the `umask` value didn't change between the creation of the two files, explain how the difference could have occurred.

4.8 When running the program in Figure 4.16, we check the available disk space with the df(1) command. Why didn't we use the du(1) command?

4.9 In Figure 4.20, we show the `unlink` function as modifying the changed-status time of the file itself. How can this happen?

4.10 In Section 4.21, how does the system's limit on the number of open files affect the `myftw` function?

4.11 In Section 4.21, our version of `ftw` never changes its directory. Modify this routine so that each time it encounters a directory, it does a `chdir` to that directory, allowing it to use the filename and not the pathname for each call to `lstat`. When all the entries in a directory have been processed, execute `chdir("..")`. Compare the time used by this version and the version in the text.

4.12 Each process also has a root directory that is used for resolution of absolute pathnames. This root directory can be changed with the `chroot` function. Look up the description for this function in your manuals. When might this function be useful?

4.13 How can you set only one of the two time values with the `utime` function?

4.14 Some versions of the finger(1) command output "New mail received ..." and "unread since ..." where ... are the corresponding times and dates. How can the program determine these two times and dates?

4.15 Examine the archive formats by the cpio(1) and tar(1) commands. (These descriptions are usually found in Section 5 of the *UNIX Programmer's Manual*.) How many of the three possible time values are saved for each file? When a file is restored, what value do you think the access time is set to, and why?

4.16 Does the UNIX System have a fundamental limitation on the depth of a directory tree? To find out, write a program that creates a directory and then changes to that directory, in a loop. Make certain that the length of the absolute pathname of the leaf of this directory is greater than your system's PATH_MAX limit. Can you call getcwd to fetch the directory's pathname? How do the standard UNIX System tools deal with this long pathname? Can you archive the directory using either tar or cpio?

4.17   In Section 3.16, we described the /dev/fd feature. For any user to be able to access these files, their permissions must be rw-rw-rw-. Some programs that create an output file delete the file first, in case it already exists, ignoring the return code:

```
unlink(path);
if ((fd = creat(path, FILE_MODE)) < 0)
    err_sys(...);
```

What happens if path is /dev/fd/1?

5

Standard I/O Library

5.1 Introduction

In this chapter, we describe the standard I/O library. This library is specified by the ISO C standard because it has been implemented on many operating systems other than the UNIX System. Additional interfaces are defined as extensions to the ISO C standard by the Single UNIX Specification.

The standard I/O library handles such details as buffer allocation and performing I/O in optimal-sized chunks, obviating our need to worry about using the correct block size (as in Section 3.9). This makes the library easy to use, but at the same time introduces another set of problems if we're not cognizant of what's going on.

> The standard I/O library was written by Dennis Ritchie around 1975. It was a major revision of the Portable I/O library written by Mike Lesk. Surprisingly, little has changed in the standard I/O library after 30 years.

5.2 Streams and `FILE` Objects

In Chapter 3, all the I/O routines centered around file descriptors. When a file is opened, a file descriptor is returned, and that descriptor is then used for all subsequent I/O operations. With the standard I/O library, the discussion centers around *streams*. (Do not confuse the standard I/O term *stream* with the STREAMS I/O system that is part of System V and standardized in the XSI STREAMS option in the Single UNIX Specification.) When we open or create a file with the standard I/O library, we say that we have associated a stream with the file.

With the ASCII character set, a single character is represented by a single byte. With international character sets, a character can be represented by more than one byte.

Standard I/O file streams can be used with single-byte and multibyte ("wide") character sets. A stream's orientation determines whether the characters that are read and written are single-byte or multibyte. Initially, when a stream is created, it has no orientation. If a multibyte I/O function (see <wchar.h>) is used on a stream without orientation, the stream's orientation is set to wide-oriented. If a byte I/O function is used on a stream without orientation, the stream's orientation is set to byte-oriented. Only two functions can change the orientation once set. The freopen function (discussed shortly) will clear a stream's orientation; the fwide function can be used to set a stream's orientation.

```
#include <stdio.h>
#include <wchar.h>

int fwide(FILE *fp, int mode);
```
Returns: positive if stream is wide-oriented,
negative if stream is byte-oriented,
or 0 if stream has no orientation

The fwide function performs different tasks, depending on the value of the *mode* argument.

- If the *mode* argument is negative, fwide will try to make the specified stream byte-oriented.

- If the *mode* argument is positive, fwide will try to make the specified stream wide-oriented.

- If the *mode* argument is zero, fwide will not try to set the orientation, but will still return a value identifying the stream's orientation.

Note that fwide will not change the orientation of a stream that is already oriented. Also note that there is no error return. Consider what would happen if the stream is invalid. The only recourse we have is to clear errno before calling fwide and check the value of errno when we return. Throughout the rest of this book, we will deal only with byte-oriented streams.

When we open a stream, the standard I/O function fopen returns a pointer to a FILE object. This object is normally a structure that contains all the information required by the standard I/O library to manage the stream: the file descriptor used for actual I/O, a pointer to a buffer for the stream, the size of the buffer, a count of the number of characters currently in the buffer, an error flag, and the like.

Application software should never need to examine a FILE object. To reference the stream, we pass its FILE pointer as an argument to each standard I/O function. Throughout this text, we'll refer to a pointer to a FILE object, the type FILE * as a *file pointer*.

Throughout this chapter, we describe the standard I/O library in the context of a UNIX system. As we mentioned, this library has already been ported to a wide variety of other operating systems. But to provide some insight about how this library can be implemented, we will talk about its typical implementation on a UNIX system.

5.3   Standard Input, Standard Output, and Standard Error

Three streams are predefined and automatically available to a process: standard input, standard output, and standard error. These streams refer to the same files as the file descriptors `STDIN_FILENO`, `STDOUT_FILENO`, and `STDERR_FILENO`, which we mentioned in Section 3.2.

These three standard I/O streams are referenced through the predefined file pointers `stdin`, `stdout`, and `stderr`. The file pointers are defined in the `<stdio.h>` header.

5.4   Buffering

The goal of the buffering provided by the standard I/O library is to use the minimum number of `read` and `write` calls. (Recall Figure 3.5, where we showed the amount of CPU time required to perform I/O using various buffer sizes.) Also, it tries to do its buffering automatically for each I/O stream, obviating the need for the application to worry about it. Unfortunately, the single aspect of the standard I/O library that generates the most confusion is its buffering.

Three types of buffering are provided:

1. Fully buffered. In this case, actual I/O takes place when the standard I/O buffer is filled. Files residing on disk are normally fully buffered by the standard I/O library. The buffer used is usually obtained by one of the standard I/O functions calling `malloc` (Section 7.8) the first time I/O is performed on a stream.

    The term *flush* describes the writing of a standard I/O buffer. A buffer can be flushed automatically by the standard I/O routines, such as when a buffer fills, or we can call the function `fflush` to flush a stream. Unfortunately, in the UNIX environment, *flush* means two different things. In terms of the standard I/O library, it means writing out the contents of a buffer, which may be partially filled. In terms of the terminal driver, such as the `tcflush` function in Chapter 18, it means to discard the data that's already stored in a buffer.

2. Line buffered. In this case, the standard I/O library performs I/O when a newline character is encountered on input or output. This allows us to output a single character at a time (with the standard I/O `fputc` function), knowing that actual I/O will take place only when we finish writing each line. Line buffering is typically used on a stream when it refers to a terminal: standard input and standard output, for example.

    Line buffering comes with two caveats. First, the size of the buffer that the standard I/O library is using to collect each line is fixed, so I/O might take place if we fill this buffer before writing a newline. Second, whenever input is requested through the standard I/O library from either (a) an unbuffered stream or (b) a line-buffered stream (that requires data to be requested from the kernel), *all* line-buffered output streams are flushed. The reason for the qualifier on (b) is that the requested data may already be in the buffer, which doesn't require data to be read from the kernel. Obviously, any input from an unbuffered stream, item (a), requires data to be obtained from the kernel.

3. Unbuffered. The standard I/O library does not buffer the characters. If we write 15 characters with the standard I/O `fputs` function, for example, we expect these 15 characters to be output as soon as possible, probably with the `write` function from Section 3.8.

   The standard error stream, for example, is normally unbuffered. This is so that any error messages are displayed as quickly as possible, regardless of whether they contain a newline.

ISO C requires the following buffering characteristics.

- Standard input and standard output are fully buffered, if and only if they do not refer to an interactive device.
- Standard error is never fully buffered.

This, however, doesn't tell us whether standard input and standard output can be unbuffered or line buffered if they refer to an interactive device and whether standard error should be unbuffered or line buffered. Most implementations default to the following types of buffering.

- Standard error is always unbuffered.
- All other streams are line buffered if they refer to a terminal device; otherwise, they are fully buffered.

> The four platforms discussed in this book follow these conventions for standard I/O buffering: standard error is unbuffered, streams open to terminal devices are line buffered, and all other streams are fully buffered.

We explore standard I/O buffering in more detail in Section 5.12 and Figure 5.11.

If we don't like these defaults for any given stream, we can change the buffering by calling either of the following two functions.

```
#include <stdio.h>

void setbuf(FILE *restrict fp, char *restrict buf);

int setvbuf(FILE *restrict fp, char *restrict buf, int mode,
            size_t size);
```
                                                Returns: 0 if OK, nonzero on error

These functions must be called *after* the stream has been opened (obviously, since each requires a valid file pointer as its first argument) but *before* any other operation is performed on the stream.

With `setbuf`, we can turn buffering on or off. To enable buffering, *buf* must point to a buffer of length BUFSIZ, a constant defined in `<stdio.h>`. Normally, the stream is then fully buffered, but some systems may set line buffering if the stream is associated with a terminal device. To disable buffering, we set *buf* to NULL.

With `setvbuf`, we specify exactly which type of buffering we want. This is done with the *mode* argument:

_IOFBF	fully buffered
_IOLBF	line buffered
_IONBF	unbuffered

If we specify an unbuffered stream, the *buf* and *size* arguments are ignored. If we specify fully buffered or line buffered, *buf* and *size* can optionally specify a buffer and its size. If the stream is buffered and *buf* is NULL, the standard I/O library will automatically allocate its own buffer of the appropriate size for the stream. By appropriate size, we mean the value specified by the constant BUFSIZ.

> Some C library implementations use the value from the st_blksize member of the stat structure (see Section 4.2) to determine the optimal standard I/O buffer size. As we will see later in this chapter, the GNU C library uses this method.

Figure 5.1 summarizes the actions of these two functions and their various options.

Function	*mode*	*buf*	Buffer and length	Type of buffering
setbuf		non-null	user *buf* of length BUFSIZ	fully buffered or line buffered
		NULL	(no buffer)	unbuffered
setvbuf	_IOFBF	non-null	user *buf* of length *size*	fully buffered
		NULL	system buffer of appropriate length	
	_IOLBF	non-null	user *buf* of length *size*	line buffered
		NULL	system buffer of appropriate length	
	_IONBF	(ignored)	(no buffer)	unbuffered

Figure 5.1 Summary of the `setbuf` and `setvbuf` functions

Be aware that if we allocate a standard I/O buffer as an automatic variable within a function, we have to close the stream before returning from the function. (We'll discuss this more in Section 7.8.) Also, some implementations use part of the buffer for internal bookkeeping, so the actual number of bytes of data that can be stored in the buffer is less than *size*. In general, we should let the system choose the buffer size and automatically allocate the buffer. When we do this, the standard I/O library automatically releases the buffer when we close the stream.

At any time, we can force a stream to be flushed.

```
#include <stdio.h>

int fflush(FILE *fp);
```
                                                            Returns: 0 if OK, EOF on error

This function causes any unwritten data for the stream to be passed to the kernel. As a special case, if *fp* is NULL, this function causes all output streams to be flushed.

5.5   Opening a Stream

The following three functions open a standard I/O stream.

```
#include <stdio.h>

FILE *fopen(const char *restrict pathname, const char *restrict type);

FILE *freopen(const char *restrict pathname, const char *restrict type,
              FILE *restrict fp);

FILE *fdopen(int filedes, const char *type);
```
                                        All three return: file pointer if OK, NULL on error

The differences in these three functions are as follows.

1. The fopen function opens a specified file.

2   The freopen function opens a specified file on a specified stream, closing the
    stream first if it is already open. If the stream previously had an orientation,
    freopen clears it. This function is typically used to open a specified file as one
    of the predefined streams: standard input, standard output, or standard error.

3. The fdopen function takes an existing file descriptor, which we could obtain
    from the open, dup, dup2, fcntl, pipe, socket, socketpair, or accept
    functions, and associates a standard I/O stream with the descriptor. This
    function is often used with descriptors that are returned by the functions that
    create pipes and network communication channels. Because these special types
    of files cannot be opened with the standard I/O fopen function, we have to call
    the device-specific function to obtain a file descriptor, and then associate this
    descriptor with a standard I/O stream using fdopen.

> Both fopen and freopen are part of ISO C; fdopen is part of POSIX.1, since ISO C doesn't
> deal with file descriptors.

ISO C specifies 15 values for the *type* argument, shown in Figure 5.2.

type	Description
r or rb	open for reading
w or wb	truncate to 0 length or create for writing
a or ab	append; open for writing at end of file, or create for writing
r+ or r+b or rb+	open for reading and writing
w+ or w+b or wb+	truncate to 0 length or create for reading and writing
a+ or a+b or ab+	open or create for reading and writing at end of file

Figure 5.2 The *type* argument for opening a standard I/O stream

Using the character b as part of the *type* allows the standard I/O system to differentiate
between a text file and a binary file. Since the UNIX kernel doesn't differentiate
between these types of files, specifying the character b as part of the *type* has no effect.

With `fdopen`, the meanings of the *type* argument differ slightly. The descriptor has already been opened, so opening for write does not truncate the file. (If the descriptor was created by the `open` function, for example, and the file already existed, the `O_TRUNC` flag would control whether or not the file was truncated. The `fdopen` function cannot simply truncate any file it opens for writing.) Also, the standard I/O append mode cannot create the file (since the file has to exist if a descriptor refers to it).

When a file is opened with a type of append, each write will take place at the then current end of file. If multiple processes open the same file with the standard I/O append mode, the data from each process will be correctly written to the file.

> Versions of `fopen` from Berkeley before 4.4BSD and the simple version shown on page 177 of Kernighan and Ritchie [1988] do not handle the append mode correctly. These versions do an `lseek` to the end of file when the stream is opened. To correctly support the append mode when multiple processes are involved, the file must be opened with the `O_APPEND` flag, which we discussed in Section 3.3. Doing an `lseek` before each write won't work either, as we discussed in Section 3.11.

When a file is opened for reading and writing (the plus sign in the *type*), the following restrictions apply.

- Output cannot be directly followed by input without an intervening `fflush`, `fseek`, `fsetpos`, or `rewind`.
- Input cannot be directly followed by output without an intervening `fseek`, `fsetpos`, or `rewind`, or an input operation that encounters an end of file.

We can summarize the six ways to open a stream from Figure 5.2 in Figure 5.3.

Restriction	r	w	a	r+	w+	a+
file must already exist	•			•		
previous contents of file discarded		•			•	
stream can be read	•			•	•	•
stream can be written		•	•	•	•	•
stream can be written only at end			•			•

Figure 5.3 Six ways to open a standard I/O stream

Note that if a new file is created by specifying a *type* of either w or a, we are not able to specify the file's access permission bits, as we were able to do with the `open` function and the `creat` function in Chapter 3.

By default, the stream that is opened is fully buffered, unless it refers to a terminal device, in which case it is line buffered. Once the stream is opened, but before we do any other operation on the stream, we can change the buffering if we want to, with the `setbuf` or `setvbuf` functions from the previous section.

An open stream is closed by calling `fclose`.

```
#include <stdio.h>

int fclose(FILE *fp);
```
                                                          Returns: 0 if OK, EOF on error

Any buffered output data is flushed before the file is closed. Any input data that may be buffered is discarded. If the standard I/O library had automatically allocated a buffer for the stream, that buffer is released.

When a process terminates normally, either by calling the `exit` function directly or by returning from the `main` function, all standard I/O streams with unwritten buffered data are flushed, and all open standard I/O streams are closed.

5.6 Reading and Writing a Stream

Once we open a stream, we can choose from among three types of unformatted I/O:

1. Character-at-a-time I/O. We can read or write one character at a time, with the standard I/O functions handling all the buffering, if the stream is buffered.

2. Line-at-a-time I/O. If we want to read or write a line at a time, we use `fgets` and `fputs`. Each line is terminated with a newline character, and we have to specify the maximum line length that we can handle when we call `fgets`. We describe these two functions in Section 5.7.

3. Direct I/O. This type of I/O is supported by the `fread` and `fwrite` functions. For each I/O operation, we read or write some number of objects, where each object is of a specified size. These two functions are often used for binary files where we read or write a structure with each operation. We describe these two functions in Section 5.9.

> The term *direct I/O*, from the ISO C standard, is known by many names: binary I/O, object-at-a-time I/O, record-oriented I/O, or structure-oriented I/O.

(We describe the formatted I/O functions, such as `printf` and `scanf`, in Section 5.11.)

Input Functions

Three functions allow us to read one character at a time.

```
#include <stdio.h>

int getc(FILE *fp);

int fgetc(FILE *fp);

int getchar(void);
```
All three return: next character if OK, EOF on end of file or error

The function `getchar` is defined to be equivalent to `getc(stdin)`. The difference between the first two functions is that `getc` can be implemented as a macro, whereas `fgetc` cannot be implemented as a macro. This means three things.

1. The argument to `getc` should not be an expression with side effects.

2. Since `fgetc` is guaranteed to be a function, we can take its address. This allows us to pass the address of `fgetc` as an argument to another function.

3. Calls to `fgetc` probably take longer than calls to `getc`, as it usually takes more time to call a function.

These three functions return the next character as an `unsigned char` converted to an `int`. The reason for specifying unsigned is so that the high-order bit, if set, doesn't cause the return value to be negative. The reason for requiring an integer return value is so that all possible character values can be returned, along with an indication that either an error occurred or the end of file has been encountered. The constant EOF in `<stdio.h>` is required to be a negative value. Its value is often –1. This representation also means that we cannot store the return value from these three functions in a character variable and compare this value later against the constant EOF.

Note that these functions return the same value whether an error occurs or the end of file is reached. To distinguish between the two, we must call either `ferror` or `feof`.

```
#include <stdio.h>

int ferror(FILE *fp);

int feof(FILE *fp);
```
                        Both return: nonzero (true) if condition is true, 0 (false) otherwise
```
void clearerr(FILE *fp);
```

In most implementations, two flags are maintained for each stream in the FILE object:

- An error flag
- An end-of-file flag

Both flags are cleared by calling `clearerr`.

After reading from a stream, we can push back characters by calling `ungetc`.

```
#include <stdio.h>

int ungetc(int c, FILE *fp);
```
                                                        Returns: *c* if OK, EOF on error

The characters that are pushed back are returned by subsequent reads on the stream in reverse order of their pushing. Be aware, however, that although ISO C allows an implementation to support any amount of pushback, an implementation is required to provide only a single character of pushback. We should not count on more than a single character.

The character that we push back does not have to be the same character that was read. We are not able to push back EOF. But when we've reached the end of file, we can push back a character. The next read will return that character, and the read after that will return EOF. This works because a successful call to `ungetc` clears the end-of-file indication for the stream.

Pushback is often used when we're reading an input stream and breaking the input into words or tokens of some form. Sometimes we need to peek at the next character to determine how to handle the current character. It's then easy to push back the character that we peeked at, for the next call to `getc` to return. If the standard I/O library didn't provide this pushback capability, we would have to store the character in a variable of our own, along with a flag telling us to use this character instead of calling getc the next time we need a character.

> When we push characters back with ungetc, they don't get written back to the underlying file or device. They are kept incore in the standard I/O library's buffer for the stream.

Output Functions

We'll find an output function that corresponds to each of the input functions that we've already described.

```
#include <stdio.h>

int putc(int c, FILE *fp);

int fputc(int c, FILE *fp);

int putchar(int c);
```
                                        All three return: *c* if OK, EOF on error

Like the input functions, putchar(c) is equivalent to putc(c, stdout), and putc can be implemented as a macro, whereas fputc cannot be implemented as a macro.

5.7   Line-at-a-Time I/O

Line-at-a-time input is provided by the following two functions.

```
#include <stdio.h>

char *fgets(char *restrict buf, int n, FILE *restrict fp);

char *gets(char *buf);
```
                              Both return: buf if OK, NULL on end of file or error

Both specify the address of the buffer to read the line into. The gets function reads from standard input, whereas fgets reads from the specified stream.

With fgets, we have to specify the size of the buffer, *n*. This function reads up through and including the next newline, but no more than *n–1* characters, into the buffer. The buffer is terminated with a null byte. If the line, including the terminating newline, is longer than *n–1*, only a partial line is returned, but the buffer is always null terminated. Another call to fgets will read what follows on the line.

The gets function should never be used. The problem is that it doesn't allow the caller to specify the buffer size. This allows the buffer to overflow, if the line is longer than the buffer, writing over whatever happens to follow the buffer in memory. For a description of how this flaw was used as part of the Internet worm of 1988, see the June 1989 issue (vol. 32, no. 6) of *Communications of the ACM*. An additional difference with gets is that it doesn't store the newline in the buffer, as does fgets.

> This difference in newline handling between the two functions goes way back in the evolution
> of the UNIX System. Even the Version 7 manual (1979) states "gets deletes a newline, fgets
> keeps it, all in the name of backward compatibility."

Even though ISO C requires an implementation to provide gets, use fgets instead.
Line-at-a-time output is provided by fputs and puts.

```
#include <stdio.h>

int fputs(const char *restrict str, FILE *restrict fp);

int puts(const char *str);
```
Both return: non-negative value if OK, EOF on error

The function fputs writes the null-terminated string to the specified stream. The null
byte at the end is not written. Note that this need not be line-at-a-time output, since the
string need not contain a newline as the last non-null character. Usually, this is the
case—the last non-null character is a newline—but it's not required.

The puts function writes the null-terminated string to the standard output, without
writing the null byte. But puts then writes a newline character to the standard output.

The puts function is not unsafe, like its counterpart gets. Nevertheless, we'll
avoid using it, to prevent having to remember whether it appends a newline. If we
always use fgets and fputs, we know that we always have to deal with the newline
character at the end of each line.

5.8 Standard I/O Efficiency

Using the functions from the previous section, we can get an idea of the efficiency of the
standard I/O system. The program in Figure 5.4 is like the one in Figure 3.4: it simply
copies standard input to standard output, using getc and putc. These two routines
can be implemented as macros.

```
#include "apue.h"

int
main(void)
{
    int     c;

    while ((c = getc(stdin)) != EOF)
        if (putc(c, stdout) == EOF)
            err_sys("output error");

    if (ferror(stdin))
        err_sys("input error");

    exit(0);
}
```

Figure 5.4 Copy standard input to standard output using getc and putc

We can make another version of this program that uses `fgetc` and `fputc`, which should be functions, not macros. (We don't show this trivial change to the source code.)

Finally, we have a version that reads and writes lines, shown in Figure 5.5.

```
#include "apue.h"

int
main(void)
{
    char    buf[MAXLINE];

    while (fgets(buf, MAXLINE, stdin) != NULL)
        if (fputs(buf, stdout) == EOF)
            err_sys("output error");

    if (ferror(stdin))
        err_sys("input error");

    exit(0);
}
```

Figure 5.5   Copy standard input to standard output using `fgets` and `fputs`

Note that we do not close the standard I/O streams explicitly in Figure 5.4 or Figure 5.5. Instead, we know that the `exit` function will flush any unwritten data and then close all open streams. (We'll discuss this in Section 8.5.) It is interesting to compare the timing of these three programs with the timing data from Figure 3.5. We show this data when operating on the same file (98.5 MB with 3 million lines) in Figure 5.6.

Function	User CPU (seconds)	System CPU (seconds)	Clock time (seconds)	Bytes of program text
best time from Figure 3.5	0.01	0.18	6.67	
fgets, fputs	2.59	0.19	7.15	139
getc, putc	10.84	0.27	12.07	120
fgetc, fputc	10.44	0.27	11.42	120
single byte time from Figure 3.5	124.89	161.65	288.64	

Figure 5.6   Timing results using standard I/O routines

For each of the three standard I/O versions, the user CPU time is larger than the best `read` version from Figure 3.5, because the character-at-a-time standard I/O versions have a loop that is executed 100 million times, and the loop in the line-at-a-time version is executed 3,144,984 times. In the `read` version, its loop is executed only 12,611 times (for a buffer size of 8,192). This difference in clock times is from the difference in user times and the difference in the times spent waiting for I/O to complete, as the system times are comparable.

The system CPU time is about the same as before, because roughly the same number of kernel requests are being made. Note that an advantage of using the standard I/O routines is that we don't have to worry about buffering or choosing the optimal I/O size. We do have to determine the maximum line size for the version that uses fgets, but that's easier than trying to choose the optimal I/O size.

The final column in Figure 5.6 is the number of bytes of text space—the machine instructions generated by the C compiler—for each of the main functions. We can see that the version using getc and putc takes the same amount of space as the one using the fgetc and fputc functions. Usually, getc and putc are implemented as macros, but in the GNU C library implementation, the macro simply expands to a function call.

The version using line-at-a-time I/O is almost twice as fast as the version using character-at-a-time I/O. If the fgets and fputs functions are implemented using getc and putc (see Section 7.7 of Kernighan and Ritchie [1988], for example), then we would expect the timing to be similar to the getc version. Actually, we might expect the line-at-a-time version to take longer, since we would be adding the overhead of 200 million extra function calls to the existing 6 million ones. What is happening with this example is that the line-at-a-time functions are implemented using memccpy(3). Often, the memccpy function is implemented in assembler instead of C, for efficiency.

The last point of interest with these timing numbers is that the fgetc version is so much faster than the BUFFSIZE=1 version from Figure 3.5. Both involve the same number of function calls—about 200 million—yet the fgetc version is almost 12 times faster in user CPU time and slightly more than 25 times faster in clock time. The difference is that the version using read executes 200 million function calls, which in turn execute 200 million system calls. With the fgetc version, we still execute 200 million function calls, but this ends up being only 25,222 system calls. System calls are usually much more expensive than ordinary function calls.

As a disclaimer, you should be aware that these timing results are valid only on the single system they were run on. The results depend on many implementation features that aren't the same on every UNIX system. Nevertheless, having a set of numbers such as these, and explaining why the various versions differ, helps us understand the system better. From this section and Section 3.9, we've learned that the standard I/O library is not much slower than calling the read and write functions directly. The approximate cost that we've seen is about 0.11 seconds of CPU time to copy a megabyte of data using getc and putc. For most nontrivial applications, the largest amount of the user CPU time is taken by the application, not by the standard I/O routines.

5.9   Binary I/O

The functions from Section 5.6 operated with one character at a time, and the functions from Section 5.7 operated with one line at a time. If we're doing binary I/O, we often would like to read or write an entire structure at a time. To do this using getc or putc, we have to loop through the entire structure, one byte at a time, reading or writing each byte. We can't use the line-at-a-time functions, since fputs stops writing when it hits a null byte, and there might be null bytes within the structure. Similarly, fgets won't work right on input if any of the data bytes are nulls or newlines. Therefore, the following two functions are provided for binary I/O.

```
#include <stdio.h>

size_t fread(void *restrict ptr, size_t size, size_t nobj,
             FILE *restrict fp);

size_t fwrite(const void *restrict ptr, size_t size, size_t nobj,
              FILE *restrict fp);
```

Both return: number of objects read or written

These functions have two common uses:

1. Read or write a binary array. For example, to write elements 2 through 5 of a floating-point array, we could write

    ```
    float    data[10];

    if (fwrite(&data[2], sizeof(float), 4, fp) != 4)
        err_sys("fwrite error");
    ```

    Here, we specify *size* as the size of each element of the array and *nobj* as the number of elements.

2. Read or write a structure. For example, we could write

    ```
    struct {
      short   count;
      long    total;
      char    name[NAMESIZE];
    } item;

    if (fwrite(&item, sizeof(item), 1, fp) != 1)
        err_sys("fwrite error");
    ```

    Here, we specify *size* as the size of structure and *nobj* as one (the number of objects to write).

The obvious generalization of these two cases is to read or write an array of structures. To do this, *size* would be the sizeof the structure, and *nobj* would be the number of elements in the array.

Both fread and fwrite return the number of objects read or written. For the read case, this number can be less than *nobj* if an error occurs or if the end of file is encountered. In this case ferror or feof must be called. For the write case, if the return value is less than the requested *nobj*, an error has occurred.

A fundamental problem with binary I/O is that it can be used to read only data that has been written on the same system. This was OK many years ago, when all the UNIX systems were PDP-11s, but the norm today is to have heterogeneous systems connected together with networks. It is common to want to write data on one system and process it on another. These two functions won't work, for two reasons.

1. The offset of a member within a structure can differ between compilers and systems, because of different alignment requirements. Indeed, some compilers have an option allowing structures to be packed tightly, to save space with a possible runtime performance penalty, or aligned accurately, to optimize runtime access of each member. This means that even on a single system, the binary layout of a structure can differ, depending on compiler options.

2. The binary formats used to store multibyte integers and floating-point values differ among machine architectures.

We'll touch on some of these issues when we discuss sockets in Chapter 16. The real solution for exchanging binary data among different systems is to use a higher-level protocol. Refer to Section 8.2 of Rago [1993] or Section 5.18 of Stevens, Fenner, & Rudoff [2004] for a description of some techniques various network protocols use to exchange binary data.

We'll return to the `fread` function in Section 8.14 when we'll use it to read a binary structure, the UNIX process accounting records.

5.10 Positioning a Stream

There are three ways to position a standard I/O stream:

1. The two functions `ftell` and `fseek`. They have been around since Version 7, but they assume that a file's position can be stored in a long integer.

2. The two functions `ftello` and `fseeko`. They were introduced in the Single UNIX Specification to allow for file offsets that might not fit in a long integer. They replace the long integer with the `off_t` data type.

3. The two functions `fgetpos` and `fsetpos`. They were introduced by ISO C. They use an abstract data type, `fpos_t`, that records a file's position. This data type can be made as big as necessary to record a file's position.

Portable applications that need to move to non-UNIX systems should use `fgetpos` and `fsetpos`.

```
#include <stdio.h>

long ftell(FILE *fp);
```

                                   Returns: current file position indicator if OK, −1L on error

```
int fseek(FILE *fp, long offset, int whence);
```

                                   Returns: 0 if OK, nonzero on error

```
void rewind(FILE *fp);
```

For a binary file, a file's position indicator is measured in bytes from the beginning of the file. The value returned by `ftell` for a binary file is this byte position. To position a binary file using `fseek`, we must specify a byte *offset* and how that offset is interpreted. The values for *whence* are the same as for the `lseek` function from Section 3.6: `SEEK_SET` means from the beginning of the file, `SEEK_CUR` means from the current file position, and `SEEK_END` means from the end of file. ISO C doesn't require an implementation to support the `SEEK_END` specification for a binary file, as some systems require a binary file to be padded at the end with zeros to make the file size a multiple of some magic number. Under the UNIX System, however, `SEEK_END` is supported for binary files.

For text files, the file's current position may not be measurable as a simple byte offset. Again, this is mainly under non-UNIX systems that might store text files in a different format. To position a text file, *whence* has to be `SEEK_SET`, and only two values for *offset* are allowed: 0—meaning rewind the file to its beginning—or a value that was returned by `ftell` for that file. A stream can also be set to the beginning of the file with the `rewind` function.

The `ftello` function is the same as `ftell`, and the `fseeko` function is the same as `fseek`, except that the type of the offset is `off_t` instead of `long`.

```
#include <stdio.h>

off_t ftello(FILE *fp);
```
                          Returns: current file position indicator if OK, (off_t) −1 on error
```
int fseeko(FILE *fp, off_t offset, int whence);
```
                                              Returns: 0 if OK, nonzero on error

Recall the discussion of the `off_t` data type in Section 3.6. Implementations can define the `off_t` type to be larger than 32 bits.

As we mentioned, the `fgetpos` and `fsetpos` functions were introduced by the ISO C standard.

```
#include <stdio.h>

int fgetpos(FILE *restrict fp, fpos_t *restrict pos);

int fsetpos(FILE *fp, const fpos_t *pos);
```
                                              Both return: 0 if OK, nonzero on error

The `fgetpos` function stores the current value of the file's position indicator in the object pointed to by *pos*. This value can be used in a later call to `fsetpos` to reposition the stream to that location.

5.11   Formatted I/O

Formatted Output

Formatted output is handled by the four `printf` functions.

```
#include <stdio.h>

int printf(const char *restrict format, ...);

int fprintf(FILE *restrict fp, const char *restrict format, ...);

        Both return: number of characters output if OK, negative value if output error

int sprintf(char *restrict buf, const char *restrict format, ...);

int snprintf(char *restrict buf, size_t n,
            const char *restrict format, ...);

    Both return: number of characters stored in array if OK, negative value if encoding error
```

The `printf` function writes to the standard output, `fprintf` writes to the specified stream, and `sprintf` places the formatted characters in the array *buf*. The `sprintf` function automatically appends a null byte at the end of the array, but this null byte is not included in the return value.

Note that it's possible for `sprintf` to overflow the buffer pointed to by *buf*. It's the caller's responsibility to ensure that the buffer is large enough. Because this can lead to buffer-overflow problems, `snprintf` was introduced. With it, the size of the buffer is an explicit parameter; any characters that would have been written past the end of the buffer are discarded instead. The `snprintf` function returns the number of characters that would have been written to the buffer had it been big enough. As with `sprintf`, the return value doesn't include the terminating null byte. If `snprintf` returns a positive value less than the buffer size *n*, then the output was not truncated. If an encoding error occurs, `snprintf` returns a negative value.

The format specification controls how the remainder of the arguments will be encoded and ultimately displayed. Each argument is encoded according to a conversion specification that starts with a percent sign (%). Except for the conversion specifications, other characters in the format are copied unmodified. A conversion specification has four optional components, shown in square brackets below:

```
%[flags][fldwidth][precision][lenmodifier]convtype
```

The flags are summarized in Figure 5.7.

The `fldwidth` component specifies a minimum field width for the conversion. If the conversion results in fewer characters, it is padded with spaces. The field width is a non-negative decimal integer or an asterisk.

The `precision` component specifies the minimum number of digits to appear for integer conversions, the minimum number of digits to appear to the right of the decimal point for floating-point conversions, or the maximum number of bytes for string conversions. The precision is a period (.) followed by a optional non-negative decimal integer or an asterisk.

Flag	Description
-	left-justify the output in the field
+	always display sign of a signed conversion
(space)	prefix by a space if no sign is generated
#	convert using alternate form (include 0x prefix for hex format, for example)
0	prefix with leading zeros instead of padding with spaces

Figure 5.7 The flags component of a conversion specification

Both the field width and precision can be an asterisk. In this case, an integer argument specifies the value to be used. The argument appears directly before the argument to converted.

The `lenmodifier` component specifies the size of the argument. Possible values are summarized in Figure 5.8.

Length modifier	Description
hh	signed or unsigned `char`
h	signed or unsigned `short`
l	signed or unsigned `long` or wide character
ll	signed or unsigned `long long`
j	`intmax_t` or `uintmax_t`
z	`size_t`
t	`ptrdiff_t`
L	`long double`

Figure 5.8 The length modifier component of a conversion specification

The `convtype` component is not optional. It controls how the argument is interpreted. The various conversion types are summarized in Figure 5.9.

Conversion type	Description
d,i	signed decimal
o	unsigned octal
u	unsigned decimal
x,X	unsigned hexadecimal
f,F	`double` floating-point number
e,E	`double` floating-point number in exponential format
g,G	interpreted as f, F, e, or E, depending on value converted
a,A	`double` floating-point number in hexadecimal exponential format
c	character (with `l` length modifier, wide character)
s	string (with `l` length modifier, wide character string)
p	pointer to a `void`
n	pointer to a signed integer into which is written the number of characters written so far
%	a % character
C	wide character (an XSI extension, equivalent to `lc`)
S	wide character string (an XSI extension, equivalent to `ls`)

Figure 5.9 The conversion type component of a conversion specification

The following four variants of the `printf` family are similar to the previous four, but the variable argument list (. . .) is replaced with *arg*.

```
#include <stdarg.h>
#include <stdio.h>

int vprintf(const char *restrict format, va_list arg);

int vfprintf(FILE *restrict fp, const char *restrict format,
             va_list arg);
```

> Both return: number of characters output if OK, negative value if output error

```
int vsprintf(char *restrict buf, const char *restrict format,
             va_list arg);

int vsnprintf(char *restrict buf, size_t n,
              const char *restrict format, va_list arg);
```

> Both return: number of characters stored in array if OK, negative value if encoding error

We use the `vsnprintf` function in the error routines in Appendix B.

Refer to Section 7.3 of Kernighan and Ritchie [1988] for additional details on handling variable-length argument lists with ISO Standard C. Be aware that the variable-length argument list routines provided with ISO C—the `<stdarg.h>` header and its associated routines—differ from the `<varargs.h>` routines that were provided with older UNIX systems.

Formatted Input

Formatted input is handled by the three `scanf` functions.

```
#include <stdio.h>

int scanf(const char *restrict format, ...);

int fscanf(FILE *restrict fp, const char *restrict format, ...);

int sscanf(const char *restrict buf, const char *restrict format,
           ...);
```

> All three return: number of input items assigned,
> EOF if input error or end of file before any conversion

The `scanf` family is used to parse an input string and convert character sequences into variables of specified types. The arguments following the format contain the addresses of the variables to initialize with the results of the conversions.

The format specification controls how the arguments are converted for assignment. The percent sign (%) indicates the start of a conversion specification. Except for the conversion specifications and white space, other characters in the format have to match the input. If a character doesn't match, processing stops, leaving the remainder of the input unread.

There are three optional components to a conversion specification, shown in square brackets below:

```
%[*][fldwidth][lenmodifier]convtype
```

The optional leading asterisk is used to suppress conversion. Input is converted as specified by the rest of the conversion specification, but the result is not stored in an argument.

The `fldwidth` component specifies the maximum field width in characters. The `lenmodifier` component specifies the size of the argument to be initialized with the result of the conversion. The same length modifiers supported by the `printf` family of functions are supported by the `scanf` family of functions (see Figure 5.8 for a list of the length modifiers).

The `convtype` field is similar to the conversion type field used by the `printf` family, but there are some differences. One difference is that results that are stored in unsigned types can optionally be signed on input. For example, –1 will scan as 4294967295 into an unsigned integer. Figure 5.10 summarizes the conversion types supported by the `scanf` family of functions.

Conversion type	Description
d	signed decimal, base 10
i	signed decimal, base determined by format of input
o	unsigned octal (input optionally signed)
u	unsigned decimal, base 10 (input optionally signed)
x	unsigned hexadecimal (input optionally signed)
a,A,e,E,f,F,g,G	floating-point number
c	character (with l length modifier, wide character)
s	string (with l length modifier, wide character string)
[	matches a sequence of listed characters, ending with]
[^	matches all characters except the ones listed, ending with]
p	pointer to a void
n	pointer to a signed integer into which is written the number of characters read so far
%	a % character
C	wide character (an XSI extension, equivalent to lc)
S	wide character string (an XSI extension, equivalent to ls)

Figure 5.10 The conversion type component of a conversion specification

As with the `printf` family, the `scanf` family also supports functions that use variable argument lists as specified by `<stdarg.h>`.

```
#include <stdarg.h>
#include <stdio.h>

int vscanf(const char *restrict format, va_list arg);

int vfscanf(FILE *restrict fp, const char *restrict format,
            va_list arg);

int vsscanf(const char *restrict buf, const char *restrict format,
            va_list arg);
```
All three return: number of input items assigned,
EOF if input error or end of file before any conversion

Refer to your UNIX system manual for additional details on the scanf family of functions.

5.12 Implementation Details

As we've mentioned, under the UNIX System, the standard I/O library ends up calling the I/O routines that we described in Chapter 3. Each standard I/O stream has an associated file descriptor, and we can obtain the descriptor for a stream by calling fileno.

> Note that fileno is not part of the ISO C standard, but an extension supported by POSIX.1.

```
#include <stdio.h>

int fileno(FILE *fp);
```
Returns: the file descriptor associated with the stream

We need this function if we want to call the dup or fcntl functions, for example.

To look at the implementation of the standard I/O library on your system, start with the header <stdio.h>. This will show how the FILE object is defined, the definitions of the per-stream flags, and any standard I/O routines, such as getc, that are defined as macros. Section 8.5 of Kernighan and Ritchie [1988] has a sample implementation that shows the flavor of many implementations on UNIX systems. Chapter 12 of Plauger [1992] provides the complete source code for an implementation of the standard I/O library. The implementation of the GNU standard I/O library is also publicly available.

Example

The program in Figure 5.11 prints the buffering for the three standard streams and for a stream that is associated with a regular file.

```
#include "apue.h"

void    pr_stdio(const char *, FILE *);

int
main(void)
{
    FILE    *fp;

    fputs("enter any character\n", stdout);
    if (getchar() == EOF)
        err_sys("getchar error");
    fputs("one line to standard error\n", stderr);

    pr_stdio("stdin",  stdin);
    pr_stdio("stdout", stdout);
    pr_stdio("stderr", stderr);

    if ((fp = fopen("/etc/motd", "r")) == NULL)
        err_sys("fopen error");
    if (getc(fp) == EOF)
        err_sys("getc error");
    pr_stdio("/etc/motd", fp);
    exit(0);
}

void
pr_stdio(const char *name, FILE *fp)
{
    printf("stream = %s, ", name);

    /*
     * The following is nonportable.
     */
    if (fp->_IO_file_flags & _IO_UNBUFFERED)
        printf("unbuffered");
    else if (fp->_IO_file_flags & _IO_LINE_BUF)
        printf("line buffered");
    else /* if neither of above */
        printf("fully buffered");
    printf(", buffer size = %d\n", fp->_IO_buf_end - fp->_IO_buf_base);
}
```

Figure 5.11 Print buffering for various standard I/O streams

Note that we perform I/O on each stream before printing its buffering status, since the first I/O operation usually causes the buffers to be allocated for a stream. The structure members `_IO_file_flags`, `_IO_buf_base`, and `_IO_buf_end` and the constants `_IO_UNBUFFERED` and `_IO_LINE_BUFFERED` are defined by the GNU standard I/O library used on Linux. Be aware that other UNIX systems may have different implementations of the standard I/O library.

If we run the program in Figure 5.11 twice, once with the three standard streams connected to the terminal and once with the three standard streams redirected to files, we get the following result:

```
$ ./a.out                              stdin, stdout, and stderr connected to terminal
enter any character
                                       we type a newline
one line to standard error
stream = stdin, line buffered, buffer size = 1024
stream = stdout, line buffered, buffer size = 1024
stream = stderr, unbuffered, buffer size = 1
stream = /etc/motd, fully buffered, buffer size = 4096
$ ./a.out < /etc/termcap > std.out 2> std.err
                                       run it again with all three streams redirected
$ cat std.err
one line to standard error
$ cat std.out
enter any character
stream = stdin, fully buffered, buffer size = 4096
stream = stdout, fully buffered, buffer size = 4096
stream = stderr, unbuffered, buffer size = 1
stream = /etc/motd, fully buffered, buffer size = 4096
```

We can see that the default for this system is to have standard input and standard output line buffered when they're connected to a terminal. The line buffer is 1,024 bytes. Note that this doesn't restrict us to 1,024-byte input and output lines; that's just the size of the buffer. Writing a 2,048-byte line to standard output will require two `write` system calls. When we redirect these two streams to regular files, they become fully buffered, with buffer sizes equal to the preferred I/O size—the `st_blksize` value from the `stat` structure—for the file system. We also see that the standard error is always unbuffered, as it should be, and that a regular file defaults to fully buffered. □

5.13 Temporary Files

The ISO C standard defines two functions that are provided by the standard I/O library to assist in creating temporary files.

```
#include <stdio.h>

char *tmpnam(char *ptr);

                                       Returns: pointer to unique pathname

FILE *tmpfile(void);

                                       Returns: file pointer if OK, NULL on error
```

The `tmpnam` function generates a string that is a valid pathname and that is not the same name as an existing file. This function generates a different pathname each time it is called, up to TMP_MAX times. TMP_MAX is defined in `<stdio.h>`.

Although ISO C defines TMP_MAX, the C standard requires only that its value be at least 25. The Single UNIX Specification, however, requires that XSI-conforming systems support a value of at least 10,000. Although this minimum value allows an implementation to use four digits (0000–9999), most implementations on UNIX systems use lowercase or uppercase characters.

If *ptr* is NULL, the generated pathname is stored in a static area, and a pointer to this area is returned as the value of the function. Subsequent calls to tmpnam can overwrite this static area. (This means that if we call this function more than once and we want to save the pathname, we have to save a copy of the pathname, not a copy of the pointer.) If *ptr* is not NULL, it is assumed that it points to an array of at least L_tmpnam characters. (The constant L_tmpnam is defined in <stdio.h>.) The generated pathname is stored in this array, and *ptr* is also returned as the value of the function.

The tmpfile function creates a temporary binary file (type wb+) that is automatically removed when it is closed or on program termination. Under the UNIX System, it makes no difference that this file is a binary file.

Example

The program in Figure 5.12 demonstrates these two functions.

```c
#include "apue.h"

int
main(void)
{
    char    name[L_tmpnam], line[MAXLINE];
    FILE    *fp;

    printf("%s\n", tmpnam(NULL));        /* first temp name */

    tmpnam(name);                        /* second temp name */
    printf("%s\n", name);

    if ((fp = tmpfile()) == NULL)        /* create temp file */
        err_sys("tmpfile error");
    fputs("one line of output\n", fp);   /* write to temp file */
    rewind(fp);                          /* then read it back */
    if (fgets(line, sizeof(line), fp) == NULL)
        err_sys("fgets error");
    fputs(line, stdout);                 /* print the line we wrote */

    exit(0);
}
```

Figure 5.12 Demonstrate tmpnam and tmpfile functions

If we execute the program in Figure 5.12, we get

```
$ ./a.out
/tmp/fileClIcwc
/tmp/filemSkHSe
one line of output
```

The standard technique often used by the tmpfile function is to create a unique pathname by calling tmpnam, then create the file, and immediately unlink it. Recall from Section 4.15 that unlinking a file does not delete its contents until the file is closed. This way, when the file is closed, either explicitly or on program termination, the contents of the file are deleted.

The Single UNIX Specification defines two additional functions as XSI extensions for dealing with temporary files. The first of these is the tempnam function.

```
#include <stdio.h>

char *tempnam(const char *directory, const char *prefix);
```
Returns: pointer to unique pathname

The tempnam function is a variation of tmpnam that allows the caller to specify both the directory and a prefix for the generated pathname. There are four possible choices for the directory, and the first one that is true is used.

1. If the environment variable TMPDIR is defined, it is used as the directory. (We describe environment variables in Section 7.9.)

2. If *directory* is not NULL, it is used as the directory.

3. The string P_tmpdir in <stdio.h> is used as the directory.

4. A local directory, usually /tmp, is used as the directory.

If the *prefix* argument is not NULL, it should be a string of up to five bytes to be used as the first characters of the filename.

This function calls the malloc function to allocate dynamic storage for the constructed pathname. We can free this storage when we're done with the pathname. (We describe the malloc and free functions in Section 7.8.)

Example

The program in Figure 5.13 shows the use of tempnam.

```
#include "apue.h"

int
main(int argc, char *argv[])
{
    if (argc != 3)
        err_quit("usage: a.out <directory> <prefix>");

    printf("%s\n", tempnam(argv[1][0] != ' ' ? argv[1] : NULL,
        argv[2][0] != ' ' ? argv[2] : NULL));

    exit(0);
}
```

Figure 5.13 Demonstrate tempnam function

Note that if either command-line argument—the directory or the prefix—begins with a blank, we pass a null pointer to the function. We can now show the various ways to use it:

```
$ ./a.out /home/sar TEMP                         specify both directory and prefix
/home/sar/TEMPsf00zi
$ ./a.out " " PFX                                 use default directory: P_tmpdir
/tmp/PFXfBw7Gi
$ TMPDIR=/var/tmp ./a.out /usr/tmp " "   use environment variable; no prefix
/var/tmp/file8fVYNi                               environment variable overrides directory
$ TMPDIR=/no/such/dir ./a.out /home/sar/tmp QQQ
/home/sar/tmp/QQQ98s8Ui                           invalid environment directory is ignored
```

As the four steps that we listed earlier for specifying the directory name are tried in order, this function also checks whether the corresponding directory name makes sense. If the directory doesn't exist (the /no/such/dir example), that case is skipped, and the next choice for the directory name is tried. From this example, we can see that for this implementation, the P_tmpdir directory is /tmp. The technique that we used to set the environment variable, specifying TMPDIR= before the program name, is used by the Bourne shell, the Korn shell, and bash.   □

The second function that XSI defines is mkstemp. It is similar to tmpfile, but returns an open file descriptor for the temporary file instead of a file pointer.

```
#include <stdlib.h>

int mkstemp(char *template);
```
                                          Returns: file descriptor if OK, −1 on error

The returned file descriptor is open for reading and writing. The name of the temporary file is selected using the *template* string. This string is a pathname whose last six characters are set to XXXXXX. The function replaces these with different characters to create a unique pathname. If mkstemp returns success, it modifies the *template* string to reflect the name of the temporary file.

Unlike tmpfile, the temporary file created by mkstemp is not removed automatically for us. If we want to remove it from the file system namespace, we need to unlink it ourselves.

There is a drawback to using tmpnam and tempnam: a window exists between the time that the unique pathname is returned and the time that an application creates a file with that name. During this timing window, another process can create a file of the same name. The tmpfile and mkstemp functions should be used instead, as they don't suffer from this problem.

> The mktemp function is similar to mkstemp, except that it creates a name suitable only for use as a temporary file. The mktemp function doesn't create a file, so it suffers from the same drawback as tmpnam and tempnam. The mktemp function is marked as a legacy interface in the Single UNIX Specification. Legacy interfaces might be withdrawn in future versions of the Single UNIX Specification, and so should be avoided.

5.14 Alternatives to Standard I/O

The standard I/O library is not perfect. Korn and Vo [1991] list numerous defects: some in the basic design, but most in the various implementations.

One inefficiency inherent in the standard I/O library is the amount of data copying that takes place. When we use the line-at-a-time functions, fgets and fputs, the data is usually copied twice: once between the kernel and the standard I/O buffer (when the corresponding read or write is issued) and again between the standard I/O buffer and our line buffer. The Fast I/O library [fio(3) in AT&T 1990a] gets around this by having the function that reads a line return a pointer to the line instead of copying the line into another buffer. Hume [1988] reports a threefold increase in the speed of a version of the grep(1) utility, simply by making this change.

Korn and Vo [1991] describe another replacement for the standard I/O library: *sfio*. This package is similar in speed to the *fio* library and normally faster than the standard I/O library. The *sfio* package also provides some new features that aren't in the others: I/O streams generalized to represent both files and regions of memory, processing modules that can be written and stacked on an I/O stream to change the operation of a stream, and better exception handling.

Krieger, Stumm, and Unrau [1992] describe another alternative that uses mapped files—the mmap function that we describe in Section 14.9. This new package is called ASI, the Alloc Stream Interface. The programming interface resembles the UNIX System memory allocation functions (malloc, realloc, and free, described in Section 7.8). As with the *sfio* package, ASI attempts to minimize the amount of data copying by using pointers.

Several implementations of the standard I/O library are available in C libraries that were designed for systems with small memory footprints, such as embedded systems. These implementations emphasize modest memory requirements over portability, speed, or functionality. Two such implementations are the uClibc C library (see http://www.uclibc.org for more information) and the newlibc C library (http://sources.redhat.com/newlib).

5.15 Summary

The standard I/O library is used by most UNIX applications. We have looked at all the functions provided by this library, as well as at some implementation details and efficiency considerations. Be aware of the buffering that takes place with this library, as this is the area that generates the most problems and confusion.

Exercises

5.1 Implement setbuf using setvbuf.

5.2 Type in the program that copies a file using line-at-a-time I/O (fgets and fputs) from Section 5.8, but use a MAXLINE of 4. What happens if you copy lines that exceed this length? Explain what is happening.

5.3   What does a return value of 0 from `printf` mean?

5.4   The following code works correctly on some machines, but not on others. What could be the problem?

```
#include     <stdio.h>

int
main(void)
{
    char    c;

    while ((c = getchar()) != EOF)
        putchar(c);
}
```

5.5   Why does `tempnam` restrict the *prefix* to five characters?

5.6   How would you use the `fsync` function (Section 3.13) with a standard I/O stream?

5.7   In the programs in Figures 1.7 and 1.10, the prompt that is printed does not contain a newline, and we don't call `fflush`. What causes the prompt to be output?

6

System Data Files and Information

6.1 Introduction

A UNIX system requires numerous data files for normal operation: the password file /etc/passwd and the group file /etc/group are two files that are frequently used by various programs. For example, the password file is used every time a user logs in to a UNIX system and every time someone executes an ls -l command.

Historically, these data files have been ASCII text files and were read with the standard I/O library. But for larger systems, a sequential scan through the password file becomes time consuming. We want to be able to store these data files in a format other than ASCII text, but still provide an interface for an application program that works with any file format. The portable interfaces to these data files are the subject of this chapter. We also cover the system identification functions and the time and date functions.

6.2 Password File

The UNIX System's password file, called the user database by POSIX.1, contains the fields shown in Figure 6.1. These fields are contained in a passwd structure that is defined in <pwd.h>.

> Note that POSIX.1 specifies only five of the ten fields in the passwd structure. Most platforms support at least seven of the fields. The BSD-derived platforms support all ten.

Description	struct passwd member	POSIX.1	FreeBSD 5.2.1	Linux 2.4.22	Mac OS X 10.3	Solaris 9
user name	`char *pw_name`	•	•	•	•	•
encrypted password	`char *pw_passwd`		•	•	•	•
numerical user ID	`uid_t pw_uid`	•	•	•	•	•
numerical group ID	`gid_t pw_gid`	•	•	•	•	•
comment field	`char *pw_gecos`		•	•	•	•
initial working directory	`char *pw_dir`	•	•	•	•	•
initial shell (user program)	`char *pw_shell`	•	•	•	•	•
user access class	`char *pw_class`		•		•	
next time to change password	`time_t pw_change`		•		•	
account expiration time	`time_t pw_expire`		•		•	

Figure 6.1 Fields in `/etc/passwd` file

Historically, the password file has been stored in `/etc/passwd` and has been an ASCII file. Each line contains the fields described in Figure 6.1, separated by colons. For example, four lines from the `/etc/passwd` file on Linux could be

```
root:x:0:0:root:/root:/bin/bash
squid:x:23:23::/var/spool/squid:/dev/null
nobody:x:65534:65534:Nobody:/home:/bin/sh
sar:x:205:105:Stephen Rago:/home/sar:/bin/bash
```

Note the following points about these entries.

- There is usually an entry with the user name `root`. This entry has a user ID of 0 (the superuser).

- The encrypted password field contains a single character as a placeholder where older versions of the UNIX System used to store the encrypted password. Because it is a security hole to store the encrypted password in a file that is readable by everyone, encrypted passwords are now kept elsewhere. We'll cover this issue in more detail in the next section when we discuss passwords.

- Some fields in a password file entry can be empty. If the encrypted password field is empty, it usually means that the user does not have a password. (This is not recommended.) The entry for `squid` has one blank field: the comment field. An empty comment field has no effect.

- The shell field contains the name of the executable program to be used as the login shell for the user. The default value for an empty shell field is usually `/bin/sh`. Note, however, that the entry for `squid` has `/dev/null` as the login shell. Obviously, this is a device and cannot be executed, so its use here is to prevent anyone from logging in to our system as user `squid`.

  > Many services have separate user IDs for the daemon processes (Chapter 13) that help implement the service. The `squid` entry is for the processes implementing the `squid` proxy cache service.

- There are several alternatives to using /dev/null to prevent a particular user from logging in to a system. It is common to see /bin/false used as the login shell. It simply exits with an unsuccessful (nonzero) status; the shell evaluates the exit status as false. It is also common to see /bin/true used to disable an account. All it does is exit with a successful (zero) status. Some systems provide the nologin command. It prints a customizable error message and exits with a nonzero exit status.

- The nobody user name can be used to allow people to log in to a system, but with a user ID (65534) and group ID (65534) that provide no privileges. The only files that this user ID and group ID can access are those that are readable or writable by the world. (This assumes that there are no files specifically owned by user ID 65534 or group ID 65534, which should be the case.)

- Some systems that provide the finger(1) command support additional information in the comment field. Each of these fields is separated by a comma: the user's name, office location, office phone number, and home phone number. Additionally, an ampersand in the comment field is replaced with the login name (capitalized) by some utilities. For example, we could have

```
sar:x:205:105:Steve Rago, SF 5-121, 555-1111, 555-2222:/home/sar:/bin/sh
```

Then we could use finger to print information about Steve Rago.

```
$ finger -p sar
Login: sar                    Name: Steve Rago
Directory: /home/sar          Shell: /bin/sh
Office:  SF 5-121,   555-1111 Home Phone:  555-2222
On since Mon Jan 19 03:57 (EST) on ttyv0 (messages off)
No Mail.
```

Even if your system doesn't support the finger command, these fields can still go into the comment field, since that field is simply a comment and not interpreted by system utilities.

Some systems provide the vipw command to allow administrators to edit the password file. The vipw command serializes changes to the password file and makes sure that any additional files are consistent with the changes made. It is also common for systems to provide similar functionality through graphical user interfaces.

POSIX.1 defines only two functions to fetch entries from the password file. These functions allow us to look up an entry given a user's login name or numerical user ID.

```
#include <pwd.h>

struct passwd *getpwuid(uid_t uid);

struct passwd *getpwnam(const char *name);
```
                                           Both return: pointer if OK, NULL on error

The getpwuid function is used by the ls(1) program to map the numerical user ID contained in an i-node into a user's login name. The getpwnam function is used by the login(1) program when we enter our login name.

Both functions return a pointer to a `passwd` structure that the functions fill in. This structure is usually a `static` variable within the function, so its contents are overwritten each time we call either of these functions.

These two POSIX.1 functions are fine if we want to look up either a login name or a user ID, but some programs need to go through the entire password file. The following three functions can be used for this.

```
#include <pwd.h>

struct passwd *getpwent(void);
```

> Returns: pointer if OK, NULL on error or end of file

```
void setpwent(void);

void endpwent(void);
```

> These three functions are not part of the base POSIX.1 standard. They are defined as XSI extensions in the Single UNIX Specification. As such, all UNIX systems are expected to provide them.

We call `getpwent` to return the next entry in the password file. As with the two POSIX.1 functions, `getpwent` returns a pointer to a structure that it has filled in. This structure is normally overwritten each time we call this function. If this is the first call to this function, it opens whatever files it uses. There is no order implied when we use this function; the entries can be in any order, because some systems use a hashed version of the file `/etc/passwd`.

The function `setpwent` rewinds whatever files it uses, and `endpwent` closes these files. When using `getpwent`, we must always be sure to close these files by calling `endpwent` when we're through. Although `getpwent` is smart enough to know when it has to open its files (the first time we call it), it never knows when we're through.

Example

Figure 6.2 shows an implementation of the function `getpwnam`.

```c
#include <pwd.h>
#include <stddef.h>
#include <string.h>

struct passwd *
getpwnam(const char *name)
{
    struct passwd  *ptr;

    setpwent();
    while ((ptr = getpwent()) != NULL)
        if (strcmp(name, ptr->pw_name) == 0)
            break;      /* found a match */
    endpwent();
    return(ptr);    /* ptr is NULL if no match found */
}
```

Figure 6.2 The `getpwnam` function

The call to `setpwent` at the beginning is self-defense: we ensure that the files are rewound, in case the caller has already opened them by calling `getpwent`. The call to `endpwent` when we're done is because neither `getpwnam` nor `getpwuid` should leave any of the files open.   □

6.3   Shadow Passwords

The encrypted password is a copy of the user's password that has been put through a one-way encryption algorithm. Because this algorithm is one-way, we can't guess the original password from the encrypted version.

Historically, the algorithm that was used (see Morris and Thompson [1979]) always generated 13 printable characters from the 64-character set [a-zA-Z0-9./]. Some newer systems use an MD5 algorithm to encrypt passwords, generating 31 characters per encrypted password. (The more characters used to store the encrypted password, the more combinations there are, and the harder it will be to guess the password by trying all possible variations.) When we place a single character in the encrypted password field, we ensure that an encrypted password will never match this value.

Given an encrypted password, we can't apply an algorithm that inverts it and returns the plaintext password. (The plaintext password is what we enter at the `Password:` prompt.) But we could guess a password, run it through the one-way algorithm, and compare the result to the encrypted password. If user passwords were randomly chosen, this brute-force approach wouldn't be too successful. Users, however, tend to choose nonrandom passwords, such as spouse's name, street names, or pet names. A common experiment is for someone to obtain a copy of the password file and try guessing the passwords. (Chapter 4 of Garfinkel et al. [2003] contains additional details and history on passwords and the password encryption scheme used on UNIX systems.)

To make it more difficult to obtain the raw materials (the encrypted passwords), systems now store the encrypted password in another file, often called the *shadow password file*. Minimally, this file has to contain the user name and the encrypted password. Other information relating to the password is also stored here (Figure 6.3).

Description	struct spwd member
user login name	`char *sp_namp`
encrypted password	`char *sp_pwdp`
days since Epoch of last password change	`int   sp_lstchg`
days until change allowed	`int   sp_min`
days before change required	`int   sp_max`
days warning for expiration	`int   sp_warn`
days before account inactive	`int   sp_inact`
days since Epoch when account expires	`int   sp_expire`
reserved	`unsigned int sp_flag`

Figure 6.3 Fields in `/etc/shadow` file

The only two mandatory fields are the user's login name and encrypted password. The other fields control how often the password is to change—known as "password aging"—and how long an account is allowed to remain active.

The shadow password file should not be readable by the world. Only a few programs need to access encrypted passwords—login(1) and passwd(1), for example—and these programs are often set-user-ID root. With shadow passwords, the regular password file, /etc/passwd, can be left readable by the world.

On Linux 2.4.22 and Solaris 9, a separate set of functions is available to access the shadow password file, similar to the set of functions used to access the password file.

```
#include <shadow.h>

struct spwd *getspnam(const char *name);

struct spwd *getspent(void);
```

                        Both return: pointer if OK, NULL on error

```
void setspent(void);

void endspent(void);
```

On FreeBSD 5.2.1 and Mac OS X 10.3, there is no shadow password structure. The additional account information is stored in the password file (refer back to Figure 6.1).

6.4   Group File

The UNIX System's group file, called the group database by POSIX.1, contains the fields shown in Figure 6.4. These fields are contained in a group structure that is defined in <grp.h>.

Description	struct group member	POSIX.1	FreeBSD 5.2.1	Linux 2.4.22	Mac OS X 10.3	Solaris 9
group name	char *gr_name	•	•	•	•	•
encrypted password	char *gr_passwd		•	•	•	•
numerical group ID	int gr_gid	•	•	•	•	•
array of pointers to individual user names	char **gr_mem	•	•	•	•	•

Figure 6.4   Fields in /etc/group file

The field gr_mem is an array of pointers to the user names that belong to this group. This array is terminated by a null pointer.

We can look up either a group name or a numerical group ID with the following two functions, which are defined by POSIX.1.

```
#include <grp.h>

struct group *getgrgid(gid_t gid);

struct group *getgrnam(const char *name);
```

                        Both return: pointer if OK, NULL on error

As with the password file functions, both of these functions normally return pointers to a static variable, which is overwritten on each call.

If we want to search the entire group file, we need some additional functions. The following three functions are like their counterparts for the password file.

```
#include <grp.h>

struct group *getgrent(void);
```
                                    Returns: pointer if OK, NULL on error or end of file
```
void setgrent(void);

void endgrent(void);
```

> These three functions are not part of the base POSIX.1 standard. They are defined as XSI extensions in the Single UNIX Specification. All UNIX Systems provide them.

The setgrent function opens the group file, if it's not already open, and rewinds it. The getgrent function reads the next entry from the group file, opening the file first, if it's not already open. The endgrent function closes the group file.

6.5   Supplementary Group IDs

The use of groups in the UNIX System has changed over time. With Version 7, each user belonged to a single group at any point in time. When we logged in, we were assigned the real group ID corresponding to the numerical group ID in our password file entry. We could change this at any point by executing newgrp(1). If the newgrp command succeeded (refer to the manual page for the permission rules), our real group ID was changed to the new group's ID, and this was used for all subsequent file access permission checks. We could always go back to our original group by executing newgrp without any arguments.

This form of group membership persisted until it was changed in 4.2BSD (circa 1983). With 4.2BSD, the concept of supplementary group IDs was introduced. Not only did we belong to the group corresponding to the group ID in our password file entry, but we also could belong to up to 16 additional groups. The file access permission checks were modified so that not only was the effective group ID compared to the file's group ID, but also all the supplementary group IDs were compared to the file's group ID.

> Supplementary group IDs are a required feature of POSIX.1. (In older versions of POSIX.1, they were optional.) The constant NGROUPS_MAX (Figure 2.10) specifies the number of supplementary group IDs. A common value is 16 (Figure 2.14).

The advantage in using supplementary group IDs is that we no longer have to change groups explicitly. It is not uncommon to belong to multiple groups (i.e., participate in multiple projects) at the same time.

Three functions are provided to fetch and set the supplementary group IDs.

```
#include <unistd.h>

int getgroups(int gidsetsize, gid_t grouplist[]);
```

                                      Returns: number of supplementary group IDs if OK, –1 on error

```
#include <grp.h>     /* on Linux */
#include <unistd.h> /* on FreeBSD, Mac OS X, and Solaris */

int setgroups(int ngroups, const gid_t grouplist[]);

#include <grp.h>     /* on Linux and Solaris */
#include <unistd.h> /* on FreeBSD and Mac OS X */

int initgroups(const char *username, gid_t basegid);
```

                                                       Both return: 0 if OK, –1 on error

Of these three functions, only getgroups is specified by POSIX.1. Because setgroups and initgroups are privileged operations, they are not part of POSIX.1. All four platforms covered in this book, however, support all three functions.

On Mac OS X 10.3, *basegid* is declared to be of type int.

The getgroups function fills in the array *grouplist* with the supplementary group IDs. Up to *gidsetsize* elements are stored in the array. The number of supplementary group IDs stored in the array is returned by the function.

As a special case, if *gidsetsize* is 0, the function returns only the number of supplementary group IDs. The array *grouplist* is not modified. (This allows the caller to determine the size of the *grouplist* array to allocate.)

The setgroups function can be called by the superuser to set the supplementary group ID list for the calling process: *grouplist* contains the array of group IDs, and *ngroups* specifies the number of elements in the array. The value of *ngroups* cannot be larger than NGROUPS_MAX.

The only use of setgroups is usually from the initgroups function, which reads the entire group file—with the functions getgrent, setgrent, and endgrent, which we described earlier—and determines the group membership for *username*. It then calls setgroups to initialize the supplementary group ID list for the user. One must be superuser to call initgroups, since it calls setgroups. In addition to finding all the groups that *username* is a member of in the group file, initgroups also includes *basegid* in the supplementary group ID list; *basegid* is the group ID from the password file for *username*.

The initgroups function is called by only a few programs: the login(1) program, for example, calls it when we log in.

6.6   Implementation Differences

We've already discussed the shadow password file supported by Linux and Solaris. FreeBSD and Mac OS X store encrypted passwords differently. Figure 6.5 summarizes how the four platforms covered in this book store user and group information.

Information	FreeBSD 5.2.1	Linux 2.4.22	Mac OS X 10.3	Solaris 9
Account information	`/etc/passwd`	`/etc/passwd`	`netinfo`	`/etc/passwd`
Encrypted passwords	`/etc/master.passwd`	`/etc/shadow`	`netinfo`	`/etc/shadow`
Hashed password files?	yes	no	no	no
Group information	`/etc/group`	`/etc/group`	`netinfo`	`/etc/group`

Figure 6.5 Account implementation differences

On FreeBSD, the shadow password file is `/etc/master.passwd`. Special commands are used to edit it, which in turn generate a copy of `/etc/passwd` from the shadow password file. In addition, hashed versions of the files are also generated: `/etc/pwd.db` is the hashed version of `/etc/passwd`, and `/etc/spwd.db` is the hashed version of `/etc/master.passwd`. These provide better performance for large installations.

On Mac OS X, however, `/etc/passwd` and `/etc/master.passwd` are used only in single-user mode (when the system is undergoing maintenance; single-user mode usually means that no system services are enabled). In multiuser mode—during normal operation—the `netinfo` directory service provides access to account information for users and groups.

Although Linux and Solaris support similar shadow password interfaces, there are some subtle differences. For example, the integer fields shown in Figure 6.3 are defined as type `int` on Solaris, but as `long int` on Linux. Another difference is the account-inactive field. Solaris defines it to be the number of days since the user last logged in to the system, whereas Linux defines it to be the number of days after which the maximum password age has been reached.

On many systems, the user and group databases are implemented using the Network Information Service (NIS). This allows administrators to edit a master copy of the databases and distribute them automatically to all servers in an organization. Client systems contact servers to look up information about users and groups. NIS+ and the Lightweight Directory Access Protocol (LDAP) provide similar functionality. Many systems control the method used to administer each type of information through the `/etc/nsswitch.conf` configuration file.

6.7   Other Data Files

We've discussed only two of the system's data files so far: the password file and the group file. Numerous other files are used by UNIX systems in normal day-to-day operation. For example, the BSD networking software has one data file for the services provided by the various network servers (/etc/services), one for the protocols (/etc/protocols), and one for the networks (/etc/networks). Fortunately, the interfaces to these various files are like the ones we've already described for the password and group files.

The general principle is that every data file has at least three functions:

1. A get function that reads the next record, opening the file if necessary. These functions normally return a pointer to a structure. A null pointer is returned when the end of file is reached. Most of the get functions return a pointer to a static structure, so we always have to copy it if we want to save it.

2. A set function that opens the file, if not already open, and rewinds the file. This function is used when we know we want to start again at the beginning of the file.

3. An end entry that closes the data file. As we mentioned earlier, we always have to call this when we're done, to close all the files.

Additionally, if the data file supports some form of keyed lookup, routines are provided to search for a record with a specific key. For example, two keyed lookup routines are provided for the password file: getpwnam looks for a record with a specific user name, and getpwuid looks for a record with a specific user ID.

Figure 6.6 shows some of these routines, which are common to UNIX systems. In this figure, we show the functions for the password files and group file, which we discussed earlier in this chapter, and some of the networking functions. There are get, set, and end functions for all the data files in this figure.

Description	Data file	Header	Structure	Additional keyed lookup functions
passwords	/etc/passwd	<pwd.h>	passwd	getpwnam, getpwuid
groups	/etc/group	<grp.h>	group	getgrnam, getgrgid
shadow	/etc/shadow	<shadow.h>	spwd	getspnam
hosts	/etc/hosts	<netdb.h>	hostent	gethostbyname, gethostbyaddr
networks	/etc/networks	<netdb.h>	netent	getnetbyname, getnetbyaddr
protocols	/etc/protocols	<netdb.h>	protoent	getprotobyname, getprotobynumber
services	/etc/services	<netdb.h>	servent	getservbyname, getservbyport

Figure 6.6 Similar routines for accessing system data files

Under Solaris, the last four data files in Figure 6.6 are symbolic links to files of the same name in the directory /etc/inet. Most UNIX System implementations have additional functions that are like these, but the additional functions tend to deal with system administration files and are specific to each implementation.

6.8   Login Accounting

Two data files that have been provided with most UNIX systems are the utmp file, which keeps track of all the users currently logged in, and the wtmp file, which keeps

track of all logins and logouts. With Version 7, one type of record was written to both
files, a binary record consisting of the following structure:

```
struct utmp {
  char   ut_line[8];  /* tty line: "ttyh0", "ttyd0", "ttyp0", ... */
  char   ut_name[8];  /* login name */
  long   ut_time;     /* seconds since Epoch */
};
```

On login, one of these structures was filled in and written to the utmp file by the login
program, and the same structure was appended to the wtmp file. On logout, the entry
in the utmp file was erased—filled with null bytes—by the init process, and a new
entry was appended to the wtmp file. This logout entry in the wtmp file had the
ut_name field zeroed out. Special entries were appended to the wtmp file to indicate
when the system was rebooted and right before and after the system's time and date
was changed. The who(1) program read the utmp file and printed its contents in a
readable form. Later versions of the UNIX System provided the last(1) command,
which read through the wtmp file and printed selected entries.

   Most versions of the UNIX System still provide the utmp and wtmp files, but as
expected, the amount of information in these files has grown. The 20-byte structure that
was written by Version 7 grew to 36 bytes with SVR2, and the extended utmp structure
with SVR4 takes over 350 bytes!

> The detailed format of these records in Solaris is given in the utmpx(4) manual page. With
> Solaris 9, both files are in the /var/adm directory. Solaris provides numerous functions
> described in getutx(3) to read and write these two files.
>
> On FreeBSD 5.2.1, Linux 2.4.22, and Mac OS X 10.3, the utmp(5) manual page gives the format
> of their versions of these login records. The pathnames of these two files are /var/run/utmp
> and /var/log/wtmp.

6.9   System Identification

POSIX.1 defines the uname function to return information on the current host and
operating system.

```
#include <sys/utsname.h>

int uname(struct utsname *name);
```

                                        Returns: non-negative value if OK, –1 on error

---

We pass the address of a utsname structure, and the function fills it in. POSIX.1 defines
only the minimum fields in the structure, which are all character arrays, and it's up to
each implementation to set the size of each array. Some implementations provide
additional fields in the structure.

```
struct utsname {
    char   sysname[];     /* name of the operating system */
    char   nodename[];    /* name of this node */
    char   release[];     /* current release of operating system */
    char   version[];     /* current version of this release */
    char   machine[];     /* name of hardware type */
};
```

Each string is null-terminated. The maximum name lengths supported by the four platforms discussed in this book are listed in Figure 6.7. The information in the utsname structure can usually be printed with the uname(1) command.

> POSIX.1 warns that the nodename element may not be adequate to reference the host on a communications network. This function is from System V, and in older days, the nodename element was adequate for referencing the host on a UUCP network.
>
> Realize also that the information in this structure does not give any information on the POSIX.1 level. This should be obtained using _POSIX_VERSION, as described in Section 2.6.
>
> Finally, this function gives us a way only to fetch the information in the structure; there is nothing specified by POSIX.1 about initializing this information.

Historically, BSD-derived systems provide the gethostname function to return only the name of the host. This name is usually the name of the host on a TCP/IP network.

```
#include <unistd.h>

int gethostname(char *name, int namelen);
```
                                                        Returns: 0 if OK, −1 on error

The *namelen* argument specifies the size of the *name* buffer. If enough space is provided, the string returned through *name* is null terminated. If insufficient room is provided, however, it is unspecified whether the string is null terminated.

The gethostname function, now defined as part of POSIX.1, specifies that the maximum host name length is HOST_NAME_MAX. The maximum name lengths supported by the four implementations covered in this book are summarized in Figure 6.7.

Interface	Maximum name length			
	FreeBSD 5.2.1	Linux 2.4.22	Mac OS X 10.3	Solaris 9
uname	256	65	256	257
gethostname	256	64	256	256

Figure 6.7 System identification name limits

If the host is connected to a TCP/IP network, the host name is normally the fully qualified domain name of the host.

There is also a hostname(1) command that can fetch or set the host name. (The host name is set by the superuser using a similar function, sethostname.) The host name is normally set at bootstrap time from one of the start-up files invoked by /etc/rc or init.

6.10   Time and Date Routines

The basic time service provided by the UNIX kernel counts the number of seconds that have passed since the Epoch: 00:00:00 January 1, 1970, Coordinated Universal Time (UTC). In Section 1.10, we said that these seconds are represented in a time_t data type, and we call them *calendar times*. These calendar times represent both the time and the date. The UNIX System has always differed from other operating systems in (a) keeping time in UTC instead of the local time, (b) automatically handling conversions, such as daylight saving time, and (c) keeping the time and date as a single quantity.

The time function returns the current time and date.

```
#include <time.h>

time_t time(time_t *calptr);
```
                                                    Returns: value of time if OK, –1 on error

The time value is always returned as the value of the function. If the argument is non-null, the time value is also stored at the location pointed to by *calptr*.

> We haven't said how the kernel's notion of the current time is initialized. Historically, on implementations derived from System V, the stime(2) function was called, whereas BSD-derived systems used settimeofday(2).
>
> The Single UNIX Specification doesn't specify how a system sets its current time.

The gettimeofday function provides greater resolution (up to a microsecond) than the time function. This is important for some applications.

```
#include <sys/time.h>

int gettimeofday(struct timeval *restrict tp, void *restrict tzp);
```
                                                    Returns: 0 always

This function is defined as an XSI extension in the Single UNIX Specification. The only legal value for *tzp* is NULL; other values result in unspecified behavior. Some platforms support the specification of a time zone through the use of *tzp*, but this is implementation-specific and not defined by the Single UNIX Specification.

The gettimeofday function stores the current time as measured from the Epoch in the memory pointed to by *tp*. This time is represented as a timeval structure, which stores seconds and microseconds:

```
struct timeval {
        time_t tv_sec;      /* seconds */
        long    tv_usec;    /* microseconds */
};
```

Once we have the integer value that counts the number of seconds since the Epoch, we normally call one of the other time functions to convert it to a human-readable time and date. Figure 6.8 shows the relationships between the various time functions.

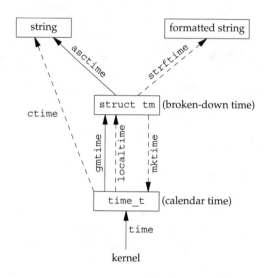

Figure 6.8 Relationship of the various time functions

(The four functions in this figure that are shown with dashed lines—`localtime`, `mktime`, `ctime`, and `strftime`—are all affected by the `TZ` environment variable, which we describe later in this section.)

The two functions `localtime` and `gmtime` convert a calendar time into what's called a broken-down time, a `tm` structure.

```
struct tm {         /* a broken-down time */
    int   tm_sec;   /* seconds after the minute: [0 - 60] */
    int   tm_min;   /* minutes after the hour: [0 - 59] */
    int   tm_hour;  /* hours after midnight: [0 - 23] */
    int   tm_mday;  /* day of the month: [1 - 31] */
    int   tm_mon;   /* months since January: [0 - 11] */
    int   tm_year;  /* years since 1900 */
    int   tm_wday;  /* days since Sunday: [0 - 6] */
    int   tm_yday;  /* days since January 1: [0 - 365] */
    int   tm_isdst; /* daylight saving time flag: <0, 0, >0 */
};
```

The reason that the seconds can be greater than 59 is to allow for a leap second. Note that all the fields except the day of the month are 0-based. The daylight saving time flag is positive if daylight saving time is in effect, 0 if it's not in effect, and negative if the information isn't available.

> In previous versions of the Single UNIX Specification, double leap seconds were allowed. Thus, the valid range of values for the tm_sec member was 0–61. The formal definition of UTC doesn't allow for double leap seconds, so the valid range for seconds is now defined to be 0–60.

```
#include <time.h>

struct tm *gmtime(const time_t *calptr);

struct tm *localtime(const time_t *calptr);
```
                                        Both return: pointer to broken-down time

The difference between `localtime` and `gmtime` is that the first converts the calendar time to the local time, taking into account the local time zone and daylight saving time flag, whereas the latter converts the calendar time into a broken-down time expressed as UTC.

The function `mktime` takes a broken-down time, expressed as a local time, and converts it into a `time_t` value.

```
#include <time.h>

time_t mktime(struct tm *tmptr);
```
                                        Returns: calendar time if OK, –1 on error

The `asctime` and `ctime` functions produce the familiar 26-byte string that is similar to the default output of the `date(1)` command:

```
Tue Feb 10 18:27:38 2004\n\0
```

```
#include <time.h>

char *asctime(const struct tm *tmptr);

char *ctime(const time_t *calptr);
```
                                        Both return: pointer to null-terminated string

The argument to `asctime` is a pointer to a broken-down string, whereas the argument to `ctime` is a pointer to a calendar time.

The final time function, `strftime`, is the most complicated. It is a `printf`-like function for time values.

```
#include <time.h>

size_t strftime(char *restrict buf, size_t maxsize,
                const char *restrict format,
                const struct tm *restrict tmptr);
```
Returns: number of characters stored in array if room, 0 otherwise

The final argument is the time value to format, specified by a pointer to a broken-down time value. The formatted result is stored in the array *buf* whose size is *maxsize* characters. If the size of the result, including the terminating null, fits in the buffer, the function returns the number of characters stored in *buf*, excluding the terminating null. Otherwise, the function returns 0.

The *format* argument controls the formatting of the time value. Like the `printf` functions, conversion specifiers are given as a percent followed by a special character. All other characters in the *format* string are copied to the output. Two percents in a row generate a single percent in the output. Unlike the `printf` functions, each conversion specified generates a different fixed-size output string—there are no field widths in the *format* string. Figure 6.9 describes the 37 ISO C conversion specifiers. The third column of this figure is from the output of `strftime` under Linux, corresponding to the time and date `Tue Feb 10 18:27:38 EST 2004`.

The only specifiers that are not self-evident are %U, %V, and %W. The %U specifier represents the week number of the year, where the week containing the first Sunday is week 1. The %W specifier represents the week number of the year, where the week containing the first Monday is week 1. The %V specifier is different. If the week containing the first day in January has four or more days in the new year, then this is treated as week 1. Otherwise, it is treated as the last week of the previous year. In both cases, Monday is treated as the first day of the week.

As with `printf`, `strftime` supports modifiers for some of the conversion specifiers. The E and O modifiers can be used to generate an alternate format if supported by the locale.

> Some systems support additional, nonstandard extensions to the *format* string for `strftime`.

We mentioned that the four functions in Figure 6.8 with dashed lines were affected by the `TZ` environment variable: `localtime`, `mktime`, `ctime`, and `strftime`. If defined, the value of this environment variable is used by these functions instead of the default time zone. If the variable is defined to be a null string, such as `TZ=`, then UTC is normally used. The value of this environment variable is often something like `TZ=EST5EDT`, but POSIX.1 allows a much more detailed specification. Refer to the Environment Variables chapter of the Single UNIX Specification [Open Group 2004] for all the details on the `TZ` variable.

> All the time and date functions described in this section, except `gettimeofday`, are defined by the ISO C standard. POSIX.1, however, added the `TZ` environment variable. On FreeBSD 5.2.1, Linux 2.4.22, and Mac OS X 10.3, more information on the `TZ` variable can be found in the `tzset(3)` manual page. On Solaris 9, this information is in the `environ(5)` manual page.

Format	Description	Example
%a	abbreviated weekday name	`Tue`
%A	full weekday name	`Tuesday`
%b	abbreviated month name	`Feb`
%B	full month name	`February`
%c	date and time	`Tue Feb 10 18:27:38 2004`
%C	year/100: [00–99]	`20`
%d	day of the month: [01–31]	`10`
%D	date [MM/DD/YY]	`02/10/04`
%e	day of month (single digit preceded by space) [1–31]	`10`
%F	ISO 8601 date format [YYYY–MM–DD]	`2004-02-10`
%g	last two digits of ISO 8601 week-based year [00–99]	`04`
%G	ISO 8601 week-based year	`2004`
%h	same as %b	`Feb`
%H	hour of the day (24-hour format): [00–23]	`18`
%I	hour of the day (12-hour format): [01–12]	`06`
%j	day of the year: [001–366]	`041`
%m	month: [01–12]	`02`
%M	minute: [00–59]	`27`
%n	newline character	
%p	AM/PM	`PM`
%r	locale's time (12-hour format)	`06:27:38 PM`
%R	same as "%H:%M"	`18:27`
%S	second: [00–60]	`38`
%t	horizontal tab character	
%T	same as "%H:%M:%S"	`18:27:38`
%u	ISO 8601 weekday [Monday=1, 1–7]	`2`
%U	Sunday week number: [00–53]	`06`
%V	ISO 8601 week number: [01–53]	`07`
%w	weekday: [0=Sunday, 0–6]	`2`
%W	Monday week number: [00–53]	`06`
%x	date	`02/10/04`
%X	time	`18:27:38`
%y	last two digits of year: [00–99]	`04`
%Y	year	`2004`
%z	offset from UTC in ISO 8601 format	`-0500`
%Z	time zone name	`EST`
%%	translates to a percent sign	`%`

Figure 6.9 Conversion specifiers for `strftime`

6.11   Summary

The password file and the group file are used on all UNIX systems. We've looked at the various functions that read these files. We've also talked about shadow passwords, which can help system security. Supplementary group IDs provide a way to participate in multiple groups at the same time. We also looked at how similar functions are provided by most systems to access other system-related data files. We discussed the

POSIX.1 functions that programs can use to identify the system on which they are running. We finished the chapter with a look at the time and date functions provided by ISO C and the Single UNIX Specification.

Exercises

6.1 If the system uses a shadow file and we need to obtain the encrypted password, how do we do it?

6.2 If you have superuser access and your system uses shadow passwords, implement the previous exercise.

6.3 Write a program that calls uname and prints all the fields in the utsname structure. Compare the output to the output from the uname(1) command.

6.4 Calculate the latest time that can be represented by the time_t data type. After it wraps around, what happens?

6.5 Write a program to obtain the current time and print it using strftime, so that it looks like the default output from date(1). Set the TZ environment variable to different values and see what happens.

7

Process Environment

7.1 Introduction

Before looking at the process control primitives in the next chapter, we need to examine the environment of a single process. In this chapter, we'll see how the `main` function is called when the program is executed, how command-line arguments are passed to the new program, what the typical memory layout looks like, how to allocate additional memory, how the process can use environment variables, and various ways for the process to terminate. Additionally, we'll look at the `longjmp` and `setjmp` functions and their interaction with the stack. We finish the chapter by examining the resource limits of a process.

7.2 `main` Function

A C program starts execution with a function called `main`. The prototype for the `main` function is

```
int main(int argc, char *argv[]);
```

where *argc* is the number of command-line arguments, and *argv* is an array of pointers to the arguments. We describe these arguments in Section 7.4.

When a C program is executed by the kernel—by one of the `exec` functions, which we describe in Section 8.10—a special start-up routine is called before the `main` function is called. The executable program file specifies this routine as the starting address for the program; this is set up by the link editor when it is invoked by the C compiler. This start-up routine takes values from the kernel—the command-line arguments and the environment—and sets things up so that the `main` function is called as shown earlier.

7.3   Process Termination

There are eight ways for a process to terminate. Normal termination occurs in five ways:

1. Return from `main`
2. Calling `exit`
3. Calling `_exit` or `_Exit`
4. Return of the last thread from its start routine (Section 11.5)
5. Calling `pthread_exit` (Section 11.5) from the last thread

Abnormal termination occurs in three ways:

6. Calling `abort` (Section 10.17)
7. Receipt of a signal (Section 10.2)
8. Response of the last thread to a cancellation request (Sections 11.5 and 12.7)

> For now, we'll ignore the three termination methods specific to threads until we discuss threads in Chapters 11 and 12.

The start-up routine that we mentioned in the previous section is also written so that if the `main` function returns, the `exit` function is called. If the start-up routine were coded in C (it is often coded in assembler) the call to `main` could look like

```
exit(main(argc, argv));
```

Exit Functions

Three functions terminate a program normally: `_exit` and `_Exit`, which return to the kernel immediately, and `exit`, which performs certain cleanup processing and then returns to the kernel.

```
#include <stdlib.h>

void exit(int status);

void _Exit(int status);

#include <unistd.h>

void _exit(int status);
```

We'll discuss the effect of these three functions on other processes, such as the children and the parent of the terminating process, in Section 8.5.

> The reason for the different headers is that `exit` and `_Exit` are specified by ISO C, whereas `_exit` is specified by POSIX.1.

Historically, the `exit` function has always performed a clean shutdown of the standard I/O library: the `fclose` function is called for all open streams. Recall from Section 5.5 that this causes all buffered output data to be flushed (written to the file).

All three exit functions expect a single integer argument, which we call the *exit status*. Most UNIX System shells provide a way to examine the exit status of a process. If (a) any of these functions is called without an exit status, (b) `main` does a `return` without a return value, or (c) the `main` function is not declared to return an integer, the exit status of the process is undefined. However, if the return type of `main` is an integer and `main` "falls off the end" (an implicit return), the exit status of the process is 0.

> This behavior is new with the 1999 version of the ISO C standard. Historically, the exit status was undefined if the end of the `main` function was reached without an explicit `return` statement or call to the `exit` function.

Returning an integer value from the `main` function is equivalent to calling `exit` with the same value. Thus

```
exit(0);
```

is the same as

```
return(0);
```

from the `main` function.

Example

The program in Figure 7.1 is the classic "hello, world" example.

```
#include     <stdio.h>

main()
{
    printf("hello, world\n");
}
```

Figure 7.1 Classic C program

When we compile and run the program in Figure 7.1, we see that the exit code is random. If we compile the same program on different systems, we are likely to get different exit codes, depending on the contents of the stack and register contents at the time that the `main` function returns:

```
$ cc hello.c
$ ./a.out
hello, world
$ echo $?                    print the exit status
13
```

Now if we enable the 1999 ISO C compiler extensions, we see that the exit code changes:

```
$ cc -std=c99 hello.c          enable gcc's 1999 ISO C extensions
hello.c:4: warning: return type defaults to `int´
$ ./a.out
hello, world
$ echo $?                      print the exit status
0
```

Note the compiler warning when we enable the 1999 ISO C extensions. This warning is printed because the type of the main function is not explicitly declared to be an integer. If we were to add this declaration, the message would go away. However, if we were to enable all recommended warnings from the compiler (with the -Wall flag), then we would see a warning message something like "control reaches end of nonvoid function."

The declaration of main as returning an integer and the use of exit instead of return produces needless warnings from some compilers and the lint(1) program. The problem is that these compilers don't know that an exit from main is the same as a return. One way around these warnings, which become annoying after a while, is to use return instead of exit from main. But doing this prevents us from using the UNIX System's grep utility to locate all calls to exit from a program. Another solution is to declare main as returning void, instead of int, and continue calling exit. This gets rid of the compiler warning but doesn't look right (especially in a programming text), and can generate other compiler warnings, since the return type of main is supposed to be a signed integer. In this text, we show main as returning an integer, since that is the definition specified by both ISO C and POSIX.1.

Different compilers vary in the verbosity of their warnings. Note that the GNU C compiler usually doesn't emit these extraneous compiler warnings unless additional warning options are used.

□

In the next chapter, we'll see how any process can cause a program to be executed, wait for the process to complete, and then fetch its exit status.

atexit Function

With ISO C, a process can register up to 32 functions that are automatically called by exit. These are called *exit handlers* and are registered by calling the atexit function.

```
#include <stdlib.h>

int atexit(void (*func)(void));

                                            Returns: 0 if OK, nonzero on error
```

This declaration says that we pass the address of a function as the argument to atexit. When this function is called, it is not passed any arguments and is not expected to return a value. The exit function calls these functions in reverse order of their registration. Each function is called as many times as it was registered.

These exit handlers first appeared in the ANSI C Standard in 1989. Systems that predate ANSI C, such as SVR3 and 4.3BSD, did not provide these exit handlers.

ISO C requires that systems support at least 32 exit handlers. The sysconf function can be used to determine the maximum number of exit handlers supported by a given platform (see Figure 2.14).

With ISO C and POSIX.1, exit first calls the exit handlers and then closes (via fclose) all open streams. POSIX.1 extends the ISO C standard by specifying that any exit handlers installed will be cleared if the program calls any of the exec family of functions. Figure 7.2 summarizes how a C program is started and the various ways it can terminate.

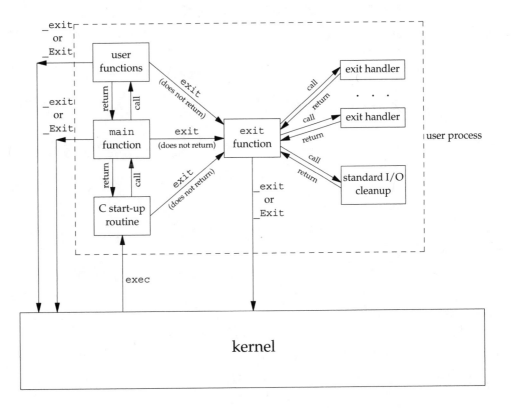

Figure 7.2 How a C program is started and how it terminates

Note that the only way a program is executed by the kernel is when one of the exec functions is called. The only way a process voluntarily terminates is when _exit or _Exit is called, either explicitly or implicitly (by calling exit). A process can also be involuntarily terminated by a signal (not shown in Figure 7.2).

Example

The program in Figure 7.3 demonstrates the use of the `atexit` function.

```
#include "apue.h"

static void my_exit1(void);
static void my_exit2(void);

int
main(void)
{
    if (atexit(my_exit2) != 0)
        err_sys("can't register my_exit2");

    if (atexit(my_exit1) != 0)
        err_sys("can't register my_exit1");
    if (atexit(my_exit1) != 0)
        err_sys("can't register my_exit1");

    printf("main is done\n");
    return(0);
}

static void
my_exit1(void)
{
    printf("first exit handler\n");
}

static void
my_exit2(void)
{
    printf("second exit handler\n");
}
```

Figure 7.3 Example of exit handlers

Executing the program in Figure 7.3 yields

```
$ ./a.out
main is done
first exit handler
first exit handler
second exit handler
```

An exit handler is called once for each time it is registered. In Figure 7.3, the first exit handler is registered twice, so it is called two times. Note that we don't call `exit`; instead, we return from `main`.   □

7.4   Command-Line Arguments

When a program is executed, the process that does the exec can pass command-line arguments to the new program. This is part of the normal operation of the UNIX system shells. We have already seen this in many of the examples from earlier chapters.

Example

The program in Figure 7.4 echoes all its command-line arguments to standard output. Note that the normal echo(1) program doesn't echo the zeroth argument.

```
#include "apue.h"

int
main(int argc, char *argv[])
{
    int     i;

    for (i = 0; i < argc; i++)          /* echo all command-line args */
        printf("argv[%d]: %s\n", i, argv[i]);
    exit(0);
}
```

Figure 7.4 Echo all command-line arguments to standard output

If we compile this program and name the executable echoarg, we have

```
$ ./echoarg arg1 TEST foo
argv[0]: ./echoarg
argv[1]: arg1
argv[2]: TEST
argv[3]: foo
```

We are guaranteed by both ISO C and POSIX.1 that argv[argc] is a null pointer. This lets us alternatively code the argument-processing loop as

```
for (i = 0; argv[i] != NULL; i++)
```                                                                    □

7.5   Environment List

Each program is also passed an *environment list*. Like the argument list, the environment list is an array of character pointers, with each pointer containing the address of a null-terminated C string. The address of the array of pointers is contained in the global variable environ:

```
extern char **environ;
```

For example, if the environment consisted of five strings, it could look like Figure 7.5. Here we explicitly show the null bytes at the end of each string. We'll call environ the

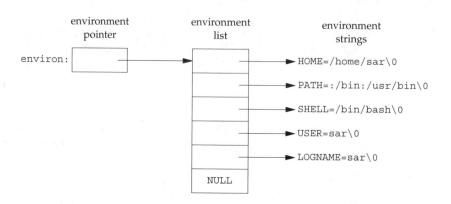

Figure 7.5 Environment consisting of five C character strings

environment pointer, the array of pointers the environment list, and the strings they point to the *environment strings*.

By convention, the environment consists of

name=value

strings, as shown in Figure 7.5. Most predefined names are entirely uppercase, but this is only a convention.

Historically, most UNIX systems have provided a third argument to the `main` function that is the address of the environment list:

```
int main(int argc, char *argv[], char *envp[]);
```

Because ISO C specifies that the `main` function be written with two arguments, and because this third argument provides no benefit over the global variable `environ`, POSIX.1 specifies that `environ` should be used instead of the (possible) third argument. Access to specific environment variables is normally through the `getenv` and `putenv` functions, described in Section 7.9, instead of through the `environ` variable. But to go through the entire environment, the `environ` pointer must be used.

7.6   Memory Layout of a C Program

Historically, a C program has been composed of the following pieces:

- Text segment, the machine instructions that the CPU executes. Usually, the text segment is sharable so that only a single copy needs to be in memory for frequently executed programs, such as text editors, the C compiler, the shells, and so on. Also, the text segment is often read-only, to prevent a program from accidentally modifying its instructions.

- Initialized data segment, usually called simply the data segment, containing variables that are specifically initialized in the program. For example, the C declaration

```
int    maxcount = 99;
```

appearing outside any function causes this variable to be stored in the initialized data segment with its initial value.

- Uninitialized data segment, often called the "bss" segment, named after an ancient assembler operator that stood for "block started by symbol." Data in this segment is initialized by the kernel to arithmetic 0 or null pointers before the program starts executing. The C declaration

```
long    sum[1000];
```

appearing outside any function causes this variable to be stored in the uninitialized data segment.

- Stack, where automatic variables are stored, along with information that is saved each time a function is called. Each time a function is called, the address of where to return to and certain information about the caller's environment, such as some of the machine registers, are saved on the stack. The newly called function then allocates room on the stack for its automatic and temporary variables. This is how recursive functions in C can work. Each time a recursive function calls itself, a new stack frame is used, so one set of variables doesn't interfere with the variables from another instance of the function.

- Heap, where dynamic memory allocation usually takes place. Historically, the heap has been located between the uninitialized data and the stack.

Figure 7.6 shows the typical arrangement of these segments. This is a logical picture of how a program looks; there is no requirement that a given implementation arrange its memory in this fashion. Nevertheless, this gives us a typical arrangement to describe. With Linux on an Intel x86 processor, the text segment starts at location 0x08048000, and the bottom of the stack starts just below 0xC0000000. (The stack grows from higher-numbered addresses to lower-numbered addresses on this particular architecture.) The unused virtual address space between the top of the heap and the top of the stack is large.

> Several more segment types exist in an a.out, containing the symbol table, debugging information, linkage tables for dynamic shared libraries, and the like. These additional sections don't get loaded as part of the program's image executed by a process.

Note from Figure 7.6 that the contents of the uninitialized data segment are not stored in the program file on disk. This is because the kernel sets it to 0 before the program starts running. The only portions of the program that need to be saved in the program file are the text segment and the initialized data.

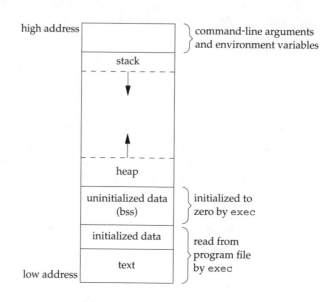

Figure 7.6 Typical memory arrangement

The size(1) command reports the sizes (in bytes) of the text, data, and bss segments. For example:

```
$ size /usr/bin/cc /bin/sh
   text     data    bss      dec     hex   filename
  79606     1536    916    82058    1408a  /usr/bin/cc
 619234    21120  18260   658614    a0cb6  /bin/sh
```

The fourth and fifth columns are the total of the three sizes, displayed in decimal and hexadecimal, respectively.

7.7   Shared Libraries

Most UNIX systems today support shared libraries. Arnold [1986] describes an early implementation under System V, and Gingell et al. [1987] describe a different implementation under SunOS. Shared libraries remove the common library routines from the executable file, instead maintaining a single copy of the library routine somewhere in memory that all processes reference. This reduces the size of each executable file but may add some runtime overhead, either when the program is first executed or the first time each shared library function is called. Another advantage of shared libraries is that library functions can be replaced with new versions without having to relink edit every program that uses the library. (This assumes that the number and type of arguments haven't changed.)

Different systems provide different ways for a program to say that it wants to use or not use the shared libraries. Options for the cc(1) and ld(1) commands are typical. As an example of the size differences, the following executable file—the classic hello.c program—was first created without shared libraries:

```
$ cc -static hello1.c          prevent gcc from using shared libraries
$ ls -l a.out
-rwxrwxr-x  1 sar       475570 Feb 18 23:17 a.out
$ size a.out
   text    data    bss     dec      hex  filename
 375657    3780   3220  382657    5d6c1  a.out
```

If we compile this program to use shared libraries, the text and data sizes of the executable file are greatly decreased:

```
$ cc hello1.c                  gcc defaults to use shared libraries
$ ls -l a.out
-rwxrwxr-x  1 sar        11410 Feb 18 23:19 a.out
$ size a.out
   text    data    bss     dec      hex  filename
    872     256      4    1132      46c  a.out
```

7.8   Memory Allocation

ISO C specifies three functions for memory allocation:

1. malloc, which allocates a specified number of bytes of memory. The initial value of the memory is indeterminate.

2. calloc, which allocates space for a specified number of objects of a specified size. The space is initialized to all 0 bits.

3. realloc, which increases or decreases the size of a previously allocated area. When the size increases, it may involve moving the previously allocated area somewhere else, to provide the additional room at the end. Also, when the size increases, the initial value of the space between the old contents and the end of the new area is indeterminate.

```
#include <stdlib.h>

void *malloc(size_t size);

void *calloc(size_t nobj, size_t size);

void *realloc(void *ptr, size_t newsize);

                        All three return: non-null pointer if OK, NULL on error

void free(void *ptr);
```

The pointer returned by the three allocation functions is guaranteed to be suitably aligned so that it can be used for any data object. For example, if the most restrictive alignment requirement on a particular system requires that doubles must start at memory locations that are multiples of 8, then all pointers returned by these three functions would be so aligned.

Because the three alloc functions return a generic void * pointer, if we #include <stdlib.h> (to obtain the function prototypes), we do not explicitly have to cast the pointer returned by these functions when we assign it to a pointer of a different type.

The function free causes the space pointed to by *ptr* to be deallocated. This freed space is usually put into a pool of available memory and can be allocated in a later call to one of the three alloc functions.

The realloc function lets us increase or decrease the size of a previously allocated area. (The most common usage is to increase an area.) For example, if we allocate room for 512 elements in an array that we fill in at runtime but find that we need room for more than 512 elements, we can call realloc. If there is room beyond the end of the existing region for the requested space, then realloc doesn't have to move anything; it simply allocates the additional area at the end and returns the same pointer that we passed it. But if there isn't room at the end of the existing region, realloc allocates another area that is large enough, copies the existing 512-element array to the new area, frees the old area, and returns the pointer to the new area. Because the area may move, we shouldn't have any pointers into this area. Exercise 4.16 shows the use of realloc with getcwd to handle any length pathname. Figure 17.36 shows an example that uses realloc to avoid arrays with fixed, compile-time sizes.

Note that the final argument to realloc is the new size of the region, not the difference between the old and new sizes. As a special case, if *ptr* is a null pointer, realloc behaves like malloc and allocates a region of the specified *newsize*.

> Older versions of these routines allowed us to realloc a block that we had freed since the last call to malloc, realloc, or calloc. This trick dates back to Version 7 and exploited the search strategy of malloc to perform storage compaction. Solaris still supports this feature, but many other platforms do not. This feature is deprecated and should not be used.

The allocation routines are usually implemented with the sbrk(2) system call. This system call expands (or contracts) the heap of the process. (Refer to Figure 7.6.) A sample implementation of malloc and free is given in Section 8.7 of Kernighan and Ritchie [1988].

Although sbrk can expand or contract the memory of a process, most versions of malloc and free never decrease their memory size. The space that we free is available for a later allocation, but the freed space is not usually returned to the kernel; that space is kept in the malloc pool.

It is important to realize that most implementations allocate a little more space than is requested and use the additional space for record keeping—the size of the allocated block, a pointer to the next allocated block, and the like. This means that writing past the end of an allocated area could overwrite this record-keeping information in a later block. These types of errors are often catastrophic, but difficult to find, because the error may not show up until much later. Also, it is possible to overwrite this record keeping by writing before the start of the allocated area.

Writing past the end or before the beginning of a dynamically-allocated buffer can corrupt more than internal record-keeping information. The memory before and after a dynamically-allocated buffer can potentially be used for other dynamically-allocated objects. These objects can be unrelated to the code corrupting them, making it even more difficult to find the source of the corruption.

Other possible errors that can be fatal are freeing a block that was already freed and calling `free` with a pointer that was not obtained from one of the three `alloc` functions. If a process calls `malloc`, but forgets to call `free`, its memory usage continually increases; this is called leakage. By not calling `free` to return unused space, the size of a process's address space slowly increases until no free space is left. During this time, performance can degrade from excess paging overhead.

Because memory allocation errors are difficult to track down, some systems provide versions of these functions that do additional error checking every time one of the three `alloc` functions or `free` is called. These versions of the functions are often specified by including a special library for the link editor. There are also publicly available sources that you can compile with special flags to enable additional runtime checking.

> FreeBSD, Mac OS X, and Linux support additional debugging through the setting of environment variables. In addition, options can be passed to the FreeBSD library through the symbolic link /etc/malloc.conf.

Alternate Memory Allocators

Many replacements for `malloc` and `free` are available. Some systems already include libraries providing alternate memory allocator implementations. Other systems provide only the standard allocator, leaving it up to software developers to download alternatives, if desired. We discuss some of the alternatives here.

libmalloc

SVR4-based systems, such as Solaris, include the `libmalloc` library, which provides a set of interfaces matching the ISO C memory allocation functions. The `libmalloc` library includes `mallopt`, a function that allows a process to set certain variables that control the operation of the storage allocator. A function called `mallinfo` is also available to provide statistics on the memory allocator.

vmalloc

Vo [1996] describes a memory allocator that allows processes to allocate memory using different techniques for different regions of memory. In addition to the functions specific to `vmalloc`, the library also provides emulations of the ISO C memory allocation functions.

quick-fit

Historically, the standard `malloc` algorithm used either a best-fit or a first-fit memory allocation strategy. Quick-fit is faster than either, but tends to use more memory. Weinstock and Wulf [1988] describe the algorithm, which is based on splitting up memory into buffers of various sizes and maintaining unused buffers on different free lists, depending on the size of the buffers. Free implementations of `malloc` and `free` based on quick-fit are readily available from several FTP sites.

`alloca` Function

One additional function is also worth mentioning. The function `alloca` has the same calling sequence as `malloc`; however, instead of allocating memory from the heap, the memory is allocated from the stack frame of the current function. The advantage is that we don't have to free the space; it goes away automatically when the function returns. The `alloca` function increases the size of the stack frame. The disadvantage is that some systems can't support `alloca`, if it's impossible to increase the size of the stack frame after the function has been called. Nevertheless, many software packages use it, and implementations exist for a wide variety of systems.

All four platforms discussed in this text provide the `alloca` function.

7.9   Environment Variables

As we mentioned earlier, the environment strings are usually of the form

name=value

The UNIX kernel never looks at these strings; their interpretation is up to the various applications. The shells, for example, use numerous environment variables. Some, such as HOME and USER, are set automatically at login, and others are for us to set. We normally set environment variables in a shell start-up file to control the shell's actions. If we set the environment variable MAILPATH, for example, it tells the Bourne shell, GNU Bourne-again shell, and Korn shell where to look for mail.

ISO C defines a function that we can use to fetch values from the environment, but this standard says that the contents of the environment are implementation defined.

```
#include <stdlib.h>

char *getenv(const char *name);
```
                    Returns: pointer to *value* associated with *name*, NULL if not found

Note that this function returns a pointer to the *value* of a *name=value* string. We should always use `getenv` to fetch a specific value from the environment, instead of accessing `environ` directly.

Some environment variables are defined by POSIX.1 in the Single UNIX Specification, whereas others are defined only if the XSI extensions are supported. Figure 7.7 lists the environment variables defined by the Single UNIX Specification and also notes which implementations support the variables. Any environment variable defined by POSIX.1 is marked with •; otherwise, it is an XSI extension. Many additional implementation-dependent environment variables are used in the four implementations described in this book. Note that ISO C doesn't define any environment variables.

Variable	POSIX.1	FreeBSD 5.2.1	Linux 2.4.22	Mac OS X 10.3	Solaris 9	Description
COLUMNS	•	•	•	•	•	terminal width
DATEMSK	XSI		•		•	`getdate`(3) template file pathname
HOME	•	•	•	•	•	home directory
LANG	•	•	•	•	•	name of locale
LC_ALL	•	•	•	•	•	name of locale
LC_COLLATE	•	•	•	•	•	name of locale for collation
LC_CTYPE	•	•	•	•	•	name of locale for character classification
LC_MESSAGES	•	•	•	•	•	name of locale for messages
LC_MONETARY	•	•	•	•	•	name of locale for monetary editing
LC_NUMERIC	•	•	•	•	•	name of locale for numeric editing
LC_TIME	•	•	•	•	•	name of locale for date/time formatting
LINES	•	•	•	•	•	terminal height
LOGNAME	•	•	•	•	•	login name
MSGVERB	XSI	•			•	`fmtmsg`(3) message components to process
NLSPATH	XSI	•	•	•	•	sequence of templates for message catalogs
PATH	•	•	•	•	•	list of path prefixes to search for executable file
PWD	•	•	•	•	•	absolute pathname of current working directory
SHELL	•	•	•	•	•	name of user's preferred shell
TERM	•	•	•	•	•	terminal type
TMPDIR	•	•	•	•	•	pathname of directory for creating temporary files
TZ	•	•	•	•	•	time zone information

Figure 7.7 Environment variables defined in the Single UNIX Specification

In addition to fetching the value of an environment variable, sometimes we may want to set an environment variable. We may want to change the value of an existing variable or add a new variable to the environment. (In the next chapter, we'll see that we can affect the environment of only the current process and any child processes that we invoke. We cannot affect the environment of the parent process, which is often a shell. Nevertheless, it is still useful to be able to modify the environment list.) Unfortunately, not all systems support this capability. Figure 7.8 shows the functions that are supported by the various standards and implementations.

Function	ISO C	POSIX.1	FreeBSD 5.2.1	Linux 2.4.22	Mac OS X 10.3	Solaris 9
getenv	•	•	•	•	•	•
putenv		XSI	•	•	•	•
setenv		•	•	•	•	
unsetenv		•	•	•	•	
clearenv				•		

Figure 7.8 Support for various environment list functions

clearenv is not part of the Single UNIX Specification. It is used to remove all entries from the environment list.

The prototypes for the middle three functions listed in Figure 7.8 are

```
#include <stdlib.h>

int putenv(char *str);
```
Returns: 0 if OK, nonzero on error

```
int setenv(const char *name, const char *value, int rewrite);

int unsetenv(const char *name);
```
Both return: 0 if OK, −1 on error

The operation of these three functions is as follows.

- The putenv function takes a string of the form *name=value* and places it in the environment list. If *name* already exists, its old definition is first removed.

- The setenv function sets *name* to *value*. If *name* already exists in the environment, then (a) if *rewrite* is nonzero, the existing definition for *name* is first removed; (b) if *rewrite* is 0, an existing definition for *name* is not removed, *name* is not set to the new *value*, and no error occurs.

- The unsetenv function removes any definition of *name*. It is not an error if such a definition does not exist.

> Note the difference between putenv and setenv. Whereas setenv must allocate memory to create the *name=value* string from its arguments, putenv is free to place the string passed to it directly into the environment. Indeed, on Linux and Solaris, the putenv implementation places the address of the string we pass to it directly into the environment list. In this case, it would be an error to pass it a string allocated on the stack, since the memory would be reused after we return from the current function.

It is interesting to examine how these functions must operate when modifying the environment list. Recall Figure 7.6: the environment list—the array of pointers to the actual *name=value* strings—and the environment strings are typically stored at the top of a process's memory space, above the stack. Deleting a string is simple; we simply find the pointer in the environment list and move all subsequent pointers down one. But adding a string or modifying an existing string is more difficult. The space at the top of the stack cannot be expanded, because it is often at the top of the address space of the process and so can't expand upward; it can't be expanded downward, because all the stack frames below it can't be moved.

1. If we're modifying an existing *name:*

    a. If the size of the new *value* is less than or equal to the size of the existing *value*, we can just copy the new string over the old string.

    b. If the size of the new *value* is larger than the old one, however, we must `malloc` to obtain room for the new string, copy the new string to this area, and then replace the old pointer in the environment list for *name* with the pointer to this allocated area.

2. If we're adding a new *name*, it's more complicated. First, we have to call `malloc` to allocate room for the *name=value* string and copy the string to this area.

    a. Then, if it's the first time we've added a new *name*, we have to call `malloc` to obtain room for a new list of pointers. We copy the old environment list to this new area and store a pointer to the *name=value* string at the end of this list of pointers. We also store a null pointer at the end of this list, of course. Finally, we set `environ` to point to this new list of pointers. Note from Figure 7.6 that if the original environment list was contained above the top of the stack, as is common, then we have moved this list of pointers to the heap. But most of the pointers in this list still point to *name=value* strings above the top of the stack.

    b. If this isn't the first time we've added new strings to the environment list, then we know that we've already allocated room for the list on the heap, so we just call `realloc` to allocate room for one more pointer. The pointer to the new *name=value* string is stored at the end of the list (on top of the previous null pointer), followed by a null pointer.

7.10 `setjmp` and `longjmp` Functions

In C, we can't `goto` a label that's in another function. Instead, we must use the `setjmp` and `longjmp` functions to perform this type of branching. As we'll see, these two functions are useful for handling error conditions that occur in a deeply nested function call.

Consider the skeleton in Figure 7.9. It consists of a main loop that reads lines from standard input and calls the function do_line to process each line. This function then calls get_token to fetch the next token from the input line. The first token of a line is assumed to be a command of some form, and a `switch` statement selects each command. For the single command shown, the function cmd_add is called.

The skeleton in Figure 7.9 is typical for programs that read commands, determine the command type, and then call functions to process each command. Figure 7.10 shows what the stack could look like after cmd_add has been called.

```
#include "apue.h"

#define TOK_ADD    5

void    do_line(char *);
void    cmd_add(void);
int     get_token(void);

int
main(void)
{
    char    line[MAXLINE];

    while (fgets(line, MAXLINE, stdin) != NULL)
        do_line(line);
    exit(0);
}

char    *tok_ptr;          /* global pointer for get_token() */

void
do_line(char *ptr)         /* process one line of input */
{
    int     cmd;

    tok_ptr = ptr;
    while ((cmd = get_token()) > 0) {
        switch (cmd) {  /* one case for each command */
        case TOK_ADD:
                cmd_add();
                break;
        }
    }
}

void
cmd_add(void)
{
    int     token;

    token = get_token();
    /* rest of processing for this command */
}

int
get_token(void)
{
    /* fetch next token from line pointed to by tok_ptr */
}
```

Figure 7.9 Typical program skeleton for command processing

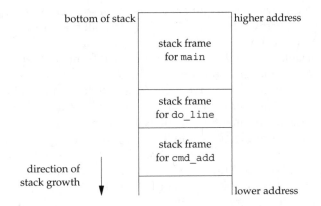

Figure 7.10 Stack frames after cmd_add has been called

Storage for the automatic variables is within the stack frame for each function. The array line is in the stack frame for main, the integer cmd is in the stack frame for do_line, and the integer token is in the stack frame for cmd_add.

As we've said, this type of arrangement of the stack is typical, but not required. Stacks do not have to grow toward lower memory addresses. On systems that don't have built-in hardware support for stacks, a C implementation might use a linked list for its stack frames.

The coding problem that's often encountered with programs like the one shown in Figure 7.9 is how to handle nonfatal errors. For example, if the cmd_add function encounters an error—say, an invalid number—it might want to print an error, ignore the rest of the input line, and return to the main function to read the next input line. But when we're deeply nested numerous levels down from the main function, this is difficult to do in C. (In this example, in the cmd_add function, we're only two levels down from main, but it's not uncommon to be five or more levels down from where we want to return to.) It becomes messy if we have to code each function with a special return value that tells it to return one level.

The solution to this problem is to use a nonlocal goto: the setjmp and longjmp functions. The adjective nonlocal is because we're not doing a normal C goto statement within a function; instead, we're branching back through the call frames to a function that is in the call path of the current function.

```
#include <setjmp.h>

int setjmp(jmp_buf env);
```

                    Returns: 0 if called directly, nonzero if returning from a call to longjmp

```
void longjmp(jmp_buf env, int val);
```

We call setjmp from the location that we want to return to, which in this example is in the main function. In this case, setjmp returns 0 because we called it directly. In the call to setjmp, the argument *env* is of the special type jmp_buf. This data type is some form of array that is capable of holding all the information required to restore the status of the stack to the state when we call longjmp. Normally, the *env* variable is a global variable, since we'll need to reference it from another function.

When we encounter an error—say, in the cmd_add function—we call longjmp with two arguments. The first is the same *env* that we used in a call to setjmp, and the second, *val*, is a nonzero value that becomes the return value from setjmp. The reason for the second argument is to allow us to have more than one longjmp for each setjmp. For example, we could longjmp from cmd_add with a *val* of 1 and also call longjmp from get_token with a *val* of 2. In the main function, the return value from setjmp is either 1 or 2, and we can test this value, if we want, and determine whether the longjmp was from cmd_add or get_token.

Let's return to the example. Figure 7.11 shows both the main and cmd_add functions. (The other two functions, do_line and get_token, haven't changed.)

```
#include "apue.h"
#include <setjmp.h>

#define TOK_ADD     5

jmp_buf jmpbuffer;

int
main(void)
{
    char    line[MAXLINE];

    if (setjmp(jmpbuffer) != 0)
        printf("error");
    while (fgets(line, MAXLINE, stdin) != NULL)
        do_line(line);
    exit(0);
}

    . . .

void
cmd_add(void)
{
    int     token;

    token = get_token();
    if (token < 0)          /* an error has occurred */
        longjmp(jmpbuffer, 1);
    /* rest of processing for this command */
}
```

Figure 7.11 Example of setjmp and longjmp

When main is executed, we call setjmp, which records whatever information it needs to in the variable jmpbuffer and returns 0. We then call do_line, which calls cmd_add, and assume that an error of some form is detected. Before the call to longjmp in cmd_add, the stack looks like that in Figure 7.10. But longjmp causes the stack to be "unwound" back to the main function, throwing away the stack frames for cmd_add and do_line (Figure 7.12). Calling longjmp causes the setjmp in main to return, but this time it returns with a value of 1 (the second argument for longjmp).

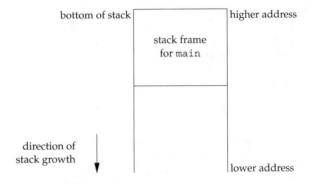

Figure 7.12 Stack frame after longjmp has been called

Automatic, Register, and Volatile Variables

We've seen what the stack looks like after calling longjmp. The next question is, "what are the states of the automatic variables and register variables in the main function?" When main is returned to by the longjmp, do these variables have values corresponding to when the setjmp was previously called (i.e., are their values rolled back), or are their values left alone so that their values are whatever they were when do_line was called (which caused cmd_add to be called, which caused longjmp to be called)? Unfortunately, the answer is "it depends." Most implementations do not try to roll back these automatic variables and register variables, but the standards say only that their values are indeterminate. If you have an automatic variable that you don't want rolled back, define it with the volatile attribute. Variables that are declared global or static are left alone when longjmp is executed.

Example

The program in Figure 7.13 demonstrates the different behavior that can be seen with automatic, global, register, static, and volatile variables after calling longjmp.

```
#include "apue.h"
#include <setjmp.h>

static void f1(int, int, int, int);
static void f2(void);

static jmp_buf   jmpbuffer;
static int       globval;

int
main(void)
{
    int          autoval;
    register int regival;
    volatile int volaval;
    static int   statval;

    globval = 1; autoval = 2; regival = 3; volaval = 4; statval = 5;

    if (setjmp(jmpbuffer) != 0) {
        printf("after longjmp:\n");
        printf("globval = %d, autoval = %d, regival = %d,"
            " volaval = %d, statval = %d\n",
            globval, autoval, regival, volaval, statval);
        exit(0);
    }

    /*
     * Change variables after setjmp, but before longjmp.
     */
    globval = 95; autoval = 96; regival = 97; volaval = 98;
    statval = 99;

    f1(autoval, regival, volaval, statval); /* never returns */
    exit(0);
}

static void
f1(int i, int j, int k, int l)
{
    printf("in f1():\n");
    printf("globval = %d, autoval = %d, regival = %d,"
        " volaval = %d, statval = %d\n", globval, i, j, k, l);
    f2();
}

static void
f2(void)
{
    longjmp(jmpbuffer, 1);
}
```

Figure 7.13 Effect of `longjmp` on various types of variables

If we compile and test the program in Figure 7.13, with and without compiler optimizations, the results are different:

```
$ cc testjmp.c                      compile without any optimization
$ ./a.out
in f1():
globval = 95, autoval = 96, regival = 97, volaval = 98, statval = 99
after longjmp:
globval = 95, autoval = 96, regival = 97, volaval = 98, statval = 99
$ cc -O testjmp.c                   compile with full optimization
$ ./a.out
in f1():
globval = 95, autoval = 96, regival = 97, volaval = 98, statval = 99
after longjmp:
globval = 95, autoval = 2, regival = 3, volaval = 98, statval = 99
```

Note that the optimizations don't affect the global, static, and volatile variables; their values after the longjmp are the last values that they assumed. The setjmp(3) manual page on one system states that variables stored in memory will have values as of the time of the longjmp, whereas variables in the CPU and floating-point registers are restored to their values when setjmp was called. This is indeed what we see when we run the program in Figure 7.13. Without optimization, all five variables are stored in memory (the register hint is ignored for regival). When we enable optimization, both autoval and regival go into registers, even though the former wasn't declared register, and the volatile variable stays in memory. The thing to realize with this example is that you must use the volatile attribute if you're writing portable code that uses nonlocal jumps. Anything else can change from one system to the next.

Some printf format strings in Figure 7.13 are longer than will fit comfortably for display in a programming text. Instead of making multiple calls to printf, we rely on ISO C's string concatenation feature, where the sequence

```
"string1" "string2"
```

is equivalent to

```
"string1string2"
```

                                                                                    □

We'll return to these two functions, setjmp and longjmp, in Chapter 10 when we discuss signal handlers and their signal versions: sigsetjmp and siglongjmp.

Potential Problem with Automatic Variables

Having looked at the way stack frames are usually handled, it is worth looking at a potential error in dealing with automatic variables. The basic rule is that an automatic variable can never be referenced after the function that declared it returns. There are numerous warnings about this throughout the UNIX System manuals.

Figure 7.14 shows a function called open_data that opens a standard I/O stream and sets the buffering for the stream.

```
#include     <stdio.h>

#define DATAFILE     "datafile"

FILE *
open_data(void)
{
    FILE     *fp;
    char     databuf[BUFSIZ];   /* setvbuf makes this the stdio buffer */

    if ((fp = fopen(DATAFILE, "r")) == NULL)
        return(NULL);
    if (setvbuf(fp, databuf, _IOLBF, BUFSIZ) != 0)
        return(NULL);
    return(fp);      /* error */
}
```

Figure 7.14 Incorrect usage of an automatic variable

The problem is that when open_data returns, the space it used on the stack will be used by the stack frame for the next function that is called. But the standard I/O library will still be using that portion of memory for its stream buffer. Chaos is sure to result. To correct this problem, the array databuf needs to be allocated from global memory, either statically (static or extern) or dynamically (one of the alloc functions).

7.11 getrlimit and setrlimit Functions

Every process has a set of resource limits, some of which can be queried and changed by the getrlimit and setrlimit functions.

```
#include <sys/resource.h>

int getrlimit(int resource, struct rlimit *rlptr);

int setrlimit(int resource, const struct rlimit *rlptr);
```
                                        Both return: 0 if OK, nonzero on error

These two functions are defined as XSI extensions in the Single UNIX Specification. The resource limits for a process are normally established by process 0 when the system is initialized and then inherited by each successive process. Each implementation has its own way of tuning the various limits.

Each call to these two functions specifies a single *resource* and a pointer to the following structure:

```
struct rlimit {
    rlim_t  rlim_cur;   /* soft limit: current limit */
    rlim_t  rlim_max;   /* hard limit: maximum value for rlim_cur */
};
```

Three rules govern the changing of the resource limits.

1. A process can change its soft limit to a value less than or equal to its hard limit.
2. A process can lower its hard limit to a value greater than or equal to its soft limit. This lowering of the hard limit is irreversible for normal users.
3. Only a superuser process can raise a hard limit.

An infinite limit is specified by the constant RLIM_INFINITY.

The *resource* argument takes on one of the following values. Figure 7.15 shows which limits are defined by the Single UNIX Specification and supported by each implementation.

RLIMIT_AS	The maximum size in bytes of a process's total available memory. This affects the sbrk function (Section 1.11) and the mmap function (Section 14.9).
RLIMIT_CORE	The maximum size in bytes of a core file. A limit of 0 prevents the creation of a core file.
RLIMIT_CPU	The maximum amount of CPU time in seconds. When the soft limit is exceeded, the SIGXCPU signal is sent to the process.
RLIMIT_DATA	The maximum size in bytes of the data segment: the sum of the initialized data, uninitialized data, and heap from Figure 7.6.
RLIMIT_FSIZE	The maximum size in bytes of a file that may be created. When the soft limit is exceeded, the process is sent the SIGXFSZ signal.
RLIMIT_LOCKS	The maximum number of file locks a process can hold. (This number also includes file leases, a Linux-specific feature. See the Linux fcntl(2) manual page for more information.)
RLIMIT_MEMLOCK	The maximum amount of memory in bytes that a process can lock into memory using mlock(2).
RLIMIT_NOFILE	The maximum number of open files per process. Changing this limit affects the value returned by the sysconf function for its _SC_OPEN_MAX argument (Section 2.5.4). See Figure 2.16 also.
RLIMIT_NPROC	The maximum number of child processes per real user ID. Changing this limit affects the value returned for _SC_CHILD_MAX by the sysconf function (Section 2.5.4).
RLIMIT_RSS	Maximum resident set size (RSS) in bytes. If available physical memory is low, the kernel takes memory from processes that exceed their RSS.
RLIMIT_SBSIZE	The maximum size in bytes of socket buffers that a user can consume at any given time.
RLIMIT_STACK	The maximum size in bytes of the stack. See Figure 7.6.
RLIMIT_VMEM	This is a synonym for RLIMIT_AS.

Limit	XSI	FreeBSD 5.2.1	Linux 2.4.22	Mac OS X 10.3	Solaris 9
RLIMIT_AS	•		•		•
RLIMIT_CORE	•	•	•	•	•
RLIMIT_CPU	•	•	•	•	•
RLIMIT_DATA	•	•	•	•	•
RLIMIT_FSIZE	•	•	•	•	•
RLIMIT_LOCKS			•		
RLIMIT_MEMLOCK		•	•	•	
RLIMIT_NOFILE	•	•	•	•	•
RLIMIT_NPROC		•	•	•	
RLIMIT_RSS		•	•	•	
RLIMIT_SBSIZE		•			
RLIMIT_STACK	•	•	•	•	•
RLIMIT_VMEM		•			•

Figure 7.15 Support for resource limits

The resource limits affect the calling process and are inherited by any of its children. This means that the setting of resource limits needs to be built into the shells to affect all our future processes. Indeed, the Bourne shell, the GNU Bourne-again shell, and the Korn shell have the built-in ulimit command, and the C shell has the built-in limit command. (The umask and chdir functions also have to be handled as shell built-ins.)

Example

The program in Figure 7.16 prints out the current soft limit and hard limit for all the resource limits supported on the system. To compile this program on all the various implementations, we have conditionally included the resource names that differ. Note also that we must use a different printf format on platforms that define rlim_t to be an unsigned long long instead of an unsigned long.

```
#include "apue.h"
#if defined(BSD) || defined(MACOS)
#include <sys/time.h>
#define FMT "%10lld  "
#else
#define FMT "%10ld  "
#endif
#include <sys/resource.h>

#define doit(name)   pr_limits(#name, name)

static void pr_limits(char *, int);

int
main(void)
{
```

```
#ifdef   RLIMIT_AS
    doit(RLIMIT_AS);
#endif
    doit(RLIMIT_CORE);
    doit(RLIMIT_CPU);
    doit(RLIMIT_DATA);
    doit(RLIMIT_FSIZE);
#ifdef   RLIMIT_LOCKS
    doit(RLIMIT_LOCKS);
#endif
#ifdef   RLIMIT_MEMLOCK
    doit(RLIMIT_MEMLOCK);
#endif
    doit(RLIMIT_NOFILE);
#ifdef   RLIMIT_NPROC
    doit(RLIMIT_NPROC);
#endif
#ifdef   RLIMIT_RSS
    doit(RLIMIT_RSS);
#endif
#ifdef   RLIMIT_SBSIZE
    doit(RLIMIT_SBSIZE);
#endif
    doit(RLIMIT_STACK);
#ifdef   RLIMIT_VMEM
    doit(RLIMIT_VMEM);
#endif
    exit(0);
}

static void
pr_limits(char *name, int resource)
{
    struct rlimit   limit;

    if (getrlimit(resource, &limit) < 0)
        err_sys("getrlimit error for %s", name);
    printf("%-14s  ", name);
    if (limit.rlim_cur == RLIM_INFINITY)
        printf("(infinite)  ");
    else
        printf(FMT, limit.rlim_cur);
    if (limit.rlim_max == RLIM_INFINITY)
        printf("(infinite)");
    else
        printf(FMT, limit.rlim_max);
    putchar((int)'\n');
}
```

Figure 7.16 Print the current resource limits

Note that we've used the ISO C string-creation operator (#) in the doit macro, to generate the string value for each resource name. When we say

```
doit(RLIMIT_CORE);
```

the C preprocessor expands this into

```
pr_limits("RLIMIT_CORE", RLIMIT_CORE);
```

Running this program under FreeBSD gives us the following:

```
$ ./a.out
RLIMIT_CORE      (infinite)   (infinite)
RLIMIT_CPU       (infinite)   (infinite)
RLIMIT_DATA      536870912     536870912
RLIMIT_FSIZE     (infinite)   (infinite)
RLIMIT_MEMLOCK   (infinite)   (infinite)
RLIMIT_NOFILE         1735          1735
RLIMIT_NPROC           867           867
RLIMIT_RSS       (infinite)   (infinite)
RLIMIT_SBSIZE    (infinite)   (infinite)
RLIMIT_STACK      67108864      67108864
RLIMIT_VMEM      (infinite)   (infinite)
```

Solaris gives us the following results:

```
$ ./a.out
RLIMIT_AS        (infinite)   (infinite)
RLIMIT_CORE      (infinite)   (infinite)
RLIMIT_CPU       (infinite)   (infinite)
RLIMIT_DATA      (infinite)   (infinite)
RLIMIT_FSIZE     (infinite)   (infinite)
RLIMIT_NOFILE          256         65536
RLIMIT_STACK       8388608    (infinite)
RLIMIT_VMEM      (infinite)   (infinite)
```

Exercise 10.11 continues the discussion of resource limits, after we've covered signals.

7.12 Summary

Understanding the environment of a C program in a UNIX system's environment is a prerequisite to understanding the process control features of the UNIX System. In this chapter, we've looked at how a process is started, how it can terminate, and how it's passed an argument list and an environment. Although both are uninterpreted by the kernel, it is the kernel that passes both from the caller of exec to the new process.

We've also examined the typical memory layout of a C program and how a process can dynamically allocate and free memory. It is worthwhile to look in detail at the functions available for manipulating the environment, since they involve memory allocation. The functions setjmp and longjmp were presented, providing a way to perform nonlocal branching within a process. We finished the chapter by describing the resource limits that various implementations provide.

Exercises

7.1 On an Intel x86 system under both FreeBSD and Linux, if we execute the program that prints "hello, world" and do not call exit or return, the termination status of the program, which we can examine with the shell, is 13. Why?

7.2 When is the output from the printfs in Figure 7.3 actually output?

7.3 Is there any way for a function that is called by main to examine the command-line arguments without (a) passing argc and argv as arguments from main to the function or (b) having main copy argc and argv into global variables?

7.4 Some UNIX system implementations purposely arrange that, when a program is executed, location 0 in the data segment is not accessible. Why?

7.5 Use the typedef facility of C to define a new data type Exitfunc for an exit handler. Redo the prototype for atexit using this data type.

7.6 If we allocate an array of longs using calloc, is the array initialized to 0? If we allocate an array of pointers using calloc, is the array initialized to null pointers?

7.7 In the output from the size command at the end of Section 7.6, why aren't any sizes given for the heap and the stack?

7.8 In Section 7.7, the two file sizes (475570 and 11410) don't equal the sums of their respective text and data sizes. Why?

7.9 In Section 7.7, why is there such a difference in the size of the executable file when using shared libraries for such a trivial program?

7.10 At the end of Section 7.10, we showed how a function can't return a pointer to an automatic variable. Is the following code correct?

```
int
f1(int val)
{
    int      *ptr;

    if (val == 0) {
        int      val;

        val = 5;
        ptr = &val;
    }
    return(*ptr + 1);
}
```

8

Process Control

8.1 Introduction

We now turn to the process control provided by the UNIX System. This includes the creation of new processes, program execution, and process termination. We also look at the various IDs that are the property of the process—real, effective, and saved; user and group IDs—and how they're affected by the process control primitives. Interpreter files and the `system` function are also covered. We conclude the chapter by looking at the process accounting provided by most UNIX systems. This lets us look at the process control functions from a different perspective.

8.2 Process Identifiers

Every process has a unique process ID, a non-negative integer. Because the process ID is the only well-known identifier of a process that is always unique, it is often used as a piece of other identifiers, to guarantee uniqueness. For example, applications sometimes include the process ID as part of a filename in an attempt to generate unique filenames.

Although unique, process IDs are reused. As processes terminate, their IDs become candidates for reuse. Most UNIX systems implement algorithms to delay reuse, however, so that newly created processes are assigned IDs different from those used by processes that terminated recently. This prevents a new process from being mistaken for the previous process to have used the same ID.

There are some special processes, but the details differ from implementation to implementation. Process ID 0 is usually the scheduler process and is often known as the *swapper*. No program on disk corresponds to this process, which is part of the kernel and is known as a system process. Process ID 1 is usually the `init` process and is invoked by the kernel at the end of the bootstrap procedure. The program file for this process was `/etc/init` in older versions of the UNIX System and is `/sbin/init` in newer versions. This process is responsible for bringing up a UNIX system after the kernel has been bootstrapped. `init` usually reads the system-dependent initialization files—the `/etc/rc*` files or `/etc/inittab` and the files in `/etc/init.d`—and brings the system to a certain state, such as multiuser. The `init` process never dies. It is a normal user process, not a system process within the kernel, like the swapper, although it does run with superuser privileges. Later in this chapter, we'll see how `init` becomes the parent process of any orphaned child process.

Each UNIX System implementation has its own set of kernel processes that provide operating system services. For example, on some virtual memory implementations of the UNIX System, process ID 2 is the *pagedaemon*. This process is responsible for supporting the paging of the virtual memory system.

In addition to the process ID, there are other identifiers for every process. The following functions return these identifiers.

```
#include <unistd.h>

pid_t getpid(void);
```
                                              Returns: process ID of calling process
```
pid_t getppid(void);
```
                                        Returns: parent process ID of calling process
```
uid_t getuid(void);
```
                                             Returns: real user ID of calling process
```
uid_t geteuid(void);
```
                                        Returns: effective user ID of calling process
```
gid_t getgid(void);
```
                                            Returns: real group ID of calling process
```
gid_t getegid(void);
```
                                       Returns: effective group ID of calling process

Note that none of these functions has an error return. We'll return to the parent process ID in the next section when we discuss the `fork` function. The real and effective user and group IDs were discussed in Section 4.4.

8.3   `fork` **Function**

An existing process can create a new one by calling the `fork` function.

```
#include <unistd.h>

pid_t fork(void);
```
Returns: 0 in child, process ID of child in parent, –1 on error

The new process created by `fork` is called the *child process*. This function is called once but returns twice. The only difference in the returns is that the return value in the child is 0, whereas the return value in the parent is the process ID of the new child. The reason the child's process ID is returned to the parent is that a process can have more than one child, and there is no function that allows a process to obtain the process IDs of its children. The reason `fork` returns 0 to the child is that a process can have only a single parent, and the child can always call `getppid` to obtain the process ID of its parent. (Process ID 0 is reserved for use by the kernel, so it's not possible for 0 to be the process ID of a child.)

Both the child and the parent continue executing with the instruction that follows the call to `fork`. The child is a copy of the parent. For example, the child gets a copy of the parent's data space, heap, and stack. Note that this is a copy for the child; the parent and the child do not share these portions of memory. The parent and the child share the text segment (Section 7.6).

Current implementations don't perform a complete copy of the parent's data, stack, and heap, since a `fork` is often followed by an `exec`. Instead, a technique called *copy-on-write* (COW) is used. These regions are shared by the parent and the child and have their protection changed by the kernel to read-only. If either process tries to modify these regions, the kernel then makes a copy of that piece of memory only, typically a "page" in a virtual memory system. Section 9.2 of Bach [1986] and Sections 5.6 and 5.7 of McKusick et al. [1996] provide more detail on this feature.

> Variations of the `fork` function are provided by some platforms. All four platforms discussed in this book support the vfork(2) variant discussed in the next section.
>
> Linux 2.4.22 also provides new process creation through the clone(2) system call. This is a generalized form of `fork` that allows the caller to control what is shared between parent and child.
>
> FreeBSD 5.2.1 provides the rfork(2) system call, which is similar to the Linux clone system call. The rfork call is derived from the Plan 9 operating system (Pike et al. [1995]).
>
> Solaris 9 provides two threads libraries: one for POSIX threads (pthreads) and one for Solaris threads. The behavior of `fork` differs between the two thread libraries. For POSIX threads, `fork` creates a process containing only the calling thread, but for Solaris threads, `fork` creates a process containing copies of all threads from the process of the calling thread. To provide similar semantics as POSIX threads, Solaris provides the fork1 function, which can be used to create a process that duplicates only the calling thread, regardless of the thread library used. Threads are discussed in detail in Chapters 11 and 12.

Example

The program in Figure 8.1 demonstrates the `fork` function, showing how changes to variables in a child process do not affect the value of the variables in the parent process.

```c
#include "apue.h"

int     glob = 6;          /* external variable in initialized data */
char    buf[] = "a write to stdout\n";

int
main(void)
{
    int     var;           /* automatic variable on the stack */
    pid_t   pid;

    var = 88;
    if (write(STDOUT_FILENO, buf, sizeof(buf)-1) != sizeof(buf)-1)
        err_sys("write error");
    printf("before fork\n");    /* we don't flush stdout */

    if ((pid = fork()) < 0) {
        err_sys("fork error");
    } else if (pid == 0) {      /* child */
        glob++;                 /* modify variables */
        var++;
    } else {
        sleep(2);               /* parent */
    }

    printf("pid = %d, glob = %d, var = %d\n", getpid(), glob, var);
    exit(0);
}
```

Figure 8.1 Example of `fork` function

If we execute this program, we get

```
$ ./a.out
a write to stdout
before fork
pid = 430, glob = 7, var = 89    child's variables were changed
pid = 429, glob = 6, var = 88    parent's copy was not changed
$ ./a.out > temp.out
$ cat temp.out
a write to stdout
before fork
pid = 432, glob = 7, var = 89
before fork
pid = 431, glob = 6, var = 88
```

In general, we never know whether the child starts executing before the parent or vice versa. This depends on the scheduling algorithm used by the kernel. If it's required that the child and parent synchronize, some form of interprocess communication is required. In the program shown in Figure 8.1, we simply have the parent put itself to sleep for 2 seconds, to let the child execute. There is no guarantee that this is adequate, and we talk about this and other types of synchronization in Section 8.9 when we discuss race conditions. In Section 10.16, we show how to use signals to synchronize a parent and a child after a fork.

When we write to standard output, we subtract 1 from the size of buf to avoid writing the terminating null byte. Although strlen will calculate the length of a string not including the terminating null byte, sizeof calculates the size of the buffer, which does include the terminating null byte. Another difference is that using strlen requires a function call, whereas sizeof calculates the buffer length at compile time, as the buffer is initialized with a known string, and its size is fixed.

Note the interaction of fork with the I/O functions in the program in Figure 8.1. Recall from Chapter 3 that the write function is not buffered. Because write is called before the fork, its data is written once to standard output. The standard I/O library, however, is buffered. Recall from Section 5.12 that standard output is line buffered if it's connected to a terminal device; otherwise, it's fully buffered. When we run the program interactively, we get only a single copy of the printf line, because the standard output buffer is flushed by the newline. But when we redirect standard output to a file, we get two copies of the printf line. In this second case, the printf before the fork is called once, but the line remains in the buffer when fork is called. This buffer is then copied into the child when the parent's data space is copied to the child. Both the parent and the child now have a standard I/O buffer with this line in it. The second printf, right before the exit, just appends its data to the existing buffer. When each process terminates, its copy of the buffer is finally flushed.   □

File Sharing

When we redirect the standard output of the parent from the program in Figure 8.1, the child's standard output is also redirected. Indeed, one characteristic of fork is that all file descriptors that are open in the parent are duplicated in the child. We say "duplicated" because it's as if the dup function had been called for each descriptor. The parent and the child share a file table entry for every open descriptor (recall Figure 3.8).

Consider a process that has three different files opened for standard input, standard output, and standard error. On return from fork, we have the arrangement shown in Figure 8.2.

It is important that the parent and the child share the same file offset. Consider a process that forks a child, then waits for the child to complete. Assume that both processes write to standard output as part of their normal processing. If the parent has its standard output redirected (by a shell, perhaps) it is essential that the parent's file offset be updated by the child when the child writes to standard output. In this case, the child can write to standard output while the parent is waiting for it; on completion of the child, the parent can continue writing to standard output, knowing that its output will be appended to whatever the child wrote. If the parent and the child did not share the same file offset, this type of interaction would be more difficult to accomplish and would require explicit actions by the parent.

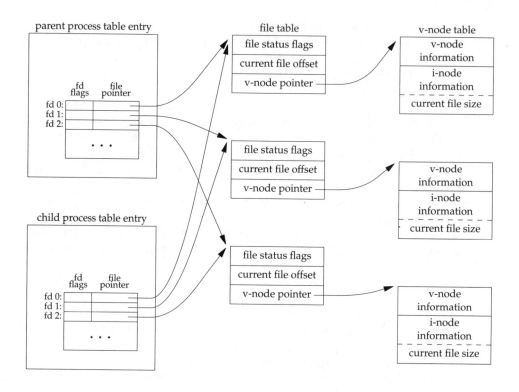

Figure 8.2 Sharing of open files between parent and child after `fork`

If both parent and child write to the same descriptor, without any form of synchronization, such as having the parent `wait` for the child, their output will be intermixed (assuming it's a descriptor that was open before the `fork`). Although this is possible—we saw it in Figure 8.2—it's not the normal mode of operation.

There are two normal cases for handling the descriptors after a `fork`.

1. The parent waits for the child to complete. In this case, the parent does not need to do anything with its descriptors. When the child terminates, any of the shared descriptors that the child read from or wrote to will have their file offsets updated accordingly.

2. Both the parent and the child go their own ways. Here, after the `fork`, the parent closes the descriptors that it doesn't need, and the child does the same thing. This way, neither interferes with the other's open descriptors. This scenario is often the case with network servers.

Besides the open files, there are numerous other properties of the parent that are inherited by the child:

- Real user ID, real group ID, effective user ID, effective group ID
- Supplementary group IDs

- Process group ID
- Session ID
- Controlling terminal
- The set-user-ID and set-group-ID flags
- Current working directory
- Root directory
- File mode creation mask
- Signal mask and dispositions
- The close-on-exec flag for any open file descriptors
- Environment
- Attached shared memory segments
- Memory mappings
- Resource limits

The differences between the parent and child are

- The return value from `fork`
- The process IDs are different
- The two processes have different parent process IDs: the parent process ID of the child is the parent; the parent process ID of the parent doesn't change
- The child's `tms_utime`, `tms_stime`, `tms_cutime`, and `tms_cstime` values are set to 0
- File locks set by the parent are not inherited by the child
- Pending alarms are cleared for the child
- The set of pending signals for the child is set to the empty set

Many of these features haven't been discussed yet—we'll cover them in later chapters.

The two main reasons for `fork` to fail are (a) if too many processes are already in the system, which usually means that something else is wrong, or (b) if the total number of processes for this real user ID exceeds the system's limit. Recall from Figure 2.10 that `CHILD_MAX` specifies the maximum number of simultaneous processes per real user ID.

There are two uses for `fork`:

1. When a process wants to duplicate itself so that the parent and child can each execute different sections of code at the same time. This is common for network servers—the parent waits for a service request from a client. When the request arrives, the parent calls `fork` and lets the child handle the request. The parent goes back to waiting for the next service request to arrive.

2. When a process wants to execute a different program. This is common for shells. In this case, the child does an `exec` (which we describe in Section 8.10) right after it returns from the `fork`.

Some operating systems combine the operations from step 2—a fork followed by an exec—into a single operation called a *spawn*. The UNIX System separates the two, as there are numerous cases where it is useful to fork without doing an exec. Also, separating the two allows the child to change the per-process attributes between the fork and the exec, such as I/O redirection, user ID, signal disposition, and so on. We'll see numerous examples of this in Chapter 15.

> The Single UNIX Specification does include spawn interfaces in the advanced real-time option group. These interfaces are not intended to be replacements for fork and exec, however. They are intended to support systems that have difficulty implementing fork efficiently, especially systems without hardware support for memory management.

8.4   vfork Function

The function vfork has the same calling sequence and same return values as fork. But the semantics of the two functions differ.

> The vfork function originated with 2.9BSD. Some consider the function a blemish, but all the platforms covered in this book support it. In fact, the BSD developers removed it from the 4.4BSD release, but all the open source BSD distributions that derive from 4.4BSD added support for it back into their own releases. The vfork function is marked as an obsolete interface in Version 3 of the Single UNIX Specification.

The vfork function is intended to create a new process when the purpose of the new process is to exec a new program (step 2 at the end of the previous section). The bare-bones shell in the program from Figure 1.7 is also an example of this type of program. The vfork function creates the new process, just like fork, without copying the address space of the parent into the child, as the child won't reference that address space; the child simply calls exec (or exit) right after the vfork. Instead, while the child is running and until it calls either exec or exit, the child runs in the address space of the parent. This optimization provides an efficiency gain on some paged virtual-memory implementations of the UNIX System. (As we mentioned in the previous section, implementations use copy-on-write to improve the efficiency of a fork followed by an exec, but no copying is still faster than some copying.)

Another difference between the two functions is that vfork guarantees that the child runs first, until the child calls exec or exit. When the child calls either of these functions, the parent resumes. (This can lead to deadlock if the child depends on further actions of the parent before calling either of these two functions.)

Example

The program in Figure 8.3 is a modified version of the program from Figure 8.1. We've replaced the call to fork with vfork and removed the write to standard output. Also, we don't need to have the parent call sleep, as we're guaranteed that it is put to sleep by the kernel until the child calls either exec or exit.

```
#include "apue.h"

int     glob = 6;          /* external variable in initialized data */

int
main(void)
{
    int     var;           /* automatic variable on the stack */
    pid_t   pid;

    var = 88;
    printf("before vfork\n");    /* we don't flush stdio */
    if ((pid = vfork()) < 0) {
        err_sys("vfork error");
    } else if (pid == 0) {       /* child */
        glob++;                  /* modify parent's variables */
        var++;
        _exit(0);                /* child terminates */
    }

    /*
     * Parent continues here.
     */
    printf("pid = %d, glob = %d, var = %d\n", getpid(), glob, var);
    exit(0);
}
```

Figure 8.3 Example of vfork function

Running this program gives us

```
$ ./a.out
before vfork
pid = 29039, glob = 7, var = 89
```

Here, the incrementing of the variables done by the child changes the values in the parent. Because the child runs in the address space of the parent, this doesn't surprise us. This behavior, however, differs from fork.

Note in Figure 8.3 that we call _exit instead of exit. As we described in Section 7.3, _exit does not perform any flushing of standard I/O buffers. If we call exit instead, the results are indeterminate. Depending on the implementation of the standard I/O library, we might see no difference in the output, or we might find that the output from the parent's printf has disappeared.

If the child calls exit, the implementation flushes the standard I/O streams. If this is the only action taken by the library, then we will see no difference with the output generated if the child called _exit. If the implementation also closes the standard I/O streams, however, the memory representing the FILE object for the standard output will be cleared out. Because the child is borrowing the parent's address space, when the parent resumes and calls printf, no output will appear and printf will return −1. Note that the parent's STDOUT_FILENO is still valid, as the child gets a copy of the parent's file descriptor array (refer back to Figure 8.2).

> Most modern implementations of exit will not bother to close the streams. Because the
> process is about to exit, the kernel will close all the file descriptors open in the process.
> Closing them in the library simply adds overhead without any benefit.
>
> □

Section 5.6 of McKusick et al. [1996] contains additional information on the implementation issues of fork and vfork. Exercises 8.1 and 8.2 continue the discussion of vfork.

8.5   exit Functions

As we described in Section 7.3, a process can terminate normally in five ways:

1. Executing a return from the main function. As we saw in Section 7.3, this is equivalent to calling exit.

2. Calling the exit function. This function is defined by ISO C and includes the calling of all exit handlers that have been registered by calling atexit and closing all standard I/O streams. Because ISO C does not deal with file descriptors, multiple processes (parents and children), and job control, the definition of this function is incomplete for a UNIX system.

3. Calling the _exit or _Exit function. ISO C defines _Exit to provide a way for a process to terminate without running exit handlers or signal handlers. Whether or not standard I/O streams are flushed depends on the implementation. On UNIX systems, _Exit and _exit are synonymous and do not flush standard I/O streams. The _exit function is called by exit and handles the UNIX system-specific details; _exit is specified by POSIX.1.

    > In most UNIX system implementations, exit(3) is a function in the standard C
    > library, whereas _exit(2) is a system call.

4. Executing a return from the start routine of the last thread in the process. The return value of the thread is not used as the return value of the process, however. When the last thread returns from its start routine, the process exits with a termination status of 0.

5. Calling the pthread_exit function from the last thread in the process. As with the previous case, the exit status of the process in this situation is always 0, regardless of the argument passed to pthread_exit. We'll say more about pthread_exit in Section 11.5.

The three forms of abnormal termination are as follows:

1. Calling abort. This is a special case of the next item, as it generates the SIGABRT signal.

2. When the process receives certain signals. (We describe signals in more detail in Chapter 10). The signal can be generated by the process itself—for example, by calling the abort function—by some other process, or by the kernel. Examples

of signals generated by the kernel include the process referencing a memory location not within its address space or trying to divide by 0.

3. The last thread responds to a cancellation request. By default, cancellation occurs in a deferred manner: one thread requests that another be canceled, and sometime later, the target thread terminates. We discuss cancellation requests in detail in Sections 11.5 and 12.7.

Regardless of how a process terminates, the same code in the kernel is eventually executed. This kernel code closes all the open descriptors for the process, releases the memory that it was using, and the like.

For any of the preceding cases, we want the terminating process to be able to notify its parent how it terminated. For the three exit functions (exit, _exit, and _Exit), this is done by passing an exit status as the argument to the function. In the case of an abnormal termination, however, the kernel, not the process, generates a termination status to indicate the reason for the abnormal termination. In any case, the parent of the process can obtain the termination status from either the wait or the waitpid function (described in the next section).

Note that we differentiate between the exit status, which is the argument to one of the three exit functions or the return value from main, and the termination status. The exit status is converted into a termination status by the kernel when _exit is finally called (recall Figure 7.2). Figure 8.4 describes the various ways the parent can examine the termination status of a child. If the child terminated normally, the parent can obtain the exit status of the child.

When we described the fork function, it was obvious that the child has a parent process after the call to fork. Now we're talking about returning a termination status to the parent. But what happens if the parent terminates before the child? The answer is that the init process becomes the parent process of any process whose parent terminates. We say that the process has been inherited by init. What normally happens is that whenever a process terminates, the kernel goes through all active processes to see whether the terminating process is the parent of any process that still exists. If so, the parent process ID of the surviving process is changed to be 1 (the process ID of init). This way, we're guaranteed that every process has a parent.

Another condition we have to worry about is when a child terminates before its parent. If the child completely disappeared, the parent wouldn't be able to fetch its termination status when and if the parent were finally ready to check if the child had terminated. The kernel keeps a small amount of information for every terminating process, so that the information is available when the parent of the terminating process calls wait or waitpid. Minimally, this information consists of the process ID, the termination status of the process, and the amount of CPU time taken by the process. The kernel can discard all the memory used by the process and close its open files. In UNIX System terminology, a process that has terminated, but whose parent has not yet waited for it, is called a *zombie*. The ps(1) command prints the state of a zombie process as Z. If we write a long-running program that forks many child processes, they become zombies unless we wait for them and fetch their termination status.

Some systems provide ways to prevent the creation of zombies, as we describe in Section 10.7.

The final condition to consider is this: what happens when a process that has been inherited by `init` terminates? Does it become a zombie? The answer is "no," because `init` is written so that whenever one of its children terminates, `init` calls one of the `wait` functions to fetch the termination status. By doing this, `init` prevents the system from being clogged by zombies. When we say "one of init's children," we mean either a process that `init` generates directly (such as `getty`, which we describe in Section 9.2) or a process whose parent has terminated and has been subsequently inherited by `init`.

8.6   `wait` and `waitpid` Functions

When a process terminates, either normally or abnormally, the kernel notifies the parent by sending the `SIGCHLD` signal to the parent. Because the termination of a child is an asynchronous event—it can happen at any time while the parent is running—this signal is the asynchronous notification from the kernel to the parent. The parent can choose to ignore this signal, or it can provide a function that is called when the signal occurs: a signal handler. The default action for this signal is to be ignored. We describe these options in Chapter 10. For now, we need to be aware that a process that calls `wait` or `waitpid` can

- Block, if all of its children are still running
- Return immediately with the termination status of a child, if a child has terminated and is waiting for its termination status to be fetched
- Return immediately with an error, if it doesn't have any child processes

If the process is calling `wait` because it received the `SIGCHLD` signal, we expect `wait` to return immediately. But if we call it at any random point in time, it can block.

```
#include <sys/wait.h>

pid_t wait(int *statloc);

pid_t waitpid(pid_t pid, int *statloc, int options);
```
                        Both return: process ID if OK, 0 (see later), or −1 on error

The differences between these two functions are as follows.

- The `wait` function can block the caller until a child process terminates, whereas `waitpid` has an option that prevents it from blocking.
- The `waitpid` function doesn't wait for the child that terminates first; it has a number of options that control which process it waits for.

If a child has already terminated and is a zombie, `wait` returns immediately with that child's status. Otherwise, it blocks the caller until a child terminates. If the caller blocks and has multiple children, `wait` returns when one terminates. We can always tell which child terminated, because the process ID is returned by the function.

For both functions, the argument *statloc* is a pointer to an integer. If this argument is not a null pointer, the termination status of the terminated process is stored in the location pointed to by the argument. If we don't care about the termination status, we simply pass a null pointer as this argument.

Traditionally, the integer status that these two functions return has been defined by the implementation, with certain bits indicating the exit status (for a normal return), other bits indicating the signal number (for an abnormal return), one bit to indicate whether a core file was generated, and so on. POSIX.1 specifies that the termination status is to be looked at using various macros that are defined in <sys/wait.h>. Four mutually exclusive macros tell us how the process terminated, and they all begin with WIF. Based on which of these four macros is true, other macros are used to obtain the exit status, signal number, and the like. The four mutually-exclusive macros are shown in Figure 8.4.

Macro	Description
WIFEXITED (*status*)	True if status was returned for a child that terminated normally. In this case, we can execute WEXITSTATUS (*status*) to fetch the low-order 8 bits of the argument that the child passed to exit, _exit, or _Exit.

WIFSIGNALED (*status*)	True if status was returned for a child that terminated abnormally, by receipt of a signal that it didn't catch. In this case, we can execute
	
	      WTERMSIG (*status*)
	
	to fetch the signal number that caused the termination.
	
	Additionally, some implementations (but not the Single UNIX Specification) define the macro
	
	      WCOREDUMP (*status*)
	
	that returns true if a core file of the terminated process was generated.

WIFSTOPPED (*status*)	True if status was returned for a child that is currently stopped. In this case, we can execute WSTOPSIG (*status*) to fetch the signal number that caused the child to stop.
WIFCONTINUED (*status*)	True if status was returned for a child that has been continued after a job control stop (XSI extension to POSIX.1; waitpid only).

Figure 8.4 Macros to examine the termination status returned by wait and waitpid

We'll discuss how a process can be stopped in Section 9.8 when we discuss job control.

Example

The function pr_exit in Figure 8.5 uses the macros from Figure 8.4 to print a description of the termination status. We'll call this function from numerous programs in the text. Note that this function handles the WCOREDUMP macro, if it is defined.

```
#include "apue.h"
#include <sys/wait.h>

void
pr_exit(int status)
{
    if (WIFEXITED(status))
        printf("normal termination, exit status = %d\n",
                WEXITSTATUS(status));
    else if (WIFSIGNALED(status))
        printf("abnormal termination, signal number = %d%s\n",
                WTERMSIG(status),
#ifdef  WCOREDUMP
                WCOREDUMP(status) ? " (core file generated)" : "");
#else
                "");
#endif
    else if (WIFSTOPPED(status))
        printf("child stopped, signal number = %d\n",
                WSTOPSIG(status));
}
```

Figure 8.5 Print a description of the exit status

FreeBSD 5.2.1, Linux 2.4.22, Mac OS X 10.3, and Solaris 9 all support the WCOREDUMP macro.

The program shown in Figure 8.6 calls the `pr_exit` function, demonstrating the various values for the termination status. If we run the program in Figure 8.6, we get

```
$ ./a.out
normal termination, exit status = 7
abnormal termination, signal number = 6 (core file generated)
abnormal termination, signal number = 8 (core file generated)
```

Unfortunately, there is no portable way to map the signal numbers from WTERMSIG into descriptive names. (See Section 10.21 for one method.) We have to look at the <signal.h> header to verify that SIGABRT has a value of 6 and that SIGFPE has a value of 8.   □

As we mentioned, if we have more than one child, wait returns on termination of any of the children. What if we want to wait for a specific process to terminate (assuming we know which process ID we want to wait for)? In older versions of the UNIX System, we would have to call wait and compare the returned process ID with the one we're interested in. If the terminated process wasn't the one we wanted, we would have to save the process ID and termination status and call wait again. We would need to continue doing this until the desired process terminated. The next time we wanted to wait for a specific process, we would go through the list of already terminated processes to see whether we had already waited for it, and if not, call wait

```
#include "apue.h"
#include <sys/wait.h>

int
main(void)
{
    pid_t    pid;
    int      status;

    if ((pid = fork()) < 0)
        err_sys("fork error");
    else if (pid == 0)                  /* child */
        exit(7);

    if (wait(&status) != pid)           /* wait for child */
        err_sys("wait error");
    pr_exit(status);                    /* and print its status */

    if ((pid = fork()) < 0)
        err_sys("fork error");
    else if (pid == 0)                  /* child */
        abort();                        /* generates SIGABRT */

    if (wait(&status) != pid)           /* wait for child */
        err_sys("wait error");
    pr_exit(status);                    /* and print its status */

    if ((pid = fork()) < 0)
        err_sys("fork error");
    else if (pid == 0)                  /* child */
        status /= 0;                    /* divide by 0 generates SIGFPE */

    if (wait(&status) != pid)           /* wait for child */
        err_sys("wait error");
    pr_exit(status);                    /* and print its status */

    exit(0);
}
```

Figure 8.6 Demonstrate various exit statuses

again. What we need is a function that waits for a specific process. This functionality (and more) is provided by the POSIX.1 waitpid function.

The interpretation of the *pid* argument for waitpid depends on its value:

pid == −1	Waits for any child process. In this respect, waitpid is equivalent to wait.
pid > 0	Waits for the child whose process ID equals *pid*.
pid == 0	Waits for any child whose process group ID equals that of the calling process. (We discuss process groups in Section 9.4.)
pid < −1	Waits for any child whose process group ID equals the absolute value of *pid*.

The `waitpid` function returns the process ID of the child that terminated and stores the child's termination status in the memory location pointed to by *statloc*. With `wait`, the only real error is if the calling process has no children. (Another error return is possible, in case the function call is interrupted by a signal. We'll discuss this in Chapter 10.) With `waitpid`, however, it's also possible to get an error if the specified process or process group does not exist or is not a child of the calling process.

The *options* argument lets us further control the operation of `waitpid`. This argument is either 0 or is constructed from the bitwise OR of the constants in Figure 8.7.

> Solaris supports one additional, but nonstandard, *option* constant. WNOWAIT has the system keep the process whose termination status is returned by `waitpid` in a wait state, so that it may be waited for again.

Constant	Description
WCONTINUED	If the implementation supports job control, the status of any child specified by *pid* that has been continued after being stopped, but whose status has not yet been reported, is returned (XSI extension to POSIX.1).
WNOHANG	The `waitpid` function will not block if a child specified by *pid* is not immediately available. In this case, the return value is 0.
WUNTRACED	If the implementation supports job control, the status of any child specified by *pid* that has stopped, and whose status has not been reported since it has stopped, is returned. The WIFSTOPPED macro determines whether the return value corresponds to a stopped child process.

Figure 8.7 The *options* constants for `waitpid`

The `waitpid` function provides three features that aren't provided by the `wait` function.

1. The `waitpid` function lets us wait for one particular process, whereas the `wait` function returns the status of any terminated child. We'll return to this feature when we discuss the `popen` function.

2. The `waitpid` function provides a nonblocking version of `wait`. There are times when we want to fetch a child's status, but we don't want to block.

3. The `waitpid` function provides support for job control with the WUNTRACED and WCONTINUED options.

Example

Recall our discussion in Section 8.5 about zombie processes. If we want to write a process so that it `forks` a child but we don't want to wait for the child to complete and we don't want the child to become a zombie until we terminate, the trick is to call `fork` twice. The program in Figure 8.8 does this.

```c
#include "apue.h"
#include <sys/wait.h>

int
main(void)
{
    pid_t   pid;

    if ((pid = fork()) < 0) {
        err_sys("fork error");
    } else if (pid == 0) {          /* first child */
        if ((pid = fork()) < 0)
            err_sys("fork error");
        else if (pid > 0)
            exit(0);    /* parent from second fork == first child */

        /*
         * We're the second child; our parent becomes init as soon
         * as our real parent calls exit() in the statement above.
         * Here's where we'd continue executing, knowing that when
         * we're done, init will reap our status.
         */
        sleep(2);
        printf("second child, parent pid = %d\n", getppid());
        exit(0);
    }

    if (waitpid(pid, NULL, 0) != pid)    /* wait for first child */
        err_sys("waitpid error");

    /*
     * We're the parent (the original process); we continue executing,
     * knowing that we're not the parent of the second child.
     */
    exit(0);
}
```

Figure 8.8 Avoid zombie processes by calling fork twice

We call sleep in the second child to ensure that the first child terminates before printing the parent process ID. After a fork, either the parent or the child can continue executing; we never know which will resume execution first. If we didn't put the second child to sleep, and if it resumed execution after the fork before its parent, the parent process ID that it printed would be that of its parent, not process ID 1.

Executing the program in Figure 8.8 gives us

```
$ ./a.out
$ second child, parent pid = 1
```

Note that the shell prints its prompt when the original process terminates, which is before the second child prints its parent process ID.   □

8.7   `waitid` Function

The XSI extension of the Single UNIX Specification includes an additional function to retrieve the exit status of a process. The `waitid` function is similar to `waitpid`, but provides extra flexibility.

```
#include <sys/wait.h>

int waitid(idtype_t idtype, id_t id, siginfo_t *infop, int options);
```
                                                        Returns: 0 if OK, −1 on error

Like `waitpid`, `waitid` allows a process to specify which children to wait for. Instead of encoding this information in a single argument combined with the process ID or process group ID, two separate arguments are used. The *id* parameter is interpreted based on the value of *idtype*. The types supported are summarized in Figure 8.9.

Constant	Description
P_PID	Wait for a particular process: *id* contains the process ID of the child to wait for.
P_PGID	Wait for any child process in a particular process group: *id* contains the process group ID of the children to wait for.
P_ALL	Wait for any child process: *id* is ignored.

Figure 8.9 The *idtype* constants for `waitid`

The *options* argument is a bitwise OR of the flags shown in Figure 8.10. These flags indicate which state changes the caller is interested in.

Constant	Description
WCONTINUED	Wait for a process that has previously stopped and has been continued, and whose status has not yet been reported.
WEXITED	Wait for processes that have exited.
WNOHANG	Return immediately instead of blocking if there is no child exit status available.
WNOWAIT	Don't destroy the child exit status. The child's exit status can be retrieved by a subsequent call to `wait`, `waitid`, or `waitpid`.
WSTOPPED	Wait for a process that has stopped and whose status has not yet been reported.

Figure 8.10 The *options* constants for `waitid`

The *infop* argument is a pointer to a `siginfo` structure. This structure contains detailed information about the signal generated that caused the state change in the child process. The `siginfo` structure is discussed further in Section 10.14.

Of the four platforms covered in this book, only Solaris provides support for `waitid`.

8.8   `wait3` and `wait4` Functions

Most UNIX system implementations provide two additional functions: `wait3` and `wait4`. Historically, these two variants descend from the BSD branch of the UNIX System. The only feature provided by these two functions that isn't provided by the `wait`, `waitid`, and `waitpid` functions is an additional argument that allows the kernel to return a summary of the resources used by the terminated process and all its child processes.

```
#include <sys/types.h>
#include <sys/wait.h>
#include <sys/time.h>
#include <sys/resource.h>

pid_t wait3(int *statloc, int options, struct rusage *rusage);

pid_t wait4(pid_t pid, int *statloc, int options, struct rusage *rusage);
```
                              Both return: process ID if OK, 0, or −1 on error

The resource information includes such statistics as the amount of user CPU time, the amount of system CPU time, number of page faults, number of signals received, and the like. Refer to the `getrusage`(2) manual page for additional details. (This resource information differs from the resource limits we described in Section 7.11.) Figure 8.11 details the various arguments supported by the `wait` functions.

Function	*pid*	*options*	*rusage*	POSIX.1	FreeBSD 5.2.1	Linux 2.4.22	Mac OS X 10.3	Solaris 9
`wait`				•	•	•	•	•
`waitid`	•	•		XSI				•
`waitpid`	•	•		•	•	•	•	•
`wait3`		•	•		•	•	•	•
`wait4`	•	•	•		•	•	•	•

Figure 8.11 Arguments supported by `wait` functions on various systems

> The `wait3` function was included in earlier versions of the Single UNIX Specification. In Version 2, `wait3` was moved to the legacy category; `wait3` was removed from the specification in Version 3.

8.9   Race Conditions

For our purposes, a race condition occurs when multiple processes are trying to do something with shared data and the final outcome depends on the order in which the processes run. The `fork` function is a lively breeding ground for race conditions, if any of the logic after the `fork` either explicitly or implicitly depends on whether the parent or child runs first after the `fork`. In general, we cannot predict which process runs first. Even if we knew which process would run first, what happens after that process starts running depends on the system load and the kernel's scheduling algorithm.

We saw a potential race condition in the program in Figure 8.8 when the second child printed its parent process ID. If the second child runs before the first child, then its parent process will be the first child. But if the first child runs first and has enough time to exit, then the parent process of the second child is init. Even calling sleep, as we did, guarantees nothing. If the system was heavily loaded, the second child could resume after sleep returns, before the first child has a chance to run. Problems of this form can be difficult to debug because they tend to work "most of the time."

A process that wants to wait for a child to terminate must call one of the wait functions. If a process wants to wait for its parent to terminate, as in the program from Figure 8.8, a loop of the following form could be used:

```
while (getppid() != 1)
    sleep(1);
```

The problem with this type of loop, called *polling*, is that it wastes CPU time, as the caller is awakened every second to test the condition.

To avoid race conditions and to avoid polling, some form of signaling is required between multiple processes. Signals can be used, and we describe one way to do this in Section 10.16. Various forms of interprocess communication (IPC) can also be used. We'll discuss some of these in Chapters 15 and 17.

For a parent and child relationship, we often have the following scenario. After the fork, both the parent and the child have something to do. For example, the parent could update a record in a log file with the child's process ID, and the child might have to create a file for the parent. In this example, we require that each process tell the other when it has finished its initial set of operations, and that each wait for the other to complete, before heading off on its own. The following code illustrates this scenario:

```
#include   "apue.h"

TELL_WAIT();      /* set things up for TELL_xxx & WAIT_xxx */

if ((pid = fork()) < 0) {
    err_sys("fork error");
} else if (pid == 0) {                    /* child */

    /* child does whatever is necessary ... */

    TELL_PARENT(getppid());    /* tell parent we're done */
    WAIT_PARENT();             /* and wait for parent */

    /* and the child continues on its way ... */

    exit(0);
}

/* parent does whatever is necessary ... */

TELL_CHILD(pid);           /* tell child we're done */
WAIT_CHILD();              /* and wait for child */

/* and the parent continues on its way ... */

exit(0);
```

We assume that the header apue.h defines whatever variables are required. The five routines TELL_WAIT, TELL_PARENT, TELL_CHILD, WAIT_PARENT, and WAIT_CHILD can be either macros or functions.

We'll show various ways to implement these TELL and WAIT routines in later chapters: Section 10.16 shows an implementation using signals; Figure 15.7 shows an implementation using pipes. Let's look at an example that uses these five routines.

Example

The program in Figure 8.12 outputs two strings: one from the child and one from the parent. The program contains a race condition because the output depends on the order in which the processes are run by the kernel and for how long each process runs.

```
#include "apue.h"

static void charatatime(char *);

int
main(void)
{
    pid_t    pid;

    if ((pid = fork()) < 0) {
        err_sys("fork error");
    } else if (pid == 0) {
        charatatime("output from child\n");
    } else {
        charatatime("output from parent\n");
    }
    exit(0);
}

static void
charatatime(char *str)
{
    char    *ptr;
    int     c;

    setbuf(stdout, NULL);               /* set unbuffered */
    for (ptr = str; (c = *ptr++) != 0; )
        putc(c, stdout);
}
```

Figure 8.12 Program with a race condition

We set the standard output unbuffered, so every character output generates a write. The goal in this example is to allow the kernel to switch between the two processes as often as possible to demonstrate the race condition. (If we didn't do this, we might never see the type of output that follows. Not seeing the erroneous output doesn't mean that the race condition doesn't exist; it simply means that we can't see it on this particular system.) The following actual output shows how the results can vary:

```
$ ./a.out
ooutput from child
utput from parent
$ ./a.out
ooutput from child
utput from parent
$ ./a.out
output from child
output from parent
```

We need to change the program in Figure 8.12 to use the TELL and WAIT functions. The program in Figure 8.13 does this. The lines preceded by a plus sign are new lines.

```
  #include "apue.h"

  static void charatatime(char *);

  int
  main(void)
  {
      pid_t    pid;

+     TELL_WAIT();
+
      if ((pid = fork()) < 0) {
          err_sys("fork error");
      } else if (pid == 0) {
+         WAIT_PARENT();          /* parent goes first */
          charatatime("output from child\n");
      } else {
          charatatime("output from parent\n");
+         TELL_CHILD(pid);
      }
      exit(0);
  }

  static void
  charatatime(char *str)
  {
      char     *ptr;
      int      c;

      setbuf(stdout, NULL);                /* set unbuffered */
      for (ptr = str; (c = *ptr++) != 0; )
          putc(c, stdout);
  }
```

Figure 8.13 Modification of Figure 8.12 to avoid race condition

When we run this program, the output is as we expect; there is no intermixing of output from the two processes.

In the program shown in Figure 8.13, the parent goes first. The child goes first if we change the lines following the `fork` to be

```
} else if (pid == 0) {
    charatatime("output from child\n");
    TELL_PARENT(getppid());
} else {
    WAIT_CHILD();              /* child goes first */
    charatatime("output from parent\n");
}
```

Exercise 8.3 continues this example.   □

8.10   exec **Functions**

We mentioned in Section 8.3 that one use of the `fork` function is to create a new process (the child) that then causes another program to be executed by calling one of the `exec` functions. When a process calls one of the `exec` functions, that process is completely replaced by the new program, and the new program starts executing at its `main` function. The process ID does not change across an `exec`, because a new process is not created; `exec` merely replaces the current process—its text, data, heap, and stack segments—with a brand new program from disk.

There are six different `exec` functions, but we'll often simply refer to "the `exec` function," which means that we could use any of the six functions. These six functions round out the UNIX System process control primitives. With `fork`, we can create new processes; and with the `exec` functions, we can initiate new programs. The `exit` function and the `wait` functions handle termination and waiting for termination. These are the only process control primitives we need. We'll use these primitives in later sections to build additional functions, such as `popen` and `system`.

```
#include <unistd.h>

int execl(const char *pathname, const char *arg0, ... /* (char *)0 */ );

int execv(const char *pathname, char *const argv[]);

int execle(const char *pathname, const char *arg0, ...
           /* (char *)0, char *const envp[] */ );

int execve(const char *pathname, char *const argv[], char *const envp[]);

int execlp(const char *filename, const char *arg0, ... /* (char *)0 */ );

int execvp(const char *filename, char *const argv[]);
```
                                          All six return: −1 on error, no return on success

The first difference in these functions is that the first four take a pathname argument, whereas the last two take a filename argument. When a *filename* argument is specified

- If *filename* contains a slash, it is taken as a pathname.

- Otherwise, the executable file is searched for in the directories specified by the PATH environment variable.

The PATH variable contains a list of directories, called path prefixes, that are separated by colons. For example, the *name=value* environment string

```
PATH=/bin:/usr/bin:/usr/local/bin/:.
```

specifies four directories to search. The last path prefix specifies the current directory. (A zero-length prefix also means the current directory. It can be specified as a colon at the beginning of the *value*, two colons in a row, or a colon at the end of the *value*.)

> There are security reasons for *never* including the current directory in the search path. See Garfinkel et al. [2003].

If either execlp or execvp finds an executable file using one of the path prefixes, but the file isn't a machine executable that was generated by the link editor, the function assumes that the file is a shell script and tries to invoke /bin/sh with the *filename* as input to the shell.

The next difference concerns the passing of the argument list (l stands for list and v stands for vector). The functions execl, execlp, and execle require each of the command-line arguments to the new program to be specified as separate arguments. We mark the end of the arguments with a null pointer. For the other three functions (execv, execvp, and execve), we have to build array of pointers to the arguments, and the address of this array is the argument to these three functions.

Before using ISO C prototypes, the normal way to show the command-line arguments for the three functions execl, execle, and execlp was

```
char *arg0, char *arg1, ..., char *argn, (char *)0
```

This specifically shows that the final command-line argument is followed by a null pointer. If this null pointer is specified by the constant 0, we must explicitly cast it to a pointer; if we don't, it's interpreted as an integer argument. If the size of an integer is different from the size of a char *, the actual arguments to the exec function will be wrong.

The final difference is the passing of the environment list to the new program. The two functions whose names end in an e (execle and execve) allow us to pass a pointer to an array of pointers to the environment strings. The other four functions, however, use the environ variable in the calling process to copy the existing environment for the new program. (Recall our discussion of the environment strings in Section 7.9 and Figure 7.8. We mentioned that if the system supported such functions as setenv and putenv, we could change the current environment and the environment of any subsequent child processes, but we couldn't affect the environment of the parent process.) Normally, a process allows its environment to be propagated to its children, but in some cases, a process wants to specify a certain environment for a child. One example of the latter is the login program when a new login shell is initiated. Normally, login creates a specific environment with only a few variables defined and lets us, through the shell start-up file, add variables to the environment when we log in.

Before using ISO C prototypes, the arguments to execle were shown as

```
char *pathname, char *arg0, ..., char *argn, (char *)0, char *envp[]
```

This specifically shows that the final argument is the address of the array of character pointers to the environment strings. The ISO C prototype doesn't show this, as all the command-line arguments, the null pointer, and the *envp* pointer are shown with the ellipsis notation (. . .).

The arguments for these six exec functions are difficult to remember. The letters in the function names help somewhat. The letter p means that the function takes a *filename* argument and uses the PATH environment variable to find the executable file. The letter l means that the function takes a list of arguments and is mutually exclusive with the letter v, which means that it takes an *argv*[] vector. Finally, the letter e means that the function takes an *envp*[] array instead of using the current environment. Figure 8.14 shows the differences among these six functions.

Function	*pathname*	*filename*	Arg list	*argv*[]	environ	*envp*[]
execl	•		•		•	
execlp		•	•		•	
execle	•		•			•
execv	•			•	•	
execvp		•		•	•	
execve	•			•		•
(letter in name)		p	l	v		e

Figure 8.14 Differences among the six exec functions

Every system has a limit on the total size of the argument list and the environment list. From Section 2.5.2 and Figure 2.8, this limit is given by ARG_MAX. This value must be at least 4,096 bytes on a POSIX.1 system. We sometimes encounter this limit when using the shell's filename expansion feature to generate a list of filenames. On some systems, for example, the command

```
grep getrlimit /usr/share/man/*/*
```

can generate a shell error of the form

```
Argument list too long
```

> Historically, the limit in older System V implementations was 5,120 bytes. Older BSD systems had a limit of 20,480 bytes. The limit in current systems is much higher. (See the output from the program in Figure 2.13, which is summarized in Figure 2.14.)

To get around the limitation in argument list size, we can use the xargs(1) command to break up long argument lists. To look for all the occurrences of getrlimit in the man pages on our system, we could use

```
find /usr/share/man -type f -print | xargs grep getrlimit
```

If the man pages on our system are compressed, however, we could try

```
find /usr/share/man -type f -print | xargs bzgrep getrlimit
```

We use the type -f option to the find command to restrict the list to contain only regular files, because the grep commands can't search for patterns in directories, and we want to avoid unnecessary error messages.

We've mentioned that the process ID does not change after an exec, but the new program inherits additional properties from the calling process:

- Process ID and parent process ID
- Real user ID and real group ID
- Supplementary group IDs
- Process group ID
- Session ID
- Controlling terminal
- Time left until alarm clock
- Current working directory
- Root directory
- File mode creation mask
- File locks
- Process signal mask
- Pending signals
- Resource limits
- Values for tms_utime, tms_stime, tms_cutime, and tms_cstime

The handling of open files depends on the value of the close-on-exec flag for each descriptor. Recall from Figure 3.6 and our mention of the FD_CLOEXEC flag in Section 3.14 that every open descriptor in a process has a close-on-exec flag. If this flag is set, the descriptor is closed across an exec. Otherwise, the descriptor is left open across the exec. The default is to leave the descriptor open across the exec unless we specifically set the close-on-exec flag using fcntl.

POSIX.1 specifically requires that open directory streams (recall the opendir function from Section 4.21) be closed across an exec. This is normally done by the opendir function calling fcntl to set the close-on-exec flag for the descriptor corresponding to the open directory stream.

Note that the real user ID and the real group ID remain the same across the exec, but the effective IDs can change, depending on the status of the set-user-ID and the set-group-ID bits for the program file that is executed. If the set-user-ID bit is set for the new program, the effective user ID becomes the owner ID of the program file. Otherwise, the effective user ID is not changed (it's not set to the real user ID). The group ID is handled in the same way.

In many UNIX system implementations, only one of these six functions, execve, is a system call within the kernel. The other five are just library functions that eventually invoke this system call. We can illustrate the relationship among these six functions as shown in Figure 8.15.

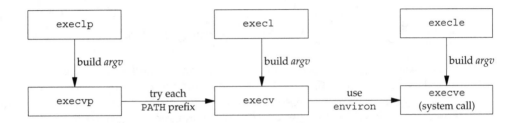

Figure 8.15 Relationship of the six exec functions

In this arrangement, the library functions execlp and execvp process the PATH environment variable, looking for the first path prefix that contains an executable file named *filename*.

Example

The program in Figure 8.16 demonstrates the exec functions.

```
#include "apue.h"
#include <sys/wait.h>

char    *env_init[] = { "USER=unknown", "PATH=/tmp", NULL };

int
main(void)
{
    pid_t   pid;

    if ((pid = fork()) < 0) {
        err_sys("fork error");
    } else if (pid == 0) {   /* specify pathname, specify environment */
        if (execle("/home/sar/bin/echoall", "echoall", "myarg1",
            "MY ARG2", (char *)0, env_init) < 0)
            err_sys("execle error");
```

```
    }

    if (waitpid(pid, NULL, 0) < 0)
        err_sys("wait error");

    if ((pid = fork()) < 0) {
        err_sys("fork error");
    } else if (pid == 0) {  /* specify filename, inherit environment */
        if (execlp("echoall", "echoall", "only 1 arg", (char *)0) < 0)
            err_sys("execlp error");
    }

    exit(0);
}
```

Figure 8.16 Example of exec functions

We first call `execle`, which requires a pathname and a specific environment. The next call is to `execlp`, which uses a filename and passes the caller's environment to the new program. The only reason the call to `execlp` works is that the directory `/home/sar/bin` is one of the current path prefixes. Note also that we set the first argument, `argv[0]` in the new program, to be the filename component of the pathname. Some shells set this argument to be the complete pathname. This is a convention only. We can set `argv[0]` to any string we like. The `login` command does this when it executes the shell. Before executing the shell, `login` adds a dash as a prefix to `argv[0]` to indicate to the shell that it is being invoked as a login shell. A login shell will execute the start-up profile commands, whereas a nonlogin shell will not.

The program `echoall` that is executed twice in the program in Figure 8.16 is shown in Figure 8.17. It is a trivial program that echoes all its command-line arguments and its entire environment list.

```
#include "apue.h"

int
main(int argc, char *argv[])
{
    int         i;
    char        **ptr;
    extern char **environ;

    for (i = 0; i < argc; i++)      /* echo all command-line args */
        printf("argv[%d]: %s\n", i, argv[i]);

    for (ptr = environ; *ptr != 0; ptr++)   /* and all env strings */
        printf("%s\n", *ptr);

    exit(0);
}
```

Figure 8.17 Echo all command-line arguments and all environment strings

When we execute the program from Figure 8.16, we get

```
$ ./a.out
argv[0]: echoall
argv[1]: myarg1
argv[2]: MY ARG2
USER=unknown
PATH=/tmp
$ argv[0]: echoall
argv[1]: only 1 arg
USER=sar
LOGNAME=sar
SHELL=/bin/bash
```
47 more lines that aren't shown
```
HOME=/home/sar
```

Note that the shell prompt appeared before the printing of `argv[0]` from the second exec. This is because the parent did not `wait` for this child process to finish.   □

8.11 Changing User IDs and Group IDs

In the UNIX System, privileges, such as being able to change the system's notion of the current date, and access control, such as being able to read or write a particular file, are based on user and group IDs. When our programs need additional privileges or need to gain access to resources that they currently aren't allowed to access, they need to change their user or group ID to an ID that has the appropriate privilege or access. Similarly, when our programs need to lower their privileges or prevent access to certain resources, they do so by changing either their user ID or group ID to an ID without the privilege or ability access to the resource.

In general, we try to use the *least-privilege* model when we design our applications. Following this model, our programs should use the least privilege necessary to accomplish any given task. This reduces the likelihood that security can be compromised by a malicious user trying to trick our programs into using their privileges in unintended ways.

We can set the real user ID and effective user ID with the `setuid` function. Similarly, we can set the real group ID and the effective group ID with the `setgid` function.

```
#include <unistd.h>

int setuid(uid_t uid);

int setgid(gid_t gid);
```
                                                        Both return: 0 if OK, −1 on error

There are rules for who can change the IDs. Let's consider only the user ID for now. (Everything we describe for the user ID also applies to the group ID.)

1. If the process has superuser privileges, the `setuid` function sets the real user ID, effective user ID, and saved set-user-ID to *uid*.

2. If the process does not have superuser privileges, but *uid* equals either the real user ID or the saved set-user-ID, `setuid` sets only the effective user ID to *uid*. The real user ID and the saved set-user-ID are not changed.

3. If neither of these two conditions is true, `errno` is set to `EPERM`, and −1 is returned.

Here, we are assuming that `_POSIX_SAVED_IDS` is true. If this feature isn't provided, then delete all preceding references to the saved set-user-ID.

> The saved IDs are a mandatory feature in the 2001 version of POSIX.1. They used to be optional in older versions of POSIX. To see whether an implementation supports this feature, an application can test for the constant `_POSIX_SAVED_IDS` at compile time or call `sysconf` with the `_SC_SAVED_IDS` argument at runtime.

We can make a few statements about the three user IDs that the kernel maintains.

1. Only a superuser process can change the real user ID. Normally, the real user ID is set by the `login(1)` program when we log in and never changes. Because `login` is a superuser process, it sets all three user IDs when it calls `setuid`.

2. The effective user ID is set by the `exec` functions only if the set-user-ID bit is set for the program file. If the set-user-ID bit is not set, the `exec` functions leave the effective user ID as its current value. We can call `setuid` at any time to set the effective user ID to either the real user ID or the saved set-user-ID. Naturally, we can't set the effective user ID to any random value.

3. The saved set-user-ID is copied from the effective user ID by `exec`. If the file's set-user-ID bit is set, this copy is saved after `exec` stores the effective user ID from the file's user ID.

Figure 8.18 summarizes the various ways these three user IDs can be changed.

ID	exec		setuid(*uid*)	
	set-user-ID bit off	set-user-ID bit on	superuser	unprivileged user
real user ID	unchanged	unchanged	set to *uid*	unchanged
effective user ID	unchanged	set from user ID of program file	set to *uid*	set to *uid*
saved set-user ID	copied from effective user ID	copied from effective user ID	set to *uid*	unchanged

Figure 8.18   Ways to change the three user IDs

Note that we can obtain only the current value of the real user ID and the effective user ID with the functions `getuid` and `geteuid` from Section 8.2. We can't obtain the current value of the saved set-user-ID.

Example

To see the utility of the saved set-user-ID feature, let's examine the operation of a program that uses it. We'll look at the man(1) program, which is used to display online manual pages. The man program can be installed either set-user-ID or set-group-ID to a specific user or group, usually one reserved for man itself. The man program can be made to read and possibly overwrite files in locations that are chosen either through a configuration file (usually /etc/man.config or /etc/manpath.config) or using a command-line option.

The man program might have to execute several other commands to process the files containing the manual page to be displayed. To prevent being tricked into running the wrong commands or overwriting the wrong files, the man command has to switch between two sets of privileges: those of the user running the man command and those of the user that owns the man executable file. The following steps take place.

1. Assuming that the man program file is owned by the user name man and has its set-user-ID bit set, when we exec it, we have

   real user ID = our user ID
   effective user ID = man
   saved set-user-ID = man

2. The man program accesses the required configuration files and manual pages. These files are owned by the user name man, but because the effective user ID is man, file access is allowed.

3. Before man runs any command on our behalf, it calls setuid(getuid()). Because we are not a superuser process, this changes only the effective user ID. We have

   real user ID = our user ID (unchanged)
   effective user ID = our user ID
   saved set-user-ID = man (unchanged)

   Now the man process is running with our user ID as its effective user ID. This means that we can access only the files to which we have normal access. We have no additional permissions. It can safely execute any filter on our behalf.

4. When the filter is done, man calls setuid(*euid*), where *euid* is the numerical user ID for the user name man. (This was saved by man by calling geteuid.) This call is allowed because the argument to setuid equals the saved set-user-ID. (This is why we need the saved set-user-ID.) Now we have

   real user ID = our user ID (unchanged)
   effective user ID = man
   saved set-user-ID = man (unchanged)

5. The man program can now operate on its files, as its effective user ID is man.

By using the saved set-user-ID in this fashion, we can use the extra privileges granted to us by the set-user-ID of the program file at the beginning of the process and at the end of the process. In between, however, the process runs with our normal permissions. If we weren't able to switch back to the saved set-user-ID at the end, we might be tempted to retain the extra permissions the whole time we were running (which is asking for trouble).

Let's look at what happens if man spawns a shell for us while it is running. (The shell is spawned using fork and exec.) Because the real user ID and the effective user ID are both our normal user ID (step 3), the shell has no extra permissions. The shell can't access the saved set-user-ID that is set to man while man is running, because the saved set-user-ID for the shell is copied from the effective user ID by exec. So in the child process that does the exec, all three user IDs are our normal user ID.

Our description of how man uses the setuid function is not correct if the program is set-user-ID to root, because a call to setuid with superuser privileges sets all three user IDs. For the example to work as described, we need setuid to set only the effective user ID.   □

setreuid and setregid Functions

Historically, BSD supported the swapping of the real user ID and the effective user ID with the setreuid function.

```
#include <unistd.h>

int setreuid(uid_t ruid, uid_t euid);

int setregid(gid_t rgid, gid_t egid);
```

Both return: 0 if OK, −1 on error

We can supply a value of −1 for any of the arguments to indicate that the corresponding ID should remain unchanged.

The rule is simple: an unprivileged user can always swap between the real user ID and the effective user ID. This allows a set-user-ID program to swap to the user's normal permissions and swap back again later for set-user-ID operations. When the saved set-user-ID feature was introduced with POSIX.1, the rule was enhanced to also allow an unprivileged user to set its effective user ID to its saved set-user-ID.

Both setreuid and setregid are XSI extensions in the Single UNIX Specification. As such, all UNIX System implementations are expected to provide support for them.

4.3BSD didn't have the saved set-user-ID feature described earlier. It used setreuid and setregid instead. This allowed an unprivileged user to swap back and forth between the two values. Be aware, however, that when programs that used this feature spawned a shell, they had to set the real user ID to the normal user ID before the exec. If they didn't do this, the real user ID could be privileged (from the swap done by setreuid) and the shell process could call setreuid to swap the two and assume the permissions of the more privileged user. As a defensive programming measure to solve this problem, programs set both the real user ID and the effective user ID to the normal user ID before the call to exec in the child.

`seteuid` and `setegid` **Functions**

POSIX.1 includes the two functions `seteuid` and `setegid`. These functions are similar to `setuid` and `setgid`, but only the effective user ID or effective group ID is changed.

```
#include <unistd.h>

int seteuid(uid_t uid);

int setegid(gid_t gid);
```
Both return: 0 if OK, −1 on error

An unprivileged user can set its effective user ID to either its real user ID or its saved set-user-ID. For a privileged user, only the effective user ID is set to *uid*. (This differs from the `setuid` function, which changes all three user IDs.)

Figure 8.19 summarizes all the functions that we've described here that modify the three user IDs.

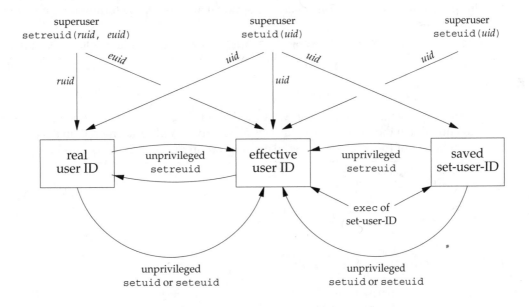

Figure 8.19 Summary of all the functions that set the various user IDs

Group IDs

Everything that we've said so far in this section also applies in a similar fashion to group IDs. The supplementary group IDs are not affected by `setgid`, `setregid`, or `setegid`.

8.12   Interpreter Files

All contemporary UNIX systems support interpreter files. These files are text files that begin with a line of the form

>   #! *pathname* [*optional-argument*]

The space between the exclamation point and the *pathname* is optional. The most common of these interpreter files begin with the line

>   #!/bin/sh

The *pathname* is normally an absolute pathname, since no special operations are performed on it (i.e., PATH is not used). The recognition of these files is done within the kernel as part of processing the exec system call. The actual file that gets executed by the kernel is not the interpreter file, but the file specified by the *pathname* on the first line of the interpreter file. Be sure to differentiate between the interpreter file—a text file that begins with #!—and the interpreter, which is specified by the *pathname* on the first line of the interpreter file.

Be aware that systems place a size limit on the first line of an interpreter file. This limit includes the #!, the *pathname*, the optional argument, the terminating newline, and any spaces.

>   On FreeBSD 5.2.1, this limit is 128 bytes. Mac OS X 10.3 extends this limit to 512 bytes. Linux 2.4.22 supports a limit of 127 bytes, whereas Solaris 9 places the limit at 1,023 bytes.

Example

Let's look at an example to see what the kernel does with the arguments to the exec function when the file being executed is an interpreter file and the optional argument on the first line of the interpreter file. The program in Figure 8.20 execs an interpreter file.

```
#include "apue.h"
#include <sys/wait.h>

int
main(void)
{
    pid_t   pid;
    if ((pid = fork()) < 0) {
        err_sys("fork error");
    } else if (pid == 0) {              /* child */
        if (execl("/home/sar/bin/testinterp",
                "testinterp", "myarg1", "MY ARG2", (char *)0) < 0)
            err_sys("execl error");
    }
    if (waitpid(pid, NULL, 0) < 0)      /* parent */
        err_sys("waitpid error");
    exit(0);
}
```

Figure 8.20 A program that execs an interpreter file

The following shows the contents of the one-line interpreter file that is executed and the result from running the program in Figure 8.20:

```
$ cat /home/sar/bin/testinterp
#!/home/sar/bin/echoarg foo
$ ./a.out
argv[0]: /home/sar/bin/echoarg
argv[1]: foo
argv[2]: /home/sar/bin/testinterp
argv[3]: myarg1
argv[4]: MY ARG2
```

The program `echoarg` (the interpreter) just echoes each of its command-line arguments. (This is the program from Figure 7.4.) Note that when the kernel `exec`s the interpreter (`/home/sar/bin/echoarg`), `argv[0]` is the *pathname* of the interpreter, `argv[1]` is the optional argument from the interpreter file, and the remaining arguments are the *pathname* (`/home/sar/bin/testinterp`) and the second and third arguments from the call to `execl` in the program shown in Figure 8.20 (`myarg1` and `MY ARG2`). Both `argv[1]` and `argv[2]` from the call to `execl` have been shifted right two positions. Note that the kernel takes the *pathname* from the `execl` call instead of the first argument (`testinterp`), on the assumption that the *pathname* might contain more information than the first argument.   □

Example

A common use for the optional argument following the interpreter *pathname* is to specify the `-f` option for programs that support this option. For example, an awk(1) program can be executed as

```
awk -f myfile
```

which tells `awk` to read the `awk` program from the file `myfile`.

> Systems derived from UNIX System V often include two versions of the `awk` language. On these systems, `awk` is often called "old `awk`" and corresponds to the original version distributed with Version 7. In contrast, `nawk` (new `awk`) contains numerous enhancements and corresponds to the language described in Aho, Kernighan, and Weinberger [1988]. This newer version provides access to the command-line arguments, which we need for the example that follows. Solaris 9 provides both versions.
>
> The `awk` program is one of the utilities included by POSIX in its 1003.2 standard, which is now part of the base POSIX.1 specification in the Single UNIX Specification. This utility is also based on the language described in Aho, Kernighan, and Weinberger [1988].
>
> The version of `awk` in Mac OS X 10.3 is based on the Bell Laboratories version that Lucent has placed in the public domain. FreeBSD 5.2.1 and Linux 2.4.22 ship with GNU `awk`, called `gawk`, which is linked to the name `awk`. The `gawk` version conforms to the POSIX standard, but also includes other extensions. Because they are more up-to-date, the version of `awk` from Bell Laboratories and `gawk` are preferred to either `nawk` or old `awk`. (The version of `awk` from Bell Laboratories is available at `http://cm.bell-labs.com/cm/cs/awkbook/index.html`.)

Using the -f option with an interpreter file lets us write

```
#!/bin/awk -f
```
(awk program follows in the interpreter file)

For example, Figure 8.21 shows /usr/local/bin/awkexample (an interpreter file).

```
#!/bin/awk -f
BEGIN {
    for (i = 0; i < ARGC; i++)
        printf "ARGV[%d] = %s\n", i, ARGV[i]
    exit
}
```

Figure 8.21 An awk program as an interpreter file

If one of the path prefixes is /usr/local/bin, we can execute the program in Figure 8.21 (assuming that we've turned on the execute bit for the file) as

```
$ awkexample file1 FILENAME2 f3
ARGV[0] = awk
ARGV[1] = file1
ARGV[2] = FILENAME2
ARGV[3] = f3
```

When /bin/awk is executed, its command-line arguments are

```
/bin/awk -f /usr/local/bin/awkexample file1 FILENAME2 f3
```

The pathname of the interpreter file (/usr/local/bin/awkexample) is passed to the interpreter. The filename portion of this pathname (what we typed to the shell) isn't adequate, because the interpreter (/bin/awk in this example) can't be expected to use the PATH variable to locate files. When it reads the interpreter file, awk ignores the first line, since the pound sign is awk's comment character.

We can verify these command-line arguments with the following commands:

```
$ /bin/su                                    become superuser
Password:                                    enter superuser password
# mv /bin/awk /bin/awk.save                  save the original program
# cp /home/sar/bin/echoarg /bin/awk          and replace it temporarily
# suspend                                    suspend the superuser shell using job control
[1] + Stopped              /bin/su
$ awkexample file1 FILENAME2 f3
argv[0]: /bin/awk
argv[1]: -f
argv[2]: /usr/local/bin/awkexample
argv[3]: file1
argv[4]: FILENAME2
argv[5]: f3
$ fg                                         resume superuser shell using job control
/bin/su
# mv /bin/awk.save /bin/awk                  restore the original program
# exit                                       and exit the superuser shell
```

In this example, the -f option for the interpreter is required. As we said, this tells awk where to look for the awk program. If we remove the -f option from the interpreter file, an error message usually results when we try to run it. The exact text of the message varies, depending on where the interpreter file is stored and whether the remaining arguments represent existing files. This is because the command-line arguments in this case are

```
/bin/awk /usr/local/bin/awkexample file1 FILENAME2 f3
```

and awk is trying to interpret the string /usr/local/bin/awkexample as an awk program. If we couldn't pass at least a single optional argument to the interpreter (-f in this case), these interpreter files would be usable only with the shells.   □

Are interpreter files required? Not really. They provide an efficiency gain for the user at some expense in the kernel (since it's the kernel that recognizes these files). Interpreter files are useful for the following reasons.

1. They hide that certain programs are scripts in some other language. For example, to execute the program in Figure 8.21, we just say

   ```
   awkexample optional-arguments
   ```

   instead of needing to know that the program is really an awk script that we would otherwise have to execute as

   ```
   awk -f awkexample optional-arguments
   ```

2. Interpreter scripts provide an efficiency gain. Consider the previous example again. We could still hide that the program is an awk script, by wrapping it in a shell script:

   ```
   awk 'BEGIN {
       for (i = 0; i < ARGC; i++)
           printf "ARGV[%d] = %s\n", i, ARGV[i]
       exit
   }' $*
   ```

   The problem with this solution is that more work is required. First, the shell reads the command and tries to execlp the filename. Because the shell script is an executable file, but isn't a machine executable, an error is returned, and execlp assumes that the file is a shell script (which it is). Then /bin/sh is executed with the pathname of the shell script as its argument. The shell correctly runs our script, but to run the awk program, the shell does a fork, exec, and wait. Thus, there is more overhead in replacing an interpreter script with a shell script.

3. Interpreter scripts let us write shell scripts using shells other than /bin/sh. When it finds an executable file that isn't a machine executable, execlp has to choose a shell to invoke, and it always uses /bin/sh. Using an interpreter script, however, we can simply write

```
#!/bin/csh
(C shell script follows in the interpreter file)
```

Again, we could wrap this all in a /bin/sh script (that invokes the C shell), as we described earlier, but more overhead is required.

None of this would work as we've shown if the three shells and awk didn't use the pound sign as their comment character.

8.13 system Function

It is convenient to execute a command string from within a program. For example, assume that we want to put a time-and-date stamp into a certain file. We could use the functions we describe in Section 6.10 to do this: call time to get the current calendar time, then call localtime to convert it to a broken-down time, and then call strftime to format the result, and write the results to the file. It is much easier, however, to say

```
system("date > file");
```

ISO C defines the system function, but its operation is strongly system dependent. POSIX.1 includes the system interface, expanding on the ISO C definition to describe its behavior in a POSIX environment.

```
#include <stdlib.h>

int system(const char *cmdstring);
```

                                                                Returns: (see below)

If cmdstring is a null pointer, system returns nonzero only if a command processor is available. This feature determines whether the system function is supported on a given operating system. Under the UNIX System, system is always available.

Because system is implemented by calling fork, exec, and waitpid, there are three types of return values.

1. If either the fork fails or waitpid returns an error other than EINTR, system returns –1 with errno set to indicate the error.

2. If the exec fails, implying that the shell can't be executed, the return value is as if the shell had executed exit(127).

3. Otherwise, all three functions—fork, exec, and waitpid—succeed, and the return value from system is the termination status of the shell, in the format specified for waitpid.

> Some older implementations of system returned an error (EINTR) if waitpid was interrupted by a caught signal. Because there is no cleanup strategy that an application can use to recover from this type of error, POSIX later added the requirement that system not return an error in this case. (We discuss interrupted system calls in Section 10.5.)

Figure 8.22 shows an implementation of the system function. The one feature that it doesn't handle is signals. We'll update this function with signal handling in Section 10.18.

```c
#include     <sys/wait.h>
#include     <errno.h>
#include     <unistd.h>

int
system(const char *cmdstring)    /* version without signal handling */
{
    pid_t   pid;
    int     status;

    if (cmdstring == NULL)
        return(1);        /* always a command processor with UNIX */

    if ((pid = fork()) < 0) {
        status = -1;      /* probably out of processes */
    } else if (pid == 0) {              /* child */
        execl("/bin/sh", "sh", "-c", cmdstring, (char *)0);
        _exit(127);       /* execl error */
    } else {                            /* parent */
        while (waitpid(pid, &status, 0) < 0) {
            if (errno != EINTR) {
                status = -1; /* error other than EINTR from waitpid() */
                break;
            }
        }
    }

    return(status);
}
```

Figure 8.22 The system function, without signal handling

The shell's -c option tells it to take the next command-line argument—*cmdstring*, in this case—as its command input instead of reading from standard input or from a given file. The shell parses this null-terminated C string and breaks it up into separate command-line arguments for the command. The actual command string that is passed to the shell can contain any valid shell commands. For example, input and output redirection using < and > can be used.

If we didn't use the shell to execute the command, but tried to execute the command ourself, it would be more difficult. First, we would want to call execlp instead of execl, to use the PATH variable, like the shell. We would also have to break up the null-terminated C string into separate command-line arguments for the call to execlp. Finally, we wouldn't be able to use any of the shell metacharacters.

Note that we call _exit instead of exit. We do this to prevent any standard I/O buffers, which would have been copied from the parent to the child across the fork, from being flushed in the child.

We can test this version of system with the program shown in Figure 8.23. (The pr_exit function was defined in Figure 8.5.)

```c
#include "apue.h"
#include <sys/wait.h>

int
main(void)
{
    int     status;

    if ((status = system("date")) < 0)
        err_sys("system() error");
    pr_exit(status);

    if ((status = system("nosuchcommand")) < 0)
        err_sys("system() error");
    pr_exit(status);

    if ((status = system("who; exit 44")) < 0)
        err_sys("system() error");
    pr_exit(status);

    exit(0);
}
```

Figure 8.23 Calling the system function

Running the program in Figure 8.23 gives us

```
$ ./a.out
Sun Mar 21 18:41:32 EST 2004
normal termination, exit status = 0      for date
sh: nosuchcommand: command not found
normal termination, exit status = 127    for nosuchcommand
sar        :0         Mar 18 19:45
sar        pts/0      Mar 18 19:45 (:0)
sar        pts/1      Mar 18 19:45 (:0)
sar        pts/2      Mar 18 19:45 (:0)
sar        pts/3      Mar 18 19:45 (:0)
normal termination, exit status = 44     for exit
```

The advantage in using system, instead of using fork and exec directly, is that system does all the required error handling and (in our next version of this function in Section 10.18) all the required signal handling.

Earlier systems, including SVR3.2 and 4.3BSD, didn't have the waitpid function available. Instead, the parent waited for the child, using a statement such as

```
while ((lastpid = wait(&status)) != pid && lastpid != -1)
    ;
```

A problem occurs if the process that calls system has spawned its own children before calling system. Because the while statement above keeps looping until the child that was generated by system terminates, if any children of the process terminate before the process identified by pid, then the process ID and termination status of these other children are discarded by the while statement. Indeed, this inability to wait for a specific child is one of the reasons given in the POSIX.1 Rationale for including the waitpid function. We'll see in Section 15.3 that the same problem occurs with the popen and pclose functions, if the system doesn't provide a waitpid function.

Set-User-ID Programs

What happens if we call system from a set-user-ID program? Doing so is a security hole and should never be done. Figure 8.24 shows a simple program that just calls system for its command-line argument.

```
#include "apue.h"

int
main(int argc, char *argv[])
{
    int     status;

    if (argc < 2)
        err_quit("command-line argument required");

    if ((status = system(argv[1])) < 0)
        err_sys("system() error");
    pr_exit(status);

    exit(0);
}
```

Figure 8.24 Execute the command-line argument using system

We'll compile this program into the executable file tsys.
Figure 8.25 shows another simple program that prints its real and effective user IDs.

```
#include "apue.h"

int
main(void)
{
    printf("real uid = %d, effective uid = %d\n", getuid(), geteuid());
    exit(0);
}
```

Figure 8.25 Print real and effective user IDs

We'll compile this program into the executable file printuids. Running both programs gives us the following:

```
$ tsys printuids                         normal execution, no special privileges
real uid = 205, effective uid = 205
normal termination, exit status = 0
$ su                                     become superuser
Password:                                enter superuser password
# chown root tsys                        change owner
# chmod u+s tsys                         make set-user-ID
# ls -l tsys                             verify file's permissions and owner
-rwsrwxr-x  1 root     16361 Mar 16 16:59 tsys
# exit                                   leave superuser shell
$ tsys printuids
real uid = 205, effective uid = 0        oops, this is a security hole
normal termination, exit status = 0
```

The superuser permissions that we gave the tsys program are retained across the fork and exec that are done by system.

> When /bin/sh is bash version 2, the previous example doesn't work, because bash will reset the effective user ID to the real user ID when they don't match.

If it is running with special permissions—either set-user-ID or set-group-ID—and wants to spawn another process, a process should use fork and exec directly, being certain to change back to normal permissions after the fork, before calling exec. The system function should *never* be used from a set-user-ID or a set-group-ID program.

> One reason for this admonition is that system invokes the shell to parse the command string, and the shell uses its IFS variable as the input field separator. Older versions of the shell didn't reset this variable to a normal set of characters when invoked. This allowed a malicious user to set IFS before system was called, causing system to execute a different program.

8.14 Process Accounting

Most UNIX systems provide an option to do process accounting. When enabled, the kernel writes an accounting record each time a process terminates. These accounting records are typically a small amount of binary data with the name of the command, the amount of CPU time used, the user ID and group ID, the starting time, and so on. We'll take a closer look at these accounting records in this section, as it gives us a chance to look at processes again and to use the fread function from Section 5.9.

> Process accounting is not specified by any of the standards. Thus, all the implementations have annoying differences. For example, the I/O counts maintained on Solaris 9 are in units of bytes, whereas FreeBSD 5.2.1 and Mac OS X 10.3 maintain units of blocks, although there is no distinction between different block sizes, making the counter effectively useless. Linux 2.4.22, on the other hand, doesn't try to maintain I/O statistics at all.

> Each implementation also has its own set of administrative commands to process raw accounting data. For example, Solaris provides runacct(1m) and acctcom(1), whereas FreeBSD provides the sa(8) command to process and summarize the raw accounting data.

A function we haven't described (acct) enables and disables process accounting. The only use of this function is from the accton(8) command (which happens to be one of the few similarities among platforms). A superuser executes `accton` with a pathname argument to enable accounting. The accounting records are written to the specified file, which is usually `/var/account/acct` on FreeBSD and Mac OS X, `/var/account/pacct` on Linux, and `/var/adm/pacct` on Solaris. Accounting is turned off by executing `accton` without any arguments.

The structure of the accounting records is defined in the header `<sys/acct.h>` and looks something like

```
typedef  u_short comp_t;   /* 3-bit base 8 exponent; 13-bit fraction */

struct   acct
{
  char    ac_flag;       /* flag (see Figure 8.26) */
  char    ac_stat;       /* termination status (signal & core flag only) */
                         /* (Solaris only) */
  uid_t   ac_uid;        /* real user ID */
  gid_t   ac_gid;        /* real group ID */
  dev_t   ac_tty;        /* controlling terminal */
  time_t  ac_btime;      /* starting calendar time */
  comp_t  ac_utime;      /* user CPU time (clock ticks) */
  comp_t  ac_stime;      /* system CPU time (clock ticks) */
  comp_t  ac_etime;      /* elapsed time (clock ticks) */
  comp_t  ac_mem;        /* average memory usage */
  comp_t  ac_io;         /* bytes transferred (by read and write) */
                         /* "blocks" on BSD systems */
  comp_t  ac_rw;         /* blocks read or written */
                         /* (not present on BSD systems) */
  char    ac_comm[8];    /* command name: [8] for Solaris, */
                         /* [10] for Mac OS X, [16] for FreeBSD, and */
                         /* [17] for Linux */
};
```

The `ac_flag` member records certain events during the execution of the process. These events are described in Figure 8.26.

ac_flag	Description	FreeBSD 5.2.1	Linux 2.4.22	Mac OS X 10.3	Solaris 9
AFORK	process is the result of `fork`, but never called exec	•	•	•	•
ASU	process used superuser privileges		•	•	•
ACOMPAT	process used compatibility mode				
ACORE	process dumped core	•	•	•	
AXSIG	process was killed by a signal	•	•	•	
AEXPND	expanded accounting entry				•

Figure 8.26 Values for `ac_flag` from accounting record

The data required for the accounting record, such as CPU times and number of characters transferred, is kept by the kernel in the process table and initialized whenever a new process is created, as in the child after a `fork`. Each accounting record is written when the process terminates. This means that the order of the records in the accounting file corresponds to the termination order of the processes, not the order in which they were started. To know the starting order, we would have to go through the accounting file and sort by the starting calendar time. But this isn't perfect, since calendar times are in units of seconds (Section 1.10), and it's possible for many processes to be started in any given second. Alternatively, the elapsed time is given in clock ticks, which are usually between 60 and 128 ticks per second. But we don't know the ending time of a process; all we know is its starting time and ending order. This means that even though the elapsed time is more accurate than the starting time, we still can't reconstruct the exact starting order of various processes, given the data in the accounting file.

The accounting records correspond to processes, not programs. A new record is initialized by the kernel for the child after a fork, not when a new program is executed. Although exec doesn't create a new accounting record, the command name changes, and the AFORK flag is cleared. This means that if we have a chain of three programs—A execs B, then B execs C, and C exits—only a single accounting record is written. The command name in the record corresponds to program C, but the CPU times, for example, are the sum for programs A, B, and C.

Example

To have some accounting data to examine, we'll create a test program to implement the diagram shown in Figure 8.27.

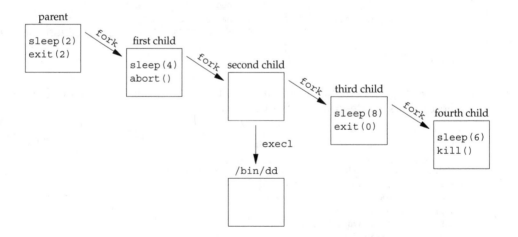

Figure 8.27 Process structure for accounting example

The source for the test program is shown in Figure 8.28. It calls fork four times. Each child does something different and then terminates.

```
#include "apue.h"

int
main(void)
{
    pid_t   pid;

    if ((pid = fork()) < 0)
        err_sys("fork error");
    else if (pid != 0) {            /* parent */
        sleep(2);
        exit(2);                    /* terminate with exit status 2 */
    }

                                    /* first child */
    if ((pid = fork()) < 0)
        err_sys("fork error");
    else if (pid != 0) {
        sleep(4);
        abort();                    /* terminate with core dump */
    }

                                    /* second child */
    if ((pid = fork()) < 0)
        err_sys("fork error");
    else if (pid != 0) {
        execl("/bin/dd", "dd", "if=/etc/termcap", "of=/dev/null", NULL);
        exit(7);                    /* shouldn't get here */
    }

                                    /* third child */
    if ((pid = fork()) < 0)
        err_sys("fork error");
    else if (pid != 0) {
        sleep(8);
        exit(0);                    /* normal exit */
    }

                                    /* fourth child */
    sleep(6);
    kill(getpid(), SIGKILL);        /* terminate w/signal, no core dump */
    exit(6);                        /* shouldn't get here */
}
```

Figure 8.28 Program to generate accounting data

We'll run the test program on Solaris and then use the program in Figure 8.29 to print out selected fields from the accounting records.

```
#include "apue.h"
#include <sys/acct.h>

#ifdef HAS_SA_STAT
#define FMT "%-*.*s  e = %6ld, chars = %7ld, stat = %3u: %c %c %c %c\n"
#else
#define FMT "%-*.*s  e = %6ld, chars = %7ld, %c %c %c %c\n"
#endif
#ifndef HAS_ACORE
#define ACORE 0
#endif
#ifndef HAS_AXSIG
#define AXSIG 0
#endif

static unsigned long
compt2ulong(comp_t comptime)     /* convert comp_t to unsigned long */
{
    unsigned long   val;
    int             exp;

    val = comptime & 0x1fff;    /* 13-bit fraction */
    exp = (comptime >> 13) & 7; /* 3-bit exponent (0-7) */
    while (exp-- > 0)
        val *= 8;
    return(val);
}
int
main(int argc, char *argv[])
{
    struct acct     acdata;
    FILE            *fp;

    if (argc != 2)
        err_quit("usage: pracct filename");
    if ((fp = fopen(argv[1], "r")) == NULL)
        err_sys("can't open %s", argv[1]);
    while (fread(&acdata, sizeof(acdata), 1, fp) == 1) {
        printf(FMT, (int)sizeof(acdata.ac_comm),
            (int)sizeof(acdata.ac_comm), acdata.ac_comm,
            compt2ulong(acdata.ac_etime), compt2ulong(acdata.ac_io),
#ifdef HAS_SA_STAT
            (unsigned char) acdata.ac_stat,
#endif
            acdata.ac_flag & ACORE ? 'D' : ' ',
            acdata.ac_flag & AXSIG ? 'X' : ' ',
            acdata.ac_flag & AFORK ? 'F' : ' ',
            acdata.ac_flag & ASU   ? 'S' : ' ');
    }
    if (ferror(fp))
        err_sys("read error");
    exit(0);
}
```

Figure 8.29 Print selected fields from system's accounting file

BSD-derived platforms don't support the `ac_stat` member, so we define the `HAS_SA_STAT` constant on the platforms that do support this member. Basing the defined symbol on the feature instead of on the platform reads better and allows us to modify the program simply by adding the additional definition to our compilation command. The alternative would be to use

```
#if defined(BSD) || defined(MACOS)
```

which becomes unwieldy as we port our application to additional platforms.

We define similar constants to determine whether the platform supports the `ACORE` and `AXSIG` accounting flags. We can't use the flag symbols themselves, because on Linux, they are defined as enum values, which we can't use in a `#ifdef` expression.

To perform our test, we do the following:

1. Become superuser and enable accounting, with the `accton` command. Note that when this command terminates, accounting should be on; therefore, the first record in the accounting file should be from this command.

2. Exit the superuser shell and run the program in Figure 8.28. This should append six records to the accounting file: one for the superuser shell, one for the test parent, and one for each of the four test children.

   A new process is not created by the `execl` in the second child. There is only a single accounting record for the second child.

3. Become superuser and turn accounting off. Since accounting is off when this `accton` command terminates, it should not appear in the accounting file.

4. Run the program in Figure 8.29 to print the selected fields from the accounting file.

The output from step 4 follows. We have appended to each line the description of the process in italics, for the discussion later.

```
accton    e =        6, chars =        0, stat =    0:       S
sh        e =     2106, chars =    15632, stat =    0:       S
dd        e =        8, chars =   273344, stat =    0:              second child
a.out     e =      202, chars =      921, stat =    0:              parent
a.out     e =      407, chars =        0, stat = 134:    F         first child
a.out     e =      600, chars =        0, stat =    9:    F         fourth child
a.out     e =      801, chars =        0, stat =    0:    F         third child
```

The elapsed time values are measured in units of clock ticks per second. From Figure 2.14, the value on this system is 100. For example, the `sleep(2)` in the parent corresponds to the elapsed time of 202 clock ticks. For the first child, the `sleep(4)` becomes 407 clock ticks. Note that the amount of time a process sleeps is not exact. (We'll return to the `sleep` function in Chapter 10.) Also, the calls to `fork` and `exit` take some amount of time.

Note that the `ac_stat` member is not the true termination status of the process, but corresponds to a portion of the termination status that we discussed in Section 8.6. The only information in this byte is a core-flag bit (usually the high-order bit) and the signal number (usually the seven low-order bits), if the process terminated abnormally. If the process terminated normally, we are not able to obtain the exit status from the accounting file. For the first child, this value is 128+6. The 128 is the core flag bit, and 6 happens to be the value on this system for SIGABRT, which is generated by the call to abort. The value 9 for the fourth child corresponds to the value of SIGKILL. We can't tell from the accounting data that the parent's argument to exit was 2 and that the third child's argument to exit was 0.

The size of the file /etc/termcap that the dd process copies in the second child is 136,663 bytes. The number of characters of I/O is just over twice this value. It is twice the value, as 136,663 bytes are read in, then 136,663 bytes are written out. Even though the output goes to the null device, the bytes are still accounted for.

The ac_flag values are as we expect. The F flag is set for all the child processes except the second child, which does the execl. The F flag is not set for the parent, because the interactive shell that executed the parent did a fork and then an exec of the a.out file. The first child process calls abort, which generates a SIGABRT signal to generate the core dump. Note that neither the X flag nor the D flag is on, as they are not supported on Solaris; the information they represent can be derived from the ac_stat field. The fourth child also terminates because of a signal, but the SIGKILL signal does not generate a core dump; it only terminates the process.

As a final note, the first child has a 0 count for the number of characters of I/O, yet this process generated a core file. It appears that the I/O required to write the core file is not charged to the process.   □

8.15   User Identification

Any process can find out its real and effective user ID and group ID. Sometimes, however, we want to find out the login name of the user who's running the program. We could call getpwuid(getuid()), but what if a single user has multiple login names, each with the same user ID? (A person might have multiple entries in the password file with the same user ID to have a different login shell for each entry.) The system normally keeps track of the name we log in under (Section 6.8), and the getlogin function provides a way to fetch that login name.

```
#include <unistd.h>

char *getlogin(void);
```
                            Returns: pointer to string giving login name if OK, NULL on error

This function can fail if the process is not attached to a terminal that a user logged in to. We normally call these processes *daemons*. We discuss them in Chapter 13.

Given the login name, we can then use it to look up the user in the password file—to determine the login shell, for example—using getpwnam.

To find the login name, UNIX systems have historically called the `ttyname` function (Section 18.9) and then tried to find a matching entry in the `utmp` file (Section 6.8). FreeBSD and Mac OS X store the login name in the session structure associated with the process table entry and provide system calls to fetch and store this name.

System V provided the `cuserid` function to return the login name. This function called `getlogin` and, if that failed, did a `getpwuid(getuid())`. The IEEE Standard 1003.1–1988 specified `cuserid`, but it called for the effective user ID to be used, instead of the real user ID. The 1990 version of POSIX.1 dropped the `cuserid` function.

The environment variable `LOGNAME` is usually initialized with the user's login name by `login(1)` and inherited by the login shell. Realize, however, that a user can modify an environment variable, so we shouldn't use `LOGNAME` to validate the user in any way. Instead, `getlogin` should be used.

8.16 Process Times

In Section 1.10, we described three times that we can measure: wall clock time, user CPU time, and system CPU time. Any process can call the `times` function to obtain these values for itself and any terminated children.

```
#include <sys/times.h>

clock_t times(struct tms *buf);
```

Returns: elapsed wall clock time in clock ticks if OK, –1 on error

This function fills in the `tms` structure pointed to by *buf*:

```
struct tms {
  clock_t  tms_utime;   /* user CPU time */
  clock_t  tms_stime;   /* system CPU time */
  clock_t  tms_cutime;  /* user CPU time, terminated children */
  clock_t  tms_cstime;  /* system CPU time, terminated children */
};
```

Note that the structure does not contain any measurement for the wall clock time. Instead, the function returns the wall clock time as the value of the function, each time it's called. This value is measured from some arbitrary point in the past, so we can't use its absolute value; instead, we use its relative value. For example, we call `times` and save the return value. At some later time, we call `times` again and subtract the earlier return value from the new return value. The difference is the wall clock time. (It is possible, though unlikely, for a long-running process to overflow the wall clock time; see Exercise 1.6.)

The two structure fields for child processes contain values only for children that we have waited for with `wait`, `waitid`, or `waitpid`.

All the `clock_t` values returned by this function are converted to seconds using the number of clock ticks per second—the `_SC_CLK_TCK` value returned by `sysconf` (Section 2.5.4).

Most implementations provide the getrusage(2) function. This function returns the CPU times and 14 other values indicating resource usage. Historically, this function originated with the BSD operating system, so BSD-derived implementations generally support more of the fields than do other implementations.

Example

The program in Figure 8.30 executes each command-line argument as a shell command string, timing the command and printing the values from the tms structure.

```
#include "apue.h"
#include <sys/times.h>

static void pr_times(clock_t, struct tms *, struct tms *);
static void do_cmd(char *);

int
main(int argc, char *argv[])
{
    int     i;

    setbuf(stdout, NULL);
    for (i = 1; i < argc; i++)
        do_cmd(argv[i]);     /* once for each command-line arg */
    exit(0);
}

static void
do_cmd(char *cmd)          /* execute and time the "cmd" */
{
    struct tms  tmsstart, tmsend;
    clock_t     start, end;
    int         status;

    printf("\ncommand: %s\n", cmd);

    if ((start = times(&tmsstart)) == -1)    /* starting values */
        err_sys("times error");

    if ((status = system(cmd)) < 0)        /* execute command */
        err_sys("system() error");

    if ((end = times(&tmsend)) == -1)        /* ending values */
        err_sys("times error");

    pr_times(end-start, &tmsstart, &tmsend);
    pr_exit(status);
}

static void
pr_times(clock_t real, struct tms *tmsstart, struct tms *tmsend)
{
    static long     clktck = 0;

    if (clktck == 0)     /* fetch clock ticks per second first time */
        if ((clktck = sysconf(_SC_CLK_TCK)) < 0)
```

```
                err_sys("sysconf error");
        printf("  real:    %7.2f\n", real / (double) clktck);
        printf("  user:    %7.2f\n",
           (tmsend->tms_utime - tmsstart->tms_utime) / (double) clktck);
        printf("  sys:     %7.2f\n",
           (tmsend->tms_stime - tmsstart->tms_stime) / (double) clktck);
        printf("  child user:  %7.2f\n",
           (tmsend->tms_cutime - tmsstart->tms_cutime) / (double) clktck);
        printf("  child sys:   %7.2f\n",
           (tmsend->tms_cstime - tmsstart->tms_cstime) / (double) clktck);
}
```

Figure 8.30 Time and execute all command-line arguments

If we run this program, we get

```
$ ./a.out "sleep 5" "date"

command: sleep 5
   real:       5.02
   user:       0.00
   sys:        0.00
   child user:     0.01
   child sys:      0.00
normal termination, exit status = 0

command: date
Mon Mar 22 00:43:58 EST 2004
   real:       0.01
   user:       0.00
   sys:        0.00
   child user:     0.01
   child sys:      0.00
normal termination, exit status = 0
```

In these two examples, all the CPU time appears in the child process, which is where the shell and the command execute.   □

8.17 Summary

A thorough understanding of the UNIX System's process control is essential for advanced programming. There are only a few functions to master: fork, the exec family, _exit, wait, and waitpid. These primitives are used in many applications. The fork function also gave us an opportunity to look at race conditions.

Our examination of the system function and process accounting gave us another look at all these process control functions. We also looked at another variation of the exec functions: interpreter files and how they operate. An understanding of the various user IDs and group IDs that are provided—real, effective, and saved—is critical to writing safe set-user-ID programs.

Given an understanding of a single process and its children, in the next chapter we examine the relationship of a process to other processes—sessions and job control. We then complete our discussion of processes in Chapter 10 when we describe signals.

Exercises

8.1   In Figure 8.3, we said that replacing the call to _exit with a call to exit might cause the standard output to be closed and printf to return −1. Modify the program to check whether your implementation behaves this way. If it does not, how can you simulate this behavior?

8.2   Recall the typical arrangement of memory in Figure 7.6. Because the stack frames corresponding to each function call are usually stored in the stack, and because after a vfork, the child runs in the address space of the parent, what happens if the call to vfork is from a function other than main and the child does a return from this function after the vfork? Write a test program to verify this, and draw a picture of what's happening.

8.3   When we execute the program in Figure 8.13 one time, as in

```
$ ./a.out
```

the output is correct. But if we execute the program multiple times, one right after the other, as in

```
$ ./a.out ; ./a.out ; ./a.out
output from parent
ooutput from parent
ouotuptut from child
put from parent
output from child
utput from child
```

the output is not correct. What's happening? How can we correct this? Can this problem happen if we let the child write its output first?

8.4   In the program shown in Figure 8.20, we call execl, specifying the *pathname* of the interpreter file. If we called execlp instead, specifying a *filename* of testinterp, and if the directory /home/sar/bin was a path prefix, what would be printed as argv[2] when the program is run?

8.5   How can a process obtain its saved set-user-ID?

8.6   Write a program that creates a zombie, and then call system to execute the ps(1) command to verify that the process is a zombie.

8.7   We mentioned in Section 8.10 that POSIX.1 requires that open directory streams be closed across an exec. Verify this as follows: call opendir for the root directory, peek at your system's implementation of the DIR structure, and print the close-on-exec flag. Then open the same directory for reading, and print the close-on-exec flag.

9

Process Relationships

9.1 Introduction

We learned in the previous chapter that there are relationships between processes. First, every process has a parent process (the initial kernel-level process is usually its own parent). The parent is notified when the child terminates, and the parent can obtain the child's exit status. We also mentioned process groups when we described the `waitpid` function (Section 8.6) and how we can wait for any process in a process group to terminate.

In this chapter, we'll look at process groups in more detail and the concept of sessions that was introduced by POSIX.1. We'll also look at the relationship between the login shell that is invoked for us when we log in and all the processes that we start from our login shell.

It is impossible to describe these relationships without talking about signals, and to talk about signals, we need many of the concepts in this chapter. If you are unfamiliar with the UNIX System signal mechanism, you may want to skim through Chapter 10 at this point.

9.2 Terminal Logins

Let's start by looking at the programs that are executed when we log in to a UNIX system. In early UNIX systems, such as Version 7, users logged in using dumb terminals that were connected to the host with hard-wired connections. The terminals were either local (directly connected) or remote (connected through a modem). In either case, these logins came through a terminal device driver in the kernel. For example, the common devices on PDP-11s were DH-11s and DZ-11s. A host had a fixed number of these terminal devices, so there was a known upper limit on the number of simultaneous logins.

As bit-mapped graphical terminals became available, windowing systems were developed to provide users with new ways to interact with host computers. Applications were developed to create "terminal windows" to emulate character-based terminals, allowing users to interact with hosts in familiar ways (i.e., via the shell command line).

Today, some platforms allow you to start a windowing system after logging in, whereas other platforms automatically start the windowing system for you. In the latter case, you might still have to log in, depending on how the windowing system is configured (some windowing systems can be configured to log you in automatically).

The procedure that we now describe is used to log in to a UNIX system using a terminal. The procedure is similar regardless of the type of terminal we use—it could be a character-based terminal, a graphical terminal emulating a simple character-based terminal, or a graphical terminal running a windowing system.

BSD Terminal Logins

This procedure has not changed much over the past 30 years. The system administrator creates a file, usually /etc/ttys, that has one line per terminal device. Each line specifies the name of the device and other parameters that are passed to the getty program. One parameter is the baud rate of the terminal, for example. When the system is bootstrapped, the kernel creates process ID 1, the init process, and it is init that brings the system up multiuser. The init process reads the file /etc/ttys and, for every terminal device that allows a login, does a fork followed by an exec of the program getty. This gives us the processes shown in Figure 9.1.

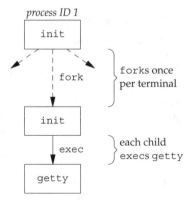

Figure 9.1 Processes invoked by init to allow terminal logins

All the processes shown in Figure 9.1 have a real user ID of 0 and an effective user ID of 0 (i.e., they all have superuser privileges). The init process also execs the getty program with an empty environment.

It is `getty` that calls `open` for the terminal device. The terminal is opened for reading and writing. If the device is a modem, the `open` may delay inside the device driver until the modem is dialed and the call is answered. Once the device is open, file descriptors 0, 1, and 2 are set to the device. Then `getty` outputs something like `login:` and waits for us to enter our user name. If the terminal supports multiple speeds, `getty` can detect special characters that tell it to change the terminal's speed (baud rate). Consult your UNIX system manuals for additional details on the `getty` program and the data files (`gettytab`) that can drive its actions.

When we enter our user name, `getty`'s job is complete, and it then invokes the `login` program, similar to

```
execle("/bin/login", "login", "-p", username, (char *)0, envp);
```

(There can be options in the `gettytab` file to have it invoke other programs, but the default is the `login` program.) `init` invokes `getty` with an empty environment; `getty` creates an environment for `login` (the `envp` argument) with the name of the terminal (something like `TERM=foo`, where the type of terminal `foo` is taken from the `gettytab` file) and any environment strings that are specified in the `gettytab`. The `-p` flag to `login` tells it to preserve the environment that it is passed and to add to that environment, not replace it. Figure 9.2 shows the state of these processes right after `login` has been invoked.

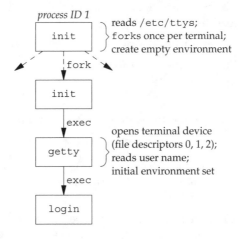

Figure 9.2 State of processes after `login` has been invoked

All the processes shown in Figure 9.2 have superuser privileges, since the original `init` process has superuser privileges. The process ID of the bottom three processes in Figure 9.2 is the same, since the process ID does not change across an `exec`. Also, all the processes other than the original `init` process have a parent process ID of 1.

The `login` program does many things. Since it has our user name, it can call `getpwnam` to fetch our password file entry. Then `login` calls `getpass`(3) to display the prompt `Password:` and read our password (with echoing disabled, of course). It calls `crypt`(3) to encrypt the password that we entered and compares the encrypted result to the pw_passwd field from our shadow password file entry. If the login attempt fails because of an invalid password (after a few tries), login calls exit with an argument of 1. This termination will be noticed by the parent (init), and it will do another fork followed by an exec of getty, starting the procedure over again for this terminal.

This is the traditional authentication procedure used on UNIX systems. Modern UNIX systems have evolved to support multiple authentication procedures. For example, FreeBSD, Linux, Mac OS X, and Solaris all support a more flexible scheme known as PAM (Pluggable Authentication Modules). PAM allows an administrator to configure the authentication methods to be used to access services that are written to use the PAM library.

If our application needs to verify that a user has the appropriate permission to perform a task, we can either hard code the authentication mechanism in the application, or we can use the PAM library to give us the equivalent functionality. The advantage to using PAM is that administrators can configure different ways to authenticate users for different tasks, based on the local site policies.

If we log in correctly, login will

- Change to our home directory (chdir)
- Change the ownership of our terminal device (chown) so we own it
- Change the access permissions for our terminal device so we have permission to read from and write to it
- Set our group IDs by calling setgid and initgroups
- Initialize the environment with all the information that login has: our home directory (HOME), shell (SHELL), user name (USER and LOGNAME), and a default path (PATH)
- Change to our user ID (setuid) and invoke our login shell, as in

  ```
  execl("/bin/sh", "-sh", (char *)0);
  ```

  The minus sign as the first character of argv[0] is a flag to all the shells that they are being invoked as a login shell. The shells can look at this character and modify their start-up accordingly.

The login program really does more than we've described here. It optionally prints the message-of-the-day file, checks for new mail, and performs other tasks. We're interested only in the features that we've described.

Recall from our discussion of the setuid function in Section 8.11 that since it is called by a superuser process, setuid changes all three user IDs: the real user ID, effective user ID, and saved set-user-ID. The call to setgid that was done earlier by login has the same effect on all three group IDs.

At this point, our login shell is running. Its parent process ID is the original init process (process ID 1), so when our login shell terminates, init is notified (it is sent a SIGCHLD signal), and it can start the whole procedure over again for this terminal. File descriptors 0, 1, and 2 for our login shell are set to the terminal device. Figure 9.3 shows this arrangement.

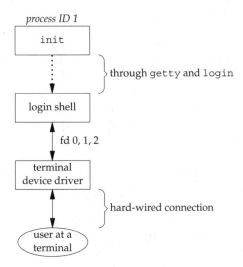

Figure 9.3 Arrangement of processes after everything is set for a terminal login

Our login shell now reads its start-up files (`.profile` for the Bourne shell and Korn shell; `.bash_profile`, `.bash_login`, or `.profile` for the GNU Bourne-again shell; and `.cshrc` and `.login` for the C shell). These start-up files usually change some of the environment variables and add many additional variables to the environment. For example, most users set their own PATH and often prompt for the actual terminal type (TERM). When the start-up files are done, we finally get the shell's prompt and can enter commands.

Mac OS X Terminal Logins

On Mac OS X, the terminal login process follows the same steps as in the BSD login process, since Mac OS X is based in part on FreeBSD. With Mac OS X, however, we are presented with a graphical-based login screen from the start.

Linux Terminal Logins

The Linux login procedure is very similar to the BSD procedure. Indeed, the Linux `login` command is derived from the 4.3BSD `login` command. The main difference between the BSD login procedure and the Linux login procedure is in the way the terminal configuration is specified.

On Linux, `/etc/inittab` contains the configuration information specifying the terminal devices for which `init` should start a `getty` process, similar to the way it is done on System V. Depending on the version of `getty` in use, the terminal characteristics are specified either on the command line (as with `agetty`) or in the file `/etc/gettydefs` (as with `mgetty`).

Solaris Terminal Logins

Solaris supports two forms of terminal logins: (a) `getty` style, as described previously for BSD, and (b) `ttymon` logins, a feature introduced with SVR4. Normally, `getty` is used for the console, and `ttymon` is used for other terminal logins.

The `ttymon` command is part of a larger facility termed SAF, the Service Access Facility. The goal of the SAF was to provide a consistent way to administer services that provide access to a system. (See Chapter 6 of Rago [1993] for more details.) For our purposes, we end up with the same picture as in Figure 9.3, with a different set of steps between `init` and the login shell. `init` is the parent of `sac` (the service access controller), which does a `fork` and `exec` of the `ttymon` program when the system enters multiuser state. The `ttymon` program monitors all the terminal ports listed in its configuration file and does a `fork` when we've entered our login name. This child of `ttymon` does an `exec` of `login`, and `login` prompts us for our password. Once this is done, `login` execs our login shell, and we're at the position shown in Figure 9.3. One difference is that the parent of our login shell is now `ttymon`, whereas the parent of the login shell from a `getty` login is `init`.

9.3   Network Logins

The main (physical) difference between logging in to a system through a serial terminal and logging in to a system through a network is that the connection between the terminal and the computer isn't point-to-point. In this case, `login` is simply a service available, just like any other network service, such as FTP or SMTP.

With the terminal logins that we described in the previous section, `init` knows which terminal devices are enabled for logins and spawns a `getty` process for each device. In the case of network logins, however, all the logins come through the kernel's network interface drivers (e.g., the Ethernet driver), and we don't know ahead of time how many of these will occur. Instead of having a process waiting for each possible login, we now have to wait for a network connection request to arrive.

To allow the same software to process logins over both terminal logins and network logins, a software driver called a *pseudo terminal* is used to emulate the behavior of a serial terminal and map terminal operations to network operations, and vice versa. (In Chapter 19, we'll talk about pseudo terminals in detail.)

BSD Network Logins

In BSD, a single process waits for most network connections: the `inetd` process, sometimes called the *Internet superserver*. In this section, we'll look at the sequence of processes involved in network logins for a BSD system. We are not interested in the detailed network programming aspects of these processes; refer to Stevens, Fenner, and Rudoff [2004] for all the details.

As part of the system start-up, `init` invokes a shell that executes the shell script `/etc/rc`. One of the daemons that is started by this shell script is `inetd`. Once the shell script terminates, the parent process of `inetd` becomes `init`; `inetd` waits for

TCP/IP connection requests to arrive at the host. When a connection request arrives for it to handle, `inetd` does a `fork` and `exec` of the appropriate program.

Let's assume that a TCP connection request arrives for the TELNET server. TELNET is a remote login application that uses the TCP protocol. A user on another host (that is connected to the server's host through a network of some form) or on the same host initiates the login by starting the TELNET client:

```
telnet hostname
```

The client opens a TCP connection to *hostname*, and the program that's started on *hostname* is called the TELNET server. The client and the server then exchange data across the TCP connection using the TELNET application protocol. What has happened is that the user who started the client program is now logged in to the server's host. (This assumes, of course, that the user has a valid account on the server's host.) Figure 9.4 shows the sequence of processes involved in executing the TELNET server, called `telnetd`.

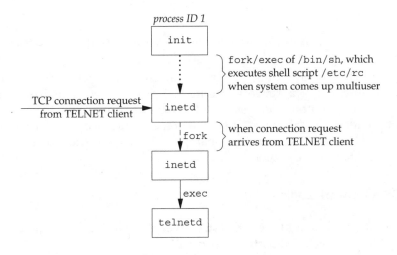

Figure 9.4 Sequence of processes involved in executing TELNET server

The `telnetd` process then opens a pseudo-terminal device and splits into two processes using `fork`. The parent handles the communication across the network connection, and the child does an `exec` of the `login` program. The parent and the child are connected through the pseudo terminal. Before doing the `exec`, the child sets up file descriptors 0, 1, and 2 to the pseudo terminal. If we log in correctly, `login` performs the same steps we described in Section 9.2: it changes to our home directory and sets our group IDs, user ID, and our initial environment. Then `login` replaces itself with our login shell by calling `exec`. Figure 9.5 shows the arrangement of the processes at this point.

Obviously, a lot is going on between the pseudo-terminal device driver and the actual user at the terminal. We'll show all the processes involved in this type of arrangement in Chapter 19 when we talk about pseudo terminals in more detail.

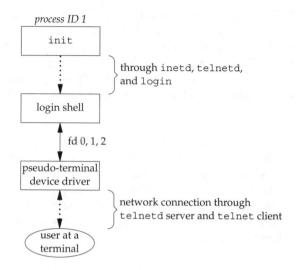

Figure 9.5 Arrangement of processes after everything is set for a network login

The important thing to understand is that whether we log in through a terminal (Figure 9.3) or a network (Figure 9.5), we have a login shell with its standard input, standard output, and standard error connected to either a terminal device or a pseudo-terminal device. We'll see in the coming sections that this login shell is the start of a POSIX.1 session, and that the terminal or pseudo terminal is the controlling terminal for the session.

Mac OS X Network Logins

Logging in to a Mac OS X system over a network is identical to a BSD system, because Mac OS X is based partially on FreeBSD.

Linux Network Logins

Network logins under Linux are the same as under BSD, except that an alternate `inetd` process is used, called the extended Internet services daemon, `xinetd`. The `xinetd` process provides a finer level of control over services it starts than does `inetd`.

Solaris Network Logins

The scenario for network logins under Solaris is almost identical to the steps under BSD and Linux. An `inetd` server is used similar to the BSD version. The Solaris version has the additional ability to run under the service access facility framework, although it is not configured to do so. Instead, the `inetd` server is started by `init`. Either way, we end up with the same overall picture as in Figure 9.5.

9.4   Process Groups

In addition to having a process ID, each process also belongs to a process group. We'll encounter process groups again when we discuss signals in Chapter 10.

A process group is a collection of one or more processes, usually associated with the same job (job control is discussed in Section 9.8), that can receive signals from the same terminal. Each process group has a unique process group ID. Process group IDs are similar to process IDs: they are positive integers and can be stored in a `pid_t` data type. The function `getpgrp` returns the process group ID of the calling process.

```
#include <unistd.h>

pid_t getpgrp(void);
```
                                   Returns: process group ID of calling process

In older BSD-derived systems, the `getpgrp` function took a *pid* argument and returned the process group for that process. The Single UNIX Specification defines the `getpgid` function as an XSI extension that mimics this behavior.

```
#include <unistd.h>

pid_t getpgid(pid_t pid);
```
                                   Returns: process group ID if OK, –1 on error

If *pid* is 0, the process group ID of the calling process is returned. Thus,

```
getpgid(0);
```

is equivalent to

```
getpgrp();
```

Each process group can have a process group leader. The leader is identified by its process group ID being equal to its process ID.

It is possible for a process group leader to create a process group, create processes in the group, and then terminate. The process group still exists, as long as at least one process is in the group, regardless of whether the group leader terminates. This is called the process group lifetime—the period of time that begins when the group is created and ends when the last remaining process leaves the group. The last remaining process in the process group can either terminate or enter some other process group.

A process joins an existing process group or creates a new process group by calling `setpgid`. (In the next section, we'll see that `setsid` also creates a new process group.)

```
#include <unistd.h>

int setpgid(pid_t pid, pid_t pgid);
```
                                   Returns: 0 if OK, –1 on error

This function sets the process group ID to *pgid* in the process whose process ID equals *pid*. If the two arguments are equal, the process specified by *pid* becomes a process group leader. If *pid* is 0, the process ID of the caller is used. Also, if *pgid* is 0, the process ID specified by *pid* is used as the process group ID.

A process can set the process group ID of only itself or any of its children. Furthermore, it can't change the process group ID of one of its children after that child has called one of the `exec` functions.

In most job-control shells, this function is called after a `fork` to have the parent set the process group ID of the child, and to have the child set its own process group ID. One of these calls is redundant, but by doing both, we are guaranteed that the child is placed into its own process group before either process assumes that this has happened. If we didn't do this, we would have a race condition, since the child's process group membership would depend on which process executes first.

When we discuss signals, we'll see how we can send a signal to either a single process (identified by its process ID) or a process group (identified by its process group ID). Similarly, the `waitpid` function from Section 8.6 lets us wait for either a single process or one process from a specified process group.

9.5   Sessions

A session is a collection of one or more process groups. For example, we could have the arrangement shown in Figure 9.6. Here we have three process groups in a single session.

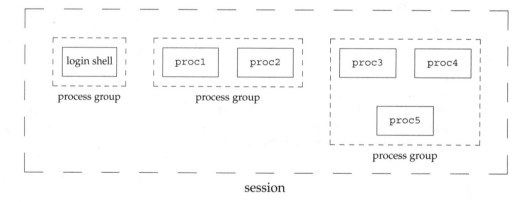

Figure 9.6   Arrangement of processes into process groups and sessions

The processes in a process group are usually placed there by a shell pipeline. For example, the arrangement shown in Figure 9.6 could have been generated by shell commands of the form

```
proc1 | proc2 &
proc3 | proc4 | proc5
```

A process establishes a new session by calling the `setsid` function.

```
#include <unistd.h>

pid_t setsid(void);
```
                                                    Returns: process group ID if OK, –1 on error

If the calling process is not a process group leader, this function creates a new session. Three things happen.

1. The process becomes the *session leader* of this new session. (A session leader is the process that creates a session.) The process is the only process in this new session.

2. The process becomes the process group leader of a new process group. The new process group ID is the process ID of the calling process.

3. The process has no controlling terminal. (We'll discuss controlling terminals in the next section.) If the process had a controlling terminal before calling `setsid`, that association is broken.

This function returns an error if the caller is already a process group leader. To ensure this is not the case, the usual practice is to call `fork` and have the parent terminate and the child continue. We are guaranteed that the child is not a process group leader, because the process group ID of the parent is inherited by the child, but the child gets a new process ID. Hence, it is impossible for the child's process ID to equal its inherited process group ID.

The Single UNIX Specification talks only about a "session leader." There is no "session ID" similar to a process ID or a process group ID. Obviously, a session leader is a single process that has a unique process ID, so we could talk about a session ID that is the process ID of the session leader. This concept of a session ID was introduced in SVR4. Historically, BSD-based systems didn't support this notion, but have since been updated to include it. The `getsid` function returns the process group ID of a process's session leader. The `getsid` function is included as an XSI extension in the Single UNIX Specification.

> Some implementations, such as Solaris, join with the Single UNIX Specification in the practice of avoiding the use of the phrase "session ID," opting instead to refer to this as the "process group ID of the session leader." The two are equivalent, since the session leader is always the leader of a process group.

```
#include <unistd.h>

pid_t getsid(pid_t pid);
```
                                                    Returns: session leader's process group ID if OK, –1 on error

If *pid* is 0, `getsid` returns the process group ID of the calling process's session leader. For security reasons, some implementations may restrict the calling process from obtaining the process group ID of the session leader if *pid* doesn't belong to the same session as the caller.

9.6 Controlling Terminal

Sessions and process groups have a few other characteristics.

- A session can have a single *controlling terminal.* This is usually the terminal device (in the case of a terminal login) or pseudo-terminal device (in the case of a network login) on which we log in.

- The session leader that establishes the connection to the controlling terminal is called the *controlling process.*

- The process groups within a session can be divided into a single *foreground process group* and one or more *background process groups.*

- If a session has a controlling terminal, it has a single foreground process group, and all other process groups in the session are background process groups.

- Whenever we type the terminal's interrupt key (often DELETE or Control-C), this causes the interrupt signal be sent to all processes in the foreground process group.

- Whenever we type the terminal's quit key (often Control-backslash), this causes the quit signal to be sent to all processes in the foreground process group.

- If a modem (or network) disconnect is detected by the terminal interface, the hang-up signal is sent to the controlling process (the session leader).

These characteristics are shown in Figure 9.7.

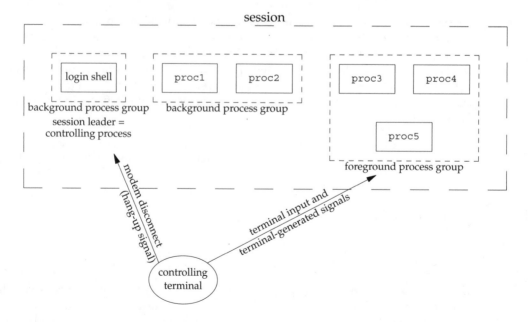

Figure 9.7 Process groups and sessions showing controlling terminal

Usually, we don't have to worry about the controlling terminal; it is established automatically when we log in.

> POSIX.1 leaves the choice of the mechanism used to allocate a controlling terminal up to each individual implementation. We'll show the actual steps in Section 19.4.
>
> Systems derived from UNIX System V allocate the controlling terminal for a session when the session leader opens the first terminal device that is not already associated with a session. This assumes that the call to open by the session leader does not specify the O_NOCTTY flag (Section 3.3).
>
> BSD-based systems allocate the controlling terminal for a session when the session leader calls ioctl with a *request* argument of TIOCSCTTY (the third argument is a null pointer). The session cannot already have a controlling terminal for this call to succeed. (Normally, this call to ioctl follows a call to setsid, which guarantees that the process is a session leader without a controlling terminal.) The POSIX.1 O_NOCTTY flag to open is not used by BSD-based systems, except in compatibility-mode support for other systems.

There are times when a program wants to talk to the controlling terminal, regardless of whether the standard input or standard output is redirected. The way a program guarantees that it is talking to the controlling terminal is to open the file /dev/tty. This special file is a synonym within the kernel for the controlling terminal. Naturally, if the program doesn't have a controlling terminal, the open of this device will fail.

The classic example is the getpass(3) function, which reads a password (with terminal echoing turned off, of course). This function is called by the crypt(1) program and can be used in a pipeline. For example,

```
crypt < salaries | lpr
```

decrypts the file salaries and pipes the output to the print spooler. Because crypt reads its input file on its standard input, the standard input can't be used to enter the password. Also, crypt is designed so that we have to enter the encryption password each time we run the program, to prevent us from saving the password in a file (which could be a security hole).

There are known ways to break the encoding used by the crypt program. See Garfinkel et al. [2003] for more details on encrypting files.

9.7 tcgetpgrp, tcsetpgrp, and tcgetsid Functions

We need a way to tell the kernel which process group is the foreground process group, so that the terminal device driver knows where to send the terminal input and the terminal-generated signals (Figure 9.7).

```
#include <unistd.h>

pid_t tcgetpgrp(int filedes);
```

Returns: process group ID of foreground process group if OK, −1 on error

```
int tcsetpgrp(int filedes, pid_t pgrpid);
```

Returns: 0 if OK, −1 on error

The function `tcgetpgrp` returns the process group ID of the foreground process group associated with the terminal open on *filedes*.

If the process has a controlling terminal, the process can call `tcsetpgrp` to set the foreground process group ID to *pgrpid*. The value of *pgrpid* must be the process group ID of a process group in the same session, and *filedes* must refer to the controlling terminal of the session.

Most applications don't call these two functions directly. They are normally called by job-control shells.

The Single UNIX Specification defines an XSI extension called `tcgetsid` to allow an application to obtain the process group ID for the session leader given a file descriptor for the controlling TTY.

```
#include <termios.h>

pid_t tcgetsid(int filedes);
```
Returns: session leader's process group ID if OK, −1 on error

Applications that need to manage controlling terminals can use `tcgetsid` to identify the session ID of the controlling terminal's session leader (which is equivalent to the session leader's process group ID).

9.8 Job Control

Job control is a feature added to BSD around 1980. This feature allows us to start multiple jobs (groups of processes) from a single terminal and to control which jobs can access the terminal and which jobs are to run in the background. Job control requires three forms of support:

1. A shell that supports job control
2. The terminal driver in the kernel must support job control
3. The kernel must support certain job-control signals

> SVR3 provided a different form of job control called *shell layers*. The BSD form of job control, however, was selected by POSIX.1 and is what we describe here. In earlier versions of the standard, job control support was optional, but POSIX.1 now requires platforms to support it.

From our perspective, using job control from a shell, we can start a job in either the foreground or the background. A job is simply a collection of processes, often a pipeline of processes. For example,

```
vi main.c
```

starts a job consisting of one process in the foreground. The commands

```
pr *.c | lpr &
make all &
```

start two jobs in the background. All the processes invoked by these background jobs are in the background.

As we said, to use the features provided by job control, we need to be using a shell that supports job control. With older systems, it was simple to say which shells supported job control and which didn't. The C shell supported job control, the Bourne shell didn't, and it was an option with the Korn shell, depending whether the host supported job control. But the C shell has been ported to systems (e.g., earlier versions of System V) that don't support job control, and the SVR4 Bourne shell, when invoked by the name jsh instead of sh, supports job control. The Korn shell continues to support job control if the host does. The Bourne-again shell also supports job control. We'll just talk generically about a shell that supports job control, versus one that doesn't, when the difference between the various shells doesn't matter.

When we start a background job, the shell assigns it a job identifier and prints one or more of the process IDs. The following script shows how the Korn shell handles this:

```
$ make all > Make.out &
[1]      1475
$ pr *.c | lpr &
[2]      1490
$                               just press RETURN
[2]  +   Done            pr *.c | lpr &
[1]  +   Done            make all > Make.out &
```

The make is job number 1 and the starting process ID is 1475. The next pipeline is job number 2 and the process ID of the first process is 1490. When the jobs are done and when we press RETURN, the shell tells us that the jobs are complete. The reason we have to press RETURN is to have the shell print its prompt. The shell doesn't print the changed status of background jobs at any random time—only right before it prints its prompt, to let us enter a new command line. If the shell didn't do this, it could output while we were entering an input line.

The interaction with the terminal driver arises because a special terminal character affects the foreground job: the suspend key (typically Control-Z). Entering this character causes the terminal driver to send the SIGTSTP signal to all processes in the foreground process group. The jobs in any background process groups aren't affected. The terminal driver looks for three special characters, which generate signals to the foreground process group.

- The interrupt character (typically DELETE or Control-C) generates SIGINT.

- The quit character (typically Control-backslash) generates SIGQUIT.

- The suspend character (typically Control-Z) generates SIGTSTP.

In Chapter 18, we'll see how we can change these three characters to be any characters we choose and how we can disable the terminal driver's processing of these special characters.

Another job control condition can arise that must be handled by the terminal driver. Since we can have a foreground job and one or more background jobs, which of these receives the characters that we enter at the terminal? Only the foreground job receives terminal input. It is not an error for a background job to try to read from the terminal, but the terminal driver detects this and sends a special signal to the background job: SIGTTIN. This signal normally stops the background job; by using the shell, we are notified of this and can bring the job into the foreground so that it can read from the terminal. The following demonstrates this:

```
$ cat > temp.foo &            start in background, but it'll read from standard input
[1]     1681
$                             we press RETURN
[1] + Stopped (SIGTTIN)         cat > temp.foo &
$ fg %1                       bring job number 1 into the foreground
cat > temp.foo                the shell tells us which job is now in the foreground
hello, world                  enter one line
^D                            type the end-of-file character
$ cat temp.foo                check that the one line was put into the file
hello, world
```

The shell starts the cat process in the background, but when cat tries to read its standard input (the controlling terminal), the terminal driver, knowing that it is a background job, sends the SIGTTIN signal to the background job. The shell detects this change in status of its child (recall our discussion of the wait and waitpid function in Section 8.6) and tells us that the job has been stopped. We then move the stopped job into the foreground with the shell's fg command. (Refer to the manual page for the shell that you are using, for all the details on its job control commands, such as fg and bg, and the various ways to identify the different jobs.) Doing this causes the shell to place the job into the foreground process group (tcsetpgrp) and send the continue signal (SIGCONT) to the process group. Since it is now in the foreground process group, the job can read from the controlling terminal.

What happens if a background job outputs to the controlling terminal? This is an option that we can allow or disallow. Normally, we use the stty(1) command to change this option. (We'll see in Chapter 18 how we can change this option from a program.) The following shows how this works:

```
$ cat temp.foo &            execute in background
[1]     1719
$ hello, world              the output from the background job appears after the prompt
                            we press RETURN
[1] +  Done        cat temp.foo &
$ stty tostop               disable ability of background jobs to output to controlling terminal
$ cat temp.foo &            try it again in the background
[1]     1721
$                           we press RETURN and find the job is stopped
[1] + Stopped(SIGTTOU)          cat temp.foo &
$ fg %1                     resume stopped job in the foreground
cat temp.foo                the shell tells us which job is now in the foreground
hello, world                and here is its output
```

When we disallow background jobs from writing to the controlling terminal, cat will block when it tries to write to its standard output, because the terminal driver identifies the write as coming from a background process and sends the job the SIGTTOU signal. As with the previous example, when we use the shell's fg command to bring the job into the foreground, the job completes.

Figure 9.8 summarizes some of the features of job control that we've been describing. The solid lines through the terminal driver box mean that the terminal I/O and the terminal-generated signals are always connected from the foreground process

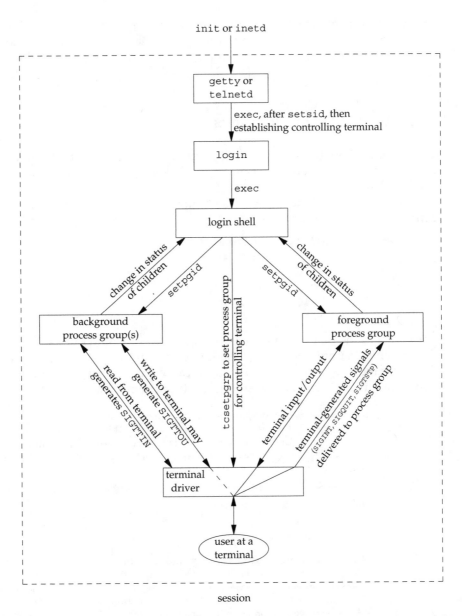

Figure 9.8 Summary of job control features with foreground and background jobs, and terminal driver

group to the actual terminal. The dashed line corresponding to the SIGTTOU signal means that whether the output from a process in the background process group appears on the terminal is an option.

Is job control necessary or desirable? Job control was originally designed and implemented before windowing terminals were widespread. Some people claim that a well-designed windowing system removes any need for job control. Some complain that the implementation of job control—requiring support from the kernel, the terminal driver, the shell, and some applications—is a hack. Some use job control with a windowing system, claiming a need for both. Regardless of your opinion, job control is a required feature of POSIX.1.

9.9   Shell Execution of Programs

Let's examine how the shells execute programs and how this relates to the concepts of process groups, controlling terminals, and sessions. To do this, we'll use the `ps` command again.

First, we'll use a shell that doesn't support job control—the classic Bourne shell running on Solaris. If we execute

```
ps -o pid,ppid,pgid,sid,comm
```

the output is

```
   PID  PPID  PGID    SID COMMAND
   949   947   949    949 sh
  1774   949   949    949 ps
```

The parent of the `ps` command is the shell, which we would expect. Both the shell and the `ps` command are in the same session and foreground process group (949). We say that 949 is the foreground process group because that is what you get when you execute a command with a shell that doesn't support job control.

> Some platforms support an option to have the `ps(1)` command print the process group ID associated with the session's controlling terminal. This value would be shown under the TPGID column. Unfortunately, the output of the `ps` command often differs among versions of the UNIX System. For example, Solaris 9 doesn't support this option. Under FreeBSD 5.2.1 and Mac OS X 10.3, the command
>
> ```
> ps -o pid,ppid,pgid,sess,tpgid,command
> ```
> and under Linux 2.4.22, the command
>
> ```
> ps -o pid,ppid,pgrp,session,tpgid,comm
> ```
> print exactly the information we want.
>
> Note that it is a misnomer to associate a process with a terminal process group ID (the TPGID column). A process does not have a terminal process control group. A process belongs to a process group, and the process group belongs to a session. The session may or may not have a controlling terminal. If the session does have a controlling terminal, then the terminal device knows the process group ID of the foreground process. This value can be set in the terminal driver with the `tcsetpgrp` function, as we show in Figure 9.8. The foreground process group ID is an attribute of the terminal, not the process. This value from the terminal device driver is what `ps` prints as the TPGID. If it finds that the session doesn't have a controlling terminal, `ps` prints −1.

If we execute the command in the background,

```
ps -o pid,ppid,pgid,sid,comm &
```

the only value that changes is the process ID of the command:

```
PID  PPID  PGID    SID COMMAND
949   947   949    949 sh
1812   949   949    949 ps
```

This shell doesn't know about job control, so the background job is not put into its own process group and the controlling terminal isn't taken away from the background job.

Let's now look at how the Bourne shell handles a pipeline. When we execute

```
ps -o pid,ppid,pgid,sid,comm | cat1
```

the output is

```
PID  PPID  PGID    SID COMMAND
949   947   949    949 sh
1823   949   949    949 cat1
1824  1823   949    949 ps
```

(The program `cat1` is just a copy of the standard `cat` program, with a different name. We have another copy of `cat` with the name `cat2`, which we'll use later in this section. When we have two copies of `cat` in a pipeline, the different names let us differentiate between the two programs.) Note that the last process in the pipeline is the child of the shell and that the first process in the pipeline is a child of the last process. It appears that the shell `forks` a copy of itself and that this copy then `forks` to make each of the previous processes in the pipeline.

If we execute the pipeline in the background,

```
ps -o pid,ppid,pgid,sid,comm | cat1 &
```

only the process IDs change. Since the shell doesn't handle job control, the process group ID of the background processes remains 949, as does the process group ID of the session.

What happens in this case if a background process tries to read from its controlling terminal? For example, suppose that we execute

```
cat > temp.foo &
```

With job control, this is handled by placing the background job into a background process group, which causes the signal SIGTTIN to be generated if the background job tries to read from the controlling terminal. The way this is handled without job control is that the shell automatically redirects the standard input of a background process to `/dev/null`, if the process doesn't redirect standard input itself. A read from `/dev/null` generates an end of file. This means that our background `cat` process immediately reads an end of file and terminates normally.

The previous paragraph adequately handles the case of a background process accessing the controlling terminal through its standard input, but what happens if a background process specifically opens `/dev/tty` and reads from the controlling terminal? The answer is "it depends," but it's probably not what we want. For example,

```
crypt < salaries | lpr &
```

is such a pipeline. We run it in the background, but the `crypt` program opens `/dev/tty`, changes the terminal characteristics (to disable echoing), reads from the device, and resets the terminal characteristics. When we execute this background pipeline, the prompt `Password:` from `crypt` is printed on the terminal, but what we enter (the encryption password) is read by the shell, which tries to execute a command of that name. The next line we enter to the shell is taken as the password, and the file is not encrypted correctly, sending junk to the printer. Here we have two processes trying to read from the same device at the same time, and the result depends on the system. Job control, as we described earlier, handles this multiplexing of a single terminal between multiple processes in a better fashion.

Returning to our Bourne shell example, if we execute three processes in the pipeline, we can examine the process control used by this shell:

```
ps -o pid,ppid,pgid,sid,comm | cat1 | cat2
```

generates the following output

```
 PID  PPID  PGID   SID COMMAND
 949   947   949   949 sh
1988   949   949   949 cat2
1989  1988   949   949 ps
1990  1988   949   949 cat1
```

> Don't be alarmed if the output on your system doesn't show the proper command names. Sometimes you might get results such as
>
> ```
>  PID  PPID  PGID   SID COMMAND
>  949   947   949   949 sh
> 1831   949   949   949 sh
> 1832  1831   949   949 ps
> 1833  1831   949   949 sh
> ```
>
> What's happening here is that the `ps` process is racing with the shell, which is forking and executing the `cat` commands. In this case, the shell hasn't yet completed the call to `exec` when `ps` has obtained the list of processes to print.

Again, the last process in the pipeline is the child of the shell, and all previous processes in the pipeline are children of the last process. Figure 9.9 shows what is happening. Since the last process in the pipeline is the child of the login shell, the shell is notified when that process (`cat2`) terminates.

Now let's examine the same examples using a job-control shell running on Linux. This shows the way these shells handle background jobs. We'll use the Bourne-again shell in this example; the results with other job-control shells are almost identical.

```
ps -o pid,ppid,pgrp,session,tpgid,comm
```

gives us

```
 PID  PPID  PGRP  SESS TPGID COMMAND
2837  2818  2837  2837  5796 bash
5796  2837  5796  2837  5796 ps
```

(Starting with this example, we show the foreground process group in a **bolder font**.) We immediately have a difference from our Bourne shell example. The Bourne-again shell places the foreground job (`ps`) into its own process group (5796). The `ps` command is the process group leader and the only process in this process group.

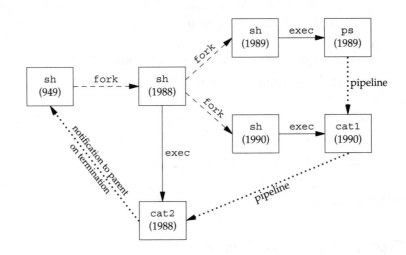

Figure 9.9 Processes in the pipeline ps | cat1 | cat2 when invoked by Bourne shell

Furthermore, this process group is the foreground process group, since it has the controlling terminal. Our login shell is a background process group while the ps command executes. Note, however, that both process groups, 2837 and 5796, are members of the same session. Indeed, we'll see that the session never changes through our examples in this section.

Executing this process in the background,

```
ps -o pid,ppid,pgrp,session,tpgid,comm &
```

gives us

```
  PID  PPID  PGRP  SESS TPGID COMMAND
 2837  2818  2837  2837  2837 bash
 5797  2837  5797  2837  2837 ps
```

Again, the ps command is placed into its own process group, but this time the process group (5797) is no longer the foreground process group. It is a background process group. The TPGID of 2837 indicates that the foreground process group is our login shell.

Executing two processes in a pipeline, as in

```
ps -o pid,ppid,pgrp,session,tpgid,comm | cat1
```

gives us

```
  PID  PPID  PGRP  SESS TPGID COMMAND
 2837  2818  2837  2837  5799 bash
 5799  2837  5799  2837  5799 ps
 5800  2837  5799  2837  5799 cat1
```

Both processes, ps and cat1, are placed into a new process group (5799), and this is the foreground process group. We can also see another difference between this example and the similar Bourne shell example. The Bourne shell created the last process in the pipeline first, and this final process was the parent of the first process. Here, the Bourne-again shell is the parent of both processes. If we execute this pipeline in the background,

```
ps -o pid,ppid,pgrp,session,tpgid,comm | cat1 &
```

the results are similar, but now `ps` and `cat1` are placed in the same background process group:

```
 PID  PPID  PGRP  SESS TPGID COMMAND
2837  2818  2837  2837  2837 bash
5801  2837  5801  2837  2837 ps
5802  2837  5801  2837  2837 cat1
```

Note that the order in which a shell creates processes can differ depending on the particular shell in use.

9.10 Orphaned Process Groups

We've mentioned that a process whose parent terminates is called an orphan and is inherited by the `init` process. We now look at entire process groups that can be orphaned and how POSIX.1 handles this situation.

Example

Consider a process that `forks` a child and then terminates. Although this is nothing abnormal (it happens all the time), what happens if the child is stopped (using job control) when the parent terminates? How will the child ever be continued, and does the child know that it has been orphaned? Figure 9.10 shows this situation: the parent process has `forked` a child that stops, and the parent is about to exit.

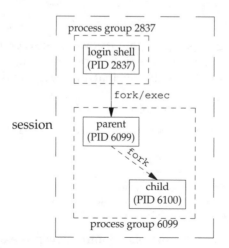

Figure 9.10 Example of a process group about to be orphaned

The program that creates this situation is shown in Figure 9.11. This program has some new features. Here, we are assuming a job-control shell. Recall from the previous section that the shell places the foreground process into its own process group (6099 in this example) and that the shell stays in its own process group (2837). The child inherits the process group of its parent (6099). After the `fork`,

- The parent sleeps for 5 seconds. This is our (imperfect) way of letting the child execute before the parent terminates.

- The child establishes a signal handler for the hang-up signal (`SIGHUP`). This is so we can see whether `SIGHUP` is sent to the child. (We discuss signal handlers in Chapter 10.)

- The child sends itself the stop signal (`SIGTSTP`) with the `kill` function. This stops the child, similar to our stopping a foreground job with our terminal's suspend character (Control-Z).

- When the parent terminates, the child is orphaned, so the child's parent process ID becomes 1, the `init` process ID.

- At this point, the child is now a member of an *orphaned process group*. The POSIX.1 definition of an orphaned process group is one in which the parent of every member is either itself a member of the group or is not a member of the group's session. Another way of wording this is that the process group is not orphaned as long as a process in the group has a parent in a different process group but in the same session. If the process group is not orphaned, there is a chance that one of those parents in a different process group but in the same session will restart a stopped process in the process group that is not orphaned. Here, the parent of every process in the group (e.g., process 1 is the parent of process 6100) belongs to another session.

- Since the process group is orphaned when the parent terminates, POSIX.1 requires that every process in the newly orphaned process group that is stopped (as our child is) be sent the hang-up signal (`SIGHUP`) followed by the continue signal (`SIGCONT`).

- This causes the child to be continued, after processing the hang-up signal. The default action for the hang-up signal is to terminate the process, so we have to provide a signal handler to catch the signal. We therefore expect the `printf` in the `sig_hup` function to appear before the `printf` in the `pr_ids` function.

Here is the output from the program shown in Figure 9.11:

```
$ ./a.out
parent: pid = 6099, ppid = 2837, pgrp = 6099, tpgrp = 6099
child: pid = 6100, ppid = 6099, pgrp = 6099, tpgrp = 6099
$ SIGHUP received, pid = 6100
child: pid = 6100, ppid = 1, pgrp = 6099, tpgrp = 2837
read error from controlling TTY, errno = 5
```

Note that our shell prompt appears with the output from the child, since two processes—our login shell and the child—are writing to the terminal. As we expect, the parent process ID of the child has become 1.

```
#include "apue.h"
#include <errno.h>

static void
sig_hup(int signo)
{
    printf("SIGHUP received, pid = %d\n", getpid());
}

static void
pr_ids(char *name)
{
    printf("%s: pid = %d, ppid = %d, pgrp = %d, tpgrp = %d\n",
        name, getpid(), getppid(), getpgrp(), tcgetpgrp(STDIN_FILENO));
    fflush(stdout);
}

int
main(void)
{
    char    c;
    pid_t   pid;

    pr_ids("parent");
    if ((pid = fork()) < 0) {
        err_sys("fork error");
    } else if (pid > 0) {      /* parent */
        sleep(5);           /* sleep to let child stop itself */
        exit(0);            /* then parent exits */
    } else {                /* child */
        pr_ids("child");
        signal(SIGHUP, sig_hup);     /* establish signal handler */
        kill(getpid(), SIGTSTP);     /* stop ourself */
        pr_ids("child");     /* prints only if we're continued */
        if (read(STDIN_FILENO, &c, 1) != 1)
            printf("read error from controlling TTY, errno = %d\n",
                errno);
        exit(0);
    }
}
```

Figure 9.11 Creating an orphaned process group

After calling pr_ids in the child, the program tries to read from standard input. As we saw earlier in this chapter, when a background process group tries to read from its controlling terminal, SIGTTIN is generated for the background process group. But here we have an orphaned process group; if the kernel were to stop it with this signal, the processes in the process group would probably never be continued. POSIX.1 specifies that the read is to return an error with errno set to EIO (whose value is 5 on this system) in this situation.

Finally, note that our child was placed in a background process group when the parent terminated, since the parent was executed as a foreground job by the shell.   □

We'll see another example of orphaned process groups in Section 19.5 with the `pty` program.

9.11 FreeBSD Implementation

Having talked about the various attributes of a process, process group, session, and controlling terminal, it's worth looking at how all this can be implemented. We'll look briefly at the implementation used by FreeBSD. Some details of the SVR4 implementation of these features can be found in Williams [1989]. Figure 9.12 shows the various data structures used by FreeBSD.

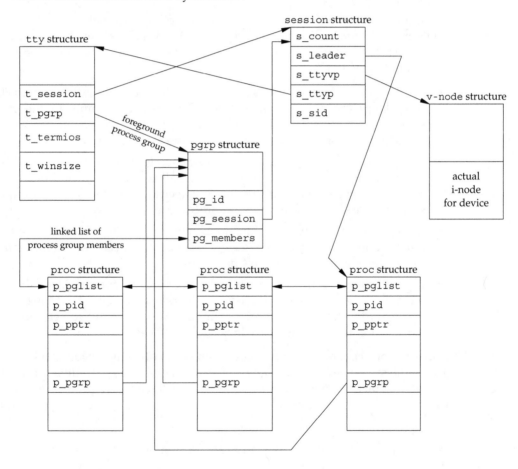

Figure 9.12 FreeBSD implementation of sessions and process groups

Let's look at all the fields that we've labeled, starting with the `session` structure. One of these structures is allocated for each session (e.g., each time `setsid` is called).

- `s_count` is the number of process groups in the session. When this counter is decremented to 0, the structure can be freed.

- `s_leader` is a pointer to the `proc` structure of the session leader.

- `s_ttyvp` is a pointer to the vnode structure of the controlling terminal.

- `s_ttyp` is a pointer to the `tty` structure of the controlling terminal.

- `s_sid` is the session ID. Recall that the concept of a session ID is not part of the Single UNIX Specification.

When `setsid` is called, a new `session` structure is allocated within the kernel. Now `s_count` is set to 1, `s_leader` is set to point to the `proc` structure of the calling process, `s_sid` is set to the process ID, and `s_ttyvp` and `s_ttyp` are set to null pointers, since the new session doesn't have a controlling terminal.

Let's move to the `tty` structure. The kernel contains one of these structures for each terminal device and each pseudo-terminal device. (We talk more about pseudo terminals in Chapter 19.)

- `t_session` points to the `session` structure that has this terminal as its controlling terminal. (Note that the `tty` structure points to the `session` structure and vice versa.) This pointer is used by the terminal to send a hang-up signal to the session leader if the terminal loses carrier (Figure 9.7).

- `t_pgrp` points to the `pgrp` structure of the foreground process group. This field is used by the terminal driver to send signals to the foreground process group. The three signals generated by entering special characters (interrupt, quit, and suspend) are sent to the foreground process group.

- `t_termios` is a structure containing all the special characters and related information for this terminal, such as baud rate, is echo on or off, and so on. We'll return to this structure in Chapter 18.

- `t_winsize` is a `winsize` structure that contains the current size of the terminal window. When the size of the terminal window changes, the `SIGWINCH` signal is sent to the foreground process group. We show how to set and fetch the terminal's current window size in Section 18.12.

Note that to find the foreground process group of a particular session, the kernel has to start with the session structure, follow `s_ttyp` to get to the controlling terminal's `tty` structure, and then follow `t_pgrp` to get to the foreground process group's `pgrp` structure. The `pgrp` structure contains the information for a particular process group.

- `pg_id` is the process group ID.

- `pg_session` points to the `session` structure for the session to which this process group belongs.

- `pg_members` is a pointer to the list of `proc` structures that are members of this process group. The `p_pglist` structure in that `proc` structure is a doubly-linked list entry that points to both the next process and the previous process in the group, and so on, until a null pointer is encountered in the `proc` structure of the last process in the group.

The `proc` structure contains all the information for a single process.

- `p_pid` contains the process ID.

- `p_pptr` is a pointer to the `proc` structure of the parent process.

- `p_pgrp` points to the `pgrp` structure of the process group to which this process belongs.

- `p_pglist` is a structure containing pointers to the next and previous processes in the process group, as we mentioned earlier.

Finally, we have the `vnode` structure. This structure is allocated when the controlling terminal device is opened. All references to `/dev/tty` in a process go through this `vnode` structure. We show the actual i-node as being part of the v-node.

9.12 Summary

This chapter has described the relationships between groups of processes: sessions, which are made up of process groups. Job control is a feature supported by most UNIX systems today, and we've described how it's implemented by a shell that supports job control. The controlling terminal for a process, `/dev/tty`, is also involved in these process relationships.

We've made numerous references to the signals that are used in all these process relationships. The next chapter continues the discussion of signals, looking at all the UNIX System signals in detail.

Exercises

9.1 Refer back to our discussion of the `utmp` and `wtmp` files in Section 6.8. Why are the logout records written by the `init` process? Is this handled the same way for a network login?

9.2 Write a small program that calls `fork` and has the child create a new session. Verify that the child becomes a process group leader and that the child no longer has a controlling terminal.

10

Signals

10.1 Introduction

Signals are software interrupts. Most nontrivial application programs need to deal with signals. Signals provide a way of handling asynchronous events: a user at a terminal typing the interrupt key to stop a program or the next program in a pipeline terminating prematurely.

Signals have been provided since the early versions of the UNIX System, but the signal model provided with systems such as Version 7 was not reliable. Signals could get lost, and it was difficult for a process to turn off selected signals when executing critical regions of code. Both 4.3BSD and SVR3 made changes to the signal model, adding what are called *reliable signals*. But the changes made by Berkeley and AT&T were incompatible. Fortunately, POSIX.1 standardized the reliable-signal routines, and that is what we describe here.

In this chapter, we start with an overview of signals and a description of what each signal is normally used for. Then we look at the problems with earlier implementations. It is often important to understand what is wrong with an implementation before seeing how to do things correctly. This chapter contains numerous examples that are not entirely correct and a discussion of the defects.

10.2 Signal Concepts

First, every signal has a name. These names all begin with the three characters SIG. For example, SIGABRT is the abort signal that is generated when a process calls the abort function. SIGALRM is the alarm signal that is generated when the timer set by the alarm function goes off. Version 7 had 15 different signals; SVR4 and 4.4BSD both have 31 different signals. FreeBSD 5.2.1, Mac OS X 10.3, and Linux 2.4.22 support 31 different signals, whereas Solaris 9 supports 38 different signals. Both Linux and Solaris, however, support additional application-defined signals as real-time extensions (the real-time extensions in POSIX aren't covered in this book; refer to Gallmeister [1995] for more information).

These names are all defined by positive integer constants (the signal number) in the header <signal.h>.

> Implementations actually define the individual signals in an alternate header file, but this header file is included by <signal.h>. It is considered bad form for the kernel to include header files meant for user-level applications, so if the applications and the kernel both need the same definitions, the information is placed in a kernel header file that is then included by the user-level header file. Thus, both FreeBSD 5.2.1 and Mac OS X 10.3 define the signals in <sys/signal.h>. Linux 2.4.22 defines the signals in <bits/signum.h>, and Solaris 9 defines them in <sys/iso/signal_iso.h>.

No signal has a signal number of 0. We'll see in Section 10.9 that the kill function uses the signal number of 0 for a special case. POSIX.1 calls this value the *null signal*.

Numerous conditions can generate a signal.

- The terminal-generated signals occur when users press certain terminal keys. Pressing the DELETE key on the terminal (or Control-C on many systems) normally causes the interrupt signal (SIGINT) to be generated. This is how to stop a runaway program. (We'll see in Chapter 18 how this signal can be mapped to any character on the terminal.)

- Hardware exceptions generate signals: divide by 0, invalid memory reference, and the like. These conditions are usually detected by the hardware, and the kernel is notified. The kernel then generates the appropriate signal for the process that was running at the time the condition occurred. For example, SIGSEGV is generated for a process that executes an invalid memory reference.

- The kill(2) function allows a process to send any signal to another process or process group. Naturally, there are limitations: we have to be the owner of the process that we're sending the signal to, or we have to be the superuser.

- The kill(1) command allows us to send signals to other processes. This program is just an interface to the kill function. This command is often used to terminate a runaway background process.

- Software conditions can generate signals when something happens about which the process should be notified. These aren't hardware-generated conditions (as is the divide-by-0 condition), but software conditions. Examples are SIGURG (generated when out-of-band data arrives over a network connection), SIGPIPE (generated when a process writes to a pipe after the reader of the pipe has terminated), and SIGALRM (generated when an alarm clock set by the process expires).

Signals are classic examples of asynchronous events. Signals occur at what appear to be random times to the process. The process can't simply test a variable (such as errno) to see whether a signal has occurred; instead, the process has to tell the kernel "if and when this signal occurs, do the following."

We can tell the kernel to do one of three things when a signal occurs. We call this the *disposition* of the signal, or the *action* associated with a signal.

1. Ignore the signal. This works for most signals, but two signals can never be ignored: SIGKILL and SIGSTOP. The reason these two signals can't be ignored is to provide the kernel and the superuser with a surefire way of either killing or stopping any process. Also, if we ignore some of the signals that are generated by a hardware exception (such as illegal memory reference or divide by 0), the behavior of the process is undefined.

2. Catch the signal. To do this, we tell the kernel to call a function of ours whenever the signal occurs. In our function, we can do whatever we want to handle the condition. If we're writing a command interpreter, for example, when the user generates the interrupt signal at the keyboard, we probably want to return to the main loop of the program, terminating whatever command we were executing for the user. If the SIGCHLD signal is caught, it means that a child process has terminated, so the signal-catching function can call waitpid to fetch the child's process ID and termination status. As another example, if the process has created temporary files, we may want to write a signal-catching function for the SIGTERM signal (the termination signal that is the default signal sent by the kill command) to clean up the temporary files. Note that the two signals SIGKILL and SIGSTOP can't be caught.

3. Let the default action apply. Every signal has a default action, shown in Figure 10.1. Note that the default action for most signals is to terminate the process.

Figure 10.1 lists the names of all the signals, an indication of which systems support the signal, and the default action for the signal. The SUS column contains • if the signal is defined as part of the base POSIX.1 specification and **XSI** if it is defined as an XSI extension to the base.

When the default action is labeled "terminate+core," it means that a memory image of the process is left in the file named core of the current working directory of the process. (Because the file is named core, it shows how long this feature has been part of the UNIX System.) This file can be used with most UNIX System debuggers to examine the state of the process at the time it terminated.

> The generation of the core file is an implementation feature of most versions of the UNIX System. Although this feature is not part of POSIX.1, it is mentioned as a potential implementation-specific action in the Single UNIX Specification's XSI extension.

> The name of the core file varies among implementations. On FreeBSD 5.2.1, for example, the core file is named *cmdname*.core, where *cmdname* is the name of the command corresponding to the process that received the signal. On Mac OS X 10.3, the core file is named core.*pid*, where *pid* is the ID of the process that received the signal. (These systems allow the core filename to be configured via a sysctl parameter.)

> Most implementations leave the core file in the current working directory of the corresponding process; Mac OS X places all core files in /cores instead.

Name	Description	ISO C	SUS	FreeBSD 5.2.1	Linux 2.4.22	Mac OS X 10.3	Solaris 9	Default action
SIGABRT	abnormal termination (abort)	•	•	•	•	•	•	terminate+core
SIGALRM	timer expired (alarm)		•	•	•	•	•	terminate
SIGBUS	hardware fault		•	•	•	•	•	terminate+core
SIGCANCEL	threads library internal use						•	ignore
SIGCHLD	change in status of child		•	•	•	•	•	ignore
SIGCONT	continue stopped process		•	•	•	•	•	continue/ignore
SIGEMT	hardware fault			•	•	•	•	terminate+core
SIGFPE	arithmetic exception	•	•	•	•	•	•	terminate+core
SIGFREEZE	checkpoint freeze						•	ignore
SIGHUP	hangup		•	•	•	•	•	terminate
SIGILL	illegal instruction	•	•	•	•	•	•	terminate+core
SIGINFO	status request from keyboard			•		•		ignore
SIGINT	terminal interrupt character	•	•	•	•	•	•	terminate
SIGIO	asynchronous I/O			•	•	•	•	terminate/ignore
SIGIOT	hardware fault			•	•	•	•	terminate+core
SIGKILL	termination		•	•	•	•	•	terminate
SIGLWP	threads library internal use						•	ignore
SIGPIPE	write to pipe with no readers		•	•	•	•	•	terminate
SIGPOLL	pollable event (poll)		XSI		•		•	terminate
SIGPROF	profiling time alarm (setitimer)		XSI	•	•	•	•	terminate
SIGPWR	power fail/restart				•		•	terminate/ignore
SIGQUIT	terminal quit character		•	•	•	•	•	terminate+core
SIGSEGV	invalid memory reference	•	•	•	•	•	•	terminate+core
SIGSTKFLT	coprocessor stack fault				•			terminate
SIGSTOP	stop		•	•	•	•	•	stop process
SIGSYS	invalid system call		XSI	•	•	•	•	terminate+core
SIGTERM	termination	•	•	•	•	•	•	terminate
SIGTHAW	checkpoint thaw						•	ignore
SIGTRAP	hardware fault		XSI	•	•	•	•	terminate+core
SIGTSTP	terminal stop character		•	•	•	•	•	stop process
SIGTTIN	background read from control tty		•	•	•	•	•	stop process
SIGTTOU	background write to control tty		•	•	•	•	•	stop process
SIGURG	urgent condition (sockets)		•	•	•	•	•	ignore
SIGUSR1	user-defined signal		•	•	•	•	•	terminate
SIGUSR2	user-defined signal		•	•	•	•	•	terminate
SIGVTALRM	virtual time alarm (setitimer)		XSI	•	•	•	•	terminate
SIGWAITING	threads library internal use						•	ignore
SIGWINCH	terminal window size change			•	•	•	•	ignore
SIGXCPU	CPU limit exceeded (setrlimit)		XSI	•	•	•	•	terminate+core/ignore
SIGXFSZ	file size limit exceeded (setrlimit)		XSI	•	•	•	•	terminate+core/ignore
SIGXRES	resource control exceeded						•	ignore

Figure 10.1 UNIX System signals

The core file will not be generated if (a) the process was set-user-ID and the current user is not the owner of the program file, or (b) the process was set-group-ID and the current user is not the group owner of the file, (c) the user does not have permission to write in the current working directory, (d) the file already exists and the user does not have permission to write to it, or (e) the file is too big (recall the RLIMIT_CORE limit in Section 7.11). The permissions of the core file (assuming that the file doesn't already exist) are usually user-read and user-write, although Mac OS X sets only user-read.

In Figure 10.1, the signals with a description "hardware fault" correspond to implementation-defined hardware faults. Many of these names are taken from the original PDP-11 implementation of the UNIX System. Check your system's manuals to determine exactly what type of error these signals correspond to.

We now describe each of these signals in more detail.

SIGABRT   This signal is generated by calling the abort function (Section 10.17). The process terminates abnormally.

SIGALRM   This signal is generated when a timer set with the alarm function expires (see Section 10.10 for more details). This signal is also generated when an interval timer set by the setitimer(2) function expires.

SIGBUS   This indicates an implementation-defined hardware fault. Implementations usually generate this signal on certain types of memory faults, as we describe in Section 14.9.

SIGCANCEL This signal is used internally by the Solaris threads library. It is not meant for general use.

SIGCHLD   Whenever a process terminates or stops, the SIGCHLD signal is sent to the parent. By default, this signal is ignored, so the parent must catch this signal if it wants to be notified whenever a child's status changes. The normal action in the signal-catching function is to call one of the wait functions to fetch the child's process ID and termination status.

Earlier releases of System V had a similar signal named SIGCLD (without the H). The semantics of this signal were different from those of other signals, and as far back as SVR2, the manual page strongly discouraged its use in new programs. (Strangely enough, this warning disappeared in the SVR3 and SVR4 versions of the manual page.) Applications should use the standard SIGCHLD signal, but be aware that many systems define SIGCLD to be the same as SIGCHLD for backward compatibility. If you maintain software that uses SIGCLD, you need to check your system's manual page to see what semantics it follows. We discuss these two signals in Section 10.7.

SIGCONT   This job-control signal is sent to a stopped process when it is continued. The default action is to continue a stopped process, but to ignore the signal if the process wasn't stopped. A full-screen editor, for example, might catch this signal and use the signal handler to make a note to redraw the terminal screen. See Section 10.20 for additional details.

SIGEMT   This indicates an implementation-defined hardware fault.

The name EMT comes from the PDP-11 "emulator trap" instruction. Not all platforms support this signal. On Linux, for example, SIGEMT is supported only for selected architectures, such as SPARC, MIPS, and PA-RISC.

SIGFPE   This signals an arithmetic exception, such as divide by 0, floating-point overflow, and so on.

SIGFREEZE   This signal is defined only by Solaris. It is used to notify processes that need to take special action before freezing the system state, such as might happen when a system goes into hibernation or suspended mode.

SIGHUP   This signal is sent to the controlling process (session leader) associated with a controlling terminal if a disconnect is detected by the terminal interface. Referring to Figure 9.12, we see that the signal is sent to the process pointed to by the s_leader field in the session structure. This signal is generated for this condition only if the terminal's CLOCAL flag is not set. (The CLOCAL flag for a terminal is set if the attached terminal is local. The flag tells the terminal driver to ignore all modem status lines. We describe how to set this flag in Chapter 18.)

               Note that the session leader that receives this signal may be in the background; see Figure 9.7 for an example. This differs from the normal terminal-generated signals (interrupt, quit, and suspend), which are always delivered to the foreground process group.

               This signal is also generated if the session leader terminates. In this case, the signal is sent to each process in the foreground process group.

               This signal is commonly used to notify daemon processes (Chapter 13) to reread their configuration files. The reason SIGHUP is chosen for this is that a daemon should not have a controlling terminal and would normally never receive this signal.

SIGILL   This signal indicates that the process has executed an illegal hardware instruction.

               4.3BSD generated this signal from the abort function. SIGABRT is now used for this.

SIGINFO   This BSD signal is generated by the terminal driver when we type the status key (often Control-T). This signal is sent to all processes in the foreground process group (refer to Figure 9.8). This signal normally causes status information on processes in the foreground process group to be displayed on the terminal.

               Linux doesn't provide support for SIGINFO except on the Alpha platform, where it is defined to be the same value as SIGPWR.

SIGINT   This signal is generated by the terminal driver when we type the interrupt key (often DELETE or Control-C). This signal is sent to all processes in the foreground process group (refer to Figure 9.8). This signal is often used to terminate a runaway program, especially when it's generating a lot of unwanted output on the screen.

SIGIO   This signal indicates an asynchronous I/O event. We discuss it in Section 14.6.2.

In Figure 10.1, we labeled the default action for SIGIO as either "terminate" or "ignore." Unfortunately, the default depends on the system. Under System V, SIGIO is identical to SIGPOLL, so its default action is to terminate the process. Under BSD, the default is to ignore the signal.

Linux 2.4.22 and Solaris 9 define SIGIO to be the same value as SIGPOLL, so the default behavior is to terminate the process. On FreeBSD 5.2.1 and Mac OS X 10.3, the default is to ignore the signal.

SIGIOT   This indicates an implementation-defined hardware fault.

The name IOT comes from the PDP-11 mnemonic for the "input/output TRAP" instruction. Earlier versions of System V generated this signal from the abort function. SIGABRT is now used for this.

On FreeBSD 5.2.1, Linux 2.4.22, Mac OS X 10.3, and Solaris 9, SIGIOT is defined to be the same value as SIGABRT.

SIGKILL   This signal is one of the two that can't be caught or ignored. It provides the system administrator with a sure way to kill any process.

SIGLWP   This signal is used internally by the Solaris threads library, and is not available for general use.

SIGPIPE   If we write to a pipeline but the reader has terminated, SIGPIPE is generated. We describe pipes in Section 15.2. This signal is also generated when a process writes to a socket of type SOCK_STREAM that is no longer connected. We describe sockets in Chapter 16.

SIGPOLL   This signal can be generated when a specific event occurs on a pollable device. We describe this signal with the poll function in Section 14.5.2. SIGPOLL originated with SVR3, and loosely corresponds to the BSD SIGIO and SIGURG signals.

On Linux and Solaris, SIGPOLL is defined to have the same value as SIGIO.

SIGPROF   This signal is generated when a profiling interval timer set by the setitimer(2) function expires.

SIGPWR   This signal is system dependent. Its main use is on a system that has an uninterruptible power supply (UPS). If power fails, the UPS takes over and the software can usually be notified. Nothing needs to be done at this point, as the system continues running on battery power. But if the battery gets low (if the power is off for an extended period), the software is usually notified again; at this point, it behooves the system to shut everything down within about 15–30 seconds. This is when SIGPWR should be sent. Most systems have the process that is notified of the low-battery condition send the SIGPWR signal to the init process, and init handles the shutdown.

Linux 2.4.22 and Solaris 9 have entries in the inittab file for this purpose: powerfail and powerwait (or powerokwait).

In Figure 10.1, we labeled the default action for SIGPWR as either "terminate" or "ignore." Unfortunately, the default depends on the system. The default on Linux is to terminate the process. On Solaris, the signal is ignored by default.

SIGQUIT   This signal is generated by the terminal driver when we type the terminal quit key (often Control-backslash). This signal is sent to all processes in the foreground process group (refer to Figure 9.8). This signal not only terminates the foreground process group (as does SIGINT), but also generates a `core` file.

SIGSEGV   This signal indicates that the process has made an invalid memory reference.

> The name SEGV stands for "segmentation violation."

SIGSTKFLT   This signal is defined only by Linux. This signal showed up in the earliest versions of Linux, intended to be used for stack faults taken by the math coprocessor. This signal is not generated by the kernel, but remains for backward compatibility.

SIGSTOP   This job-control signal stops a process. It is like the interactive stop signal (SIGTSTP), but SIGSTOP cannot be caught or ignored.

SIGSYS   This signals an invalid system call. Somehow, the process executed a machine instruction that the kernel thought was a system call, but the parameter with the instruction that indicates the type of system call was invalid. This might happen if you build a program that uses a new system call and you then try to run the same binary on an older version of the operating system where the system call doesn't exist.

SIGTERM   This is the termination signal sent by the `kill(1)` command by default.

SIGTHAW   This signal is defined only by Solaris and is used to notify processes that need to take special action when the system resumes operation after being suspended.

SIGTRAP   This indicates an implementation-defined hardware fault.

> The signal name comes from the PDP-11 TRAP instruction. Implementations often use this signal to transfer control to a debugger when a breakpoint instruction is executed.

SIGTSTP   This interactive stop signal is generated by the terminal driver when we type the terminal suspend key (often Control-Z). This signal is sent to all processes in the foreground process group (refer to Figure 9.8).

> Unfortunately, the term *stop* has different meanings. When discussing job control and signals, we talk about stopping and continuing jobs. The terminal driver, however, has historically used the term *stop* to refer to stopping and starting the terminal output using the Control-S and Control-Q characters. Therefore, the terminal driver calls the character that generates the interactive stop signal the suspend character, not the stop character.

SIGTTIN   This signal is generated by the terminal driver when a process in a background process group tries to read from its controlling terminal. (Refer to the discussion of this topic in Section 9.8.) As special cases, if either (a) the reading process is ignoring or blocking this signal or (b) the process group of the reading process is orphaned, then the signal is not generated; instead, the read operation returns an error with `errno` set to EIO.

SIGTTOU   This signal is generated by the terminal driver when a process in a background process group tries to write to its controlling terminal. (Refer to the discussion of this topic in Section 9.8.) Unlike the SIGTTIN signal just described, a process has a choice of allowing background writes to the controlling terminal. We describe how to change this option in Chapter 18.

If background writes are not allowed, then like the SIGTTIN signal, there are two special cases: if either (a) the writing process is ignoring or blocking this signal or (b) the process group of the writing process is orphaned, then the signal is not generated; instead, the write operation returns an error with `errno` set to EIO.

Regardless of whether background writes are allowed, certain terminal operations (other than writing) can also generate the SIGTTOU signal: `tcsetattr`, `tcsendbreak`, `tcdrain`, `tcflush`, `tcflow`, and `tcsetpgrp`. We describe these terminal operations in Chapter 18.

SIGURG   This signal notifies the process that an urgent condition has occurred. This signal is optionally generated when out-of-band data is received on a network connection.

SIGUSR1   This is a user-defined signal, for use in application programs.

SIGUSR2   This is another user-defined signal, similar to SIGUSR1, for use in application programs.

SIGVTALRM   This signal is generated when a virtual interval timer set by the `setitimer`(2) function expires.

SIGWAITING   This signal is used internally by the Solaris threads library, and is not available for general use.

SIGWINCH   The kernel maintains the size of the window associated with each terminal and pseudo terminal. A process can get and set the window size with the `ioctl` function, which we describe in Section 18.12. If a process changes the window size from its previous value using the `ioctl` set-window-size command, the kernel generates the SIGWINCH signal for the foreground process group.

SIGXCPU   The Single UNIX Specification supports the concept of resource limits as an XSI extension; refer to Section 7.11. If the process exceeds its soft CPU time limit, the SIGXCPU signal is generated.

In Figure 10.1, we labeled the default action for SIGXCPU as either "terminate with a core file" or "ignore." Unfortunately, the default depends on the operating system. Linux 2.4.22 and Solaris 9 support a default action of terminate with a core file, whereas FreeBSD 5.2.1 and Mac OS X 10.3 support a default action of ignore. The Single UNIX Specification requires that the default action be to terminate the process abnormally. Whether a core file is generated is left up to the implementation.

SIGXFSZ   This signal is generated if the process exceeds its soft file size limit; refer to Section 7.11.

Just as with SIGXCPU, the default action taken with SIGXFSZ depends on the operating system. On Linux 2.4.22 and Solaris 9, the default is to terminate the process and create a core file. On FreeBSD 5.2.1 and Mac OS X 10.3, the default is to be ignored. The Single UNIX Specification requires that the default action be to terminate the process abnormally. Whether a core file is generated is left up to the implementation.

SIGXRES   This signal is defined only by Solaris. This signal is optionally used to notify processes that have exceeded a preconfigured resource value. The Solaris resource control mechanism is a general facility for controlling the use of shared resources among independent application sets.

10.3   signal Function

The simplest interface to the signal features of the UNIX System is the signal function.

```
#include <signal.h>

void (*signal(int signo, void (*func)(int)))(int);
```

Returns: previous disposition of signal (see following) if OK, SIG_ERR on error

The signal function is defined by ISO C, which doesn't involve multiple processes, process groups, terminal I/O, and the like. Therefore, its definition of signals is vague enough to be almost useless for UNIX systems.

Implementations derived from UNIX System V support the signal function, but it provides the old unreliable-signal semantics. (We describe these older semantics in Section 10.4.) This function provides backward compatibility for applications that require the older semantics. New applications should not use these unreliable signals.

4.4BSD also provides the signal function, but it is defined in terms of the sigaction function (which we describe in Section 10.14), so using it under 4.4BSD provides the newer reliable-signal semantics. FreeBSD 5.2.1 and Mac OS X 10.3 follow this strategy.

Solaris 9 has roots in both System V and BSD, but it chooses to follow the System V semantics for the signal function.

On Linux 2.4.22, the semantic of signal can follow either the BSD or System V semantics, depending on the version of the C library and how you compile your application.

Because the semantics of signal differ among implementations, it is better to use the sigaction function instead. When we describe the sigaction function in Section 10.14, we provide an implementation of signal that uses it. All the examples in this text use the signal function that we show in Figure 10.18.

The *signo* argument is just the name of the signal from Figure 10.1. The value of *func* is (a) the constant SIG_IGN, (b) the constant SIG_DFL, or (c) the address of a function to be called when the signal occurs. If we specify SIG_IGN, we are telling the system to ignore the signal. (Remember that we cannot ignore the two signals SIGKILL and SIGSTOP.) When we specify SIG_DFL, we are setting the action associated with the signal to its default value (see the final column in Figure 10.1). When we specify the address of a function to be called when the signal occurs, we are arranging to "catch" the signal. We call the function either the *signal handler* or the *signal-catching function*.

The prototype for the signal function states that the function requires two arguments and returns a pointer to a function that returns nothing (void). The signal function's first argument, *signo*, is an integer. The second argument is a pointer to a function that takes a single integer argument and returns nothing. The function whose address is returned as the value of signal takes a single integer argument (the final (int)). In plain English, this declaration says that the signal handler is passed a single integer argument (the signal number) and that it returns nothing. When we call signal to establish the signal handler, the second argument is a pointer to the function. The return value from signal is the pointer to the previous signal handler.

> Many systems call the signal handler with additional, implementation-dependent arguments. We discuss this further in Section 10.14.

The perplexing signal function prototype shown at the beginning of this section can be made much simpler through the use of the following typedef [Plauger 1992]:

```
typedef void Sigfunc(int);
```

Then the prototype becomes

```
Sigfunc *signal(int, Sigfunc *);
```

We've included this typedef in apue.h (Appendix B) and use it with the functions in this chapter.

If we examine the system's header <signal.h>, we probably find declarations of the form

```
#define SIG_ERR    (void (*)())-1
#define SIG_DFL    (void (*)())0
#define SIG_IGN    (void (*)())1
```

These constants can be used in place of the "pointer to a function that takes an integer argument and returns nothing," the second argument to signal, and the return value from signal. The three values used for these constants need not be −1, 0, and 1. They must be three values that can never be the address of any declarable function. Most UNIX systems use the values shown.

Example

Figure 10.2 shows a simple signal handler that catches either of the two user-defined signals and prints the signal number. In Section 10.10, we describe the pause function, which simply suspends the calling process until a signal is received.

```
#include "apue.h"

static void sig_usr(int);    /* one handler for both signals */

int
main(void)
{
    if (signal(SIGUSR1, sig_usr) == SIG_ERR)
        err_sys("can't catch SIGUSR1");
    if (signal(SIGUSR2, sig_usr) == SIG_ERR)
        err_sys("can't catch SIGUSR2");
    for ( ; ; )
        pause();
}

static void
sig_usr(int signo)           /* argument is signal number */
{
    if (signo == SIGUSR1)
        printf("received SIGUSR1\n");
    else if (signo == SIGUSR2)
        printf("received SIGUSR2\n");
    else
        err_dump("received signal %d\n", signo);
}
```

Figure 10.2 Simple program to catch SIGUSR1 and SIGUSR2

We invoke the program in the background and use the kill(1) command to send it signals. Note that the term *kill* in the UNIX System is a misnomer. The kill(1) command and the kill(2) function just send a signal to a process or process group. Whether or not that signal terminates the process depends on which signal is sent and whether the process has arranged to catch the signal.

```
$ ./a.out &                      start process in background
[1]      7216                     job-control shell prints job number and process ID
$ kill -USR1 7216                 send it SIGUSR1
received SIGUSR1
$ kill -USR2 7216                 send it SIGUSR2
received SIGUSR2
$ kill 7216                       now send it SIGTERM
[1]+  Terminated        ./a.out
```

When we send the SIGTERM signal, the process is terminated, since it doesn't catch the signal, and the default action for the signal is termination.   □

Program Start-Up

When a program is executed, the status of all signals is either default or ignore. Normally, all signals are set to their default action, unless the process that calls exec is ignoring the signal. Specifically, the exec functions change the disposition of any signals being caught to their default action and leave the status of all other signals alone. (Naturally, a signal that is being caught by a process that calls exec cannot be caught by the same function in the new program, since the address of the signal-catching function in the caller probably has no meaning in the new program file that is executed.)

One specific example is how an interactive shell treats the interrupt and quit signals for a background process. With a shell that doesn't support job control, when we execute a process in the background, as in

```
cc main.c &
```

the shell automatically sets the disposition of the interrupt and quit signals in the background process to be ignored. This is so that if we type the interrupt character, it doesn't affect the background process. If this weren't done and we typed the interrupt character, it would terminate not only the foreground process, but also all the background processes.

Many interactive programs that catch these two signals have code that looks like

```
void sig_int(int), sig_quit(int);

if (signal(SIGINT, SIG_IGN) != SIG_IGN)
    signal(SIGINT, sig_int);
if (signal(SIGQUIT, SIG_IGN) != SIG_IGN)
    signal(SIGQUIT, sig_quit);
```

Doing this, the process catches the signal only if the signal is not currently being ignored.

These two calls to signal also show a limitation of the signal function: we are not able to determine the current disposition of a signal without changing the disposition. We'll see later in this chapter how the sigaction function allows us to determine a signal's disposition without changing it.

Process Creation

When a process calls fork, the child inherits the parent's signal dispositions. Here, since the child starts off with a copy of the parent's memory image, the address of a signal-catching function has meaning in the child.

10.4 Unreliable Signals

In earlier versions of the UNIX System (such as Version 7), signals were unreliable. By this we mean that signals could get lost: a signal could occur and the process would never know about it. Also, a process had little control over a signal: a process could catch the signal or ignore it. Sometimes, we would like to tell the kernel to block a signal: don't ignore it, just remember if it occurs, and tell us later when we're ready.

> Changes were made with 4.2BSD to provide what are called *reliable signals*. A different set of changes was then made in SVR3 to provide reliable signals under System V. POSIX.1 chose the BSD model to standardize.

One problem with these early versions is that the action for a signal was reset to its default each time the signal occurred. (In the previous example, when we ran the program in Figure 10.2, we avoided this detail by catching each signal only once.) The classic example from programming books that described these earlier systems concerns how to handle the interrupt signal. The code that was described usually looked like

```
int      sig_int();          /* my signal handling function */

    ...

    signal(SIGINT, sig_int); /* establish handler */
    ...

sig_int()
{
    signal(SIGINT, sig_int); /* reestablish handler for next time */
    ...                      /* process the signal ... */
}
```

(The reason the signal handler is declared as returning an integer is that these early systems didn't support the ISO C void data type.)

The problem with this code fragment is that there is a window of time—after the signal has occurred, but before the call to signal in the signal handler—when the interrupt signal could occur another time. This second signal would cause the default action to occur, which for this signal terminates the process. This is one of those conditions that works correctly most of the time, causing us to think that it is correct, when it isn't.

Another problem with these earlier systems is that the process was unable to turn a signal off when it didn't want the signal to occur. All the process could do was ignore the signal. There are times when we would like to tell the system "prevent the following signals from occurring, but remember if they do occur." The classic example that demonstrates this flaw is shown by a piece of code that catches a signal and sets a flag for the process that indicates that the signal occurred:

```
int    sig_int_flag;              /* set nonzero when signal occurs */

main()
{
    int     sig_int();            /* my signal handling function */
    ...
    signal(SIGINT, sig_int);      /* establish handler */
    ...
    while (sig_int_flag == 0)
        pause();                  /* go to sleep, waiting for signal */
    ...
}

sig_int()
{
    signal(SIGINT, sig_int);      /* reestablish handler for next time */
    sig_int_flag = 1;             /* set flag for main loop to examine */
}
```

Here, the process is calling the `pause` function to put it to sleep until a signal is caught. When the signal is caught, the signal handler just sets the flag `sig_int_flag` to a nonzero value. The process is automatically awakened by the kernel after the signal handler returns, notices that the flag is nonzero, and does whatever it needs to do. But there is a window of time when things can go wrong. If the signal occurs after the test of `sig_int_flag`, but before the call to `pause`, the process could go to sleep forever (assuming that the signal is never generated again). This occurrence of the signal is lost. This is another example of some code that isn't right, yet it works most of the time. Debugging this type of problem can be difficult.

10.5   Interrupted System Calls

A characteristic of earlier UNIX systems is that if a process caught a signal while the process was blocked in a "slow" system call, the system call was interrupted. The system call returned an error and `errno` was set to `EINTR`. This was done under the assumption that since a signal occurred and the process caught it, there is a good chance that something has happened that should wake up the blocked system call.

> Here, we have to differentiate between a system call and a function. It is a system call within the kernel that is interrupted when a signal is caught.

To support this feature, the system calls are divided into two categories: the "slow" system calls and all the others. The slow system calls are those that can block forever. Included in this category are

- Reads that can block the caller forever if data isn't present with certain file types (pipes, terminal devices, and network devices)

- Writes that can block the caller forever if the data can't be accepted immediately by these same file types

- Opens that block until some condition occurs on certain file types (such as an open of a terminal device that waits until an attached modem answers the phone)

- The `pause` function (which by definition puts the calling process to sleep until a signal is caught) and the `wait` function

- Certain `ioctl` operations

- Some of the interprocess communication functions (Chapter 15)

The notable exception to these slow system calls is anything related to disk I/O. Although a read or a write of a disk file can block the caller temporarily (while the disk driver queues the request and then the request is executed), unless a hardware error occurs, the I/O operation always returns and unblocks the caller quickly.

One condition that is handled by interrupted system calls, for example, is when a process initiates a read from a terminal device and the user at the terminal walks away from the terminal for an extended period. In this example, the process could be blocked for hours or days and would remain so unless the system was taken down.

POSIX.1 semantics for interrupted reads and writes changed with the 2001 version of the standard. Earlier versions gave implementations a choice for how to deal with reads and writes that have processed partial amounts of data. If read has received and transferred data to an application's buffer, but has not yet received all that the application requested and is then interrupted, the operating system could either fail the system call with errno set to EINTR or allow the system call to succeed, returning the partial amount of data received. Similarly, if write is interrupted after transferring some of the data in an application's buffer, the operation system could either fail the system call with errno set to EINTR or allow the system call to succeed, returning the partial amount of data written. Historically, implementations derived from System V fail the system call, whereas BSD-derived implementations return partial success. With the 2001 version of the POSIX.1 standard, the BSD-style semantics are required.

The problem with interrupted system calls is that we now have to handle the error return explicitly. The typical code sequence (assuming a read operation and assuming that we want to restart the read even if it's interrupted) would be

```
again:
    if ((n = read(fd, buf, BUFFSIZE)) < 0) {
        if (errno == EINTR)
            goto again;      /* just an interrupted system call */
        /* handle other errors */
    }
```

To prevent applications from having to handle interrupted system calls, 4.2BSD introduced the automatic restarting of certain interrupted system calls. The system calls that were automatically restarted are ioctl, read, readv, write, writev, wait, and waitpid. As we've mentioned, the first five of these functions are interrupted by a signal only if they are operating on a slow device; wait and waitpid are always interrupted when a signal is caught. Since this caused a problem for some applications that didn't want the operation restarted if it was interrupted, 4.3BSD allowed the process to disable this feature on a per signal basis.

POSIX.1 allows an implementation to restart system calls, but it is not required. The Single UNIX Specification defines the SA_RESTART flag as an XSI extension to sigaction to allow applications to request that interrupted system calls be restarted.

System V has never restarted system calls by default. BSD, on the other hand, restarts them if interrupted by signals. By default, FreeBSD 5.2.1, Linux 2.4.22, and Mac OS X 10.3 restart system calls interrupted by signals. The default on Solaris 9, however, is to return an error (EINTR) instead.

One of the reasons 4.2BSD introduced the automatic restart feature is that sometimes we don't know that the input or output device is a slow device. If the program we write can be used interactively, then it might be reading or writing a slow device, since terminals fall into this category. If we catch signals in this program, and if the system doesn't provide the restart capability, then we have to test every read or write for the interrupted error return and reissue the read or write.

Figure 10.3 summarizes the signal functions and their semantics provided by the various implementations.

We don't discuss the older sigset and sigvec functions. Their use has been superceded by the sigaction function; they are included only for completeness. In contrast, some implementations promote the signal function as a simplified interface to sigaction.

Functions	System	Signal handler remains installed	Ability to block signals	Automatic restart of interrupted system calls?
signal	ISO C, POSIX.1	unspecified	unspecified	unspecified
	V7, SVR2, SVR3, SVR4, Solaris			never
	4.2BSD	•	•	always
	4.3BSD, 4.4BSD, FreeBSD, Linux, Mac OS X	•	•	default
sigset	XSI	•	•	unspecified
	SVR3, SVR4, Linux, Solaris	•	•	never
sigvec	4.2BSD	•	•	always
	4.3BSD, 4.4BSD, FreeBSD, Mac OS X	•	•	default
sigaction	POSIX.1	•	•	unspecified
	XSI, 4.4BSD, SVR4, FreeBSD, Mac OS X, Linux, Solaris	•	•	optional

Figure 10.3 Features provided by various signal implementations

Be aware that UNIX systems from other vendors can have values different from those shown in this figure. For example, sigaction under SunOS 4.1.2 restarts an interrupted system call by default, different from the platforms listed in Figure 10.3.

In Figure 10.18, we provide our own version of the signal function that automatically tries to restart interrupted system calls (other than for the SIGALRM signal). In Figure 10.19, we provide another function, signal_intr, that tries to never do the restart.

We talk more about interrupted system calls in Section 14.5 with regard to the select and poll functions.

10.6 Reentrant Functions

When a signal that is being caught is handled by a process, the normal sequence of instructions being executed by the process is temporarily interrupted by the signal handler. The process then continues executing, but the instructions in the signal handler are now executed. If the signal handler returns (instead of calling exit or longjmp, for example), then the normal sequence of instructions that the process was executing when the signal was caught continues executing. (This is similar to what happens when a hardware interrupt occurs.) But in the signal handler, we can't tell where the process was executing when the signal was caught. What if the process was in the middle of allocating additional memory on its heap using malloc, and we call `malloc` from the signal handler? Or, what if the process was in the middle of a call to a function, such as `getpwnam` (Section 6.2), that stores its result in a static location, and we call the same function from the signal handler? In the `malloc` example, havoc can result for the process, since `malloc` usually maintains a linked list of all its allocated areas, and it may have been in the middle of changing this list. In the case of `getpwnam`, the information returned to the normal caller can get overwritten with the information returned to the signal handler.

The Single UNIX Specification specifies the functions that are guaranteed to be reentrant. Figure 10.4 lists these reentrant functions.

abort	_exit	lseek	setgid	symlink
accept	fchmod	lstat	setpgid	sysconf
access	fchown	mkdir	setsid	tcdrain
aio_error	fcntl	mkfifo	setsockopt	tcflow
aio_return	fdatasync	open	setuid	tcflush
aio_suspend	fork	pathconf	shutdown	tcgetattr
alarm	fpathconf	pause	sigaction	tcgetpgrp
bind	fstat	pipe	sigaddset	tcsendbreak
cfgetispeed	fsync	poll	sigdelset	tcsetattr
cfgetospeed	ftruncate	posix_trace_event	sigemptyset	tcsetpgrp
cfsetispeed	getegid	pselect	sigfillset	time
cfsetospeed	geteuid	raise	sigismember	timer_getoverrun
chdir	getgid	read	signal	timer_gettime
chmod	getgroups	readlink	sigpause	timer_settime
chown	getpeername	recv	sigpending	times
clock_gettime	getpgrp	recvfrom	sigprocmask	umask
close	getpid	recvmsg	sigqueue	uname
connect	getppid	rename	sigset	unlink
creat	getsockname	rmdir	sigsuspend	utime
dup	getsockopt	select	sleep	wait
dup2	getuid	sem_post	sockatmark	waitpid
execle	kill	send	socket	write
execve	link	sendmsg	socketpair	
_Exit	listen	sendto	stat	

Figure 10.4 Reentrant functions that may be called from a signal handler

Most functions that are not in Figure 10.4 are missing because (a) they are known to use static data structures, (b) they call `malloc` or `free`, or (c) they are part of the standard I/O library. Most implementations of the standard I/O library use global data structures in a nonreentrant way. Note that even though we call `printf` from signal handlers in some of our examples, it is not guaranteed to produce the expected results, since the signal hander can interrupt a call to `printf` from our main program.

Be aware that even if we call a function listed in Figure 10.4 from a signal handler, there is only one `errno` variable per thread (recall the discussion of `errno` and threads in Section 1.7), and we might modify its value. Consider a signal handler that is invoked right after `main` has set `errno`. If the signal handler calls `read`, for example, this call can change the value of `errno`, wiping out the value that was just stored in `main`. Therefore, as a general rule, when calling the functions listed in Figure 10.4 from a signal handler, we should save and restore `errno`. (Be aware that a commonly caught signal is `SIGCHLD`, and its signal handler usually calls one of the `wait` functions. All the `wait` functions can change `errno`.)

Note that `longjmp` (Section 7.10) and `siglongjmp` (Section 10.15) are missing from Figure 10.4, because the signal may have occurred while the main routine was updating a data structure in a nonreentrant way. This data structure could be left half updated if we call `siglongjmp` instead of returning from the signal handler. If it is going to do such things as update global data structures, as we describe here, while catching signals that cause `sigsetjmp` to be executed, an application needs to block the signals while updating the data structures.

Example

Figure 10.5 shows a program that calls the nonreentrant function `getpwnam` from a signal handler that is called every second. We describe the `alarm` function in Section 10.10. We use it here to generate a `SIGALRM` signal every second.

```
#include "apue.h"
#include <pwd.h>

static void
my_alarm(int signo)
{
    struct passwd   *rootptr;

    printf("in signal handler\n");
    if ((rootptr = getpwnam("root")) == NULL)
            err_sys("getpwnam(root) error");
    alarm(1);
}

int
main(void)
{
    struct passwd   *ptr;

    signal(SIGALRM, my_alarm);
    alarm(1);
    for ( ; ; ) {
        if ((ptr = getpwnam("sar")) == NULL)
            err_sys("getpwnam error");
        if (strcmp(ptr->pw_name, "sar") != 0)
            printf("return value corrupted!, pw_name = %s\n",
                    ptr->pw_name);
    }
}
```

Figure 10.5 Call a nonreentrant function from a signal handler

When this program was run, the results were random. Usually, the program would be terminated by a `SIGSEGV` signal when the signal handler returned after several iterations. An examination of the `core` file showed that the `main` function had called getpwnam, but that some internal pointers had been corrupted when the signal handler called the same function. Occasionally, the program would run for several seconds before crashing with a SIGSEGV error. When the main function did run correctly after the signal had been caught, the return value was sometimes corrupted and sometimes fine. Once (on Mac OS X), messages were printed from the malloc library routine warning about freeing pointers not allocated through malloc.

As shown by this example, if we call a nonreentrant function from a signal handler, the results are unpredictable.   □

10.7 SIGCLD Semantics

Two signals that continually generate confusion are SIGCLD and SIGCHLD. First, SIGCLD (without the H) is the System V name, and this signal has different semantics from the BSD signal, named SIGCHLD. The POSIX.1 signal is also named SIGCHLD.

The semantics of the BSD SIGCHLD signal are normal, in that its semantics are similar to those of all other signals. When the signal occurs, the status of a child has changed, and we need to call one of the wait functions to determine what has happened.

System V, however, has traditionally handled the SIGCLD signal differently from other signals. SVR4-based systems continue this questionable tradition (i.e., compatibility constraint) if we set its disposition using either signal or sigset (the older, SVR3-compatible functions to set the disposition of a signal). This older handling of SIGCLD consists of the following.

1. If the process specifically sets its disposition to SIG_IGN, children of the calling process will not generate zombie processes. Note that this is different from its default action (SIG_DFL), which from Figure 10.1 is to be ignored. Instead, on termination, the status of these child processes is discarded. If it subsequently calls one of the wait functions, the calling process will block until all its children have terminated, and then wait returns −1 with errno set to ECHILD. (The default disposition of this signal is to be ignored, but this default will not cause the preceding semantics to occur. Instead, we specifically have to set its disposition to SIG_IGN.)

> POSIX.1 does not specify what happens when SIGCHLD is ignored, so this behavior is allowed. The Single UNIX Specification includes an XSI extension specifying that this behavior be supported for SIGCHLD.

> 4.4BSD always generates zombies if SIGCHLD is ignored. If we want to avoid zombies, we have to wait for our children. FreeBSD 5.2.1 works like 4.4BSD. Mac OS X 10.3, however, doesn't create zombies when SIGCHLD is ignored.

> With SVR4, if either signal or sigset is called to set the disposition of SIGCHLD to be ignored, zombies are never generated. Solaris 9 and Linux 2.4.22 follow SVR4 in this behavior.

> With sigaction, we can set the SA_NOCLDWAIT flag (Figure 10.16) to avoid zombies. This action is supported on all four platforms: FreeBSD 5.2.1, Linux 2.4.22, Mac OS X 10.3, and Solaris 9.

2. If we set the disposition of SIGCLD to be caught, the kernel immediately checks whether any child processes are ready to be waited for and, if so, calls the SIGCLD handler.

Item 2 changes the way we have to write a signal handler for this signal, as illustrated in the following example.

Example

Recall from Section 10.4 that the first thing to do on entry to a signal handler is to call signal again, to reestablish the handler. (This action was to minimize the window of time when the signal is reset back to its default and could get lost.) We show this in Figure 10.6. This program doesn't work on some platforms. If we compile and run it under a traditional System V platform, such as OpenServer 5 or UnixWare 7, the output

```
#include     "apue.h"
#include     <sys/wait.h>

static void sig_cld(int);

int
main()
{
    pid_t   pid;

    if (signal(SIGCLD, sig_cld) == SIG_ERR)
        perror("signal error");
    if ((pid = fork()) < 0) {
        perror("fork error");
    } else if (pid == 0) {        /* child */
        sleep(2);
        _exit(0);
    }
    pause();     /* parent */
    exit(0);
}

static void
sig_cld(int signo)  /* interrupts pause() */
{
    pid_t   pid;
    int     status;

    printf("SIGCLD received\n");
    if (signal(SIGCLD, sig_cld) == SIG_ERR) /* reestablish handler */
        perror("signal error");
    if ((pid = wait(&status)) < 0)        /* fetch child status */
        perror("wait error");
    printf("pid = %d\n", pid);
}
```

Figure 10.6 System V SIGCLD handler that doesn't work

is a continual string of SIGCLD received lines. Eventually, the process runs out of stack space and terminates abnormally.

> FreeBSD 5.2.1 and Mac OS X 10.3 don't exhibit this problem, because BSD-based systems generally don't support historic System V semantics for SIGCLD. Linux 2.4.22 also doesn't exhibit this problem, because it doesn't call the SIGCHLD signal handler when a process arranges to catch SIGCHLD and child processes are ready to be waited for, even though SIGCLD and SIGCHLD are defined to be the same value. Solaris 9, on the other hand, does call the signal handler in this situation, but includes extra code in the kernel to avoid this problem.
>
> Although the four platforms described in this book solve this problem, realize that platforms (such as UnixWare) still exist that haven't addressed it.

The problem with this program is that the call to signal at the beginning of the signal handler invokes item 2 from the preceding discussion—the kernel checks whether a child needs to be waited for (which there is, since we're processing a SIGCLD signal), so it generates another call to the signal handler. The signal handler calls signal, and the whole process starts over again.

To fix this program, we have to move the call to signal after the call to wait. By doing this, we call signal after fetching the child's termination status; the signal is generated again by the kernel only if some other child has since terminated.

> POSIX.1 states that when we establish a signal handler for SIGCHLD and there exists a terminated child we have not yet waited for, it is unspecified whether the signal is generated. This allows the behavior described previously. But since POSIX.1 does not reset a signal's disposition to its default when the signal occurs (assuming that we're using the POSIX.1 sigaction function to set its disposition), there is no need for us to ever establish a signal handler for SIGCHLD within that handler.
>
> □

Be cognizant of the SIGCHLD semantics for your implementation. Be especially aware of some systems that #define SIGCHLD to be SIGCLD or vice versa. Changing the name may allow you to compile a program that was written for another system, but if that program depends on the other semantics, it may not work.

> On the four platforms described in this text, SIGCLD is equivalent to SIGCHLD.

10.8 Reliable-Signal Terminology and Semantics

We need to define some of the terms used throughout our discussion of signals. First, a signal is *generated* for a process (or sent to a process) when the event that causes the signal occurs. The event could be a hardware exception (e.g., divide by 0), a software condition (e.g., an alarm timer expiring), a terminal-generated signal, or a call to the kill function. When the signal is generated, the kernel usually sets a flag of some form in the process table.

We say that a signal is *delivered* to a process when the action for a signal is taken. During the time between the generation of a signal and its delivery, the signal is said to be *pending*.

A process has the option of *blocking* the delivery of a signal. If a signal that is blocked is generated for a process, and if the action for that signal is either the default action or to catch the signal, then the signal remains pending for the process until the process either (a) unblocks the signal or (b) changes the action to ignore the signal. The system determines what to do with a blocked signal when the signal is delivered, not when it's generated. This allows the process to change the action for the signal before it's delivered. The sigpending function (Section 10.13) can be called by a process to determine which signals are blocked and pending.

What happens if a blocked signal is generated more than once before the process unblocks the signal? POSIX.1 allows the system to deliver the signal either once or more than once. If the system delivers the signal more than once, we say that the signals are queued. Most UNIX systems, however, do *not* queue signals unless they support the real-time extensions to POSIX.1. Instead, the UNIX kernel simply delivers the signal once.

> The manual pages for SVR2 claimed that the SIGCLD signal was queued while the process was executing its SIGCLD signal handler. Although this might have been true on a conceptual level, the actual implementation was different. Instead, the signal was regenerated by the kernel as we described in Section 10.7. In SVR3, the manual was changed to indicate that the SIGCLD signal was ignored while the process was executing its signal handler for SIGCLD. The SVR4 manual removed any mention of what happens to SIGCLD signals that are generated while a process is executing its SIGCLD signal handler.

> The SVR4 sigaction(2) manual page in AT&T [1990e] claims that the SA_SIGINFO flag (Figure 10.16) causes signals to be reliably queued. This is wrong. Apparently, this feature was partially implemented within the kernel, but it is not enabled in SVR4. Curiously, the SVID doesn't make the same claims of reliable queuing.

What happens if more than one signal is ready to be delivered to a process? POSIX.1 does not specify the order in which the signals are delivered to the process. The Rationale for POSIX.1 does suggest, however, that signals related to the current state of the process be delivered before other signals. (SIGSEGV is one such signal.)

Each process has a *signal mask* that defines the set of signals currently blocked from delivery to that process. We can think of this mask as having one bit for each possible signal. If the bit is on for a given signal, that signal is currently blocked. A process can examine and change its current signal mask by calling sigprocmask, which we describe in Section 10.12.

Since it is possible for the number of signals to exceed the number of bits in an integer, POSIX.1 defines a data type, called sigset_t, that holds a *signal set*. The signal mask, for example, is stored in one of these signal sets. We describe five functions that operate on signal sets in Section 10.11.

10.9 kill and raise Functions

The kill function sends a signal to a process or a group of processes. The raise function allows a process to send a signal to itself.

> raise was originally defined by ISO C. POSIX.1 includes it to align itself with the ISO C standard, but POSIX.1 extends the specification of raise to deal with threads (we discuss how threads interact with signals in Section 12.8). Since ISO C does not deal with multiple processes, it could not define a function, such as kill, that requires a process ID argument.

```
#include <signal.h>

int kill(pid_t pid, int signo);

int raise(int signo);
```
                                                        Both return: 0 if OK, −1 on error

The call

```
    raise(signo);
```

is equivalent to the call

```
    kill(getpid(), signo);
```

There are four different conditions for the *pid* argument to `kill`.

pid > 0   The signal is sent to the process whose process ID is *pid*.

pid == 0   The signal is sent to all processes whose process group ID equals the
                process group ID of the sender and for which the sender has permission
                to send the signal. Note that the term *all processes* excludes an
                implementation-defined set of system processes. For most UNIX
                systems, this set of system processes includes the kernel processes and
                init (pid 1).

pid < 0   The signal is sent to all processes whose process group ID equals the
                absolute value of *pid* and for which the sender has permission to send the
                signal. Again, the set of all processes excludes certain system processes,
                as described earlier.

pid == −1   The signal is sent to all processes on the system for which the sender has
                permission to send the signal. As before, the set of processes excludes
                certain system processes.

As we've mentioned, a process needs permission to send a signal to another
process. The superuser can send a signal to any process. For other users, the basic rule
is that the real or effective user ID of the sender has to equal the real or effective user ID
of the receiver. If the implementation supports _POSIX_SAVED_IDS (as POSIX.1 now
requires), the saved set-user-ID of the receiver is checked instead of its effective user ID.
There is also one special case for the permission testing: if the signal being sent is
SIGCONT, a process can send it to any other process in the same session.

POSIX.1 defines signal number 0 as the null signal. If the *signo* argument is 0, then
the normal error checking is performed by `kill`, but no signal is sent. This is often
used to determine if a specific process still exists. If we send the process the null signal
and it doesn't exist, `kill` returns −1 and `errno` is set to ESRCH. Be aware, however,
that UNIX systems recycle process IDs after some amount of time, so the existence of a
process with a given process ID does not mean that it's the process that you think it is.

Also understand that the test for process existence is not atomic. By the time that
`kill` returns the answer to the caller, the process in question might have exited, so the
answer is of limited value.

If the call to kill causes the signal to be generated for the calling process and if the signal is not blocked, either *signo* or some other pending, unblocked signal is delivered to the process before kill returns. (Additional conditions occur with threads; see Section 12.8 for more information.)

10.10 alarm and pause Functions

The alarm function allows us to set a timer that will expire at a specified time in the future. When the timer expires, the SIGALRM signal is generated. If we ignore or don't catch this signal, its default action is to terminate the process.

```
#include <unistd.h>

unsigned int alarm(unsigned int seconds);
```
                                 Returns: 0 or number of seconds until previously set alarm

The *seconds* value is the number of clock seconds in the future when the signal should be generated. Be aware that when that time occurs, the signal is generated by the kernel, but there could be additional time before the process gets control to handle the signal, because of processor scheduling delays.

> Earlier UNIX System implementations warned that the signal could also be sent up to 1 second early. POSIX.1 does not allow this.

There is only one of these alarm clocks per process. If, when we call alarm, a previously registered alarm clock for the process has not yet expired, the number of seconds left for that alarm clock is returned as the value of this function. That previously registered alarm clock is replaced by the new value.

If a previously registered alarm clock for the process has not yet expired and if the *seconds* value is 0, the previous alarm clock is canceled. The number of seconds left for that previous alarm clock is still returned as the value of the function.

Although the default action for SIGALRM is to terminate the process, most processes that use an alarm clock catch this signal. If the process then wants to terminate, it can perform whatever cleanup is required before terminating. If we intend to catch SIGALRM, we need to be careful to install its signal handler before calling alarm. If we call alarm first and are sent SIGALRM before we can install the signal handler, our process will terminate.

The pause function suspends the calling process until a signal is caught.

```
#include <unistd.h>

int pause(void);
```
                                                       Returns: −1 with errno set to EINTR

The only time pause returns is if a signal handler is executed and that handler returns. In that case, pause returns −1 with errno set to EINTR.

Example

Using `alarm` and `pause`, we can put a process to sleep for a specified amount of time. The `sleep1` function in Figure 10.7 appears to do this (but it has problems, as we shall see shortly).

```
#include     <signal.h>
#include     <unistd.h>

static void
sig_alrm(int signo)
{
    /* nothing to do, just return to wake up the pause */
}

unsigned int
sleep1(unsigned int nsecs)
{
    if (signal(SIGALRM, sig_alrm) == SIG_ERR)
        return(nsecs);
    alarm(nsecs);            /* start the timer */
    pause();                 /* next caught signal wakes us up */
    return(alarm(0));        /* turn off timer, return unslept time */
}
```

Figure 10.7 Simple, incomplete implementation of `sleep`

This function looks like the `sleep` function, which we describe in Section 10.19, but this simple implementation has three problems.

1. If the caller already has an alarm set, that alarm is erased by the first call to `alarm`. We can correct this by looking at the return value from the first call to `alarm`. If the number of seconds until some previously set alarm is less than the argument, then we should wait only until the previously set alarm expires. If the previously set alarm will go off after ours, then before returning we should reset this alarm to occur at its designated time in the future.

2. We have modified the disposition for `SIGALRM`. If we're writing a function for others to call, we should save the disposition when we're called and restore it when we're done. We can correct this by saving the return value from `signal` and resetting the disposition before we return.

3. There is a race condition between the first call to `alarm` and the call to `pause`. On a busy system, it's possible for the alarm to go off and the signal handler to be called before we call `pause`. If that happens, the caller is suspended forever in the call to `pause` (assuming that some other signal isn't caught).

Earlier implementations of `sleep` looked like our program, with problems 1 and 2 corrected as described. There are two ways to correct problem 3. The first uses `setjmp`, which we show in the next example. The other uses `sigprocmask` and `sigsuspend`, and we describe it in Section 10.19.   □

Example

The SVR2 implementation of sleep used setjmp and longjmp (Section 7.10) to avoid the race condition described in problem 3 of the previous example. A simple version of this function, called sleep2, is shown in Figure 10.8. (To reduce the size of this example, we don't handle problems 1 and 2 described earlier.)

```c
#include    <setjmp.h>
#include    <signal.h>
#include    <unistd.h>

static jmp_buf  env_alrm;

static void
sig_alrm(int signo)
{
    longjmp(env_alrm, 1);
}

unsigned int
sleep2(unsigned int nsecs)
{
    if (signal(SIGALRM, sig_alrm) == SIG_ERR)
        return(nsecs);
    if (setjmp(env_alrm) == 0) {
        alarm(nsecs);           /* start the timer */
        pause();                /* next caught signal wakes us up */
    }
    return(alarm(0));           /* turn off timer, return unslept time */
}
```

Figure 10.8 Another (imperfect) implementation of sleep

The sleep2 function avoids the race condition from Figure 10.7. Even if the pause is never executed, the sleep2 function returns when the SIGALRM occurs.

There is, however, another subtle problem with the sleep2 function that involves its interaction with other signals. If the SIGALRM interrupts some other signal handler, when we call longjmp, we abort the other signal handler. Figure 10.9 shows this scenario. The loop in the SIGINT handler was written so that it executes for longer than 5 seconds on one of the systems used by the author. We simply want it to execute longer than the argument to sleep2. The integer k is declared volatile to prevent an optimizing compiler from discarding the loop. Executing the program shown in Figure 10.9 gives us

```
$ ./a.out
^?                          we type the interrupt character
sig_int starting
sleep2 returned: 0
```

We can see that the longjmp from the sleep2 function aborted the other signal handler, sig_int, even though it wasn't finished. This is what you'll encounter if you mix the SVR2 sleep function with other signal handling. See Exercise 10.3.   □

```
#include "apue.h"

unsigned int    sleep2(unsigned int);
static void     sig_int(int);

int
main(void)
{
    unsigned int    unslept;

    if (signal(SIGINT, sig_int) == SIG_ERR)
        err_sys("signal(SIGINT) error");
    unslept = sleep2(5);
    printf("sleep2 returned: %u\n", unslept);
    exit(0);
}

static void
sig_int(int signo)
{
    int             i, j;
    volatile int    k;

    /*
     * Tune these loops to run for more than 5 seconds
     * on whatever system this test program is run.
     */
    printf("\nsig_int starting\n");
    for (i = 0; i < 300000; i++)
        for (j = 0; j < 4000; j++)
            k += i * j;
    printf("sig_int finished\n");
}
```

Figure 10.9 Calling `sleep2` from a program that catches other signals

The purpose of these two examples, the `sleep1` and `sleep2` functions, is to show the pitfalls in dealing naively with signals. The following sections will show ways around all these problems, so we can handle signals reliably, without interfering with other pieces of code.

Example

A common use for `alarm`, in addition to implementing the `sleep` function, is to put an upper time limit on operations that can block. For example, if we have a `read` operation on a device that can block (a "slow" device, as described in Section 10.5), we might want the `read` to time out after some amount of time. The program in Figure 10.10 does this, reading one line from standard input and writing it to standard output.

```
#include "apue.h"

static void sig_alrm(int);

int
main(void)
{
    int     n;
    char    line[MAXLINE];

    if (signal(SIGALRM, sig_alrm) == SIG_ERR)
        err_sys("signal(SIGALRM) error");

    alarm(10);
    if ((n = read(STDIN_FILENO, line, MAXLINE)) < 0)
        err_sys("read error");
    alarm(0);

    write(STDOUT_FILENO, line, n);
    exit(0);
}

static void
sig_alrm(int signo)
{
    /* nothing to do, just return to interrupt the read */
}
```

Figure 10.10 Calling read with a timeout

This sequence of code is common in UNIX applications, but this program has two problems.

1. The program in Figure 10.10 has one of the same flaws that we described in Figure 10.7: a race condition between the first call to alarm and the call to read. If the kernel blocks the process between these two function calls for longer than the alarm period, the read could block forever. Most operations of this type use a long alarm period, such as a minute or more, making this unlikely; nevertheless, it is a race condition.

2. If system calls are automatically restarted, the read is not interrupted when the SIGALRM signal handler returns. In this case, the timeout does nothing.

Here, we specifically want a slow system call to be interrupted. POSIX.1 does not give us a portable way to do this; however, the XSI extension in the Single UNIX Specification does. We'll discuss this more in Section 10.14.   □

Example

Let's redo the preceding example using longjmp. This way, we don't need to worry about whether a slow system call is interrupted.

```
#include "apue.h"
#include <setjmp.h>

static void     sig_alrm(int);
static jmp_buf  env_alrm;

int
main(void)
{
    int     n;
    char    line[MAXLINE];

    if (signal(SIGALRM, sig_alrm) == SIG_ERR)
        err_sys("signal(SIGALRM) error");
    if (setjmp(env_alrm) != 0)
        err_quit("read timeout");

    alarm(10);
    if ((n = read(STDIN_FILENO, line, MAXLINE)) < 0)
        err_sys("read error");
    alarm(0);

    write(STDOUT_FILENO, line, n);
    exit(0);
}

static void
sig_alrm(int signo)
{
    longjmp(env_alrm, 1);
}
```

Figure 10.11 Calling `read` with a timeout, using `longjmp`

This version works as expected, regardless of whether the system restarts interrupted system calls. Realize, however, that we still have the problem of interactions with other signal handlers, as in Figure 10.8.   □

If we want to set a time limit on an I/O operation, we need to use `longjmp`, as shown previously, realizing its possible interaction with other signal handlers. Another option is to use the `select` or `poll` functions, described in Sections 14.5.1 and 14.5.2.

10.11 Signal Sets

We need a data type to represent multiple signals—a *signal set*. We'll use this with such functions as `sigprocmask` (in the next section) to tell the kernel not to allow any of the signals in the set to occur. As we mentioned earlier, the number of different signals can exceed the number of bits in an integer, so in general, we can't use an integer to represent the set with one bit per signal. POSIX.1 defines the data type `sigset_t` to contain a signal set and the following five functions to manipulate signal sets.

```
#include <signal.h>

int sigemptyset(sigset_t *set);

int sigfillset(sigset_t *set);

int sigaddset(sigset_t *set, int signo);

int sigdelset(sigset_t *set, int signo);
```

All four return: 0 if OK, −1 on error

```
int sigismember(const sigset_t *set, int signo);
```

Returns: 1 if true, 0 if false, −1 on error

The function `sigemptyset` initializes the signal set pointed to by *set* so that all signals are excluded. The function `sigfillset` initializes the signal set so that all signals are included. All applications have to call either `sigemptyset` or `sigfillset` once for each signal set, before using the signal set, because we cannot assume that the C initialization for external and static variables (0) corresponds to the implementation of signal sets on a given system.

Once we have initialized a signal set, we can add and delete specific signals in the set. The function `sigaddset` adds a single signal to an existing set, and `sigdelset` removes a single signal from a set. In all the functions that take a signal set as an argument, we always pass the address of the signal set as the argument.

Implementation

If the implementation has fewer signals than bits in an integer, a signal set can be implemented using one bit per signal. For the remainder of this section, assume that an implementation has 31 signals and 32-bit integers. The `sigemptyset` function zeros the integer, and the `sigfillset` function turns on all the bits in the integer. These two functions can be implemented as macros in the `<signal.h>` header:

```
#define sigemptyset(ptr)    (*(ptr) = 0)
#define sigfillset(ptr)     (*(ptr) = ~(sigset_t)0, 0)
```

Note that `sigfillset` must return 0, in addition to setting all the bits on in the signal set, so we use C's comma operator, which returns the value after the comma as the value of the expression.

Using this implementation, `sigaddset` turns on a single bit and `sigdelset` turns off a single bit; `sigismember` tests a certain bit. Since no signal is ever numbered 0, we subtract 1 from the signal number to obtain the bit to manipulate. Figure 10.12 shows implementations of these functions.

```
#include     <signal.h>
#include     <errno.h>

/* <signal.h> usually defines NSIG to include signal number 0 */
#define SIGBAD(signo)    ((signo) <= 0 || (signo) >= NSIG)

int
sigaddset(sigset_t *set, int signo)
{
    if (SIGBAD(signo)) { errno = EINVAL; return(-1); }

    *set |= 1 << (signo - 1);          /* turn bit on */
    return(0);
}

int
sigdelset(sigset_t *set, int signo)
{
    if (SIGBAD(signo)) { errno = EINVAL; return(-1); }

    *set &= ~(1 << (signo - 1));     /* turn bit off */
    return(0);
}

int
sigismember(const sigset_t *set, int signo)
{
    if (SIGBAD(signo)) { errno = EINVAL; return(-1); }

    return(((*set & (1 << (signo - 1))) != 0);
}
```

Figure 10.12 An implementation of `sigaddset`, `sigdelset`, and `sigismember`

We might be tempted to implement these three functions as one-line macros in the
`<signal.h>` header, but POSIX.1 requires us to check the signal number argument for
validity and to set `errno` if it is invalid. This is more difficult to do in a macro than in a
function.

10.12 `sigprocmask` Function

Recall from Section 10.8 that the signal mask of a process is the set of signals currently
blocked from delivery to that process. A process can examine its signal mask, change its
signal mask, or perform both operations in one step by calling the following function.

```
#include <signal.h>

int sigprocmask(int how, const sigset_t *restrict set,
                sigset_t *restrict oset);
```
Returns: 0 if OK, −1 on error

First, if *oset* is a non-null pointer, the current signal mask for the process is returned through *oset*.

Second, if *set* is a non-null pointer, the *how* argument indicates how the current signal mask is modified. Figure 10.13 describes the possible values for *how*. SIG_BLOCK is an inclusive-OR operation, whereas SIG_SETMASK is an assignment. Note that SIGKILL and SIGSTOP can't be blocked.

how	Description
SIG_BLOCK	The new signal mask for the process is the union of its current signal mask and the signal set pointed to by *set*. That is, *set* contains the additional signals that we want to block.
SIG_UNBLOCK	The new signal mask for the process is the intersection of its current signal mask and the complement of the signal set pointed to by *set*. That is, *set* contains the signals that we want to unblock.
SIG_SETMASK	The new signal mask for the process is replaced by the value of the signal set pointed to by *set*.

Figure 10.13 Ways to change current signal mask using sigprocmask

If *set* is a null pointer, the signal mask of the process is not changed, and *how* is ignored.

After calling sigprocmask, if any unblocked signals are pending, at least one of these signals is delivered to the process before sigprocmask returns.

> The sigprocmask function is defined only for single-threaded processes. A separate function is provided to manipulate a thread's signal mask in a multithreaded process. We'll discuss this in Section 12.8.

Example

Figure 10.14 shows a function that prints the names of the signals in the signal mask of the calling process. We call this function from the programs shown in Figure 10.20 and Figure 10.22.

```
#include "apue.h"
#include <errno.h>

void
pr_mask(const char *str)
{
    sigset_t    sigset;
    int         errno_save;

    errno_save = errno;      /* we can be called by signal handlers */
    if (sigprocmask(0, NULL, &sigset) < 0)
        err_sys("sigprocmask error");

    printf("%s", str);
```

```
    if (sigismember(&sigset, SIGINT))    printf("SIGINT ");
    if (sigismember(&sigset, SIGQUIT))   printf("SIGQUIT ");
    if (sigismember(&sigset, SIGUSR1))   printf("SIGUSR1 ");
    if (sigismember(&sigset, SIGALRM))   printf("SIGALRM ");

    /* remaining signals can go here  */

    printf("\n");
    errno = errno_save;
}
```

Figure 10.14 Print the signal mask for the process

To save space, we don't test the signal mask for every signal that we listed in
Figure 10.1. (See Exercise 10.9.)   □

10.13 `sigpending` Function

The `sigpending` function returns the set of signals that are blocked from delivery and
currently pending for the calling process. The set of signals is returned through the *set*
argument.

```
#include <signal.h>

int sigpending(sigset_t *set);
```
                                                 Returns: 0 if OK, −1 on error

Example

Figure 10.15 shows many of the signal features that we've been describing.

```
#include "apue.h"

static void sig_quit(int);

int
main(void)
{
    sigset_t    newmask, oldmask, pendmask;

    if (signal(SIGQUIT, sig_quit) == SIG_ERR)
        err_sys("can't catch SIGQUIT");

    /*
     * Block SIGQUIT and save current signal mask.
     */
    sigemptyset(&newmask);
    sigaddset(&newmask, SIGQUIT);
```

```
        if (sigprocmask(SIG_BLOCK, &newmask, &oldmask) < 0)
            err_sys("SIG_BLOCK error");

        sleep(5);    /* SIGQUIT here will remain pending */

        if (sigpending(&pendmask) < 0)
            err_sys("sigpending error");
        if (sigismember(&pendmask, SIGQUIT))
            printf("\nSIGQUIT pending\n");

        /*
         * Reset signal mask which unblocks SIGQUIT.
         */
        if (sigprocmask(SIG_SETMASK, &oldmask, NULL) < 0)
            err_sys("SIG_SETMASK error");
        printf("SIGQUIT unblocked\n");

        sleep(5);    /* SIGQUIT here will terminate with core file */
        exit(0);
}

static void
sig_quit(int signo)
{
        printf("caught SIGQUIT\n");
        if (signal(SIGQUIT, SIG_DFL) == SIG_ERR)
            err_sys("can't reset SIGQUIT");
}
```

Figure 10.15 Example of signal sets and `sigprocmask`

The process blocks SIGQUIT, saving its current signal mask (to reset later), and then
goes to sleep for 5 seconds. Any occurrence of the quit signal during this period is
blocked and won't be delivered until the signal is unblocked. At the end of the
5-second sleep, we check whether the signal is pending and unblock the signal.

   Note that we saved the old mask when we blocked the signal. To unblock the
signal, we did a SIG_SETMASK of the old mask. Alternatively, we could SIG_UNBLOCK
only the signal that we had blocked. Be aware, however, if we write a function that can
be called by others and if we need to block a signal in our function, we can't use
SIG_UNBLOCK to unblock the signal. In this case, we have to use SIG_SETMASK and
reset the signal mask to its prior value, because it's possible that the caller had
specifically blocked this signal before calling our function. We'll see an example of this
in the system function in Section 10.18.

   If we generate the quit signal during this sleep period, the signal is now pending
and unblocked, so it is delivered before sigprocmask returns. We'll see this occur
because the printf in the signal handler is output before the printf that follows the
call to sigprocmask.

   The process then goes to sleep for another 5 seconds. If we generate the quit signal
during this sleep period, the signal should terminate the process, since we reset the

handling of the signal to its default when we caught it. In the following output, the terminal prints `^\` when we input Control-backslash, the terminal quit character:

```
$ ./a.out
^\                              generate signal once (before 5 seconds are up)
SIGQUIT pending                 after return from sleep
caught SIGQUIT                  in signal handler
SIGQUIT unblocked               after return from sigprocmask
^\Quit (coredump)               generate signal again
$ ./a.out
^\^\^\^\^\^\^\^\^\^\             generate signal 10 times (before 5 seconds are up)
SIGQUIT pending
caught SIGQUIT                  signal is generated only once
SIGQUIT unblocked
^\Quit (coredump)               generate signal again
```

The message `Quit(coredump)` is printed by the shell when it sees that its child terminated abnormally. Note that when we run the program the second time, we generate the quit signal ten times while the process is asleep, yet the signal is delivered only once to the process when it's unblocked. This demonstrates that signals are not queued on this system.   □

10.14 `sigaction` Function

The `sigaction` function allows us to examine or modify (or both) the action associated with a particular signal. This function supersedes the `signal` function from earlier releases of the UNIX System. Indeed, at the end of this section, we show an implementation of `signal` using `sigaction`.

```
#include <signal.h>

int sigaction(int signo, const struct sigaction *restrict act,
              struct sigaction *restrict oact);
```
                                                            Returns: 0 if OK, −1 on error

The argument *signo* is the signal number whose action we are examining or modifying. If the *act* pointer is non-null, we are modifying the action. If the *oact* pointer is non-null, the system returns the previous action for the signal through the *oact* pointer. This function uses the following structure:

```
struct sigaction {
  void      (*sa_handler)(int);     /* addr of signal handler, */
                                    /* or SIG_IGN, or SIG_DFL */
  sigset_t sa_mask;                 /* additional signals to block */
  int      sa_flags;                /* signal options, Figure 10.16 */

  /* alternate handler */
  void      (*sa_sigaction)(int, siginfo_t *, void *);
};
```

When changing the action for a signal, if the `sa_handler` field contains the address of a signal-catching function (as opposed to the constants `SIG_IGN` or `SIG_DFL`), then the `sa_mask` field specifies a set of signals that are added to the signal mask of the process before the signal-catching function is called. If and when the signal-catching function returns, the signal mask of the process is reset to its previous value. This way, we are able to block certain signals whenever a signal handler is invoked. The operating system includes the signal being delivered in the signal mask when the handler is invoked. Hence, we are guaranteed that whenever we are processing a given signal, another occurrence of that same signal is blocked until we're finished processing the first occurrence. Recall from Section 10.8 that additional occurrences of the same signal are usually not queued. If the signal occurs five times while it is blocked, when we unblock the signal, the signal-handling function for that signal will usually be invoked only one time.

Once we install an action for a given signal, that action remains installed until we explicitly change it by calling `sigaction`. Unlike earlier systems with their unreliable signals, POSIX.1 requires that a signal handler remain installed until explicitly changed.

The `sa_flags` field of the *act* structure specifies various options for the handling of this signal. Figure 10.16 details the meaning of these options when set. The SUS column contains • if the flag is defined as part of the base POSIX.1 specification, and **XSI** if it is defined as an XSI extension to the base.

The `sa_sigaction` field is an alternate signal handler used when the `SA_SIGINFO` flag is used with `sigaction`. Implementations might use the same storage for both the `sa_sigaction` field and the `sa_handler` field, so applications can use only one of these fields at a time.

Normally, the signal handler is called as

```
void handler(int signo);
```

but if the `SA_SIGINFO` flag is set, the signal handler is called as

```
void handler(int signo, siginfo_t *info, void *context);
```

The `siginfo_t` structure contains information about why the signal was generated. An example of what it might look like is shown below. All POSIX.1-compliant implementations must include at least the `si_signo` and `si_code` members. Additionally, implementations that are XSI compliant contain at least the following fields:

```
struct siginfo {
  int     si_signo;  /* signal number */
  int     si_errno;  /* if nonzero, errno value from <errno.h> */
  int     si_code;   /* additional info (depends on signal) */
  pid_t   si_pid;    /* sending process ID */
  uid_t   si_uid;    /* sending process real user ID */
  void    *si_addr;  /* address that caused the fault */
  int     si_status; /* exit value or signal number */
  long    si_band;   /* band number for SIGPOLL */
  /* possibly other fields also */
};
```

Option	SUS	FreeBSD 5.2.1	Linux 2.4.22	Mac OS X 10.3	Solaris 9	Description
SA_INTERRUPT			•			System calls interrupted by this signal are not automatically restarted (the XSI default for sigaction). See Section 10.5 for more information.
SA_NOCLDSTOP	•	•	•	•	•	If *signo* is SIGCHLD, do not generate this signal when a child process stops (job control). This signal is still generated, of course, when a child terminates (but see the SA_NOCLDWAIT option below). As an XSI extension, SIGCHLD won't be sent when a stopped child continues if this flag is set.
SA_NOCLDWAIT	XSI	•	•	•	•	If *signo* is SIGCHLD, this option prevents the system from creating zombie processes when children of the calling process terminate. If it subsequently calls wait, the calling process blocks until all its child processes have terminated and then returns −1 with errno set to ECHILD. (Recall Section 10.7.)
SA_NODEFER	XSI	•	•	•	•	When this signal is caught, the signal is not automatically blocked by the system while the signal-catching function executes (unless the signal is also included in sa_mask). Note that this type of operation corresponds to the earlier unreliable signals.
SA_ONSTACK	XSI	•	•	•	•	If an alternate stack has been declared with sigaltstack(2), this signal is delivered to the process on the alternate stack.
SA_RESETHAND	XSI	•	•	•	•	The disposition for this signal is reset to SIG_DFL, and the SA_SIGINFO flag is cleared on entry to the signal-catching function. Note that this type of operation corresponds to the earlier unreliable signals. The disposition for the two signals SIGILL and SIGTRAP can't be reset automatically, however. Setting this flag causes sigaction to behave as if SA_NODEFER is also set.
SA_RESTART	XSI	•	•	•	•	System calls interrupted by this signal are automatically restarted. (Refer to Section 10.5.)
SA_SIGINFO	•	•	•	•	•	This option provides additional information to a signal handler: a pointer to a siginfo structure and a pointer to an identifier for the process context.

Figure 10.16 Option flags (sa_flags) for the handling of each signal

Figure 10.17 shows values of si_code for various signals, as defined by the Single
UNIX Specification. Note that implementations may define additional code values.

Signal	Code	Reason
SIGILL	ILL_ILLOPC	illegal opcode
	ILL_ILLOPN	illegal operand
	ILL_ILLADR	illegal addressing mode
	ILL_ILLTRP	illegal trap
	ILL_PRVOPC	privileged opcode
	ILL_PRVREG	privileged register
	ILL_COPROC	coprocessor error
	ILL_BADSTK	internal stack error
SIGFPE	FPE_INTDIV	integer divide by zero
	FPE_INTOVF	integer overflow
	FPE_FLTDIV	floating-point divide by zero
	FPE_FLTOVF	floating-point overflow
	FPE_FLTUND	floating-point underflow
	FPE_FLTRES	floating-point inexact result
	FPE_FLTINV	invalid floating-point operation
	FPE_FLTSUB	subscript out of range
SIGSEGV	SEGV_MAPERR	address not mapped to object
	SEGV_ACCERR	invalid permissions for mapped object
SIGBUS	BUS_ADRALN	invalid address alignment
	BUS_ADRERR	nonexistent physical address
	BUS_OBJERR	object-specific hardware error
SIGTRAP	TRAP_BRKPT	process breakpoint trap
	TRAP_TRACE	process trace trap
SIGCHLD	CLD_EXITED	child has exited
	CLD_KILLED	child has terminated abnormally (no core)
	CLD_DUMPED	child has terminated abnormally with core
	CLD_TRAPPED	traced child has trapped
	CLD_STOPPED	child has stopped
	CLD_CONTINUED	stopped child has continued
SIGPOLL	POLL_IN	data can be read
	POLL_OUT	data can be written
	POLL_MSG	input message available
	POLL_ERR	I/O error
	POLL_PRI	high-priority message available
	POLL_HUP	device disconnected
Any	SI_USER	signal sent by kill
	SI_QUEUE	signal sent by sigqueue (real-time extension)
	SI_TIMER	expiration of a timer set by timer_settime (real-time extension)
	SI_ASYNCIO	completion of asynchronous I/O request (real-time extension)
	SI_MESGQ	arrival of a message on a message queue (real-time extension)

Figure 10.17 siginfo_t code values

If the signal is SIGCHLD, then the si_pid, si_status, and si_uid field will be
set. If the signal is SIGILL or SIGSEGV, then the si_addr contains the address
responsible for the fault, although the address might not be accurate. If the signal is
SIGPOLL, then the si_band field will contain the priority band for STREAMS

messages that generate the POLL_IN, POLL_OUT, or POLL_MSG events. (For a complete discussion of priority bands, see Rago [1993].) The si_errno field contains the error number corresponding to the condition that caused the signal to be generated, although its use is implementation defined.

The *context* argument to the signal handler is a typeless pointer that can be cast to a ucontext_t structure identifying the process context at the time of signal delivery.

> When an implementation supports the real-time signal extensions, signal handlers established with the SA_SIGINFO flag will result in signals being queued reliably. A separate range of reserved signals is available for real-time application use. The siginfo structure can contain application-specific data if the signal is generated by sigqueue. We do not discuss the real-time extensions further. Refer to Gallmeister [1995] for more details.

Example—signal Function

Let's now implement the signal function using sigaction. This is what many platforms do (and what a note in the POSIX.1 Rationale states was the intent of POSIX). Systems with binary compatibility constraints, on the other hand, might provide a signal function that supports the older, unreliable-signal semantics. Unless you specifically require these older, unreliable semantics (for backward compatibility), you should use the following implementation of signal or call sigaction directly. (As you might guess, an implementation of signal with the old semantics could call sigaction specifying SA_RESETHAND and SA_NODEFER.) All the examples in this text that call signal call the function shown in Figure 10.18.

```
#include "apue.h"

/* Reliable version of signal(), using POSIX sigaction().  */
Sigfunc *
signal(int signo, Sigfunc *func)
{
    struct sigaction    act, oact;

    act.sa_handler = func;
    sigemptyset(&act.sa_mask);
    act.sa_flags = 0;
    if (signo == SIGALRM) {
#ifdef   SA_INTERRUPT
        act.sa_flags |= SA_INTERRUPT;
#endif
    } else {
#ifdef   SA_RESTART
        act.sa_flags |= SA_RESTART;
#endif
    }
    if (sigaction(signo, &act, &oact) < 0)
        return(SIG_ERR);
    return(oact.sa_handler);
}
```

Figure 10.18 An implementation of signal using sigaction

Note that we must use `sigemptyset` to initialize the `sa_mask` member of the structure. We're not guaranteed that

```
act.sa_mask = 0;
```

does the same thing.

We intentionally try to set the `SA_RESTART` flag for all signals other than `SIGALRM`, so that any system call interrupted by these other signals is automatically restarted. The reason we don't want `SIGALRM` restarted is to allow us to set a timeout for I/O operations. (Recall the discussion of Figure 10.10.)

Some older systems, such as SunOS, define the `SA_INTERRUPT` flag. These systems restart interrupted system calls by default, so specifying this flag causes system calls to be interrupted. Linux defines the `SA_INTERRUPT` flag for compatibility with applications that use it, but the default is to not restart system calls when the signal handler is installed with `sigaction`. The XSI extension of the Single UNIX Specification specifies that the `sigaction` function not restart interrupted system calls unless the `SA_RESTART` flag is specified.   □

Example—`signal_intr` Function

Figure 10.19 shows a version of the `signal` function that tries to prevent any interrupted system calls from being restarted.

```
#include "apue.h"

Sigfunc *
signal_intr(int signo, Sigfunc *func)
{
    struct sigaction    act, oact;

    act.sa_handler = func;
    sigemptyset(&act.sa_mask);
    act.sa_flags = 0;
#ifdef  SA_INTERRUPT
    act.sa_flags |= SA_INTERRUPT;
#endif
    if (sigaction(signo, &act, &oact) < 0)
        return(SIG_ERR);
    return(oact.sa_handler);
}
```

Figure 10.19 The `signal_intr` function

For improved portability, we specify the `SA_INTERRUPT` flag, if defined by the system, to prevent interrupted system calls from being restarted.   □

10.15 `sigsetjmp` and `siglongjmp` Functions

In Section 7.10, we described the `setjmp` and `longjmp` functions, which can be used for nonlocal branching. The `longjmp` function is often called from a signal handler to return to the main loop of a program, instead of returning from the handler. We saw this in Figures 10.8 and 10.11.

There is a problem in calling longjmp, however. When a signal is caught, the signal-catching function is entered with the current signal automatically being added to the signal mask of the process. This prevents subsequent occurrences of that signal from interrupting the signal handler. If we longjmp out of the signal handler, what happens to the signal mask for the process?

> Under FreeBSD 5.2.1 and Mac OS X 10.3, setjmp and longjmp save and restore the signal mask. Linux 2.4.22 and Solaris 9, however, do not do this. FreeBSD and Mac OS X provide the functions _setjmp and _longjmp, which do not save and restore the signal mask.

To allow either form of behavior, POSIX.1 does not specify the effect of setjmp and longjmp on signal masks. Instead, two new functions, sigsetjmp and siglongjmp, are defined by POSIX.1. These two functions should always be used when branching from a signal handler.

```
#include <setjmp.h>

int sigsetjmp(sigjmp_buf env, int savemask);
```

                    Returns: 0 if called directly, nonzero if returning from a call to siglongjmp

```
void siglongjmp(sigjmp_buf env, int val);
```

The only difference between these functions and the setjmp and longjmp functions is that sigsetjmp has an additional argument. If *savemask* is nonzero, then sigsetjmp also saves the current signal mask of the process in *env*. When siglongjmp is called, if the *env* argument was saved by a call to sigsetjmp with a nonzero *savemask*, then siglongjmp restores the saved signal mask.

Example

The program in Figure 10.20 demonstrates how the signal mask that is installed by the system when a signal handler is invoked automatically includes the signal being caught. The program also illustrates the use of the sigsetjmp and siglongjmp functions.

```
#include "apue.h"
#include <setjmp.h>
#include <time.h>

static void                     sig_usr1(int), sig_alrm(int);
static sigjmp_buf               jmpbuf;
static volatile sig_atomic_t    canjump;

int
main(void)
{
    if (signal(SIGUSR1, sig_usr1) == SIG_ERR)
        err_sys("signal(SIGUSR1) error");
```

```
        if (signal(SIGALRM, sig_alrm) == SIG_ERR)
            err_sys("signal(SIGALRM) error");
        pr_mask("starting main: ");       /* Figure 10.14 */

        if (sigsetjmp(jmpbuf, 1)) {
            pr_mask("ending main: ");
            exit(0);
        }
        canjump = 1;    /* now sigsetjmp() is OK */

        for ( ; ; )
            pause();
}

static void
sig_usr1(int signo)
{
    time_t   starttime;

    if (canjump == 0)
        return;     /* unexpected signal, ignore */

    pr_mask("starting sig_usr1: ");
    alarm(3);                   /* SIGALRM in 3 seconds */
    starttime = time(NULL);
    for ( ; ; )                 /* busy wait for 5 seconds */
        if (time(NULL) > starttime + 5)
            break;
    pr_mask("finishing sig_usr1: ");

    canjump = 0;
    siglongjmp(jmpbuf, 1);   /* jump back to main, don't return */
}

static void
sig_alrm(int signo)
{
    pr_mask("in sig_alrm: ");
}
```

Figure 10.20 Example of signal masks, sigsetjmp, and siglongjmp

This program demonstrates another technique that should be used whenever siglongjmp is called from a signal handler. We set the variable canjump to a nonzero value only after we've called sigsetjmp. This variable is also examined in the signal handler, and siglongjmp is called only if the flag canjump is nonzero. This provides protection against the signal handler being called at some earlier or later time, when the jump buffer isn't initialized by sigsetjmp. (In this trivial program, we terminate quickly after the siglongjmp, but in larger programs, the signal handler may remain installed long after the siglongjmp.) Providing this type of protection usually isn't required with longjmp in normal C code (as opposed to a signal handler). Since a signal can occur at *any* time, however, we need the added protection in a signal handler.

Here, we use the data type sig_atomic_t, which is defined by the ISO C standard to be the type of variable that can be written without being interrupted. By this we mean that a variable of this type should not extend across page boundaries on a system with virtual memory and can be accessed with a single machine instruction, for example. We always include the ISO type qualifier volatile for these data types too, since the variable is being accessed by two different threads of control: the main function and the asynchronously executing signal handler. Figure 10.21 shows a time line for this program.

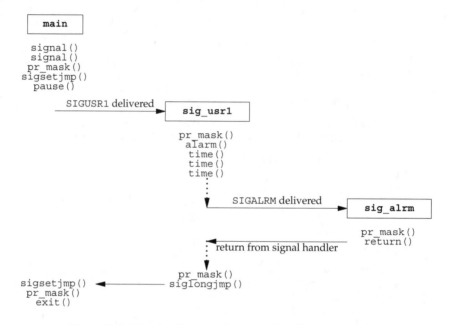

Figure 10.21 Time line for example program handling two signals

We can divide Figure 10.21 into three parts: the left part (corresponding to main), the center part (sig_usr1), and the right part (sig_alrm). While the process is executing in the left part, its signal mask is 0 (no signals are blocked). While executing in the center part, its signal mask is SIGUSR1. While executing in the right part, its signal mask is SIGUSR1 | SIGALRM.

Let's examine the output when the program in Figure 10.20 is executed:

```
$ ./a.out &                        start process in background
starting main:
[1]    531                         the job-control shell prints its process ID
$ kill -USR1 531                   send the process SIGUSR1
starting sig_usr1: SIGUSR1
$ in sig_alrm: SIGUSR1 SIGALRM
finishing sig_usr1: SIGUSR1
ending main:
                                   just press RETURN

[1] +  Done             ./a.out &
```

The output is as we expect: when a signal handler is invoked, the signal being caught is added to the current signal mask of the process. The original mask is restored when the signal handler returns. Also, `siglongjmp` restores the signal mask that was saved by `sigsetjmp`.

If we change the program in Figure 10.20 so that the calls to `sigsetjmp` and `siglongjmp` are replaced with calls to `setjmp` and `longjmp` on Linux (or `_setjmp` and `_longjmp` on FreeBSD), the final line of output becomes

```
ending main: SIGUSR1
```

This means that the `main` function is executing with the `SIGUSR1` signal blocked, after the call to `setjmp`. This probably isn't what we want.   □

10.16 `sigsuspend` **Function**

We have seen how we can change the signal mask for a process to block and unblock selected signals. We can use this technique to protect critical regions of code that we don't want interrupted by a signal. What if we want to unblock a signal and then pause, waiting for the previously blocked signal to occur? Assuming that the signal is `SIGINT`, the incorrect way to do this is

```
sigset_t    newmask, oldmask;

sigemptyset(&newmask);
sigaddset(&newmask, SIGINT);

/* block SIGINT and save current signal mask */
if (sigprocmask(SIG_BLOCK, &newmask, &oldmask) < 0)
    err_sys("SIG_BLOCK error");

/* critical region of code */

/* reset signal mask, which unblocks SIGINT */
if (sigprocmask(SIG_SETMASK, &oldmask, NULL) < 0)
    err_sys("SIG_SETMASK error");

/* window is open */
pause();  /* wait for signal to occur */

/* continue processing */
```

If the signal is sent to the process while it is blocked, the signal delivery will be deferred until the signal is unblocked. To the application, this can look as if the signal occurs between the unblocking and the `pause` (depending on how the kernel implements signals). If this happens, or if the signal does occur between the unblocking and the pause, we have a problem. Any occurrence of the signal in this window of time is lost in the sense that we might not see the signal again, in which case the `pause` will block indefinitely. This is another problem with the earlier unreliable signals.

To correct this problem, we need a way to both reset the signal mask and put the process to sleep in a single atomic operation. This feature is provided by the `sigsuspend` function.

```
#include <signal.h>

int sigsuspend(const sigset_t *sigmask);
```
Returns: −1 with errno set to EINTR

The signal mask of the process is set to the value pointed to by *sigmask*. Then the process is suspended until a signal is caught or until a signal occurs that terminates the process. If a signal is caught and if the signal handler returns, then sigsuspend returns, and the signal mask of the process is set to its value before the call to sigsuspend.

Note that there is no successful return from this function. If it returns to the caller, it always returns −1 with errno set to EINTR (indicating an interrupted system call).

Example

Figure 10.22 shows the correct way to protect a critical region of code from a specific signal.

```
#include "apue.h"

static void sig_int(int);

int
main(void)
{
    sigset_t    newmask, oldmask, waitmask;

    pr_mask("program start: ");

    if (signal(SIGINT, sig_int) == SIG_ERR)
        err_sys("signal(SIGINT) error");
    sigemptyset(&waitmask);
    sigaddset(&waitmask, SIGUSR1);
    sigemptyset(&newmask);
    sigaddset(&newmask, SIGINT);

    /*
     * Block SIGINT and save current signal mask.
     */
    if (sigprocmask(SIG_BLOCK, &newmask, &oldmask) < 0)
        err_sys("SIG_BLOCK error");

    /*
     * Critical region of code.
     */
    pr_mask("in critical region: ");

    /*
     * Pause, allowing all signals except SIGUSR1.
```

```
        */
        if (sigsuspend(&waitmask) != -1)
            err_sys("sigsuspend error");

        pr_mask("after return from sigsuspend: ");

        /*
         * Reset signal mask which unblocks SIGINT.
         */
        if (sigprocmask(SIG_SETMASK, &oldmask, NULL) < 0)
            err_sys("SIG_SETMASK error");

        /*
         * And continue processing ...
         */
        pr_mask("program exit: ");

        exit(0);
}

static void
sig_int(int signo)
{
        pr_mask("\nin sig_int: ");
}
```

Figure 10.22 Protecting a critical region from a signal

Note that when sigsuspend returns, it sets the signal mask to its value before the call. In this example, the SIGINT signal will be blocked. We therefore reset the signal mask to the value that we saved earlier (oldmask).

Running the program from Figure 10.22 produces the following output:

```
$ ./a.out
program start:
in critical region: SIGINT
^?                                      type the interrupt character
in sig_int: SIGINT SIGUSR1
after return from sigsuspend: SIGINT
program exit:
```

We added SIGUSR1 to the mask installed when we called sigsuspend so that when the signal handler ran, we could tell that the mask had actually changed. We can see that when sigsuspend returns, it restores the signal mask to its value before the call. □

Example

Another use of sigsuspend is to wait for a signal handler to set a global variable. In the program shown in Figure 10.23, we catch both the interrupt signal and the quit signal, but want to wake up the main routine only when the quit signal is caught.

```
#include "apue.h"

volatile sig_atomic_t    quitflag;    /* set nonzero by signal handler */

static void
sig_int(int signo)   /* one signal handler for SIGINT and SIGQUIT */
{
    if (signo == SIGINT)
        printf("\ninterrupt\n");
    else if (signo == SIGQUIT)
        quitflag = 1;    /* set flag for main loop */
}

int
main(void)
{
    sigset_t    newmask, oldmask, zeromask;

    if (signal(SIGINT, sig_int) == SIG_ERR)
        err_sys("signal(SIGINT) error");
    if (signal(SIGQUIT, sig_int) == SIG_ERR)
        err_sys("signal(SIGQUIT) error");

    sigemptyset(&zeromask);
    sigemptyset(&newmask);
    sigaddset(&newmask, SIGQUIT);

    /*
     * Block SIGQUIT and save current signal mask.
     */
    if (sigprocmask(SIG_BLOCK, &newmask, &oldmask) < 0)
        err_sys("SIG_BLOCK error");

    while (quitflag == 0)
        sigsuspend(&zeromask);

    /*
     * SIGQUIT has been caught and is now blocked; do whatever.
     */
    quitflag = 0;

    /*
     * Reset signal mask which unblocks SIGQUIT.
     */
    if (sigprocmask(SIG_SETMASK, &oldmask, NULL) < 0)
        err_sys("SIG_SETMASK error");

    exit(0);
}
```

Figure 10.23 Using sigsuspend to wait for a global variable to be set

Sample output from this program is

```
$ ./a.out
^?                          type the interrupt character
interrupt
^?                          type the interrupt character again
interrupt
^?                          and again
interrupt
^?                          and again
interrupt
^?                          and again
interrupt
^?                          and again
interrupt
^?                          and again
interrupt
^\ $                        now terminate with quit character
```

For portability between non-POSIX systems that support ISO C, and POSIX.1 systems, the only thing we should do within a signal handler is assign a value to a variable of type sig_atomic_t, and nothing else. POSIX.1 goes further and specifies a list of functions that are safe to call from within a signal handler (Figure 10.4), but if we do this, our code may not run correctly on non-POSIX systems.

Example

As another example of signals, we show how signals can be used to synchronize a parent and child. Figure 10.24 shows implementations of the five routines TELL_WAIT, TELL_PARENT, TELL_CHILD, WAIT_PARENT, and WAIT_CHILD from Section 8.9.

```c
#include "apue.h"

static volatile sig_atomic_t sigflag; /* set nonzero by sig handler */
static sigset_t newmask, oldmask, zeromask;

static void
sig_usr(int signo)   /* one signal handler for SIGUSR1 and SIGUSR2 */
{
    sigflag = 1;
}

void
TELL_WAIT(void)
{
    if (signal(SIGUSR1, sig_usr) == SIG_ERR)
        err_sys("signal(SIGUSR1) error");
    if (signal(SIGUSR2, sig_usr) == SIG_ERR)
        err_sys("signal(SIGUSR2) error");
    sigemptyset(&zeromask);
    sigemptyset(&newmask);
```

```
        sigaddset(&newmask, SIGUSR1);
        sigaddset(&newmask, SIGUSR2);

        /*
         * Block SIGUSR1 and SIGUSR2, and save current signal mask.
         */
        if (sigprocmask(SIG_BLOCK, &newmask, &oldmask) < 0)
            err_sys("SIG_BLOCK error");
    }

void
TELL_PARENT(pid_t pid)
{
    kill(pid, SIGUSR2);      /* tell parent we're done */
}

void
WAIT_PARENT(void)
{
    while (sigflag == 0)
        sigsuspend(&zeromask);   /* and wait for parent */
    sigflag = 0;

    /*
     * Reset signal mask to original value.
     */
    if (sigprocmask(SIG_SETMASK, &oldmask, NULL) < 0)
        err_sys("SIG_SETMASK error");
}

void
TELL_CHILD(pid_t pid)
{
    kill(pid, SIGUSR1);          /* tell child we're done */
}

void
WAIT_CHILD(void)
{
    while (sigflag == 0)
        sigsuspend(&zeromask);   /* and wait for child */
    sigflag = 0;

    /*
     * Reset signal mask to original value.
     */
    if (sigprocmask(SIG_SETMASK, &oldmask, NULL) < 0)
        err_sys("SIG_SETMASK error");
}
```

Figure 10.24 Routines to allow a parent and child to synchronize

We use the two user-defined signals: SIGUSR1 is sent by the parent to the child, and SIGUSR2 is sent by the child to the parent. In Figure 15.7, we show another implementation of these five functions using pipes.   □

The sigsuspend function is fine if we want to go to sleep while waiting for a signal to occur (as we've shown in the previous two examples), but what if we want to call other system functions while we're waiting? Unfortunately, this problem has no bulletproof solution unless we use multiple threads and dedicate a separate thread to handling signals, as we discuss in Section 12.8.

Without using threads, the best we can do is to set a global variable in the signal handler when the signal occurs. For example, if we catch both SIGINT and SIGALRM and install the signal handlers using the signal_intr function, the signals will interrupt any slow system call that is blocked. The signals are most likely to occur when we're blocked in a call to the select function (Section 14.5.1), waiting for input from a slow device. (This is especially true for SIGALRM, since we set the alarm clock to prevent us from waiting forever for input.) The code to handle this looks similar to the following:

```
if (intr_flag)        /* flag set by our SIGINT handler */
    handle_intr();
if (alrm_flag)        /* flag set by our SIGALRM handler */
    handle_alrm();

/* signals occurring in here are lost */

while (select( ... ) < 0) {
    if (errno == EINTR) {
        if (alrm_flag)
            handle_alrm();
        else if (intr_flag)
            handle_intr();
    } else {
        /* some other error */
    }
}
```

We test each of the global flags before calling select and again if select returns an interrupted system call error. The problem occurs if either signal is caught between the first two if statements and the subsequent call to select. Signals occurring in here are lost, as indicated by the code comment. The signal handlers are called, and they set the appropriate global variable, but the select never returns (unless some data is ready to be read).

What we would like to be able to do is the following sequence of steps, in order.

1. Block SIGINT and SIGALRM.

2. Test the two global variables to see whether either signal has occurred and, if so, handle the condition.

3. Call `select` (or any other system function, such as `read`) and unblock the two signals, as an atomic operation.

The `sigsuspend` function helps us only if step 3 is a `pause` operation.

10.17 `abort` Function

We mentioned earlier that the `abort` function causes abnormal program termination.

```
#include <stdlib.h>

void abort(void);
```
                                                                        This function never returns

This function sends the `SIGABRT` signal to the caller. (Processes should not ignore this signal.) ISO C states that calling `abort` will deliver an unsuccessful termination notification to the host environment by calling `raise(SIGABRT)`.

ISO C requires that if the signal is caught and the signal handler returns, `abort` still doesn't return to its caller. If this signal is caught, the only way the signal handler can't return is if it calls `exit`, `_exit`, `_Exit`, `longjmp`, or `siglongjmp`. (Section 10.15 discusses the differences between `longjmp` and `siglongjmp`.) POSIX.1 also specifies that `abort` overrides the blocking or ignoring of the signal by the process.

The intent of letting the process catch the `SIGABRT` is to allow it to perform any cleanup that it wants to do before the process terminates. If the process doesn't terminate itself from this signal handler, POSIX.1 states that, when the signal handler returns, `abort` terminates the process.

The ISO C specification of this function leaves it up to the implementation as to whether output streams are flushed and whether temporary files (Section 5.13) are deleted. POSIX.1 goes further and requires that if the call to `abort` terminates the process, then the effect on the open standard I/O streams in the process will be the same as if the process had called `fclose` on each stream before terminating.

> Earlier versions of System V generated the `SIGIOT` signal from the `abort` function. Furthermore, it was possible for a process to ignore this signal or to catch it and return from the signal handler, in which case `abort` returned to its caller.
>
> 4.3BSD generated the `SIGILL` signal. Before doing this, the 4.3BSD function unblocked the signal and reset its disposition to `SIG_DFL` (terminate with core file). This prevented a process from either ignoring the signal or catching it.
>
> Historically, implementations of `abort` differ in how they deal with standard I/O streams. For defensive programming and improved portability, if we want standard I/O streams to be flushed, we specifically do it before calling `abort`. We do this in the `err_dump` function (Appendix B).
>
> Since most UNIX System implementations of `tmpfile` call `unlink` immediately after creating the file, the ISO C warning about temporary files does not usually concern us.

Example

Figure 10.25 shows an implementation of the `abort` function as specified by POSIX.1.

```c
#include <signal.h>
#include <stdio.h>
#include <stdlib.h>
#include <unistd.h>

void
abort(void)              /* POSIX-style abort() function */
{
    sigset_t            mask;
    struct sigaction    action;

    /*
     * Caller can't ignore SIGABRT, if so reset to default.
     */
    sigaction(SIGABRT, NULL, &action);
    if (action.sa_handler == SIG_IGN) {
        action.sa_handler = SIG_DFL;
        sigaction(SIGABRT, &action, NULL);
    }
    if (action.sa_handler == SIG_DFL)
        fflush(NULL);                   /* flush all open stdio streams */

    /*
     * Caller can't block SIGABRT; make sure it's unblocked.
     */
    sigfillset(&mask);
    sigdelset(&mask, SIGABRT);  /* mask has only SIGABRT turned off */
    sigprocmask(SIG_SETMASK, &mask, NULL);
    kill(getpid(), SIGABRT);    /* send the signal */

    /*
     * If we're here, process caught SIGABRT and returned.
     */
    fflush(NULL);                       /* flush all open stdio streams */
    action.sa_handler = SIG_DFL;
    sigaction(SIGABRT, &action, NULL);  /* reset to default */
    sigprocmask(SIG_SETMASK, &mask, NULL);  /* just in case ... */
    kill(getpid(), SIGABRT);                /* and one more time */
    exit(1);    /* this should never be executed ... */
}
```

Figure 10.25 Implementation of POSIX.1 abort

We first see whether the default action will occur; if so, we flush all the standard I/O streams. This is not equivalent to an `fclose` on all the open streams (since it just flushes them and doesn't close them), but when the process terminates, the system closes all open files. If the process catches the signal and returns, we flush all the streams again, since the process could have generated more output. The only condition we don't handle is if the process catches the signal and calls _exit or _Exit. In this case, any unflushed standard I/O buffers in memory are discarded. We assume that a caller that does this doesn't want the buffers flushed.

Recall from Section 10.9 that if calling kill causes the signal to be generated for the caller, and if the signal is not blocked (which we guarantee in Figure 10.25), then the signal (or some other pending, unlocked signal) is delivered to the process before kill returns. We block all signals except SIGABRT, so we know that if the call to kill returns, the process caught the signal and the signal handler returned.   □

10.18 system Function

In Section 8.13, we showed an implementation of the system function. That version, however, did not do any signal handling. POSIX.1 requires that system ignore SIGINT and SIGQUIT and block SIGCHLD. Before showing a version that correctly handles these signals, let's see why we need to worry about signal handling.

Example

The program shown in Figure 10.26 uses the version of system from Section 8.13 to invoke the ed(1) editor. (This editor has been part of UNIX systems for a long time. We use it here because it is an interactive program that catches the interrupt and quit signals. If we invoke ed from a shell and type the interrupt character, it catches the interrupt signal and prints a question mark. The ed program also sets the disposition of the quit signal so that it is ignored.) The program in Figure 10.26 catches both SIGINT and SIGCHLD. If we invoke the program, we get

```
$ ./a.out
a                            append text to the editor's buffer
Here is one line of text
.                            period on a line by itself stops append mode
1,$p                         print first through last lines of buffer to see what's there
Here is one line of text
w temp.foo                   write the buffer to a file
25                           editor says it wrote 25 bytes
q                            and leave the editor
caught SIGCHLD
```

When the editor terminates, the system sends the SIGCHLD signal to the parent (the a.out process). We catch it and return from the signal handler. But if it is catching the SIGCHLD signal, the parent should be doing so because it has created its own children, so that it knows when its children have terminated. The delivery of this signal in the parent should be blocked while the system function is executing. Indeed, this is what POSIX.1 specifies. Otherwise, when the child created by system terminates, it would fool the caller of system into thinking that one of its own children terminated. The

```
#include "apue.h"

static void
sig_int(int signo)
{
    printf("caught SIGINT\n");
}

static void
sig_chld(int signo)
{
    printf("caught SIGCHLD\n");
}

int
main(void)
{
    if (signal(SIGINT, sig_int) == SIG_ERR)
        err_sys("signal(SIGINT) error");
    if (signal(SIGCHLD, sig_chld) == SIG_ERR)
        err_sys("signal(SIGCHLD) error");
    if (system("/bin/ed") < 0)
        err_sys("system() error");
    exit(0);
}
```

Figure 10.26 Using system to invoke the ed editor

caller would then use one of the wait functions to get the termination status of the child, thus preventing the system function from being able to obtain the child's termination status for its return value.

If we run the program again, this time sending the editor an interrupt signal, we get

```
$ ./a.out
a                          append text to the editor's buffer
hello, world
.                          period on a line by itself stops append mode
1,$p                       print first through last lines to see what's there
hello, world
w temp.foo                 write the buffer to a file
13                         editor says it wrote 13 bytes
^?                         type the interrupt character
?                          editor catches signal, prints question mark
caught SIGINT              and so does the parent process
q                          leave editor
caught SIGCHLD
```

Recall from Section 9.6 that typing the interrupt character causes the interrupt signal to be sent to all the processes in the foreground process group. Figure 10.27 shows the arrangement of the processes when the editor is running.

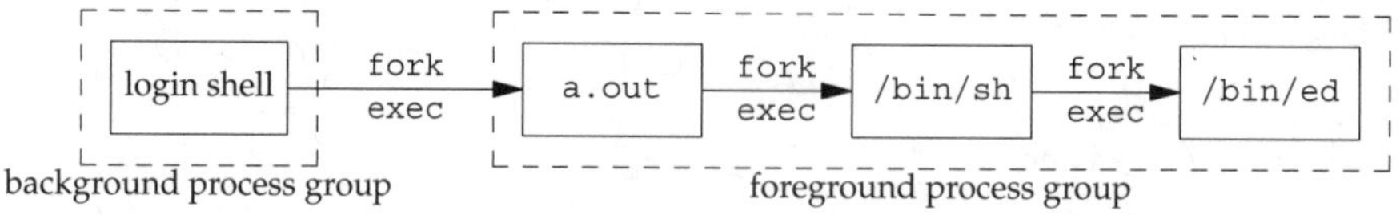

Figure 10.27 Foreground and background process groups for Figure 10.26

In this example, SIGINT is sent to all three foreground processes. (The shell ignores it.) As we can see from the output, both the a.out process and the editor catch the signal. But when we're running another program with the system function, we shouldn't have both the parent and the child catching the two terminal-generated signals: interrupt and quit. These two signals should really be sent to the program that is running: the child. Since the command that is executed by system can be an interactive command (as is the ed program in this example) and since the caller of system gives up control while the program executes, waiting for it to finish, the caller of system should not be receiving these two terminal-generated signals. This is why POSIX.1 specifies that the system function should ignore these two signals while waiting for the command to complete.   □

Example

Figure 10.28 shows an implementation of the system function with the required signal handling.

```
#include     <sys/wait.h>
#include     <errno.h>
#include     <signal.h>
#include     <unistd.h>

int
system(const char *cmdstring)    /* with appropriate signal handling */
{
    pid_t              pid;
    int                status;
    struct sigaction   ignore, saveintr, savequit;
    sigset_t           chldmask, savemask;

    if (cmdstring == NULL)
        return(1);       /* always a command processor with UNIX */

    ignore.sa_handler = SIG_IGN;     /* ignore SIGINT and SIGQUIT */
    sigemptyset(&ignore.sa_mask);
    ignore.sa_flags = 0;
    if (sigaction(SIGINT, &ignore, &saveintr) < 0)
        return(-1);
    if (sigaction(SIGQUIT, &ignore, &savequit) < 0)
        return(-1);
    sigemptyset(&chldmask);                 /* now block SIGCHLD */
    sigaddset(&chldmask, SIGCHLD);
```

```
    if (sigprocmask(SIG_BLOCK, &chldmask, &savemask) < 0)
        return(-1);

    if ((pid = fork()) < 0) {
        status = -1;        /* probably out of processes */
    } else if (pid == 0) {              /* child */
        /* restore previous signal actions & reset signal mask */
        sigaction(SIGINT, &saveintr, NULL);
        sigaction(SIGQUIT, &savequit, NULL);
        sigprocmask(SIG_SETMASK, &savemask, NULL);

        execl("/bin/sh", "sh", "-c", cmdstring, (char *)0);
        _exit(127);         /* exec error */
    } else {                            /* parent */
        while (waitpid(pid, &status, 0) < 0)
            if (errno != EINTR) {
                status = -1; /* error other than EINTR from waitpid() */
                break;
            }
    }

    /* restore previous signal actions & reset signal mask */
    if (sigaction(SIGINT, &saveintr, NULL) < 0)
        return(-1);
    if (sigaction(SIGQUIT, &savequit, NULL) < 0)
        return(-1);
    if (sigprocmask(SIG_SETMASK, &savemask, NULL) < 0)
        return(-1);

    return(status);
}
```

Figure 10.28 Correct POSIX.1 implementation of system function

If we link the program in Figure 10.26 with this implementation of the system function, the resulting binary differs from the last (flawed) one in the following ways.

1. No signal is sent to the calling process when we type the interrupt or quit character.

2. When the ed command exits, SIGCHLD is not sent to the calling process. Instead, it is blocked until we unblock it in the last call to sigprocmask, after the system function retrieves the child's termination status by calling waitpid.

> POSIX.1 states that if wait or waitpid returns the status of a child process while SIGCHLD is pending, then SIGCHLD should not be delivered to the process unless the status of another child process is also available. None of the four implementations discussed in this book implements this semantic. Instead, SIGCHLD remains pending after the system function calls waitpid; when the signal is unblocked, it is delivered to the caller. If we called wait in the sig_chld function in Figure 10.26, it would return –1 with errno set to ECHILD, since the system function already retrieved the termination status of the child.

Many older texts show the ignoring of the interrupt and quit signals as follows:

```
if ((pid = fork()) < 0) {
    err_sys("fork error");
} else if (pid == 0) {
    /* child */
    execl(...);
    _exit(127);
}

/* parent */
old_intr = signal(SIGINT, SIG_IGN);
old_quit = signal(SIGQUIT, SIG_IGN);
waitpid(pid, &status, 0)
signal(SIGINT, old_intr);
signal(SIGQUIT, old_quit);
```

The problem with this sequence of code is that we have no guarantee after the fork whether the parent or child runs first. If the child runs first and the parent doesn't run for some time after, it's possible for an interrupt signal to be generated before the parent is able to change its disposition to be ignored. For this reason, in Figure 10.28, we change the disposition of the signals before the fork.

Note that we have to reset the dispositions of these two signals in the child before the call to execl. This allows execl to change their dispositions to the default, based on the caller's dispositions, as we described in Section 8.10.   □

Return Value from system

Beware of the return value from system. It is the termination status of the shell, which isn't always the termination status of the command string. We saw some examples in Figure 8.23, and the results were as we expected: if we execute a simple command, such as date, the termination status is 0. Executing the shell command exit 44 gave us a termination status of 44. What happens with signals?

Let's run the program in Figure 8.24 and send some signals to the command that's executing:

```
$ tsys "sleep 30"
^?normal termination, exit status = 130    we type the interrupt key
$ tsys "sleep 30"
^\sh: 946 Quit                             we type the quit key
normal termination, exit status = 131
```

When we terminate the sleep with the interrupt signal, the pr_exit function (Figure 8.5) thinks that it terminated normally. The same thing happens when we kill the sleep with the quit key. What is happening here is that the Bourne shell has a poorly documented feature that its termination status is 128 plus the signal number, when the command it was executing is terminated by a signal. We can see this with the shell interactively.

```
$ sh                                      make sure we're running the Bourne shell
$ sh -c "sleep 30"
^?                                        type the interrupt key
$ echo $?                                 print termination status of last command
130
$ sh -c "sleep 30"
^\sh: 962 Quit - core dumped             type the quit key
$ echo $?                                 print termination status of last command
131
$ exit                                    leave Bourne shell
```

On the system being used, SIGINT has a value of 2 and SIGQUIT has a value of 3, giving us the shell's termination statuses of 130 and 131.

Let's try a similar example, but this time we'll send a signal directly to the shell and see what gets returned by system:

```
$ tsys "sleep 30" &                       start it in background this time
9257
$ ps -f                                   look at the process IDs
     UID    PID   PPID  TTY       TIME CMD
     sar   9260    949  pts/5    0:00 ps -f
     sar   9258   9257  pts/5    0:00 sh -c sleep 60
     sar    949    947  pts/5    0:01 /bin/sh
     sar   9257    949  pts/5    0:00 tsys sleep 60
     sar   9259   9258  pts/5    0:00 sleep 60
$ kill -KILL 9258                         kill the shell itself
abnormal termination, signal number = 9
```

Here, we can see that the return value from system reports an abnormal termination only when the shell itself abnormally terminates.

When writing programs that use the system function, be sure to interpret the return value correctly. If you call fork, exec, and wait yourself, the termination status is not the same as if you call system.

10.19 sleep Function

We've used the sleep function in numerous examples throughout the text, and we showed two flawed implementations of it in Figures 10.7 and 10.8.

```
#include <unistd.h>

unsigned int sleep(unsigned int seconds);
```
                                          Returns: 0 or number of unslept seconds

This function causes the calling process to be suspended until either

1. The amount of wall clock time specified by *seconds* has elapsed.

2. A signal is caught by the process and the signal handler returns.

As with an `alarm` signal, the actual return may be at a time later than requested, because of other system activity.

In case 1, the return value is 0. When `sleep` returns early, because of some signal being caught (case 2), the return value is the number of unslept seconds (the requested time minus the actual time slept).

Although `sleep` can be implemented with the `alarm` function (Section 10.10), this isn't required. If `alarm` is used, however, there can be interactions between the two functions. The POSIX.1 standard leaves all these interactions unspecified. For example, if we do an `alarm(10)` and 3 wall clock seconds later do a `sleep(5)`, what happens? The `sleep` will return in 5 seconds (assuming that some other signal isn't caught in that time), but will another `SIGALRM` be generated 2 seconds later? These details depend on the implementation.

Solaris 9 implements `sleep` using `alarm`. The Solaris `sleep(3)` manual page says that a previously scheduled alarm is properly handled. For example, in the preceding scenario, before `sleep` returns, it will reschedule the alarm to happen 2 seconds later; `sleep` returns 0 in this case. (Obviously, `sleep` must save the address of the signal handler for `SIGALRM` and reset it before returning.) Also, if we do an `alarm(6)` and 3 wall clock seconds later do a `sleep(5)`, the `sleep` returns in 3 seconds (when the alarm goes off), not in 5 seconds. Here, the return value from `sleep` is 2 (the number of unslept seconds).

FreeBSD 5.2.1, Linux 2.4.22, and Mac OS X 10.3, on the other hand, use another technique: the delay is provided by `nanosleep(2)`. This function is specified to be a high-resolution delay by the real-time extensions in the Single UNIX Specification. This function allows the implementation of `sleep` to be independent of signals.

For portability, you shouldn't make any assumptions about the implementation of `sleep`, but if you have any intentions of mixing calls to `sleep` with any other timing functions, you need to be aware of possible interactions.

Example

Figure 10.29 shows an implementation of the POSIX.1 `sleep` function. This function is a modification of Figure 10.7, which handles signals reliably, avoiding the race condition in the earlier implementation. We still do not handle any interactions with previously set alarms. (As we mentioned, these interactions are explicitly undefined by POSIX.1.)

```
#include "apue.h"

static void
sig_alrm(int signo)
{
    /* nothing to do, just returning wakes up sigsuspend() */
}

unsigned int
sleep(unsigned int nsecs)
{
    struct sigaction    newact, oldact;
    sigset_t            newmask, oldmask, suspmask;
```

```
unsigned int        unslept;

/* set our handler, save previous information */
newact.sa_handler = sig_alrm;
sigemptyset(&newact.sa_mask);
newact.sa_flags = 0;
sigaction(SIGALRM, &newact, &oldact);

/* block SIGALRM and save current signal mask */
sigemptyset(&newmask);
sigaddset(&newmask, SIGALRM);
sigprocmask(SIG_BLOCK, &newmask, &oldmask);

alarm(nsecs);

suspmask = oldmask;
sigdelset(&suspmask, SIGALRM);   /* make sure SIGALRM isn't blocked */
sigsuspend(&suspmask);           /* wait for any signal to be caught */

/* some signal has been caught, SIGALRM is now blocked */

unslept = alarm(0);
sigaction(SIGALRM, &oldact, NULL);   /* reset previous action */

/* reset signal mask, which unblocks SIGALRM */
sigprocmask(SIG_SETMASK, &oldmask, NULL);
return(unslept);
}
```

Figure 10.29 Reliable implementation of `sleep`

It takes more code to write this reliable implementation than what is shown in Figure 10.7. We don't use any form of nonlocal branching (as we did in Figure 10.8 to avoid the race condition between the `alarm` and `pause`), so there is no effect on other signal handlers that may be executing when the `SIGALRM` is handled.   □

10.20 Job-Control Signals

Of the signals shown in Figure 10.1, POSIX.1 considers six to be job-control signals:

SIGCHLD   Child process has stopped or terminated.

SIGCONT   Continue process, if stopped.

SIGSTOP   Stop signal (can't be caught or ignored).

SIGTSTP   Interactive stop signal.

SIGTTIN   Read from controlling terminal by member of a background process group.

SIGTTOU   Write to controlling terminal by member of a background process group.

Except for SIGCHLD, most application programs don't handle these signals: interactive shells usually do all the work required to handle these signals. When we type the suspend character (usually Control-Z), SIGTSTP is sent to all processes in the foreground process group. When we tell the shell to resume a job in the foreground or background, the shell sends all the processes in the job the SIGCONT signal. Similarly, if SIGTTIN or SIGTTOU is delivered to a process, the process is stopped by default, and the job-control shell recognizes this and notifies us.

An exception is a process that is managing the terminal: the vi(1) editor, for example. It needs to know when the user wants to suspend it, so that it can restore the terminal's state to the way it was when vi was started. Also, when it resumes in the foreground, the vi editor needs to set the terminal state back to the way it wants it, and it needs to redraw the terminal screen. We see how a program such as vi handles this in the example that follows.

There are some interactions between the job-control signals. When any of the four stop signals (SIGTSTP, SIGSTOP, SIGTTIN, or SIGTTOU) is generated for a process, any pending SIGCONT signal for that process is discarded. Similarly, when the SIGCONT signal is generated for a process, any pending stop signals for that same process are discarded.

Note that the default action for SIGCONT is to continue the process, if it is stopped; otherwise, the signal is ignored. Normally, we don't have to do anything with this signal. When SIGCONT is generated for a process that is stopped, the process is continued, even if the signal is blocked or ignored.

Example

The program in Figure 10.30 demonstrates the normal sequence of code used when a program handles job control. This program simply copies its standard input to its standard output, but comments are given in the signal handler for typical actions performed by a program that manages a screen. When the program in Figure 10.30 starts, it arranges to catch the SIGTSTP signal only if the signal's disposition is SIG_DFL. The reason is that when the program is started by a shell that doesn't support job control (/bin/sh, for example), the signal's disposition should be set to SIG_IGN. In fact, the shell doesn't explicitly ignore this signal; init sets the disposition of the three job-control signals (SIGTSTP, SIGTTIN, and SIGTTOU) to SIG_IGN. This disposition is then inherited by all login shells. Only a job-control shell should reset the disposition of these three signals to SIG_DFL.

When we type the suspend character, the process receives the SIGTSTP signal, and the signal handler is invoked. At this point, we would do any terminal-related processing: move the cursor to the lower-left corner, restore the terminal mode, and so on. We then send ourself the same signal, SIGTSTP, after resetting its disposition to its default (stop the process) and unblocking the signal. We have to unblock it since we're currently handling that same signal, and the system blocks it automatically while it's being caught. At this point, the system stops the process. It is continued only when it receives (usually from the job-control shell, in response to an interactive fg command) a

```
#include "apue.h"

#define BUFFSIZE    1024

static void sig_tstp(int);

int
main(void)
{
    int     n;
    char    buf[BUFFSIZE];

    /*
     * Only catch SIGTSTP if we're running with a job-control shell.
     */
    if (signal(SIGTSTP, SIG_IGN) == SIG_DFL)
        signal(SIGTSTP, sig_tstp);

    while ((n = read(STDIN_FILENO, buf, BUFFSIZE)) > 0)
        if (write(STDOUT_FILENO, buf, n) != n)
            err_sys("write error");

    if (n < 0)
        err_sys("read error");

    exit(0);
}

static void
sig_tstp(int signo) /* signal handler for SIGTSTP */
{
    sigset_t    mask;

    /* ... move cursor to lower left corner, reset tty mode ... */

    /*
     * Unblock SIGTSTP, since it's blocked while we're handling it.
     */
    sigemptyset(&mask);
    sigaddset(&mask, SIGTSTP);
    sigprocmask(SIG_UNBLOCK, &mask, NULL);

    signal(SIGTSTP, SIG_DFL);    /* reset disposition to default */

    kill(getpid(), SIGTSTP);     /* and send the signal to ourself */

    /* we won't return from the kill until we're continued */

    signal(SIGTSTP, sig_tstp);   /* reestablish signal handler */

    /* ... reset tty mode, redraw screen ... */
}
```

Figure 10.30 How to handle `SIGTSTP`

SIGCONT signal. We don't catch SIGCONT. Its default disposition is to continue the stopped process; when this happens, the program continues as though it returned from the kill function. When the program is continued, we reset the disposition for the SIGTSTP signal and do whatever terminal processing we want (we could redraw the screen, for example).   □

10.21 Additional Features

In this section, we describe some additional implementation-dependent features of signals.

Signal Names

Some systems provide the array

```
extern char *sys_siglist[];
```

The array index is the signal number, giving a pointer to the character string name of the signal.

> FreeBSD 5.2.1, Linux 2.4.22, and Mac OS X 10.3 all provide this array of signal names. Solaris 9 does, too, but it uses the name _sys_siglist instead.

These systems normally provide the function psignal also.

```
#include <signal.h>

void psignal(int signo, const char *msg);
```

The string msg (which is normally the name of the program) is output to the standard error, followed by a colon and a space, followed by a description of the signal, followed by a newline. This function is similar to perror (Section 1.7).

Another common function is strsignal. This function is similar to strerror (also described in Section 1.7).

```
#include <string.h>

char *strsignal(int signo);
```
                                                            Returns: a pointer to a string describing the signal

Given a signal number, strsignal will return a string that describes the signal. This string can be used by applications to print error messages about signals received.

> All the platforms discussed in this book provide the psignal and strsignal functions, but differences do occur. On Solaris 9, strsignal will return a null pointer if the signal number is invalid, whereas FreeBSD 5.2.1, Linux 2.4.22, and Mac OS X 10.3 return a string indicating that the signal number is unrecognized. Also, to get the function prototype for psignal on Solaris, you need to include <siginfo.h>.

Signal Mappings

Solaris provides a couple of functions to map a signal number to a signal name and vice versa.

```
#include <signal.h>

int sig2str(int signo, char *str);

int str2sig(const char *str, int *signop);
```
Both return: 0 if OK, −1 on error

These functions are useful when writing interactive programs that need to accept and print signal names and numbers.

The `sig2str` function translates the given signal number into a string and stores the result in the memory pointed to by *str*. The caller must ensure that the memory is large enough to hold the longest string, including the terminating null byte. Solaris provides the constant `SIG2STR_MAX` in `<signal.h>` to define the maximum string length. The string consists of the signal name without the "SIG" prefix. For example, translating `SIGKILL` would result in the string "KILL" being stored in the *str* memory buffer.

The `str2sig` function translates the given name into a signal number. The signal number is stored in the integer pointed to by *signop*. The name can be either the signal name without the "SIG" prefix or a string representation of the decimal signal number (i.e., "9").

Note that `sig2str` and `str2sig` depart from common practice and don't set `errno` when they fail.

10.22 Summary

Signals are used in most nontrivial applications. An understanding of the hows and whys of signal handling is essential to advanced UNIX System programming. This chapter has been a long and thorough look at UNIX System signals. We started by looking at the warts in previous implementations of signals and how they manifest themselves. We then proceeded to the POSIX.1 reliable-signal concept and all the related functions. Once we covered all these details, we were able to provide implementations of the POSIX.1 abort, `system`, and `sleep` functions. We finished with a look at the job-control signals and the ways that we can convert between signal names and signal numbers.

Exercises

10.1   In Figure 10.2, remove the `for (;;)` statement. What happens and why?

10.2   Implement the `sig2str` function described in Section 10.21.

10.3   Draw pictures of the stack frames when we run the program from Figure 10.9.

10.4   In Figure 10.11, we showed a technique that's often used to set a timeout on an I/O operation using `setjmp` and `longjmp`. The following code has also been seen:

```
signal(SIGALRM, sig_alrm);
alarm(60);
if (setjmp(env_alrm) != 0) {
    /* handle timeout */
    ...
}
...
```

What else is wrong with this sequence of code?

10.5   Using only a single timer (either `alarm` or the higher-precision `setitimer`), provide a set of functions that allows a process to set any number of timers.

10.6   Write the following program to test the parent–child synchronization functions in Figure 10.24. The process creates a file and writes the integer 0 to the file. The process then calls `fork`, and the parent and child alternate incrementing the counter in the file. Each time the counter is incremented, print which process (parent or child) is doing the increment.

10.7   In the function shown in Figure 10.25, if the caller catches SIGABRT and returns from the signal handler, why do we go to the trouble of resetting the disposition to its default and call `kill` the second time, instead of simply calling `_exit`?

10.8   Why do you think the `siginfo` structure (Section 10.14) includes the real user ID, instead of the effective user ID, in the `si_uid` field?

10.9   Rewrite the function in Figure 10.14 to handle all the signals from Figure 10.1. The function should consist of a single loop that iterates once for every signal in the current signal mask (not once for every possible signal).

10.10 Write a program that calls `sleep(60)` in an infinite loop. Every five times through the loop (every 5 minutes), fetch the current time of day and print the `tm_sec` field. Run the program overnight and explain the results. How would a program such as the BSD `cron` daemon, which runs every minute on the minute, handle this?

10.11 Modify Figure 3.4 as follows: (a) change BUFFSIZE to 100; (b) catch the SIGXFSZ signal using the `signal_intr` function, printing a message when it's caught, and returning from the signal handler; and (c) print the return value from `write` if the requested number of bytes weren't written. Modify the soft RLIMIT_FSIZE resource limit (Section 7.11) to 1,024 bytes and run your new program, copying a file that is larger than 1,024 bytes. (Try to set the soft resource limit from your shell. If you can't do this from your shell, call `setrlimit` directly from the program.) Run this program on the different systems that you have access to. What happens and why?

10.12 Write a program that calls `fwrite` with a large buffer (a few hundred megabytes). Before calling `fwrite`, call `alarm` to schedule a signal in 1 second. In your signal handler, print that the signal was caught and return. Does the call to `fwrite` complete? What's happening?

11

Threads

11.1 Introduction

We discussed processes in earlier chapters. We learned about the environment of a UNIX process, the relationships between processes, and ways to control processes. We saw that a limited amount of sharing can occur between related processes.

In this chapter, we'll look inside a process further to see how we can use multiple *threads of control* (or simply *threads*) to perform multiple tasks within the environment of a single process. All threads within a single process have access to the same process components, such as file descriptors and memory.

Any time you try to share a single resource among multiple users, you have to deal with consistency. We'll conclude the chapter with a look at the synchronization mechanisms available to prevent multiple threads from viewing inconsistencies in their shared resources.

11.2 Thread Concepts

A typical UNIX process can be thought of as having a single thread of control: each process is doing only one thing at a time. With multiple threads of control, we can design our programs to do more than one thing at a time within a single process, with each thread handling a separate task. This approach can have several benefits.

- We can simplify code that deals with asynchronous events by assigning a separate thread to handle each event type. Each thread can then handle its event using a synchronous programming model. A synchronous programming model is much simpler than an asynchronous one.

- Multiple processes have to use complex mechanisms provided by the operating system to share memory and file descriptors, as we will see in Chapters 15 and 17. Threads, on the other hand, automatically have access to the same memory address space and file descriptors.

- Some problems can be partitioned so that overall program throughput can be improved. A single process that has multiple tasks to perform implicitly serializes those tasks, because there is only one thread of control. With multiple threads of control, the processing of independent tasks can be interleaved by assigning a separate thread per task. Two tasks can be interleaved only if they don't depend on the processing performed by each other.

- Similarly, interactive programs can realize improved response time by using multiple threads to separate the portions of the program that deal with user input and output from the other parts of the program.

Some people associate multithreaded programming with multiprocessor systems. The benefits of a multithreaded programming model can be realized even if your program is running on a uniprocessor. A program can be simplified using threads regardless of the number of processors, because the number of processors doesn't affect the program structure. Furthermore, as long as your program has to block when serializing tasks, you can still see improvements in response time and throughput when running on a uniprocessor, because some threads might be able to run while others are blocked.

A thread consists of the information necessary to represent an execution context within a process. This includes a *thread ID* that identifies the thread within a process, a set of register values, a stack, a scheduling priority and policy, a signal mask, an `errno` variable (recall Section 1.7), and thread-specific data (Section 12.6). Everything within a process is sharable among the threads in a process, including the text of the executable program, the program's global and heap memory, the stacks, and the file descriptors.

The threads interface we're about to see is from POSIX.1-2001. The threads interface, also known as "pthreads" for "POSIX threads," is an optional feature in POSIX.1-2001. The feature test macro for POSIX threads is `_POSIX_THREADS`. Applications can either use this in an `#ifdef` test to determine at compile time whether threads are supported or call `sysconf` with the `_SC_THREADS` constant to determine at runtime whether threads are supported.

11.3 Thread Identification

Just as every process has a process ID, every thread has a thread ID. Unlike the process ID, which is unique in the system, the thread ID has significance only within the context of the process to which it belongs.

Recall that a process ID, represented by the `pid_t` data type, is a non-negative integer. A thread ID is represented by the `pthread_t` data type. Implementations are allowed to use a structure to represent the `pthread_t` data type, so portable implementations can't treat them as integers. Therefore, a function must be used to compare two thread IDs.

```
#include <pthread.h>

int pthread_equal(pthread_t tid1, pthread_t tid2);
```

Returns: nonzero if equal, 0 otherwise

Linux 2.4.22 uses an unsigned long integer for the pthread_t data type. Solaris 9 represents the pthread_t data type as an unsigned integer. FreeBSD 5.2.1 and Mac OS X 10.3 use a pointer to the pthread structure for the pthread_t data type.

A consequence of allowing the pthread_t data type to be a structure is that there is no portable way to print its value. Sometimes, it is useful to print thread IDs during program debugging, but there is usually no need to do so otherwise. At worst, this results in nonportable debug code, so it is not much of a limitation.

A thread can obtain its own thread ID by calling the pthread_self function.

```
#include <pthread.h>

pthread_t pthread_self(void);
```

Returns: the thread ID of the calling thread

This function can be used with pthread_equal when a thread needs to identify data structures that are tagged with its thread ID. For example, a master thread might place work assignments on a queue and use the thread ID to control which jobs go to each worker thread. This is illustrated in Figure 11.1. A single master thread places new jobs on a work queue. A pool of three worker threads removes jobs from the queue. Instead of allowing each thread to process whichever job is at the head of the queue, the master thread controls job assignment by placing the ID of the thread that should process the job in each job structure. Each worker thread then removes only jobs that are tagged with its own thread ID.

11.4 Thread Creation

The traditional UNIX process model supports only one thread of control per process. Conceptually, this is the same as a threads-based model whereby each process is made up of only one thread. With pthreads, when a program runs, it also starts out as a single process with a single thread of control. As the program runs, its behavior should be indistinguishable from the traditional process, until it creates more threads of control. Additional threads can be created by calling the pthread_create function.

```
#include <pthread.h>

int pthread_create(pthread_t *restrict tidp,
                   const pthread_attr_t *restrict attr,
                   void *(*start_rtn)(void *), void *restrict arg);
```

Returns: 0 if OK, error number on failure

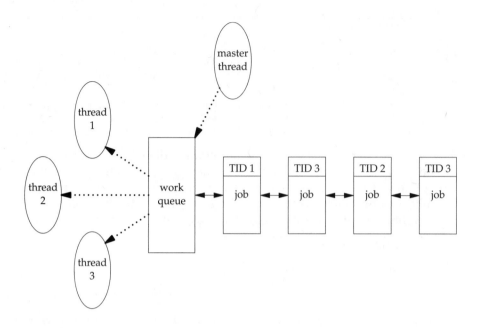

Figure 11.1   Work queue example

The memory location pointed to by *tidp* is set to the thread ID of the newly created thread when pthread_create returns successfully. The *attr* argument is used to customize various thread attributes. We'll cover thread attributes in Section 12.3, but for now, we'll set this to NULL to create a thread with the default attributes.

The newly created thread starts running at the address of the *start_rtn* function. This function takes a single argument, *arg*, which is a typeless pointer. If you need to pass more than one argument to the *start_rtn* function, then you need to store them in a structure and pass the address of the structure in *arg*.

When a thread is created, there is no guarantee which runs first: the newly created thread or the calling thread. The newly created thread has access to the process address space and inherits the calling thread's floating-point environment and signal mask; however, the set of pending signals for the thread is cleared.

Note that the pthread functions usually return an error code when they fail. They don't set errno like the other POSIX functions. The per thread copy of errno is provided only for compatibility with existing functions that use it. With threads, it is cleaner to return the error code from the function, thereby restricting the scope of the error to the function that caused it, instead of relying on some global state that is changed as a side effect of the function.

Example

Although there is no portable way to print the thread ID, we can write a small test program that does, to gain some insight into how threads work. The program in

Figure 11.2 creates one thread and prints the process and thread IDs of the new thread and the initial thread.

```c
#include "apue.h"
#include <pthread.h>

pthread_t ntid;

void
printids(const char *s)
{
    pid_t       pid;
    pthread_t   tid;

    pid = getpid();
    tid = pthread_self();
    printf("%s pid %u tid %u (0x%x)\n", s, (unsigned int)pid,
        (unsigned int)tid, (unsigned int)tid);
}

void *
thr_fn(void *arg)
{
    printids("new thread: ");
    return((void *)0);
}

int
main(void)
{
    int     err;

    err = pthread_create(&ntid, NULL, thr_fn, NULL);
    if (err != 0)
        err_quit("can't create thread: %s\n", strerror(err));
    printids("main thread:");
    sleep(1);
    exit(0);
}
```

Figure 11.2   Printing thread IDs

This example has two oddities, necessary to handle races between the main thread and the new thread. (We'll learn better ways to deal with these later in this chapter.) The first is the need to sleep in the main thread. If it doesn't sleep, the main thread might exit, thereby terminating the entire process before the new thread gets a chance to run. This behavior is dependent on the operating system's threads implementation and scheduling algorithms.

The second oddity is that the new thread obtains its thread ID by calling pthread_self instead of reading it out of shared memory or receiving it as an argument to its thread-start routine. Recall that pthread_create will return the thread ID of the newly created thread through the first parameter (*tidp*). In our example, the main thread stores this in `ntid`, but the new thread can't safely use it. If the new thread runs before the main thread returns from calling `pthread_create`, then the new thread will see the uninitialized contents of `ntid` instead of the thread ID.

Running the program in Figure 11.2 on Solaris gives us

```
$ ./a.out
main thread: pid 7225 tid 1 (0x1)
new thread:  pid 7225 tid 4 (0x4)
```

As we expect, both threads have the same process ID, but different thread IDs. Running the program in Figure 11.2 on FreeBSD gives us

```
$ ./a.out
main thread: pid 14954 tid 134529024 (0x804c000)
new thread:  pid 14954 tid 134530048 (0x804c400)
```

As we expect, both threads have the same process ID. If we look at the thread IDs as decimal integers, the values look strange, but if we look at them in hexadecimal, they make more sense. As we noted earlier, FreeBSD uses a pointer to the thread data structure for its thread ID.

We would expect Mac OS X to be similar to FreeBSD; however, the thread ID for the main thread is from a different address range than the thread IDs for threads created with `pthread_create`:

```
$ ./a.out
main thread: pid 779 tid 2684396012 (0xa000a1ec)
new thread:  pid 779 tid 25166336 (0x1800200)
```

Running the same program on Linux gives us slightly different results:

```
$ ./a.out
new thread:  pid 6628 tid 1026 (0x402)
main thread: pid 6626 tid 1024 (0x400)
```

The Linux thread IDs look more reasonable, but the process IDs don't match. This is an artifact of the Linux threads implementation, where the `clone` system call is used to implement `pthread_create`. The `clone` system call creates a child process that can share a configurable amount of its parent's execution context, such as file descriptors and memory.

Note also that the output from the main thread appears before the output from the thread we create, except on Linux. This illustrates that we can't make any assumptions about how threads will be scheduled.   □

11.5 Thread Termination

If any thread within a process calls `exit`, `_Exit`, or `_exit`, then the entire process terminates. Similarly, when the default action is to terminate the process, a signal sent to a thread will terminate the entire process (we'll talk more about the interactions between signals and threads in Section 12.8).

A single thread can exit in three ways, thereby stopping its flow of control, without terminating the entire process.

1. The thread can simply return from the start routine. The return value is the thread's exit code.

2. The thread can be canceled by another thread in the same process.

3. The thread can call `pthread_exit`.

```
#include <pthread.h>

void pthread_exit(void *rval_ptr);
```

The *rval_ptr* is a typeless pointer, similar to the single argument passed to the start routine. This pointer is available to other threads in the process by calling the `pthread_join` function.

```
#include <pthread.h>

int pthread_join(pthread_t thread, void **rval_ptr);
```
                                     Returns: 0 if OK, error number on failure

The calling thread will block until the specified thread calls `pthread_exit`, returns from its start routine, or is canceled. If the thread simply returned from its start routine, *rval_ptr* will contain the return code. If the thread was canceled, the memory location specified by *rval_ptr* is set to PTHREAD_CANCELED.

By calling `pthread_join`, we automatically place the thread with which we're joining in the detached state (discussed shortly) so that its resources can be recovered. If the thread was already in the detached state, `pthread_join` can fail, returning EINVAL, although this is implementation-specific.

If we're not interested in a thread's return value, we can set *rval_ptr* to NULL. In this case, calling `pthread_join` allows us to wait for the specified thread, but does not retrieve the thread's termination status.

Example

Figure 11.3 shows how to fetch the exit code from a thread that has terminated.

```
#include "apue.h"
#include <pthread.h>

void *
thr_fn1(void *arg)
{
    printf("thread 1 returning\n");
    return((void *)1);
}

void *
thr_fn2(void *arg)
{
    printf("thread 2 exiting\n");
```

```
        pthread_exit((void *)2);
}

int
main(void)
{
    int         err;
    pthread_t   tid1, tid2;
    void        *tret;

    err = pthread_create(&tid1, NULL, thr_fn1, NULL);
    if (err != 0)
        err_quit("can't create thread 1: %s\n", strerror(err));
    err = pthread_create(&tid2, NULL, thr_fn2, NULL);
    if (err != 0)
        err_quit("can't create thread 2: %s\n", strerror(err));
    err = pthread_join(tid1, &tret);
    if (err != 0)
        err_quit("can't join with thread 1: %s\n", strerror(err));
    printf("thread 1 exit code %d\n", (int)tret);
    err = pthread_join(tid2, &tret);
    if (err != 0)
        err_quit("can't join with thread 2: %s\n", strerror(err));
    printf("thread 2 exit code %d\n", (int)tret);
    exit(0);
}
```

Figure 11.3   Fetching the thread exit status

Running the program in Figure 11.3 gives us

```
$ ./a.out
thread 1 returning
thread 2 exiting
thread 1 exit code 1
thread 2 exit code 2
```

As we can see, when a thread exits by calling pthread_exit or by simply returning from the start routine, the exit status can be obtained by another thread by calling pthread_join.   □

The typeless pointer passed to pthread_create and pthread_exit can be used to pass more than a single value. The pointer can be used to pass the address of a structure containing more complex information. Be careful that the memory used for the structure is still valid when the caller has completed. If the structure was allocated on the caller's stack, for example, the memory contents might have changed by the time the structure is used. For example, if a thread allocates a structure on its stack and passes a pointer to this structure to pthread_exit, then the stack might be destroyed and its memory reused for something else by the time the caller of pthread_join tries to use it.

Example

The program in Figure 11.4 shows the problem with using an automatic variable (allocated on the stack) as the argument to pthread_exit.

```c
#include "apue.h"
#include <pthread.h>

struct foo {
    int a, b, c, d;
};

void
printfoo(const char *s, const struct foo *fp)
{
    printf(s);
    printf("  structure at 0x%x\n", (unsigned)fp);
    printf("  foo.a = %d\n", fp->a);
    printf("  foo.b = %d\n", fp->b);
    printf("  foo.c = %d\n", fp->c);
    printf("  foo.d = %d\n", fp->d);
}

void *
thr_fn1(void *arg)
{
    struct foo  foo = {1, 2, 3, 4};

    printfoo("thread 1:\n", &foo);
    pthread_exit((void *)&foo);
}

void *
thr_fn2(void *arg)
{
    printf("thread 2: ID is %d\n", pthread_self());
    pthread_exit((void *)0);
}

int
main(void)
{
    int          err;
    pthread_t    tid1, tid2;
    struct foo   *fp;

    err = pthread_create(&tid1, NULL, thr_fn1, NULL);
    if (err != 0)
        err_quit("can't create thread 1: %s\n", strerror(err));
    err = pthread_join(tid1, (void *)&fp);
    if (err != 0)
        err_quit("can't join with thread 1: %s\n", strerror(err));
    sleep(1);
    printf("parent starting second thread\n");
```

```
        err = pthread_create(&tid2, NULL, thr_fn2, NULL);
        if (err != 0)
            err_quit("can't create thread 2: %s\n", strerror(err));
        sleep(1);
        printfoo("parent:\n", fp);
        exit(0);
    }
```

Figure 11.4   Incorrect use of `pthread_exit` argument

When we run this program on Linux, we get

```
$ ./a.out
thread 1:
  structure at 0x409a2abc
  foo.a = 1
  foo.b = 2
  foo.c = 3
  foo.d = 4
parent starting second thread
thread 2: ID is 32770
parent:
  structure at 0x409a2abc
  foo.a = 0
  foo.b = 32770
  foo.c = 1075430560
  foo.d = 1073937284
```

Of course, the results vary, depending on the memory architecture, the compiler, and the implementation of the threads library. The results on FreeBSD are similar:

```
$ ./a.out
thread 1:
  structure at 0xbfafefc0
  foo.a = 1
  foo.b = 2
  foo.c = 3
  foo.d = 4
parent starting second thread
thread 2: ID is 134534144
parent:
  structure at 0xbfafefc0
  foo.a = 0
  foo.b = 134534144
  foo.c = 3
  foo.d = 671642590
```

As we can see, the contents of the structure (allocated on the stack of thread *tid1*) have changed by the time the main thread can access the structure. Note how the stack of the second thread (*tid2*) has overwritten the first thread's stack. To solve this problem, we can either use a global structure or allocate the structure using `malloc`.   □

One thread can request that another in the same process be canceled by calling the pthread_cancel function.

```
#include <pthread.h>

int pthread_cancel(pthread_t tid);
```
                                               Returns: 0 if OK, error number on failure

In the default circumstances, pthread_cancel will cause the thread specified by *tid* to behave as if it had called pthread_exit with an argument of PTHREAD_CANCELED. However, a thread can elect to ignore or otherwise control how it is canceled. We will discuss this in detail in Section 12.7. Note that pthread_cancel doesn't wait for the thread to terminate. It merely makes the request.

A thread can arrange for functions to be called when it exits, similar to the way that the atexit function (Section 7.3) can be used by a process to arrange that functions can be called when the process exits. The functions are known as *thread cleanup handlers*. More than one cleanup handler can be established for a thread. The handlers are recorded in a stack, which means that they are executed in the reverse order from that with which they were registered.

```
#include <pthread.h>

void pthread_cleanup_push(void (*rtn)(void *), void *arg);

void pthread_cleanup_pop(int execute);
```

The pthread_cleanup_push function schedules the cleanup function, *rtn*, to be called with the single argument, *arg*, when the thread performs one of the following actions:

- Makes a call to pthread_exit
- Responds to a cancellation request
- Makes a call to pthread_cleanup_pop with a nonzero *execute* argument

If the *execute* argument is set to zero, the cleanup function is not called. In either case, pthread_cleanup_pop removes the cleanup handler established by the last call to pthread_cleanup_push.

A restriction with these functions is that, because they can be implemented as macros, they must be used in matched pairs within the same scope in a thread. The macro definition of pthread_cleanup_push can include a { character, in which case the matching } character is in the pthread_cleanup_pop definition.

Example

Figure 11.5 shows how to use thread cleanup handlers. Although the example is somewhat contrived, it illustrates the mechanics involved. Note that although we never intend to pass zero as an argument to the thread start-up routines, we still need to match calls to pthread_cleanup_pop with the calls to pthread_cleanup_push; otherwise, the program might not compile.

```
#include "apue.h"
#include <pthread.h>

void
cleanup(void *arg)
{
    printf("cleanup: %s\n", (char *)arg);
}

void *
thr_fn1(void *arg)
{
    printf("thread 1 start\n");
    pthread_cleanup_push(cleanup, "thread 1 first handler");
    pthread_cleanup_push(cleanup, "thread 1 second handler");
    printf("thread 1 push complete\n");
    if (arg)
        return((void *)1);
    pthread_cleanup_pop(0);
    pthread_cleanup_pop(0);
    return((void *)1);
}

void *
thr_fn2(void *arg)
{
    printf("thread 2 start\n");
    pthread_cleanup_push(cleanup, "thread 2 first handler");
    pthread_cleanup_push(cleanup, "thread 2 second handler");
    printf("thread 2 push complete\n");
    if (arg)
        pthread_exit((void *)2);
    pthread_cleanup_pop(0);
    pthread_cleanup_pop(0);
    pthread_exit((void *)2);
}

int
main(void)
{
    int         err;
    pthread_t   tid1, tid2;
    void        *tret;

    err = pthread_create(&tid1, NULL, thr_fn1, (void *)1);
    if (err != 0)
        err_quit("can't create thread 1: %s\n", strerror(err));
    err = pthread_create(&tid2, NULL, thr_fn2, (void *)1);
    if (err != 0)
        err_quit("can't create thread 2: %s\n", strerror(err));
    err = pthread_join(tid1, &tret);
    if (err != 0)
```

```
            err_quit("can't join with thread 1: %s\n", strerror(err));
        printf("thread 1 exit code %d\n", (int)tret);
        err = pthread_join(tid2, &tret);
        if (err != 0)
            err_quit("can't join with thread 2: %s\n", strerror(err));
        printf("thread 2 exit code %d\n", (int)tret);
        exit(0);
    }
}
```

Figure 11.5   Thread cleanup handler

Running the program in Figure 11.5 gives us

```
$ ./a.out
thread 1 start
thread 1 push complete
thread 2 start
thread 2 push complete
cleanup: thread 2 second handler
cleanup: thread 2 first handler
thread 1 exit code 1
thread 2 exit code 2
```

From the output, we can see that both threads start properly and exit, but that only the second thread's cleanup handlers are called. Thus, if the thread terminates by returning from its start routine, its cleanup handlers are not called, although this behavior varies among implementations. Also note that the cleanup handlers are called in the reverse order from which they were installed.   □

By now, you should begin to see similarities between the thread functions and the process functions. Figure 11.6 summarizes the similar functions.

Process primitive	Thread primitive	Description
fork	pthread_create	create a new flow of control
exit	pthread_exit	exit from an existing flow of control
waitpid	pthread_join	get exit status from flow of control
atexit	pthread_cleanup_push	register function to be called at exit from flow of control
getpid	pthread_self	get ID for flow of control
abort	pthread_cancel	request abnormal termination of flow of control

Figure 11.6   Comparison of process and thread primitives

By default, a thread's termination status is retained until pthread_join is called for that thread. A thread's underlying storage can be reclaimed immediately on termination if that thread has been *detached*. When a thread is already detached, the pthread_join function can't be used to wait for its termination status. A call to pthread_join for a detached thread usually fails, returning EINVAL or ESRCH, but it can also succeed sometimes, depending on timing and implementation. We can detach a thread by calling pthread_detach.

```
#include <pthread.h>

int pthread_detach(pthread_t tid);
```
                                                    Returns: 0 if OK, error number on failure

As we will see in the next chapter, we can create a thread that is already in the detached state by modifying the thread attributes we pass to `pthread_create`.

11.6 Thread Synchronization

When multiple threads of control share the same memory, we need to make sure that each thread sees a consistent view of its data. If each thread uses variables that other threads don't read or modify, no consistency problems exist. Similarly, if a variable is read-only, there is no consistency problem with more than one thread reading its value at the same time. However, when one thread can modify a variable that other threads can read or modify, we need to synchronize the threads to ensure that they don't use an invalid value when accessing the variable's memory contents.

When one thread modifies a variable, other threads can potentially see inconsistencies when reading the value of the variable. On processor architectures in which the modification takes more than one memory cycle, this can happen when the memory read is interleaved between the memory write cycles. Of course, this behavior is architecture dependent, but portable programs can't make any assumptions about what type of processor architecture is being used.

Figure 11.7 shows a hypothetical example of two threads reading and writing the same variable. In this example, thread A reads the variable and then writes a new value to it, but the write operation takes two memory cycles. If thread B reads the same variable between the two write cycles, it will see an inconsistent value.

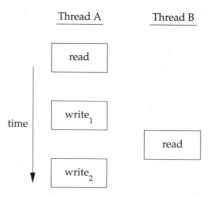

Figure 11.7   Interleaved memory cycles with two threads

To solve this problem, the threads have to use a lock that will allow only one thread to access the variable at a time. Figure 11.8 shows this synchronization. If it wants to read the variable, thread B acquires a lock. Similarly, when thread A updates the variable, it acquires the same lock. Thus, thread B will be unable to read the variable until thread A releases the lock.

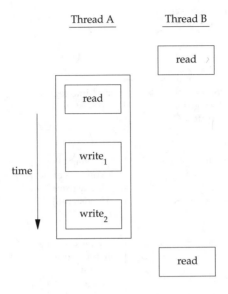

Figure 11.8   Two threads synchronizing memory access

You also need to synchronize two or more threads that might try to modify the same variable at the same time. Consider the case in which you increment a variable (Figure 11.9). The increment operation is usually broken down into three steps.

1. Read the memory location into a register.

2. Increment the value in the register.

3. Write the new value back to the memory location.

If two threads try to increment the same variable at almost the same time without synchronizing with each other, the results can be inconsistent. You end up with a value that is either one or two greater than before, depending on the value observed when the second thread starts its operation. If the second thread performs step 1 before the first thread performs step 3, the second thread will read the same initial value as the first thread, increment it, and write it back, with no net effect.

If the modification is atomic, then there isn't a race. In the previous example, if the increment takes only one memory cycle, then no race exists. If our data always appears to be *sequentially consistent*, then we need no additional synchronization. Our operations are sequentially consistent when multiple threads can't observe inconsistencies in our data. In modern computer systems, memory accesses take multiple bus cycles, and multiprocessors generally interleave bus cycles among multiple processors, so we aren't guaranteed that our data is sequentially consistent.

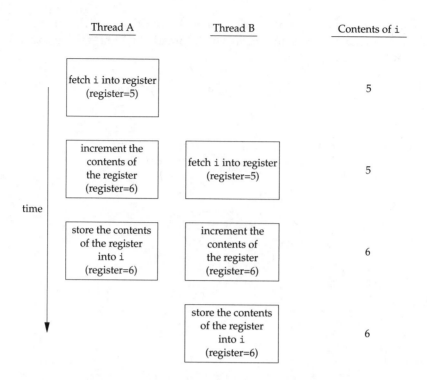

Figure 11.9   Two unsynchronized threads incrementing the same variable

In a sequentially consistent environment, we can explain modifications to our data as a sequential step of operations taken by the running threads. We can say such things as "Thread A incremented the variable, then thread B incremented the variable, so its value is two greater than before" or "Thread B incremented the variable, then thread A incremented the variable, so its value is two greater than before." No possible ordering of the two threads can result in any other value of the variable.

Besides the computer architecture, races can arise from the ways in which our programs use variables, creating places where it is possible to view inconsistencies. For example, we might increment a variable and then make a decision based on its value. The combination of the increment step and the decision-making step aren't atomic, so this opens a window where inconsistencies can arise.

Mutexes

We can protect our data and ensure access by only one thread at a time by using the pthreads mutual-exclusion interfaces. A *mutex* is basically a lock that we set (lock) before accessing a shared resource and release (unlock) when we're done. While it is set, any other thread that tries to set it will block until we release it. If more than one thread is blocked when we unlock the mutex, then all threads blocked on the lock will be made runnable, and the first one to run will be able to set the lock. The others will see that the mutex is still locked and go back to waiting for it to become available again. In this way, only one thread will proceed at a time.

This mutual-exclusion mechanism works only if we design our threads to follow the same data-access rules. The operating system doesn't serialize access to data for us. If we allow one thread to access a shared resource without first acquiring a lock, then inconsistencies can occur even though the rest of our threads do acquire the lock before attempting to access the shared resource.

A mutex variable is represented by the `pthread_mutex_t` data type. Before we can use a mutex variable, we must first initialize it by either setting it to the constant `PTHREAD_MUTEX_INITIALIZER` (for statically-allocated mutexes only) or calling `pthread_mutex_init`. If we allocate the mutex dynamically (by calling `malloc`, for example), then we need to call `pthread_mutex_destroy` before freeing the memory.

```
#include <pthread.h>

int pthread_mutex_init(pthread_mutex_t *restrict mutex,
                       const pthread_mutexattr_t *restrict attr);

int pthread_mutex_destroy(pthread_mutex_t *mutex);
```
                                        Both return: 0 if OK, error number on failure

To initialize a mutex with the default attributes, we set *attr* to NULL. We will discuss nondefault mutex attributes in Section 12.4.

To lock a mutex, we call `pthread_mutex_lock`. If the mutex is already locked, the calling thread will block until the mutex is unlocked. To unlock a mutex, we call `pthread_mutex_unlock`.

```
#include <pthread.h>

int pthread_mutex_lock(pthread_mutex_t *mutex);

int pthread_mutex_trylock(pthread_mutex_t *mutex);

int pthread_mutex_unlock(pthread_mutex_t *mutex);
```
                                        All return: 0 if OK, error number on failure

If a thread can't afford to block, it can use `pthread_mutex_trylock` to lock the mutex conditionally. If the mutex is unlocked at the time `pthread_mutex_trylock` is called, then `pthread_mutex_trylock` will lock the mutex without blocking and return 0. Otherwise, `pthread_mutex_trylock` will fail, returning EBUSY without locking the mutex.

Example

Figure 11.10 illustrates a mutex used to protect a data structure. When more than one thread needs to access a dynamically-allocated object, we can embed a reference count in the object to ensure that we don't free its memory before all threads are done using it.

```
#include <stdlib.h>
#include <pthread.h>

struct foo {
    int             f_count;
    pthread_mutex_t f_lock;
    /* ... more stuff here ... */
};

struct foo *
foo_alloc(void) /* allocate the object */
{
    struct foo *fp;

    if ((fp = malloc(sizeof(struct foo))) != NULL) {
        fp->f_count = 1;
        if (pthread_mutex_init(&fp->f_lock, NULL) != 0) {
            free(fp);
            return(NULL);
        }
        /* ... continue initialization ... */
    }
    return(fp);
}

void
foo_hold(struct foo *fp) /* add a reference to the object */
{
    pthread_mutex_lock(&fp->f_lock);
    fp->f_count++;
    pthread_mutex_unlock(&fp->f_lock);
}

void
foo_rele(struct foo *fp) /* release a reference to the object */
{
    pthread_mutex_lock(&fp->f_lock);
    if (--fp->f_count == 0) { /* last reference */
        pthread_mutex_unlock(&fp->f_lock);
        pthread_mutex_destroy(&fp->f_lock);
        free(fp);
    } else {
        pthread_mutex_unlock(&fp->f_lock);
    }
}
```

Figure 11.10 Using a mutex to protect a data structure

We lock the mutex before incrementing the reference count, decrementing the reference count, and checking whether the reference count reaches zero. No locking is necessary when we initialize the reference count to 1 in the foo_alloc function, because the allocating thread is the only reference to it so far. If we were to place the structure on a list at this point, it could be found by other threads, so we would need to lock it first.

Before using the object, threads are expected to add a reference count to it. When they are done, they must release the reference. When the last reference is released, the object's memory is freed.   □

Deadlock Avoidance

A thread will deadlock itself if it tries to lock the same mutex twice, but there are less obvious ways to create deadlocks with mutexes. For example, when we use more than one mutex in our programs, a deadlock can occur if we allow one thread to hold a mutex and block while trying to lock a second mutex at the same time that another thread holding the second mutex tries to lock the first mutex. Neither thread can proceed, because each needs a resource that is held by the other, so we have a deadlock.

Deadlocks can be avoided by carefully controlling the order in which mutexes are locked. For example, assume that you have two mutexes, A and B, that you need to lock at the same time. If all threads always lock mutex A before mutex B, no deadlock can occur from the use of the two mutexes (but you can still deadlock on other resources). Similarly, if all threads always lock mutex B before mutex A, no deadlock will occur. You'll have the potential for a deadlock only when one thread attempts to lock the mutexes in the opposite order from another thread.

Sometimes, an application's architecture makes it difficult to apply a lock ordering. If enough locks and data structures are involved that the functions you have available can't be molded to fit a simple hierarchy, then you'll have to try some other approach. In this case, you might be able to release your locks and try again at a later time. You can use the `pthread_mutex_trylock` interface to avoid deadlocking in this case. If you are already holding locks and `pthread_mutex_trylock` is successful, then you can proceed. If it can't acquire the lock, however, you can release the locks you already hold, clean up, and try again later.

Example

In this example, we update Figure 11.10 to show the use of two mutexes. We avoid deadlocks by ensuring that when we need to acquire two mutexes at the same time, we always lock them in the same order. The second mutex protects a hash list that we use to keep track of the `foo` data structures. Thus, the `hashlock` mutex protects both the `fh` hash table and the `f_next` hash link field in the `foo` structure. The `f_lock` mutex in the `foo` structure protects access to the remainder of the `foo` structure's fields.

```
#include <stdlib.h>
#include <pthread.h>

#define NHASH 29
#define HASH(fp)  (((unsigned long)fp)%NHASH)
```

```
struct foo *fh[NHASH];

pthread_mutex_t hashlock = PTHREAD_MUTEX_INITIALIZER;

struct foo {
    int             f_count;
    pthread_mutex_t f_lock;
    struct foo      *f_next; /* protected by hashlock */
    int             f_id;
    /* ... more stuff here ... */
};

struct foo *
foo_alloc(void) /* allocate the object */
{
    struct foo  *fp;
    int         idx;

    if ((fp = malloc(sizeof(struct foo))) != NULL) {
        fp->f_count = 1;
        if (pthread_mutex_init(&fp->f_lock, NULL) != 0) {
            free(fp);
            return(NULL);
        }
        idx = HASH(fp);
        pthread_mutex_lock(&hashlock);
        fp->f_next = fh[idx];
        fh[idx] = fp;
        pthread_mutex_lock(&fp->f_lock);
        pthread_mutex_unlock(&hashlock);
        /* ... continue initialization ... */
        pthread_mutex_unlock(&fp->f_lock);
    }
    return(fp);
}

void
foo_hold(struct foo *fp) /* add a reference to the object */
{
    pthread_mutex_lock(&fp->f_lock);
    fp->f_count++;
    pthread_mutex_unlock(&fp->f_lock);
}

struct foo *
foo_find(int id) /* find an existing object */
{
    struct foo  *fp;
    int         idx;

    pthread_mutex_lock(&hashlock);
    for (idx = 0; idx < NHASH; idx++) {
```

```
            for (fp = fh[idx]; fp != NULL; fp = fp->f_next) {
                if (fp->f_id == id) {
                    foo_hold(fp);
                    pthread_mutex_unlock(&hashlock);
                    return(fp);
                }
            }
        }
        pthread_mutex_unlock(&hashlock);
        return(NULL);
}

void
foo_rele(struct foo *fp) /* release a reference to the object */
{
        struct foo  *tfp;
        int          idx;

        pthread_mutex_lock(&fp->f_lock);
        if (fp->f_count == 1) { /* last reference */
            pthread_mutex_unlock(&fp->f_lock);
            pthread_mutex_lock(&hashlock);
            pthread_mutex_lock(&fp->f_lock);
            /* need to recheck the condition */
            if (fp->f_count != 1) {
                fp->f_count--;
                pthread_mutex_unlock(&fp->f_lock);
                pthread_mutex_unlock(&hashlock);
                return;
            }
            /* remove from list */
            idx = HASH(fp);
            tfp = fh[idx];
            if (tfp == fp) {
                fh[idx] = fp->f_next;
            } else {
                while (tfp->f_next != fp)
                    tfp = tfp->f_next;
                tfp->f_next = fp->f_next;
            }
            pthread_mutex_unlock(&hashlock);
            pthread_mutex_unlock(&fp->f_lock);
            pthread_mutex_destroy(&fp->f_lock);
            free(fp);
        } else {
            fp->f_count--;
            pthread_mutex_unlock(&fp->f_lock);
        }
}
```

Figure 11.11 Using two mutexes

Comparing Figure 11.11 with Figure 11.10, we see that our allocation function now locks the hash list lock, adds the new structure to a hash bucket, and before unlocking the hash list lock, locks the mutex in the new structure. Since the new structure is placed on a global list, other threads can find it, so we need to block them if they try to access the new structure, until we are done initializing it.

The `foo_find` function locks the hash list lock and searches for the requested structure. If it is found, we increase the reference count and return a pointer to the structure. Note that we honor the lock ordering by locking the hash list lock in `foo_find` before `foo_hold` locks the `foo` structure's `f_lock` mutex.

Now with two locks, the `foo_rele` function is more complicated. If this is the last reference, we need to unlock the structure mutex so that we can acquire the hash list lock, since we'll need to remove the structure from the hash list. Then we reacquire the structure mutex. Because we could have blocked since the last time we held the structure mutex, we need to recheck the condition to see whether we still need to free the structure. If another thread found the structure and added a reference to it while we blocked to honor the lock ordering, we simply need to decrement the reference count, unlock everything, and return.

This locking is complex, so we need to revisit our design. We can simplify things considerably by using the hash list lock to protect the structure reference count, too. The structure mutex can be used to protect everything else in the `foo` structure. Figure 11.12 reflects this change.

```c
#include <stdlib.h>
#include <pthread.h>

#define NHASH 29
#define HASH(fp)  (((unsigned long)fp)%NHASH)

struct foo *fh[NHASH];
pthread_mutex_t hashlock = PTHREAD_MUTEX_INITIALIZER;

struct foo {
    int             f_count; /* protected by hashlock */
    pthread_mutex_t f_lock;
    struct foo     *f_next; /* protected by hashlock */
    int             f_id;
    /* ... more stuff here ... */
};

struct foo *
foo_alloc(void) /* allocate the object */
{
    struct foo *fp;
    int         idx;

    if ((fp = malloc(sizeof(struct foo))) != NULL) {
        fp->f_count = 1;
        if (pthread_mutex_init(&fp->f_lock, NULL) != 0) {
            free(fp);
            return(NULL);
```

```
            }
            idx = HASH(fp);
            pthread_mutex_lock(&hashlock);
            fp->f_next = fh[idx];
            fh[idx] = fp;
            pthread_mutex_lock(&fp->f_lock);
            pthread_mutex_unlock(&hashlock);
            /* ... continue initialization ... */
        }
        return(fp);
}

void
foo_hold(struct foo *fp) /* add a reference to the object */
{
        pthread_mutex_lock(&hashlock);
        fp->f_count++;
        pthread_mutex_unlock(&hashlock);
}

struct foo *
foo_find(int id) /* find a existing object */
{
        struct foo   *fp;
        int          idx;

        pthread_mutex_lock(&hashlock);
        for (idx = 0; idx < NHASH; idx++) {
            for (fp = fh[idx]; fp != NULL; fp = fp->f_next) {
                if (fp->f_id == id) {
                    fp->f_count++;
                    pthread_mutex_unlock(&hashlock);
                    return(fp);
                }
            }
        }
        pthread_mutex_unlock(&hashlock);
        return(NULL);
}

void
foo_rele(struct foo *fp) /* release a reference to the object */
{
        struct foo   *tfp;
        int          idx;

        pthread_mutex_lock(&hashlock);
        if (--fp->f_count == 0) { /* last reference, remove from list */
            idx = HASH(fp);
            tfp = fh[idx];
            if (tfp == fp) {
                fh[idx] = fp->f_next;
```

```
        } else {
            while (tfp->f_next != fp)
                tfp = tfp->f_next;
            tfp->f_next = fp->f_next;
        }
        pthread_mutex_unlock(&hashlock);
        pthread_mutex_destroy(&fp->f_lock);
        free(fp);
    } else {
        pthread_mutex_unlock(&hashlock);
    }
}
```

Figure 11.12 Simplified locking

Note how much simpler the program in Figure 11.12 is compared to the program in Figure 11.11. The lock-ordering issues surrounding the hash list and the reference count go away when we use the same lock for both purposes. Multithreaded software design involves these types of tradeoffs. If your locking granularity is too coarse, you end up with too many threads blocking behind the same locks, with little improvement possible from concurrency. If your locking granularity is too fine, then you suffer bad performance from excess locking overhead, and you end up with complex code. As a programmer, you need to find the correct balance between code complexity and performance, and still satisfy your locking requirements.   □

Reader–Writer Locks

Reader–writer locks are similar to mutexes, except that they allow for higher degrees of parallelism. With a mutex, the state is either locked or unlocked, and only one thread can lock it at a time. Three states are possible with a reader–writer lock: locked in read mode, locked in write mode, and unlocked. Only one thread at a time can hold a reader–writer lock in write mode, but multiple threads can hold a reader–writer lock in read mode at the same time.

When a reader–writer lock is write-locked, all threads attempting to lock it block until it is unlocked. When a reader–writer lock is read-locked, all threads attempting to lock it in read mode are given access, but any threads attempting to lock it in write mode block until all the threads have relinquished their read locks. Although implementations vary, reader–writer locks usually block additional readers if a lock is already held in read mode and a thread is blocked trying to acquire the lock in write mode. This prevents a constant stream of readers from starving waiting writers.

Reader–writer locks are well suited for situations in which data structures are read more often than they are modified. When a reader–writer lock is held in write mode, the data structure it protects can be modified safely, since only one thread at a time can hold the lock in write mode. When the reader–writer lock is held in read mode, the data structure it protects can be read by multiple threads, as long as the threads first acquire the lock in read mode.

Reader–writer locks are also called shared–exclusive locks. When a reader–writer lock is read-locked, it is said to be locked in shared mode. When it is write-locked, it is said to be locked in exclusive mode.

As with mutexes, reader–writer locks must be initialized before use and destroyed before freeing their underlying memory.

```
#include <pthread.h>

int pthread_rwlock_init(pthread_rwlock_t *restrict rwlock,
                        const pthread_rwlockattr_t *restrict attr);

int pthread_rwlock_destroy(pthread_rwlock_t *rwlock);
```
                                      Both return: 0 if OK, error number on failure

A reader–writer lock is initialized by calling `pthread_rwlock_init`. We can pass a null pointer for *attr* if we want the reader–writer lock to have the default attributes. We discuss reader–writer lock attributes in Section 12.4.

Before freeing the memory backing a reader–writer lock, we need to call `pthread_rwlock_destroy` to clean it up. If `pthread_rwlock_init` allocated any resources for the reader–writer lock, `pthread_rwlock_destroy` frees those resources. If we free the memory backing a reader–writer lock without first calling `pthread_rwlock_destroy`, any resources assigned to the lock will be lost.

To lock a reader–writer lock in read mode, we call `pthread_rwlock_rdlock`. To write-lock a reader–writer lock, we call `pthread_rwlock_wrlock`. Regardless of how we lock a reader–writer lock, we can call `pthread_rwlock_unlock` to unlock it.

```
#include <pthread.h>

int pthread_rwlock_rdlock(pthread_rwlock_t *rwlock);

int pthread_rwlock_wrlock(pthread_rwlock_t *rwlock);

int pthread_rwlock_unlock(pthread_rwlock_t *rwlock);
```
                                        All return: 0 if OK, error number on failure

Implementations might place a limit on the number of times a reader–writer lock can be locked in shared mode, so we need to check the return value of `pthread_rwlock_rdlock`. Even though `pthread_rwlock_wrlock` and `pthread_rwlock_unlock` have error returns, we don't need to check them if we design our locking properly. The only error returns defined are when we use them improperly, such as with an uninitialized lock, or when we might deadlock by attempting to acquire a lock we already own.

The Single UNIX Specification also defines conditional versions of the reader–writer locking primitives.

```
#include <pthread.h>

int pthread_rwlock_tryrdlock(pthread_rwlock_t *rwlock);

int pthread_rwlock_trywrlock(pthread_rwlock_t *rwlock);
```
                                      Both return: 0 if OK, error number on failure

When the lock can be acquired, these functions return 0. Otherwise, they return the error EBUSY. These functions can be used in situations in which conforming to a lock hierarchy isn't enough to avoid a deadlock, as we discussed previously.

Example

The program in Figure 11.13 illustrates the use of reader–writer locks. A queue of job requests is protected by a single reader–writer lock. This example shows a possible implementation of Figure 11.1, whereby multiple worker threads obtain jobs assigned to them by a single master thread.

```c
#include <stdlib.h>
#include <pthread.h>

struct job {
    struct job *j_next;
    struct job *j_prev;
    pthread_t  j_id;   /* tells which thread handles this job */
    /* ... more stuff here ... */
};

struct queue {
    struct job        *q_head;
    struct job        *q_tail;
    pthread_rwlock_t q_lock;
};

/*
 * Initialize a queue.
 */
int
queue_init(struct queue *qp)
{
    int err;

    qp->q_head = NULL;
    qp->q_tail = NULL;
    err = pthread_rwlock_init(&qp->q_lock, NULL);
    if (err != 0)
        return(err);
    /* ... continue initialization ... */

    return(0);
}

/*
 * Insert a job at the head of the queue.
 */
void
job_insert(struct queue *qp, struct job *jp)
{
    pthread_rwlock_wrlock(&qp->q_lock);
    jp->j_next = qp->q_head;
```

```
        jp->j_prev = NULL;
        if (qp->q_head != NULL)
            qp->q_head->j_prev = jp;
        else
            qp->q_tail = jp;        /* list was empty */
        qp->q_head = jp;
        pthread_rwlock_unlock(&qp->q_lock);
}

/*
 * Append a job on the tail of the queue.
 */
void
job_append(struct queue *qp, struct job *jp)
{
        pthread_rwlock_wrlock(&qp->q_lock);
        jp->j_next = NULL;
        jp->j_prev = qp->q_tail;
        if (qp->q_tail != NULL)
            qp->q_tail->j_next = jp;
        else
            qp->q_head = jp;        /* list was empty */
        qp->q_tail = jp;
        pthread_rwlock_unlock(&qp->q_lock);
}

/*
 * Remove the given job from a queue.
 */
void
job_remove(struct queue *qp, struct job *jp)
{
        pthread_rwlock_wrlock(&qp->q_lock);
        if (jp == qp->q_head) {
            qp->q_head = jp->j_next;
            if (qp->q_tail == jp)
                qp->q_tail = NULL;
            else
                jp->j_next->j_prev = jp->j_prev;
        } else if (jp == qp->q_tail) {
            qp->q_tail = jp->j_prev;
            if (qp->q_head == jp)
                qp->q_head = NULL;
            else
                jp->j_prev->j_next = jp->j_next;
        } else {
            jp->j_prev->j_next = jp->j_next;
            jp->j_next->j_prev = jp->j_prev;
        }
        pthread_rwlock_unlock(&qp->q_lock);
}
```

```
/*
 * Find a job for the given thread ID.
 */
struct job *
job_find(struct queue *qp, pthread_t id)
{
    struct job *jp;

    if (pthread_rwlock_rdlock(&qp->q_lock) != 0)
        return(NULL);

    for (jp = qp->q_head; jp != NULL; jp = jp->j_next)
        if (pthread_equal(jp->j_id, id))
            break;

    pthread_rwlock_unlock(&qp->q_lock);
    return(jp);
}
```

Figure 11.13 Using reader–writer locks

In this example, we lock the queue's reader–writer lock in write mode whenever we need to add a job to the queue or remove a job from the queue. Whenever we search the queue, we grab the lock in read mode, allowing all the worker threads to search the queue concurrently. Using a reader–writer lock will improve performance in this case only if threads search the queue much more frequently than they add or remove jobs.

The worker threads take only those jobs that match their thread ID off the queue. Since the job structures are used only by one thread at a time, they don't need any extra locking.   □

Condition Variables

Condition variables are another synchronization mechanism available to threads. Condition variables provide a place for threads to rendezvous. When used with mutexes, condition variables allow threads to wait in a race-free way for arbitrary conditions to occur.

The condition itself is protected by a mutex. A thread must first lock the mutex to change the condition state. Other threads will not notice the change until they acquire the mutex, because the mutex must be locked to be able to evaluate the condition.

Before a condition variable is used, it must first be initialized. A condition variable, represented by the pthread_cond_t data type, can be initialized in two ways. We can assign the constant PTHREAD_COND_INITIALIZER to a statically-allocated condition variable, but if the condition variable is allocated dynamically, we can use the pthread_cond_init function to initialize it.

We can use the pthread_cond_destroy function to deinitialize a condition variable before freeing its underlying memory.

```
#include <pthread.h>

int pthread_cond_init(pthread_cond_t *restrict cond,
                      pthread_condattr_t *restrict attr);

int pthread_cond_destroy(pthread_cond_t *cond);
```

                                     Both return: 0 if OK, error number on failure

Unless you need to create a conditional variable with nondefault attributes, the *attr* argument to pthread_cond_init can be set to NULL. We will discuss condition variable attributes in Section 12.4.

We use pthread_cond_wait to wait for a condition to be true. A variant is provided to return an error code if the condition hasn't been satisfied in the specified amount of time.

```
#include <pthread.h>

int pthread_cond_wait(pthread_cond_t *restrict cond,
                      pthread_mutex_t *restrict mutex);

int pthread_cond_timedwait(pthread_cond_t *restrict cond,
                           pthread_mutex_t *restrict mutex,
                           const struct timespec *restrict timeout);
```

                                     Both return: 0 if OK, error number on failure

The mutex passed to pthread_cond_wait protects the condition. The caller passes it locked to the function, which then atomically places the calling thread on the list of threads waiting for the condition and unlocks the mutex. This closes the window between the time that the condition is checked and the time that the thread goes to sleep waiting for the condition to change, so that the thread doesn't miss a change in the condition. When pthread_cond_wait returns, the mutex is again locked.

The pthread_cond_timedwait function works the same as the pthread_cond_wait function with the addition of the timeout. The timeout value specifies how long we will wait. It is specified by the timespec structure, where a time value is represented by a number of seconds and partial seconds. Partial seconds are specified in units of nanoseconds:

```
struct timespec {
        time_t tv_sec;    /* seconds */
        long   tv_nsec;   /* nanoseconds */
};
```

Using this structure, we need to specify how long we are willing to wait as an absolute time instead of a relative time. For example, if we are willing to wait 3 minutes, instead of translating 3 minutes into a timespec structure, we need to translate now+3 minutes into a timespec structure.

We can use gettimeofday (Section 6.10) to get the current time expressed as a timeval structure and translate this into a timespec structure. To obtain the absolute time for the timeout value, we can use the following function:

```
void
maketimeout(struct timespec *tsp, long minutes)
{
    struct timeval now;

    /* get the current time */
    gettimeofday(&now);
    tsp->tv_sec = now.tv_sec;
    tsp->tv_nsec = now.tv_usec * 1000; /* usec to nsec */
    /* add the offset to get timeout value */
    tsp->tv_sec += minutes * 60;
}
```

If the timeout expires without the condition occurring, pthread_cond_timedwait will reacquire the mutex and return the error ETIMEDOUT. When it returns from a successful call to pthread_cond_wait or pthread_cond_timedwait, a thread needs to reevaluate the condition, since another thread might have run and already changed the condition.

There are two functions to notify threads that a condition has been satisfied. The pthread_cond_signal function will wake up one thread waiting on a condition, whereas the pthread_cond_broadcast function will wake up all threads waiting on a condition.

> The POSIX specification allows for implementations of pthread_cond_signal to wake up more than one thread, to make the implementation simpler.

```
#include <pthread.h>

int pthread_cond_signal(pthread_cond_t *cond);

int pthread_cond_broadcast(pthread_cond_t *cond);
```
                                    Both return: 0 if OK, error number on failure

When we call pthread_cond_signal or pthread_cond_broadcast, we are said to be *signaling* the thread or condition. We have to be careful to signal the threads only after changing the state of the condition.

Example

Figure 11.14 shows an example of how to use condition variables and mutexes together to synchronize threads.

```
#include <pthread.h>

struct msg {
    struct msg *m_next;
    /* ... more stuff here ... */
};
```

```
struct msg *workq;
pthread_cond_t qready = PTHREAD_COND_INITIALIZER;
pthread_mutex_t qlock = PTHREAD_MUTEX_INITIALIZER;

void
process_msg(void)
{
    struct msg *mp;

    for (;;) {
        pthread_mutex_lock(&qlock);
        while (workq == NULL)
            pthread_cond_wait(&qready, &qlock);
        mp = workq;
        workq = mp->m_next;
        pthread_mutex_unlock(&qlock);
        /* now process the message mp */
    }
}
void
enqueue_msg(struct msg *mp)
{
    pthread_mutex_lock(&qlock);
    mp->m_next = workq;
    workq = mp;
    pthread_mutex_unlock(&qlock);
    pthread_cond_signal(&qready);
}
```

Figure 11.14 Using condition variables

The condition is the state of the work queue. We protect the condition with a mutex and evaluate the condition in a `while` loop. When we put a message on the work queue, we need to hold the mutex, but we don't need to hold the mutex when we signal the waiting threads. As long as it is okay for a thread to pull the message off the queue before we call `cond_signal`, we can do this after releasing the mutex. Since we check the condition in a `while` loop, this doesn't present a problem: a thread will wake up, find that the queue is still empty, and go back to waiting again. If the code couldn't tolerate this race, we would need to hold the mutex when we signal the threads.   □

11.7 Summary

In this chapter, we introduced the concept of threads and discussed the POSIX.1 primitives available to create and destroy them. We also introduced the problem of thread synchronization. We discussed three fundamental synchronization mechanisms—mutexes, reader–writer locks, and condition variables—and we saw how to use them to protect shared resources.

Exercises

11.1 Modify the example shown in Figure 11.4 to pass the structure between the threads properly.

11.2 In the example shown in Figure 11.13, what additional synchronization (if any) is necessary to allow the master thread to change the thread ID associated with a pending job? How would this affect the `job_remove` function?

11.3 Apply the techniques shown in Figure 11.14 to the worker thread example (Figure 11.1 and Figure 11.13) to implement the worker thread function. Don't forget to update the `queue_init` function to initialize the condition variable and change the the `job_insert` and `job_append` functions to signal the worker threads. What difficulties arise?

11.4 Which sequence of steps is correct?

   1. Lock a mutex (`pthread_mutex_lock`).
   2. Change the condition protected by the mutex.
   3. Signal threads waiting on the condition (`pthread_cond_broadcast`).
   4. Unlock the mutex (`pthread_mutex_unlock`).

or

   1. Lock a mutex (`pthread_mutex_lock`).
   2. Change the condition protected by the mutex.
   3. Unlock the mutex (`pthread_mutex_unlock`).
   4. Signal threads waiting on the condition (`pthread_cond_broadcast`).

12

Thread Control

12.1 Introduction

In Chapter 11, we learned the basics about threads and thread synchronization. In this chapter, we will learn the details of controlling thread behavior. We will look at thread attributes and synchronization primitive attributes, which we ignored in the previous chapter in favor of the default behaviors.

We will follow this with a look at how threads can keep data private from other threads in the same process. Then we will wrap up the chapter with a look at how some process-based system calls interact with threads.

12.2 Thread Limits

We discussed the `sysconf` function in Section 2.5.4. The Single UNIX Specification defines several limits associated with the operation of threads, which we didn't show in Figure 2.10. As with other system limits, the thread limits can be queried using `sysconf`. Figure 12.1 summarizes these limits.

As with the other limits reported by `sysconf`, use of these limits is intended to promote application portability among different operating system implementations. For example, if your application requires that you create four threads for every file you manage, you might have to limit the number of files you can manage concurrently if the system won't let you create enough threads.

Name of limit	Description	*name* argument
PTHREAD_DESTRUCTOR_ITERATIONS	maximum number of times an implementation will try to destroy the thread-specific data when a thread exits (Section 12.6)	_SC_THREAD_DESTRUCTOR_ITERATIONS
PTHREAD_KEYS_MAX	maximum number of keys that can be created by a process (Section 12.6)	_SC_THREAD_KEYS_MAX
PTHREAD_STACK_MIN	minimum number of bytes that can be used for a thread's stack (Section 12.3)	_SC_THREAD_STACK_MIN
PTHREAD_THREADS_MAX	maximum number of threads that can be created in a process (Section 12.3)	_SC_THREAD_THREADS_MAX

Figure 12.1 Thread limits and *name* arguments to `sysconf`

Figure 12.2 shows the values of the thread limits for the four implementations described in this book. When the implementation doesn't define the corresponding sysconf symbol (starting with _SC_), "no symbol" is listed. If the implementation's limit is indeterminate, "no limit" is listed. This doesn't mean that the value is unlimited, however. An "unsupported" entry means that the implementation defines the corresponding sysconf limit symbol, but the sysconf function doesn't recognize it.

> Note that although an implementation may not provide access to these limits, that doesn't mean that the limits don't exist. It just means that the implementation doesn't provide us with a way to get at them using sysconf.

Limit	FreeBSD 5.2.1	Linux 2.4.22	Mac OS X 10.3	Solaris 9
PTHREAD_DESTRUCTOR_ITERATIONS	no symbol	unsupported	no symbol	no limit
PTHREAD_KEYS_MAX	no symbol	unsupported	no symbol	no limit
PTHREAD_STACK_MIN	no symbol	unsupported	no symbol	4,096
PTHREAD_THREADS_MAX	no symbol	unsupported	no symbol	no limit

Figure 12.2 Examples of thread configuration limits

12.3 Thread Attributes

In all the examples in which we called `pthread_create` in Chapter 11, we passed in a null pointer instead of passing in a pointer to a `pthread_attr_t` structure. We can use the `pthread_attr_t` structure to modify the default attributes, and associate these attributes with threads that we create. We use the `pthread_attr_init` function to initialize the `pthread_attr_t` structure. After calling `pthread_attr_init`, the `pthread_attr_t` structure contains the default values for all the thread attributes supported by the implementation. To change individual attributes, we need to call other functions, as described later in this section.

```
#include <pthread.h>

int pthread_attr_init(pthread_attr_t *attr);

int pthread_attr_destroy(pthread_attr_t *attr);
```
Both return: 0 if OK, error number on failure

To deinitialize a `pthread_attr_t` structure, we call `pthread_attr_destroy`. If an implementation of `pthread_attr_init` allocated any dynamic memory for the attribute object, `pthread_attr_destroy` will free that memory. In addition, `pthread_attr_destroy` will initialize the attribute object with invalid values, so if it is used by mistake, `pthread_create` will return an error.

The `pthread_attr_t` structure is opaque to applications. This means that applications aren't supposed to know anything about its internal structure, thus promoting application portability. Following this model, POSIX.1 defines separate functions to query and set each attribute.

The thread attributes defined by POSIX.1 are summarized in Figure 12.3. POSIX.1 defines additional attributes in the real-time threads option, but we don't discuss those here. In Figure 12.3, we also show which platforms support each thread attribute. If the attribute is accessible through an obsolete interface, we show **ob** in the table entry.

Name	Description	FreeBSD 5.2.1	Linux 2.4.22	Mac OS X 10.3	Solaris 9
detachstate	detached thread attribute	•	•	•	•
guardsize	guard buffer size in bytes at end of thread stack		•	•	•
stackaddr	lowest address of thread stack	**ob**	•	•	**ob**
stacksize	size in bytes of thread stack	•	•	•	•

Figure 12.3 POSIX.1 thread attributes

In Section 11.5, we introduced the concept of detached threads. If we are no longer interested in an existing thread's termination status, we can use `pthread_detach` to allow the operating system to reclaim the thread's resources when the thread exits.

If we know that we don't need the thread's termination status at the time we create the thread, we can arrange for the thread to start out in the detached state by modifying the *detachstate* thread attribute in the `pthread_attr_t` structure. We can use the `pthread_attr_setdetachstate` function to set the *detachstate* thread attribute to one of two legal values: `PTHREAD_CREATE_DETACHED` to start the thread in the detached state or `PTHREAD_CREATE_JOINABLE` to start the thread normally, so its termination status can be retrieved by the application.

```
#include <pthread.h>

int pthread_attr_getdetachstate(const pthread_attr_t *restrict attr,
                                int *detachstate);

int pthread_attr_setdetachstate(pthread_attr_t *attr, int detachstate);

                                  Both return: 0 if OK, error number on failure
```

We can call `pthread_attr_getdetachstate` to obtain the current *detachstate* attribute. The integer pointed to by the second argument is set to either `PTHREAD_CREATE_DETACHED` or `PTHREAD_CREATE_JOINABLE`, depending on the value of the attribute in the given `pthread_attr_t` structure.

Example

Figure 12.4 shows a function that can be used to create a thread in the detached state.

```
#include "apue.h"
#include <pthread.h>

int
makethread(void * (*fn)(void *), void *arg)
{
    int             err;
    pthread_t       tid;
    pthread_attr_t  attr;

    err = pthread_attr_init(&attr);
    if (err != 0)
        return(err);
    err = pthread_attr_setdetachstate(&attr, PTHREAD_CREATE_DETACHED);
    if (err == 0)
        err = pthread_create(&tid, &attr, fn, arg);
    pthread_attr_destroy(&attr);
    return(err);
}
```

Figure 12.4   Creating a thread in the detached state

Note that we ignore the return value from the call to `pthread_attr_destroy`. In this case, we initialized the thread attributes properly, so `pthread_attr_destroy` shouldn't fail. Nonetheless, if it does fail, cleaning up would be difficult: we would have to destroy the thread we just created, which is possibly already running, asynchronous to the execution of this function. By ignoring the error return from `pthread_attr_destroy`, the worst that can happen is that we leak a small amount of memory if `pthread_attr_init` allocated any. But if `pthread_attr_init` succeeded in initializing the thread attributes and then `pthread_attr_destroy` failed to clean up, we have no recovery strategy anyway, because the attributes structure is opaque to the application. The only interface defined to clean up the structure is `pthread_attr_destroy`, and it just failed.   □

Support for thread stack attributes is optional for a POSIX-conforming operating system, but is required if the system is to conform to the XSI. At compile time, you can check whether your system supports each thread stack attribute using the `_POSIX_THREAD_ATTR_STACKADDR` and `_POSIX_THREAD_ATTR_STACKSIZE` symbols. If one is defined, then the system supports the corresponding thread stack attribute. You can also check at runtime, by using the `_SC_THREAD_ATTR_STACKADDR` and `_SC_THREAD_ATTR_STACKSIZE` parameters to the `sysconf` function.

POSIX.1 defines several interfaces to manipulate thread stack attributes. Two older functions, `pthread_attr_getstackaddr` and `pthread_attr_setstackaddr`, are marked as obsolete in Version 3 of the Single UNIX Specification, although many pthreads implementations still provide them. The preferred way to query and modify a thread's stack attributes is to use the newer functions `pthread_attr_getstack` and `pthread_attr_setstack`. These functions clear up ambiguities present in the definition of the older interfaces.

```
#include <pthread.h>

int pthread_attr_getstack(const pthread_attr_t *restrict attr,
                          void **restrict stackaddr,
                          size_t *restrict stacksize);

int pthread_attr_setstack(pthread_attr_t *attr,
                          void *stackaddr, size_t stacksize);
```
                                        Both return: 0 if OK, error number on failure

These two functions are used to manage both the *stackaddr* and the *stacksize* thread attributes.

With a process, the amount of virtual address space is fixed. Since there is only one stack, its size usually isn't a problem. With threads, however, the same amount of virtual address space must be shared by all the thread stacks. You might have to reduce your default thread stack size if your application uses so many threads that the cumulative size of their stacks exceeds the available virtual address space. On the other hand, if your threads call functions that allocate large automatic variables or call functions many stack frames deep, you might need more than the default stack size.

If you run out of virtual address space for thread stacks, you can use `malloc` or `mmap` (see Section 14.9) to allocate space for an alternate stack and use `pthread_attr_setstack` to change the stack location of threads you create. The address specified by the *stackaddr* parameter is the lowest addressable address in the range of memory to be used as the thread's stack, aligned at the proper boundary for the processor architecture.

The *stackaddr* thread attribute is defined as the lowest memory address for the stack. This is not necessarily the start of the stack, however. If stacks grow from higher address to lower addresses for a given processor architecture, the *stackaddr* thread attribute will be the end of the stack instead of the beginning.

The drawback with `pthread_attr_getstackaddr` and `pthread_attr_setstackaddr` is that the *stackaddr* parameter was underspecified. It could have been interpreted as the start of the stack or as the lowest memory address of the memory extent to use as the stack. On architectures in which the stacks grow down from higher memory addresses to lower addresses, if the *stackaddr* parameter is the lowest memory address of the stack, then you need to know the stack size to determine the start of the stack. The `pthread_attr_getstack` and `pthread_attr_setstack` functions correct these shortcomings.

An application can also get and set the *stacksize* thread attribute using the `pthread_attr_getstacksize` and `pthread_attr_setstacksize` functions.

```
#include <pthread.h>

int pthread_attr_getstacksize(const pthread_attr_t *restrict attr,
                              size_t *restrict stacksize);

int pthread_attr_setstacksize(pthread_attr_t *attr, size_t stacksize);
```
                                    Both return: 0 if OK, error number on failure

The `pthread_attr_setstacksize` function is useful when you want to change the default stack size but don't want to deal with allocating the thread stacks on your own.

The *guardsize* thread attribute controls the size of the memory extent after the end of the thread's stack to protect against stack overflow. By default, this is set to PAGESIZE bytes. We can set the *guardsize* thread attribute to 0 to disable this feature: no guard buffer will be provided in this case. Also, if we change the *stackaddr* thread attribute, the system assumes that we will be managing our own stacks and disables stack guard buffers, just as if we had set the *guardsize* thread attribute to 0.

```
#include <pthread.h>

int pthread_attr_getguardsize(const pthread_attr_t *restrict attr,
                              size_t *restrict guardsize);

int pthread_attr_setguardsize(pthread_attr_t *attr, size_t guardsize);
```
                                    Both return: 0 if OK, error number on failure

If the *guardsize* thread attribute is modified, the operating system might round it up to an integral multiple of the page size. If the thread's stack pointer overflows into the guard area, the application will receive an error, possibly with a signal.

The Single UNIX Specification defines several other optional thread attributes as part of the real-time threads option. We will not discuss them here.

More Thread Attributes

Threads have other attributes not represented by the `pthread_attr_t` structure:

- The cancelability state (discussed in Section 12.7)
- The cancelability type (also discussed in Section 12.7)
- The concurrency level

The concurrency level controls the number of kernel threads or processes on top of which the user-level threads are mapped. If an implementation keeps a one-to-one mapping between kernel-level threads and user-level threads, then changing the concurrency level will have no effect, since it is possible for all user-level threads to be scheduled. If the implementation multiplexes user-level threads on top of kernel-level threads or processes, however, you might be able to improve performance by increasing the number of user-level threads that can run at a given time. The `pthread_setconcurrency` function can be used to provide a hint to the system of the desired level of concurrency.

```
#include <pthread.h>

int pthread_getconcurrency(void);
```
                                              Returns: current concurrency level
```
int pthread_setconcurrency(int level);
```
                                              Returns: 0 if OK, error number on failure

The `pthread_getconcurrency` function returns the current concurrency level. If the operating system is controlling the concurrency level (i.e., if no prior call to `pthread_setconcurrency` has been made), then `pthread_getconcurrency` will return 0.

The concurrency level specified by `pthread_setconcurrency` is only a hint to the system. There is no guarantee that the requested concurrency level will be honored. You can tell the system that you want it to decide for itself what concurrency level to use by passing a *level* of 0. Thus, an application can undo the effects of a prior call to `pthread_setconcurrency` with a nonzero value of *level* by calling it again with *level* set to 0.

12.4 Synchronization Attributes

Just as threads have attributes, so too do their synchronization objects. In this section, we discuss the attributes of mutexes, reader–writer locks, and condition variables.

Mutex Attributes

We use `pthread_mutexattr_init` to initialize a `pthread_mutexattr_t` structure and `pthread_mutexattr_destroy` to deinitialize one.

```
#include <pthread.h>

int pthread_mutexattr_init(pthread_mutexattr_t *attr);

int pthread_mutexattr_destroy(pthread_mutexattr_t *attr);
```
                                              Both return: 0 if OK, error number on failure

The `pthread_mutexattr_init` function will initialize the `pthread_mutexattr_t` structure with the default mutex attributes. Two attributes of interest are the *process-shared* attribute and the *type* attribute. Within POSIX.1, the *process-shared* attribute is optional; you can test whether a platform supports it by checking whether the `_POSIX_THREAD_PROCESS_SHARED` symbol is defined. You can also check at runtime by passing the `_SC_THREAD_PROCESS_SHARED` parameter to the `sysconf` function. Although this option is not required to be provided by POSIX-conforming operating systems, the Single UNIX Specification requires that XSI-conforming operating systems do support this option.

Within a process, multiple threads can access the same synchronization object. This is the default behavior, as we saw in Chapter 11. In this case, the *process-shared* mutex attribute is set to `PTHREAD_PROCESS_PRIVATE`.

As we shall see in Chapters 14 and 15, mechanisms exist that allow independent processes to map the same extent of memory into their independent address spaces. Access to shared data by multiple processes usually requires synchronization, just as does access to shared data by multiple threads. If the *process-shared* mutex attribute is set to `PTHREAD_PROCESS_SHARED`, a mutex allocated from a memory extent shared between multiple processes may be used for synchronization by those processes.

We can use the `pthread_mutexattr_getpshared` function to query a `pthread_mutexattr_t` structure for its *process-shared* attribute. We can change the *process-shared* attribute with the `pthread_mutexattr_setpshared` function.

```
#include <pthread.h>

int pthread_mutexattr_getpshared(const pthread_mutexattr_t *
                                        restrict attr,
                                        int *restrict pshared);

int pthread_mutexattr_setpshared(pthread_mutexattr_t *attr,
                                        int pshared);
```

Both return: 0 if OK, error number on failure

The *process-shared* mutex attribute allows the pthread library to provide more efficient mutex implementations when the attribute is set to `PTHREAD_PROCESS_PRIVATE`, which is the default case with multithreaded applications. Then the pthread library can restrict the more expensive implementation to the case in which mutexes are shared among processes.

The *type* mutex attribute controls the characteristics of the mutex. POSIX.1 defines four types. The `PTHREAD_MUTEX_NORMAL` type is a standard mutex that doesn't do any special error checking or deadlock detection. The `PTHREAD_MUTEX_ERRORCHECK` mutex type provides error checking.

The `PTHREAD_MUTEX_RECURSIVE` mutex type allows the same thread to lock it multiple times without first unlocking it. A recursive mutex maintains a lock count and isn't released until it is unlocked the same number of times it is locked. So if you lock a recursive mutex twice and then unlock it, the mutex remains locked until it is unlocked a second time.

Finally, the `PTHREAD_MUTEX_DEFAULT` type can be used to request default
semantics. Implementations are free to map this to one of the other types. On Linux,
for example, this type is mapped to the normal mutex type.

The behavior of the four types is shown in Figure 12.5. The "Unlock when not
owned" column refers to one thread unlocking a mutex that was locked by a different
thread. The "Unlock when unlocked" column refers to what happens when a thread
unlocks a mutex that is already unlocked, which usually is a coding mistake.

Mutex type	Relock without unlock?	Unlock when not owned?	Unlock when unlocked?
`PTHREAD_MUTEX_NORMAL`	deadlock	undefined	undefined
`PTHREAD_MUTEX_ERRORCHECK`	returns error	returns error	returns error
`PTHREAD_MUTEX_RECURSIVE`	allowed	returns error	returns error
`PTHREAD_MUTEX_DEFAULT`	undefined	undefined	undefined

Figure 12.5 Mutex type behavior

We can use `pthread_mutexattr_gettype` to get the mutex *type* attribute and
`pthread_mutexattr_settype` to change the mutex *type* attribute.

```
#include <pthread.h>

int pthread_mutexattr_gettype(const pthread_mutexattr_t *
                              restrict attr, int *restrict type);

int pthread_mutexattr_settype(pthread_mutexattr_t *attr, int type);
```
                                    Both return: 0 if OK, error number on failure

Recall from Section 11.6 that a mutex is used to protect the condition that is
associated with a condition variable. Before blocking the thread, the
`pthread_cond_wait` and the `pthread_cond_timedwait` functions release the
mutex associated with the condition. This allows other threads to acquire the mutex,
change the condition, release the mutex, and signal the condition variable. Since the
mutex must be held to change the condition, it is not a good idea to use a recursive
mutex. If a recursive mutex is locked multiple times and used in a call to
`pthread_cond_wait`, the condition can never be satisfied, because the unlock done by
`pthread_cond_wait` doesn't release the mutex.

Recursive mutexes are useful when you need to adapt existing single-threaded
interfaces to a multithreaded environment, but can't change the interfaces to your
functions because of compatibility constraints. However, using recursive locks can be
tricky, and they should be used only when no other solution is possible.

Example

Figure 12.6 illustrates a situation in which a recursive mutex might seem to solve a
concurrency problem. Assume that `func1` and `func2` are existing functions in a
library whose interfaces can't be changed, because applications exist that call them, and
the applications can't be changed.

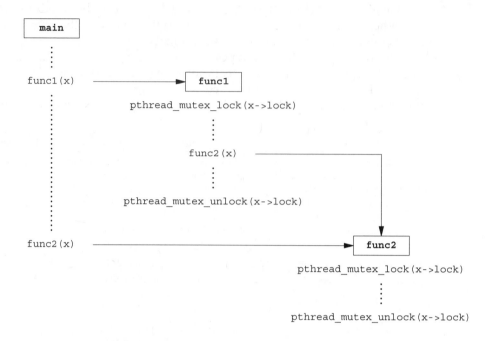

Figure 12.6 Recursive locking opportunity

To keep the interfaces the same, we embed a mutex in the data structure whose address (x) is passed in as an argument. This is possible only if we have provided an allocator function for the structure, so the application doesn't know about its size (assuming we must increase its size when we add a mutex to it).

> This is also possible if we originally defined the structure with enough padding to allow us now to replace some pad fields with a mutex. Unfortunately, most programmers are unskilled at predicting the future, so this is not a common practice.

If both `func1` and `func2` must manipulate the structure and it is possible to access it from more than one thread at a time, then `func1` and `func2` must lock the mutex before manipulating the data. If `func1` must call `func2`, we will deadlock if the mutex type is not recursive. We could avoid using a recursive mutex if we could release the mutex before calling `func2` and reacquire it after `func2` returns, but this opens a window where another thread can possibly grab control of the mutex and change the data structure in the middle of `func1`. This may not be acceptable, depending on what protection the mutex is intended to provide.

Figure 12.7 shows an alternative to using a recursive mutex in this case. We can leave the interfaces to `func1` and `func2` unchanged and avoid a recursive mutex by providing a private version of `func2`, called `func2_locked`. To call `func2_locked`, we must hold the mutex embedded in the data structure whose address we pass as the argument. The body of `func2_locked` contains a copy of `func2`, and `func2` now simply acquires the mutex, calls `func2_locked`, and then releases the mutex.

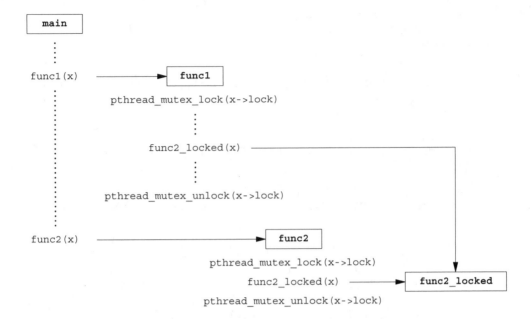

Figure 12.7 Avoiding a recursive locking opportunity

If we didn't have to leave the interfaces to the library functions unchanged, we could have added a second parameter to each function to indicate whether the structure is locked by the caller. It is usually better to leave the interfaces unchanged if we can, however, instead of polluting it with implementation artifacts.

The strategy of providing locked and unlocked versions of functions is usually applicable in simple situations. In more complex situations, such as when the library needs to call a function outside the library, which then might call back into the library, we need to rely on recursive locks.   □

Example

The program in Figure 12.8 illustrates another situation in which a recursive mutex is necessary. Here, we have a "timeout" function that allows us to schedule another function to be run at some time in the future. Assuming that threads are an inexpensive resource, we can create a thread for each pending timeout. The thread waits until the time has been reached, and then it calls the function we've requested.

The problem arises when we can't create a thread or when the scheduled time to run the function has already passed. In these cases, we simply call the requested function now, from the current context. Since the function acquires the same lock that we currently hold, a deadlock will occur unless the lock is recursive.

```
#include "apue.h"
#include <pthread.h>
#include <time.h>
#include <sys/time.h>

extern int makethread(void *(*)(void *), void *);

struct to_info {
    void    (*to_fn)(void *);    /* function */
    void    *to_arg;             /* argument */
    struct timespec to_wait;     /* time to wait */
};

#define SECTONSEC  1000000000    /* seconds to nanoseconds */
#define USECTONSEC 1000          /* microseconds to nanoseconds */

void *
timeout_helper(void *arg)
{
    struct to_info  *tip;

    tip = (struct to_info *)arg;
    nanosleep(&tip->to_wait, NULL);
    (*tip->to_fn)(tip->to_arg);
    return(0);
}

void
timeout(const struct timespec *when, void (*func)(void *), void *arg)
{
    struct timespec now;
    struct timeval  tv;
    struct to_info  *tip;
    int             err;

    gettimeofday(&tv, NULL);
    now.tv_sec = tv.tv_sec;
    now.tv_nsec = tv.tv_usec * USECTONSEC;
    if ((when->tv_sec > now.tv_sec) ||
      (when->tv_sec == now.tv_sec && when->tv_nsec > now.tv_nsec)) {
        tip = malloc(sizeof(struct to_info));
        if (tip != NULL) {
            tip->to_fn = func;
            tip->to_arg = arg;
            tip->to_wait.tv_sec = when->tv_sec - now.tv_sec;
            if (when->tv_nsec >= now.tv_nsec) {
                tip->to_wait.tv_nsec = when->tv_nsec - now.tv_nsec;
            } else {
                tip->to_wait.tv_sec--;
                tip->to_wait.tv_nsec = SECTONSEC - now.tv_nsec +
                  when->tv_nsec;
```

```
                    }
                    err = makethread(timeout_helper, (void *)tip);
                    if (err == 0)
                        return;
                }
        }

        /*
         * We get here if (a) when <= now, or (b) malloc fails, or
         * (c) we can't make a thread, so we just call the function now.
         */
        (*func)(arg);
}

pthread_mutexattr_t attr;
pthread_mutex_t mutex;

void
retry(void *arg)
{
    pthread_mutex_lock(&mutex);
    /* perform retry steps ... */
    pthread_mutex_unlock(&mutex);
}

int
main(void)
{
    int             err, condition, arg;
    struct timespec when;

    if ((err = pthread_mutexattr_init(&attr)) != 0)
        err_exit(err, "pthread_mutexattr_init failed");
    if ((err = pthread_mutexattr_settype(&attr,
      PTHREAD_MUTEX_RECURSIVE)) != 0)
        err_exit(err, "can't set recursive type");
    if ((err = pthread_mutex_init(&mutex, &attr)) != 0)
        err_exit(err, "can't create recursive mutex");
    /* ... */
    pthread_mutex_lock(&mutex);
    /* ... */
    if (condition) {
        /* calculate target time "when" */
        timeout(&when, retry, (void *)arg);
    }
    /* ... */
    pthread_mutex_unlock(&mutex);
    /* ... */
    exit(0);
}
```

Figure 12.8   Using a recursive mutex

We use the `makethread` function from Figure 12.4 to create a thread in the detached state. We want the function to run in the future, and we don't want to wait around for the thread to complete.

We could call `sleep` to wait for the timeout to expire, but that gives us only second granularity. If we want to wait for some time other than an integral number of seconds, we need to use `nanosleep(2)`, which provides similar functionality.

> Although `nanosleep` is required to be implemented only in the real-time extensions of the Single UNIX Specification, all the platforms discussed in this text support it.

The caller of `timeout` needs to hold a mutex to check the condition and to schedule the `retry` function as an atomic operation. The `retry` function will try to lock the same mutex. Unless the mutex is recursive, a deadlock will occur if the `timeout` function calls `retry` directly.   □

Reader–Writer Lock Attributes

Reader–writer locks also have attributes, similar to mutexes. We use `pthread_rwlockattr_init` to initialize a `pthread_rwlockattr_t` structure and `pthread_rwlockattr_destroy` to deinitialize the structure.

```
#include <pthread.h>

int pthread_rwlockattr_init(pthread_rwlockattr_t *attr);

int pthread_rwlockattr_destroy(pthread_rwlockattr_t *attr);
```
                                          Both return: 0 if OK, error number on failure

The only attribute supported for reader–writer locks is the *process-shared* attribute. It is identical to the mutex *process-shared* attribute. Just as with the mutex *process-shared* attributes, a pair of functions is provided to get and set the *process-shared* attributes of reader–writer locks.

```
#include <pthread.h>

int pthread_rwlockattr_getpshared(const pthread_rwlockattr_t *
                                  restrict attr,
                                  int *restrict pshared);

int pthread_rwlockattr_setpshared(pthread_rwlockattr_t *attr,
                                  int pshared);
```
                                          Both return: 0 if OK, error number on failure

Although POSIX defines only one reader–writer lock attribute, implementations are free to define additional, nonstandard ones.

Condition Variable Attributes

Condition variables have attributes, too. There is a pair of functions for initializing and deinitializing them, similar to mutexes and reader–writer locks.

```
#include <pthread.h>

int pthread_condattr_init(pthread_condattr_t *attr);

int pthread_condattr_destroy(pthread_condattr_t *attr);
```
Both return: 0 if OK, error number on failure

Just as with the other synchronization primitives, condition variables support the *process-shared* attribute.

```
#include <pthread.h>

int pthread_condattr_getpshared(const pthread_condattr_t *
                                restrict attr,
                                int *restrict pshared);

int pthread_condattr_setpshared(pthread_condattr_t *attr,
                                int pshared);
```
Both return: 0 if OK, error number on failure

12.5 Reentrancy

We discussed reentrant functions and signal handlers in Section 10.6. Threads are similar to signal handlers when it comes to reentrancy. With both signal handlers and threads, multiple threads of control can potentially call the same function at the same time.

If a function can be safely called by multiple threads at the same time, we say that the function is *thread-safe*. All functions defined in the Single UNIX Specification are guaranteed to be thread-safe, except those listed in Figure 12.9. In addition, the ctermid and tmpnam functions are not guaranteed to be thread-safe if they are passed a null pointer. Similarly, there is no guarantee that wcrtomb and wcsrtombs are thread-safe when they are passed a null pointer for their mbstate_t argument.

Implementations that support thread-safe functions will define the _POSIX_THREAD_SAFE_FUNCTIONS symbol in <unistd.h>. Applications can also use the _SC_THREAD_SAFE_FUNCTIONS argument with sysconf to check for support of thread-safe functions at runtime. All XSI-conforming implementations are required to support thread-safe functions.

When it supports the thread-safe functions feature, an implementation provides alternate, thread-safe versions of some of the POSIX.1 functions that aren't thread-safe. Figure 12.10 lists the thread-safe versions of these functions. Many functions are not

asctime	ecvt	gethostent	getutxline	putc_unlocked
basename	encrypt	getlogin	gmtime	putchar_unlocked
catgets	endgrent	getnetbyaddr	hcreate	putenv
crypt	endpwent	getnetbyname	hdestroy	pututxline
ctime	endutxent	getnetent	hsearch	rand
dbm_clearerr	fcvt	getopt	inet_ntoa	readdir
dbm_close	ftw	getprotobyname	l64a	setenv
dbm_delete	gcvt	getprotobynumber	lgamma	setgrent
dbm_error	getc_unlocked	getprotoent	lgammaf	setkey
dbm_fetch	getchar_unlocked	getpwent	lgammal	setpwent
dbm_firstkey	getdate	getpwnam	localeconv	setutxent
dbm_nextkey	getenv	getpwuid	localtime	strerror
dbm_open	getgrent	getservbyname	lrand48	strtok
dbm_store	getgrgid	getservbyport	mrand48	ttyname
dirname	getgrnam	getservent	nftw	unsetenv
dlerror	gethostbyaddr	getutxent	nl_langinfo	wcstombs
drand48	gethostbyname	getutxid	ptsname	wctomb

Figure 12.9 Functions *not* guaranteed to be thread-safe by POSIX.1

thread-safe, because they return data stored in a static memory buffer. They are made thread-safe by changing their interfaces to require that the caller provide its own buffer.

The functions listed in Figure 12.10 are named the same as their non-thread-safe relatives, but with an _r appended at the end of the name, signifying that these versions are reentrant.

If a function is reentrant with respect to multiple threads, we say that it is thread-safe. This doesn't tell us, however, whether the function is reentrant with respect to signal handlers. We say that a function that is safe to be reentered from an asynchronous signal handler is *async-signal safe*. We saw the async-signal safe functions in Figure 10.4 when we discussed reentrant functions in Section 10.6.

acstime_r	gmtime_r
ctime_r	localtime_r
getgrgid_r	rand_r
getgrnam_r	readdir_r
getlogin_r	strerror_r
getpwnam_r	strtok_r
getpwuid_r	ttyname_r

Figure 12.10 Alternate thread-safe functions

In addition to the functions listed in Figure 12.10, POSIX.1 provides a way to manage FILE objects in a thread-safe way. You can use flockfile and ftrylockfile to obtain a lock associated with a given FILE object. This lock is recursive: you can acquire it again, while you already hold it, without deadlocking. Although the exact implementation of the lock is unspecified, it is required that all standard I/O routines that manipulate FILE objects behave as if they call flockfile and funlockfile internally.

```
#include <stdio.h>

int ftrylockfile(FILE *fp);
```

Returns: 0 if OK, nonzero if lock can't be acquired

```
void flockfile(FILE *fp);

void funlockfile(FILE *fp);
```

Although the standard I/O routines might be implemented to be thread-safe from the perspective of their own internal data structures, it is still useful to expose the locking to applications. This allows applications to compose multiple calls to standard I/O functions into atomic sequences. Of course, when dealing with multiple FILE objects, you need to beware of potential deadlocks and to order your locks carefully.

If the standard I/O routines acquire their own locks, then we can run into serious performance degradation when doing character-at-a-time I/O. In this situation, we end up acquiring and releasing a lock for every character read or written. To avoid this overhead, unlocked versions of the character-based standard I/O routines are available.

```
#include <stdio.h>

int getchar_unlocked(void);

int getc_unlocked(FILE *fp);
```

Both return: the next character if OK, EOF on end of file or error

```
int putchar_unlocked(int c);

int putc_unlocked(int c, FILE *fp);
```

Both return: c if OK, EOF on error

These four functions should not be called unless surrounded by calls to flockfile (or ftrylockfile) and funlockfile. Otherwise, unpredictable results can occur (i.e., the types of problems that result from unsynchronized access to data by multiple threads of control).

Once you lock the FILE object, you can make multiple calls to these functions before releasing the lock. This amortizes the locking overhead across the amount of data read or written.

Example

Figure 12.11 shows a possible implementation of getenv (Section 7.9). This version is not reentrant. If two threads call it at the same time, they will see inconsistent results, because the string returned is stored in a single static buffer that is shared by all threads calling getenv.

```
#include <limits.h>
#include <string.h>

static char envbuf[ARG_MAX];

extern char **environ;

char *
getenv(const char *name)
{
    int i, len;

    len = strlen(name);
    for (i = 0; environ[i] != NULL; i++) {
        if ((strncmp(name, environ[i], len) == 0) &&
            (environ[i][len] == '=')) {
            strcpy(envbuf, &environ[i][len+1]);
            return(envbuf);
        }
    }
    return(NULL);
}
```

Figure 12.11 A nonreentrant version of `getenv`

We show a reentrant version of getenv in Figure 12.12. This version is called
getenv_r. It uses the pthread_once function (described in Section 12.6) to ensure
that the thread_init function is called only once per process.

```
#include <string.h>
#include <errno.h>
#include <pthread.h>
#include <stdlib.h>

extern char **environ;

pthread_mutex_t env_mutex;
static pthread_once_t init_done = PTHREAD_ONCE_INIT;

static void
thread_init(void)
{
    pthread_mutexattr_t attr;

    pthread_mutexattr_init(&attr);
    pthread_mutexattr_settype(&attr, PTHREAD_MUTEX_RECURSIVE);
    pthread_mutex_init(&env_mutex, &attr);
    pthread_mutexattr_destroy(&attr);
}
```

```
int
getenv_r(const char *name, char *buf, int buflen)
{
    int i, len, olen;

    pthread_once(&init_done, thread_init);
    len = strlen(name);
    pthread_mutex_lock(&env_mutex);
    for (i = 0; environ[i] != NULL; i++) {
        if ((strncmp(name, environ[i], len) == 0) &&
          (environ[i][len] == '=')) {
            olen = strlen(&environ[i][len+1]);
            if (olen >= buflen) {
                pthread_mutex_unlock(&env_mutex);
                return(ENOSPC);
            }
            strcpy(buf, &environ[i][len+1]);
            pthread_mutex_unlock(&env_mutex);
            return(0);
        }
    }
    pthread_mutex_unlock(&env_mutex);
    return(ENOENT);
}
```

Figure 12.12 A reentrant (thread-safe) version of getenv

To make getenv_r reentrant, we changed the interface so that the caller must provide its own buffer. Thus, each thread can use a different buffer to avoid interfering with the others. Note, however, that this is not enough to make getenv_r thread-safe. To make getenv_r thread-safe, we need to protect against changes to the environment while we are searching for the requested string. We can use a mutex to serialize access to the environment list by getenv_r and putenv.

We could have used a reader–writer lock to allow multiple concurrent calls to getenv_r, but the added concurrency probably wouldn't improve the performance of our program by very much, for two reasons. First, the environment list usually isn't very long, so we won't hold the mutex for too long while we scan the list. Second, calls to getenv and putenv are infrequent, so if we improve their performance, we won't affect the overall performance of the program very much.

If we make getenv_r thread-safe, that doesn't mean that it is reentrant with respect to signal handlers. If we use a nonrecursive mutex, we run the risk that a thread will deadlock itself if it calls getenv_r from a signal handler. If the signal handler interrupts the thread while it is executing getenv_r, we will already be holding env_mutex locked, so another attempt to lock it will block, causing the thread to deadlock. Thus, we must use a recursive mutex to prevent other threads from changing the data structures while we look at them, and also prevent deadlocks from signal handlers. The problem is that the pthread functions are not guaranteed to be async-signal safe, so we can't use them to make another function async-signal safe. □

12.6 Thread-Specific Data

Thread-specific data, also known as thread-private data, is a mechanism for storing and finding data associated with a particular thread. The reason we call the data thread-specific, or thread-private, is that we'd like each thread to access its own separate copy of the data, without worrying about synchronizing access with other threads.

Many people went to a lot of trouble designing a threads model that promotes sharing process data and attributes. So why would anyone want to promote interfaces that prevent sharing in this model? There are two reasons.

First, sometimes we need to maintain data on a per thread basis. Since there is no guarantee that thread IDs are small, sequential integers, we can't simply allocate an array of per thread data and use the thread ID as the index. Even if we could depend on small, sequential thread IDs, we'd like a little extra protection so that one thread can't mess with another's data.

The second reason for thread-private data is to provide a mechanism for adapting process-based interfaces to a multithreaded environment. An obvious example of this is errno. Recall the discussion of errno in Section 1.7. Older interfaces (before the advent of threads) defined errno as an integer accessible globally within the context of a process. System calls and library routines set errno as a side effect of failing. To make it possible for threads to use these same system calls and library routines, errno is redefined as thread-private data. Thus, one thread making a call that sets errno doesn't affect the value of errno for the other threads in the process.

Recall that all threads in a process have access to the entire address space of the process. Other than using registers, there is no way for one thread to prevent another from accessing its data. This is true even for thread-specific data. Even though the underlying implementation doesn't prevent access, the functions provided to manage thread-specific data promote data separation among threads.

Before allocating thread-specific data, we need to create a *key* to associate with the data. The key will be used to gain access to the thread-specific data. We use pthread_key_create to create a key.

```
#include <pthread.h>

int pthread_key_create(pthread_key_t *keyp,
                        void (*destructor)(void *));
```
                                            Returns: 0 if OK, error number on failure

The key created is stored in the memory location pointed to by *keyp*. The same key can be used by all threads in the process, but each thread will associate a different thread-specific data address with the key. When the key is created, the data address for each thread is set to a null value.

In addition to creating a key, pthread_key_create associates an optional destructor function with the key. When the thread exits, if the data address has been set to a non-null value, the destructor function is called with the data address as the only argument. If *destructor* is null, then no destructor function is associated with the key. When the thread exits normally, by calling pthread_exit or by returning, the

destructor is called. But if the thread calls `exit,` `_exit,` `_Exit,` or `abort,` or otherwise
exits abnormally, the destructor is not called.

Threads usually use `malloc` to allocate memory for their thread-specific data. The
destructor function usually frees the memory that was allocated. If the thread exited
without freeing the memory, then the memory would be lost: leaked by the process.

A thread can allocate multiple keys for thread-specific data. Each key can have a
destructor associated with it. There can be a different destructor function for each key,
or they can all use the same function. Each operating system implementation can place
a limit on the number of keys a process can allocate (recall `PTHREAD_KEYS_MAX` from
Figure 12.1).

When a thread exits, the destructors for its thread-specific data are called in an
implementation-defined order. It is possible for the destructor function to call another
function that might create new thread-specific data and associate it with the key. After
all destructors are called, the system will check whether any non-null thread-specific
values were associated with the keys and, if so, call the destructors again. This process
will repeat until either all keys for the thread have null thread-specific data values or a
maximum of `PTHREAD_DESTRUCTOR_ITERATIONS` (Figure 12.1) attempts have been
made.

We can break the association of a key with the thread-specific data values for all
threads by calling `pthread_key_delete`.

```
#include <pthread.h>

int pthread_key_delete(pthread_key_t *key);
```
                                        Returns: 0 if OK, error number on failure

Note that calling `pthread_key_delete` will not invoke the destructor function
associated with the key. To free any memory associated with the key's thread-specific
data values, we need to take additional steps in the application.

We need to ensure that a key we allocate doesn't change because of a race during
initialization. Code like the following can result in two threads both calling
`pthread_key_create`:

```
void destructor(void *);

pthread_key_t key;
int init_done = 0;

int
threadfunc(void *arg)
{
    if (!init_done) {
        init_done = 1;
        err = pthread_key_create(&key, destructor);
    }
    ...
}
```

Depending on how the system schedules threads, some threads might see one key value, whereas other threads might see a different value. The way to solve this race is to use pthread_once.

```
#include <pthread.h>

pthread_once_t initflag = PTHREAD_ONCE_INIT;

int pthread_once(pthread_once_t *initflag, void (*initfn)(void));
```
Returns: 0 if OK, error number on failure

The *initflag* must be a nonlocal variable (i.e., global or static) and initialized to PTHREAD_ONCE_INIT.

If each thread calls pthread_once, the system guarantees that the initialization routine, *initfn*, will be called only once, on the first call to pthread_once. The proper way to create a key without a race is as follows:

```
void destructor(void *);

pthread_key_t key;
pthread_once_t init_done = PTHREAD_ONCE_INIT;

void
thread_init(void)
{
    err = pthread_key_create(&key, destructor);
}

int
threadfunc(void *arg)
{
    pthread_once(&init_done, thread_init);
    ...
}
```

Once a key is created, we can associate thread-specific data with the key by calling pthread_setspecific. We can obtain the address of the thread-specific data with pthread_getspecific.

```
#include <pthread.h>

void *pthread_getspecific(pthread_key_t key);
```
Returns: thread-specific data value or NULL if no value
has been associated with the key

```
int pthread_setspecific(pthread_key_t key, const void *value);
```
Returns: 0 if OK, error number on failure

If no thread-specific data has been associated with a key, pthread_getspecific will return a null pointer. We can use this to determine whether we need to call pthread_setspecific.

Example

In Figure 12.11, we showed a hypothetical implementation of getenv. We came up with a new interface to provide the same functionality, but in a thread-safe way (Figure 12.12). But what would happen if we couldn't modify our application programs to use the new interface? In that case, we could use thread-specific data to maintain a per thread copy of the data buffer used to hold the return string. This is shown in Figure 12.13.

```c
#include <limits.h>
#include <string.h>
#include <pthread.h>
#include <stdlib.h>

static pthread_key_t key;
static pthread_once_t init_done = PTHREAD_ONCE_INIT;
pthread_mutex_t env_mutex = PTHREAD_MUTEX_INITIALIZER;

extern char **environ;

static void
thread_init(void)
{
    pthread_key_create(&key, free);
}

char *
getenv(const char *name)
{
    int     i, len;
    char    *envbuf;

    pthread_once(&init_done, thread_init);
    pthread_mutex_lock(&env_mutex);
    envbuf = (char *)pthread_getspecific(key);
    if (envbuf == NULL) {
        envbuf = malloc(ARG_MAX);
        if (envbuf == NULL) {
            pthread_mutex_unlock(&env_mutex);
            return(NULL);
        }
        pthread_setspecific(key, envbuf);
    }
    len = strlen(name);
    for (i = 0; environ[i] != NULL; i++) {
        if ((strncmp(name, environ[i], len) == 0) &&
```

```
                    (environ[i][len] == '=')) {
                        strcpy(envbuf, &environ[i][len+1]);
                        pthread_mutex_unlock(&env_mutex);
                        return(envbuf);
                    }
                }
                pthread_mutex_unlock(&env_mutex);
                return(NULL);
        }
```

Figure 12.13 A thread-safe, compatible version of getenv

We use pthread_once to ensure that only one key is created for the thread-specific data we will use. If pthread_getspecific returns a null pointer, we need to allocate the memory buffer and associate it with the key. Otherwise, we use the memory buffer returned by pthread_getspecific. For the destructor function, we use free to free the memory previously allocated by malloc. The destructor function will be called with the value of the thread-specific data only if the value is non-null.

Note that although this version of getenv is thread-safe, it is not async-signal safe. Even if we made the mutex recursive, we could not make it reentrant with respect to signal handlers, because it calls malloc, which itself is not async-signal safe.   □

12.7 Cancel Options

Two thread attributes that are not included in the pthread_attr_t structure are the *cancelability state* and the *cancelability type*. These attributes affect the behavior of a thread in response to a call to pthread_cancel (Section 11.5).

The *cancelability state* attribute can be either PTHREAD_CANCEL_ENABLE or PTHREAD_CANCEL_DISABLE. A thread can change its *cancelability state* by calling pthread_setcancelstate.

```
#include <pthread.h>

int pthread_setcancelstate(int state, int *oldstate);
```
                                          Returns: 0 if OK, error number on failure

In one atomic operation, pthread_setcancelstate sets the current *cancelability state* to *state* and stores the previous *cancelability state* in the memory location pointed to by *oldstate*.

Recall from Section 11.5 that a call to pthread_cancel doesn't wait for a thread to terminate. In the default case, a thread will continue to execute after a cancellation request is made, until the thread reaches a *cancellation point*. A cancellation point is a place where the thread checks to see whether it has been canceled, and then acts on the request. POSIX.1 guarantees that cancellation points will occur when a thread calls any of the functions listed in Figure 12.14.

accept	mq_timedsend	putpmsg	sigsuspend
aio_suspend	msgrcv	pwrite	sigtimedwait
clock_nanosleep	msgsnd	read	sigwait
close	msync	readv	sigwaitinfo
connect	nanosleep	recv	sleep
creat	open	recvfrom	system
fcntl2	pause	recvmsg	tcdrain
fsync	poll	select	usleep
getmsg	pread	sem_timedwait	wait
getpmsg	pthread_cond_timedwait	sem_wait	waitid
lockf	pthread_cond_wait	send	waitpid
mq_receive	pthread_join	sendmsg	write
mq_send	pthread_testcancel	sendto	writev
mq_timedreceive	putmsg	sigpause	

Figure 12.14 Cancellation points defined by POSIX.1

A thread starts with a default *cancelability state* of PTHREAD_CANCEL_ENABLE. When the state is set to PTHREAD_CANCEL_DISABLE, a call to pthread_cancel will not kill the thread. Instead, the cancellation request remains pending for the thread. When the state is enabled again, the thread will act on any pending cancellation requests at the next cancellation point.

In addition to the functions listed in Figure 12.14, POSIX.1 specifies the functions listed in Figure 12.15 as optional cancellation points.

> Note that several of the functions listed in Figure 12.15 are not discussed further in this text. Many are optional in the Single UNIX Specification.

If your application doesn't call one of the functions in Figure 12.14 or Figure 12.15 for a long period of time (if it is compute-bound, for example), then you can call pthread_testcancel to add your own cancellation points to the program.

```
#include <pthread.h>

void pthread_testcancel(void);
```

When you call pthread_testcancel, if a cancellation request is pending and if cancellation has not been disabled, the thread will be canceled. When cancellation is disabled, however, calls to pthread_testcancel have no effect.

The default cancellation type we have been describing is known as *deferred cancellation*. After a call to pthread_cancel, the actual cancellation doesn't occur until the thread hits a cancellation point. We can change the cancellation type by calling pthread_setcanceltype.

```
#include <pthread.h>

int pthread_setcanceltype(int type, int *oldtype);
```
                                        Returns: 0 if OK, error number on failure

catclose	ftell	getwc	printf
catgets	ftello	getwchar	putc
catopen	ftw	getwd	putc_unlocked
closedir	fwprintf	glob	putchar
closelog	fwrite	iconv_close	putchar_unlocked
ctermid	fwscanf	iconv_open	puts
dbm_close	getc	ioctl	pututxline
dbm_delete	getc_unlocked	lseek	putwc
dbm_fetch	getchar	mkstemp	putwchar
dbm_nextkey	getchar_unlocked	nftw	readdir
dbm_open	getcwd	opendir	readdir_r
dbm_store	getdate	openlog	remove
dlclose	getgrent	pclose	rename
dlopen	getgrgid	perror	rewind
endgrent	getgrgid_r	popen	rewinddir
endhostent	getgrnam	posix_fadvise	scanf
endnetent	getgrnam_r	posix_fallocate	seekdir
endprotoent	gethostbyaddr	posix_madvise	semop
endpwent	gethostbyname	posix_spawn	setgrent
endservent	gethostent	posix_spawnp	sethostent
endutxent	gethostname	posix_trace_clear	setnetent
fclose	getlogin	posix_trace_close	setprotoent
fcntl	getlogin_r	posix_trace_create	setpwent
fflush	getnetbyaddr	posix_trace_create_withlog	setservent
fgetc	getnetbyname	posix_trace_eventtypelist_getnext_id	setutxent
fgetpos	getnetent	posix_trace_eventtypelist_rewind	strerror
fgets	getprotobyname	posix_trace_flush	syslog
fgetwc	getprotobynumber	posix_trace_get_attr	tmpfile
fgetws	getprotoent	posix_trace_get_filter	tmpnam
fopen	getpwent	posix_trace_get_status	ttyname
fprintf	getpwnam	posix_trace_getnext_event	ttyname_r
fputc	getpwnam_r	posix_trace_open	ungetc
fputs	getpwuid	posix_trace_rewind	ungetwc
fputwc	getpwuid_r	posix_trace_set_filter	unlink
fputws	gets	posix_trace_shutdown	vfprintf
fread	getservbyname	posix_trace_timedgetnext_event	vfwprintf
freopen	getservbyport	posix_typed_mem_open	vprintf
fscanf	getservent	pthread_rwlock_rdlock	vwprintf
fseek	getutxent	pthread_rwlock_timedrdlock	wprintf
fseeko	getutxid	pthread_rwlock_timedwrlock	wscanf
fsetpos	getutxline	pthread_rwlock_wrlock	

Figure 12.15 Optional cancellation points defined by POSIX.1

The *type* parameter can be either PTHREAD_CANCEL_DEFERRED or PTHREAD_CANCEL_ASYNCHRONOUS. The pthread_setcanceltype function sets the cancellation type to *type* and returns the previous type in the integer pointed to by *oldtype*.

Asynchronous cancellation differs from deferred cancellation in that the thread can be canceled at any time. The thread doesn't necessarily need to hit a cancellation point for it to be canceled.

12.8 Threads and Signals

Dealing with signals can be complicated even with a process-based paradigm. Introducing threads into the picture makes things even more complicated.

Each thread has its own signal mask, but the signal disposition is shared by all threads in the process. This means that individual threads can block signals, but when a thread modifies the action associated with a given signal, all threads share the action. Thus, if one thread chooses to ignore a given signal, another thread can undo that choice by restoring the default disposition or installing a signal handler for the signal.

Signals are delivered to a single thread in the process. If the signal is related to a hardware fault, the signal is usually sent to the thread whose action caused the event. Other signals, on the other hand, are delivered to an arbitrary thread.

In Section 10.12, we discussed how processes can use sigprocmask to block signals from delivery. The behavior of sigprocmask is undefined in a multithreaded process. Threads have to use pthread_sigmask instead.

```
#include <signal.h>

int pthread_sigmask(int how, const sigset_t *restrict set,
                    sigset_t *restrict oset);
```
Returns: 0 if OK, error number on failure

The pthread_sigmask function is identical to sigprocmask, except that pthread_sigmask works with threads and returns an error code on failure instead of setting errno and returning −1.

A thread can wait for one or more signals to occur by calling sigwait.

```
#include <signal.h>

int sigwait(const sigset_t *restrict set, int *restrict signop);
```
Returns: 0 if OK, error number on failure

The *set* argument specifies the set of signals for which the thread is waiting. On return, the integer to which *signop* points will contain the number of the signal that was delivered.

If one of the signals specified in the set is pending at the time sigwait is called, then sigwait will return without blocking. Before returning, sigwait removes the signal from the set of signals pending for the process. To avoid erroneous behavior, a thread must block the signals it is waiting for before calling sigwait. The sigwait function will atomically unblock the signals and wait until one is delivered. Before returning, sigwait will restore the thread's signal mask. If the signals are not blocked at the time that sigwait is called, then a timing window is opened up where one of the signals can be delivered to the thread before it completes its call to sigwait.

The advantage to using sigwait is that it can simplify signal handling by allowing us to treat asynchronously-generated signals in a synchronous manner. We can prevent the signals from interrupting the threads by adding them to each thread's signal mask. Then we can dedicate specific threads to handling the signals. These dedicated threads can make function calls without having to worry about which functions are safe to call from a signal handler, because they are being called from normal thread context, not from a traditional signal handler interrupting a normal thread's execution.

If multiple threads are blocked in calls to sigwait for the same signal, only one of the threads will return from sigwait when the signal is delivered. If a signal is being caught (the process has established a signal handler by using sigaction, for example) and a thread is waiting for the same signal in a call to sigwait, it is left up to the implementation to decide which way to deliver the signal. In this case, the implementation could either allow sigwait to return or invoke the signal handler, but not both.

To send a signal to a process, we call kill (Section 10.9). To send a signal to a thread, we call pthread_kill.

```
#include <signal.h>

int pthread_kill(pthread_t thread, int signo);
```
                                            Returns: 0 if OK, error number on failure

---

We can pass a *signo* value of 0 to check for existence of the thread. If the default action for a signal is to terminate the process, then sending the signal to a thread will still kill the entire process.

Note that alarm timers are a process resource, and all threads share the same set of alarms. Thus, it is not possible for multiple threads in a process to use alarm timers without interfering (or cooperating) with one another (this is the subject of Exercise 12.6).

Example

Recall that in Figure 10.23, we waited for the signal handler to set a flag indicating that the main program should exit. The only threads of control that could run were the main thread and the signal handler, so blocking the signals was sufficient to avoid missing a change to the flag. With threads, we need to use a mutex to protect the flag, as we show in the program in Figure 12.16.

```
#include "apue.h"
#include <pthread.h>

int         quitflag;   /* set nonzero by thread */
sigset_t    mask;

pthread_mutex_t lock = PTHREAD_MUTEX_INITIALIZER;
pthread_cond_t waitloc = PTHREAD_COND_INITIALIZER;

void *
thr_fn(void *arg)
{
    int err, signo;

    for (;;) {
```

```
                err = sigwait(&mask, &signo);
                if (err != 0)
                    err_exit(err, "sigwait failed");
                switch (signo) {
                case SIGINT:
                    printf("\ninterrupt\n");
                    break;

                case SIGQUIT:
                    pthread_mutex_lock(&lock);
                    quitflag = 1;
                    pthread_mutex_unlock(&lock);
                    pthread_cond_signal(&waitloc);
                    return(0);

                default:
                    printf("unexpected signal %d\n", signo);
                    exit(1);
                }
        }
}

int
main(void)
{
    int         err;
    sigset_t    oldmask;
    pthread_t   tid;

    sigemptyset(&mask);
    sigaddset(&mask, SIGINT);
    sigaddset(&mask, SIGQUIT);
    if ((err = pthread_sigmask(SIG_BLOCK, &mask, &oldmask)) != 0)
        err_exit(err, "SIG_BLOCK error");

    err = pthread_create(&tid, NULL, thr_fn, 0);
    if (err != 0)
        err_exit(err, "can't create thread");

    pthread_mutex_lock(&lock);
    while (quitflag == 0)
        pthread_cond_wait(&waitloc, &lock);
    pthread_mutex_unlock(&lock);

    /* SIGQUIT has been caught and is now blocked; do whatever */
    quitflag = 0;

    /* reset signal mask which unblocks SIGQUIT */
    if (sigprocmask(SIG_SETMASK, &oldmask, NULL) < 0)
        err_sys("SIG_SETMASK error");
    exit(0);
}
```

Figure 12.16 Synchronous signal handling

Instead of relying on a signal handler that interrupts the main thread of control, we dedicate a separate thread of control to handle the signals. We change the value of quitflag under the protection of a mutex so that the main thread of control can't miss the wake-up call made when we call pthread_cond_signal. We use the same mutex in the main thread of control to check the value of the flag, and atomically release the mutex and wait for the condition.

Note that we block SIGINT and SIGQUIT in the beginning of the main thread. When we create the thread to handle signals, the thread inherits the current signal mask. Since sigwait will unblock the signals, only one thread is available to receive signals. This enables us to code the main thread without having to worry about interrupts from these signals.

If we run this program, we get output similar to that from Figure 10.23:

```
$ ./a.out
^?                           type the interrupt character
interrupt
^?                           type the interrupt character again
interrupt
^?                           and again
interrupt
^\ $                         now terminate with quit character
```

Linux implements threads as separate processes, sharing resources using clone(2). Because of this, the behavior of threads on Linux differs from that on other implementations when it comes to signals. In the POSIX.1 thread model, asynchronous signals are sent to a process, and then an individual thread within the process is selected to receive the signal, based on which threads are not currently blocking the signal. On Linux, an asynchronous signal is sent to a particular thread, and since each thread executes as a separate process, the system is unable to select a thread that isn't currently blocking the signal. The result is that the thread may not notice the signal. Thus, programs like the one in Figure 12.16 work when the signal is generated from the terminal driver, which signals the process group, but when you try to send a signal to the process using kill, it doesn't work as expected on Linux.

12.9   Threads and fork

When a thread calls fork, a copy of the entire process address space is made for the child. Recall the discussion of copy-on-write in Section 8.3. The child is an entirely different process from the parent, and as long as neither one makes changes to its memory contents, copies of the memory pages can be shared between parent and child.

By inheriting a copy of the address space, the child also inherits the state of every mutex, reader–writer lock, and condition variable from the parent process. If the parent consists of more than one thread, the child will need to clean up the lock state if it isn't going to call exec immediately after fork returns.

Inside the child process, only one thread exists. It is made from a copy of the thread that called fork in the parent. If the threads in the parent process hold any locks, the locks will also be held in the child process. The problem is that the child process doesn't contain copies of the threads holding the locks, so there is no way for the child to know which locks are held and need to be unlocked.

This problem can be avoided if the child calls one of the `exec` functions directly after returning from `fork`. In this case, the old address space is discarded, so the lock state doesn't matter. This is not always possible, however, so if the child needs to continue processing, we need to use a different strategy.

To clean up the lock state, we can establish *fork handlers* by calling the function `pthread_atfork`.

```
#include <pthread.h>

int pthread_atfork(void (*prepare)(void), void (*parent)(void),
                   void (*child)(void));
```
Returns: 0 if OK, error number on failure

With `pthread_atfork`, we can install up to three functions to help clean up the locks. The *prepare* fork handler is called in the parent before `fork` creates the child process. This fork handler's job is to acquire all locks defined by the parent. The *parent* fork handler is called in the context of the parent after `fork` has created the child process, but before `fork` has returned. This fork handler's job is to unlock all the locks acquired by the *prepare* fork handler. The *child* fork handler is called in the context of the child process before returning from `fork`. Like the *parent* fork handler, the *child* fork handler too must release all the locks acquired by the *prepare* fork handler.

Note that the locks are not locked once and unlocked twice, as it may appear. When the child address space is created, it gets a copy of all locks that the parent defined. Because the *prepare* fork handler acquired all the locks, the memory in the parent and the memory in the child start out with identical contents. When the parent and the child unlock their "copy" of the locks, new memory is allocated for the child, and the memory contents from the parent are copied to the child's memory (copy-on-write), so we are left with a situation that looks as if the parent locked all its copies of the locks and the child locked all its copies of the locks. The parent and the child end up unlocking duplicate locks stored in different memory locations, as if the following sequence of events occurred.

1. The parent acquired all its locks.
2. The child acquired all its locks.
3. The parent released its locks.
4. The child released its locks.

We can call `pthread_atfork` multiple times to install more than one set of fork handlers. If we don't have a need to use one of the handlers, we can pass a null pointer for the particular handler argument, and it will have no effect. When multiple fork handlers are used, the order in which the handlers are called differs. The *parent* and *child* fork handlers are called in the order in which they were registered, whereas the *prepare* fork handlers are called in the opposite order from which they were registered. This allows multiple modules to register their own fork handlers and still honor the locking hierarchy.

For example, assume that module A calls functions from module B and that each module has its own set of locks. If the locking hierarchy is A before B, module B must install its fork handlers before module A. When the parent calls `fork`, the following steps are taken, assuming that the child process runs before the parent.

1. The *prepare* fork handler from module A is called to acquire all module A's locks.
2. The *prepare* fork handler from module B is called to acquire all module B's locks.
3. A child process is created.
4. The *child* fork handler from module B is called to release all module B's locks in the child process.
5. The *child* fork handler from module A is called to release all module A's locks in the child process.
6. The `fork` function returns to the child.
7. The *parent* fork handler from module B is called to release all module B's locks in the parent process.
8. The *parent* fork handler from module A is called to release all module A's locks in the parent process.
9. The `fork` function returns to the parent.

If the fork handlers serve to clean up the lock state, what cleans up the state of condition variables? On some implementations, condition variables might not need any cleaning up. However, an implementation that uses a lock as part of the implementation of condition variables will require cleaning up. The problem is that no interface exists to allow us to do this. If the lock is embedded in the condition variable data structure, then we can't use condition variables after calling `fork`, because there is no portable way to clean up its state. On the other hand, if an implementation uses a global lock to protect all condition variable data structures in a process, then the implementation itself can clean up the lock in the `fork` library routine. Application programs shouldn't rely on implementation details like this, however.

Example

The program in Figure 12.17 illustrates the use of `pthread_atfork` and fork handlers.

```
#include "apue.h"
#include <pthread.h>

pthread_mutex_t lock1 = PTHREAD_MUTEX_INITIALIZER;
pthread_mutex_t lock2 = PTHREAD_MUTEX_INITIALIZER;

void
prepare(void)
{
    printf("preparing locks...\n");
    pthread_mutex_lock(&lock1);
    pthread_mutex_lock(&lock2);
}
```

```
void
parent(void)
{
    printf("parent unlocking locks...\n");
    pthread_mutex_unlock(&lock1);
    pthread_mutex_unlock(&lock2);
}

void
child(void)
{
    printf("child unlocking locks...\n");
    pthread_mutex_unlock(&lock1);
    pthread_mutex_unlock(&lock2);
}

void *
thr_fn(void *arg)
{
    printf("thread started...\n");
    pause();
    return(0);
}

int
main(void)
{
    int        err;
    pid_t      pid;
    pthread_t  tid;

#if defined(BSD) || defined(MACOS)
    printf("pthread_atfork is unsupported\n");
#else
    if ((err = pthread_atfork(prepare, parent, child)) != 0)
        err_exit(err, "can't install fork handlers");
    err = pthread_create(&tid, NULL, thr_fn, 0);
    if (err != 0)
        err_exit(err, "can't create thread");
    sleep(2);
    printf("parent about to fork...\n");
    if ((pid = fork()) < 0)
        err_quit("fork failed");
    else if (pid == 0)   /* child */
        printf("child returned from fork\n");
    else        /* parent */
        printf("parent returned from fork\n");
#endif
    exit(0);
}
```

Figure 12.17 pthread_atfork example

We define two mutexes, `lock1` and `lock2`. The *prepare* fork handler acquires them both, the *child* fork handler releases them in the context of the child process, and the *parent* fork handler releases them in the context of the parent process.

When we run this program, we get the following output:

```
$ ./a.out
thread started...
parent about to fork...
preparing locks...
child unlocking locks...
child returned from fork
parent unlocking locks...
parent returned from fork
```

As we can see, the *prepare* fork handler runs after `fork` is called, the *child* fork handler runs before `fork` returns in the child, and the *parent* fork handler runs before `fork` returns in the parent.   □

12.10 Threads and I/O

We introduced the `pread` and `pwrite` functions in Section 3.11. These functions are helpful in a multithreaded environment, because all threads in a process share the same file descriptors.

Consider two threads reading from or writing to the same file descriptor at the same time.

Thread A	Thread B
`lseek(fd, 300, SEEK_SET);`	`lseek(fd, 700, SEEK_SET);`
`read(fd, buf1, 100);`	`read(fd, buf2, 100);`

If thread A executes the `lseek` and then thread B calls `lseek` before thread A calls `read`, then both threads will end up reading the same record. Clearly, this isn't what was intended.

To solve this problem, we can use `pread` to make the setting of the offset and the reading of the data one atomic operation.

Thread A	Thread B
`pread(fd, buf1, 100, 300);`	`pread(fd, buf2, 100, 700);`

Using `pread`, we can ensure that thread A reads the record at offset 300, whereas thread B reads the record at offset 700. We can use `pwrite` to solve the problem of concurrent threads writing to the same file.

12.11 Summary

Threads provide an alternate model for partitioning concurrent tasks in UNIX systems. Threads promote sharing among separate threads of control, but present unique synchronization problems. In this chapter, we looked at how we can fine-tune our threads and their synchronization primitives. We discussed reentrancy with threads. We also looked at how threads interact with some of the process-oriented system calls.

Exercises

12.1 Run the program in Figure 12.17 on a Linux system, but redirect the output into a file. Explain the results.

12.2 Implement `putenv_r`, a reentrant version of `putenv`. Make sure that your implementation is async-signal safe as well as thread-safe.

12.3 Can you make the program in Figure 12.13 async-signal safe by blocking signals at the beginning of the function and restoring the previous signal mask before returning? Explain.

12.4 Write a program to exercise the version of `getenv` from Figure 12.13. Compile and run the program on FreeBSD. What happens? Explain.

12.5 Given that you can create multiple threads to perform different tasks within a program, explain why you might still need to use `fork`.

12.6 Reimplement the program in Figure 10.29 to make it thread-safe without using `nanosleep`.

12.7 After calling `fork`, could we safely reinitialize a condition variable in the child process by first destroying the condition variable with `pthread_cond_destroy` and then initializing it with `pthread_cond_init`?

13

Daemon Processes

13.1 Introduction

Daemons are processes that live for a long time. They are often started when the system is bootstrapped and terminate only when the system is shut down. Because they don't have a controlling terminal, we say that they run in the background. UNIX systems have numerous daemons that perform day-to-day activities.

In this chapter, we look at the process structure of daemons and how to write a daemon. Since a daemon does not have a controlling terminal, we need to see how a daemon can report error conditions when something goes wrong.

> For a discussion of the historical background of the term *daemon* as it applies to computer systems, see Raymond [1996].

13.2 Daemon Characteristics

Let's look at some common system daemons and how they relate to the concepts of process groups, controlling terminals, and sessions that we described in Chapter 9. The ps(1) command prints the status of various processes in the system. There are a multitude of options—consult your system's manual for all the details. We'll execute

```
ps -axj
```

under BSD-based systems to see the information we need for this discussion. The -a option shows the status of processes owned by others, and -x shows processes that don't have a controlling terminal. The -j option displays the job-related information: the session ID, process group ID, controlling terminal, and terminal process group ID.

Under System V–based systems, a similar command is `ps -efjc`. (In an attempt to improve security, some UNIX systems don't allow us to use `ps` to look at any processes other than our own.) The output from `ps` looks like

```
  PPID    PID  PGID    SID TTY TPGID UID   COMMAND
     0      1     0      0 ?     -1   0   init
     1      2     1      1 ?     -1   0   [keventd]
     1      3     1      1 ?     -1   0   [kapmd]
     0      5     1      1 ?     -1   0   [kswapd]
     0      6     1      1 ?     -1   0   [bdflush]
     0      7     1      1 ?     -1   0   [kupdated]
     1   1009  1009   1009 ?     -1  32   portmap
     1   1048  1048   1048 ?     -1   0   syslogd -m 0
     1   1335  1335   1335 ?     -1   0   xinetd -pidfile /var/run/xinetd.pid
     1   1403     1      1 ?     -1   0   [nfsd]
     1   1405     1      1 ?     -1   0   [lockd]
  1405   1406     1      1 ?     -1   0   [rpciod]
     1   1853  1853   1853 ?     -1   0   crond
     1   2182  2182   2182 ?     -1   0   /usr/sbin/cupsd
```

We have removed a few columns that don't interest us, such as the accumulated CPU time. The column headings, in order, are the parent process ID, process ID, process group ID, session ID, terminal name, terminal process group ID (the foreground process group associated with the controlling terminal), user ID, and command string.

> The system that this `ps` command was run on (Linux) supports the notion of a session ID, which we mentioned with the `setsid` function in Section 9.5. The session ID is simply the process ID of the session leader. A BSD-based system, however, will print the address of the `session` structure corresponding to the process group that the process belongs to (Section 9.11).

The system processes you see will depend on the operating system implementation. Anything with a parent process ID of 0 is usually a kernel process started as part of the system bootstrap procedure. (An exception to this is `init`, since it is a user-level command started by the kernel at boot time.) Kernel processes are special and generally exist for the entire lifetime of the system. They run with superuser privileges and have no controlling terminal and no command line.

Process 1 is usually `init`, as we described in Section 8.2. It is a system daemon responsible for, among other things, starting system services specific to various run levels. These services are usually implemented with the help of their own daemons.

On Linux, the `keventd` daemon provides process context for running scheduled functions in the kernel. The `kapmd` daemon provides support for the advanced power management features available with various computer systems. The `kswapd` daemon is also known as the pageout daemon. It supports the virtual memory subsystem by writing dirty pages to disk slowly over time, so the pages can be reclaimed.

The Linux kernel flushes cached data to disk using two additional daemons: `bdflush` and `kupdated`. The `bdflush` daemon flushes dirty buffers from the buffer cache back to disk when available memory reaches a low-water mark. The `kupdated` daemon flushes dirty pages back to disk at regular intervals to decrease data loss in the event of a system failure.

The portmapper daemon, `portmap`, provides the service of mapping RPC (Remote Procedure Call) program numbers to network port numbers. The `syslogd` daemon is available to any program to log system messages for an operator. The messages may be printed on a console device and also written to a file. (We describe the `syslog` facility in Section 13.4.)

We talked about the `inetd` daemon (`xinetd`) in Section 9.3. It listens on the system's network interfaces for incoming requests for various network servers. The `nfsd`, `lockd`, and `rpciod` daemons provide support for the Network File System (NFS).

The `cron` daemon (`crond`) executes commands at specified dates and times. Numerous system administration tasks are handled by having programs executed regularly by `cron`. The `cupsd` daemon is a print spooler; it handles print requests on the system.

Note that most of the daemons run with superuser privilege (a user ID of 0). None of the daemons has a controlling terminal: the terminal name is set to a question mark, and the terminal foreground process group is −1. The kernel daemons are started without a controlling terminal. The lack of a controlling terminal in the user-level daemons is probably the result of the daemons having called `setsid`. All the user-level daemons are process group leaders and session leaders and are the only processes in their process group and session. Finally, note that the parent of most of these daemons is the `init` process.

13.3 Coding Rules

Some basic rules to coding a daemon prevent unwanted interactions from happening. We state these rules and then show a function, `daemonize`, that implements them.

1. The first thing to do is call `umask` to set the file mode creation mask to 0. The file mode creation mask that's inherited could be set to deny certain permissions. If the daemon process is going to create files, it may want to set specific permissions. For example, if it specifically creates files with group-read and group-write enabled, a file mode creation mask that turns off either of these permissions would undo its efforts.

2. Call `fork` and have the parent `exit`. This does several things. First, if the daemon was started as a simple shell command, having the parent terminate makes the shell think that the command is done. Second, the child inherits the process group ID of the parent but gets a new process ID, so we're guaranteed that the child is not a process group leader. This is a prerequisite for the call to `setsid` that is done next.

3. Call `setsid` to create a new session. The three steps listed in Section 9.5 occur. The process (a) becomes a session leader of a new session, (b) becomes the process group leader of a new process group, and (c) has no controlling terminal.

Under System V–based systems, some people recommend calling `fork` again at this point and having the parent terminate. The second child continues as the daemon. This guarantees that the daemon is not a session leader, which prevents it from acquiring a controlling terminal under the System V rules (Section 9.6). Alternatively, to avoid acquiring a controlling terminal, be sure to specify `O_NOCTTY` whenever opening a terminal device.

4. Change the current working directory to the root directory. The current working directory inherited from the parent could be on a mounted file system. Since daemons normally exist until the system is rebooted, if the daemon stays on a mounted file system, that file system cannot be unmounted.

   Alternatively, some daemons might change the current working directory to some specific location, where they will do all their work. For example, line printer spooling daemons often change to their spool directory.

5. Unneeded file descriptors should be closed. This prevents the daemon from holding open any descriptors that it may have inherited from its parent (which could be a shell or some other process). We can use our `open_max` function (Figure 2.16) or the `getrlimit` function (Section 7.11) to determine the highest descriptor and close all descriptors up to that value.

6. Some daemons open file descriptors 0, 1, and 2 to `/dev/null` so that any library routines that try to read from standard input or write to standard output or standard error will have no effect. Since the daemon is not associated with a terminal device, there is nowhere for output to be displayed; nor is there anywhere to receive input from an interactive user. Even if the daemon was started from an interactive session, the daemon runs in the background, and the login session can terminate without affecting the daemon. If other users log in on the same terminal device, we wouldn't want output from the daemon showing up on the terminal, and the users wouldn't expect their input to be read by the daemon.

Example

Figure 13.1 shows a function that can be called from a program that wants to initialize itself as a daemon.

```
#include "apue.h"
#include <syslog.h>
#include <fcntl.h>
#include <sys/resource.h>

void
daemonize(const char *cmd)
{
    int                 i, fd0, fd1, fd2;
    pid_t               pid;
    struct rlimit       rl;
    struct sigaction    sa;
```

```
/*
 * Clear file creation mask.
 */
umask(0);

/*
 * Get maximum number of file descriptors.
 */
if (getrlimit(RLIMIT_NOFILE, &rl) < 0)
    err_quit("%s: can't get file limit", cmd);

/*
 * Become a session leader to lose controlling TTY.
 */
if ((pid = fork()) < 0)
    err_quit("%s: can't fork", cmd);
else if (pid != 0) /* parent */
    exit(0);
setsid();

/*
 * Ensure future opens won't allocate controlling TTYs.
 */
sa.sa_handler = SIG_IGN;
sigemptyset(&sa.sa_mask);
sa.sa_flags = 0;
if (sigaction(SIGHUP, &sa, NULL) < 0)
    err_quit("%s: can't ignore SIGHUP");
if ((pid = fork()) < 0)
    err_quit("%s: can't fork", cmd);
else if (pid != 0) /* parent */
    exit(0);

/*
 * Change the current working directory to the root so
 * we won't prevent file systems from being unmounted.
 */
if (chdir("/") < 0)
    err_quit("%s: can't change directory to /");

/*
 * Close all open file descriptors.
 */
if (rl.rlim_max == RLIM_INFINITY)
    rl.rlim_max = 1024;
for (i = 0; i < rl.rlim_max; i++)
    close(i);

/*
 * Attach file descriptors 0, 1, and 2 to /dev/null.
 */
```

```
fd0 = open("/dev/null", O_RDWR);
fd1 = dup(0);
fd2 = dup(0);

/*
 * Initialize the log file.
 */
openlog(cmd, LOG_CONS, LOG_DAEMON);
if (fd0 != 0 || fd1 != 1 || fd2 != 2) {
    syslog(LOG_ERR, "unexpected file descriptors %d %d %d",
      fd0, fd1, fd2);
    exit(1);
}
}
```

Figure 13.1   Initialize a daemon process

If the `daemonize` function is called from a `main` program that then goes to sleep, we can check the status of the daemon with the `ps` command:

```
$ ./a.out
$ ps -axj
 PPID    PID   PGID    SID TTY TPGID UID    COMMAND
    1   3346   3345   3345 ?     -1 501     ./a.out
$ ps -axj | grep 3345
    1   3346   3345   3345 ?     -1 501     ./a.out
```

We can also use `ps` to verify that no active process exists with ID 3345. This means that our daemon is in an orphaned process group (Section 9.10) and is not a session leader and thus has no chance of allocating a controlling terminal. This is a result of performing the second `fork` in the `daemonize` function. We can see that our daemon has been initialized correctly.   □

13.4   Error Logging

One problem a daemon has is how to handle error messages. It can't simply write to standard error, since it shouldn't have a controlling terminal. We don't want all the daemons writing to the console device, since on many workstations, the console device runs a windowing system. We also don't want each daemon writing its own error messages into a separate file. It would be a headache for anyone administering the system to keep up with which daemon writes to which log file and to check these files on a regular basis. A central daemon error-logging facility is required.

> The BSD `syslog` facility was developed at Berkeley and used widely in 4.2BSD. Most systems derived from BSD support `syslog`.
>
> Until SVR4, System V never had a central daemon logging facility.
>
> The `syslog` function is included as an XSI extension in the Single UNIX Specification.

The BSD `syslog` facility has been widely used since 4.2BSD. Most daemons use this facility. Figure 13.2 illustrates its structure.

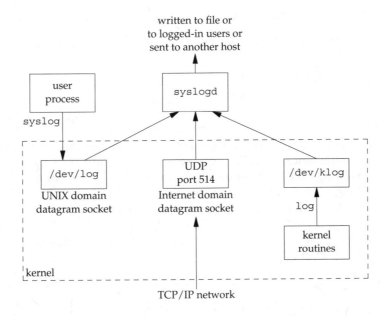

Figure 13.2 The BSD `syslog` facility

There are three ways to generate log messages:

1. Kernel routines can call the `log` function. These messages can be read by any user process that `opens` and `reads` the `/dev/klog` device. We won't describe this function any further, since we're not interested in writing kernel routines.

2. Most user processes (daemons) call the `syslog`(3) function to generate log messages. We describe its calling sequence later. This causes the message to be sent to the UNIX domain datagram socket `/dev/log`.

3. A user process on this host, or on some other host that is connected to this host by a TCP/IP network, can send log messages to UDP port 514. Note that the `syslog` function never generates these UDP datagrams: they require explicit network programming by the process generating the log message.

Refer to Stevens, Fenner, and Rudoff [2004] for details on UNIX domain sockets and UDP sockets.

Normally, the `syslogd` daemon reads all three forms of log messages. On start-up, this daemon reads a configuration file, usually `/etc/syslog.conf`, which determines where different classes of messages are to be sent. For example, urgent messages can be sent to the system administrator (if logged in) and printed on the console, whereas warnings may be logged to a file.

Our interface to this facility is through the `syslog` function.

```
#include <syslog.h>

void openlog(const char *ident, int option, int facility);

void syslog(int priority, const char *format, ...);

void closelog(void);

int setlogmask(int maskpri);
```
                                    Returns: previous log priority mask value

Calling `openlog` is optional. If it's not called, the first time `syslog` is called, `openlog` is called automatically. Calling `closelog` is also optional—it just closes the descriptor that was being used to communicate with the `syslogd` daemon.

Calling `openlog` lets us specify an *ident* that is added to each log message. This is normally the name of the program (`cron`, `inetd`, etc.). The *option* argument is a bitmask specifying various options. Figure 13.3 describes the available options, including a bullet in the XSI column if the option is included in the `openlog` definition in the Single UNIX Specification.

option	XSI	Description
LOG_CONS	•	If the log message can't be sent to `syslogd` via the UNIX domain datagram, the message is written to the console instead.
LOG_NDELAY	•	Open the UNIX domain datagram socket to the `syslogd` daemon immediately; don't wait until the first message is logged. Normally, the socket is not opened until the first message is logged.
LOG_NOWAIT	•	Do not wait for child processes that might have been created in the process of logging the message. This prevents conflicts with applications that catch `SIGCHLD`, since the application might have retrieved the child's status by the time that `syslog` calls `wait`.
LOG_ODELAY	•	Delay the open of the connection to the `syslogd` daemon until the first message is logged.
LOG_PERROR		Write the log message to standard error in addition to sending it to `syslogd`. (Unavailable on Solaris.)
LOG_PID	•	Log the process ID with each message. This is intended for daemons that `fork` a child process to handle different requests (as compared to daemons, such as `syslogd`, that never call `fork`).

Figure 13.3 The *option* argument for `openlog`

The *facility* argument for `openlog` is taken from Figure 13.4. Note that the Single UNIX Specification defines only a subset of the facility codes typically available on a given platform. The reason for the *facility* argument is to let the configuration file specify that messages from different facilities are to be handled differently. If we don't call `openlog`, or if we call it with a *facility* of 0, we can still specify the facility as part of the *priority* argument to `syslog`.

facility	XSI	Description
LOG_AUTH		authorization programs: login, su, getty, ...
LOG_AUTHPRIV		same as LOG_AUTH, but logged to file with restricted permissions
LOG_CRON		cron and at
LOG_DAEMON		system daemons: inetd, routed, ...
LOG_FTP		the FTP daemon (ftpd)
LOG_KERN		messages generated by the kernel
LOG_LOCAL0	•	reserved for local use
LOG_LOCAL1	•	reserved for local use
LOG_LOCAL2	•	reserved for local use
LOG_LOCAL3	•	reserved for local use
LOG_LOCAL4	•	reserved for local use
LOG_LOCAL5	•	reserved for local use
LOG_LOCAL6	•	reserved for local use
LOG_LOCAL7	•	reserved for local use
LOG_LPR		line printer system: lpd, lpc, ...
LOG_MAIL		the mail system
LOG_NEWS		the Usenet network news system
LOG_SYSLOG		the syslogd daemon itself
LOG_USER	•	messages from other user processes (default)
LOG_UUCP		the UUCP system

Figure 13.4 The *facility* argument for openlog

level	Description
LOG_EMERG	emergency (system is unusable) (highest priority)
LOG_ALERT	condition that must be fixed immediately
LOG_CRIT	critical condition (e.g., hard device error)
LOG_ERR	error condition
LOG_WARNING	warning condition
LOG_NOTICE	normal, but significant condition
LOG_INFO	informational message
LOG_DEBUG	debug message (lowest priority)

Figure 13.5 The syslog *level*s (ordered)

We call syslog to generate a log message. The *priority* argument is a combination of the *facility* shown in Figure 13.4 and a *level*, shown in Figure 13.5. These *level*s are ordered by priority, from highest to lowest.

The *format* argument and any remaining arguments are passed to the vsprintf function for formatting. Any occurrence of the two characters %m in the *format* are first replaced with the error message string (strerror) corresponding to the value of errno.

The setlogmask function can be used to set the log priority mask for the process. This function returns the previous mask. When the log priority mask is set, messages are not logged unless their priority is set in the log priority mask. Note that attempts to set the log priority mask to 0 will have no effect.

The logger(1) program is also provided by many systems as a way to send log messages to the syslog facility. Some implementations allow optional arguments to this program, specifying the *facility*, *level*, and *ident*, although the Single UNIX Specification doesn't define any options. The logger command is intended for a shell script running noninteractively that needs to generate log messages.

Example

In a (hypothetical) line printer spooler daemon, you might encounter the sequence

```
openlog("lpd", LOG_PID, LOG_LPR);
syslog(LOG_ERR, "open error for %s: %m", filename);
```

The first call sets the *ident* string to the program name, specifies that the process ID should always be printed, and sets the default *facility* to the line printer system. The call to syslog specifies an error condition and a message string. If we had not called openlog, the second call could have been

```
syslog(LOG_ERR | LOG_LPR, "open error for %s: %m", filename);
```

Here, we specify the *priority* argument as a combination of a *level* and a *facility*.   □

In addition to syslog, many platforms provide a variant that handles variable argument lists.

```
#include <syslog.h>
#include <stdarg.h>

void vsyslog(int priority, const char *format, va_list arg);
```

All four platforms described in this book provide vsyslog, but it is not included in the Single UNIX Specification.

Most syslogd implementations will queue messages for a short time. If a duplicate message arrives during this time, the syslog daemon will not write it to the log. Instead, the daemon will print out a message similar to "last message repeated *N* times."

13.5   Single-Instance Daemons

Some daemons are implemented so that only a single copy of the daemon should be running at a time for proper operation. The daemon might need exclusive access to a device, for example. In the case of the cron daemon, if multiple instances were running, each copy might try to start a single scheduled operation, resulting in duplicate operations and probably an error.

If the daemon needs to access a device, the device driver will sometimes prevent multiple opens of the corresponding device node in /dev. This restricts us to one copy of the daemon running at a time. If no such device is available, however, we need to do the work ourselves.

The file- and record-locking mechanism provides the basis for one way to ensure that only one copy of a daemon is running. (We discuss file and record locking in Section 14.3.) If each daemon creates a file and places a write lock on the entire file, only one such write lock will be allowed to be created. Successive attempts to create write locks will fail, serving as an indication to successive copies of the daemon that another instance is already running.

File and record locking provides a convenient mutual-exclusion mechanism. If the daemon obtains a write-lock on an entire file, the lock will be removed automatically if the daemon exits. This simplifies recovery, removing the need for us to clean up from the previous instance of the daemon.

Example

The function shown in Figure 13.6 illustrates the use of file and record locking to ensure that only one copy of a daemon is running.

```c
#include <unistd.h>
#include <stdlib.h>
#include <fcntl.h>
#include <syslog.h>
#include <string.h>
#include <errno.h>
#include <stdio.h>
#include <sys/stat.h>

#define LOCKFILE "/var/run/daemon.pid"
#define LOCKMODE (S_IRUSR|S_IWUSR|S_IRGRP|S_IROTH)

extern int lockfile(int);

int
already_running(void)
{
    int     fd;
    char    buf[16];

    fd = open(LOCKFILE, O_RDWR|O_CREAT, LOCKMODE);
    if (fd < 0) {
        syslog(LOG_ERR, "can't open %s: %s", LOCKFILE, strerror(errno));
        exit(1);
    }
    if (lockfile(fd) < 0) {
        if (errno == EACCES || errno == EAGAIN) {
            close(fd);
            return(1);
        }
        syslog(LOG_ERR, "can't lock %s: %s", LOCKFILE, strerror(errno));
        exit(1);
    }
    ftruncate(fd, 0);
```

```
        sprintf(buf, "%ld", (long)getpid());
        write(fd, buf, strlen(buf)+1);
        return(0);
}
```

Each copy of the daemon will try to create a file and write its process ID in it. This will allow administrators to identify the process easily. If the file is already locked, the `lockfile` function will fail with `errno` set to `EACCES` or `EAGAIN`, so we return 1, indicating that the daemon is already running. Otherwise, we truncate the file, write our process ID to it, and return 0.

We need to truncate the file, because the previous instance of the daemon might have had a process ID larger than ours, with a larger string length. For example, if the previous instance of the daemon was process ID 12345, and the new instance is process ID 9999, when we write the process ID to the file, we will be left with 99995 in the file. Truncating the file prevents data from the previous daemon appearing as if it applies to the current daemon.   □

13.6 Daemon Conventions

Several common conventions are followed by daemons in the UNIX System.

- If the daemon uses a lock file, the file is usually stored in `/var/run`. Note, however, that the daemon might need superuser permissions to create a file here. The name of the file is usually *name*`.pid`, where *name* is the name of the daemon or the service. For example, the name of the `cron` daemon's lock file is `/var/run/crond.pid`.

- If the daemon supports configuration options, they are usually stored in `/etc`. The configuration file is named *name*`.conf`, where *name* is the name of the daemon or the name of the service. For example, the configuration for the `syslogd` daemon is `/etc/syslog.conf`.

- Daemons can be started from the command line, but they are usually started from one of the system initialization scripts (`/etc/rc*` or `/etc/init.d/*`). If the daemon should be restarted automatically when it exits, we can arrange for `init` to restart it if we include a `respawn` entry for it in `/etc/inittab`.

- If a daemon has a configuration file, the daemon reads it when it starts, but usually won't look at it again. If an administrator changes the configuration, the daemon would need to be stopped and restarted to account for the configuration changes. To avoid this, some daemons will catch `SIGHUP` and reread their configuration files when they receive the signal. Since they aren't associated with terminals and are either session leaders without controlling terminals or members of orphaned process groups, daemons have no reason to expect to receive `SIGHUP`. Thus, they can safely reuse it.

Example

The program shown in Figure 13.7 shows one way a daemon can reread its configuration file. The program uses `sigwait` and multiple threads, as discussed in Section 12.8.

```c
#include "apue.h"
#include <pthread.h>
#include <syslog.h>

sigset_t    mask;

extern int already_running(void);

void
reread(void)
{
    /* ... */
}

void *
thr_fn(void *arg)
{
    int err, signo;

    for (;;) {
        err = sigwait(&mask, &signo);
        if (err != 0) {
            syslog(LOG_ERR, "sigwait failed");
            exit(1);
        }

        switch (signo) {
        case SIGHUP:
            syslog(LOG_INFO, "Re-reading configuration file");
            reread();
            break;

        case SIGTERM:
            syslog(LOG_INFO, "got SIGTERM; exiting");
            exit(0);

        default:
            syslog(LOG_INFO, "unexpected signal %d\n", signo);
        }
    }
    return(0);
}

int
main(int argc, char *argv[])
```

```
{
    int               err;
    pthread_t         tid;
    char              *cmd;
    struct sigaction  sa;

    if ((cmd = strrchr(argv[0], '/')) == NULL)
        cmd = argv[0];
    else
        cmd++;

    /*
     * Become a daemon.
     */
    daemonize(cmd);

    /*
     * Make sure only one copy of the daemon is running.
     */
    if (already_running()) {
        syslog(LOG_ERR, "daemon already running");
        exit(1);
    }

    /*
     * Restore SIGHUP default and block all signals.
     */
    sa.sa_handler = SIG_DFL;
    sigemptyset(&sa.sa_mask);
    sa.sa_flags = 0;
    if (sigaction(SIGHUP, &sa, NULL) < 0)
        err_quit("%s: can't restore SIGHUP default");
    sigfillset(&mask);
    if ((err = pthread_sigmask(SIG_BLOCK, &mask, NULL)) != 0)
        err_exit(err, "SIG_BLOCK error");

    /*
     * Create a thread to handle SIGHUP and SIGTERM.
     */
    err = pthread_create(&tid, NULL, thr_fn, 0);
    if (err != 0)
        err_exit(err, "can't create thread");

    /*
     * Proceed with the rest of the daemon.
     */
    /* ... */
    exit(0);
}
```

Figure 13.7 Daemon rereading configuration files

We call `daemonize` from Figure 13.1 to initialize the daemon. When it returns, we call `already_running` from Figure 13.6 to ensure that only one copy of the daemon is running. At this point, SIGHUP is still ignored, so we need to reset the disposition to the default behavior; otherwise, the thread calling `sigwait` may never see the signal.

We block all signals, as is recommended for multithreaded programs, and create a thread to handle signals. The thread's only job is to wait for SIGHUP and SIGTERM. When it receives SIGHUP, the thread calls `reread` to reread its configuration file. When it receives SIGTERM, the thread logs a message and exits.

Recall from Figure 10.1 that the default action for SIGHUP and SIGTERM is to terminate the process. Because we block these signals, the daemon will not die when one of them is sent to the process. Instead, the thread calling `sigwait` will return with an indication that the signal has been received.   □

Example

As noted in Section 12.8, Linux threads behave differently with respect to signals. Because of this, identifying the proper process to signal in Figure 13.7 will be difficult. In addition, we aren't guaranteed that the daemon will react as we expect, because of the implementation differences.

The program in Figure 13.8 shows how a daemon can catch SIGHUP and reread its configuration file without using multiple threads.

```
#include "apue.h"
#include <syslog.h>
#include <errno.h>

extern int lockfile(int);
extern int already_running(void);

void
reread(void)
{
    /* ... */
}

void
sigterm(int signo)
{
    syslog(LOG_INFO, "got SIGTERM; exiting");
    exit(0);
}

void
sighup(int signo)
{
    syslog(LOG_INFO, "Re-reading configuration file");
    reread();
}
```

```
int
main(int argc, char *argv[])
{
    char            *cmd;
    struct sigaction    sa;

    if ((cmd = strrchr(argv[0], '/')) == NULL)
        cmd = argv[0];
    else
        cmd++;

    /*
     * Become a daemon.
     */
    daemonize(cmd);

    /*
     * Make sure only one copy of the daemon is running.
     */
    if (already_running()) {
        syslog(LOG_ERR, "daemon already running");
        exit(1);
    }

    /*
     * Handle signals of interest.
     */
    sa.sa_handler = sigterm;
    sigemptyset(&sa.sa_mask);
    sigaddset(&sa.sa_mask, SIGHUP);
    sa.sa_flags = 0;
    if (sigaction(SIGTERM, &sa, NULL) < 0) {
        syslog(LOG_ERR, "can't catch SIGTERM: %s", strerror(errno));
        exit(1);
    }
    sa.sa_handler = sighup;
    sigemptyset(&sa.sa_mask);
    sigaddset(&sa.sa_mask, SIGTERM);
    sa.sa_flags = 0;
    if (sigaction(SIGHUP, &sa, NULL) < 0) {
        syslog(LOG_ERR, "can't catch SIGHUP: %s", strerror(errno));
        exit(1);
    }

    /*
     * Proceed with the rest of the daemon.
     */
    /* ... */
    exit(0);
}
```

Figure 13.8 Alternate implementation of daemon rereading configuration files

After initializing the daemon, we install signal handlers for SIGHUP and SIGTERM. We can either place the reread logic in the signal handler or just set a flag in the handler and have the main thread of the daemon do all the work instead.   □

13.7 Client–Server Model

A common use for a daemon process is as a server process. Indeed, in Figure 13.2, we can call the syslogd process a server that has messages sent to it by user processes (clients) using a UNIX domain datagram socket.

In general, a *server* is a process that waits for a *client* to contact it, requesting some type of service. In Figure 13.2, the service being provided by the syslogd server is the logging of an error message.

In Figure 13.2, the communication between the client and the server is one-way. The client sends its service request to the server; the server sends nothing back to the client. In the upcoming chapters, we'll see numerous examples of two-way communication between a client and a server. The client sends a request to the server, and the server sends a reply back to the client.

13.8 Summary

Daemon processes are running all the time on most UNIX systems. Initializing our own process to run as a daemon takes some care and an understanding of the process relationships that we described in Chapter 9. In this chapter, we developed a function that can be called by a daemon process to initialize itself correctly.

We also discussed the ways a daemon can log error messages, since a daemon normally doesn't have a controlling terminal. We discussed several conventions that daemons follow on most UNIX systems and showed examples of how to implement some of these conventions.

Exercises

13.1 As we might guess from Figure 13.2, when the syslog facility is initialized, either by calling openlog directly or on the first call to syslog, the special device file for the UNIX domain datagram socket, /dev/log, has to be opened. What happens if the user process (the daemon) calls chroot before calling openlog?

13.2 List all the daemons active on your system, and identify the function of each one.

13.3 Write a program that calls the daemonize function in Figure 13.1. After calling this function, call getlogin (Section 8.15) to see whether the process has a login name now that it has become a daemon. Print the results to a file.

14

Advanced I/O

14.1 Introduction

This chapter covers numerous topics and functions that we lump under the term *advanced I/O*: nonblocking I/O, record locking, System V STREAMS, I/O multiplexing (the `select` and `poll` functions), the `readv` and `writev` functions, and memory-mapped I/O (`mmap`). We need to cover these topics before describing interprocess communication in Chapter 15, Chapter 17, and many of the examples in later chapters.

14.2 Nonblocking I/O

In Section 10.5, we said that the system calls are divided into two categories: the "slow" ones and all the others. The slow system calls are those that can block forever. They include

- Reads that can block the caller forever if data isn't present with certain file types (pipes, terminal devices, and network devices)
- Writes that can block the caller forever if the data can't be accepted immediately by these same file types (no room in the pipe, network flow control, etc.)
- Opens that block until some condition occurs on certain file types (such as an open of a terminal device that waits until an attached modem answers the phone, or an open of a FIFO for writing-only when no other process has the FIFO open for reading)
- Reads and writes of files that have mandatory record locking enabled

- Certain `ioctl` operations
- Some of the interprocess communication functions (Chapter 15)

We also said that system calls related to disk I/O are not considered slow, even though the read or write of a disk file can block the caller temporarily.

Nonblocking I/O lets us issue an I/O operation, such as an `open`, `read`, or `write`, and not have it block forever. If the operation cannot be completed, the call returns immediately with an error noting that the operation would have blocked.

There are two ways to specify nonblocking I/O for a given descriptor.

1. If we call `open` to get the descriptor, we can specify the `O_NONBLOCK` flag (Section 3.3).

2. For a descriptor that is already open, we call `fcntl` to turn on the `O_NONBLOCK` file status flag (Section 3.14). Figure 3.11 shows a function that we can call to turn on any of the file status flags for a descriptor.

> Earlier versions of System V used the flag `O_NDELAY` to specify nonblocking mode. These versions of System V returned a value of 0 from the `read` function if there wasn't any data to be read. Since this use of a return value of 0 overlapped with the normal UNIX System convention of 0 meaning the end of file, POSIX.1 chose to provide a nonblocking flag with a different name and different semantics. Indeed, with these older versions of System V, when we get a return of 0 from `read`, we don't know whether the call would have blocked or whether the end of file was encountered. We'll see that POSIX.1 requires that `read` return −1 with `errno` set to `EAGAIN` if there is no data to read from a nonblocking descriptor. Some platforms derived from System V support both the older `O_NDELAY` and the POSIX.1 `O_NONBLOCK`, but in this text, we'll use only the POSIX.1 feature. The older `O_NDELAY` is for backward compatibility and should not be used in new applications.
>
> 4.3BSD provided the `FNDELAY` flag for `fcntl`, and its semantics were slightly different. Instead of affecting only the file status flags for the descriptor, the flags for either the terminal device or the socket were also changed to be nonblocking, affecting all users of the terminal or socket, not only the users sharing the same file table entry (4.3BSD nonblocking I/O worked only on terminals and sockets). Also, 4.3BSD returned `EWOULDBLOCK` if an operation on a nonblocking descriptor could not complete without blocking. Today, BSD-based systems provide the POSIX.1 `O_NONBLOCK` flag and define `EWOULDBLOCK` to be the same as `EAGAIN`. These systems provide nonblocking semantics consistent with other POSIX-compatible systems: changes in file status flags affect all users of the same file table entry, but are independent of accesses to the same device through other file table entries. (Refer to Figures 3.6 and 3.8.)

Example

Let's look at an example of nonblocking I/O. The program in Figure 14.1 reads up to 500,000 bytes from the standard input and attempts to write it to the standard output. The standard output is first set nonblocking. The output is in a loop, with the results of each `write` being printed on the standard error. The function `clr_fl` is similar to the function `set_fl` that we showed in Figure 3.11. This new function simply clears one or more of the flag bits.

```
#include "apue.h"
#include <errno.h>
#include <fcntl.h>

char      buf[500000];

int
main(void)
{
    int      ntowrite, nwrite;
    char     *ptr;

    ntowrite = read(STDIN_FILENO, buf, sizeof(buf));
    fprintf(stderr, "read %d bytes\n", ntowrite);

    set_fl(STDOUT_FILENO, O_NONBLOCK);    /* set nonblocking */

    ptr = buf;
    while (ntowrite > 0) {
        errno = 0;
        nwrite = write(STDOUT_FILENO, ptr, ntowrite);
        fprintf(stderr, "nwrite = %d, errno = %d\n", nwrite, errno);

        if (nwrite > 0) {
            ptr += nwrite;
            ntowrite -= nwrite;
        }
    }

    clr_fl(STDOUT_FILENO, O_NONBLOCK);    /* clear nonblocking */

    exit(0);
}
```

Figure 14.1 Large nonblocking `write`

If the standard output is a regular file, we expect the `write` to be executed once:

```
$ ls -l /etc/termcap                                      print file size
-rw-r--r--  1 root      702559 Feb 23  2002 /etc/termcap
$ ./a.out < /etc/termcap > temp.file                      try a regular file first
read 500000 bytes
nwrite = 500000, errno = 0                                a single write
$ ls -l temp.file                                         verify size of output file
-rw-rw-r--  1 sar       500000 Jul  8 04:19 temp.file
```

But if the standard output is a terminal, we expect the `write` to return a partial count sometimes and an error at other times. This is what we see:

```
$ ./a.out < /etc/termcap 2>stderr.out          output to terminal
                                                lots of output to terminal ...
$ cat stderr.out
read 500000 bytes
nwrite = 216041, errno = 0
nwrite = -1, errno = 11                         1,497 of these errors
 . . .
nwrite = 16015, errno = 0
nwrite = -1, errno = 11                         1,856 of these errors
 . . .
nwrite = 32081, errno = 0
nwrite = -1, errno = 11                         1,654 of these errors
 . . .
nwrite = 48002, errno = 0
nwrite = -1, errno = 11                         1,460 of these errors
 . . .
                                                and so on ...
nwrite = 7949, errno = 0
```

On this system, the errno of 11 is EAGAIN. The amount of data accepted by the terminal driver varies from system to system. The results will also vary depending on how you are logged in to the system: on the system console, on a hardwired terminal, on network connection using a pseudo terminal. If you are running a windowing system on your terminal, you are also going through a pseudo-terminal device.   □

In this example, the program issues thousands of write calls, even though only between 10 and 20 are needed to output the data. The rest just return an error. This type of loop, called *polling*, is a waste of CPU time on a multiuser system. In Section 14.5, we'll see that I/O multiplexing with a nonblocking descriptor is a more efficient way to do this.

Sometimes, we can avoid using nonblocking I/O by designing our applications to use multiple threads (see Chapter 11). We can allow individual threads to block in I/O calls if we can continue to make progress in other threads. This can sometimes simplify the design, as we shall see in Chapter 21; sometimes, however, the overhead of synchronization can add more complexity than is saved from using threads.

14.3 Record Locking

What happens when two people edit the same file at the same time? In most UNIX systems, the final state of the file corresponds to the last process that wrote the file. In some applications, however, such as a database system, a process needs to be certain that it alone is writing to a file. To provide this capability for processes that need it, commercial UNIX systems provide record locking. (In Chapter 20, we develop a database library that uses record locking.)

Record locking is the term normally used to describe the ability of a process to prevent other processes from modifying a region of a file while the first process is reading or modifying that portion of the file. Under the UNIX System, the adjective "record" is a misnomer, since the UNIX kernel does not have a notion of records in a file. A better term is *byte-range locking*, since it is a range of a file (possibly the entire file) that is locked.

History

One of the criticisms of early UNIX systems was that they couldn't be used to run database systems, because there was no support for locking portions of files. As UNIX systems found their way into business computing environments, various groups added support record locking (differently, of course).

Early Berkeley releases supported only the flock function. This function locks only entire files, not regions of a file.

Record locking was added to System V Release 3 through the fcntl function. The lockf function was built on top of this, providing a simplified interface. These functions allowed callers to lock arbitrary byte ranges in a file, from the entire file down to a single byte within the file.

POSIX.1 chose to standardize on the fcntl approach. Figure 14.2 shows the forms of record locking provided by various systems. Note that the Single UNIX Specification includes lockf in the XSI extension.

System	Advisory	Mandatory	fcntl	lockf	flock
SUS	•		•	XSI	
FreeBSD 5.2.1	•		•	•	•
Linux 2.4.22	•	•	•	•	•
Mac OS X 10.3	•		•	•	•
Solaris 9	•	•	•	•	•

Figure 14.2 Forms of record locking supported by various UNIX systems

We describe the difference between advisory locking and mandatory locking later in this section. In this text, we describe only the POSIX.1 fcntl locking.

> Record locking was originally added to Version 7 in 1980 by John Bass. The system call entry into the kernel was a function named locking. This function provided mandatory record locking and propagated through many versions of System III. Xenix systems picked up this function, and some Intel-based System V derivatives, such as OpenServer 5, still support it in a Xenix-compatibility library.

fcntl Record Locking

Let's repeat the prototype for the fcntl function from Section 3.14.

```
#include <fcntl.h>

int fcntl(int filedes, int cmd, ... /* struct flock *flockptr */ );
```
                        Returns: depends on *cmd* if OK (see following), –1 on error

For record locking, *cmd* is F_GETLK, F_SETLK, or F_SETLKW. The third argument (which we'll call *flockptr*) is a pointer to an flock structure.

```
struct flock {
  short  l_type;   /* F_RDLCK, F_WRLCK, or F_UNLCK */
  off_t  l_start;  /* offset in bytes, relative to l_whence */
  short  l_whence; /* SEEK_SET, SEEK_CUR, or SEEK_END */
  off_t  l_len;    /* length, in bytes; 0 means lock to EOF */
  pid_t  l_pid;    /* returned with F_GETLK */
};
```

This structure describes

- The type of lock desired: F_RDLCK (a shared read lock), F_WRLCK (an exclusive write lock), or F_UNLCK (unlocking a region)
- The starting byte offset of the region being locked or unlocked (l_start and l_whence)
- The size of the region in bytes (l_len)
- The ID (l_pid) of the process holding the lock that can block the current process (returned by F_GETLK only)

There are numerous rules about the specification of the region to be locked or unlocked.

- The two elements that specify the starting offset of the region are similar to the last two arguments of the lseek function (Section 3.6). Indeed, the l_whence member is specified as SEEK_SET, SEEK_CUR, or SEEK_END.
- Locks can start and extend beyond the current end of file, but cannot start or extend before the beginning of the file.
- If l_len is 0, it means that the lock extends to the largest possible offset of the file. This allows us to lock a region starting anywhere in the file, up through and including any data that is appended to the file. (We don't have to try to guess how many bytes might be appended to the file.)
- To lock the entire file, we set l_start and l_whence to point to the beginning of the file and specify a length (l_len) of 0. (There are several ways to specify the beginning of the file, but most applications specify l_start as 0 and l_whence as SEEK_SET.)

We mentioned two types of locks: a shared read lock (l_type of F_RDLCK) and an exclusive write lock (F_WRLCK). The basic rule is that any number of processes can have a shared read lock on a given byte, but only one process can have an exclusive write lock on a given byte. Furthermore, if there are one or more read locks on a byte, there can't be any write locks on that byte; if there is an exclusive write lock on a byte, there can't be any read locks on that byte. We show this compatibility rule in Figure 14.3.

| | Request for | |
	read lock	write lock
no locks	OK	OK
one or more read locks	OK	denied
one write lock	denied	denied

Region currently has

Figure 14.3 Compatibility between different lock types

The compatibility rule applies to lock requests made from different processes, not to multiple lock requests made by a single process. If a process has an existing lock on a range of a file, a subsequent attempt to place a lock on the same range by the same process will replace the existing lock with the new one. Thus, if a process has a write lock on bytes 16–32 of a file and then tries to place a read lock on bytes 16–32, the request will succeed (assuming that we're not racing with any other processes trying to lock the same portion of the file), and the write lock will be replaced by a read lock.

To obtain a read lock, the descriptor must be open for reading; to obtain a write lock, the descriptor must be open for writing.

We can now describe the three commands for the fcntl function.

F_GETLK   Determine whether the lock described by *flockptr* is blocked by some other lock. If a lock exists that would prevent ours from being created, the information on that existing lock overwrites the information pointed to by *flockptr*. If no lock exists that would prevent ours from being created, the structure pointed to by *flockptr* is left unchanged except for the l_type member, which is set to F_UNLCK.

F_SETLK   Set the lock described by *flockptr*. If we are trying to obtain a read lock (l_type of F_RDLCK) or a write lock (l_type of F_WRLCK) and the compatibility rule prevents the system from giving us the lock (Figure 14.3), fcntl returns immediately with errno set to either EACCES or EAGAIN.

> Although POSIX allows an implementation to return either error code, all four implementations described in this text return EAGAIN if the locking request cannot be satisfied.

This command is also used to clear the lock described by *flockptr* (l_type of F_UNLCK).

F_SETLKW   This command is a blocking version of F_SETLK. (The W in the command name means *wait*.) If the requested read lock or write lock cannot be granted because another process currently has some part of the requested region locked, the calling process is put to sleep. The process wakes up either when the lock becomes available or when interrupted by a signal.

Be aware that testing for a lock with F_GETLK and then trying to obtain that lock with F_SETLK or F_SETLKW is not an atomic operation. We have no guarantee that, between the two fcntl calls, some other process won't come in and obtain the same lock. If we don't want to block while waiting for a lock to become available to us, we must handle the possible error returns from F_SETLK.

> Note that POSIX.1 doesn't specify what happens when one process read-locks a range of a file, a second process blocks while trying to get a write lock on the same range, and a third processes then attempts to get another read lock on the range. If the third process is allowed to place a read lock on the range just because the range is already read-locked, then the implementation might starve processes with pending write locks. This means that as additional requests to read lock the same range arrive, the time that the process with the pending write-lock request has to wait is extended. If the read-lock requests arrive quickly enough without a lull in the arrival rate, then the writer could wait for a long time.

When setting or releasing a lock on a file, the system combines or splits adjacent areas as required. For example, if we lock bytes 100 through 199 and then unlock byte 150, the kernel still maintains the locks on bytes 100 through 149 and bytes 151 through 199. Figure 14.4 illustrates the byte-range locks in this situation.

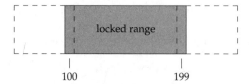

File after locking bytes 100 through 199

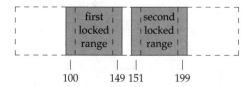

File after unlocking byte 150

Figure 14.4 File byte-range lock diagram

If we were to lock byte 150, the system would coalesce the adjacent locked regions into a single region from byte 100 through 199. The resulting picture would be the first diagram in Figure 14.4, the same as when we started.

Example—Requesting and Releasing a Lock

To save ourselves from having to allocate an flock structure and fill in all the elements each time, the function lock_reg in Figure 14.5 handles all these details.

```
#include "apue.h"
#include <fcntl.h>

int
lock_reg(int fd, int cmd, int type, off_t offset, int whence, off_t len)
{
    struct flock    lock;

    lock.l_type = type;       /* F_RDLCK, F_WRLCK, F_UNLCK */
    lock.l_start = offset;    /* byte offset, relative to l_whence */
    lock.l_whence = whence;   /* SEEK_SET, SEEK_CUR, SEEK_END */
    lock.l_len = len;         /* #bytes (0 means to EOF) */

    return(fcntl(fd, cmd, &lock));
}
```

Figure 14.5 Function to lock or unlock a region of a file

Since most locking calls are to lock or unlock a region (the command F_GETLK is rarely used), we normally use one of the following five macros, which are defined in apue.h (Appendix B).

```
#define read_lock(fd, offset, whence, len) \
            lock_reg((fd), F_SETLK, F_RDLCK, (offset), (whence), (len))
#define readw_lock(fd, offset, whence, len) \
            lock_reg((fd), F_SETLKW, F_RDLCK, (offset), (whence), (len))
#define write_lock(fd, offset, whence, len) \
            lock_reg((fd), F_SETLK, F_WRLCK, (offset), (whence), (len))
#define writew_lock(fd, offset, whence, len) \
            lock_reg((fd), F_SETLKW, F_WRLCK, (offset), (whence), (len))
#define un_lock(fd, offset, whence, len) \
            lock_reg((fd), F_SETLK, F_UNLCK, (offset), (whence), (len))
```

We have purposely defined the first three arguments to these macros in the same order as the lseek function.   □

Example—Testing for a Lock

Figure 14.6 defines the function lock_test that we'll use to test for a lock.

```
#include "apue.h"
#include <fcntl.h>

pid_t
lock_test(int fd, int type, off_t offset, int whence, off_t len)
{
    struct flock    lock;
```

```
lock.l_type = type;      /* F_RDLCK or F_WRLCK */
lock.l_start = offset;   /* byte offset, relative to l_whence */
lock.l_whence = whence;  /* SEEK_SET, SEEK_CUR, SEEK_END */
lock.l_len = len;        /* #bytes (0 means to EOF) */

if (fcntl(fd, F_GETLK, &lock) < 0)
    err_sys("fcntl error");

if (lock.l_type == F_UNLCK)
    return(0);        /* false, region isn't locked by another proc */
return(lock.l_pid); /* true, return pid of lock owner */
}
```

Figure 14.6 Function to test for a locking condition

If a lock exists that would block the request specified by the arguments, this function returns the process ID of the process holding the lock. Otherwise, the function returns 0 (false). We normally call this function from the following two macros (defined in apue.h):

```
#define is_read_lockable(fd, offset, whence, len) \
        (lock_test((fd), F_RDLCK, (offset), (whence), (len)) == 0)
#define is_write_lockable(fd, offset, whence, len) \
        (lock_test((fd), F_WRLCK, (offset), (whence), (len)) == 0)
```

Note that the lock_test function can't be used by a process to see whether it is currently holding a portion of a file locked. The definition of the F_GETLK command states that the information returned applies to an existing lock that would prevent us from creating our own lock. Since the F_SETLK and F_SETLKW commands always replace a process's existing lock if it exists, we can never block on our own lock; thus, the F_GETLK command will never report our own lock.   □

Example—Deadlock

Deadlock occurs when two processes are each waiting for a resource that the other has locked. The potential for deadlock exists if a process that controls a locked region is put to sleep when it tries to lock another region that is controlled by a different process.

Figure 14.7 shows an example of deadlock. The child locks byte 0 and the parent locks byte 1. Then each tries to lock the other's already locked byte. We use the parent–child synchronization routines from Section 8.9 (TELL_xxx and WAIT_xxx) so that each process can wait for the other to obtain its lock. Running the program in Figure 14.7 gives us

```
$ ./a.out
parent: got the lock, byte 1
child: got the lock, byte 0
child: writew_lock error: Resource deadlock avoided
parent: got the lock, byte 0
```

```
#include "apue.h"
#include <fcntl.h>

static void
lockabyte(const char *name, int fd, off_t offset)
{
    if (writew_lock(fd, offset, SEEK_SET, 1) < 0)
        err_sys("%s: writew_lock error", name);
    printf("%s: got the lock, byte %ld\n", name, offset);
}

int
main(void)
{
    int     fd;
    pid_t   pid;

    /*
     * Create a file and write two bytes to it.
     */
    if ((fd = creat("templock", FILE_MODE)) < 0)
        err_sys("creat error");
    if (write(fd, "ab", 2) != 2)
        err_sys("write error");

    TELL_WAIT();
    if ((pid = fork()) < 0) {
        err_sys("fork error");
    } else if (pid == 0) {                  /* child */
        lockabyte("child", fd, 0);
        TELL_PARENT(getppid());
        WAIT_PARENT();
        lockabyte("child", fd, 1);
    } else {                                /* parent */
        lockabyte("parent", fd, 1);
        TELL_CHILD(pid);
        WAIT_CHILD();
        lockabyte("parent", fd, 0);
    }
    exit(0);
}
```

Figure 14.7 Example of deadlock detection

When a deadlock is detected, the kernel has to choose one process to receive the
error return. In this example, the child was chosen, but this is an implementation detail.
On some systems, the child always receives the error. On other systems, the parent
always gets the error. On some systems, you might even see the errors split between the
child and the parent as multiple lock attempts are made.   □

Implied Inheritance and Release of Locks

Three rules govern the automatic inheritance and release of record locks.

1. Locks are associated with a process and a file. This has two implications. The first is obvious: when a process terminates, all its locks are released. The second is far from obvious: whenever a descriptor is closed, any locks on the file referenced by that descriptor for that process are released. This means that if we do

    ```
    fd1 = open(pathname, ...);
    read_lock(fd1, ...);
    fd2 = dup(fd1);
    close(fd2);
    ```

    after the close(fd2), the lock that was obtained on fd1 is released. The same thing would happen if we replaced the dup with open, as in

    ```
    fd1 = open(pathname, ...);
    read_lock(fd1, ...);
    fd2 = open(pathname, ...)
    close(fd2);
    ```

    to open the same file on another descriptor.

2. Locks are never inherited by the child across a fork. This means that if a process obtains a lock and then calls fork, the child is considered another process with regard to the lock that was obtained by the parent. The child has to call fcntl to obtain its own locks on any descriptors that were inherited across the fork. This makes sense because locks are meant to prevent multiple processes from writing to the same file at the same time. If the child inherited locks across a fork, both the parent and the child could write to the same file at the same time.

3. Locks are inherited by a new program across an exec. Note, however, that if the close-on-exec flag is set for a file descriptor, all locks for the underlying file are released when the descriptor is closed as part of an exec.

FreeBSD Implementation

Let's take a brief look at the data structures used in the FreeBSD implementation. This should help clarify rule 1, that locks are associated with a process and a file.

Consider a process that executes the following statements (ignoring error returns):

```
fd1 = open(pathname, ...);
write_lock(fd1, 0, SEEK_SET, 1);       /* parent write locks byte 0 */
if ((pid = fork()) > 0) {              /* parent */
    fd2 = dup(fd1);
    fd3 = open(pathname, ...);
} else if (pid == 0) {
    read_lock(fd1, 1, SEEK_SET, 1); /* child read locks byte 1 */
}
pause();
```

Figure 14.8 shows the resulting data structures after both the parent and the child have
paused.

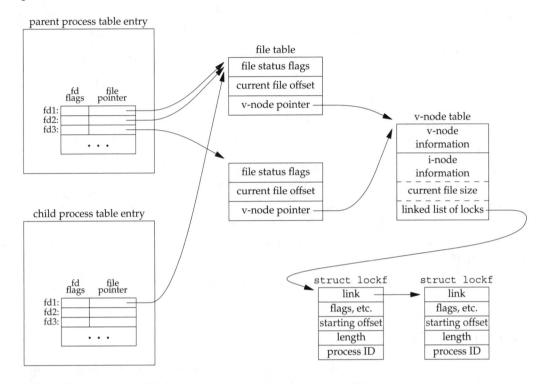

Figure 14.8 The FreeBSD data structures for record locking

We've shown the data structures that result from the open, fork, and dup earlier
(Figures 3.8 and 8.2). What is new are the lockf structures that are linked together
from the i-node structure. Note that each lockf structure describes one locked region
(defined by an offset and length) for a given process. We show two of these structures:
one for the parent's call to write_lock and one for the child's call to read_lock.
Each structure contains the corresponding process ID.

In the parent, closing any one of fd1, fd2, or fd3 causes the parent's lock to be
released. When any one of these three file descriptors is closed, the kernel goes through
the linked list of locks for the corresponding i-node and releases the locks held by the
calling process. The kernel can't tell (and doesn't care) which descriptor of the three
was used by the parent to obtain the lock.

Example

In the program in Figure 13.6, we saw how a daemon can use a lock on a file to ensure
that only one copy of the daemon is running. Figure 14.9 shows the implementation of
the lockfile function used by the daemon to place a write lock on a file.

```
#include <unistd.h>
#include <fcntl.h>

int
lockfile(int fd)
{
    struct flock fl;

    fl.l_type = F_WRLCK;
    fl.l_start = 0;
    fl.l_whence = SEEK_SET;
    fl.l_len = 0;
    return(fcntl(fd, F_SETLK, &fl));
}
```

Figure 14.9 Place a write lock on an entire file

Alternatively, we could define the `lockfile` function in terms of the `write_lock` function:

```
#define lockfile(fd) write_lock((fd), 0, SEEK_SET, 0)
```

□

Locks at End of File

Use caution when locking or unlocking relative to the end of file. Most implementations convert an `l_whence` value of `SEEK_CUR` or `SEEK_END` into an absolute file offset, using `l_start` and the file's current position or current length. Often, however, we need to specify a lock relative to the file's current position or current length, because we can't call `lseek` to obtain the current file offset, since we don't have a lock on the file. (There's a chance that another process could change the file's length between the call to `lseek` and the lock call.)

Consider the following sequence of steps:

```
writew_lock(fd, 0, SEEK_END, 0);
write(fd, buf, 1);
un_lock(fd, 0, SEEK_END);
write(fd, buf, 1);
```

This sequence of code might not do what you expect. It obtains a write lock from the current end of the file onward, covering any future data we might append to the file. Assuming that we are at end of file when we perform the first `write`, that will extend the file by one byte, and that byte will be locked. The unlock that follows has the effect of removing the locks for future writes that append data to the file, but it leaves a lock on the last byte in the file. When the second write occurs, the end of file is extended by one byte, but this byte is not locked. The state of the file locks for this sequence of steps is shown in Figure 14.10

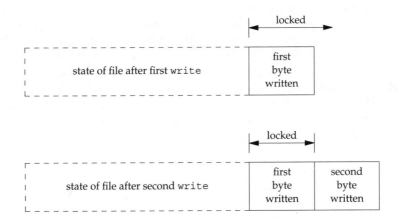

Figure 14.10 File range lock diagram

When a portion of a file is locked, the kernel converts the offset specified into an absolute file offset. In addition to specifying an absolute file offset (SEEK_SET), fcntl allows us to specify this offset relative to a point in the file: current (SEEK_CUR) or end of file (SEEK_END). The kernel needs to remember the locks independent of the current file offset or end of file, because the current offset and end of file can change, and changes to these attributes shouldn't affect the state of existing locks.

If we intended to remove the lock covering the byte we wrote in the first write, we could have specified the length as −1. Negative-length values represent the bytes before the specified offset.

Advisory versus Mandatory Locking

Consider a library of database access routines. If all the functions in the library handle record locking in a consistent way, then we say that any set of processes using these functions to access a database are *cooperating processes*. It is feasible for these database access functions to use advisory locking if they are the only ones being used to access the database. But advisory locking doesn't prevent some other process that has write permission for the database file from writing whatever it wants to the database file. This rogue process would be an uncooperating process, since it's not using the accepted method (the library of database functions) to access the database.

Mandatory locking causes the kernel to check every open, read, and write to verify that the calling process isn't violating a lock on the file being accessed. Mandatory locking is sometimes called *enforcement-mode locking*.

> We saw in Figure 14.2 that Linux 2.4.22 and Solaris 9 provide mandatory record locking, but FreeBSD 5.2.1 and Mac OS X 10.3 do not. Mandatory record locking is not part of the Single UNIX Specification. On Linux, if you want mandatory locking, you need to enable it on a per file system basis by using the -o mand option to the mount command.

Mandatory locking is enabled for a particular file by turning on the set-group-ID bit and turning off the group-execute bit. (Recall Figure 4.12.) Since the set-group-ID bit makes no sense when the group-execute bit is off, the designers of SVR3 chose this way to specify that the locking for a file is to be mandatory locking and not advisory locking.

What happens to a process that tries to read or write a file that has mandatory locking enabled and the specified part of the file is currently read-locked or write-locked by another process? The answer depends on the type of operation (read or write), the type of lock held by the other process (read lock or write lock), and whether the descriptor for the read or write is nonblocking. Figure 14.11 shows the eight possibilities.

Type of existing lock on region held by other process	Blocking descriptor, tries to		Nonblocking descriptor, tries to	
	read	write	read	write
read lock	OK	blocks	OK	EAGAIN
write lock	blocks	blocks	EAGAIN	EAGAIN

Figure 14.11   Effect of mandatory locking on reads and writes by other processes

In addition to the read and write functions in Figure 14.11, the open function can also be affected by mandatory record locks held by another process. Normally, open succeeds, even if the file being opened has outstanding mandatory record locks. The next read or write follows the rules listed in Figure 14.11. But if the file being opened has outstanding mandatory record locks (either read locks or write locks), and if the flags in the call to open specify either O_TRUNC or O_CREAT, then open returns an error of EAGAIN immediately, regardless of whether O_NONBLOCK is specified.

> Only Solaris treats the O_CREAT flag as an error case. Linux allows the O_CREAT flag to be specified when opening a file with an outstanding mandatory lock. Generating the open error for O_TRUNC makes sense, because the file cannot be truncated if it is read-locked or write-locked by another process. Generating the error for O_CREAT, however, makes little sense; this flag says to create the file only if it doesn't already exist, but it has to exist to be record-locked by another process.

This handling of locking conflicts with open can lead to surprising results. While developing the exercises in this section, a test program was run that opened a file (whose mode specified mandatory locking), established a read lock on an entire file, and then went to sleep for a while. (Recall from Figure 14.11 that a read lock should prevent writing to the file by other processes.) During this sleep period, the following behavior was seen in other typical UNIX System programs.

- The same file could be edited with the ed editor, and the results written back to disk! The mandatory record locking had no effect at all. Using the system call trace feature provided by some versions of the UNIX System, it was seen that ed wrote the new contents to a temporary file, removed the original file, and then renamed the temporary file to be the original file. The mandatory record locking has no effect on the unlink function, which allowed this to happen.

Under Solaris, the system call trace of a process is obtained by the truss(1) command. FreeBSD and Mac OS X use the ktrace(1) and kdump(1) commands. Linux provides the strace(1) command for tracing the system calls made by a process.

- The vi editor was never able to edit the file. It could read the file's contents, but whenever we tried to write new data to the file, EAGAIN was returned. If we tried to append new data to the file, the write blocked. This behavior from vi is what we expect.

- Using the Korn shell's > and >> operators to overwrite or append to the file resulted in the error "cannot create."

- Using the same two operators with the Bourne shell resulted in an error for >, but the >> operator just blocked until the mandatory lock was removed, and then proceeded. (The difference in the handling of the append operator is because the Korn shell opens the file with O_CREAT and O_APPEND, and we mentioned earlier that specifying O_CREAT generates an error. The Bourne shell, however, doesn't specify O_CREAT if the file already exists, so the open succeeds but the next write blocks.)

Results will vary, depending on the version of the operating system you are using. The bottom line with this exercise is to be wary of mandatory record locking. As seen with the ed example, it can be circumvented.

Mandatory record locking can also be used by a malicious user to hold a read lock on a file that is publicly readable. This can prevent anyone from writing to the file. (Of course, the file has to have mandatory record locking enabled for this to occur, which may require the user be able to change the permission bits of the file.) Consider a database file that is world readable and has mandatory record locking enabled. If a malicious user were to hold a read lock on the entire file, the file could not be written to by other processes.

Example

The program in Figure 14.12 determines whether mandatory locking is supported by a system.

```
#include "apue.h"
#include <errno.h>
#include <fcntl.h>
#include <sys/wait.h>

int
main(int argc, char *argv[])
{
    int             fd;
    pid_t           pid;
    char            buf[5];
    struct stat     statbuf;
```

```c
    if (argc != 2) {
        fprintf(stderr, "usage: %s filename\n", argv[0]);
        exit(1);
    }
    if ((fd = open(argv[1], O_RDWR | O_CREAT | O_TRUNC, FILE_MODE)) < 0)
        err_sys("open error");
    if (write(fd, "abcdef", 6) != 6)
        err_sys("write error");

    /* turn on set-group-ID and turn off group-execute */
    if (fstat(fd, &statbuf) < 0)
        err_sys("fstat error");
    if (fchmod(fd, (statbuf.st_mode & ~S_IXGRP) | S_ISGID) < 0)
        err_sys("fchmod error");

    TELL_WAIT();

    if ((pid = fork()) < 0) {
        err_sys("fork error");
    } else if (pid > 0) {    /* parent */
        /* write lock entire file */
        if (write_lock(fd, 0, SEEK_SET, 0) < 0)
            err_sys("write_lock error");

        TELL_CHILD(pid);

        if (waitpid(pid, NULL, 0) < 0)
            err_sys("waitpid error");
    } else {                 /* child */
        WAIT_PARENT();       /* wait for parent to set lock */

        set_fl(fd, O_NONBLOCK);

        /* first let's see what error we get if region is locked */
        if (read_lock(fd, 0, SEEK_SET, 0) != -1)    /* no wait */
            err_sys("child: read_lock succeeded");
        printf("read_lock of already-locked region returns %d\n",
          errno);

        /* now try to read the mandatory locked file */
        if (lseek(fd, 0, SEEK_SET) == -1)
            err_sys("lseek error");
        if (read(fd, buf, 2) < 0)
            err_ret("read failed (mandatory locking works)");
        else
            printf("read OK (no mandatory locking), buf = %2.2s\n",
              buf);
    }
    exit(0);
}
```

Figure 14.12   Determine whether mandatory locking is supported

This program creates a file and enables mandatory locking for the file. The program then splits into parent and child, with the parent obtaining a write lock on the entire file. The child first sets its descriptor nonblocking and then attempts to obtain a read lock on the file, expecting to get an error. This lets us see whether the system returns EACCES or EAGAIN. Next, the child rewinds the file and tries to read from the file. If mandatory locking is provided, the read should return EACCES or EAGAIN (since the descriptor is nonblocking). Otherwise, the read returns the data that it read. Running this program under Solaris 9 (which supports mandatory locking) gives us

```
$ ./a.out temp.lock
read_lock of already-locked region returns 11
read failed (mandatory locking works): Resource temporarily unavailable
```

If we look at either the system's headers or the intro(2) manual page, we see that an errno of 11 corresponds to EAGAIN. Under FreeBSD 5.2.1, we get

```
$ ./a.out temp.lock
read_lock of already-locked region returns 35
read OK (no mandatory locking), buf = ab
```

Here, an errno of 35 corresponds to EAGAIN. Mandatory locking is not supported.   □

Example

Let's return to the first question of this section: what happens when two people edit the same file at the same time? The normal UNIX System text editors do not use record locking, so the answer is still that the final result of the file corresponds to the last process that wrote the file.

Some versions of the vi editor use advisory record locking. Even if we were using one of these versions of vi, it still doesn't prevent users from running another editor that doesn't use advisory record locking.

If the system provides mandatory record locking, we could modify our favorite editor to use it (if we have the sources). Not having the source code to the editor, we might try the following. We write our own program that is a front end to vi. This program immediately calls fork, and the parent just waits for the child to complete. The child opens the file specified on the command line, enables mandatory locking, obtains a write lock on the entire file, and then executes vi. While vi is running, the file is write-locked, so other users can't modify it. When vi terminates, the parent's wait returns, and our front end terminates.

A small front-end program of this type can be written, but it doesn't work. The problem is that it is common for most editors to read their input file and then close it. A lock is released on a file whenever a descriptor that references that file is closed. This means that when the editor closes the file after reading its contents, the lock is gone. There is no way to prevent this in the front-end program.   □

We'll use record locking in Chapter 20 in our database library to provide concurrent access to multiple processes. We'll also provide some timing measurements to see what effect record locking has on a process.

14.4 STREAMS

The STREAMS mechanism is provided by System V as a general way to interface
communication drivers into the kernel. We need to discuss STREAMS to understand
the terminal interface in System V, the use of the `poll` function for I/O multiplexing
(Section 14.5.2), and the implementation of STREAMS-based pipes and named pipes
(Sections 17.2 and 17.2.1).

> Be careful not to confuse this usage of the word *stream* with our previous usage of it in the
> standard I/O library (Section 5.2). The streams mechanism was developed by Dennis Ritchie
> [Ritchie 1984] as a way of cleaning up the traditional character I/O system (c-lists) and to
> accommodate networking protocols. The streams mechanism was later added to SVR3, after
> enhancing it a bit and capitalizing the name. Complete support for STREAMS (i.e., a
> STREAMS-based terminal I/O system) was provided with SVR4. The SVR4 implementation is
> described in [AT&T 1990d]. Rago [1993] discusses both user-level STREAMS programming
> and kernel-level STREAMS programming.

> STREAMS is an optional feature in the Single UNIX Specification (included as the XSI
> STREAMS Option Group). Of the four platforms discussed in this text, only Solaris provides
> native support for STREAMS. A STREAMS subsystem is available for Linux, but you need to
> add it yourself. It is not usually included by default.

A stream provides a full-duplex path between a user process and a device driver.
There is no need for a stream to talk to a hardware device; a stream can also be used
with a pseudo-device driver. Figure 14.13 shows the basic picture for what is called a
simple stream.

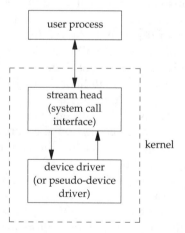

Figure 14.13 A simple stream

Beneath the stream head, we can push processing modules onto the stream. This is
done using an `ioctl` command. Figure 14.14 shows a stream with a single processing
module. We also show the connection between these boxes with two arrows to stress
the full-duplex nature of streams and to emphasize that the processing in one direction
is separate from the processing in the other direction.

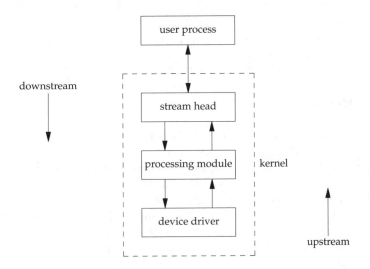

Figure 14.14 A stream with a processing module

Any number of processing modules can be pushed onto a stream. We use the term *push*, because each new module goes beneath the stream head, pushing any previously pushed modules down. (This is similar to a last-in, first-out stack.) In Figure 14.14, we have labeled the downstream and upstream sides of the stream. Data that we write to a stream head is sent downstream. Data read by the device driver is sent upstream.

STREAMS modules are similar to device drivers in that they execute as part of the kernel, and they are normally link edited into the kernel when the kernel is built. If the system supports dynamically-loadable kernel modules (as do Linux and Solaris), then we can take a STREAMS module that has not been link edited into the kernel and try to push it onto a stream; however, there is no guarantee that arbitrary combinations of modules and drivers will work properly together.

We access a stream with the functions from Chapter 3: `open`, `close`, `read`, `write`, and `ioctl`. Additionally, three new functions were added to the SVR3 kernel to support STREAMS (`getmsg`, `putmsg`, and `poll`), and another two (`getpmsg` and `putpmsg`) were added with SVR4 to handle messages with different priority bands within a stream. We describe these five new functions later in this section.

The *pathname* that we `open` for a stream normally lives beneath the `/dev` directory. Simply looking at the device name using `ls -l`, we can't tell whether the device is a STREAMS device. All STREAMS devices are character special files.

Although some STREAMS documentation implies that we can write processing modules and push them willy-nilly onto a stream, the writing of these modules requires the same skills and care as writing a device driver. Generally, only specialized applications or functions push and pop STREAMS modules.

Before STREAMS, terminals were handled with the existing c-list mechanism. (Section 10.3.1 of Bach [1986] and Section 10.6 of McKusick et al. [1996] describe c-lists in SVR2 and 4.4BSD, respectively.) Adding other character-based devices to the kernel usually involved writing a device driver and putting everything into the driver. Access to the new device was typically through the raw device, meaning that every user `read` or `write` ended up directly in the device driver. The STREAMS mechanism cleans up this way of interacting, allowing the data to flow between the stream head and the driver in STREAMS messages and allowing any number of intermediate processing modules to operate on the data.

STREAMS Messages

All input and output under STREAMS is based on messages. The stream head and the user process exchange messages using `read`, `write`, `ioctl`, `getmsg`, `getpmsg`, `putmsg`, and `putpmsg`. Messages are also passed up and down a stream between the stream head, the processing modules, and the device driver.

Between the user process and the stream head, a message consists of a message type, optional control information, and optional data. We show in Figure 14.15 how the various message types are generated by the arguments to `write`, `putmsg`, and `putpmsg`. The control information and data are specified by `strbuf` structures:

```
struct strbuf
   int   maxlen;   /* size of buffer */
   int   len;      /* number of bytes currently in buffer */
   char *buf;      /* pointer to buffer */
};
```

When we send a message with `putmsg` or `putpmsg`, `len` specifies the number of bytes of data in the buffer. When we receive a message with `getmsg` or `getpmsg`, `maxlen` specifies the size of the buffer (so the kernel won't overflow the buffer), and `len` is set by the kernel to the amount of data stored in the buffer. We'll see that a zero-length message is OK and that a `len` of –1 can specify that there is no control or data.

Why do we need to pass both control information and data? Providing both allows us to implement service interfaces between a user process and a stream. Olander, McGrath, and Israel [1986] describe the original implementation of service interfaces in System V. Chapter 5 of AT&T [1990d] describes service interfaces in detail, along with a simple example. Probably the best-known service interface, described in Chapter 4 of Rago [1993], is the System V Transport Layer Interface (TLI), which provides an interface to the networking system.

Another example of control information is sending a connectionless network message (a datagram). To send the message, we need to specify the contents of the message (the data) and the destination address for the message (the control information). If we couldn't send control and data together, some ad hoc scheme would be required. For example, we could specify the address using an `ioctl`, followed by a `write` of the data. Another technique would be to require that the address occupy the first N bytes of the data that is written using `write`. Separating the control information from the data, and providing functions that handle both (`putmsg` and `getmsg`) is a cleaner way to handle this.

There are about 25 different types of messages, but only a few of these are used between the user process and the stream head. The rest are passed up and down a stream within the kernel. (These message types are of interest to people writing

STREAMS processing modules, but can safely be ignored by people writing user-level code.) We'll encounter only three of these message types with the functions we use (read, write, getmsg, getpmsg, putmsg, and putpmsg):

- M_DATA (user data for I/O)
- M_PROTO (protocol control information)
- M_PCPROTO (high-priority protocol control information)

Every message on a stream has a queueing priority:

- High-priority messages (highest priority)
- Priority band messages
- Ordinary messages (lowest priority)

Ordinary messages are simply priority band messages with a band of 0. Priority band messages have a band of 1–255, with a higher band specifying a higher priority. High-priority messages are special in that only one is queued by the stream head at a time. Additional high-priority messages are discarded when one is already on the stream head's read queue.

Each STREAMS module has two input queues. One receives messages from the module above (messages moving downstream from the stream head toward the driver), and one receives messages from the module below (messages moving upstream from the driver toward the stream head). The messages on an input queue are arranged by priority. We show in Figure 14.15 how the arguments to write, putmsg, and putpmsg cause these various priority messages to be generated.

There are other types of messages that we don't consider. For example, if the stream head receives an M_SIG message from below, it generates a signal. This is how a terminal line discipline module sends the terminal-generated signals to the foreground process group associated with a controlling terminal.

putmsg and putpmsg Functions

A STREAMS message (control information or data, or both) is written to a stream using either putmsg or putpmsg. The difference in these two functions is that the latter allows us to specify a priority band for the message.

```
#include <stropts.h>

int putmsg(int filedes, const struct strbuf *ctlptr,
           const struct strbuf *dataptr, int flag);

int putpmsg(int filedes, const struct strbuf *ctlptr,
            const struct strbuf *dataptr, int band, int flag);

                                    Both return: 0 if OK, –1 on error
```

We can also write to a stream, which is equivalent to a putmsg without any control information and with a flag of 0.

These two functions can generate the three different priorities of messages: ordinary, priority band, and high priority. Figure 14.15 details the combinations of the arguments to these two functions that generate the various types of messages.

Function	Control?	Data?	*band*	*flag*	Message type generated
write	N/A	yes	N/A	N/A	M_DATA (ordinary)
putmsg	no	no	N/A	0	no message sent, returns 0
putmsg	no	yes	N/A	0	M_DATA (ordinary)
putmsg	yes	yes or no	N/A	0	M_PROTO (ordinary)
putmsg	yes	yes or no	N/A	RS_HIPRI	M_PCPROTO (high-priority)
putmsg	no	yes or no	N/A	RS_HIPRI	error, EINVAL
putpmsg	yes or no	yes or no	0–255	0	error, EINVAL
putpmsg	no	no	0–255	MSG_BAND	no message sent, returns 0
putpmsg	no	yes	0	MSG_BAND	M_DATA (ordinary)
putpmsg	no	yes	1–255	MSG_BAND	M_DATA (priority band)
putpmsg	yes	yes or no	0	MSG_BAND	M_PROTO (ordinary)
putpmsg	yes	yes or no	1–255	MSG_BAND	M_PROTO (priority band)
putpmsg	yes	yes or no	0	MSG_HIPRI	M_PCPROTO (high-priority)
putpmsg	no	yes or no	0	MSG_HIPRI	error, EINVAL
putpmsg	yes or no	yes or no	nonzero	MSG_HIPRI	error, EINVAL

Figure 14.15 Type of STREAMS message generated for `write`, `putmsg`, and `putpmsg`

The notation "N/A" means *not applicable*. In this figure, a "no" for the control portion of the message corresponds to either a null *ctlptr* argument or *ctlptr–>len* being –1. A "yes" for the control portion corresponds to *ctlptr* being non-null and *ctlptr–>len* being greater than or equal to 0. The data portion of the message is handled equivalently (using *dataptr* instead of *ctlptr*).

STREAMS `ioctl` Operations

In Section 3.15, we said that the `ioctl` function is the catchall for anything that can't be done with the other I/O functions. The STREAMS system continues this tradition.

Between Linux and Solaris, there are almost 40 different operations that can be performed on a stream using `ioctl`. Most of these operations are documented in the `streamio(7)` manual page. The header `<stropts.h>` must be included in C code that uses any of these operations. The second argument for `ioctl`, *request*, specifies which of the operations to perform. All the *request*s begin with `I_`. The third argument depends on the *request*. Sometimes, the third argument is an integer value; sometimes, it's a pointer to an integer or a structure.

Example—`isastream` Function

We sometimes need to determine if a descriptor refers to a stream or not. This is similar to calling the `isatty` function to determine if a descriptor refers to a terminal device (Section 18.9). Linux and Solaris provide the `isastream` function.

```
#include <stropts.h>

int isastream(int filedes);
```
                                        Returns: 1 (true) if STREAMS device, 0 (false) otherwise

Like isatty, this is usually a trivial function that merely tries an ioctl that is
valid only on a STREAMS device. Figure 14.16 shows one possible implementation of
this function. We use the I_CANPUT ioctl command, which checks if the band
specified by the third argument (0 in the example) is writable. If the ioctl succeeds,
the stream is not changed.

```
#include      <stropts.h>
#include      <unistd.h>

int
isastream(int fd)
{
    return(ioctl(fd, I_CANPUT, 0) != -1);
}
```

Figure 14.16 Check if descriptor is a STREAMS device

We can use the program in Figure 14.17 to test this function.

```
#include "apue.h"
#include <fcntl.h>

int
main(int argc, char *argv[])
{
    int      i, fd;

    for (i = 1; i < argc; i++) {
        if ((fd = open(argv[i], O_RDONLY)) < 0) {
            err_ret("%s: can't open", argv[i]);
            continue;
        }

        if (isastream(fd) == 0)
            err_ret("%s: not a stream", argv[i]);
        else
            err_msg("%s: streams device", argv[i]);
    }

    exit(0);
}
```

Figure 14.17 Test the isastream function

Running this program on Solaris 9 shows the various errors returned by the `ioctl` function:

```
$ ./a.out /dev/tty /dev/fb /dev/null /etc/motd
/dev/tty: streams device
/dev/fb: not a stream: Invalid argument
/dev/null: not a stream: No such device or address
/etc/motd: not a stream: Inappropriate ioctl for device
```

Note that /dev/tty is a STREAMS device, as we expect under Solaris. The character special file /dev/fb is not a STREAMS device, but it supports other `ioctl` requests. These devices return EINVAL when the `ioctl` request is unknown. The character special file /dev/null does not support any `ioctl` operations, so the error ENODEV is returned. Finally, /etc/motd is a regular file, not a character special file, so the classic error ENOTTY is returned. We never receive the error we might expect: ENOSTR ("Device is not a stream").

> The message for ENOTTY used to be "Not a typewriter," a historical artifact because the UNIX kernel returns ENOTTY whenever an `ioctl` is attempted on a descriptor that doesn't refer to a character special device. This message has been updated on Solaris to "Inappropriate ioctl for device."
>
> □

Example

If the `ioctl` *request* is I_LIST, the system returns the names of all the modules on the stream—the ones that have been pushed onto the stream, including the topmost driver. (We say topmost because in the case of a multiplexing driver, there may be more than one driver. Chapter 12 of Rago [1993] discusses multiplexing drivers in detail.) The third argument must be a pointer to a `str_list` structure:

```
struct str_list {
    int             sl_nmods;   /* number of entries in array */
    struct str_mlist *sl_modlist; /* ptr to first element of array */
};
```

We have to set sl_modlist to point to the first element of an array of str_mlist structures and set sl_nmods to the number of entries in the array:

```
struct str_mlist {
    char  l_name[FMNAMESZ+1];   /* null terminated module name */
};
```

The constant FMNAMESZ is defined in the header <sys/conf.h> and is often 8. The extra byte in l_name is for the terminating null byte.

If the third argument to the `ioctl` is 0, the count of the number of modules is returned (as the value of `ioctl`) instead of the module names. We'll use this to determine the number of modules and then allocate the required number of str_mlist structures.

Figure 14.18 illustrates the I_LIST operation. Since the returned list of names doesn't differentiate between the modules and the driver, when we print the module names, we know that the final entry in the list is the driver at the bottom of the stream.

```
#include "apue.h"
#include <fcntl.h>
#include <stropts.h>
#include <sys/conf.h>

int
main(int argc, char *argv[])
{
    int                 fd, i, nmods;
    struct str_list     list;

    if (argc != 2)
        err_quit("usage: %s <pathname>", argv[0]);

    if ((fd = open(argv[1], O_RDONLY)) < 0)
        err_sys("can't open %s", argv[1]);
    if (isastream(fd) == 0)
        err_quit("%s is not a stream", argv[1]);

    /*
     * Fetch number of modules.
     */
    if ((nmods = ioctl(fd, I_LIST, (void *) 0)) < 0)
        err_sys("I_LIST error for nmods");
    printf("#modules = %d\n", nmods);

    /*
     * Allocate storage for all the module names.
     */
    list.sl_modlist = calloc(nmods, sizeof(struct str_mlist));
    if (list.sl_modlist == NULL)
        err_sys("calloc error");
    list.sl_nmods = nmods;

    /*
     * Fetch the module names.
     */
    if (ioctl(fd, I_LIST, &list) < 0)
        err_sys("I_LIST error for list");

    /*
     * Print the names.
     */
    for (i = 1; i <= nmods; i++)
        printf("  %s: %s\n", (i == nmods) ? "driver" : "module",
            list.sl_modlist++->l_name);

    exit(0);
}
```

Figure 14.18 List the names of the modules on a stream

If we run the program in Figure 14.18 from both a network login and a console login, to see which STREAMS modules are pushed onto the controlling terminal, we get the following:

```
$ who
sar          console      May  1 18:27
sar          pts/7        Jul 12 06:53
$ ./a.out /dev/console
#modules = 5
   module: redirmod
   module: ttcompat
   module: ldterm
   module: ptem
   driver: pts
$ ./a.out /dev/pts/7
#modules = 4
   module: ttcompat
   module: ldterm
   module: ptem
   driver: pts
```

The modules are the same in both cases, except that the console has an extra module on top that helps with virtual console redirection. On this computer, a windowing system was running on the console, so /dev/console actually refers to a pseudo terminal instead of to a hardwired device. We'll return to the pseudo terminal case in Chapter 19.   □

`write` to STREAMS Devices

In Figure 14.15 we said that a `write` to a STREAMS device generates an M_DATA message. Although this is generally true, there are some additional details to consider. First, with a stream, the topmost processing module specifies the minimum and maximum packet sizes that can be sent downstream. (We are unable to query the module for these values.) If we `write` more than the maximum, the stream head normally breaks the data into packets of the maximum size, with one final packet that can be smaller than the maximum.

The next thing to consider is what happens if we `write` zero bytes to a stream. Unless the stream refers to a pipe or FIFO, a zero-length message is sent downstream. With a pipe or FIFO, the default is to ignore the zero-length `write`, for compatibility with previous versions. We can change this default for pipes and FIFOs using an `ioctl` to set the write mode for the stream.

Write Mode

Two `ioctl` commands fetch and set the write mode for a stream. Setting *request* to I_GWROPT requires that the third argument be a pointer to an integer, and the current write mode for the stream is returned in that integer. If *request* is I_SWROPT, the third argument is an integer whose value becomes the new write mode for the stream. As with the file descriptor flags and the file status flags (Section 3.14), we should always fetch the current write mode value and modify it rather than set the write mode to some absolute value (possibly turning off some other bits that were enabled).

Currently, only two write mode values are defined.

SNDZERO   A zero-length write to a pipe or FIFO will cause a zero-length message to be sent downstream. By default, this zero-length write sends no message.

SNDPIPE   Causes SIGPIPE to be sent to the calling process that calls either write or putmsg after an error has occurred on a stream.

A stream also has a read mode, and we'll look at it after describing the getmsg and getpmsg functions.

getmsg and getpmsg Functions

STREAMS messages are read from a stream head using read, getmsg, or getpmsg.

```
#include <stropts.h>

int getmsg(int filedes, struct strbuf *restrict ctlptr,
           struct strbuf *restrict dataptr, int *restrict flagptr);

int getpmsg(int filedes, struct strbuf *restrict ctlptr,
            struct strbuf *restrict dataptr, int *restrict bandptr,
            int *restrict flagptr);
```
                                        Both return: non-negative value if OK, −1 on error

Note that *flagptr* and *bandptr* are pointers to integers. The integer pointed to by these two pointers must be set before the call to specify the type of message desired, and the integer is also set on return to the type of message that was read.

If the integer pointed to by *flagptr* is 0, getmsg returns the next message on the stream head's read queue. If the next message is a high-priority message, the integer pointed to by *flagptr* is set to RS_HIPRI on return. If we want to receive only high-priority messages, we must set the integer pointed to by *flagptr* to RS_HIPRI before calling getmsg.

A different set of constants is used by getpmsg. We can set the integer pointed to by *flagptr* to MSG_HIPRI to receive only high-priority messages. We can set the integer to MSG_BAND and then set the integer pointed to by *bandptr* to a nonzero priority value to receive only messages from that band, or higher (including high-priority messages). If we only want to receive the first available message, we can set the integer pointed to by *flagptr* to MSG_ANY; on return, the integer will be overwritten with either MSG_HIPRI or MSG_BAND, depending on the type of message received. If the message we retrieved was not a high-priority message, the integer pointed to by *bandptr* will contain the message's priority band.

If *ctlptr* is null or *ctlptr−>maxlen* is −1, the control portion of the message will remain on the stream head's read queue, and we will not process it. Similarly, if *dataptr* is null or *dataptr−>maxlen* is −1, the data portion of the message is not processed and remains on the stream head's read queue. Otherwise, we will retrieve as much control and data portions of the message as our buffers will hold, and any remainder will be left on the head of the queue for the next call.

If the call to `getmsg` or `getpmsg` retrieves a message, the return value is 0. If part of the control portion of the message is left on the stream head read queue, the constant `MORECTL` is returned. Similarly, if part of the data portion of the message is left on the queue, the constant `MOREDATA` is returned. If both control and data are left, the return value is (`MORECTL`|`MOREDATA`).

Read Mode

We also need to consider what happens if we `read` from a STREAMS device. There are two potential problems.

1. What happens to the record boundaries associated with the messages on a stream?

2. What happens if we call `read` and the next message on the stream has control information?

The default handling for condition 1 is called byte-stream mode. In this mode, a `read` takes data from the stream until the requested number of bytes has been read or until there is no more data. The message boundaries associated with the STREAMS messages are ignored in this mode. The default handling for condition 2 causes the `read` to return an error if there is a control message at the front of the queue. We can change either of these defaults.

Using `ioctl`, if we set *request* to `I_GRDOPT`, the third argument is a pointer to an integer, and the current read mode for the stream is returned in that integer. A *request* of `I_SRDOPT` takes the integer value of the third argument and sets the read mode to that value. The read mode is specified by one of the following three constants:

`RNORM`	Normal, byte-stream mode (the default), as described previously.
`RMSGN`	Message-nondiscard mode. A `read` takes data from a stream until the requested number of bytes have been read or until a message boundary is encountered. If the `read` uses a partial message, the rest of the data in the message is left on the stream for a subsequent `read`.
`RMSGD`	Message-discard mode. This is like the nondiscard mode, but if a partial message is used, the remainder of the message is discarded.

Three additional constants can be specified in the read mode to set the behavior of `read` when it encounters messages containing protocol control information on a stream:

`RPROTNORM`	Protocol-normal mode: `read` returns an error of `EBADMSG`. This is the default.
`RPROTDAT`	Protocol-data mode: `read` returns the control portion as data.
`RPROTDIS`	Protocol-discard mode: `read` discards the control information but returns any data in the message.

Only one of the message read modes and one of the protocol read modes can be set at a time. The default read mode is (RNORM | RPROTNORM).

Example

The program in Figure 14.19 is the same as the one in Figure 3.4, but recoded to use getmsg instead of read.

```c
#include "apue.h"
#include <stropts.h>

#define BUFFSIZE    4096

int
main(void)
{
    int             n, flag;
    char            ctlbuf[BUFFSIZE], datbuf[BUFFSIZE];
    struct strbuf   ctl, dat;

    ctl.buf = ctlbuf;
    ctl.maxlen = BUFFSIZE;
    dat.buf = datbuf;
    dat.maxlen = BUFFSIZE;
    for ( ; ; ) {
        flag = 0;          /* return any message */
        if ((n = getmsg(STDIN_FILENO, &ctl, &dat, &flag)) < 0)
            err_sys("getmsg error");
        fprintf(stderr, "flag = %d, ctl.len = %d, dat.len = %d\n",
          flag, ctl.len, dat.len);
        if (dat.len == 0)
            exit(0);
        else if (dat.len > 0)
            if (write(STDOUT_FILENO, dat.buf, dat.len) != dat.len)
                err_sys("write error");
    }
}
```

Figure 14.19 Copy standard input to standard output using getmsg

If we run this program under Solaris, where both pipes and terminals are implemented using STREAMS, we get the following output:

```
$ echo hello, world | ./a.out          requires STREAMS-based pipes
flag = 0, ctl.len = -1, dat.len = 13
hello, world
flag = 0, ctl.len = 0, dat.len = 0      indicates a STREAMS hangup
$ ./a.out                               requires STREAMS-based terminals
this is line 1
flag = 0, ctl.len = -1, dat.len = 15
```

```
this is line 1
and line 2
flag = 0, ctl.len = -1, dat.len = 11
and line 2
^D                                          type the terminal EOF character
flag = 0, ctl.len = -1, dat.len = 0         tty end of file is not the same as a hangup
$ ./a.out < /etc/motd
getmsg error: Not a stream device
```

When the pipe is closed (when echo terminates), it appears to the program in Figure 14.19 as a STREAMS hangup, with both the control length and the data length set to 0. (We discuss pipes in Section 15.2.) With a terminal, however, typing the end-of-file character causes only the data length to be returned as 0. This terminal end of file is not the same as a STREAMS hangup. As expected, when we redirect standard input to be a non-STREAMS device, getmsg returns an error.   □

14.5   I/O Multiplexing

When we read from one descriptor and write to another, we can use blocking I/O in a loop, such as

```
while ((n = read(STDIN_FILENO, buf, BUFSIZ)) > 0)
    if (write(STDOUT_FILENO, buf, n) != n)
        err_sys("write error");
```

We see this form of blocking I/O over and over again. What if we have to read from two descriptors? In this case, we can't do a blocking read on either descriptor, as data may appear on one descriptor while we're blocked in a read on the other. A different technique is required to handle this case.

Let's look at the structure of the telnet(1) command. In this program, we read from the terminal (standard input) and write to a network connection, and we read from the network connection and write to the terminal (standard output). At the other end of the network connection, the telnetd daemon reads what we typed and presents it to a shell as if we were logged in to the remote machine. The telnetd daemon sends any output generated by the commands we type back to us through the telnet command, to be displayed on our terminal. Figure 14.20 shows a picture of this.

Figure 14.20 Overview of telnet program

The telnet process has two inputs and two outputs. We can't do a blocking read on either of the inputs, as we never know which input will have data for us.

One way to handle this particular problem is to divide the process in two pieces (using `fork`), with each half handling one direction of data. We show this in Figure 14.21. (The `cu(1)` command provided with System V's `uucp` communication package was structured like this.)

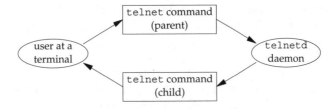

Figure 14.21 The `telnet` program using two processes

If we use two processes, we can let each process do a blocking `read`. But this leads to a problem when the operation terminates. If an end of file is received by the child (the network connection is disconnected by the `telnetd` daemon), then the child terminates, and the parent is notified by the `SIGCHLD` signal. But if the parent terminates (the user enters an end of file at the terminal), then the parent has to tell the child to stop. We can use a signal for this (`SIGUSR1`, for example), but it does complicate the program somewhat.

Instead of two processes, we could use two threads in a single process. This avoids the termination complexity, but requires that we deal with synchronization between the threads, which could add more complexity than it saves.

We could use nonblocking I/O in a single process by setting both descriptors nonblocking and issuing a `read` on the first descriptor. If data is present, we read it and process it. If there is no data to read, the call returns immediately. We then do the same thing with the second descriptor. After this, we wait for some amount of time (a few seconds, perhaps) and then try to read from the first descriptor again. This type of loop is called *polling*. The problem is that it wastes CPU time. Most of the time, there won't be data to read, so we waste time performing the `read` system calls. We also have to guess how long to wait each time around the loop. Although it works on any system that supports nonblocking I/O, polling should be avoided on a multitasking system.

Another technique is called *asynchronous I/O*. To do this, we tell the kernel to notify us with a signal when a descriptor is ready for I/O. There are two problems with this. First, not all systems support this feature (it is an optional facility in the Single UNIX Specification). System V provides the `SIGPOLL` signal for this technique, but this signal works only if the descriptor refers to a STREAMS device. BSD has a similar signal, `SIGIO`, but it has similar limitations: it works only on descriptors that refer to terminal devices or networks. The second problem with this technique is that there is only one of these signals per process (`SIGPOLL` or `SIGIO`). If we enable this signal for two descriptors (in the example we've been talking about, reading from two descriptors), the occurrence of the signal doesn't tell us which descriptor is ready. To determine which descriptor is ready, we still need to set each nonblocking and try them in sequence. We describe asynchronous I/O briefly in Section 14.6.

A better technique is to use *I/O multiplexing*. To do this, we build a list of the descriptors that we are interested in (usually more than one descriptor) and call a function that doesn't return until one of the descriptors is ready for I/O. On return from the function, we are told which descriptors are ready for I/O.

Three functions—poll, pselect, and select—allow us to perform I/O multiplexing. Figure 14.22 summarizes which platforms support them. Note that select is defined by the base POSIX.1 standard, but poll is an XSI extension to the base.

System	poll	pselect	select	<sys/select.h>
SUS	XSI	•	•	•
FreeBSD 5.2.1	•	•	•	
Linux 2.4.22	•	•	•	•
Mac OS X 10.3	•	•	•	
Solaris 9	•	•	•	•

Figure 14.22 I/O multiplexing supported by various UNIX systems

POSIX specifies that <sys/select> be included to pull the information for select into your program. Historically, however, we have had to include three other header files, and some of the implementations haven't yet caught up to the standard. Check the select manual page to see what your system supports. Older systems require that you include <sys/types.h>, <sys/time.h>, and <unistd.h>.

I/O multiplexing was provided with the select function in 4.2BSD. This function has always worked with any descriptor, although its main use has been for terminal I/O and network I/O. SVR3 added the poll function when the STREAMS mechanism was added. Initially, however, poll worked only with STREAMS devices. In SVR4, support was added to allow poll to work on any descriptor.

14.5.1 `select` and `pselect` Functions

The select function lets us do I/O multiplexing under all POSIX-compatible platforms. The arguments we pass to select tell the kernel

- Which descriptors we're interested in.

- What conditions we're interested in for each descriptor. (Do we want to read from a given descriptor? Do we want to write to a given descriptor? Are we interested in an exception condition for a given descriptor?)

- How long we want to wait. (We can wait forever, wait a fixed amount of time, or not wait at all.)

On the return from select, the kernel tells us

- The total count of the number of descriptors that are ready

- Which descriptors are ready for each of the three conditions (read, write, or exception condition)

With this return information, we can call the appropriate I/O function (usually `read` or `write`) and know that the function won't block.

```
#include <sys/select.h>

int select(int maxfdp1, fd_set *restrict readfds,
           fd_set *restrict writefds, fd_set *restrict exceptfds,
           struct timeval *restrict tvptr);
```
                                Returns: count of ready descriptors, 0 on timeout, −1 on error

Let's look at the last argument first. This specifies how long we want to wait:

```
struct timeval {
  long  tv_sec;   /* seconds */
  long  tv_usec;  /* and microseconds */
};
```

There are three conditions.

tvptr == NULL

> Wait forever. This infinite wait can be interrupted if we catch a signal. Return is made when one of the specified descriptors is ready or when a signal is caught. If a signal is caught, `select` returns −1 with `errno` set to EINTR.

tvptr–>*tv_sec* == 0 && *tvptr*–>*tv_usec* == 0

> Don't wait at all. All the specified descriptors are tested, and return is made immediately. This is a way to poll the system to find out the status of multiple descriptors, without blocking in the `select` function.

tvptr–>*tv_sec* != 0 || *tvptr*–>*tv_usec* != 0

> Wait the specified number of seconds and microseconds. Return is made when one of the specified descriptors is ready or when the timeout value expires. If the timeout expires before any of the descriptors is ready, the return value is 0. (If the system doesn't provide microsecond resolution, the *tvptr*–>*tv_usec* value is rounded up to the nearest supported value.) As with the first condition, this wait can also be interrupted by a caught signal.

> > POSIX.1 allows an implementation to modify the `timeval` structure, so after `select` returns, you can't rely on the structure containing the same values it did before calling `select`. FreeBSD 5.2.1, Mac OS X 10.3, and Solaris 9 all leave the structure unchanged, but Linux 2.4.22 will update it with the time remaining if `select` returns before the timeout value expires.

The middle three arguments—*readfds*, *writefds*, and *exceptfds*—are pointers to *descriptor sets*. These three sets specify which descriptors we're interested in and for which conditions (readable, writable, or an exception condition). A descriptor set is stored in an `fd_set` data type. This data type is chosen by the implementation so that it can hold one bit for each possible descriptor. We can consider it to be just a big array of bits, as shown in Figure 14.23.

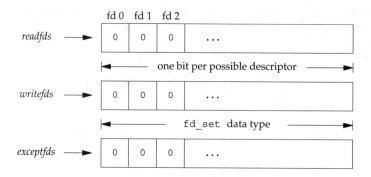

Figure 14.23 Specifying the read, write, and exception descriptors for select

The only thing we can do with the `fd_set` data type is allocate a variable of this type, assign a variable of this type to another variable of the same type, or use one of the following four functions on a variable of this type.

```
#include <sys/select.h>

int FD_ISSET(int fd, fd_set *fdset);
```

                                           Returns: nonzero if *fd* is in set, 0 otherwise

```
void FD_CLR(int fd, fd_set *fdset);
void FD_SET(int fd, fd_set *fdset);
void FD_ZERO(fd_set *fdset);
```

These interfaces can be implemented as either macros or functions. An `fd_set` is set to all zero bits by calling `FD_ZERO`. To turn on a single bit in a set, we use `FD_SET`. We can clear a single bit by calling `FD_CLR`. Finally, we can test whether a given bit is turned on in the set with `FD_ISSET`.

After declaring a descriptor set, we must zero the set using `FD_ZERO`. We then set bits in the set for each descriptor that we're interested in, as in

```
fd_set    rset;
int       fd;

FD_ZERO(&rset);
FD_SET(fd, &rset);
FD_SET(STDIN_FILENO, &rset);
```

On return from `select`, we can test whether a given bit in the set is still on using `FD_ISSET`:

```
if (FD_ISSET(fd, &rset)) {
    ...
}
```

Any (or all) of the middle three arguments to `select` (the pointers to the descriptor sets) can be null pointers if we're not interested in that condition. If all three pointers are NULL, then we have a higher precision timer than provided by `sleep`. (Recall from Section 10.19 that `sleep` waits for an integral number of seconds. With `select`, we can wait for intervals less than 1 second; the actual resolution depends on the system's clock.) Exercise 14.6 shows such a function.

The first argument to `select`, *maxfdp1*, stands for "maximum file descriptor plus 1." We calculate the highest descriptor that we're interested in, considering all three of the descriptor sets, add 1, and that's the first argument. We could just set the first argument to FD_SETSIZE, a constant in `<sys/select.h>` that specifies the maximum number of descriptors (often 1,024), but this value is too large for most applications. Indeed, most applications probably use between 3 and 10 descriptors. (Some applications need many more descriptors, but these UNIX programs are atypical.) By specifying the highest descriptor that we're interested in, we can prevent the kernel from going through hundreds of unused bits in the three descriptor sets, looking for bits that are turned on.

As an example, Figure 14.24 shows what two descriptor sets look like if we write

```
fd_set   readset, writeset;

FD_ZERO(&readset);
FD_ZERO(&writeset);
FD_SET(0, &readset);
FD_SET(3, &readset);
FD_SET(1, &writeset);
FD_SET(2, &writeset);
select(4, &readset, &writeset, NULL, NULL);
```

The reason we have to add 1 to the maximum descriptor number is that descriptors start at 0, and the first argument is really a count of the number of descriptors to check (starting with descriptor 0).

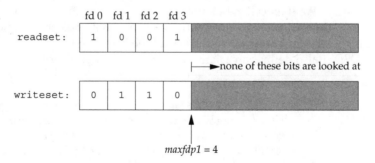

Figure 14.24 Example descriptor sets for `select`

There are three possible return values from `select`.

1. A return value of −1 means that an error occurred. This can happen, for example, if a signal is caught before any of the specified descriptors are ready. In this case, none of the descriptor sets will be modified.

2. A return value of 0 means that no descriptors are ready. This happens if the time limit expires before any of the descriptors are ready. When this happens, all the descriptor sets will be zeroed out.

3. A positive return value specifies the number of descriptors that are ready. This value is the sum of the descriptors ready in all three sets, so if the same descriptor is ready to be read *and* written, it will be counted twice in the return value. The only bits left on in the three descriptor sets are the bits corresponding to the descriptors that are ready.

We now need to be more specific about what "ready" means.

- A descriptor in the read set (*readfds*) is considered ready if a `read` from that descriptor won't block.

- A descriptor in the write set (*writefds*) is considered ready if a `write` to that descriptor won't block.

- A descriptor in the exception set (*exceptfds*) is considered ready if an exception condition is pending on that descriptor. Currently, an exception condition corresponds to either the arrival of out-of-band data on a network connection or certain conditions occurring on a pseudo terminal that has been placed into packet mode. (Section 15.10 of Stevens [1990] describes this latter condition.)

- File descriptors for regular files always return ready for reading, writing, and exception conditions.

It is important to realize that whether a descriptor is blocking or not doesn't affect whether `select` blocks. That is, if we have a nonblocking descriptor that we want to read from and we call `select` with a timeout value of 5 seconds, `select` will block for up to 5 seconds. Similarly, if we specify an infinite timeout, `select` blocks until data is ready for the descriptor or until a signal is caught.

If we encounter the end of file on a descriptor, that descriptor is considered readable by `select`. We then call `read` and it returns 0, the way to signify end of file on UNIX systems. (Many people incorrectly assume that `select` indicates an exception condition on a descriptor when the end of file is reached.)

POSIX.1 also defines a variant of `select` called `pselect`.

```
#include <sys/select.h>

int pselect(int maxfdp1, fd_set *restrict readfds,
            fd_set *restrict writefds, fd_set *restrict exceptfds,
            const struct timespec *restrict tsptr,
            const sigset_t *restrict sigmask);
```
Returns: count of ready descriptors, 0 on timeout, −1 on error

The `pselect` function is identical to `select`, with the following exceptions.

- The timeout value for `select` is specified by a `timeval` structure, but for `pselect`, a `timespec` structure is used. (Recall the definition of the `timespec` structure in Section 11.6.) Instead of seconds and microseconds, the `timespec` structure represents the timeout value in seconds and nanoseconds. This provides a higher-resolution timeout if the platform supports that fine a level of granularity.

• The timeout value for `pselect` is declared `const`, and we are guaranteed that its value will not change as a result of calling `pselect`.

• An optional signal mask argument is available with `pselect`. If *sigmask* is null, `pselect` behaves as `select` does with respect to signals. Otherwise, *sigmask* points to a signal mask that is atomically installed when `pselect` is called. On return, the previous signal mask is restored.

14.5.2 `poll` Function

The `poll` function is similar to `select`, but the programmer interface is different. As we'll see, `poll` is tied to the STREAMS system, since it originated with System V, although we are able to use it with any type of file descriptor.

```
#include <poll.h>

int poll(struct pollfd fdarray[], nfds_t nfds, int timeout);
```
                                    Returns: count of ready descriptors, 0 on timeout, –1 on error

With `poll`, instead of building a set of descriptors for each condition (readability, writability, and exception condition), as we did with `select`, we build an array of `pollfd` structures, with each array element specifying a descriptor number and the conditions that we're interested in for that descriptor:

```
struct pollfd {
    int     fd;        /* file descriptor to check, or <0 to ignore */
    short   events;    /* events of interest on fd */
    short   revents;   /* events that occurred on fd */
};
```

The number of elements in the *fdarray* array is specified by *nfds*.

> Historically, there have been differences in how the *nfds* parameter was declared. SVR3 specified the number of elements in the array as an `unsigned long`, which seems excessive. In the SVR4 manual [AT&T 1990d], the prototype for `poll` showed the data type of the second argument as `size_t`. (Recall the primitive system data types, Figure 2.20.) But the actual prototype in the `<poll.h>` header still showed the second argument as an `unsigned long`. The Single UNIX Specification defines the new type `nfds_t` to allow the implementation to select the appropriate type and hide the details from applications. Note that this type has to be large enough to hold an integer, since the return value represents the number of entries in the array with satisfied events.
>
> The SVID corresponding to SVR4 [AT&T 1989] showed the first argument to `poll` as `struct pollfd fdarray[]`, whereas the SVR4 manual page [AT&T 1990d] showed this argument as `struct pollfd *fdarray`. In the C language, both declarations are equivalent. We use the first declaration to reiterate that `fdarray` points to an array of structures and not a pointer to a single structure.

To tell the kernel what events we're interested in for each descriptor, we have to set the `events` member of each array element to one or more of the values in Figure 14.25. On return, the `revents` member is set by the kernel, specifying which events have occurred for each descriptor. (Note that `poll` doesn't change the `events` member. This differs from `select`, which modifies its arguments to indicate what is ready.)

Name	Input to events?	Result from revents?	Description
POLLIN	•	•	Data other than high priority can be read without blocking (equivalent to POLLRDNORM | POLLRDBAND).
POLLRDNORM	•	•	Normal data (priority band 0) can be read without blocking.
POLLRDBAND	•	•	Data from a nonzero priority band can be read without blocking.
POLLPRI	•	•	High-priority data can be read without blocking.
POLLOUT	•	•	Normal data can be written without blocking.
POLLWRNORM	•	•	Same as POLLOUT.
POLLWRBAND	•	•	Data for a nonzero priority band can be written without blocking.
POLLERR		•	An error has occurred.
POLLHUP		•	A hangup has occurred.
POLLNVAL		•	The descriptor does not reference an open file.

Figure 14.25 The `events` and `revents` flags for `poll`

The first four rows of Figure 14.25 test for readability, the next three test for writability, and the final three are for exception conditions. The last three rows in Figure 14.25 are set by the kernel on return. These three values are returned in `revents` when the condition occurs, even if they weren't specified in the `events` field.

When a descriptor is hung up (POLLHUP), we can no longer write to the descriptor. There may, however, still be data to be read from the descriptor.

The final argument to `poll` specifies how long we want to wait. As with `select`, there are three cases.

timeout == −1

Wait forever. (Some systems define the constant INFTIM in `<stropts.h>` as −1.) We return when one of the specified descriptors is ready or when a signal is caught. If a signal is caught, `poll` returns −1 with `errno` set to EINTR.

timeout == 0

Don't wait. All the specified descriptors are tested, and we return immediately. This is a way to poll the system to find out the status of multiple descriptors, without blocking in the call to `poll`.

timeout > 0

Wait *timeout* milliseconds. We return when one of the specified descriptors is ready or when the *timeout* expires. If the *timeout* expires before any of the descriptors is ready, the return value is 0. (If your system doesn't provide millisecond resolution, *timeout* is rounded up to the nearest supported value.)

It is important to realize the difference between an end of file and a hangup. If we're entering data from the terminal and type the end-of-file character, POLLIN is turned on so we can read the end-of-file indication (read returns 0). POLLHUP is not turned on in revents. If we're reading from a modem and the telephone line is hung up, we'll receive the POLLHUP notification.

As with select, whether a descriptor is blocking or not doesn't affect whether poll blocks.

Interruptibility of select and poll

When the automatic restarting of interrupted system calls was introduced with 4.2BSD (Section 10.5), the select function was never restarted. This characteristic continues with most systems even if the SA_RESTART option is specified. But under SVR4, if SA_RESTART was specified, even select and poll were automatically restarted. To prevent this from catching us when we port software to systems derived from SVR4, we'll always use the signal_intr function (Figure 10.19) if the signal could interrupt a call to select or poll.

> None of the implementations described in this book restart poll or select when a signal is received, even if the SA_RESTART flag is used.

14.6 Asynchronous I/O

Using select and poll, as described in the previous section, is a synchronous form of notification. The system doesn't tell us anything until we ask (by calling either select or poll). As we saw in Chapter 10, signals provide an asynchronous form of notification that something has happened. All systems derived from BSD and System V provide some form of asynchronous I/O, using a signal (SIGPOLL in System V; SIGIO in BSD) to notify the process that something of interest has happened on a descriptor.

> We saw that select and poll work with any descriptors. But with asynchronous I/O, we now encounter restrictions. On systems derived from System V, asynchronous I/O works only with STREAMS devices and STREAMS pipes. On systems derived from BSD, asynchronous I/O works only with terminals and networks.

One limitation of asynchronous I/O is that there is only one signal per process. If we enable more than one descriptor for asynchronous I/O, we cannot tell which descriptor the signal corresponds to when the signal is delivered.

> The Single UNIX Specification includes an optional generic asynchronous I/O mechanism, adopted from the real-time draft standard. It is unrelated to the mechanisms we describe here. This mechanism solves a lot of the limitations that exist with these older asynchronous I/O mechanisms, but we will not discuss it further.

14.6.1 System V Asynchronous I/O

In System V, asynchronous I/O is part of the STREAMS system and works only with STREAMS devices and STREAMS pipes. The System V asynchronous I/O signal is SIGPOLL.

To enable asynchronous I/O for a STREAMS device, we have to call `ioctl` with a second argument (*request*) of `I_SETSIG`. The third argument is an integer value formed from one or more of the constants in Figure 14.26. These constants are defined in `<stropts.h>`.

Constant	Description
S_INPUT	A message other than a high-priority message has arrived.
S_RDNORM	An ordinary message has arrived.
S_RDBAND	A message with a nonzero priority band has arrived.
S_BANDURG	If this constant is specified with S_RDBAND, the SIGURG signal is generated instead of SIGPOLL when a nonzero priority band message has arrived.
S_HIPRI	A high-priority message has arrived.
S_OUTPUT	The write queue is no longer full.
S_WRNORM	Same as S_OUTPUT.
S_WRBAND	We can send a nonzero priority band message.
S_MSG	A STREAMS signal message that contains the SIGPOLL signal has arrived.
S_ERROR	An M_ERROR message has arrived.
S_HANGUP	An M_HANGUP message has arrived.

Figure 14.26 Conditions for generating SIGPOLL signal

In Figure 14.26, whenever we say "has arrived," we mean "has arrived at the stream head's read queue."

In addition to calling `ioctl` to specify the conditions that should generate the SIGPOLL signal, we also have to establish a signal handler for this signal. Recall from Figure 10.1 that the default action for SIGPOLL is to terminate the process, so we should establish the signal handler before calling `ioctl`.

14.6.2 BSD Asynchronous I/O

Asynchronous I/O in BSD-derived systems is a combination of two signals: SIGIO and SIGURG. The former is the general asynchronous I/O signal, and the latter is used only to notify the process that out-of-band data has arrived on a network connection.

To receive the SIGIO signal, we need to perform three steps.

1.   Establish a signal handler for SIGIO, by calling either `signal` or `sigaction`.
2.   Set the process ID or process group ID to receive the signal for the descriptor, by calling `fcntl` with a command of F_SETOWN (Section 3.14).
3.   Enable asynchronous I/O on the descriptor by calling `fcntl` with a command of F_SETFL to set the O_ASYNC file status flag (Figure 3.9).

Step 3 can be performed only on descriptors that refer to terminals or networks, which is a fundamental limitation of the BSD asynchronous I/O facility.

For the SIGURG signal, we need perform only steps 1 and 2. SIGURG is generated only for descriptors that refer to network connections that support out-of-band data.

14.7 `readv` and `writev` Functions

The `readv` and `writev` functions let us read into and write from multiple noncontiguous buffers in a single function call. These operations are called *scatter read* and *gather write*.

```
#include <sys/uio.h>

ssize_t readv(int filedes, const struct iovec *iov, int iovcnt);

ssize_t writev(int filedes, const struct iovec *iov, int iovcnt);
```
                        Both return: number of bytes read or written, −1 on error

The second argument to both functions is a pointer to an array of `iovec` structures:

```
struct iovec {
  void    *iov_base;   /* starting address of buffer */
  size_t  iov_len;     /* size of buffer */
};
```

The number of elements in the *iov* array is specified by *iovcnt*. It is limited to `IOV_MAX` (Recall Figure 2.10). Figure 14.27 shows a picture relating the arguments to these two functions and the `iovec` structure.

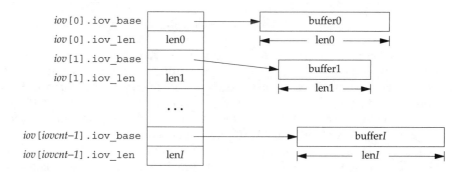

Figure 14.27 The `iovec` structure for `readv` and `writev`

The `writev` function gathers the output data from the buffers in order: *iov[0]*, *iov[1]*, through *iov[iovcnt−1]*; `writev` returns the total number of bytes output, which should normally equal the sum of all the buffer lengths.

The `readv` function scatters the data into the buffers in order, always filling one buffer before proceeding to the next. `readv` returns the total number of bytes that were read. A count of 0 is returned if there is no more data and the end of file is encountered.

These two functions originated in 4.2BSD and were later added to SVR4. These two functions are included in the XSI extension of the Single UNIX Specification.

Although the Single UNIX Specification defines the buffer address to be a `void *`, many implementations that predate the standard still use a `char *` instead.

Example

In Section 20.8, in the function _db_writeidx, we need to write two buffers consecutively to a file. The second buffer to output is an argument passed by the caller, and the first buffer is one we create, containing the length of the second buffer and a file offset of other information in the file. There are three ways we can do this.

1. Call write twice, once for each buffer.
2. Allocate a buffer of our own that is large enough to contain both buffers, and copy both into the new buffer. We then call write once for this new buffer.
3. Call writev to output both buffers.

The solution we use in Section 20.8 is to use writev, but it's instructive to compare it to the other two solutions.

Figure 14.28 shows the results from the three methods just described.

	Linux (Intel x86)			Mac OS X (PowerPC)		
Operation	User	System	Clock	User	System	Clock
two writes	1.29	3.15	7.39	1.60	17.40	19.84
buffer copy, then one write	1.03	1.98	6.47	1.10	11.09	12.54
one writev	0.70	2.72	6.41	0.86	13.58	14.72

Figure 14.28 Timing results comparing writev and other techniques

The test program that we measured output a 100-byte header followed by 200 bytes of data. This was done 1,048,576 times, generating a 300-megabyte file. The test program has three separate cases—one for each of the techniques measured in Figure 14.28. We used times (Section 8.16) to obtain the user CPU time, system CPU time, and wall clock time before and after the writes. All three times are shown in seconds.

As we expect, the system time increases when we call write twice, compared to calling either write or writev once. This correlates with the results in Figure 3.5.

Next, note that the sum of the CPU times (user plus system) is less when we do a buffer copy followed by a single write compared to a single call to writev. With the single write, we copy the buffers to a staging buffer at user level, and then the kernel will copy the data to its internal buffers when we call write. With writev, we should do less copying, because the kernel only needs to copy the data directly into its staging buffers. The fixed cost of using writev for such small amounts of data, however, is greater than the benefit. As the amount of data we need to copy increases, the more expensive it will be to copy the buffers in our program, and the writev alternative will be more attractive.

Be careful not to infer too much about the relative performance of Linux to Mac OS X from the numbers shown in Figure 14.28. The two computers were very different: they had different processor architectures, different amounts of RAM, and disks with different speeds. To do an apples-to-apples comparison of one operating system to another, we need to use the same hardware for each operating system.

□

In summary, we should always try to use the fewest number of system calls necessary to get the job done. If we are writing small amounts of data, we will find it less expensive to copy the data ourselves and use a single `write` instead of using `writev`. We might find, however, that the performance benefits aren't worth the extra complexity cost needed to manage our own staging buffers.

14.8 `readn` and `writen` Functions

Pipes, FIFOs, and some devices, notably terminals, networks, and STREAMS devices, have the following two properties.

1. A `read` operation may return less than asked for, even though we have not encountered the end of file. This is not an error, and we should simply continue reading from the device.

2. A `write` operation can also return less than we specified. This may be caused by flow control constraints by downstream modules, for example. Again, it's not an error, and we should continue writing the remainder of the data. (Normally, this short return from a `write` occurs only with a nonblocking descriptor or if a signal is caught.)

We'll never see this happen when reading or writing a disk file, except when the file system runs out of space or we hit our quota limit and we can't write all that we requested.

Generally, when we read from or write to a pipe, network device, or terminal, we need to take these characteristics into consideration. We can use the following two functions to read or write N bytes of data, letting these functions handle a possible return value that's less than requested. These two functions simply call `read` or `write` as many times as required to read or write the entire N bytes of data.

```
#include "apue.h"

ssize_t readn(int filedes, void *buf, size_t nbytes);

ssize_t writen(int filedes, void *buf, size_t nbytes);
```
                        Both return: number of bytes read or written, −1 on error

> We define these functions as a convenience for later examples, similar to the error-handling routines used in many of the examples in this text. The readn and writen functions are not part of any standard.

We call `writen` whenever we're writing to one of the file types that we mentioned, but we call `readn` only when we know ahead of time that we will be receiving a certain number of bytes. Figure 14.29 shows implementations of `readn` and `writen` that we will use in later examples.

Note that if we encounter an error and have previously read or written any data, we return the amount of data transferred instead of the error. Similarly, if we reach end of

file while reading, we return the number of bytes copied to the caller's buffer if we
already read some data successfully and have not yet satisfied the amount requested.

```c
#include "apue.h"

ssize_t                 /* Read "n" bytes from a descriptor  */
readn(int fd, void *ptr, size_t n)
{
    size_t      nleft;
    ssize_t     nread;

    nleft = n;
    while (nleft > 0) {
        if ((nread = read(fd, ptr, nleft)) < 0) {
            if (nleft == n)
                return(-1); /* error, return -1 */
            else
                break;      /* error, return amount read so far */
        } else if (nread == 0) {
            break;          /* EOF */
        }
        nleft -= nread;
        ptr   += nread;
    }
    return(n - nleft);      /* return >= 0 */
}

ssize_t                 /* Write "n" bytes to a descriptor  */
writen(int fd, const void *ptr, size_t n)
{
    size_t      nleft;
    ssize_t     nwritten;

    nleft = n;
    while (nleft > 0) {
        if ((nwritten = write(fd, ptr, nleft)) < 0) {
            if (nleft == n)
                return(-1); /* error, return -1 */
            else
                break;      /* error, return amount written so far */
        } else if (nwritten == 0) {
            break;
        }
        nleft -= nwritten;
        ptr   += nwritten;
    }
    return(n - nleft);      /* return >= 0 */
}
```

Figure 14.29 The readn and writen functions

14.9 Memory-Mapped I/O

Memory-mapped I/O lets us map a file on disk into a buffer in memory so that, when we fetch bytes from the buffer, the corresponding bytes of the file are read. Similarly, when we store data in the buffer, the corresponding bytes are automatically written to the file. This lets us perform I/O without using `read` or `write`.

> Memory-mapped I/O has been in use with virtual memory systems for many years. In 1981, 4.1BSD provided a different form of memory-mapped I/O with its `vread` and `vwrite` functions. These two functions were then removed in 4.2BSD and were intended to be replaced with the `mmap` function. The `mmap` function, however, was not included with 4.2BSD (for reasons described in Section 2.5 of McKusick et al. [1996]). Gingell, Moran, and Shannon [1987] describe one implementation of `mmap`. The `mmap` function is included in the memory-mapped files option in the Single UNIX Specification and is required on all XSI-conforming systems; most UNIX systems support it.

To use this feature, we have to tell the kernel to map a given file to a region in memory. This is done by the `mmap` function.

```
#include <sys/mman.h>

void *mmap(void *addr, size_t len, int prot, int flag, int filedes,
           off_t off);
```
                    Returns: starting address of mapped region if OK, `MAP_FAILED` on error

The *addr* argument lets us specify the address of where we want the mapped region to start. We normally set this to 0 to allow the system to choose the starting address. The return value of this function is the starting address of the mapped area.

The *filedes* argument is the file descriptor specifying the file that is to be mapped. We have to open this file before we can map it into the address space. The *len* argument is the number of bytes to map, and *off* is the starting offset in the file of the bytes to map. (Some restrictions on the value of *off* are described later.)

The *prot* argument specifies the protection of the mapped region.

prot	Description
PROT_READ	Region can be read.
PROT_WRITE	Region can be written.
PROT_EXEC	Region can be executed.
PROT_NONE	Region cannot be accessed.

Figure 14.30 Protection of memory-mapped region

We can specify the protection as either `PROT_NONE` or the bitwise OR of any combination of `PROT_READ`, `PROT_WRITE`, and `PROT_EXEC`. The protection specified for a region can't allow more access than the `open` mode of the file. For example, we can't specify `PROT_WRITE` if the file was opened read-only.

Before looking at the *flag* argument, let's see what's going on here. Figure 14.31 shows a memory-mapped file. (Recall the memory layout of a typical process,

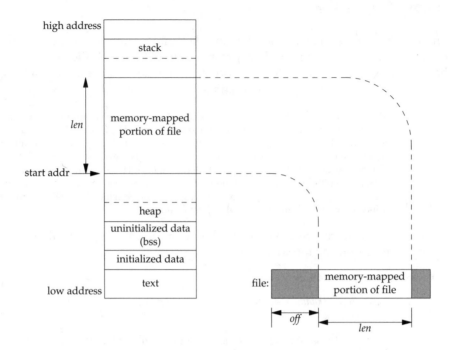

Figure 14.31 Example of a memory-mapped file

Figure 7.6.) In this figure, "start addr" is the return value from mmap. We have shown the mapped memory being somewhere between the heap and the stack: this is an implementation detail and may differ from one implementation to the next.

The *flag* argument affects various attributes of the mapped region.

MAP_FIXED   The return value must equal *addr*. Use of this flag is discouraged, as it hinders portability. If this flag is not specified and if *addr* is nonzero, then the kernel uses *addr* as a hint of where to place the mapped region, but there is no guarantee that the requested address will be used. Maximum portability is obtained by specifying *addr* as 0.

> Support for the MAP_FIXED flag is optional on POSIX-conforming systems, but required on XSI-conforming systems.

MAP_SHARED   This flag describes the disposition of store operations into the mapped region by this process. This flag specifies that store operations modify the mapped file—that is, a store operation is equivalent to a write to the file. Either this flag or the next (MAP_PRIVATE), but not both, must be specified.

MAP_PRIVATE   This flag says that store operations into the mapped region cause a private copy of the mapped file to be created. All successive references to the mapped region then reference the copy. (One use of this flag is for a debugger that maps the text portion of a program file but allows the user to modify the instructions. Any modifications affect the copy, not the original program file.)

Each implementation has additional MAP_xxx flag values, which are specific to that implementation. Check the mmap(2) manual page on your system for details.

The value of *off* and the value of *addr* (if MAP_FIXED is specified) are required to be multiples of the system's virtual memory page size. This value can be obtained from the sysconf function (Section 2.5.4) with an argument of _SC_PAGESIZE or _SC_PAGE_SIZE. Since *off* and *addr* are often specified as 0, this requirement is not a big deal.

Since the starting offset of the mapped file is tied to the system's virtual memory page size, what happens if the length of the mapped region isn't a multiple of the page size? Assume that the file size is 12 bytes and that the system's page size is 512 bytes. In this case, the system normally provides a mapped region of 512 bytes, and the final 500 bytes of this region are set to 0. We can modify the final 500 bytes, but any changes we make to them are not reflected in the file. Thus, we cannot append to a file with mmap. We must first grow the file, as we will see in Figure 14.32.

Two signals are normally used with mapped regions. SIGSEGV is the signal normally used to indicate that we have tried to access memory that is not available to us. This signal can also be generated if we try to store into a mapped region that we specified to mmap as read-only. The SIGBUS signal can be generated if we access a portion of the mapped region that does not make sense at the time of the access. For example, assume that we map a file using the file's size, but before we reference the mapped region, the file's size is truncated by some other process. If we then try to access the memory-mapped region corresponding to the end portion of the file that was truncated, we'll receive SIGBUS.

A memory-mapped region is inherited by a child across a fork (since it's part of the parent's address space), but for the same reason, is not inherited by the new program across an exec.

We can change the permissions on an existing mapping by calling mprotect.

```
#include <sys/mman.h>

int mprotect(void *addr, size_t len, int prot);
```

Returns: 0 if OK, −1 on error

The legal values for *prot* are the same as those for mmap (Figure 14.30). The address argument must be an integral multiple of the system's page size.

> The mprotect function is included as part of the memory protection option in the Single UNIX Specification, but all XSI-conforming systems are required to support it.

If the pages in a shared mapping have been modified, we can call msync to flush the changes to the file that backs the mapping. The msync function is similar to fsync (Section 3.13), but works on memory-mapped regions.

```
#include <sys/mman.h>

int msync(void *addr, size_t len, int flags);
```
                                                              Returns: 0 if OK, −1 on error

If the mapping is private, the file mapped is not modified. As with the other memory-mapped functions, the address must be aligned on a page boundary.

The *flags* argument allows us some control over how the memory is flushed. We can specify the MS_ASYNC flag to simply schedule the pages to be written. If we want to wait for the writes to complete before returning, we can use the MS_SYNC flag. Either MS_ASYNC or MS_SYNC must be specified.

An optional flag, MS_INVALIDATE, lets us tell the operating system to discard any pages that are out of sync with the underlying storage. Some implementations will discard all pages in the specified range when we use this flag, but this behavior is not required.

A memory-mapped region is automatically unmapped when the process terminates or by calling munmap directly. Closing the file descriptor *filedes* does not unmap the region.

```
#include <sys/mman.h>

int munmap(caddr_t addr, size_t len);
```
                                                              Returns: 0 if OK, −1 on error

munmap does not affect the object that was mapped—that is, the call to munmap does not cause the contents of the mapped region to be written to the disk file. The updating of the disk file for a MAP_SHARED region happens automatically by the kernel's virtual memory algorithm as we store into the memory-mapped region. Modifications to memory in a MAP_PRIVATE region are discarded when the region is unmapped.

Example

The program in Figure 14.32 copies a file (similar to the cp(1) command) using memory-mapped I/O.

```c
#include "apue.h"
#include <fcntl.h>
#include <sys/mman.h>

int
main(int argc, char *argv[])
{
    int         fdin, fdout;
    void        *src, *dst;
    struct stat statbuf;

    if (argc != 3)
```

```
            err_quit("usage: %s <fromfile> <tofile>", argv[0]);

    if ((fdin = open(argv[1], O_RDONLY)) < 0)
        err_sys("can't open %s for reading", argv[1]);

    if ((fdout = open(argv[2], O_RDWR | O_CREAT | O_TRUNC,
        FILE_MODE)) < 0)
        err_sys("can't creat %s for writing", argv[2]);

    if (fstat(fdin, &statbuf) < 0)    /* need size of input file */
        err_sys("fstat error");

    /* set size of output file */
    if (lseek(fdout, statbuf.st_size - 1, SEEK_SET) == -1)
        err_sys("lseek error");
    if (write(fdout, "", 1) != 1)
        err_sys("write error");

    if ((src = mmap(0, statbuf.st_size, PROT_READ, MAP_SHARED,
        fdin, 0)) == MAP_FAILED)
        err_sys("mmap error for input");

    if ((dst = mmap(0, statbuf.st_size, PROT_READ | PROT_WRITE,
        MAP_SHARED, fdout, 0)) == MAP_FAILED)
        err_sys("mmap error for output");

    memcpy(dst, src, statbuf.st_size);   /* does the file copy */
    exit(0);
}
```

Figure 14.32 Copy a file using memory-mapped I/O

We first open both files and then call fstat to obtain the size of the input file. We need this size for the call to mmap for the input file, and we also need to set the size of the output file. We call lseek and then write one byte to set the size of the output file. If we don't set the output file's size, the call to mmap for the output file is OK, but the first reference to the associated memory region generates SIGBUS. We might be tempted to use ftruncate to set the size of the output file, but not all systems extend the size of a file with this function. (See Section 4.13.)

> Extending a file with ftruncate works on the four platforms discussed in this text.

We then call mmap for each file, to map the file into memory, and finally call memcpy to copy from the input buffer to the output buffer. As the bytes of data are fetched from the input buffer (src), the input file is automatically read by the kernel; as the data is stored in the output buffer (dst), the data is automatically written to the output file.

> Exactly when the data is written to the file is dependent on the system's page management algorithms. Some systems have daemons that write dirty pages to disk slowly over time. If we want to ensure that the data is safely written to the file, we need to call msync with the MS_SYNC flag before exiting.

Let's compare this memory-mapped file copy to a copy that is done by calling `read` and `write` (with a buffer size of 8,192). Figure 14.33 shows the results. The times are given in seconds, and the size of the file being copied was 300 megabytes.

Operation	Linux 2.4.22 (Intel x86)			Solaris 9 (SPARC)		
	User	System	Clock	User	System	Clock
`read/write`	0.04	1.02	39.76	0.18	9.70	41.66
`mmap/memcpy`	0.64	1.31	24.26	1.68	7.94	28.53

Figure 14.33 Timing results comparing `read/write` versus `mmap/memcpy`

For Solaris 9, the total CPU time (user + system) is almost the same for both types of copies: 9.88 seconds versus 9.62 seconds. For Linux 2.4.22, the total CPU time is almost doubled when we use `mmap` and `memcpy` (1.06 seconds versus 1.95 seconds). The difference is probably because the two systems implement process time accounting differently.

As far as elapsed time is concerned, the version with `mmap` and `memcpy` is faster than the version with `read` and `write`. This makes sense, because we're doing less work with `mmap` and `memcpy`. With `read` and `write`, we copy the data from the kernel's buffer to the application's buffer (`read`), and then copy the data from the application's buffer to the kernel's buffer (`write`). With `mmap` and `memcpy`, we copy the data directly from one kernel buffer mapped into our address space into another kernel buffer mapped into our address space.   □

Memory-mapped I/O is faster when copying one regular file to another. There are limitations. We can't use it to copy between certain devices (such as a network device or a terminal device), and we have to be careful if the size of the underlying file could change after we map it. Nevertheless, some applications can benefit from memory-mapped I/O, as it can often simplify the algorithms, since we manipulate memory instead of reading and writing a file. One example that can benefit from memory-mapped I/O is the manipulation of a frame buffer device that references a bit-mapped display.

Krieger, Stumm, and Unrau [1992] describe an alternative to the standard I/O library (Chapter 5) that uses memory-mapped I/O.

We return to memory-mapped I/O in Section 15.9, showing an example of how it can be used to provide shared memory between related processes.

14.10 Summary

In this chapter, we've described numerous advanced I/O functions, most of which are used in the examples in later chapters:

- Nonblocking I/O—issuing an I/O operation without letting it block

- Record locking (which we'll look at in more detail through an example, the database library in Chapter 20)

- System V STREAMS (which we'll need in Chapter 17 to understand STREAMS-based pipes, passing file descriptors, and System V client–server connections)

- I/O multiplexing—the `select` and `poll` functions (we'll use these in many of the later examples)

- The `readv` and `writev` functions (also used in many of the later examples)

- Memory-mapped I/O (`mmap`)

Exercises

14.1 Write a test program that illustrates your system's behavior when a process is blocked trying to write-lock a range of a file and additional read-lock requests are made. Is the process requesting a write lock starved by the processes read-locking the file?

14.2 Take a look at your system's headers and examine the implementation of `select` and the four `FD_` macros.

14.3 The system headers usually have a built-in limit on the maximum number of descriptors that the `fd_set` data type can handle. Assume that we need to increase this limit to handle up to 2,048 descriptors. How can we do this?

14.4 Compare the functions provided for signal sets (Section 10.11) and the `fd_set` descriptor sets. Also compare the implementation of the two on your system.

14.5 How many types of information does `getmsg` return?

14.6 Implement the function `sleep_us`, which is similar to `sleep`, but waits for a specified number of microseconds. Use either `select` or `poll`. Compare this function to the BSD `usleep` function.

14.7 Can you implement the functions `TELL_WAIT`, `TELL_PARENT`, `TELL_CHILD`, `WAIT_PARENT`, and `WAIT_CHILD` from Figure 10.24 using advisory record locking instead of signals? If so, code and test your implementation.

14.8 Determine the capacity of a pipe using nonblocking writes. Compare this value with the value of `PIPE_BUF` from Chapter 2.

14.9 Recall Figure 14.28. Determine the break-even point on your system where using `writev` is faster than copying the data yourself and using a single `write`.

14.10 Run the program in Figure 14.32 to copy a file and determine whether the last-access time for the input file is updated.

14.11 In the program from Figure 14.32, `close` the input file after calling `mmap` to verify that closing the descriptor does not invalidate the memory-mapped I/O.

15

Interprocess Communication

15.1 Introduction

In Chapter 8, we described the process control primitives and saw how to invoke multiple processes. But the only way for these processes to exchange information is by passing open files across a `fork` or an `exec` or through the file system. We'll now describe other techniques for processes to communicate with each other: IPC, or interprocess communication.

In the past, UNIX System IPC was a hodgepodge of various approaches, few of which were portable across all UNIX system implementations. Through the POSIX and The Open Group (formerly X/Open) standardization efforts, the situation has improved, but differences still exist. Figure 15.1 summarizes the various forms of IPC that are supported by the four implementations discussed in this text.

Note that the Single UNIX Specification (the "SUS" column) allows an implementation to support full-duplex pipes, but requires only half-duplex pipes. An implementation that supports full-duplex pipes will still work with correctly written applications that assume that the underlying operating system supports only half-duplex pipes. We use "(full)" instead of a bullet to show implementations that support half-duplex pipes by using full-duplex pipes.

In Figure 15.1, we show a bullet where basic functionality is supported. For full-duplex pipes, if the feature can be provided through UNIX domain sockets (Section 17.3), we show "UDS" in the column. Some implementations support the feature with pipes and UNIX domain sockets, so these entries have both "UDS" and a bullet.

As we mentioned in Section 14.4, support for STREAMS is optional in the Single UNIX Specification. Named full-duplex pipes are provided as mounted STREAMS-based pipes and so are also optional in the Single UNIX Specification. On

IPC type	SUS	FreeBSD 5.2.1	Linux 2.4.22	Mac OS X 10.3	Solaris 9
half-duplex pipes	•	(full)	•	•	(full)
FIFOs	•	•	•	•	•
full-duplex pipes	allowed	•, UDS	opt, UDS	UDS	•, UDS
named full-duplex pipes	XSI option	UDS	opt, UDS	UDS	•, UDS
message queues	XSI	•	•		•
semaphores	XSI	•	•	•	•
shared memory	XSI	•	•	•	•
sockets	•	•	•	•	•
STREAMS	XSI option		opt		•

Figure 15.1 Summary of UNIX System IPC

Linux, support for STREAMS is available in a separate, optional package called "LiS" (for Linux STREAMS). We show "opt" where the platform provides support for the feature through an optional package—one that is not usually installed by default.

The first seven forms of IPC in Figure 15.1 are usually restricted to IPC between processes on the same host. The final two rows—sockets and STREAMS—are the only two that are generally supported for IPC between processes on different hosts.

We have divided the discussion of IPC into three chapters. In this chapter, we examine classical IPC: pipes, FIFOs, message queues, semaphores, and shared memory. In the next chapter, we take a look at network IPC using the sockets mechanism. In Chapter 17, we take a look at some advanced features of IPC.

15.2   Pipes

Pipes are the oldest form of UNIX System IPC and are provided by all UNIX systems. Pipes have two limitations.

1. Historically, they have been half duplex (i.e., data flows in only one direction). Some systems now provide full-duplex pipes, but for maximum portability, we should never assume that this is the case.

2. Pipes can be used only between processes that have a common ancestor. Normally, a pipe is created by a process, that process calls `fork`, and the pipe is used between the parent and the child.

We'll see that FIFOs (Section 15.5) get around the second limitation, and that UNIX domain sockets (Section 17.3) and named STREAMS-based pipes (Section 17.2.2) get around both limitations.

Despite these limitations, half-duplex pipes are still the most commonly used form of IPC. Every time you type a sequence of commands in a pipeline for the shell to execute, the shell creates a separate process for each command and links the standard output of one to the standard input of the next using a pipe.

A pipe is created by calling the `pipe` function.

```
#include <unistd.h>

int pipe(int filedes[2]);
```
                                                              Returns: 0 if OK, −1 on error

Two file descriptors are returned through the *filedes* argument: *filedes[0]* is open for reading, and *filedes[1]* is open for writing. The output of *filedes[1]* is the input for *filedes[0]*.

> Pipes are implemented using UNIX domain sockets in 4.3BSD, 4.4BSD, and Mac OS X 10.3. Even though UNIX domain sockets are full duplex by default, these operating systems hobble the sockets used with pipes so that they operate in half-duplex mode only.
>
> POSIX.1 allows for an implementation to support full-duplex pipes. For these implementations, *filedes[0]* and *filedes[1]* are open for both reading and writing.

Two ways to picture a half-duplex pipe are shown in Figure 15.2. The left half of the figure shows the two ends of the pipe connected in a single process. The right half of the figure emphasizes that the data in the pipe flows through the kernel.

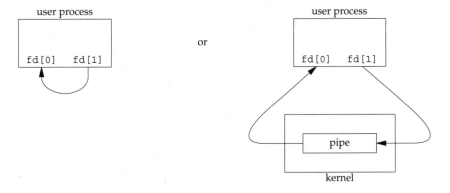

Figure 15.2 Two ways to view a half-duplex pipe

The `fstat` function (Section 4.2) returns a file type of FIFO for the file descriptor of either end of a pipe. We can test for a pipe with the `S_ISFIFO` macro.

> POSIX.1 states that the `st_size` member of the `stat` structure is undefined for pipes. But when the `fstat` function is applied to the file descriptor for the read end of the pipe, many systems store in `st_size` the number of bytes available for reading in the pipe. This is, however, nonportable.

A pipe in a single process is next to useless. Normally, the process that calls `pipe` then calls `fork`, creating an IPC channel from the parent to the child or vice versa. Figure 15.3 shows this scenario.

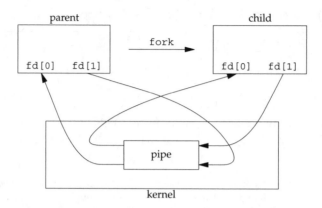

Figure 15.3 Half-duplex pipe after a `fork`

What happens after the `fork` depends on which direction of data flow we want. For a pipe from the parent to the child, the parent closes the read end of the pipe (`fd[0]`), and the child closes the write end (`fd[1]`). Figure 15.4 shows the resulting arrangement of descriptors.

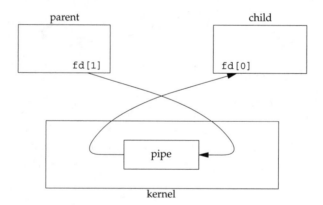

Figure 15.4 Pipe from parent to child

For a pipe from the child to the parent, the parent closes `fd[1]`, and the child closes `fd[0]`.

When one end of a pipe is closed, the following two rules apply.

1. If we `read` from a pipe whose write end has been closed, `read` returns 0 to indicate an end of file after all the data has been read. (Technically, we should say that this end of file is not generated until there are no more writers for the pipe. It's possible to duplicate a pipe descriptor so that multiple processes have the pipe open for writing. Normally, however, there is a single reader and a single writer for a pipe. When we get to FIFOs in the next section, we'll see that often there are multiple writers for a single FIFO.)

2. If we write to a pipe whose read end has been closed, the signal SIGPIPE is
    generated. If we either ignore the signal or catch it and return from the signal
    handler, write returns −1 with errno set to EPIPE.

When we're writing to a pipe (or FIFO), the constant PIPE_BUF specifies the
kernel's pipe buffer size. A write of PIPE_BUF bytes or less will not be interleaved
with the writes from other processes to the same pipe (or FIFO). But if multiple
processes are writing to a pipe (or FIFO), and if we write more than PIPE_BUF bytes,
the data might be interleaved with the data from the other writers. We can determine
the value of PIPE_BUF by using pathconf or fpathconf (recall Figure 2.11).

Example

Figure 15.5 shows the code to create a pipe between a parent and its child and to send
data down the pipe.

```
#include "apue.h"

int
main(void)
{
    int     n;
    int     fd[2];
    pid_t   pid;
    char    line[MAXLINE];

    if (pipe(fd) < 0)
        err_sys("pipe error");
    if ((pid = fork()) < 0) {
        err_sys("fork error");
    } else if (pid > 0) {        /* parent */
        close(fd[0]);
        write(fd[1], "hello world\n", 12);
    } else {                     /* child */
        close(fd[1]);
        n = read(fd[0], line, MAXLINE);
        write(STDOUT_FILENO, line, n);
    }
    exit(0);
}
```

Figure 15.5 Send data from parent to child over a pipe

□

In the previous example, we called read and write directly on the pipe
descriptors. What is more interesting is to duplicate the pipe descriptors onto standard
input or standard output. Often, the child then runs some other program, and that
program can either read from its standard input (the pipe that we created) or write to its
standard output (the pipe).

Example

Consider a program that displays some output that it has created, one page at a time. Rather than reinvent the pagination done by several UNIX system utilities, we want to invoke the user's favorite pager. To avoid writing all the data to a temporary file and calling `system` to display that file, we want to pipe the output directly to the pager. To do this, we create a pipe, `fork` a child process, set up the child's standard input to be the read end of the pipe, and `exec` the user's pager program. Figure 15.6 shows how to do this. (This example takes a command-line argument to specify the name of a file to display. Often, a program of this type would already have the data to display to the terminal in memory.)

```c
#include "apue.h"
#include <sys/wait.h>

#define DEF_PAGER    "/bin/more"       /* default pager program */

int
main(int argc, char *argv[])
{
    int     n;
    int     fd[2];
    pid_t   pid;
    char    *pager, *argv0;
    char    line[MAXLINE];
    FILE    *fp;

    if (argc != 2)
        err_quit("usage: a.out <pathname>");

    if ((fp = fopen(argv[1], "r")) == NULL)
        err_sys("can't open %s", argv[1]);
    if (pipe(fd) < 0)
        err_sys("pipe error");

    if ((pid = fork()) < 0) {
        err_sys("fork error");
    } else if (pid > 0) {                                    /* parent */
        close(fd[0]);          /* close read end */

        /* parent copies argv[1] to pipe */
        while (fgets(line, MAXLINE, fp) != NULL) {
            n = strlen(line);
            if (write(fd[1], line, n) != n)
                err_sys("write error to pipe");
        }
        if (ferror(fp))
            err_sys("fgets error");

        close(fd[1]);    /* close write end of pipe for reader */

        if (waitpid(pid, NULL, 0) < 0)
            err_sys("waitpid error");
```

```
            exit(0);
        } else {                                              /* child */
            close(fd[1]);     /* close write end */
            if (fd[0] != STDIN_FILENO) {
                if (dup2(fd[0], STDIN_FILENO) != STDIN_FILENO)
                    err_sys("dup2 error to stdin");
                close(fd[0]);    /* don't need this after dup2 */
            }

            /* get arguments for execl() */
            if ((pager = getenv("PAGER")) == NULL)
                pager = DEF_PAGER;
            if ((argv0 = strrchr(pager, '/')) != NULL)
                argv0++;              /* step past rightmost slash */
            else
                argv0 = pager;   /* no slash in pager */

            if (execl(pager, argv0, (char *)0) < 0)
                err_sys("execl error for %s", pager);
        }
        exit(0);
    }
```

Figure 15.6 Copy file to pager program

Before calling fork, we create a pipe. After the fork, the parent closes its read end, and the child closes its write end. The child then calls dup2 to have its standard input be the read end of the pipe. When the pager program is executed, its standard input will be the read end of the pipe.

When we duplicate a descriptor onto another (fd[0] onto standard input in the child), we have to be careful that the descriptor doesn't already have the desired value. If the descriptor already had the desired value and we called dup2 and close, the single copy of the descriptor would be closed. (Recall the operation of dup2 when its two arguments are equal, discussed in Section 3.12). In this program, if standard input had not been opened by the shell, the fopen at the beginning of the program should have used descriptor 0, the lowest unused descriptor, so fd[0] should never equal standard input. Nevertheless, whenever we call dup2 and close to duplicate a descriptor onto another, we'll always compare the descriptors first, as a defensive programming measure.

Note how we try to use the environment variable PAGER to obtain the name of the user's pager program. If this doesn't work, we use a default. This is a common usage of environment variables.   □

Example

Recall the five functions TELL_WAIT, TELL_PARENT, TELL_CHILD, WAIT_PARENT, and WAIT_CHILD from Section 8.9. In Figure 10.24, we showed an implementation using signals. Figure 15.7 shows an implementation using pipes.

```c
#include "apue.h"

static int  pfd1[2], pfd2[2];

void
TELL_WAIT(void)
{
    if (pipe(pfd1) < 0 || pipe(pfd2) < 0)
        err_sys("pipe error");
}

void
TELL_PARENT(pid_t pid)
{
    if (write(pfd2[1], "c", 1) != 1)
        err_sys("write error");
}

void
WAIT_PARENT(void)
{
    char    c;

    if (read(pfd1[0], &c, 1) != 1)
        err_sys("read error");

    if (c != 'p')
        err_quit("WAIT_PARENT: incorrect data");
}

void
TELL_CHILD(pid_t pid)
{
    if (write(pfd1[1], "p", 1) != 1)
        err_sys("write error");
}

void
WAIT_CHILD(void)
{
    char    c;

    if (read(pfd2[0], &c, 1) != 1)
        err_sys("read error");

    if (c != 'c')
        err_quit("WAIT_CHILD: incorrect data");
}
```

Figure 15.7 Routines to let a parent and child synchronize

We create two pipes before the fork, as shown in Figure 15.8. The parent writes the character "p" across the top pipe when TELL_CHILD is called, and the child writes the character "c" across the bottom pipe when TELL_PARENT is called. The corresponding WAIT_xxx functions do a blocking read for the single character.

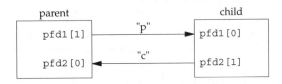

Figure 15.8 Using two pipes for parent–child synchronization

Note that each pipe has an extra reader, which doesn't matter. That is, in addition to the child reading from pfd1[0], the parent also has this end of the top pipe open for reading. This doesn't affect us, since the parent doesn't try to read from this pipe. □

15.3 popen **and** pclose **Functions**

Since a common operation is to create a pipe to another process, to either read its output or send it input, the standard I/O library has historically provided the popen and pclose functions. These two functions handle all the dirty work that we've been doing ourselves: creating a pipe, forking a child, closing the unused ends of the pipe, executing a shell to run the command, and waiting for the command to terminate.

```
#include <stdio.h>

FILE *popen(const char *cmdstring, const char *type);
```
                                     Returns: file pointer if OK, NULL on error
```
int pclose(FILE *fp);
```
                          Returns: termination status of cmdstring, or –1 on error

The function popen does a fork and exec to execute the *cmdstring*, and returns a standard I/O file pointer. If *type* is "r", the file pointer is connected to the standard output of *cmdstring* (Figure 15.9).

Figure 15.9 Result of fp = popen(*cmdstring*, "r")

If *type* is "w", the file pointer is connected to the standard input of *cmdstring*, as shown in Figure 15.10.

Figure 15.10 Result of fp = popen(*cmdstring*, "w")

One way to remember the final argument to popen is to remember that, like fopen, the returned file pointer is readable if *type* is "r" or writable if *type* is "w".

The pclose function closes the standard I/O stream, waits for the command to terminate, and returns the termination status of the shell. (We described the termination status in Section 8.6. The system function, described in Section 8.13, also returns the termination status.) If the shell cannot be executed, the termination status returned by pclose is as if the shell had executed exit(127).

The *cmdstring* is executed by the Bourne shell, as in

```
sh -c cmdstring
```

This means that the shell expands any of its special characters in *cmdstring*. This allows us to say, for example,

```
fp = popen("ls *.c", "r");
```

or

```
fp = popen("cmd 2>&1", "r");
```

Example

Let's redo the program from Figure 15.6, using popen. This is shown in Figure 15.11.

```
#include "apue.h"
#include <sys/wait.h>

#define PAGER    "${PAGER:-more}" /* environment variable, or default */

int
main(int argc, char *argv[])
{
    char    line[MAXLINE];
    FILE    *fpin, *fpout;

    if (argc != 2)
        err_quit("usage: a.out <pathname>");
    if ((fpin = fopen(argv[1], "r")) == NULL)
        err_sys("can't open %s", argv[1]);

    if ((fpout = popen(PAGER, "w")) == NULL)
        err_sys("popen error");

    /* copy argv[1] to pager */
```

```
            while (fgets(line, MAXLINE, fpin) != NULL) {
                if (fputs(line, fpout) == EOF)
                    err_sys("fputs error to pipe");
            }
            if (ferror(fpin))
                err_sys("fgets error");
            if (pclose(fpout) == -1)
                err_sys("pclose error");

            exit(0);
        }
```

Figure 15.11 Copy file to pager program using popen

Using popen reduces the amount of code we have to write.

The shell command ${PAGER:-more} says to use the value of the shell variable
PAGER if it is defined and non-null; otherwise, use the string more.   □

Example—popen and pclose Functions

Figure 15.12 shows our version of popen and pclose.

```
#include "apue.h"
#include <errno.h>
#include <fcntl.h>
#include <sys/wait.h>

/*
 * Pointer to array allocated at run-time.
 */
static pid_t    *childpid = NULL;

/*
 * From our open_max(), Figure 2.16.
 */
static int      maxfd;

FILE *
popen(const char *cmdstring, const char *type)
{
    int     i;
    int     pfd[2];
    pid_t   pid;
    FILE    *fp;

    /* only allow "r" or "w" */
    if ((type[0] != 'r' && type[0] != 'w') || type[1] != 0) {
        errno = EINVAL;         /* required by POSIX */
        return(NULL);
    }
```

```
        if (childpid == NULL) {        /* first time through */
            /* allocate zeroed out array for child pids */
            maxfd = open_max();
            if ((childpid = calloc(maxfd, sizeof(pid_t))) == NULL)
                return(NULL);
        }

        if (pipe(pfd) < 0)
            return(NULL);    /* errno set by pipe() */

        if ((pid = fork()) < 0) {
            return(NULL);    /* errno set by fork() */
        } else if (pid == 0) {                          /* child */
            if (*type == 'r') {
                close(pfd[0]);
                if (pfd[1] != STDOUT_FILENO) {
                    dup2(pfd[1], STDOUT_FILENO);
                    close(pfd[1]);
                }
            } else {
                close(pfd[1]);
                if (pfd[0] != STDIN_FILENO) {
                    dup2(pfd[0], STDIN_FILENO);
                    close(pfd[0]);
                }
            }

            /* close all descriptors in childpid[] */
            for (i = 0; i < maxfd; i++)
                if (childpid[i] > 0)
                    close(i);

            execl("/bin/sh", "sh", "-c", cmdstring, (char *)0);
            _exit(127);
        }

        /* parent continues... */
        if (*type == 'r') {
            close(pfd[1]);
            if ((fp = fdopen(pfd[0], type)) == NULL)
                return(NULL);
        } else {
            close(pfd[0]);
            if ((fp = fdopen(pfd[1], type)) == NULL)
                return(NULL);
        }

        childpid[fileno(fp)] = pid; /* remember child pid for this fd */
        return(fp);
    }
```

```
int
pclose(FILE *fp)
{
    int     fd, stat;
    pid_t   pid;

    if (childpid == NULL) {
        errno = EINVAL;
        return(-1);      /* popen() has never been called */
    }

    fd = fileno(fp);
    if ((pid = childpid[fd]) == 0) {
        errno = EINVAL;
        return(-1);      /* fp wasn't opened by popen() */
    }

    childpid[fd] = 0;
    if (fclose(fp) == EOF)
        return(-1);

    while (waitpid(pid, &stat, 0) < 0)
        if (errno != EINTR)
            return(-1); /* error other than EINTR from waitpid() */

    return(stat);    /* return child's termination status */
}
```

Figure 15.12 The popen and pclose functions

Although the core of popen is similar to the code we've used earlier in this chapter, there are many details that we need to take care of. First, each time popen is called, we have to remember the process ID of the child that we create and either its file descriptor or FILE pointer. We choose to save the child's process ID in the array childpid, which we index by the file descriptor. This way, when pclose is called with the FILE pointer as its argument, we call the standard I/O function fileno to get the file descriptor, and then have the child process ID for the call to waitpid. Since it's possible for a given process to call popen more than once, we dynamically allocate the childpid array (the first time popen is called), with room for as many children as there are file descriptors.

Calling pipe and fork and then duplicating the appropriate descriptors for each process is similar to what we did earlier in this chapter.

POSIX.1 requires that popen close any streams that are still open in the child from previous calls to popen. To do this, we go through the childpid array in the child, closing any descriptors that are still open.

What happens if the caller of pclose has established a signal handler for SIGCHLD? The call to waitpid from pclose would return an error of EINTR. Since the caller is allowed to catch this signal (or any other signal that might interrupt the call to waitpid), we simply call waitpid again if it is interrupted by a caught signal.

Note that if the application calls `waitpid` and obtains the exit status of the child created by `popen`, we will call `waitpid` when the application calls `pclose`, find that the child no longer exists, and return –1 with `errno` set to `ECHILD`. This is the behavior required by POSIX.1 in this situation.

> Some early versions of `pclose` returned an error of `EINTR` if a signal interrupted the `wait`. Also, some early versions of `pclose` blocked or ignored the signals `SIGINT`, `SIGQUIT`, and `SIGHUP` during the `wait`. This is not allowed by POSIX.1.
>
>   □

Note that `popen` should never be called by a set-user-ID or set-group-ID program. When it executes the command, `popen` does the equivalent of

```
execl("/bin/sh", "sh", "-c", command, NULL);
```

which executes the shell and *command* with the environment inherited by the caller. A malicious user can manipulate the environment so that the shell executes commands other than those intended, with the elevated permissions granted by the set-ID file mode.

One thing that `popen` is especially well suited for is executing simple filters to transform the input or output of the running command. Such is the case when a command wants to build its own pipeline.

Example

Consider an application that writes a prompt to standard output and reads a line from standard input. With `popen`, we can interpose a program between the application and its input to transform the input. Figure 15.13 shows the arrangement of processes.

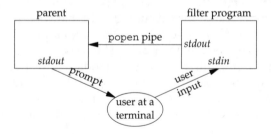

Figure 15.13   Transforming input using popen

The transformation could be pathname expansion, for example, or providing a history mechanism (remembering previously entered commands).

Figure 15.14 shows a simple filter to demonstrate this operation. The filter copies standard input to standard output, converting any uppercase character to lowercase. The reason we're careful to `fflush` standard output after writing a newline is discussed in the next section when we talk about coprocesses.

```
#include "apue.h"
#include <ctype.h>

int
main(void)
{
    int        c;

    while ((c = getchar()) != EOF) {
        if (isupper(c))
            c = tolower(c);
        if (putchar(c) == EOF)
            err_sys("output error");
        if (c == '\n')
            fflush(stdout);
    }
    exit(0);
}
```

Figure 15.14 Filter to convert uppercase characters to lowercase

We compile this filter into the executable file `myuclc`, which we then invoke from the program in Figure 15.15 using popen.

```
#include "apue.h"
#include <sys/wait.h>

int
main(void)
{
    char    line[MAXLINE];
    FILE    *fpin;

    if ((fpin = popen("myuclc", "r")) == NULL)
        err_sys("popen error");
    for ( ; ; ) {
        fputs("prompt> ", stdout);
        fflush(stdout);
        if (fgets(line, MAXLINE, fpin) == NULL) /* read from pipe */
            break;
        if (fputs(line, stdout) == EOF)
            err_sys("fputs error to pipe");
    }
    if (pclose(fpin) == -1)
        err_sys("pclose error");
    putchar('\n');
    exit(0);
}
```

Figure 15.15 Invoke uppercase/lowercase filter to read commands

We need to call fflush after writing the prompt, because the standard output is normally line buffered, and the prompt does not contain a newline.   □

15.4   Coprocesses

A UNIX system filter is a program that reads from standard input and writes to standard output. Filters are normally connected linearly in shell pipelines. A filter becomes a *coprocess* when the same program generates the filter's input and reads the filter's output.

The Korn shell provides coprocesses [Bolsky and Korn 1995]. The Bourne shell, the Bourne-again shell, and the C shell don't provide a way to connect processes together as coprocesses. A coprocess normally runs in the background from a shell, and its standard input and standard output are connected to another program using a pipe. Although the shell syntax required to initiate a coprocess and connect its input and output to other processes is quite contorted (see pp. 62–63 of Bolsky and Korn [1995] for all the details), coprocesses are also useful from a C program.

Whereas popen gives us a one-way pipe to the standard input or from the standard output of another process, with a coprocess, we have two one-way pipes to the other process: one to its standard input and one from its standard output. We want to write to its standard input, let it operate on the data, and then read from its standard output.

Example

Let's look at coprocesses with an example. The process creates two pipes: one is the standard input of the coprocess, and the other is the standard output of the coprocess. Figure 15.16 shows this arrangement.

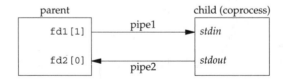

Figure 15.16 Driving a coprocess by writing its standard input and reading its standard output

The program in Figure 15.17 is a simple coprocess that reads two numbers from its standard input, computes their sum, and writes the sum to its standard output. (Coprocesses usually do more interesting work than we illustrate here. This example is admittedly contrived so that we can study the plumbing needed to connect the processes.)

```
#include "apue.h"

int
main(void)
{
    int     n, int1, int2;
    char    line[MAXLINE];

    while ((n = read(STDIN_FILENO, line, MAXLINE)) > 0) {
        line[n] = 0;            /* null terminate */
        if (sscanf(line, "%d%d", &int1, &int2) == 2) {
            sprintf(line, "%d\n", int1 + int2);
            n = strlen(line);
            if (write(STDOUT_FILENO, line, n) != n)
                err_sys("write error");
        } else {
            if (write(STDOUT_FILENO, "invalid args\n", 13) != 13)
                err_sys("write error");
        }
    }
    exit(0);
}
```

Figure 15.17 Simple filter to add two numbers

We compile this program and leave the executable in the file add2.

The program in Figure 15.18 invokes the add2 coprocess after reading two numbers from its standard input. The value from the coprocess is written to its standard output.

```
#include "apue.h"

static void sig_pipe(int);       /* our signal handler */

int
main(void)
{
    int     n, fd1[2], fd2[2];
    pid_t   pid;
    char    line[MAXLINE];

    if (signal(SIGPIPE, sig_pipe) == SIG_ERR)
        err_sys("signal error");

    if (pipe(fd1) < 0 || pipe(fd2) < 0)
        err_sys("pipe error");

    if ((pid = fork()) < 0) {
        err_sys("fork error");
    } else if (pid > 0) {                                /* parent */
        close(fd1[0]);
        close(fd2[1]);
```

```
        while (fgets(line, MAXLINE, stdin) != NULL) {
            n = strlen(line);
            if (write(fd1[1], line, n) != n)
                err_sys("write error to pipe");
            if ((n = read(fd2[0], line, MAXLINE)) < 0)
                err_sys("read error from pipe");
            if (n == 0) {
                err_msg("child closed pipe");
                break;
            }
            line[n] = 0;       /* null terminate */
            if (fputs(line, stdout) == EOF)
                err_sys("fputs error");
        }

        if (ferror(stdin))
            err_sys("fgets error on stdin");
        exit(0);
    } else {                                    /* child */
        close(fd1[1]);
        close(fd2[0]);
        if (fd1[0] != STDIN_FILENO) {
            if (dup2(fd1[0], STDIN_FILENO) != STDIN_FILENO)
                err_sys("dup2 error to stdin");
            close(fd1[0]);
        }

        if (fd2[1] != STDOUT_FILENO) {
            if (dup2(fd2[1], STDOUT_FILENO) != STDOUT_FILENO)
                err_sys("dup2 error to stdout");
            close(fd2[1]);
        }
        if (execl("./add2", "add2", (char *)0) < 0)
            err_sys("execl error");
    }
    exit(0);
}

static void
sig_pipe(int signo)
{
    printf("SIGPIPE caught\n");
    exit(1);
}
```

Figure 15.18 Program to drive the add2 filter

Here, we create two pipes, with the parent and the child closing the ends they don't need. We have to use two pipes: one for the standard input of the coprocess and one for its standard output. The child then calls dup2 to move the pipe descriptors onto its standard input and standard output, before calling execl.

If we compile and run the program in Figure 15.18, it works as expected. Furthermore, if we `kill` the `add2` coprocess while the program in Figure 15.18 is waiting for our input and then enter two numbers, the signal handler is invoked when the program writes to the pipe that has no reader. (See Exercise 15.4.)

Recall from Figure 15.1 that not all systems provide full-duplex pipes using the `pipe` function. In Figure 17.4, we provide another version of this example using a single full-duplex pipe instead of two half-duplex pipes, for those systems that support full-duplex pipes.   □

Example

In the coprocess `add2` (Figure 15.17), we purposely used low-level I/O (UNIX system calls): `read` and `write`. What happens if we rewrite this coprocess to use standard I/O? Figure 15.19 shows the new version.

```c
#include "apue.h"

int
main(void)
{
    int     int1, int2;
    char    line[MAXLINE];

    while (fgets(line, MAXLINE, stdin) != NULL) {
        if (sscanf(line, "%d%d", &int1, &int2) == 2) {
            if (printf("%d\n", int1 + int2) == EOF)
                err_sys("printf error");
        } else {
            if (printf("invalid args\n") == EOF)
                err_sys("printf error");
        }
    }
    exit(0);
}
```

Figure 15.19 Filter to add two numbers, using standard I/O

If we invoke this new coprocess from the program in Figure 15.18, it no longer works. The problem is the default standard I/O buffering. When the program in Figure 15.19 is invoked, the first `fgets` on the standard input causes the standard I/O library to allocate a buffer and choose the type of buffering. Since the standard input is a pipe, the standard I/O library defaults to fully buffered. The same thing happens with the standard output. While `add2` is blocked reading from its standard input, the program in Figure 15.18 is blocked reading from the pipe. We have a deadlock.

Here, we have control over the coprocess that's being run. We can change the program in Figure 15.19 by adding the following four lines before the `while` loop:

```
if (setvbuf(stdin, NULL, _IOLBF, 0) != 0)
    err_sys("setvbuf error");
if (setvbuf(stdout, NULL, _IOLBF, 0) != 0)
    err_sys("setvbuf error");
```

These lines cause `fgets` to return when a line is available and cause `printf` to do an `fflush` when a newline is output (refer back to Section 5.4 for the details on standard I/O buffering). Making these explicit calls to `setvbuf` fixes the program in Figure 15.19.

If we aren't able to modify the program that we're piping the output into, other techniques are required. For example, if we use `awk(1)` as a coprocess from our program (instead of the `add2` program), the following won't work:

```
#! /bin/awk -f
{ print $1 + $2 }
```

The reason this won't work is again the standard I/O buffering. But in this case, we cannot change the way `awk` works (unless we have the source code for it). We are unable to modify the executable of `awk` in any way to change the way the standard I/O buffering is handled.

The solution for this general problem is to make the coprocess being invoked (`awk` in this case) think that its standard input and standard output are connected to a terminal. That causes the standard I/O routines in the coprocess to line buffer these two I/O streams, similar to what we did with the explicit calls to `setvbuf` previously. We use pseudo terminals to do this in Chapter 19.   □

15.5   FIFOs

FIFOs are sometimes called named pipes. Pipes can be used only between related processes when a common ancestor has created the pipe. (An exception to this is mounted STREAMS-based pipes, which we discuss in Section 17.2.2.) With FIFOs, however, unrelated processes can exchange data.

We saw in Chapter 4 that a FIFO is a type of file. One of the encodings of the `st_mode` member of the `stat` structure (Section 4.2) indicates that a file is a FIFO. We can test for this with the `S_ISFIFO` macro.

Creating a FIFO is similar to creating a file. Indeed, the *pathname* for a FIFO exists in the file system.

```
#include <sys/stat.h>

int mkfifo(const char *pathname, mode_t mode);
```
                                                        Returns: 0 if OK, –1 on error

The specification of the *mode* argument for the `mkfifo` function is the same as for the `open` function (Section 3.3). The rules for the user and group ownership of the new FIFO are the same as we described in Section 4.6.

Once we have used mkfifo to create a FIFO, we open it using open. Indeed, the normal file I/O functions (close, read, write, unlink, etc.) all work with FIFOs.

> Applications can create FIFOs with the mknod function. Because POSIX.1 originally didn't include mknod, the mkfifo function was invented specifically for POSIX.1. The mknod function is now included as an XSI extension. On most systems, the mkfifo function calls mknod to create the FIFO.
>
> POSIX.1 also includes support for the mkfifo(1) command. All four platforms discussed in this text provide this command. This allows a FIFO to be created using a shell command and then accessed with the normal shell I/O redirection.

When we open a FIFO, the nonblocking flag (O_NONBLOCK) affects what happens.

- In the normal case (O_NONBLOCK not specified), an open for read-only blocks until some other process opens the FIFO for writing. Similarly, an open for write-only blocks until some other process opens the FIFO for reading.

- If O_NONBLOCK is specified, an open for read-only returns immediately. But an open for write-only returns −1 with errno set to ENXIO if no process has the FIFO open for reading.

As with a pipe, if we write to a FIFO that no process has open for reading, the signal SIGPIPE is generated. When the last writer for a FIFO closes the FIFO, an end of file is generated for the reader of the FIFO.

It is common to have multiple writers for a given FIFO. This means that we have to worry about atomic writes if we don't want the writes from multiple processes to be interleaved. (We'll see a way around this problem in Section 17.2.2.) As with pipes, the constant PIPE_BUF specifies the maximum amount of data that can be written atomically to a FIFO.

There are two uses for FIFOs.

1. FIFOs are used by shell commands to pass data from one shell pipeline to another without creating intermediate temporary files.

2. FIFOs are used as rendezvous points in client–server applications to pass data between the clients and the servers.

We discuss each of these uses with an example.

Example—Using FIFOs to Duplicate Output Streams

FIFOs can be used to duplicate an output stream in a series of shell commands. This prevents writing the data to an intermediate disk file (similar to using pipes to avoid intermediate disk files). But whereas pipes can be used only for linear connections between processes, a FIFO has a name, so it can be used for nonlinear connections.

Consider a procedure that needs to process a filtered input stream twice. Figure 15.20 shows this arrangement.

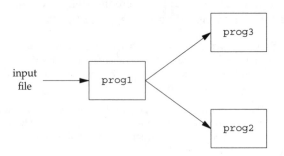

Figure 15.20 Procedure that processes a filtered input stream twice

With a FIFO and the UNIX program tee(1), we can accomplish this procedure without using a temporary file. (The tee program copies its standard input to both its standard output and to the file named on its command line.)

```
mkfifo fifo1
prog3 < fifo1 &
prog1 < infile | tee fifo1 | prog2
```

We create the FIFO and then start prog3 in the background, reading from the FIFO. We then start prog1 and use tee to send its input to both the FIFO and prog2. Figure 15.21 shows the process arrangement.

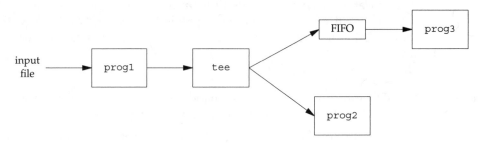

Figure 15.21 Using a FIFO and tee to send a stream to two different processes

□

Example—Client–Server Communication Using a FIFO

Another use for FIFOs is to send data between a client and a server. If we have a server that is contacted by numerous clients, each client can write its request to a well-known FIFO that the server creates. (By "well-known" we mean that the pathname of the FIFO is known to all the clients that need to contact the server.) Figure 15.22 shows this arrangement. Since there are multiple writers for the FIFO, the requests sent by the clients to the server need to be less than PIPE_BUF bytes in size. This prevents any interleaving of the client writes.

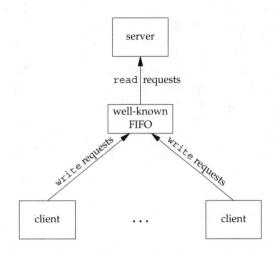

Figure 15.22 Clients sending requests to a server using a FIFO

The problem in using FIFOs for this type of client–server communication is how to send replies back from the server to each client. A single FIFO can't be used, as the clients would never know when to read their response versus responses for other clients. One solution is for each client to send its process ID with the request. The server then creates a unique FIFO for each client, using a pathname based on the client's process ID. For example, the server can create a FIFO with the name /tmp/serv1.XXXXX, where XXXXX is replaced with the client's process ID. Figure 15.23 shows this arrangement.

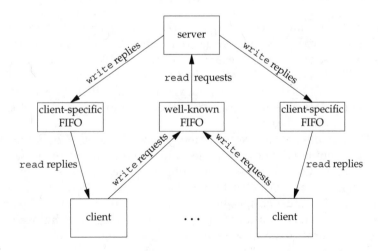

Figure 15.23 Client–server communication using FIFOs

This arrangement works, although it is impossible for the server to tell whether a client crashes. This causes the client-specific FIFOs to be left in the file system. The server also must catch SIGPIPE, since it's possible for a client to send a request and terminate before reading the response, leaving the client-specific FIFO with one writer (the server) and no reader. We'll see a more elegant approach to this problem when we discuss mounted STREAMS-based pipes and connld in Section 17.2.2.

With the arrangement shown in Figure 15.23, if the server opens its well-known FIFO read-only (since it only reads from it) each time the number of clients goes from 1 to 0, the server will read an end of file on the FIFO. To prevent the server from having to handle this case, a common trick is just to have the server open its well-known FIFO for read–write. (See Exercise 15.10.)   □

15.6   XSI IPC

The three types of IPC that we call XSI IPC—message queues, semaphores, and shared memory—have many similarities. In this section, we cover these similar features; in the following sections, we look at the specific functions for each of the three IPC types.

> The XSI IPC functions are based closely on the System V IPC functions. These three types of IPC originated in the 1970s in an internal AT&T version of the UNIX System called "Columbus UNIX." These IPC features were later added to System V. They are often criticized for inventing their own namespace instead of using the file system.

> Recall from Figure 15.1 that message queues, semaphores, and shared memory are defined as XSI extensions in the Single UNIX Specification.

15.6.1   Identifiers and Keys

Each *IPC structure* (message queue, semaphore, or shared memory segment) in the kernel is referred to by a non-negative integer *identifier*. To send or fetch a message to or from a message queue, for example, all we need know is the identifier for the queue. Unlike file descriptors, IPC identifiers are not small integers. Indeed, when a given IPC structure is created and then removed, the identifier associated with that structure continually increases until it reaches the maximum positive value for an integer, and then wraps around to 0.

The identifier is an internal name for an IPC object. Cooperating processes need an external naming scheme to be able to rendezvous using the same IPC object. For this purpose, an IPC object is associated with a *key* that acts as an external name.

Whenever an IPC structure is being created (by calling msgget, semget, or shmget), a key must be specified. The data type of this key is the primitive system data type key_t, which is often defined as a long integer in the header <sys/types.h>. This key is converted into an identifier by the kernel.

There are various ways for a client and a server to rendezvous at the same IPC structure.

1. The server can create a new IPC structure by specifying a key of IPC_PRIVATE and store the returned identifier somewhere (such as a file) for the client to obtain. The key IPC_PRIVATE guarantees that the server creates a new IPC structure. The disadvantage to this technique is that file system operations are required for the server to write the integer identifier to a file, and then for the clients to retrieve this identifier later.

    The IPC_PRIVATE key is also used in a parent–child relationship. The parent creates a new IPC structure specifying IPC_PRIVATE, and the resulting identifier is then available to the child after the fork. The child can pass the identifier to a new program as an argument to one of the exec functions.

2. The client and the server can agree on a key by defining the key in a common header, for example. The server then creates a new IPC structure specifying this key. The problem with this approach is that it's possible for the key to already be associated with an IPC structure, in which case the get function (msgget, semget, or shmget) returns an error. The server must handle this error, deleting the existing IPC structure, and try to create it again.

3. The client and the server can agree on a pathname and project ID (the project ID is a character value between 0 and 255) and call the function ftok to convert these two values into a key. This key is then used in step 2. The only service provided by ftok is a way of generating a key from a pathname and project ID.

```
#include <sys/ipc.h>

key_t ftok(const char *path, int id);
```
                                                    Returns: key if OK, (key_t)−1 on error

The *path* argument must refer to an existing file. Only the lower 8 bits of *id* are used when generating the key.

The key created by ftok is usually formed by taking parts of the st_dev and st_ino fields in the stat structure (Section 4.2) corresponding to the given pathname and combining them with the project ID. If two pathnames refer to two different files, then ftok usually returns two different keys for the two pathnames. However, because both i-node numbers and keys are often stored in long integers, there can be information loss creating a key. This means that two different pathnames to different files can generate the same key if the same project ID is used.

The three get functions (msgget, semget, and shmget) all have two similar arguments: a *key* and an integer *flag*. A new IPC structure is created (normally, by a server) if either *key* is IPC_PRIVATE or *key* is not currently associated with an IPC structure of the particular type and the IPC_CREAT bit of *flag* is specified. To reference an existing queue (normally done by a client), *key* must equal the key that was specified when the queue was created, and IPC_CREAT must not be specified.

Note that it's never possible to specify IPC_PRIVATE to reference an existing queue, since this special *key* value always creates a new queue. To reference an existing queue that was created with a *key* of IPC_PRIVATE, we must know the associated identifier and then use that identifier in the other IPC calls (such as `msgsnd` and `msgrcv`), bypassing the `get` function.

If we want to create a new IPC structure, making sure that we don't reference an existing one with the same identifier, we must specify a *flag* with both the `IPC_CREAT` and `IPC_EXCL` bits set. Doing this causes an error return of `EEXIST` if the IPC structure already exists. (This is similar to an `open` that specifies the `O_CREAT` and `O_EXCL` flags.)

15.6.2 Permission Structure

XSI IPC associates an `ipc_perm` structure with each IPC structure. This structure defines the permissions and owner and includes at least the following members:

```
struct ipc_perm {
  uid_t  uid;  /* owner's effective user id */
  gid_t  gid;  /* owner's effective group id */
  uid_t  cuid; /* creator's effective user id */
  gid_t  cgid; /* creator's effective group id */
  mode_t mode; /* access modes */
    .
    .
    .
};
```

Each implementation includes additional members. See `<sys/ipc.h>` on your system for the complete definition.

All the fields are initialized when the IPC structure is created. At a later time, we can modify the `uid`, `gid`, and `mode` fields by calling `msgctl`, `semctl`, or `shmctl`. To change these values, the calling process must be either the creator of the IPC structure or the superuser. Changing these fields is similar to calling `chown` or `chmod` for a file.

The values in the `mode` field are similar to the values we saw in Figure 4.6, but there is nothing corresponding to execute permission for any of the IPC structures. Also, message queues and shared memory use the terms *read* and *write*, but semaphores use the terms *read* and *alter*. Figure 15.24 shows the six permissions for each form of IPC.

Permission	Bit
user-read	0400
user-write (alter)	0200
group-read	0040
group-write (alter)	0020
other-read	0004
other-write (alter)	0002

Figure 15.24 XSI IPC permissions

Some implementations define symbolic constants to represent each permission, however, these constants are not standardized by the Single UNIX Specification.

15.6.3 Configuration Limits

All three forms of XSI IPC have built-in limits that we may encounter. Most of these limits can be changed by reconfiguring the kernel. We describe the limits when we describe each of the three forms of IPC.

> Each platform provides its own way to report and modify a particular limit. FreeBSD 5.2.1, Linux 2.4.22, and Mac OS X 10.3 provide the `sysctl` command to view and modify kernel configuration parameters. On Solaris 9, changes to kernel configuration parameters are made by modifying the file `/etc/system` and rebooting.
>
> On Linux, you can display the IPC-related limits by running `ipcs -l`. On FreeBSD, the equivalent command is `ipcs -T`. On Solaris, you can discover the tunable parameters by running `sysdef -i`.

15.6.4 Advantages and Disadvantages

A fundamental problem with XSI IPC is that the IPC structures are systemwide and do not have a reference count. For example, if we create a message queue, place some messages on the queue, and then terminate, the message queue and its contents are not deleted. They remain in the system until specifically read or deleted by some process calling `msgrcv` or `msgctl`, by someone executing the `ipcrm(1)` command, or by the system being rebooted. Compare this with a pipe, which is completely removed when the last process to reference it terminates. With a FIFO, although the name stays in the file system until explicitly removed, any data left in a FIFO is removed when the last process to reference the FIFO terminates.

Another problem with XSI IPC is that these IPC structures are not known by names in the file system. We can't access them and modify their properties with the functions we described in Chapters 3 and 4. Almost a dozen new system calls (`msgget`, `semop`, `shmat`, and so on) were added to the kernel to support these IPC objects. We can't see the IPC objects with an `ls` command, we can't remove them with the `rm` command, and we can't change their permissions with the `chmod` command. Instead, two new commands—`ipcs(1)` and `ipcrm(1)`—were added.

Since these forms of IPC don't use file descriptors, we can't use the multiplexed I/O functions (`select` and `poll`) with them. This makes it harder to use more than one of these IPC structures at a time or to use any of these IPC structures with file or device I/O. For example, we can't have a server wait for a message to be placed on one of two message queues without some form of busy–wait loop.

An overview of a transaction processing system built using System V IPC is given in Andrade, Carges, and Kovach [1989]. They claim that the namespace used by System V IPC (the identifiers) is an advantage, not a problem as we said earlier, because using identifiers allows a process to send a message to a message queue with a single function call (`msgsnd`), whereas other forms of IPC normally require an `open`, `write`, and `close`. This argument is false. Clients still have to obtain the identifier for the server's queue somehow, to avoid using a key and calling `msgget`. The identifier assigned to a particular queue depends on how many other message queues exist when the queue is created and how many times the table in the kernel assigned to the new queue has been used since the kernel was bootstrapped. This is a dynamic value that can't be guessed or stored in a header. As we mentioned in Section 15.6.1, minimally a server has to write the assigned queue identifier to a file for its clients to read.

Other advantages listed by these authors for message queues are that they're reliable, flow controlled, record oriented, and can be processed in other than first-in, first-out order. As we saw in Section 14.4, the STREAMS mechanism also possesses all these properties, although an `open` is required before sending data to a stream, and a `close` is required when we're finished. Figure 15.25 compares some of the features of these various forms of IPC.

IPC type	Connectionless?	Reliable?	Flow control?	Records?	Message types or priorities?
message queues	no	yes	yes	yes	yes
STREAMS	no	yes	yes	yes	yes
UNIX domain stream socket	no	yes	yes	no	no
UNIX domain datagram socket	yes	yes	no	yes	no
FIFOs (non-STREAMS)	no	yes	yes	no	no

Figure 15.25 Comparison of features of various forms of IPC

(We describe stream and datagram sockets in Chapter 16. We describe UNIX domain sockets in Section 17.3.) By "connectionless," we mean the ability to send a message without having to call some form of an open function first. As described previously, we don't consider message queues connectionless, since some technique is required to obtain the identifier for a queue. Since all these forms of IPC are restricted to a single host, all are reliable. When the messages are sent across a network, the possibility of messages being lost becomes a concern. "Flow control" means that the sender is put to sleep if there is a shortage of system resources (buffers) or if the receiver can't accept any more messages. When the flow control condition subsides, the sender should automatically be awakened.

One feature that we don't show in Figure 15.25 is whether the IPC facility can automatically create a unique connection to a server for each client. We'll see in Chapter 17 that STREAMS and UNIX stream sockets provide this capability.

The next three sections describe each of the three forms of XSI IPC in detail.

15.7   Message Queues

A message queue is a linked list of messages stored within the kernel and identified by a message queue identifier. We'll call the message queue just a *queue* and its identifier a *queue ID*.

> The Single UNIX Specification includes an alternate IPC message queue implementation in the message-passing option of its real-time extensions. We do not cover the real-time extensions in this text.

A new queue is created or an existing queue opened by `msgget`. New messages are added to the end of a queue by `msgsnd`. Every message has a positive long integer type field, a non-negative length, and the actual data bytes (corresponding to the length), all of which are specified to msgsnd when the message is added to a queue. Messages are fetched from a queue by msgrcv. We don't have to fetch the messages in a first-in, first-out order. Instead, we can fetch messages based on their type field.

Each queue has the following msqid_ds structure associated with it:

```
struct msqid_ds {
    struct ipc_perm   msg_perm;       /* see Section 15.6.2 */
    msgqnum_t         msg_qnum;       /* # of messages on queue */
    msglen_t          msg_qbytes;     /* max # of bytes on queue */
    pid_t             msg_lspid;      /* pid of last msgsnd() */
    pid_t             msg_lrpid;      /* pid of last msgrcv() */
    time_t            msg_stime;      /* last-msgsnd() time */
    time_t            msg_rtime;      /* last-msgrcv() time */
    time_t            msg_ctime;      /* last-change time */
        .
        .
        .
};
```

This structure defines the current status of the queue. The members shown are the ones defined by the Single UNIX Specification. Implementations include additional fields not covered by the standard.

Figure 15.26 lists the system limits that affect message queues. We show "notsup" where the platform doesn't support the feature. We show "derived" whenever a limit is derived from other limits. For example, the maximum number of messages in a Linux system is based on the maximum number of queues and the maximum amount of data allowed on the queues. If the minimum message size is 1 byte, that would limit the number of messages systemwide to *maximum # queues * maximum size of a queue*. Given the limits in Figure 15.26, Linux has an upper bound of 262,144 messages with the default configuration. (Even though a message can contain zero bytes of data, Linux treats it as if it contained 1 byte, to limit the number of messages queued.)

Description	Typical values			
	FreeBSD 5.2.1	Linux 2.4.22	Mac OS X 10.3	Solaris 9
Size in bytes of largest message we can send	2,048	8,192	notsup	2,048
The maximum size in bytes of a particular queue (i.e., the sum of all the messages on the queue)	2,048	16,384	notsup	4,096
The maximum number of messages queues, systemwide	40	16	notsup	50
The maximum number of messages, systemwide	40	derived	notsup	40

Figure 15.26 System limits that affect message queues

Recall from Figure 15.1 that Mac OS X 10.3 doesn't support XSI message queues. Since Mac OS X is based in part on FreeBSD, and FreeBSD supports message queues, it is possible for Mac OS X to support them, too. Indeed, a good Internet search engine will provide pointers to a third-party port of XSI message queues for Mac OS X.

The first function normally called is msgget to either open an existing queue or create a new queue.

```
#include <sys/msg.h>

int msgget(key_t key, int flag);
```
Returns: message queue ID if OK, −1 on error

In Section 15.6.1, we described the rules for converting the *key* into an identifier and discussed whether a new queue is created or an existing queue is referenced. When a new queue is created, the following members of the `msqid_ds` structure are initialized.

- The `ipc_perm` structure is initialized as described in Section 15.6.2. The `mode` member of this structure is set to the corresponding permission bits of *flag*. These permissions are specified with the values from Figure 15.24.

- `msg_qnum`, `msg_lspid`, `msg_lrpid`, `msg_stime`, and `msg_rtime` are all set to 0.

- `msg_ctime` is set to the current time.

- `msg_qbytes` is set to the system limit.

On success, `msgget` returns the non-negative queue ID. This value is then used with the other three message queue functions.

The `msgctl` function performs various operations on a queue. This function and the related functions for semaphores and shared memory (`semctl` and `shmctl`) are the `ioctl`-like functions for XSI IPC (i.e., the garbage-can functions).

```
#include <sys/msg.h>

int msgctl(int msqid, int cmd, struct msqid_ds *buf);
```
Returns: 0 if OK, −1 on error

The *cmd* argument specifies the command to be performed on the queue specified by *msqid*.

IPC_STAT   Fetch the `msqid_ds` structure for this queue, storing it in the structure pointed to by *buf*.

IPC_SET   Copy the following fields from the structure pointed to by *buf* to the `msqid_ds` structure associated with this queue: `msg_perm.uid`, `msg_perm.gid`, `msg_perm.mode`, and `msg_qbytes`. This command can be executed only by a process whose effective user ID equals `msg_perm.cuid` or `msg_perm.uid` or by a process with superuser privileges. Only the superuser can increase the value of `msg_qbytes`.

IPC_RMID   Remove the message queue from the system and any data still on the queue. This removal is immediate. Any other process still using the message queue will get an error of `EIDRM` on its next attempted operation on the queue. This command can be executed only by a process whose effective user ID equals `msg_perm.cuid` or `msg_perm.uid` or by a process with superuser privileges.

We'll see that these three commands (IPC_STAT, IPC_SET, and IPC_RMID) are also provided for semaphores and shared memory.

Data is placed onto a message queue by calling msgsnd.

```
#include <sys/msg.h>

int msgsnd(int msqid, const void *ptr, size_t nbytes, int flag);
```
Returns: 0 if OK, –1 on error

As we mentioned earlier, each message is composed of a positive long integer type field, a non-negative length (nbytes), and the actual data bytes (corresponding to the length). Messages are always placed at the end of the queue.

The ptr argument points to a long integer that contains the positive integer message type, and it is immediately followed by the message data. (There is no message data if nbytes is 0.) If the largest message we send is 512 bytes, we can define the following structure:

```
struct mymesg {
    long  mtype;        /* positive message type */
    char  mtext[512]; /* message data, of length nbytes */
};
```

The ptr argument is then a pointer to a mymesg structure. The message type can be used by the receiver to fetch messages in an order other than first in, first out.

> Some platforms support both 32-bit and 64-bit environments. This affects the size of long integers and pointers. For example, on 64-bit SPARC systems, Solaris allows both 32-bit and 64-bit applications to coexist. If a 32-bit application were to exchange this structure over a pipe or a socket with a 64-bit application, problems would arise, because the size of a long integer is 4 bytes in a 32-bit application, but 8 bytes in a 64-bit application. This means that a 32-bit application will expect that the mtext field will start 4 bytes after the start of the structure, whereas a 64-bit application will expect the mtext field to start 8 bytes after the start of the structure. In this situation, part of the 64-bit application's mtype field will appear as part of the mtext field to the 32-bit application, and the first 4 bytes in the 32-bit application's mtext field will be interpreted as a part of the mtype field by the 64-bit application.

> This problem doesn't happen with XSI message queues, however. Solaris implements the 32-bit version of the IPC system calls with different entry points than the 64-bit version of the IPC system calls. The system calls know how to deal with a 32-bit application communicating with a 64-bit application, and treat the type field specially to avoid it interfering with the data portion of the message. The only potential problem is a loss of information when a 64-bit application sends a message with a value in the 8-byte type field that is larger than will fit in a 32-bit application's 4-byte type field. In this case, the 32-bit application will see a truncated type value.

A flag value of IPC_NOWAIT can be specified. This is similar to the nonblocking I/O flag for file I/O (Section 14.2). If the message queue is full (either the total number of messages on the queue equals the system limit, or the total number of bytes on the queue equals the system limit), specifying IPC_NOWAIT causes msgsnd to return immediately with an error of EAGAIN. If IPC_NOWAIT is not specified, we are blocked until there is room for the message, the queue is removed from the system, or a signal is caught and the signal handler returns. In the second case, an error of EIDRM is returned ("identifier removed"); in the last case, the error returned is EINTR.

Note how ungracefully the removal of a message queue is handled. Since a reference count is not maintained with each message queue (as there is for open files), the removal of a queue simply generates errors on the next queue operation by processes still using the queue. Semaphores handle this removal in the same fashion. In contrast, when a file is removed, the file's contents are not deleted until the last open descriptor for the file is closed.

When `msgsnd` returns successfully, the `msqid_ds` structure associated with the message queue is updated to indicate the process ID that made the call (`msg_lspid`), the time that the call was made (`msg_stime`), and that one more message is on the queue (`msg_qnum`).

Messages are retrieved from a queue by `msgrcv`.

```
#include <sys/msg.h>

ssize_t msgrcv(int msqid, void *ptr, size_t nbytes, long type, int flag);
```
Returns: size of data portion of message if OK, −1 on error

As with `msgsnd`, the *ptr* argument points to a long integer (where the message type of the returned message is stored) followed by a data buffer for the actual message data. *nbytes* specifies the size of the data buffer. If the returned message is larger than *nbytes* and the `MSG_NOERROR` bit in *flag* is set, the message is truncated. (In this case, no notification is given to us that the message was truncated, and the remainder of the message is discarded.) If the message is too big and this *flag* value is not specified, an error of `E2BIG` is returned instead (and the message stays on the queue).

The *type* argument lets us specify which message we want.

type == 0   The first message on the queue is returned.

type > 0   The first message on the queue whose message type equals *type* is returned.

type < 0   The first message on the queue whose message type is the lowest value less than or equal to the absolute value of *type* is returned.

A nonzero *type* is used to read the messages in an order other than first in, first out. For example, the *type* could be a priority value if the application assigns priorities to the messages. Another use of this field is to contain the process ID of the client if a single message queue is being used by multiple clients and a single server (as long as a process ID fits in a long integer).

We can specify a *flag* value of `IPC_NOWAIT` to make the operation nonblocking, causing `msgrcv` to return −1 with `errno` set to `ENOMSG` if a message of the specified type is not available. If `IPC_NOWAIT` is not specified, the operation blocks until a message of the specified type is available, the queue is removed from the system (−1 is returned with `errno` set to `EIDRM`), or a signal is caught and the signal handler returns (causing `msgrcv` to return −1 with `errno` set to `EINTR`).

When `msgrcv` succeeds, the kernel updates the `msqid_ds` structure associated with the message queue to indicate the caller's process ID (`msg_lrpid`), the time of the call (`msg_rtime`), and that one less message is on the queue (`msg_qnum`).

Example—Timing Comparison of Message Queues versus Stream Pipes

If we need a bidirectional flow of data between a client and a server, we can use either message queues or full-duplex pipes. (Recall from Figure 15.1 that full-duplex pipes are available through the UNIX domain sockets mechanism (Section 17.3), although some platforms provide a full-duplex pipe mechanism through the `pipe` function.)

Figure 15.27 shows a timing comparison of three of these techniques on Solaris: message queues, STREAMS-based pipes, and UNIX domain sockets. The tests consisted of a program that created the IPC channel, called `fork`, and then sent about 200 megabytes of data from the parent to the child. The data was sent using 100,000 calls to `msgsnd`, with a message length of 2,000 bytes for the message queue, and 100,000 calls to `write`, with a length of 2,000 bytes for the STREAMS-based pipe and UNIX domain socket. The times are all in seconds.

Operation	User	System	Clock
message queue	0.57	3.63	4.22
STREAMS pipe	0.50	3.21	3.71
UNIX domain socket	0.43	4.45	5.59

Figure 15.27 Timing comparison of IPC alternatives on Solaris

These numbers show us that message queues, originally implemented to provide higher-than-normal-speed IPC, are no longer that much faster than other forms of IPC (in fact, STREAMS-based pipes are faster than message queues). (When message queues were implemented, the only other form of IPC available was half-duplex pipes.) When we consider the problems in using message queues (Section 15.6.4), we come to the conclusion that we shouldn't use them for new applications.   □

15.8 Semaphores

A semaphore isn't a form of IPC similar to the others that we've described (pipes, FIFOs, and message queues). A semaphore is a counter used to provide access to a shared data object for multiple processes.

> The Single UNIX Specification includes an alternate set of semaphore interfaces in the semaphore option of its real-time extensions. We do not discuss these interfaces in this text.

To obtain a shared resource, a process needs to do the following:

1. Test the semaphore that controls the resource.

2. If the value of the semaphore is positive, the process can use the resource. In this case, the process decrements the semaphore value by 1, indicating that it has used one unit of the resource.

3. Otherwise, if the value of the semaphore is 0, the process goes to sleep until the semaphore value is greater than 0. When the process wakes up, it returns to step 1.

When a process is done with a shared resource that is controlled by a semaphore, the semaphore value is incremented by 1. If any other processes are asleep, waiting for the semaphore, they are awakened.

To implement semaphores correctly, the test of a semaphore's value and the decrementing of this value must be an atomic operation. For this reason, semaphores are normally implemented inside the kernel.

A common form of semaphore is called a *binary semaphore*. It controls a single resource, and its value is initialized to 1. In general, however, a semaphore can be initialized to any positive value, with the value indicating how many units of the shared resource are available for sharing.

XSI semaphores are, unfortunately, more complicated than this. Three features contribute to this unnecessary complication.

1. A semaphore is not simply a single non-negative value. Instead, we have to define a semaphore as a set of one or more semaphore values. When we create a semaphore, we specify the number of values in the set.

2. The creation of a semaphore (semget) is independent of its initialization (semctl). This is a fatal flaw, since we cannot atomically create a new semaphore set and initialize all the values in the set.

3. Since all forms of XSI IPC remain in existence even when no process is using them, we have to worry about a program that terminates without releasing the semaphores it has been allocated. The *undo* feature that we describe later is supposed to handle this.

The kernel maintains a semid_ds structure for each semaphore set:

```
struct semid_ds {
    struct ipc_perm   sem_perm;  /* see Section 15.6.2 */
    unsigned short    sem_nsems; /* # of semaphores in set */
    time_t            sem_otime; /* last-semop() time */
    time_t            sem_ctime; /* last-change time */
      .
      .
      .
};
```

The Single UNIX Specification defines the fields shown, but implementations can define additional members in the semid_ds structure.

Each semaphore is represented by an anonymous structure containing at least the following members:

```
struct {
    unsigned short   semval;   /* semaphore value, always >= 0 */
    pid_t            sempid;   /* pid for last operation */
    unsigned short   semncnt;  /* # processes awaiting semval>curval */
    unsigned short   semzcnt;  /* # processes awaiting semval==0 */
      .
      .
      .
};
```

Figure 15.28 lists the system limits (Section 15.6.3) that affect semaphore sets.

Description	Typical values			
	FreeBSD 5.2.1	Linux 2.4.22	Mac OS X 10.3	Solaris 9
The maximum value of any semaphore	32,767	32,767	32,767	32,767
The maximum value of any semaphore's adjust-on-exit value	16,384	32,767	16,384	16,384
The maximum number of semaphore sets, systemwide	10	128	87,381	10
The maximum number of semaphores, systemwide	60	32,000	87,381	60
The maximum number of semaphores per semaphore set	60	250	87,381	25
The maximum number of undo structures, systemwide	30	32,000	87,381	30
The maximum number of undo entries per undo structures	10	32	10	10
The maximum number of operations per semop call	100	32	100	10

Figure 15.28 System limits that affect semaphores

The first function to call is semget to obtain a semaphore ID.

```
#include <sys/sem.h>

int semget(key_t key, int nsems, int flag);
```
Returns: semaphore ID if OK, −1 on error

In Section 15.6.1, we described the rules for converting the *key* into an identifier and discussed whether a new set is created or an existing set is referenced. When a new set is created, the following members of the semid_ds structure are initialized.

- The ipc_perm structure is initialized as described in Section 15.6.2. The mode member of this structure is set to the corresponding permission bits of *flag*. These permissions are specified with the values from Figure 15.24.

- sem_otime is set to 0.

- sem_ctime is set to the current time.

- sem_nsems is set to *nsems*.

The number of semaphores in the set is *nsems*. If a new set is being created (typically in the server), we must specify *nsems*. If we are referencing an existing set (a client), we can specify *nsems* as 0.

The semctl function is the catchall for various semaphore operations.

```
#include <sys/sem.h>

int semctl(int semid, int semnum, int cmd,
           ... /* union semun arg */);
```
Returns: (see following)

The fourth argument is optional, depending on the command requested, and if present, is of type semun, a union of various command-specific arguments:

```
union semun {
    int                val;    /* for SETVAL */
    struct semid_ds   *buf;    /* for IPC_STAT and IPC_SET */
    unsigned short    *array; /* for GETALL and SETALL */
};
```

Note that the optional argument is the actual union, not a pointer to the union.

The *cmd* argument specifies one of the following ten commands to be performed on the set specified by *semid*. The five commands that refer to one particular semaphore value use *semnum* to specify one member of the set. The value of *semnum* is between 0 and *nsems–1*, inclusive.

IPC_STAT   Fetch the `semid_ds` structure for this set, storing it in the structure pointed to by *arg.buf*.

IPC_SET   Set the `sem_perm.uid`, `sem_perm.gid`, and `sem_perm.mode` fields from the structure pointed to by *arg.buf* in the `semid_ds` structure associated with this set. This command can be executed only by a process whose effective user ID equals `sem_perm.cuid` or `sem_perm.uid` or by a process with superuser privileges.

IPC_RMID   Remove the semaphore set from the system. This removal is immediate. Any other process still using the semaphore will get an error of `EIDRM` on its next attempted operation on the semaphore. This command can be executed only by a process whose effective user ID equals `sem_perm.cuid` or `sem_perm.uid` or by a process with superuser privileges.

GETVAL   Return the value of `semval` for the member *semnum*.

SETVAL   Set the value of `semval` for the member *semnum*. The value is specified by *arg.val*.

GETPID   Return the value of `sempid` for the member *semnum*.

GETNCNT   Return the value of `semncnt` for the member *semnum*.

GETZCNT   Return the value of `semzcnt` for the member *semnum*.

GETALL   Fetch all the semaphore values in the set. These values are stored in the array pointed to by *arg.array*.

SETALL   Set all the semaphore values in the set to the values pointed to by *arg.array*.

For all the GET commands other than GETALL, the function returns the corresponding value. For the remaining commands, the return value is 0.

The function `semop` atomically performs an array of operations on a semaphore set.

```
#include <sys/sem.h>

int semop(int semid, struct sembuf semoparray[], size_t nops);
```
                                                    Returns: 0 if OK, −1 on error

The *semoparray* argument is a pointer to an array of semaphore operations, represented by `sembuf` structures:

```
struct sembuf {
  unsigned short  sem_num;  /* member # in set (0, 1, ..., nsems-1) */
  short           sem_op;   /* operation (negative, 0, or positive) */
  short           sem_flg;  /* IPC_NOWAIT, SEM_UNDO */
};
```

The *nops* argument specifies the number of operations (elements) in the array.

The operation on each member of the set is specified by the corresponding `sem_op` value. This value can be negative, 0, or positive. (In the following discussion, we refer to the "undo" flag for a semaphore. This flag corresponds to the `SEM_UNDO` bit in the corresponding `sem_flg` member.)

1. The easiest case is when `sem_op` is positive. This case corresponds to the returning of resources by the process. The value of `sem_op` is added to the semaphore's value. If the undo flag is specified, `sem_op` is also subtracted from the semaphore's adjustment value for this process.

2. If `sem_op` is negative, we want to obtain resources that the semaphore controls.

   If the semaphore's value is greater than or equal to the absolute value of `sem_op` (the resources are available), the absolute value of `sem_op` is subtracted from the semaphore's value. This guarantees that the resulting value for the semaphore is greater than or equal to 0. If the undo flag is specified, the absolute value of `sem_op` is also added to the semaphore's adjustment value for this process.

   If the semaphore's value is less than the absolute value of `sem_op` (the resources are not available), the following conditions apply.

   a. If `IPC_NOWAIT` is specified, `semop` returns with an error of `EAGAIN`.

   b. If `IPC_NOWAIT` is not specified, the `semncnt` value for this semaphore is incremented (since the caller is about to go to sleep), and the calling process is suspended until one of the following occurs.

      i. The semaphore's value becomes greater than or equal to the absolute value of `sem_op` (i.e., some other process has released some resources). The value of `semncnt` for this semaphore is decremented (since the calling process is done waiting), and the absolute value of `sem_op` is subtracted from the semaphore's value. If the undo flag is specified, the absolute value of `sem_op` is also added to the semaphore's adjustment value for this process.

      ii. The semaphore is removed from the system. In this case, the function returns an error of `EIDRM`.

      iii. A signal is caught by the process, and the signal handler returns. In this case, the value of `semncnt` for this semaphore is decremented (since the calling process is no longer waiting), and the function returns an error of EINTR.

3. If sem_op is 0, this means that the calling process wants to wait until the semaphore's value becomes 0.

    If the semaphore's value is currently 0, the function returns immediately.

    If the semaphore's value is nonzero, the following conditions apply.

    a. If IPC_NOWAIT is specified, return is made with an error of EAGAIN.

    b. If IPC_NOWAIT is not specified, the semzcnt value for this semaphore is incremented (since the caller is about to go to sleep), and the calling process is suspended until one of the following occurs.

        i.   The semaphore's value becomes 0. The value of semzcnt for this semaphore is decremented (since the calling process is done waiting).

        ii. The semaphore is removed from the system. In this case, the function returns an error of EIDRM.

        iii. A signal is caught by the process, and the signal handler returns. In this case, the value of semzcnt for this semaphore is decremented (since the calling process is no longer waiting), and the function returns an error of EINTR.

The semop function operates atomically; it does either all the operations in the array or none of them.

Semaphore Adjustment on exit

As we mentioned earlier, it is a problem if a process terminates while it has resources allocated through a semaphore. Whenever we specify the SEM_UNDO flag for a semaphore operation and we allocate resources (a sem_op value less than 0), the kernel remembers how many resources we allocated from that particular semaphore (the absolute value of sem_op). When the process terminates, either voluntarily or involuntarily, the kernel checks whether the process has any outstanding semaphore adjustments and, if so, applies the adjustment to the corresponding semaphore.

If we set the value of a semaphore using semctl, with either the SETVAL or SETALL commands, the adjustment value for that semaphore in all processes is set to 0.

Example—Timing Comparison of Semaphores versus Record Locking

If we are sharing a single resource among multiple processes, we can use either a semaphore or record locking. It's interesting to compare the timing differences between the two techniques.

With a semaphore, we create a semaphore set consisting of a single member and initialize the semaphore's value to 1. To allocate the resource, we call `semop` with a `sem_op` of −1; to release the resource, we perform a `sem_op` of +1. We also specify `SEM_UNDO` with each operation, to handle the case of a process that terminates without releasing its resource.

With record locking, we create an empty file and use the first byte of the file (which need not exist) as the lock byte. To allocate the resource, we obtain a write lock on the byte; to release it, we unlock the byte. The properties of record locking guarantee that if a process terminates while holding a lock, then the lock is automatically released by the kernel.

Figure 15.29 shows the time required to perform these two locking techniques on Linux. In each case, the resource was allocated and then released 100,000 times. This was done simultaneously by three different processes. The times in Figure 15.29 are the totals in seconds for all three processes.

Operation	User	System	Clock
semaphores with undo	0.38	0.48	0.86
advisory record locking	0.41	0.95	1.36

Figure 15.29 Timing comparison of locking alternatives on Linux

On Linux, there is about a 60 percent penalty in the elapsed time for record locking compared to semaphore locking.

Even though record locking is slower than semaphore locking, if we're locking a single resource (such as a shared memory segment) and don't need all the fancy features of XSI semaphores, record locking is preferred. The reasons are that it is much simpler to use, and the system takes care of any lingering locks when a process terminates.   □

15.9 Shared Memory

Shared memory allows two or more processes to share a given region of memory. This is the fastest form of IPC, because the data does not need to be copied between the client and the server. The only trick in using shared memory is synchronizing access to a given region among multiple processes. If the server is placing data into a shared memory region, the client shouldn't try to access the data until the server is done. Often, semaphores are used to synchronize shared memory access. (But as we saw at the end of the previous section, record locking can also be used.)

> The Single UNIX Specification includes an alternate set of interfaces to access shared memory in the shared memory objects option of its real-time extensions. We do not cover the real-time extensions in this text.

The kernel maintains a structure with at least the following members for each shared memory segment:

```
struct shmid_ds {
    struct ipc_perm  shm_perm;    /* see Section 15.6.2 */
    size_t           shm_segsz;   /* size of segment in bytes */
    pid_t            shm_lpid;    /* pid of last shmop() */
    pid_t            shm_cpid;    /* pid of creator */
    shmatt_t         shm_nattch;  /* number of current attaches */
    time_t           shm_atime;   /* last-attach time */
    time_t           shm_dtime;   /* last-detach time */
    time_t           shm_ctime;   /* last-change time */
        .
        .
        .
};
```

(Each implementation adds other structure members as needed to support shared memory segments.)

The type shmatt_t is defined to be an unsigned integer at least as large as an unsigned short. Figure 15.30 lists the system limits (Section 15.6.3) that affect shared memory.

Description	Typical values			
	FreeBSD 5.2.1	Linux 2.4.22	Mac OS X 10.3	Solaris 9
The maximum size in bytes of a shared memory segment	33,554,432	33,554,432	4,194,304	8,388,608
The minimum size in bytes of a shared memory segment	1	1	1	1
The maximum number of shared memory segments, systemwide	192	4,096	32	100
The maximum number of shared memory segments, per process	128	4,096	8	6

Figure 15.30 System limits that affect shared memory

The first function called is usually shmget, to obtain a shared memory identifier.

```
#include <sys/shm.h>

int shmget(key_t key, size_t size, int flag);
                                   Returns: shared memory ID if OK, −1 on error
```

In Section 15.6.1, we described the rules for converting the *key* into an identifier and whether a new segment is created or an existing segment is referenced. When a new segment is created, the following members of the shmid_ds structure are initialized.

- The ipc_perm structure is initialized as described in Section 15.6.2. The mode member of this structure is set to the corresponding permission bits of *flag*. These permissions are specified with the values from Figure 15.24.

- shm_lpid, shm_nattch, shm_atime, and shm_dtime are all set to 0.

- shm_ctime is set to the current time.

- shm_segsz is set to the *size* requested.

The *size* parameter is the size of the shared memory segment in bytes. Implementations will usually round up the size to a multiple of the system's page size, but if an application specifies *size* as a value other than an integral multiple of the system's page size, the remainder of the last page will be unavailable for use. If a new segment is being created (typically in the server), we must specify its *size*. If we are referencing an existing segment (a client), we can specify *size* as 0. When a new segment is created, the contents of the segment are initialized with zeros.

The shmctl function is the catchall for various shared memory operations.

```
#include <sys/shm.h>

int shmctl(int shmid, int cmd, struct shmid_ds *buf);
```

Returns: 0 if OK, −1 on error

The *cmd* argument specifies one of the following five commands to be performed, on the segment specified by *shmid*.

IPC_STAT   Fetch the shmid_ds structure for this segment, storing it in the structure pointed to by *buf*.

IPC_SET   Set the following three fields from the structure pointed to by *buf* in the shmid_ds structure associated with this shared memory segment: shm_perm.uid, shm_perm.gid, and shm_perm.mode. This command can be executed only by a process whose effective user ID equals shm_perm.cuid or shm_perm.uid or by a process with superuser privileges.

IPC_RMID   Remove the shared memory segment set from the system. Since an attachment count is maintained for shared memory segments (the shm_nattch field in the shmid_ds structure), the segment is not removed until the last process using the segment terminates or detaches it. Regardless of whether the segment is still in use, the segment's identifier is immediately removed so that shmat can no longer attach the segment. This command can be executed only by a process whose effective user ID equals shm_perm.cuid or shm_perm.uid or by a process with superuser privileges.

Two additional commands are provided by Linux and Solaris, but are not part of the Single UNIX Specification.

SHM_LOCK   Lock the shared memory segment in memory. This command can be executed only by the superuser.

SHM_UNLOCK Unlock the shared memory segment. This command can be executed only by the superuser.

Once a shared memory segment has been created, a process attaches it to its address space by calling shmat.

```
#include <sys/shm.h>

void *shmat(int shmid, const void *addr, int flag);
```
                    Returns: pointer to shared memory segment if OK, −1 on error

The address in the calling process at which the segment is attached depends on the *addr* argument and whether the SHM_RND bit is specified in *flag*.

- If *addr* is 0, the segment is attached at the first available address selected by the kernel. This is the recommended technique.

- If *addr* is nonzero and SHM_RND is not specified, the segment is attached at the address given by *addr*.

- If *addr* is nonzero and SHM_RND is specified, the segment is attached at the address given by *(addr − (addr* modulus SHMLBA*))*. The SHM_RND command stands for "round." SHMLBA stands for "low boundary address multiple" and is always a power of 2. What the arithmetic does is round the address down to the next multiple of SHMLBA.

Unless we plan to run the application on only a single type of hardware (which is highly unlikely today), we should not specify the address where the segment is to be attached. Instead, we should specify an *addr* of 0 and let the system choose the address.

If the SHM_RDONLY bit is specified in *flag*, the segment is attached read-only. Otherwise, the segment is attached read–write.

The value returned by shmat is the address at which the segment is attached, or −1 if an error occurred. If shmat succeeds, the kernel will increment the shm_nattch counter in the shmid_ds structure associated with the shared memory segment.

When we're done with a shared memory segment, we call shmdt to detach it. Note that this does not remove the identifier and its associated data structure from the system. The identifier remains in existence until some process (often a server) specifically removes it by calling shmctl with a command of IPC_RMID.

```
#include <sys/shm.h>

int shmdt(void *addr);
```
                                                     Returns: 0 if OK, −1 on error

The *addr* argument is the value that was returned by a previous call to shmat. If successful, shmdt will decrement the shm_nattch counter in the associated shmid_ds structure.

Example

Where a kernel places shared memory segments that are attached with an address of 0 is highly system dependent. Figure 15.31 shows a program that prints some information on where one particular system places various types of data.

```c
#include "apue.h"
#include <sys/shm.h>

#define ARRAY_SIZE  40000
#define MALLOC_SIZE 100000
#define SHM_SIZE    100000
#define SHM_MODE    0600    /* user read/write */

char    array[ARRAY_SIZE];  /* uninitialized data = bss */

int
main(void)
{
    int     shmid;
    char    *ptr, *shmptr;

    printf("array[] from %lx to %lx\n", (unsigned long)&array[0],
      (unsigned long)&array[ARRAY_SIZE]);
    printf("stack around %lx\n", (unsigned long)&shmid);

    if ((ptr = malloc(MALLOC_SIZE)) == NULL)
        err_sys("malloc error");
    printf("malloced from %lx to %lx\n", (unsigned long)ptr,
      (unsigned long)ptr+MALLOC_SIZE);

    if ((shmid = shmget(IPC_PRIVATE, SHM_SIZE, SHM_MODE)) < 0)
        err_sys("shmget error");
    if ((shmptr = shmat(shmid, 0, 0)) == (void *)-1)
        err_sys("shmat error");
    printf("shared memory attached from %lx to %lx\n",
      (unsigned long)shmptr, (unsigned long)shmptr+SHM_SIZE);

    if (shmctl(shmid, IPC_RMID, 0) < 0)
        err_sys("shmctl error");

    exit(0);
}
```

Figure 15.31 Print where various types of data are stored

Running this program on an Intel-based Linux system gives us the following output:

```
$ ./a.out
array[] from 804a080 to 8053cc0
stack around bffff9e4
malloced from 8053cc8 to 806c368
shared memory attached from 40162000 to 4017a6a0
```

Figure 15.32 shows a picture of this, similar to what we said was a typical memory layout in Figure 7.6. Note that the shared memory segment is placed well below the stack.   □

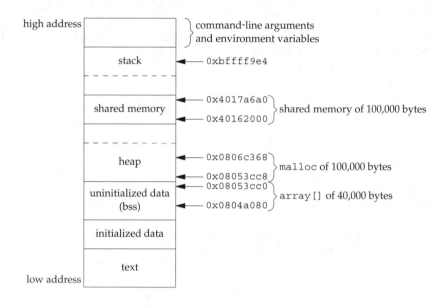

Figure 15.32 Memory layout on an Intel-based Linux system

Recall that the mmap function (Section 14.9) can be used to map portions of a file into the address space of a process. This is conceptually similar to attaching a shared memory segment using the shmat XSI IPC function. The main difference is that the memory segment mapped with mmap is backed by a file, whereas no file is associated with an XSI shared memory segment.

Example—Memory Mapping of /dev/zero

Shared memory can be used between unrelated processes. But if the processes are related, some implementations provide a different technique.

> The following technique works on FreeBSD 5.2.1, Linux 2.4.22, and Solaris 9. Mac OS X 10.3 currently doesn't support the mapping of character devices into the address space of a process.

The device /dev/zero is an infinite source of 0 bytes when read. This device also accepts any data that is written to it, ignoring the data. Our interest in this device for IPC arises from its special properties when it is memory mapped.

- An unnamed memory region is created whose size is the second argument to mmap, rounded up to the nearest page size on the system.

- The memory region is initialized to 0.

- Multiple processes can share this region if a common ancestor specifies the MAP_SHARED flag to mmap.

The program in Figure 15.33 is an example that uses this special device.

```
#include "apue.h"
#include <fcntl.h>
#include <sys/mman.h>

#define NLOOPS      1000
#define SIZE        sizeof(long)    /* size of shared memory area */

static int
update(long *ptr)
{
    return((*ptr)++);   /* return value before increment */
}

int
main(void)
{
    int     fd, i, counter;
    pid_t   pid;
    void    *area;

    if ((fd = open("/dev/zero", O_RDWR)) < 0)
        err_sys("open error");
    if ((area = mmap(0, SIZE, PROT_READ | PROT_WRITE, MAP_SHARED,
      fd, 0)) == MAP_FAILED)
        err_sys("mmap error");
    close(fd);      /* can close /dev/zero now that it's mapped */

    TELL_WAIT();

    if ((pid = fork()) < 0) {
        err_sys("fork error");
    } else if (pid > 0) {           /* parent */
        for (i = 0; i < NLOOPS; i += 2) {
            if ((counter = update((long *)area)) != i)
                err_quit("parent: expected %d, got %d", i, counter);

            TELL_CHILD(pid);
            WAIT_CHILD();
        }
    } else {                        /* child */
        for (i = 1; i < NLOOPS + 1; i += 2) {
            WAIT_PARENT();

            if ((counter = update((long *)area)) != i)
                err_quit("child: expected %d, got %d", i, counter);

            TELL_PARENT(getppid());
        }
    }

    exit(0);
}
```

Figure 15.33 IPC between parent and child using memory mapped I/O of /dev/zero

The program opens the /dev/zero device and calls mmap, specifying a size of a long integer. Note that once the region is mapped, we can close the device. The process then creates a child. Since MAP_SHARED was specified in the call to mmap, writes to the memory-mapped region by one process are seen by the other process. (If we had specified MAP_PRIVATE instead, this example wouldn't work.)

The parent and the child then alternate running, incrementing a long integer in the shared memory-mapped region, using the synchronization functions from Section 8.9. The memory-mapped region is initialized to 0 by mmap. The parent increments it to 1, then the child increments it to 2, then the parent increments it to 3, and so on. Note that we have to use parentheses when we increment the value of the long integer in the update function, since we are incrementing the value and not the pointer.

The advantage of using /dev/zero in the manner that we've shown is that an actual file need not exist before we call mmap to create the mapped region. Mapping /dev/zero automatically creates a mapped region of the specified size. The disadvantage of this technique is that it works only between related processes. With related processes, however, it is probably simpler and more efficient to use threads (Chapters 11 and 12). Note that regardless of which technique is used, we still need to synchronize access to the shared data.   □

Example—Anonymous Memory Mapping

Many implementations provide anonymous memory mapping, a facility similar to the /dev/zero feature. To use this facility, we specify the MAP_ANON flag to mmap and specify the file descriptor as –1. The resulting region is anonymous (since it's not associated with a pathname through a file descriptor) and creates a memory region that can be shared with descendant processes.

> The anonymous memory-mapping facility is supported by all four platforms discussed in this text. Note, however, that Linux defines the MAP_ANONYMOUS flag for this facility, but defines the MAP_ANON flag to be the same value for improved application portability.

To modify the program in Figure 15.33 to use this facility, we make three changes: (a) remove the open of /dev/zero, (b) remove the close of fd, and (c) change the call to mmap to the following:

```
if ((area = mmap(0, SIZE, PROT_READ | PROT_WRITE,
                 MAP_ANON | MAP_SHARED, -1, 0)) == MAP_FAILED)
```

In this call, we specify the MAP_ANON flag and set the file descriptor to –1. The rest of the program from Figure 15.33 is unchanged.   □

The last two examples illustrate sharing memory among multiple related processes. If shared memory is required between unrelated processes, there are two alternatives. Applications can use the XSI shared memory functions, or they can use mmap to map the same file into their address spaces using the MAP_SHARED flag.

15.10 Client–Server Properties

Let's detail some of the properties of clients and servers that are affected by the various types of IPC used between them. The simplest type of relationship is to have the client `fork` and `exec` the desired server. Two half-duplex pipes can be created before the `fork` to allow data to be transferred in both directions. Figure 15.16 is an example of this. The server that is executed can be a set-user-ID program, giving it special privileges. Also, the server can determine the real identity of the client by looking at its real user ID. (Recall from Section 8.10 that the real user ID and real group ID don't change across an `exec`.)

With this arrangement, we can build an *open server*. (We show an implementation of this client–server in Section 17.5.) It opens files for the client instead of the client calling the `open` function. This way, additional permission checking can be added, above and beyond the normal UNIX system user/group/other permissions. We assume that the server is a set-user-ID program, giving it additional permissions (root permission, perhaps). The server uses the real user ID of the client to determine whether to give it access to the requested file. This way, we can build a server that allows certain users permissions that they don't normally have.

In this example, since the server is a child of the parent, all the server can do is pass back the contents of the file to the parent. Although this works fine for regular files, it can't be used for special device files, for example. We would like to be able to have the server open the requested file and pass back the file descriptor. Whereas a parent can pass a child an open descriptor, a child cannot pass a descriptor back to the parent (unless special programming techniques are used, which we cover in Chapter 17).

We showed the next type of server in Figure 15.23. The server is a daemon process that is contacted using some form of IPC by all clients. We can't use pipes for this type of client–server. A form of named IPC is required, such as FIFOs or message queues. With FIFOs, we saw that an individual per client FIFO is also required if the server is to send data back to the client. If the client–server application sends data only from the client to the server, a single well-known FIFO suffices. (The System V line printer spooler used this form of client–server arrangement. The client was the `lp(1)` command, and the server was the `lpsched` daemon process. A single FIFO was used, since the flow of data was only from the client to the server. Nothing was sent back to the client.)

Multiple possibilities exist with message queues.

1. A single queue can be used between the server and all the clients, using the type field of each message to indicate the message recipient. For example, the clients can send their requests with a type field of 1. Included in the request must be the client's process ID. The server then sends the response with the type field set to the client's process ID. The server receives only the messages with a type field of 1 (the fourth argument for `msgrcv`), and the clients receive only the messages with a type field equal to their process IDs.

2. Alternatively, an individual message queue can be used for each client. Before sending the first request to a server, each client creates its own message queue

with a key of IPC_PRIVATE. The server also has its own queue, with a key or identifier known to all clients. The client sends its first request to the server's well-known queue, and this request must contain the message queue ID of the client's queue. The server sends its first response to the client's queue, and all future requests and responses are exchanged on this queue.

One problem with this technique is that each client-specific queue usually has only a single message on it: a request for the server or a response for a client. This seems wasteful of a limited systemwide resource (a message queue), and a FIFO can be used instead. Another problem is that the server has to read messages from multiple queues. Neither select nor poll works with message queues.

Either of these two techniques using message queues can be implemented using shared memory segments and a synchronization method (a semaphore or record locking).

The problem with this type of client–server relationship (the client and the server being unrelated processes) is for the server to identify the client accurately. Unless the server is performing a nonprivileged operation, it is essential that the server know who the client is. This is required, for example, if the server is a set-user-ID program. Although all these forms of IPC go through the kernel, there is no facility provided by them to have the kernel identify the sender.

With message queues, if a single queue is used between the client and the server (so that only a single message is on the queue at a time, for example), the msg_lspid of the queue contains the process ID of the other process. But when writing the server, we want the effective user ID of the client, not its process ID. There is no portable way to obtain the effective user ID, given the process ID. (Naturally, the kernel maintains both values in the process table entry, but other than rummaging around through the kernel's memory, we can't obtain one, given the other.)

We'll use the following technique in Section 17.3 to allow the server to identify the client. The same technique can be used with FIFOs, message queues, semaphores, or shared memory. For the following description, assume that FIFOs are being used, as in Figure 15.23. The client must create its own FIFO and set the file access permissions of the FIFO so that only user-read and user-write are on. We assume that the server has superuser privileges (or else it probably wouldn't care about the client's true identity), so the server can still read and write to this FIFO. When the server receives the client's first request on the server's well-known FIFO (which must contain the identity of the client-specific FIFO), the server calls either stat or fstat on the client-specific FIFO. The server assumes that the effective user ID of the client is the owner of the FIFO (the st_uid field of the stat structure). The server verifies that only the user-read and user-write permissions are enabled. As another check, the server should also look at the three times associated with the FIFO (the st_atime, st_mtime, and st_ctime fields of the stat structure) to verify that they are recent (no older than 15 or 30 seconds, for example). If a malicious client can create a FIFO with someone else as the owner and set the file's permission bits to user-read and user-write only, then the system has other fundamental security problems.

To use this technique with XSI IPC, recall that the `ipc_perm` structure associated with each message queue, semaphore, and shared memory segment identifies the creator of the IPC structure (the `cuid` and `cgid` fields). As with the example using FIFOs, the server should require the client to create the IPC structure and have the client set the access permissions to user-read and user-write only. The times associated with the IPC structure should also be verified by the server to be recent (since these IPC structures hang around until explicitly deleted).

We'll see in Section 17.2.2 that a far better way of doing this authentication is for the kernel to provide the effective user ID and effective group ID of the client. This is done by the STREAMS subsystem when file descriptors are passed between processes.

15.11 Summary

We've detailed numerous forms of interprocess communication: pipes, named pipes (FIFOs), and the three forms of IPC commonly called XSI IPC (message queues, semaphores, and shared memory). Semaphores are really a synchronization primitive, not true IPC, and are often used to synchronize access to a shared resource, such as a shared memory segment. With pipes, we looked at the implementation of the `popen` function, at coprocesses, and the pitfalls that can be encountered with the standard I/O library's buffering.

After comparing the timing of message queues versus full-duplex pipes, and semaphores versus record locking, we can make the following recommendations: learn pipes and FIFOs, since these two basic techniques can still be used effectively in numerous applications. Avoid using message queues and semaphores in any new applications. Full-duplex pipes and record locking should be considered instead, as they are far simpler. Shared memory still has its use, although the same functionality can be provided through the use of the `mmap` function (Section 14.9).

In the next chapter, we will look at network IPC, which can allow processes to communicate across machine boundaries.

Exercises

15.1 In the program shown in Figure 15.6, remove the `close` right before the `waitpid` at the end of the parent code. Explain what happens.

15.2 In the program in Figure 15.6, remove the `waitpid` at the end of the parent code. Explain what happens.

15.3 What happens if the argument to `popen` is a nonexistent command? Write a small program to test this.

15.4 In the program shown in Figure 15.18, remove the signal handler, execute the program, and then terminate the child. After entering a line of input, how can you tell that the parent was terminated by `SIGPIPE`?

15.5 In the program in Figure 15.18, use the standard I/O library for reading and writing the pipes instead of `read` and `write`.

15.6   The Rationale for POSIX.1 gives as one of the reasons for adding the `waitpid` function that most pre-POSIX.1 systems can't handle the following:

```
if ((fp = popen("/bin/true", "r")) == NULL)
    ...
if ((rc = system("sleep 100")) == -1)
    ...
if (pclose(fp) == -1)
    ...
```

What happens in this code if `waitpid` isn't available and `wait` is used instead?

15.7   Explain how `select` and `poll` handle an input descriptor that is a pipe, when the pipe is closed by the writer. To determine the answer, write two small test programs: one using `select` and one using `poll`.

Redo this exercise, looking at an output descriptor that is a pipe, when the read end is closed.

15.8   What happens if the *cmdstring* executed by `popen` with a *type* of `"r"` writes to its standard error?

15.9   Since `popen` invokes a shell to execute its *cmdstring* argument, what happens when `cmdstring` terminates? (Hint: draw all the processes involved.)

15.10 POSIX.1 specifically states that opening a FIFO for read–write is undefined. Although most UNIX systems allow this, show another method for opening a FIFO for both reading and writing, without blocking.

15.11 Unless a file contains sensitive or confidential data, allowing other users to read the file causes no harm. (It is usually considered antisocial, however, to go snooping around in other people's files.) But what happens if a malicious process reads a message from a message queue that is being used by a server and several clients? What information does the malicious process need to know to read the message queue?

15.12 Write a program that does the following. Execute a loop five times: create a message queue, print the queue identifier, delete the message queue. Then execute the next loop five times: create a message queue with a key of `IPC_PRIVATE`, and place a message on the queue. After the program terminates, look at the message queues using `ipcs(1)`. Explain what is happening with the queue identifiers.

15.13 Describe how to build a linked list of data objects in a shared memory segment. What would you store as the list pointers?

15.14 Draw a time line of the program in Figure 15.33 showing the value of the variable `i` in both the parent and child, the value of the long integer in the shared memory region, and the value returned by the `update` function. Assume that the child runs first after the `fork`.

15.15 Redo the program in Figure 15.33 using the XSI shared memory functions from Section 15.9 instead of the shared memory-mapped region.

15.16 Redo the program in Figure 15.33 using the XSI semaphore functions from Section 15.8 to alternate between the parent and the child.

15.17 Redo the program in Figure 15.33 using advisory record locking to alternate between the parent and the child.

16

Network IPC: Sockets

16.1 Introduction

In the previous chapter, we looked at pipes, FIFOs, message queues, semaphores, and shared memory: the classical methods of IPC provided by various UNIX systems. These mechanisms allow processes running on the same computer to communicate with one another. In this chapter, we look at the mechanisms that allow processes running on different computers (connected to a common network) to communicate with one another: network IPC.

In this chapter, we describe the socket network IPC interface, which can be used by processes to communicate with other processes, regardless of where they are running: on the same machine or on different machines. Indeed, this was one of the design goals of the socket interface. The same interfaces can be used for both intermachine communication and intramachine communication. Although the socket interface can be used to communicate using many different network protocols, we will restrict our discussion to the TCP/IP protocol suite in this chapter, since it is the de facto standard for communicating over the Internet.

The socket API as specified by POSIX.1 is based on the 4.4BSD socket interface. Although minor changes have been made over the years, the current socket interface closely resembles the interface when it was originally introduced in 4.2BSD in the early 1980s.

This chapter is only an overview of the socket API. Stevens, Fenner, and Rudoff [2004] discuss the socket interface in detail in the definitive text on network programming in the UNIX System.

16.2   Socket Descriptors

A socket is an abstraction of a communication endpoint. Just as they would use file descriptors to access a file, applications use socket descriptors to access sockets. Socket descriptors are implemented as file descriptors in the UNIX System. Indeed, many of the functions that deal with file descriptors, such as `read` and `write`, will work with a socket descriptor.

To create a socket, we call the `socket` function.

```
#include <sys/socket.h>

int socket(int domain, int type, int protocol);
```
                                          Returns: file (socket) descriptor if OK, –1 on error

The *domain* argument determines the nature of the communication, including the address format (described in more detail in the next section). Figure 16.1 summarizes the domains specified by POSIX.1. The constants start with AF_ (for *address family*) because each domain has its own format for representing an address.

Domain	Description
AF_INET	IPv4 Internet domain
AF_INET6	IPv6 Internet domain
AF_UNIX	UNIX domain
AF_UNSPEC	unspecified

Figure 16.1   Socket communication domains

We discuss the UNIX domain in Section 17.3. Most systems define the AF_LOCAL domain also, which is an alias for AF_UNIX. The AF_UNSPEC domain is a wildcard that represents "any" domain. Historically, some platforms provide support for additional network protocols, such as AF_IPX for the NetWare protocol family, but domain constants for these protocols are not defined by the POSIX.1 standard.

The *type* argument determines the type of the socket, which further determines the communication characteristics. The socket types defined by POSIX.1 are summarized in Figure 16.2, but implementations are free to add support for additional types.

Type	Description
SOCK_DGRAM	fixed-length, connectionless, unreliable messages
SOCK_RAW	datagram interface to IP (optional in POSIX.1)
SOCK_SEQPACKET	fixed-length, sequenced, reliable, connection-oriented messages
SOCK_STREAM	sequenced, reliable, bidirectional, connection-oriented byte streams

Figure 16.2   Socket types

The *protocol* argument is usually zero, to select the default protocol for the given domain and socket type. When multiple protocols are supported for the same domain and socket type, we can use the *protocol* argument to select a particular protocol. The default protocol for a SOCK_STREAM socket in the AF_INET communication domain is TCP (Transmission Control Protocol). The default protocol for a SOCK_DGRAM socket in the AF_INET communication domain is UDP (User Datagram Protocol).

With a datagram (SOCK_DGRAM) interface, no logical connection needs to exist between peers for them to communicate. All you need to do is send a message addressed to the socket being used by the peer process.

A datagram, therefore, provides a connectionless service. A byte stream (SOCK_STREAM), on the other hand, requires that, before you can exchange data, you set up a logical connection between your socket and the socket belonging to the peer you want to communicate with.

A datagram is a self-contained message. Sending a datagram is analogous to mailing someone a letter. You can mail many letters, but you can't guarantee the order of delivery, and some might get lost along the way. Each letter contains the address of the recipient, making the letter independent from all the others. Each letter can even go to different recipients.

In contrast, using a connection-oriented protocol for communicating with a peer is like making a phone call. First, you need to establish a connection by placing a phone call, but after the connection is in place, you can communicate bidirectionally with each other. The connection is a peer-to-peer communication channel over which you talk. Your words contain no addressing information, as a point-to-point virtual connection exists between both ends of the call, and the connection itself implies a particular source and destination.

With a SOCK_STREAM socket, applications are unaware of message boundaries, since the socket provides a byte stream service. This means that when we read data from a socket, it might not return the same number of bytes written by the process sending us data. We will eventually get everything sent to us, but it might take several function calls.

A SOCK_SEQPACKET socket is just like a SOCK_STREAM socket except that we get a message-based service instead of a byte-stream service. This means that the amount of data received from a SOCK_SEQPACKET socket is the same amount as was written. The Stream Control Transmission Protocol (SCTP) provides a sequential packet service in the Internet domain.

A SOCK_RAW socket provides a datagram interface directly to the underlying network layer (which means IP in the Internet domain). Applications are responsible for building their own protocol headers when using this interface, because the transport protocols (TCP and UDP, for example) are bypassed. Superuser privileges are required to create a raw socket to prevent malicious applications from creating packets that might bypass established security mechanisms.

Calling socket is similar to calling open. In both cases, you get a file descriptor that can be used for I/O. When you are done using the file descriptor, you call close to relinquish access to the file or socket and free up the file descriptor for reuse.

Although a socket descriptor is actually a file descriptor, you can't use a socket descriptor with every function that accepts a file descriptor argument. Figure 16.3 summarizes most of the functions we've described so far that are used with file descriptors and describes how they behave when used with a socket descriptor. Unspecified and implementation-defined behavior usually means that the function doesn't work with socket descriptors. For example, lseek doesn't work with sockets, since sockets don't support the concept of a file offset.

Function	Behavior with socket
close (Section 3.3)	deallocates the socket
dup, dup2 (Section 3.12)	duplicates the file descriptor as normal
fchdir (Section 4.22)	fails with errno set to ENOTDIR
fchmod (Section 4.9)	unspecified
fchown (Section 4.11)	implementation defined
fcntl (Section 3.14)	some commands supported, including F_DUPFD, F_GETFD, F_GETFL, F_GETOWN, F_SETFD, F_SETFL, and F_SETOWN
fdatasync, fsync (Section 3.13)	implementation defined
fstat (Section 4.2)	some stat structure members supported, but how left up to the implementation
ftruncate (Section 4.13)	unspecified
getmsg, getpmsg (Section 14.4)	works if sockets are implemented with STREAMS (i.e., on Solaris)
ioctl (Section 3.15)	some commands work, depending on underlying device driver
lseek (Section 3.6)	implementation defined (usually fails with errno set to ESPIPE)
mmap (Section 14.9)	unspecified
poll (Section 14.5.2)	works as expected
putmsg, putpmsg (Section 14.4)	works if sockets are implemented with STREAMS (i.e., on Solaris)
read (Section 3.7) and readv (Section 14.7)	equivalent to recv (Section 16.5) without any flags
select (Section 14.5.1)	works as expected
write (Section 3.8) and writev (Section 14.7)	equivalent to send (Section 16.5) without any flags

Figure 16.3 How file descriptor functions act with sockets

Communication on a socket is bidirectional. We can disable I/O on a socket with the shutdown function.

```
#include <sys/socket.h>

int shutdown(int sockfd, int how);
```
                                                        Returns: 0 if OK, −1 on error

If *how* is SHUT_RD, then reading from the socket is disabled. If *how* is SHUT_WR, then we can't use the socket for transmitting data. We can use SHUT_RDWR to disable both data transmission and reception.

Given that we can close a socket, why is shutdown needed? There are several reasons. First, close will deallocate the network endpoint only when the last active reference is closed. This means that if we duplicate the socket (with dup, for example), the socket won't be deallocated until we close the last file descriptor referring to it. The shutdown function allows us to deactivate a socket independently of the number of active file descriptors referencing it. Second, it is sometimes convenient to shut a socket down in one direction only. For example, we can shut a socket down for writing if we want the process we are communicating with to be able to determine when we are done transmitting data, while still allowing us to use the socket to receive data sent to us by the process.

16.3 Addressing

In the previous section, we learned how to create and destroy a socket. Before we learn to do something useful with a socket, we need to learn how to identify the process that we want to communicate with. Identifying the process has two components. The machine's network address helps us identify the computer on the network we wish to contact, and the service helps us identify the particular process on the computer.

16.3.1 Byte Ordering

When communicating with processes running on the same computer, we generally don't have to worry about byte ordering. The byte order is a characteristic of the processor architecture, dictating how bytes are ordered within larger data types, such as integers. Figure 16.4 shows how the bytes within a 32-bit integer are numbered.

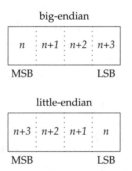

Figure 16.4 Byte order in a 32-bit integer

If the processor architecture supports *big-endian* byte order, then the highest byte address occurs in the least significant byte (LSB). *Little-endian* byte order is the opposite: the least significant byte contains the lowest byte address. Note that regardless of the byte ordering, the most significant byte (MSB) is always on the left, and the least significant byte is always on the right. Thus, if we were to assign a 32-bit integer the value 0x04030201, the most significant byte would contain 4, and the least significant byte would contain 1, regardless of the byte ordering. If we were then to cast a character pointer (cp) to the address of the integer, we would see a difference from the byte ordering. On a little-endian processor, cp[0] would refer to the least significant byte and contain 1; cp[3] would refer to the most significant byte and contain 4. Compare that to a big-endian processor, where cp[0] would contain 4, referring to the most significant byte, and cp[3] would contain 1, referring to the least significant byte. Figure 16.5 summarizes the byte ordering for the four platforms discussed in this text.

Operating system	Processor architecture	Byte order
FreeBSD 5.2.1	Intel Pentium	little-endian
Linux 2.4.22	Intel Pentium	little-endian
Mac OS X 10.3	PowerPC	big-endian
Solaris 9	Sun SPARC	big-endian

Figure 16.5 Byte order for test platforms

To confuse matters further, some processors can be configured for either little-endian or big-endian operation.

Network protocols specify a byte ordering so that heterogeneous computer systems can exchange protocol information without confusing the byte ordering. The TCP/IP protocol suite uses big-endian byte order. The byte ordering becomes visible to applications when they exchange formatted data. With TCP/IP, addresses are presented in network byte order, so applications sometimes need to translate them between the processor's byte order and the network byte order. This is common when printing an address in a human-readable form, for example.

Four common functions are provided to convert between the processor byte order and the network byte order for TCP/IP applications.

```
#include <arpa/inet.h>

uint32_t htonl(uint32_t hostint32);
```
Returns: 32-bit integer in network byte order

```
uint16_t htons(uint16_t hostint16);
```
Returns: 16-bit integer in network byte order

```
uint32_t ntohl(uint32_t netint32);
```
Returns: 32-bit integer in host byte order

```
uint16_t ntohs(uint16_t netint16);
```
Returns: 16-bit integer in host byte order

The h is for "host" byte order, and the n is for "network" byte order. The l is for "long" (i.e., 4-byte) integer, and the s is for "short" (i.e., 2-byte) integer. These four functions are defined in <arpa/inet.h>, although some older systems define them in <netinet/in.h>.

16.3.2 Address Formats

An address identifies a socket endpoint in a particular communication domain. The address format is specific to the particular domain. So that addresses with different formats can be passed to the socket functions, the addresses are cast to a generic sockaddr address structure:

```
struct sockaddr {
  sa_family_t    sa_family;   /* address family */
  char           sa_data[];   /* variable-length address */
  .
  .
  .
};
```

Implementations are free to add additional members and define a size for the sa_data member. For example, on Linux, the structure is defined as

```
struct sockaddr {
  sa_family_t  sa_family;    /* address family */
  char         sa_data[14];  /* variable-length address */
};
```

But on FreeBSD, the structure is defined as

```
struct sockaddr {
  unsigned char  sa_len;      /* total length */
  sa_family_t    sa_family;   /* address family */
  char           sa_data[14]; /* variable-length address */
};
```

Internet addresses are defined in <netinet/in.h>. In the IPv4 Internet domain (AF_INET), a socket address is represented by a sockaddr_in structure:

```
struct in_addr {
  in_addr_t      s_addr;      /* IPv4 address */
};

struct sockaddr_in {
  sa_family_t    sin_family;  /* address family */
  in_port_t      sin_port;    /* port number */
  struct in_addr sin_addr;    /* IPv4 address */
};
```

The in_port_t data type is defined to be a uint16_t. The in_addr_t data type is defined to be a uint32_t. These integer data types specify the number of bits in the data type and are defined in <stdint.h>.

In contrast to the AF_INET domain, the IPv6 Internet domain (AF_INET6) socket address is represented by a sockaddr_in6 structure:

```
struct in6_addr {
  uint8_t        s6_addr[16]; /* IPv6 address */
};
```

```
struct sockaddr_in6 {
  sa_family_t     sin6_family;    /* address family */
  in_port_t       sin6_port;      /* port number */
  uint32_t        sin6_flowinfo;  /* traffic class and flow info */
  struct in6_addr sin6_addr;      /* IPv6 address */
  uint32_t        sin6_scope_id;  /* set of interfaces for scope */
};
```

These are the definitions required by the Single UNIX Specification. Individual implementations are free to add additional fields. For example, on Linux, the sockaddr_in structure is defined as

```
struct sockaddr_in {
  sa_family_t     sin_family;     /* address family */
  in_port_t       sin_port;       /* port number */
  struct in_addr  sin_addr;       /* IPv4 address */
  unsigned char   sin_zero[8];    /* filler */
};
```

where the sin_zero member is a filler field that should be set to all-zero values.

Note that although the sockaddr_in and sockaddr_in6 structures are quite different, they are both passed to the socket routines cast to a sockaddr structure. In Section 17.3, we will see that the structure of a UNIX domain socket address is different from both of the Internet domain socket address formats.

It is sometimes necessary to print an address in a format that is understandable by a person instead of a computer. The BSD networking software included the inet_addr and inet_ntoa functions to convert between the binary address format and a string in dotted-decimal notation (a.b.c.d). These functions, however, work only with IPv4 addresses. Two new functions—inet_ntop and inet_pton—support similar functionality and work with both IPv4 and IPv6 addresses.

```
#include <arpa/inet.h>

const char *inet_ntop(int domain, const void *restrict addr,
                      char *restrict str, socklen_t size);
```

                    Returns: pointer to address string on success, NULL on error

```
int inet_pton(int domain, const char *restrict str,
              void *restrict addr);
```

                    Returns: 1 on success, 0 if the format is invalid, or −1 on error

---

The inet_ntop function converts a binary address in network byte order into a text string; inet_pton converts a text string into a binary address in network byte order. Only two domain values are supported: AF_INET and AF_INET6.

For inet_ntop, the size parameter specifies the size of the buffer (str) to hold the text string. Two constants are defined to make our job easier: INET_ADDRSTRLEN is large enough to hold a text string representing an IPv4 address, and INET6_ADDRSTRLEN is large enough to hold a text string representing an IPv6 address. For inet_pton, the addr buffer needs to be large enough to hold a 32-bit address if domain is AF_INET or large enough to hold a 128-bit address if domain is AF_INET6.

16.3.3 Address Lookup

Ideally, an application won't have to be aware of the internal structure of a socket address. If an application simply passes socket addresses around as `sockaddr` structures and doesn't rely on any protocol-specific features, then the application will work with many different protocols that provide the same type of service.

Historically, the BSD networking software has provided interfaces to access the various network configuration information. In Section 6.7, we briefly discussed the networking data files and the functions used to access them. In this section, we discuss them in a little more detail and introduce the newer functions used to look up addressing information.

The network configuration information returned by these functions can be kept in a number of places. They can be kept in static files (`/etc/hosts`, `/etc/services`, etc.), or they can be managed by a name service, such as DNS (Domain Name System) or NIS (Network Information Service). Regardless of where the information is kept, the same functions can be used to access it.

The hosts known by a given computer system are found by calling `gethostent`.

```
#include <netdb.h>

struct hostent *gethostent(void);
```
Returns: pointer if OK, NULL on error

```
void sethostent(int stayopen);

void endhostent(void);
```

If the host database file isn't already open, `gethostent` will open it. The `gethostent` function returns the next entry in the file. The `sethostent` function will open the file or rewind it if it is already open. The `endhostent` function will close the file.

When `gethostent` returns, we get a pointer to a `hostent` structure which might point to a static data buffer that is overwritten each time we call `gethostent`. The `hostent` structure is defined to have at least the following members:

```
struct hostent {
  char   *h_name;       /* name of host */
  char   **h_aliases;   /* pointer to alternate host name array */
  int     h_addrtype;   /* address type */
  int     h_length;     /* length in bytes of address */
  char   **h_addr_list; /* pointer to array of network addresses */
  .
  .
  .
};
```

The addresses returned are in network byte order.

Two additional functions—`gethostbyname` and `gethostbyaddr`—originally were included with the `hostent` functions, but are now considered to be obsolete. We'll see replacements for them shortly.

We can get network names and numbers with a similar set of interfaces.

```
#include <netdb.h>

struct netent *getnetbyaddr(uint32_t net, int type);

struct netent *getnetbyname(const char *name);

struct netent *getnetent(void);
```

All return: pointer if OK, NULL on error

```
void setnetent(int stayopen);

void endnetent(void);
```

The `netent` structure contains at least the following fields:

```
struct netent {
  char      *n_name;       /* network name */
  char      **n_aliases;   /* alternate network name array pointer */
  int       n_addrtype;    /* address type */
  uint32_t  n_net;         /* network number */
  .
  .
  .
};
```

The network number is returned in network byte order. The address type is one of the address family constants (`AF_INET`, for example).

We can map between protocol names and numbers with the following functions.

```
#include <netdb.h>

struct protoent *getprotobyname(const char *name);

struct protoent *getprotobynumber(int proto);

struct protoent *getprotoent(void);
```

All return: pointer if OK, NULL on error

```
void setprotoent(int stayopen);

void endprotoent(void);
```

The `protoent` structure as defined by POSIX.1 has at least the following members:

```
struct protoent {
  char   *p_name;       /* protocol name */
  char   **p_aliases;   /* pointer to alternate protocol name array */
  int    p_proto;       /* protocol number */
  .
  .
  .
};
```

Services are represented by the port number portion of the address. Each service is offered on a unique, well-known port number. We can map a service name to a port number with `getservbyname`, map a port number to a service name with `getservbyport`, or scan the services database sequentially with `getservent`.

```
#include <netdb.h>

struct servent *getservbyname(const char *name, const char *proto);

struct servent *getservbyport(int port, const char *proto);

struct servent *getservent(void);
```

All return: pointer if OK, NULL on error

```
void setservent(int stayopen);

void endservent(void);
```

The `servent` structure is defined to have at least the following members:

```
struct servent {
  char   *s_name;      /* service name */
  char   **s_aliases;  /* pointer to alternate service name array */
  int    s_port;       /* port number */
  char   *s_proto;     /* name of protocol */
   .
   .
   .
};
```

POSIX.1 defines several new functions to allow an application to map from a host name and a service name to an address and vice versa. These functions replace the older `gethostbyname` and `gethostbyaddr` functions.

The `getaddrinfo` function allows us to map a host name and a service name to an address.

```
#include <sys/socket.h>
#include <netdb.h>

int getaddrinfo(const char *restrict host,
                const char *restrict service,
                const struct addrinfo *restrict hint,
                struct addrinfo **restrict res);
```

Returns: 0 if OK, nonzero error code on error

```
void freeaddrinfo(struct addrinfo *ai);
```

We need to provide the host name, the service name, or both. If we provide only one name, the other should be a null pointer. The host name can be either a node name or the host address in dotted-decimal notation.

The `getaddrinfo` function returns a linked list of `addrinfo` structures. We can use `freeaddrinfo` to free one or more of these structures, depending on how many structures are linked together using the `ai_next` field.

The `addrinfo` structure is defined to include at least the following members:

```
struct addrinfo {
    int               ai_flags;       /* customize behavior */
    int               ai_family;      /* address family */
    int               ai_socktype;    /* socket type */
    int               ai_protocol;    /* protocol */
    socklen_t         ai_addrlen;     /* length in bytes of address */
    struct sockaddr   *ai_addr;       /* address */
    char              *ai_canonname;  /* canonical name of host */
    struct addrinfo   *ai_next;       /* next in list */
    .
    .
    .
};
```

We can supply an optional *hint* to select addresses that meet certain criteria. The hint is a template used for filtering addresses and uses only the `ai_family`, `ai_flags`, `ai_protocol`, and `ai_socktype` fields. The remaining integer fields must be set to 0, and the pointer fields must be null. Figure 16.6 summarizes the flags we can use in the `ai_flags` field to customize how addresses and names are treated.

Flag	Description
AI_ADDRCONFIG	Query for whichever address type (IPv4 or IPv6) is configured.
AI_ALL	Look for both IPv4 and IPv6 addresses (used only with AI_V4MAPPED).
AI_CANONNAME	Request a canonical name (as opposed to an alias).
AI_NUMERICHOST	Return the host address in numeric format.
AI_NUMERICSERV	Return the service as a port number.
AI_PASSIVE	Socket address is intended to be bound for listening.
AI_V4MAPPED	If no IPv6 addresses are found, return IPv4 addresses mapped in IPv6 format.

Figure 16.6 Flags for `addrinfo` structure

If `getaddrinfo` fails, we can't use `perror` or `strerror` to generate an error message. Instead, we need to call `gai_strerror` to convert the error code returned into an error message.

```
#include <netdb.h>

const char *gai_strerror(int error);
```
                        Returns: a pointer to a string describing the error

The `getnameinfo` function converts an address into a host name and a service name.

```
#include <sys/socket.h>
#include <netdb.h>

int getnameinfo(const struct sockaddr *restrict addr,
                socklen_t alen, char *restrict host,
                socklen_t hostlen, char *restrict service,
                socklen_t servlen, unsigned int flags);
```
                        Returns: 0 if OK, nonzero on error

The socket address (*addr*) is translated into a host name and a service name. If *host* is non-null, it points to a buffer *hostlen* bytes long that will be used to return the host name. Similarly, if *service* is non-null, it points to a buffer *servlen* bytes long that will be used to return the service name.

The *flags* argument gives us some control over how the translation is done. Figure 16.7 summarizes the supported flags.

Flag	Description
NI_DGRAM	The service is datagram based instead of stream based.
NI_NAMEREQD	If the host name can't be found, treat this as an error.
NI_NOFQDN	Return only the node name portion of the fully-qualified domain name for local hosts.
NI_NUMERICHOST	Return the numeric form of the host address instead of the name.
NI_NUMERICSERV	Return the numeric form of the service address (i.e., the port number) instead of the name.

Figure 16.7 Flags for the getnameinfo function

Example

Figure 16.8 illustrates the use of the getaddrinfo function.

```c
#include "apue.h"
#include <netdb.h>
#include <arpa/inet.h>
#if defined(BSD) || defined(MACOS)
#include <sys/socket.h>
#include <netinet/in.h>
#endif

void
print_family(struct addrinfo *aip)
{
    printf(" family ");
    switch (aip->ai_family) {
    case AF_INET:
        printf("inet");
        break;
    case AF_INET6:
        printf("inet6");
        break;
    case AF_UNIX:
        printf("unix");
        break;
    case AF_UNSPEC:
        printf("unspecified");
        break;
    default:
        printf("unknown");
    }
```

```
        }

void
print_type(struct addrinfo *aip)
{
    printf(" type ");
    switch (aip->ai_socktype) {
    case SOCK_STREAM:
        printf("stream");
        break;
    case SOCK_DGRAM:
        printf("datagram");
        break;
    case SOCK_SEQPACKET:
        printf("seqpacket");
        break;
    case SOCK_RAW:
        printf("raw");
        break;
    default:
        printf("unknown (%d)", aip->ai_socktype);
    }
}

void
print_protocol(struct addrinfo *aip)
{
    printf(" protocol ");
    switch (aip->ai_protocol) {
    case 0:
        printf("default");
        break;
    case IPPROTO_TCP:
        printf("TCP");
        break;
    case IPPROTO_UDP:
        printf("UDP");
        break;
    case IPPROTO_RAW:
        printf("raw");
        break;
    default:
        printf("unknown (%d)", aip->ai_protocol);
    }
}

void
print_flags(struct addrinfo *aip)
{
    printf("flags");
    if (aip->ai_flags == 0) {
        printf(" 0");
```

```
            } else {
                if (aip->ai_flags & AI_PASSIVE)
                    printf(" passive");
                if (aip->ai_flags & AI_CANONNAME)
                    printf(" canon");
                if (aip->ai_flags & AI_NUMERICHOST)
                    printf(" numhost");
#if defined(AI_NUMERICSERV)
                if (aip->ai_flags & AI_NUMERICSERV)
                    printf(" numserv");
#endif
#if defined(AI_V4MAPPED)
                if (aip->ai_flags & AI_V4MAPPED)
                    printf(" v4mapped");
#endif
#if defined(AI_ALL)
                if (aip->ai_flags & AI_ALL)
                    printf(" all");
#endif
            }
}

int
main(int argc, char *argv[])
{
    struct addrinfo     *ailist, *aip;
    struct addrinfo     hint;
    struct sockaddr_in  *sinp;
    const char          *addr;
    int                 err;
    char                abuf[INET_ADDRSTRLEN];

    if (argc != 3)
        err_quit("usage: %s nodename service", argv[0]);
    hint.ai_flags = AI_CANONNAME;
    hint.ai_family = 0;
    hint.ai_socktype = 0;
    hint.ai_protocol = 0;
    hint.ai_addrlen = 0;
    hint.ai_canonname = NULL;
    hint.ai_addr = NULL;
    hint.ai_next = NULL;
    if ((err = getaddrinfo(argv[1], argv[2], &hint, &ailist)) != 0)
        err_quit("getaddrinfo error: %s", gai_strerror(err));
    for (aip = ailist; aip != NULL; aip = aip->ai_next) {
        print_flags(aip);
        print_family(aip);
        print_type(aip);
        print_protocol(aip);
        printf("\n\thost %s", aip->ai_canonname?aip->ai_canonname:"-");
        if (aip->ai_family == AF_INET) {
```

```
               sinp = (struct sockaddr_in *)aip->ai_addr;
               addr = inet_ntop(AF_INET, &sinp->sin_addr, abuf,
                   INET_ADDRSTRLEN);
               printf(" address %s", addr?addr:"unknown");
               printf(" port %d", ntohs(sinp->sin_port));
           }
           printf("\n");
       }
       exit(0);
   }
```

Figure 16.8 Print host and service information

This program illustrates the use of the `getaddrinfo` function. If multiple protocols provide the given service for the given host, the program will print more than one entry. In this example, we print out the address information only for the protocols that work with IPv4 (`ai_family` equals `AF_INET`). If we wanted to restrict the output to the `AF_INET` protocol family, we could set the `ai_family` field in the hint.

When we run the program on one of the test systems, we get

```
$ ./a.out harry nfs
flags canon family inet type stream protocol TCP
     host harry address 192.168.1.105 port 2049
flags canon family inet type datagram protocol UDP
     host harry address 192.168.1.105 port 2049
```
                                                                              □

16.3.4 Associating Addresses with Sockets

The address associated with a client's socket is of little interest, and we can let the system choose a default address for us. For a server, however, we need to associate a well-known address with the server's socket on which client requests will arrive. Clients need a way to discover the address to use to contact a server, and the simplest scheme is for a server to reserve an address and register it in `/etc/services` or with a name service.

We use the `bind` function to associate an address with a socket.

```
#include <sys/socket.h>

int bind(int sockfd, const struct sockaddr *addr, socklen_t len);
```
                                              Returns: 0 if OK, –1 on error

---

There are several restrictions on the address we can use:

- The address we specify must be valid for the machine on which the process is running; we can't specify an address belonging to some other machine.

- The address must match the format supported by the address family we used to create the socket.

- The port number in the address cannot be less than 1,024 unless the process has the appropriate privilege (i.e., is the superuser).

- Usually, only one socket endpoint can be bound to a given address, although some protocols allow duplicate bindings.

For the Internet domain, if we specify the special IP address INADDR_ANY, the socket endpoint will be bound to all the system's network interfaces. This means that we can receive packets from any of the network interface cards installed in the system. We'll see in the next section that the system will choose an address and bind it to our socket for us if we call connect or listen without first binding an address to the socket.

We can use the getsockname function to discover the address bound to a socket.

```
#include <sys/socket.h>

int getsockname(int sockfd, struct sockaddr *restrict addr,
                socklen_t *restrict alenp);
```
                                                        Returns: 0 if OK, −1 on error

Before calling getsockname, we set *alenp* to point to an integer containing the size of the sockaddr buffer. On return, the integer is set to the size of the address returned. If the address won't fit in the buffer provided, the address is silently truncated. If no address is currently bound to the socket, the results are undefined.

If the socket is connected to a peer, we can find out the peer's address by calling the getpeername function.

```
#include <sys/socket.h>

int getpeername(int sockfd, struct sockaddr *restrict addr,
                socklen_t *restrict alenp);
```
                                                        Returns: 0 if OK, −1 on error

Other than returning the peer's address, the getpeername function is identical to the getsockname function.

16.4 Connection Establishment

If we're dealing with a connection-oriented network service (SOCK_STREAM or SOCK_SEQPACKET), then before we can exchange data, we need to create a connection between the socket of the process requesting the service (the client) and the process providing the service (the server). We use the connect function to create a connection.

```
#include <sys/socket.h>

int connect(int sockfd, const struct sockaddr *addr, socklen_t len);
```
                                                        Returns: 0 if OK, −1 on error

The address we specify with connect is the address of the server with which we wish to communicate. If *sockfd* is not bound to an address, connect will bind a default address for the caller.

When we try to connect to a server, the connect request might fail for several reasons. The machine to which we are trying to connect must be up and running, the server must be bound to the address we are trying to contact, and there must be room in the server's pending connect queue (we'll learn more about this shortly). Thus, applications must be able to handle connect error returns that might be caused by transient conditions.

Example

Figure 16.9 shows one way to handle transient connect errors. This is likely with a server that is running on a heavily loaded system.

```
#include "apue.h"
#include <sys/socket.h>

#define MAXSLEEP 128

int
connect_retry(int sockfd, const struct sockaddr *addr, socklen_t alen)
{
    int nsec;

    /*
     * Try to connect with exponential backoff.
     */
    for (nsec = 1; nsec <= MAXSLEEP; nsec <<= 1) {
        if (connect(sockfd, addr, alen) == 0) {
            /*
             * Connection accepted.
             */
            return(0);
        }

        /*
         * Delay before trying again.
         */
        if (nsec <= MAXSLEEP/2)
            sleep(nsec);
    }
    return(-1);
}
```

Figure 16.9 Connect with retry

This function shows what is known as an *exponential backoff* algorithm. If the call to connect fails, the process goes to sleep for a short time and then tries again, increasing the delay each time through the loop, up to a maximum delay of about 2 minutes.   □

If the socket descriptor is in nonblocking mode, which we discuss further in Section 16.8, `connect` will return −1 with `errno` set to the special error code `EINPROGRESS` if the connection can't be established immediately. The application can use either `poll` or `select` to determine when the file descriptor is writable. At this point, the connection is complete.

The `connect` function can also be used with a connectionless network service (`SOCK_DGRAM`). This might seem like a contradiction, but it is an optimization instead. If we call `connect` with a `SOCK_DGRAM` socket, the destination address of all messages we send is set to the address we specified in the `connect` call, relieving us from having to provide the address every time we transmit a message. In addition, we will receive datagrams only from the address we've specified.

A server announces that it is willing to accept connect requests by calling the `listen` function.

```
#include <sys/socket.h>

int listen(int sockfd, int backlog);
```
                                                              Returns: 0 if OK, −1 on error

The *backlog* argument provides a hint to the system of the number of outstanding connect requests that it should enqueue on behalf of the process. The actual value is determined by the system, but the upper limit is specified as `SOMAXCONN` in `<sys/socket.h>`.

> On Solaris, the `SOMAXCONN` value in `<sys/socket.h>` is ignored. The particular maximum depends on the implementation of each protocol. For TCP, the default is 128.

Once the queue is full, the system will reject additional connect requests, so the *backlog* value must be chosen based on the expected load of the server and the amount of processing it must do to accept a connect request and start the service.

Once a server has called `listen`, the socket used can receive connect requests. We use the `accept` function to retrieve a connect request and convert that into a connection.

```
#include <sys/socket.h>

int accept(int sockfd, struct sockaddr *restrict addr,
           socklen_t *restrict len);
```
                                              Returns: file (socket) descriptor if OK, −1 on error

The file descriptor returned by `accept` is a socket descriptor that is connected to the client that called `connect`. This new socket descriptor has the same socket type and address family as the original socket (*sockfd*). The original socket passed to `accept` is not associated with the connection, but instead remains available to receive additional connect requests.

If we don't care about the client's identity, we can set the *addr* and *len* parameters to `NULL`. Otherwise, before calling `accept`, we need to set the *addr* parameter to a buffer large enough to hold the address and set the integer pointed to by *len* to the size of the buffer. On return, accept will fill in the client's address in the buffer and update the integer pointed to by *len* to reflect the size of the address.

If no connect requests are pending, accept will block until one arrives. If *sockfd* is in nonblocking mode, accept will return −1 and set errno to either EAGAIN or EWOULDBLOCK.

All four platforms discussed in this text define EAGAIN to be the same as EWOULDBLOCK.

If a server calls accept and no connect request is present, the server will block until one arrives. Alternatively, a server can use either poll or select to wait for a connect request to arrive. In this case, a socket with pending connect requests will appear to be readable.

Example

Figure 16.10 shows a function we can use to allocate and initialize a socket for use by a server process.

```c
#include "apue.h"
#include <errno.h>
#include <sys/socket.h>

int
initserver(int type, const struct sockaddr *addr, socklen_t alen,
  int qlen)
{
    int fd;
    int err = 0;

    if ((fd = socket(addr->sa_family, type, 0)) < 0)
        return(-1);
    if (bind(fd, addr, alen) < 0) {
        err = errno;
        goto errout;
    }
    if (type == SOCK_STREAM || type == SOCK_SEQPACKET) {
        if (listen(fd, qlen) < 0) {
            err = errno;
            goto errout;
        }
    }
    return(fd);

errout:
    close(fd);
    errno = err;
    return(-1);
}
```

Figure 16.10 Initialize a socket endpoint for use by a server

We'll see that TCP has some strange rules regarding address reuse that make this example inadequate. Figure 16.20 shows a version of this function that bypasses these rules, solving the major drawback with this version.   □

16.5 Data Transfer

Since a socket endpoint is represented as a file descriptor, we can use `read` and `write` to communicate with a socket, as long as it is connected. Recall that a datagram socket can be "connected" if we set the default peer address using the `connect` function. Using `read` and `write` with socket descriptors is significant, because it means that we can pass socket descriptors to functions that were originally designed to work with local files. We can also arrange to pass the socket descriptors to child processes that execute programs that know nothing about sockets.

Although we can exchange data using `read` and `write`, that is about all we can do with these two functions. If we want to specify options, receive packets from multiple clients, or send out-of-band data, we need to use one of the six socket functions designed for data transfer.

Three functions are available for sending data, and three are available for receiving data. First, we'll look at the ones used to send data.

The simplest one is `send`. It is similar to `write`, but allows us to specify flags to change how the data we want to transmit is treated.

```
#include <sys/socket.h>

ssize_t send(int sockfd, const void *buf, size_t nbytes, int flags);
```
Returns: number of bytes sent if OK, −1 on error

Like `write`, the socket has to be connected to use `send`. The *buf* and *nbytes* arguments have the same meaning as they do with `write`.

Unlike `write`, however, `send` supports a fourth *flags* argument. Two flags are defined by the Single UNIX Specification, but it is common for implementations to support additional ones. They are summarized in Figure 16.11.

Flag	Description	POSIX.1	FreeBSD 5.2.1	Linux 2.4.22	Mac OS X 10.3	Solaris 9
MSG_DONTROUTE	Don't route packet outside of local network.		•	•	•	•
MSG_DONTWAIT	Enable nonblocking operation (equivalent to using O_NONBLOCK).		•	•	•	
MSG_EOR	This is the end of record if supported by protocol.	•	•	•	•	
MSG_OOB	Send out-of-band data if supported by protocol (see Section 16.7).	•	•	•	•	•

Figure 16.11 Flags used with `send` socket calls

If send returns success, it doesn't necessarily mean that the process at the other end of the connection receives the data. All we are guaranteed is that when send succeeds, the data has been delivered to the network drivers without error.

With a protocol that supports message boundaries, if we try to send a single message larger than the maximum supported by the protocol, send will fail with errno set to EMSGSIZE. With a byte-stream protocol, send will block until the entire amount of data has been transmitted.

The sendto function is similar to send. The difference is that sendto allows us to specify a destination address to be used with connectionless sockets.

```
#include <sys/socket.h>

ssize_t sendto(int sockfd, const void *buf, size_t nbytes, int flags,
               const struct sockaddr *destaddr, socklen_t destlen);
```
                          Returns: number of bytes sent if OK, −1 on error

With a connection-oriented socket, the destination address is ignored, as the destination is implied by the connection. With a connectionless socket, we can't use send unless the destination address is first set by calling connect, so sendto gives us an alternate way to send a message.

We have one more choice when transmitting data over a socket. We can call sendmsg with a msghdr structure to specify multiple buffers from which to transmit data, similar to the writev function (Section 14.7).

```
#include <sys/socket.h>

ssize_t sendmsg(int sockfd, const struct msghdr *msg, int flags);
```
                          Returns: number of bytes sent if OK, −1 on error

POSIX.1 defines the msghdr structure to have at least the following members:

```
struct msghdr {
    void          *msg_name;        /* optional address */
    socklen_t      msg_namelen;     /* address size in bytes */
    struct iovec  *msg_iov;         /* array of I/O buffers */
    int            msg_iovlen;      /* number of elements in array */
    void          *msg_control;     /* ancillary data */
    socklen_t      msg_controllen;  /* number of ancillary bytes */
    int            msg_flags;       /* flags for received message */
      .
      .
      .
};
```

We saw the iovec structure in Section 14.7. We'll see the use of ancillary data in Section 17.4.2.

The recv function is similar to read, but allows us to specify some options to control how we receive the data.

```
#include <sys/socket.h>

ssize_t recv(int sockfd, void *buf, size_t nbytes, int flags);
```

Returns: length of message in bytes,
0 if no messages are available and peer has done an orderly shutdown,
or −1 on error

The flags that can be passed to `recv` are summarized in Figure 16.12. Only three are defined by the Single UNIX Specification.

Flag	Description	POSIX.1	FreeBSD 5.2.1	Linux 2.4.22	Mac OS X 10.3	Solaris 9
MSG_OOB	Retrieve out-of-band data if supported by protocol (see Section 16.7).	•	•	•	•	•
MSG_PEEK	Return packet contents without consuming packet.	•	•	•	•	•
MSG_TRUNC	Request that the real length of the packet be returned, even if it was truncated.			•		
MSG_WAITALL	Wait until all data is available (SOCK_STREAM only).	•	•	•	•	•

Figure 16.12 Flags used with `recv` socket calls

When we specify the `MSG_PEEK` flag, we can peek at the next data to be read without actually consuming it. The next call to `read` or one of the `recv` functions will return the same data we peeked at.

With `SOCK_STREAM` sockets, we can receive less data than we requested. The `MSG_WAITALL` flag inhibits this behavior, preventing `recv` from returning until all the data we requested has been received. With `SOCK_DGRAM` and `SOCK_SEQPACKET` sockets, the `MSG_WAITALL` flag provides no change in behavior, because these message-based socket types already return an entire message in a single read.

If the sender has called `shutdown` (Section 16.2) to end transmission, or if the network protocol supports orderly shutdown by default and the sender has closed the socket, then `recv` will return 0 when we have received all the data.

If we are interested in the identity of the sender, we can use `recvfrom` to obtain the source address from which the data was sent.

```
#include <sys/socket.h>

ssize_t recvfrom(int sockfd, void *restrict buf, size_t len, int flags,
                 struct sockaddr *restrict addr,
                 socklen_t *restrict addrlen);
```

Returns: length of message in bytes,
0 if no messages are available and peer has done an orderly shutdown,
or −1 on error

If *addr* is non-null, it will contain the address of the socket endpoint from which the data was sent. When calling recvfrom, we need to set the *addrlen* parameter to point to an integer containing the size in bytes of the socket buffer to which *addr* points. On return, the integer is set to the actual size of the address in bytes.

Because it allows us to retrieve the address of the sender, recvfrom is usually used with connectionless sockets. Otherwise, recvfrom behaves identically to recv.

To receive data into multiple buffers, similar to readv (Section 14.7), or if we want to receive ancillary data (Section 17.4.2), we can use recvmsg.

```
#include <sys/socket.h>

ssize_t recvmsg(int sockfd, struct msghdr *msg, int flags);
```

Returns: length of message in bytes,
0 if no messages are available and peer has done an orderly shutdown,
or −1 on error

The msghdr structure (which we saw used with sendmsg) is used by recvmsg to specify the input buffers to be used to receive the data. We can set the *flags* argument to change the default behavior of recvmsg. On return, the msg_flags field of the msghdr structure is set to indicate various characteristics of the data received. (The msg_flags field is ignored on entry to recvmsg). The possible values on return from recvmsg are summarized in Figure 16.13. We'll see an example that uses recvmsg in Chapter 17.

Flag	Description	POSIX.1	FreeBSD 5.2.1	Linux 2.4.22	Mac OS X 10.3	Solaris 9
MSG_CTRUNC	Control data was truncated.	•	•	•	•	•
MSG_DONTWAIT	recvmsg was called in nonblocking mode.			•		•
MSG_EOR	End of record was received.	•	•	•	•	•
MSG_OOB	Out-of-band data was received.	•	•	•	•	•
MSG_TRUNC	Normal data was truncated.	•	•	•	•	•

Figure 16.13 Flags returned in msg_flags by recvmsg

Example—Connection-Oriented Client

Figure 16.14 shows a client command that communicates with a server to obtain the output from a system's uptime command. We call this service "remote uptime" (or "ruptime" for short).

```
#include "apue.h"
#include <netdb.h>
#include <errno.h>
#include <sys/socket.h>

#define MAXADDRLEN  256
```

```
#define BUFLEN        128

extern int connect_retry(int, const struct sockaddr *, socklen_t);

void
print_uptime(int sockfd)
{
    int     n;
    char    buf[BUFLEN];

    while ((n = recv(sockfd, buf, BUFLEN, 0)) > 0)
        write(STDOUT_FILENO, buf, n);
    if (n < 0)
        err_sys("recv error");
}

int
main(int argc, char *argv[])
{
    struct addrinfo *ailist, *aip;
    struct addrinfo hint;
    int             sockfd, err;

    if (argc != 2)
        err_quit("usage: ruptime hostname");
    hint.ai_flags = 0;
    hint.ai_family = 0;
    hint.ai_socktype = SOCK_STREAM;
    hint.ai_protocol = 0;
    hint.ai_addrlen = 0;
    hint.ai_canonname = NULL;
    hint.ai_addr = NULL;
    hint.ai_next = NULL;
    if ((err = getaddrinfo(argv[1], "ruptime", &hint, &ailist)) != 0)
        err_quit("getaddrinfo error: %s", gai_strerror(err));
    for (aip = ailist; aip != NULL; aip = aip->ai_next) {
        if ((sockfd = socket(aip->ai_family, SOCK_STREAM, 0)) < 0)
            err = errno;
        if (connect_retry(sockfd, aip->ai_addr, aip->ai_addrlen) < 0) {
            err = errno;
        } else {
            print_uptime(sockfd);
            exit(0);
        }
    }
    fprintf(stderr, "can't connect to %s: %s\n", argv[1],
      strerror(err));
    exit(1);
}
```

Figure 16.14   Client command to get uptime from server

This program connects to a server, reads the string sent by the server, and prints the string on the standard output. Since we're using a SOCK_STREAM socket, we can't be guaranteed that we will read the entire string in one call to recv, so we need to repeat the call until it returns 0.

The getaddrinfo function might return more than one candidate address for us to use if the server supports multiple network interfaces or multiple network protocols. We try each one in turn, giving up when we find one that allows us to connect to the service. We use the connect_retry function from Figure 16.9 to establish a connection with the server.   □

Example—Connection-Oriented Server

Figure 16.15 shows the server that provides the uptime command's output to the client program from Figure 16.14.

```c
#include "apue.h"
#include <netdb.h>
#include <errno.h>
#include <syslog.h>
#include <sys/socket.h>

#define BUFLEN   128
#define QLEN 10

#ifndef HOST_NAME_MAX
#define HOST_NAME_MAX 256
#endif

extern int initserver(int, struct sockaddr *, socklen_t, int);

void
serve(int sockfd)
{
    int     clfd;
    FILE    *fp;
    char    buf[BUFLEN];

    for (;;) {
        clfd = accept(sockfd, NULL, NULL);
        if (clfd < 0) {
            syslog(LOG_ERR, "ruptimed: accept error: %s",
              strerror(errno));
            exit(1);
        }
        if ((fp = popen("/usr/bin/uptime", "r")) == NULL) {
            sprintf(buf, "error: %s\n", strerror(errno));
            send(clfd, buf, strlen(buf), 0);
        } else {
            while (fgets(buf, BUFLEN, fp) != NULL)
                send(clfd, buf, strlen(buf), 0);
```

```
                    pclose(fp);
                }
            close(clfd);
        }
}

int
main(int argc, char *argv[])
{
    struct addrinfo *ailist, *aip;
    struct addrinfo hint;
    int             sockfd, err, n;
    char            *host;

    if (argc != 1)
        err_quit("usage: ruptimed");
#ifdef _SC_HOST_NAME_MAX
    n = sysconf(_SC_HOST_NAME_MAX);
    if (n < 0)   /* best guess */
#endif
        n = HOST_NAME_MAX;
    host = malloc(n);
    if (host == NULL)
        err_sys("malloc error");
    if (gethostname(host, n) < 0)
        err_sys("gethostname error");
    daemonize("ruptimed");
    hint.ai_flags = AI_CANONNAME;
    hint.ai_family = 0;
    hint.ai_socktype = SOCK_STREAM;
    hint.ai_protocol = 0;
    hint.ai_addrlen = 0;
    hint.ai_canonname = NULL;
    hint.ai_addr = NULL;
    hint.ai_next = NULL;
    if ((err = getaddrinfo(host, "ruptime", &hint, &ailist)) != 0) {
        syslog(LOG_ERR, "ruptimed: getaddrinfo error: %s",
          gai_strerror(err));
        exit(1);
    }
    for (aip = ailist; aip != NULL; aip = aip->ai_next) {
        if ((sockfd = initserver(SOCK_STREAM, aip->ai_addr,
          aip->ai_addrlen, QLEN)) >= 0) {
            serve(sockfd);
            exit(0);
        }
    }
    exit(1);
}
```

Figure 16.15 Server program to provide system uptime

To find out its address, the server needs to get the name of the host on which it is running. Some systems don't define the _SC_HOST_NAME_MAX constant, so we use HOST_NAME_MAX in this case. If the system doesn't define HOST_NAME_MAX, we define it ourselves. POSIX.1 states that the minimum value for the host name is 255 bytes, not including the terminating null, so we define HOST_NAME_MAX to be 256 to include the terminating null.

The server gets the host name by calling gethostname and looks up the address for the remote uptime service. Multiple addresses can be returned, but we simply choose the first one for which we can establish a passive socket endpoint. Handling multiple addresses is left as an exercise.

We use the initserver function from Figure 16.10 to initialize the socket endpoint on which we will wait for connect requests to arrive. (Actually, we use the version from Figure 16.20; we'll see why when we discuss socket options in Section 16.6.)   □

Example—Alternate Connection-Oriented Server

Previously, we stated that using file descriptors to access sockets was significant, because it allowed programs that knew nothing about networking to be used in a networked environment. The version of the server shown in Figure 16.16 illustrates this point. Instead of reading the output of the uptime command and sending it to the client, the server arranges to have the standard output and standard error of the uptime command be the socket endpoint connected to the client.

```
#include "apue.h"
#include <netdb.h>
#include <errno.h>
#include <syslog.h>
#include <fcntl.h>
#include <sys/socket.h>
#include <sys/wait.h>

#define QLEN 10

#ifndef HOST_NAME_MAX
#define HOST_NAME_MAX 256
#endif

extern int initserver(int, struct sockaddr *, socklen_t, int);

void
serve(int sockfd)
{
    int     clfd, status;
    pid_t   pid;

    for (;;) {
        clfd = accept(sockfd, NULL, NULL);
        if (clfd < 0) {
            syslog(LOG_ERR, "ruptimed: accept error: %s",
              strerror(errno));
```

```
                exit(1);
            }
        if ((pid = fork()) < 0) {
            syslog(LOG_ERR, "ruptimed: fork error: %s",
              strerror(errno));
            exit(1);
        } else if (pid == 0) {   /* child */
            /*
             * The parent called daemonize (Figure 13.1), so
             * STDIN_FILENO, STDOUT_FILENO, and STDERR_FILENO
             * are already open to /dev/null.  Thus, the call to
             * close doesn't need to be protected by checks that
             * clfd isn't already equal to one of these values.
             */
            if (dup2(clfd, STDOUT_FILENO) != STDOUT_FILENO ||
              dup2(clfd, STDERR_FILENO) != STDERR_FILENO) {
                syslog(LOG_ERR, "ruptimed: unexpected error");
                exit(1);
            }
            close(clfd);
            execl("/usr/bin/uptime", "uptime", (char *)0);
            syslog(LOG_ERR, "ruptimed: unexpected return from exec: %s",
              strerror(errno));
        } else {            /* parent */
            close(clfd);
            waitpid(pid, &status, 0);
        }
    }
}

int
main(int argc, char *argv[])
{
    struct addrinfo *ailist, *aip;
    struct addrinfo hint;
    int             sockfd, err, n;
    char            *host;

    if (argc != 1)
        err_quit("usage: ruptimed");
#ifdef _SC_HOST_NAME_MAX
    n = sysconf(_SC_HOST_NAME_MAX);
    if (n < 0)   /* best guess */
#endif
        n = HOST_NAME_MAX;
    host = malloc(n);
    if (host == NULL)
        err_sys("malloc error");
    if (gethostname(host, n) < 0)
        err_sys("gethostname error");
    daemonize("ruptimed");
```

```
        hint.ai_flags = AI_CANONNAME;
        hint.ai_family = 0;
        hint.ai_socktype = SOCK_STREAM;
        hint.ai_protocol = 0;
        hint.ai_addrlen = 0;
        hint.ai_canonname = NULL;
        hint.ai_addr = NULL;
        hint.ai_next = NULL;
        if ((err = getaddrinfo(host, "ruptime", &hint, &ailist)) != 0) {
            syslog(LOG_ERR, "ruptimed: getaddrinfo error: %s",
              gai_strerror(err));
            exit(1);
        }
        for (aip = ailist; aip != NULL; aip = aip->ai_next) {
            if ((sockfd = initserver(SOCK_STREAM, aip->ai_addr,
              aip->ai_addrlen, QLEN)) >= 0) {
                serve(sockfd);
                exit(0);
            }
        }
        exit(1);
}
```

Figure 16.16 Server program illustrating command writing directly to socket

Instead of using popen to run the uptime command and reading the output from the pipe connected to the command's standard output, we use fork to create a child process and then use dup2 to arrange that the child's copy of STDIN_FILENO is open to /dev/null and that both STDOUT_FILENO and STDERR_FILENO are open to the socket endpoint. When we execute uptime, the command writes the results to its standard output, which is connected to the socket, and the data is sent back to the ruptime client command.

The parent can safely close the file descriptor connected to the client, because the child still has it open. The parent waits for the child to complete before proceeding, so that the child doesn't become a zombie. Since it shouldn't take too long to run the uptime command, the parent can afford to wait for the child to exit before accepting the next connect request. This strategy might not be appropriate if the child takes a long time, however.   □

The previous examples have used connection-oriented sockets. But how do we choose the appropriate type? When do we use a connection-oriented socket, and when do we use a connectionless socket? The answer depends on how much work we want to do and what kind of tolerance we have for errors.

With a connectionless socket, packets can arrive out of order, so if we can't fit all our data in one packet, we will have to worry about ordering in our application. The maximum packet size is a characteristic of the communication protocol. Also, with a connectionless socket, the packets can be lost. If our application can't tolerate this loss, we should use connection-oriented sockets.

Tolerating packet loss means that we have two choices. If we intend to have reliable communication with our peer, we have to number our packets and request retransmission from the peer application when we detect a missing packet. We will also have to identify duplicate packets and discard them, since a packet might be delayed and appear to be lost, but show up after we have requested retransmission.

The other choice we have is to deal with the error by letting the user retry the command. For simple applications, this might be adequate, but for complex applications, this usually isn't a viable alternative, so it is generally better to use connection-oriented sockets in this case.

The drawbacks to connection-oriented sockets are that more work and time are needed to establish a connection, and each connection consumes more resources from the operating system.

Example—Connectionless Client

The program in Figure 16.17 is a version of the `uptime` client command that uses the datagram socket interface.

```c
#include "apue.h"
#include <netdb.h>
#include <errno.h>
#include <sys/socket.h>

#define BUFLEN      128
#define TIMEOUT     20

void
sigalrm(int signo)
{
}

void
print_uptime(int sockfd, struct addrinfo *aip)
{
    int     n;
    char    buf[BUFLEN];

    buf[0] = 0;
    if (sendto(sockfd, buf, 1, 0, aip->ai_addr, aip->ai_addrlen) < 0)
        err_sys("sendto error");
    alarm(TIMEOUT);
    if ((n = recvfrom(sockfd, buf, BUFLEN, 0, NULL, NULL)) < 0) {
        if (errno != EINTR)
            alarm(0);
        err_sys("recv error");
    }
    alarm(0);
    write(STDOUT_FILENO, buf, n);
}
```

```
int
main(int argc, char *argv[])
{
    struct addrinfo    *ailist, *aip;
    struct addrinfo    hint;
    int                sockfd, err;
    struct sigaction   sa;

    if (argc != 2)
        err_quit("usage: ruptime hostname");
    sa.sa_handler = sigalrm;
    sa.sa_flags = 0;
    sigemptyset(&sa.sa_mask);
    if (sigaction(SIGALRM, &sa, NULL) < 0)
        err_sys("sigaction error");
    hint.ai_flags = 0;
    hint.ai_family = 0;
    hint.ai_socktype = SOCK_DGRAM;
    hint.ai_protocol = 0;
    hint.ai_addrlen = 0;
    hint.ai_canonname = NULL;
    hint.ai_addr = NULL;
    hint.ai_next = NULL;
    if ((err = getaddrinfo(argv[1], "ruptime", &hint, &ailist)) != 0)
        err_quit("getaddrinfo error: %s", gai_strerror(err));

    for (aip = ailist; aip != NULL; aip = aip->ai_next) {
        if ((sockfd = socket(aip->ai_family, SOCK_DGRAM, 0)) < 0) {
            err = errno;
        } else {
            print_uptime(sockfd, aip);
            exit(0);
        }
    }

    fprintf(stderr, "can't contact %s: %s\n", argv[1], strerror(err));
    exit(1);
}
```

Figure 16.17 Client command using datagram service

The `main` function for the datagram-based client is similar to the one for the connection-oriented client, with the addition of installing a signal handler for `SIGALRM`. We use the `alarm` function to avoid blocking indefinitely in the call to `recvfrom`.

With the connection-oriented protocol, we needed to connect to the server before exchanging data. The arrival of the connect request was enough for the server to determine that it needed to provide service to a client. But with the datagram-based protocol, we need a way to notify the server that we want it to perform its service on our behalf. In this example, we simply send the server a 1-byte message. The server will receive it, get our address from the packet, and use this address to transmit its response. If the server offered multiple services, we could use this request message to indicate the service we want, but since the server does only one thing, the content of the 1-byte message doesn't matter.

If the server isn't running, the client will block indefinitely in the call to recvfrom. With the connection-oriented example, the connect call will fail if the server isn't running. To avoid blocking indefinitely, we set an alarm clock before calling recvfrom.

□

Example—Connectionless Server

The program in Figure 16.18 is the datagram version of the uptime server.

```c
#include "apue.h"
#include <netdb.h>
#include <errno.h>
#include <syslog.h>
#include <sys/socket.h>

#define BUFLEN      128
#define MAXADDRLEN  256

#ifndef HOST_NAME_MAX
#define HOST_NAME_MAX 256
#endif

extern int initserver(int, struct sockaddr *, socklen_t, int);

void
serve(int sockfd)
{
    int        n;
    socklen_t  alen;
    FILE       *fp;
    char       buf[BUFLEN];
    char       abuf[MAXADDRLEN];

    for (;;) {
        alen = MAXADDRLEN;
        if ((n = recvfrom(sockfd, buf, BUFLEN, 0,
          (struct sockaddr *)abuf, &alen)) < 0) {
            syslog(LOG_ERR, "ruptimed: recvfrom error: %s",
              strerror(errno));
            exit(1);
        }
        if ((fp = popen("/usr/bin/uptime", "r")) == NULL) {
            sprintf(buf, "error: %s\n", strerror(errno));
            sendto(sockfd, buf, strlen(buf), 0,
                (struct sockaddr *)abuf, alen);
        } else {
            if (fgets(buf, BUFLEN, fp) != NULL)
                sendto(sockfd, buf, strlen(buf), 0,
```

```
                            (struct sockaddr *)abuf, alen);
                pclose(fp);
            }
        }
    }

    int
    main(int argc, char *argv[])
    {
        struct addrinfo *ailist, *aip;
        struct addrinfo hint;
        int             sockfd, err, n;
        char            *host;

        if (argc != 1)
            err_quit("usage: ruptimed");
    #ifdef _SC_HOST_NAME_MAX
        n = sysconf(_SC_HOST_NAME_MAX);
        if (n < 0)   /* best guess */
    #endif
            n = HOST_NAME_MAX;
        host = malloc(n);
        if (host == NULL)
            err_sys("malloc error");
        if (gethostname(host, n) < 0)
            err_sys("gethostname error");
        daemonize("ruptimed");
        hint.ai_flags = AI_CANONNAME;
        hint.ai_family = 0;
        hint.ai_socktype = SOCK_DGRAM;
        hint.ai_protocol = 0;
        hint.ai_addrlen = 0;
        hint.ai_canonname = NULL;
        hint.ai_addr = NULL;
        hint.ai_next = NULL;
        if ((err = getaddrinfo(host, "ruptime", &hint, &ailist)) != 0) {
            syslog(LOG_ERR, "ruptimed: getaddrinfo error: %s",
              gai_strerror(err));
            exit(1);
        }
        for (aip = ailist; aip != NULL; aip = aip->ai_next) {
            if ((sockfd = initserver(SOCK_DGRAM, aip->ai_addr,
              aip->ai_addrlen, 0)) >= 0) {
                serve(sockfd);
                exit(0);
            }
        }
        exit(1);
    }
```

Figure 16.18 Server providing system uptime over datagrams

The server blocks in `recvfrom` for a request for service. When a request arrives, we save the requester's address and use `popen` to run the `uptime` command. We send the output back to the client using the `sendto` function, with the destination address set to the requester's address.   □

16.6 Socket Options

The socket mechanism provides two socket-option interfaces for us to control the behavior of sockets. One interface is used to set an option, and another interface allows us to query the state of an option. We can get and set three kinds of options:

1. Generic options that work with all socket types

2. Options that are managed at the socket level, but depend on the underlying protocols for support

3. Protocol-specific options unique to each individual protocol

The Single UNIX Specification defines only the socket-layer options (the first two option types in the preceding list).

We can set a socket option with the `setsockopt` function.

```
#include <sys/socket.h>

int setsockopt(int sockfd, int level, int option, const void *val,
               socklen_t len);
```
Returns: 0 if OK, −1 on error

The *level* argument identifies the protocol to which the option applies. If the option is a generic socket-level option, then *level* is set to `SOL_SOCKET`. Otherwise, *level* is set to the number of the protocol that controls the option. Examples are `IPPROTO_TCP` for TCP options and `IPPROTO_IP` for IP options. Figure 16.19 summarizes the generic socket-level options defined by the Single UNIX Specification.

The *val* argument points to a data structure or an integer, depending on the option. Some options are on/off switches. If the integer is nonzero, then the option is enabled. If the integer is zero, then the option is disabled. The *len* argument specifies the size of the object to which *val* points.

We can find out the current value of an option with the `getsockopt` function.

```
#include <sys/socket.h>

int getsockopt(int sockfd, int level, int option, void *restrict val,
               socklen_t *restrict lenp);
```
Returns: 0 if OK, −1 on error

Note that the *lenp* argument is a pointer to an integer. Before calling `getsockopt`, we set the integer to the size of the buffer where the option is to be copied. If the actual size

Option	Type of *val* argument	Description
SO_ACCEPTCONN	int	Return whether a socket is enabled for listening (getsockopt only).
SO_BROADCAST	int	Broadcast datagrams if *val is nonzero.
SO_DEBUG	int	Debugging in network drivers enabled if *val is nonzero.
SO_DONTROUTE	int	Bypass normal routing if *val is nonzero.
SO_ERROR	int	Return and clear pending socket error (getsockopt only).
SO_KEEPALIVE	int	Periodic keep-alive messages enabled if *val is nonzero.
SO_LINGER	struct linger	Delay time when unsent messages exist and socket is closed.
SO_OOBINLINE	int	Out-of-band data placed inline with normal data if *val is nonzero.
SO_RCVBUF	int	The size in bytes of the receive buffer.
SO_RCVLOWAT	int	The minimum amount of data in bytes to return on a receive call.
SO_RCVTIMEO	struct timeval	The timeout value for a socket receive call.
SO_REUSEADDR	int	Reuse addresses in bind if *val is nonzero.
SO_SNDBUF	int	The size in bytes of the send buffer.
SO_SNDLOWAT	int	The minimum amount of data in bytes to transmit in a send call.
SO_SNDTIMEO	struct timeval	The timeout value for a socket send call.
SO_TYPE	int	Identify the socket type (getsockopt only).

Figure 16.19 Socket options

of the option is greater than this size, the option is silently truncated. If the actual size of the option is less than or equal to this size, then the integer is updated with the actual size on return.

Example

The function in Figure 16.10 fails to operate properly when the server terminates and we try to restart it immediately. Normally, the implementation of TCP will prevent us from binding the same address until a timeout expires, which is usually on the order of several minutes. Luckily, the SO_REUSEADDR socket option allows us to bypass this restriction, as illustrated in Figure 16.20.

```
#include "apue.h"
#include <errno.h>
#include <sys/socket.h>

int
initserver(int type, const struct sockaddr *addr, socklen_t alen,
  int qlen)
{
    int fd, err;
```

```
        int reuse = 1;
        if ((fd = socket(addr->sa_family, type, 0)) < 0)
            return(-1);
        if (setsockopt(fd, SOL_SOCKET, SO_REUSEADDR, &reuse,
          sizeof(int)) < 0) {
            err = errno;
            goto errout;
        }
        if (bind(fd, addr, alen) < 0) {
            err = errno;
            goto errout;
        }
        if (type == SOCK_STREAM || type == SOCK_SEQPACKET) {
            if (listen(fd, qlen) < 0) {
                err = errno;
                goto errout;
            }
        }
        return(fd);
errout:
    close(fd);
    errno = err;
    return(-1);
}
```

Figure 16.20 Initialize a socket endpoint for use by a server with address reuse

To enable the SO_REUSEADDR option, we set an integer to a nonzero value and pass the address of the integer as the *val* argument to setsockopt. We set the *len* argument to the size of an integer to indicate the size of the object to which *val* points.   □

16.7 Out-of-Band Data

Out-of-band data is an optional feature supported by some communication protocols, allowing higher-priority delivery of data than normal. Out-of-band data is sent ahead of any data that is already queued for transmission. TCP supports out-of-band data, but UDP doesn't. The socket interface to out-of-band data is heavily influenced by TCP's implementation of out-of-band data.

TCP refers to out-of-band data as "urgent" data. TCP supports only a single byte of urgent data, but allows urgent data to be delivered out of band from the normal data delivery mechanisms. To generate urgent data, we specify the MSG_OOB flag to any of the three send functions. If we send more than one byte with the MSG_OOB flag, the last byte will be treated as the urgent-data byte.

When urgent data is received, we are sent the SIGURG signal if we have arranged for signal generation by the socket. In Sections 3.14 and 14.6.2, we saw that we could use the F_SETOWN command to fcntl to set the ownership of a socket. If the third argument to `fcntl` is positive, it specifies a process ID. If it is a negative value other than −1, it represents the process group ID. Thus, we can arrange that our process receive signals from a socket by calling

```
fcntl(sockfd, F_SETOWN, pid);
```

The `F_GETOWN` command can be used to retrieve the current socket ownership. As with the `F_SETOWN` command, a negative value represents a process group ID, and a positive value represents a process ID. Thus, the call

```
owner = fcntl(sockfd, F_GETOWN, 0);
```

will return with `owner` equal to the ID of the process configured to receive signals from the socket if `owner` is positive and with the absolute value of `owner` equal to the ID of the process group configured to receive signals from the socket if `owner` is negative.

TCP supports the notion of an *urgent mark*: the point in the normal data stream where the urgent data would go. We can choose to receive the urgent data inline with the normal data if we use the `SO_OOBINLINE` socket option. To help us identify when we have reached the urgent mark, we can use the `sockatmark` function.

```
#include <sys/socket.h>

int sockatmark(int sockfd);
```
Returns: 1 if at mark, 0 if not at mark, −1 on error

When the next byte to be read is where the urgent mark is located, `sockatmark` will return 1.

When out-of-band data is present in a socket's read queue, the `select` function (Section 14.5.1) will return the file descriptor as having an exception condition pending. We can choose to receive the urgent data inline with the normal data, or we can use the `MSG_OOB` flag with one of the `recv` functions to receive the urgent data ahead of any other queue data. TCP queues only one byte of urgent data. If another urgent byte arrives before we receive the current one, the existing one is discarded.

16.8   Nonblocking and Asynchronous I/O

Normally, the `recv` functions will block when no data is immediately available. Similarly, the `send` functions will block when there is not enough room in the socket's output queue to send the message. This behavior changes when the socket is in nonblocking mode. In this case, these functions will fail instead of blocking, setting `errno` to either `EWOULDBLOCK` or `EAGAIN`. When this happens, we can use either `poll` or `select` to determine when we can receive or transmit data.

The real-time extensions in the Single UNIX Specification include support for a generic asynchronous I/O mechanism. The socket mechanism has its own way of handling asynchronous I/O, but this isn't standardized in the Single UNIX Specification. Some texts refer to the classic socket-based asynchronous I/O mechanism as "signal-based I/O" to distinguish it from the asynchronous I/O mechanism in the real-time extensions.

With socket-based asynchronous I/O, we can arrange to be sent the SIGIO signal when we can read data from a socket or when space becomes available in a socket's write queue. Enabling asynchronous I/O is a two-step process.

1. Establish socket ownership so signals can be delivered to the proper processes.

2. Inform the socket that we want it to signal us when I/O operations won't block.

We can accomplish the first step in three ways.

1. Use the F_SETOWN command with fcntl.

2. Use the FIOSETOWN command with ioctl.

3. Use the SIOCSPGRP command with ioctl.

To accomplish the second step, we have two choices.

1. Use the F_SETFL command with fcntl and enable the O_ASYNC file flag.

2. Use the FIOASYNC command with ioctl.

We have several options, but they are not universally supported. Figure 16.21 summarizes the support for these options provided by the platforms discussed in this text. We show • where support is provided and † where support depends on the particular domain. For example, on Linux, the UNIX domain sockets don't support FIOSETOWN or SIOCSPGRP.

Mechanism	POSIX.1	FreeBSD 5.2.1	Linux 2.4.22	Mac OS X 10.3	Solaris 9
fcntl(fd, F_SETOWN, pid) ioctl(fd, FIOSETOWN, pid) ioctl(fd, SIOCSPGRP, pid)	•	• • •	• † †	• • •	• • •
fcntl(fd, F_SETFL, flags|O_ASYNC) ioctl(fd, FIOASYNC, &n);		• •	• •	• •	 •

Figure 16.21 Socket asynchronous I/O management commands

16.9 Summary

In this chapter, we looked at the IPC mechanisms that allow processes to communicate with other processes on different machines as well as within the same machine. We discussed how socket endpoints are named and how we can discover the addresses to use when contacting servers.

We presented examples of clients and servers that use connectionless (i.e., datagram-based) sockets and connection-oriented sockets. We briefly discussed asynchronous and nonblocking socket I/O and the interfaces used to manage socket options.

In the next chapter, we will look at some advanced IPC topics, including how we can use sockets to pass file descriptors between processes running on the same machine.

Exercises

16.1 Write a program to determine your system's byte ordering.

16.2 Write a program to print out which `stat` structure members are supported for sockets on at least two different platforms, and describe how the results differ.

16.3 The program in Figure 16.15 provides service on only a single endpoint. Modify the program to support service on multiple endpoints (each with a different address) at the same time.

16.4 Write a client program and a server program to return the number of processes currently running on a specified host computer.

16.5 In the program in Figure 16.16, the server waits for the child to execute the `uptime` command and exit before accepting the next connect request. Redesign the server so that the time to service one request doesn't delay the processing of incoming connect requests.

16.6 Write two library routines: one to enable asynchronous I/O on a socket and one to disable asynchronous I/O on a socket. Use Figure 16.21 to make sure that the functions work on all platforms with as many socket types as possible.

17

Advanced IPC

17.1 Introduction

In the previous two chapters, we discussed various forms of IPC, including pipes and sockets. In this chapter, we look at two advanced forms of IPC—STREAMS-based pipes and UNIX domain sockets—and what we can do with them. With these forms of IPC, we can pass open file descriptors between processes, servers can associate names with their file descriptors, and clients can use these names to rendezvous with the servers. We'll also see how the operating system provides a unique IPC channel per client. Many of the ideas that form the basis for the techniques described in this chapter come from the paper by Presotto and Ritchie [1990].

17.2 STREAMS-Based Pipes

A STREAMS-based pipe ("STREAMS pipe," for short) is a bidirectional (full-duplex) pipe. To obtain bidirectional data flow between a parent and a child, only a single STREAMS pipe is required.

> Recall from Section 15.1 that STREAMS pipes are supported by Solaris and are available in an optional add-on package with Linux.

Figure 17.1 shows the two ways to view a STREAMS pipe. The only difference between this picture and Figure 15.2 is that the arrows have heads on both ends; since the STREAMS pipe is full duplex, data can flow in both directions.

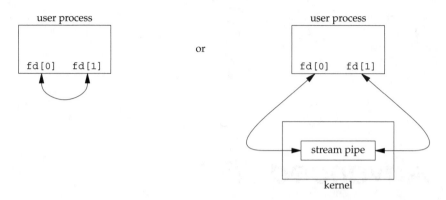

Figure 17.1 Two ways to view a STREAMS pipe

If we look inside a STREAMS pipe (Figure 17.2), we see that it is simply two stream heads, with each write queue (WQ) pointing at the other's read queue (RQ). Data written to one end of the pipe is placed in messages on the other's read queue.

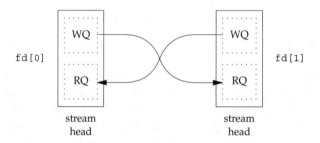

Figure 17.2 Inside a STREAMS pipe

Since a STREAMS pipe is a stream, we can push a STREAMS module onto either end of the pipe to process data written to the pipe (Figure 17.3). But if we push a module on one end, we can't pop it off the other end. If we want to remove it, we need to remove it from the same end on which it was pushed.

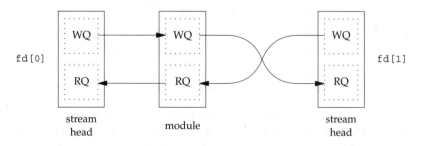

Figure 17.3 Inside a STREAMS pipe with a module

Assuming that we don't do anything fancy, such as pushing modules, a STREAMS pipe behaves just like a non-STREAMS pipe, except that it supports most of the STREAMS ioctl commands described in streamio(7). In Section 17.2.2, we'll see an example of pushing a module on a STREAMS pipe to provide unique connections when we give the pipe a name in the file system.

Example

Let's redo the coprocess example, Figure 15.18, with a single STREAMS pipe. Figure 17.4 shows the new main function. The add2 coprocess is the same (Figure 15.17). We call a new function, s_pipe, to create a single STREAMS pipe. (We show versions of this function for both STREAMS pipes and UNIX domain sockets shortly.)

```c
#include "apue.h"

static void sig_pipe(int);        /* our signal handler */

int
main(void)
{
    int     n;
    int     fd[2];
    pid_t   pid;
    char    line[MAXLINE];

    if (signal(SIGPIPE, sig_pipe) == SIG_ERR)
        err_sys("signal error");

    if (s_pipe(fd) < 0)           /* need only a single stream pipe */
        err_sys("pipe error");

    if ((pid = fork()) < 0) {
        err_sys("fork error");
    } else if (pid > 0) {                         /* parent */
        close(fd[1]);
        while (fgets(line, MAXLINE, stdin) != NULL) {
            n = strlen(line);
            if (write(fd[0], line, n) != n)
                err_sys("write error to pipe");
            if ((n = read(fd[0], line, MAXLINE)) < 0)
                err_sys("read error from pipe");
            if (n == 0) {
                err_msg("child closed pipe");
                break;
            }
            line[n] = 0;    /* null terminate */
            if (fputs(line, stdout) == EOF)
                err_sys("fputs error");
        }
    }
```

```
            if (ferror(stdin))
                err_sys("fgets error on stdin");
            exit(0);
    } else {                                        /* child */
            close(fd[0]);
            if (fd[1] != STDIN_FILENO &&
              dup2(fd[1], STDIN_FILENO) != STDIN_FILENO)
                err_sys("dup2 error to stdin");
            if (fd[1] != STDOUT_FILENO &&
              dup2(fd[1], STDOUT_FILENO) != STDOUT_FILENO)
                err_sys("dup2 error to stdout");
            if (execl("./add2", "add2", (char *)0) < 0)
                err_sys("execl error");
    }
    exit(0);
}

static void
sig_pipe(int signo)
{
    printf("SIGPIPE caught\n");
    exit(1);
}
```

Figure 17.4 Program to drive the add2 filter, using a STREAMS pipe

The parent uses only fd[0], and the child uses only fd[1]. Since each end of the STREAMS pipe is full duplex, the parent reads and writes fd[0], and the child duplicates fd[1] to both standard input and standard output. Figure 17.5 shows the resulting descriptors. Note that this example also works with full-duplex pipes that are not based on STREAMS, because it doesn't make use of any STREAMS features other than the full-duplex nature of STREAMS-based pipes.

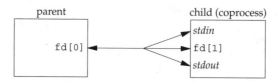

Figure 17.5 Arrangement of descriptors for coprocess

> Rago [1993] covers STREAMS-based pipes in more detail. Recall from Figure 15.1 that FreeBSD supports full-duplex pipes, but these pipes are not based on the STREAMS mechanism.
>
> □

We define the function s_pipe to be similar to the standard pipe function. Both functions take the same argument, but the descriptors returned by s_pipe are open for reading and writing.

Example—STREAMS-Based `s_pipe` Function

Figure 17.6 shows the STREAMS-based version of the `s_pipe` function. This version
simply calls the standard `pipe` function, which creates a full-duplex pipe.

```
#include "apue.h"

/*
 * Returns a STREAMS-based pipe, with the two file descriptors
 * returned in fd[0] and fd[1].
 */
int
s_pipe(int fd[2])
{
    return(pipe(fd));
}
```

Figure 17.6 STREAMS version of the s_pipe function

□

17.2.1 Naming STREAMS Pipes

Normally, pipes can be used only between related processes: child processes inheriting
pipes from their parent processes. In Section 15.5, we saw that unrelated processes can
communicate using FIFOs, but this provides only a one-way communication path. The
STREAMS mechanism provides a way for processes to give a pipe a name in the file
system. This bypasses the problem of dealing with unidirectional FIFOs.

We can use the `fattach` function to give a STREAMS pipe a name in the file
system.

```
#include <stropts.h>

int fattach(int filedes, const char *path);
```
                                                          Returns: 0 if OK, −1 on error

The *path* argument must refer to an existing file, and the calling process must either own
the file and have write permissions to it or be running with superuser privileges.

Once a STREAMS pipe is attached to the file system namespace, the underlying file
is inaccessible. Any process that opens the name will gain access to the pipe, not the
underlying file. Any processes that had the underlying file open before `fattach` was
called, however, can continue to access the underlying file. Indeed, these processes
generally will be unaware that the name now refers to a different file.

Figure 17.7 shows a pipe attached to the pathname `/tmp/pipe`. Only one end of
the pipe is attached to a name in the file system. The other end is used to communicate
with processes that open the attached filename. Even though it can attach any kind of
STREAMS file descriptor to a name in the file system, the `fattach` function is most
commonly used to give a name to a STREAMS pipe.

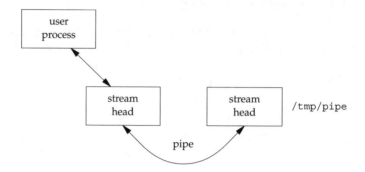

Figure 17.7 A pipe mounted on a name in the file system

A process can call `fdetach` to undo the association between a STREAMS file and the name in the file system.

```
#include <stropts.h>

int fdetach(const char *path);
```
                                                    Returns: 0 if OK, –1 on error

After `fdetach` is called, any processes that had accessed the STREAMS pipe by opening the *path* will still continue to access the stream, but subsequent opens of the *path* will access the original file residing in the file system.

17.2.2 Unique Connections

Although we can attach one end of a STREAMS pipe to the file system namespace, we still have problems if multiple processes want to communicate with a server using the named STREAMS pipe. Data from one client will be interleaved with data from the other clients writing to the pipe. Even if we guarantee that the clients write less than PIPE_BUF bytes so that the writes are atomic, we have no way to write back to an individual client and guarantee that the intended client will read the message. With multiple clients reading from the same pipe, we cannot control which one will be scheduled and actually read what we send.

The `connld` STREAMS module solves this problem. Before attaching a STREAMS pipe to a name in the file system, a server process can push the `connld` module on the end of the pipe that is to be attached. This results in the configuration shown in Figure 17.8.

In Figure 17.8, the server process has attached one end of its pipe to the path `/tmp/pipe`. We show a dotted line to indicate a client process in the middle of opening the attached STREAMS pipe. Once the open completes, we have the configuration shown in Figure 17.9.

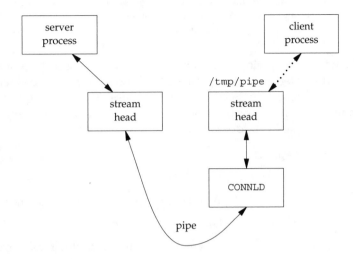

Figure 17.8 Setting up connld for unique connections

The client process never receives an open file descriptor for the end of the pipe that it opened. Instead, the operating system creates a new pipe and returns one end to the client process as the result of opening /tmp/pipe. The system sends the other end of the new pipe to the server process by passing its file descriptor over the existing (attached) pipe, resulting in a unique connection between the client process and the server process. We'll see the mechanics of passing file descriptors using STREAMS pipes in Section 17.4.1.

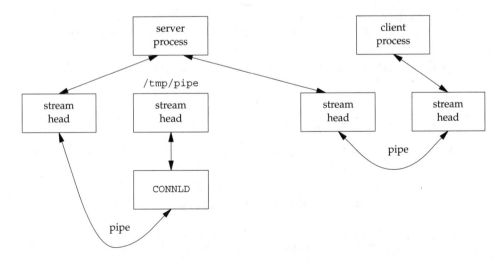

Figure 17.9 Using connld to make unique connections

The `fattach` function is built on top of the `mount` system call. This facility is known as *mounted streams*. Mounted streams and the `connld` module were developed by Presotto and Ritchie [1990] for the Research UNIX system. These mechanisms were then picked up by SVR4.

We will now develop three functions that can be used to create unique connections between unrelated processes. These functions mimic the connection-oriented socket functions discussed in Section 16.4. We use STREAMS pipes for the underlying communication mechanism here, but we'll see alternate implementations of these functions that use UNIX domain sockets in Section 17.3.

```
#include "apue.h"

int serv_listen(const char *name);
```
> Returns: file descriptor to listen on if OK, negative value on error
```
int serv_accept(int listenfd, uid_t *uidptr);
```
> Returns: new file descriptor if OK, negative value on error
```
int cli_conn(const char *name);
```
> Returns: file descriptor if OK, negative value on error

The `serv_listen` function (Figure 17.10) can be used by a server to announce its willingness to listen for client connect requests on a well-known name (some pathname in the file system). Clients will use this name when they want to connect to the server. The return value is the server's end of the STREAMS pipe.

```
#include "apue.h"
#include <fcntl.h>
#include <stropts.h>

/* pipe permissions: user rw, group rw, others rw */
#define FIFO_MODE   (S_IRUSR|S_IWUSR|S_IRGRP|S_IWGRP|S_IROTH|S_IWOTH)

/*
 * Establish an endpoint to listen for connect requests.
 * Returns fd if all OK, <0 on error
 */
int
serv_listen(const char *name)
{
    int     tempfd;
    int     fd[2];

    /*
     * Create a file: mount point for fattach().
     */
    unlink(name);
    if ((tempfd = creat(name, FIFO_MODE)) < 0)
        return(-1);
    if (close(tempfd) < 0)
        return(-2);
```

```
        if (pipe(fd) < 0)
            return(-3);
        /*
         * Push connld & fattach() on fd[1].
         */
        if (ioctl(fd[1], I_PUSH, "connld") < 0) {
            close(fd[0]);
            close(fd[1]);
            return(-4);
        }
        if (fattach(fd[1], name) < 0) {
            close(fd[0]);
            close(fd[1]);
            return(-5);
        }
        close(fd[1]);    /* fattach holds this end open */
        return(fd[0]);   /* fd[0] is where client connections arrive */
    }
```

Figure 17.10 The serv_listen function using STREAMS pipes

The serv_accept function (Figure 17.11) is used by a server to wait for a client's connect request to arrive. When one arrives, the system automatically creates a new STREAMS pipe, and the function returns one end to the server. Additionally, the effective user ID of the client is stored in the memory to which *uidptr* points.

```
#include "apue.h"
#include <stropts.h>

/*
 * Wait for a client connection to arrive, and accept it.
 * We also obtain the client's user ID.
 * Returns new fd if all OK, <0 on error.
 */
int
serv_accept(int listenfd, uid_t *uidptr)
{
    struct strrecvfd    recvfd;

    if (ioctl(listenfd, I_RECVFD, &recvfd) < 0)
        return(-1);      /* could be EINTR if signal caught */
    if (uidptr != NULL)
        *uidptr = recvfd.uid;   /* effective uid of caller */
    return(recvfd.fd);   /* return the new descriptor */
}
```

Figure 17.11 The serv_accept function using STREAMS pipes

A client calls cli_conn (Figure 17.12) to connect to a server. The *name* argument specified by the client must be the same name that was advertised by the server's call to serv_listen. On return, the client gets a file descriptor connected to the server.

```
#include "apue.h"
#include <fcntl.h>
#include <stropts.h>

/*
 * Create a client endpoint and connect to a server.
 * Returns fd if all OK, <0 on error.
 */
int
cli_conn(const char *name)
{
    int     fd;

    /* open the mounted stream */
    if ((fd = open(name, O_RDWR)) < 0)
        return(-1);
    if (isastream(fd) == 0) {
        close(fd);
        return(-2);
    }
    return(fd);
}
```

Figure 17.12 The `cli_conn` function using STREAMS pipes

We double-check that the returned descriptor refers to a STREAMS device, in case the server has not been started but the pathname still exists in the file system. In Section 17.6, we'll see how these three functions are used.

17.3 UNIX Domain Sockets

UNIX domain sockets are used to communicate with processes running on the same machine. Although Internet domain sockets can be used for this same purpose, UNIX domain sockets are more efficient. UNIX domain sockets only copy data; they have no protocol processing to perform, no network headers to add or remove, no checksums to calculate, no sequence numbers to generate, and no acknowledgements to send.

UNIX domain sockets provide both stream and datagram interfaces. The UNIX domain datagram service is reliable, however. Messages are neither lost nor delivered out of order. UNIX domain sockets are like a cross between sockets and pipes. You can use the network-oriented socket interfaces with them, or you can use the `socketpair` function to create a pair of unnamed, connected, UNIX domain sockets.

```
#include <sys/socket.h>

int socketpair(int domain, int type, int protocol, int sockfd[2]);
```
                                                          Returns: 0 if OK, −1 on error

Although the interface is sufficiently general to allow `socketpair` to be used with arbitrary domains, operating systems typically provide support only for the UNIX domain.

Example—`s_pipe` Function Using UNIX Domain Sockets

Figure 17.13 shows the socket-based version of the s_pipe function previously shown in Figure 17.6. The function creates a pair of connected UNIX domain stream sockets.

```
#include "apue.h"
#include <sys/socket.h>

/*
 * Returns a full-duplex "stream" pipe (a UNIX domain socket)
 * with the two file descriptors returned in fd[0] and fd[1].
 */
int
s_pipe(int fd[2])
{
    return(socketpair(AF_UNIX, SOCK_STREAM, 0, fd));
}
```

Figure 17.13 Socket version of the s_pipe function

Some BSD-based systems use UNIX domain sockets to implement pipes. But when `pipe` is called, the write end of the first descriptor and the read end of the second descriptor are both closed. To get a full-duplex pipe, we must call `socketpair` directly.   □

17.3.1 Naming UNIX Domain Sockets

Although the `socketpair` function creates sockets that are connected to each other, the individual sockets don't have names. This means that they can't be addressed by unrelated processes.

In Section 16.3.4, we learned how to bind an address to an Internet domain socket. Just as with Internet domain sockets, UNIX domain sockets can be named and used to advertise services. The address format used with UNIX domain sockets differs from Internet domain sockets, however.

Recall from Section 16.3 that socket address formats differ from one implementation to the next. An address for a UNIX domain socket is represented by a `sockaddr_un` structure. On Linux 2.4.22 and Solaris 9, the `sockaddr_un` structure is defined in the header `<sys/un.h>` as follows:

```
struct sockaddr_un {
    sa_family_t  sun_family;      /* AF_UNIX */
    char         sun_path[108];   /* pathname */
};
```

On FreeBSD 5.2.1 and Mac OS X 10.3, however, the sockaddr_un structure is defined
as

```
struct sockaddr_un {
    unsigned char   sun_len;        /* length including null */
    sa_family_t     sun_family;     /* AF_UNIX */
    char            sun_path[104];  /* pathname */
};
```

The sun_path member of the sockaddr_un structure contains a pathname.
When we bind an address to a UNIX domain socket, the system creates a file of type
S_IFSOCK with the same name.

This file exists only as a means of advertising the socket name to clients. The file
can't be opened or otherwise used for communication by applications.

If the file already exists when we try to bind the same address, the bind request
will fail. When we close the socket, this file is not automatically removed, so we need to
make sure that we unlink it before our application exits.

Example

The program in Figure 17.14 shows an example of binding an address to a UNIX
domain socket.

```
#include "apue.h"
#include <sys/socket.h>
#include <sys/un.h>

int
main(void)
{
    int fd, size;
    struct sockaddr_un un;

    un.sun_family = AF_UNIX;
    strcpy(un.sun_path, "foo.socket");
    if ((fd = socket(AF_UNIX, SOCK_STREAM, 0)) < 0)
        err_sys("socket failed");
    size = offsetof(struct sockaddr_un, sun_path) + strlen(un.sun_path);
    if (bind(fd, (struct sockaddr *)&un, size) < 0)
        err_sys("bind failed");
    printf("UNIX domain socket bound\n");
    exit(0);
}
```

Figure 17.14 Binding an address to a UNIX domain socket

When we run this program, the bind request succeeds, but if we run the program a
second time, we get an error, because the file already exists. The program won't
succeed again until we remove the file.

```
$ ./a.out                                          run the program
UNIX domain socket bound
$ ls -l foo.socket                                 look at the socket file
srwxrwxr-x  1 sar         0 Aug 22 12:43 foo.socket
$ ./a.out                                          try to run the program again
bind failed: Address already in use
$ rm foo.socket                                    remove the socket file
$ ./a.out                                          run the program a third time
UNIX domain socket bound                           now it succeeds
```

The way we determine the size of the address to bind is to determine the offset of the sun_path member in the sockaddr_un structure and add to this the length of the pathname, not including the terminating null byte. Since implementations vary in what members precede sun_path in the sockaddr_un structure, we use the offsetof macro from <stddef.h> (included by apue.h) to calculate the offset of the sun_path member from the start of the structure. If you look in <stddef.h>, you'll see a definition similar to the following:

```
#define offsetof(TYPE, MEMBER)   ((int)&((TYPE *)0)->MEMBER)
```

The expression evaluates to an integer, which is the starting address of the member, assuming that the structure begins at address 0.   ☐

17.3.2 Unique Connections

A server can arrange for unique UNIX domain connections to clients using the standard bind, listen, and accept functions. Clients use connect to contact the server; after the connect request is accepted by the server, a unique connection exists between the client and the server. This style of operation is the same that we illustrated with Internet domain sockets in Figures 16.14 and 16.15.

Figure 17.15 shows the UNIX domain socket version of the serv_listen function.

```
#include "apue.h"
#include <sys/socket.h>
#include <sys/un.h>
#include <errno.h>

#define QLEN    10

/*
 * Create a server endpoint of a connection.
 * Returns fd if all OK, <0 on error.
 */
int
serv_listen(const char *name)
{
    int                 fd, len, err, rval;
    struct sockaddr_un  un;

    /* create a UNIX domain stream socket */
    if ((fd = socket(AF_UNIX, SOCK_STREAM, 0)) < 0)
        return(-1);
```

```
        unlink(name);   /* in case it already exists */

        /* fill in socket address structure */
        memset(&un, 0, sizeof(un));
        un.sun_family = AF_UNIX;
        strcpy(un.sun_path, name);
        len = offsetof(struct sockaddr_un, sun_path) + strlen(name);

        /* bind the name to the descriptor */
        if (bind(fd, (struct sockaddr *)&un, len) < 0) {
            rval = -2;
            goto errout;
        }

        if (listen(fd, QLEN) < 0) { /* tell kernel we're a server */
            rval = -3;
            goto errout;
        }
        return(fd);

errout:
    err = errno;
    close(fd);
    errno = err;
    return(rval);
}
```

Figure 17.15 The serv_listen function for UNIX domain sockets

First, we create a single UNIX domain socket by calling socket. We then fill in a
sockaddr_un structure with the well-known pathname to be assigned to the socket.
This structure is the argument to bind. Note that we don't need to set the sun_len
field present on some platforms, because the operating system sets this for us using the
address length we pass to the bind function.

Finally, we call listen (Section 16.4) to tell the kernel that the process will be
acting as a server awaiting connections from clients. When a connect request from a
client arrives, the server calls the serv_accept function (Figure 17.16).

```
#include "apue.h"
#include <sys/socket.h>
#include <sys/un.h>
#include <time.h>
#include <errno.h>

#define STALE   30  /* client's name can't be older than this (sec) */

/*
 * Wait for a client connection to arrive, and accept it.
 * We also obtain the client's user ID from the pathname
 * that it must bind before calling us.
 * Returns new fd if all OK, <0 on error
 */
```

```
int
serv_accept(int listenfd, uid_t *uidptr)
{
    int                 clifd, err, rval;
    socklen_t           len;
    time_t              staletime;
    struct sockaddr_un  un;
    struct stat         statbuf;

    len = sizeof(un);
    if ((clifd = accept(listenfd, (struct sockaddr *)&un, &len)) < 0)
        return(-1);         /* often errno=EINTR, if signal caught */

    /* obtain the client's uid from its calling address */
    len -= offsetof(struct sockaddr_un, sun_path); /* len of pathname */
    un.sun_path[len] = 0;               /* null terminate */
    if (stat(un.sun_path, &statbuf) < 0) {
        rval = -2;
        goto errout;
    }
#ifdef  S_ISSOCK    /* not defined for SVR4 */
    if (S_ISSOCK(statbuf.st_mode) == 0) {
        rval = -3;          /* not a socket */
        goto errout;
    }
#endif
    if ((statbuf.st_mode & (S_IRWXG | S_IRWXO)) ||
        (statbuf.st_mode & S_IRWXU) != S_IRWXU) {
            rval = -4;      /* is not rwx------ */
            goto errout;
    }

    staletime = time(NULL) - STALE;
    if (statbuf.st_atime < staletime ||
        statbuf.st_ctime < staletime ||
        statbuf.st_mtime < staletime) {
            rval = -5;      /* i-node is too old */
            goto errout;
    }

    if (uidptr != NULL)
        *uidptr = statbuf.st_uid;   /* return uid of caller */
    unlink(un.sun_path);            /* we're done with pathname now */
    return(clifd);

errout:
    err = errno;
    close(clifd);
    errno = err;
    return(rval);
}
```

Figure 17.16 The serv_accept function for UNIX domain sockets

The server blocks in the call to `accept`, waiting for a client to call `cli_conn`. When `accept` returns, its return value is a brand new descriptor that is connected to the client. (This is somewhat similar to what the `connld` module does with the STREAMS subsystem.) Additionally, the pathname that the client assigned to its socket (the name that contained the client's process ID) is also returned by `accept`, through the second argument (the pointer to the `sockaddr_un` structure). We null terminate this pathname and call `stat`. This lets us verify that the pathname is indeed a socket and that the permissions allow only user-read, user-write, and user-execute. We also verify that the three times associated with the socket are no older than 30 seconds. (Recall from Section 6.10 that the `time` function returns the current time and date in seconds past the Epoch.)

If all these checks are OK, we assume that the identity of the client (its effective user ID) is the owner of the socket. Although this check isn't perfect, it's the best we can do with current systems. (It would be better if the kernel returned the effective user ID to `accept` as the `I_RECVFD` `ioctl` command does.)

The client initiates the connection to the server by calling the `cli_conn` function (Figure 17.17).

```
#include "apue.h"
#include <sys/socket.h>
#include <sys/un.h>
#include <errno.h>

#define CLI_PATH    "/var/tmp/"     /* +5 for pid = 14 chars */
#define CLI_PERM    S_IRWXU         /* rwx for user only */

/*
 * Create a client endpoint and connect to a server.
 * Returns fd if all OK, <0 on error.
 */
int
cli_conn(const char *name)
{
    int                 fd, len, err, rval;
    struct sockaddr_un  un;

    /* create a UNIX domain stream socket */
    if ((fd = socket(AF_UNIX, SOCK_STREAM, 0)) < 0)
        return(-1);

    /* fill socket address structure with our address */
    memset(&un, 0, sizeof(un));
    un.sun_family = AF_UNIX;
    sprintf(un.sun_path, "%s%05d", CLI_PATH, getpid());
    len = offsetof(struct sockaddr_un, sun_path) + strlen(un.sun_path);

    unlink(un.sun_path);        /* in case it already exists */
    if (bind(fd, (struct sockaddr *)&un, len) < 0) {
        rval = -2;
        goto errout;
    }
    if (chmod(un.sun_path, CLI_PERM) < 0) {
```

```
                rval = -3;
                goto errout;
        }
        /* fill socket address structure with server's address */
        memset(&un, 0, sizeof(un));
        un.sun_family = AF_UNIX;
        strcpy(un.sun_path, name);
        len = offsetof(struct sockaddr_un, sun_path) + strlen(name);
        if (connect(fd, (struct sockaddr *)&un, len) < 0) {
                rval = -4;
                goto errout;
        }
        return(fd);
errout:
    err = errno;
    close(fd);
    errno = err;
    return(rval);
}
```

Figure 17.17 The `cli_conn` function for UNIX domain sockets

We call `socket` to create the client's end of a UNIX domain socket. We then fill in a `sockaddr_un` structure with a client-specific name.

We don't let the system choose a default address for us, because the server would be unable to distinguish one client from another. Instead, we bind our own address, a step we usually don't take when developing a client program that uses sockets.

The last five characters of the pathname we bind are made from the process ID of the client. We call `unlink`, just in case the pathname already exists. We then call `bind` to assign a name to the client's socket. This creates a socket file in the file system with the same name as the bound pathname. We call `chmod` to turn off all permissions other than user-read, user-write, and user-execute. In `serv_accept`, the server checks these permissions and the user ID of the socket to verify the client's identity.

We then have to fill in another `sockaddr_un` structure, this time with the well-known pathname of the server. Finally, we call the `connect` function to initiate the connection with the server.

17.4 Passing File Descriptors

The ability to pass an open file descriptor between processes is powerful. It can lead to different ways of designing client–server applications. It allows one process (typically a server) to do everything that is required to open a file (involving such details as translating a network name to a network address, dialing a modem, negotiating locks for the file, etc.) and simply pass back to the calling process a descriptor that can be used with all the I/O functions. All the details involved in opening the file or device are hidden from the client.

We must be more specific about what we mean by "passing an open file descriptor" from one process to another. Recall Figure 3.7, which showed two processes that have opened the same file. Although they share the same v-node, each process has its own file table entry.

When we pass an open file descriptor from one process to another, we want the passing process and the receiving process to share the same file table entry. Figure 17.18 shows the desired arrangement.

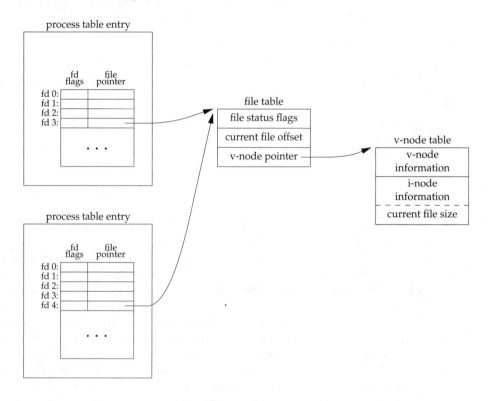

Figure 17.18 Passing an open file from the top process to the bottom process

Technically, we are passing a pointer to an open file table entry from one process to another. This pointer is assigned the first available descriptor in the receiving process. (Saying that we are passing an open descriptor mistakenly gives the impression that the descriptor number in the receiving process is the same as in the sending process, which usually isn't true.) Having two processes share an open file table is exactly what happens after a fork (recall Figure 8.2).

What normally happens when a descriptor is passed from one process to another is that the sending process, after passing the descriptor, then closes the descriptor. Closing the descriptor by the sender doesn't really close the file or device, since the descriptor is still considered open by the receiving process (even if the receiver hasn't specifically received the descriptor yet).

We define the following three functions that we use in this chapter to send and receive file descriptors. Later in this section, we'll show the code for these three functions for both STREAMS and sockets.

```
#include "apue.h"

int send_fd(int fd, int fd_to_send);

int send_err(int fd, int status, const char *errmsg);
```
                                                    Both return: 0 if OK, −1 on error
```
int recv_fd(int fd, ssize_t (*userfunc)(int, const void *, size_t));
```
                                    Returns: file descriptor if OK, negative value on error

A process (normally a server) that wants to pass a descriptor to another process calls either `send_fd` or `send_err`. The process waiting to receive the descriptor (the client) calls `recv_fd`.

The `send_fd` function sends the descriptor *fd_to_send* across using the STREAMS pipe or UNIX domain socket represented by *fd*.

> We'll use the term *s-pipe* to refer to a bidirectional communication channel that could be implemented as either a STREAMS pipe or a UNIX domain stream socket.

The `send_err` function sends the *errmsg* using *fd*, followed by the *status* byte. The value of *status* must be in the range −1 through −255.

Clients call `recv_fd` to receive a descriptor. If all is OK (the sender called `send_fd`), the non-negative descriptor is returned as the value of the function. Otherwise, the value returned is the *status* that was sent by `send_err` (a negative value in the range −1 through −255). Additionally, if an error message was sent by the server, the client's *userfunc* is called to process the message. The first argument to *userfunc* is the constant `STDERR_FILENO`, followed by a pointer to the error message and its length. The return value from *userfunc* is the number of bytes written or a negative number on error. Often, the client specifies the normal `write` function as the *userfunc*.

We implement our own protocol that is used by these three functions. To send a descriptor, `send_fd` sends two bytes of 0, followed by the actual descriptor. To send an error, `send_err` sends the *errmsg*, followed by a byte of 0, followed by the absolute value of the *status* byte (1 through 255). The `recv_fd` function reads everything on the s-pipe until it encounters a null byte. Any characters read up to this point are passed to the caller's *userfunc*. The next byte read by `recv_fd` is the status byte. If the status byte is 0, a descriptor was passed; otherwise, there is no descriptor to receive.

The function `send_err` calls the `send_fd` function after writing the error message to the s-pipe. This is shown in Figure 17.19.

```
#include "apue.h"

/*
 * Used when we had planned to send an fd using send_fd(),
 * but encountered an error instead.  We send the error back
 * using the send_fd()/recv_fd() protocol.
 */
```

```
int
send_err(int fd, int errcode, const char *msg)
{
    int     n;

    if ((n = strlen(msg)) > 0)
        if (writen(fd, msg, n) != n)      /* send the error message */
            return(-1);

    if (errcode >= 0)
        errcode = -1;   /* must be negative */

    if (send_fd(fd, errcode) < 0)
        return(-1);

    return(0);
}
```

Figure 17.19 The send_err function

In the next two sections, we'll look at the implementation of the send_fd and recv_fd functions.

17.4.1 Passing File Descriptors over STREAMS-Based Pipes

With STREAMS pipes, file descriptors are exchanged using two ioctl commands: I_SENDFD and I_RECVFD. To send a descriptor, we set the third argument for ioctl to the actual descriptor. This is shown in Figure 17.20.

```
#include "apue.h"
#include <stropts.h>

/*
 * Pass a file descriptor to another process.
 * If fd<0, then -fd is sent back instead as the error status.
 */
int
send_fd(int fd, int fd_to_send)
{
    char    buf[2];     /* send_fd()/recv_fd() 2-byte protocol */

    buf[0] = 0;             /* null byte flag to recv_fd() */
    if (fd_to_send < 0) {
        buf[1] = -fd_to_send;   /* nonzero status means error */
        if (buf[1] == 0)
            buf[1] = 1; /* -256, etc. would screw up protocol */
    } else {
        buf[1] = 0;     /* zero status means OK */
    }

    if (write(fd, buf, 2) != 2)
        return(-1);
```

```
          if (fd_to_send >= 0)
              if (ioctl(fd, I_SENDFD, fd_to_send) < 0)
                  return(-1);
      return(0);
}
```

Figure 17.20 The send_fd function for STREAMS pipes

When we receive a descriptor, the third argument for `ioctl` is a pointer to a `strrecvfd` structure:

```
struct strrecvfd {
    int    fd;        /* new descriptor */
    uid_t  uid;       /* effective user ID of sender */
    gid_t  gid;       /* effective group ID of sender */
    char   fill[8];
};
```

The `recv_fd` function reads the STREAMS pipe until the first byte of the 2-byte protocol (the null byte) is received. When we issue the `I_RECVFD` ioctl command, the next message on the stream head's read queue must be a descriptor from an `I_SENDFD` call, or we get an error. This function is shown in Figure 17.21.

```
#include "apue.h"
#include <stropts.h>

/*
 * Receive a file descriptor from another process (a server).
 * In addition, any data received from the server is passed
 * to (*userfunc)(STDERR_FILENO, buf, nbytes).  We have a
 * 2-byte protocol for receiving the fd from send_fd().
 */
int
recv_fd(int fd, ssize_t (*userfunc)(int, const void *, size_t))
{
    int                newfd, nread, flag, status;
    char               *ptr;
    char               buf[MAXLINE];
    struct strbuf      dat;
    struct strrecvfd   recvfd;

    status = -1;
    for ( ; ; ) {
        dat.buf = buf;
        dat.maxlen = MAXLINE;
        flag = 0;
        if (getmsg(fd, NULL, &dat, &flag) < 0)
            err_sys("getmsg error");
        nread = dat.len;
        if (nread == 0) {
            err_ret("connection closed by server");
```

```
                    return(-1);
            }
            /*
             * See if this is the final data with null & status.
             * Null must be next to last byte of buffer, status
             * byte is last byte.  Zero status means there must
             * be a file descriptor to receive.
             */
            for (ptr = buf; ptr < &buf[nread]; ) {
                if (*ptr++ == 0) {
                    if (ptr != &buf[nread-1])
                        err_dump("message format error");
                    status = *ptr & 0xFF;    /* prevent sign extension */
                    if (status == 0) {
                        if (ioctl(fd, I_RECVFD, &recvfd) < 0)
                            return(-1);
                        newfd = recvfd.fd;   /* new descriptor */
                    } else {
                        newfd = -status;
                    }
                    nread -= 2;
                }
            }
            if (nread > 0)
                if ((*userfunc)(STDERR_FILENO, buf, nread) != nread)
                    return(-1);

            if (status >= 0)      /* final data has arrived */
                return(newfd);    /* descriptor, or -status */
        }
    }
```

Figure 17.21 The `recv_fd` function for STREAMS pipes

17.4.2 Passing File Descriptors over UNIX Domain Sockets

To exchange file descriptors using UNIX domain sockets, we call the sendmsg(2) and
recvmsg(2) functions (Section 16.5). Both functions take a pointer to a msghdr
structure that contains all the information on what to send or receive. The structure on
your system might look similar to the following:

```
struct msghdr {
    void          *msg_name;        /* optional address */
    socklen_t      msg_namelen;     /* address size in bytes */
    struct iovec  *msg_iov;         /* array of I/O buffers */
    int            msg_iovlen;      /* number of elements in array */
    void          *msg_control;     /* ancillary data */
    socklen_t      msg_controllen;  /* number of ancillary bytes */
    int            msg_flags;       /* flags for received message */
};
```

The first two elements are normally used for sending datagrams on a network connection, where the destination address can be specified with each datagram. The next two elements allow us to specify an array of buffers (scatter read or gather write), as we described for the `readv` and `writev` functions (Section 14.7). The `msg_flags` field contains flags describing the message received, as summarized in Figure 16.13.

Two elements deal with the passing or receiving of control information. The `msg_control` field points to a `cmsghdr` (control message header) structure, and the `msg_controllen` field contains the number of bytes of control information.

```
struct cmsghdr {
    socklen_t   cmsg_len;    /* data byte count, including header */
    int         cmsg_level;  /* originating protocol */
    int         cmsg_type;   /* protocol-specific type */
    /* followed by the actual control message data */
};
```

To send a file descriptor, we set `cmsg_len` to the size of the `cmsghdr` structure, plus the size of an integer (the descriptor). The `cmsg_level` field is set to `SOL_SOCKET`, and `cmsg_type` is set to `SCM_RIGHTS`, to indicate that we are passing access rights. (SCM stands for *socket-level control message*.) Access rights can be passed only across a UNIX domain socket. The descriptor is stored right after the `cmsg_type` field, using the macro `CMSG_DATA` to obtain the pointer to this integer.

Three macros are used to access the control data, and one macro is used to help calculate the value to be used for `cmsg_len`.

```
#include <sys/socket.h>

unsigned char *CMSG_DATA(struct cmsghdr *cp);
```

                                      Returns: pointer to data associated with `cmsghdr` structure

```
struct cmsghdr *CMSG_FIRSTHDR(struct msghdr *mp);
```

                                      Returns: pointer to first `cmsghdr` structure associated
                                            with the `msghdr` structure, or NULL if none exists

```
struct cmsghdr *CMSG_NXTHDR(struct msghdr *mp,
                            struct cmsghdr *cp);
```

                                      Returns: pointer to next `cmsghdr` structure associated with
                                            the `msghdr` structure given the current `cmsghdr`
                                                  structure, or NULL if we're at the last one

```
unsigned int CMSG_LEN(unsigned int nbytes);
```

                                      Returns: size to allocate for data object *nbytes* large

The Single UNIX Specification defines the first three macros, but omits `CMSG_LEN`.

The `CMSG_LEN` macro returns the number of bytes needed to store a data object of size *nbytes*, after adding the size of the `cmsghdr` structure, adjusting for any alignment constraints required by the processor architecture, and rounding up.

The program in Figure 17.22 is the `send_fd` function for UNIX domain sockets.

```c
#include "apue.h"
#include <sys/socket.h>

/* size of control buffer to send/recv one file descriptor */
#define CONTROLLEN  CMSG_LEN(sizeof(int))

static struct cmsghdr   *cmptr = NULL;  /* malloc'ed first time */

/*
 * Pass a file descriptor to another process.
 * If fd<0, then -fd is sent back instead as the error status.
 */
int
send_fd(int fd, int fd_to_send)
{
    struct iovec    iov[1];
    struct msghdr   msg;
    char            buf[2]; /* send_fd()/recv_fd() 2-byte protocol */

    iov[0].iov_base = buf;
    iov[0].iov_len  = 2;
    msg.msg_iov     = iov;
    msg.msg_iovlen  = 1;
    msg.msg_name    = NULL;
    msg.msg_namelen = 0;
    if (fd_to_send < 0) {
        msg.msg_control    = NULL;
        msg.msg_controllen = 0;
        buf[1] = -fd_to_send;   /* nonzero status means error */
        if (buf[1] == 0)
            buf[1] = 1; /* -256, etc. would screw up protocol */
    } else {
        if (cmptr == NULL && (cmptr = malloc(CONTROLLEN)) == NULL)
            return(-1);
        cmptr->cmsg_level  = SOL_SOCKET;
        cmptr->cmsg_type   = SCM_RIGHTS;
        cmptr->cmsg_len    = CONTROLLEN;
        msg.msg_control    = cmptr;
        msg.msg_controllen = CONTROLLEN;
        *(int *)CMSG_DATA(cmptr) = fd_to_send;       /* the fd to pass */
        buf[1] = 0;     /* zero status means OK */
    }
    buf[0] = 0;             /* null byte flag to recv_fd() */
    if (sendmsg(fd, &msg, 0) != 2)
        return(-1);
    return(0);
}
```

Figure 17.22 The send_fd function for UNIX domain sockets

In the sendmsg call, we send both the protocol data (the null and the status byte) and the descriptor.

To receive a descriptor (Figure 17.23), we allocate enough room for a cmsghdr structure and a descriptor, set msg_control to point to the allocated area, and call recvmsg. We use the CMSG_LEN macro to calculate the amount of space needed.

We read from the socket until we read the null byte that precedes the final status byte. Everything up to this null byte is an error message from the sender. This is shown in Figure 17.23.

```
#include "apue.h"
#include <sys/socket.h>        /* struct msghdr */

/* size of control buffer to send/recv one file descriptor */
#define CONTROLLEN  CMSG_LEN(sizeof(int))

static struct cmsghdr   *cmptr = NULL;          /* malloc'ed first time */

/*
 * Receive a file descriptor from a server process.  Also, any data
 * received is passed to (*userfunc)(STDERR_FILENO, buf, nbytes).
 * We have a 2-byte protocol for receiving the fd from send_fd().
 */
int
recv_fd(int fd, ssize_t (*userfunc)(int, const void *, size_t))
{
    int             newfd, nr, status;
    char            *ptr;
    char            buf[MAXLINE];
    struct iovec    iov[1];
    struct msghdr   msg;

    status = -1;
    for ( ; ; ) {
        iov[0].iov_base = buf;
        iov[0].iov_len  = sizeof(buf);
        msg.msg_iov       = iov;
        msg.msg_iovlen    = 1;
        msg.msg_name      = NULL;
        msg.msg_namelen   = 0;
        if (cmptr == NULL && (cmptr = malloc(CONTROLLEN)) == NULL)
            return(-1);
        msg.msg_control    = cmptr;
        msg.msg_controllen = CONTROLLEN;
        if ((nr = recvmsg(fd, &msg, 0)) < 0) {
            err_sys("recvmsg error");
        } else if (nr == 0) {
            err_ret("connection closed by server");
            return(-1);
        }

        /*
         * See if this is the final data with null & status.  Null
```

```
      * is next to last byte of buffer; status byte is last byte.
      * Zero status means there is a file descriptor to receive.
      */
     for (ptr = buf; ptr < &buf[nr]; ) {
         if (*ptr++ == 0) {
             if (ptr != &buf[nr-1])
                 err_dump("message format error");
             status = *ptr & 0xFF;    /* prevent sign extension */
             if (status == 0) {
                 if (msg.msg_controllen != CONTROLLEN)
                     err_dump("status = 0 but no fd");
                 newfd = *(int *)CMSG_DATA(cmptr);
             } else {
                 newfd = -status;
             }
             nr -= 2;
         }
     }
     if (nr > 0 && (*userfunc)(STDERR_FILENO, buf, nr) != nr)
         return(-1);
     if (status >= 0)      /* final data has arrived */
         return(newfd);    /* descriptor, or -status */
    }
}
```

Figure 17.23 The recv_fd function for UNIX domain sockets

Note that we are always prepared to receive a descriptor (we set msg_control and msg_controllen before each call to recvmsg), but only if msg_controllen is nonzero on return did we receive a descriptor.

When it comes to passing file descriptors, one difference between UNIX domain sockets and STREAMS pipes is that we get the identity of the sending process with STREAMS pipes. Some versions of UNIX domain sockets provide similar functionality, but their interfaces differ.

> FreeBSD 5.2.1 and Linux 2.4.22 provide support for sending credentials over UNIX domain sockets, but they do it differently. Mac OS X 10.3 is derived in part from FreeBSD, but has credential passing disabled. Solaris 9 doesn't support sending credentials over UNIX domain sockets.

With FreeBSD, credentials are transmitted as a cmsgcred structure:

```
#define CMGROUP_MAX 16

struct cmsgcred {
    pid_t   cmcred_pid;                    /* sender's process ID */
    uid_t   cmcred_uid;                    /* sender's real UID */
    uid_t   cmcred_euid;                   /* sender's effective UID */
    gid_t   cmcred_gid;                    /* sender's real GID */
    short   cmcred_ngroups;                /* number of groups */
    gid_t   cmcred_groups[CMGROUP_MAX];    /* groups */
};
```

When we transmit credentials, we need to reserve space only for the `cmsgcred` structure. The kernel will fill it in for us to prevent an application from pretending to have a different identity.

On Linux, credentials are transmitted as a `ucred` structure:

```
struct ucred {
    uint32_t  pid;  /* sender's process ID */
    uint32_t  uid;  /* sender's user ID */
    uint32_t  gid;  /* sender's group ID */
};
```

Unlike FreeBSD, Linux requires that we initialize this structure before transmission. The kernel will ensure that applications either use values that correspond to the caller or have the appropriate privilege to use other values.

Figure 17.24 shows the `send_fd` function updated to include the credentials of the sending process.

```
#include "apue.h"
#include <sys/socket.h>

#if defined(SCM_CREDS)            /* BSD interface */
#define CREDSTRUCT      cmsgcred
#define SCM_CREDTYPE    SCM_CREDS
#elif defined(SCM_CREDENTIALS)  /* Linux interface */
#define CREDSTRUCT      ucred
#define SCM_CREDTYPE    SCM_CREDENTIALS
#else
#error passing credentials is unsupported!
#endif

/* size of control buffer to send/recv one file descriptor */
#define RIGHTSLEN   CMSG_LEN(sizeof(int))
#define CREDSLEN    CMSG_LEN(sizeof(struct CREDSTRUCT))
#define CONTROLLEN  (RIGHTSLEN + CREDSLEN)

static struct cmsghdr  *cmptr = NULL;  /* malloc'ed first time */

/*
 * Pass a file descriptor to another process.
 * If fd<0, then -fd is sent back instead as the error status.
 */
int
send_fd(int fd, int fd_to_send)
{
    struct CREDSTRUCT  *credp;
    struct cmsghdr     *cmp;
    struct iovec       iov[1];
    struct msghdr      msg;
    char               buf[2]; /* send_fd/recv_ufd 2-byte protocol */

    iov[0].iov_base = buf;
    iov[0].iov_len  = 2;
    msg.msg_iov     = iov;
    msg.msg_iovlen  = 1;
```

```
        msg.msg_name     = NULL;
        msg.msg_namelen = 0;
        msg.msg_flags = 0;
        if (fd_to_send < 0) {
            msg.msg_control     = NULL;
            msg.msg_controllen = 0;
            buf[1] = -fd_to_send;   /* nonzero status means error */
            if (buf[1] == 0)
                buf[1] = 1; /* -256, etc. would screw up protocol */
        } else {
            if (cmptr == NULL && (cmptr = malloc(CONTROLLEN)) == NULL)
                return(-1);
            msg.msg_control     = cmptr;
            msg.msg_controllen = CONTROLLEN;
            cmp = cmptr;
            cmp->cmsg_level   = SOL_SOCKET;
            cmp->cmsg_type    = SCM_RIGHTS;
            cmp->cmsg_len     = RIGHTSLEN;
            *(int *)CMSG_DATA(cmp) = fd_to_send;    /* the fd to pass */

            cmp = CMSG_NXTHDR(&msg, cmp);
            cmp->cmsg_level   = SOL_SOCKET;
            cmp->cmsg_type    = SCM_CREDTYPE;
            cmp->cmsg_len     = CREDSLEN;
            credp = (struct CREDSTRUCT *)CMSG_DATA(cmp);
#if defined(SCM_CREDENTIALS)
            credp->uid = geteuid();
            credp->gid = getegid();
            credp->pid = getpid();
#endif
            buf[1] = 0;      /* zero status means OK */
        }
        buf[0] = 0;              /* null byte flag to recv_ufd() */
        if (sendmsg(fd, &msg, 0) != 2)
            return(-1);
        return(0);
    }
```

Figure 17.24 Sending credentials over UNIX domain sockets

Note that we need to initialize the credentials structure only on Linux.

The function in Figure 17.25 is a modified version of `recv_fd`, called `recv_ufd`, that returns the user ID of the sender through a reference parameter.

```
#include "apue.h"
#include <sys/socket.h>       /* struct msghdr */
#include <sys/un.h>

#if defined(SCM_CREDS)              /* BSD interface */
#define CREDSTRUCT      cmsgcred
#define CR_UID          cmcred_uid
#define CREDOPT         LOCAL_PEERCRED
```

```
#define SCM_CREDTYPE     SCM_CREDS
#elif defined(SCM_CREDENTIALS)  /* Linux interface */
#define CREDSTRUCT       ucred
#define CR_UID           uid
#define CREDOPT          SO_PASSCRED
#define SCM_CREDTYPE     SCM_CREDENTIALS
#else
#error passing credentials is unsupported!
#endif

/* size of control buffer to send/recv one file descriptor */
#define RIGHTSLEN    CMSG_LEN(sizeof(int))
#define CREDSLEN     CMSG_LEN(sizeof(struct CREDSTRUCT))
#define CONTROLLEN   (RIGHTSLEN + CREDSLEN)

static struct cmsghdr   *cmptr = NULL;        /* malloc'ed first time */

/*
 * Receive a file descriptor from a server process.  Also, any data
 * received is passed to (*userfunc)(STDERR_FILENO, buf, nbytes).
 * We have a 2-byte protocol for receiving the fd from send_fd().
 */
int
recv_ufd(int fd, uid_t *uidptr,
         ssize_t (*userfunc)(int, const void *, size_t))
{
    struct cmsghdr      *cmp;
    struct CREDSTRUCT   *credp;
    int                 newfd, nr, status;
    char                *ptr;
    char                buf[MAXLINE];
    struct iovec        iov[1];
    struct msghdr       msg;
    const int           on = 1;

    status = -1;
    newfd = -1;
    if (setsockopt(fd, SOL_SOCKET, CREDOPT, &on, sizeof(int)) < 0) {
        err_ret("setsockopt failed");
        return(-1);
    }
    for ( ; ; ) {
        iov[0].iov_base = buf;
        iov[0].iov_len  = sizeof(buf);
        msg.msg_iov     = iov;
        msg.msg_iovlen  = 1;
        msg.msg_name    = NULL;
        msg.msg_namelen = 0;
        if (cmptr == NULL && (cmptr = malloc(CONTROLLEN)) == NULL)
            return(-1);
        msg.msg_control    = cmptr;
        msg.msg_controllen = CONTROLLEN;
        if ((nr = recvmsg(fd, &msg, 0)) < 0) {
```

```
                err_sys("recvmsg error");
        } else if (nr == 0) {
            err_ret("connection closed by server");
            return(-1);
        }
        /*
         * See if this is the final data with null & status.  Null
         * is next to last byte of buffer; status byte is last byte.
         * Zero status means there is a file descriptor to receive.
         */
        for (ptr = buf; ptr < &buf[nr]; ) {
            if (*ptr++ == 0) {
                if (ptr != &buf[nr-1])
                    err_dump("message format error");
                status = *ptr & 0xFF;    /* prevent sign extension */
                if (status == 0) {
                    if (msg.msg_controllen != CONTROLLEN)
                        err_dump("status = 0 but no fd");

                    /* process the control data */
                    for (cmp = CMSG_FIRSTHDR(&msg);
                       cmp != NULL; cmp = CMSG_NXTHDR(&msg, cmp)) {
                        if (cmp->cmsg_level != SOL_SOCKET)
                            continue;
                        switch (cmp->cmsg_type) {
                        case SCM_RIGHTS:
                            newfd = *(int *)CMSG_DATA(cmp);
                            break;
                        case SCM_CREDTYPE:
                            credp = (struct CREDSTRUCT *)CMSG_DATA(cmp);
                            *uidptr = credp->CR_UID;
                        }
                    }
                } else {
                    newfd = -status;
                }
                nr -= 2;
            }
        }
        if (nr > 0 && (*userfunc)(STDERR_FILENO, buf, nr) != nr)
            return(-1);
        if (status >= 0)    /* final data has arrived */
            return(newfd);  /* descriptor, or -status */
    }
}
```

Figure 17.25 Receiving credentials over UNIX domain sockets

On FreeBSD, we specify SCM_CREDS to transmit credentials; on Linux, we use
SCM_CREDENTIALS.

17.5   An Open Server, Version 1

Using file descriptor passing, we now develop an open server: a program that is executed by a process to open one or more files. But instead of sending the contents of the file back to the calling process, the server sends back an open file descriptor. This lets the server work with any type of file (such as a device or a socket) and not simply regular files. It also means that a minimum of information is exchanged using IPC: the filename and open mode from the client to the server, and the returned descriptor from the server to the client. The contents of the file are not exchanged using IPC.

There are several advantages in designing the server to be a separate executable program (either one that is executed by the client, as we develop in this section, or a daemon server, which we develop in the next section).

- The server can easily be contacted by any client, similar to the client calling a library function. We are not hard coding a particular service into the application, but designing a general facility that others can reuse.
- If we need to change the server, only a single program is affected. Conversely, updating a library function can require that all programs that call the function be updated (i.e., relinked with the link editor). Shared libraries can simplify this updating (Section 7.7).
- The server can be a set-user-ID program, providing it with additional permissions that the client does not have. Note that a library function (or shared library function) can't provide this capability.

The client process creates an s-pipe (either a STREAMS-based pipe or a UNIX domain socket pair) and then calls `fork` and `exec` to invoke the server. The client sends requests across the s-pipe, and the server sends back responses across the s-pipe.

We define the following application protocol between the client and the server.

1. The client sends a request of the form "open *<pathname>* *<openmode>*\0" across the s-pipe to the server. The *<openmode>* is the numeric value, in ASCII decimal, of the second argument to the `open` function. This request string is terminated by a null byte.
2. The server sends back an open descriptor or an error by calling either `send_fd` or `send_err`.

This is an example of a process sending an open descriptor to its parent. In Section 17.6, we'll modify this example to use a single daemon server, where the server sends a descriptor to a completely unrelated process.

We first have the header, `open.h` (Figure 17.26), which includes the standard headers and defines the function prototypes.

```
#include "apue.h"
#include <errno.h>

#define CL_OPEN "open"          /* client's request for server */

int     csopen(char *, int);
```

Figure 17.26 The `open.h` header

The `main` function (Figure 17.27) is a loop that reads a pathname from standard input and copies the file to standard output. The function calls `csopen` to contact the open server and return an open descriptor.

```
#include     "open.h"
#include     <fcntl.h>

#define BUFFSIZE     8192

int
main(int argc, char *argv[])
{
    int     n, fd;
    char    buf[BUFFSIZE], line[MAXLINE];

    /* read filename to cat from stdin */
    while (fgets(line, MAXLINE, stdin) != NULL) {
        if (line[strlen(line) - 1] == '\n')
            line[strlen(line) - 1] = 0; /* replace newline with null */

        /* open the file */
        if ((fd = csopen(line, O_RDONLY)) < 0)
            continue;    /* csopen() prints error from server */

        /* and cat to stdout */
        while ((n = read(fd, buf, BUFFSIZE)) > 0)
            if (write(STDOUT_FILENO, buf, n) != n)
                err_sys("write error");
        if (n < 0)
            err_sys("read error");
        close(fd);
    }

    exit(0);
}
```

Figure 17.27 The client `main` function, version 1

The function `csopen` (Figure 17.28) does the `fork` and `exec` of the server, after creating the s-pipe.

```
#include     "open.h"
#include     <sys/uio.h>      /* struct iovec */

/*
 * Open the file by sending the "name" and "oflag" to the
 * connection server and reading a file descriptor back.
 */
int
csopen(char *name, int oflag)
{
    pid_t           pid;
    int             len;
```

```
char            buf[10];
struct iovec    iov[3];
static int      fd[2] = { -1, -1 };

if (fd[0] < 0) {      /* fork/exec our open server first time */
    if (s_pipe(fd) < 0)
        err_sys("s_pipe error");
    if ((pid = fork()) < 0) {
        err_sys("fork error");
    } else if (pid == 0) {        /* child */
        close(fd[0]);
        if (fd[1] != STDIN_FILENO &&
          dup2(fd[1], STDIN_FILENO) != STDIN_FILENO)
            err_sys("dup2 error to stdin");
        if (fd[1] != STDOUT_FILENO &&
          dup2(fd[1], STDOUT_FILENO) != STDOUT_FILENO)
            err_sys("dup2 error to stdout");
        if (execl("./opend", "opend", (char *)0) < 0)
            err_sys("execl error");
    }
    close(fd[1]);                      /* parent */
}
sprintf(buf, " %d", oflag);       /* oflag to ascii */
iov[0].iov_base = CL_OPEN " ";          /* string concatenation */
iov[0].iov_len  = strlen(CL_OPEN) + 1;
iov[1].iov_base = name;
iov[1].iov_len  = strlen(name);
iov[2].iov_base = buf;
iov[2].iov_len  = strlen(buf) + 1;   /* +1 for null at end of buf */
len = iov[0].iov_len + iov[1].iov_len + iov[2].iov_len;
if (writev(fd[0], &iov[0], 3) != len)
    err_sys("writev error");

/* read descriptor, returned errors handled by write() */
return(recv_fd(fd[0], write));
}
```

Figure 17.28 The csopen function, version 1

The child closes one end of the pipe, and the parent closes the other. For the server that it executes, the child also duplicates its end of the pipe onto its standard input and standard output. (Another option would have been to pass the ASCII representation of the descriptor fd[1] as an argument to the server.)

The parent sends to the server the request containing the pathname and open mode. Finally, the parent calls recv_fd to return either the descriptor or an error. If an error is returned by the server, write is called to output the message to standard error.

Now let's look at the open server. It is the program opend that is executed by the client in Figure 17.28. First, we have the opend.h header (Figure 17.29), which includes the standard headers and declares the global variables and function prototypes.

```
#include "apue.h"
#include <errno.h>

#define CL_OPEN "open"              /* client's request for server */

extern char   errmsg[];   /* error message string to return to client */
extern int    oflag;      /* open() flag: O_xxx ... */
extern char *pathname;    /* of file to open() for client */

int      cli_args(int, char **);
void     request(char *, int, int);
```

Figure 17.29   The opend.h header, version 1

The main function (Figure 17.30) reads the requests from the client on the s-pipe (its standard input) and calls the function request.

```
#include     "opend.h"

char     errmsg[MAXLINE];
int      oflag;
char     *pathname;

int
main(void)
{
    int      nread;
    char     buf[MAXLINE];

    for ( ; ; ) {   /* read arg buffer from client, process request */
        if ((nread = read(STDIN_FILENO, buf, MAXLINE)) < 0)
            err_sys("read error on stream pipe");
        else if (nread == 0)
            break;       /* client has closed the stream pipe */
        request(buf, nread, STDOUT_FILENO);
    }
    exit(0);
}
```

Figure 17.30   The server main function, version 1

The function request in Figure 17.31 does all the work. It calls the function buf_args to break up the client's request into a standard argv-style argument list and calls the function cli_args to process the client's arguments. If all is OK, open is called to open the file, and then send_fd sends the descriptor back to the client across the s-pipe (its standard output). If an error is encountered, send_err is called to send back an error message, using the client–server protocol that we described earlier.

```
#include     "opend.h"
#include     <fcntl.h>

void
request(char *buf, int nread, int fd)
{
```

```
    int     newfd;
    if (buf[nread-1] != 0) {
        sprintf(errmsg, "request not null terminated: %*.*s\n",
          nread, nread, buf);
        send_err(fd, -1, errmsg);
        return;
    }
    if (buf_args(buf, cli_args) < 0) {  /* parse args & set options */
        send_err(fd, -1, errmsg);
        return;
    }
    if ((newfd = open(pathname, oflag)) < 0) {
        sprintf(errmsg, "can't open %s: %s\n", pathname,
          strerror(errno));
        send_err(fd, -1, errmsg);
        return;
    }
    if (send_fd(fd, newfd) < 0)       /* send the descriptor */
        err_sys("send_fd error");
    close(newfd);          /* we're done with descriptor */
}
```

Figure 17.31 The request function, version 1

The client's request is a null-terminated string of white-space-separated arguments. The function buf_args in Figure 17.32 breaks this string into a standard argv-style argument list and calls a user function to process the arguments. We'll use the buf_args function later in this chapter. We use the ISO C function strtok to tokenize the string into separate arguments.

```
#include "apue.h"

#define MAXARGC     50  /* max number of arguments in buf */
#define WHITE   " \t\n" /* white space for tokenizing arguments */

/*
 * buf[] contains white-space-separated arguments.  We convert it to an
 * argv-style array of pointers, and call the user's function (optfunc)
 * to process the array.  We return -1 if there's a problem parsing buf,
 * else we return whatever optfunc() returns.  Note that user's buf[]
 * array is modified (nulls placed after each token).
 */
int
buf_args(char *buf, int (*optfunc)(int, char **))
{
    char    *ptr, *argv[MAXARGC];
    int     argc;

    if (strtok(buf, WHITE) == NULL)      /* an argv[0] is required */
        return(-1);
    argv[argc = 0] = buf;
```

```
    while ((ptr = strtok(NULL, WHITE)) != NULL) {
        if (++argc >= MAXARGC-1)      /* -1 for room for NULL at end */
            return(-1);
        argv[argc] = ptr;
    }
    argv[++argc] = NULL;

    /*
     * Since argv[] pointers point into the user's buf[],
     * user's function can just copy the pointers, even
     * though argv[] array will disappear on return.
     */
    return((*optfunc)(argc, argv));
}
```

Figure 17.32 The buf_args function

The server's function that is called by buf_args is cli_args (Figure 17.33). It verifies that the client sent the right number of arguments and stores the pathname and open mode in global variables.

```
#include    "opend.h"

/*
 * This function is called by buf_args(), which is called by
 * request().  buf_args() has broken up the client's buffer
 * into an argv[]-style array, which we now process.
 */
int
cli_args(int argc, char **argv)
{
    if (argc != 3 || strcmp(argv[0], CL_OPEN) != 0) {
        strcpy(errmsg, "usage: <pathname> <oflag>\n");
        return(-1);
    }
    pathname = argv[1];      /* save ptr to pathname to open */
    oflag = atoi(argv[2]);
    return(0);
}
```

Figure 17.33 The cli_args function

This completes the open server that is invoked by a fork and exec from the client. A single s-pipe is created before the fork and is used to communicate between the client and the server. With this arrangement, we have one server per client.

17.6 An Open Server, Version 2

In the previous section, we developed an open server that was invoked by a fork and exec by the client, demonstrating how we can pass file descriptors from a child to a parent. In this section, we develop an open server as a daemon process. One server handles all clients. We expect this design to be more efficient, since a `fork` and `exec` are avoided. We still use an s-pipe between the client and the server and demonstrate passing file descriptors between unrelated processes. We'll use the three functions `serv_listen`, `serv_accept`, and `cli_conn` introduced in Section 17.2.2. This server also demonstrates how a single server can handle multiple clients, using both the `select` and `poll` functions from Section 14.5.

The client is similar to the client from Section 17.5. Indeed, the file `main.c` is identical (Figure 17.27). We add the following line to the `open.h` header (Figure 17.26):

```
#define CS_OPEN "/home/sar/opend"   /* server's well-known name */
```

The file `open.c` does change from Figure 17.28, since we now call `cli_conn` instead of doing the `fork` and `exec`. This is shown in Figure 17.34.

```
#include     "open.h"
#include     <sys/uio.h>        /* struct iovec */

/*
 * Open the file by sending the "name" and "oflag" to the
 * connection server and reading a file descriptor back.
 */
int
csopen(char *name, int oflag)
{
    int          len;
    char         buf[10];
    struct iovec iov[3];
    static int   csfd = -1;

    if (csfd < 0) {      /* open connection to conn server */
        if ((csfd = cli_conn(CS_OPEN)) < 0)
            err_sys("cli_conn error");
    }

    sprintf(buf, " %d", oflag);       /* oflag to ascii */
    iov[0].iov_base = CL_OPEN " ";   /* string concatenation */
    iov[0].iov_len  = strlen(CL_OPEN) + 1;
    iov[1].iov_base = name;
    iov[1].iov_len  = strlen(name);
    iov[2].iov_base = buf;
    iov[2].iov_len  = strlen(buf) + 1;   /* null always sent */
    len = iov[0].iov_len + iov[1].iov_len + iov[2].iov_len;
    if (writev(csfd, &iov[0], 3) != len)
        err_sys("writev error");

    /* read back descriptor; returned errors handled by write() */
    return(recv_fd(csfd, write));
}
```

Figure 17.34 The `csopen` function, version 2

The protocol from the client to the server remains the same.

Next, we'll look at the server. The header `opend.h` (Figure 17.35) includes the standard headers and declares the global variables and the function prototypes.

```
#include "apue.h"
#include <errno.h>

#define CS_OPEN "/home/sar/opend"    /* well-known name */
#define CL_OPEN "open"               /* client's request for server */

extern int    debug;      /* nonzero if interactive (not daemon) */
extern char   errmsg[];   /* error message string to return to client */
extern int    oflag;      /* open flag: O_xxx ... */
extern char  *pathname;   /* of file to open for client */

typedef struct {    /* one Client struct per connected client */
  int    fd;        /* fd, or -1 if available */
  uid_t uid;
} Client;

extern Client   *client;          /* ptr to malloc'ed array */
extern int       client_size;     /* # entries in client[] array */

int     cli_args(int, char **);
int     client_add(int, uid_t);
void    client_del(int);
void    loop(void);
void    request(char *, int, int, uid_t);
```

Figure 17.35 The `opend.h` header, version 2

Since this server handles all clients, it must maintain the state of each client connection. This is done with the `client` array declared in the `opend.h` header. Figure 17.36 defines three functions that manipulate this array.

```
#include      "opend.h"

#define NALLOC  10        /* # client structs to alloc/realloc for */

static void
client_alloc(void)        /* alloc more entries in the client[] array */
{
    int     i;

    if (client == NULL)
        client = malloc(NALLOC * sizeof(Client));
    else
        client = realloc(client, (client_size+NALLOC)*sizeof(Client));
    if (client == NULL)
        err_sys("can't alloc for client array");

    /* initialize the new entries */
    for (i = client_size; i < client_size + NALLOC; i++)
        client[i].fd = -1;  /* fd of -1 means entry available */

    client_size += NALLOC;
```

```
}
/*
 * Called by loop() when connection request from a new client arrives.
 */
int
client_add(int fd, uid_t uid)
{
    int     i;

    if (client == NULL)      /* first time we're called */
        client_alloc();
again:
    for (i = 0; i < client_size; i++) {
        if (client[i].fd == -1) {    /* find an available entry */
            client[i].fd = fd;
            client[i].uid = uid;
            return(i);   /* return index in client[] array */
        }
    }

    /* client array full, time to realloc for more */
    client_alloc();
    goto again;       /* and search again (will work this time) */
}
/*
 * Called by loop() when we're done with a client.
 */
void
client_del(int fd)
{
    int     i;

    for (i = 0; i < client_size; i++) {
        if (client[i].fd == fd) {
            client[i].fd = -1;
            return;
        }
    }
    log_quit("can't find client entry for fd %d", fd);
}
```

Figure 17.36 Functions to manipulate `client` array

The first time `client_add` is called, it calls `client_alloc`, which calls `malloc` to allocate space for ten entries in the array. After these ten entries are all in use, a later call to `client_add` causes `realloc` to allocate additional space. By dynamically allocating space this way, we have not limited the size of the `client` array at compile time to some value that we guessed and put into a header. These functions call the `log_` functions (Appendix B) if an error occurs, since we assume that the server is a daemon.

The `main` function (Figure 17.37) defines the global variables, processes the command-line options, and calls the function `loop`. If we invoke the server with the `-d` option, the server runs interactively instead of as a daemon. This is used when testing the server.

```c
#include    "opend.h"
#include    <syslog.h>

int     debug, oflag, client_size, log_to_stderr;
char    errmsg[MAXLINE];
char    *pathname;
Client  *client = NULL;

int
main(int argc, char *argv[])
{
    int     c;

    log_open("open.serv", LOG_PID, LOG_USER);

    opterr = 0;        /* don't want getopt() writing to stderr */
    while ((c = getopt(argc, argv, "d")) != EOF) {
        switch (c) {
        case 'd':         /* debug */
            debug = log_to_stderr = 1;
            break;

        case '?':
            err_quit("unrecognized option: -%c", optopt);
        }
    }

    if (debug == 0)
        daemonize("opend");

    loop();     /* never returns */
}
```

Figure 17.37 The server `main` function, version 2

The function `loop` is the server's infinite loop. We'll show two versions of this function. Figure 17.38 shows one version that uses `select`; Figure 17.39 shows another version that uses `poll`.

```c
#include    "opend.h"
#include    <sys/time.h>
#include    <sys/select.h>

void
loop(void)
{
    int     i, n, maxfd, maxi, listenfd, clifd, nread;
    char    buf[MAXLINE];
```

```
uid_t   uid;
fd_set  rset, allset;

FD_ZERO(&allset);

/* obtain fd to listen for client requests on */
if ((listenfd = serv_listen(CS_OPEN)) < 0)
    log_sys("serv_listen error");
FD_SET(listenfd, &allset);
maxfd = listenfd;
maxi = -1;

for ( ; ; ) {
    rset = allset;  /* rset gets modified each time around */
    if ((n = select(maxfd + 1, &rset, NULL, NULL, NULL)) < 0)
        log_sys("select error");

    if (FD_ISSET(listenfd, &rset)) {
        /* accept new client request */
        if ((clifd = serv_accept(listenfd, &uid)) < 0)
            log_sys("serv_accept error: %d", clifd);
        i = client_add(clifd, uid);
        FD_SET(clifd, &allset);
        if (clifd > maxfd)
            maxfd = clifd;  /* max fd for select() */
        if (i > maxi)
            maxi = i;    /* max index in client[] array */
        log_msg("new connection: uid %d, fd %d", uid, clifd);
        continue;
    }

    for (i = 0; i <= maxi; i++) {    /* go through client[] array */
        if ((clifd = client[i].fd) < 0)
            continue;
        if (FD_ISSET(clifd, &rset)) {
            /* read argument buffer from client */
            if ((nread = read(clifd, buf, MAXLINE)) < 0) {
                log_sys("read error on fd %d", clifd);
            } else if (nread == 0) {
                log_msg("closed: uid %d, fd %d",
                  client[i].uid, clifd);
                client_del(clifd);  /* client has closed cxn */
                FD_CLR(clifd, &allset);
                close(clifd);
            } else {     /* process client's request */
                request(buf, nread, clifd, client[i].uid);
            }
        }
    }
}
}
```

Figure 17.38 The `loop` function using `select`

This function calls `serv_listen` to create the server's endpoint for the client connections. The remainder of the function is a loop that starts with a call to `select`. Two conditions can be true after `select` returns.

1. The descriptor `listenfd` can be ready for reading, which means that a new client has called `cli_conn`. To handle this, we call `serv_accept` and then update the `client` array and associated bookkeeping information for the new client. (We keep track of the highest descriptor number for the first argument to `select`. We also keep track of the highest index in use in the `client` array.)

2. An existing client's connection can be ready for reading. This means that the client has either terminated or sent a new request. We find out about a client termination by `read` returning 0 (end of file). If `read` returns a value greater than 0, there is a new request to process, which we handle by calling `request`.

We keep track of which descriptors are currently in use in the `allset` descriptor set. As new clients connect to the server, the appropriate bit is turned on in this descriptor set. The appropriate bit is turned off when the client terminates.

We always know when a client terminates, whether the termination is voluntary or not, since all the client's descriptors (including the connection to the server) are automatically closed by the kernel. This differs from the XSI IPC mechanisms.

The `loop` function that uses `poll` is shown in Figure 17.39.

```
#include     "opend.h"
#include     <poll.h>
#if !defined(BSD) && !defined(MACOS)
#include     <stropts.h>
#endif

void
loop(void)
{
    int             i, maxi, listenfd, clifd, nread;
    char            buf[MAXLINE];
    uid_t           uid;
    struct pollfd   *pollfd;

    if ((pollfd = malloc(open_max() * sizeof(struct pollfd))) == NULL)
        err_sys("malloc error");

    /* obtain fd to listen for client requests on */
    if ((listenfd = serv_listen(CS_OPEN)) < 0)
        log_sys("serv_listen error");
    client_add(listenfd, 0);    /* we use [0] for listenfd */
    pollfd[0].fd = listenfd;
    pollfd[0].events = POLLIN;
    maxi = 0;

    for ( ; ; ) {
        if (poll(pollfd, maxi + 1, -1) < 0)
            log_sys("poll error");

        if (pollfd[0].revents & POLLIN) {
```

```
                    /* accept new client request */
                    if ((clifd = serv_accept(listenfd, &uid)) < 0)
                        log_sys("serv_accept error: %d", clifd);
                    i = client_add(clifd, uid);
                    pollfd[i].fd = clifd;
                    pollfd[i].events = POLLIN;
                    if (i > maxi)
                        maxi = i;
                    log_msg("new connection: uid %d, fd %d", uid, clifd);
                }

            for (i = 1; i <= maxi; i++) {
                if ((clifd = client[i].fd) < 0)
                    continue;
                if (pollfd[i].revents & POLLHUP) {
                    goto hungup;
                } else if (pollfd[i].revents & POLLIN) {
                    /* read argument buffer from client */
                    if ((nread = read(clifd, buf, MAXLINE)) < 0) {
                        log_sys("read error on fd %d", clifd);
                    } else if (nread == 0) {
hungup:
                        log_msg("closed: uid %d, fd %d",
                          client[i].uid, clifd);
                        client_del(clifd);   /* client has closed conn */
                        pollfd[i].fd = -1;
                        close(clifd);
                    } else {          /* process client's request */
                        request(buf, nread, clifd, client[i].uid);
                    }
                }
            }
        }
    }
```

Figure 17.39 The `loop` function using `poll`

To allow for as many clients as there are possible open descriptors, we dynamically allocate space for the array of `pollfd` structures. (Recall the `open_max` function from Figure 2.16.)

We use the first entry (index 0) of the `client` array for the `listenfd` descriptor. That way, a client's index in the `client` array is the same index that we use in the `pollfd` array. The arrival of a new client connection is indicated by a `POLLIN` on the `listenfd` descriptor. As before, we call `serv_accept` to accept the connection.

For an existing client, we have to handle two different events from `poll`: a client termination is indicated by `POLLHUP`, and a new request from an existing client is indicated by `POLLIN`. Recall from Exercise 15.7 that the hang-up message can arrive at the stream head while there is still data to be read from the stream. With a pipe, we want to read all the data before processing the hangup. But with this server, when we receive the hangup from the client, we can `close` the connection (the stream) to the client, effectively throwing away any data still on the stream. There is no reason to process any requests still on the stream, since we can't send any responses back.

As with the `select` version of this function, new requests from a client are handled by calling the `request` function (Figure 17.40). This function is similar to the earlier version (Figure 17.31). It calls the same function, `buf_args` (Figure 17.32), that calls `cli_args` (Figure 17.33), but since it runs from a daemon process, it logs error messages instead of printing them on the standard error stream.

```c
#include     "opend.h"
#include     <fcntl.h>

void
request(char *buf, int nread, int clifd, uid_t uid)
{
    int      newfd;

    if (buf[nread-1] != 0) {
        sprintf(errmsg,
          "request from uid %d not null terminated: %*.*s\n",
          uid, nread, nread, buf);
        send_err(clifd, -1, errmsg);
        return;
    }
    log_msg("request: %s, from uid %d", buf, uid);

    /* parse the arguments, set options */
    if (buf_args(buf, cli_args) < 0) {
        send_err(clifd, -1, errmsg);
        log_msg(errmsg);
        return;
    }

    if ((newfd = open(pathname, oflag)) < 0) {
        sprintf(errmsg, "can't open %s: %s\n",
          pathname, strerror(errno));
        send_err(clifd, -1, errmsg);
        log_msg(errmsg);
        return;
    }

    /* send the descriptor */
    if (send_fd(clifd, newfd) < 0)
        log_sys("send_fd error");
    log_msg("sent fd %d over fd %d for %s", newfd, clifd, pathname);
    close(newfd);         /* we're done with descriptor */
}
```

Figure 17.40   The `request` function, version 2

This completes the second version of the open server, using a single daemon to handle all the client requests.

17.7 Summary

The key points in this chapter are the ability to pass file descriptors between processes and the ability of a server to accept unique connections from clients. We've seen how to do this using both STREAMS pipes and UNIX domain sockets. Although all platforms provide support for UNIX domain sockets (refer back to Figure 15.1), we've seen that there are differences in each implementation, which makes it more difficult for us to develop portable applications.

We presented two versions of an open server. One version was invoked directly by the client, using `fork` and `exec`. The second was a daemon server that handled all client requests. Both versions used the file descriptor passing and receiving functions. The final version also used the client–server connection functions introduced in Section 17.2.2 and the I/O multiplexing functions from Section 14.5.

Exercises

17.1 Recode Figure 17.4 to use the standard I/O library instead of `read` and `write` on the STREAMS pipe.

17.2 Write the following program using the file descriptor passing functions from this chapter and the parent–child synchronization routines from Section 8.9. The program calls `fork`, and the child `open`s an existing file and passes the open descriptor to the parent. The child then positions the file using `lseek` and notifies the parent. The parent reads the file's current offset and prints it for verification. If the file was passed from the child to the parent as we described, they should be sharing the same file table entry, so each time the child changes the file's current offset, that change should also affect the parent's descriptor. Have the child position the file to a different offset and notify the parent again.

17.3 In Figures 17.29 and 17.30, we differentiated between declaring and defining the global variables. What is the difference?

17.4 Recode the `buf_args` function (Figure 17.32), removing the compile-time limit on the size of the `argv` array. Use dynamic memory allocation.

17.5 Describe ways to optimize the function `loop` in Figure 17.38 and Figure 17.39. Implement your optimizations.

18

Terminal I/O

18.1 Introduction

The handling of terminal I/O is a messy area, regardless of the operating system. The UNIX System is no exception. The manual page for terminal I/O is usually one of the longest in most editions of the programmer's manuals.

With the UNIX System, a schism formed in the late 1970s when System III developed a different set of terminal routines from those of Version 7. The System III style of terminal I/O continued through System V, and the Version 7 style became the standard for the BSD-derived systems. As with signals, this difference between the two worlds has been conquered by POSIX.1. In this chapter, we look at all the POSIX.1 terminal functions and some of the platform-specific additions.

Part of the complexity of the terminal I/O system occurs because people use terminal I/O for so many different things: terminals, hardwired lines between computers, modems, printers, and so on.

18.2 Overview

Terminal I/O has two modes:

1. Canonical mode input processing. In this mode, terminal input is processed as lines. The terminal driver returns at most one line per read request.

2. Noncanonical mode input processing. The input characters are not assembled into lines.

If we don't do anything special, canonical mode is the default. For example, if the shell redirects standard input to the terminal and we use `read` and `write` to copy standard input to standard output, the terminal is in canonical mode, and each `read` returns at most one line. Programs that manipulate the entire screen, such as the `vi` editor, use noncanonical mode, since the commands may be single characters and are not terminated by newlines. Also, this editor doesn't want processing by the system of the special characters, since they may overlap with the editor commands. For example, the Control-D character is often the end-of-file character for the terminal, but it's also a `vi` command to scroll down one-half screen.

> The Version 7 and older BSD-style terminal drivers supported three modes for terminal input: (a) cooked mode (the input is collected into lines, and the special characters are processed), (b) raw mode (the input is not assembled into lines, and there is no processing of special characters), and (c) cbreak mode (the input is not assembled into lines, but some of the special characters are processed). Figure 18.20 shows a POSIX.1 function that places a terminal in cbreak or raw mode.

POSIX.1 defines 11 special input characters, 9 of which we can change. We've been using some of these throughout the text: the end-of-file character (usually Control-D) and the suspend character (usually Control-Z), for example. Section 18.3 describes each of these characters.

We can think of a terminal device as being controlled by a terminal driver, usually within the kernel. Each terminal device has an input queue and an output queue, shown in Figure 18.1.

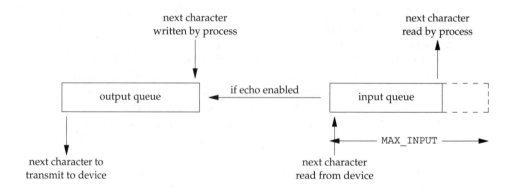

Figure 18.1 Logical picture of input and output queues for a terminal device

There are several points to consider from this picture.

- If echoing is enabled, there is an implied link between the input queue and the output queue.

- The size of the input queue, `MAX_INPUT` (see Figure 2.11), is finite. When the input queue for a particular device fills, the system behavior is implementation dependent. Most UNIX systems echo the bell character when this happens.

- There is another input limit, MAX_CANON, that we don't show here. This limit is the maximum number of bytes in a canonical input line.

- Although the size of the output queue is finite, no constants defining that size are accessible to the program, because when the output queue starts to fill up, the kernel simply puts the writing process to sleep until room is available.

- We'll see how the tcflush flush function allows us to flush either the input queue or the output queue. Similarly, when we describe the tcsetattr function, we'll see how we can tell the system to change the attributes of a terminal device only after the output queue is empty. (We want to do this, for example, if we're changing the output attributes.) We can also tell the system to discard everything in the input queue when changing the terminal attributes. (We want to do this if we're changing the input attributes or changing between canonical and noncanonical modes, so that previously entered characters aren't interpreted in the wrong mode.)

Most UNIX systems implement all the canonical processing in a module called the *terminal line discipline*. We can think of this module as a box that sits between the kernel's generic read and write functions and the actual device driver (see Figure 18.2).

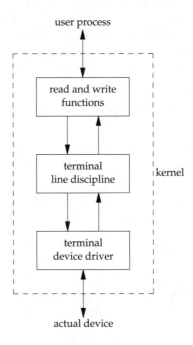

Figure 18.2 Terminal line discipline

Note the similarity of this picture and the diagram of a stream shown in Figure 14.14. We'll return to this picture in Chapter 19, when we discuss pseudo terminals.

All the terminal device characteristics that we can examine and change are contained in a `termios` structure. This structure is defined in the header `<termios.h>`, which we use throughout this chapter:

```
struct termios {
    tcflag_t  c_iflag;      /* input flags */
    tcflag_t  c_oflag;      /* output flags */
    tcflag_t  c_cflag;      /* control flags */
    tcflag_t  c_lflag;      /* local flags */
    cc_t      c_cc[NCCS];   /* control characters */
};
```

Roughly speaking, the input flags control the input of characters by the terminal device driver (strip eighth bit on input, enable input parity checking, etc.), the output flags control the driver output (perform output processing, map newline to CR/LF, etc.), the control flags affect the RS-232 serial lines (ignore modem status lines, one or two stop bits per character, etc.), and the local flags affect the interface between the driver and the user (echo on or off, visually erase characters, enable terminal-generated signals, job control stop signal for background output, etc.).

The type `tcflag_t` is big enough to hold each of the flag values and is often defined as an `unsigned int` or an `unsigned long`. The `c_cc` array contains all the special characters that we can change. `NCCS` is the number of elements in this array and is typically between 15 and 20 (since most implementations of the UNIX System support more than the 11 POSIX-defined special characters). The `cc_t` type is large enough to hold each special character and is typically an `unsigned char`.

> Versions of System V that predated the POSIX standard had a header named `<termio.h>` and a structure named `termio`. POSIX.1 added an s to the names, to differentiate them from their predecessors.

Figures 18.3 through 18.6 list all the terminal flags that we can change to affect the characteristics of a terminal device. Note that even though the Single UNIX Specification defines a common subset that all platforms start from, all the implementations have their own additions. Most of these additions come from the historical differences between the systems. We'll discuss each of these flag values in detail in Section 18.5.

Given all the options available, how do we examine and change these characteristics of a terminal device? Figure 18.7 summarizes the various functions defined by the Single UNIX Specification that operate on terminal devices. (All the functions listed are part of the base POSIX specification, except for `tcgetsid`, which is an XSI extension. We described `tcgetpgrp`, `tcgetsid`, and `tcsetpgrp` in Section 9.7.)

Note that the Single UNIX Specification doesn't use the classic `ioctl` on terminal devices. Instead, it uses the 13 functions shown in Figure 18.7. The reason is that the `ioctl` function for terminal devices uses a different data type for its final argument, which depends on the action being performed. This makes type checking of the arguments impossible.

Although only 13 functions operate on terminal devices, the first two functions in Figure 18.7 (`tcgetattr` and `tcsetattr`) manipulate almost 70 different flags (see Figures 18.3 through 18.6). The handling of terminal devices is complicated by the large number of options available for terminal devices and trying to determine which options are required for a particular device (be it a terminal, modem, printer, or whatever).

Flag	Description	POSIX.1	FreeBSD 5.2.1	Linux 2.4.22	Mac OS X 10.3	Solaris 9
CBAUDEXT	extended baud rate					•
CCAR_OFLOW	DCD flow control of output		•		•	
CCTS_OFLOW	CTS flow control of output		•		•	•
CDSR_OFLOW	DSR flow control of output		•		•	
CDTR_IFLOW	DTR flow control of input		•		•	
CIBAUDEXT	extended input baud rate					•
CIGNORE	ignore control flags		•		•	
CLOCAL	ignore modem status lines	•	•	•	•	•
CREAD	enable receiver	•	•	•	•	•
CRTSCTS	enable hardware flow control		•	•	•	•
CRTS_IFLOW	RTS flow control of input		•		•	•
CRTSXOFF	enable input hardware flow control					•
CSIZE	character size mask	•	•	•	•	•
CSTOPB	send two stop bits, else one	•	•	•	•	•
HUPCL	hang up on last close	•	•	•	•	•
MDMBUF	same as CCAR_OFLOW		•		•	
PARENB	parity enable	•	•	•	•	•
PAREXT	mark or space parity					•
PARODD	odd parity, else even	•	•	•	•	•

Figure 18.3 `c_cflag` terminal flags

Flag	Description	POSIX.1	FreeBSD 5.2.1	Linux 2.4.22	Mac OS X 10.3	Solaris 9
BRKINT	generate SIGINT on BREAK	•	•	•	•	•
ICRNL	map CR to NL on input	•	•	•	•	•
IGNBRK	ignore BREAK condition	•	•	•	•	•
IGNCR	ignore CR	•	•	•	•	•
IGNPAR	ignore characters with parity errors	•	•	•	•	•
IMAXBEL	ring bell on input queue full		•	•	•	•
INLCR	map NL to CR on input	•	•	•	•	•
INPCK	enable input parity checking	•	•	•	•	•
ISTRIP	strip eighth bit off input characters	•	•	•	•	•
IUCLC	map uppercase to lowercase on input			•		•
IXANY	enable any characters to restart output	XSI	•	•	•	•
IXOFF	enable start/stop input flow control	•	•	•	•	•
IXON	enable start/stop output flow control	•	•	•	•	•
PARMRK	mark parity errors	•	•	•	•	•

Figure 18.4 `c_iflag` terminal flags

Flag	Description	POSIX.1	FreeBSD 5.2.1	Linux 2.4.22	Mac OS X 10.3	Solaris 9
ALTWERASE	use alternate WERASE algorithm		•		•	
ECHO	enable echo	•	•	•	•	•
ECHOCTL	echo control chars as ^(Char)		•	•	•	•
ECHOE	visually erase chars	•	•	•	•	•
ECHOK	echo kill	•	•	•	•	•
ECHOKE	visual erase for kill		•	•	•	•
ECHONL	echo NL	•	•	•	•	•
ECHOPRT	visual erase mode for hard copy		•	•	•	•
EXTPROC	external character processing		•		•	
FLUSHO	output being flushed		•	•	•	•
ICANON	canonical input	•	•	•	•	•
IEXTEN	enable extended input char processing	•	•	•	•	•
ISIG	enable terminal-generated signals	•	•	•	•	•
NOFLSH	disable flush after interrupt or quit	•	•	•	•	•
NOKERNINFO	no kernel output from STATUS		•		•	
PENDIN	retype pending input		•	•	•	•
TOSTOP	send SIGTTOU for background output	•	•	•	•	•
XCASE	canonical upper/lower presentation			•		•

Figure 18.5 c_lflag terminal flags

Flag	Description	POSIX.1	FreeBSD 5.2.1	Linux 2.4.22	Mac OS X 10.3	Solaris 9
BSDLY	backspace delay mask	XSI		•		•
CMSPAR	mark or space parity			•		
CRDLY	CR delay mask	XSI		•		•
FFDLY	form feed delay mask	XSI		•		•
NLDLY	NL delay mask	XSI		•		•
OCRNL	map CR to NL on output	XSI	•	•		•
OFDEL	fill is DEL, else NUL	XSI		•		•
OFILL	use fill character for delay	XSI		•		•
OLCUC	map lowercase to uppercase on output			•		•
ONLCR	map NL to CR-NL	XSI	•	•	•	•
ONLRET	NL performs CR function	XSI	•	•		•
ONOCR	no CR output at column 0	XSI	•	•		•
ONOEOT	discard EOTs (^D) on output		•		•	
OPOST	perform output processing	•	•	•	•	•
OXTABS	expand tabs to spaces		•		•	
TABDLY	horizontal tab delay mask	XSI		•		•
VTDLY	vertical tab delay mask	XSI		•		•

Figure 18.6 c_oflag terminal flags

Function	Description
`tcgetattr` `tcsetattr`	fetch attributes (`termios` structure) set attributes (`termios` structure)

`cfgetispeed`
`cfgetospeed`
`cfsetispeed`
`cfsetospeed`
	get input speed
	get output speed
	set input speed
	set output speed

`tcdrain`
`tcflow`
`tcflush`
`tcsendbreak`
	wait for all output to be transmitted
	suspend transmit or receive
	flush pending input and/or output
	send BREAK character

`tcgetpgrp`
`tcsetpgrp`
`tcgetsid`
	get foreground process group ID
	set foreground process group ID
	get process group ID of session leader for controlling
	TTY (XSI extension)

Figure 18.7 Summary of terminal I/O functions

The relationships among the 13 functions shown in Figure 18.7 are shown in Figure 18.8.

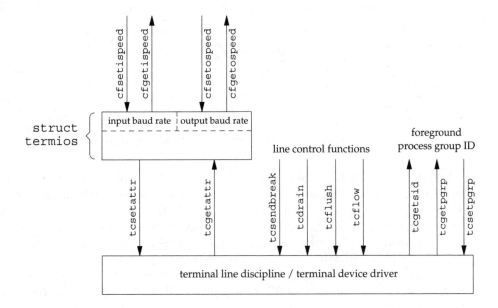

Figure 18.8 Relationships among the terminal-related functions

POSIX.1 doesn't specify where in the `termios` structure the baud rate information is stored; that is an implementation detail. Some systems, such as Linux and Solaris, store this information in the `c_cflag` field. BSD-derived systems, such as FreeBSD and Mac OS X, have two separate fields in the structure: one for the input speed and one for the output speed.

18.3   Special Input Characters

POSIX.1 defines 11 characters that are handled specially on input. Implementations define additional special characters. Figure 18.9 summarizes these special characters.

Character	Description	c_cc subscript	Enabled by field	Enabled by flag	Typical value	POSIX.1	FreeBSD 5.2.1	Linux 2.4.22	Mac OS X 10.3	Solaris 9
CR	carriage return	(can't change)	c_lflag	ICANON	\r	•	•	•	•	•
DISCARD	discard output	VDISCARD	c_lflag	IEXTEN	^O		•	•	•	•
DSUSP	delayed suspend (SIGTSTP)	VDSUSP	c_lflag	ISIG	^Y		•		•	•
EOF	end of file	VEOF	c_lflag	ICANON	^D	•	•	•	•	•
EOL	end of line	VEOL	c_lflag	ICANON		•	•	•	•	•
EOL2	alternate end of line	VEOL2	c_lflag	ICANON			•	•	•	•
ERASE	backspace one character	VERASE	c_lflag	ICANON	^H, ^?	•	•	•	•	•
ERASE2	alternate backspace character	VERASE2	c_lflag	ICANON	^H, ^?		•			
INTR	interrupt signal (SIGINT)	VINTR	c_lflag	ISIG	^?, ^C	•	•	•	•	•
KILL	erase line	VKILL	c_lflag	ICANON	^U	•	•	•	•	•
LNEXT	literal next	VLNEXT	c_lflag	IEXTEN	^V		•	•	•	•
NL	line feed (newline)	(can't change)	c_lflag	ICANON	\n	•	•	•	•	•
QUIT	quit signal (SIGQUIT)	VQUIT	c_lflag	ISIG	^\	•	•	•	•	•
REPRINT	reprint all input	VREPRINT	c_lflag	ICANON	^R		•	•	•	•
START	resume output	VSTART	c_iflag	IXON/IXOFF	^Q	•	•	•	•	•
STATUS	status request	VSTATUS	c_lflag	ICANON	^T		•		•	
STOP	stop output	VSTOP	c_iflag	IXON/IXOFF	^S	•	•	•	•	•
SUSP	suspend signal (SIGTSTP)	VSUSP	c_lflag	ISIG	^Z	•	•	•	•	•
WERASE	backspace one word	VWERASE	c_lflag	ICANON	^W		•	•	•	•

Figure 18.9 Summary of special terminal input characters

Of the 11 POSIX.1 special characters, we can change 9 of them to almost any value that we like. The exceptions are the newline and carriage return characters (\n and \r, respectively) and perhaps the STOP and START characters (depends on the implementation). To do this, we modify the appropriate entry in the c_cc array of the termios structure. The elements in this array are referred to by name, with each name beginning with a V (the third column in Figure 18.9).

POSIX.1 allows us to disable these characters. If we set the value of an entry in the c_cc array to the value of _POSIX_VDISABLE, then we disable the corresponding special character.

In older versions of the Single UNIX Specification, support for _POSIX_VDISABLE was optional. It is now required.

All four platforms discussed in this text support this feature. Linux 2.4.22 and Solaris 9 define _POSIX_VDISABLE as 0; FreeBSD 5.2.1 and Mac OS X 10.3 define it as 0xff.

Some earlier UNIX systems disabled a feature if the corresponding special input character was 0.

Example

Before describing all the special characters in detail, let's look at a small program that
changes them. The program in Figure 18.10 disables the interrupt character and sets the
end-of-file character to Control-B.

```c
#include "apue.h"
#include <termios.h>

int
main(void)
{
    struct termios  term;
    long            vdisable;

    if (isatty(STDIN_FILENO) == 0)
        err_quit("standard input is not a terminal device");

    if ((vdisable = fpathconf(STDIN_FILENO, _PC_VDISABLE)) < 0)
        err_quit("fpathconf error or _POSIX_VDISABLE not in effect");

    if (tcgetattr(STDIN_FILENO, &term) < 0) /* fetch tty state */
        err_sys("tcgetattr error");

    term.c_cc[VINTR] = vdisable;    /* disable INTR character */
    term.c_cc[VEOF]  = 2;           /* EOF is Control-B */

    if (tcsetattr(STDIN_FILENO, TCSAFLUSH, &term) < 0)
        err_sys("tcsetattr error");

    exit(0);
}
```

Figure 18.10 Disable interrupt character and change end-of-file character

Note the following in this program.

- We modify the terminal characters only if standard input is a terminal device.
  We call `isatty` (Section 18.9) to check this.

- We fetch the `_POSIX_VDISABLE` value using `fpathconf`.

- The function `tcgetattr` (Section 18.4) fetches a `termios` structure from the
  kernel. After we've modified this structure, we call `tcsetattr` to set the
  attributes. The only attributes that change are the ones we specifically modified.

- Disabling the interrupt key is different from ignoring the interrupt signal. The
  program in Figure 18.10 simply disables the special character that causes the
  terminal driver to generate `SIGINT`. We can still use the `kill` function to send
  the signal to the process.   □

We now describe each of the special characters in more detail. We call these the special input characters, but two of the characters, STOP and START (Control-S and Control-Q), are also handled specially when output. Note that when recognized by the terminal driver and processed specially, most of these special characters are then discarded: they are not returned to the process in a read operation. The exceptions to this are the newline characters (NL, EOL, EOL2) and the carriage return (CR).

CR
The carriage return character. We cannot change this character. This character is recognized on input in canonical mode. When both ICANON (canonical mode) and ICRNL (map CR to NL) are set and IGNCR (ignore CR) is not set, the CR character is translated to NL and has the same effect as a NL character. This character is returned to the reading process (perhaps after being translated to a NL).

DISCARD
The discard character. This character, recognized on input in extended mode (IEXTEN), causes subsequent output to be discarded until another DISCARD character is entered or the discard condition is cleared (see the FLUSHO option). This character is discarded when processed (i.e., it is not passed to the process).

DSUSP
The delayed-suspend job-control character. This character is recognized on input in extended mode (IEXTEN) if job control is supported and if the ISIG flag is set. Like the SUSP character, this delayed-suspend character generates the SIGTSTP signal that is sent to all processes in the foreground process group (refer to Figure 9.7). But the delayed-suspend character generates a signal only when a process reads from the controlling terminal, not when the character is typed. This character is discarded when processed (i.e., it is not passed to the process).

EOF
The end-of-file character. This character is recognized on input in canonical mode (ICANON). When we type this character, all bytes waiting to be read are immediately passed to the reading process. If no bytes are waiting to be read, a count of 0 is returned. Entering an EOF character at the beginning of the line is the normal way to indicate an end of file to a program. This character is discarded when processed in canonical mode (i.e., it is not passed to the process).

EOL
The additional line delimiter character, like NL. This character is recognized on input in canonical mode (ICANON) and is returned to the reading process; however, this character is not normally used.

EOL2
Another line delimiter character, like NL. This character is treated identically to the EOL character.

ERASE
The erase character (backspace). This character is recognized on input in canonical mode (ICANON) and erases the previous character in the line, not erasing beyond the beginning of the line. This character is discarded when processed in canonical mode (i.e., it is not passed to the process).

ERASE2   The alternate erase character (backspace). This character is treated exactly like the erase character (ERASE).

INTR   The interrupt character. This character is recognized on input if the ISIG flag is set and generates the SIGINT signal that is sent to all processes in the foreground process group (refer to Figure 9.7). This character is discarded when processed (i.e., it is not passed to the process).

KILL   The kill character. (The name "kill" is overused; recall the kill function used to send a signal to a process. This character should be called the line-erase character; it has nothing to do with signals.) It is recognized on input in canonical mode (ICANON). It erases the entire line and is discarded when processed (i.e., it is not passed to the process).

LNEXT   The literal-next character. This character is recognized on input in extended mode (IEXTEN) and causes any special meaning of the next character to be ignored. This works for all special characters listed in this section. We can use this character to type any character to a program. The LNEXT character is discarded when processed, but the next character entered is passed to the process.

NL   The newline character, which is also called the line delimiter. We cannot change this character. This character is recognized on input in canonical mode (ICANON). This character is returned to the reading process.

QUIT   The quit character. This character is recognized on input if the ISIG flag is set. The quit character generates the SIGQUIT signal, which is sent to all processes in the foreground process group (refer to Figure 9.7). This character is discarded when processed (i.e., it is not passed to the process).

         Recall from Figure 10.1 that the difference between INTR and QUIT is that the QUIT character not only terminates the process by default, but also generates a core file.

REPRINT The reprint character. This character is recognized on input in extended, canonical mode (both IEXTEN and ICANON flags set) and causes all unread input to be output (reechoed). This character is discarded when processed (i.e., it is not passed to the process).

START   The start character. This character is recognized on input if the IXON flag is set and is automatically generated as output if the IXOFF flag is set. A received START character with IXON set causes stopped output (from a previously entered STOP character) to restart. In this case, the START character is discarded when processed (i.e., it is not passed to the process).

         When IXOFF is set, the terminal driver automatically generates a START character to resume input that it had previously stopped, when the new input will not overflow the input buffer.

STATUS   The BSD status-request character. This character is recognized on input in
           extended, canonical mode (both IEXTEN and ICANON flags set) and
           generates the SIGINFO signal, which is sent to all processes in the
           foreground process group (refer to Figure 9.7). Additionally, if the
           NOKERNINFO flag is not set, status information on the foreground process
           group is also displayed on the terminal. This character is discarded when
           processed (i.e., it is not passed to the process).

STOP   The stop character. This character is recognized on input if the IXON flag is
           set and is automatically generated as output if the IXOFF flag is set. A
           received STOP character with IXON set stops the output. In this case, the
           STOP character is discarded when processed (i.e., it is not passed to the
           process). The stopped output is restarted when a START character is
           entered.

           When IXOFF is set, the terminal driver automatically generates a STOP
           character to prevent the input buffer from overflowing.

SUSP   The suspend job-control character. This character is recognized on input if
           job control is supported and if the ISIG flag is set. The suspend character
           generates the SIGTSTP signal, which is sent to all processes in the
           foreground process group (refer to Figure 9.7). This character is discarded
           when processed (i.e., it is not passed to the process).

WERASE   The word-erase character. This character is recognized on input in
           extended, canonical mode (both IEXTEN and ICANON flags set) and causes
           the previous word to be erased. First, it skips backward over any white
           space (spaces or tabs), then backward over the previous token, leaving the
           cursor positioned where the first character of the previous token was
           located. Normally, the previous token ends when a white space character is
           encountered. We can change this, however, by setting the ALTWERASE flag.
           This flag causes the previous token to end when the first nonalphanumeric
           character is encountered. The word-erase character is discarded when
           processed (i.e., it is not passed to the process).

Another "character" that we need to define for terminal devices is the BREAK
character. BREAK is not really a character, but rather a condition that occurs during
asynchronous serial data transmission. A BREAK condition is signaled to the device
driver in various ways, depending on the serial interface.

> Most old serial terminals have a key labeled BREAK that generates the BREAK condition,
> which is why most people think of BREAK as a character. Some newer terminal keyboards
> don't have a BREAK key. On PCs, the break key might be mapped for other purpose. For
> example, the Windows command interpreter can be interrupted by typing Control-BREAK.

For asynchronous serial data transmission, a BREAK is a sequence of zero-valued
bits that continues for longer than the time required to send one byte. The entire
sequence of zero-valued bits is considered a single BREAK. In Section 18.8, we'll see
how to send a BREAK with the tcsendbreak function.

18.4   Getting and Setting Terminal Attributes

To get and set a `termios` structure, we call two functions: `tcgetattr` and `tcsetattr`. This is how we examine and modify the various option flags and special characters to make the terminal operate the way we want it to.

```
#include <termios.h>

int tcgetattr(int filedes, struct termios *termptr);

int tcsetattr(int filedes, int opt, const struct termios *termptr);
```
                                                    Both return: 0 if OK, −1 on error

Both functions take a pointer to a `termios` structure and either return the current terminal attributes or set the terminal's attributes. Since these two functions operate only on terminal devices, `errno` is set to `ENOTTY` and −1 is returned if *filedes* does not refer to a terminal device.

The argument *opt* for `tcsetattr` lets us specify when we want the new terminal attributes to take effect. This argument is specified as one of the following constants.

`TCSANOW`   The change occurs immediately.

`TCSADRAIN`   The change occurs after all output has been transmitted. This option should be used if we are changing the output parameters.

`TCSAFLUSH`   The change occurs after all output has been transmitted. Furthermore, when the change takes place, all input data that has not been read is discarded (flushed).

The return status of `tcsetattr` confuses the programming. This function returns OK if it was able to perform *any* of the requested actions, even if it couldn't perform all the requested actions. If the function returns OK, it is our responsibility to see whether all the requested actions were performed. This means that after we call `tcsetattr` to set the desired attributes, we need to call `tcgetattr` and compare the actual terminal's attributes to the desired attributes to detect any differences.

18.5   Terminal Option Flags

In this section, we list all the various terminal option flags, expanding the descriptions of all the options from Figures 18.3 through 18.6. This list is alphabetical and indicates in which of the four terminal flag fields the option appears. (The field a given option is controlled by is usually not apparent from the option name alone.) We also note whether each option is defined by the Single UNIX Specification and list the platforms that support it.

All the flags listed specify one or more bits that we turn on or clear, unless we call the flag a *mask*. A mask defines multiple bits grouped together from which a set of values is defined. We have a defined name for the mask and a name for each value. For example, to set the character size, we first zero the bits using the character-size mask CSIZE, and then set one of the values CS5, CS6, CS7, or CS8.

The six delay values supported by Linux and Solaris are also masks: BSDLY, CRDLY, FFDLY, NLDLY, TABDLY, and VTDLY. Refer to the termio(7I) manual page on Solaris for the length of each delay value. In all cases, a delay mask of 0 means no delay. If a delay is specified, the OFILL and OFDEL flags determine whether the driver does an actual delay or whether fill characters are transmitted instead.

Example

Figure 18.11 demonstrates the use of these masks to extract a value and to set a value.

```c
#include "apue.h"
#include <termios.h>

int
main(void)
{
    struct termios  term;

    if (tcgetattr(STDIN_FILENO, &term) < 0)
        err_sys("tcgetattr error");

    switch (term.c_cflag & CSIZE) {
    case CS5:
        printf("5 bits/byte\n");
        break;
    case CS6:
        printf("6 bits/byte\n");
        break;
    case CS7:
        printf("7 bits/byte\n");
        break;
    case CS8:
        printf("8 bits/byte\n");
        break;
    default:
        printf("unknown bits/byte\n");
    }

    term.c_cflag &= ~CSIZE;      /* zero out the bits */
    term.c_cflag |= CS8;         /* set 8 bits/byte */
    if (tcsetattr(STDIN_FILENO, TCSANOW, &term) < 0)
        err_sys("tcsetattr error");

    exit(0);
}
```

Figure 18.11 Example of tcgetattr and tcsetattr

We now describe each of the flags.

ALTWERASE   (c_lflag, FreeBSD, Mac OS X) If set, an alternate word-erase algorithm is used when the WERASE character is entered. Instead of moving backward until the previous white space character, this flag causes the WERASE character to move backward until the first nonalphanumeric character is encountered.

BRKINT   (c_iflag, POSIX.1, FreeBSD, Linux, Mac OS X, Solaris) If this flag is set and IGNBRK is not set, the input and output queues are flushed when a BREAK is received, and a SIGINT signal is generated. This signal is generated for the foreground process group if the terminal device is a controlling terminal.

If neither IGNBRK nor BRKINT is set, then a BREAK is read as a single character \0, unless PARMRK is set, in which case the BREAK is read as the 3-byte sequence \377, \0, \0.

BSDLY   (c_oflag, XSI, Linux, Solaris) Backspace delay mask. The values for the mask are BS0 or BS1.

CBAUDEXT   (c_cflag, Solaris) Extended baud rates. Used to enable baud rates greater than B38400. (We discuss baud rates in Section 18.7.)

CCAR_OFLOW   (c_cflag, FreeBSD, Mac OS X) Enable hardware flow control of the output using the RS-232 modem carrier signal (DCD, known as Data-Carrier-Detect). This is the same as the old MDMBUF flag.

CCTS_OFLOW   (c_cflag, FreeBSD, Mac OS X, Solaris) Enable hardware flow control of the output using the Clear-To-Send (CTS) RS-232 signal.

CDSR_OFLOW   (c_cflag, FreeBSD, Mac OS X) Flow control the output according to the Data-Set-Ready (DSR) RS-232 signal.

CDTR_IFLOW   (c_cflag, FreeBSD, Mac OS X) Flow control the input according to the Data-Terminal-Ready (DTR) RS-232 signal.

CIBAUDEXT   (c_cflag, Solaris) Extended input baud rates. Used to enable input baud rates greater than B38400. (We discuss baud rates in Section 18.7.)

CIGNORE   (c_cflag, FreeBSD, Mac OS X) Ignore control flags.

CLOCAL   (c_cflag, POSIX.1, FreeBSD, Linux, Mac OS X, Solaris) If set, the modem status lines are ignored. This usually means that the device is directly attached. When this flag is not set, an open of a terminal device usually blocks until the modem answers a call and establishes a connection, for example.

CMSPAR   (c_oflag, Linux) Select mark or space parity. If PARODD is set, the parity bit is always 1 (mark parity). Otherwise, the parity bit is always 0 (space parity).

CRDLY   (c_oflag, XSI, Linux, Solaris) Carriage return delay mask. The values for the mask are CR0, CR1, CR2, or CR3.

CREAD
: (c_cflag, POSIX.1, FreeBSD, Linux, Mac OS X, Solaris) If set, the receiver is enabled, and characters can be received.

CRTSCTS
: (c_cflag, FreeBSD, Linux, Mac OS X, Solaris) Behavior depends on platform. For Solaris, enables outbound hardware flow control if set. On the other three platforms, enables both inbound and outbound hardware flow control (equivalent to CCTS_OFLOW | CRTS_IFLOW).

CRTS_IFLOW
: (c_cflag, FreeBSD, Mac OS X, Solaris) Request-To-Send (RTS) flow control of input.

CRTSXOFF
: (c_cflag, Solaris) If set, inbound hardware flow control is enabled. The state of the Request-To-Send RS-232 signal controls the flow control.

CSIZE
: (c_cflag, POSIX.1, FreeBSD, Linux, Mac OS X, Solaris) This field is a mask that specifies the number of bits per byte for both transmission and reception. This size does not include the parity bit, if any. The values for the field defined by this mask are CS5, CS6, CS7, and CS8, for 5, 6, 7, and 8 bits per byte, respectively.

CSTOPB
: (c_cflag, POSIX.1, FreeBSD, Linux, Mac OS X, Solaris) If set, two stop bits are used; otherwise, one stop bit is used.

ECHO
: (c_lflag, POSIX.1, FreeBSD, Linux, Mac OS X, Solaris) If set, input characters are echoed back to the terminal device. Input characters can be echoed in either canonical or noncanonical mode.

ECHOCTL
: (c_lflag, FreeBSD, Linux, Mac OS X, Solaris) If set and if ECHO is set, ASCII control characters (those characters in the range 0 through octal 37, inclusive) other than the ASCII TAB, the ASCII NL, and the START and STOP characters are echoed as ^X, where X is the character formed by adding octal 100 to the control character. This means that the ASCII Control-A character (octal 1) is echoed as ^A. Also, the ASCII DELETE character (octal 177) is echoed as ^?. If this flag is not set, the ASCII control characters are echoed as themselves. As with the ECHO flag, this flag affects the echoing of control characters in both canonical and noncanonical modes.

   Be aware that some systems echo the EOF character differently, since its typical value is Control-D. (Control-D is the ASCII EOT character, which can cause some terminals to hang up.) Check your manual.

ECHOE
: (c_lflag, POSIX.1, FreeBSD, Linux, Mac OS X, Solaris) If set and if ICANON is set, the ERASE character erases the last character in the current line from the display. This is usually done in the terminal driver by writing the three-character sequence backspace, space, backspace.

   If the WERASE character is supported, ECHOE causes the previous word to be erased using one or more of the same three-character sequence.

   If the ECHOPRT flag is supported, the actions described here for ECHOE assume that the ECHOPRT flag is not set.

ECHOK   (c_lflag, POSIX.1, FreeBSD, Linux, Mac OS X, Solaris) If set and if
                ICANON is set, the KILL character erases the current line from the
                display or outputs the NL character (to emphasize that the entire line
                was erased).

                If the ECHOKE flag is supported, this description of ECHOK assumes that
                ECHOKE is not set.

ECHOKE   (c_lflag, FreeBSD, Linux, Mac OS X, Solaris) If set and if ICANON is
                set, the KILL character is echoed by erasing each character on the line.
                The way in which each character is erased is selected by the ECHOE and
                ECHOPRT flags.

ECHONL   (c_lflag, POSIX.1, FreeBSD, Linux, Mac OS X, Solaris) If set and if
                ICANON is set, the NL character is echoed, even if ECHO is not set.

ECHOPRT   (c_lflag, FreeBSD, Linux, Mac OS X, Solaris) If set and if both
                ICANON and ECHO are set, then the ERASE character (and WERASE
                character, if supported) cause all the characters being erased to be
                printed as they are erased. This is often useful on a hard-copy terminal
                to see exactly which characters are being deleted.

EXTPROC   (c_lflag, FreeBSD, Mac OS X) If set, canonical character processing is
                performed external to the operating system. This can be the case if the
                serial communication peripheral card can offload the host processor by
                doing some of the line discipline processing. This can also be the case
                when using pseudo terminals (Chapter 19).

FFDLY   (c_oflag, XSI, Linux, Solaris) Form feed delay mask. The values for
                the mask are FF0 or FF1.

FLUSHO   (c_lflag, FreeBSD, Linux, Mac OS X, Solaris) If set, output is being
                flushed. This flag is set when we type the DISCARD character; the flag
                is cleared when we type another DISCARD character. We can also set or
                clear this condition by setting or clearing this terminal flag.

HUPCL   (c_cflag, POSIX.1, FreeBSD, Linux, Mac OS X, Solaris) If set, the
                modem control lines are lowered (i.e., the modem connection is broken)
                when the last process closes the device.

ICANON   (c_lflag, POSIX.1, FreeBSD, Linux, Mac OS X, Solaris) If set, canonical
                mode is in effect (Section 18.10). This enables the following characters:
                EOF, EOL, EOL2, ERASE, KILL, REPRINT, STATUS, and WERASE. The
                input characters are assembled into lines.

                If canonical mode is not enabled, read requests are satisfied directly
                from the input queue. A read does not return until at least MIN bytes
                have been received or the timeout value TIME has expired between
                bytes. Refer to Section 18.11 for additional details.

ICRNL   (c_iflag, POSIX.1, FreeBSD, Linux, Mac OS X, Solaris) If set and if
             IGNCR is not set, a received CR character is translated into a NL
             character.

IEXTEN   (c_lflag, POSIX.1, FreeBSD, Linux, Mac OS X, Solaris) If set, the
             extended, implementation-defined special characters are recognized and
             processed.

IGNBRK   (c_iflag, POSIX.1, FreeBSD, Linux, Mac OS X, Solaris) When set, a
             BREAK condition on input is ignored. See BRKINT for a way to have a
             BREAK condition either generate a SIGINT signal or be read as data.

IGNCR   (c_iflag, POSIX.1, FreeBSD, Linux, Mac OS X, Solaris) If set, a
             received CR character is ignored. If this flag is not set, it is possible to
             translate the received CR into a NL character if the ICRNL flag is set.

IGNPAR   (c_iflag, POSIX.1, FreeBSD, Linux, Mac OS X, Solaris) When set, an
             input byte with a framing error (other than a BREAK) or an input byte
             with a parity error is ignored.

IMAXBEL   (c_iflag, FreeBSD, Linux, Mac OS X, Solaris) Ring bell when input
             queue is full.

INLCR   (c_iflag, POSIX.1, FreeBSD, Linux, Mac OS X, Solaris) If set, a
             received NL character is translated into a CR character.

INPCK   (c_iflag, POSIX.1, FreeBSD, Linux, Mac OS X, Solaris) When set,
             input parity checking is enabled. If INPCK is not set, input parity
             checking is disabled.

             Parity "generation and detection" and "input parity checking" are two
             different things. The generation and detection of parity bits is controlled
             by the PARENB flag. Setting this flag usually causes the device driver for
             the serial interface to generate parity for outgoing characters and to
             verify the parity of incoming characters. The flag PARODD determines
             whether the parity should be odd or even. If an input character arrives
             with the wrong parity, then the state of the INPCK flag is checked. If this
             flag is set, then the IGNPAR flag is checked (to see whether the input
             byte with the parity error should be ignored); if the byte should not be
             ignored, then the PARMRK flag is checked to see what characters should
             be passed to the reading process.

ISIG   (c_lflag, POSIX.1, FreeBSD, Linux, Mac OS X, Solaris) If set, the input
             characters are compared against the special characters that cause the
             terminal-generated signals to be generated (INTR, QUIT, SUSP, and
             DSUSP); if equal, the corresponding signal is generated.

ISTRIP   (c_iflag, POSIX.1, FreeBSD, Linux, Mac OS X, Solaris) When set,
             valid input bytes are stripped to 7 bits. When this flag is not set, all
             8 bits are processed.

IUCLC   (c_iflag, Linux, Solaris) Map uppercase to lowercase on input.

IXANY   (c_iflag, XSI, FreeBSD, Linux, Mac OS X, Solaris) Enable any characters to restart output.

IXOFF   (c_iflag, POSIX.1, FreeBSD, Linux, Mac OS X, Solaris) If set, start–stop input control is enabled. When it notices that the input queue is getting full, the terminal driver outputs a STOP character. This character should be recognized by the device that is sending the data and cause the device to stop. Later, when the characters on the input queue have been processed, the terminal driver will output a START character. This should cause the device to resume sending data.

IXON   (c_iflag, POSIX.1, FreeBSD, Linux, Mac OS X, Solaris) If set, start–stop output control is enabled. When the terminal driver receives a STOP character, output stops. While the output is stopped, the next START character resumes the output. If this flag is not set, the START and STOP characters are read by the process as normal characters.

MDMBUF   (c_cflag, FreeBSD, Mac OS X) Flow control the output according to the modem carrier flag. This is the old name for the CCAR_OFLOW flag.

NLDLY   (c_oflag, XSI, Linux, Solaris) Newline delay mask. The values for the mask are NL0 or NL1.

NOFLSH   (c_lflag, POSIX.1, FreeBSD, Linux, Mac OS X, Solaris) By default, when the terminal driver generates the SIGINT and SIGQUIT signals, both the input and output queues are flushed. Also, when it generates the SIGSUSP signal, the input queue is flushed. If the NOFLSH flag is set, this normal flushing of the queues does not occur when these signals are generated.

NOKERNINFO   (c_lflag, FreeBSD, Mac OS X) When set, this flag prevents the STATUS character from printing information on the foreground process group. Regardless of this flag, however, the STATUS character still causes the SIGINFO signal to be sent to the foreground process group.

OCRNL   (c_oflag, XSI, FreeBSD, Linux, Solaris) If set, map CR to NL on output.

OFDEL   (c_oflag, XSI, Linux, Solaris) If set, the output fill character is ASCII DEL; otherwise, it's ASCII NUL. See the OFILL flag.

OFILL   (c_oflag, XSI, Linux, Solaris) If set, fill characters (either ASCII DEL or ASCII NUL; see the OFDEL flag) are transmitted for a delay, instead of using a timed delay. See the six delay masks: BSDLY, CRDLY, FFDLY, NLDLY, TABDLY, and VTDLY.

OLCUC   (c_oflag, Linux, Solaris) If set, map lowercase characters to uppercase characters on output.

ONLCR   (c_oflag, XSI, FreeBSD, Linux, Mac OS X, Solaris) If set, map NL to CR-NL on output.

ONLRET   (c_oflag, XSI, FreeBSD, Linux, Solaris) If set, the NL character is assumed to perform the carriage return function on output.

ONOCR   (c_oflag, XSI, FreeBSD, Linux, Solaris) If set, a CR is not output at column 0.

ONOEOT   (c_oflag, FreeBSD, Mac OS X) If set, EOT (^D) characters are discarded on output. This may be necessary on some terminals that interpret the Control-D as a hangup.

OPOST   (c_oflag, POSIX.1, FreeBSD, Linux, Mac OS X, Solaris) If set, implementation-defined output processing takes place. Refer to Figure 18.6 for the various implementation-defined flags for the c_oflag word.

OXTABS   (c_oflag, FreeBSD, Mac OS X) If set, tabs are expanded to spaces on output. This produces the same effect as setting the horizontal tab delay (TABDLY) to XTABS or TAB3.

PARENB   (c_cflag, POSIX.1, FreeBSD, Linux, Mac OS X, Solaris) If set, parity generation is enabled for outgoing characters, and parity checking is performed on incoming characters. The parity is odd if PARODD is set; otherwise, it is even parity. See also the discussion of the INPCK, IGNPAR, and PARMRK flags.

PAREXT   (c_cflag, Solaris) Select mark or space parity. If PARODD is set, the parity bit is always 1 (mark parity). Otherwise, the parity bit is always 0 (space parity).

PARMRK   (c_iflag, POSIX.1, FreeBSD, Linux, Mac OS X, Solaris) When set and if IGNPAR is not set, a byte with a framing error (other than a BREAK) or a byte with a parity error is read by the process as the three-character sequence \377, \0, X, where X is the byte received in error. If ISTRIP is not set, a valid \377 is passed to the process as \377, \377. If neither IGNPAR nor PARMRK is set, a byte with a framing error (other than a BREAK) or with a parity error is read as a single character \0.

PARODD   (c_cflag, POSIX.1, FreeBSD, Linux, Mac OS X, Solaris) If set, the parity for outgoing and incoming characters is odd parity. Otherwise, the parity is even parity. Note that the PARENB flag controls the generation and detection of parity.

           The PARODD flag also controls whether mark or space parity is used when either the CMSPAR or PAREXT flag is set.

PENDIN   (c_lflag, FreeBSD, Linux, Mac OS X, Solaris) If set, any input that has not been read is reprinted by the system when the next character is input. This action is similar to what happens when we type the REPRINT character.

TABDLY   (c_oflag, XSI, Linux, Solaris) Horizontal tab delay mask. The values
                for the mask are TAB0, TAB1, TAB2, or TAB3.

                The value XTABS is equal to TAB3. This value causes the system to
                expand tabs into spaces. The system assumes a tab stop every eight
                spaces, and we can't change this assumption.

TOSTOP   (c_lflag, POSIX.1, FreeBSD, Linux, Mac OS X, Solaris) If set and if the
                implementation supports job control, the SIGTTOU signal is sent to the
                process group of a background process that tries to write to its
                controlling terminal. By default, this signal stops all the processes in the
                process group. This signal is not generated by the terminal driver if the
                background process that is writing to the controlling terminal is either
                ignoring or blocking the signal.

VTDLY   (c_oflag, XSI, Linux, Solaris) Vertical tab delay mask. The values for
                the mask are VT0 or VT1.

XCASE   (c_lflag, Linux, Solaris) If set and if ICANON is also set, the terminal is
                assumed to be uppercase only, and all input is converted to lowercase.
                To input an uppercase character, precede it with a backslash. Similarly,
                an uppercase character is output by the system by being preceded by a
                backslash. (This option flag is obsolete today, since most, if not all,
                uppercase-only terminals have disappeared.)

18.6   stty Command

All the options described in the previous section can be examined and changed from
within a program, with the tcgetattr and tcsetattr functions (Section 18.4) or
from the command line (or a shell script), with the stty(1) command. This command
is simply an interface to the first six functions that we listed in Figure 18.7. If we
execute this command with its -a option, it displays all the terminal options:

```
$ stty -a
speed 9600 baud; 25 rows; 80 columns;
lflags: icanon isig iexten echo echoe -echok echoke -echonl echoctl
        -echoprt -altwerase -noflsh -tostop -flusho pendin -nokerninfo
        -extproc
iflags: -istrip icrnl -inlcr -igncr ixon -ixoff ixany imaxbel -ignbrk
        brkint -inpck -ignpar -parmrk
oflags: opost onlcr -ocrnl -oxtabs -onocr -onlret
cflags: cread cs8 -parenb -parodd hupcl -clocal -cstopb -crtscts
        -dsrflow -dtrflow -mdmbuf
cchars: discard = ^O; dsusp = ^Y; eof = ^D; eol = <undef>;
        eol2 = <undef>; erase = ^H; erase2 = ^?; intr = ^C; kill = ^U;
        lnext = ^V; min = 1; quit = ^\; reprint = ^R; start = ^Q;
        status = ^T; stop = ^S; susp = ^Z; time = 0; werase = ^W;
```

Option names preceded by a hyphen are disabled. The last four lines display the current settings for each of the terminal special characters (Section 18.3). The first line displays the number of rows and columns for the current terminal window; we discuss this in Section 18.12.

> The `stty` command uses its standard input to get and set the terminal option flags. Although some older implementations used standard output, POSIX.1 requires that the standard input be used. All four implementations discussed in this text provide versions of `stty` that operate on standard input. This means that we can type
>
>   stty -a </dev/tty1a
>
> if we are interested in discovering the settings on the terminal named `tty1a`.

18.7 Baud Rate Functions

The term *baud rate* is a historical term that should be referred to today as "bits per second." Although most terminal devices use the same baud rate for both input and output, the capability exists to set the two to different values, if the hardware allows this.

```
#include <termios.h>

speed_t cfgetispeed(const struct termios *termptr);

speed_t cfgetospeed(const struct termios *termptr);
```
                                                    Both return: baud rate value
```
int cfsetispeed(struct termios *termptr, speed_t speed);

int cfsetospeed(struct termios *termptr, speed_t speed);
```
                                                    Both return: 0 if OK, −1 on error

The return value from the two `cfget` functions and the *speed* argument to the two `cfset` functions are one of the following constants: B50, B75, B110, B134, B150, B200, B300, B600, B1200, B1800, B2400, B4800, B9600, B19200, or B38400. The constant B0 means "hang up." When B0 is specified as the output baud rate when `tcsetattr` is called, the modem control lines are no longer asserted.

> Most systems define additional baud rate values, such as B57600 and B115200.

To use these functions, we must realize that the input and output baud rates are stored in the device's `termios` structure, as shown in Figure 18.8. Before calling either of the `cfget` functions, we first have to obtain the device's `termios` structure using `tcgetattr`. Similarly, after calling either of the two `cfset` functions, all we've done is set the baud rate in a `termios` structure. For this change to affect the device, we have to call `tcsetattr`. If there is an error in either of the baud rates that we set, we may not find out about the error until we call `tcsetattr`.

The four baud rate functions exist to insulate applications from differences in the way that implementations represent baud rates in the `termios` structure. BSD-derived platforms tend to store baud rates as numeric values equal to the rates (i.e., 9,600 baud is stored as the value 9,600), whereas Linux and System V–derived platforms tend to encode the baud rate in a bitmask. The speed values we get from the `cfget` functions and pass to the `cfset` functions are untranslated from their representation as they are stored in the `termios` structure.

18.8 Line Control Functions

The following four functions provide line control capability for terminal devices. All four require that *filedes* refer to a terminal device; otherwise, an error is returned with errno set to ENOTTY.

```
#include <termios.h>

int tcdrain(int filedes);

int tcflow(int filedes, int action);

int tcflush(int filedes, int queue);

int tcsendbreak(int filedes, int duration);
```
All four return: 0 if OK, −1 on error

The `tcdrain` function waits for all output to be transmitted. The `tcflow` function gives us control over both input and output flow control. The *action* argument must be one of the following four values:

TCOOFF   Output is suspended.

TCOON   Output that was previously suspended is restarted.

TCIOFF   The system transmits a STOP character, which should cause the terminal device to stop sending data.

TCION   The system transmits a START character, which should cause the terminal device to resume sending data.

The `tcflush` function lets us flush (throw away) either the input buffer (data that has been received by the terminal driver, which we have not read) or the output buffer (data that we have written, which has not yet been transmitted). The *queue* argument must be one of the following three constants:

TCIFLUSH   The input queue is flushed.

TCOFLUSH   The output queue is flushed.

TCIOFLUSH   Both the input and the output queues are flushed.

The `tcsendbreak` function transmits a continuous stream of zero bits for a specified duration. If the *duration* argument is 0, the transmission lasts between 0.25 seconds and 0.5 seconds. POSIX.1 specifies that if *duration* is nonzero, the transmission time is implementation dependent.

18.9   Terminal Identification

Historically, the name of the controlling terminal in most versions of the UNIX System has been `/dev/tty`. POSIX.1 provides a runtime function that we can call to determine the name of the controlling terminal.

```
#include <stdio.h>

char *ctermid(char *ptr);
```
Returns: pointer to name of controlling terminal
on success, pointer to empty string on error

If *ptr* is non-null, it is assumed to point to an array of at least `L_ctermid` bytes, and the name of the controlling terminal of the process is stored in the array. The constant `L_ctermid` is defined in `<stdio.h>`. If *ptr* is a null pointer, the function allocates room for the array (usually as a static variable). Again, the name of the controlling terminal of the process is stored in the array.

In both cases, the starting address of the array is returned as the value of the function. Since most UNIX systems use `/dev/tty` as the name of the controlling terminal, this function is intended to aid portability to other operating systems.

All four platforms described in this text return the string `/dev/tty` when we call `ctermid`.

Example—`ctermid` Function

Figure 18.12 shows an implementation of the POSIX.1 `ctermid` function.

```
#include     <stdio.h>
#include     <string.h>

static char ctermid_name[L_ctermid];

char *
ctermid(char *str)
{
    if (str == NULL)
        str = ctermid_name;
    return(strcpy(str, "/dev/tty"));     /* strcpy() returns str */
}
```

Figure 18.12 Implementation of POSIX.1 `ctermid` function

Note that we can't protect against overrunning the caller's buffer, because we have no way to determine its size.   □

Two functions that are more interesting for a UNIX system are `isatty`, which returns true if a file descriptor refers to a terminal device, and `ttyname`, which returns the pathname of the terminal device that is open on a file descriptor.

```
#include <unistd.h>

int isatty(int filedes);
```
                              Returns: 1 (true) if terminal device, 0 (false) otherwise

```
char *ttyname(int filedes);
```
                              Returns: pointer to pathname of terminal, NULL on error

Example—`isatty` Function

The `isatty` function is trivial to implement, as we show in Figure 18.13. We simply try one of the terminal-specific functions (that doesn't change anything if it succeeds) and look at the return value.

```
#include    <termios.h>

int
isatty(int fd)
{
    struct termios  ts;

    return(tcgetattr(fd, &ts) != -1); /* true if no error (is a tty) */
}
```

Figure 18.13 Implementation of POSIX.1 `isatty` function

We test our `isatty` function with the program in Figure 18.14.

```
#include "apue.h"

int
main(void)
{
    printf("fd 0: %s\n", isatty(0) ? "tty" : "not a tty");
    printf("fd 1: %s\n", isatty(1) ? "tty" : "not a tty");
    printf("fd 2: %s\n", isatty(2) ? "tty" : "not a tty");
    exit(0);
}
```

Figure 18.14 Test the `isatty` function

When we run the program from Figure 18.14, we get the following output:

```
$ ./a.out
fd 0: tty
fd 1: tty
fd 2: tty
$ ./a.out </etc/passwd 2>/dev/null
fd 0: not a tty
fd 1: tty
fd 2: not a tty
```

☐

Example—`ttyname` Function

The `ttyname` function (Figure 18.15) is longer, as we have to search all the device entries, looking for a match.

```
#include    <sys/stat.h>
#include    <dirent.h>
#include    <limits.h>
#include    <string.h>
#include    <termios.h>
#include    <unistd.h>
#include    <stdlib.h>

struct devdir {
    struct devdir   *d_next;
    char            *d_name;
};

static struct devdir    *head;
static struct devdir    *tail;
static char             pathname[_POSIX_PATH_MAX + 1];

static void
add(char *dirname)
{
    struct devdir   *ddp;
    int             len;

    len = strlen(dirname);

    /*
     * Skip ., .., and /dev/fd.
     */
    if ((dirname[len-1] == '.') && (dirname[len-2] == '/' ||
      (dirname[len-2] == '.' && dirname[len-3] == '/')))
        return;
    if (strcmp(dirname, "/dev/fd") == 0)
        return;
    ddp = malloc(sizeof(struct devdir));
    if (ddp == NULL)
```

```
            return;
        ddp->d_name = strdup(dirname);
        if (ddp->d_name == NULL) {
            free(ddp);
            return;
        }
        ddp->d_next = NULL;
        if (tail == NULL) {
            head = ddp;
            tail = ddp;
        } else {
            tail->d_next = ddp;
            tail = ddp;
        }
}

static void
cleanup(void)
{
    struct devdir   *ddp, *nddp;

    ddp = head;
    while (ddp != NULL) {
        nddp = ddp->d_next;
        free(ddp->d_name);
        free(ddp);
        ddp = nddp;
    }
    head = NULL;
    tail = NULL;
}

static char *
searchdir(char *dirname, struct stat *fdstatp)
{
    struct stat     devstat;
    DIR             *dp;
    int             devlen;
    struct dirent   *dirp;

    strcpy(pathname, dirname);
    if ((dp = opendir(dirname)) == NULL)
        return(NULL);
    strcat(pathname, "/");
    devlen = strlen(pathname);
    while ((dirp = readdir(dp)) != NULL) {
        strncpy(pathname + devlen, dirp->d_name,
          _POSIX_PATH_MAX - devlen);

        /*
         * Skip aliases.
         */
```

```
            if (strcmp(pathname, "/dev/stdin") == 0 ||
              strcmp(pathname, "/dev/stdout") == 0 ||
              strcmp(pathname, "/dev/stderr") == 0)
                continue;
            if (stat(pathname, &devstat) < 0)
                continue;
            if (S_ISDIR(devstat.st_mode)) {
                add(pathname);
                continue;
            }
            if (devstat.st_ino == fdstatp->st_ino &&
              devstat.st_dev == fdstatp->st_dev) {   /* found a match */
                closedir(dp);
                return(pathname);
            }
        }
    }
    closedir(dp);
    return(NULL);
}

char *
ttyname(int fd)
{
    struct stat      fdstat;
    struct devdir    *ddp;
    char             *rval;

    if (isatty(fd) == 0)
        return(NULL);
    if (fstat(fd, &fdstat) < 0)
        return(NULL);
    if (S_ISCHR(fdstat.st_mode) == 0)
        return(NULL);

    rval = searchdir("/dev", &fdstat);
    if (rval == NULL) {
        for (ddp = head; ddp != NULL; ddp = ddp->d_next)
            if ((rval = searchdir(ddp->d_name, &fdstat)) != NULL)
                break;
    }
    cleanup();
    return(rval);
}
```

Figure 18.15 Implementation of POSIX.1 ttyname function

The technique is to read the /dev directory, looking for an entry with the same device number and i-node number. Recall from Section 4.23 that each file system has a unique device number (the st_dev field in the stat structure, from Section 4.2), and each directory entry in that file system has a unique i-node number (the st_ino field in the `stat` structure). We assume in this function that when we hit a matching device number and matching i-node number, we've located the desired directory entry. We could also verify that the two entries have matching `st_rdev` fields (the major and minor device numbers for the terminal device) and that the directory entry is also a character special file. But since we've already verified that the file descriptor argument is both a terminal device and a character special file, and since a matching device number and i-node number is unique on a UNIX system, there is no need for the additional comparisons.

The name of our terminal might reside in a subdirectory in `/dev`. Thus, we might need to search the entire file system tree under `/dev`. We skip several directories that might produce incorrect or odd-looking results: `/dev/.`, `/dev/..`, and `/dev/fd`. We also skip the aliases `/dev/stdin`, `/dev/stdout`, and `/dev/stderr`, since they are symbolic links to files in `/dev/fd`.

We can test this implementation with the program shown in Figure 18.16.

```
#include "apue.h"

int
main(void)
{
    char *name;

    if (isatty(0)) {
        name = ttyname(0);
        if (name == NULL)
            name = "undefined";
    } else {
        name = "not a tty";
    }
    printf("fd 0: %s\n", name);
    if (isatty(1)) {
        name = ttyname(1);
        if (name == NULL)
            name = "undefined";
    } else {
        name = "not a tty";
    }
    printf("fd 1: %s\n", name);
    if (isatty(2)) {
        name = ttyname(2);
        if (name == NULL)
            name = "undefined";
    } else {
        name = "not a tty";
    }
    printf("fd 2: %s\n", name);
    exit(0);
}
```

Figure 18.16 Test the `ttyname` function

Running the program from Figure 18.16 gives us

```
$ ./a.out < /dev/console 2> /dev/null
fd 0: /dev/console
fd 1: /dev/ttyp3
fd 2: not a tty
```

□

18.10 Canonical Mode

Canonical mode is simple: we issue a read, and the terminal driver returns when a line has been entered. Several conditions cause the read to return.

- The read returns when the requested number of bytes have been read. We don't have to read a complete line. If we read a partial line, no information is lost; the next read starts where the previous read stopped.

- The read returns when a line delimiter is encountered. Recall from Section 18.3 that the following characters are interpreted as end of line in canonical mode: NL, EOL, EOL2, and EOF. Also, recall from Section 18.5 that if ICRNL is set and if IGNCR is not set, then the CR character also terminates a line, since it acts just like the NL character.

  Realize that of these five line delimiters, one (EOF) is discarded by the terminal driver when it's processed. The other four are returned to the caller as the last character of the line.

- The read also returns if a signal is caught and if the function is not automatically restarted (Section 10.5).

Example—`getpass` Function

We now show the function `getpass`, which reads a password of some type from the user at a terminal. This function is called by the `login`(1) and `crypt`(1) programs. To read the password, the function must turn off echoing, but it can leave the terminal in canonical mode, as whatever we type as the password forms a complete line. Figure 18.17 shows a typical implementation on a UNIX system.

There are several points to consider in this example.

- Instead of hardwiring `/dev/tty` into the program, we call the function `ctermid` to open the controlling terminal.

- We read and write only to the controlling terminal and return an error if we can't open this device for reading and writing. There are other conventions to use. The BSD version of `getpass` reads from standard input and writes to standard error if the controlling terminal can't be opened for reading and writing. The System V version always writes to standard error but reads only from the controlling terminal.

```
#include    <signal.h>
#include    <stdio.h>
#include    <termios.h>

#define MAX_PASS_LEN    8        /* max #chars for user to enter */

char *
getpass(const char *prompt)
{
    static char        buf[MAX_PASS_LEN + 1];  /* null byte at end */
    char               *ptr;
    sigset_t           sig, osig;
    struct termios     ts, ots;
    FILE               *fp;
    int                c;

    if ((fp = fopen(ctermid(NULL), "r+")) == NULL)
        return(NULL);
    setbuf(fp, NULL);

    sigemptyset(&sig);
    sigaddset(&sig, SIGINT);          /* block SIGINT */
    sigaddset(&sig, SIGTSTP);         /* block SIGTSTP */
    sigprocmask(SIG_BLOCK, &sig, &osig);   /* and save mask */

    tcgetattr(fileno(fp), &ts);       /* save tty state */
    ots = ts;                         /* structure copy */
    ts.c_lflag &= ~(ECHO | ECHOE | ECHOK | ECHONL);
    tcsetattr(fileno(fp), TCSAFLUSH, &ts);
    fputs(prompt, fp);

    ptr = buf;
    while ((c = getc(fp)) != EOF && c != '\n')
        if (ptr < &buf[MAX_PASS_LEN])
            *ptr++ = c;
    *ptr = 0;                /* null terminate */
    putc('\n', fp);          /* we echo a newline */

    tcsetattr(fileno(fp), TCSAFLUSH, &ots); /* restore TTY state */
    sigprocmask(SIG_SETMASK, &osig, NULL);  /* restore mask */
    fclose(fp);              /* done with /dev/tty */
    return(buf);
}
```

Figure 18.17 Implementation of getpass function

- We block the two signals SIGINT and SIGTSTP. If we didn't do this, entering the INTR character would abort the program and leave the terminal with echoing disabled. Similarly, entering the SUSP character would stop the program and return to the shell with echoing disabled. We choose to block the signals while we have echoing disabled. If they are generated while we're reading the password, they are held until we return. There are other ways to handle these signals. Some versions just ignore SIGINT (saving its previous action) while in getpass, resetting the action for this signal to its previous value before returning. This means that any occurrence of the signal while it's ignored is lost. Other versions catch SIGINT (saving its previous action) and if the signal is caught, send themselves the signal with the kill function after resetting the terminal state and signal action. None of the versions of getpass catch, ignore, or block SIGQUIT, so entering the QUIT character aborts the program and probably leaves the terminal with echoing disabled.

- Be aware that some shells, notably the Korn shell, turn echoing back on whenever they read interactive input. These shells are the ones that provide command-line editing and therefore manipulate the state of the terminal every time we enter an interactive command. So, if we invoke this program under one of these shells and abort it with the QUIT character, it may reenable echoing for us. Other shells that don't provide this form of command-line editing, such as the Bourne shell, will abort the program and leave the terminal in no-echo mode. If we do this to our terminal, the stty command can reenable echoing.

- We use standard I/O to read and write the controlling terminal. We specifically set the stream to be unbuffered; otherwise, there might be some interactions between the writing and reading of the stream (we would need some calls to fflush). We could have also used unbuffered I/O (Chapter 3), but we would have to simulate the getc function using read.

- We store only up to eight characters as the password. Any additional characters that are entered are ignored.

The program in Figure 18.18 calls getpass and prints what we enter to let us verify that the ERASE and KILL characters work (as they should in canonical mode).

```
#include "apue.h"

char    *getpass(const char *);

int
main(void)
{
    char    *ptr;

    if ((ptr = getpass("Enter password:")) == NULL)
        err_sys("getpass error");
    printf("password: %s\n", ptr);

    /* now use password (probably encrypt it) ... */

    while (*ptr != 0)
        *ptr++ = 0;      /* zero it out when we're done with it */
    exit(0);
}
```

Figure 18.18 Call the getpass function

Whenever a program that calls `getpass` is done with the cleartext password, the program should zero it out in memory, just to be safe. If the program were to generate a `core` file that others might be able to read or if some other process were somehow able to read our memory, they might be able to read the cleartext password. (By "cleartext," we mean the password that we type at the prompt that is printed by `getpass`. Most UNIX system programs then modify this cleartext password into an "encrypted" password. The field `pw_passwd` in the password file, for example, contains the encrypted password, not the cleartext password.)   □

18.11 Noncanonical Mode

Noncanonical mode is specified by turning off the `ICANON` flag in the `c_lflag` field of the `termios` structure. In noncanonical mode, the input data is not assembled into lines. The following special characters (Section 18.3) are not processed: ERASE, KILL, EOF, NL, EOL, EOL2, CR, REPRINT, STATUS, and WERASE.

As we said, canonical mode is easy: the system returns up to one line at a time. But with noncanonical mode, how does the system know when to return data to us? If it returned one byte at a time, overhead would be excessive. (Recall Figure 3.5, which showed the overhead in reading one byte at a time. Each time we doubled the amount of data returned, we halved the system call overhead.) The system can't always return multiple bytes at a time, since sometimes we don't know how much data to read until we start reading it.

The solution is to tell the system to return when either a specified amount of data has been read or after a given amount of time has passed. This technique uses two variables in the `c_cc` array in the `termios` structure: MIN and TIME. These two elements of the array are indexed by the names `VMIN` and `VTIME`.

MIN specifies the minimum number of bytes before a `read` returns. TIME specifies the number of tenths of a second to wait for data to arrive. There are four cases.

Case A: MIN > 0, TIME > 0

> TIME specifies an interbyte timer that is started only when the first byte is received. If MIN bytes are received before the timer expires, `read` returns MIN bytes. If the timer expires before MIN bytes are received, `read` returns the bytes received. (At least one byte is returned if the timer expires, because the timer is not started until the first byte is received.) In this case, the caller blocks until the first byte is received. If data is already available when `read` is called, it is as if the data had been received immediately after the `read`.

Case B: MIN > 0, TIME == 0

> The `read` does not return until MIN bytes have been received. This can cause a `read` to block indefinitely.

Case C: MIN == 0, TIME > 0

> TIME specifies a read timer that is started when read is called. (Compare this
> to case A, in which a nonzero TIME represented an interbyte timer that was not
> started until the first byte was received.) The read returns when a single byte
> is received or when the timer expires. If the timer expires, read returns 0.

Case D: MIN == 0, TIME == 0

> If some data is available, read returns up to the number of bytes requested. If
> no data is available, read returns 0 immediately.

Realize in all these cases that MIN is only a minimum. If the program requests more
than MIN bytes of data, it's possible to receive up to the requested amount. This also
applies to cases C and D, in which MIN is 0.

Figure 18.19 summarizes the four cases for noncanonical input. In this figure, *nbytes*
is the third argument to read (the maximum number of bytes to return).

	MIN > 0	MIN == 0
TIME > 0	**A:** read returns [MIN, *nbytes*] before timer expires; read returns [1, MIN) if timer expires. (TIME = interbyte timer. Caller can block indefinitely.)	**C:** read returns [1, *nbytes*] before timer expires; read returns 0 if timer expires. (TIME = read timer.)
TIME == 0	**B:** read returns [MIN, *nbytes*] when available. (Caller can block indefinitely.)	**D:** read returns [0, *nbytes*] immediately.

Figure 18.19   Four cases for noncanonical input

> Be aware that POSIX.1 allows the subscripts VMIN and VTIME to have the same values as VEOF
> and VEOL, respectively. Indeed, Solaris does this for backward compatibility with older
> versions of System V. This creates a portability problem, however. In going from
> noncanonical to canonical mode, we must now restore VEOF and VEOL also. If VMIN equals
> VEOF and we don't restore their values, when we set VMIN to its typical value of 1, the
> end-of-file character becomes Control-A. The easiest way around this problem is to save the
> entire termios structure when going into noncanonical mode and restore it when going back
> to canonical mode.

Example

The program in Figure 18.20 defines the tty_cbreak and tty_raw functions that set
the terminal in *cbreak mode* and *raw mode*. (The terms *cbreak* and *raw* come from the
Version 7 terminal driver.) We can reset the terminal to its original state (the state before
either of these functions was called) by calling the function tty_reset.

If we've called tty_cbreak, we need to call tty_reset before calling tty_raw.
The same goes for calling tty_cbreak after calling tty_raw. This improves the
chances that the terminal will be left in a usable state if we encounter any errors.

Two additional functions are also provided: `tty_atexit` can be established as an exit handler to ensure that the terminal mode is reset by `exit`, and `tty_termios` returns a pointer to the original canonical mode `termios` structure.

```
#include "apue.h"
#include <termios.h>
#include <errno.h>

static struct termios        save_termios;
static int                   ttysavefd = -1;
static enum { RESET, RAW, CBREAK } ttystate = RESET;

int
tty_cbreak(int fd)    /* put terminal into a cbreak mode */
{
    int             err;
    struct termios  buf;

    if (ttystate != RESET) {
        errno = EINVAL;
        return(-1);
    }
    if (tcgetattr(fd, &buf) < 0)
        return(-1);
    save_termios = buf; /* structure copy */

    /*
     * Echo off, canonical mode off.
     */
    buf.c_lflag &= ~(ECHO | ICANON);

    /*
     * Case B: 1 byte at a time, no timer.
     */
    buf.c_cc[VMIN] = 1;
    buf.c_cc[VTIME] = 0;
    if (tcsetattr(fd, TCSAFLUSH, &buf) < 0)
        return(-1);

    /*
     * Verify that the changes stuck.  tcsetattr can return 0 on
     * partial success.
     */
    if (tcgetattr(fd, &buf) < 0) {
        err = errno;
        tcsetattr(fd, TCSAFLUSH, &save_termios);
        errno = err;
        return(-1);
    }
    if ((buf.c_lflag & (ECHO | ICANON)) || buf.c_cc[VMIN] != 1 ||
      buf.c_cc[VTIME] != 0) {
```

```
        /*
         * Only some of the changes were made.  Restore the
         * original settings.
         */
        tcsetattr(fd, TCSAFLUSH, &save_termios);
        errno = EINVAL;
        return(-1);
    }

    ttystate = CBREAK;
    ttysavefd = fd;
    return(0);
}

int
tty_raw(int fd)         /* put terminal into a raw mode */
{
    int             err;
    struct termios  buf;

    if (ttystate != RESET) {
        errno = EINVAL;
        return(-1);
    }
    if (tcgetattr(fd, &buf) < 0)
        return(-1);
    save_termios = buf; /* structure copy */

    /*
     * Echo off, canonical mode off, extended input
     * processing off, signal chars off.
     */
    buf.c_lflag &= ~(ECHO | ICANON | IEXTEN | ISIG);

    /*
     * No SIGINT on BREAK, CR-to-NL off, input parity
     * check off, don't strip 8th bit on input, output
     * flow control off.
     */
    buf.c_iflag &= ~(BRKINT | ICRNL | INPCK | ISTRIP | IXON);

    /*
     * Clear size bits, parity checking off.
     */
    buf.c_cflag &= ~(CSIZE | PARENB);

    /*
     * Set 8 bits/char.
     */
    buf.c_cflag |= CS8;

    /*
```

```
         * Output processing off.
         */
        buf.c_oflag &= ~(OPOST);

        /*
         * Case B: 1 byte at a time, no timer.
         */
        buf.c_cc[VMIN] = 1;
        buf.c_cc[VTIME] = 0;
        if (tcsetattr(fd, TCSAFLUSH, &buf) < 0)
            return(-1);

        /*
         * Verify that the changes stuck.  tcsetattr can return 0 on
         * partial success.
         */
        if (tcgetattr(fd, &buf) < 0) {
            err = errno;
            tcsetattr(fd, TCSAFLUSH, &save_termios);
            errno = err;
            return(-1);
        }
        if ((buf.c_lflag & (ECHO | ICANON | IEXTEN | ISIG)) ||
          (buf.c_iflag & (BRKINT | ICRNL | INPCK | ISTRIP | IXON)) ||
          (buf.c_cflag & (CSIZE | PARENB | CS8)) != CS8 ||
          (buf.c_oflag & OPOST) || buf.c_cc[VMIN] != 1 ||
          buf.c_cc[VTIME] != 0) {
            /*
             * Only some of the changes were made.  Restore the
             * original settings.
             */
            tcsetattr(fd, TCSAFLUSH, &save_termios);
            errno = EINVAL;
            return(-1);
        }

        ttystate = RAW;
        ttysavefd = fd;
        return(0);
}

int
tty_reset(int fd)           /* restore terminal's mode */
{
        if (ttystate == RESET)
            return(0);
        if (tcsetattr(fd, TCSAFLUSH, &save_termios) < 0)
            return(-1);
        ttystate = RESET;
        return(0);
}
```

```
void
tty_atexit(void)              /* can be set up by atexit(tty_atexit) */
{
    if (ttysavefd >= 0)
        tty_reset(ttysavefd);
}

struct termios *
tty_termios(void)             /* let caller see original tty state */
{
    return(&save_termios);
}
```

Figure 18.20 Set terminal mode to cbreak or raw

Our definition of cbreak mode is the following:

- Noncanonical mode. As we mentioned at the beginning of this section, this mode turns off some input character processing. It does not turn off signal handling, so the user can always type one of the terminal-generated signals. Be aware that the caller should catch these signals, or there's a chance that the signal will terminate the program, and the terminal will be left in cbreak mode.

  As a general rule, whenever we write a program that changes the terminal mode, we should catch most signals. This allows us to reset the terminal mode before terminating.

- Echo off.

- One byte at a time input. To do this, we set MIN to 1 and TIME to 0. This is case B from Figure 18.19. A read won't return until at least one byte is available.

We define raw mode as follows:

- Noncanonical mode. We also turn off processing of the signal-generating characters (ISIG) and the extended input character processing (IEXTEN). Additionally, we disable a BREAK character from generating a signal, by turning off BRKINT.

- Echo off.

- We disable the CR-to-NL mapping on input (ICRNL), input parity detection (INPCK), the stripping of the eighth bit on input (ISTRIP), and output flow control (IXON).

- Eight-bit characters (CS8), and parity checking is disabled (PARENB).

- All output processing is disabled (OPOST).

- One byte at a time input (MIN = 1, TIME = 0).

The program in Figure 18.21 tests raw and cbreak modes.

```
#include "apue.h"

static void
sig_catch(int signo)
{
    printf("signal caught\n");
    tty_reset(STDIN_FILENO);
    exit(0);
}

int
main(void)
{
    int     i;
    char    c;

    if (signal(SIGINT, sig_catch) == SIG_ERR)    /* catch signals */
        err_sys("signal(SIGINT) error");
    if (signal(SIGQUIT, sig_catch) == SIG_ERR)
        err_sys("signal(SIGQUIT) error");
    if (signal(SIGTERM, sig_catch) == SIG_ERR)
        err_sys("signal(SIGTERM) error");

    if (tty_raw(STDIN_FILENO) < 0)
        err_sys("tty_raw error");
    printf("Enter raw mode characters, terminate with DELETE\n");
    while ((i = read(STDIN_FILENO, &c, 1)) == 1) {
        if ((c &= 255) == 0177)    /* 0177 = ASCII DELETE */
            break;
        printf("%o\n", c);
    }
    if (tty_reset(STDIN_FILENO) < 0)
        err_sys("tty_reset error");
    if (i <= 0)
        err_sys("read error");
    if (tty_cbreak(STDIN_FILENO) < 0)
        err_sys("tty_cbreak error");
    printf("\nEnter cbreak mode characters, terminate with SIGINT\n");
    while ((i = read(STDIN_FILENO, &c, 1)) == 1) {
        c &= 255;
        printf("%o\n", c);
    }
    if (tty_reset(STDIN_FILENO) < 0)
        err_sys("tty_reset error");
    if (i <= 0)
        err_sys("read error");

    exit(0);
}
```

Figure 18.21 Test raw and cbreak terminal modes

Running the program in Figure 18.21, we can see what happens with these two terminal modes:

```
$ ./a.out
Enter raw mode characters, terminate with DELETE
                                                4
                                            33
                                        133
                                      61
                                   70
                                176
```

type DELETE

```
Enter cbreak mode characters, terminate with SIGINT
1                              type Control-A
10                             type backspace
signal caught                  type interrupt key
```

In raw mode, the characters entered were Control-D (04) and the special function key F7. On the terminal being used, this function key generated five characters: *ESC* (033), *[* (0133), *1* (061), *8* (070), and *~* (0176). Note that with the output processing turned off in raw mode (~OPOST), we do not get a carriage return output after each character. Also note that special-character processing is disabled in cbreak mode (so, for example, Control-D, the end-of-file character, and backspace aren't handled specially), whereas the terminal-generated signals are still processed.   □

18.12 Terminal Window Size

Most UNIX systems provide a way to keep track of the current terminal window size and to have the kernel notify the foreground process group when the size changes. The kernel maintains a winsize structure for every terminal and pseudo terminal:

```
struct winsize {
  unsigned short  ws_row;     /* rows, in characters */
  unsigned short  ws_col;     /* columns, in characters */
  unsigned short  ws_xpixel;  /* horizontal size, pixels (unused) */
  unsigned short  ws_ypixel;  /* vertical size, pixels (unused) */
};
```

The rules for this structure are as follows.

- We can fetch the current value of this structure using an ioctl (Section 3.15) of TIOCGWINSZ.

- We can store a new value of this structure in the kernel using an ioctl of TIOCSWINSZ. If this new value differs from the current value stored in the kernel, a SIGWINCH signal is sent to the foreground process group. (Note from Figure 10.1 that the default action for this signal is to be ignored.)

- Other than storing the current value of the structure and generating a signal when the value changes, the kernel does nothing else with this structure. Interpreting the structure is entirely up to the application.

The reason for providing this feature is to notify applications (such as the vi editor) when the window size changes. When it receives the signal, the application can fetch the new size and redraw the screen.

Example

Figure 18.22 shows a program that prints the current window size and goes to sleep. Each time the window size changes, SIGWINCH is caught and the new size is printed. We have to terminate this program with a signal.

```
#include "apue.h"
#include <termios.h>
#ifndef TIOCGWINSZ
#include <sys/ioctl.h>
#endif

static void
pr_winsize(int fd)
{
    struct winsize  size;

    if (ioctl(fd, TIOCGWINSZ, (char *) &size) < 0)
        err_sys("TIOCGWINSZ error");
    printf("%d rows, %d columns\n", size.ws_row, size.ws_col);
}

static void
sig_winch(int signo)
{
    printf("SIGWINCH received\n");
    pr_winsize(STDIN_FILENO);
}

int
main(void)
{
    if (isatty(STDIN_FILENO) == 0)
        exit(1);
    if (signal(SIGWINCH, sig_winch) == SIG_ERR)
        err_sys("signal error");
    pr_winsize(STDIN_FILENO);    /* print initial size */
    for ( ; ; )                  /* and sleep forever */
        pause();
}
```

Figure 18.22 Print window size

Running the program in Figure 18.22 on a windowed terminal gives us

```
$ ./a.out
35 rows, 80 columns          initial size
SIGWINCH received            change window size: signal is caught
40 rows, 123 columns
SIGWINCH received            and again
42 rows, 33 columns
^? $                         type the interrupt key to terminate
```
                                                                                                              □

18.13 `termcap`, `terminfo`, **and** `curses`

`termcap` stands for "terminal capability," and it refers to the text file `/etc/termcap`
and a set of routines to read this file. The `termcap` scheme was developed at Berkeley
to support the `vi` editor. The `termcap` file contains descriptions of various terminals:
what features the terminal supports (how many lines and rows, whether the terminal
support backspace, etc.) and how to make the terminal perform certain operations (clear
the screen, move the cursor to a given location, etc.). Taking this information out of the
compiled program and placing it into a text file that can easily be edited allows the `vi`
editor to run on many different terminals.

The routines that support the `termcap` file were then extracted from the `vi` editor
and placed into a separate `curses` library. Many features were added to make this
library usable for any program that wanted to manipulate the screen.

The `termcap` scheme was not perfect. As more and more terminals were added to
the data file, it took longer to scan the file, looking for a specific terminal. The data file
also used two-character names to identify the various terminal attributes. These
deficiencies led to development of the `terminfo` scheme and its associated `curses`
library. The terminal descriptions in `terminfo` are basically compiled versions of a
textual description and can be located faster at runtime. `terminfo` appeared with
SVR2 and has been in all System V releases since then.

> Historically, System V–based systems used `terminfo`, and BSD-derived systems used
> `termcap`, but it is now common for systems to provide both. Mac OS X, however, supports
> only `terminfo`.

A description of `terminfo` and the `curses` library is provided by Goodheart [1991],
but this is currently out of print. Strang [1986] describes the Berkeley version of the
`curses` library. Strang, Mui, and O'Reilly [1988] provide a description of `termcap` and
`terminfo`.

> The ncurses library, a free version that is compatible with the SVR4 `curses` interface, can be
> found at `http://invisible-island.net/ncurses/ncurses.html`.

Neither `termcap` nor `terminfo`, by itself, addresses the problems we've been
looking at in this chapter: changing the terminal's mode, changing one of the terminal
special characters, handling the window size, and so on. What they do provide is a way
to perform typical operations (clear the screen, move the cursor) on a wide variety of

terminals. On the other hand, curses does help with some of the details that we've addressed in this chapter. Functions are provided by curses to set raw mode, set cbreak mode, turn echo on and off, and the like. But the curses library is designed for character-based dumb terminals, which have mostly been replaced by pixel-based graphics terminals today.

18.14 Summary

Terminals have many features and options, most of which we're able to change to suit our needs. In this chapter, we've described numerous functions that change a terminal's operation: special input characters and the option flags. We've looked at all the terminal special characters and the many options that can be set or reset for a terminal device.

There are two modes of terminal input—canonical (line at a time) and noncanonical. We showed examples of both modes and provided functions that map between the POSIX.1 terminal options and the older BSD cbreak and raw modes. We also described how to fetch and change the window size of a terminal.

Exercises

18.1 Write a program that calls tty_raw and terminates (without resetting the terminal mode). If your system provides the reset(1) command (all four systems described in this text do), use it to restore the terminal mode.

18.2 The PARODD flag in the c_cflag field allows us to specify even or odd parity. The BSD tip program, however, also allows the parity bit to be 0 or 1. How does it do this?

18.3 If your system's stty(1) command outputs the MIN and TIME values, do the following exercise. Log in to the system twice and start the vi editor from one login. Use the stty command from your other login to determine what values vi sets MIN and TIME to (since vi sets the terminal to noncanonical mode). (If you are running a windowing system on your terminal, you can do this same test by logging in once and using two separate windows instead.)

19

Pseudo Terminals

19.1 Introduction

In Chapter 9, we saw that terminal logins come in through a terminal device, automatically providing terminal semantics. A terminal line discipline (Figure 18.2) exists between the terminal and the programs that we run, so we can set the terminal's special characters (backspace, line erase, interrupt, etc.) and the like. When a login arrives on a network connection, however, a terminal line discipline is not automatically provided between the incoming network connection and the login shell. Figure 9.5 showed that a *pseudo-terminal* device driver is used to provide terminal semantics.

In addition to network logins, pseudo terminals have other uses that we explore in this chapter. We start with an overview on how to use pseudo terminals, followed by a discussion of specific use cases. We then provide functions to create pseudo terminals on various platforms and then use these functions to write a program that we call `pty`. We'll show various uses of this program: making a transcript of all the character input and output on the terminal (the `script(1)` program) and running coprocesses to avoid the buffering problems we encountered in the program from Figure 15.19.

19.2 Overview

The term *pseudo terminal* implies that it looks like a terminal to an application program, but it's not a real terminal. Figure 19.1 shows the typical arrangement of the processes involved when a pseudo terminal is being used. The key points in this figure are the following.

- Normally, a process opens the pseudo-terminal master and then calls `fork`. The child establishes a new session, opens the corresponding pseudo-terminal slave,

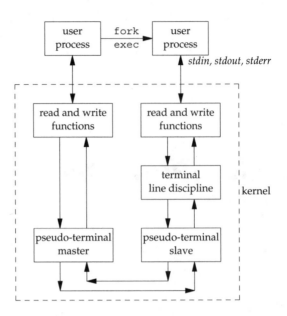

Figure 19.1 Typical arrangement of processes using a pseudo terminal

duplicates the file descriptor to the standard input, standard output, and standard error, and then calls `exec`. The pseudo-terminal slave becomes the controlling terminal for the child process.

- It appears to the user process above the slave that its standard input, standard output, and standard error are a terminal device. The process can issue all the terminal I/O functions from Chapter 18 on these descriptors. But since there is not a real terminal device beneath the slave, functions that don't make sense (change the baud rate, send a break character, set odd parity, etc.) are just ignored.

- Anything written to the master appears as input to the slave and vice versa. Indeed, all the input to the slave comes from the user process above the pseudo-terminal master. This behaves like a bidirectional pipe, but with the terminal line discipline module above the slave, we have additional capabilities over a plain pipe.

Figure 19.1 shows what a pseudo terminal looks like on a FreeBSD, Mac OS X, or Linux system. In Sections 19.3.2 and 19.3.3, we show how to open these devices.

Under Solaris, a pseudo terminal is built using the STREAMS subsystem (Section 14.4). Figure 19.2 details the arrangement of the pseudo-terminal STREAMS modules under Solaris. The two STREAMS modules that are shown as dashed boxes are optional. The `pckt` and `ptem` modules help provide semantics specific to pseudo terminals. The other two modules (`ldterm` and `ttcompat`) provide line discipline processing.

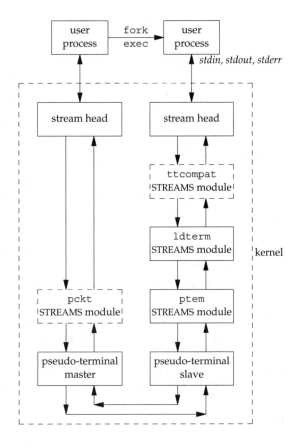

Figure 19.2 Arrangement of pseudo terminals under Solaris

Note that the three STREAMS modules above the slave are the same as the output from the program shown in Figure 14.18 for a network login. In Section 19.3.1, we show how to build this arrangement of STREAMS modules.

From this point on, we'll simplify the figures by not showing the "read and write functions" from Figure 19.1 or the "stream head" from Figure 19.2. We'll also use the abbreviation PTY for pseudo terminal and lump all the STREAMS modules above the slave PTY in Figure 19.2 into a box called "terminal line discipline," as in Figure 19.1.

We'll now examine some of the typical uses of pseudo terminals.

Network Login Servers

Pseudo terminals are built into servers that provide network logins. The typical examples are the telnetd and rlogind servers. Chapter 15 of Stevens [1990] details the steps involved in the rlogin service. Once the login shell is running on the remote host, we have the arrangement shown in Figure 19.3. A similar arrangement is used by the telnetd server.

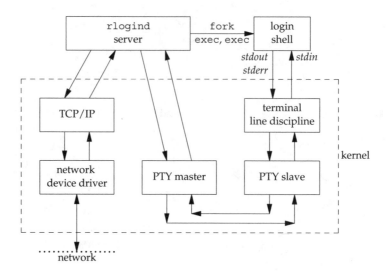

Figure 19.3 Arrangement of processes for rlogind server

We show two calls to exec between the rlogind server and the login shell, because the login program is usually between the two to validate the user.

A key point in this figure is that the process driving the PTY master is normally reading and writing another I/O stream at the same time. In this example, the other I/O stream is the TCP/IP box. This implies that the process must be using some form of I/O multiplexing (Section 14.5), such as select or poll, or must be divided into two processes or threads.

script **Program**

The script(1) program that is supplied with most UNIX systems makes a copy in a file of everything that is input and output during a terminal session. The program does this by placing itself between the terminal and a new invocation of our login shell. Figure 19.4 details the interactions involved in the script program. Here, we specifically show that the script program is normally run from a login shell, which then waits for script to terminate.

While script is running, everything output by the terminal line discipline above the PTY slave is copied to the script file (usually called typescript). Since our keystrokes are normally echoed by that line discipline module, the script file also contains our input. The script file won't contain any passwords that we enter, however, since passwords aren't echoed.

> While writing the first edition of this book, Rich Stevens used the script program to capture the output of the example programs. This avoided typographical errors that could have occurred if he had copied the program output by hand. The drawback to using script, however, is having to deal with control characters that are present in the script file.

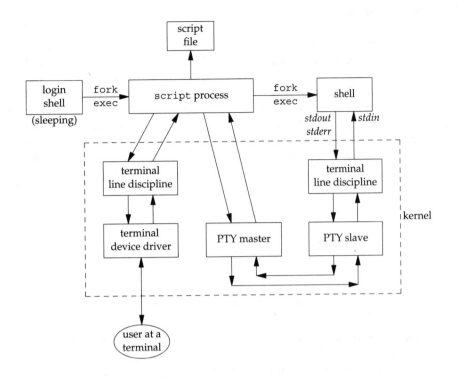

Figure 19.4 The script program

    After developing the general pty program in Section 19.5, we'll see that a trivial shell script turns it into a version of the script program.

expect Program

    Pseudo terminals can be used to drive interactive programs in noninteractive modes. Numerous programs are hardwired to require a terminal to run. One example is the passwd(1) command, which requires that the user enter a password in response to a prompt.

    Rather than modify all the interactive programs to support a batch mode of operation, a better solution is to provide a way to drive any interactive program from a script. The expect program [Libes 1990, 1991, 1994] provides a way to do this. It uses pseudo terminals to run other programs, similar to the pty program in Section 19.5. But expect also provides a programming language to examine the output of the program being run to make decisions about what to send the program as input. When an interactive program is being run from a script, we can't just copy everything from the script to the program and vice versa. Instead, we have to send the program some input, look at its output, and decide what to send it next.

Running Coprocesses

In the coprocess example in Figure 15.19, we couldn't invoke a coprocess that used the standard I/O library for its input and output, because when we talked to the coprocess across a pipe, the standard I/O library fully buffered the standard input and standard output, leading to a deadlock. If the coprocess is a compiled program for which we don't have the source code, we can't add fflush statements to solve this problem. Figure 15.16 showed a process driving a coprocess. What we need to do is place a pseudo terminal between the two processes, as shown in Figure 19.5, to trick the coprocess into thinking that it is being driven from a terminal instead of from another process.

Figure 19.5 Driving a coprocess using a pseudo terminal

Now the standard input and standard output of the coprocess look like a terminal device, so the standard I/O library will set these two streams to be line buffered.

The parent can obtain a pseudo terminal between itself and the coprocess in two ways. (The parent in this case could be either the program in Figure 15.18, which used two pipes to communicate with the coprocess, or the program in Figure 17.4, which used a single STREAMS pipe.) One way is for the parent to call the pty_fork function directly (Section 19.4) instead of calling fork. Another is to exec the pty program (Section 19.5) with the coprocess as its argument. We'll look at these two solutions after showing the pty program.

Watching the Output of Long-Running Programs

If we have a program that runs for a long time, we can easily run it in the background using any of the standard shells. But if we redirect its standard output to a file, and if it doesn't generate much output, we can't easily monitor its progress, because the standard I/O library will fully buffer its standard output. All that we'll see are blocks of output written by the standard I/O library to the output file, possibly in chunks as large as 8,192 bytes.

If we have the source code, we can insert calls to fflush. Alternatively, we can run the program under the pty program, making its standard I/O library think that its standard output is a terminal. Figure 19.6 shows this arrangement, where we have called the slow output program slowout. The fork/exec arrow from the login shell to the pty process is shown as a dashed arrow to reiterate that the pty process is running as a background job.

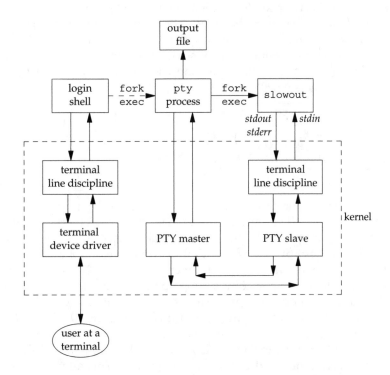

Figure 19.6 Running a slow output program using a pseudo terminal

19.3 Opening Pseudo-Terminal Devices

The way we open a pseudo-terminal device differs among platforms. The Single UNIX Specification includes several functions as XSI extensions in an attempt to unify the methods. These extensions are based on the functions originally provided to manage STREAMS-based pseudo terminals in System V Release 4.

The `posix_openpt` function is provided as a portable way to open an available pseudo-terminal master device.

```
#include <stdlib.h>
#include <fcntl.h>

int posix_openpt(int oflag);
```
                        Returns: file descriptor of next available PTY master if OK, −1 on error

The *oflag* argument is a bitmask that specifies how the master device is to be opened, similar to the same argument used with open(2). Not all open flags are supported, however. With `posix_openpt`, we can specify O_RDWR to open the master device for reading and writing, and we can specify O_NOCTTY to prevent the master device from becoming a controlling terminal for the caller. All other open flags result in unspecified behavior.

Before a slave pseudo-terminal device can be used, its permissions need to be set so that it is accessible to applications. The grantpt function does just this. It sets the user ID of the slave's device node to be the caller's real user ID and sets the node's group ID to an unspecified value, usually some group that has access to terminal devices. The permissions are set to allow read and write access to individual owners and write access to group owners (0620).

```
#include <stdlib.h>

int grantpt(int filedes);

int unlockpt(int filedes);
```
                                               Both return: 0 on success, −1 on error

To change permission on the slave device node, grantpt might need to fork and exec a set-user-ID program (/usr/lib/pt_chmod on Solaris, for example). Thus, the behavior is unspecified if the caller is catching SIGCHLD.

The unlockpt function is used to grant access to the slave pseudo-terminal device, thereby allowing applications to open the device. By preventing others from opening the slave device, applications setting up the devices have an opportunity to initialize the slave and master devices properly before they can be used.

Note that in both grantpt and unlockpt, the file descriptor argument is the file descriptor associated with the master pseudo-terminal device.

The ptsname function is used to find the pathname of the slave pseudo-terminal device, given the file descriptor of the master. This allows applications to identify the slave independent of any particular conventions that might be followed by a given platform. Note that the name returned might be stored in static memory, so it can be overwritten on successive calls.

```
#include <stdlib.h>

char *ptsname(int filedes);
```
                                    Returns: pointer to name of PTY slave if OK, NULL on error

Figure 19.7 summarizes the pseudo-terminal functions in the Single UNIX Specification and indicates which functions are supported by the platforms discussed in this text.

> On FreeBSD, unlockpt does nothing; the O_NOCTTY flag is defined only for compatibility with applications that call posix_openpt. FreeBSD does not allocate a controlling terminal as a side effect of opening a terminal device, so the O_NOCTTY flag has no effect.

Function	Description	XSI	FreeBSD 5.2.1	Linux 2.4.22	Mac OS X 10.3	Solaris 9
grantpt	Change permissions of slave PTY device.	•	•	•		•
posix_openpt	Open a master PTY device.	•	•	•		
ptsname	Return name of slave PTY device.	•	•	•	•	•
unlockpt	Allow slave PTY device to be opened.	•	•	•	•	•

Figure 19.7 XSI pseudo-terminal functions

Even though the Single UNIX Specification has tried to improve portability in this area, implementations are still catching up, as illustrated by Figure 19.7. Thus, we provide two functions that handle all the details: `ptym_open` to open the next available PTY master device and `ptys_open` to open the corresponding slave device.

```
#include "apue.h"

int ptym_open(char *pts_name, int pts_namesz);
```
                                  Returns: file descriptor of PTY master if OK, –1 on error
```
int ptys_open(char *pts_name);
```
                                  Returns: file descriptor of PTY slave if OK, –1 on error

Normally, we don't call these two functions directly; the function `pty_fork` (Section 19.4) calls them and also `fork`s a child process.

The `ptym_open` function determines the next available PTY master and opens the device. The caller must allocate an array to hold the name of either the master or the slave; if the call succeeds, the name of the corresponding slave is returned through *pts_name*. This name is then passed to `ptys_open`, which opens the slave device. The length of the buffer in bytes is passed in *pts_namesz* so that the `ptym_open` function doesn't copy a string that is longer than the buffer.

The reason for providing two functions to open the two devices will become obvious when we show the `pty_fork` function. Normally, a process calls `ptym_open` to open the master and obtain the name of the slave. The process then `fork`s, and the child calls `ptys_open` to open the slave after calling `setsid` to establish a new session. This is how the slave becomes the controlling terminal for the child.

19.3.1 STREAMS-Based Pseudo Terminals

The details of the STREAMS implementation of pseudo terminals under Solaris are covered in Appendix C of Sun Microsystems [2002]. The next available PTY master device is accessed through a STREAMS *clone device*. A clone device is a special device that returns an unused device when it is opened. (STREAMS clone opens are discussed in detail in Rago [1993].)

The STREAMS-based PTY master clone device is `/dev/ptmx`. When we open it, the clone open routine automatically determines the first unused PTY master device and opens that unused device. (We'll see in the next section that, under BSD-based systems, we have to find the first unused PTY master ourselves.)

```
#include "apue.h"
#include <errno.h>
#include <fcntl.h>
#include <stropts.h>

int
ptym_open(char *pts_name, int pts_namesz)
{
    char    *ptr;
```

```
    int     fdm;

    /*
     * Return the name of the master device so that on failure
     * the caller can print an error message.  Null terminate
     * to handle case where strlen("/dev/ptmx") > pts_namesz.
     */
    strncpy(pts_name, "/dev/ptmx", pts_namesz);
    pts_name[pts_namesz - 1] = '\0';
    if ((fdm = open(pts_name, O_RDWR)) < 0)
        return(-1);
    if (grantpt(fdm) < 0) {      /* grant access to slave */
        close(fdm);
        return(-2);
    }
    if (unlockpt(fdm) < 0) {     /* clear slave's lock flag */
        close(fdm);
        return(-3);
    }
    if ((ptr = ptsname(fdm)) == NULL) { /* get slave's name */
        close(fdm);
        return(-4);
    }

    /*
     * Return name of slave.  Null terminate to handle
     * case where strlen(ptr) > pts_namesz.
     */
    strncpy(pts_name, ptr, pts_namesz);
    pts_name[pts_namesz - 1] = '\0';
    return(fdm);                 /* return fd of master */
}

int
ptys_open(char *pts_name)
{
    int     fds, setup;

    /*
     * The following open should allocate a controlling terminal.
     */
    if ((fds = open(pts_name, O_RDWR)) < 0)
        return(-5);

    /*
     * Check if stream is already set up by autopush facility.
     */
    if ((setup = ioctl(fds, I_FIND, "ldterm")) < 0) {
        close(fds);
        return(-6);
    }
    if (setup == 0) {
```

```
            if (ioctl(fds, I_PUSH, "ptem") < 0) {
                close(fds);
                return(-7);
            }
            if (ioctl(fds, I_PUSH, "ldterm") < 0) {
                close(fds);
                return(-8);
            }
            if (ioctl(fds, I_PUSH, "ttcompat") < 0) {
                close(fds);
                return(-9);
            }
        }
        return(fds);
    }
```

Figure 19.8 STREAMS-based pseudo-terminal open functions

We first open the clone device /dev/ptmx to get a file descriptor for the PTY master. Opening this master device automatically locks out the corresponding slave device.

We then call grantpt to change permissions of the slave device. On Solaris, it changes the ownership of the slave to the real user ID, changes the group ownership to the group tty, and changes the permissions to allow only user-read, user-write, and group-write. The reason for setting the group ownership to tty and enabling group-write permission is that the programs wall(1) and write(1) are set-group-ID to the group tty. Calling grantpt executes the program /usr/lib/pt_chmod, which is set-user-ID to root so that it can modify the ownership and permissions of the slave.

The function unlockpt is called to clear an internal lock on the slave device. We have to do this before we can open the slave. Additionally, we must call ptsname to obtain the name of the slave device. This name is of the form /dev/pts/*NNN*.

The next function in the file is ptys_open, which does the actual open of the slave device. Solaris follows the historical System V behavior: if the caller is a session leader that does not already have a controlling terminal, this call to open allocates the PTY slave as the controlling terminal. If we didn't want this to happen, we could specify the O_NOCTTY flag for open.

After opening the slave device, we might need to push three STREAMS modules onto the slave's stream. Together, the pseudo terminal emulation module (ptem) and the terminal line discipline module (ldterm) act like a real terminal. The ttcompat module provides compatibility for older V7, 4BSD, and Xenix ioctl calls. It's an optional module, but since it's automatically pushed for console logins and network logins (see the output from the program shown in Figure 14.18), we push it onto the slave's stream.

The reason that we might not need to push these three modules is that they might be there already. The STREAMS system supports a facility known as *autopush*, which allows an administrator to configure a list of modules to be pushed onto a stream whenever a particular device is opened (see Rago [1993] for more details). We use the I_FIND ioctl command to see whether ldterm is already on the stream. If so, we assume that the stream has been configured by the autopush mechanism and avoid pushing the modules a second time.

The result of calling `ptym_open` and `ptys_open` is two file descriptors open in the calling process: one for the master and one for the slave.

19.3.2 BSD-Based Pseudo Terminals

Under BSD-based systems and Linux-based systems, we provide our own versions of the XSI functions, which we can optionally include in our library, depending on which functions (if any) are provided by the underlying platform.

In our version of `posix_openpt`, we have to determine the first available PTY master device. To do this, we start at /dev/ptyp0 and keep trying until we successfully open a PTY master or until we run out of devices. We can get two different errors from open: EIO means that the device is already in use; ENOENT means that the device doesn't exist. In the latter case, we can terminate the search, as all pseudo terminals are in use. Once we are able to open a PTY master, say /dev/pty*MN*, the name of the corresponding slave is /dev/tty*MN*. On Linux, if the name of the PTY master is /dev/pty/m*XX*, then the name of the corresponding PTY slave is /dev/pty/s*XX*.

```
#include "apue.h"
#include <errno.h>
#include <fcntl.h>
#include <grp.h>

#ifndef _HAS_OPENPT
int
posix_openpt(int oflag)
{
    int     fdm;
    char    *ptr1, *ptr2;
    char    ptm_name[16];

    strcpy(ptm_name, "/dev/ptyXY");
    /* array index:    0123456789   (for references in following code) */
    for (ptr1 = "pqrstuvwxyzPQRST"; *ptr1 != 0; ptr1++) {
        ptm_name[8] = *ptr1;
        for (ptr2 = "0123456789abcdef"; *ptr2 != 0; ptr2++) {
            ptm_name[9] = *ptr2;

            /*
             * Try to open the master.
             */
            if ((fdm = open(ptm_name, oflag)) < 0) {
                if (errno == ENOENT)    /* different from EIO */
                    return(-1);         /* out of pty devices */
                else
                    continue;           /* try next pty device */
            }
            return(fdm);            /* got it, return fd of master */
```

```
            }
        }
        errno = EAGAIN;
        return(-1);      /* out of pty devices */
}
#endif

#ifndef _HAS_PTSNAME
char *
ptsname(int fdm)
{
    static char pts_name[16];
    char        *ptm_name;

    ptm_name = ttyname(fdm);
    if (ptm_name == NULL)
        return(NULL);
    strncpy(pts_name, ptm_name, sizeof(pts_name));
    pts_name[sizeof(pts_name) - 1] = '\0';
    if (strncmp(pts_name, "/dev/pty/", 9) == 0)
        pts_name[9] = 's';  /* change /dev/pty/mXX to /dev/pty/sXX */
    else
        pts_name[5] = 't';  /* change "pty" to "tty" */
    return(pts_name);
}
#endif

#ifndef _HAS_GRANTPT
int
grantpt(int fdm)
{
    struct group    *grptr;
    int             gid;
    char            *pts_name;

    pts_name = ptsname(fdm);
    if ((grptr = getgrnam("tty")) != NULL)
        gid = grptr->gr_gid;
    else
        gid = -1;        /* group tty is not in the group file */

    /*
     * The following two calls won't work unless we're the superuser.
     */
    if (chown(pts_name, getuid(), gid) < 0)
        return(-1);
    return(chmod(pts_name, S_IRUSR | S_IWUSR | S_IWGRP));
}
#endif

#ifndef _HAS_UNLOCKPT
int
unlockpt(int fdm)
```

```
{
    return(0); /* nothing to do */
}
#endif

int
ptym_open(char *pts_name, int pts_namesz)
{
    char    *ptr;
    int     fdm;

    /*
     * Return the name of the master device so that on failure
     * the caller can print an error message.  Null terminate
     * to handle case where string length > pts_namesz.
     */
    strncpy(pts_name, "/dev/ptyXX", pts_namesz);
    pts_name[pts_namesz - 1] = '\0';
    if ((fdm = posix_openpt(O_RDWR)) < 0)
        return(-1);
    if (grantpt(fdm) < 0) {        /* grant access to slave */
        close(fdm);
        return(-2);
    }
    if (unlockpt(fdm) < 0) {     /* clear slave's lock flag */
        close(fdm);
        return(-3);
    }
    if ((ptr = ptsname(fdm)) == NULL) { /* get slave's name */
        close(fdm);
        return(-4);
    }

    /*
     * Return name of slave.  Null terminate to handle
     * case where strlen(ptr) > pts_namesz.
     */
    strncpy(pts_name, ptr, pts_namesz);
    pts_name[pts_namesz - 1] = '\0';
    return(fdm);                 /* return fd of master */
}

int
ptys_open(char *pts_name)
{
    int fds;

    if ((fds = open(pts_name, O_RDWR)) < 0)
        return(-5);
    return(fds);
}
```

Figure 19.9 Pseudo-terminal open functions for BSD and Linux

In our version of `grantpt`, we call `chown` and `chmod` but realize that these two functions won't work unless the calling process has superuser permissions. If it is important that the ownership and protection be changed, these two function calls need to be placed into a set-user-ID root executable, similar to the way Solaris implements it.

The function `ptys_open` in Figure 19.9 simply opens the slave device. No other initialization is necessary. The `open` of the slave PTY under BSD-based systems does not have the side effect of allocating the device as the controlling terminal. In Section 19.4, we'll see how to allocate the controlling terminal under BSD-based systems.

> Our version of `posix_openpt` tries 16 different groups of 16 PTY master devices: `/dev/ptyp0` through `/dev/ptyTf`. The actual number of PTY devices available depends on two factors: (a) the number configured into the kernel, and (b) the number of special device files that have been created in the `/dev` directory. The number available to any program is the lesser of (a) or (b).

19.3.3 Linux-Based Pseudo Terminals

Linux supports the BSD method for accessing pseudo terminals, so the same functions shown in Figure 19.9 will also work on Linux. However, Linux also supports a clone-style interface to pseudo terminals using `/dev/ptmx` (but this is not a STREAMS device). The clone interface requires extra steps to identify and unlock a slave device. The functions we can use to access these pseudo terminals on Linux are shown in Figure 19.10.

```
#include "apue.h"
#include <fcntl.h>

#ifndef _HAS_OPENPT
int
posix_openpt(int oflag)
{
    int     fdm;

    fdm = open("/dev/ptmx", oflag);
    return(fdm);
}
#endif

#ifndef _HAS_PTSNAME
char *
ptsname(int fdm)
{
    int         sminor;
    static char pts_name[16];

    if (ioctl(fdm, TIOCGPTN, &sminor) < 0)
        return(NULL);
    snprintf(pts_name, sizeof(pts_name), "/dev/pts/%d", sminor);
    return(pts_name);
```

```
}
#endif

#ifndef _HAS_GRANTPT
int
grantpt(int fdm)
{
    char            *pts_name;

    pts_name = ptsname(fdm);
    return(chmod(pts_name, S_IRUSR | S_IWUSR | S_IWGRP));
}
#endif

#ifndef _HAS_UNLOCKPT
int
unlockpt(int fdm)
{
    int lock = 0;

    return(ioctl(fdm, TIOCSPTLCK, &lock));
}
#endif

int
ptym_open(char *pts_name, int pts_namesz)
{
    char    *ptr;
    int     fdm;

    /*
     * Return the name of the master device so that on failure
     * the caller can print an error message.  Null terminate
     * to handle case where string length > pts_namesz.
     */
    strncpy(pts_name, "/dev/ptmx", pts_namesz);
    pts_name[pts_namesz - 1] = '\0';

    fdm = posix_openpt(O_RDWR);
    if (fdm < 0)
        return(-1);
    if (grantpt(fdm) < 0) {     /* grant access to slave */
        close(fdm);
        return(-2);
    }
    if (unlockpt(fdm) < 0) {    /* clear slave's lock flag */
        close(fdm);
        return(-3);
    }
    if ((ptr = ptsname(fdm)) == NULL) { /* get slave's name */
        close(fdm);
        return(-4);
    }
```

```
    /*
     * Return name of slave.  Null terminate to handle case
     * where strlen(ptr) > pts_namesz.
     */
    strncpy(pts_name, ptr, pts_namesz);
    pts_name[pts_namesz - 1] = '\0';
    return(fdm);                    /* return fd of master */
}

int
ptys_open(char *pts_name)
{
    int fds;

    if ((fds = open(pts_name, O_RDWR)) < 0)
        return(-5);
    return(fds);
}
```

Figure 19.10 Pseudo-terminal open functions for Linux

On Linux, the PTY slave device is already owned by group tty, so all we need to do in grantpt is ensure that the permissions are correct.

19.4 pty_fork **Function**

We now use the two functions from the previous section, ptym_open and ptys_open, to write a new function that we call pty_fork. This new function combines the opening of the master and the slave with a call to fork, establishing the child as a session leader with a controlling terminal.

```
#include "apue.h"
#include <termios.h>
#include <sys/ioctl.h>   /* find struct winsize on BSD systems */

pid_t pty_fork(int *ptrfdm, char *slave_name, int slave_namesz,
               const struct termios *slave_termios,
               const struct winsize *slave_winsize);
```
$\qquad\qquad$ Returns: 0 in child, process ID of child in parent, −1 on error

The file descriptor of the PTY master is returned through the *ptrfdm* pointer.

If *slave_name* is non-null, the name of the slave device is stored at that location. The caller has to allocate the storage pointed to by this argument.

If the pointer *slave_termios* is non-null, the system uses the referenced structure to initialize the terminal line discipline of the slave. If this pointer is null, the system sets the slave's termios structure to an implementation-defined initial state. Similarly, if the *slave_winsize* pointer is non-null, the referenced structure initializes the slave's window size. If this pointer is null, the winsize structure is normally initialized to 0.

Figure 19.11 shows the code for this function. It works on all four platforms described in this text, calling the appropriate `ptym_open` and `ptys_open` functions.

After opening the PTY master, `fork` is called. As we mentioned before, we want to wait to call `ptys_open` until in the child and after calling `setsid` to establish a new session. When it calls `setsid`, the child is not a process group leader, so the three steps listed in Section 9.5 occur: (a) a new session is created with the child as the session leader, (b) a new process group is created for the child, and (c) the child loses any association it might have had with its previous controlling terminal. Under Linux and Solaris, the slave becomes the controlling terminal of this new session when `ptys_open` is called. Under FreeBSD and Mac OS X, we have to call `ioctl` with an argument of `TIOCSCTTY` to allocate the controlling terminal. (Linux also supports the `TIOCSCTTY` ioctl command.) The two structures `termios` and `winsize` are then initialized in the child. Finally, the slave file descriptor is duplicated onto standard input, standard output, and standard error in the child. This means that whatever process the caller `execs` from the child will have these three descriptors connected to the slave PTY (its controlling terminal).

After the call to `fork`, the parent just returns the PTY master descriptor and the process ID of the child. In the next section, we use the `pty_fork` function in the `pty` program.

```c
#include "apue.h"
#include <termios.h>
#ifndef TIOCGWINSZ
#include <sys/ioctl.h>
#endif

pid_t
pty_fork(int *ptrfdm, char *slave_name, int slave_namesz,
         const struct termios *slave_termios,
         const struct winsize *slave_winsize)
{
    int      fdm, fds;
    pid_t    pid;
    char     pts_name[20];

    if ((fdm = ptym_open(pts_name, sizeof(pts_name))) < 0)
        err_sys("can't open master pty: %s, error %d", pts_name, fdm);

    if (slave_name != NULL) {
        /*
         * Return name of slave.  Null terminate to handle case
         * where strlen(pts_name) > slave_namesz.
         */
        strncpy(slave_name, pts_name, slave_namesz);
        slave_name[slave_namesz - 1] = '\0';
    }

    if ((pid = fork()) < 0) {
        return(-1);
```

```
        } else if (pid == 0) {        /* child */
            if (setsid() < 0)
                err_sys("setsid error");

            /*
             * System V acquires controlling terminal on open().
             */
            if ((fds = ptys_open(pts_name)) < 0)
                err_sys("can't open slave pty");
            close(fdm);      /* all done with master in child */

#if defined(TIOCSCTTY)
            /*
             * TIOCSCTTY is the BSD way to acquire a controlling terminal.
             */
            if (ioctl(fds, TIOCSCTTY, (char *)0) < 0)
                err_sys("TIOCSCTTY error");
#endif
            /*
             * Set slave's termios and window size.
             */
            if (slave_termios != NULL) {
                if (tcsetattr(fds, TCSANOW, slave_termios) < 0)
                    err_sys("tcsetattr error on slave pty");
            }
            if (slave_winsize != NULL) {
                if (ioctl(fds, TIOCSWINSZ, slave_winsize) < 0)
                    err_sys("TIOCSWINSZ error on slave pty");
            }

            /*
             * Slave becomes stdin/stdout/stderr of child.
             */
            if (dup2(fds, STDIN_FILENO) != STDIN_FILENO)
                err_sys("dup2 error to stdin");
            if (dup2(fds, STDOUT_FILENO) != STDOUT_FILENO)
                err_sys("dup2 error to stdout");
            if (dup2(fds, STDERR_FILENO) != STDERR_FILENO)
                err_sys("dup2 error to stderr");
            if (fds != STDIN_FILENO && fds != STDOUT_FILENO &&
              fds != STDERR_FILENO)
                close(fds);
            return(0);       /* child returns 0 just like fork() */
        } else {                       /* parent */
            *ptrfdm = fdm;   /* return fd of master */
            return(pid);     /* parent returns pid of child */
        }
    }
```

Figure 19.11 The pty_fork function

19.5   `pty` **Program**

The goal in writing the `pty` program is to be able to type

```
pty prog arg1 arg2
```

instead of

```
prog arg1 arg2
```

When we use `pty` to execute another program, that program is executed in a session of its own, connected to a pseudo terminal.

Let's look at the source code for the `pty` program. The first file (Figure 19.12) contains the `main` function. It calls the `pty_fork` function from the previous section.

```c
#include "apue.h"
#include <termios.h>
#ifndef TIOCGWINSZ
#include <sys/ioctl.h>  /* for struct winsize */
#endif

#ifdef LINUX
#define OPTSTR "+d:einv"
#else
#define OPTSTR "d:einv"
#endif

static void set_noecho(int);    /* at the end of this file */
void        do_driver(char *);  /* in the file driver.c */
void        loop(int, int);     /* in the file loop.c */

int
main(int argc, char *argv[])
{
    int             fdm, c, ignoreeof, interactive, noecho, verbose;
    pid_t           pid;
    char            *driver;
    char            slave_name[20];
    struct termios  orig_termios;
    struct winsize  size;

    interactive = isatty(STDIN_FILENO);
    ignoreeof = 0;
    noecho = 0;
    verbose = 0;
    driver = NULL;

    opterr = 0;     /* don't want getopt() writing to stderr */
    while ((c = getopt(argc, argv, OPTSTR)) != EOF) {
        switch (c) {
        case 'd':          /* driver for stdin/stdout */
            driver = optarg;
            break;
```

```
        case 'e':        /* noecho for slave pty's line discipline */
            noecho = 1;
            break;

        case 'i':        /* ignore EOF on standard input */
            ignoreeof = 1;
            break;

        case 'n':        /* not interactive */
            interactive = 0;
            break;

        case 'v':        /* verbose */
            verbose = 1;
            break;

        case '?':
            err_quit("unrecognized option: -%c", optopt);
        }
    }
    if (optind >= argc)
        err_quit("usage: pty [ -d driver -einv ] program [ arg ... ]");

    if (interactive) {  /* fetch current termios and window size */
        if (tcgetattr(STDIN_FILENO, &orig_termios) < 0)
            err_sys("tcgetattr error on stdin");
        if (ioctl(STDIN_FILENO, TIOCGWINSZ, (char *) &size) < 0)
            err_sys("TIOCGWINSZ error");
        pid = pty_fork(&fdm, slave_name, sizeof(slave_name),
            &orig_termios, &size);
    } else {
        pid = pty_fork(&fdm, slave_name, sizeof(slave_name),
            NULL, NULL);
    }

    if (pid < 0) {
        err_sys("fork error");
    } else if (pid == 0) {        /* child */
        if (noecho)
            set_noecho(STDIN_FILENO);    /* stdin is slave pty */

        if (execvp(argv[optind], &argv[optind]) < 0)
            err_sys("can't execute: %s", argv[optind]);
    }

    if (verbose) {
        fprintf(stderr, "slave name = %s\n", slave_name);
        if (driver != NULL)
            fprintf(stderr, "driver = %s\n", driver);
    }

    if (interactive && driver == NULL) {
        if (tty_raw(STDIN_FILENO) < 0)  /* user's tty to raw mode */
```

```
                err_sys("tty_raw error");
        if (atexit(tty_atexit) < 0)      /* reset user's tty on exit */
                err_sys("atexit error");
    }

    if (driver)
        do_driver(driver);   /* changes our stdin/stdout */

    loop(fdm, ignoreeof);    /* copies stdin -> ptym, ptym -> stdout */

    exit(0);
}

static void
set_noecho(int fd)        /* turn off echo (for slave pty) */
{
    struct termios  stermios;

    if (tcgetattr(fd, &stermios) < 0)
        err_sys("tcgetattr error");

    stermios.c_lflag &= ~(ECHO | ECHOE | ECHOK | ECHONL);

    /*
     * Also turn off NL to CR/NL mapping on output.
     */
    stermios.c_oflag &= ~(ONLCR);

    if (tcsetattr(fd, TCSANOW, &stermios) < 0)
        err_sys("tcsetattr error");
}
```

Figure 19.12 The main function for the pty program

In the next section, we'll look at the various command-line options when we examine different uses of the pty program. The getopt function helps us parse command-line arguments in a consistent manner. We'll discuss getopt in more detail in Chapter 21.

Before calling pty_fork, we fetch the current values for the termios and winsize structures, passing these as arguments to pty_fork. This way, the PTY slave assumes the same initial state as the current terminal.

After returning from pty_fork, the child optionally turns off echoing for the slave PTY and then calls execvp to execute the program specified on the command line. All remaining command-line arguments are passed as arguments to this program.

The parent optionally sets the user's terminal to raw mode. In this case, the parent also sets an exit handler to reset the terminal state when exit is called. We describe the do_driver function in the next section.

The parent then calls the function loop (Figure 19.13), which copies everything received from the standard input to the PTY master and everything from the PTY master to standard output. For variety, we have coded it in two processes this time, although a single process using select, poll, or multiple threads would also work.

```c
#include "apue.h"

#define BUFFSIZE    512

static void sig_term(int);
static volatile sig_atomic_t     sigcaught;  /* set by signal handler */

void
loop(int ptym, int ignoreeof)
{
    pid_t   child;
    int     nread;
    char    buf[BUFFSIZE];

    if ((child = fork()) < 0) {
        err_sys("fork error");
    } else if (child == 0) {     /* child copies stdin to ptym */
        for ( ; ; ) {
            if ((nread = read(STDIN_FILENO, buf, BUFFSIZE)) < 0)
                err_sys("read error from stdin");
            else if (nread == 0)
                break;        /* EOF on stdin means we're done */
            if (writen(ptym, buf, nread) != nread)
                err_sys("writen error to master pty");
        }

        /*
         * We always terminate when we encounter an EOF on stdin,
         * but we notify the parent only if ignoreeof is 0.
         */
        if (ignoreeof == 0)
            kill(getppid(), SIGTERM);   /* notify parent */
        exit(0);    /* and terminate; child can't return */
    }

    /*
     * Parent copies ptym to stdout.
     */
    if (signal_intr(SIGTERM, sig_term) == SIG_ERR)
        err_sys("signal_intr error for SIGTERM");

    for ( ; ; ) {
        if ((nread = read(ptym, buf, BUFFSIZE)) <= 0)
            break;        /* signal caught, error, or EOF */
        if (writen(STDOUT_FILENO, buf, nread) != nread)
            err_sys("writen error to stdout");
    }

    /*
     * There are three ways to get here: sig_term() below caught the
     * SIGTERM from the child, we read an EOF on the pty master (which
     * means we have to signal the child to stop), or an error.
     */
```

```
        if (sigcaught == 0) /* tell child if it didn't send us the signal */
            kill(child, SIGTERM);
        /*
         * Parent returns to caller.
         */
}

/*
 * The child sends us SIGTERM when it gets EOF on the pty slave or
 * when read() fails.  We probably interrupted the read() of ptym.
 */
static void
sig_term(int signo)
{
    sigcaught = 1;          /* just set flag and return */
}
```

Figure 19.13 The loop function

Note that, with two processes, when one terminates, it has to notify the other. We use the SIGTERM signal for this notification.

19.6 Using the pty Program

We'll now look at various examples with the pty program, seeing the need for the command-line options.

If our shell is the Korn shell, we can execute

```
pty ksh
```

and get a brand new invocation of the shell, running under a pseudo terminal.

If the file ttyname is the program we showed in Figure 18.16, we can run the pty program as follows:

```
$ who
sar    :0        Oct   5 18:07
sar    pts/0     Oct   5 18:07
sar    pts/1     Oct   5 18:07
sar    pts/2     Oct   5 18:07
sar    pts/3     Oct   5 18:07
sar    pts/4     Oct   5 18:07      pts/4 is the highest PTY currently in use
$ pty ttyname                       run program in Figure 18.16 from PTY
fd 0: /dev/pts/5                     pts/5 is the next available PTY
fd 1: /dev/pts/5
fd 2: /dev/pts/5
```

utmp File

In Section 6.8, we described the utmp file that records all users currently logged in to a UNIX system. The question is whether a user running a program on a pseudo terminal is considered logged in. In the case of remote logins, telnetd and rlogind, obviously an entry should be made in the utmp file for the user logged in on the pseudo terminal. There is little agreement, however, whether users running a shell on a pseudo terminal from a window system or from a program, such as script, should have entries made in the utmp file. Some systems record these and some don't. If a system doesn't record these in the utmp file, the who(1) program normally won't show the corresponding pseudo terminals as being used.

Unless the utmp file has other-write permission enabled (which is considered to be a security hole), random programs that use pseudo terminals won't be able to write to this file.

Job Control Interaction

If we run a job-control shell under pty, it works normally. For example,

```
pty ksh
```

runs the Korn shell under pty. We can run programs under this new shell and use job control just as we do with our login shell. But if we run an interactive program other than a job-control shell under pty, as in

```
pty cat
```

everything is fine until we type the job-control suspend character. At that point, the job-control character is echoed as ^Z and is ignored. Under earlier BSD-based systems, the cat process terminates, the pty process terminates, and we're back to our original shell. To understand what's going on here, we need to examine all the processes involved, their process groups, and sessions. Figure 19.14 shows the arrangement when pty cat is running.

When we type the suspend character (Control-Z), it is recognized by the line discipline module beneath the cat process, since pty puts the terminal (beneath the pty parent) into raw mode. But the kernel won't stop the cat process, because it belongs to an orphaned process group (Section 9.10). The parent of cat is the pty parent, and it belongs to another session.

Historically, implementations have handled this condition differently. POSIX.1 says only that the SIGTSTP signal can't be delivered to the process. Systems derived from 4.3BSD delivered SIGKILL instead, which the process can't even catch. In 4.4BSD, this behavior was changed to conform to POSIX.1. Instead of sending SIGKILL, the 4.4BSD kernel silently discards the SIGTSTP signal if it has the default disposition and is to be delivered to a process in an orphaned process group. Most current implementations follow this behavior.

When we use pty to run a job-control shell, the jobs invoked by this new shell are never members of an orphaned process group, because the job-control shell always belongs to the same session. In that case, the Control-Z that we type is sent to the process invoked by the shell, not to the shell itself.

The only way to avoid this inability of the process invoked by pty to handle job-control signals is to add yet another command-line flag to pty, telling it to recognize

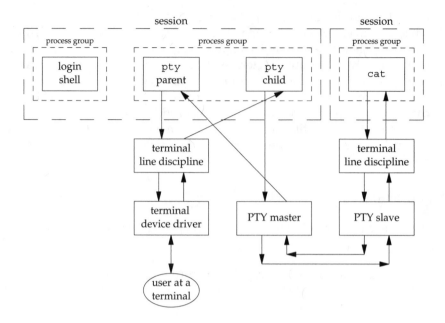

Figure 19.14 Process groups and sessions for `pty cat`

the job control suspend character itself (in the `pty` child) instead of letting the character get all the way through to the other line discipline.

Watching the Output of Long-Running Programs

Another example of job-control interaction with the `pty` program is with the example in Figure 19.6. If we run the program that generates output slowly as

```
pty slowout > file.out &
```

the `pty` process is stopped immediately when the child tries to read from its standard input (the terminal). The reason is that the job is a background job and gets job-control stopped when it tries to access the terminal. If we redirect standard input so that `pty` doesn't try to read from the terminal, as in

```
pty slowout < /dev/null > file.out &
```

the `pty` program stops immediately because it reads an end of file on its standard input and terminates. The solution for this problem is the `-i` option, which says to ignore an end of file on the standard input:

```
pty -i slowout < /dev/null > file.out &
```

This flag causes the `pty` child in Figure 19.13 to exit when the end of file is encountered, but the child doesn't tell the parent to terminate. Instead, the parent continues copying the PTY slave output to standard output (the file `file.out` in the example).

script Program

Using the pty program, we can implement the script(1) program as the following shell script:

```
#!/bin/sh
pty "${SHELL:-/bin/sh}" | tee typescript
```

Once we run this shell script, we can execute the ps command to see all the process relationships. Figure 19.15 details these relationships.

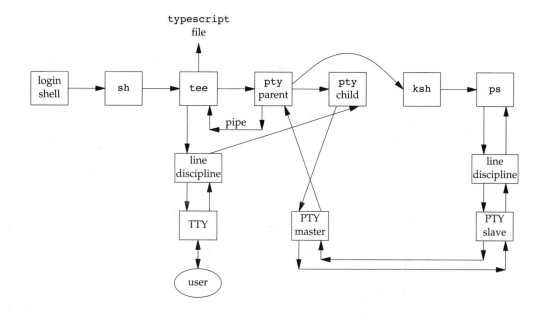

Figure 19.15 Arrangement of processes for script shell script

In this example, we assume that the SHELL variable is the Korn shell (probably /bin/ksh). As we mentioned earlier, script copies only what is output by the new shell (and any processes that it invokes), but since the line discipline module above the PTY slave normally has echo enabled, most of what we type also gets written to the typescript file.

Running Coprocesses

In Figure 15.18, the coprocess couldn't use the standard I/O functions, because standard input and standard output do not refer to a terminal, so the standard I/O functions treat them as fully buffered. If we run the coprocess under pty by replacing the line

```
        if (execl("./add2", "add2", (char *)0) < 0)
```

with

```
        if (execl("./pty", "pty", "-e", "add2", (char *)0) < 0)
```

the program now works, even if the coprocess uses standard I/O.

Figure 19.16 shows the arrangement of processes when we run the coprocess with a pseudo terminal as its input and output. It is an expansion of Figure 19.5, showing all the process connections and data flow. The box labeled "driving program" is the program from Figure 15.8, with the execl changed as described previously.

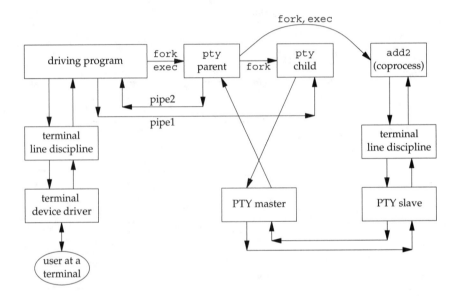

Figure 19.16 Running a coprocess with a pseudo terminal as its input and output

This example shows the need for the -e (no echo) option for the pty program. The pty program is not running interactively, because its standard input is not connected to a terminal. In Figure 19.12, the interactive flag defaults to false, since the call to isatty returns false. This means that the line discipline above the actual terminal remains in a canonical mode with echo enabled. By specifying the -e option, we turn off echo in the line discipline module above the PTY slave. If we don't do this, everything we type is echoed twice—by both line discipline modules.

We also have the -e option turn off the ONLCR flag in the termios structure to prevent all the output from the coprocess from being terminated with a carriage return and a newline.

Testing this example on different systems showed another problem that we alluded to in Section 14.8 when we described the readn and writen functions. The amount of data returned by a read, when the descriptor refers to something other than an ordinary disk file, can differ between implementations. This coprocess example using pty gave unexpected results that were tracked down to the read function on the pipe in the program from Figure 15.8 returning less than a line. The solution was to not use the program shown in Figure 15.8, but to use the version of this program from Exercise 15.5 that was modified to use the standard I/O library, with the standard I/O streams for the both pipes set to line buffering. By doing this, the fgets function does as many reads as required to obtain a complete line. The while loop in Figure 15.8 assumes that each line sent to the coprocess causes one line to be returned.

Driving Interactive Programs Noninteractively

Although it's tempting to think that pty can run any coprocess, even a coprocess that is interactive, it doesn't work. The problem is that pty just copies everything on its standard input to the PTY and everything from the PTY to its standard output, never looking at what it sends or what it gets back.

As an example, we can run the telnet command under pty talking directly to the remote host:

```
pty telnet 192.168.1.3
```

Doing this provides no benefit over just typing telnet 192.168.1.3, but we would like to run the telnet program from a script, perhaps to check some condition on the remote host. If the file telnet.cmd contains the four lines

```
sar
passwd
uptime
exit
```

the first line is the user name we use to log in to the remote host, the second line is the password, the third line is a command we'd like to run, and the fourth line terminates the session. But if we run this script as

```
pty -i < telnet.cmd telnet 192.168.1.3
```

it doesn't do what we want. What happens is that the contents of the file telnet.cmd are sent to the remote host before it has a chance to prompt us for an account name and password. When it turns off echoing to read the password, login uses the tcsetattr option, which discards any data already queued. Thus, the data we send is thrown away.

When we run the telnet program interactively, we wait for the remote host to prompt for a password before we type it, but the pty program doesn't know to do this. This is why it takes a more sophisticated program than pty, such as expect, to drive an interactive program from a script file.

Even running pty from the program in Figure 15.8, as we showed earlier, doesn't help, because the program in Figure 15.8 assumes that each line it writes to the pipe generates exactly one line on the other pipe. With an interactive program, one line of input may generate many lines of output. Furthermore, the program in Figure 15.8

always sent a line to the coprocess before reading from it. This won't work when we want to read from the coprocess before sending it anything.

There are a few ways to proceed from here to be able to drive an interactive program from a script. We could add a command language and interpreter to pty, but a reasonable command language would probably be ten times larger than the pty program. Another option is to take a command language and use the pty_fork function to invoke interactive programs. This is what the expect program does.

We'll take a different path and just provide an option (-d) to allow pty to be connected to a driver process for its input and output. The standard output of the driver is pty's standard input and vice versa. This is similar to a coprocess, but on "the other side" of pty. The resulting arrangement of processes is almost identical to Figure 19.16, but in the current scenario, pty does the fork and exec of the driver process. Also, instead of two half-duplex pipes, we'll use a single bidirectional pipe between pty and the driver process.

Figure 19.17 shows the source for the do_driver function, which is called by the main function of pty (Figure 19.12) when the -d option is specified.

```c
#include "apue.h"

void
do_driver(char *driver)
{
    pid_t   child;
    int     pipe[2];

    /*
     * Create a stream pipe to communicate with the driver.
     */
    if (s_pipe(pipe) < 0)
        err_sys("can't create stream pipe");

    if ((child = fork()) < 0) {
        err_sys("fork error");
    } else if (child == 0) {        /* child */
        close(pipe[1]);

        /* stdin for driver */
        if (dup2(pipe[0], STDIN_FILENO) != STDIN_FILENO)
            err_sys("dup2 error to stdin");

        /* stdout for driver */
        if (dup2(pipe[0], STDOUT_FILENO) != STDOUT_FILENO)
            err_sys("dup2 error to stdout");
        if (pipe[0] != STDIN_FILENO && pipe[0] != STDOUT_FILENO)
            close(pipe[0]);

        /* leave stderr for driver alone */
        execlp(driver, driver, (char *)0);
        err_sys("execlp error for: %s", driver);
    }
```

```
    close(pipe[0]);        /* parent */
    if (dup2(pipe[1], STDIN_FILENO) != STDIN_FILENO)
        err_sys("dup2 error to stdin");
    if (dup2(pipe[1], STDOUT_FILENO) != STDOUT_FILENO)
        err_sys("dup2 error to stdout");
    if (pipe[1] != STDIN_FILENO && pipe[1] != STDOUT_FILENO)
        close(pipe[1]);

    /*
     * Parent returns, but with stdin and stdout connected
     * to the driver.
     */
}
```

Figure 19.17 The do_driver function for the pty program

By writing our own driver program that is invoked by pty, we can drive interactive programs in any way desired. Even though it has its standard input and standard output connected to pty, the driver process can still interact with the user by reading and writing /dev/tty. This solution still isn't as general as the expect program, but it provides a useful option to pty for fewer than 50 lines of code.

19.7 Advanced Features

Pseudo terminals have some additional capabilities that we briefly mention here. These capabilities are further documented in Sun Microsystems [2002] and the BSD pty(4) manual page.

Packet Mode

Packet mode lets the PTY master learn of state changes in the PTY slave. On Solaris, this mode is enabled by pushing the STREAMS module pckt onto the PTY master side. We showed this optional module in Figure 19.2. On FreeBSD, Linux, and Mac OS X, this mode is enabled with the TIOCPKT ioctl command.

The details of packet mode differ between Solaris and the other platforms. Under Solaris, the process reading the PTY master has to call getmsg to fetch the messages from the stream head, because the pckt module converts certain events into nondata STREAMS messages. With the other platforms, each read from the PTY master returns a status byte followed by optional data.

Regardless of the implementation details, the purpose of packet mode is to inform the process reading the PTY master when the following events occur at the line discipline module above the PTY slave: when the read queue is flushed, when the write queue is flushed, whenever output is stopped (e.g., Control-S), whenever output is restarted, whenever XON/XOFF flow control is enabled after being disabled, and whenever XON/XOFF flow control is disabled after being enabled. These events are used, for example, by the rlogin client and rlogind server.

Remote Mode

A PTY master can set the PTY slave into remote mode by issuing an `ioctl` of `TIOCREMOTE`. Although FreeBSD 5.2.1, Mac OS X 10.3, and Solaris 9 use the same command to enable and disable this feature, under Solaris the third argument to `ioctl` is an integer, whereas with FreeBSD and Mac OS X, it is a pointer to an integer. (Linux 2.4.22 doesn't support this command.)

When it sets this mode, the PTY master is telling the PTY slave's line discipline module not to perform any processing of the data that it receives from the PTY master, regardless of the canonical/noncanonical flag in the slave's `termios` structure. Remote mode is intended for an application, such as a window manager, that does its own line editing.

Window Size Changes

The process above the PTY master can issue the `ioctl` of `TIOCSWINSZ` to set the window size of the slave. If the new size differs from the current size, a `SIGWINCH` signal is sent to the foreground process group of the PTY slave.

Signal Generation

The process reading and writing the PTY master can send signals to the process group of the PTY slave. Under Solaris 9, this is done with an `ioctl` of `TIOCSIGNAL`, with the third argument set to the signal number. With FreeBSD 5.2.1 and Mac OS X 10.3, the `ioctl` is `TIOCSIG`, and the third argument is a pointer to the integer signal number. (Linux 2.4.22 doesn't support this `ioctl` command either.)

19.8 Summary

We started this chapter with an overview of how to use pseudo terminals and a look at some use cases. We continued by examining the code required to open a pseudo terminal under the four platforms discussed in this text. We then used this code to provide the generic `pty_fork` function that can be used by many different applications. We used this function as the basis for a small program (`pty`), which we then used to explore many of the properties of pseudo terminals.

Pseudo terminals are used daily on most UNIX systems to provide network logins. We've examined other uses for pseudo terminals, from the `script` program to driving interactive programs from a batch script.

Exercises

19.1 When we remotely log in to a BSD system using either `telnet` or `rlogin`, the ownership of the PTY slave and its permissions are set, as we described in Section 19.3.2. How does this happen?

19.2 Modify the function `grantpt` from Figure 19.9 to invoke a set-user-ID program to change the ownership and protection of the PTY slave device on a BSD system (similar to what the Solaris version of the `grantpt` function does).

19.3 Use the `pty` program to determine the values used by your system to initialize a slave PTY's `termios` structure and `winsize` structure.

19.4 Recode the `loop` function (Figure 19.13) as a single process using either `select` or `poll`.

19.5 In the child process after `pty_fork` returns, standard input, standard output, and standard error are all open for read–write. Can you change standard input to be read-only and the other two to be write-only?

19.6 In Figure 19.14, identify which process groups are foreground and which are background, and identify the session leaders.

19.7 In Figure 19.14, in what order do the processes terminate when we type the end-of-file character? Verify this with process accounting, if possible.

19.8 The `script`(1) program normally adds to the beginning of the output file a line with the starting time, and to the end of the output file another line with the ending time. Add these features to the simple shell script that we showed.

19.9 Explain why the contents of the file `data` are output to the terminal in the following example, when the program `ttyname` only generates output and never reads its input.

```
$ cat data              a file with two lines
hello,
world
$ pty -i < data ttyname -i says ignore eof on stdin
hello,                  where did these two lines come from?
world
fd 0: /dev/ttyp5        we expect these three lines from ttyname
fd 1: /dev/ttyp5
fd 2: /dev/ttyp5
```

19.10 Write a program that calls `pty_fork` and have the child exec another program that you must write. The new program that the child execs must catch `SIGTERM` and `SIGWINCH`. When it catches a signal, the program should print that it did; for the latter signal, it should also print the terminal's window size. Then have the parent process send the `SIGTERM` signal to the process group of the PTY slave with the `ioctl` we described in Section 19.7. Read back from the slave to verify that the signal was caught. Follow this with the parent setting the window size of the PTY slave and read back the slave's output again. Have the parent `exit` and determine whether the slave process also terminates; if so, how does it terminate?

20

A Database Library

20.1 Introduction

During the early 1980s, the UNIX System was considered a hostile environment for running multiuser database systems. (See Stonebraker [1981] and Weinberger [1982].) Earlier systems, such as Version 7, did indeed present large obstacles, since they did not provide any form of IPC (other than half-duplex pipes) and did not provide any form of byte-range locking. Many of these deficiencies were remedied, however. By the late 1980s, the UNIX System had evolved to provide a suitable environment for running reliable, multiuser database systems. Since then, numerous commercial firms have offered these types of database systems.

In this chapter, we develop a simple, multiuser database library of C functions that any program can call to fetch and store records in a database. This library of C functions is usually only one part of a complete database system. We do not develop the other pieces, such as a query language, leaving these items to the many textbooks on database systems. Our interest is the UNIX System interface a database library requires and how that interface relates to the topics we've already covered (such as record—byte-range—locking, in Section 14.3).

20.2 History

One popular library of database functions in the UNIX System is the dbm(3) library. This library was developed by Ken Thompson and uses a dynamic hashing scheme. It was originally provided with Version 7, appears in all BSD releases, and was also provided in SVR4's BSD-compatibility library [AT&T 1990c]. The BSD developers extended the dbm library and called it ndbm. The ndbm library was included in BSD as well as in SVR4. The ndbm functions are standardized in the XSI extensions of the Single UNIX Specification.

Seltzer and Yigit [1991] provide a detailed history of the dynamic hashing algorithm used by the dbm library and other implementations of this library, including gdbm, the GNU version of the dbm library. Unfortunately, a basic limitation of all these implementations is that none allows concurrent updating of the database by multiple processes. These implementations provide no type of concurrency controls (such as record locking).

4.4BSD provided a new db(3) library that supports three forms of access: (a) record oriented, (b) hashing, and (c) a B-tree. Again, no form of concurrency was provided (as was plainly stated in the BUGS section of the db(3) manual page).

> Sleepycat Software (http://www.sleepycat.com) provides versions of the db library that do support concurrent access, locking, and transactions.

Most commercial database libraries do provide the concurrency controls required for multiple processes to update a database simultaneously. These systems typically use advisory locking, as we described in Section 14.3, but they often implement their own locking primitives to avoid the overhead of a system call to acquire an uncontested lock. These commercial systems usually implement their database using B+ trees [Comer 1979] or some dynamic hashing technique, such as linear hashing [Litwin 1980] or extendible hashing [Fagin et al. 1979].

Figure 20.1 summarizes the database libraries commonly found in the four operating systems described in this book. Note that on Linux, the gdbm library provides support for both dbm and ndbm functions.

Library	POSIX.1	FreeBSD 5.2.1	Linux 2.4.22	Mac OS X 10.3	Solaris 9
dbm			gdbm		•
ndbm	XSI	•	gdbm	•	•
db		•	•	•	•

Figure 20.1 Support for database libraries on various platforms

20.3 The Library

The library we develop in this chapter will be similar to the ndbm library, but we'll add the concurrency control mechanisms to allow multiple processes to update the same database at the same time. We first describe the C interface to the database library, then in the next section describe the actual implementation.

When we open a database, we are returned a handle (an opaque pointer) representing the database. We'll pass this handle to the remaining database functions.

```
#include "apue_db.h"

DBHANDLE db_open(const char *pathname, int oflag, ... /* int mode */);
                                        Returns: database handle if OK, NULL on error

void db_close(DBHANDLE db);
```

If db_open is successful, two files are created: *pathname.idx* is the index file, and *pathname.dat* is the data file. The *oflag* argument is used as the second argument to open (Section 3.3) to specify how the files are to be opened (read-only, read–write, create file if it doesn't exist, etc.). The *mode* argument is used as the third argument to open (the file access permissions) if the database files are created.

When we're done with a database, we call db_close. It closes the index file and the data file and releases any memory that it allocated for internal buffers.

When we store a new record in the database, we have to specify the key for the record and the data associated with the key. If the database contained personnel records, the key could be the employee ID, and the data could be the employee's name, address, telephone number, date of hire, and the like. Our implementation requires that the key for each record be unique. (We can't have two employee records with the same employee ID, for example.)

```
#include "apue_db.h"

int db_store(DBHANDLE db, const char *key, const char *data,
             int flag);
```
Returns: 0 if OK, nonzero on error (see following)

The *key* and *data* arguments are null-terminated character strings. The only restriction on these two strings is that neither can contain null bytes. They may contain, for example, newlines.

The *flag* argument can be DB_INSERT (to insert a new record), DB_REPLACE (to replace an existing record), or DB_STORE (to either insert or replace, whichever is appropriate). These three constants are defined in the apue_db.h header. If we specify either DB_INSERT or DB_STORE and the record does not exist, a new record is inserted. If we specify either DB_REPLACE or DB_STORE and the record already exists, the existing record is replaced with the new record. If we specify DB_REPLACE and the record doesn't exist, we set errno to ENOENT and return −1 without adding the new record. If we specify DB_INSERT and the record already exists, no record is inserted. In this case, the return value is 1 to distinguish this from a normal error return (−1).

We can fetch any record from the database by specifying its *key*.

```
#include "apue_db.h"

char *db_fetch(DBHANDLE db, const char *key);
```
Returns: pointer to data if OK, NULL if record not found

The return value is a pointer to the data that was stored with the *key*, if the record is found. We can also delete a record from the database by specifying its *key*.

```
#include "apue_db.h"

int db_delete(DBHANDLE db, const char *key);
```
Returns: 0 if OK, −1 if record not found

In addition to fetching a record by specifying its key, we can go through the entire database, reading each record in turn. To do this, we first call db_rewind to rewind the database to the first record and then call db_nextrec in a loop to read each sequential record.

```
#include "apue_db.h"

void db_rewind(DBHANDLE db);

char *db_nextrec(DBHANDLE db, char *key);
```

Returns: pointer to data if OK, NULL on end of file

If *key* is a non-null pointer, db_nextrec returns the key by copying it to the memory starting at that location.

There is no order to the records returned by db_nextrec. All we're guaranteed is that we'll read each record in the database once. If we store three records with keys of A, B, and C, in that order, we have no idea in which order db_nextrec will return the three records. It might return B, then A, then C, or some other (apparently random) order. The actual order depends on the implementation of the database.

These seven functions provide the interface to the database library. We now describe the actual implementation that we have chosen.

20.4 Implementation Overview

Database access libraries often use two files to store the information: an index file and a data file. The index file contains the actual index value (the key) and a pointer to the corresponding data record in the data file. Numerous techniques can be used to organize the index file so that it can be searched quickly and efficiently for any key: hashing and B+ trees are popular. We have chosen to use a fixed-size hash table with chaining for the index file. We mentioned in the description of db_open that we create two files: one with a suffix of .idx and one with a suffix of .dat.

We store the key and the index as null-terminated character strings; they cannot contain arbitrary binary data. Some database systems store numerical data in a binary format (1, 2, or 4 bytes for an integer, for example) to save storage space. This complicates the functions and requires more work to make the database files portable between different systems. For example, if a network has two systems that use different formats for storing binary integers, we need to handle this if we want both systems to access the database. (It is not at all uncommon today to have systems with different architectures sharing files on a network.) Storing all the records, both keys and data, as character strings simplifies everything. It does require additional disk space, but that is a small cost for portability.

With db_store, only one record for each key is allowed. Some database systems allow a key to have multiple records and then provide a way to access all the records associated with a given key. Additionally, we have only a single index file, meaning that each data record can have only a single key (we don't support secondary keys).

Some database systems allow each record to have multiple keys and often use one index file per key. Each time a new record is inserted or deleted, all index files must be updated accordingly. (An example of a file with multiple indexes is an employee file. We could have one index whose key is the employee ID and another whose key is the employee's Social Security number. Having an index whose key is the employee name could be a problem, as names need not be unique.)

Figure 20.2 shows a general picture of the database implementation.

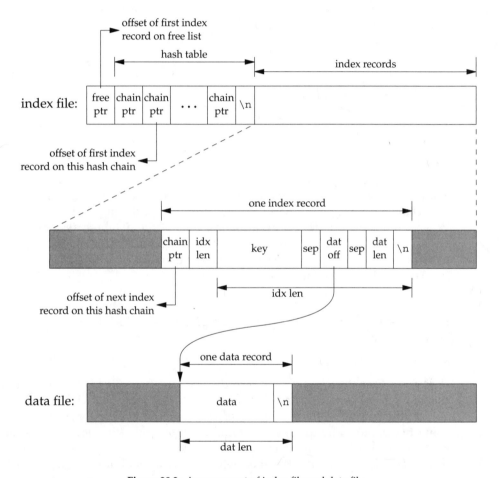

Figure 20.2 Arrangement of index file and data file

The index file consists of three portions: the free-list pointer, the hash table, and the index records. In Figure 20.2, all the fields called *ptr* are simply file offsets stored as an ASCII number.

To find a record in the database, given its key, db_fetch calculates the hash value of the key, which leads to one hash chain in the hash table. (The *chain ptr* field could be 0, indicating an empty chain.) We then follow this hash chain, which is a linked list of all the index records with this hash value. When we encounter a *chain ptr* value of 0, we've hit the end of the hash chain.

Let's look at an actual database file. The program in Figure 20.3 creates a new database and writes three records to it. Since we store all the fields in the database as ASCII characters, we can look at the actual index file and data file using any of the standard UNIX System tools:

```
$ ls -l db4.*
-rw-r--r--  1 sar          28 Oct 19 21:33 db4.dat
-rw-r--r--  1 sar          72 Oct 19 21:33 db4.idx
$ cat db4.idx
    0   53   35     0
    0   10Alpha:0:6
    0   10beta:6:14
   17   11gamma:20:8
$ cat db4.dat
data1
Data for beta
record3
```

To keep this example small, we have set the size of each *ptr* field to four ASCII characters; the number of hash chains is three. Since each *ptr* is a file offset, a four-character field limits the total size of the index file and data file to 10,000 bytes. When we do some performance measurements of the database system in Section 20.9, we set the size of each *ptr* field to six characters (allowing file sizes up to 1 million bytes), and the number of hash chains to more than 100.

The first line in the index file

```
    0   53   35     0
```

is the free-list pointer (0, the free list is empty) and the three hash chain pointers: 53, 35, and 0. The next line

```
    0   10Alpha:0:6
```

shows the format of each index record. The first field (0) is the four-character chain pointer. This record is the end of its hash chain. The next field (10) is the four-character *idx len*, the length of the remainder of this index record. We read each index record using two reads: one to read the two fixed-size fields (the *chain ptr* and *idx len*) and another to read the remaining (variable-length) portion. The remaining three fields—*key, dat off,* and *dat len*—are delimited by a separator character (a colon in this case). We need the separator character, since each of these three fields is variable length. The separator character can't appear in the key. Finally, a newline terminates the index record. The newline isn't required, since *idx len* contains the length of the record. We store the newline to separate each index record so we can use the normal UNIX System tools, such as cat and more, with the index file. The *key* is the value that we specified when we wrote the record to the database. The data offset (0) and data length (6) refer to the data file. We can see that the data record does start at offset 0 in the data file and has a length of 6 bytes. (As with the index file, we automatically append a newline to

```
#include "apue.h"
#include "apue_db.h"
#include <fcntl.h>

int
main(void)
{
    DBHANDLE    db;

    if ((db = db_open("db4", O_RDWR | O_CREAT | O_TRUNC,
      FILE_MODE)) == NULL)
        err_sys("db_open error");

    if (db_store(db, "Alpha", "data1", DB_INSERT) != 0)
        err_quit("db_store error for alpha");
    if (db_store(db, "beta", "Data for beta", DB_INSERT) != 0)
        err_quit("db_store error for beta");
    if (db_store(db, "gamma", "record3", DB_INSERT) != 0)
        err_quit("db_store error for gamma");

    db_close(db);
    exit(0);
}
```

Figure 20.3 Create a database and write three records to it

each data record, so we can use the normal UNIX System tools with the file. This newline at the end is not returned to the caller by db_fetch.)

If we follow the three hash chains in this example, we see that the first record on the first hash chain is at offset 53 (gamma). The next record on this chain is at offset 17 (alpha), and this is the last record on the chain. The first record on the second hash chain is at offset 35 (beta), and it's the last record on the chain. The third hash chain is empty.

Note that the order of the keys in the index file and the order of their corresponding records in the data file is the same as the order of the calls to db_store in Figure 20.3. Since the O_TRUNC flag was specified for db_open, the index file and the data file were both truncated and the database initialized from scratch. In this case, db_store just appends the new index records and data records to the end of the corresponding file. We'll see later that db_store can also reuse portions of these two files that correspond to deleted records.

The choice of a fixed-size hash table for the index is a compromise. It allows fast access as long as each hash chain isn't too long. We want to be able to search for any key quickly, but we don't want to complicate the data structures by using either a B-tree or dynamic hashing. Dynamic hashing has the advantage that any data record can be located with only two disk accesses (see Litwin [1980] or Fagin et al. [1979] for details). B-trees have the advantage of traversing the database in (sorted) key order (something that we can't do with the db_nextrec function using a hash table.)

20.5 Centralized or Decentralized?

Given multiple processes accessing the same database, we can implement the functions
in two ways:

1. Centralized. Have a single process that is the database manager, and have it be
    the only process that accesses the database. The functions contact this central
    process using some form of IPC.

2. Decentralized. Have each function apply the required concurrency controls
    (locking) and then issue its own I/O function calls.

Database systems have been built using each of these techniques. Given adequate
locking routines, the decentralized implementation is usually faster, because IPC is
avoided. Figure 20.4 depicts the operation of the centralized approach.

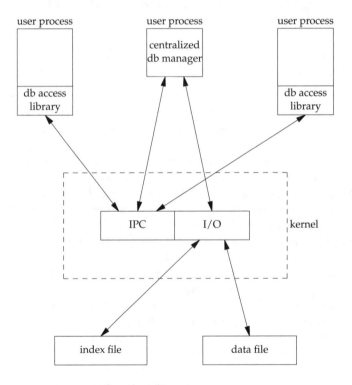

Figure 20.4 Centralized approach for database access

We purposely show the IPC going through the kernel, as most forms of message
passing under the UNIX System operate this way. (Shared memory, as described in
Section 15.9, avoids this copying of the data.) We see with the centralized approach that
a record is read by the central process and then passed to the requesting process using

IPC. This is a disadvantage of this design. Note that the centralized database manager is the only process that does I/O with the database files.

The centralized approach has the advantage that customer tuning of its operation may be possible. For example, we might be able to assign different priorities to different processes through the centralized process. This could affect the scheduling of I/O operations by the centralized process. With the decentralized approach, this is more difficult to do. We are usually at the mercy of the kernel's disk I/O scheduling policy and locking policy; that is, if three processes are waiting for a lock to become available, which process gets the lock next?

Another advantage of the centralized approach is that recovery is easier than with the decentralized approach. All the state information is in one place in the centralized approach, so if the database processes are killed, we have only one place to look to identify the outstanding transactions we need to resolve to restore the database to a consistent state.

The decentralized approach is shown in Figure 20.5. This is the design that we'll implement in this chapter.

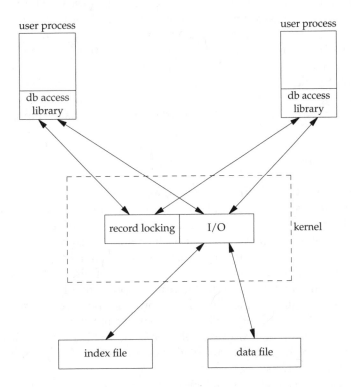

Figure 20.5 Decentralized approach for database access

The user processes that call the functions in the database library to perform I/O are considered cooperating processes, since they use byte-range locking to provide concurrent access.

20.6 Concurrency

We purposely chose a two-file implementation (an index file and a data file) because that is a common implementation technique. It requires us to handle the locking interactions of both files. But there are numerous ways to handle the locking of these two files.

Coarse-Grained Locking

The simplest form of locking is to use one of the two files as a lock for the entire database and to require the caller to obtain this lock before operating on the database. We call this *coarse-grained locking*. For example, we can say that the process with a read lock on byte 0 of the index file has read access to the entire database. A process with a write lock on byte 0 of the index file has write access to the entire database. We can use the normal UNIX System byte-range locking semantics to allow any number of readers at one time, but only one writer at a time. (Recall Figure 14.3.) The functions db_fetch and db_nextrec require a read lock, and db_delete, db_store, and db_open all require a write lock. (The reason db_open requires a write lock is that if the file is being created, it has to write the empty free list and hash chains at the front of the index file.)

The problem with coarse-grained locking is that it doesn't allow the maximum amount of concurrency. If a process is adding a record to one hash chain, another process should be able to read a record on a different hash chain.

Fine-Grained Locking

We enhance coarse-grained locking to allow more concurrency and call this *fine-grained locking*. We first require a reader or a writer to obtain a read lock or a write lock on the hash chain for a given record. We allow any number of readers at one time on any hash chain but only a single writer on a hash chain. Next, a writer needing to access the free list (either db_delete or db_store) must obtain a write lock on the free list. Finally, whenever it appends a new record to the end of either the index file or the data file, db_store has to obtain a write lock on that portion of the file.

We expect fine-grained locking to provide more concurrency than coarse-grained locking. In Section 20.9, we'll show some actual measurements. In Section 20.8, we show the source code to our implementation of fine-grained locking and discuss the details of implementing locking. (Coarse-grained locking is merely a simplification of the locking that we show.)

In the source code, we call read, readv, write, and writev directly. We do not use the standard I/O library. Although it is possible to use byte-range locking with the standard I/O library, careful handling of buffering is required. We don't want an fgets, for example, to return data that was read into a standard I/O buffer 10 minutes ago if the data was modified by another process 5 minutes ago.

Our discussion of concurrency is predicated on the simple needs of the database library. Commercial systems often have additional requirements. See Chapter 16 of Date [2004] for additional details on concurrency.

20.7 Building the Library

The database library consists of two files: a public C header file and a C source file. We can build a static library using the commands

```
gcc -I../include -Wall -c db.c
ar rsv libapue_db.a db.o
```

Applications that want to link with `libapue_db.a` will also need to link with `libapue.a`, since we use some of our common functions in the database library.

If, on the other hand, we want to build a dynamic shared library version of the database library, we can use the following commands:

```
gcc -I../include -Wall -fPIC -c db.c
gcc -shared -Wl,-soname,libapue_db.so.1 -o libapue_db.so.1 \
    -L../lib -lapue -lc db.o
```

The resulting shared library, `libapue_db.so.1`, needs to be placed in a common directory where the dynamic linker/loader can find it. Alternatively, we can place it in a private directory and modify our `LD_LIBRARY_PATH` environment variable to include the private directory in the search path of the dynamic linker/loader.

> The steps used to build shared libraries vary among platforms. Here, we have shown how to do it on a Linux system with the GNU C compiler.

20.8 Source Code

We start with the `apue_db.h` header shown first. This header is included by the library source code and all applications that call the library.

For the remainder of this text, we depart from the style of the previous examples in several ways. First, because the source code example is longer than usual, we number the lines. This makes it easier to link the discussion with the corresponding source code. Second, we place the description of the source code immediately below the source code on the same page.

> This style was inspired by John Lions in his book documenting the UNIX Version 6 operating system source code [Lions 1977, 1996]. It simplifies the task of studying large amounts of source code.

Note that we do not bother to number blank lines. Although this departs from the normal behavior of such tools as `pr(1)`, we have nothing interesting to say about blank lines.

```
 1   #ifndef _APUE_DB_H
 2   #define _APUE_DB_H

 3   typedef    void *  DBHANDLE;

 4   DBHANDLE  db_open(const char *, int, ...);
 5   void      db_close(DBHANDLE);
 6   char      *db_fetch(DBHANDLE, const char *);
 7   int       db_store(DBHANDLE, const char *, const char *, int);
 8   int       db_delete(DBHANDLE, const char *);
 9   void      db_rewind(DBHANDLE);
10   char      *db_nextrec(DBHANDLE, char *);

11   /*
12    * Flags for db_store().
13    */
14   #define DB_INSERT    1    /* insert new record only */
15   #define DB_REPLACE   2    /* replace existing record */
16   #define DB_STORE     3    /* replace or insert */

17   /*
18    * Implementation limits.
19    */
20   #define IDXLEN_MIN    6    /* key, sep, start, sep, length, \n */
21   #define IDXLEN_MAX 1024    /* arbitrary */
22   #define DATLEN_MIN    2    /* data byte, newline */
23   #define DATLEN_MAX 1024    /* arbitrary */

24   #endif /* _APUE_DB_H */
```

[1–3]   We use the _APUE_DB_H symbol to ensure that the contents of the header file are included only once. The DBHANDLE type represents an active reference to the database and is used to isolate applications from the implementation details of the database. Compare this technique with the way the standard I/O library exposes the FILE structure to applications.

[4–10] Next, we declare the prototypes for the database library's public functions. Since this header is included by applications that want to use the library, we don't declare the prototypes for the library's private functions here.

[11–24] The legal flags that can be passed to the db_store function are defined next, followed by fundamental limits of the implementation. These limits can be changed, if desired, to support bigger databases.

The minimum index record length is specified by IDXLEN_MIN. This represents a 1-byte key, a 1-byte separator, a 1-byte starting offset, another 1-byte separator, a 1-byte length, and a terminating newline character. (Recall the format of an index record from Figure 20.2.) An index record will usually be larger than IDXLEN_MIN bytes, but this is the bare minimum size.

The next file is db.c, the C source file for the library. For simplicity, we include all functions in a single file. This has the advantage that we can hide private functions by declaring them static.

```
1    #include "apue.h"
2    #include "apue_db.h"
3    #include <fcntl.h>        /* open & db_open flags */
4    #include <stdarg.h>
5    #include <errno.h>
6    #include <sys/uio.h>      /* struct iovec */

7    /*
8     * Internal index file constants.
9     * These are used to construct records in the
10    * index file and data file.
11    */
12   #define IDXLEN_SZ    4       /* index record length (ASCII chars) */
13   #define SEP         ':'      /* separator char in index record */
14   #define SPACE       ' '      /* space character */
15   #define NEWLINE     '\n'     /* newline character */

16   /*
17    * The following definitions are for hash chains and free
18    * list chain in the index file.
19    */
20   #define PTR_SZ       6       /* size of ptr field in hash chain */
21   #define PTR_MAX 999999       /* max file offset = 10**PTR_SZ - 1 */
22   #define NHASH_DEF   137      /* default hash table size */
23   #define FREE_OFF     0       /* free list offset in index file */
24   #define HASH_OFF PTR_SZ      /* hash table offset in index file */

25   typedef unsigned long  DBHASH; /* hash values */
26   typedef unsigned long  COUNT;  /* unsigned counter */
```

[1–6]   We include apue.h because we use some of the functions from our private library. In turn, apue.h includes several standard header files, including <stdio.h> and <unistd.h>. We include <stdarg.h> because the db_open function uses the variable-argument functions declared by <stdarg.h>.

[7–26] The size of an index record is specified by IDXLEN_SZ. We use some characters, such as colon and newline, as delimiters in the database. We use the space character as "white out" when we delete a record.

Some of the values that we have defined as constants could also be made variable, with some added complexity in the implementation. For example, we set the size of the hash table to 137 entries. A better technique would be to let the caller specify this as an argument to db_open, based on the expected size of the database. We would then have to store this size at the beginning of the index file.

```
27    /*
28     * Library's private representation of the database.
29     */
30    typedef struct {
31      int     idxfd;   /* fd for index file */
32      int     datfd;   /* fd for data file */
33      char    *idxbuf; /* malloc'ed buffer for index record */
34      char    *datbuf; /* malloc'ed buffer for data record*/
35      char    *name;   /* name db was opened under */
36      off_t   idxoff;  /* offset in index file of index record */
37                       /* key is at (idxoff + PTR_SZ + IDXLEN_SZ) */
38      size_t  idxlen;  /* length of index record */
39                       /* excludes IDXLEN_SZ bytes at front of record */
40                       /* includes newline at end of index record */
41      off_t   datoff;  /* offset in data file of data record */
42      size_t  datlen;  /* length of data record */
43                       /* includes newline at end */
44      off_t   ptrval;  /* contents of chain ptr in index record */
45      off_t   ptroff;  /* chain ptr offset pointing to this idx record */
46      off_t   chainoff; /* offset of hash chain for this index record */
47      off_t   hashoff;  /* offset in index file of hash table */
48      DBHASH  nhash;    /* current hash table size */
49      COUNT   cnt_delok;   /* delete OK */
50      COUNT   cnt_delerr;  /* delete error */
51      COUNT   cnt_fetchok; /* fetch OK */
52      COUNT   cnt_fetcherr; /* fetch error */
53      COUNT   cnt_nextrec; /* nextrec */
54      COUNT   cnt_stor1;   /* store: DB_INSERT, no empty, appended */
55      COUNT   cnt_stor2;   /* store: DB_INSERT, found empty, reused */
56      COUNT   cnt_stor3;   /* store: DB_REPLACE, diff len, appended */
57      COUNT   cnt_stor4;   /* store: DB_REPLACE, same len, overwrote */
58      COUNT   cnt_storerr; /* store error */
59    } DB;
```

[27–48] The DB structure is where we keep all the information for each open database. The DBHANDLE value that is returned by db_open and used by all the other functions is really just a pointer to one of these structures, but we hide that from the callers.

Since we store pointers and lengths as ASCII in the database, we convert these to numeric values and save them in the DB structure. We also save the hash table size even though it is fixed, just in case we decide to enhance the library to allow callers to specify the size when the database is created (see Exercise 20.7).

[49–59] The last ten fields in the DB structure count both successful and unsuccessful operations. If we want to analyze the performance of our database, we can write a function to return these statistics, but for now, we only maintain the counters.

```
60   /*
61    * Internal functions.
62    */
63   static DB      *_db_alloc(int);
64   static void     _db_dodelete(DB *);
65   static int      _db_find_and_lock(DB *, const char *, int);
66   static int      _db_findfree(DB *, int, int);
67   static void     _db_free(DB *);
68   static DBHASH   _db_hash(DB *, const char *);
69   static char    *_db_readdat(DB *);
70   static off_t    _db_readidx(DB *, off_t);
71   static off_t    _db_readptr(DB *, off_t);
72   static void     _db_writedat(DB *, const char *, off_t, int);
73   static void     _db_writeidx(DB *, const char *, off_t, int, off_t);
74   static void     _db_writeptr(DB *, off_t, off_t);

75   /*
76    * Open or create a database.  Same arguments as open(2).
77    */
78   DBHANDLE
79   db_open(const char *pathname, int oflag, ...)
80   {
81       DB          *db;
82       int          len, mode;
83       size_t       i;
84       char         asciiptr[PTR_SZ + 1],
85                    hash[(NHASH_DEF + 1) * PTR_SZ + 2];
86                        /* +2 for newline and null */
87       struct stat statbuff;

88       /*
89        * Allocate a DB structure, and the buffers it needs.
90        */
91       len = strlen(pathname);
92       if ((db = _db_alloc(len)) == NULL)
93           err_dump("db_open: _db_alloc error for DB");
```

[60–74] We have chosen to name all the user-callable (public) functions starting with
db_ and all the internal (private) functions starting with _db_. The public
functions were declared in the library's header file, apue_db.h. We declare
the internal functions as static so they are visible only to functions residing
in the same file (the file containing the library implementation).

[75–93] The db_open function has the same arguments as open(2). If the caller wants
to create the database files, the optional third argument specifies the file
permissions. The db_open function opens the index file and the data file,
initializing the index file, if necessary. The function starts by calling
_db_alloc to allocate and initialize a DB structure.

```
94      db->nhash   = NHASH_DEF;/* hash table size */
95      db->hashoff = HASH_OFF; /* offset in index file of hash table */
96      strcpy(db->name, pathname);
97      strcat(db->name, ".idx");

98      if (oflag & O_CREAT) {
99          va_list ap;

100         va_start(ap, oflag);
101         mode = va_arg(ap, int);
102         va_end(ap);

103         /*
104          * Open index file and data file.
105          */
106         db->idxfd = open(db->name, oflag, mode);
107         strcpy(db->name + len, ".dat");
108         db->datfd = open(db->name, oflag, mode);
109     } else {
110         /*
111          * Open index file and data file.
112          */
113         db->idxfd = open(db->name, oflag);
114         strcpy(db->name + len, ".dat");
115         db->datfd = open(db->name, oflag);
116     }

117     if (db->idxfd < 0 || db->datfd < 0) {
118         _db_free(db);
119         return(NULL);
120     }
```

[94–97] We continue to initialize the DB structure. The pathname passed in by the
         caller specifies the prefix of the database filenames. We append the suffix
         .idx to create the name for the database index file.

[98–108] If the caller wants to create the database files, we use the variable argument
         functions from <stdarg.h> to find the optional third argument. Then we
         use open to create and open the index file and data file. Note that the
         filename of the data file starts with the same prefix as the index file but has
         .dat as a suffix instead.

[109–116] If the caller doesn't specify the O_CREAT flag, then we're opening existing
         database files. In this case, we simply call open with two arguments.

[117–120] If we hit an error opening or creating either database file, we call _db_free
         to clean up the DB structure and then return NULL to the caller. If one open
         succeeded and one failed, _db_free will take care of closing the open file
         descriptor, as we shall see shortly.

```
121        if ((oflag & (O_CREAT | O_TRUNC)) == (O_CREAT | O_TRUNC)) {
122            /*
123             * If the database was created, we have to initialize
124             * it.  Write lock the entire file so that we can stat
125             * it, check its size, and initialize it, atomically.
126             */
127            if (writew_lock(db->idxfd, 0, SEEK_SET, 0) < 0)
128                err_dump("db_open: writew_lock error");

129            if (fstat(db->idxfd, &statbuff) < 0)
130                err_sys("db_open: fstat error");

131            if (statbuff.st_size == 0) {
132                /*
133                 * We have to build a list of (NHASH_DEF + 1) chain
134                 * ptrs with a value of 0.  The +1 is for the free
135                 * list pointer that precedes the hash table.
136                 */
137                sprintf(asciiptr, "%*d", PTR_SZ, 0);
```

[121–130] We encounter locking if the database is being created. Consider two processes trying to create the same database at about the same time. Assume that the first process calls fstat and is blocked by the kernel after fstat returns. The second process calls db_open, finds that the length of the index file is 0, and initializes the free list and hash chain. The second process then writes one record to the database. At this point, the second process is blocked, and the first process continues executing right after the call to fstat. The first process finds the size of the index file to be 0 (since fstat was called before the second process initialized the index file), so the first process initializes the free list and hash chain, wiping out the record that the second process stored in the database. The way to prevent this is to use locking. We use the macros readw_lock, writew_lock, and un_lock from Section 14.3.

[131–137] If the size of the index file is 0, we have just created it, so we need to initialize the free list and hash chain pointers it contains. Note that we use the format string %*d to convert a database pointer from an integer to an ASCII string. (We'll use this type of format again in _db_writeidx and _db_writeptr.) This format tells sprintf to take the PTR_SZ argument and use it as the minimum field width for the next argument, which is 0 in this instance (here we are initializing the pointers to 0, since we are creating a new database). This has the effect of forcing the string created to be at least PTR_SZ characters (padded on the left with spaces). In _db_writeidx and _db_writeptr, we will pass a pointer value instead of zero, but we will first verify that the pointer value isn't greater than PTR_MAX, to guarantee that every pointer string we write to the database occupies exactly PTR_SZ (6) characters.

```
138                    hash[0] = 0;
139                    for (i = 0; i < NHASH_DEF + 1; i++)
140                        strcat(hash, asciiptr);
141                    strcat(hash, "\n");
142                    i = strlen(hash);
143                    if (write(db->idxfd, hash, i) != i)
144                        err_dump("db_open: index file init write error");
145                }
146                if (un_lock(db->idxfd, 0, SEEK_SET, 0) < 0)
147                    err_dump("db_open: un_lock error");
148            }
149        db_rewind(db);
150        return(db);
151    }
152    /*
153     * Allocate & initialize a DB structure and its buffers.
154     */
155    static DB *
156    _db_alloc(int namelen)
157    {
158        DB      *db;
159        /*
160         * Use calloc, to initialize the structure to zero.
161         */
162        if ((db = calloc(1, sizeof(DB))) == NULL)
163            err_dump("_db_alloc: calloc error for DB");
164        db->idxfd = db->datfd = -1;                /* descriptors */
165        /*
166         * Allocate room for the name.
167         * +5 for ".idx" or ".dat" plus null at end.
168         */
169        if ((db->name = malloc(namelen + 5)) == NULL)
170            err_dump("_db_alloc: malloc error for name");
```

[138–151] We continue to initialize the newly created database. We build the hash table and write it to the index file. Then we unlock the index file, reset the database file pointers, and return a pointer to the DB structure as the opaque handle for the caller to use with the other database functions.

[152–164] The _db_alloc function is called by db_open to allocate storage for the DB structure, an index buffer, and a data buffer. We use calloc to allocate memory to hold the DB structure and ensure that it is initialized to all zeros. Since this has the side effect of setting the database file descriptors to zero, we need to reset them to −1 to indicate that they are not yet valid.

[165–170] We allocate space to hold the name of the database file. We use this buffer to create both filenames by changing the suffix to refer to either the index file or the data file, as we saw in db_open.

```
171        /*
172         * Allocate an index buffer and a data buffer.
173         * +2 for newline and null at end.
174         */
175        if ((db->idxbuf = malloc(IDXLEN_MAX + 2)) == NULL)
176            err_dump("_db_alloc: malloc error for index buffer");
177        if ((db->datbuf = malloc(DATLEN_MAX + 2)) == NULL)
178            err_dump("_db_alloc: malloc error for data buffer");
179        return(db);
180    }
181    /*
182     * Relinquish access to the database.
183     */
184    void
185    db_close(DBHANDLE h)
186    {
187        _db_free((DB *)h);   /* closes fds, free buffers & struct */
188    }
189    /*
190     * Free up a DB structure, and all the malloc'ed buffers it
191     * may point to.  Also close the file descriptors if still open.
192     */
193    static void
194    _db_free(DB *db)
195    {
196        if (db->idxfd >= 0)
197            close(db->idxfd);
198        if (db->datfd >= 0)
199            close(db->datfd);
```

[171–180] We allocate space for buffers for the index and data files. The buffer sizes are defined in apue_db.h. An enhancement to the database library would be to allow these buffers to expand as required. We could keep track of the size of these two buffers and call realloc whenever we find we need a bigger buffer. Finally, we return a pointer to the DB structure that we allocated.

[181–188] The db_close function is a wrapper that casts a database handle to a DB structure pointer, passing it to _db_free to release any resources and free the DB structure.

[189–199] The _db_free function is called by db_open if an error occurs while opening the index file or data file and is also called by db_close when an application is done using the database. If the file descriptor for the database index file is valid, we close it. The same is done with the file descriptor for the data file. (Recall that when we allocate a new DB structure in _db_alloc, we initialize each file descriptor to −1. If we are unable to open one of the database files, the corresponding file descriptor will still be set to −1, and we will avoid trying to close it.)

```
200      if (db->idxbuf != NULL)
201            free(db->idxbuf);
202      if (db->datbuf != NULL)
203            free(db->datbuf);
204      if (db->name != NULL)
205            free(db->name);
206      free(db);
207   }

208   /*
209    * Fetch a record.  Return a pointer to the null-terminated data.
210    */
211   char *
212   db_fetch(DBHANDLE h, const char *key)
213   {
214      DB        *db = h;
215      char      *ptr;

216      if (_db_find_and_lock(db, key, 0) < 0) {
217          ptr = NULL;                    /* error, record not found */
218          db->cnt_fetcherr++;
219      } else {
220          ptr = _db_readdat(db);   /* return pointer to data */
221          db->cnt_fetchok++;
222      }

223      /*
224       * Unlock the hash chain that _db_find_and_lock locked.
225       */
226      if (un_lock(db->idxfd, db->chainoff, SEEK_SET, 1) < 0)
227          err_dump("db_fetch: un_lock error");
228      return(ptr);
229   }
```

[200–207] Next, we free any dynamically-allocated buffers. We can safely pass a null pointer to free, so we don't need to check the value of each buffer pointer beforehand, but we do so anyway because we consider it better style to free only those objects that we allocated. (Not all deallocator functions are as forgiving as free.) Finally, we free the memory backing the DB structure.

[208–218] The db_fetch function is used to read a record given its key. We first try to find the record by calling _db_find_and_lock. If the record can't be found, we set the return value (ptr) to NULL and increment the count of unsuccessful record searches. Because _db_find_and_lock returns with the database index file locked, we can't return until we unlock it.

[219–229] If the record is found, we call _db_readdat to read the corresponding data record and increment the count of the successful record searches. Before returning, we unlock the index file by calling un_lock. Then we return a pointer to the record found (or NULL if the record wasn't found).

```
230    /*
231     * Find the specified record.  Called by db_delete, db_fetch,
232     * and db_store.  Returns with the hash chain locked.
233     */
234    static int
235    _db_find_and_lock(DB *db, const char *key, int writelock)
236    {
237      off_t   offset, nextoffset;
238      /*
239       * Calculate the hash value for this key, then calculate the
240       * byte offset of corresponding chain ptr in hash table.
241       * This is where our search starts.  First we calculate the
242       * offset in the hash table for this key.
243       */
244      db->chainoff = (_db_hash(db, key) * PTR_SZ) + db->hashoff;
245      db->ptroff = db->chainoff;
246      /*
247       * We lock the hash chain here.  The caller must unlock it
248       * when done.  Note we lock and unlock only the first byte.
249       */
250      if (writelock) {
251          if (writew_lock(db->idxfd, db->chainoff, SEEK_SET, 1) < 0)
252              err_dump("_db_find_and_lock: writew_lock error");
253      } else {
254          if (readw_lock(db->idxfd, db->chainoff, SEEK_SET, 1) < 0)
255              err_dump("_db_find_and_lock: readw_lock error");
256      }
257      /*
258       * Get the offset in the index file of first record
259       * on the hash chain (can be 0).
260       */
261      offset = _db_readptr(db, db->ptroff);
```

[230–237] The _db_find_and_lock function is used internally by the library to find a record given its key. We set the writelock parameter to a nonzero value if we want to acquire a write lock on the index file while we search for the record. If we set writelock to zero, we read-lock the index file while we search it.

[238–256] We prepare to traverse a hash chain in _db_find_and_lock. We convert the key into a hash value, which we use to calculate the starting address of the hash chain in the file (chainoff). We wait for the lock to be granted before going through the hash chain. Note that we lock only the first byte in the start of the hash chain. This increases concurrency by allowing multiple processes to search different hash chains at the same time.

[257–261] We call _db_readptr to read the first pointer in the hash chain. If this returns zero, the hash chain is empty.

```
262     while (offset != 0) {
263         nextoffset = _db_readidx(db, offset);
264         if (strcmp(db->idxbuf, key) == 0)
265             break;          /* found a match */
266         db->ptroff = offset; /* offset of this (unequal) record */
267         offset = nextoffset; /* next one to compare */
268     }
269     /*
270      * offset == 0 on error (record not found).
271      */
272     return(offset == 0 ? -1 : 0);
273 }

274 /*
275  * Calculate the hash value for a key.
276  */
277 static DBHASH
278 _db_hash(DB *db, const char *key)
279 {
280     DBHASH      hval = 0;
281     char        c;
282     int         i;

283     for (i = 1; (c = *key++) != 0; i++)
284         hval += c * i;      /* ascii char times its 1-based index */
285     return(hval % db->nhash);
286 }
```

[262–268] In the while loop, we go through each index record on the hash chain, comparing keys. We call _db_readidx to read each index record. It populates the idxbuf field with the key of the current record. If _db_readidx returns zero, we've reached the last entry in the chain.

[269–273] If offset is zero after the loop, we've reached the end of a hash chain without finding a matching key, so we return −1. Otherwise, we found a match (and exited the loop with the break statement), so we return success (0). In this case, the ptroff field contains the address of the previous index record, datoff contains the address of the data record, and datlen contains the size of the data record. As we make our way through the hash chain, we save the previous index record that points to the current index record. We'll use this when we delete a record, since we have to modify the chain pointer of the previous record to delete the current record.

[274–286] _db_hash calculates the hash value for a given key. It multiplies each ASCII character times its 1-based index and divides the result by the number of hash table entries. The remainder from the division is the hash value for this key. Recall that the number of hash table entries is 137, which is a prime number. According to Knuth [1998], prime hashes generally provide good distribution characteristics.

```
287    /*
288     * Read a chain ptr field from anywhere in the index file:
289     * the free list pointer, a hash table chain ptr, or an
290     * index record chain ptr.
291     */
292    static off_t
293    _db_readptr(DB *db, off_t offset)
294    {
295        char    asciiptr[PTR_SZ + 1];

296        if (lseek(db->idxfd, offset, SEEK_SET) == -1)
297            err_dump("_db_readptr: lseek error to ptr field");
298        if (read(db->idxfd, asciiptr, PTR_SZ) != PTR_SZ)
299            err_dump("_db_readptr: read error of ptr field");
300        asciiptr[PTR_SZ] = 0;           /* null terminate */
301        return(atol(asciiptr));
302    }

303    /*
304     * Read the next index record.  We start at the specified offset
305     * in the index file.  We read the index record into db->idxbuf
306     * and replace the separators with null bytes.  If all is OK we
307     * set db->datoff and db->datlen to the offset and length of the
308     * corresponding data record in the data file.
309     */
310    static off_t
311    _db_readidx(DB *db, off_t offset)
312    {
313        ssize_t                 i;
314        char                    *ptr1, *ptr2;
315        char                    asciiptr[PTR_SZ + 1], asciilen[IDXLEN_SZ + 1];
316        struct iovec    iov[2];
```

[287–302] _db_readptr reads any one of three different chain pointers: (a) the pointer
at the beginning of the index file that points to the first index record on the
free list, (b) the pointers in the hash table that point to the first index record
on each hash chain, and (c) the pointers that are stored at the beginning of
each index record (whether the index record is part of a hash chain or on the
free list). We convert the pointer from ASCII to a long integer before
returning it. No locking is done by this function; that is up to the caller.

[303–316] The _db_readidx function is used to read the record at the specified offset
from the index file. On success, the function will return the offset of the next
record in the list. In this case, the function will populate several fields in the
DB structure: idxoff contains the offset of the current record in the index
file, ptrval contains the offset of the next index entry in the list, idxlen
contains the length of the current index record, idxbuf contains the actual
index record, datoff contains the offset of the record in the data file, and
datlen contains the length of the data record.

```
317     /*
318      * Position index file and record the offset.  db_nextrec
319      * calls us with offset==0, meaning read from current offset.
320      * We still need to call lseek to record the current offset.
321      */
322     if ((db->idxoff = lseek(db->idxfd, offset,
323       offset == 0 ? SEEK_CUR : SEEK_SET)) == -1)
324         err_dump("_db_readidx: lseek error");

325     /*
326      * Read the ascii chain ptr and the ascii length at
327      * the front of the index record.  This tells us the
328      * remaining size of the index record.
329      */
330     iov[0].iov_base = asciiptr;
331     iov[0].iov_len  = PTR_SZ;
332     iov[1].iov_base = asciilen;
333     iov[1].iov_len  = IDXLEN_SZ;
334     if ((i = readv(db->idxfd, &iov[0], 2)) != PTR_SZ + IDXLEN_SZ) {
335         if (i == 0 && offset == 0)
336             return(-1);       /* EOF for db_nextrec */
337         err_dump("_db_readidx: readv error of index record");
338     }

339     /*
340      * This is our return value; always >= 0.
341      */
342     asciiptr[PTR_SZ] = 0;          /* null terminate */
343     db->ptrval = atol(asciiptr); /* offset of next key in chain */

344     asciilen[IDXLEN_SZ] = 0;       /* null terminate */
345     if ((db->idxlen = atoi(asciilen)) < IDXLEN_MIN ||
346       db->idxlen > IDXLEN_MAX)
347         err_dump("_db_readidx: invalid length");
```

[317–324] We start by seeking to the index file offset provided by the caller. We record the offset in the DB structure, so even if the caller wants to read the record at the current file offset (by setting offset to 0), we still need to call lseek to determine the current offset. Since an index record will never be stored at offset 0 in the index file, we can safely overload the value of 0 to mean "read from the current offset."

[325–338] We call readv to read the two fixed-length fields at the beginning of the index record: the chain pointer to the next index record and the size of the variable-length index record that follows.

[339–347] We convert the offset of the next record to an integer and store it in the ptrval field (this will be used as the return value for this function). Then we convert the length of the index record into an integer and save it in the idxlen field.

```
348     /*
349      * Now read the actual index record.  We read it into the key
350      * buffer that we malloced when we opened the database.
351      */
352     if ((i = read(db->idxfd, db->idxbuf, db->idxlen)) != db->idxlen)
353         err_dump("_db_readidx: read error of index record");
354     if (db->idxbuf[db->idxlen-1] != NEWLINE)      /* sanity check */
355         err_dump("_db_readidx: missing newline");
356     db->idxbuf[db->idxlen-1] = 0;    /* replace newline with null */

357     /*
358      * Find the separators in the index record.
359      */
360     if ((ptr1 = strchr(db->idxbuf, SEP)) == NULL)
361         err_dump("_db_readidx: missing first separator");
362     *ptr1++ = 0;                      /* replace SEP with null */

363     if ((ptr2 = strchr(ptr1, SEP)) == NULL)
364         err_dump("_db_readidx: missing second separator");
365     *ptr2++ = 0;                      /* replace SEP with null */

366     if (strchr(ptr2, SEP) != NULL)
367         err_dump("_db_readidx: too many separators");

368     /*
369      * Get the starting offset and length of the data record.
370      */
371     if ((db->datoff = atol(ptr1)) < 0)
372         err_dump("_db_readidx: starting offset < 0");
373     if ((db->datlen = atol(ptr2)) <= 0 || db->datlen > DATLEN_MAX)
374         err_dump("_db_readidx: invalid length");
375     return(db->ptrval);      /* return offset of next key in chain */
376 }
```

[348–356] We read the variable-length index record into the idxbuf field in the DB structure. The record should be terminated with a newline, which we replace with a null byte. If the index file is corrupt, we terminate and drop core by calling err_dump.

[357–367] We separate the index record into three fields: the key, the offset of the corresponding data record, and the length of the data record. The strchr function finds the first occurrence of the specified character in the given string. Here we look for the character that separates fields in the record (SEP, which we define to be a colon).

[368–376] We convert the data record offset and length into integers and store them in the DB structure. Then we return the offset of the next record in the hash chain. Note that we do not read the data record. That is left to the caller. In db_fetch, for example, we don't read the data record until _db_find_and_lock has read the index record that matches the key that we're looking for.

```
377    /*
378     * Read the current data record into the data buffer.
379     * Return a pointer to the null-terminated data buffer.
380     */
381    static char *
382    _db_readdat(DB *db)
383    {
384        if (lseek(db->datfd, db->datoff, SEEK_SET) == -1)
385            err_dump("_db_readdat: lseek error");
386        if (read(db->datfd, db->datbuf, db->datlen) != db->datlen)
387            err_dump("_db_readdat: read error");
388        if (db->datbuf[db->datlen-1] != NEWLINE)      /* sanity check */
389            err_dump("_db_readdat: missing newline");
390        db->datbuf[db->datlen-1] = 0; /* replace newline with null */
391        return(db->datbuf);       /* return pointer to data record */
392    }
393    /*
394     * Delete the specified record.
395     */
396    int
397    db_delete(DBHANDLE h, const char *key)
398    {
399        DB      *db = h;
400        int     rc = 0;           /* assume record will be found */
401        if (_db_find_and_lock(db, key, 1) == 0) {
402            _db_dodelete(db);
403            db->cnt_delok++;
404        } else {
405            rc = -1;              /* not found */
406            db->cnt_delerr++;
407        }
408        if (un_lock(db->idxfd, db->chainoff, SEEK_SET, 1) < 0)
409            err_dump("db_delete: un_lock error");
410        return(rc);
411    }
```

[377–392] The _db_readdat function populates the datbuf field in the DB structure with the contents of the data record, expecting that the datoff and datlen fields have been properly initialized already.

[393–411] The db_delete function is used to delete a record given its key. We use _db_find_and_lock to determine whether the record exists in the database. If it does, we call _db_dodelete to do the work needed to delete the record. The third argument to _db_find_and_lock controls whether the chain is read-locked or write-locked. Here we are requesting a write lock, since we will potentially change the list. Since _db_find_and_lock returns with the lock still held, we need to unlock it, regardless of whether the record was found.

```
412     /*
413      * Delete the current record specified by the DB structure.
414      * This function is called by db_delete and db_store, after
415      * the record has been located by _db_find_and_lock.
416      */
417     static void
418     _db_dodelete(DB *db)
419     {
420         int     i;
421         char    *ptr;
422         off_t   freeptr, saveptr;

423         /*
424          * Set data buffer and key to all blanks.
425          */
426         for (ptr = db->datbuf, i = 0; i < db->datlen - 1; i++)
427             *ptr++ = SPACE;
428         *ptr = 0;    /* null terminate for _db_writedat */
429         ptr = db->idxbuf;
430         while (*ptr)
431             *ptr++ = SPACE;

432         /*
433          * We have to lock the free list.
434          */
435         if (writew_lock(db->idxfd, FREE_OFF, SEEK_SET, 1) < 0)
436             err_dump("_db_dodelete: writew_lock error");

437         /*
438          * Write the data record with all blanks.
439          */
440         _db_writedat(db, db->datbuf, db->datoff, SEEK_SET);
```

[412–431] The _db_dodelete function does all the work necessary to delete a record from the database. (This function is also called by db_store.) Most of the function just updates two linked lists: the free list and the hash chain for this key. When a record is deleted, we set its key and data record to blanks. This fact is used by db_nextrec, which we'll examine later in this section.

[432–440] We call writew_lock to write-lock the free list. This is to prevent two processes that are deleting records at the same time, on two different hash chains, from interfering with each other. Since we'll add the deleted record to the free list, which changes the free-list pointer, only one process at a time can be doing this.

We write the all-blank data record by calling _db_writedat. Note that there is no need for _db_writedat to lock the data file in this case. Since db_delete has write-locked the hash chain for this record, we know that no other process is reading or writing this particular data record.

```
441      /*
442       * Read the free list pointer.  Its value becomes the
443       * chain ptr field of the deleted index record.  This means
444       * the deleted record becomes the head of the free list.
445       */
446      freeptr = _db_readptr(db, FREE_OFF);

447      /*
448       * Save the contents of index record chain ptr,
449       * before it's rewritten by _db_writeidx.
450       */
451      saveptr = db->ptrval;

452      /*
453       * Rewrite the index record.  This also rewrites the length
454       * of the index record, the data offset, and the data length,
455       * none of which has changed, but that's OK.
456       */
457      _db_writeidx(db, db->idxbuf, db->idxoff, SEEK_SET, freeptr);

458      /*
459       * Write the new free list pointer.
460       */
461      _db_writeptr(db, FREE_OFF, db->idxoff);

462      /*
463       * Rewrite the chain ptr that pointed to this record being
464       * deleted.  Recall that _db_find_and_lock sets db->ptroff to
465       * point to this chain ptr.  We set this chain ptr to the
466       * contents of the deleted record's chain ptr, saveptr.
467       */
468      _db_writeptr(db, db->ptroff, saveptr);
469      if (un_lock(db->idxfd, FREE_OFF, SEEK_SET, 1) < 0)
470          err_dump("_db_dodelete: un_lock error");
471  }
```

[441–461]   We read the free-list pointer and then update the index record so that its next record pointer is set to the first record on the free list. (If the free list was empty, this new chain pointer is 0.) We have already cleared the key. Then we update the free-list pointer with the offset of the index record we are deleting. This means that the free list is handled on a last-in, first-out basis; that is, deleted records are added to the front of the free list (although we remove entries from the free list on a first-fit basis).

We don't have a separate free list for each file. When we add a deleted index record to the free list, the index record still points to the deleted data record. There are better ways to do this, in exchange for added complexity.

[462–471]   We update the previous record in the hash chain to point to the record after the one we are deleting, thus removing the deleted record from the hash chain. Finally, we unlock the free list.

```
472  /*
473   * Write a data record.  Called by _db_dodelete (to write
474   * the record with blanks) and db_store.
475   */
476  static void
477  _db_writedat(DB *db, const char *data, off_t offset, int whence)
478  {
479      struct iovec    iov[2];
480      static char     newline = NEWLINE;

481      /*
482       * If we're appending, we have to lock before doing the lseek
483       * and write to make the two an atomic operation.  If we're
484       * overwriting an existing record, we don't have to lock.
485       */
486      if (whence == SEEK_END) /* we're appending, lock entire file */
487          if (writew_lock(db->datfd, 0, SEEK_SET, 0) < 0)
488              err_dump("_db_writedat: writew_lock error");

489      if ((db->datoff = lseek(db->datfd, offset, whence)) == -1)
490          err_dump("_db_writedat: lseek error");
491      db->datlen = strlen(data) + 1;  /* datlen includes newline */

492      iov[0].iov_base = (char *) data;
493      iov[0].iov_len  = db->datlen - 1;
494      iov[1].iov_base = &newline;
495      iov[1].iov_len  = 1;
496      if (writev(db->datfd, &iov[0], 2) != db->datlen)
497          err_dump("_db_writedat: writev error of data record");

498      if (whence == SEEK_END)
499          if (un_lock(db->datfd, 0, SEEK_SET, 0) < 0)
500              err_dump("_db_writedat: un_lock error");
501  }
```

[472–491] We call _db_writedat to write a data record. When we delete a record, we use _db_writedat to overwrite the record with blanks; _db_writedat doesn't need to lock the data file, because db_delete has write-locked the hash chain for this record. Thus, no other process could be reading or writing this particular data record. When we cover db_store later in this section, we'll encounter the case in which _db_writedat is appending to the data file and has to lock it.

We seek to the location where we want to write the data record. The amount to write is the record size plus 1 byte for the terminating newline we add.

[492–501] We set up the iovec array and call writev to write the data record and newline. We can't assume that the caller's buffer has room at the end for us to append the newline, so we write the newline from a separate buffer. If we are appending a record to the file, we release the lock we acquired earlier.

```
502    /*
503     * Write an index record.  _db_writedat is called before
504     * this function to set the datoff and datlen fields in the
505     * DB structure, which we need to write the index record.
506     */
507    static void
508    _db_writeidx(DB *db, const char *key,
509                     off_t offset, int whence, off_t ptrval)
510    {
511        struct iovec    iov[2];
512        char            asciiptrlen[PTR_SZ + IDXLEN_SZ +1];
513        int             len;
514        char            *fmt;

515        if ((db->ptrval = ptrval) < 0 || ptrval > PTR_MAX)
516            err_quit("_db_writeidx: invalid ptr: %d", ptrval);
517        if (sizeof(off_t) == sizeof(long long))
518            fmt = "%s%c%lld%c%d\n";
519        else
520            fmt = "%s%c%ld%c%d\n";
521        sprintf(db->idxbuf, fmt, key, SEP, db->datoff, SEP, db->datlen);
522        if ((len = strlen(db->idxbuf)) < IDXLEN_MIN || len > IDXLEN_MAX)
523            err_dump("_db_writeidx: invalid length");
524        sprintf(asciiptrlen, "%*ld%*d", PTR_SZ, ptrval, IDXLEN_SZ, len);

525        /*
526         * If we're appending, we have to lock before doing the lseek
527         * and write to make the two an atomic operation.  If we're
528         * overwriting an existing record, we don't have to lock.
529         */
530        if (whence == SEEK_END)      /* we're appending */
531            if (writew_lock(db->idxfd, ((db->nhash+1)*PTR_SZ)+1,
532                SEEK_SET, 0) < 0)
533                    err_dump("_db_writeidx: writew_lock error");
```

[502–524] The _db_writeidx function is called to write an index record. After validating the next pointer in the chain, we create the index record and store the second half of it in idxbuf. We need the size of this portion of the index record to create the first half of the index record, which we store in the local variable asciiptrlen.

Note that we select the format string passed to sprintf based on the size of the off_t data type. Even a 32-bit system can provide 64-bit file offsets, so we can't make any assumptions about the size of the off_t data type.

[525–533] As with _db_writedat, this function deals with locking only when a new index record is being appended to the index file. When _db_dodelete calls this function, we're rewriting an existing index record. In this case, the caller has write-locked the hash chain, so no additional locking is required.

```
534     /*
535      * Position the index file and record the offset.
536      */
537     if ((db->idxoff = lseek(db->idxfd, offset, whence)) == -1)
538         err_dump("_db_writeidx: lseek error");

539     iov[0].iov_base = asciiptrlen;
540     iov[0].iov_len  = PTR_SZ + IDXLEN_SZ;
541     iov[1].iov_base = db->idxbuf;
542     iov[1].iov_len  = len;
543     if (writev(db->idxfd, &iov[0], 2) != PTR_SZ + IDXLEN_SZ + len)
544         err_dump("_db_writeidx: writev error of index record");

545     if (whence == SEEK_END)
546         if (un_lock(db->idxfd, ((db->nhash+1)*PTR_SZ)+1,
547             SEEK_SET, 0) < 0)
548             err_dump("_db_writeidx: un_lock error");
549 }

550     /*
551      * Write a chain ptr field somewhere in the index file:
552      * the free list, the hash table, or in an index record.
553      */
554 static void
555 _db_writeptr(DB *db, off_t offset, off_t ptrval)
556 {
557     char    asciiptr[PTR_SZ + 1];

558     if (ptrval < 0 || ptrval > PTR_MAX)
559         err_quit("_db_writeptr: invalid ptr: %d", ptrval);
560     sprintf(asciiptr, "%*ld", PTR_SZ, ptrval);

561     if (lseek(db->idxfd, offset, SEEK_SET) == -1)
562         err_dump("_db_writeptr: lseek error to ptr field");
563     if (write(db->idxfd, asciiptr, PTR_SZ) != PTR_SZ)
564         err_dump("_db_writeptr: write error of ptr field");
565 }
```

[534–549] We seek to the location where we want to write the index record and save this offset in the `idxoff` field of the `DB` structure. Since we built the index record in two separate buffers, we use `writev` to store it in the index file. If we were appending to the file, we release the lock we acquired before seeking. This makes the seek and the write an atomic operation from the perspective of concurrently running processes appending new records to the same database.

[550–565] `_db_writeptr` is used to write a chain pointer to the index file. We validate that the chain pointer is within bounds, then convert it to an ASCII string. We seek to the specified offset in the index file and write the pointer.

```
566    /*
567     * Store a record in the database.  Return 0 if OK, 1 if record
568     * exists and DB_INSERT specified, -1 on error.
569     */
570    int
571    db_store(DBHANDLE h, const char *key, const char *data, int flag)
572    {
573        DB      *db = h;
574        int     rc, keylen, datlen;
575        off_t   ptrval;

576        if (flag != DB_INSERT && flag != DB_REPLACE &&
577          flag != DB_STORE) {
578            errno = EINVAL;
579            return(-1);
580        }
581        keylen = strlen(key);
582        datlen = strlen(data) + 1;        /* +1 for newline at end */
583        if (datlen < DATLEN_MIN || datlen > DATLEN_MAX)
584            err_dump("db_store: invalid data length");

585        /*
586         * _db_find_and_lock calculates which hash table this new record
587         * goes into (db->chainoff), regardless of whether it already
588         * exists or not. The following calls to _db_writeptr change the
589         * hash table entry for this chain to point to the new record.
590         * The new record is added to the front of the hash chain.
591         */
592        if (_db_find_and_lock(db, key, 1) < 0) { /* record not found */
593            if (flag == DB_REPLACE) {
594                rc = -1;
595                db->cnt_storerr++;
596                errno = ENOENT;       /* error, record does not exist */
597                goto doreturn;
598            }
```

[566–584] We use db_store to add a record to the database. We first validate the flag value we are passed. Then we make sure that the length of the data record is valid. If it isn't, we drop core and exit. This is OK for an example, but if we were building a production-quality library, we'd return an error status instead, which would give the application a chance to recover.

[585–598] We call _db_find_and_lock to see if the record already exists. It is OK if the record doesn't exist and either DB_INSERT or DB_STORE is specified, or if the record already exists and either DB_REPLACE or DB_STORE is specified. If we're replacing an existing record, that implies that the keys are identical but that the data records probably differ. Note that the final argument to _db_find_and_lock specifies that the hash chain must be write-locked, as we will probably be modifying this hash chain.

```
599          /*
600           * _db_find_and_lock locked the hash chain for us; read
601           * the chain ptr to the first index record on hash chain.
602           */
603          ptrval = _db_readptr(db, db->chainoff);

604          if (_db_findfree(db, keylen, datlen) < 0) {
605              /*
606               * Can't find an empty record big enough. Append the
607               * new record to the ends of the index and data files.
608               */
609              _db_writedat(db, data, 0, SEEK_END);
610              _db_writeidx(db, key, 0, SEEK_END, ptrval);

611              /*
612               * db->idxoff was set by _db_writeidx.  The new
613               * record goes to the front of the hash chain.
614               */
615              _db_writeptr(db, db->chainoff, db->idxoff);
616              db->cnt_stor1++;
617          } else {
618              /*
619               * Reuse an empty record. _db_findfree removed it from
620               * the free list and set both db->datoff and db->idxoff.
621               * Reused record goes to the front of the hash chain.
622               */
623              _db_writedat(db, data, db->datoff, SEEK_SET);
624              _db_writeidx(db, key, db->idxoff, SEEK_SET, ptrval);
625              _db_writeptr(db, db->chainoff, db->idxoff);
626              db->cnt_stor2++;
627          }
```

[599–603] After we call _db_find_and_lock, the code divides into four cases. In the first two, no record was found, so we are adding a new record. We read the offset of the first entry on the hash list.

[604–616] Case 1: we call _db_findfree to search the free list for a deleted record with the same size key and same size data. If no such record is found, we have to append the new record to the ends of the index and data files. We call _db_writedat to write the data part, _db_writeidx to write the index part, and _db_writeptr to place the new record on the front of the hash chain. We increment a count (cnt_stor1) of the number of times we executed this case to allow us to characterize the behavior of the database.

[617–627] Case 2: _db_findfree found an empty record with the correct sizes and removed it from the free list (we'll see the implementation of _db_findfree shortly). We write the data and index portions of the new record and add the record to the front of the hash chain as we did in case 1. The cnt_stor2 field counts how many times we've executed this case.

```
628        } else {                                    /* record found */
629            if (flag == DB_INSERT) {
630                rc = 1;        /* error, record already in db */
631                db->cnt_storerr++;
632                goto doreturn;
633            }

634            /*
635             * We are replacing an existing record.  We know the new
636             * key equals the existing key, but we need to check if
637             * the data records are the same size.
638             */
639            if (datlen != db->datlen) {
640                _db_dodelete(db);    /* delete the existing record */

641                /*
642                 * Reread the chain ptr in the hash table
643                 * (it may change with the deletion).
644                 */
645                ptrval = _db_readptr(db, db->chainoff);

646                /*
647                 * Append new index and data records to end of files.
648                 */
649                _db_writedat(db, data, 0, SEEK_END);
650                _db_writeidx(db, key, 0, SEEK_END, ptrval);

651                /*
652                 * New record goes to the front of the hash chain.
653                 */
654                _db_writeptr(db, db->chainoff, db->idxoff);
655                db->cnt_stor3++;
656            } else {
```

[628–633] Now we reach the two cases in which a record with the same key already exists in the database. If the caller isn't replacing the record, we set the return code to indicate that a record exists, increment the count of the number of store errors, and jump to the end of the function, where we handle the common return logic.

[634–656] Case 3: an existing record is being replaced, and the length of the new data record differs from the length of the existing one. We call _db_dodelete to delete the existing record. Recall that this places the deleted record at the head of the free list. Then we append the new record to the ends of the data and index files by calling _db_writedat and _db_writeidx. (There are other ways to handle this case. We could try to find a deleted record that has the correct data size.) The new record is added to the front of the hash chain by calling _db_writeptr. The cnt_stor3 counter in the DB structure records the number of times we've executed this case.

```
657                    /*
658                     * Same size data, just replace data record.
659                     */
660                    _db_writedat(db, data, db->datoff, SEEK_SET);
661                    db->cnt_stor4++;
662                }
663            }
664        rc = 0;        /* OK */

665    doreturn: /* unlock hash chain locked by _db_find_and_lock */
666        if (un_lock(db->idxfd, db->chainoff, SEEK_SET, 1) < 0)
667            err_dump("db_store: un_lock error");
668        return(rc);
669    }

670    /*
671     * Try to find a free index record and accompanying data record
672     * of the correct sizes.  We're only called by db_store.
673     */
674    static int
675    _db_findfree(DB *db, int keylen, int datlen)
676    {
677        int     rc;
678        off_t   offset, nextoffset, saveoffset;

679        /*
680         * Lock the free list.
681         */
682        if (writew_lock(db->idxfd, FREE_OFF, SEEK_SET, 1) < 0)
683            err_dump("_db_findfree: writew_lock error");

684        /*
685         * Read the free list pointer.
686         */
687        saveoffset = FREE_OFF;
688        offset = _db_readptr(db, saveoffset);
```

[657–663] Case 4: An existing record is being replaced, and the length of the new data
         record equals the length of the existing data record. This is the easiest case;
         we simply rewrite the data record and increment the counter (cnt_stor4)
         for this case.

[664–669] In the normal case, we set the return code to indicate success and fall
         through to the common return logic. We unlock the hash chain that was
         locked as a result of calling _db_find_and_lock and return to the caller.

[670–688] The _db_findfree function tries to find a free index record and associated
         data record of the specified sizes. We need to write-lock the free list to avoid
         interfering with any other processes using the free list. After locking the free
         list, we get the pointer address at the head of the list.

```
689        while (offset != 0) {
690            nextoffset = _db_readidx(db, offset);
691            if (strlen(db->idxbuf) == keylen && db->datlen == datlen)
692                break;        /* found a match */
693            saveoffset = offset;
694            offset = nextoffset;
695        }

696        if (offset == 0) {
697            rc = -1;      /* no match found */
698        } else {
699            /*
700             * Found a free record with matching sizes.
701             * The index record was read in by _db_readidx above,
702             * which sets db->ptrval.  Also, saveoffset points to
703             * the chain ptr that pointed to this empty record on
704             * the free list.  We set this chain ptr to db->ptrval,
705             * which removes the empty record from the free list.
706             */
707            _db_writeptr(db, saveoffset, db->ptrval);
708            rc = 0;

709            /*
710             * Notice also that _db_readidx set both db->idxoff
711             * and db->datoff.  This is used by the caller, db_store,
712             * to write the new index record and data record.
713             */
714        }

715        /*
716         * Unlock the free list.
717         */
718        if (un_lock(db->idxfd, FREE_OFF, SEEK_SET, 1) < 0)
719            err_dump("_db_findfree: un_lock error");
720        return(rc);
721    }
```

[689–695] The `while` loop in `_db_findfree` goes through the free list, looking for a record with matching key and data sizes. In this simple implementation, we reuse a deleted record only if the key length and data length equal the lengths for the new record being inserted. There are a variety of better ways to reuse this deleted space, in exchange for added complexity.

[696–714] If we can't find an available record of the requested key and data sizes, we set the return code to indicate failure. Otherwise, we write the previous record's chain pointer to point to the next chain pointer value of the record we have found. This removes the record from the free list.

[715–721] Once we are done with the free list, we release the write lock. Then we return the status to the caller.

```
722  /*
723   * Rewind the index file for db_nextrec.
724   * Automatically called by db_open.
725   * Must be called before first db_nextrec.
726   */
727  void
728  db_rewind(DBHANDLE h)
729  {
730      DB       *db = h;
731      off_t    offset;

732      offset = (db->nhash + 1) * PTR_SZ;   /* +1 for free list ptr */

733      /*
734       * We're just setting the file offset for this process
735       * to the start of the index records; no need to lock.
736       * +1 below for newline at end of hash table.
737       */
738      if ((db->idxoff = lseek(db->idxfd, offset+1, SEEK_SET)) == -1)
739          err_dump("db_rewind: lseek error");
740  }

741  /*
742   * Return the next sequential record.
743   * We just step our way through the index file, ignoring deleted
744   * records.  db_rewind must be called before this function is
745   * called the first time.
746   */
747  char *
748  db_nextrec(DBHANDLE h, char *key)
749  {
750      DB       *db = h;
751      char     c;
752      char     *ptr;
```

[722–740] The db_rewind function is used to reset the database to "the beginning;" we set the file offset for the index file to point to the first record in the index file (immediately following the hash table). (Recall the structure of the index file from Figure 20.2.)

[741–752] The db_nextrec function returns the next record in the database. The return value is a pointer to the data buffer. If the caller provides a non-null value for the key parameter, the corresponding key is copied to this address. The caller is responsible for allocating a buffer big enough to store the key. A buffer whose size is IDXLEN_MAX bytes is large enough to hold any key.

Records are returned sequentially, in the order that they happen to be stored in the database file. Thus, the records are not sorted by key value. Also, because we do not follow the hash chains, we can come across records that have been deleted, but we will not return these to the caller.

```
753      /*
754       * We read lock the free list so that we don't read
755       * a record in the middle of its being deleted.
756       */
757      if (readw_lock(db->idxfd, FREE_OFF, SEEK_SET, 1) < 0)
758          err_dump("db_nextrec: readw_lock error");

759      do {
760          /*
761           * Read next sequential index record.
762           */
763          if (_db_readidx(db, 0) < 0) {
764              ptr = NULL;        /* end of index file, EOF */
765              goto doreturn;
766          }

767          /*
768           * Check if key is all blank (empty record).
769           */
770          ptr = db->idxbuf;
771          while ((c = *ptr++) != 0  &&  c == SPACE)
772              ;    /* skip until null byte or nonblank */
773      } while (c == 0);   /* loop until a nonblank key is found */

774      if (key != NULL)
775          strcpy(key, db->idxbuf);    /* return key */
776      ptr = _db_readdat(db);  /* return pointer to data buffer */
777      db->cnt_nextrec++;

778  doreturn:
779      if (un_lock(db->idxfd, FREE_OFF, SEEK_SET, 1) < 0)
780          err_dump("db_nextrec: un_lock error");
781      return(ptr);
782  }
```

[753–758] We first need to read-lock the free list so that no other processes can remove a record while we are reading it.

[759–773] We call _db_readidx to read the next record. We pass in an offset of 0 to tell _db_readidx to continue reading from the current offset. Since we are reading the index file sequentially, we can come across records that have been deleted. We want to return only valid records, so we skip any record whose key is all spaces (recall that _db_dodelete clears a key by setting it to all spaces).

[774–782] When we find a valid key, we copy it to the caller's buffer if one was supplied. Then we read the data record and set the return value to point to the internal buffer containing the data record. We increment a statistics counter, unlock the free list, and return the pointer to the data record.

The normal use of `db_rewind` and `db_nextrec` is in a loop of the form

```
db_rewind(db);
while ((ptr = db_nextrec(db, key)) != NULL) {
    /* process record */
}
```

As we warned earlier, there is no order to the returned records; they are not in key order.

If the database is being modified while `db_nextrec` is called from a loop, the records returned by `db_nextrec` are simply a snapshot of a changing database at some point in time. `db_nextrec` always returns a "correct" record when it is called; that is, it won't return a record that was deleted. But it is possible for a record returned by `db_nextrec` to be deleted immediately after `db_nextrec` returns. Similarly, if a deleted record is reused right after `db_nextrec` skips over the deleted record, we won't see that new record unless we rewind the database and go through it again. If it's important to obtain an accurate "frozen" snapshot of the database using `db_nextrec`, there must be no insertions or deletions going on at the same time.

Look at the locking used by `db_nextrec`. We're not going through any hash chain, and we can't determine the hash chain that a record belongs on. Therefore, it is possible for an index record to be in the process of being deleted when `db_nextrec` is reading the record. To prevent this, `db_nextrec` read-locks the free list, thereby avoiding any interaction with `_db_dodelete` and `_db_findfree`.

Before we conclude our study of the `db.c` source file, we need to describe the locking when new index records or data records are appended to the end of the file. In cases 1 and 3, `db_store` calls both `_db_writeidx` and `_db_writedat` with a third argument of 0 and a fourth argument of `SEEK_END`. This fourth argument is the flag to these two functions, indicating that the new record is being appended to the file. The technique used by `_db_writeidx` is to write-lock the index file from the end of the hash chain to the end of file. This won't interfere with any other readers or writers of the database (since they will lock a hash chain), but it does prevent other callers of `db_store` from trying to append at the same time. The technique used by `_db_writedat` is to write-lock the entire data file. Again, this won't interfere with other readers or writers of the database (since they don't even try to lock the data file), but it does prevent other callers of `db_store` from trying to append to the data file at the same time. (See Exercise 20.3.)

20.9 Performance

To test the database library and to obtain some timing measurements of the database access patterns of typical applications, a test program was written. This program takes two command-line arguments: the number of children to create and the number of database records (*nrec*) for each child to write to the database. The program then creates an empty database (by calling `db_open`), forks the number of child processes, and waits for all the children to terminate. Each child performs the following steps.

1. Write *nrec* records to the database.

2. Read the *nrec* records back by key value.

3. Perform the following loop *nrec* × 5 times.

   a. Read a random record.

   b. Every 37 times through the loop, delete a random record.

   c. Every 11 times through the loop, insert a new record and read the record back.

   d. Every 17 times through the loop, replace a random record with a new record. Every other one of these replacements is a record with the same size data, and the alternate is a record with a longer data portion.

4. Delete all the records that this child wrote. Every time a record is deleted, ten random records are looked up.

The number of operations performed on the database is counted by the `cnt_xxx` variables in the `DB` structure, which were incremented in the functions. The number of operations differs from one child to the next, since the random-number generator used to select records is initialized in each child to the child's process ID. A typical count of the operations performed in each child, when *nrec* is 500, is shown in Figure 20.6.

Operation	Count
`db_store`, `DB_INSERT`, no empty record, appended	678
`db_store`, `DB_INSERT`, empty record reused	164
`db_store`, `DB_REPLACE`, different data length, appended	97
`db_store`, `DB_REPLACE`, equal data length	109
`db_store`, record not found	19
`db_fetch`, record found	8,114
`db_fetch`, record not found	732
`db_delete`, record found	842
`db_delete`, record not found	110

Figure 20.6 Typical count of operations performed by each child when *nrec* is 500

We performed about ten times more fetches than stores or deletions, which is probably typical of many database applications.

Each child is doing these operations (fetching, storing, and deleting) only with the records that the child wrote. The concurrency controls are being exercised because all the children are operating on the same database (albeit different records in the same database). The total number of records in the database increases in proportion to the number of children. (With one child, *nrec* records are originally written to the database. With two children, *nrec* × 2 records are originally written, and so on.)

To test the concurrency provided by coarse-grained locking versus fine-grained locking and to compare the three types of locking (no locking, advisory locking, and mandatory locking), we ran three versions of the test program. The first version used the source code shown in Section 20.8, which we've called fine-grained locking. The second version changed the locking calls to implement coarse-grained locking, as described in Section 20.6. The third version had all locking calls removed, so we could measure the overhead involved in locking. We can run the first and second versions (fine-grained locking and coarse-grained locking) using either advisory or mandatory locking, by changing the permission bits on the database files. (In all the tests reported in this section, we measured the times for mandatory locking using only the implementation of fine-grained locking.)

All the timing tests in this section were done on a SPARC system running Solaris 9.

Single-Process Results

Figure 20.7 shows the results when only a single child process ran, with an *nrec* of 500, 1,000, and 2,000.

	No locking			Advisory locking						Mandatory locking		
				Coarse-grained locking			Fine-grained locking			Fine-grained locking		
nrec	User	Sys	Clock	User	Sys	Clock	User	Sys	Clock	User	Sys	Clock
500	0.42	0.89	1.31	0.42	1.17	1.59	0.41	1.04	1.45	0.46	1.49	1.95
1,000	1.51	3.89	5.41	1.64	4.13	5.78	1.63	4.12	5.76	1.73	6.34	8.07
2,000	3.91	10.06	13.98	4.09	10.30	14.39	4.03	10.63	14.66	4.47	16.21	20.70

Figure 20.7 Single child, varying *nrec*, different locking techniques

The last 12 columns give the corresponding times in seconds. In all cases, the user CPU time plus the system CPU time approximately equals the clock time. This set of tests was CPU-limited and not disk-limited.

The six columns under "Advisory locking" are almost equal for each row. This makes sense because for a single process, there is no difference between coarse-grained locking and fine-grained locking.

Comparing no locking versus advisory locking, we see that adding the locking calls adds between 2 percent and 31 percent to the system CPU time. Even though the locks are never used (since only a single process is running), the system call overhead in the calls to fcntl adds time. Also note that the user CPU time is about the same for all four versions of locking. Since the user code is almost equivalent (except for the number of calls to fcntl), this makes sense.

The final point to note from Figure 20.7 is that mandatory locking adds between 43 percent and 54 percent to the system CPU time, compared to advisory locking. Since the number of locking calls is the same for advisory fine-grained locking and mandatory fine-grained locking, the additional system call overhead must be in the reads and writes.

The final test was to try the no-locking program with multiple children. The results, as expected, were random errors. Normally, records that were added to the database couldn't be found, and the test program aborted. Different errors occurred every time the test program was run. This illustrates a classic race condition: multiple processes updating the same file without using any form of locking.

Multiple-Process Results

The next set of measurements looks mainly at the differences between coarse-grained locking and fine-grained locking. As we said earlier, intuitively, we expect fine-grained locking to provide additional concurrency, since there is less time that portions of the database are locked from other processes. Figure 20.8 shows the results for an *nrec* of 500, varying the number of children from 1 to 12.

	Advisory locking							Mandatory locking			
	Coarse-grained locking			Fine-grained locking			Δ	Fine-grained locking			Δ
#Proc	User	Sys	Clock	User	Sys	Clock	Clock	User	Sys	Clock	Percent
1	0.41	1.00	1.42	0.41	1.05	1.47	0.05	0.47	1.40	1.87	33
2	1.10	2.81	3.92	1.11	2.80	3.92	0.00	1.15	4.06	5.22	45
3	2.17	5.27	7.44	2.19	5.18	7.37	−0.07	2.31	7.67	9.99	48
4	3.36	8.55	11.91	3.26	8.67	11.94	0.03	3.51	12.69	16.20	46
5	4.72	13.08	17.80	4.99	12.64	17.64	−0.16	4.91	19.21	24.14	52
6	6.45	17.96	24.42	6.83	17.29	24.14	−0.28	7.03	26.59	33.66	54
7	8.46	23.12	31.62	8.67	22.96	31.65	0.03	9.25	35.47	44.74	54
8	10.83	29.68	40.55	11.00	29.39	40.41	−0.14	11.67	45.90	57.63	56
9	13.35	36.81	50.23	13.43	36.28	49.76	−0.47	14.45	58.02	72.49	60
10	16.35	45.28	61.66	16.09	44.10	60.23	−1.43	17.43	70.90	88.37	61
11	18.97	54.24	73.24	19.13	51.70	70.87	−2.37	20.62	84.98	105.69	64
12	22.92	63.54	86.51	22.94	61.28	84.29	−2.22	24.41	101.68	126.20	66

Figure 20.8 Comparison of various locking techniques, *nrec* = 500

All times are in seconds and are the total for the parent and all its children. There are many items to consider from this data.

The eighth column, labeled "Δ clock," is the difference in seconds between the clock times from advisory coarse-grained locking to advisory fine-grained locking. This is the measurement of how much concurrency we obtain by going from coarse-grained locking to fine-grained locking. On the system used for these tests, coarse-grained locking is roughly the same until we have more than seven processes. Even after seven processes, the decrease in clock time using fine-grained locking isn't that great (less than 3 percent), which makes us wonder whether the additional code required to implement fine-grained locking is worth the effort.

We would like the clock time to decrease from coarse-grained to fine-grained locking, as it eventually does, but we expect the system time to remain higher for fine-grained locking, for any number of processes. The reason we expect this is that with fine-grained locking, we are issuing more fcntl calls than with coarse-grained locking. If we total the number of fcntl calls in Figure 20.6 for coarse-grained locking and fine-grained locking, we have an average of 21,730 for coarse-grained locking and 25,292 for fine-grained locking. (To get these numbers, realize that each operation in Figure 20.6 requires two calls to fcntl for coarse-grained locking and that the first three calls to db_store along with record deletion [record found] each require four calls to fcntl for fine-grained locking.) We expect this increase of 16 percent in the number of calls to fcntl to result in an increased system time for fine-grained locking.

Therefore, the slight decrease in system time for fine-grained locking, when the number of processes exceeds seven, is puzzling.

The reason for the decrease is that with coarse-grained locking, we hold locks for longer periods of time, thus increasing the likelihood that other processes will block on a lock. With fine-grained locking, the locking is done over shorter intervals, so there is less chance that processes will block. If we analyze the system behavior running 12 database processes, we will see that there is three times as much process switching with coarse-grained locking as with fine-grained locking. This means that processes block on locks less often with fine-grained locking.

The final column, labeled "Δ percent," is the percentage increase in the system CPU time from advisory fine-grained locking to mandatory fine-grained locking. These percentages verify what we saw in Figure 20.7, that mandatory locking adds significantly (between 33 percent and 66 percent) to the system time.

Since the user code for all these tests is almost identical (there are some additional fcntl calls for both advisory fine-grained and mandatory fine-grained locking), we expect the user CPU times to be the same across any row.

The values in the first row of Figure 20.8 are similar to those for an *nrec* of 500 in Figure 20.7. This corresponds to our expectation.

Figure 20.9 is a graph of the data from Figure 20.8 for advisory fine-grained locking. We plot the clock time as the number of processes goes from 1 to 12. We also plot the user CPU time divided by the number of processes and the system CPU time divided by the number of processes.

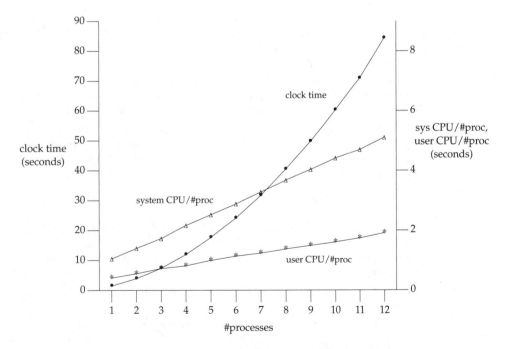

Figure 20.9 Values from Figure 20.8 for advisory fine-grained locking

Note that both CPU times, divided by the number of processes, are linear but that the plot of the clock time is nonlinear. The probable reason is the added amount of CPU time used by the operating system to switch between processes as the number of processes increases. This operating system overhead would show up as an increased clock time, but shouldn't affect the CPU times of the individual processes.

The reason the user CPU time increases with the number of processes is that there are more records in the database. Each hash chain is getting longer, so it takes the _db_find_and_lock function longer, on the average, to find a record.

20.10 Summary

This chapter has taken a long look at the design and implementation of a database library. Although we've kept the library small and simple for presentation purposes, it contains the record locking required to allow concurrent access by multiple processes.

We've also looked at the performance of this library with various numbers of processes using no locking, advisory locking (fine-grained and coarse-grained), and mandatory locking. We saw that advisory locking adds less than 10 percent to the clock time over no locking and that mandatory locking adds another 33 percent to 66 percent over advisory locking.

Exercises

20.1   The locking in _db_dodelete is somewhat conservative. For example, we could allow more concurrency by not write-locking the free list until we really need to; that is, the call to writew_lock could be moved between the calls to _db_writedat and _db_readptr. What happens if we do this?

20.2   If db_nextrec did not read-lock the free list and a record that it was reading was also in the process of being deleted, describe how db_nextrec could return the correct key but an all-blank (hence incorrect) data record. (Hint: look at _db_dodelete.)

20.3   At the end of Section 20.8, we described the locking performed by _db_writeidx and _db_writedat. We said that this locking didn't interfere with other readers and writers except those making calls to db_store. Is this true if mandatory locking is being used?

20.4   How would you integrate the fsync function into this database library?

20.5   In db_store, we write the data record before the index record. What happens if you do it in the opposite order?

20.6   Create a new database and write some number of records to the database. Write a program that calls db_nextrec to read each record in the database, and call _db_hash to calculate the hash value for each record. Print a histogram of the number of records on each hash chain. Is the hashing function in _db_hash adequate?

20.7   Modify the database functions so that the number of hash chains in the index file can be specified when the database is created.

20.8   Compare the performance of the database functions when the database is (a) on the same host as the test program and (b) on a different host accessed via NFS. Does the record locking provided by the database library still work?

21

Communicating with a
Network Printer

21.1 Introduction

We now develop a program that can communicate with a network printer. These printers are connected to multiple computers via Ethernet and often support PostScript files as well as plaintext files. Applications generally use the Internet Printing Protocol (IPP) to communicate with these printers, although some support alternate communication protocols.

We are about to describe two programs: a print spooler daemon that sends jobs to a printer and a command to submit print jobs to the spooler daemon. Since the print spooler has to do multiple things (communicate with clients submitting jobs, communicate with the printer, read files, scan directories, etc.), this gives us a chance to use many of the functions from earlier chapters. For example, we use threads (Chapters 11 and 12) to simplify the design of the print spooler and sockets (Chapter 16) to communicate between the program used to schedule a file to be printed and the print spooler, and also between the print spooler and the network printer.

21.2 The Internet Printing Protocol

IPP specifies the communication rules for building network-based printing systems. By embedding an IPP server inside a printer with an Ethernet card, the printer can service requests from many computer systems. These computer systems need not be located on the same physical network, however. IPP is built on top of standard Internet protocols, so any computer that can create a TCP/IP connection to the printer can submit a print job.

Specifically, IPP is built on top of HTTP, the Hypertext Transfer Protocol (Section 21.3). HTTP, in turn, is built on top of TCP/IP. The structure of an IPP message is shown in Figure 21.1.

Ethernet header	IP header	TCP header	HTTP header	IPP header	data to be printed

Figure 21.1 Structure of an IPP message

IPP is a request–response protocol. A client sends a request message to a server, and the server answers with a response message. The IPP header contains a field that indicates the requested operation. Operations are defined to submit print jobs, cancel print jobs, get job attributes, get printer attributes, pause and restart the printer, place a job on hold, and release a held job.

Figure 21.2 shows the structure of an IPP message header. The first 2 bytes are the IPP version number. For protocol version 1.1, each byte has a value of 1. For a protocol request, the next 2 bytes contain a value identifying the requested operation. For a protocol response, these 2 bytes contain a status code instead.

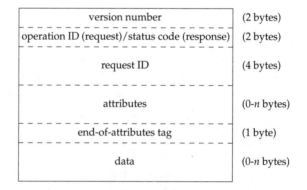

version number	(2 bytes)
operation ID (request)/status code (response)	(2 bytes)
request ID	(4 bytes)
attributes	(0-n bytes)
end-of-attributes tag	(1 byte)
data	(0-n bytes)

Figure 21.2 Structure of an IPP header

The next 4 bytes contain an integer identifying the request. Optional attributes follow this, terminated by an end-of-attributes tag. Any data that might be associated with the request follows immediately after the end-of-attributes tag.

In the header, integers are stored as signed, two's-complement, binary values in big-endian byte order (i.e., network byte order). Attributes are stored in groups. Each group starts with a single byte identifying the group. Within each group, an attribute is generally represented as a 1-byte tag, followed by a 2-byte name length, followed by the name of the attribute, followed by a 2-byte value length, and finally the value itself. The value can be encoded as a string, a binary integer, or a more complex structure, such as a date/timestamp.

Figure 21.3 shows how the `attributes-charset` attribute would be encoded with a value of `utf-8`.

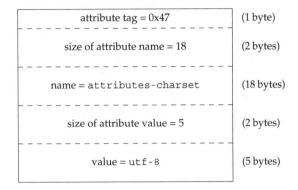

attribute tag = 0x47	(1 byte)
size of attribute name = 18	(2 bytes)
name = attributes-charset	(18 bytes)
size of attribute value = 5	(2 bytes)
value = utf-8	(5 bytes)

Figure 21.3 Sample IPP attribute encoding

Depending on the operation requested, some attributes are required to be provided in the request message, whereas others are optional. For example, Figure 21.4 shows the attributes defined for a print-job request.

Attribute	Status	Description
attributes-charset	required	The character set used by attributes of type text or name
attributes-natural-language	required	The natural language used by attributes of type text or name
printer-uri	required	The printer's Universal Resource Identifier
requesting-user-name	optional	Name of user submitting job (used for authentication, if enabled)
job-name	optional	Name of job used to distinguish between multiple jobs
ipp-attribute-fidelity	optional	If true, tells printer to reject job if all attributes can't be met; otherwise, printer does its best to print the job
document-name	optional	The name of the document (suitable for printing in a banner, for example)
document-format	optional	The format of the document (plaintext, PostScript, etc.)
document-natural-language	optional	The natural language of the document
compression	optional	The algorithm used to compress the document data
job-k-octets	optional	Size of the document in 1,024-octet units
job-impressions	optional	Number of impressions (images imposed on a page) submitted in this job
job-media-sheets	optional	Number of sheets printed by this job

Figure 21.4 Attributes of print-job request

The IPP header contains a mixture of text and binary data. Attribute names are stored as text, but sizes are stored as binary integers. This complicates the process of building and parsing the header, since we need to worry about such things as network byte order and whether our host processor can address an integer on an arbitrary byte boundary. A better alternative would have been to design the header to contain text only. This simplifies processing at the cost of slightly larger protocol messages.

IPP is specified in a series of documents (Requests For Comments, or RFCs) available at `http://www.pwg.org/ipp`. The main documents are listed in Figure 21.5, although many other documents are available to further specify administrative procedures, job attributes, and the like.

RFC	Title
2567	Design Goals for an Internet Printing Protocol
2568	Rationale for the Structure of the Model and Protocol for the Internet Printing Protocol
2911	Internet Printing Protocol/1.1: Model and Semantics
2910	Internet Printing Protocol/1.1: Encoding and Transport
3196	Internet Printing Protocol/1.1: Implementor's Guide

Figure 21.5 Primary IPP RFCs

21.3   The Hypertext Transfer Protocol

Version 1.1 of HTTP is specified in RFC 2616. HTTP is also a request–response protocol. A request message contains a start line, followed by header lines, a blank line, and an optional entity body. The entity body contains the IPP header and data in this case.

HTTP headers are ASCII, with each line terminated by a carriage return (\r) and a line feed (\n). The start line consists of a *method* that indicates what operation the client is requesting, a Uniform Resource Locator (URL) that describes the server and protocol, and a string indicating the HTTP version. The only method used by IPP is POST, which is used to send data to a server.

The header lines specify attributes, such as the format and length of the entity body. A header line consists of an attribute name followed by a colon, optional white space, and the attribute value, and is terminated by a carriage return and a line feed. For example, to specify that the entity body contains an IPP message, we include the header line

```
Content-Type: application/ipp
```

The start line in an HTTP response message contains a version string followed by a numeric status code and a status message, terminated by a carriage return and a line feed. The remainder of the HTTP response message has the same format as the request message: headers followed by a blank line and an optional entity body.

The following is a sample HTTP header for a print request for the author's printer:

```
POST /phaser860/ipp HTTP/1.1^M
Content-Length: 21931^M
Content-Type: application/ipp^M
Host: phaser860:ipp^M
^M
```

The ^M at the end of the each line is the carriage return that precedes the line feed. The line feed doesn't show up as a printable character. Note that the last line of the header is empty, except for the carriage return and line feed.

21.4 Printer Spooling

The programs that we develop in this chapter form the basis of a simple printer spooler. A simple user command sends a file to the printer spooler; the spooler saves it to disk, queues the request, and ultimately sends the file to the printer.

All UNIX Systems provide at least one print spooling system. FreeBSD ships LPD, the BSD print spooling system (see lpd(8) and Chapter 13 of Stevens [1990]). Linux and Mac OS X include CUPS, the Common UNIX Printing System (see cupsd(8)). Solaris ships with the standard System V printer spooler (see lp(1) and lpsched(1M)). In this chapter, our interest is not in these spooling systems per se, but in communicating with a network printer. We need to develop a spooling system to solve the problem of multiuser access to a single resource (the printer).

We use a simple command that reads a file and sends it to the printer spooler daemon. The command has one option to force the file to be treated as plaintext (the default assumes that the file is PostScript). We call this command print.

In our printer spooler daemon, printd, we use multiple threads to divide up the work that the daemon needs to accomplish.

- One thread listens on a socket for new print requests arriving from clients running the print command.

- A separate thread is spawned for each client to copy the file to be printed to a spooling area.

- One thread communicates with the printer, sending it queued jobs one at a time.

- One thread handles signals.

Figure 21.6 shows how these components fit together.

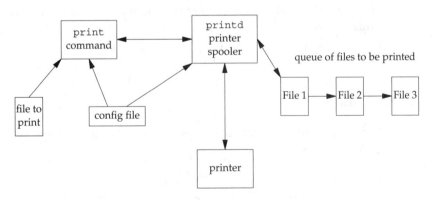

Figure 21.6 Printer spooling components

The print configuration file is /etc/printer.conf. It identifies the host name of the server running the printer spooling daemon and the host name of the network printer. The spooling daemon is identified by a line starting with the printserver keyword, followed by white space and the host name of the server. The printer is identified by a line starting with the `printer` keyword, followed by white space and the host name of the printer.

A sample printer configuration file might contain the following lines:

```
printserver    blade
printer        phaser860
```

where `blade` is the host name of the computer system running the printer spooling daemon, and `phaser860` is the host name of the network printer.

Security

Programs that run with superuser privileges have the potential to open a computer system up to attack. Such programs usually aren't more vulnerable than any other program, but when compromised can lead to attackers obtaining full access to your system.

The printer spooling daemon in this chapter starts out with superuser privileges in this example to be able to bind a socket to a privileged TCP port number. To make the daemon less vulnerable to attack, we can

- Design the daemon to conform to the principles of least privilege (Section 8.11). After we obtain a socket bound to a privileged port address, we can change the user and group IDs of the daemon to something other that `root` (`lp`, for example). All the files and directories used to store queued print jobs should be owned by this nonprivileged user. This way, the daemon, if compromised, will provide the attacker with access only to the printing subsystem. This is still a concern, but it is far less serious than an attacker getting full access to your system.

- Audit the daemon's source code for all known potential vulnerabilities, such as buffer overruns.

- Log unexpected or suspicious behavior so that an administrator can take note and investigate further.

21.5 Source Code

The source code for this chapter comprises five files, not including some of the common library routines we've used in earlier chapters:

`ipp.h`	Header file containing IPP definitions
`print.h`	Header containing common constants, data structure definitions, and utility routine declarations
`util.c`	Utility routines used by the two programs
`print.c`	The C source file for the command used to print a file
`printd.c`	The C source file for the printer spooling daemon

We will study each file in the order listed.

We start with the `ipp.h` header file.

```
 1   #ifndef _IPP_H
 2   #define _IPP_H

 3   /*
 4    * Defines parts of the IPP protocol between the scheduler
 5    * and the printer.  Based on RFC2911 and RFC2910.
 6    */

 7   /*
 8    * Status code classes.
 9    */
10   #define STATCLASS_OK(x)      ((x) >= 0x0000 && (x) <= 0x00ff)
11   #define STATCLASS_INFO(x)    ((x) >= 0x0100 && (x) <= 0x01ff)
12   #define STATCLASS_REDIR(x)   ((x) >= 0x0200 && (x) <= 0x02ff)
13   #define STATCLASS_CLIERR(x)  ((x) >= 0x0400 && (x) <= 0x04ff)
14   #define STATCLASS_SRVERR(x)  ((x) >= 0x0500 && (x) <= 0x05ff)

15   /*
16    * Status codes.
17    */
18   #define STAT_OK           0x0000  /* success */
19   #define STAT_OK_ATTRIGN   0x0001  /* OK; some attrs ignored */
20   #define STAT_OK_ATTRCON   0x0002  /* OK; some attrs conflicted */

21   #define STAT_CLI_BADREQ   0x0400  /* invalid client request */
22   #define STAT_CLI_FORBID   0x0401  /* request is forbidden */
23   #define STAT_CLI_NOAUTH   0x0402  /* authentication required */
24   #define STAT_CLI_NOPERM   0x0403  /* client not authorized */
25   #define STAT_CLI_NOTPOS   0x0404  /* request not possible */
26   #define STAT_CLI_TIMOUT   0x0405  /* client too slow */
27   #define STAT_CLI_NOTFND   0x0406  /* no object found for URI */
28   #define STAT_CLI_OBJGONE  0x0407  /* object no longer available */
29   #define STAT_CLI_TOOBIG   0x0408  /* requested entity too big */
30   #define STAT_CLI_TOOLNG   0x0409  /* attribute value too large */
31   #define STAT_CLI_BADFMT   0x040a  /* unsupported doc format */
32   #define STAT_CLI_NOTSUP   0x040b  /* attributes not supported */
33   #define STAT_CLI_NOSCHM   0x040c  /* URI scheme not supported */
34   #define STAT_CLI_NOCHAR   0x040d  /* charset not supported */
35   #define STAT_CLI_ATTRCON  0x040e  /* attributes conflicted */
36   #define STAT_CLI_NOCOMP   0x040f  /* compression not supported */
37   #define STAT_CLI_COMPERR  0x0410  /* data can't be decompressed */
38   #define STAT_CLI_FMTERR   0x0411  /* document format error */
39   #define STAT_CLI_ACCERR   0x0412  /* error accessing data */
```

[1–14] We start the `ipp.h` header with the standard `#ifdef` to prevent errors when it is included twice in the same file. Then we define the classes of IPP status codes (see Section 13 in RFC 2911).

[15–39] We define specific status codes based on RFC 2911. We don't use these codes in the program shown here; their use is left as an exercise (See Exercise 21.1).

```
40    #define STAT_SRV_INTERN    0x0500   /* unexpected internal error */
41    #define STAT_SRV_NOTSUP    0x0501   /* operation not supported */
42    #define STAT_SRV_UNAVAIL   0x0502   /* service unavailable */
43    #define STAT_SRV_BADVER    0x0503   /* version not supported */
44    #define STAT_SRV_DEVERR    0x0504   /* device error */
45    #define STAT_SRV_TMPERR    0x0505   /* temporary error */
46    #define STAT_SRV_REJECT    0x0506   /* server not accepting jobs */
47    #define STAT_SRV_TOOBUSY   0x0507   /* server too busy */
48    #define STAT_SRV_CANCEL    0x0508   /* job has been canceled */
49    #define STAT_SRV_NOMULTI   0x0509   /* multi-doc jobs unsupported */

50    /*
51     * Operation IDs
52     */
53    #define OP_PRINT_JOB         0x02
54    #define OP_PRINT_URI         0x03
55    #define OP_VALIDATE_JOB      0x04
56    #define OP_CREATE_JOB        0x05
57    #define OP_SEND_DOC          0x06
58    #define OP_SEND_URI          0x07
59    #define OP_CANCEL_JOB        0x08
60    #define OP_GET_JOB_ATTR      0x09
61    #define OP_GET_JOBS          0x0a
62    #define OP_GET_PRINTER_ATTR  0x0b
63    #define OP_HOLD_JOB          0x0c
64    #define OP_RELEASE_JOB       0x0d
65    #define OP_RESTART_JOB       0x0e
66    #define OP_PAUSE_PRINTER     0x10
67    #define OP_RESUME_PRINTER    0x11
68    #define OP_PURGE_JOBS        0x12

69    /*
70     * Attribute Tags.
71     */
72    #define TAG_OPERATION_ATTR   0x01   /* operation attributes tag */
73    #define TAG_JOB_ATTR         0x02   /* job attributes tag */
74    #define TAG_END_OF_ATTR      0x03   /* end of attributes tag */
75    #define TAG_PRINTER_ATTR     0x04   /* printer attributes tag */
76    #define TAG_UNSUPP_ATTR      0x05   /* unsupported attributes tag */
```

[40–49] We continue to define status codes. The ones in the range 0x500 to 0x5ff are server error codes. All codes are described in Sections 13.1.1 through 13.1.5 in RFC 2911.

[50–68] We define the various operation IDs next. There is one ID for each task defined by IPP (see Section 4.4.15 in RFC 2911). In our example, we will use only the print-job operation.

[69–76] The attribute tags delimit the attribute groups in the IPP request and response messages. The tag values are defined in Section 3.5.1 of RFC 2910.

```
 77     /*
 78      * Value Tags.
 79      */
 80     #define TAG_UNSUPPORTED        0x10 /* unsupported value */
 81     #define TAG_UNKNOWN            0x12 /* unknown value */
 82     #define TAG_NONE               0x13 /* no value */
 83     #define TAG_INTEGER            0x21 /* integer */
 84     #define TAG_BOOLEAN            0x22 /* boolean */
 85     #define TAG_ENUM               0x23 /* enumeration */
 86     #define TAG_OCTSTR             0x30 /* octetString */
 87     #define TAG_DATETIME           0x31 /* dateTime */
 88     #define TAG_RESOLUTION         0x32 /* resolution */
 89     #define TAG_INTRANGE           0x33 /* rangeOfInteger */
 90     #define TAG_TEXTWLANG          0x35 /* textWithLanguage */
 91     #define TAG_NAMEWLANG          0x36 /* nameWithLanguage */
 92     #define TAG_TEXTWOLANG         0x41 /* textWithoutLanguage */
 93     #define TAG_NAMEWOLANG         0x42 /* nameWithoutLanguage */
 94     #define TAG_KEYWORD            0x44 /* keyword */
 95     #define TAG_URI                0x45 /* URI */
 96     #define TAG_URISCHEME          0x46 /* uriScheme */
 97     #define TAG_CHARSET            0x47 /* charset */
 98     #define TAG_NATULANG           0x48 /* naturalLanguage */
 99     #define TAG_MIMETYPE           0x49 /* mimeMediaType */

100     struct ipp_hdr {
101       int8_t  major_version;  /* always 1 */
102       int8_t  minor_version;  /* always 1 */
103       union {
104           int16_t op; /* operation ID */
105           int16_t st; /* status */
106       } u;
107       int32_t request_id;       /* request ID */
108       char    attr_group[1];  /* start of optional attributes group */
109       /* optional data follows */
110     };

111     #define operation u.op
112     #define status u.st

113     #endif /* _IPP_H */
```

[77–99]   The value tags indicate the format of individual attributes and parameters. They are defined in Section 3.5.2 of RFC 2910.

[100–113] We define the structure of an IPP header. Request messages start with the same header as response messages, except that the operation ID in the request is replaced by a status code in the response.

We end the header file with a #endif to match the #ifdef at the start of the file.

The next file is the `print.h` header.

```
 1   #ifndef _PRINT_H
 2   #define _PRINT_H
 3   /*
 4    * Print server header file.
 5    */
 6   #include <sys/socket.h>
 7   #include <arpa/inet.h>
 8   #if defined(BSD) || defined(MACOS)
 9   #include <netinet/in.h>
10   #endif
11   #include <netdb.h>
12   #include <errno.h>

13   #define CONFIG_FILE      "/etc/printer.conf"
14   #define SPOOLDIR         "/var/spool/printer"
15   #define JOBFILE          "jobno"
16   #define DATADIR          "data"
17   #define REQDIR           "reqs"

18   #define FILENMSZ         64
19   #define FILEPERM         (S_IRUSR|S_IWUSR)
20   #define USERNM_MAX       64
21   #define JOBNM_MAX        256
22   #define MSGLEN_MAX       512

23   #ifndef HOST_NAME_MAX
24   #define HOST_NAME_MAX    256
25   #endif

26   #define IPP_PORT         631
27   #define QLEN             10
28   #define IBUFSZ           512     /* IPP header buffer size */
29   #define HBUFSZ           512     /* HTTP header buffer size */
30   #define IOBUFSZ          8192    /* data buffer size */
```

[1–12]   We include all header files that an application might need if it included this header. This makes it easy for applications to include `print.h` without having to track down all the header dependencies.

[13–17]   We define the files and directories for the implementation. Copies of the files to be printed will be stored in the directory `/var/spool/printer/data`; control information for each request will be stored in the directory `/var/spool/printer/reqs`. The file containing the next job number is `/var/spool/printer/jobno`.

[18–30]   Next, we define limits and constants. `FILEPERM` is the permissions used when creating copies of files submitted to be printed. The permissions are restrictive because we don't want ordinary users to be able to read one another's files while they are waiting to be printed. IPP is defined to use port 631. The `QLEN` is the backlog parameter we pass to `listen` (see Section 16.4 for details).

```
31   #ifndef ETIME
32   #define ETIME ETIMEDOUT
33   #endif

34   extern int getaddrlist(const char *, const char *,
35     struct addrinfo **);
36   extern char *get_printserver(void);
37   extern struct addrinfo *get_printaddr(void);
38   extern ssize_t tread(int, void *, size_t, unsigned int);
39   extern ssize_t treadn(int, void *, size_t, unsigned int);
40   extern int connect_retry(int, const struct sockaddr *, socklen_t);
41   extern int initserver(int, struct sockaddr *, socklen_t, int);

42   /*
43    * Structure describing a print request.
44    */
45   struct printreq {
46     long size;                    /* size in bytes */
47     long flags;                   /* see below */
48     char usernm[USERNM_MAX];      /* user's name */
49     char jobnm[JOBNM_MAX];        /* job's name */
50   };

51   /*
52    * Request flags.
53    */
54   #define PR_TEXT         0x01    /* treat file as plain text */

55   /*
56    * The response from the spooling daemon to the print command.
57    */
58   struct printresp {
59     long retcode;                 /* 0=success, !0=error code */
60     long jobid;                   /* job ID */
61     char msg[MSGLEN_MAX];         /* error message */
62   };

63   #endif /* _PRINT_H */
```

[31–33] Some platforms don't define the error ETIME, so we define it to an alternate error code that makes sense for these systems.

[34–41] Next, we declare all the public routines contained in util.c (we'll look at these next). Note that the connect_retry function, from Figure 16.9, and the initserver function, from Figure 16.20, are not included in util.c.

[42–63] The printreq and printresp structures define the protocol between the print command and the printer spooling daemon. The print command sends the printreq structure defining the user name, job name, and file size to the printer spooling daemon. The spooling daemon responds with a printresp structure consisting of a return code, a job ID, and an error message if the request failed.

The next file we will look at is `util.c`, the file containing utility routines.

```
 1    #include "apue.h"
 2    #include "print.h"
 3    #include <ctype.h>
 4    #include <sys/select.h>

 5    #define MAXCFGLINE  512
 6    #define MAXKWLEN     16
 7    #define MAXFMTLEN    16

 8    /*
 9     * Get the address list for the given host and service and
10     * return through ailistpp.  Returns 0 on success or an error
11     * code on failure.  Note that we do not set errno if we
12     * encounter an error.
13     *
14     * LOCKING: none.
15     */
16    int
17    getaddrlist(const char *host, const char *service,
18      struct addrinfo **ailistpp)
19    {
20        int              err;
21        struct addrinfo hint;

22        hint.ai_flags = AI_CANONNAME;
23        hint.ai_family = AF_INET;
24        hint.ai_socktype = SOCK_STREAM;
25        hint.ai_protocol = 0;
26        hint.ai_addrlen = 0;
27        hint.ai_canonname = NULL;
28        hint.ai_addr = NULL;
29        hint.ai_next = NULL;
30        err = getaddrinfo(host, service, &hint, ailistpp);
31        return(err);
32    }
```

[1–7]   We first define the limits needed by the functions in this file. `MAXCFGLINE` is the maximum size of a line in the printer configuration file, `MAXKWLEN` is the maximum size of a keyword in the configuration file, and `MAXFMTLEN` is the maximum size of the format string we pass to `sscanf`.

[8–32]   The first function is `getaddrlist`. It is a wrapper for `getaddrinfo` (Section 16.3.3), since we always call `getaddrinfo` with the same hint structure. Note that we need no mutex locking in this function. The `LOCKING` comment at the beginning of each function is intended only for documenting multithreaded locking. This comment lists the assumptions, if any, that are made regarding the locking, tells which locks the function might acquire or release, and tells which locks must be held to call the function.

```
33    /*
34     * Given a keyword, scan the configuration file for a match
35     * and return the string value corresponding to the keyword.
36     *
37     * LOCKING: none.
38     */
39    static char *
40    scan_configfile(char *keyword)
41    {
42        int            n, match;
43        FILE           *fp;
44        char           keybuf[MAXKWLEN], pattern[MAXFMTLEN];
45        char           line[MAXCFGLINE];
46        static char    valbuf[MAXCFGLINE];

47        if ((fp = fopen(CONFIG_FILE, "r")) == NULL)
48            log_sys("can't open %s", CONFIG_FILE);
49        sprintf(pattern, "%%%ds %%%ds", MAXKWLEN-1, MAXCFGLINE-1);
50        match = 0;
51        while (fgets(line, MAXCFGLINE, fp) != NULL) {
52            n = sscanf(line, pattern, keybuf, valbuf);
53            if (n == 2 && strcmp(keyword, keybuf) == 0) {
54                match = 1;
55                break;
56            }
57        }
58        fclose(fp);
59        if (match != 0)
60            return(valbuf);
61        else
62            return(NULL);
63    }
```

[33–46] The scan_configfile function searches through the printer configuration file for the specified keyword.

[47–63] We open the configuration file for reading and build the format string corresponding to the search pattern. The notation %%%ds builds a format specifier that limits the string size so we don't overrun the buffers used to store the strings on the stack. We read the file one line at a time and scan for two strings separated by white space; if we find them, we compare the first string with the keyword. If we find a match or we reach the end of the file, the loop ends and we close the file. If the keyword matches, we return a pointer to the buffer containing the string after the keyword; otherwise, we return NULL.

The string returned is stored in a static buffer (valbuf), which can be overwritten on successive calls. Thus, scan_configfile can't be called by a multithreaded application unless we take care to avoid calling it from multiple threads at the same time.

```
64    /*
65     * Return the host name running the print server or NULL on error.
66     *
67     * LOCKING: none.
68     */
69    char *
70    get_printserver(void)
71    {
72        return(scan_configfile("printserver"));
73    }

74    /*
75     * Return the address of the network printer or NULL on error.
76     *
77     * LOCKING: none.
78     */
79    struct addrinfo *
80    get_printaddr(void)
81    {
82        int             err;
83        char            *p;
84        struct addrinfo *ailist;

85        if ((p = scan_configfile("printer")) != NULL) {
86            if ((err = getaddrlist(p, "ipp", &ailist)) != 0) {
87                log_msg("no address information for %s", p);
88                return(NULL);
89            }
90            return(ailist);
91        }
92        log_msg("no printer address specified");
93        return(NULL);
94    }
```

[64–73] The get_printserver function is simply a wrapper function that calls scan_configfile to find the name of the computer system where the printer spooling daemon is running.

[74–94] We use the get_printaddr function to get the address of the network printer. It is similar to the previous function except that when we find the name of the printer in the configuration file, we use the name to find the corresponding network address.

Both get_printserver and get_printaddr call scan_configfile. If it can't open the printer configuration file, scan_configfile calls log_sys to print an error message and exit. Although get_printserver is meant to be called from a client command and get_printaddr is meant to be called from the daemon, having both call log_sys is OK, because we can arrange for the log functions to print to the standard error instead of to the log file by setting a global variable.

```
 95    /*
 96     * "Timed" read - timout specifies the # of seconds to wait before
 97     * giving up (5th argument to select controls how long to wait for
 98     * data to be readable).  Returns # of bytes read or -1 on error.
 99     *
100     * LOCKING: none.
101     */
102    ssize_t
103    tread(int fd, void *buf, size_t nbytes, unsigned int timout)
104    {
105        int             nfds;
106        fd_set          readfds;
107        struct timeval  tv;

108        tv.tv_sec = timout;
109        tv.tv_usec = 0;
110        FD_ZERO(&readfds);
111        FD_SET(fd, &readfds);
112        nfds = select(fd+1, &readfds, NULL, NULL, &tv);
113        if (nfds <= 0) {
114            if (nfds == 0)
115                errno = ETIME;
116            return(-1);
117        }
118        return(read(fd, buf, nbytes));
119    }
```

[95–107]   We provide a function called tread to read a specified number of bytes, but
           block for at most *timout* seconds before giving up. This function is useful
           when reading from a socket or a pipe. If we don't receive data before the
           specified time limit, we return –1 with errno set to ETIME. If data is
           available within the time limit, we return at most *nbytes* bytes of data, but we
           can return less than requested if all the data doesn't arrive in time.

           We will use tread to prevent denial-of-service attacks on the printer
           spooling daemon. A malicious user might repeatedly try to connect to the
           daemon without sending it data, just to prevent other users from being able
           to submit print jobs. By giving up after a reasonable amount of time, we
           prevent this from happening. The tricky part is selecting a suitable timeout
           value that is large enough to prevent premature failures when the system is
           under load and tasks are taking longer to complete. If we choose a value too
           large, however, we might enable denial-of-service attacks by allowing the
           daemon to consume too many resources to process the pending requests.

[108–119] We use select to wait for the specified file descriptor to be readable. If the
           time limit expires before data is available to be read, select returns 0, so
           we set errno to ETIME in this case. If select fails or times out, we return
           –1. Otherwise, we return whatever data is available.

```
120    /*
121     * "Timed" read - timout specifies the number of seconds to wait
122     * per read call before giving up, but read exactly nbytes bytes.
123     * Returns number of bytes read or -1 on error.
124     *
125     * LOCKING: none.
126     */
127    ssize_t
128    treadn(int fd, void *buf, size_t nbytes, unsigned int timout)
129    {
130      size_t   nleft;
131      ssize_t  nread;
132
133      nleft = nbytes;
134      while (nleft > 0) {
135          if ((nread = tread(fd, buf, nleft, timout)) < 0) {
136              if (nleft == nbytes)
137                  return(-1); /* error, return -1 */
138              else
139                  break;       /* error, return amount read so far */
140          } else if (nread == 0) {
141              break;           /* EOF */
142          }
143          nleft -= nread;
144          buf += nread;
145      }
146      return(nbytes - nleft);       /* return >= 0 */
147    }
```

[120–146] We also provide a variation of tread, called treadn, that reads exactly the number of bytes requested. This is similar to the readn function described in Section 14.8, but with the addition of the timeout parameter.

To read exactly *nbytes* bytes, we have to be prepared to make multiple calls to read. The difficult part is trying to apply a single timeout value to multiple calls to read. We don't want to use an alarm, because signals can be messy to deal with in multithreaded applications. We can't rely on the system updating the timeval structure on return from select to indicate the amount of time left, because many platforms do not support this (Section 14.5.1). Thus, we compromise and define the timeout value in this case to apply to an individual read call. Instead of limiting the total amount of time we wait, it limits the amount of time we'll wait in every iteration of the loop. The maximum time we can wait is bounded by (*nbytes* × *timout*) seconds (worst case, we'll receive only 1 byte at a time).

We use nleft to record the number of bytes remaining to be read. If tread fails and we have received data in a previous iteration, we break out of the while loop and return the number of bytes read; otherwise, we return −1.

The command used to submit a print job is shown next. The C source file is `print.c`.

```
1    /*
2     * The client command for printing documents.  Opens the file
3     * and sends it to the printer spooling daemon.  Usage:
4     *      print [-t] filename
5     */
6    #include "apue.h"
7    #include "print.h"
8    #include <fcntl.h>
9    #include <pwd.h>

10   /*
11    * Needed for logging funtions.
12    */
13   int log_to_stderr = 1;

14   void submit_file(int, int, const char *, size_t, int);

15   int
16   main(int argc, char *argv[])
17   {
18       int            fd, sockfd, err, text, c;
19       struct stat    sbuf;
20       char           *host;
21       struct addrinfo *ailist, *aip;

22       err = 0;
23       text = 0;
24       while ((c = getopt(argc, argv, "t")) != -1) {
25           switch (c) {
26           case 't':
27               text = 1;
28               break;

29           case '?':
30               err = 1;
31               break;
32           }
33       }
```

[1–14]   We need to define an integer called `log_to_stderr` to be able to use the log functions in our library. If set to a nonzero value, error messages will be sent to the standard error stream instead of to a log file. Although we don't use any logging functions in `print.c`, we do link `util.o` with `print.o` to build the executable `print` command, and `util.c` contains functions for both user commands and daemons.

[15–33] We support one option, `-t`, to force the file to be printed as text (instead of as a PostScript program, for example). We use the `getopt`(3) function to process the command options.

```
34        if (err || (optind != argc - 1))
35            err_quit("usage: print [-t] filename");
36        if ((fd = open(argv[optind], O_RDONLY)) < 0)
37            err_sys("print: can't open %s", argv[1]);
38        if (fstat(fd, &sbuf) < 0)
39            err_sys("print: can't stat %s", argv[1]);
40        if (!S_ISREG(sbuf.st_mode))
41            err_quit("print: %s must be a regular file\n", argv[1]);

42        /*
43         * Get the hostname of the host acting as the print server.
44         */
45        if ((host = get_printserver()) == NULL)
46            err_quit("print: no print server defined");
47        if ((err = getaddrlist(host, "print", &ailist)) != 0)
48            err_quit("print: getaddrinfo error: %s", gai_strerror(err));

49        for (aip = ailist; aip != NULL; aip = aip->ai_next) {
50            if ((sockfd = socket(AF_INET, SOCK_STREAM, 0)) < 0) {
51                err = errno;
52            } else if (connect_retry(sockfd, aip->ai_addr,
53              aip->ai_addrlen) < 0) {
54                err = errno;
```

[34–41] When `getopt` completes processing the command options, it leaves the variable `optind` set to the index of the first nonoptional argument. If this is any value other than the index of the last argument, then the wrong number of arguments was specified (we support only one nonoptional argument). Our error processing includes checks to ensure that we can open the file to be printed and that it is a regular file (as opposed to a directory or other type of file).

[42–48] We get the name of the printer spooling daemon by calling the `get_printserver` function from `util.c` and then translate the host name into a network address by calling `getaddrlist` (also from `util.c`).

Note that we specify the service as "print." As part of installing the printer spooling daemon on a system, we need to make sure that `/etc/services` (or the equivalent database) has an entry for the printer service. When we select a port number for the daemon, it would be a good idea to select one that is privileged, to prevent malicious users from writing applications that pretend to be a printer spooling daemon but instead steal copies of the files we try to print. This means that the port number should be less than 1,024 (recall Section 16.3.4) and that our daemon will have to run with superuser privileges to allow it to bind to a reserved port.

[49–54] We try to connect to the daemon using one address at a time from the list returned by `getaddrinfo`. We will try to send the file to the daemon using the first address to which we can connect.

```
55                } else {
56                     submit_file(fd, sockfd, argv[1], sbuf.st_size, text);
57                     exit(0);
58                }
59            }
60        errno = err;
61        err_ret("print: can't contact %s", host);
62        exit(1);
63    }
64    /*
65     * Send a file to the printer daemon.
66     */
67    void
68    submit_file(int fd, int sockfd, const char *fname, size_t nbytes,
69                    int text)
70    {
71        int                nr, nw, len;
72        struct passwd      *pwd;
73        struct printreq    req;
74        struct printresp   res;
75        char               buf[IOBUFSZ];
76        /*
77         * First build the header.
78         */
79        if ((pwd = getpwuid(geteuid())) == NULL)
80            strcpy(req.usernm, "unknown");
81        else
82            strcpy(req.usernm, pwd->pw_name);
83        req.size = htonl(nbytes);
84        if (text)
85            req.flags = htonl(PR_TEXT);
86        else
87            req.flags = 0;
```

[55–63] If we can make a connection, we call submit_file to transmit the file to the printer spooling daemon. If we can't connect to any of the addresses, we print an error message and exit. We use err_ret and exit instead of making a single call to err_sys to avoid a compiler warning, because the last line in main wouldn't be a return statement or a call to exit.

[64–87] submit_file sends a print request to the daemon and reads the response. First, we build the printreq request header. We use geteuid to get the caller's effective user ID and pass this to getpwuid to look for the user in the system's password file. We copy the user's name to the request header or use the string unknown if we can't identify the user. We store the size of the file to be printed in the header after converting it to network byte order. Then we do the same with the PR_TEXT flag if the file is to be printed as plaintext.

```
 88        if ((len = strlen(fname)) >= JOBNM_MAX) {
 89            /*
 90             * Truncate the filename (+-5 accounts for the leading
 91             * four characters and the terminating null).
 92             */
 93            strcpy(req.jobnm, "... ");
 94            strncat(req.jobnm, &fname[len-JOBNM_MAX+5], JOBNM_MAX-5);
 95        } else {
 96            strcpy(req.jobnm, fname);
 97        }
 98        /*
 99         * Send the header to the server.
100         */
101        nw = writen(sockfd, &req, sizeof(struct printreq));
102        if (nw != sizeof(struct printreq)) {
103            if (nw < 0)
104                err_sys("can't write to print server");
105            else
106                err_quit("short write (%d/%d) to print server",
107                    nw, sizeof(struct printreq));
108        }
109        /*
110         * Now send the file.
111         */
112        while ((nr = read(fd, buf, IOBUFSZ)) != 0) {
113            nw = writen(sockfd, buf, nr);
114            if (nw != nr) {
115                if (nw < 0)
116                    err_sys("can't write to print server");
117                else
118                    err_quit("short write (%d/%d) to print server",
119                        nw, nr);
120            }
121        }
```

[88–108]   We set the job name to the name of the file being printed. If the name is longer than will fit in the message, we truncate the beginning portion of the name and prepend an ellipsis to indicate that there were more characters than would fit in the field. Then we send the request header to the daemon using writen. If the write fails or if we transmit less than we expect, we print an error message and exit.

[109–121]   After sending the header to the daemon, we send the file to be printed. We read the file IOBUFSZ bytes at a time and use writen to send the data to the daemon. As with the header, if the write fails or we write less than we expect, we print an error message and exit.

```
122        /*
123         * Read the response.
124         */
125        if ((nr = readn(sockfd, &res, sizeof(struct printresp))) !=
126          sizeof(struct printresp))
127            err_sys("can't read response from server");
128        if (res.retcode != 0) {
129            printf("rejected: %s\n", res.msg);
130            exit(1);
131        } else {
132            printf("job ID %ld\n", ntohl(res.jobid));
133        }
134        exit(0);
135    }
```

[122–135] After we send the file to be printed to the daemon, we read the daemon's response. If the request failed, the return code (retcode) will be nonzero, so we print the textual error message included in the response. If the request succeeded, we print the job ID so that the user knows how to refer to the request in the future. (Writing a command to cancel the print request is left as an exercise; the job ID can be used in the cancellation request to identify the job to be removed from the print queue.)

Note that a successful response from the daemon does not mean that the printer was able to print the file. It merely means that the daemon successfully added the print job to the queue.

Most of what we have seen in print.c was discussed in earlier chapters. The only topic that we haven't covered is the getopt function, although we saw it earlier in the pty program from Chapter 19.

It is important that all commands on a system follow the same conventions, because this makes them easier to use. If someone is familiar with the way command-line options are formed with one command, it would create more chances for mistakes if another command followed different conventions.

This problem is sometimes visible when dealing with white space on the command line. Some commands require that an option be separated from its argument by white space, but other commands require the argument to follow immediate after its option, without any intervening spaces. Without a consistent set of rules to follow, users either have to memorize the syntax of all commands or resort to a trial-and-error process when invoking them.

The Single UNIX Specification includes a set of conventions and guidelines that promote consistent command-line syntax. They include such suggestions as "Restrict each command-line option to a single alphanumeric character" and "All options should be preceded by a – character."

Luckily, the getopt function exists to help command developers process command-line options in a consistent manner.

```
#include <fcntl.h>

int getopt(int argc, const * const argv[], const char *options);

extern int optind, opterr, optopt;
extern char *optarg;
```

Returns: the next option character, or
−1 when all options have been processed

The *argc* and *argv* arguments are the same ones passed to the main function of the program. The *options* argument is a string containing the option characters supported by the command. If an option character is followed by a colon, then the option takes an argument. Otherwise, the option exists by itself. For example, if the usage statement for a command was

```
command [-i] [-u username] [-z] filename
```

we would pass "iu:z" as the *options* string to getopt.

The normal use of getopt is in a loop that terminates when getopt returns −1. During each iteration of the loop, getopt will return the next option processed. It is up to the application to sort out any conflict in options, however; getopt simply parses the options and enforces a standard format.

When it encounters an invalid option, getopt returns a question mark instead of the character. If an option's argument is missing, getopt will also return a question mark, but if the first character in the options string is a colon, getopt returns a colon instead. The special pattern -- will cause getopt to stop processing options and return −1. This allows users to provide command arguments that start with a minus sign but aren't options. For example, if you have a file named -bar, you can't remove it by typing

```
rm -bar
```

because rm will try to interpret -bar as options. The way to remove the file is to type

```
rm -- -bar
```

The getopt function supports four external variables.

optarg   If an option takes an argument, getopt sets optarg to point to the option's argument string when an option is processed.

opterr   If an option error is encountered, getopt will print an error message by default. To disable this behavior, applications can set opterr to 0.

optind   The index in the argv array of the next string to be processed. It starts out at 1 and is incremented for each argument processed by getopt.

optopt   If an error is encountered during options processing, getopt will set optopt to point to the option string that caused the error.

The last file we will look at is the C source file for the printer spooling daemon.

```
 1    /*
 2     * Print server daemon.
 3     */
 4    #include "apue.h"
 5    #include "print.h"
 6    #include "ipp.h"
 7    #include <fcntl.h>
 8    #include <dirent.h>
 9    #include <ctype.h>
10    #include <pwd.h>
11    #include <pthread.h>
12    #include <strings.h>
13    #include <sys/select.h>
14    #include <sys/uio.h>

15    /*
16     * These are for the HTTP response from the printer.
17     */
18    #define HTTP_INFO(x)    ((x) >= 100 && (x) <= 199)
19    #define HTTP_SUCCESS(x) ((x) >= 200 && (x) <= 299)

20    /*
21     * Describes a print job.
22     */
23    struct job {
24        struct job        *next;       /* next in list */
25        struct job        *prev;       /* previous in list */
26        long              jobid;       /* job ID */
27        struct printreq   req;         /* copy of print request */
28    };

29    /*
30     * Describes a thread processing a client request.
31     */
32    struct worker_thread {
33        struct worker_thread  *next;    /* next in list */
34        struct worker_thread  *prev;    /* previous in list */
35        pthread_t             tid;      /* thread ID */
36        int                   sockfd;   /* socket */
37    };
```

[1–19] The printer spooling daemon includes the IPP header file that we saw earlier, because the daemon needs to communicate with the printer using this protocol. The HTTP_INFO and HTTP_SUCCESS macros define the status of the HTTP request (recall that IPP is built on top of HTTP).

[20–37] The job and worker_thread structures are used by the spooling daemon to keep track of print jobs and threads accepting print requests, respectively.

```
38    /*
39     * Needed for logging.
40     */
41    int                     log_to_stderr = 0;

42    /*
43     * Printer-related stuff.
44     */
45    struct addrinfo         *printer;
46    char                    *printer_name;
47    pthread_mutex_t         configlock = PTHREAD_MUTEX_INITIALIZER;
48    int                     reread;

49    /*
50     * Thread-related stuff.
51     */
52    struct worker_thread    *workers;
53    pthread_mutex_t         workerlock = PTHREAD_MUTEX_INITIALIZER;
54    sigset_t                mask;

55    /*
56     * Job-related stuff.
57     */
58    struct job              *jobhead, *jobtail;
59    int                     jobfd;
```

[38–41] Our logging functions require that we define the log_to_stderr variable
and set it to 0 to force log messages to be sent to the system log instead of to
the standard error. In print.c, we defined log_to_stderr and set it to 1,
even though we don't use the log functions in the user command. We could
have avoided this by splitting the utility functions into two separate files: one
for the server and one for the client commands.

[42–48] We use the global variable printer to hold the network address of the printer.
We store the host name of the printer in printer_name. The configlock
mutex protects access to the reread variable, which is used to indicate that
the daemon needs to reread the configuration file, presumably because an
administrator changed the printer or its network address.

[49–54] Next, we define the thread-related variables. We use workers as the head of a
doubly-linked list of threads that are receiving files from clients. This list is
protected by the mutex workerlock. The signal mask used by the threads is
held in the variable mask.

[55–59] For the list of pending jobs, we define jobhead to be the start of the list and
jobtail to be the tail of the list. This list is also doubly linked, but we need
to add jobs to the end of the list, so we need to remember a pointer to the list
tail. With the list of worker threads, the order doesn't matter, so we can add
them to the head of the list and don't need to remember the tail pointer.
jobfd is the file descriptor for the job file.

```
60    long                     nextjob;
61    pthread_mutex_t          joblock = PTHREAD_MUTEX_INITIALIZER;
62    pthread_cond_t           jobwait = PTHREAD_COND_INITIALIZER;
63    /*
64     * Function prototypes.
65     */
66    void       init_request(void);
67    void       init_printer(void);
68    void       update_jobno(void);
69    long       get_newjobno(void);
70    void       add_job(struct printreq *, long);
71    void       replace_job(struct job *);
72    void       remove_job(struct job *);
73    void       build_qonstart(void);
74    void       *client_thread(void *);
75    void       *printer_thread(void *);
76    void       *signal_thread(void *);
77    ssize_t    readmore(int, char **, int, int *);
78    int        printer_status(int, struct job *);
79    void       add_worker(pthread_t, int);
80    void       kill_workers(void);
81    void       client_cleanup(void *);
82    /*
83     * Main print server thread.  Accepts connect requests from
84     * clients and spawns additional threads to service requests.
85     *
86     * LOCKING: none.
87     */
88    int
89    main(int argc, char *argv[])
90    {
91        pthread_t            tid;
92        struct addrinfo      *ailist, *aip;
93        int                  sockfd, err, i, n, maxfd;
94        char                 *host;
95        fd_set               rendezvous, rset;
96        struct sigaction     sa;
97        struct passwd        *pwdp;
```

[60–62] nextjob is the ID of the next print job to be received. The joblock mutex protects the linked list of jobs, as well as the condition represented by the jobwait condition variable.

[63–81] We declare the function prototypes for the remaining functions in this file. Doing this up front allows us to place the functions in the file without worrying about the order in which each is called.

[82–97] The main function for the printer spooling daemon has two tasks to perform: initialize the daemon and then process connect requests from clients.

```
98      if (argc != 1)
99          err_quit("usage: printd");
100     daemonize("printd");

101     sigemptyset(&sa.sa_mask);
102     sa.sa_flags = 0;
103     sa.sa_handler = SIG_IGN;
104     if (sigaction(SIGPIPE, &sa, NULL) < 0)
105         log_sys("sigaction failed");
106     sigemptyset(&mask);
107     sigaddset(&mask, SIGHUP);
108     sigaddset(&mask, SIGTERM);
109     if ((err = pthread_sigmask(SIG_BLOCK, &mask, NULL)) != 0)
110         log_sys("pthread_sigmask failed");
111     init_request();
112     init_printer();

113  #ifdef _SC_HOST_NAME_MAX
114     n = sysconf(_SC_HOST_NAME_MAX);
115     if (n < 0)   /* best guess */
116  #endif
117         n = HOST_NAME_MAX;

118     if ((host = malloc(n)) == NULL)
119         log_sys("malloc error");
120     if (gethostname(host, n) < 0)
121         log_sys("gethostname error");
```

[98–100]   The daemon doesn't have any options, so if argc is not 1, we call err_quit to print an error message and exit. We call the daemonize function from Figure 13.1 to become a daemon. After this point, we can't print error messages to standard error; we need to log them instead.

[101–112]   We arrange to ignore SIGPIPE. We will be writing to socket file descriptors, and we don't want a write error to trigger SIGPIPE, because the default action is to kill the process. Next, we set the signal mask of the thread to include SIGHUP and SIGTERM. All threads we create will inherit this signal mask. We'll use SIGHUP to tell the daemon to reread the configuration file and SIGTERM to tell the daemon to clean up and exit gracefully. We call init_request to initialize the job requests and ensure that only one copy of the daemon is running, and we call init_printer to initialize the printer information (we'll see both of these functions shortly).

[113–121]   If the platform defines the _SC_HOST_NAME_MAX symbol, we call sysconf to get the maximum size of a host name. If sysconf fails or the limit is undefined, we use HOST_NAME_MAX as a best guess. Sometimes, this is defined for us by the platform, but if it isn't, we chose our own value in print.h. We allocate memory to hold the host name and call gethostname to retrieve it.

```
122         if ((err = getaddrlist(host, "print", &ailist)) != 0) {
123             log_quit("getaddrinfo error: %s", gai_strerror(err));
124             exit(1);
125         }
126         FD_ZERO(&rendezvous);
127         maxfd = -1;
128         for (aip = ailist; aip != NULL; aip = aip->ai_next) {
129             if ((sockfd = initserver(SOCK_STREAM, aip->ai_addr,
130               aip->ai_addrlen, QLEN)) >= 0) {
131                 FD_SET(sockfd, &rendezvous);
132                 if (sockfd > maxfd)
133                     maxfd = sockfd;
134             }
135         }
136         if (maxfd == -1)
137             log_quit("service not enabled");

138         pwdp = getpwnam("lp");
139         if (pwdp == NULL)
140             log_sys("can't find user lp");
141         if (pwdp->pw_uid == 0)
142             log_quit("user lp is privileged");
143         if (setuid(pwdp->pw_uid) < 0)
144             log_sys("can't change IDs to user lp");
```

[122–135] Next, we try to find the network address that the daemon is supposed to use
to provide printer spooling service. We clear the rendezvous fd_set
variable that we will use with select to wait for client connect requests.
We initialize the maximum file descriptor to –1 so that the first file descriptor
we allocate is sure to be greater than maxfd. For each network address on
which we need to provide service, we call initserver (from Figure 16.20)
to allocate and initialize a socket. If initserver succeeds, we add the file
descriptor to the fd_set; if it is greater than the maximum, we set maxfd
equal to the socket file descriptor.

[136–137] If maxfd is still –1 after stepping through the list of addrinfo structures,
we can't enable the printer spooling service, so we log a message and exit.

[138–144] Our daemon needs superuser privileges to bind a socket to a reserved port
number. Now that this is done, we can lower its privileges by changing its
user ID to the one associated with user lp (recall the security discussion in
Section 21.4). We want to follow the principles of least privilege to avoid
exposing the system to any potential vulnerabilities in the daemon. We call
getpwnam to find the password entry associated with user lp. If no such
user account exists, or if it exists with the same user ID as the superuser, we
log a message and exit. Otherwise, we call setuid to change both the real
and effective user IDs to the user ID for lp. To avoid exposing our system,
we choose to provide no service at all if we can't reduce our privileges.

```
145        pthread_create(&tid, NULL, printer_thread, NULL);
146        pthread_create(&tid, NULL, signal_thread, NULL);
147        build_qonstart();

148        log_msg("daemon initialized");

149        for (;;) {
150            rset = rendezvous;
151            if (select(maxfd+1, &rset, NULL, NULL, NULL) < 0)
152                log_sys("select failed");
153            for (i = 0; i <= maxfd; i++) {
154                if (FD_ISSET(i, &rset)) {

155                    /*
156                     * Accept the connection and handle
157                     * the request.
158                     */
159                    sockfd = accept(i, NULL, NULL);
160                    if (sockfd < 0)
161                        log_ret("accept failed");
162                    pthread_create(&tid, NULL, client_thread,
163                        (void *)sockfd);
164                }
165            }
166        }
167        exit(1);
168    }
```

[145–148] We call `pthread_create` twice to create one thread to handle signals and one thread to communicate with the printer. (By restricting printer communication to one thread, we can simplify the locking of the printer-related data structures.) Then we call `build_qonstart` to search the directories in `/var/spool/printer` for any pending jobs. For each job that we find on disk, we will create a structure to let the printer thread know that it should send the file to the printer. At this point, we are done setting up the daemon, so we log a message to indicate that the daemon has initialized successfully.

[149–168] We copy the `rendezvous fd_set` structure to `rset` and call `select` to wait for one of the file descriptors to become readable. We have to copy `rendezvous`, because `select` will modify the `fd_set` structure that we pass to it to include only those file descriptors that satisfy the event. Since the sockets have been initialized for use by a server, a readable file descriptor means that a connect request is pending. After `select` returns, we check `rset` for a readable file descriptor. If we find one, we call `accept` to accept the connection. If this fails, we log a message and continue checking for more readable file descriptors. Otherwise, we create a thread to handle the client connection. The `main` thread loops, farming requests out to other threads for processing, and should never reach the `exit` statement.

```
169     /*
170      * Initialize the job ID file.  Use a record lock to prevent
171      * more than one printer daemon from running at a time.
172      *
173      * LOCKING: none, except for record-lock on job ID file.
174      */
175     void
176     init_request(void)
177     {
178         int      n;
179         char     name[FILENMSZ];
180         sprintf(name, "%s/%s", SPOOLDIR, JOBFILE);
181         jobfd = open(name, O_CREAT|O_RDWR, S_IRUSR|S_IWUSR);
182         if (write_lock(jobfd, 0, SEEK_SET, 0) < 0)
183             log_quit("daemon already running");
184         /*
185          * Reuse the name buffer for the job counter.
186          */
187         if ((n = read(jobfd, name, FILENMSZ)) < 0)
188             log_sys("can't read job file");
189         if (n == 0)
190             nextjob = 1;
191         else
192             nextjob = atol(name);
193     }
```

[169–183] The init_request function does two things: it places a record lock on the job file, /var/spool/printer/jobno, and it reads the file to determine the next job number to assign. We place a write lock on the entire file to indicate that the daemon is running. If someone tries to start additional copies of the printer spooling daemon while one is already running, these additional daemons will fail to obtain the write lock and will exit. Thus, only one copy of the daemon can be running at a time. (Recall that we used this technique in Figure 13.6; we discussed the write_lock macro in Section 14.3.)

[184–193] The job file contains an ASCII integer string representing the next job number. If the file was just created and therefore is empty, we set nextjob to 1. Otherwise, we use atol to convert the string to an integer and use this as the next job number. We leave jobfd open to the job file so that we can update the job number as jobs are created. We can't close the file, because this would release the write lock that we've placed on it.

On a system where a long integer is 64 bits wide, we need a buffer at least 21 bytes in size to fit a string representing the largest possible long integer. We are safe reusing the filename buffer, because FILENMSZ is defined to be 64 in print.h.

```
194     /*
195      * Initialize printer information.
196      *
197      * LOCKING: none.
198      */
199     void
200     init_printer(void)
201     {
202         printer = get_printaddr();
203         if (printer == NULL) {
204             log_msg("no printer device registered");
205             exit(1);
206         }
207         printer_name = printer->ai_canonname;
208         if (printer_name == NULL)
209             printer_name = "printer";
210         log_msg("printer is %s", printer_name);
211     }

212     /*
213      * Update the job ID file with the next job number.
214      *
215      * LOCKING: none.
216      */
217     void
218     update_jobno(void)
219     {
220         char    buf[32];

221         lseek(jobfd, 0, SEEK_SET);
222         sprintf(buf, "%ld", nextjob);
223         if (write(jobfd, buf, strlen(buf)) < 0)
224             log_sys("can't update job file");
225     }
```

[194–211] The init_printer function is used to set the printer name and address. We get the printer address by calling get_printaddr (from util.c). If this fails, we log a message and exit. We can't do this by calling log_sys, because get_printaddr can fail without setting errno. When it fails and does set errno, however, get_printaddr logs its own error message. We set the printer name to the ai_canonname field in the addrinfo structure. If this field is null, we set the printer name to a default value of printer. Note that we log the name of the printer we are using to aid administrators in diagnosing problems with the spooling system.

[212–225] The update_jobno function is used to write the next job number to the job file, /var/spool/printer/jobno. First, we seek to the beginning of the file. Then we convert the integer job number into a string and write it to the file. If the write fails, we log an error message and exit.

```
226    /*
227     * Get the next job number.
228     *
229     * LOCKING: acquires and releases joblock.
230     */
231    long
232    get_newjobno(void)
233    {
234        long    jobid;

235        pthread_mutex_lock(&joblock);
236        jobid = nextjob++;
237        if (nextjob <= 0)
238            nextjob = 1;
239        pthread_mutex_unlock(&joblock);
240        return(jobid);
241    }

242    /*
243     * Add a new job to the list of pending jobs.    Then signal
244     * the printer thread that a job is pending.
245     *
246     * LOCKING: acquires and releases joblock.
247     */
248    void
249    add_job(struct printreq *reqp, long jobid)
250    {
251        struct job  *jp;

252        if ((jp = malloc(sizeof(struct job))) == NULL)
253            log_sys("malloc failed");
254        memcpy(&jp->req, reqp, sizeof(struct printreq));
```

[226–241] The get_newjobno function is used to get the next job number. We first lock the joblock mutex. We increment the nextjob variable and handle the case where it wraps around. Then we unlock the mutex and return the value nextjob had before we incremented it. Multiple threads can call get_newjobno at the same time; we need to serialize access to the next job number so that each thread gets a unique job number. (Refer to Figure 11.9 to see what could happen if we don't serialize the threads in this case.)

[242–254] The add_job function is used to add a new print request to the end of the list of pending print jobs. We start by allocating space for the job structure. If this fails, we log a message and exit. At this point, the print request is stored safely on disk; when the printer spooling daemon is restarted, it will pick the request up. After we allocate memory for the new job, we copy the request structure from the client into the job structure. Recall from print.h that a job structure consists of a pair of list pointers, a job ID, and a copy of the printreq structure sent to us by the client print command.

```
255        jp->jobid = jobid;
256        jp->next = NULL;
257        pthread_mutex_lock(&joblock);
258        jp->prev = jobtail;
259        if (jobtail == NULL)
260            jobhead = jp;
261        else
262            jobtail->next = jp;
263        jobtail = jp;
264        pthread_mutex_unlock(&joblock);
265        pthread_cond_signal(&jobwait);
266    }

267    /*
268     * Replace a job back on the head of the list.
269     *
270     * LOCKING: acquires and releases joblock.
271     */
272    void
273    replace_job(struct job *jp)
274    {
275        pthread_mutex_lock(&joblock);
276        jp->prev = NULL;
277        jp->next = jobhead;
278        if (jobhead == NULL)
279            jobtail = jp;
280        else
281            jobhead->prev = jp;
282        jobhead = jp;
283        pthread_mutex_unlock(&joblock);
284    }
```

[255–266] We save the job ID and lock the `joblock` mutex to gain exclusive access to the linked list of print jobs. We are about to add the new job structure to the end of the list. We set the new structure's previous pointer to the last job on the list. If the list is empty, we set `jobhead` to point to the new structure. Otherwise, we set the next pointer in the last entry on the list to point to the new structure. Then we set `jobtail` to point to the new structure. We unlock the mutex and signal the printer thread that another job is available.

[267–284] The `replace_job` function is used to insert a job at the head of the pending job list. We acquire the `joblock` mutex, set the previous pointer in the `job` structure to null, and set the next pointer in the `job` structure to point to the head of the list. If the list is empty, we set `jobtail` to point to the `job` structure we are replacing. Otherwise, we set the previous pointer in the first `job` structure on the list to point to the `job` structure we are replacing. Then we set the `jobhead` pointer to the `job` structure we are replacing. Finally, we release the `joblock` mutex.

```
285    /*
286     * Remove a job from the list of pending jobs.
287     *
288     * LOCKING: caller must hold joblock.
289     */
290    void
291    remove_job(struct job *target)
292    {
293        if (target->next != NULL)
294            target->next->prev = target->prev;
295        else
296            jobtail = target->prev;
297        if (target->prev != NULL)
298            target->prev->next = target->next;
299        else
300            jobhead = target->next;
301    }

302    /*
303     * Check the spool directory for pending jobs on start-up.
304     *
305     * LOCKING: none.
306     */
307    void
308    build_qonstart(void)
309    {
310        int            fd, err, nr;
311        long           jobid;
312        DIR            *dirp;
313        struct dirent  *entp;
314        struct printreq req;
315        char           dname[FILENMSZ], fname[FILENMSZ];

316        sprintf(dname, "%s/%s", SPOOLDIR, REQDIR);
317        if ((dirp = opendir(dname)) == NULL)
318            return;
```

[285–301] remove_job removes a job from the list of pending jobs given a pointer to the job to be removed. The caller must already hold the joblock mutex. If the next pointer is non-null, we set the next entry's previous pointer to the target's previous pointer. Otherwise, the entry is the last one on the list, so we set jobtail to the target's previous pointer. If the target's previous pointer is non-null, we set the previous entry's next pointer equal to the target's next pointer. Otherwise, this is the first entry in the list, so we set jobhead to point to the next entry in the list after the target.

[302–318] When the daemon starts, it calls build_qonstart to build an in-memory list of print jobs from the disk files stored in /var/spool/printer/reqs. If we can't open the directory, no print jobs are pending, so we return.

```
319     while ((entp = readdir(dirp)) != NULL) {
320         /*
321          * Skip "." and ".."
322          */
323         if (strcmp(entp->d_name, ".") == 0 ||
324           strcmp(entp->d_name, "..") == 0)
325             continue;

326         /*
327          * Read the request structure.
328          */
329         sprintf(fname, "%s/%s/%s", SPOOLDIR, REQDIR, entp->d_name);
330         if ((fd = open(fname, O_RDONLY)) < 0)
331             continue;
332         nr = read(fd, &req, sizeof(struct printreq));
333         if (nr != sizeof(struct printreq)) {
334             if (nr < 0)
335                 err = errno;
336             else
337                 err = EIO;
338             close(fd);
339             log_msg("build_qonstart: can't read %s: %s",
340               fname, strerror(err));
341             unlink(fname);
342             sprintf(fname, "%s/%s/%s", SPOOLDIR, DATADIR,
343               entp->d_name);
344             unlink(fname);
345             continue;
346         }
347         jobid = atol(entp->d_name);
348         log_msg("adding job %ld to queue", jobid);
349         add_job(&req, jobid);
350     }
351     closedir(dirp);
352 }
```

[319–325] We read each entry in the directory, one at a time. We skip the entries for dot and dot-dot.

[326–346] For each entry, we create the full pathname of the file and open it for reading. If the open call fails, we just skip the file. Otherwise, we read the printreq structure stored in it. If we don't read the entire structure, we close the file, log a message, and unlink the file. Then we create the full pathname of the corresponding data file and unlink it, too.

[347–352] If we were able to read a complete printreq structure, we convert the filename into a job ID (the name of the file is its job ID), log a message, and then add the request to the list of pending print jobs. When we are done reading the directory, readdir will return NULL, and we close the directory and return.

```
353  /*
354   * Accept a print job from a client.
355   *
356   * LOCKING: none.
357   */
358  void *
359  client_thread(void *arg)
360  {
361      int                 n, fd, sockfd, nr, nw, first;
362      long                jobid;
363      pthread_t           tid;
364      struct printreq     req;
365      struct printresp    res;
366      char                name[FILENMSZ];
367      char                buf[IOBUFSZ];

368      tid = pthread_self();
369      pthread_cleanup_push(client_cleanup, (void *)tid);
370      sockfd = (int)arg;
371      add_worker(tid, sockfd);

372      /*
373       * Read the request header.
374       */
375      if ((n = treadn(sockfd, &req, sizeof(struct printreq), 10)) !=
376          sizeof(struct printreq)) {
377          res.jobid = 0;
378          if (n < 0)
379              res.retcode = htonl(errno);
380          else
381              res.retcode = htonl(EIO);
382          strncpy(res.msg, strerror(res.retcode), MSGLEN_MAX);
383          writen(sockfd, &res, sizeof(struct printresp));
384          pthread_exit((void *)1);
385      }
```

[353–371] The client_thread is spawned from the main thread when a connect request is accepted. Its job is to receive the file to be printed from the client print command. We create a separate thread for each client print request.

The first thing we do is install a thread cleanup handler (see Section 11.5 for a discussion of thread cleanup handlers). The cleanup handler is client_cleanup, which we will see later. It takes a single argument: our thread ID. Then we call add_worker to create a worker_thread structure and add it to the list of active client threads.

[372–385] At this point, we are done with the thread's initialization tasks, so we read the request header from the client. If the client sends less than we expect or we encounter an error, we respond with a message indicating the reason for the error and call pthread_exit to terminate the thread.

```
386        req.size = ntohl(req.size);
387        req.flags = ntohl(req.flags);
388        /*
389         * Create the data file.
390         */
391        jobid = get_newjobno();
392        sprintf(name, "%s/%s/%ld", SPOOLDIR, DATADIR, jobid);
393        fd = creat(name, FILEPERM);
394        if (fd < 0) {
395            res.jobid = 0;
396            res.retcode = htonl(errno);
397            log_msg("client_thread: can't create %s: %s", name,
398              strerror(res.retcode));
399            strncpy(res.msg, strerror(res.retcode), MSGLEN_MAX);
400            writen(sockfd, &res, sizeof(struct printresp));
401            pthread_exit((void *)1);
402        }
403        /*
404         * Read the file and store it in the spool directory.
405         * Try to figure out if the file is a PostScript file
406         * or a plain text file.
407         */
408        first = 1;
409        while ((nr = tread(sockfd, buf, IOBUFSZ, 20)) > 0) {
410            if (first) {
411                first = 0;
412                if (strncmp(buf, "%!PS", 4) != 0)
413                    req.flags |= PR_TEXT;
414            }
```

[386–402] We convert the integer fields in the request header to host byte order and call get_newjobno to reserve the next job ID for this print request. We create the job data file, named /var/spool/printer/data/*jobid*, where *jobid* is the request's job ID. We use permissions that prevent others from being able read the files (FILEPERM is defined as S_IRUSR|S_IWUSR in print.h). If we can't create the file, we log an error message, send a failure response back to the client, and terminate the thread by calling pthread_exit.

[403–414] We read the file contents from the client, with the intent of writing the contents out to our private copy of the data file. But before we write anything, we need to check if this is a PostScript file the first time through the loop. If the file doesn't begin with the pattern %!PS, we can assume that the file is plaintext, so we set the PR_TEXT flag in the request header in this case. (Recall that the client can also set this flag if the -t flag is included when the print command is executed.) Although PostScript programs are not required to start with the pattern %!PS, the document formatting guidelines (Adobe Systems [1999]) strongly recommends that they do.

```
415            nw = write(fd, buf, nr);
416            if (nw != nr) {
417                res.jobid = 0;
418                if (nw < 0)
419                    res.retcode = htonl(errno);
420                else
421                    res.retcode = htonl(EIO);
422                log_msg("client_thread: can't write %s: %s", name,
423                  strerror(res.retcode));
424                close(fd);
425                strncpy(res.msg, strerror(res.retcode), MSGLEN_MAX);
426                writen(sockfd, &res, sizeof(struct printresp));
427                unlink(name);
428                pthread_exit((void *)1);
429            }
430        }
431        close(fd);

432        /*
433         * Create the control file.  Then write the
434         * print request information to the control
435         * file.
436         */
437        sprintf(name, "%s/%s/%ld", SPOOLDIR, REQDIR, jobid);
438        fd = creat(name, FILEPERM);
439        if (fd < 0) {
440            res.jobid = 0;
441            res.retcode = htonl(errno);
442            log_msg("client_thread: can't create %s: %s", name,
443              strerror(res.retcode));
444            strncpy(res.msg, strerror(res.retcode), MSGLEN_MAX);
445            writen(sockfd, &res, sizeof(struct printresp));
446            sprintf(name, "%s/%s/%ld", SPOOLDIR, DATADIR, jobid);
447            unlink(name);
448            pthread_exit((void *)1);
449        }
```

[415–431] We write the data that we read from the client to the data file. If write fails, we log an error message, close the file descriptor for the data file, send an error message back to the client, delete the data file, and terminate the thread by calling pthread_exit. Note that we do not explicitly close the socket file descriptor. This is done for us by our thread cleanup handler as part of the processing that occurs when we call pthread_exit.

When we receive all the data to be printed, we close the file descriptor for the data file.

[432–449] Next, we create a file, /var/spool/printer/reqs/*jobid*, to remember the print request. If this fails, we log an error message, send an error response to the client, remove the data file, and terminate the thread.

```
450        nw = write(fd, &req, sizeof(struct printreq));
451        if (nw != sizeof(struct printreq)) {
452            res.jobid = 0;
453            if (nw < 0)
454                res.retcode = htonl(errno);
455            else
456                res.retcode = htonl(EIO);
457            log_msg("client_thread: can't write %s: %s", name,
458                strerror(res.retcode));
459            close(fd);
460            strncpy(res.msg, strerror(res.retcode), MSGLEN_MAX);
461            writen(sockfd, &res, sizeof(struct printresp));
462            unlink(name);
463            sprintf(name, "%s/%s/%ld", SPOOLDIR, DATADIR, jobid);
464            unlink(name);
465            pthread_exit((void *)1);
466        }
467        close(fd);

468        /*
469         * Send response to client.
470         */
471        res.retcode = 0;
472        res.jobid = htonl(jobid);
473        sprintf(res.msg, "request ID %ld", jobid);
474        writen(sockfd, &res, sizeof(struct printresp));

475        /*
476         * Notify the printer thread, clean up, and exit.
477         */
478        log_msg("adding job %ld to queue", jobid);
479        add_job(&req, jobid);
480        pthread_cleanup_pop(1);
481        return((void *)0);
482    }
```

[450–466] We write the `printreq` structure to the control file. On error, we log a
message, close the descriptor for the control file, send a failure response back
to the client, remove the data and control files, and terminate the thread.

[467–474] We close the file descriptor for the control file and send a message containing
the job ID and a successful status (`retcode` set to 0) back to the client.

[475–482] We call `add_job` to add the received job to the list of pending print jobs and
call `pthread_cleanup_pop` to complete the cleanup processing. The
thread terminates when we return.

Note that before the thread exits, we must close any file descriptors we no
longer need. Unlike process termination, file descriptors are not closed
automatically when a thread ends if other threads exist in the process. If we
didn't close unneeded file descriptors, we'd eventually run out of resources.

```
483    /*
484     * Add a worker to the list of worker threads.
485     *
486     * LOCKING: acquires and releases workerlock.
487     */
488    void
489    add_worker(pthread_t tid, int sockfd)
490    {
491      struct worker_thread    *wtp;

492      if ((wtp = malloc(sizeof(struct worker_thread))) == NULL) {
493          log_ret("add_worker: can't malloc");
494          pthread_exit((void *)1);
495      }
496      wtp->tid = tid;
497      wtp->sockfd = sockfd;
498      pthread_mutex_lock(&workerlock);
499      wtp->prev = NULL;
500      wtp->next = workers;
501      if (workers == NULL)
502          workers = wtp;
503      else
504          workers->prev = wtp;
505      pthread_mutex_unlock(&workerlock);
506    }

507    /*
508     * Cancel (kill) all outstanding workers.
509     *
510     * LOCKING: acquires and releases workerlock.
511     */
512    void
513    kill_workers(void)
514    {
515      struct worker_thread    *wtp;

516      pthread_mutex_lock(&workerlock);
517      for (wtp = workers; wtp != NULL; wtp = wtp->next)
518          pthread_cancel(wtp->tid);
519      pthread_mutex_unlock(&workerlock);
520    }
```

[483–506] add_worker adds a worker_thread structure to the list of active threads. We allocate memory for the structure, initialize it, lock the workerlock mutex, add the structure to the head of the list, and unlock the mutex.

[507–520] The kill_workers function walks the list of worker threads and cancels each one. We hold the workerlock mutex while we walk the list. Recall that pthread_cancel merely schedules a thread for cancellation; actual cancellation happens when each thread reaches the next cancellation point.

```
521    /*
522     * Cancellation routine for the worker thread.
523     *
524     * LOCKING: acquires and releases workerlock.
525     */
526    void
527    client_cleanup(void *arg)
528    {
529        struct worker_thread    *wtp;
530        pthread_t               tid;

531        tid = (pthread_t)arg;
532        pthread_mutex_lock(&workerlock);
533        for (wtp = workers; wtp != NULL; wtp = wtp->next) {
534            if (wtp->tid == tid) {
535                if (wtp->next != NULL)
536                    wtp->next->prev = wtp->prev;
537                if (wtp->prev != NULL)
538                    wtp->prev->next = wtp->next;
539                else
540                    workers = wtp->next;
541                break;
542            }
543        }
544        pthread_mutex_unlock(&workerlock);
545        if (wtp != NULL) {
546            close(wtp->sockfd);
547            free(wtp);
548        }
549    }
```

[521–543] The client_cleanup function is the thread cleanup handler for the
         worker threads that communicate with client commands. This function is
         called when the thread calls pthread_exit, calls pthread_cleanup_pop
         with a nonzero argument, or responds to a cancellation request. The
         argument is the thread ID of the thread terminating.

         We lock the workerlock mutex and search the list of worker threads until
         we find a matching thread ID. When we find a match, we remove the
         worker thread structure from the list and stop the search.

[544–549] We unlock the workerlock mutex, close the socket file descriptor used by
         the thread to communicate with the client, and free the memory backing the
         worker_thread structure.

         Since we try to acquire the workerlock mutex, if a thread reaches a
         cancellation point while the kill_workers function is still walking the list,
         we will have to wait until kill_workers releases the mutex before we can
         proceed.

```
550     /*
551      * Deal with signals.
552      *
553      * LOCKING: acquires and releases configlock.
554      */
555     void *
556     signal_thread(void *arg)
557     {
558         int     err, signo;

559         for (;;) {
560             err = sigwait(&mask, &signo);
561             if (err != 0)
562                 log_quit("sigwait failed: %s", strerror(err));
563             switch (signo) {
564             case SIGHUP:
565                 /*
566                  * Schedule to re-read the configuration file.
567                  */
568                 pthread_mutex_lock(&configlock);
569                 reread = 1;
570                 pthread_mutex_unlock(&configlock);
571                 break;

572             case SIGTERM:
573                 kill_workers();
574                 log_msg("terminate with signal %s", strsignal(signo));
575                 exit(0);

576             default:
577                 kill_workers();
578                 log_quit("unexpected signal %d", signo);
579             }
580         }
581     }
```

[550–563] The signal_thread function is run by the thread that is responsible for handling signals. In the main function, we initialized the signal mask to include SIGHUP and SIGTERM. Here, we call sigwait to wait for one of these signals to occur. If sigwait fails, we log an error message and exit.

[564–571] If we receive SIGHUP, we acquire the configlock mutex, set the reread variable to 1, and release the mutex. This tells the printer daemon to reread the configuration file on the next iteration in its processing loop.

[572–575] If we receive SIGTERM, we call kill_workers to kill all the worker threads, log a message, and call exit to terminate the process.

[576–581] If we receive a signal we are not expecting, we kill the worker threads and call log_quit to log a message and exit.

```
582   /*
583    * Add an option to the IPP header.
584    *
585    * LOCKING: none.
586    */
587   char *
588   add_option(char *cp, int tag, char *optname, char *optval)
589   {
590       int      n;
591       union {
592           int16_t s;
593           char c[2];
594       }        u;

595       *cp++ = tag;
596       n = strlen(optname);
597       u.s = htons(n);
598       *cp++ = u.c[0];
599       *cp++ = u.c[1];
600       strcpy(cp, optname);
601       cp += n;
602       n = strlen(optval);
603       u.s = htons(n);
604       *cp++ = u.c[0];
605       *cp++ = u.c[1];
606       strcpy(cp, optval);
607       return(cp + n);
608   }
```

[582–594] The add_option function is used to add an option to the IPP header that we build to send to the printer. Recall from Figure 21.3 that the format of an attribute is a 1-byte tag describing the type of the attribute, followed by the length of the attribute name stored in binary as a 2-byte integer, followed by the name, the size of the attribute value, and finally the value itself.

IPP makes no attempt to control the alignment of the binary integers embedded in the header. Some processor architectures, such as the SPARC, can't load an integer from an arbitrary address. This means that we can't store the integers in the header by casting a pointer to an int16_t to the address in the header where the integer is to be stored. Instead, we need to copy the integer 1 byte at a time. This is why we define the union containing a 16-bit integer and 2 bytes.

[595–608] We store the tag in the header and convert the length of the attribute name to network byte order. We copy the length 1 byte at a time to the header. Then we copy the attribute name. We repeat this process for the attribute value and return the address in the header where the next part of the header should begin.

```
609    /*
610     * Single thread to communicate with the printer.
611     *
612     * LOCKING: acquires and releases joblock and configlock.
613     */
614    void *
615    printer_thread(void *arg)
616    {
617        struct job        *jp;
618        int               hlen, ilen, sockfd, fd, nr, nw;
619        char              *icp, *hcp;
620        struct ipp_hdr    *hp;
621        struct stat       sbuf;
622        struct iovec      iov[2];
623        char              name[FILENMSZ];
624        char              hbuf[HBUFSZ];
625        char              ibuf[IBUFSZ];
626        char              buf[IOBUFSZ];
627        char              str[64];

628        for (;;) {
629            /*
630             * Get a job to print.
631             */
632            pthread_mutex_lock(&joblock);
633            while (jobhead == NULL) {
634                log_msg("printer_thread: waiting...");
635                pthread_cond_wait(&jobwait, &joblock);
636            }
637            remove_job(jp = jobhead);
638            log_msg("printer_thread: picked up job %ld", jp->jobid);
639            pthread_mutex_unlock(&joblock);

640            update_jobno();
```

[609–627] The printer_thread function is run by the thread that communicates with the network printer. We'll use icp and ibuf to build the IPP header. We'll use hcp and hbuf to build the HTTP header. We need to build the headers in separate buffers. The HTTP header includes a length field in ASCII, and we won't know how much space to reserve for it until we assemble the IPP header. We'll use writev to write these two headers in one call.

[628–640] The printer thread runs in an infinite loop that waits for jobs to transmit to the printer. We use the joblock mutex to protect the list of jobs. If a job is not pending, we use pthread_cond_wait to wait for one to arrive. When a job is ready, we remove it from the list by calling remove_job. We still hold the mutex at this point, so we release it and call update_jobno to write the next job number to /var/spool/printer/jobno.

```
641         /*
642          * Check for a change in the config file.
643          */
644         pthread_mutex_lock(&configlock);
645         if (reread) {
646             freeaddrinfo(printer);
647             printer = NULL;
648             printer_name = NULL;
649             reread = 0;
650             pthread_mutex_unlock(&configlock);
651             init_printer();
652         } else {
653             pthread_mutex_unlock(&configlock);
654         }

655         /*
656          * Send job to printer.
657          */
658         sprintf(name, "%s/%s/%ld", SPOOLDIR, DATADIR, jp->jobid);
659         if ((fd = open(name, O_RDONLY)) < 0) {
660             log_msg("job %ld canceled - can't open %s: %s",
661                 jp->jobid, name, strerror(errno));
662             free(jp);
663             continue;
664         }
665         if (fstat(fd, &sbuf) < 0) {
666             log_msg("job %ld canceled - can't fstat %s: %s",
667                 jp->jobid, name, strerror(errno));
668             free(jp);
669             close(fd);
670             continue;
671         }
```

[641–654] Now that we have a job to print, we check for a change in the configuration file. We lock the configlock mutex and check the reread variable. If it is nonzero, then we free the old printer addrinfo list, clear the pointers, unlock the mutex, and call init_printer to reinitialize the printer information. Since only this context looks at and potentially changes the printer information after the main thread initialized it, we don't need any synchronization other than using the configlock mutex to protect the state of the reread flag.

Note that although we acquire and release two different mutex locks in this function, we never hold both at the same time, so we don't need to establish a lock hierarchy (Section 11.6).

[655–671] If we can't open the data file, we log a message, free the job structure, and continue. After opening the file, we call fstat to find the size of the file. If this fails, we log a message, clean up, and continue.

```
672         if ((sockfd = socket(AF_INET, SOCK_STREAM, 0)) < 0) {
673             log_msg("job %ld deferred - can't create socket: %s",
674               jp->jobid, strerror(errno));
675             goto defer;
676         }
677         if (connect_retry(sockfd, printer->ai_addr,
678           printer->ai_addrlen) < 0) {
679             log_msg("job %ld deferred - can't contact printer: %s",
680               jp->jobid, strerror(errno));
681             goto defer;
682         }

683         /*
684          * Set up the IPP header.
685          */
686         icp = ibuf;
687         hp = (struct ipp_hdr *)icp;
688         hp->major_version = 1;
689         hp->minor_version = 1;
690         hp->operation = htons(OP_PRINT_JOB);
691         hp->request_id = htonl(jp->jobid);
692         icp += offsetof(struct ipp_hdr, attr_group);
693         *icp++ = TAG_OPERATION_ATTR;
694         icp = add_option(icp, TAG_CHARSET, "attributes-charset",
695           "utf-8");
696         icp = add_option(icp, TAG_NATULANG,
697           "attributes-natural-language", "en-us");
698         sprintf(str, "http://%s:%d", printer_name, IPP_PORT);
699         icp = add_option(icp, TAG_URI, "printer-uri", str);
```

[672–682] We open a stream socket to communicate with the printer. If the socket call fails, we jump down to defer, where we will clean up, delay, and try again later. If we can create a socket, we call connect_retry to connect to the printer.

[683–699] Next, we set up the IPP header. The operation is a print-job request. We use htons to convert the 2-byte operation ID from host to network byte order and htonl to convert the 4-byte job ID from host to network byte order. After the initial portion of the header, we set the tag value to indicate that operation attributes follow. We call add_option to add attributes to the message. Figure 21.4 lists the required and optional attributes for print-job requests. The first three are required. We specify the character set to be UTF-8, which the printer must support. We specify the language as en-us, which represents U.S. English. Another required attribute is the printer Universal Resource Identifier (URI). We set it to http://*printer_name*:631. (We really should ask the printer for a list of supported URIs and select one from that list, but that would complicate this example without adding much value.)

```
700         icp = add_option(icp, TAG_NAMEWOLANG,
701             "requesting-user-name", jp->req.usernm);
702         icp = add_option(icp, TAG_NAMEWOLANG, "job-name",
703             jp->req.jobnm);
704         if (jp->req.flags & PR_TEXT) {
705             icp = add_option(icp, TAG_MIMETYPE, "document-format",
706                 "text/plain");
707         } else {
708             icp = add_option(icp, TAG_MIMETYPE, "document-format",
709                 "application/postscript");
710         }
711         *icp++ = TAG_END_OF_ATTR;
712         ilen = icp - ibuf;

713         /*
714          * Set up the HTTP header.
715          */
716         hcp = hbuf;
717         sprintf(hcp, "POST /%s/ipp HTTP/1.1\r\n", printer_name);
718         hcp += strlen(hcp);
719         sprintf(hcp, "Content-Length: %ld\r\n",
720             (long)sbuf.st_size + ilen);
721         hcp += strlen(hcp);
722         strcpy(hcp, "Content-Type: application/ipp\r\n");
723         hcp += strlen(hcp);
724         sprintf(hcp, "Host: %s:%d\r\n", printer_name, IPP_PORT);
725         hcp += strlen(hcp);
726         *hcp++ = '\r';
727         *hcp++ = '\n';
728         hlen = hcp - hbuf;
```

[700–712] The `requesting-user-name` attribute is recommended, but not required. The `job-name` attribute is optional. Recall that the `print` command sends the name of the file being printed as the job name, which can help users distinguish among multiple pending jobs. The last attribute we supply is the `document-format`. If we omit it, the printer will assume that the file conforms to the printer's default format. For a PostScript printer, this is probably PostScript, but some printers can autosense the format and choose between PostScript and text or PostScript and PCL (HP's Printer Command Language). If the `PR_TEXT` flag is set, we specify the document format as `text/plain`. Otherwise, we set it to `application/postscript`. Then we delimit the end of the attributes portion of the header with an end-of-attributes tag and calculate the size of the IPP header.

[713–728] Now that we know the IPP header size, we can set up the HTTP header. We set the `Context-Length` to the size in bytes of the IPP header plus the size of the file to be printed. The `Content-Type` is `application/ipp`. We mark the end of the HTTP header with a carriage return and a line feed.

```
729        /*
730         * Write the headers first.   Then send the file.
731         */
732        iov[0].iov_base = hbuf;
733        iov[0].iov_len = hlen;
734        iov[1].iov_base = ibuf;
735        iov[1].iov_len = ilen;
736        if ((nw = writev(sockfd, iov, 2)) != hlen + ilen) {
737            log_ret("can't write to printer");
738            goto defer;
739        }
740        while ((nr = read(fd, buf, IOBUFSZ)) > 0) {
741            if ((nw = write(sockfd, buf, nr)) != nr) {
742                if (nw < 0)
743                    log_ret("can't write to printer");
744                else
745                    log_msg("short write (%d/%d) to printer", nw, nr);
746                goto defer;
747            }
748        }
749        if (nr < 0) {
750            log_ret("can't read %s", name);
751            goto defer;
752        }

753        /*
754         * Read the response from the printer.
755         */
756        if (printer_status(sockfd, jp)) {
757            unlink(name);
758            sprintf(name, "%s/%s/%ld", SPOOLDIR, REQDIR, jp->jobid);
759            unlink(name);
760            free(jp);
761            jp = NULL;
762        }
```

[729–739] We set the first element of the iovec array to refer to the HTTP header and the second element to refer to the IPP header. Then we use writev to send both headers to the printer. If the write fails, we log a message and jump to defer, where we will clean up and delay before trying again.

[740–752] Next, we send the data file to the printer. We read the data file in IOBUFSZ chunks and write it to the socket connected to the printer. If either read or write fails, we log a message and jump to defer.

[753–762] After sending the entire file to be printed, we call printer_status to receive the printer's response to our print request. If printer_status succeeds, it returns a positive value, and we delete the data and control files. Then we free the job structure, set its pointer to NULL, and fall through to the defer label.

```
763   defer:
764         close(fd);
765         if (sockfd >= 0)
766             close(sockfd);
767         if (jp != NULL) {
768             replace_job(jp);
769             sleep(60);
770         }
771     }
772   }
773   /*
774    * Read data from the printer, possibly increasing the buffer.
775    * Returns offset of end of data in buffer or -1 on failure.
776    *
777    * LOCKING: none.
778    */
779   ssize_t
780   readmore(int sockfd, char **bpp, int off, int *bszp)
781   {
782     ssize_t nr;
783     char    *bp = *bpp;
784     int     bsz = *bszp;
785     if (off >= bsz) {
786         bsz += IOBUFSZ;
787         if ((bp = realloc(*bpp, bsz)) == NULL)
788             log_sys("readmore: can't allocate bigger read buffer");
789         *bszp = bsz;
790         *bpp = bp;
791     }
792     if ((nr = tread(sockfd, &bp[off], bsz-off, 1)) > 0)
793         return(off+nr);
794     else
795         return(-1);
796   }
```

[763–772] At the defer label, we close the file descriptor for the open data file. If the socket descriptor is valid, we close it. On error, we place the job back on the head of the pending job list and delay for 1 minute. On success, jp is NULL, so we simply go back to the top of the loop to get the next job to print.

[773–796] The readmore function is used to read part of the response message from the printer. If we're at the end of the buffer, we reallocate a bigger buffer and return the new starting buffer address and buffer size through the bpp and bszp parameters, respectively. In either case, we read as much as the buffer will hold, starting at the end of the data already in the buffer. We return the new offset in the buffer corresponding to the end of the data read. If the read fails or the timeout expires, we return –1.

```
797    /*
798     * Read and parse the response from the printer.  Return 1
799     * if the request was successful, and 0 otherwise.
800     *
801     * LOCKING: none.
802     */
803    int
804    printer_status(int sockfd, struct job *jp)
805    {
806        int             i, success, code, len, found, bufsz;
807        long            jobid;
808        ssize_t         nr;
809        char            *statcode, *reason, *cp, *contentlen;
810        struct ipp_hdr  *hp;
811        char            *bp;

812        /*
813         * Read the HTTP header followed by the IPP response header.
814         * They can be returned in multiple read attempts.  Use the
815         * Content-Length specifier to determine how much to read.
816         */
817        success = 0;
818        bufsz = IOBUFSZ;
819        if ((bp = malloc(IOBUFSZ)) == NULL)
820            log_sys("printer_status: can't allocate read buffer");

821        while ((nr = tread(sockfd, bp, IOBUFSZ, 5)) > 0) {
822            /*
823             * Find the status.  Response starts with "HTTP/x.y"
824             * so we can skip the first 8 characters.
825             */
826            cp = bp + 8;
827            while (isspace((int)*cp))
828                cp++;
829            statcode = cp;
830            while (isdigit((int)*cp))
831                cp++;
832            if (cp == statcode) { /* Bad format; log it and move on */
833                log_msg(bp);
```

[797–811] The printer_status function reads the printer's response to a print-job request. We don't know how the printer will respond; it might send a response in multiple messages, send the complete response in one message, or include intermediate acknowledgements, such as HTTP 100 Continue messages. We need to handle all these possibilities.

[812–833] We allocate a buffer and read from the printer, expecting a response to be available within about 5 seconds. We skip the HTTP/1.1 and any white space that starts the message. The numeric status code should follow. If it doesn't, we log the contents of the message.

```
834            } else {
835                *cp++ = '\0';
836                reason = cp;
837                while (*cp != '\r' && *cp != '\n')
838                    cp++;
839                *cp = '\0';
840                code = atoi(statcode);
841                if (HTTP_INFO(code))
842                    continue;
843                if (!HTTP_SUCCESS(code)) { /* probable error: log it */
844                    bp[nr] = '\0';
845                    log_msg("error: %s", reason);
846                    break;
847                }
848                /*
849                 * The HTTP request was okay, but we still
850                 * need to check the IPP status.  First
851                 * search for the Content-Length specifier.
852                 */
853                i = cp - bp;
854                for (;;) {
855                    while (*cp != 'C' && *cp != 'c' && i < nr) {
856                        cp++;
857                        i++;
858                    }
859                    if (i >= nr &&   /* get more header */
860                      ((nr = readmore(sockfd, &bp, i, &bufsz)) < 0))
861                        goto out;
862                    cp = &bp[i];
```

[834–839] If we have found a numeric status code in the response, we convert the first nondigit character to a null byte. The reason string (a text message) should follow. We search for the terminating carriage return or line feed, also terminating the text string with a null byte.

[840–847] We convert the code to an integer. If this is an informational message only, we ignore it and continue the loop so we end up reading more. We expect to see either a success message or an error message. If we get an error message, we log the error and break out of the loop.

[848–862] If the HTTP request was successful, we need to check the IPP status. We search through the message until we find the Content-Length attribute, so we look for a C or c. HTTP header keywords are case-insensitive, so we need to check both lowercase and uppercase characters.

If we run out of buffer space, we read some more. Since readmore calls realloc, which might change the address of the buffer, we need to reset cp to point to the correct place in the buffer.

```
863              if (strncasecmp(cp, "Content-Length:", 15) == 0) {
864                  cp += 15;
865                  while (isspace((int)*cp))
866                      cp++;
867                  contentlen = cp;
868                  while (isdigit((int)*cp))
869                      cp++;
870                  *cp++ = '\0';
871                  i = cp - bp;
872                  len = atoi(contentlen);
873                  break;
874              } else {
875                  cp++;
876                  i++;
877              }
878          }
879          if (i >= nr &&   /* get more header */
880            ((nr = readmore(sockfd, &bp, i, &bufsz)) < 0))
881              goto out;
882          cp = &bp[i];

883          found = 0;
884          while (!found) {   /* look for end of HTTP header */
885              while (i < nr - 2) {
886                  if (*cp == '\n' && *(cp + 1) == '\r' &&
887                    *(cp + 2) == '\n') {
888                      found = 1;
889                      cp += 3;
890                      i += 3;
891                      break;
892                  }
893                  cp++;
894                  i++;
895              }
896              if (i >= nr &&   /* get more header */
897                ((nr = readmore(sockfd, &bp, i, &bufsz)) < 0))
898                  goto out;
899              cp = &bp[i];
900          }
```

[863–882] If we find the Content-Length attribute string, we search for its value. We convert this numeric string into an integer, break out of the for loop, and read more from the printer if we've exhausted the contents of the buffer. If we reach the end of the buffer without finding the Content-Length attribute, we continue in the loop and read some more from the printer.

[883–900] Once we get the length of the message as specified by the Content-Length attribute, we search for the end of the HTTP header (a blank line). If we find it, we set the found flag and skip past the blank line in the message.

```
901                 if (nr - i < len && /* get more header */
902                     ((nr = readmore(sockfd, &bp, i, &bufsz)) < 0))
903                     goto out;
904                 cp = &bp[i];

905                 hp = (struct ipp_hdr *)cp;
906                 i = ntohs(hp->status);
907                 jobid = ntohl(hp->request_id);
908                 if (jobid != jp->jobid) {
909                     /*
910                      * Different jobs.  Ignore it.
911                      */
912                     log_msg("jobid %ld status code %d", jobid, i);
913                     break;
914                 }

915                 if (STATCLASS_OK(i))
916                     success = 1;
917                 break;
918             }
919         }

920     out:
921         free(bp);
922         if (nr < 0) {
923             log_msg("jobid %ld: error reading printer response: %s",
924                 jobid, strerror(errno));
925         }
926         return(success);
927     }
```

[901–904] We continue searching for the end of the HTTP header. If we run out of space in the buffer, we read more. When we find the end of the HTTP header, we calculate the number of bytes that the HTTP header consumed. If the amount we've read minus the size of the HTTP header is not equal to the amount of data in the IPP message (the value we calculated from the content length), then we read some more.

[905–927] We get the status and job ID from the IPP header in the message. Both are stored as integers in network byte order, so we need to convert them to the host byte order by calling ntohs and ntohl. If the job IDs don't match, then this is not our response, so we log a message and break out of the outer while loop. If the IPP status indicates success, then we save the return value and break out of the loop. We return 1 if the print request was successful and 0 if it failed.

This concludes our look at the extended example in this chapter. The programs in this chapter were tested with a Xerox Phaser 860 network-attached PostScript printer. Unfortunately, this printer doesn't recognize the text/plain document format, but it does support the ability to autosense between plaintext and PostScript. Therefore, with this printer, we can print PostScript files and text files, but we cannot print the source to a PostScript program as plaintext unless we use some other utility, such as a2ps(1) to encapsulate the PostScript program.

21.6 Summary

This chapter has examined in detail two complete programs: a print spooler daemon that sends a print job to a network printer and a command that can be used to submit a job to be printed to the spooling daemon. This has given us a chance to see lots of features that we described in earlier chapters used in a real program: threads, I/O multiplexing, file I/O, socket I/O, and signals.

Exercises

21.1 Translate the IPP error code values listed in ipp.h into error messages. Then modify the print spooler daemon to log a message at the end of the printer_status function when the IPP header indicates a printer error.

21.2 Add support to the print command and the printd daemon to allow users to request double-sided printing. Do the same for landscape and portrait page orientation.

21.3 Modify the print spooler daemon so that when it starts, it contacts the printer to find out what features are supported by the printer so that the daemon doesn't request an option that isn't supported.

21.4 Write a command to report on the status of pending print jobs.

21.5 Write a command to cancel a pending print job.

21.6 Add support for multiple printers to the printer spooler. Include a way to move print jobs from one printer to another.

Appendix A

Function Prototypes

This appendix contains the function prototypes for the standard ISO C, POSIX, and UNIX System functions described in the text. Often, we want to see only the arguments to a function ("Which argument is the file pointer for fgets?") or only the return value ("Does sprintf return a pointer or a count?"). These prototypes also show which headers need to be included to obtain the definitions of any special constants and to obtain the ISO C function prototype to help detect any compile-time errors.

The page number reference for each function prototype appears to the right of the first header file listed for the function. The page number reference gives the page containing the prototype for the function. That page should be consulted for additional information on the function.

Some functions are supported by only a few of the platforms described in this text. In addition, some platforms support function flags that other platforms don't support. In these cases, we usually list the platforms for which support is provided. In a few cases, however, we list platforms that lack support.

```
void      abort(void);
                    <stdlib.h>                                    p. 340
                    This function never returns

int       accept(int sockfd, struct sockaddr *restrict addr,
                  socklen_t *restrict len);
                    <sys/socket.h>                                p. 563
                    Returns: file (socket) descriptor if OK, −1 on error
```

```
int        access(const char *pathname, int mode);
                    <unistd.h>                                          p. 95
                    mode: R_OK, W_OK, X_OK, F_OK
                    Returns: 0 if OK, −1 on error
unsigned
int        alarm(unsigned int seconds);
                    <unistd.h>                                          p. 313
                    Returns: 0 or number of seconds until previously set alarm

char       *asctime(const struct tm *tmptr);
                    <time.h>                                            p. 175
                    Returns: pointer to null-terminated string

int        atexit(void (*func)(void));
                    <stdlib.h>                                          p. 182
                    Returns: 0 if OK, nonzero on error

int        bind(int sockfd, const struct sockaddr *addr, socklen_t len);
                    <sys/socket.h>                                      p. 560
                    Returns: 0 if OK, −1 on error

void       *calloc(size_t nobj, size_t size);
                    <stdlib.h>                                          p. 189
                    Returns: non-null pointer if OK, NULL on error

speed_t    cfgetispeed(const struct termios *termptr);
                    <termios.h>                                         p. 652
                    Returns: baud rate value

speed_t    cfgetospeed(const struct termios *termptr);
                    <termios.h>                                         p. 652
                    Returns: baud rate value

int        cfsetispeed(struct termios *termptr, speed_t speed);
                    <termios.h>                                         p. 652
                    Returns: 0 if OK, −1 on error

int        cfsetospeed(struct termios *termptr, speed_t speed);
                    <termios.h>                                         p. 652
                    Returns: 0 if OK, −1 on error

int        chdir(const char *pathname);
                    <unistd.h>                                          p. 125
                    Returns: 0 if OK, −1 on error

int        chmod(const char *pathname, mode_t mode);
                    <sys/stat.h>                                        p. 99
                    mode: S_IS[UG]ID, S_ISVTX, S_I[RWX](USR|GRP|OTH)
                    Returns: 0 if OK, −1 on error
```

```
int       chown(const char *pathname, uid_t owner, gid_t group);
                      <unistd.h>                                        p. 102
                      Returns: 0 if OK, –1 on error

void      clearerr(FILE *fp);
                      <stdio.h>                                         p. 141

int       close(int filedes);
                      <unistd.h>                                        p. 63
                      Returns: 0 if OK, –1 on error

int       closedir(DIR *dp);
                      <dirent.h>                                        p. 120
                      Returns: 0 if OK, –1 on error

void      closelog(void);
                      <syslog.h>                                        p. 430
unsigned
char      *CMSG_DATA(struct cmsghdr *cp);
                      <sys/socket.h>                                    p. 607
                      Returns: pointer to data associated with cmsghdr structure
struct
cmsghdr   *CMSG_FIRSTHDR(struct msghdr *mp);
                      <sys/socket.h>                                    p. 607
                      Returns: pointer to first cmsghdr structure associated with the msghdr
                              structure, or NULL if none exists
unsigned
int       CMSG_LEN(unsigned int nbytes);
                      <sys/socket.h>                                    p. 607
                      Returns: size to allocate for data object nbytes large
struct
cmsghdr   *CMSG_NXTHDR(struct msghdr *mp, struct cmsghdr *cp);
                      <sys/socket.h>                                    p. 607
                      Returns: pointer to next cmsghdr structure associated with the msghdr
                              structure given the current cmsghdr structure, or NULL if we're
                              at the last one

int       connect(int sockfd, const struct sockaddr *addr, socklen_t len);
                      <sys/socket.h>                                    p. 561
                      Returns: 0 if OK, –1 on error

int       creat(const char *pathname, mode_t mode);
                      <fcntl.h>                                         p. 62
                      mode: S_IS[UG]ID, S_ISVTX, S_I[RWX](USR|GRP|OTH)
                      Returns: file descriptor opened for write-only if OK, –1 on error

char      *ctermid(char *ptr);
                      <stdio.h>                                         p. 654
                      Returns: pointer to name of controlling terminal on success, pointer to
                              empty string on error
```

```
char       *ctime(const time_t *calptr);
                         <time.h>                                                p. 175
                         Returns: pointer to null-terminated string

int        dup(int filedes);
                         <unistd.h>                                              p. 76
                         Returns: new file descriptor if OK, −1 on error

int        dup2(int filedes, int filedes2);
                         <unistd.h>                                              p. 76
                         Returns: new file descriptor if OK, −1 on error

void       endgrent(void);
                         <grp.h>                                                 p. 167

void       endhostent(void);
                         <netdb.h>                                               p. 553

void       endnetent(void);
                         <netdb.h>                                               p. 554

void       endprotoent(void);
                         <netdb.h>                                               p. 554

void       endpwent(void);
                         <pwd.h>                                                 p. 164

void       endservent(void);
                         <netdb.h>                                               p. 555

void       endspent(void);
                         <shadow.h>                                              p. 166
                         Platforms: Linux 2.4.22, Solaris 9

int        execl(const char *pathname, const char *arg0, ... /* (char *) 0 */ );
                         <unistd.h>                                              p. 231
                         Returns: −1 on error, no return on success

int        execle(const char *pathname, const char *arg0, ... /* (char *) 0,
               char *const envp[] */ );
                         <unistd.h>                                              p. 231
                         Returns: −1 on error, no return on success

int        execlp(const char *filename, const char *arg0, ... /* (char *) 0 */ );
                         <unistd.h>                                              p. 231
                         Returns: −1 on error, no return on success

int        execv(const char *pathname, char *const argv[]);
                         <unistd.h>                                              p. 231
                         Returns: −1 on error, no return on success
```

int   **execve**(const char *pathname*, char *const *argv*[], char *const *envp*[]);
                          <unistd.h>   p. 231
                          Returns: −1 on error, no return on success

int   **execvp**(const char *filename*, char *const *argv*[]);
                          <unistd.h>   p. 231
                          Returns: −1 on error, no return on success

void   **_Exit**(int *status*);
                          <stdlib.h>   p. 180
                          This function never returns

void   **_exit**(int *status*);
                          <unistd.h>   p. 180
                          This function never returns

void   **exit**(int *status*);
                          <stdlib.h>   p. 180
                          This function never returns

int   **fattach**(int *filedes*, const char *path*);
                          <stropts.h>   p. 589
                          Returns: 0 if OK, −1 on error
                          Platforms: Linux 2.4.22, Solaris 9

int   **fchdir**(int *filedes*);
                          <unistd.h>   p. 125
                          Returns: 0 if OK, −1 on error

int   **fchmod**(int *filedes*, mode_t *mode*);
                          <sys/stat.h>   p. 99
                          mode: S_IS[UG]ID, S_ISVTX, S_I[RWX](USR|GRP|OTH)
                          Returns: 0 if OK, −1 on error

int   **fchown**(int *filedes*, uid_t *owner*, gid_t *group*);
                          <unistd.h>   p. 102
                          Returns: 0 if OK, −1 on error

int   **fclose**(FILE **fp*);
                          <stdio.h>   p. 139
                          Returns: 0 if OK, EOF on error

int   **fcntl**(int *filedes*, int *cmd*, ... /* int *arg* */);
                          <fcntl.h>   p. 78
                          cmd: F_DUPFD, F_GETFD, F_SETFD, F_GETFL, F_SETFL,
                                 F_GETOWN, F_SETOWN, F_GETLK, F_SETLK, F_SETLKW
                          Returns: depends on *cmd* if OK, −1 on error

int   **fdatasync**(int *filedes*);
                              <unistd.h>   p. 77
                              Returns: 0 if OK, –1 on error
                              Platforms: Linux 2.4.22, Solaris 9

void   **FD_CLR**(int *fd*, fd_set **fdset*);
                              <sys/select.h>   p. 476

int   **fdetach**(const char **path*);
                              <stropts.h>   p. 590
                              Returns: 0 if OK, –1 on error
                              Platforms: Linux 2.4.22, Solaris 9

int   **FD_ISSET**(int *fd*, fd_set **fdset*);
                              <sys/select.h>   p. 476
                              Returns: nonzero if *fd* is in set, 0 otherwise

FILE   ***fdopen**(int *filedes*, const char **type*);
                              <stdio.h>   p. 138
                              type: "r", "w", "a", "r+", "w+", "a+",
                              Returns: file pointer if OK, NULL on error

void   **FD_SET**(int *fd*, fd_set **fdset*);
                              <sys/select.h>   p. 476

void   **FD_ZERO**(fd_set **fdset*);
                              <sys/select.h>   p. 476

int   **feof**(FILE **fp*);
                              <stdio.h>   p. 141
                              Returns: nonzero (true) if end of file on stream, 0 (false) otherwise

int   **ferror**(FILE **fp*);
                              <stdio.h>   p. 141
                              Returns: nonzero (true) if error on stream, 0 (false) otherwise

int   **fflush**(FILE **fp*);
                              <stdio.h>   p. 137
                              Returns: 0 if OK, EOF on error

int   **fgetc**(FILE **fp*);
                              <stdio.h>   p. 140
                              Returns: next character if OK, EOF on end of file or error

int   **fgetpos**(FILE *restrict *fp*, fpos_t *restrict *pos*);
                              <stdio.h>   p. 148
                              Returns: 0 if OK, nonzero on error

char   ***fgets**(char *restrict *buf*, int *n*, FILE *restrict *fp*);
        <stdio.h>   p. 142
        Returns: buf if OK, NULL on end of file or error

int   **fileno**(FILE *fp);
        <stdio.h>   p. 153
        Returns: file descriptor associated with the stream

void   **flockfile**(FILE *fp);
        <stdio.h>   p. 403

FILE   ***fopen**(const char *restrict *pathname*, const char *restrict *type*);
        <stdio.h>   p. 138
        type: "r", "w", "a", "r+", "w+", "a+",
        Returns: file pointer if OK, NULL on error

pid_t   **fork**(void);
        <unistd.h>   p. 211
        Returns: 0 in child, process ID of child in parent, −1 on error

long   **fpathconf**(int *filedes*, int *name*);
        <unistd.h>   p. 41
        name: _PC_ASYNC_IO, _PC_CHOWN_RESTRICTED,
          _PC_FILESIZEBITS, _PC_LINK_MAX, _PC_MAX_CANON,
          _PC_MAX_INPUT, _PC_NAME_MAX, _PC_NO_TRUNC,
          _PC_PATH_MAX, 'u'_PC_PIPE_BUF, _PC_PRIO_IO,
          _PC_SYNC_IO, _PC_SYMLINK_MAX, _PC_VDISABLE
        Returns: corresponding value if OK, −1 on error

int   **fprintf**(FILE *restrict *fp*, const char *restrict *format*, ...);
        <stdio.h>   p. 149
        Returns: number of characters output if OK, negative value if output error

int   **fputc**(int *c*, FILE *fp);
        <stdio.h>   p. 142
        Returns: c if OK, EOF on error

int   **fputs**(const char *restrict *str*, FILE *restrict *fp*);
        <stdio.h>   p. 143
        Returns: non-negative value if OK, EOF on error

size_t   **fread**(void *restrict *ptr*, size_t *size*, size_t *nobj*, FILE *restrict *fp*);
        <stdio.h>   p. 146
        Returns: number of objects read

void   **free**(void *ptr);
        <stdlib.h>   p. 189

```
void        freeaddrinfo(struct addrinfo *ai);
                        <sys/socket.h>                          p. 555
                        <netdb.h>


FILE        *freopen(const char *restrict pathname, const char *restrict type,
                FILE *restrict fp);
                        <stdio.h>                               p. 138
                        type: "r", "w", "a", "r+", "w+", "a+",
                        Returns: file pointer if OK, NULL on error


int         fscanf(FILE *restrict fp, const char *restrict format, ...);
                        <stdio.h>                               p. 151
                        Returns: number of input items assigned, EOF if input error or end of file
                            before any conversion


int         fseek(FILE *fp, long offset, int whence);
                        <stdio.h>                               p. 147
                        whence: SEEK_SET, SEEK_CUR, SEEK_END
                        Returns: 0 if OK, nonzero on error


int         fseeko(FILE *fp, off_t offset, int whence);
                        <stdio.h>                               p. 148
                        whence: SEEK_SET, SEEK_CUR, SEEK_END
                        Returns: 0 if OK, nonzero on error


int         fsetpos(FILE *fp, const fpos_t *pos);
                        <stdio.h>                               p. 148
                        Returns: 0 if OK, nonzero on error


int         fstat(int filedes, struct stat *buf);
                        <sys/stat.h>                            p. 87
                        Returns: 0 if OK, -1 on error


int         fsync(int filedes);
                        <unistd.h>                              p. 77
                        Returns: 0 if OK, -1 on error


long        ftell(FILE *fp);
                        <stdio.h>                               p. 147
                        Returns: current file position indicator if OK, -1L on error


off_t       ftello(FILE *fp);
                        <stdio.h>                               p. 148
                        Returns: current file position indicator if OK, (off_t)-1 on error


key_t       ftok(const char *path, int id);
                        <sys/ipc.h>                             p. 519
                        Returns: key if OK, (key_t)-1 on error
```

int   **ftruncate**(int *filedes*, off_t *length*);
                                                 <unistd.h>   p. 105
                                                 Returns: 0 if OK, −1 on error

int   **ftrylockfile**(FILE *fp*);
         <stdio.h>   p. 403
         Returns: 0 if OK, nonzero if lock can't be acquired

void   **funlockfile**(FILE *fp*);
         <stdio.h>   p. 403

int   **fwide**(FILE *fp*, int *mode*);
         <stdio.h>   p. 134
         <wchar.h>
         Returns: positive if stream is wide oriented, negative if stream is
                  byte oriented, or 0 if stream has no orientation

size_t   **fwrite**(const void *restrict *ptr*, size_t *size*, size_t *nobj*,
             FILE *restrict *fp*);
         <stdio.h>   p. 146
         Returns: number of objects written

const
char   ***gai_strerror**(int *error*);
         <netdb.h>   p. 556
         Returns: a pointer to a string describing the error

int   **getaddrinfo**(const char *restrict *host*, const char *restrict *service*,
             const struct addrinfo *restrict *hint*,
             struct addrinfo **restrict *res*);
         <sys/socket.h>   p. 555
         <netdb.h>
         Returns: 0 if OK, nonzero error code on error

int   **getc**(FILE *fp*);
         <stdio.h>   p. 140
          Returns: next character if OK, EOF on end of file or error

int   **getchar**(void);
         <stdio.h>   p. 140
          Returns: next character if OK, EOF on end of file or error

int   **getchar_unlocked**(void);
         <stdio.h>   p. 403
          Returns: the next character if OK, EOF on end of file or error

int   **getc_unlocked**(FILE *fp*);
         <stdio.h>   p. 403
          Returns: the next character if OK, EOF on end of file or error

```
char        *getcwd(char *buf, size_t size);
```
                               <unistd.h>   p. 126
                               Returns: *buf* if OK, NULL on error


```
gid_t       getegid(void);
```
                               <unistd.h>   p. 210
                               Returns: effective group ID of calling process


```
char        *getenv(const char *name);
```
                               <stdlib.h>   p. 192
                               Returns: pointer to *value* associated with *name*, NULL if not found


```
uid_t       geteuid(void);
```
                               <unistd.h>   p. 210
                               Returns: effective user ID of calling process


```
gid_t       getgid(void);
```
                               <unistd.h>   p. 210
                               Returns: real group ID of calling process

```
struct
group       *getgrent(void);
```
                               <grp.h>   p. 167
                               Returns: pointer if OK, NULL on error or end of file

```
struct
group       *getgrgid(gid_t gid);
```
                               <grp.h>   p. 166
                               Returns: pointer if OK, NULL on error

```
struct
group       *getgrnam(const char *name);
```
                               <grp.h>   p. 166
                               Returns: pointer if OK, NULL on error


```
int         getgroups(int gidsetsize, gid_t grouplist[]);
```
                               <unistd.h>   p. 168
                               Returns: number of supplementary group IDs if OK, −1 on error

```
struct
hostent     *gethostent(void);
```
                               <netdb.h>   p. 553
                               Returns: pointer if OK, NULL on error


```
int         gethostname(char *name, int namelen);
```
                               <unistd.h>   p. 172
                               Returns: 0 if OK, −1 on error


```
char        *getlogin(void);
```
                               <unistd.h>   p. 256
                               Returns: pointer to string giving login name if OK, NULL on error

int   **getmsg**(int *filedes*, struct strbuf *restrict *ctlptr*,
                   struct strbuf *restrict *dataptr*, int *restrict *flagptr*);

<stropts.h>   p. 469
flagptr: 0, RS_HIPRI
Returns: non-negative value if OK, −1 on error
Platforms: Linux 2.4.22, Solaris 9

int   **getnameinfo**(const struct sockaddr *restrict *addr*, socklen_t *alen*,
                   char *restrict *host*, socklen_t *hostlen*, char *restrict *service*,
                   socklen_t *servlen*, unsigned int *flags*);

<sys/socket.h>   p. 556
<netdb.h>
Returns: 0 if OK, nonzero on error

struct
netent   ***getnetbyaddr**(uint32_t *net*, int *type*);

<netdb.h>   p. 554
Returns: pointer if OK, NULL on error

struct
netent   ***getnetbyname**(const char *name*);

<netdb.h>   p. 554
Returns: pointer if OK, NULL on error

struct
netent   ***getnetent**(void);

<netdb.h>   p. 554
Returns: pointer if OK, NULL on error

int   **getopt**(int *argc*, const * const *argv[]*, const char *options*);

<fcntl.h>   p. 774
extern int optind, opterr, optopt;
extern char *optarg;
Returns: the next option character, or −1 when all options have been
         processed

int   **getpeername**(int *sockfd*, struct sockaddr *restrict *addr*,
                   socklen_t *restrict *alenp*);

<sys/socket.h>   p. 561
Returns: 0 if OK, −1 on error

pid_t   **getpgid**(pid_t *pid*);

<unistd.h>   p. 269
Returns: process group ID if OK, −1 on error

pid_t   **getpgrp**(void);

<unistd.h>   p. 269
Returns: process group ID of calling process

pid_t   **getpid**(void);

<unistd.h>   p. 210
Returns: process ID of calling process

```
int        getpmsg(int filedes, struct strbuf *restrict ctlptr,
                   struct strbuf *restrict dataptr, int *restrict bandptr,
                   int *restrict flagptr);
```
                            `<stropts.h>`   p. 469

    flagptr: 0, MSG_HIPRI, MSG_BAND, MSG_ANY
    Returns: non-negative value if OK, −1 on error
    Platforms: Linux 2.4.22, Solaris 9

```
pid_t      getppid(void);
```
    `<unistd.h>`   p. 210
    Returns: parent process ID of calling process

```
struct
protoent  *getprotobyname(const char *name);
```
    `<netdb.h>`   p. 554
    Returns: pointer if OK, NULL on error

```
struct
protoent  *getprotobynumber(int proto);
```
    `<netdb.h>`   p. 554
    Returns: pointer if OK, NULL on error

```
struct
protoent  *getprotoent(void);
```
    `<netdb.h>`   p. 554
    Returns: pointer if OK, NULL on error

```
struct
passwd    *getpwent(void);
```
    `<pwd.h>`   p. 164
    Returns: pointer if OK, NULL on error or end of file

```
struct
passwd    *getpwnam(const char *name);
```
    `<pwd.h>`   p. 163
    Returns: pointer if OK, NULL on error

```
struct
passwd    *getpwuid(uid_t uid);
```
    `<pwd.h>`   p. 163
    Returns: pointer if OK, NULL on error

```
int        getrlimit(int resource, struct rlimit *rlptr);
```
    `<sys/resource.h>`   p. 202
    Returns: 0 if OK, nonzero on error

```
char      *gets(char *buf);
```
    `<stdio.h>`   p. 142
    Returns: buf if OK, NULL on end of file or error

```
struct
servent   *getservbyname(const char *name, const char *proto);
```
    `<netdb.h>`   p. 555
    Returns: pointer if OK, NULL on error

```
struct
servent  *getservbyport(int port, const char *proto);
```
                    <netdb.h>   p. 555
                    Returns: pointer if OK, NULL on error

```
struct
servent  *getservent(void);
```
                    <netdb.h>   p. 555
                    Returns: pointer if OK, NULL on error

```
pid_t    getsid(pid_t pid);
```
                    <unistd.h>   p. 271
                    Returns: session leader's process group ID if OK, −1 on error

```
int      getsockname(int sockfd, struct sockaddr *restrict addr,
                    socklen_t *restrict alenp);
```
                    <sys/socket.h>   p. 561
                    Returns: 0 if OK, −1 on error

```
int      getsockopt(int sockfd, int level, int option, void *restrict val,
                    socklen_t *restrict lenp);
```
                    <sys/socket.h>   p. 579
                    Returns: 0 if OK, −1 on error

```
struct
spwd     *getspent(void);
```
                    <shadow.h>   p. 166
                    Returns: pointer if OK, NULL on error
                    Platforms: Linux 2.4.22, Solaris 9

```
struct
spwd     *getspnam(const char *name);
```
                    <shadow.h>   p. 166
                    Returns: pointer if OK, NULL on error
                    Platforms: Linux 2.4.22, Solaris 9

```
int      gettimeofday(struct timeval *restrict tp, void *restrict tzp);
```
                    <sys/time.h>   p. 173
                    Returns: 0 always

```
uid_t    getuid(void);
```
                    <unistd.h>   p. 210
                    Returns: real user ID of calling process

```
struct
tm       *gmtime(const time_t *calptr);
```
                    <time.h>   p. 175
                    Returns: pointer to broken-down time

```
int      grantpt(int filedes);
```
                    <stdlib.h>   p. 682
                    Returns: 0 on success, −1 on error
                    Platforms: FreeBSD 5.2.1, Linux 2.4.22, Solaris 9

uint32_t   **htonl**(uint32_t *hostint32*);

                                         `<arpa/inet.h>`   p. 550
                                         Returns: 32-bit integer in network byte order

uint16_t   **htons**(uint16_t *hostint16*);

                                         `<arpa/inet.h>`   p. 550
                                         Returns: 16-bit integer in network byte order

const
char   *__**inet_ntop**__(int *domain*, const void *restrict *addr*, char *restrict *str*,
                      socklen_t *size*);

                                         `<arpa/inet.h>`   p. 552
                                         Returns: pointer to address string on success, NULL on error

int   **inet_pton**(int *domain*, const char *restrict *str*, void *restrict *addr*);

                                         `<arpa/inet.h>`   p. 552
                                         Returns: 1 on success, 0 if the format is invalid, or −1 on error

int   **initgroups**(const char *username*, gid_t *basegid*);

                                         `<grp.h>`   /* Linux & Solaris */   p. 168
                                         `<unistd.h>` /* FreeBSD & Mac OS X */
                                         Returns: 0 if OK, −1 on error

int   **ioctl**(int *filedes*, int *request*, ...);

                                         `<unistd.h>`   /* System V */   p. 83
                                         `<sys/ioctl.h>` /* BSD and Linux */
                                         `<stropts.h>`   /* XSI STREAMS */
                                         Returns: −1 on error, something else if OK

int   **isastream**(int *filedes*);

                                         `<stropts.h>`   p. 465
                                         Returns: 1 (true) if STREAMS device, 0 (false) otherwise
                                         Platforms: Linux 2.4.22, Solaris 9

int   **isatty**(int *filedes*);

                                         `<unistd.h>`   p. 655
                                         Returns: 1 (true) if terminal device, 0 (false) otherwise

int   **kill**(pid_t *pid*, int *signo*);

                                         `<signal.h>`   p. 312
                                         Returns: 0 if OK, −1 on error

int   **lchown**(const char *pathname*, uid_t *owner*, gid_t *group*);

                                         `<unistd.h>`   p. 102
                                         Returns: 0 if OK, −1 on error

int   **link**(const char *existingpath*, const char *newpath*);

                                         `<unistd.h>`   p. 109
                                         Returns: 0 if OK, −1 on error

```
int        listen(int sockfd, int backlog);
                         <sys/socket.h>                              p. 563
                         Returns: 0 if OK, -1 on error

struct
tm         *localtime(const time_t *calptr);
                         <time.h>                                    p. 175
                         Returns: pointer to broken-down time


void       longjmp(jmp_buf env, int val);
                         <setjmp.h>                                  p. 197
                         This function never returns


off_t      lseek(int filedes, off_t offset, int whence);
                         <unistd.h>                                  p. 63
                         whence: SEEK_SET, SEEK_CUR, SEEK_END
                         Returns: new file offset if OK, -1 on error


int        lstat(const char *restrict pathname, struct stat *restrict buf);
                         <sys/stat.h>                                p. 87
                         Returns: 0 if OK, -1 on error


void       *malloc(size_t size);
                         <stdlib.h>                                  p. 189
                         Returns: non-null pointer if OK, NULL on error


int        mkdir(const char *pathname, mode_t mode);
                         <sys/stat.h>                                p. 119
                         mode: S_IS[UG]ID, S_ISVTX, S_I[RWX](USR|GRP|OTH)
                         Returns: 0 if OK, -1 on error


int        mkfifo(const char *pathname, mode_t mode);
                         <sys/stat.h>                                p. 514
                         mode: S_IS[UG]ID, S_ISVTX, S_I[RWX](USR|GRP|OTH)
                         Returns: 0 if OK, -1 on error


int        mkstemp(char *template);
                         <stdlib.h>                                  p. 158
                         Returns: file descriptor if OK, -1 on error


time_t     mktime(struct tm *tmptr);
                         <time.h>                                    p. 175
                         Returns: calendar time if OK, -1 on error


caddr_t    mmap(void *addr, size_t len, int prot, int flag, int filedes, off_t off);
                         <sys/mman.h>                                p. 487
                         prot: PROT_READ, PROT_WRITE, PROT_EXEC, PROT_NONE
                         flag: MAP_FIXED, MAP_SHARED, MAP_PRIVATE
                         Returns: starting address of mapped region if OK, MAP_FAILED on error
```

```
int        mprotect(void *addr, size_t len, int prot);
                    <sys/mman.h>                                              p. 489
                    Returns: 0 if OK, −1 on error

int        msgctl(int msqid, int cmd, struct msqid_ds *buf);
                    <sys/msg.h>                                               p. 524
                    cmd: IPC_STAT, IPC_SET, IPC_RMID
                    Returns: 0 if OK, −1 on error
                    Platforms: FreeBSD 5.2.1, Linux 2.4.22, Solaris 9

int        msgget(key_t key, int flag);
                    <sys/msg.h>                                               p. 524
                    flag: 0, IPC_CREAT, IPC_EXCL
                    Returns: message queue ID if OK, −1 on error
                    Platforms: FreeBSD 5.2.1, Linux 2.4.22, Solaris 9

ssize_t    msgrcv(int msqid, void *ptr, size_t nbytes, long type, int flag);
                    <sys/msg.h>                                               p. 526
                    flag: 0, IPC_NOWAIT, MSG_NOERROR
                    Returns: size of data portion of message if OK, −1 on error
                    Platforms: FreeBSD 5.2.1, Linux 2.4.22, Solaris 9

int        msgsnd(int msqid, const void *ptr, size_t nbytes, int flag);
                    <sys/msg.h>                                               p. 525
                    flag: 0, IPC_NOWAIT
                    Returns: 0 if OK, −1 on error
                    Platforms: FreeBSD 5.2.1, Linux 2.4.22, Solaris 9

int        msync(void *addr, size_t len, int flags);
                    <sys/mman.h>                                              p. 490
                    Returns: 0 if OK, −1 on error

int        munmap(caddr_t addr, size_t len);
                    <sys/mman.h>                                              p. 490
                    Returns: 0 if OK, −1 on error

uint32_t   ntohl(uint32_t netint32);
                    <arpa/inet.h>                                             p. 550
                    Returns: 32-bit integer in host byte order

uint16_t   ntohs(uint16_t netint16);
                    <arpa/inet.h>                                             p. 550
                    Returns: 16-bit integer in host byte order

int        open(const char *pathname, int oflag, ... /* mode_t mode */ );
                    <fcntl.h>                                                 p. 60
                    oflag: O_RDONLY, O_WRONLY, O_RDWR;
                           O_APPEND, O_CREAT, O_DSYNC, O_EXCL, O_NOCTTY,
                           O_NONBLOCK, O_RSYNC, O_SYNC, O_TRUNC
                    mode: S_IS[UG]ID, S_ISVTX, S_I[RWX](USR|GRP|OTH)
                    Returns: file descriptor if OK, −1 on error
                    Platforms: O_FSYNC flag on FreeBSD 5.2.1 and Mac OS X 10.3
```

DIR   ***opendir**(const char *pathname);

                                       <direct.h>   p. 120

                                       Returns: pointer if OK, NULL on error

void   **openlog**(char *ident, int option, int facility);

                 <syslog.h>   p. 430

                 option: LOG_CONS, LOG_NDELAY, LOG_NOWAIT, LOG_ODELAY,
                           LOG_PERROR, LOG_PID
              facility: LOG_AUTH, LOG_AUTHPRIV, LOG_CRON, LOG_DAEMON,
                           LOG_FTP, LOG_KERN, LOG_LOCAL[0-7], LOG_LPR,
                           LOG_MAIL, LOG_NEWS, LOG_SYSLOG, LOG_USER, LOG_UUCP

long   **pathconf**(const char *pathname, int name);

                 <unistd.h>   p. 41

                 name: _PC_ASYNC_IO, _PC_CHOWN_RESTRICTED,
                       _PC_FILESIZEBITS, _PC_LINK_MAX, _PC_MAX_CANON,
                       _PC_MAX_INPUT, _PC_NAME_MAX, _PC_NO_TRUNC,
                       _PC_PATH_MAX, _PC_PIPE_BUF, _PC_PRIO_IO,
                       _PC_SYMLINK_MAX, _PC_SYNC_IO, _PC_VDISABLE
                 Returns: corresponding value if OK, −1 on error

int   **pause**(void);

                 <unistd.h>   p. 313

                 Returns: −1 with errno set to EINTR

int   **pclose**(FILE *fp);

                 <stdio.h>   p. 503

                 Returns: termination status of popen cmdstring, or −1 on error

void   **perror**(const char *msg);

                 <stdio.h>   p. 15

int   **pipe**(int filedes[2]);

                 <unistd.h>   p. 497

                 Returns: 0 if OK, −1 on error

int   **poll**(struct pollfd fdarray[], nfds_t nfds, int timeout);

                 <poll.h>   p. 479

                 Returns: count of ready descriptors, 0 on timeout, −1 on error
                 Platforms: FreeBSD 5.2.1, Linux 2.4.22, Solaris 9

FILE   ***popen**(const char *cmdstring, const char *type);

                 <stdio.h>   p. 503

                 type: "r", "w"
                 Returns: file pointer if OK, NULL on error

int   **posix_openpt**(int oflag);

                 <stdlib.h>   p. 681

                 <fcntl.h>
                 oflag: O_RWDR, O_NOCTTY
                 Returns: file descriptor of next available PTY master if OK, −1 on error
                 Platforms: FreeBSD 5.2.1

ssize_t   **pread**(int *filedes*, void **buf*, size_t *nbytes*, off_t *offset*);
                                          <unistd.h>   p. 75
                                          Returns: number of bytes read, 0 if end of file, −1 on error

int   **printf**(const char *restrict *format*, ...);
                                          <stdio.h>   p. 149
                                          Returns: number of characters output if OK, negative value if output error

int   **pselect**(int *maxfdp1*, fd_set *restrict *readfds*, fd_set *restrict *writefds*,
                     fd_set *restrict *exceptfds*, const struct timespec *restrict *tsptr*,
                     const sigset_t *restrict *sigmask*);
                                            <sys/select.h>   p. 478
                                          Returns: count of ready descriptors, 0 on timeout, −1 on error
                                          Platforms: FreeBSD 5.2.1, Linux 2.4.22, Mac OS X 10.3

void   **psignal**(int *signo*, const char **msg*);
                                          <signal.h>   p. 352
                                          <siginfo.h>   /* on Solaris */

int   **pthread_atfork**(void (**prepare*) (void), void (**parent*) (void),
                        void (**child*) (void));
                                          <pthread.h>   p. 417
                                          Returns: 0 if OK, error number on failure

int   **pthread_attr_destroy**(pthread_attr_t **attr*);
                                          <pthread.h>   p. 389
                                          Returns: 0 if OK, error number on failure

int   **pthread_attr_getdetachstate**(const pthread_attr_t *restrict *attr*,
                                          int **detachstate*);
                                          <pthread.h>   p. 390
                                          Returns: 0 if OK, error number on failure

int   **pthread_attr_getguardsize**(const pthread_attr_t *restrict *attr*,
                                          size_t *restrict *guardsize*);
                                          <pthread.h>   p. 392
                                          Returns: 0 if OK, error number on failure

int   **pthread_attr_getstack**(const pthread_attr_t *restrict *attr*, void
                              **restrict *stackaddr*, size_t *restrict *stacksize*);
                                          <pthread.h>   p. 391
                                            Returns: 0 if OK, error number on failure

int   **pthread_attr_getstacksize**(const pthread_attr_t *restrict *attr*,
                                          size_t *restrict *stacksize*);
                                          <pthread.h>   p. 392
                                          Returns: 0 if OK, error number on failure

int   **pthread_attr_init**(pthread_attr_t **attr*);
                                          <pthread.h>   p. 389
                                          Returns: 0 if OK, error number on failure

int   **pthread_attr_setdetachstate**(pthread_attr_t *attr, int *detachstate*);
                              <pthread.h>   p. 390
                              Returns: 0 if OK, error number on failure

int   **pthread_attr_setguardsize**(pthread_attr_t *attr, size_t *guardsize*);
                              <pthread.h>   p. 392
                              Returns: 0 if OK, error number on failure

int   **pthread_attr_setstack**(const pthread_attr_t *attr, void *stackaddr*,
                              size_t *stacksize*);
                              <pthread.h>   p. 391
                              Returns: 0 if OK, error number on failure

int   **pthread_attr_setstacksize**(pthread_attr_t *attr, size_t *stacksize*);
                              <pthread.h>   p. 392
                              Returns: 0 if OK, error number on failure

int   **pthread_cancel**(pthread_t *tid*);
                              <pthread.h>   p. 365
                              Returns: 0 if OK, error number on failure

void   **pthread_cleanup_pop**(int *execute*);
                              <pthread.h>   p. 365

void   **pthread_cleanup_push**(void (*rtn*)(void *), void *arg*);
                              <pthread.h>   p. 365

int   **pthread_condattr_destroy**(pthread_condattr_t *attr*);
                              <pthread.h>   p. 401
                              Returns: 0 if OK, error number on failure

int   **pthread_condattr_getpshared**(const pthread_condattr_t *restrict *attr*,
                              int *restrict *pshared*);
                              <pthread.h>   p. 401
                              Returns: 0 if OK, error number on failure

int   **pthread_condattr_init**(pthread_condattr_t *attr*);
                              <pthread.h>   p. 401
                              Returns: 0 if OK, error number on failure

int   **pthread_condattr_setpshared**(pthread_condattr_t *attr, int *pshared*);
                              <pthread.h>   p. 401
                              Returns: 0 if OK, error number on failure

int   **pthread_cond_broadcast**(pthread_cond_t *cond*);
                              <pthread.h>   p. 384
                              Returns: 0 if OK, error number on failure

int   **pthread_cond_destroy**(pthread_cond_t *cond*);
                              <pthread.h>   p. 383
                              Returns: 0 if OK, error number on failure

```
int         pthread_cond_init(pthread_cond_t *restrict cond,
                        pthread_condattr_t *restrict attr);
```
<pthread.h>   p. 383
Returns: 0 if OK, error number on failure


```
int         pthread_cond_signal(pthread_cond_t *cond);
```
<pthread.h>   p. 384
Returns: 0 if OK, error number on failure


```
int         pthread_cond_timedwait(pthread_cond_t *restrict cond,
                        pthread_mutex_t *restrict mutex,
                        const struct timespec *restrict timeout);
```
<pthread.h>   p. 383
Returns: 0 if OK, error number on failure


```
int         pthread_cond_wait(pthread_cond_t *restrict cond,
                        pthread_mutex_t *restrict mutex);
```
<pthread.h>   p. 383
Returns: 0 if OK, error number on failure


```
int         pthread_create(pthread_t *restrict tidp,
                    const pthread_attr_t *restrict attr,
                    void *(*start_rtn)(void), void *restrict arg);
```
<pthread.h>   p. 357
Returns: 0 if OK, error number on failure


```
int         pthread_detach(pthread_t tid);
```
<pthread.h>   p. 368
Returns: 0 if OK, error number on failure


```
int         pthread_equal(pthread_t tid1, pthread_t tid2);
```
<pthread.h>   p. 357
Returns: nonzero if equal, 0 otherwise


```
void        pthread_exit(void *rval_ptr);
```
<pthread.h>   p. 361


```
int         pthread_getconcurrency(void);
```
<pthread.h>   p. 393
Returns: current concurrency level


```
void        *pthread_getspecific(pthread_key_t key);
```
<pthread.h>   p. 408
Returns: thread-specific data value or NULL if no value has been
         associated with the key


```
int         pthread_join(pthread_t thread, void **rval_ptr);
```
<pthread.h>   p. 361
Returns: 0 if OK, error number on failure

int   **pthread_key_create**(pthread_key_t *`keyp`, void (*`destructor`)(void *);
                 <pthread.h>   p. 406
                 Returns: 0 if OK, error number on failure

int   **pthread_key_delete**(pthread_key_t *`key`);
                 <pthread.h>   p. 407
                 Returns: 0 if OK, error number on failure

int   **pthread_kill**(pthread_t *`thread`, int *`signo`);
                 <signal.h>   p. 414
                 Returns: 0 if OK, error number on failure

int   **pthread_mutexattr_destroy**(pthread_mutexattr_t *`attr`);
                 <pthread.h>   p. 393
                 Returns: 0 if OK, error number on failure

int   **pthread_mutexattr_getpshared**(const pthread_mutexattr_t *restrict `attr`,
                                int *restrict `pshared`);
                 <pthread.h>   p. 394
                 Returns: 0 if OK, error number on failure

int   **pthread_mutexattr_gettype**(const pthread_mutexattr_t *restrict `attr`,
                                int *restrict `type`);
                 <pthread.h>   p. 395
                 Returns: 0 if OK, error number on failure

int   **pthread_mutexattr_init**(pthread_mutexattr_t *`attr`);
                 <pthread.h>   p. 393
                 Returns: 0 if OK, error number on failure

int   **pthread_mutexattr_setpshared**(pthread_mutexattr_t *`attr`, int `pshared`);
                 <pthread.h>   p. 394
                 Returns: 0 if OK, error number on failure

int   **pthread_mutexattr_settype**(pthread_mutexattr_t *`attr`, int `type`);
                 <pthread.h>   p. 395
                 Returns: 0 if OK, error number on failure

int   **pthread_mutex_destroy**(pthread_mutex_t *`mutex`);
                 <pthread.h>   p. 371
                 Returns: 0 if OK, error number on failure

int   **pthread_mutex_init**(pthread_mutex_t *restrict `mutex`,
                          const pthread_mutexattr_t *restrict `attr`);
                 <pthread.h>   p. 371
                 Returns: 0 if OK, error number on failure

int   **pthread_mutex_lock**(pthread_mutex_t *`mutex`);
                 <pthread.h>   p. 371
                 Returns: 0 if OK, error number on failure

```
int        pthread_mutex_trylock(pthread_mutex_t *mutex);
                      <pthread.h>                                   p. 371
                      Returns: 0 if OK, error number on failure


int        pthread_mutex_unlock(pthread_mutex_t *mutex);
                      <pthread.h>                                   p. 371
                      Returns: 0 if OK, error number on failure


int        pthread_once(pthread_once_t *initflag, void (*initfn)(void);
                      <pthread.h>                                   p. 408
                      pthread_once_t initflag = PTHREAD_ONCE_INIT;
                      Returns: 0 if OK, error number on failure


int        pthread_rwlockattr_destroy(pthread_rwlockattr_t *attr);
                      <pthread.h>                                   p. 400
                      Returns: 0 if OK, error number on failure


int        pthread_rwlockattr_getpshared(const pthread_rwlockattr_t *restrict attr,
                                    int *restrict pshared);
                      <pthread.h>                                   p. 400
                      Returns: 0 if OK, error number on failure


int        pthread_rwlockattr_init(pthread_rwlockattr_t *attr);
                      <pthread.h>                                   p. 400
                      Returns: 0 if OK, error number on failure


int        pthread_rwlockattr_setpshared(pthread_rwlockattr_t *attr, int pshared);
                      <pthread.h>                                   p. 400
                      Returns: 0 if OK, error number on failure


int        pthread_rwlock_destroy(pthread_rwlock_t *rwlock);
                      <pthread.h>                                   p. 379
                      Returns: 0 if OK, error number on failure


int        pthread_rwlock_init(pthread_rwlock_t *restrict rwlock,
                      const pthread_rwlockattr_t *restrict attr);
                      <pthread.h>                                   p. 379
                      Returns: 0 if OK, error number on failure


int        pthread_rwlock_rdlock(pthread_rwlock_t *rwlock);
                      <pthread.h>                                   p. 379
                      Returns: 0 if OK, error number on failure


int        pthread_rwlock_tryrdlock(pthread_rwlock_t *rwlock);
                      <pthread.h>                                   p. 379
                      Returns: 0 if OK, error number on failure


int        pthread_rwlock_trywrlock(pthread_rwlock_t *rwlock);
                      <pthread.h>                                   p. 379
                      Returns: 0 if OK, error number on failure
```

int   **pthread_rwlock_unlock**(pthread_rwlock_t *rwlock);
                            <pthread.h>   p. 379
                            Returns: 0 if OK, error number on failure

int   **pthread_rwlock_wrlock**(pthread_rwlock_t *rwlock);
                            <pthread.h>   p. 379
                            Returns: 0 if OK, error number on failure

pthread_t **pthread_self**(void);
                            <pthread.h>   p. 357
                            Returns: thread ID of the calling thread

int   **pthread_setcancelstate**(int state, int *oldstate);
                            <pthread.h>   p. 410
                            Returns: 0 if OK, error number on failure

int   **pthread_setcanceltype**(int type, int *oldtype);
                            <pthread.h>   p. 411
                            Returns: 0 if OK, error number on failure

int   **pthread_setconcurrency**(int level);
                            <pthread.h>   p. 393
                            Returns: 0 if OK, error number on failure

int   **pthread_setspecific**(pthread_key_t key, const void *value);
                            <pthread.h>   p. 408
                            Returns: 0 if OK, error number on failure

int   **pthread_sigmask**(int how, const sigset_t *restrict set,
                            sigset_t *restrict oset);
                            <signal.h>   p. 413
                            Returns: 0 if OK, error number on failure

void   **pthread_testcancel**(void);
                            <pthread.h>   p. 411

char   ***ptsname**(int filedes);
                            <stdlib.h>   p. 682
                            Returns: pointer to name of PTY slave if OK, NULL on error
                            Platforms: FreeBSD 5.2.1, Linux 2.4.22, Solaris 9

int   **putc**(int c, FILE *fp);
                            <stdio.h>   p. 142
                            Returns: c if OK, EOF on error

int   **putchar**(int c);
                            <stdio.h>   p. 142
                            Returns: c if OK, EOF on error

```
int        putchar_unlocked(int c);
```
> `<stdio.h>`   p. 403
> Returns: *c* if OK, EOF on error

```
int        putc_unlocked(int c, FILE *fp);
```
> `<stdio.h>`   p. 403
> Returns: *c* if OK, EOF on error

```
int        putenv(char *str);
```
> `<stdlib.h>`   p. 194
> Returns: 0 if OK, nonzero on error

```
int        putmsg(int filedes, const struct strbuf *ctlptr,
                  const struct strbuf *dataptr, int flag);
```
> `<stropts.h>`   p. 463
> *flag*: 0, RS_HIPRI
> Returns: 0 if OK, −1 on error
> Platforms: Linux 2.4.22, Solaris 9

```
int        putpmsg(int filedes, const struct strbuf *ctlptr,
                   const struct strbuf *dataptr, int band, int flag);
```
> `<stropts.h>`   p. 463
> *flag*: 0, MSG_HIPRI, MSG_BAND
> Returns: 0 if OK, −1 on error
> Platforms: Linux 2.4.22, Solaris 9

```
int        puts(const char *str);
```
> `<stdio.h>`   p. 143
> Returns: non-negative value if OK, EOF on error

```
ssize_t    pwrite(int filedes, const void *buf, size_t nbytes, off_t offset);
```
> `<unistd.h>`   p. 75
> Returns: number of bytes written if OK, −1 on error

```
int        raise(int signo);
```
> `<signal.h>`   p. 312
> Returns: 0 if OK, −1 on error

```
ssize_t    read(int filedes, void *buf, size_t nbytes);
```
> `<unistd.h>`   p. 67
> Returns: number of bytes read if OK, 0 if end of file, −1 on error

```
struct
dirent     *readdir(DIR *dp);
```
> `<dirent.h>`   p. 120
> Returns: pointer if OK, NULL at end of directory or error

```
int        readlink(const char *restrict pathname, char *restrict buf,
                    size_t bufsize);
```
> `<unistd.h>`   p. 115
> Returns: number of bytes read if OK, −1 on error

ssize_t   **readv**(int *filedes*, const struct iovec *iov*, int *iovcnt*);
                      <sys/uio.h>   p. 483
                      Returns: number of bytes read if OK, −1 on error

void   ***realloc**(void *ptr*, size_t *newsize*);
                      <stdlib.h>   p. 189
                      Returns: non-null pointer if OK, NULL on error

ssize_t   **recv**(int *sockfd*, void *buf*, size_t *nbytes*, int *flags*);
                      <sys/socket.h>   p. 567
                      flags: 0, MSG_PEEK, MSG_OOB, MSG_WAITALL
                      Returns: length of message in bytes, 0 if no messages are available
                              and peer has done an orderly shutdown, or −1 on error
                      Platforms: MSG_TRUNC flag on Linux 2.4.22

ssize_t   **recvfrom**(int *sockfd*, void *restrict *buf*, size_t *len*, int *flags*,
                    struct sockaddr *restrict *addr*, socklen_t *restrict *addrlen*);
                      <sys/socket.h>   p. 567
                      flags: 0, MSG_PEEK, MSG_OOB, MSG_WAITALL
                      Returns: length of message in bytes, 0 if no messages are available
                              and peer has done an orderly shutdown, or −1 on error
                      Platforms: MSG_TRUNC flag on Linux 2.4.22

ssize_t   **recvmsg**(int *sockfd*, struct msghdr *msg*, int *flags*);
                      <sys/socket.h>   p. 568
                      flags: 0, MSG_PEEK, MSG_OOB, MSG_WAITALL
                      Returns: length of message in bytes, 0 if no messages are available
                              and peer has done an orderly shutdown, or −1 on error
                      Platforms: MSG_TRUNC flag on Linux 2.4.22

int   **remove**(const char *pathname*);
                      <stdio.h>   p. 111
                      Returns: 0 if OK, −1 on error

int   **rename**(const char *oldname*, const char *newname*);
                      <stdio.h>   p. 111
                      Returns: 0 if OK, −1 on error

void   **rewind**(FILE *fp*);
                      <stdio.h>   p. 147

void   **rewinddir**(DIR *dp*);
                      <dirent.h>   p. 120

int   **rmdir**(const char *pathname*);
                      <unistd.h>   p. 120
                      Returns: 0 if OK, −1 on error

int   **scanf**(const char *restrict *format*, ...);
                      <stdio.h>   p. 151
                      Returns: number of input items assigned, EOF if input error or
                              end of file before any conversion

```
void       seekdir(DIR *dp, long loc);
                       <dirent.h>                                          p. 120
```

```
int        select(int maxfdp1, fd_set *restrict readfds, fd_set *restrict writefds,
                   fd_set *restrict exceptfds, struct timeval *restrict tvptr);
                       <sys/select.h>                                      p. 475
                   Returns: count of ready descriptors, 0 on timeout, −1 on error
```

```
int        semctl(int semid, int semnum, int cmd, ... /* union semun arg */ );
                       <sys/sem.h>                                         p. 529
                   cmd: IPC_STAT, IPC_SET, IPC_RMID, GETPID, GETNCNT,
                        GETZCNT, GETVAL, SETVAL, GETALL, SETALL
                   Returns: (depends on command)
```

```
int        semget(key_t key, int nsems, int flag);
                       <sys/sem.h>                                         p. 529
                   flag: 0, IPC_CREAT, IPC_EXCL
                   Returns: semaphore ID if OK, −1 on error
```

```
int        semop(int semid, struct sembuf semoparray[], size_t nops);
                       <sys/sem.h>                                         p. 530
                   Returns: 0 if OK, −1 on error
```

```
ssize_t    send(int sockfd, const void *buf, size_t nbytes, int flags);
                       <sys/socket.h>                                      p. 565
                   flags: 0, MSG_DONTROUTE, MSG_EOR, MSG_OOB
                   Returns: number of bytes sent if OK, −1 on error
                   Platforms: MSG_DONTWAIT flag on FreeBSD 5.2.1, Linux 2.4.22, Mac OS X 10.3
                        MSG_EOR flag not on Solaris 9
```

```
ssize_t    sendmsg(int sockfd, const struct msghdr *msg, int flags);
                       <sys/socket.h>                                      p. 566
                   flags: 0, MSG_DONTROUTE, MSG_EOR, MSG_OOB
                   Returns: number of bytes sent if OK, −1 on error
                   Platforms: MSG_DONTWAIT flag on FreeBSD 5.2.1, Linux 2.4.22, Mac OS X 10.3
                        MSG_EOR flag not on Solaris 9
```

```
ssize_t    sendto(int sockfd, const void *buf, size_t nbytes, int flags,
                   const struct sockaddr *destaddr, socklen_t destlen);
                       <sys/socket.h>                                      p. 566
                   flags: 0, MSG_DONTROUTE, MSG_EOR, MSG_OOB
                   Returns: number of bytes sent if OK, −1 on error
                   Platforms: MSG_DONTWAIT flag on FreeBSD 5.2.1, Linux 2.4.22, Mac OS X 10.3
                        MSG_EOR flag not on Solaris 9
```

```
void       setbuf(FILE *restrict fp, char *restrict buf);
                       <stdio.h>                                           p. 136
```

```
int        setegid(gid_t gid);
                       <unistd.h>                                          p. 241
                   Returns: 0 if OK, −1 on error
```

int   **setenv**(const char *_name_, const char *_value_, int _rewrite_);
                      <stdlib.h>   p. 194
                      Returns: 0 if OK, nonzero on error

int   **seteuid**(uid_t _uid_);
                      <unistd.h>   p. 241
                      Returns: 0 if OK, −1 on error

int   **setgid**(gid_t _gid_);
                      <unistd.h>   p. 237
                      Returns: 0 if OK, −1 on error

void   **setgrent**(void);
                      <grp.h>   p. 167

int   **setgroups**(int _ngroups_, const gid_t _grouplist_[]);
                      <grp.h>   /* on Linux */   p. 168
                      <unistd.h> /* on FreeBSD, Mac OS X, and Solaris */
                      Returns: 0 if OK, −1 on error

void   **sethostent**(int _stayopen_);
                      <netdb.h>   p. 553

int   **setjmp**(jmp_buf _env_);
                      <setjmp.h>   p. 197
                      Returns: 0 if called directly, nonzero if returning from a call to longjmp

int   **setlogmask**(int _maskpri_);
                      <syslog.h>   p. 430
                      Returns: previous log priority mask value

void   **setnetent**(int _stayopen_);
                      <netdb.h>   p. 554

int   **setpgid**(pid_t _pid_, pid_t _pgid_);
                      <unistd.h>   p. 269
                      Returns: 0 if OK, −1 on error

void   **setprotoent**(int _stayopen_);
                      <netdb.h>   p. 554

void   **setpwent**(void);
                      <pwd.h>   p. 164

int   **setregid**(gid_t _rgid_, gid_t _egid_);
                      <unistd.h>   p. 240
                      Returns: 0 if OK, −1 on error

int   **setreuid**(uid_t _ruid_, uid_t _euid_);
                      <unistd.h>   p. 240
                      Returns: 0 if OK, −1 on error

```
int        setrlimit(int resource, const struct rlimit *rlptr);
                        <sys/resource.h>                              p. 202
                        Returns: 0 if OK, nonzero on error


void       setservent(int stayopen);
                        <netdb.h>                                     p. 555


pid_t      setsid(void);
                        <unistd.h>                                    p. 271
                        Returns: process group ID if OK, -1 on error


int        setsockopt(int sockfd, int level, int option, const void *val,
                      socklen_t len);
                        <sys/socket.h>                                p. 579
                        Returns: 0 if OK, -1 on error


void       setspent(void);
                        <shadow.h>                                    p. 166
                        Platforms: Linux 2.4.22, Solaris 9


int        setuid(uid_t uid);
                        <unistd.h>                                    p. 237
                        Returns: 0 if OK, -1 on error


int        setvbuf(FILE *restrict fp, char *restrict buf, int mode, size_t size);
                        <stdio.h>                                     p. 136
                        mode: _IOFBF, _IOLBF, _IONBF
                        Returns: 0 if OK, nonzero on error


void       *shmat(int shmid, const void *addr, int flag);
                        <sys/shm.h>                                   p. 536
                        flag: 0, SHM_RND, SHM_RDONLY
                        Returns: pointer to shared memory segment if OK, -1 on error


int        shmctl(int shmid, int cmd, struct shmid_ds *buf);
                        <sys/shm.h>                                   p. 535
                        cmd: IPC_STAT, IPC_SET, IPC_RMID,
                             SHM_LOCK, SHM_UNLOCK
                        Returns: 0 if OK, -1 on error


int        shmdt(void *addr);
                        <sys/shm.h>                                   p. 536
                        Returns: 0 if OK, -1 on error


int        shmget(key_t key, int size, int flag);
                        <sys/shm.h>                                   p. 534
                        flag: 0, IPC_CREAT, IPC_EXCL
                        Returns: shared memory ID if OK, -1 on error
```

int   **shutdown**(int *sockfd*, int *how*);
                            <sys/socket.h>   p. 548
                            how: SHUT_RD, SHUT_WR, SHUT_RDWR
                            Returns: 0 if OK, −1 on error

int   **sig2str**(int *signo*, char **str*);
                            <signal.h>   p. 353
                            Returns: 0 if OK, −1 on error
                            Platforms: Solaris 9

int   **sigaction**(int *signo*, const struct sigaction *restrict *act*,
                       struct sigaction *restrict *oact*);
                            <signal.h>   p. 324
                            Returns: 0 if OK, −1 on error

int   **sigaddset**(sigset_t **set*, int *signo*);
                            <signal.h>   p. 319
                            Returns: 0 if OK, −1 on error

int   **sigdelset**(sigset_t **set*, int *signo*);
                            <signal.h>   p. 319
                            Returns: 0 if OK, −1 on error

int   **sigemptyset**(sigset_t **set*);
                            <signal.h>   p. 319
                            Returns: 0 if OK, −1 on error

int   **sigfillset**(sigset_t **set*);
                            <signal.h>   p. 319
                            Returns: 0 if OK, −1 on error

int   **sigismember**(const sigset_t **set*, int *signo*);
                            <signal.h>   p. 319
                            Returns: 1 if true, 0 if false, −1 on error

void   **siglongjmp**(sigjmp_buf *env*, int *val*);
                            <setjmp.h>   p. 330
                            This function never returns

void   (***signal**(int *signo*, void (*func)(int)))(int);
                            <signal.h>   p. 298
                            Returns: previous disposition of signal if OK, SIG_ERR on error

int   **sigpending**(sigset_t **set*);
                            <signal.h>   p. 322
                            Returns: 0 if OK, −1 on error

```
int         sigprocmask(int how, const sigset_t *restrict set,
                        sigset_t *restrict oset);
                        <signal.h>                                       p. 320
                        how: SIG_BLOCK, SIG_UNBLOCK, SIG_SETMASK
                        Returns: 0 if OK, −1 on error

int         sigsetjmp(sigjmp_buf env, int savemask);
                        <setjmp.h>                                       p. 330
                        Returns: 0 if called directly, nonzero if returning from a call
                                 to siglongjmp

int         sigsuspend(const sigset_t *sigmask);
                        <signal.h>                                       p. 334
                        Returns: −1 with errno set to EINTR

int         sigwait(const sigset_t *restrict set, int *restrict signop);
                        <signal.h>                                       p. 413
                        Returns: 0 if OK, error number on failure
unsigned
int         sleep(unsigned int seconds);
                        <unistd.h>                                       p. 347
                        Returns: 0 or number of unslept seconds

int         snprintf(char *restrict buf, size_t n, const char *restrict format, ...);
                        <stdio.h>                                        p. 149
                        Returns: number of characters stored in array if OK, negative
                                 value if encoding error

int         sockatmark(int sockfd);
                        <sys/socket.h>                                   p. 582
                        Returns: 1 if at mark, 0 if not at mark, −1 on error

int         socket(int domain, int type, int protocol);
                        <sys/socket.h>                                   p. 546
                        type: SOCK_STREAM, SOCK_DGRAM, SOCK_SEQPACKET,
                        Returns: file (socket) descriptor if OK, −1 on error

int         socketpair(int domain, int type, int protocol, int sockfd[2]);
                        <sys/socket.h>                                   p. 594
                        type: SOCK_STREAM, SOCK_DGRAM, SOCK_SEQPACKET,
                        Returns: 0 if OK, −1 on error

int         sprintf(char *restrict buf, const char *restrict format, ...);
                        <stdio.h>                                        p. 149
                        Returns: number of characters stored in array if OK, negative
                                 value if encoding error

int         sscanf(const char *restrict buf, const char *restrict format, ...);
                        <stdio.h>                                        p. 151
                        Returns: number of input items assigned, EOF if input error or
                                 end of file before any conversion
```

int   **stat**(const char *restrict *pathname*, struct stat *restrict *buf*);
                                <sys/stat.h>   p. 87
                                Returns: 0 if OK, −1 on error

int   **str2sig**(const char *str*, int *signop*);
                                <signal.h>   p. 353
                                Returns: 0 if OK, −1 on error
                                Platforms: Solaris 9

char   ***strerror**(int *errnum*);
                                <string.h>   p. 15
                                Returns: pointer to message string

size_t   **strftime**(char *restrict *buf*, size_t *maxsize*, const char *restrict *format*,
                  const struct tm *restrict *tmptr*);
                                <time.h>   p. 176
                                Returns: number of characters stored in array if room, 0 otherwise

char   ***strsignal**(int *signo*);
                                <string.h>   p. 352
                                Returns: a pointer to a string describing the signal

int   **symlink**(const char *actualpath*, const char *sympath*);
                                <unistd.h>   p. 115
                                Returns: 0 if OK, −1 on error

void   **sync**(void);
                                <unistd.h>   p. 77

long   **sysconf**(int *name*);
                                <unistd.h>   p. 41
                                name: _SC_ARG_MAX, _SC_ATEXIT_MAX, _SC_CHILD_MAX,
                                    _SC_CLK_TCK, _SC_COLL_WEIGHTS_MAX,
                                    _SC_HOST_NAME_MAX, _SC_IOV_MAX, _SC_JOB_CONTROL,
                                    _SC_LINE_MAX, _SC_LOGIN_NAME_MAX, _SC_NGROUPS_MAX,
                                    _SC_OPEN_MAX, _SC_PAGESIZE, _SC_PAGE_SIZE,
                                    _SC_READER_WRITER_LOCKS, _SC_RE_DUP_MAX,
                                    _SC_SAVED_IDS, _SC_SHELL, _SC_STREAM_MAX,
                                    _SC_SYMLOOP_MAX, _SC_TTY_NAME_MAX, _SC_TZNAME_MAX,
                                    _SC_VERSION, _SC_XOPEN_CRYPT, _SC_XOPEN_LEGACY,
                                    _SC_XOPEN_REALTIME, _SC_XOPEN_REALTIME_THREADS,
                                    _SC_XOPEN_VERSION
                                Returns: corresponding value if OK, −1 on error

void   **syslog**(int *priority*, char *format*, ...);
                                <syslog.h>   p. 430

int   **system**(const char *cmdstring*);
                                <stdlib.h>   p. 246
                                Returns: termination status of shell

int   **tcdrain**(int *filedes*);

                        \<termios.h\>   p. 653
                        Returns: 0 if OK, −1 on error

int   **tcflow**(int *filedes*, int *action*);

                        \<termios.h\>   p. 653
                        action: TCOOFF, TCOON, TCIOFF, TCION
                        Returns: 0 if OK, −1 on error

int   **tcflush**(int *filedes*, int *queue*);

                        \<termios.h\>   p. 653
                        queue: TCIFLUSH, TCOFLUSH, TCIOFLUSH
                        Returns: 0 if OK, −1 on error

int   **tcgetattr**(int *filedes*, struct termios **termptr*);

                        \<termios.h\>   p. 643
                        Returns: 0 if OK, −1 on error

pid_t   **tcgetpgrp**(int *filedes*);

                        \<unistd.h\>   p. 273
                        Returns: process group ID of foreground process group if OK, −1 on error

pid_t   **tcgetsid**(int *filedes*);

                        \<termios.h\>   p. 274
                        Returns: session leader's process group ID if OK, −1 on error

int   **tcsendbreak**(int *filedes*, int *duration*);

                        \<termios.h\>   p. 653
                        Returns: 0 if OK, −1 on error

int   **tcsetattr**(int *filedes*, int *opt*, const struct termios **termptr*);

                        \<termios.h\>   p. 643
                        opt: TCSANOW, TCSADRAIN, TCSAFLUSH
                        Returns: 0 if OK, −1 on error

int   **tcsetpgrp**(int *filedes*, pid_t *pgrpid*);

                        \<unistd.h\>   p. 273
                        Returns: 0 if OK, −1 on error

long   **telldir**(DIR **dp*);

                        \<dirent.h\>   p. 120
                        Returns: current location in directory associated with *dp*

char   **tempnam*(const char **directory*, const char **prefix*);

                        \<stdio.h\>   p. 157
                        Returns: pointer to unique pathname

time_t   **time**(time_t **calptr*);

                        \<time.h\>   p. 173
                        Returns: value of time if OK, −1 on error

```
clock_t    times(struct tms *buf);
```
<sys/times.h>   p. 257
Returns: elapsed wall clock time in clock ticks if OK, −1 on error

```
FILE       *tmpfile(void);
```
<stdio.h>   p. 155
Returns: file pointer if OK, NULL on error

```
char       *tmpnam(char *ptr);
```
<stdio.h>   p. 155
Returns: pointer to unique pathname

```
int        truncate(const char *pathname, off_t length);
```
<unistd.h>   p. 105
Returns: 0 if OK, −1 on error

```
char       *ttyname(int filedes);
```
<unistd.h>   p. 655
Returns: pointer to pathname of terminal, NULL on error

```
mode_t     umask(mode_t cmask);
```
<sys/stat.h>   p. 97
Returns: previous file mode creation mask

```
int        uname(struct utsname *name);
```
<sys/utsname.h>   p. 171
Returns: non-negative value if OK, −1 on error

```
int        ungetc(int c, FILE *fp);
```
<stdio.h>   p. 141
Returns: c if OK, EOF on error

```
int        unlink(const char *pathname);
```
<unistd.h>   p. 109
Returns: 0 if OK, −1 on error

```
int        unlockpt(int filedes);
```
<stdlib.h>   p. 682
Returns: 0 on success, −1 on error
Platforms: FreeBSD 5.2.1, Linux 2.4.22, Solaris 9

```
void       unsetenv(const char *name);
```
<stdlib.h>   p. 194

```
int        utime(const char *pathname, const struct utimbuf *times);
```
<utime.h>   p. 116
Returns: 0 if OK, −1 on error

```
int        vfprintf(FILE *restrict fp, const char *restrict format, va_list arg);
```
<stdarg.h>   p. 151
<stdio.h>
Returns: number of characters output if OK, negative
              value if output error

```
int        vfscanf(FILE *restrict fp, const char *restrict format, va_list arg);
```
<stdarg.h>   p. 151
<stdio.h>
Returns: number of input items assigned, EOF if input error or end of file
              before any conversion

```
int        vprintf(const char *restrict format, va_list arg);
```
<stdarg.h>
<stdio.h>   p. 151
Returns: number of characters output if OK, negative
              value if output error

```
int        vscanf(const char *restrict format, va_list arg);
```
<stdarg.h>
<stdio.h>   p. 151
Returns: number of input items assigned, EOF if input error or end of file
              before any conversion

```
int        vsnprintf(char *restrict buf, size_t n, const char *restrict format,
              va_list arg);
```
<stdarg.h>
<stdio.h>   p. 151
Returns: number of characters stored in array if OK, negative
              value if encoding error

```
int        vsprintf(char *restrict buf, const char *restrict format, va_list arg);
```
<stdarg.h>   p. 151
<stdio.h>
Returns: number of characters stored in array if OK, negative
              value if encoding error

```
int        vsscanf(const char *restrict buf, const char *restrict format,
              va_list arg);
```
<stdarg.h>   p. 151
<stdio.h>
Returns: number of input items assigned, EOF if input error or end of file
              before any conversion

```
void       vsyslog(int priority, const char *format, va_list arg);
```
<syslog.h>   p. 432
<stdarg.h>

```
pid_t      wait(int *statloc);
```
<sys/wait.h>   p. 220
Returns: process ID if OK, 0, or –1 on error

int   **waitid**(idtype_t *idtype*, id_t *id*, siginfo_t **infop*, int *options*);
                     <sys/wait.h>   p. 220
                     idtype: P_PID, P_PGID, P_ALL
                     options: WCONTINUED, WEXITED, WNOHANG, WNOWAIT, WSTOPPED
                     Returns: 0 if OK, −1 on error
                     Platforms: Solaris 9

pid_t   **waitpid**(pid_t *pid*, int **statloc*, int *options*);
                     <sys/wait.h>   p. 220
                     options: 0, WCONTINUED, WNOHANG, WUNTRACED
                     Returns: process ID if OK, 0, or −1 on error

pid_t   **wait3**(int **statloc*, int *options*, struct rusage **rusage*);
                     <sys/types.h>   p. 227
                     <sys/wait.h>
                     <sys/time.h>
                     <sys/resource.h>
                     options: 0, WNOHANG, WUNTRACED
                     Returns: process ID if OK, 0, or −1 on error

pid_t   **wait4**(pid_t *pid*, int **statloc*, int *options*, struct rusage **rusage*);
                     <sys/types.h>   p. 227
                     <sys/wait.h>
                     <sys/time.h>
                     <sys/resource.h>
                     options: 0, WNOHANG, WUNTRACED
                     Returns: process ID if OK, 0, or −1 on error

ssize_t   **write**(int *filedes*, const void **buf*, size_t *nbytes*);
                     <unistd.h>   p. 68
                     Returns: number of bytes written if OK, −1 on error

ssize_t   **writev**(int *filedes*, const struct iovec **iov*, int *iovcnt*);
                     <sys/uio.h>   p. 483
                     Returns: number of bytes written if OK, −1 on error

Appendix B

Miscellaneous Source Code

B.1   Our Header File

Most programs in the text include the header apue.h, shown in Figure B.1. It defines constants (such as MAXLINE) and prototypes for our own functions.

Most programs need to include the following headers: <stdio.h>, <stdlib.h> (for the exit function prototype), and <unistd.h> (for all the standard UNIX function prototypes). So our header automatically includes these system headers, along with <string.h>. This also reduces the size of all the program listings in the text.

```
/* Our own header, to be included before all standard system headers */

#ifndef _APUE_H
#define _APUE_H

#if defined(SOLARIS)          /* Solaris 9 */
#define _XOPEN_SOURCE   500 /* Single UNIX Specification, Version 2 */
#define CMSG_LEN(x) _CMSG_DATA_ALIGN(sizeof(struct cmsghdr)+(x))
#elif !defined(BSD)
#define _XOPEN_SOURCE   600 /* Single UNIX Specification, Version 3 */
#endif

#include <sys/types.h>       /* some systems still require this */
#include <sys/stat.h>
#include <sys/termios.h>     /* for winsize */
#ifndef TIOCGWINSZ
#include <sys/ioctl.h>
#endif
```

```
#ifdef MACOS
#include <sys/uio.h>
#endif

#include <stdio.h>       /* for convenience */
#include <stdlib.h>      /* for convenience */
#include <stddef.h>      /* for offsetof */
#include <string.h>      /* for convenience */
#include <unistd.h>      /* for convenience */
#include <signal.h>      /* for SIG_ERR */

#define MAXLINE 4096                 /* max line length */

/*
 * Default file access permissions for new files.
 */
#define FILE_MODE    (S_IRUSR | S_IWUSR | S_IRGRP | S_IROTH)

/*
 * Default permissions for new directories.
 */
#define DIR_MODE     (FILE_MODE | S_IXUSR | S_IXGRP | S_IXOTH)

typedef void    Sigfunc(int);    /* for signal handlers */

#if defined(SIG_IGN) && !defined(SIG_ERR)
#define SIG_ERR ((Sigfunc *)-1)
#endif

#define min(a,b)     ((a) < (b) ? (a) : (b))
#define max(a,b)     ((a) > (b) ? (a) : (b))

/*
 * Prototypes for our own functions.
 */
char    *path_alloc(int *);                     /* Figure 2.15 */
long     open_max(void);                        /* Figure 2.16 */

void     clr_fl(int, int);                      /* Figure 3.11 */
void     set_fl(int, int);                      /* Figure 3.11 */

void     pr_exit(int);                          /* Figure 8.5 */

void     pr_mask(const char *);                 /* Figure 10.14 */
Sigfunc *signal_intr(int, Sigfunc *);           /* Figure 10.19 */

void     daemonize(const char *);               /* Figure 13.1 */

void     sleep_us(unsigned int);                /* Exercise 14.6 */
ssize_t  readn(int, void *, size_t);            /* Figure 14.29 */
ssize_t  writen(int, const void *, size_t); /* Figure 14.29 */
```

```
int        s_pipe(int *);                    /* Figures 17.6 and 17.13 */
int        recv_fd(int, ssize_t (*func)(int,
                   const void *, size_t));/* Figures 17.21 and 17.23 */
int        send_fd(int, int);                /* Figures 17.20 and 17.22 */
int        send_err(int, int,
                   const char *);            /* Figure 17.19 */
int        serv_listen(const char *);        /* Figures 17.10 and 17.15 */
int        serv_accept(int, uid_t *);        /* Figures 17.11 and 17.16 */
int        cli_conn(const char *);           /* Figures 17.12 and 17.17 */
int        buf_args(char *, int (*func)(int,
                   char **));                /* Figure 17.32 */

int        tty_cbreak(int);                  /* Figure 18.20 */
int        tty_raw(int);                     /* Figure 18.20 */
int        tty_reset(int);                   /* Figure 18.20 */
void       tty_atexit(void);                 /* Figure 18.20 */
struct termios  *tty_termios(void);          /* Figure 18.20 */

int        ptym_open(char *, int);     /* Figures 19.8, 19.9, and 19.10 */
int        ptys_open(char *);          /* Figures 19.8, 19.9, and 19.10 */
#ifdef  TIOCGWINSZ
pid_t      pty_fork(int *, char *, int, const struct termios *,
                   const struct winsize *);        /* Figure 19.11 */
#endif

int        lock_reg(int, int, int, off_t, int, off_t); /* Figure 14.5 */

#define read_lock(fd, offset, whence, len) \
           lock_reg((fd), F_SETLK, F_RDLCK, (offset), (whence), (len))
#define readw_lock(fd, offset, whence, len) \
           lock_reg((fd), F_SETLKW, F_RDLCK, (offset), (whence), (len))
#define write_lock(fd, offset, whence, len) \
           lock_reg((fd), F_SETLK, F_WRLCK, (offset), (whence), (len))
#define writew_lock(fd, offset, whence, len) \
           lock_reg((fd), F_SETLKW, F_WRLCK, (offset), (whence), (len))
#define un_lock(fd, offset, whence, len) \
           lock_reg((fd), F_SETLK, F_UNLCK, (offset), (whence), (len))

pid_t   lock_test(int, int, off_t, int, off_t);      /* Figure 14.6 */

#define is_read_lockable(fd, offset, whence, len) \
           (lock_test((fd), F_RDLCK, (offset), (whence), (len)) == 0)
#define is_write_lockable(fd, offset, whence, len) \
           (lock_test((fd), F_WRLCK, (offset), (whence), (len)) == 0)

void       err_dump(const char *, ...);           /* Appendix B */
void       err_msg(const char *, ...);
void       err_quit(const char *, ...);
void       err_exit(int, const char *, ...);
void       err_ret(const char *, ...);
void       err_sys(const char *, ...);
```

```
void     log_msg(const char *, ...);              /* Appendix B */
void     log_open(const char *, int, int);
void     log_quit(const char *, ...);
void     log_ret(const char *, ...);
void     log_sys(const char *, ...);

void     TELL_WAIT(void);            /* parent/child from Section 8.9 */
void     TELL_PARENT(pid_t);
void     TELL_CHILD(pid_t);
void     WAIT_PARENT(void);
void     WAIT_CHILD(void);

#endif   /* _APUE_H */
```

Figure B.1 Our header: apue.h

The reasons we include our header before all the normal system headers are to allow us to define anything that might be required by headers before they are included, control the order in which header files are included, and allow us to redefine anything that needs to be fixed up to hide the differences between systems.

B.2   Standard Error Routines

Two sets of error functions are used in most of the examples throughout the text to handle error conditions. One set begins with err_ and outputs an error message to standard error. The other set begins with log_ and is for daemon processes (Chapter 13) that probably have no controlling terminal.

The reason for our own error functions is to let us write our error handling with a single line of C code, as in

```
if (error condition)
        err_dump (printf format with any number of arguments) ;
```

instead of

```
if (error condition) {
        char  buf[200];

        sprintf(buf,  printf format with any number of arguments) ;
        perror(buf);
        abort();
}
```

Our error functions use the variable-length argument list facility from ISO C. See Section 7.3 of Kernighan and Ritchie [1988] for additional details. Be aware that this ISO C facility differs from the varargs facility provided by earlier systems (such as SVR3 and 4.3BSD). The names of the macros are the same, but the arguments to some of the macros have changed.

Figure B.2 summarizes the differences between the various error functions.

Function	Adds string from `strerror`?	Parameter to `strerror`	Terminate?
`err_dump`	yes	errno	`abort();`
`err_exit`	yes	explicit parameter	`exit(1);`
`err_msg`	no		`return;`
`err_quit`	no		`exit(1);`
`err_ret`	yes	errno	`return;`
`err_sys`	yes	errno	`exit(1);`
`log_msg`	no		`return;`
`log_quit`	no		`exit(2);`
`log_ret`	yes	errno	`return;`
`log_sys`	yes	errno	`exit(2);`

Figure B.2 Our standard error functions

Figure B.3 shows the error functions that output to standard error.

```
#include "apue.h"
#include <errno.h>        /* for definition of errno */
#include <stdarg.h>       /* ISO C variable aruments */

static void err_doit(int, int, const char *, va_list);

/*
 * Nonfatal error related to a system call.
 * Print a message and return.
 */
void
err_ret(const char *fmt, ...)
{
    va_list     ap;

    va_start(ap, fmt);
    err_doit(1, errno, fmt, ap);
    va_end(ap);
}

/*
 * Fatal error related to a system call.
 * Print a message and terminate.
 */
void
err_sys(const char *fmt, ...)
{
    va_list     ap;

    va_start(ap, fmt);
    err_doit(1, errno, fmt, ap);
    va_end(ap);
    exit(1);
}
```

```
/*
 * Fatal error unrelated to a system call.
 * Error code passed as explict parameter.
 * Print a message and terminate.
 */
void
err_exit(int error, const char *fmt, ...)
{
    va_list     ap;

    va_start(ap, fmt);
    err_doit(1, error, fmt, ap);
    va_end(ap);
    exit(1);
}

/*
 * Fatal error related to a system call.
 * Print a message, dump core, and terminate.
 */
void
err_dump(const char *fmt, ...)
{
    va_list     ap;

    va_start(ap, fmt);
    err_doit(1, errno, fmt, ap);
    va_end(ap);
    abort();            /* dump core and terminate */
    exit(1);            /* shouldn't get here */
}

/*
 * Nonfatal error unrelated to a system call.
 * Print a message and return.
 */
void
err_msg(const char *fmt, ...)
{
    va_list     ap;

    va_start(ap, fmt);
    err_doit(0, 0, fmt, ap);
    va_end(ap);
}

/*
 * Fatal error unrelated to a system call.
 * Print a message and terminate.
 */
void
err_quit(const char *fmt, ...)
```

```
{
    va_list     ap;

    va_start(ap, fmt);
    err_doit(0, 0, fmt, ap);
    va_end(ap);
    exit(1);
}

/*
 * Print a message and return to caller.
 * Caller specifies "errnoflag".
 */
static void
err_doit(int errnoflag, int error, const char *fmt, va_list ap)
{
    char    buf[MAXLINE];

    vsnprintf(buf, MAXLINE-1, fmt, ap);
    if (errnoflag)
        snprintf(buf+strlen(buf), MAXLINE-strlen(buf)-1, ": %s",
            strerror(error));
    strcat(buf, "\n");
    fflush(stdout);        /* in case stdout and stderr are the same */
    fputs(buf, stderr);
    fflush(NULL);          /* flushes all stdio output streams */
}
```

Figure B.3 Error functions that output to standard error

Figure B.4 shows the log_XXX error functions. These require the caller to define the variable log_to_stderr and set it nonzero if the process is not running as a daemon. In this case, the error messages are sent to standard error. If the log_to_stderr flag is 0, the syslog facility (Section 13.4) is used.

```
/*
 * Error routines for programs that can run as a daemon.
 */

#include "apue.h"
#include <errno.h>        /* for definition of errno */
#include <stdarg.h>       /* ISO C variable arguments */
#include <syslog.h>

static void log_doit(int, int, const char *, va_list ap);

/*
 * Caller must define and set this: nonzero if
 * interactive, zero if daemon
 */
extern int  log_to_stderr;
```

```
/*
 * Initialize syslog(), if running as daemon.
 */
void
log_open(const char *ident, int option, int facility)
{
    if (log_to_stderr == 0)
        openlog(ident, option, facility);
}

/*
 * Nonfatal error related to a system call.
 * Print a message with the system's errno value and return.
 */
void
log_ret(const char *fmt, ...)
{
    va_list     ap;

    va_start(ap, fmt);
    log_doit(1, LOG_ERR, fmt, ap);
    va_end(ap);
}

/*
 * Fatal error related to a system call.
 * Print a message and terminate.
 */
void
log_sys(const char *fmt, ...)
{
    va_list     ap;

    va_start(ap, fmt);
    log_doit(1, LOG_ERR, fmt, ap);
    va_end(ap);
    exit(2);
}

/*
 * Nonfatal error unrelated to a system call.
 * Print a message and return.
 */
void
log_msg(const char *fmt, ...)
{
    va_list     ap;

    va_start(ap, fmt);
    log_doit(0, LOG_ERR, fmt, ap);
    va_end(ap);
}
```

```
/*
 * Fatal error unrelated to a system call.
 * Print a message and terminate.
 */
void
log_quit(const char *fmt, ...)
{
    va_list     ap;

    va_start(ap, fmt);
    log_doit(0, LOG_ERR, fmt, ap);
    va_end(ap);
    exit(2);
}

/*
 * Print a message and return to caller.
 * Caller specifies "errnoflag" and "priority".
 */
static void
log_doit(int errnoflag, int priority, const char *fmt, va_list ap)
{
    int     errno_save;
    char    buf[MAXLINE];

    errno_save = errno;     /* value caller might want printed */
    vsnprintf(buf, MAXLINE-1, fmt, ap);
    if (errnoflag)
        snprintf(buf+strlen(buf), MAXLINE-strlen(buf)-1, ": %s",
            strerror(errno_save));
    strcat(buf, "\n");
    if (log_to_stderr) {
        fflush(stdout);
        fputs(buf, stderr);
        fflush(stderr);
    } else {
        syslog(priority, buf);
    }
}
```

Figure B.4 Error functions for daemons

Appendix C

Solutions to Selected Exercises

Chapter 1

1.1 For this exercise, we use the following two arguments for the `ls`(1) command: `-i` prints the i-node number of the file or directory (we say more about i-nodes in Section 4.14), and `-d` prints information about a directory instead of information on all the files in the directory.

Execute the following:

```
$ ls -ldi /etc/. /etc/..                  -i says print i-node number
   162561 drwxr-xr-x  66 root    4096 Feb  5 03:59 /etc/./
        2 drwxr-xr-x  19 root    4096 Jan 15 07:25 /etc/../
$ ls -ldi /. /..                          both . and .. have i-node number 2
        2 drwxr-xr-x  19 root    4096 Jan 15 07:25 /./
        2 drwxr-xr-x  19 root    4096 Jan 15 07:25 /../
```

1.2 The UNIX System is a multiprogramming, or multitasking, system. Other processes were running at the time this program was run.

1.3 Since the *msg* argument to `perror` is a pointer, `perror` could modify the string that *msg* points to. The qualifier `const`, however, says that `perror` does not modify what the pointer points to. On the other hand, the error number argument to `strerror` is an integer, and since C passes all arguments by value, the `strerror` function couldn't modify this value even if it wanted to. (If the handling of function arguments in C is not clear, you should review Section 5.2 of Kernighan and Ritchie [1988].)

1.4   It is possible for the calls to `fflush`, `fprintf`, and `vprintf` to modify `errno`. If they did modify its value and we didn't save it, the error message finally printed would be incorrect.

1.5   During the year 2038. We can solve the problem by making the `time_t` data type a 64-bit integer. If it is currently a 32-bit integer, applications will have to be recompiled to work properly. But the problem is worse. Some file systems and backup media store times in 32-bit integers. These would need to be updated as well, but we still need to be able to read the old format.

1.6   Approximately 248 days.

Chapter 2

2.1   The following technique is used by FreeBSD. The primitive data types that can appear in multiple headers are defined in the header `<machine/_types.h>`. For example:

```
#ifndef _MACHINE__TYPES_H_
#define _MACHINE__TYPES_H_

typedef int              __int32_t;
typedef unsigned int     __uint32_t;
...

typedef __uint32_t       __size_t;
...

#endif  /* _MACHINE__TYPES_H_ */
```

In each of the headers that can define the `size_t` primitive system data type, we have the sequence

```
#ifndef _SIZE_T_DECLARED
typedef __size_t         size_t;
#define _SIZE_T_DECLARED
#endif
```

This way, the `typedef` for `size_t` is executed only once.

2.3   If `OPEN_MAX` is indeterminite or ridiculously large (i.e., equal to `LONG_MAX`), we can use `getrlimit` to get the per process maximum for open file descriptors. Since the per process limit can be modified, we can't cache the value obtained from the previous call (it might have changed). See Figure C.1.

```
#include "apue.h"
#include <limits.h>
#include <sys/resource.h>

#define OPEN_MAX_GUESS   256

long
open_max(void)
{
    long openmax;
    struct rlimit rl;

    if ((openmax = sysconf(_SC_OPEN_MAX)) < 0 ||
      openmax == LONG_MAX) {
        if (getrlimit(RLIMIT_NOFILE, &rl) < 0)
            err_sys("can't get file limit");
        if (rl.rlim_max == RLIM_INFINITY)
            openmax = OPEN_MAX_GUESS;
        else
            openmax = rl.rlim_max;
    }
    return(openmax);
}
```

Figure C.1 Alternate method for identifying the largest possible file descriptor

Chapter 3

3.1 All disk I/O goes through the kernel's block buffers (also called the kernel's buffer cache). The exception to this is I/O on a raw disk device, which we aren't considering. Chapter 3 of Bach [1986] describes the operation of this buffer cache. Since the data that we read or write is buffered by the kernel, the term *unbuffered I/O* refers to the lack of automatic buffering in the user process with these two functions. Each read or write invokes a single system call.

3.3 Each call to open gives us a new file table entry. But since both opens reference the same file, both file table entries point to the same v-node table entry. The call to dup references the existing file table entry. We show this in Figure C.2. An F_SETFD on fd1 affects only the file descriptor flags for fd1. But an F_SETFL on fd1 affects the file table entry that both fd1 and fd2 point to.

3.4 If fd is 1, then the dup2(fd, 1) returns 1 without closing descriptor 1. (Remember our discussion of this in Section 3.12.) After the three calls to dup2, all three descriptors point to the same file table entry. Nothing needs to be closed.

If fd is 3, however, after the three calls to dup2, four descriptors are pointing to the same file table entry. In this case, we need to close descriptor 3.

process table entry

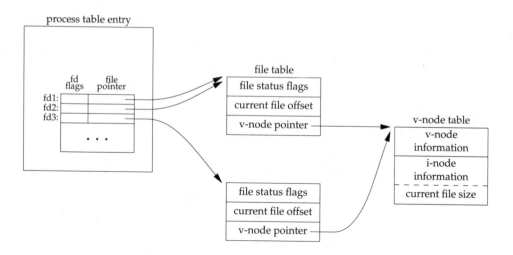

Figure C.2 Result of dup and open

3.5   Since the shells process their command line from left to right, the command

```
./a.out > outfile 2>&1
```

first sets standard output to `outfile` and then dups standard output onto descriptor 2 (standard error). The result is that standard output and standard error are set to the same file. Descriptors 1 and 2 both point to the same file table entry. With

```
./a.out 2>&1 > outfile
```

however, the dup is executed first, causing descriptor 2 to be the terminal (assuming that the command is run interactively). Then standard output is redirected to the file `outfile`. The result is that descriptor 1 points to the file table entry for `outfile`, and descriptor 2 points to the file table entry for the terminal.

3.6   You can still `lseek` and `read` anywhere in the file, but a `write` automatically resets the file offset to the end of file before the data is written. This makes it impossible to `write` anywhere other than at the end of file.

Chapter 4

4.1   If `stat` is called, it always tries to follow a symbolic link (Figure 4.17), so the program will never print a file type of "symbolic link." For the example shown in the text, where `/dev/cdrom` is a symbolic link to `cdroms/cdrom0` (which itself is a symbolic link to `../scsi/host0/bus0/target0/lun0/cd`), `stat` reports that `/dev/cdrom` is a block special file, not a symbolic link. If the symbolic link points to a nonexistent file, `stat` returns an error.

4.2   All permissions are turned off:

```
$ umask 777
$ date > temp.foo
$ ls -l temp.foo
---------- 1 sar           0 Feb  5 14:06 temp.foo
```

4.3   The following shows what happens when user-read permission is turned off:

```
$ date > foo
$ chmod u-r foo                turn off user-read permission
$ ls -l foo                    verify the file's permissions
--w-r--r-- 1 sar          29 Feb  5 14:21 foo
$ cat foo                      and try to read it
cat: foo: Permission denied
```

4.4   If we try, using either open or creat, to create a file that already exists, the file's access permission bits are not changed. We can verify this by running the program from Figure 4.9:

```
$ rm foo bar               delete the files in case they already exist
$ date > foo               create them with some data
$ date > bar
$ chmod a-r foo bar        turn off all read permissions
$ ls -l foo bar            verify their permissions
--w------- 1 sar          29 Feb  5 14:25 bar
--w------- 1 sar          29 Feb  5 14:25 foo
$ ./a.out                  run program from Figure 4.9
$ ls -l foo bar            check permissions and sizes
--w------- 1 sar           0 Feb  5 14:26 bar
--w------- 1 sar           0 Feb  5 14:26 foo
```

Note that the permissions didn't change but that the files were truncated.

4.5   The size of a directory should never be 0, since there should always be entries for dot and dot-dot. The size of a symbolic link is the number of characters in the pathname contained in the symbolic link, and this pathname must always contain at least one character.

4.7   The kernel has a default setting for the file access permission bits when it creates a new core file. In this example, it was rw-r--r--. This default value may or may not be modified by the umask value. The shell also has a default setting for the file access permission bits when it creates a new file for redirection. In this example, it was rw-rw-rw-, and this value is always modified by our current umask. In this example, our umask was 02.

4.8   We can't use du, because it requires either the name of the file, as in

```
du tempfile
```

or a directory name, as in

```
du .
```

But when the unlink function returns, the directory entry for tempfile is gone.

The du . command just shown would not account for the space still taken by tempfile. We have to use the df command in this example to see the actual amount of free space on the file system.

4.9   If the link being removed is not the last link to the file, the file is not removed. In this case, the changed-status time of the file is updated. But if the link being removed is the last link to the file, it makes no sense to update this time, because all the information about the file (the i-node) is removed with the file.

4.10 We recursively call our function dopath after opening a directory with opendir. Assuming that opendir uses a single file descriptor, this means that each time we descend one level, we use another descriptor. (We assume that the descriptor isn't closed until we're finished with a directory and call closedir.) This limits the depth of the file system tree that we can traverse to the maximum number of open descriptors for the process. Note that the ftw function as specified in the XSI extensions of the Single UNIX Specification allows the caller to specify the number of descriptors to use, implying that it can close and reuse descriptors.

4.12 The chroot function is used by the Internet File Transfer Program (FTP) to aid in security. Users without accounts on a system (termed *anonymous FTP*) are placed in a separate directory, and a chroot is done to that directory. This prevents the user from accessing any file outside this new root directory.

In addition, chroot can be used to build a copy of a file system hierarchy at a new location and then modify this new copy without changing the original file system. This could be used, for example, to test the installation of new software packages.

Only the superuser can execute chroot, and once you change the root of a process, it (and all its descendants) can never get back to the original root.

4.13 First, call stat to fetch the three times for the file; then call utime to set the desired value. The value that we don't want to change in the call to utime should be the corresponding value from stat.

4.14 The finger(1) command calls stat on the mailbox. The last-modification time is the time that mail was last received, and the last-access time is when the mail was last read.

4.15 Both cpio and tar store only the modification time (st_mtime) on the archive. The access time isn't stored, because its value corresponds to the time the archive was created, since the file has to be read to be archived. The -a option to cpio has it reset the access time of each input file after the file has been read. This way, the creation of the archive doesn't change the access time. (Resetting the access time, however, does modify the changed-status time.) The changed-status time isn't stored on the archive, because we can't set this value on extraction even if it was archived. (The utime function can change only the access time and the modification time.)

When the archive is read back (extracted), tar, by default, restores the modification time to the value on the archive. The m option to tar tells it to not restore the modification time from the archive; instead, the modification time is set to the time of extraction. In all cases with `tar`, the access time after extraction will be the time of extraction.

On the other hand, `cpio` sets the access time and the modification time to the time of extraction. By default, it doesn't try to set the modification time to the value on the archive. The `-m` option to `cpio` has it set both the access time and the modification time to the value that was archived.

4.16 The kernel has no inherent limit on the depth of a directory tree. But many commands will fail on pathnames that exceed `PATH_MAX`. The program shown in Figure C.3 creates a directory tree that is 100 levels deep, with each level being a 45-character name. We are able to create this structure on all platforms; however, we cannot obtain the absolute pathname of the directory at the 100th level using `getcwd` on all platforms. On Linux 2.4.22 and Solaris 9, we can never get `getcwd` to succeed while in the directory at the end of this long path. The program is able to retrieve the pathname on FreeBSD 5.2.1 and Mac OS X 10.3, but we have to call `realloc` numerous times to obtain a buffer that is large enough. Running this program on FreeBSD 5.2.1 gives us

```
$ ./a.out
getcwd failed, size = 1025: Result too large
getcwd failed, size = 1125: Result too large
 . . .                        33 more lines
getcwd failed, size = 4525: Result too large
length = 4610
```
                          the 4,610-byte pathname is printed here

We are not able to archive this directory, however, using either `tar` or `cpio`. Both complain of a filename that is too long.

4.17 The `/dev` directory has all write permissions turned off to prevent a normal user from removing the filenames in the directory. This means that the `unlink` fails.

Chapter 5

5.2 The `fgets` function reads up through and including the next newline *or* until the buffer is full (leaving room, of course, for the terminating null). Also, `fputs` writes everything in the buffer until it hits a null byte; it doesn't care whether a newline is in the buffer. So, if `MAXLINE` is too small, both functions still work; they're just called more often than they would be if the buffer were larger.

If either of these functions removed or added the newline (as `gets` and `puts` do), we would have to ensure that our buffer was big enough for the largest line.

5.3 The function call

```
printf("");
```

returns 0, since no characters are output.

```c
#include "apue.h"
#include <fcntl.h>

#define DEPTH   100             /* directory depth */
#define MYHOME  "/home/sar"
#define NAME    "alonglonglonglonglonglonglonglonglonglongname"
#define MAXSZ   8192

int
main(void)
{
    int     i, size;
    char    *path;

    if (chdir(MYHOME) < 0)
        err_sys("chdir error");

    for (i = 0; i < DEPTH; i++) {
        if (mkdir(NAME, DIR_MODE) < 0)
            err_sys("mkdir failed, i = %d", i);
        if (chdir(NAME) < 0)
            err_sys("chdir failed, i = %d", i);
    }
    if (creat("afile", FILE_MODE) < 0)
        err_sys("creat error");

    /*
     * The deep directory is created, with a file at the leaf.
     * Now let's try to obtain its pathname.
     */
    path = path_alloc(&size);
    for ( ; ; ) {
        if (getcwd(path, size) != NULL) {
            break;
        } else {
            err_ret("getcwd failed, size = %d", size);
            size += 100;
            if (size > MAXSZ)
                err_quit("giving up");
            if ((path = realloc(path, size)) == NULL)
                err_sys("realloc error");
        }
    }
    printf("length = %d\n%s\n", strlen(path), path);

    exit(0);
}
```

Figure C.3   Create a deep directory tree

5.4 This is a common error. The return value from `getc` and `getchar` is an `int`, not a `char`. EOF is often defined to be −1, so if the system uses signed characters, the code normally works. But if the system uses unsigned characters, after the EOF returned by `getchar` is stored as an unsigned character, the character's value no longer equals −1, so the loop never terminates. The four platforms described in this book all use signed characters, so the example code works on these platforms.

5.5 A 5-character prefix, a 4-character per process unique identifier, and a 5-character per system unique identifier (the process ID) equals 14 characters, the original UNIX System limit on the length of a filename.

5.6 Call `fsync` after each call to `fflush`. The argument to `fsync` is obtained with the `fileno` function. Calling `fsync` without calling `fflush` might do nothing if all the data were still in memory buffers.

5.7 Standard input and standard output are both line buffered when a program is run interactively. When `fgets` is called, standard output is flushed automatically.

Chapter 6

6.1 The functions to access the shadow password file on Linux and Solaris are discussed in Section 6.3. We can't use the value returned in the pw_passwd field by the functions described in Section 6.2 to compare an encrypted password, since that field is not the encrypted password. Instead, we need to find the user's entry in the shadow file and use its encrypted password field.

On FreeBSD and Mac OS X, the password file is shadowed automatically. In the passwd structure returned by getpwnam and getpwuid, the pw_passwd field contains the encrypted password (only if the caller's effective user ID is 0 on FreeBSD, however).

6.2 The program in Figure C.4 prints the encrypted password on Linux and Solaris. Unless this program is run with superuser permissions, the call to getspnam fails with an error of EACCES.

```
#include "apue.h"
#include <shadow.h>

int
main(void)        /* Linux/Solaris version */
{
    struct spwd *ptr;

    if ((ptr = getspnam("sar")) == NULL)
        err_sys("getspnam error");
    printf("sp_pwdp = %s\n", ptr->sp_pwdp == NULL ||
      ptr->sp_pwdp[0] == 0 ?  "(null)" : ptr->sp_pwdp);
    exit(0);
}
```

Figure C.4 Print encrypted password under Linux and Solaris

Under FreeBSD, the program in Figure C.5 prints the encrypted password if the program is run with superuser permissions. Otherwise, the value returned in pw_passwd is an asterisk. On Mac OS X, the encrypted password is printed regardless of the permissions with which it is run.

```
#include "apue.h"
#include <pwd.h>

int
main(void)        /* FreeBSD/Mac OS X version */
{
    struct passwd   *ptr;

    if ((ptr = getpwnam("sar")) == NULL)
        err_sys("getpwnam error");
    printf("pw_passwd = %s\n", ptr->pw_passwd == NULL ||
      ptr->pw_passwd[0] == 0 ?  "(null)" : ptr->pw_passwd);
    exit(0);
}
```

Figure C.5 Print encrypted password under FreeBSD and Mac OS X

6.5   The program shown in Figure C.6 prints the date in a format similar to date.

```
#include "apue.h"
#include <time.h>

int
main(void)
{
    time_t       caltime;
    struct tm    *tm;
    char         line[MAXLINE];

    if ((caltime = time(NULL)) == -1)
        err_sys("time error");
    if ((tm = localtime(&caltime)) == NULL)
        err_sys("localtime error");
    if (strftime(line, MAXLINE, "%a %b %d %X %Z %Y\n", tm) == 0)
        err_sys("strftime error");
    fputs(line, stdout);
    exit(0);
}
```

Figure C.6 Print the time and date in a format similar to date(1)

Running this program gives us

```
$ ./a.out                        author's default is US/Eastern
Sun Feb 06 16:53:57 EST 2005
$ TZ=US/Mountain ./a.out         U.S. Mountain time zone
Sun Feb 06 14:53:57 MST 2005
$ TZ=Japan ./a.out               Japan
Mon Feb 07 06:53:57 JST 2005
```

Chapter 7

7.1   It appears that the return value from `printf` (the number of characters output) becomes the return value of `main`. Not all systems exhibit this property.

7.2   When the program is run interactively, standard output is usually line buffered, so the actual output occurs when each newline is output. If standard output were directed to a file, however, it would probably be fully buffered, and the actual output wouldn't occur until the standard I/O cleanup is performed.

7.3   On most UNIX systems, there is no way to do this. Copies of `argc` and `argv` are not kept in global variables like `environ` is.

7.4   This provides a way to terminate the process when it tries to dereference a null pointer, a common C programming error.

7.5   The definitions are

```
typedef void    Exitfunc(void);

int atexit(Exitfunc *func);
```

7.6   `calloc` initializes the memory that it allocates to all zero bits. ISO C does not guarantee that this is the same as either a floating-point 0 or a null pointer.

7.7   The heap and the stack aren't allocated until a program is executed by one of the `exec` functions (described in Section 8.10).

7.8   The executable file (`a.out`) contains symbol table information that can be helpful in debugging a `core` file. To remove this information, the `strip`(1) command is used. Stripping the two `a.out` files reduces their size to 381,976 and 2,912 bytes.

7.9   When shared libraries are not used, a large portion of the executable file is occupied by the standard I/O library.

7.10 The code is incorrect, since it references the automatic integer `val` through a pointer after the automatic variable is no longer in existence. Automatic variables declared after the left brace that starts a compound statement disappear after the matching right brace.

Chapter 8

8.1   To simulate the behavior of the child closing the standard output when it exits, add the following line before calling `exit` in the child:

```
fclose(stdout);
```

To see the effects of doing this, replace the call to `printf` with the lines

```
i = printf("pid = %d, glob = %d, var = %d\n",
    getpid(), glob, var);
sprintf(buf, "%d\n", i);
write(STDOUT_FILENO, buf, strlen(buf));
```

You need to define the variables `i` and `buf` also.

This assumes that the standard I/O stream `stdout` is closed when the child calls `exit`, not the file descriptor `STDOUT_FILENO`. Some versions of the standard I/O library close the file descriptor associated with standard output, which would cause the `write` to standard output to also fail. In this case, dup standard output to another descriptor, and use this new descriptor for the `write`.

8.2   Consider Figure C.7.

```c
#include "apue.h"

static void f1(void), f2(void);

int
main(void)
{
    f1();
    f2();
    _exit(0);
}

static void
f1(void)
{
    pid_t    pid;

    if ((pid = vfork()) < 0)
        err_sys("vfork error");
    /* child and parent both return */
}

static void
f2(void)
{
    char    buf[1000];         /* automatic variables */
    int     i;

    for (i = 0; i < sizeof(buf); i++)
        buf[i] = 0;
}
```

Figure C.7   Incorrect use of `vfork`

When `vfork` is called, the parent's stack pointer points to the stack frame for the `f1` function that calls `vfork`. Figure C.8 shows this.

`vfork` causes the child to execute first, and the child returns from `f1`. The child then calls `f2`, and its stack frame overwrites the previous stack frame for `f1`. The child then zeros out the automatic variable `buf`, setting 1,000 bytes of the stack frame to 0. The child returns from `f2` and then calls `_exit`, but the contents of

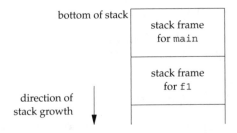

Figure C.8 Stack frames when vfork is called

the stack beneath the stack frame for main have been changed. The parent then resumes after the call to vfork and does a return from f1. The return information is often stored in the stack frame, and that information has probably been modified by the child. After the parent resumes, what happens with this example depends on many implementation features of your UNIX system (where in the stack frame the return information is stored, what information in the stack frame is wiped out when the automatic variables are modified, and so on). The normal result is a core file, but your results may differ.

8.3 In Figure 8.13, we have the parent output first. When the parent is done, the child writes its output, but we let the parent terminate. Whether the parent terminates or whether the child finishes its output first depends on the kernel's scheduling of the two processes (another race condition). When the parent terminates, the shell starts up the next program, and this next program can interfere with the output from the previous child.

We can prevent this from happening by not letting the parent terminate until the child has also finished its output. Replace the code following the fork with the following:

```
else if (pid == 0) {
    WAIT_PARENT();              /* parent goes first */
    charatatime("output from child\n");
    TELL_PARENT(getppid()); /* tell parent we're done */
} else {
    charatatime("output from parent\n");
    TELL_CHILD(pid);           /* tell child we're done */
    WAIT_CHILD();              /* wait for child to finish */
}
```

We won't see this happen if we let the child go first, since the shell doesn't start the next program until the parent terminates.

8.4 The same value (/home/sar/bin/testinterp) is printed for argv[2]. The reason is that execlp ends up calling execve with the same *pathname* as when we call execl directly. Recall Figure 8.15.

8.5 A function is not provided to return the saved set-user-ID. Instead, we must save the effective user ID when the process is started.

8.6 The program in Figure C.9 creates a zombie.

```
#include "apue.h"

#ifdef SOLARIS
#define PSCMD    "ps -a -o pid,ppid,s,tty,comm"
#else
#define PSCMD    "ps -o pid,ppid,state,tty,command"
#endif

int
main(void)
{
    pid_t    pid;

    if ((pid = fork()) < 0)
        err_sys("fork error");
    else if (pid == 0)        /* child */
        exit(0);

    /* parent */
    sleep(4);
    system(PSCMD);

    exit(0);
}
```

Figure C.9 Create a zombie and look at its status with ps

Zombies are usually designated by ps(1) with a status of Z:

```
$ ./a.out
  PID  PPID S TT          COMMAND
 3395  3264 S pts/3       bash
29520  3395 S pts/3       ./a.out
29521 29520 Z pts/3       [a.out] <defunct>
29522 29520 R pts/3       ps -o pid,ppid,state,tty,command
```

Chapter 9

9.1 The init process learns when a terminal user logs out, because init is the parent of the login shell and receives the SIGCHLD signal when the login shell terminates.

For a network login, however, init is not involved. Instead, the login entries in the utmp and wtmp files, and their corresponding logout entries, are usually written by the process that handles the login and detects the logout (telnetd in our example).

Chapter 10

10.1 The program terminates the first time we send it a signal. The reason is that the pause function returns whenever a signal is caught.

10.3 Figure C.10 shows the stack frames.

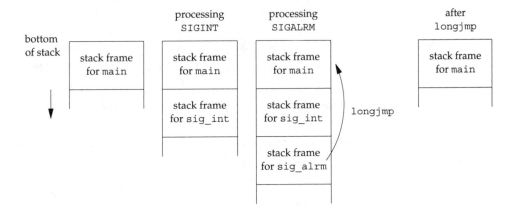

Figure C.10 Stack frames before and after longjmp

The longjmp from sig_alrm back to main effectively aborts the call to sig_int.

10.4 We again have a race condition, this time between the first call to alarm and the call to setjmp. If the process is blocked by the kernel between these two function calls, the alarm goes off, the signal handler is called, and longjmp is called. But since setjmp was never called, the buffer env_alrm is not set. The operation of longjmp is undefined if its jump buffer has not been initialized by setjmp.

10.5 See "Implementing Software Timers" by Don Libes (*C Users Journal*, vol. 8, no. 11, Nov. 1990) for an example.

10.7 If we simply called _exit, the termination status of the process would not show that it was terminated by the SIGABRT signal.

10.8 If the signal was sent by a process owned by some other user, the process has to be set-user-ID to either root or to the owner of the receiving process, or the kill won't work. Therefore, the real user ID provides more information to the receiver of the signal.

10.10 On one system used by the author, the value for the number of seconds increased by 1 about every 60–90 minutes. This skew occurs because each call to sleep schedules an event for a time in the future, but is not awakened exactly when that event occurs (because of CPU scheduling). In addition, a finite amount of time is required for our process to start running and call sleep again.

A program such as the `cron` daemon has to fetch the current time every minute, as well as to set its first sleep period so that it wakes up at the beginning of the next minute. (Convert the current time to the local time and look at the `tm_sec` value.) Every minute, it sets the next sleep period so that it'll wake up at the next minute. Most of the calls will probably be `sleep(60)`, with an occasional `sleep(59)` to resynchronize with the next minute. But if at some point the process takes a long time executing commands or if the system gets heavily loaded and scheduling delays hold up the process, the sleep value can be much less than 60.

10.11 Under Linux 2.4.22 and Solaris 9, the signal handler for `SIGXFSZ` is never called. But `write` returns a count of 24 as soon as the file's size reaches 1,024 bytes.

When the file's size has reached 1,000 bytes under FreeBSD 5.2.1 and Mac OS X 10.3, the signal handler is called on the next attempt to write 100 bytes, and the `write` call returns –1 with `errno` set to `EFBIG` ("File too big").

10.12 The results depend on the implementation of the standard I/O library: how the `fwrite` function handles an interrupted `write`.

Chapter 11

11.1 A version of the program that allocates the memory dynamically instead of using an automatic variable is shown in Figure C.11.

```
#include "apue.h"
#include <pthread.h>

struct foo {
    int a, b, c, d;
};

void
printfoo(const char *s, const struct foo *fp)
{
    printf(s);
    printf("  structure at 0x%x\n", (unsigned)fp);
    printf("  foo.a = %d\n", fp->a);
    printf("  foo.b = %d\n", fp->b);
    printf("  foo.c = %d\n", fp->c);
    printf("  foo.d = %d\n", fp->d);
}

void *
thr_fn1(void *arg)
{
    struct foo *fp;

    if ((fp = malloc(sizeof(struct foo))) == NULL)
        err_sys("can't allocate memory");
    fp->a = 1;
```

```
        fp->b = 2;
        fp->c = 3;
        fp->d = 4;
        printfoo("thread:\n", fp);
        return((void *)fp);
    }
int
main(void)
{
    int err;
    pthread_t tid1;
    struct foo *fp;

    err = pthread_create(&tid1, NULL, thr_fn1, NULL);
    if (err != 0)
        err_exit(err, "can't create thread 1");
    err = pthread_join(tid1, (void *)&fp);
    if (err != 0)
        err_exit(err, "can't join with thread 1");
    printfoo("parent:\n", fp);
    exit(0);
}
```

Figure C.11 Correct use of thread return value

11.2 To change the thread ID of a pending job, the reader–writer lock must be held in write mode to prevent anyone from searching the list while the ID is being changed. The problem with the way the interfaces are currently defined is that the ID of a job can change between the time that the job is found with job_find and the job is removed from the list by calling job_remove. This problem can be solved by embedding a reference count and a mutex inside the job structure and having job_find increment the reference count. The code that changes the ID can then avoid any job in the list that has a nonzero reference count.

11.3 First of all, the list is protected by a reader–writer lock, but the condition variable needs a mutex to protect the condition. Second, the condition each thread should wait to be satisfied is that there is a job for it to process, so we need to create a per thread data structure to represent this condition. Alternatively, we can embed the mutex and condition variable in the queue structure, but this means that all worker threads will wait on the same condition. If there are many worker threads, we can run into a *thundering herd* problem, whereby many threads are awakened without work to do, resulting in a waste of CPU resources and increased lock contention.

11.4 It depends on the circumstances. In general, both can be correct, but each alternative has drawbacks. In the first sequence, the waiting threads will be scheduled to run after we call pthread_cond_broadcast. If the program is running on a multiprocessor, some threads will run and immediately block because we are still holding the mutex (recall that pthread_cond_wait returns with the mutex held). In the second sequence, a running thread can acquire the mutex between steps 3 and 4, invalidate the condition, and release the mutex. Then, when we call `pthread_cond_broadcast`, the condition will no longer be true, and the threads will run needlessly. This is why the awakened threads must recheck the condition and not assume that it is true merely because `pthread_cond_wait` returned.

Chapter 12

12.1 This is not a multithreading problem, as one might first guess. The standard I/O routines are indeed thread-safe. When we call `fork`, each process gets a copy of the standard I/O data structures. When we run the program with standard output attached to a terminal, the output is line buffered, so every time we print a line, the standard I/O library writes it to our terminal. However, if we redirect the standard output to a file, then the standard output is fully buffered. The output is written when the buffer fills or the process closes the stream. When we `fork` in this example, the buffer contains several printed lines not yet written, so when the parent and the child finally flush their copies of the buffer, the initial duplicate contents are written to the file.

12.3 Theoretically, if we arrange for all signals to be blocked when the signal handler runs, we should be able to make a function async-signal-safe. The problem is that we don't know whether any of the functions we call might unmask a signal that we've blocked, thereby making it possible for the function to be reentered through another signal handler.

12.4 On FreeBSD 5.2.1, we get a continuous spray of error messages, and after a while, the program drops core. With `gdb`, we are able to see that the program was stuck in an infinite loop during initialization. The program initialization calls thread initialization functions, which call `malloc`. The `malloc` function, in turn, calls `getenv` to find the value of the `MALLOC_OPTIONS` environment variable. Our implementation of `getenv` calls pthread functions, which then try to call the thread initialization functions. Eventually, we hit an error and get stuck in a similar infinite loop after `abort` is called. After half a million or so stack frames, the process exits, generating a core dump.

12.5 We still need `fork` if we want to run a program from within another program (i.e., before calling `exec`).

12.6 Figure C.12 shows a thread-safe `sleep` implementation that uses `select` to delay for the specified amount of time. It is thread-safe because it doesn't use any unprotected global or static data and calls only other thread-safe functions.

12.7 The implementation of a condition variable most likely uses a mutex to protect its internal structure. Because this is an implementation detail and therefore hidden, there is no portable way for us to acquire and release the lock in the fork handlers. Since we can't determine the state of the internal lock in a condition variable after calling `fork`, it is unsafe for us to use the condition variable in the child process.

```
#include <unistd.h>
#include <time.h>
#include <sys/select.h>

unsigned
sleep(unsigned nsec)
{
    int n;
    unsigned slept;
    time_t start, end;
    struct timeval tv;

    tv.tv_sec = nsec;
    tv.tv_usec = 0;
    time(&start);
    n = select(0, NULL, NULL, NULL, &tv);
    if (n == 0)
        return(0);
    time(&end);
    slept = end - start;
    if (slept >= nsec)
        return(0);
    return(nsec - slept);
}
```

Figure C.12 A thread-safe implementation of `sleep`

Chapter 13

13.1   If it calls `chroot`, the process will not be able to open `/dev/log`. The solution is for the daemon to call `openlog` with an *option* of `LOG_NDELAY`, before calling `chroot`. This opens the special device file (the UNIX domain datagram socket), yielding a descriptor that is still valid, even after a call to `chroot`. This scenario is encountered in daemons, such as `ftpd` (the File Transfer Protocol daemon), that specifically call `chroot` for security reasons but still need to call `syslog` to log error conditions.

13.3   Figure C.13 shows a solution. The results depend on the platform. Recall that `daemonize` closes all open file descriptors and then reopens the first three to `/dev/null`. This means that the process won't have a controlling terminal, so `getlogin` won't be able to look in the `utmp` file for the process's login entry. Thus, on Linux 2.4.22 and Solaris 9, we find that a daemon has no login name.

Under FreeBSD 5.2.1 and Mac OS X 10.3, however, the login name is maintained in the process table and copied across a `fork`. This means that the process can always get the login name, unless the parent didn't have one to start out (such as `init` when the system is bootstrapped).

```
#include "apue.h"

int
main(void)
{
    FILE *fp;
    char *p;

    daemonize("getlog");
    p = getlogin();
    fp = fopen("/tmp/getlog.out", "w");
    if (fp != NULL) {
        if (p == NULL)
            fprintf(fp, "no login name\n");
        else
            fprintf(fp, "login name: %s\n", p);
    }
    exit(0);
}
```

Figure C.13 Call daemonize and then obtain login name

Chapter 14

14.1   The test program is shown in Figure C.14

```
#include "apue.h"
#include <fcntl.h>
#include <errno.h>

void
sigint(int signo)
{
}

int
main(void)
{
    pid_t pid1, pid2, pid3;
    int fd;

    setbuf(stdout, NULL);
    signal_intr(SIGINT, sigint);

    /*
     * Create a file.
     */
    if ((fd = open("lockfile", O_RDWR|O_CREAT, 0666)) < 0)
        err_sys("can't open/create lockfile");

    /*
     * Read-lock the file.
     */
```

```
    if ((pid1 = fork()) < 0) {
        err_sys("fork failed");
    } else if (pid1 == 0) { /* child */
        if (lock_reg(fd, F_SETLK, F_RDLCK, 0, SEEK_SET, 0) < 0)
            err_sys("child 1: can't read-lock file");
        printf("child 1: obtained read lock on file\n");
        pause();
        printf("child 1: exit after pause\n");
        exit(0);
    } else {           /* parent */
        sleep(2);
    }

    /*
     * Parent continues ... read-lock the file again.
     */
    if ((pid2 = fork()) < 0) {
        err_sys("fork failed");
    } else if (pid2 == 0) { /* child */
        if (lock_reg(fd, F_SETLK, F_RDLCK, 0, SEEK_SET, 0) < 0)
            err_sys("child 2: can't read-lock file");
        printf("child 2: obtained read lock on file\n");
        pause();
        printf("child 2: exit after pause\n");
        exit(0);
    } else {           /* parent */
        sleep(2);
    }

    /*
     * Parent continues ... block while trying to write-lock
     * the file.
     */
    if ((pid3 = fork()) < 0) {
        err_sys("fork failed");
    } else if (pid3 == 0) { /* child */
        if (lock_reg(fd, F_SETLK, F_WRLCK, 0, SEEK_SET, 0) < 0)
            printf("child 3: can't set write lock: %s\n",
              strerror(errno));
        printf("child 3 about to block in write-lock...\n");
        if (lock_reg(fd, F_SETLKW, F_WRLCK, 0, SEEK_SET, 0) < 0)
            err_sys("child 3: can't write-lock file");
        printf("child 3 returned and got write lock????\n");
        pause();
        printf("child 3: exit after pause\n");
        exit(0);
    } else {           /* parent */
        sleep(2);
    }

    /*
     * See if a pending write lock will block the next
```

```
        * read-lock attempt.
        */
      if (lock_reg(fd, F_SETLK, F_RDLCK, 0, SEEK_SET, 0) < 0)
          printf("parent: can't set read lock: %s\n",
            strerror(errno));
      else
          printf("parent: obtained additional read lock while"
            " write lock is pending\n");
      printf("killing child 1...\n");
      kill(pid1, SIGINT);
      printf("killing child 2...\n");
      kill(pid2, SIGINT);
      printf("killing child 3...\n");
      kill(pid3, SIGINT);
      exit(0);
}
```

Figure C.14   Determine record-locking behavior

On all four systems described in this book, the behavior is the same: additional readers can starve pending writers. Running the program gives us

```
child 1: obtained read lock on file
child 2: obtained read lock on file
child 3: can't set write lock: Resource temporarily unavailable
child 3 about to block in write-lock...
parent: obtained additional read lock while write lock is pending
killing child 1...
child 1: exit after pause
killing child 2...
child 2: exit after pause
killing child 3...
child 3: can't write-lock file: Interrupted system call
```

14.2   Most systems define the fd_set data type to be a structure that contains a single member: an array of long integers. One bit in this array corresponds to each descriptor. The four FD_ macros then manipulate this array of longs, turning specific bits on and off and testing specific bits.

One reason that the data type is defined to be a structure containing an array and not simply an array is to allow variables of type fd_set to be assigned to one another with the C assignment statement.

14.3   Most systems allow us to define the constant FD_SETSIZE before including the header <sys/select.h>. For example, we can write

```
#define FD_SETSIZE  2048
#include <sys/select.h>
```

to define the fd_set data type to accommodate 2,048 descriptors. This works on FreeBSD 5.2.1, Mac OS X 10.3, and Solaris 9. Linux 2.4.22 implements things differently.

14.4 The following table lists the functions that do similar things.

FD_ZERO	sigemptyset
FD_SET	sigaddset
FD_CLR	sigdelset
FD_ISSET	sigismember

There is not an FD_xxx function that corresponds to sigfillset. With signal sets, the pointer to the set is always the first argument, and the signal number is the second argument. With descriptor sets, the descriptor number is the first argument, and the pointer to the set is the next argument.

14.5 Up to five types of information are returned by getmsg: the data itself, the length of the data, the control information, the length of the control information, and the flags.

14.6 Figure C.15 shows an implementation using select.

```
#include "apue.h"
#include <sys/select.h>

void
sleep_us(unsigned int nusecs)
{
    struct timeval  tval;

    tval.tv_sec = nusecs / 1000000;
    tval.tv_usec = nusecs % 1000000;
    select(0, NULL, NULL, NULL, &tval);
}
```

Figure C.15 Implementation of sleep_us using select

Figure C.16 shows an implementation using poll.

```
#include <poll.h>

void
sleep_us(unsigned int nusecs)
{
    struct pollfd   dummy;
    int             timeout;

    if ((timeout = nusecs / 1000) <= 0)
        timeout = 1;
    poll(&dummy, 0, timeout);
}
```

Figure C.16 Implementation of sleep_us using poll

As the BSD usleep(3) manual page states, usleep uses the setitimer interval timer and performs eight system calls each time it's called. It correctly interacts with other timers set by the calling process, and it is not interrupted if a signal is caught.

14.7 No. What we would like to do is have `TELL_WAIT` create a temporary file and use 1 byte for the parent's lock and 1 byte for the child's lock. `WAIT_CHILD` would have the parent wait to obtain a lock on the child's byte, and `TELL_PARENT` would have the child release the lock on the child's byte. The problem, however, is that calling `fork` releases all the locks in the child, so the child can't start off with any locks of its own.

14.8 A solution is shown in Figure C.17.

```
#include "apue.h"
#include <fcntl.h>

int
main(void)
{
    int i, n;
    int fd[2];

    if (pipe(fd) < 0)
        err_sys("pipe error");
    set_fl(fd[1], O_NONBLOCK);
    /*
     * Write 1 byte at a time until pipe is full.
     */
    for (n = 0; ; n++) {
        if ((i = write(fd[1], "a", 1)) != 1) {
            printf("write ret %d, ", i);
            break;
        }
    }
    printf("pipe capacity = %d\n", n);
    exit(0);
}
```

Figure C.17 Calculation of pipe capacity using nonlocking writes

The following table shows the values calculated for our four platforms.

Platform	Pipe Capacity (bytes)
FreeBSD 5.2.1	16,384
Linux 2.4.22	4,096
Mac OS X 10.3	8,192
Solaris 9	9,216

These values can differ from the corresponding `PIPE_BUF` values, because `PIPE_BUF` is defined to be the maximum amount of data that can be written to a pipe *atomically*. Here, we calculate the amount of data that a pipe can hold independent of any atomicity constraints.

14.10 Whether the program in Figure 14.32 updates the last-access time for the input file depends on the operating system and the type of file system on which the file resides.

Chapter 15

15.1 If the write end of the pipe is never closed, the reader never sees an end of file. The pager program blocks forever reading from its standard input.

15.2 The parent terminates right after writing the last line to the pipe. The read end of the pipe is automatically closed when the parent terminates. But the parent is probably running ahead of the child by one pipe buffer, since the child (the pager program) is waiting for us to look at a page of output. If we're running a shell, such as the Korn shell, with interactive command-line editing enabled, the shell probably changes the terminal mode when our parent terminates and the shell prints a prompt. This undoubtedly interferes with the pager program, which has also modified the terminal mode. (Most pager programs set the terminal to noncanonical mode when awaiting input to proceed to the next page.)

15.3 The popen function returns a file pointer because the shell is executed. But the shell can't execute the nonexistent command, so it prints

```
sh: line 1: ./a.out: No such file or directory
```

on the standard error and terminates with an exit status of 127. pclose returns the termination status of the command as it is returned by waitpid.

15.4 When the parent terminates, look at its termination status with the shell. For the Bourne shell, Bourne-again shell, and Korn shell, the command is echo $?. The number printed is 128 plus the signal number.

15.5 First add the declaration

```
FILE    *fpin, *fpout;
```

Then use fdopen to associate the pipe descriptors with a standard I/O stream, and set the streams to be line buffered. Do this before the while loop that reads from standard input:

```
if ((fpin = fdopen(fd2[0], "r")) == NULL)
    err_sys("fdopen error");
if ((fpout = fdopen(fd1[1], "w")) == NULL)
    err_sys("fdopen error");
if (setvbuf(fpin, NULL, _IOLBF, 0) < 0)
    err_sys("setvbuf error");
if (setvbuf(fpout, NULL, _IOLBF, 0) < 0)
    err_sys("setvbuf error");
```

The write and read in the while loop are replaced with

```
if (fputs(line, fpout) == EOF)
    err_sys("fputs error to pipe");
if (fgets(line, MAXLINE, fpin) == NULL) {
    err_msg("child closed pipe");
    break;
}
```

15.6 The `system` function calls `wait`, and the first child to terminate is the child generated by `popen`. Since that's not the child that `system` created, it calls `wait` again and blocks until the `sleep` is done. Then `system` returns. When `pclose` calls `wait`, an error is returned, since there are no more children to `wait` for. Then `pclose` returns an error.

15.7 The `select` function indicates that the descriptor is readable. When we call `read` after all the data has been read, it returns 0 to indicate the end of file. But with `poll` (assuming a STREAMS-based pipe), the `POLLHUP` event is returned, and this event may be returned while there is still data to be read. Once we have read all the data, however, `read` returns 0 to indicate the end of file. After all the data has been read, the `POLLIN` event is not returned, even though we need to issue a `read` to receive the end-of-file notification (the return of 0).

With an output descriptor that refers to a pipe that has been closed by the reader, `select` indicates that the descriptor is writable. But when we call `write`, the `SIGPIPE` signal is generated. If we either ignore this signal or return from its signal handler, `write` returns an error of `EPIPE`. With `poll`, however, if the pipe is STREAMS based, `poll` returns with a `POLLHUP` event for the descriptor.

15.8 Anything written by the child to standard error appears wherever the parent's standard error would appear. To send standard error back to the parent, include the shell redirection `2>&1` in the *cmdstring*.

15.9 The `popen` function `forks` a child, and the child executes the shell. The shell in turn calls `fork`, and the child of the shell executes the command string. When *cmdstring* terminates, the shell is waiting for this to happen. The shell then exits, which is what the `waitpid` in `pclose` is waiting for.

15.10 The trick is to open the FIFO twice: once for reading and once for writing. We never use the descriptor that is opened for writing, but leaving that descriptor open prevents an end of file from being generated when the number of clients goes from 1 to 0. Opening the FIFO twice requires some care, as a nonblocking open is required. We have to do a nonblocking, read-only open first, followed by a blocking open for write-only. (If we tried a nonblocking open for write-only first, it would return an error.) We then turn off nonblocking for the read descriptor. Figure C.18 shows the code for this.

```
#include "apue.h"
#include <fcntl.h>

#define FIFO    "temp.fifo"

int
main(void)
{
    int     fdread, fdwrite;

    unlink(FIFO);
    if (mkfifo(FIFO, FILE_MODE) < 0)
        err_sys("mkfifo error");
    if ((fdread = open(FIFO, O_RDONLY | O_NONBLOCK)) < 0)
```

```
        err_sys("open error for reading");
if ((fdwrite = open(FIFO, O_WRONLY)) < 0)
        err_sys("open error for writing");
clr_fl(fdread, O_NONBLOCK);
exit(0);
}
```

Figure C.18 Opening a FIFO for reading and writing, without blocking

15.11 Randomly reading a message from an active queue would interfere with the client–server protocol, as either a client request or a server's response would be lost. To read the queue, all that is needed is for the process to know the identifier for the queue and for the queue to allow world-read access.

15.13 We never store actual addresses in a shared memory segment, since it's possible for the server and all the clients to attach the segment at different addresses. Instead, when a linked list is built in a shared memory segment, the list pointers should be stored as offsets to other objects in the shared memory segment. These offsets are formed by subtracting the start of the shared memory segment from the actual address of the object.

15.14 Figure C.19 shows the relevant events.

Parent i set to	Child i set to	Shared value set to	update returns	Comment
		0		initialized by mmap
	1			child runs first, then is blocked
0				parent runs
		1		
			0	then parent is blocked
		2		child resumes
			1	
	3			then child is blocked
2				parent resumes
		3		
			2	then parent is blocked
		4		
			3	
	5			then child is blocked
4				parent resumes

Figure C.19 Alternation between parent and child in Figure 15.33

Chapter 16

16.1 Figure C.20 shows a program that prints the system's byte order.

16.3 For each endpoint we will be listening on, we need to bind the proper address and record an entry in an `fd_set` structure corresponding to each file descriptor.

```
#include <stdio.h>
#include <stdlib.h>
#include <inttypes.h>

int
main(void)
{
    uint32_t i;
    unsigned char *cp;

    i = 0x04030201;
    cp = (unsigned char *)&i;
    if (*cp == 1)
        printf("little-endian\n");
    else if (*cp == 4)
        printf("big-endian\n");
    else
        printf("who knows?\n");
    exit(0);
}
```

Figure C.20   Determine byte order on system

We will use `select` to wait for connect requests to arrive on multiple endpoints. Recall from Section 16.4 that a passive endpoint will appear to be readable when a connect request arrives on it. When a connect request does arrive, we will accept the request and process it as before.

16.5   In the `main` procedure, we need to arrange to catch `SIGCHLD` by calling our `signal` function (Figure 10.18), which will use `sigaction` to install the handler specifying the restartable system call option. Next, we need to remove the call to `waitpid` from our `serve` function. After `forking` the child to service the request, the parent closes the new file descriptor and resumes listening for additional connect requests. Finally, we need a signal handler for `SIGCHLD`, as follows:

```
void
sigchld(int signo)
{
    while (waitpid((pid_t)-1, NULL, WNOHANG) > 0)
        ;
}
```

16.6   To enable asynchronous socket I/O, we need to establish socket ownership using the `F_SETOWN` fcntl command, and then enable asynchronous signaling using the `FIOASYNC` ioctl command. To disable asynchronous socket I/O, we simply need to disable asynchronous signaling. The reason we mix `fcntl` and `ioctl` commands is to find the methods that are most portable. The code is shown in Figure C.21.

```
#include "apue.h"
#include <errno.h>
#include <fcntl.h>
#include <sys/socket.h>
#include <sys/ioctl.h>
#if defined(BSD) || defined(MACOS) || defined(SOLARIS)
#include <sys/filio.h>
#endif

int
setasync(int sockfd)
{
    int n;

    if (fcntl(sockfd, F_SETOWN, getpid()) < 0)
        return(-1);
    n = 1;
    if (ioctl(sockfd, FIOASYNC, &n) < 0)
        return(-1);
    return(0);
}

int
clrasync(int sockfd)
{
    int n;

    n = 0;
    if (ioctl(sockfd, FIOASYNC, &n) < 0)
        return(-1);
    return(0);
}
```

Figure C.21 Enable and disable asynchronous socket I/O

Chapter 17

17.3 A *declaration* specifies the attributes (such as the data type) of a set of identifiers. If the declaration also causes storage to be allocated, it is called a *definition*.

In the opend.h header, we declare the three global variables with the extern storage class. These declarations do not cause storage to be allocated for the variables. In the main.c file, we define the three global variables. Sometimes, we'll also initialize a global variable when we define it, but we typically let the C default apply.

17.5 Both select and poll return the number of ready descriptors as the value of the function. The loop that goes through the client array can terminate when the number of ready descriptors have been processed.

Chapter 18

18.1 Note that you have to terminate the `reset` command with a line feed character, not a return, since the terminal is in noncanonical mode.

18.2 It builds a table for each of the 128 characters and sets the high-order bit (the parity bit) according to the user's specification. It then uses 8-bit I/O, handling the parity generation itself.

18.3 If you happen to be on a windowing terminal, you don't need to log in twice. You can do this experiment between two separate windows. Under Solaris, execute `stty -a` with standard input redirected from the terminal window running `vi`. This shows that `vi` sets MIN to 1 and TIME to 1. A call to `read` will wait for at least one character to be typed, but after that character is entered, `read` waits only one-tenth of a second for additional characters before returning.

Chapter 19

19.1 Both servers, `telnetd` and `rlogind`, run with superuser privileges, so their calls to `chown` and `chmod` succeed.

19.3 Execute `pty -n stty -a` to prevent the slave's `termios` structure and `winsize` structure from being initialized.

19.5 Unfortunately, the `F_SETFL` command of `fcntl` doesn't allow the read–write status to be changed.

19.6 There are three process groups: (1) the login shell, (2) the `pty` parent and child, and (3) the `cat` process. The first two process groups constitute a session with the login shell as the session leader. The second session contains only the `cat` process. The first process group (the login shell) is a background process group, and the other two are foreground process groups.

19.7 First, `cat` terminates when it receives the end of file from its line discipline. This causes the PTY slave to terminate, which causes the PTY master to terminate. This in turn generates an end of file for the `pty` parent that's reading from the PTY master. The parent sends `SIGTERM` to the child, so the child terminates next. (The child doesn't catch this signal.) Finally, the parent calls `exit(0)` at the end of the `main` function.

The relevant output from the program shown in Figure 8.29 is

```
cat      e =    270, chars =    274, stat =   0:
pty      e =    262, chars =     40, stat =  15: F       X
pty      e =    288, chars =    188, stat =   0:
```

19.8 This can be done with the shell's `echo` command and the `date(1)` command, all in a subshell:

```sh
#!/bin/sh
( echo "Script started on " `date`;
  pty "${SHELL:-/bin/sh}";
  echo "Script done on " `date` ) | tee typescript
```

19.9 The line discipline above the PTY slave has echo enabled, so whatever `pty` reads
on its standard input and writes to the PTY master gets echoed by default. This
echoing is done by the line discipline module above the slave even though the
program (`ttyname`) never reads the data.

Chapter 20

20.1 Our conservative locking in `_db_dodelete` is to avoid race conditions with
`db_nextrec`. If the call to `_db_writedat` were not protected with a write lock,
it would be possible to erase the data record while `db_nextrec` was reading that
data record: `db_nextrec` would read an index record, determine that it was not
blank, and then read the data record, which could be erased by `_db_dodelete`
between the calls to `_db_readidx` and `_db_readdat` in `db_nextrec`.

20.2 Assume that `db_nextrec` calls `_db_readidx`, which reads the key into the
index buffer for the process. This process is then stopped by the kernel, and
another process runs. This other process calls `db_delete`, and the record being
read by the other process is deleted. Both its key and its data are rewritten in the
two files as all blanks. The first process resumes and calls `_db_readdat` (from
`db_nextrec`) and reads the all-blank data record. The read lock by `db_nextrec`
allows it to do the read of the index record, followed by the read of the data
record, as an atomic operation (with regard to other cooperating processes using
the same database).

20.3 With mandatory locking, other readers and writers are affected. Other reads and
writes are blocked by the kernel until the locks placed by `_db_writeidx` and
`_db_writedat` are removed.

20.5 By writing the data record before the index record, we protect ourselves from
generating a corrupt record if the process should be killed in between the two
writes. If the process were to write the index record first, but be killed before
writing the data record, then we'd have a valid index record that pointed to
invalid data.

Chapter 21

21.5 Here are some hints. There are two places to check for queued jobs: the printer
spooling daemon's queue and the network printer's internal queue. Take care to
prevent one user from being able to cancel someone else's print job. Of course,
the superuser should be able to cancel any job.

Bibliography

Accetta, M., Baron, R., Bolosky, W., Golub, D., Rashid, R., Tevanian, A., and Young, M. 1986. "Mach: A New Kernel Foundation for UNIX Development," *Proceedings of the 1986 Summer USENIX Conference*, pp. 93–113, Atlanta, GA.

> A paper introducing the Mach operating system.

Adobe Systems Inc. 1999. *PostScript Language Reference Manual, Third Edition.* Addison-Wesley, Reading, MA.

> The language reference manual for PostScript.

Aho, A. V., Kernighan, B. W., and Weinberger, P. J. 1988. *The AWK Programming Language.* Addison-Wesley, Reading, MA.

> A complete book on the awk programming language. The version of awk described in this book is sometimes called "nawk" (for new awk).

Andrade, J. M., Carges, M. T., and Kovach, K. R. 1989. "Building a Transaction Processing System on UNIX Systems," *Proceedings of the 1989 USENIX Transaction Processing Workshop*, vol. May, pp. 13–22, Pittsburgh, PA.

> A description of the AT&T Tuxedo Transaction Processing System.

Arnold, J. Q. 1986. "Shared Libraries on UNIX System V," *Proceedings of the 1986 Summer USENIX Conference*, pp. 395–404, Atlanta, GA.

> Describes the implementation of shared libraries in SVR3.

AT&T. 1989. *System V Interface Definition, Third Edition.* Addison-Wesley, Reading, MA.

> This four-volume set specifies the source code interface and runtime behavior of System V. The third edition corresponds to SVR4. A fifth volume, containing updated versions of commands and functions from volumes 1–4, was published in 1991. Currently out of print.

AT&T. 1990a. *UNIX Research System Programmer's Manual, Tenth Edition, Volume I.* Saunders College Publishing, Fort Worth, TX.

> The version of the *UNIX Programmer's Manual* for the 10th Edition of the Research UNIX System (V10). This volume contains the traditional UNIX System manual pages (Sections 1–9).

AT&T. 1990b. *UNIX Research System Papers, Tenth Edition, Volume II.* Saunders College Publishing, Fort Worth, TX.

> Volume II for the 10th Edition of the Research UNIX System (V10) contains 40 papers describing various aspects of the system.

AT&T. 1990c. *UNIX System V Release 4 BSD/XENIX Compatibility Guide.* Prentice-Hall, Englewood Cliffs, NJ.

> Contains manual pages describing the compatibility library.

AT&T. 1990d. *UNIX System V Release 4 Programmer's Guide: STREAMS.* Prentice-Hall, Englewood Cliffs, NJ.

> Describes the STREAMS system in SVR4.

AT&T. 1990e. *UNIX System V Release 4 Programmer's Reference Manual.* Prentice-Hall, Englewood Cliffs, NJ.

> This is the programmer's reference manual for the SVR4 implementation for the Intel 80386 processor. It contains Sections 1 (commands), 2 (system calls), 3 (subroutines), 4 (file formats), and 5 (miscellaneous facilities).

AT&T. 1991. *UNIX System V Release 4 System Administrator's Reference Manual.* Prentice-Hall, Englewood Cliffs, NJ.

> This is the system administrator's reference manual for the SVR4 implementation for the Intel 80386 processor. It contains Sections 1 (commands), 4 (file formats), 5 (miscellaneous facilities), and 7 (special files).

Bach, M. J. 1986. *The Design of the UNIX Operating System.* Prentice-Hall, Englewood Cliffs, NJ.

> A book on the details of the design and implementation of the UNIX operating system. Although actual UNIX System source code is not provided in this text (since it was proprietary to AT&T at the time), many of the algorithms and data structures used by the UNIX kernel are presented and discussed. This book describes SVR2.

Bolsky, M. I., and Korn, D. G. 1995. *The New KornShell Command and Programming Language, Second Edition.* Prentice-Hall, Englewood Cliffs, NJ.

> A book describing how to use the Korn shell, both as a command interpreter and as a programming language.

Chen, D., Barkley, R. E., and Lee, T. P. 1990. "Insuring Improved VM Performance: Some No-Fault Policies," *Proceedings of the 1990 Winter USENIX Conference,* pp. 11–22, Washington, D.C.

> Describes changes made to the virtual memory implementation of SVR4 to improve its performance, especially for fork and exec.

Comer, D. E. 1979. "The Ubiquitous B-Tree," *ACM Computing Surveys,* vol. 11, no. 2, pp. 121–137 (June).

> A good, comprehensive paper on B-trees.

Date, C. J. 2004. *An Introduction to Database Systems, Eighth Edition.* Addison-Wesley, Boston, MA.

> A comprehensive overview of database systems.

Fagin, R., Nievergelt, J., Pippenger, N., and Strong, H. R. 1979. "Extendible Hashing—A Fast Access Method for Dynamic Files," *ACM Transactions on Databases,* vol. 4, no. 3, pp. 315–344 (September).

> A paper describing the extendible hashing technique.

Fowler, G. S., Korn, D. G., and Vo, K. P. 1989. "An Efficient File Hierarchy Walker," *Proceeding of the 1989 Summer USENIX Conference*, pp. 173–188, Baltimore, MD.

> Describes an alternate library function to traverse a file system hierarchy.

Gallmeister, B. O. 1995. *POSIX.4: Programming for the Real World*. O'Reilly & Associates, Sebastopol, CA.

> Describes the real-time interfaces in the POSIX standard.

Garfinkel, S., Spafford, G., and Schwartz, A. 2003. *Practical UNIX & Internet Security, Third Edition*. O'Reilly & Associates, Sebastopol, CA.

> A detailed book on UNIX System security.

Gingell, R. A., Lee, M., Dang, X. T., and Weeks, M. S. 1987. "Shared Libraries in SunOS," *Proceedings of the 1987 Summer USENIX Conference*, pp. 131–145, Phoenix, AZ.

> Describes the implementation of shared libraries in SunOS.

Gingell, R. A., Moran, J. P., and Shannon, W. A. 1987. "Virtual Memory Architecture in SunOS," *Proceedings of the 1987 Summer USENIX Conference*, pp. 81–94, Phoenix, AZ.

> Describes the initial implementation of the mmap function and related issues in the virtual memory design.

Goodheart, B. 1991. *UNIX Curses Explained*. Prentice-Hall, Englewood Cliffs, NJ.

> A complete reference on terminfo and the curses library. Currently out of print.

Hume, A. G. 1988. "A Tale of Two Greps," *Software Practice and Experience*, vol. 18, no. 11, pp. 1063–1072.

> An interesting paper that discusses performance improvements in grep.

IEEE. 1990. *Information Technology—Portable Operating System Interface (POSIX) Part 1: System Application Program Interface (API) [C Language]*. IEEE (Dec.).

> This was the first of the POSIX standards, and it defined the C language systems interface standard, based on the UNIX operating system. It is often called POSIX.1. It is now part of the Single UNIX Specification published by the The Open Group [2004].

ISO. 1999. *International Standard ISO/IEC 9899—Programming Language C*. ISO/IEC.

> The official standard for the C language and the standard libraries.
>
> PDF versions of this standard can be purchased online at either http://www.ansi.org or http://www.iso.org.

Kernighan, B. W., and Pike, R. 1984. *The UNIX Programming Environment*. Prentice-Hall, Englewood Cliffs, NJ.

> A general reference for additional details on UNIX programming. This book covers numerous UNIX commands and utilities, such as grep, sed, awk, and the Bourne shell.

Kernighan, B. W., and Ritchie, D. M. 1988. *The C Programming Language, Second Edition*. Prentice-Hall, Englewood Cliffs, NJ.

> A book on the ANSI standard version of the C programming language. Appendix B contains a description of the libraries defined by the ANSI standard.

Kleiman, S. R. 1986. "Vnodes: An Architecture for Multiple File System Types in Sun Unix," *Proceedings of the 1986 Summer USENIX Conference*, pp. 238–247, Atlanta, GA.

> A description of the original v-node implementation.

Knuth, D. E. 1998. *The Art of Computer Programming, Volume 3: Sorting and Searching, Second Edition.* Addison-Wesley, Boston, MA.

> Describes sorting and searching algorithms.

Korn, D. G., and Vo, K. P. 1991. "SFIO: Safe/Fast String/File IO," *Proceedings of the 1991 Summer USENIX Conference*, pp. 235–255, Nashville, TN.

> A description of an alternative to the standard I/O library. The library is available at http://www.research.att.com/sw/tools/sfio.

Krieger, O., Stumm, M., and Unrau, R. 1992. "Exploiting the Advantages of Mapped Files for Stream I/O," *Proceedings of the 1992 Winter USENIX Conference*, pp. 27–42, San Francisco, CA.

> An alternative to the standard I/O library based on mapped files.

Leffler, S. J., McKusick, M. K., Karels, M. J., and Quarterman, J. S. 1989. *The Design and Implementation of the 4.3BSD UNIX Operating System.* Addison-Wesley, Reading, MA.

> An entire book on the 4.3BSD operating system. This book describes the Tahoe release of 4.3BSD. Currently out of print.

Lennert, D. 1987. "How to Write a UNIX Daemon," *;login:*, vol. 12, no. 4, pp. 17–23 (July/August).

> Describes how to write a daemon in the UNIX System.

Libes, D. 1990. "expect: Curing Those Uncontrollable Fits of Interaction," *Proceedings of the 1990 Summer USENIX Conference*, pp. 183–192, Anaheim, CA.

> A description of the expect program and its implementation.

Libes, D. 1991. "expect: Scripts for Controlling Interactive Processes," *Computing Systems*, vol. 4, no. 2, pp. 99–125 (Spring).

> This paper presents numerous expect scripts.

Libes, D. 1994. *Exploring Expect.* O'Reilly & Associates, Sebastopol, CA.

> A complete book on using the expect program.

Lions, J. 1977. *A Commentary on the UNIX Operating System.* AT&T Bell Laboratories, Murray Hill, NJ.

> Describes the source code of the 6th Edition UNIX System. Available only to AT&T employees, contractors, and interns, although copies leaked outside of AT&T.

Lions, J. 1996. *Lions' Commentary on UNIX 6th Edition.* Peer-to-Peer Communications, San Jose, CA.

> Describes the 6th Edition UNIX System in a publicly available version of the 1977 classic.

Litwin, W. 1980. "Linear Hashing: A New Tool for File and Table Addressing," *Proceedings of the 6th International Conference on Very Large Databases*, pp. 212–223, Montreal, Canada.

> A paper describing the linear hashing technique.

McKusick, M. K., Bostic, K., Karels, M. J., and Quarterman, J. S. 1996. *The Design and Implementation of the 4.4BSD Operating System.* Addison-Wesley, Reading, MA.

> An entire book on the 4.4BSD operating system.

McKusick, M. K., and Neville-Neil, G. V. 2005. *The Design and Implementation of the FreeBSD Operating System.* Addison-Wesley, Boston, MA.

> An entire book on the FreeBSD operating system, version 5.2.

Mauro, J., and McDougall, R. 2001. *Solaris Internals.* Prentice-Hall, Upper Saddle River, NJ.

> A book on the internals of the Solaris operating system. Covers Solaris versions 2.5.1, 2.6, and 2.7 (also known as Solaris 7).

Morris, R., and Thompson, K. 1979. "UNIX Password Security," *Communications of the ACM,* vol. 22, no. 11, pp. 594–597 (Nov.).

> A description of the history of the design of the password scheme used in UNIX Systems.

Nemeth, E., Snyder, G., Seebass, S., and Hein, T. R. 2001. *UNIX System Administration Handbook, Third Edition.* Prentice-Hall, Upper Saddle River, NJ.

> A book with many details on administering a UNIX system.

Olander, D. J., McGrath, G. J., and Israel, R. K. 1986. "A Framework for Networking in System V," *Proceedings of the 1986 Summer USENIX Conference,* pp. 38–45, Atlanta, GA.

> Describes the original implementation of service interfaces, STREAMS, and TLI for System V.

The Open Group. 2004. *The Single UNIX Specification, Version 3.* The Open Group, Berkshire, UK.

> The POSIX and X/Open standards combined into a single reference.
>
> The HTML version can be viewed for free online at http://www.opengroup.org. Alternatively, a CD-ROM containing the whole standard is available for purchase.

Pike, R., Presotto, D., Dorward, S., Flandrena, B., Thompson, K., Trickey, H., and Winterbottom, P. 1995. "Plan 9 from Bell Labs," *Plan 9 Programmer's Manual Volume 2.* AT&T, Reading, MA.

> A description of the Plan 9 operating system, developed in the same department where the UNIX System was invented.

Plauger, P. J. 1992. *The Standard C Library.* Prentice-Hall, Englewood Cliffs, NJ.

> A complete book on the ANSI C library. It contains a complete C implementation of the library.

Presotto, D. L., and Ritchie, D. M. 1990. "Interprocess Communication in the Ninth Edition UNIX System," *Software Practice and Experience,* vol. 20, no. S1, pp. S1/3–S1/17 (June).

> Describes the IPC facilities provided by the Ninth Edition Research UNIX System, developed at AT&T Bell Laboratories. The features are built on the stream input–output system and include full-duplex pipes, the ability to pass file descriptors between processes, and unique client connections to servers. A copy of this paper also appears in AT&T [1990b].

Rago, S. A. 1993. *UNIX System V Network Programming.* Addison-Wesley, Reading, MA.

> A book that describes the networking programming environment of UNIX System V Release 4, which is based on STREAMS.

Raymond, E. S., ed. 1996. *The New Hacker's Dictionary, Third Edition.* MIT Press, Cambridge, MA.

> Lots of computer hacker terms defined.

Ritchie, D. M. 1984. "A Stream Input-Output System," *AT&T Bell Laboratories Technical Journal,* vol. 63, no. 8, pp. 1897–1910 (Oct.).

> The original paper on Streams.

Salus, P. H. 1994. *A Quarter Century of UNIX.* Addison-Wesley, Reading, MA.

> A history of the UNIX System from 1969 to 1994.

Seltzer, M., and Olson, M. 1992. "LIBTP: Portable Modular Transactions for UNIX," *Proceedings of the 1992 Winter USENIX Conference,* pp. 9–25, San Francisco, CA.

> A modification of the db(3) library from 4.4BSD that implements transactions.

Seltzer, M., and Yigit, O. 1991. "A New Hashing Package for UNIX," *Proceedings of the 1991 Winter USENIX Conference*, pp. 173–184, Dallas, TX.

> A description of the dbm(3) library and its implementations, and a newer hashing package.

Stevens, W. R. 1990. *UNIX Network Programming*. Prentice-Hall, Englewood Cliffs, NJ.

> A detailed book on network programming under the UNIX System. The contents of the first edition of this book differ greatly from later editions.

Stevens, W. R., Fenner, B., and Rudoff, A. M. 2004. *UNIX Network Programming, Volume 1, Third Edition*. Addison-Wesley, Boston, MA.

> A detailed book on network programming under UNIX System. Redesigned and split into two volumes in the second edition and updated in the third edition.

Stonebraker, M. R. 1981. "Operating System Support for Database Management," *Communications of the ACM*, vol. 24, no. 7, pp. 412–418 (July).

> Describes operating system services and how they affect database operation.

Strang, J. 1986. *Programming with curses*. O'Reilly & Associates, Sebastopol, CA.

> A book on the Berkeley version of curses.

Strang, J., Mui, L., and O'Reilly, T. 1988. *termcap & terminfo, Third Edition*. O'Reilly & Associates, Sebastopol, CA.

> A book on termcap and terminfo.

Sun Microsystems. 2002. *STREAMS Programming Guide*. Sun Microsystems, Santa Clara, CA.

> Describes STREAMS programming on the Solaris platform.

Thompson, K. 1978. "UNIX Implementation," *The Bell System Technical Journal*, vol. 57, no. 6, pp. 1931–1946 (July–Aug.).

> Describes some of the implementation details of Version 7.

Vo, Kiem-Phong. 1996. "Vmalloc: A General and Efficient Memory Allocator," *Software Practice and Experience*, vol. 26, no. 3, pp. 357–374.

> Describes a flexible memory allocator.

Weinberger, P. J. 1982. "Making UNIX Operating Systems Safe for Databases," *The Bell System Technical Journal*, vol. 61, no. 9, pp. 2407–2422 (Nov.).

> Describes some problems in implementing databases in early UNIX systems.

Weinstock, C. B., and Wulf, W. A. 1988. "Quick Fit: An Efficient Algorithm for Heap Storage Allocation," *SIGPLAN Notices*, vol. 23, no. 10, pp. 141–148.

> Describes a memory allocation algorithm suitable for a wide variety of applications.

Williams, T. 1989. "Session Management in System V Release 4," *Proceedings of the 1989 Winter USENIX Conference*, pp. 365–375, San Diego, CA.

> Describes the session architecture in SVR4, on which the POSIX.1 interfaces were based. This includes process groups, job control, and controlling terminals. Also describes the security concerns of existing approaches.

X/Open. 1989. *X/Open Portability Guide*. Prentice-Hall, Englewood Cliffs, NJ.

> A set of seven volumes covering commands and utilities (Vol. 1), system interfaces and headers (Vol. 2), supplementary definitions (Vol. 3), programming languages (Vol. 4), data management (Vol. 5), window management (Vol. 6), networking services (Vol. 7). Although out of print, this has been replaced by the Single UNIX Specification [Open Group 2004].

Index

The function subentries labeled "definition of" point to where the function prototype appears and, when applicable, to the source code for the function. Functions defined in the text that are used in later examples, such as the set_fl function in Figure 3.11, are included in this index. The definitions of external functions that are part of the larger examples (Chapters 17, 19, 20, and 21) are also included in this index, to help in going through these larger examples. Also, significant functions and constants that occur in any of the examples in the text, such as select and poll, are also included in this index. Trivial functions that occur in almost every example, such as exit, are not referenced when they occur in examples.

#!, *see* interpreter files
., *see* current directory
.., *see* parent directory
2.9BSD, 216
386BSD, xxvii, 34–35
4.1BSD, 487
4.2BSD, 18, 112, 119–120, 167, 428–429, 474, 481, 483, 487, 545
4.3BSD, xxvii, 33–34, 36, 183, 240, 248, 265, 442, 497, 699, 846, 888
  Reno, xxvii, 34, 72
  Tahoe, xxvii, 34, 888
4.4BSD, xxii, xxvii, 21, 34, 105, 112, 119, 139, 216, 462, 497, 545, 699, 710, 888

a2ps program, 805
abort function, 180, 218, 223, 253, 256, 289, 293–295, 306, 340–342, 353, 407, 848, 870
  definition of, 340–341
absolute pathname, 5, 7, 43, 49, 126, 131, 242, 859
accept function, 138, 306, 411, 563–564, 570, 572, 597, 599–600, 780
  definition of, 563
access function, 95–97, 113, 116, 306
  definition of, 95
accounting
  login, 170–171
  process, 250–256
acct function, 250

acct structure, 251, 254
acctcom program, 250
accton program, 250–251, 255
ACOMPAT constant, 251
ACORE constant, 251, 254–255
acstime_r function, 402
add_job function, 783, 790
add_option function, 794, 797
addressing, socket, 549–561
addrinfo structure, 555–559, 569, 571, 573, 576,
    578, 779, 782, 796
add_worker function, 787, 791
adjustment on exit, semaphore, 532–533
Adobe Systems, 885
advisory record locking, 455
AES (Application Environment Specification), 32
AEXPND constant, 251
AF_INET constant, 547, 551–552, 554, 557,
    559–560
AF_INET6 constant, 551–552, 557
AF_IPX constant, 546
AF_LOCAL constant, 546
AFORK constant, 251–252, 254
AF_UNIX constant, 546, 557, 595–598, 600–601
AF_UNSPEC constant, 546, 557
agetty program, 265
Aho, A. V., 243, 885
AI_ALL constant, 559
AI_CANONNAME constant, 559, 571, 574, 578
AI_NUMERICHOST constant, 559
AI_NUMERICSERV constant, 559
aio_error function, 306
<aio.h> header, 30
aio_return function, 306
aio_suspend function, 306, 411
AI_PASSIVE constant, 559
AI_V4MAPPED constant, 556, 559
AIX, 36
alarm function, 289, 293, 306–307, 310, 313–318,
    331, 348–349, 354, 575–576, 867
    definition of, 313
alloca function, 192
already_running function, definition of, 433
ALTWERASE constant, 636, 642, 645
American National Standards Institute, see ANSI
Andrade, J. M., 521, 885
ANSI (American National Standards Institute), 25
ANSI C, xxvi–xxvii
Apple Computer, xxii
Application Environment Specification, see AES
apue_db.h header, 711, 719, 723, 727
apue.h header, 6, 9–10, 229, 299, 449–450, 597,
    721, 843–846

Architecture, UNIX, 1–2
argc variable, 778
ARG_MAX constant, 39, 42, 46, 48, 233, 404
arguments, command-line, 185
argv variable, 774
Arnold J. Q., 188, 885
<arpa/inet.h> header, 29, 550
asctime function, 175, 402
    definition of, 175
<assert.h> header, 27
ASU constant, 251, 254
asynchronous I/O, 473, 481–482
asynchronous socket I/O, 582–583
at program, 431
atexit function, 42, 182, 184, 207, 218, 365, 696,
    863
    definition of, 182
ATEXIT_MAX constant, 40, 42, 48, 51
atol function, 781
atomic operation, 39, 43, 57, 61, 74–75, 77, 109, 139,
    333, 340, 448, 515, 528, 530, 532, 883
AT&T, xix, 5, 33–34, 159, 311, 460, 462, 479,
    885–886
automatic variables, 187, 197, 199, 201, 207
avoidance, deadlock, 373
awk program, 44–46, 243–246, 514, 887
AXSIG constant, 251, 254–255

B0 constant, 652
B110 constant, 652
B115200 constant, 652
B1200 constant, 652
B134 constant, 652
B150 constant, 652
B1800 constant, 652
B19200 constant, 652
B200 constant, 652
B2400 constant, 652
B300 constant, 652
B38400 constant, 652
B4800 constant, 652
B50 constant, 652
B57600 constant, 652
B600 constant, 652
B75 constant, 652
B9600 constant, 652
Bach, M. J., xix, xxviii, 70, 77, 104, 108, 211, 461,
    855, 886
background process group, 272, 275, 277, 279,
    281–282, 284–285, 296–297, 344, 349, 882
backoff, exponential, 562

Barkley, R. E., 886
basename function, 402
bash program, 81, 158, 250
.bash_login file, 265
.bash_profile file, 265
Bass, J., 445
baud rate, terminal I/O, 652–653
Berkeley Software Distribution, *see* BSD
bibliography, alphabetical, 885–890
big-endian byte order, 549
bind function, 306, 560, 564, 580–581, 596–598,
    600–601
    definition of, 560
/bin/false program, 163
/bin/true program, 163
<bits/signum.h> header, 290
block special file, 89, 128–129
Bolsky, M. I., 510, 886
Bostic, K., xxviii, 33, 70, 104, 108, 461, 487, 888
    Keith, 211, 218
Bourne, S. R., 3
Bourne shell, 3, 52, 86, 158, 192, 204, 265, 275, 278,
    346, 457, 504, 510, 662, 877, 887
Bourne-again shell, 3, 51–52, 81, 86, 192, 204, 265,
    275, 510
BREAK character, 637, 642, 645, 648, 650, 654, 668
BRKINT constant, 635, 645, 648, 666–668
BS0 constant, 645
BS1 constant, 645
BSD (Berkeley Software Distribution), 34, 62, 83,
    262, 265–266, 268–269, 271, 273–274, 442,
    473, 481–482, 493, 552–553, 595, 683,
    685–686, 689, 691, 699, 706–707
BSD Networking Release 1.0, xxvii, 34
BSD Networking Release 2.0, xxvii, 34
BSD/386, xxvii
BSDLY constant, 637, 644–645, 649
bss segment, 187
buf_args function, 618–620, 628–629, 845
    definition of, 619
buffer cache, 77
buffering, standard I/O, 135–137, 213, 217, 247,
    342, 513–514, 680, 718
BUFSIZ constant, 49, 137, 202
build_qonstart function, 780, 785
BUS_ADRALN constant, 327
BUS_ADRERR constant, 327
BUS_OBJERR constant, 327
byte order
    big-endian, 549
    little-endian, 549
byte ordering, 549–550

C, ANSI, xxvi–xxvii
    ISO, 25–26, 887
C shell, 3, 52, 204, 265, 275, 510
c99 program, 56, 67
cache
    buffer, 77
    page, 77
caddr_t data type, 57
CAE (Common Application Environment), 32
calendar time, 20, 24, 57, 117, 173–175, 246,
    251–252
calloc function, 189–190, 207, 467, 506, 726, 863
    definition of, 189
cancellation point, 410–411
canonical mode, terminal I/O, 660–663
Carges, M. T., 521, 885
cat program, 85, 104, 114, 276, 279, 699, 714, 882
catclose function, 412
catgets function, 402, 412
catopen function, 412
CBAUDEXT constant, 635, 645
cbreak terminal mode, 632, 664, 668, 673
cc program, 6, 55, 189
CCAR_OFLOW constant, 635, 645, 649
cc_t data type, 634
CCTS_OFLOW constant, 635, 645
cc(1) program, 6
cd program, 126
CDSR_OFLOW constant, 635, 645
CDTR_IFLOW constant, 635, 645
cfgetispeed function, 306, 637, 652
    definition of, 652
cfgetospeed function, 306, 637, 652
    definition of, 652
cfsetispeed function, 306, 637, 652
    definition of, 652
cfsetospeed function, 306, 637, 652
    definition of, 652
character special file, 89, 128–129, 461, 466, 659
CHAR_BIT constant, 38
CHARCLASS_NAME_MAX constant, 39, 48
CHAR_MAX constant, 38
CHAR_MIN constant, 38
chdir function, 7, 113, 125–127, 131, 204, 264, 306,
    427, 860
    definition of, 125
Chen, D., 886
CHILD_MAX constant, 39, 42, 48, 215
chmod function, 99–101, 113, 117, 306, 520,
    600–601, 687, 689–690, 882
    definition of, 99
chmod program, 93, 521

chown function, 54, 102–103, 112–113, 117, 264,
        306, 520, 687, 689, 882
    definition of, 102
chroot function, 131, 439, 858, 871
CIBAUDEXT constant, 635, 645
CIGNORE constant, 635, 645
Clark, J. J., xxviii
CLD_CONTINUED constant, 327
CLD_DUMPED constant, 327
CLD_EXITED constant, 327
CLD_KILLED constant, 327
CLD_STOPPED constant, 327
CLD_TRAPPED constant, 327
clearenv function, 194
clearerr function, 141
    definition of, 141
cli_args function, 618–620, 628
    definition of, 620
cli_conn function, 592–593, 600, 621, 626, 845
    definition of, 592, 594, 600
client_add function, 623, 625–627
    definition of, 623
client_alloc function, 623
    definition of, 622
client_cleanup function, 787, 792
client_del function, 625, 627
    definition of, 623
client–server
    model, 439, 541–543
client_thread function, 787
CLOCAL constant, 294, 635, 645
clock function, 57
clock tick, 20, 42, 48, 57, 251–252, 257
clock_gettime function, 306
clock_nanosleep function, 411
CLOCKS_PER_SEC constant, 57
clock_t data type, 20, 57, 257
clone device, STREAMS, 683
clone function, 211, 360, 416
close function, 8, 51, 59, 63, 77, 115, 118, 306, 411,
        427, 433, 452, 461, 493, 499–501, 506, 511–512,
        515, 521–522, 539–540, 543, 547–548, 564,
        571, 573, 581, 587–588, 592–594, 598–599,
        601, 616–617, 619, 625, 627–628, 684–685,
        688, 690, 693, 704–705
    definition of, 63
closedir function, 5, 7, 120–125, 412, 658, 858
    definition of, 120
closelog function, 412, 430
    definition of, 430
close-on-exec flag, 76, 79, 234, 452
clrasync function, definition of, 881

clr_fl function, 81, 442–443, 844, 879
clri program, 114
cmsgcred structure, 610–613
CMSG_DATA function, 607–608, 610, 612, 614
    definition of, 607
CMSG_FIRSTHDR function, 607, 614
    definition of, 607
cmsghdr structure, 607–609, 611, 613
CMSG_LEN function, 607–609, 611, 613
    definition of, 607
CMSG_NXTHDR function, 607, 612, 614
    definition of, 607
CMSPAR constant, 637, 645, 650
codes, option, 31
COLL_WEIGHTS_MAX constant, 39, 42, 48
COLUMNS environment variable, 193
Comer, D. E., 710, 886
command-line arguments, 185
Common Application Environment, see CAE
Common Open Software Environment, see COSE
communication, network printer, 753–805
<complex.h> header, 27
comp_t data type, 57
Computing Science Research Group, see CSRG
cond_signal function, 385
connect function, 306, 411, 561–563, 565–566,
        577, 597, 601
    definition of, 561
connection establishment, 561–565
connect_retry function, 569, 763, 797
    definition of, 562
connld STREAMS module, 518, 590, 592, 600
controlling
    process, 272, 294
    terminal, 61, 215, 234, 251, 268, 271–274, 276,
        278–279, 281, 284, 286–287, 294, 296–297,
        349, 423–425, 428, 439, 463, 468, 640, 645, 651,
        654, 660, 662, 676, 683, 685, 689, 691–692, 846,
        890
cooked terminal mode, 632
cooperating processes, 455, 717, 883
Coordinated Universal Time, see UTC
coprocesses, 510–514, 680, 701
copy-on-write, 211, 417
core dump, 70, 870
core file, 104, 116, 256, 291, 293, 296, 307, 340, 641,
        663, 857, 863, 865
COSE (Common Open Software Environment), 32
cp program, 131, 490
cpio program, 117, 131–132, 858–859
<cpio.h> header, 30
CR terminal character, 638, 640, 663

CR0 constant, 645
CR1 constant, 645
CR2 constant, 645
CR3 constant, 645
CRDLY constant, 637, 644–645, 649
CREAD constant, 635, 646
creat function, 59, 62–63, 65, 75, 85, 95, 97, 110,
        113, 117, 139, 306, 411, 451, 592, 857, 860
    definition of, 62
creation mask, file mode, 97–98, 119, 131, 215, 234,
        425
cron program, 354, 425, 430–432, 434, 868
CRTSCTS constant, 635, 646
CRTS_IFLOW constant, 635, 646
CRTSXOFF constant, 635, 646
crypt function, 263, 273, 279–280, 402
crypt program, 273, 660
CS5 constant, 644, 646
CS6 constant, 644, 646
CS7 constant, 644, 646
CS8 constant, 644, 646, 666–668
.cshrc file, 265
CSIZE constant, 635, 644, 646, 666–667
csopen function, 615–616
    definition of, 616, 621
CSRG (Computing Science Research Group), xx,
        xxii, 35
CSTOPB constant, 635, 646
ctermid function, 401, 412, 654, 660–661
    definition of, 654
ctime function, 174–176, 402
    definition of, 175
ctime_r function, 402
<ctype.h> header, 27
cu program, 473
cupsd program, 425, 757
curses library, 672–673, 887, 890
cuserid function, 257

daemon, 423–439
    coding, 425–428
    conventions, 434–439
    error logging, 428–432
daemonize function, 425, 428, 439, 571, 573, 578,
        624, 778, 844, 871–872
    definition of, 426
Dang, X. T., 188, 887
Darwin, xxiii, 35
data, out-of-band, 581–582
data segment
    initialized, 187

uninitialized, 187
data transfer, 565–579
data types, primitive system, 56
database library, 709–752
    coarse-grained locking, 718
    concurrency, 718–719
    fine-grained locking, 718
    implementation, 712–715
    performance, 747–752
    source code, 719–747
database transactions, 889
Date, C. J., 719, 886
date functions, time and, 173–176
date program, 175, 178, 346, 862, 882
DATEMSK environment variable, 193
db library, 710, 889
DB structure, 722–724, 726–728, 731–734, 739, 742,
        748
_db_alloc function, 723, 726–727
db_close function, 710–711, 715, 727
    definition of, 710
db_delete function, 711, 718, 734–735, 737, 883
    definition of, 711
_db_dodelete function, 734–735, 738, 742,
        746–747, 752, 883
db_fetch function, 711, 713, 715, 718, 728, 733
    definition of, 711
_db_find_and_lock function, 728–729,
        733–734, 740–741, 743, 752
_db_findfree function, 741, 743–744, 747
_db_free function, 724, 727
DBHANDLE data type, 715
_db_hash function, 730, 752
DB_INSERT constant, 711, 715, 740
dbm library, 709–710, 890
dbm_clearerr function, 402
dbm_close function, 402, 412
dbm_delete function, 402, 412
dbm_error function, 402
dbm_fetch function, 402, 412
dbm_firstkey function, 402
dbm_nextkey function, 402, 412
dbm_open function, 402, 412
dbm_store function, 402, 412
db_nextrec function, 712, 715, 718, 735, 745, 747,
        752, 883
    definition of, 712
db_open function, 710–712, 715, 718, 721–723,
        725–727, 747
    definition of, 710
_db_readdat function, 728, 734, 883
_db_readidx function, 730–731, 746, 883

_db_readptr function, 729, 731, 752
DB_REPLACE constant, 711, 740
db_rewind function, 712, 745, 747
    definition of, 712
DB_STORE constant, 711, 740
db_store function, 711–712, 715, 718, 720, 735,
        737, 740, 747, 750, 752
    definition of, 711
_db_writedat function, 735, 737–738, 741–742,
        747, 752, 883
_db_writeidx function, 484, 725, 738, 741–742,
        747, 752, 883
_db_writeptr function, 725, 739, 741–742
dcheck program, 114
dd program, 256
deadlock, 216, 373, 450, 513, 680
    avoidance, 373
    record locking, 450
delayed write, 77
descriptor set, 475, 477, 493, 875
detachstate attribute, 389–390
/dev/fb device, 466
/dev/fd device, 84–85, 132, 656
/dev/fd/0 device, 85
/dev/fd/1 device, 85, 132
/dev/fd/2 device, 85
devfs file system, 129
device number
    major, 56–57, 127, 129, 659
    minor, 56–57, 127, 129, 659
device special file, 127–129
device, STREAMS clone, 683
/dev/klog device, 429
/dev/kmem device, 65
/dev/log device, 429, 439, 871
/dev/null device, 69, 82, 279, 466
/dev/ptmx device, 683–685, 689–690
/dev/pts device, 689
/dev/pty device, 686–687
/dev/stderr device, 85, 658
/dev/stdin device, 85, 658
/dev/stdout device, 85, 658
dev_t data type, 57, 127–128
/dev/tty device, 273, 279, 287, 466, 654, 660, 705
/dev/zero device, 538–540
df program, 131, 858
DIR structure, 7, 121, 260, 657
directories
    files and, 4–7
    reading, 120–125
directory, 4
    file, 88

home, 2, 7, 125, 193, 264, 267
    ownership, 95
    parent, 4, 101, 116, 119
    root, 4, 7, 24, 129, 131, 215, 234, 260, 858
    working, 7, 13, 43, 49, 107, 125–126, 162, 193,
        215, 234, 291, 426
dirent structure, 5, 7, 121, 123, 657
<dirent.h> header, 29, 121
dirname function, 402
DISCARD terminal character, 638, 640, 647
dlclose function, 412
dlerror function, 402
<dlfcn.h> header, 30
dlopen function, 412
do_driver function, 696, 704
    definition of, 704
Dorward, S., 211, 889
DOS, 55
dot, see current directory
dot-dot, see parent directory
drand48 function, 402
DSUSP terminal character, 638, 640, 648
du program, 104, 131, 857–858
Duff, T., 84
dup function, 51, 59, 70, 73, 76–77, 138, 153, 213,
        306, 428, 452–453, 548, 855–856, 864
    definition of, 76
dup2 function, 62, 76–77, 86, 138, 306, 501, 506,
        512, 548, 573–574, 588, 617, 693, 704–705, 855
    definition of, 76

E2BIG error, 526
EACCES error, 14–15, 433–434, 447, 459, 861
EAGAIN error, 16, 433–434, 442, 444, 447, 456–457,
        459, 525, 531–532, 564, 582, 687
EBADF error, 51
EBADMSG error, 470
EBUSY error, 16, 371, 380
ECHILD error, 308, 326, 345, 508
ECHO constant, 636, 646–647, 661, 665–667, 696
echo program, 185
ECHOCTL constant, 636, 646
ECHOE constant, 636, 646–647, 661, 696
ECHOK constant, 636, 647, 661, 696
ECHOKE constant, 636, 647
ECHONL constant, 636, 647, 661, 696
ECHOPRT constant, 636, 646–647
ecvt function, 402
ed program, 342, 344–345, 456–457
EEXIST error, 112, 520
EFBIG error, 868

effective
  group ID, 91–92, 94–95, 101, 103, 130, 167, 210,
      214, 237, 241, 520, 543, 605
  user ID, 91–92, 94–95, 99, 103, 117, 130, 210,
      214, 235, 237–241, 257, 262, 264, 312, 354, 520,
      524, 530, 535, 542–543, 593, 600, 605, 771, 861,
      866
efficiency
  I/O, 68–70
  standard I/O, 143–145
EIDRM error, 524–526, 530–532
EINPROGRESS error, 563
EINTR error, 16, 246–247, 303–304, 313, 334, 345,
      475, 480, 507–508, 525–526, 532, 575
EINVAL error, 42, 47, 320, 361, 367, 464, 466, 505,
      507, 665–667
EIO error, 284, 297, 686
Ellis, M., xxviii
ELOOP error, 113–114
EMSGSIZE error, 566
ENAMETOOLONG error, 62
encrypt function, 402
endgrent function, 167–168, 402, 412
  definition of, 167
endhostent function, 412, 553
  definition of, 553
endnetent function, 412, 554
  definition of, 554
endprotoent function, 412, 554
  definition of, 554
endpwent function, 164–165, 402, 412
  definition of, 164
endservent function, 412, 555
  definition of, 555
endspent function, 166
  definition of, 166
endutxent function, 402, 412
ENFILE error, 16
ENOBUFS error, 16
ENODEV error, 466
ENOENT error, 15, 405, 686, 711
ENOLCK error, 16
ENOMEM error, 16
ENOMSG error, 526
ENOSPC error, 16, 405
ENOSR error, 16
ENOSTR error, 466
ENOTDIR error, 548
ENOTTY error, 466, 643, 653
environ variable, 185–186, 193, 195, 232, 236,
      404–405, 409, 863
environment list, 185–186, 215, 233, 262–264

environment variable, 192–195
  COLUMNS, 193
  DATEMSK, 193
  HOME, 192–193, 264
  IFS, 250
  LANG, 41, 193
  LC_ALL, 193
  LC_COLLATE, 42, 193
  LC_CTYPE, 193
  LC_MESSAGES, 193
  LC_MONETARY, 193
  LC_NUMERIC, 193
  LC_TIME, 193
  LD_LIBRARY_PATH, 719
  LINES, 193
  LOGNAME, 193, 257, 264
  MAILPATH, 192
  MALLOC_OPTIONS, 870
  MSGVERB, 193
  NLSPATH, 193
  PAGER, 501, 504–505
  PATH, 93, 193, 232–233, 235, 242, 244, 247,
      264–265
  PWD, 193
  SHELL, 193, 264, 701
  TERM, 193, 263, 265
  TMPDIR, 157–158, 193
  TZ, 174, 176, 178, 193, 862
  USER, 192, 264
ENXIO error, 515
EOF constant, 10, 141, 143–144, 154, 160, 507, 509,
      512–513, 587, 624, 694, 861
EOF terminal character, 638, 640, 646–647, 660, 663
EOL terminal character, 638, 640, 647, 660, 663
EOL2 terminal character, 638, 640, 647, 660, 663
EPERM error, 238
EPIPE error, 499, 878
Epoch, 20, 22, 117, 171, 173–174, 600
ERANGE error, 49
ERASE terminal character, 638, 640, 646–647,
      662–663
ERASE2 terminal character, 638, 641
err_dump function, 340, 733, 845, 847
  definition of, 848
err_exit function, 845, 847
  definition of, 848
err_msg function, 845, 847
  definition of, 848
errno variable, 14–15, 24, 42, 49, 54, 62, 64, 77,
      112–113, 134, 238, 246, 284, 290, 297, 303–304,
      306–308, 312–313, 320, 326, 334, 345, 353,
      356, 358, 406, 413, 431, 434, 442, 444, 447, 459,
      475, 480, 499, 508, 515, 526, 548, 563–564, 566,
      582, 643, 653, 711, 767, 782, 847, 854, 868

`<errno.h>` header, 14, 16, 27
error
    handling, 14–16
    logging, daemon, 428–432
    recovery, 16
    routines, standard, 846–851
`err_quit` function, 7, 778, 845, 847, 860
    definition of, 848
`err_ret` function, 771, 845, 847, 860
    definition of, 847
`err_sys` function, 7, 771, 845, 847
    definition of, 847
ESPIPE error, 64, 548
ESRCH error, 312, 367
`/etc/gettydefs` file, 265
`/etc/group` file, 17–18, 161, 169–170
`/etc/hosts` file, 170
`/etc/inittab` file, 265
`/etc/master.passwd` file, 169
`/etc/motd` device, 466
`/etc/networks` file, 170
`/etc/passwd` file, 2, 92, 125, 161–162, 164, 166, 169–170
`/etc/protocols` file, 170
`/etc/pwd.db` file, 169
`/etc/rc` file, 173, 266
`/etc/services` file, 170
`/etc/shadow` file, 92, 169–170
`/etc/spwd.db` file, 169
`/etc/syslog.conf` file, 429
`/etc/termcap` file, 672
`/etc/ttys` file, 262
ETIME error, 763, 767
ETIMEDOUT error, 384
EWOULDBLOCK error, 16, 442, 564, 582
exec function, 10–12, 22, 39, 42, 78, 94, 113, 116–117, 179, 183, 185, 206, 211, 215–216, 231–240, 242–243, 245–246, 248, 250, 252, 256, 259–260, 262–264, 266–267, 270, 280, 300–301, 347, 416–417, 452, 489, 495, 500, 503, 519, 541, 615–616, 620–621, 629, 676, 678, 680, 682, 692, 704, 707, 863, 870, 886
execl function, 231–233, 242–243, 247, 253, 255–256, 260, 264, 345–346, 501, 506, 512, 573, 588, 617, 702, 865
    definition of, 231
execle function, 231–233, 235–236, 263, 306
    definition of, 231
execlp function, 11–13, 19, 231–233, 235–236, 245, 247, 260, 704, 865
    definition of, 231
execv function, 231–233

    definition of, 231
execve function, 231–233, 235, 306, 865
    definition of, 231
execvp function, 231–233, 235, 695–696
    definition of, 231
exercises, solutions to, 853–883
`_exit` function, 180, 183, 217–221, 247, 259–260, 306, 340, 342, 345, 354, 360, 407, 864, 867
`_Exit` function, 180, 183, 218–219, 221, 306, 340, 342, 360, 407
    definition of, 180
`_exit` function, definition of, 180
exit function, 7, 140, 144, 180–184, 207, 213, 216–221, 228, 231, 246–247, 252–253, 255–256, 260, 264, 305, 340–341, 360, 407, 425, 504, 665, 696, 707, 771, 780, 793, 843, 863–864, 882
    definition of, 180
exit handler, 182
expect program, 679, 703–705, 888
exponential backoff, 562
ext2 file system, 69, 82, 95, 119
ext3 file system, 95, 119
EXTPROC constant, 636, 647

Fagin, R., 710, 715, 886
fatal error, 16
fattach function, 589, 592–593
    definition of, 589
fchdir function, 125–127, 548
    definition of, 125
fchmod function, 99–101, 112, 117, 306, 458, 548
    definition of, 99
fchown function, 102–103, 117, 306, 548
    definition of, 102
fclose function, 138–140, 181, 183, 340–341, 412, 507, 661
    definition of, 139
fcntl function, 59, 73, 76–83, 86, 105, 138, 153, 203, 234, 306, 411–412, 442, 445, 447–450, 452, 454–455, 482, 548, 581–583, 749–751, 880–882
    definition of, 78
`<fcntl.h>` header, 29, 60
fcvt function, 402
fdatasync function, 77–78, 82–83, 306, 548
    definition of, 77
FD_CLOEXEC constant, 78–79, 234
FD_CLR function, 476, 625, 875
    definition of, 476
fdetach function, 590

definition of, 590
FD_ISSET function, 476, 625, 875
    definition of, 476
fdopen function, 138–140, 506, 877
    definition of, 138
fd_set data type, 57, 475–476, 493, 625, 779–780,
    874, 879
FD_SET function, 476, 625, 875
    definition of, 476
FD_SETSIZE constant, 477, 874
F_DUPFD constant, 77–79, 548
FD_ZERO function, 476, 625, 875
    definition of, 476
feature test macro, 55–56, 81
Fenner, B., 147, 266, 429, 545, 890
<fenv.h> header, 27
feof function, 141, 146
    definition of, 141
ferror function, 10, 141, 143–144, 146, 254, 500,
    505, 512, 588
    definition of, 141
FF0 constant, 647
FF1 constant, 647
FFDLY constant, 637, 644, 647, 649
fflush function, 135, 137, 139, 160, 341, 412,
    508–510, 514, 662, 680, 849, 851, 854, 861
    definition of, 137
F_FREESP constant, 105
fgetc function, 140–141, 144–145, 412
    definition of, 140
F_GETFD constant, 78–79, 548
F_GETFL constant, 78–81, 548
F_GETLK constant, 78, 446–450
F_GETOWN constant, 78–79, 548, 582
fgetpos function, 147–148, 412
    definition of, 148
fgets function, 9, 11–12, 19, 140, 142–145, 156,
    159, 196, 198, 412, 500, 505, 509, 512–514, 570,
    577, 587, 616, 703, 718, 807, 859, 861, 877
    definition of, 142
fgetwc function, 412
fgetws function, 412
FIFOs, 89, 496, 514–518, 589
file
    access permissions, 92–94, 130
    block special, 89, 128–129
    character special, 89, 128–129, 461, 466, 659
    descriptor passing, 543, 601–614
    descriptor passing, socket, 606–614
    descriptor passing, STREAMS, 604–606
    descriptors, 8–10, 59–60
    device special, 127–129

directory, 88
group, 166–167
holes, 65–66, 104–105
mode creation mask, 97–98, 119, 131, 215, 234,
    425
offset, 63–65, 71–74, 76, 213–214, 454, 484,
    713–714, 856
ownership, 95
pointer, 134
regular, 88
sharing, 70–73, 213
size, 103–105
times, 115–116, 493
truncation, 105
types, 88–91
FILE structure, 121, 133–134, 141, 153–154, 156,
    202, 217, 254, 402–403, 500, 504–505, 507,
    509, 577, 661, 720, 872
file system, 4, 105–108
    devfs, 129
    ext2, 69, 82, 95, 119
    ext3, 95, 119
    HSFS, 105
    PCFS, 48, 55, 105
    S5, 62
    UFS, 48, 55, 62, 105, 108, 119
filename, 4
    truncation, 62
FILENAME_MAX constant, 38
fileno function, 153, 506–507, 661, 861
    definition of, 153
_FILE_OFFSET_BITS constant, 67
FILEPERM constant, 762, 788
files and directories, 4–7
FILESIZEBITS constant, 39, 43, 48
find program, 116, 125, 234
finger program, 131, 163, 858
FIOASYNC constant, 583, 880–881
FIOSETOWN constant, 583
FIPS, 33
Flandrena, B., 211, 889
<float.h> header, 27, 38
flock function, 445
flock structure, 446, 448–449, 454
flockfile function, 402–403
    definition of, 403
FLUSHO constant, 636, 640, 647
FMNAMESZ constant, 466
fmtmsg function, 193
<fmtmsg.h> header, 30
FNDELAY constant, 442
<fnmatch.h> header, 29

F_OK constant, 96
foo_alloc function, 372
foo_find function, 376
foo_hold function, 376
foo_rele function, 376
fopen function, 5, 134, 138–140, 154, 202, 254,
    412, 500–501, 504, 661, 872
    definition of, 138
FOPEN_MAX constant, 38, 42
foreground process group, 272–278, 280–281, 286,
    294, 296–297, 343, 350, 424–425, 463,
    640–642, 645, 649, 670, 706, 882
foreground process group ID, 274, 278, 637
fork function, 11–12, 19, 22, 73, 210–219,
    223–225, 227–231, 235–236, 240, 242,
    245–248, 250–253, 255–256, 259, 262, 264,
    266–267, 270–271, 279, 282–284, 287, 301,
    306, 309, 345–347, 354, 416–421, 425–428,
    430, 451–453, 458–459, 473, 489, 495–501,
    503, 506–507, 511, 519, 527, 539, 541, 544,
    573–574, 587, 602, 615–617, 620–621, 629,
    675, 680, 682–683, 691–692, 697, 704, 747,
    865–866, 870–871, 873, 876, 878, 880, 886
    definition of, 211
fork1 function, 211
Fowler, G. S., 125, 887, 890
fpathconf function, 37, 39–48, 52–54, 103, 121,
    306, 499, 639
    definition of, 41
FPE_FLTDIV constant, 327
FPE_FLTINV constant, 327
FPE_FLTOVF constant, 327
FPE_FLTRES constant, 327
FPE_FLTSUB constant, 327
FPE_FLTUND constant, 327
FPE_INTDIV constant, 327
FPE_INTOVF constant, 327
fpos_t data type, 57, 147
fprintf function, 149, 412, 854
    definition of, 149
fputc function, 135, 142, 144–145, 412
    definition of, 142
fputs function, 136, 140, 142–145, 154, 156, 159,
    412, 505, 509, 512, 587, 661, 849, 851, 859, 862,
    877
    definition of, 143
fputwc function, 412
fputws function, 412
F_RDLCK constant, 446–447, 449–450, 845,
    873–874
fread function, 140, 145–147, 250, 254, 412
    definition of, 146

free function, 157, 159, 189–192, 306, 372,
    374–376, 378, 410, 657, 728
    definition of, 189
freeaddrinfo function, 555
    definition of, 555
FreeBSD, xxii–xxiii, 3, 21, 26–27, 29–30, 35–36, 38,
    48, 55, 58, 60, 62, 65, 78–79, 84, 95, 101–103,
    112, 119, 122, 128, 162, 166, 169, 171–172, 176,
    191, 193–194, 204, 206–207, 211, 222, 227,
    242–243, 250–251, 257, 264–265, 268, 278,
    285, 290–292, 295, 298, 304–305, 308, 310,
    326, 330, 333, 348, 352, 357, 360, 364, 445,
    452–453, 457, 459, 474–475, 496, 521, 523,
    529, 534, 538, 550–551, 566–568, 583, 588,
    596, 610–611, 614, 635–638, 645–651, 676,
    682–683, 692, 705–706, 710, 876, 888
freopen function, 134, 138–140, 412
    definition of, 138
fscanf function, 151, 412
    definition of, 151
fsck program, 114
fseek function, 139, 147–148, 412
    definition of, 147
fseeko function, 147–148, 412
    definition of, 148
F_SETFD constant, 78–79, 81, 86, 548, 855
F_SETFL constant, 78–79, 81, 86, 482, 548, 583,
    855, 882
F_SETLK constant, 78, 446–448, 450, 454, 845,
    873–874
F_SETLKW constant, 78, 446–448, 450, 845, 873
F_SETOWN constant, 78–79, 482, 548, 581–583,
    880–881
fsetpos function, 139, 147–148, 412
    definition of, 148
fstat function, 4, 87–88, 112, 306, 458, 491, 497,
    542, 548, 658, 725, 796
    definition of, 87
fsync function, 59, 77–78, 82–83, 160, 306, 411,
    489, 548, 752, 861
    definition of, 77
ftell function, 147–148, 412
    definition of, 147
ftello function, 147–148, 412
    definition of, 148
ftok function, 519
    definition of, 519
ftpd program, 431, 871
ftruncate function, 105, 117, 306, 491, 548
    definition of, 105
ftrylockfile function, 402–403
    definition of, 403

fts function, 122
ftw function, 113–114, 120–125, 131, 402, 412, 858
<ftw.h> header, 30
full-duplex pipes, 496
    named, 496
function prototypes, 807–841
functions, system calls versus, 21–23
F_UNLCK constant, 446–447, 449–450, 845
funlockfile function, 402–403
    definition of, 403
fwide function, 134
    definition of, 134
fwprintf function, 412
fwrite function, 140, 145–147, 354, 412, 868
    definition of, 146
F_WRLCK constant, 446–447, 449–450, 454, 845,
    873
fwscanf function, 412

gai_strerror function, 556, 571, 574, 576, 578
    definition of, 556
Gallmeister, B. O., 887
Garfinkel, S., 165, 232, 273, 887
gather write, 483, 607
gawk program, 243
gcc program, 6, 26, 56
gcvt function, 402
gdb program, 870
gdbm library, 710
generic pointer, 68, 190
getaddrinfo function, 555–557, 559–560,
    569–571, 574, 576, 578, 764, 770
    definition of, 555
getaddrlist function, 764, 770
GETALL constant, 530
getc function, 10, 140–143, 145, 153–154, 412,
    661–662, 861
    definition of, 140
getchar function, 140, 154, 160, 412, 509, 861
    definition of, 140
getchar_unlocked function, 402–403, 412
    definition of, 403
getconf program, 67
getc_unlocked function, 402–403, 412
    definition of, 403
getcwd function, 49, 125–127, 132, 190, 412,
    859–860
    definition of, 126
getdate function, 193, 402, 412
getegid function, 210, 306
    definition of, 210

getenv function, 186, 192–194, 402–405, 409–410,
    421, 501, 870
    definition of, 192
getenv_r function, 404–405
geteuid function, 210, 238–239, 249, 306, 612, 771
    definition of, 210
getgid function, 17, 210, 306
    definition of, 210
getgrent function, 167–168, 402, 412
    definition of, 167
getgrgid function, 166, 402, 412
    definition of, 166
getgrgid_r function, 402, 412
getgrnam function, 166, 402, 412, 687
    definition of, 166
getgrnam_r function, 402, 412
getgroups function, 168, 306
    definition of, 168
gethostbyaddr function, 402, 412, 553, 555
gethostbyname function, 402, 412, 553, 555
gethostent function, 402, 412, 553
    definition of, 553
gethostname function, 39, 42, 172, 412, 571–573,
    578, 778
    definition of, 172
getlogin function, 256–257, 402, 412, 439,
    871–872
    definition of, 256
getlogin_r function, 402, 412
getmsg function, 411, 461–463, 469–472, 493, 548,
    605, 705, 875
    definition of, 469
getnameinfo function, 556
    definition of, 556
GETNCNT constant, 530
getnetbyaddr function, 402, 412, 554
    definition of, 554
getnetbyname function, 402, 412, 554
    definition of, 554
getnetent function, 402, 412, 554
    definition of, 554
get_newjobno function, 783, 788
getopt function, 402, 624, 694, 696, 770, 773–774
    definition of, 774
getpass function, 263, 273, 660, 662–663
    definition of, 661
getpeername function, 306, 561
    definition of, 561
getpgid function, 269
    definition of, 269
getpgrp function, 269, 306
    definition of, 269

GETPID constant, 530
getpid function, 11, 210, 212, 217, 253, 284, 306,
    341, 351, 359, 434, 612, 881
    definition of, 210
getpmsg function, 411, 461–463, 469–470, 548
    definition of, 469
getppid function, 210–211, 306, 451, 697
    definition of, 210
get_printaddr function, 766, 782
get_printserver function, 766, 770
getprotobyname function, 402, 412, 554
    definition of, 554
getprotobynumber function, 402, 412, 554
    definition of, 554
getprotoent function, 402, 412, 554
    definition of, 554
getpwent function, 164–165, 402, 412
    definition of, 164
getpwnam function, 161–165, 170, 256, 263,
    306–308, 402, 412, 779, 861–862
    definition of, 163–164
getpwnam_r function, 402, 412
getpwuid function, 161–165, 170, 256–257, 402,
    412, 771, 861
    definition of, 163
getpwuid_r function, 402, 412
getrlimit function, 52, 202, 205, 426–427,
    854–855
    definition of, 202
getrusage function, 227, 258
gets function, 142–143, 412, 859
    definition of, 142
getservbyname function, 402, 412, 555
    definition of, 555
getservbyport function, 402, 412, 555
    definition of, 555
getservent function, 402, 412, 555
    definition of, 555
getsid function, 271
    definition of, 271
getsockname function, 306, 561
    definition of, 561
getsockopt function, 306, 579–580
    definition of, 579
getspent function, 166
    definition of, 166
getspnam function, 166, 861
    definition of, 166
gettimeofday function, 173, 176, 383, 398
    definition of, 173
getty program, 220, 262–266, 431
gettytab file, 263

getuid function, 17, 210, 238–239, 249, 256–257,
    306, 687
    definition of, 210
getutxent function, 402, 412
getutxid function, 402, 412
getutxline function, 402, 412
GETVAL constant, 530
getwc function, 412
getwchar function, 412
getwd function, 412
GETZCNT constant, 530
GID, see group ID
gid_t data type, 57
Gingell, R. A., 188, 487, 887
Gitlin, J. E., xxviii
glob function, 412
global variables, 201
<glob.h> header, 29
gmtime function, 174–175, 402
    definition of, 175
gmtime_r function, 402
GNU, 2, 265, 719
GNU Public License, 35
_GNU_SOURCE constant, 91
Godsil, J. M., xxviii
Goodheart, B., 672, 887
goto, nonlocal, 195–202, 329–333
Grandi, S., xxviii
grantpt function, 682–685, 688–691, 707
    definition of, 682, 687, 690
grep program, 20, 159, 182, 234, 887
group file, 166–167
group ID, 17, 237–241
    effective, 91–92, 94–95, 101, 103, 130, 167, 210,
        214, 237, 241, 520, 543, 605
    real, 91–92, 95, 167, 210, 214, 234–235, 237, 251,
        541
    supplementary, 18, 39, 91–92, 94, 101, 103,
        167–168, 214, 234, 241
group structure, 166, 687
<grp.h> header, 29, 166, 170
guardsize attribute, 389, 392

hack, 278
half-duplex pipes, 496
hard link, 4, 107, 109, 112, 114
hcreate function, 402
hdestroy function, 402
headers
    optional, 30
    POSIX required, 29

standard, 27
    XSI extension, 30
heap, 187
Hein, T. R., xxviii, 889
Hewlett-Packard, 36, 798
Hogue, J. E., xxviii
holes, file, 65–66, 104–105
home directory, 2, 7, 125, 193, 264, 267
HOME environment variable, 192–193, 264
Honeyman, P., xxviii
hostent structure, 553
hostname program, 173
HOST_NAME_MAX constant, 39, 42, 48, 172,
    570–573, 577–578, 778
HP-UX, 36
hsearch function, 402
HSFS file system, 105
htonl function, 550, 797
    definition of, 550
htons function, 550, 797
    definition of, 550
HTTP (Hypertext Transfer Protocol), 756
Hume, A. G., 159, 887
HUPCL constant, 635, 647
Hypertext Transfer Protocol, see HTTP

IBM (International Business Machines), 36
ICANON constant, 636, 638, 640–642, 646–647, 651,
    663, 665–667
I_CANPUT constant, 465
iconv_close function, 412
<iconv.h> header, 30
iconv_open function, 412
ICRNL constant, 635, 640, 648, 660, 666–668
identifiers
    IPC, 518–520
    process, 209–210
IDXLEN_MAX constant, 745
IEC, 25
IEEE (Institute for Electrical and Electronic
    Engineers), xx, 26–27, 887
IEXTEN constant, 636, 638, 640–642, 648, 666–668
I_FIND constant, 684–685
IFS environment variable, 250
IGNBRK constant, 635, 645, 648
IGNCR constant, 635, 640, 648, 660
IGNPAR constant, 635, 648, 650
I_GRDOPT constant, 470
I_GWROPT constant, 468
I_LIST constant, 466–467
ILL_BADSTK constant, 327

ILL_COPROC constant, 327
ILL_ILLADR constant, 327
ILL_ILLOPC constant, 327
ILL_ILLOPN constant, 327
ILL_ILLTRP constant, 327
ILL_PRVOPC constant, 327
ILL_PRVREG constant, 327
IMAXBEL constant, 635, 648
implementation differences, password, 169
implementations, UNIX System, 33
INADDR_ANY constant, 561
in_addr_t data type, 551
incore, 70
INET6_ADDRSTRLEN constant, 552
inet_addr function, 552
INET_ADDRSTRLEN constant, 552, 559–560
inetd program, 266–268, 425, 430–431
inet_ntoa function, 402, 552
inet_ntop function, 552, 560
    definition of, 552
inet_pton function, 552
    definition of, 552
INFTIM constant, 480
init program, 171, 173, 210, 219–220, 228,
    262–266, 268, 282–283, 287, 295, 312, 350,
    425, 434, 866, 871
initgroups function, 168, 264
    definition of, 168
initialized data segment, 187
init_printer function, 778, 782, 796
init_request function, 778, 781
initserver function, 570–572, 574, 577–578,
    763, 779
    definition of, 564, 580
inittab file, 295
INLCR constant, 635, 648
i-node, 57, 71–72, 88, 101, 105, 107–108, 112,
    115–117, 120–121, 128–129, 163, 287, 453,
    658, 853, 858
ino_t data type, 57, 107
INPCK constant, 635, 648, 650, 666–668
in_port_t data type, 551
Institute for Electrical and Electronic Engineers, see
    IEEE
int16_t data type, 794
International Business Machines, see IBM
International Standards Organization, see ISO
Internet Printing Protocol, see IPP
Internet worm, 142
interpreter file, 242–246, 260
interprocess communication, see IPC
interrupted system calls, 303–305, 317–318, 326,
    329, 339, 481

INT_MAX constant, 38
INT_MIN constant, 38
INTR terminal character, 638, 641, 648, 661
<inttypes.h> header, 27
I/O
    asynchronous, 473, 481–482
    asynchronous socket, 582–583
    efficiency, 68–70
    library, standard, 9, 133–160
    memory-mapped, 487–492
    multiplexing, 472–481
    nonblocking, 441–444
    nonblocking socket, 563–564, 582–583
    terminal, 631–673
    unbuffered, 8, 59–86
IOBUFSZ constant, 799
ioctl function, 59, 83–84, 86, 273, 297, 303–304,
        412, 442, 460–462, 464–468, 470, 482, 524,
        548, 583, 587, 593, 600, 604–606, 634,
        670–671, 684–685, 689–690, 692–693, 695,
        705–707, 880–881
    definition of, 83
ioctl operations, STREAMS, 464
_IOFBF constant, 137
_IOLBF constant, 137, 202
_IO_LINE_BUFFERED constant, 154
_IONBF constant, 137
_IO_UNBUFFERED constant, 154
iovec structure, 40–42, 483, 566, 608–609, 611,
        613, 617, 621, 737, 799
IOV_MAX constant, 40, 42, 48, 483
IPC (interprocess communication), 495–544,
        585–629
    identifiers, 518–520
    key, 518–520, 524, 529, 534
    XSI, 518–522
IPC_CREAT constant, 519–520
IPC_EXCL constant, 520
IPC_NOWAIT constant, 525–526, 531–532
ipc_perm structure, 520, 524, 529, 534, 543
IPC_PRIVATE constant, 519, 537, 542, 544
ipcrm program, 521
IPC_RMID constant, 524–525, 530, 535–537
ipcs program, 521, 544
IPC_SET constant, 524–525, 530, 535
IPC_STAT constant, 524–525, 530, 535
IPP (Internet Printing Protocol), 753–756
ipp.h header, 805
IPPROTO_IP constant, 579
IPPROTO_RAW constant, 558
IPPROTO_TCP constant, 558, 579
IPPROTO_UDP constant, 558

I_PUSH constant, 593, 685
I_RECVFD constant, 593, 600, 604–606
IRIX, 36
isastream function, 464–465, 467, 594
    definition of, 465
isatty function, 464–465, 639, 655, 658–659, 671,
        694, 702
    definition of, 655
I_SENDFD constant, 604–605
I_SETSIG constant, 482
ISIG constant, 636, 638, 640–642, 648, 666–668
ISO (International Standards Organization), xx,
        xxvii, 25–27, 887
ISO C, 25–26, 887
<iso646.h> header, 27
Israel, R. K., 462, 889
I_SRDOPT constant, 470
ISTRIP constant, 635, 648, 650, 666–668
is_write_lockable function, 450, 845
I_SWROPT constant, 468
IUCLC constant, 635, 649
IXANY constant, 635, 649
IXOFF constant, 635, 641–642, 649
IXON constant, 635, 641–642, 649, 666–668

jmp_buf data type, 198, 200, 315, 318
job control, 274–278
    shell, 270, 274, 280, 283, 300, 333, 350, 699
    signals, 349–352
job_find function, 869
job_remove function, 869
Jolitz, W. F., 34
Joy, W. N., 3, 71
jsh program, 275

Karels, M. J., 33–34, 70, 104, 108, 211, 218, 461, 487,
        888
kdump program, 457
kernel, 1
Kernighan, B. W., xx, xxviii, 26, 139, 145, 151, 153,
        190, 243, 846, 854, 885, 887
key, IPC, 518–520, 524, 529, 534
key_t data type, 518
kill function, 18, 253, 283–284, 290, 300, 306,
        310–313, 327, 338, 341–342, 351–352, 354,
        414, 416, 639, 641, 662, 697–698, 867, 874
    definition of, 312
kill program, 290–291, 296, 300, 513

KILL terminal character, 638, 641, 647, 662–663
kill_workers function, 791–793
Kleiman, S. R., 71, 887
Knuth, D. E., 730, 888
Korn, D. G., 3, 125, 159, 510, 886–888, 890
Korn shell, 3, 52, 86, 158, 192, 204, 265, 275, 457,
        510, 662, 698–699, 701, 877, 886
Kovach, K. R., 521, 885
Krieger, O., 159, 492, 888
ktrace program, 457

l64a function, 402
LANG environment variable, 41, 193
<langinfo.h> header, 30
last program, 171
layers, shell, 274
LC_ALL environment variable, 193
LC_COLLATE environment variable, 42, 193
LC_CTYPE environment variable, 193
lchown function, 102–103, 112–113, 117
    definition of, 102
LC_MESSAGES environment variable, 193
LC_MONETARY environment variable, 193
LC_NUMERIC environment variable, 193
L_ctermid constant, 654
LC_TIME environment variable, 193
ld program, 189
LDAP (Lightweight Directory Access Protocol),
        169
LD_LIBRARY_PATH environment variable, 719
ldterm STREAMS module, 468, 676, 685
leakage, memory, 191
least privilege, 237, 758, 779
Lee, M., 188, 887
Lee, T. P., 886
Leffler, S. J., 34, 888
Lennert, D., 888
Lesk, M. E., 133
lgamma function, 402
lgammaf function, 402
lgammal function, 402
Libes, D., 679, 867, 888
<libgen.h> header, 30
libraries, shared, 188–189, 207, 719, 863, 885
Lightweight Directory Access Protocol, see LDAP
limit program, 52, 204
limits, 36–52
    C, 38
    POSIX, 38–40
    resource, 202–206, 215, 234, 297, 354
    runtime indeterminate, 48–52

XSI, 40–41
<limits.h> header, 27, 38–40, 48–49
Linderman, J. P., xxviii
line control, terminal I/O, 653–654
LINE_MAX constant, 39, 42, 48
LINES environment variable, 193
link count, 43, 57, 107–109, 120
link function, 75, 107–114, 117, 306
    definition of, 109
link, hard, 4, 107, 109, 112, 114
    symbolic, 88–89, 102–103, 107, 110, 112–114,
        121, 127, 131, 170, 856–857
LINK_MAX constant, 39, 43, 48, 107
lint program, 182
Linux, xxi, xxiii, 2–3, 14, 21, 26–27, 29–30, 35–36,
        38, 40, 48, 51, 55, 58, 60, 62, 69–72, 82–84, 91,
        95, 101–103, 112, 114, 119, 122, 128, 154, 162,
        166, 169, 171–172, 176, 187, 191, 193–194,
        203–204, 207, 211, 222, 227, 242–243,
        250–251, 255, 264–265, 268, 278, 280, 290,
        292–296, 298, 304–305, 308, 310, 326,
        329–330, 333, 348, 352, 357, 360, 364, 424, 437,
        445, 455–457, 460–461, 464, 474–475, 484,
        492, 496, 521, 523, 529, 533–535, 537–538,
        540, 550–552, 566–568, 583, 585, 595,
        610–612, 614, 635–638, 644–651, 653, 676,
        683, 686, 689, 691–692, 705–706, 710, 719, 876
Linux STREAMS, 496
Lions, J., 888
LiS, 496
listen function, 306, 561, 563–564, 581, 597–598,
        762
    definition of, 563
little-endian byte order, 549
Litwin, W., 710, 715, 888
LLONG_MAX constant, 38
LLONG_MIN constant, 38
ln program, 107
LNEXT terminal character, 638, 641
locale, 42
localeconv function, 402
<locale.h> header, 27
LOCAL_PEERCRED constant, 612
localtime function, 174–176, 246, 402, 862
    definition of, 175
localtime_r function, 402
lockf function, 411, 445
lockf structure, 453
lockfile function, 433
    definition of, 454
locking
    database library, coarse-grained, 718

database library, fine-grained, 718
locking function, 445
lock_reg function, 448, 845, 873–874
  definition of, 449
lock_test function, 449–450, 845
  definition of, 449
log function, 429
LOG_ALERT constant, 431
LOG_AUTH constant, 431
LOG_AUTHPRIV constant, 431
LOG_CONS constant, 428, 430
LOG_CRIT constant, 431
LOG_CRON constant, 431
LOG_DAEMON constant, 428, 431
LOG_DEBUG constant, 431
LOG_EMERG constant, 431
LOG_ERR constant, 431, 433, 435–436, 438,
    570–574, 577–578, 850–851
LOG_FTP constant, 431
logger program, 432
login accounting, 170–171
.login file, 265
login name, 2, 17, 125, 163, 171, 193, 256–257, 266,
    439, 871
  root, 16
login program, 163, 166, 168, 171, 233, 236, 238,
    257, 263–267, 431, 660, 678, 703
LOG_INFO constant, 431, 435, 437
LOGIN_NAME_MAX constant, 39, 42, 48
logins
  network, 266–268
  terminal, 261–266
LOG_KERN constant, 431
LOG_LOCAL0 constant, 431
LOG_LOCAL1 constant, 431
LOG_LOCAL2 constant, 431
LOG_LOCAL3 constant, 431
LOG_LOCAL4 constant, 431
LOG_LOCAL5 constant, 431
LOG_LOCAL6 constant, 431
LOG_LOCAL7 constant, 431
LOG_LPR constant, 431
LOG_MAIL constant, 431
log_msg function, 846–847
  definition of, 850
LOGNAME environment variable, 193, 257, 264
LOG_NDELAY constant, 430, 871
LOG_NEWS constant, 431
LOG_NOTICE constant, 431
log_open function, 624, 846
  definition of, 850
LOG_PERROR constant, 430

LOG_PID constant, 430, 624
log_quit function, 793, 846–847
  definition of, 851
log_ret function, 846–847
  definition of, 850
log_sys function, 766, 782, 846–847
  definition of, 850
LOG_SYSLOG constant, 431
log_to_stderr variable, 624, 776, 849–851
LOG_USER constant, 431, 624
LOG_WARNING constant, 431
LONG_BIT constant, 40
longjmp function, 179, 195, 197–201, 206, 305,
    307, 315, 317–318, 329–331, 333, 340, 354, 867
  definition of, 197
_longjmp function, 330, 333
LONG_MAX constant, 38, 51, 58, 854–855
LONG_MIN constant, 38
loop function, 624, 626, 629, 696, 707
  definition of, 626, 697
lp program, 541, 757
lpc program, 431
lpd program, 431, 757
lpsched program, 541, 757
lrand48 function, 402
ls program, 5–6, 8, 13, 100–101, 104, 114, 116, 121,
    125, 129, 131, 161, 163, 521, 853
lseek function, 8, 57, 59, 63–67, 72–75, 84, 86,
    139, 148, 306, 412, 420, 446, 449, 454, 458, 491,
    548, 629, 732, 856
  definition of, 63
lstat function, 87–88, 90–91, 113–114, 123, 131,
    306
  definition of, 87
L_tmpnam constant, 156
Lucchina, P., xxviii

Mac OS X, xxii, 3, 16, 26–27, 29–30, 35–36, 38, 48,
    54–55, 58, 60, 62, 78–79, 82, 84, 95, 101–103,
    112, 119, 122, 128, 162, 166, 168–169, 171–172,
    176, 191, 193–194, 204, 222, 227, 242–243,
    250–251, 257, 264–265, 268, 278, 290–293,
    295, 298, 304–305, 308, 310, 326, 330, 348, 352,
    357, 360, 445, 457, 474–475, 484, 496–497,
    521, 523, 529, 534, 538, 550, 566–568, 583, 596,
    610, 635–638, 645–651, 676, 683, 692,
    705–706, 710, 876
Mach, xxii–xxiii, 35, 885
<machine/_types.h> header, 854
macro, feature test, 55–56, 81
MAILPATH environment variable, 192

main function, 7, 140, 145, 179–182, 184, 186,
    197–199, 207, 218–219, 231, 260, 306–308,
    332–333, 428, 587, 616, 618, 624, 694, 704, 771,
    774, 777, 780, 787, 793, 796, 863, 865, 867, 880,
    882
major device number, 56–57, 127, 129, 659
major function, 128–129
make program, 275
makethread function, 400
mallinfo function, 191
malloc function, 21–23, 50, 126, 135, 157, 159,
    189–192, 195, 305–306, 308, 364, 371–372,
    374, 376, 391, 398, 407, 409–410, 537, 571, 573,
    578, 608–609, 612–613, 622–623, 626, 656,
    868, 870
    definition of, 189
MALLOC_OPTIONS environment variable, 870
mallopt function, 191
man program, 239–240
mandatory record locking, 455
Mandrake, xxiii
MAP_ANON constant, 540
MAP_ANONYMOUS constant, 540
MAP_FAILED constant, 491, 539
MAP_FIXED constant, 488–489
MAP_PRIVATE constant, 488, 490, 540
MAP_SHARED constant, 488, 490–491, 538–540
<math.h> header, 27
Mauro, J., 70, 105, 108, 889
MAX_CANON constant, 39, 43, 46, 48, 633
MAX_INPUT constant, 39, 43, 48, 632
MAXPATHLEN constant, 49
MB_LEN_MAX constant, 38
mbstate_t structure, 401
McDougall, R., 70, 105, 108, 889
McGrath, G. J., 462, 889
McIlroy, M. D., xxviii
McKusick, M. K., xxviii, 33–34, 70, 104, 108, 211,
    218, 461, 487, 888
M_DATA STREAMS message type, 463–464, 468
MDMBUF constant, 635, 645, 649
memccpy function, 145
memcpy function, 491–492
memory
    allocation, 189–192
    layout, 186–188
    leakage, 191
    shared, 496, 533–540
memory-mapped I/O, 487–492
M_ERROR STREAMS message type, 482
message queues, 496, 522–527
    timing, 527

messages, STREAMS, 462
mgetty program, 265
M_HANGUP STREAMS message type, 482
MIN terminal value, 647, 663–664, 668, 673, 882
minor device number, 56–57, 127, 129, 659
minor function, 128–129
mkdir function, 95, 112–114, 116–117, 119–120,
    306, 860
    definition of, 119
mkdir program, 119
mkfifo function, 112–113, 116–117, 306, 514–515,
    878
    definition of, 514
mkfifo program, 515
mknod function, 112–113, 119, 515
mkstemp function, 155–159, 412
    definition of, 158
mktemp function, 158
mktime function, 174–176
    definition of, 175
mlock function, 203
mmap function, 159, 203, 391, 441, 487–489,
    491–493, 538–540, 543, 548, 887
    definition of, 487
modem, xx, xxiii, 261, 263, 272, 294, 303, 441, 481,
    631, 634–635, 645, 647, 649, 652
mode_t data type, 57
<monetary.h> header, 30
Moran, J. P., 487, 887
more program, 505, 714
MORECTL constant, 470
MOREDATA constant, 470
Morris, R., 165, 889
mount function, 592
mount program, 95, 119, 129, 455
mounted STREAMS-based pipes, 495, 514, 518
M_PCPROTO STREAMS message type, 463–464
mprotect function, 489
    definition of, 489
M_PROTO STREAMS message type, 463–464
mq_receive function, 411
mq_send function, 411
mq_timedreceive function, 411
mq_timedsend function, 411
<mqueue.h> header, 30
mrand48 function, 402
MS_ASYNC constant, 490
MSG_ANY constant, 469
MSG_BAND constant, 464, 469
msgctl function, 520–521, 524
    definition of, 524
MSG_CTRUNC constant, 568

MSG_DONTROUTE constant, 566
MSG_DONTWAIT constant, 566, 568
MSG_EOR constant, 566, 568
msgget function, 518–519, 521–524
    definition of, 524
msghdr structure, 566, 568, 606, 608–609, 611, 613
MSG_HIPRI constant, 464, 469
MSG_NOERROR constant, 526
MSG_OOB constant, 566–568, 581–582
MSG_PEEK constant, 567
msgrcv function, 411, 520–521, 523, 526, 541
    definition of, 526
msgsnd function, 411, 520–523, 525–527
    definition of, 525
MSG_TRUNC constant, 567–568
MSGVERB environment variable, 193
MSG_WAITALL constant, 567
M_SIG STREAMS message type, 463
MS_INVALIDATE constant, 490
msqid_ds structure, 523–524, 526
MS_SYNC constant, 490–491
msync function, 411, 489–491
    definition of, 490
Mui, L., 672, 890
multiplexing, I/O, 472–481
munmap function, 490
    definition of, 490
mv program, 107
myftw function, 123, 131

named full-duplex pipes, 496
NAME_MAX constant, 39, 43, 48, 54, 62, 121
nanosleep function, 348, 398, 400, 411, 421
Nataros, S., xxviii
nawk program, 243
NCCS constant, 634
ndbm library, 709–710
<ndbm.h> header, 30
Nemeth, E., xxviii, 889
<netdb.h> header, 29, 170
netent structure, 554
<net/if.h> header, 29
<netinet/in.h> header, 29, 550–551
<netinet/tcp.h> header, 29
netinfo, 169
Network File System, Sun Microsystems, see NFS
Network Information Service, see NIS
network logins, 266–268
network printer communication, 753–805
Neville-Neil, G. V., 70, 104, 108, 888
newgrp program, 167

nfds_t data type, 479
_NFILE constant, 50
NFS (Network File System, Sun Microsystems), 72, 752
nftw function, 121–122, 402, 412
NGROUPS_MAX constant, 39, 42, 48, 167–168
Nievergelt, J., 710, 715, 886
NIS (Network Information Service), 169
NIS+, 169
NL terminal character, 638, 640–641, 647, 660, 663
NL0 constant, 649
NL1 constant, 649
NL_ARGMAX constant, 41
NLDLY constant, 637, 644, 649
nlink_t data type, 57, 107
nl_langinfo function, 402
NL_LANGMAX constant, 41
NL_MSGMAX constant, 41
NL_NMAX constant, 41
NL_SETMAX constant, 41
NLSPATH environment variable, 193
NL_TEXTMAX constant, 41
<nl_types.h> header, 30
nobody login name, 162–163
NOFILE constant, 50
NOFLSH constant, 636, 649
NOKERNINFO constant, 636, 642, 649
nologin program, 163
nonblocking
    I/O, 441–444
    socket I/O, 563–564, 582–583
noncanonical mode, terminal I/O, 663–670
nonfatal error, 16
nonlocal goto, 195–202, 329–333
ntohl function, 550, 804
    definition of, 550
ntohs function, 550, 560, 804
    definition of, 550
NULL constant, 786
null signal, 290, 312
NZERO constant, 41

O_ACCMODE constant, 79–80
O_APPEND constant, 60, 63, 68, 72, 74, 79–80, 139, 457
O_ASYNC constant, 79, 482, 583
O_CREAT constant, 61, 63, 75, 85, 112, 117, 433, 456–458, 491, 520, 715, 724, 872
OCRNL constant, 637, 649
od program, 66
O_DSYNC constant, 61–62, 79

O_EXCL constant, 61, 75, 112, 520
OFDEL constant, 637, 644, 649
off_t data type, 57, 64–67, 147–148, 738
OFILL constant, 637, 644, 649
O_FSYNC constant, 62, 79–80
Olander, D. J., 462, 889
OLCUC constant, 637, 649
Olson, M., 889
O_NDELAY constant, 36, 61, 442
ONLCR constant, 637, 650, 696, 702
ONLRET constant, 637, 650
ONOCR constant, 637, 650
O_NOCTTY constant, 61, 273, 426, 681–682, 685
ONOEOT constant, 637, 650
O_NONBLOCK constant, 36, 61, 79–80, 442–443,
        456, 458, 515, 565, 876, 878–879
open function, 8, 14, 59–63, 74–75, 79, 85–86,
        94–97, 105, 110, 112–115, 117–118, 127,
        138–139, 260, 263, 273, 306, 411, 428–429, 433,
        442, 452–453, 455–458, 461, 465, 467, 487,
        491, 514–515, 518, 520–522, 539–541, 544,
        547, 594, 615, 618–619, 628–629, 645, 681,
        684–686, 688–689, 691, 711, 723–724, 786,
        855, 857, 872, 878–879
    definition of, 60
Open Software Foundation, *see* OSF
opend.h header, 617, 622, 881
opendir function, 5, 7, 113, 120–125, 234, 260,
        412, 657, 858
    definition of, 120
openlog function, 412, 428, 430, 432, 439, 850, 871
    definition of, 430
OPEN_MAX constant, 39, 42, 48, 50–52, 58, 60, 854
open_max function, 426, 506, 626–627, 844
    definition of, 51, 855
OpenServer, 309, 445
OPOST constant, 637, 650, 666–668, 670
optarg variable, 774
opterr variable, 774
optind variable, 770
option codes, 31
options, 52–55
    socket, 579–581
optopt variable, 774
ordering, byte, 549–550
O_RDONLY constant, 60, 79–80, 94, 96, 465, 467,
        491, 616, 878
O_RDWR constant, 60, 79–80, 94, 118, 428, 433, 458,
        491, 539, 594, 681, 684, 688, 690–691, 715, 872
O'Reilly, T., 672, 890
orientation, stream, 134
orphaned process group, 282–285, 428, 699

O_RSYNC constant, 61–62, 79
OSF (Open Software Foundation), 32
O_SYNC constant, 61–62, 79–80, 82–83
O_TRUNC constant, 61, 63, 94, 105, 117–118, 139,
        456, 458, 491, 715
out-of-band data, 581–582
ownership
    directory, 95
    file, 95
O_WRONLY constant, 60, 79–80, 94, 879
OXTABS constant, 637, 650

packet mode, pseudo terminal, 705
page cache, 77
page size, 535
pagedaemon process, 210
PAGER environment variable, 501, 504–505
PAGESIZE constant, 39, 42, 48, 392
PAGE_SIZE constant, 40, 42, 48
P_ALL constant, 226
PARENB constant, 635, 648, 650, 666–668
parent
    directory, 4, 101, 116, 119
    process ID, 210, 215, 219, 225, 228, 234, 263–264,
        283, 424
PAREXT constant, 635, 650
parity, terminal I/O, 648
PARMRK constant, 635, 645, 648, 650
PARODD constant, 635, 645, 648, 650, 673
Partridge, C., xxviii
passing, file descriptor, 543, 601–614
    socket file descriptor, 606–614
    STREAMS file descriptor, 604–606
passwd program, 92, 166, 679
passwd structure, 161, 164, 307, 861–862
password
    file, 161–165
    implementation differences, 169
    shadow, 165–166, 178, 861
PATH environment variable, 93, 193, 232–233, 235,
        242, 244, 247, 264–265
path_alloc function, 123, 127, 844, 860
    definition of, 49
pathconf function, 37, 39–50, 52–55, 103, 113,
        306, 499
    definition of, 41
PATH_MAX constant, 39, 43, 48–49, 62, 132, 859
pathname, 5
    absolute, 5, 7, 43, 49, 126, 131, 242, 859
    relative, 5, 7, 43, 49, 125
    truncation, 62

pause function, 299–300, 303, 306, 309, 313–318, 331, 333, 340, 349, 411, 419, 671, 867, 873
    definition of, 313
_PC_ASYNC_IO constant, 54
_PC_CHOWN_RESTRICTED constant, 54
_PC_FILESIZEBITS constant, 43
PCFS file system, 48, 55, 105
pckt STREAMS module, 676, 705
_PC_LINK_MAX constant, 43
pclose function, 249, 412, 503–510, 571, 578, 877–878
    definition of, 503, 507
_PC_MAX_CANON constant, 43, 46
_PC_MAX_INPUT constant, 43
_PC_NAME_MAX constant, 43
_PC_NO_TRUNC constant, 54–55
_PC_PATH_MAX constant, 43, 50
_PC_PIPE_BUF constant, 43
_PC_PRIO_IO constant, 54
_PC_SYMLINK_MAX constant, 43
_PC_SYNC_IO constant, 54
_PC_VDISABLE constant, 54, 639
PENDIN constant, 636, 650
Pentium, xxiii
permissions, file access, 92–94, 130
perror function, 15–16, 24, 309, 352, 412, 556, 853
    definition of, 15
pgrp structure, 286–287
PID, see process ID
pid_t data type, 57, 269, 356
Pike, R., 211, 887, 889
pipe function, 116–117, 138, 306, 497, 499–500, 502, 506–507, 511, 513, 527, 588–589, 593, 595, 876
    definition of, 497
PIPE_BUF constant, 39, 43, 48, 493, 499, 515–516, 590, 876
pipes, 496–503
    full-duplex, 496
    half-duplex, 496
    mounted STREAMS-based, 495, 514, 518
    named full-duplex, 496
    STREAMS-based, 585–594
Pippenger, N., 710, 715, 886
Plan 9 operating system, 211, 889
Plauger, P. J., 26, 153, 299, 889
pointer, generic, 68, 190
poll function, 295, 305–306, 318, 411, 441, 460–461, 474, 479–481, 493, 521, 542, 544, 548, 563–564, 582, 621, 624, 626–627, 678, 696, 707, 875, 878, 881
    definition of, 479

POLL_ERR constant, 327
POLLERR constant, 480
pollfd structure, 479, 626–627, 875
<poll.h> header, 30, 479
POLL_HUP constant, 327
POLLHUP constant, 480–481, 627, 878
POLL_IN constant, 327–328
POLLIN constant, 480, 626–627, 878
polling, 228, 444, 473
POLL_MSG constant, 327–328
POLLNVAL constant, 480
POLL_OUT constant, 327–328
POLLOUT constant, 480
POLL_PRI constant, 327
POLLPRI constant, 480
POLLRDBAND constant, 480
POLLRDNORM constant, 480
POLLWRBAND constant, 480
POLLWRNORM constant, 480
popen function, 23, 224, 231, 249, 412, 503–510, 543–544, 570, 574, 577, 579, 877–878
    definition of, 503, 505
Portable Operating System Environment for Computer Environments, IEEE, see POSIX
portmap program, 425
POSIX (Portable Operating System Environment for Computer Environments, IEEE), xix, xxvii, 26–29, 34, 246
POSIX.1, xxii, xxvii, 27, 84, 243, 342, 507–508, 515, 545, 710, 887
POSIX.2, 243
_POSIX2_LINE_MAX constant, 41
_POSIX_ARG_MAX constant, 39
_POSIX_ASYNC_IO constant, 54
_POSIX_CHILD_MAX constant, 39
_POSIX_CHOWN_RESTRICTED constant, 54–55, 103
_POSIX_C_SOURCE constant, 55, 81
posix_fadvise function, 412
posix_fallocate function, 412
_POSIX_HOST_NAME_MAX constant, 39
_POSIX_JOB_CONTROL constant, 53, 55
_POSIX_LINK_MAX constant, 39
_POSIX_LOGIN_NAME_MAX constant, 39
posix_madvise function, 412
_POSIX_MAX_CANON constant, 39
_POSIX_MAX_INPUT constant, 39
_POSIX_NAME_MAX constant, 39
_POSIX_NGROUPS_MAX constant, 39
_POSIX_NO_TRUNC constant, 54–55, 62
_POSIX_OPEN_MAX constant, 39–40
posix_openpt function, 681–683, 686, 688–690

definition of, 681, 686, 689
_POSIX_PATH_MAX constant, 39–40, 656–657
_POSIX_PIPE_BUF constant, 39
_POSIX_PRIO_IO constant, 54
_POSIX_READER_WRITER_LOCKS constant, 53
_POSIX_RE_DUP_MAX constant, 39
_POSIX_SAVED_IDS constant, 53, 55, 92, 238, 312
_POSIX_SHELL constant, 53
_POSIX_SOURCE constant, 55
posix_spawn function, 412
posix_spawnp function, 412
_POSIX_SSIZE_MAX constant, 39
_POSIX_STREAM_MAX constant, 39
_POSIX_SYMLINK_MAX constant, 39
_POSIX_SYMLOOP_MAX constant, 39
_POSIX_SYNC_IO constant, 54
_POSIX_THREAD_ATTR_STACKADDR constant, 391
_POSIX_THREAD_ATTR_STACKSIZE constant, 391
_POSIX_THREAD_PROCESS_SHARED constant, 394
_POSIX_THREADS constant, 54–55, 356
_POSIX_THREAD_SAFE_FUNCTIONS constant, 401
posix_trace_clear function, 412
posix_trace_close function, 412
posix_trace_create function, 412
posix_trace_create_withlog function, 412
posix_trace_event function, 306
posix_trace_eventtypelist_getnext_id function, 412
posix_trace_eventtypelist_rewind function, 412
posix_trace_flush function, 412
posix_trace_get_attr function, 412
posix_trace_get_filter function, 412
posix_trace_getnext_event function, 412
posix_trace_get_status function, 412
posix_trace_open function, 412
posix_trace_rewind function, 412
posix_trace_set_filter function, 412
posix_trace_shutdown function, 412
posix_trace_timedgetnext_event function, 412
_POSIX_TTY_NAME_MAX constant, 39
posix_typed_mem_open function, 412
_POSIX_TZNAME_MAX constant, 39
_POSIX_V6_ILP32_OFF32 constant, 67
_POSIX_V6_ILP32_OFFBIG constant, 67
_POSIX_V6_LP64_OFF64 constant, 67
_POSIX_V6_LP64_OFFBIG constant, 67

_POSIX_VDISABLE constant, 54–55, 638–639
_POSIX_VERSION constant, 53, 55, 172
PowerPC, xxiii
P_PGID constant, 226
PPID, *see* parent process ID
P_PID constant, 226
pr program, 719
pread function, 74–75, 411, 420
    definition of, 75
Presotto, D. L., xxviii, 211, 585, 592, 889
pr_exit function, 221–223, 248–249, 258, 346, 844
    definition of, 222
primitive system data types, 56
print program, 757, 763, 783, 787–788, 798, 805
printd program, 757, 805
printer communication, network, 753–805
printer spooling, 757–758
    source code, 758–805
printer_status function, 799, 801, 805
printer_thread function, 795
printf function, 10, 21, 41, 140, 149, 151–152, 160, 175–176, 201, 204, 207, 213, 217, 260, 283, 306, 323, 412, 514, 863
    definition of, 149
print.h header, 778, 783, 788
printreq structure, 763, 771, 783, 786, 790
printresp structure, 763
privilege, least, 237, 758, 779
pr_mask function, 331, 334–335, 844
    definition of, 321
proc structure, 286–287
process, 10
    accounting, 250–256
    control, 11, 209–260
    ID, 10, 210, 234
    ID, parent, 210, 215, 219, 225, 228, 234, 263–264, 283, 424
    identifiers, 209–210
    relationships, 261–287
    system, 210, 312
    termination, 180–184
    time, 20, 24, 57, 257–259
process group, 269–270
    background, 272, 275, 277, 279, 281–282, 284–285, 296–297, 344, 349, 882
    foreground, 272–278, 280–281, 286, 294, 296–297, 343, 350, 424–425, 463, 640–642, 645, 649, 670, 706, 882
    ID, 215, 234
    ID, foreground, 274, 278, 637
    ID, session, 279

ID, terminal, 278, 423–424
leader, 269–271, 280, 287, 425, 692
lifetime, 269
orphaned, 282–285, 428, 699
processes, cooperating, 455, 717, 883
process-shared attribute, 394
.profile file, 265
program, 10
PROT_EXEC constant, 487
PROT_NONE constant, 487
protoent structure, 554
prototypes, function, 807–841
PROT_READ constant, 487, 491, 539
PROT_WRITE constant, 487, 491, 539
PR_TEXT constant, 771, 788, 798
ps program, 219, 260, 278, 280–282, 423–424, 428, 701, 866
pselect function, 306, 474, 478–479
definition of, 478
pseudo terminal, 675–707
packet mode, 705
remote mode, 706
signal generation, 706
window size, 706
psignal function, 352
definition of, 352
ptem STREAMS module, 468, 676, 685
pthread structure, 357
pthread_atfork function, 417–419
definition of, 417
pthread_attr_destroy function, 389–390
definition of, 389
pthread_attr_getdetachstate function, 390
definition of, 390
pthread_attr_getguardsize function, 392
definition of, 392
pthread_attr_getstack function, 391–392
definition of, 391
pthread_attr_getstackaddr function, 391
pthread_attr_getstacksize function, 392
definition of, 392
pthread_attr_init function, 388–390
definition of, 389
pthread_attr_setdetachstate function, 389–390
definition of, 390
pthread_attr_setguardsize function, 392
definition of, 392
pthread_attr_setstack function, 391–392
definition of, 391
pthread_attr_setstackaddr function, 391
pthread_attr_setstacksize function, 392

definition of, 392
pthread_attr_t data type, 388–390, 392, 410
pthread_cancel function, 365, 410–411, 791
definition of, 365
PTHREAD_CANCEL_ASYNCHRONOUS constant, 412
PTHREAD_CANCEL_DEFERRED constant, 412
PTHREAD_CANCEL_DISABLE constant, 410–411
PTHREAD_CANCELED constant, 361, 365
PTHREAD_CANCEL_ENABLE constant, 410–411
pthread_cleanup_pop function, 365–366, 790, 792
definition of, 365
pthread_cleanup_push function, 365–366
definition of, 365
pthread_condattr_destroy function, 401
definition of, 401
pthread_condattr_getpshared function, 401
definition of, 401
pthread_condattr_init function, 401
definition of, 401
pthread_condattr_setpshared function, 401
definition of, 401
pthread_cond_broadcast function, 384, 386, 869–870
definition of, 384
pthread_cond_destroy function, 382–383, 421
definition of, 383
pthread_cond_init function, 382–383, 421
definition of, 383
PTHREAD_COND_INITIALIZER constant, 382, 385, 414
pthread_cond_signal function, 384–385, 415–416
definition of, 384
pthread_cond_t data type, 382, 385, 414
pthread_cond_timedwait function, 383–384, 395, 411
definition of, 383
pthread_cond_wait function, 383–385, 395, 411, 415, 795, 869–870
definition of, 383
pthread_create function, 357–360, 362–364, 366, 368, 388–390, 415, 419, 436, 780, 869
definition of, 357
PTHREAD_CREATE_DETACHED constant, 389–390
PTHREAD_CREATE_JOINABLE constant, 389–390
PTHREAD_DESTRUCTOR_ITERATIONS constant, 388, 407
pthread_detach function, 367–368, 389
definition of, 368
pthread_equal function, 357, 382
definition of, 357

`pthread_exit` function, 180, 218, 361–363, 365–366, 406, 787–789, 792
    definition of, 361
`pthread_getconcurrency` function, 393
    definition of, 393
`pthread_getspecific` function, 408–410
    definition of, 408
`<pthread.h>` header, 30
`pthread_join` function, 361–363, 366–367, 411, 869
    definition of, 361
`pthread_key_create` function, 406–407, 409
    definition of, 406
`pthread_key_delete` function, 407
    definition of, 407
`PTHREAD_KEYS_MAX` constant, 388, 407
`pthread_key_t` data type, 409
`pthread_kill` function, 414
    definition of, 414
`pthread_mutexattr_destroy` function, 393, 404
    definition of, 393
`pthread_mutexattr_getpshared` function, 394
    definition of, 394
`pthread_mutexattr_gettype` function, 395
    definition of, 395
`pthread_mutexattr_init` function, 393–394, 399, 404
    definition of, 393
`pthread_mutexattr_setpshared` function, 394
    definition of, 394
`pthread_mutexattr_settype` function, 395, 399, 404
    definition of, 395
`pthread_mutexattr_t` data type, 393–394, 399, 404
`PTHREAD_MUTEX_DEFAULT` constant, 395
`pthread_mutex_destroy` function, 371–372, 375, 378
    definition of, 371
`PTHREAD_MUTEX_ERRORCHECK` constant, 394–395
`pthread_mutex_init` function, 371–372, 374, 376, 399, 404
    definition of, 371
`PTHREAD_MUTEX_INITIALIZER` constant, 371, 374, 376, 385, 409, 414, 418
`pthread_mutex_lock` function, 371–372, 374–375, 377, 385–386, 399, 405, 409, 415, 418–419

    definition of, 371
`PTHREAD_MUTEX_NORMAL` constant, 394–395
`PTHREAD_MUTEX_RECURSIVE` constant, 394–395, 399, 404
`pthread_mutex_t` data type, 371–372, 374, 376, 385, 399, 404, 409, 414, 418
`pthread_mutex_trylock` function, 371, 373
    definition of, 371
`pthread_mutex_unlock` function, 371–372, 374–375, 377–378, 385–386, 399, 405, 409–410, 415, 419
    definition of, 371
`pthread_once` function, 404–405, 408, 410
    definition of, 408
`PTHREAD_ONCE_INIT` constant, 404, 408–409
`pthread_once_init` function, 409
`pthread_once_t` data type, 404, 409
`PTHREAD_PROCESS_PRIVATE` constant, 394
`PTHREAD_PROCESS_SHARED` constant, 394
`pthread_rwlockattr_destroy` function, 400
    definition of, 400
`pthread_rwlockattr_getpshared` function, 400
    definition of, 400
`pthread_rwlockattr_init` function, 400
    definition of, 400
`pthread_rwlockattr_setpshared` function, 400
    definition of, 400
`pthread_rwlockattr_t` data type, 400
`pthread_rwlock_destroy` function, 379
    definition of, 379
`pthread_rwlock_init` function, 379–380
    definition of, 379
`pthread_rwlock_rdlock` function, 379, 382, 412
    definition of, 379
`pthread_rwlock_t` data type, 380
`pthread_rwlock_timedrdlock` function, 412
`pthread_rwlock_timedwrlock` function, 412
`pthread_rwlock_tryrdlock` function, 379
    definition of, 379
`pthread_rwlock_trywrlock` function, 379
    definition of, 379
`pthread_rwlock_unlock` function, 379, 381–382
    definition of, 379
`pthread_rwlock_wrlock` function, 379–381, 412
    definition of, 379
pthreads, 27, 211
`pthread_self` function, 357, 359, 363

definition of, 357
pthread_setcancelstate function, 410
  definition of, 410
pthread_setcanceltype function, 411–412
  definition of, 411
pthread_setconcurrency function, 393
  definition of, 393
pthread_setspecific function, 408–409
  definition of, 408
pthread_sigmask function, 413, 436
  definition of, 413
PTHREAD_STACK_MIN constant, 388
pthread_t data type, 356–357, 359, 362–363,
    366, 380, 390, 415, 419, 436, 869
pthread_testcancel function, 411
  definition of, 411
PTHREAD_THREADS_MAX constant, 388
P_tmpdir constant, 157–158
ptrdiff_t data type, 57
pts STREAMS module, 468
ptsname function, 402, 682–685, 687–688, 690
  definition of, 682, 687, 689
pty program, 285, 675, 679–680, 692, 694–707,
    773, 882–883
pty_fork function, 680, 683, 691–696, 704,
    706–707
  definition of, 691–692
ptym_open function, 683, 686, 691–692, 845
  definition of, 683, 688, 690
ptys_fork function, 845
ptys_open function, 683, 685–686, 689, 691–693,
    845
  definition of, 683–684, 688, 691
putc function, 10, 142–143, 145, 229–230, 412, 661
  definition of, 142
putchar function, 142, 160, 412, 509
  definition of, 142
putchar_unlocked function, 402–403, 412
  definition of, 403
putc_unlocked function, 402–403, 412
  definition of, 403
putenv function, 186, 194, 232, 402, 405, 421
  definition of, 194
putenv_r function, 421
putmsg function, 411, 461–463, 469, 548
  definition of, 463
putpmsg function, 411, 461–463, 548
  definition of, 463
puts function, 142–143, 412, 859
  definition of, 143
pututxline function, 402, 412
putwc function, 412

putwchar function, 412
PWD environment variable, 193
<pwd.h> header, 29, 161, 170
pwrite function, 74–75, 411, 420
  definition of, 75

Quarterman, J. S., 33–34, 70, 104, 108, 211, 218, 461,
    487, 888
QUIT terminal character, 638, 641, 648, 662

race conditions, 227–231, 314, 749, 865, 867
Rago, J. E., xxiii
Rago, S. A., xxviii, 83, 147, 266, 460, 462, 889
raise function, 306, 311–313, 340
  definition of, 312
rand function, 402
rand_r function, 402
raw terminal mode, 632, 664, 668, 673, 696, 699
Raymond, E. S., 889
read function, 8–10, 20, 57, 59, 61, 67–69, 75,
    84–86, 104, 115, 117, 120, 135, 144–145, 159,
    284, 304, 306, 316–318, 340, 351, 411, 420, 429,
    442–443, 455–456, 458–459, 461–463,
    469–473, 475, 478, 481, 485–487, 492,
    498–499, 502–503, 511–513, 515, 518, 543,
    546, 548, 565–567, 587, 616, 618, 625–627,
    629, 632, 662–664, 668–669, 697, 702–703,
    705, 714, 718, 768, 799–800, 855–856,
    877–878, 882
  definition of, 67
read mode, STREAMS, 470
read, scatter, 483, 607
readdir function, 5, 7, 120–125, 402, 412, 657, 786
  definition of, 120
readdir_r function, 402, 412
reading directories, 120–125
readlink function, 113, 115, 306
  definition of, 115
read_lock function, 449, 453, 458, 845
readmore function, 800, 802
readn function, 485–486, 702, 768, 844
  definition of, 485–486
readv function, 40–42, 304, 411, 441, 483–485,
    493, 548, 568, 607, 718, 732
  definition of, 483
readw_lock function, 449, 725, 845
real
  group ID, 91–92, 95, 167, 210, 214, 234–235, 237,
    251, 541

user ID, 39, 42, 91–92, 95, 203, 210, 214–215, 234–235, 237–241, 251, 257, 262, 264, 312, 354, 541, 685, 867
realloc function, 49, 159, 189–190, 195, 622–623, 727, 802, 859–860
   definition of, 189
record locking, 444–459
   advisory, 455
   deadlock, 450
   mandatory, 455
   timing, semaphore locking versus, 533
recv function, 306, 411, 548, 566–570, 582
   definition of, 567
recv_fd function, 603–605, 612, 617, 621, 845
   definition of, 603, 605, 609
recvfrom function, 306, 411, 567–568, 575–577, 579
   definition of, 567
recvmsg function, 306, 411, 568, 606, 609–610, 613
   definition of, 568
recv_ufd function, 612
   definition of, 613
redirmod STREAMS module, 468
RE_DUP_MAX constant, 39, 42, 48
reentrant functions, 305–308
regcomp function, 39, 42
regexec function, 39, 42
<regex.h> header, 29
register variables, 199
regular file, 88
relative pathname, 5, 7, 43, 49, 125
reliable signals, 310–311
remote mode, pseudo terminal, 706
remove function, 108–113, 117, 412
   definition of, 111
remove_job function, 785, 795
rename function, 108–113, 117, 306, 412
   definition of, 111
replace_job function, 784
REPRINT terminal character, 638, 641, 647, 650, 663
request function, 618, 625–628
   definition of, 618, 628
reset program, 673, 882
resource limits, 202–206, 215, 234, 297, 354
restarted system calls, 304–305, 317–318, 326, 329, 481, 660
restrict keyword, 26, 87, 115, 136, 138, 142–143, 146, 148–149, 151, 153, 173, 176, 320, 324, 357, 371, 379, 383, 390–392, 394–395, 400–401, 413, 469, 475, 478, 552, 555–556, 561, 563, 567, 579

rewind function, 139, 147–148, 156, 412
   definition of, 147
rewinddir function, 120–125, 412
   definition of, 120
rfork function, 211
Ritchie, D. M., xx, 26, 133, 139, 145, 151, 153, 190, 460, 585, 592, 846, 854, 887, 889
RLIM_INFINITY constant, 203, 427
rlimit structure, 202, 205, 426, 855
RLIMIT_AS constant, 203–205
RLIMIT_CORE constant, 203–205, 293
RLIMIT_CPU constant, 203–205
RLIMIT_DATA constant, 203–205
RLIMIT_FSIZE constant, 203–205, 354
RLIMIT_INFINITY constant, 205, 855
RLIMIT_LOCKS constant, 203–205
RLIMIT_MEMLOCK constant, 203–205
RLIMIT_NOFILE constant, 203–205, 427, 855
RLIMIT_NPROC constant, 203–205
RLIMIT_RSS constant, 203–205
RLIMIT_SBSIZE constant, 203–205
RLIMIT_STACK constant, 203–205
RLIMIT_VMEM constant, 203–205
rlim_t data type, 57, 204
rlogin program, 677, 705–706
rlogind program, 677–678, 699, 705, 882
rm program, 521, 774
rmdir function, 111–112, 116–117, 119–120, 306
   definition of, 120
RMSGD constant, 470
RMSGN constant, 470
RNORM constant, 470
R_OK constant, 96
root
   directory, 4, 7, 24, 129, 131, 215, 234, 260, 858
   login name, 16
routed program, 431
RPROTDAT constant, 470
RPROTDIS constant, 470
RPROTNORM constant, 470
RS-232, 634, 645–646
RS_HIPRI constant, 464, 469
Rudoff, A. M., 147, 266, 429, 545, 890
runacct program, 250

S5 file system, 62
sa program, 250
sac program, 266
Sacksen, J., xxviii
SAF (Service Access Facility), 266
SA_INTERRUPT constant, 326, 328–329

Salus, P. H., xxviii, 889
SA_NOCLDSTOP constant, 326
SA_NOCLDWAIT constant, 308, 326
SA_NODEFER constant, 326, 328
Santa Cruz Operation, *see* SCO
SA_ONSTACK constant, 326
SA_RESETHAND constant, 326, 328
SA_RESTART constant, 304, 326, 328–329, 481
SA_SIGINFO constant, 311, 325–326, 328
saved
    set-group-ID, 53, 91–92
    set-user-ID, 53, 91–92, 238–241, 260, 264, 312,
      866
S_BANDURG constant, 482
sbrk function, 21–23, 190, 203
scan_configfile function, 765–766
scanf function, 41, 140, 151–153, 412
    definition of, 151
_SC_ARG_MAX constant, 42, 46
_SC_ATEXIT_MAX constant, 42
scatter read, 483, 607
_SC_CHILD_MAX constant, 42, 203
_SC_CLK_TCK constant, 42, 257–258
_SC_COLL_WEIGHTS_MAX constant, 42
SCHAR_MAX constant, 38
SCHAR_MIN constant, 38
<sched.h> header, 30
_SC_HOST_NAME_MAX constant, 42, 571–573, 578,
    778
Schwartz, A., 165, 232, 273, 887
_SC_IOV_MAX constant, 42
_SC_JOB_CONTROL constant, 53–54
_SC_LINE_MAX constant, 42
_SC_LOGIN_NAME_MAX constant, 42
SCM_CREDENTIALS constant, 611–614
SCM_CREDS constant, 611, 613–614
SCM_CREDTYPE constant, 612, 614
SCM_RIGHTS constant, 607–608, 612, 614
_SC_NGROUPS_MAX constant, 42
SCO (Santa Cruz Operation), 36
_SC_OPEN_MAX constant, 42, 51, 203, 855
_SC_PAGESIZE constant, 42, 489
_SC_PAGE_SIZE constant, 42, 489
_SC_READER_WRITER_LOCKS constant, 53
_SC_RE_DUP_MAX constant, 42
script program, 675, 678–679, 699, 701, 706–707
_SC_SAVED_IDS constant, 53–54, 92, 238
_SC_SHELL constant, 53
_SC_STREAM_MAX constant, 42
_SC_SYMLOOP_MAX constant, 42
_SC_THREAD_ATTR_STACKADDR constant, 391
_SC_THREAD_ATTR_STACKSIZE constant, 391

_SC_THREAD_DESTRUCTOR_ITERATIONS
    constant, 388
_SC_THREAD_KEYS_MAX constant, 388
_SC_THREAD_PROCESS_SHARED constant, 394
_SC_THREADS constant, 356
_SC_THREAD_SAFE_FUNCTIONS constant, 401
_SC_THREAD_STACK_MIN constant, 388
_SC_THREAD_THREADS_MAX constant, 388
_SC_TTY_NAME_MAX constant, 42
_SC_TZNAME_MAX constant, 42
_SC_V6_ILP32_OFF32 constant, 67
_SC_V6_ILP32_OFFBIG constant, 67
_SC_V6_LP64_OFF64 constant, 67
_SC_V6_LP64_OFFBIG constant, 67
_SC_VERSION constant, 49, 53
_SC_XOPEN_CRYPT constant, 53
_SC_XOPEN_LEGACY constant, 53
_SC_XOPEN_REALTIME constant, 53
_SC_XOPEN_REALTIME_THREADS constant, 53
_SC_XOPEN_VERSION constant, 53–54
<search.h> header, 30
sed program, 887
Seebass, S., 889
seek function, 64
SEEK_CUR constant, 64, 148, 446, 454–455
seekdir function, 120–125, 412
    definition of, 120
SEEK_END constant, 64, 148, 446, 454–455, 747
SEEK_SET constant, 64, 148, 446, 454–455, 458,
    491, 873–874
SEGV_ACCERR constant, 327
SEGV_MAPERR constant, 327
select function, 305–306, 318, 339–340, 411, 441,
    474–481, 493, 521, 542, 544, 548, 563–564,
    582, 621, 624–626, 628, 678, 696, 707,
    767–768, 779–780, 870–871, 875, 878,
    880–881
    definition of, 475
Seltzer, M., 710, 889–890
semaphore, 496, 527–533
    adjustment on exit, 532–533
    locking versus record locking timing, 533
<semaphore.h> header, 30
sembuf structure, 531
semctl function, 520, 524, 528–529, 532
    definition of, 529
semget function, 518–519, 528–529
    definition of, 529
semid_ds structure, 528–530
semop function, 412, 521, 529–533
    definition of, 530
sem_post function, 306

`sem_timedwait` function, 411
`semun` union, 529
`SEM_UNDO` constant, 531–533
`sem_wait` function, 411
`send` function, 306, 411, 548, 565–566, 570, 581–582
    definition of, 565
`send_err` function, 603, 615, 618–619, 628, 845
    definition of, 603–604
`send_fd` function, 603–604, 608, 611, 615, 618–619, 628, 845
    definition of, 603–604, 608, 611
`sendmsg` function, 306, 411, 566, 568, 606, 608–609, 612
    definition of, 566
`sendto` function, 306, 411, 566, 575, 577, 579
    definition of, 566
`S_ERROR` constant, 482
`serv_accept` function, 592–593, 598, 601, 621, 625–627, 845
    definition of, 592–593, 599
`servent` structure, 555
Service Access Facility, *see* SAF
`serv_listen` function, 592–593, 597, 621, 625–626, 845
    definition of, 592, 597
session, 270–271
    ID, 215, 234, 271, 286, 423–424
    leader, 271–273, 286, 294, 424–425, 428, 685, 691–692, 707, 882
    process group ID, 279
`session` structure, 286, 294, 424
set
    descriptor, 475, 477, 493, 875
    signal, 311, 318–320, 493, 875
`SETALL` constant, 530, 532
`setasync` function, definition of, 881
`setbuf` function, 136–137, 139, 159, 229–230, 661, 872
    definition of, 136
`setegid` function, 241
    definition of, 241
`setenv` function, 194, 232, 402
    definition of, 194
`seteuid` function, 241
    definition of, 241
`set_fl` function, 82, 442–443, 458, 844, 876
    definition of, 81
`setgid` function, 237, 241, 264, 306
    definition of, 237
`setgrent` function, 167–168, 402, 412
    definition of, 167

set-group-ID, 91–92, 95, 100–101, 103, 119, 130, 215, 235, 292, 456, 508, 685
    saved, 53, 91–92
`setgroups` function, 168
    definition of, 168
`sethostent` function, 412, 553
    definition of, 553
`sethostname` function, 173
`setitimer` function, 293, 295, 297, 354, 875
`setjmp` function, 179, 195, 197–201, 206, 314–315, 318, 329–330, 333, 354, 867
    definition of, 197
`_setjmp` function, 330, 333
`<setjmp.h>` header, 27
`setkey` function, 402
`setlogmask` function, 430–431
    definition of, 430
`setnetent` function, 412, 554
    definition of, 554
`setpgid` function, 269, 306
    definition of, 269
`setprotoent` function, 412, 554
    definition of, 554
`setpwent` function, 164–165, 402, 412
    definition of, 164
`setregid` function, 240–241
    definition of, 240
`setreuid` function, 240
    definition of, 240
`setrlimit` function, 52, 202, 354
    definition of, 202
`setservent` function, 412, 555
    definition of, 555
`setsid` function, 269, 271, 273, 286, 306, 424–425, 427, 683, 692–693
    definition of, 271
`setsockopt` function, 306, 579, 581, 613
    definition of, 579
`setspent` function, 166
    definition of, 166
`settimeofday` function, 173
`setuid` function, 92, 237–241, 264, 306, 779
    definition of, 237
set-user-ID, 91–92, 95, 97, 100–101, 103, 119, 130, 166, 215, 235, 238–240, 249, 292, 508, 541–542, 615, 685, 689, 707, 867
    saved, 53, 91–92, 238–241, 260, 264, 312, 866
`setutxent` function, 402, 412
`SETVAL` constant, 530, 532
`setvbuf` function, 136–137, 139, 159, 202, 514, 877
    definition of, 136
SGI (Silicon Graphics, Inc.), 36

SGID, *see* set-group-ID
shadow passwords, 165–166, 178, 861
<shadow.h> header, 170
S_HANGUP constant, 482
Shannon, W. A., 487, 887
shared
    libraries, 188–189, 207, 719, 863, 885
    memory, 496, 533–540
sharing, file, 70–73, 213
shell, *see* Bourne shell, Bourne-again shell, C shell,
    Korn shell
SHELL environment variable, 193, 264, 701
shell, job-control, 270, 274, 280, 283, 300, 333, 350,
    699
shell layers, 274
shells, 3
S_HIPRI constant, 482
shmat function, 521, 535–538
    definition of, 536
shmatt_t data type, 534
shmctl function, 520, 524, 535–537
    definition of, 535
shmdt function, 536
    definition of, 536
shmget function, 518–519, 534, 537
    definition of, 534
shmid_ds structure, 534–536
SHMLBA constant, 536
SHM_LOCK constant, 535
SHM_RDONLY constant, 536
SHM_RND constant, 536
SHRT_MAX constant, 38
SHRT_MIN constant, 38
shutdown function, 306, 548–549, 567
    definition of, 548
SHUT_RD constant, 548
SHUT_RDWR constant, 548
SHUT_WR constant, 548
SI_ASYNCIO constant, 327
S_IFBLK constant, 124
S_IFCHR constant, 124
S_IFDIR constant, 124
S_IFIFO constant, 124
S_IFLNK constant, 107, 124
S_IFMT constant, 91
S_IFREG constant, 124
S_IFSOCK constant, 124, 596
sig2str function, 353
    definition of, 353
SIG2STR_MAX constant, 353
SIGABRT signal, 218, 222–223, 256, 289, 292–295,
    340–342, 354, 867

sigaction function, 57, 298, 301, 304–306, 308,
    310–311, 324–329, 341, 344–345, 349, 414,
    427, 436, 438, 482, 576, 880
    definition of, 324
sigaction structure, 324, 328–329, 341, 344, 348,
    426, 436, 438, 576
sigaddset function, 306, 319, 322, 334, 336, 338,
    344, 349, 351, 415, 438, 661, 875
    definition of, 319–320
SIGALRM signal, 289–290, 292–293, 305, 307,
    313–315, 317–318, 322, 328–329, 331–332,
    339, 348–349, 576
sigaltstack function, 326
sig_atomic_t data type, 57, 330, 332, 336–337,
    697
SIG_BLOCK constant, 321, 323, 334, 336, 338, 345,
    349, 415, 436, 661
SIGBUS signal, 292–293, 327, 489, 491
SIGCANCEL signal, 292–293
SIGCHLD signal, 220, 264, 291–293, 307–308, 310,
    326–327, 342–345, 349–350, 430, 473, 507,
    682, 866, 880
    semantics, 308–310
SIGCLD signal, 293, 308–311
SIGCONT signal, 276, 283, 292–293, 312, 349–350,
    352
sigdelset function, 306, 319, 341, 349, 875
    definition of, 319–320
SIG_DFL constant, 299, 308, 325–326, 340–341,
    350–351, 436
sigemptyset function, 306, 319, 322, 328–329,
    334, 336–337, 344, 349, 351, 415, 427, 436, 438,
    576, 661, 875
    definition of, 319
SIGEMT signal, 292–293
SIG_ERR constant, 19, 300, 309, 315–318, 322–323,
    328–331, 334, 336–337, 343, 511, 587, 669, 671,
    697, 844
sigfillset function, 306, 319, 341, 436, 875
    definition of, 319
SIGFPE signal, 18, 222–223, 292, 294, 327
SIGFREEZE signal, 292, 294
Sigfunc data type, 328–329, 844
SIGHUP signal, 283–284, 292, 294, 427, 434–439,
    508, 778, 793
SIG_IGN constant, 299, 308, 325, 341, 344, 350,
    427, 844
SIGILL signal, 292, 294, 326–327, 340
SIGINFO signal, 292, 294, 642, 649
siginfo structure, 226, 326, 328, 354
<siginfo.h> header, 352
siginfo_t structure, 325

SIGINT signal, 18–19, 275, 290, 292, 294, 296,
    315–316, 322, 333–336, 339, 342–345, 347,
    415–416, 508, 639, 641, 645, 648–649,
    661–662, 669, 872, 874
SIGIO signal, 79, 292, 294–295, 473, 481–482, 583
SIGIOT signal, 292, 295, 340
sigismember function, 306, 319, 322–323, 875
    definition of, 319–320
sigjmp_buf data type, 330
SIGKILL signal, 253, 256, 291–292, 295, 299, 321,
    353, 699
siglongjmp function, 201, 307, 329–333, 340
    definition of, 330
SIGLWP signal, 292, 295
signal function, 18–19, 57, 284, 298–302,
    304–310, 314–318, 322–324, 328–331, 334,
    336–337, 343, 351, 482, 511, 587, 669, 671, 880
    definition of, 298, 328
signal mask, 311
signal set, 311, 318–320, 493, 875
<signal.h> header, 27, 222, 290, 299, 319–320,
    353
signal_intr function, 305, 329, 339, 354, 481,
    697, 844, 872
    definition of, 329
signals, 18–19, 289–354
    blocking, 310
    delivery, 310
    generation, 310
    generation, pseudo terminal, 706
    job-control, 349–352
    null, 290, 312
    pending, 310
    queueing, 311, 324
    reliable, 310–311
    unreliable, 301–303
signal_thread function, 793
sigpause function, 306, 411
sigpending function, 306, 311, 322–324
    definition of, 322
SIGPIPE signal, 290, 292, 295, 469, 499, 511–512,
    515, 518, 543, 587–588, 778, 878
SIGPOLL signal, 292, 295, 327, 473, 481–482
sigprocmask function, 306, 311, 314, 318,
    320–323, 334–336, 338, 341, 345, 349, 351,
    413, 415, 661
    definition of, 320
SIGPROF signal, 292, 295
SIGPWR signal, 292, 294–295
sigqueue function, 306, 327–328
SIGQUIT signal, 275, 292, 296, 322–323, 336, 342,
    344–345, 347, 415–416, 508, 641, 649, 662, 669

SIGSEGV signal, 290, 292, 296, 307–308, 311, 327,
    489
sigset function, 304–306, 308
sigsetjmp function, 201, 307, 329–333
    definition of, 330
SIG_SETMASK constant, 321, 323, 335–336, 338,
    341, 345, 349, 415, 661
sigset_t data type, 57, 311, 319, 321–322, 334,
    336–337, 341, 344, 348, 351, 414–415, 661
SIGSTKFLT signal, 292, 296
SIGSTOP signal, 291–292, 296, 299, 321, 349–350
SIGSUSP signal, 649
sigsuspend function, 306, 314, 333–340, 349, 411
    definition of, 334
SIGSYS signal, 292, 296
SIGTERM signal, 291–292, 296, 300, 435, 437–439,
    669, 697–698, 707, 778, 793, 882
SIGTHAW signal, 292, 296
sigtimedwait function, 411
SIGTRAP signal, 292, 296, 326–327
SIGTSTP signal, 275, 283–284, 292, 296, 349–352,
    640, 642, 661, 699
SIGTTIN signal, 275–276, 279, 284, 292, 296–297,
    349–350
SIGTTOU signal, 276–277, 292, 297, 349–350, 651
SIG_UNBLOCK constant, 321, 323, 351
SIGURG signal, 79, 290, 292, 295, 297, 482, 581
SIGUSR1 signal, 292, 297, 300, 322, 330, 332–335,
    337–339, 473
SIGUSR2 signal, 292, 297, 300, 337–339
sigvec function, 304–305
SIGVTALRM signal, 292, 297
sigwait function, 411, 413–416, 435, 437, 793
    definition of, 413
sigwaitinfo function, 411
SIGWAITING signal, 292, 297
SIGWINCH signal, 286, 292, 297, 670–671, 706–707
SIGXCPU signal, 203, 292, 297–298
SIGXFSZ signal, 203, 292, 298, 354, 868
SIGXRES signal, 292, 298
Silicon Graphics, Inc., *see* SGI
SI_MESGQ constant, 327
Single UNIX Specification, *see* SUS
    Version 3, *see* SUSv3
single-instance daemons, 432–434
S_INPUT constant, 482
SIOCSPGRP constant, 583
SI_QUEUE constant, 327
S_IRGRP constant, 93, 97, 100, 130, 433, 592, 844
S_IROTH constant, 93, 97, 100, 130, 433, 592, 844
S_IRUSR constant, 93, 97, 100, 130, 433, 592, 687,
    690, 844

S_IRWXG constant, 100, 599
S_IRWXO constant, 100, 599
S_IRWXU constant, 100, 599
S_ISBLK function, 89–90, 129
S_ISCHR function, 89–90, 129, 658
S_ISDIR function, 89–91, 123, 658
S_ISFIFO function, 89–90, 497, 514
S_ISGID constant, 92, 100, 130, 458
S_ISLNK function, 89–90
S_ISREG function, 89–90
S_ISSOCK function, 89–91, 599
S_ISUID constant, 92, 100, 130
S_ISVTX constant, 100–102, 130
SI_TIMER constant, 327
SI_USER constant, 327
S_IWGRP constant, 93, 97, 100, 130, 592, 687, 690
S_IWOTH constant, 93, 97, 100, 130, 592
S_IWUSR constant, 93, 97, 100, 130, 433, 592, 687, 690, 844
S_IXGRP constant, 93, 100, 130, 458, 844
S_IXOTH constant, 93, 100, 130, 844
S_IXUSR constant, 93, 100, 130, 844
size, file, 103–105
size program, 188–189, 207
sizeof operator, 213
size_t data type, 57–58, 68, 479, 854
sleep function, 212, 216, 225, 228, 253, 255, 284, 306, 309, 314–316, 323, 346–349, 353–354, 359, 363–364, 400, 411, 419, 477, 493, 562, 866–868, 870, 873, 878
    definition of, 347–348, 871
sleep_us function, 493, 844
    definition of, 875
S_MSG constant, 482
SNDPIPE constant, 469
SNDZERO constant, 469
snprintf function, 149, 689, 849, 851
    definition of, 149
Snyder, G., 889
sockaddr structure, 551–553, 561–562, 564, 577–578, 580, 596, 598–601
sockaddr_in structure, 551–552, 559
sockaddr_in6 structure, 551–552
sockaddr_un structure, 595–601
sockatmark function, 306, 582
    definition of, 582
SOCK_DGRAM constant, 547, 558, 563, 567, 576, 578
socket
    addressing, 549–561
    descriptors, 546–549
    file descriptor passing, 606–614
    I/O, asynchronous, 582–583

I/O, nonblocking, 563–564, 582–583
    mechanism, 89, 496, 545–584
    options, 579–581
socket function, 138, 306, 546–547, 564, 569, 576, 581, 597–598, 600–601, 797
    definition of, 546
socketpair function, 138, 306, 594–595
    definition of, 594
sockets, UNIX domain, 594–601
    timing, 527
socklen_t data type, 562, 564, 577, 580
SOCK_RAW constant, 547, 558
SOCK_SEQPACKET constant, 547, 558, 561, 564, 567, 581
SOCK_STREAM constant, 295, 547, 558, 561, 564, 567, 569–571, 574, 581, 595–597, 600
Solaris, xxi, xxiii, 3–4, 26–27, 29–30, 35–36, 38, 48, 55–58, 60, 62, 72, 84, 95, 101–105, 112–113, 119, 121–122, 128, 162, 166, 169–172, 176, 190–191, 193–194, 204, 206, 227, 264, 266, 268, 271, 278, 290, 292–298, 304–305, 308, 310, 326, 330, 348, 352–353, 357, 360, 430, 445, 455–457, 459–461, 464, 466, 471, 474–475, 492, 496, 521, 523, 525, 527, 529, 534–535, 538, 548, 550, 563, 566–568, 583, 585, 595, 610, 635–638, 644–651, 664, 676–677, 682–683, 685, 689, 692, 705–707, 710, 749, 876, 889
SOL_SOCKET constant, 579, 581, 607–608, 612–614
solutions to exercises, 853–883
SOMAXCONN constant, 563
SO_OOBINLINE constant, 582
SO_PASSCRED constant, 613
SO_REUSEADDR constant, 580–581
source code, availability, xxvi
S_OUTPUT constant, 482
Spafford, G., 165, 232, 273, 887
spawn function, 216
<spawn.h> header, 30
s-pipe, 603, 615–616, 618, 620–621
s_pipe function, 587–589, 595, 617, 704, 845
    definition of, 589, 595
spooling, printer, 757–758
sprintf function, 149, 511, 570, 577, 600, 617, 619, 621, 628, 725, 738, 807
    definition of, 149
spwd structure, 861
squid login name, 162
S_RDBAND constant, 482
S_RDNORM constant, 482
sscanf function, 151, 511, 513, 764
    definition of, 151
SSIZE_MAX constant, 39, 68

`ssize_t` data type, 39, 57, 68
stack, 187, 197
`stackaddr` attribute, 389, 391
`stacksize` attribute, 389, 391
standard error, 8, 135, 572
standard error routines, 846–851
standard input, 8, 135
standard I/O
    alternatives, 159
    buffering, 135–137, 213, 217, 247, 342, 513–514,
        680, 718
    efficiency, 143–145
    implementation, 153–155
    library, 9, 133–160
    streams, 133–134
    versus unbuffered I/O, timing, 144
standard output, 8, 135, 572
standards, 25–33
    conflicts, 56–57
START terminal character, 638, 640–642, 646, 649,
    653
`stat` function, 4, 7, 62, 87–88, 91–92, 100,
    113–114, 116, 118, 121, 128, 130–131, 306, 542,
    548, 584, 599–600, 658, 856, 858
    definition of, 87
`stat` structure, 87–89, 92, 103, 107, 130, 137, 155,
    457, 490, 497, 514, 519, 542, 599, 657–659
static variables, 201
STATUS terminal character, 638, 642, 647, 649, 663
`<stdarg.h>` header, 27, 151–152, 721, 724
`<stdbool.h>` header, 27
`__STDC__` constant, 56
`<stddef.h>` header, 27, 597
`stderr` variable, 135, 443, 695, 849
`STDERR_FILENO` constant, 60, 135, 573–574, 603,
    606, 610, 614, 693
`stdin` variable, 10, 135, 144, 196, 198, 512–513,
    588, 616
`STDIN_FILENO` constant, 8–9, 60, 64, 69, 135, 284,
    351, 443, 471, 501, 506, 511–512, 574, 588,
    617–618, 639, 644, 669, 671, 693–695, 697,
    704–705
`<stdint.h>` header, 27, 551
`<stdio.h>` header, 10, 27, 38, 50, 135, 137, 141,
    153, 155–157, 654, 721, 843
`<stdlib.h>` header, 27, 190, 843
`stdout` variable, 10, 135, 144, 229–230, 849, 864,
    872
`STDOUT_FILENO` constant, 8–9, 60, 69, 135, 212,
    217, 351, 443, 471, 499, 506, 511–512, 569,
    573–575, 588, 616–618, 693, 697, 704–705, 864
Stevens, D. A., xxviii

Stevens, E. M., xxviii
Stevens, S. H., xxviii
Stevens, W. R., xx–xxii, xxviii, 147, 266, 429, 478,
    545, 677, 757, 890
sticky bit, 100–102, 109, 130
`stime` function, 173
Stonebraker, M. R., 709, 890
STOP terminal character, 638, 640–642, 646, 649,
    653
`str2sig` function, 353
    definition of, 353
`strace` program, 457
Strang, J., 672, 890
`strbuf` structure, 462, 471, 605
`strchr` function, 733
stream orientation, 134
`STREAM_MAX` constant, 38–39, 42, 48
STREAMS, 30–32, 83–84, 86, 133, 328, 441,
    460–474, 479, 481–482, 485, 493, 495–496,
    514, 518, 522, 527, 543, 548, 585, 600, 603–604,
    610, 615, 629, 676–677, 680–681, 683, 685,
    689, 705, 878, 889
    clone device, 683
    file descriptor passing, 604–606
    `ioctl` operations, 464
    Linux, 496
    messages, 462
    read mode, 470
    write mode, 468
STREAMS module
    `connld`, 518, 590, 592, 600
    `ldterm`, 468, 676, 685
    `pckt`, 676, 705
    `ptem`, 468, 676, 685
    `pts`, 468
    `redirmod`, 468
    `ttcompat`, 468, 676, 685
streams, standard I/O, 133–134
STREAMS-based pipes, 585–594
    mounted, 495, 514, 518
    timing, 527
`strerror` function, 15–16, 24, 352, 402, 412, 431,
    433, 438, 556, 569–570, 572–573, 576–577,
    619, 628, 847, 849, 851, 853–854, 873–874
    definition of, 15
`strerror_r` function, 402
`strftime` function, 174–176, 178, 246, 862
    definition of, 176
`<string.h>` header, 27, 843
`<strings.h>` header, 30
`strip` program, 863
`strlen` function, 11, 213

str_list structure, 466–467
str_mlist structure, 466–467
Strong, H. R., 710, 715, 886
<stropts.h> header, 30, 464, 480, 482
strrecvfd structure, 593, 605
strsignal function, 352
    definition of, 352
strtok function, 402, 619–620
strtok_r function, 402
stty program, 276, 651–652, 662, 673, 882
Stumm, M., 159, 492, 888
S_TYPEISMQ function, 89
S_TYPEISSEM function, 89
S_TYPEISSHM function, 89
su program, 431
submit_file function, 771
SUID, see set-user-ID
Sun Microsystems, xxiii, 33, 71, 683, 705, 890
SunOS, xxvii, 33, 188, 305, 329, 533
superuser, 16
supplementary group ID, 18, 39, 91–92, 94, 101,
        103, 167–168, 214, 234, 241
SUS (Single UNIX Specification), xxii, 28–33, 41,
        52–56, 58–59, 61, 66–67, 74, 83, 88, 99–100,
        102, 105, 121–122, 125–126, 133, 147,
        156–158, 164, 167, 173, 175–176, 178,
        193–194, 202–203, 216, 221, 226–227, 240,
        243, 269, 271, 274, 286, 291, 297–298, 304, 306,
        308, 317, 327, 329, 348, 379, 387, 391–392, 394,
        401, 411, 428, 430, 432, 445, 455, 460, 473, 479,
        481, 483, 487, 489, 495–496, 518, 520,
        522–523, 527–528, 533, 535, 552, 565, 567,
        579, 582, 607, 634, 638, 643, 681–683, 709, 773,
        858, 887, 890
SUSP terminal character, 638, 640, 642, 648, 661
SUSv3 (Single UNIX Specification, Version 3), 32,
        36, 49, 56
SVID (System V Interface Definition), xix, 32, 34,
        885
SVR2, 62, 171, 462, 672
SVR3, 119, 183, 274, 456, 460–461, 474, 479, 846
SVR3.0, xxvii
SVR3.1, xxvii
SVR3.2, xxvii, 36, 248
SVR4, xxvii, 3, 21, 33–37, 48, 72, 112, 171, 191, 266,
        271, 285, 428, 460–461, 474, 479, 481, 483, 592,
        681, 709
swapper process, 210
S_WRBAND constant, 482
S_WRNORM constant, 482
symbolic link, 88–89, 102–103, 107, 110, 112–114,
        121, 127, 131, 170, 856–857

symlink function, 115, 306
    definition of, 115
SYMLINK_MAX constant, 39, 43, 48
SYMLOOP_MAX constant, 39, 42, 48
sync function, 59, 77–78
    definition of, 77
sync program, 77
synchronization mechanisms, 82–83
synchronous write, 61, 82–83
<sys/acct.h> header, 251
sysconf function, 20, 37, 39–54, 57–58, 66, 92,
        183, 203, 238, 257–258, 306, 356, 387–388,
        391, 394, 401, 489, 571, 573, 578, 778, 855
    definition of, 41
<sys/conf.h> header, 466
sysctl program, 291, 521
sysdef program, 521
<sys/disklabel.h> header, 84
<sys/filio.h> header, 84
<sys/ipc.h> header, 30, 520
<sys/iso/signal_iso.h> header, 290
syslog function, 412, 425, 428–433, 435–439,
        570–574, 577–578, 849, 851, 871
    definition of, 430
syslogd program, 425, 429–430, 432, 434, 439
<syslog.h> header, 30
<sys/mkdev.h> header, 128
<sys/mman.h> header, 29
<sys/msg.h> header, 30
<sys/mtio.h> header, 84
<sys/param.h> header, 49–50
<sys/resource.h> header, 30
<sys/select> header, 474
<sys/select.h> header, 29, 477, 874
<sys/sem.h> header, 30
<sys/shm.h> header, 30
sys_siglist variable, 352
<sys/signal.h> header, 290
<sys/socket.h> header, 29, 563
<sys/sockio.h> header, 84
<sys/stat.h> header, 29, 91
<sys/statvfs.h> header, 30
<sys/sysmacros.h> header, 128
system calls, 1, 21
    interrupted, 303–305, 317–318, 326, 329, 339,
        481
    restarted, 304–305, 317–318, 326, 329, 481, 660
    tracing, 457
    versus functions, 21–23
system function, 23, 119, 209, 231, 246–250,
        258–260, 323, 342–347, 353, 411, 500, 504, 866,
        878

definition of, 246–247, 344
  return value, 346
system identification, 171–173
system process, 210, 312
System V, xxi, 83, 441–442, 445, 460, 462, 473, 479,
    481, 493, 681, 685
System V Interface Definition, *see* SVID
<sys/timeb.h> header, 30
<sys/time.h> header, 30, 474
<sys/times.h> header, 29
<sys/ttycom.h> header, 84
<sys/types.h> header, 29, 56, 128, 474, 518
<sys/uio.h> header, 30
<sys/un.h> header, 29, 595
<sys/utsname.h> header, 29
<sys/wait.h> header, 29, 221
sysyconf function, 57

TAB0 constant, 651
TAB1 constant, 651
TAB2 constant, 651
TAB3 constant, 650–651
TABDLY constant, 637, 644, 649–651
Tankus, E., xxviii
tar program, 117, 125, 131–132, 858–859
<tar.h> header, 29
tcdrain function, 297, 306, 411, 637, 653
  definition of, 653
tcflag_t data type, 634
tcflow function, 297, 306, 637, 653
  definition of, 653
tcflush function, 135, 297, 306, 633, 637, 653
  definition of, 653
tcgetattr function, 306, 635, 637, 639, 643–644,
    651–652, 655, 661, 665–667, 695–696
  definition of, 643
tcgetpgrp function, 273–274, 306, 634, 637
  definition of, 273
tcgetsid function, 273–274, 634, 637
  definition of, 274
TCIFLUSH constant, 653
TCIOFF constant, 653
TCIOFLUSH constant, 653
TCION constant, 653
TCOFLUSH constant, 653
TCOOFF constant, 653
TCOON constant, 653
TCSADRAIN constant, 643
TCSAFLUSH constant, 639, 643, 661, 665–667
TCSANOW constant, 643–644, 693, 696
tcsendbreak function, 297, 306, 637, 642,
    653–654

definition of, 653
tcsetattr function, 297, 306, 633, 635, 637, 639,
    643–644, 651–652, 661, 665–667, 693, 696, 703
  definition of, 643
tcsetpgrp function, 273–274, 276, 278, 297, 306,
    634, 637
  definition of, 273
tee program, 516
tell function, 64
TELL_CHILD function, 229–230, 337, 451, 458,
    493, 501, 503, 539, 846
  definition of, 338, 502
telldir function, 120–125
  definition of, 120
TELL_PARENT function, 229, 337, 451, 493, 501,
    503, 539, 846, 876
  definition of, 338, 502
TELL_WAIT function, 229–230, 337, 451, 458, 493,
    501, 539, 846, 876
  definition of, 337, 502
telnet program, 472, 703, 706
telnetd program, 267, 472–473, 677, 699, 866,
    882
tempnam function, 155–160
  definition of, 157
TENEX C shell, 3
TERM environment variable, 193, 263, 265
termcap, 672–673, 890
terminal
  baud rate, 652–653
  canonical mode, 660–663
  controlling, 61, 215, 234, 251, 268, 271–274, 276,
    278–279, 281, 284, 286–287, 294, 296–297,
    349, 423–425, 428, 439, 463, 468, 640, 645, 651,
    654, 660, 662, 676, 683, 685, 689, 691–692, 846,
    890
  identification, 654–660
  I/O, 631–673
  line control, 653–654
  logins, 261–266
  mode, cbreak, 632, 664, 668, 673
  mode, cooked, 632
  mode, raw, 632, 664, 668, 673, 696, 699
  noncanonical mode, 663–670
  options, 643–651
  parity, 648
  process group ID, 278, 423–424
  special input characters, 638–642
  window size, 286, 297, 670–672, 691, 706–707
termination, process, 180–184
terminfo, 672–673, 887, 890
termio structure, 634

`<termio.h>` header, 634
termios structure, 286, 634, 637–639, 643–644,
    652–653, 655, 661, 663–666, 668, 691–692,
    694, 696, 702, 706–707, 845, 882
`<termios.h>` header, 29, 84, 634
text segment, 186
`<tgmath.h>` header, 27
The Open Group, xxii, 32, 176, 887
Thompson, K., 71, 165, 211, 709, 889–890
thread_init function, 404
threads, 13, 27, 211, 355–386, 540
    concepts, 355–357
    control, 387–421
    creation, 357–360
    synchronization, 368–385
    termination, 360–368
thundering herd, 869
tick, clock, 20, 42, 48, 57, 251–252, 257
time
    and date functions, 173–176
    calendar, 20, 24, 57, 117, 173–175, 246, 251–252
    process, 20, 24, 57, 257–259
    values, 20
time function, 173, 246, 306, 331, 599–600, 862,
    871
    definition of, 173
time program, 20
TIME terminal value, 647, 663–664, 668, 673, 882
`<time.h>` header, 27, 57
timer_getoverrun function, 306
timer_gettime function, 306
timer_settime function, 306, 327
times, file, 115–116, 493
times function, 42, 57, 257–258, 306, 484
    definition of, 257
timespec structure, 383, 398–399, 478
time_t data type, 20, 57, 173, 175, 178, 854
timeval structure, 173, 383, 398, 475, 478, 768,
    871, 875
timing
    message queues, 527
    read buffer sizes, 70
    read/write versus mmap, 492
    semaphore locking versus record locking, 533
    standard I/O versus unbuffered I/O, 144
    STREAMS-based pipes, 527
    synchronization mechanisms, 82–83
    UNIX domain sockets, 527
    writev versus other techniques, 484
TIOCGPTN constant, 689
TIOCGWINSZ constant, 670–671, 695, 845
TIOCPKT constant, 705

TIOCPTLCK constant, 690
TIOCREMOTE constant, 706
TIOCSCTTY constant, 273, 692–693
TIOCSIG constant, 706
TIOCSIGNAL constant, 706
TIOCSWINSZ constant, 670, 693, 706
tip program, 673
TLI (Transport Layer Interface, System V), 889
tm structure, 174, 862
TMPDIR environment variable, 157–158, 193
tmpfile function, 155–159, 340, 412
    definition of, 155
TMP_MAX constant, 38, 155–156
tmpnam function, 38, 155–159, 401, 412
    definition of, 155
tms structure, 257–258
Torvalds, L., 35
TOSTOP constant, 636, 651
touch program, 117
`<trace.h>` header, 30
tracing system calls, 457
transactions, database, 889
Transport Layer Interface, System V, see TLI
TRAP_BRKPT constant, 327
TRAP_TRACE constant, 327
tread function, 767–768
treadn function, 768
Trickey, H., 211, 889
truncate function, 105, 113, 117, 433
    definition of, 105
truncation
    file, 105
    filename, 62
    pathname, 62
truss program, 457
ttcompat STREAMS module, 468, 676, 685
tty structure, 286
tty_atexit function, 665, 696, 845
    definition of, 668
tty_cbreak function, 664, 669, 845
    definition of, 665
ttymon program, 266
ttyname function, 127, 257, 402, 412, 655–656,
    659, 687
    definition of, 655, 658
TTY_NAME_MAX constant, 39, 42, 48
ttyname_r function, 402, 412
tty_raw function, 664, 669, 673, 695, 845
    definition of, 666
tty_reset function, 664, 669, 845
    definition of, 667
tty_termios function, 665, 845

definition of, 668
type attribute, 394
typescript file, 678, 701
TZ environment variable, 174, 176, 178, 193, 862
TZNAME_MAX constant, 39, 42, 48

UCHAR_MAX constant, 38
<ucontext.h> header, 30
ucontext_t structure, 328
ucred structure, 611, 613
UFS file system, 48, 55, 62, 105, 108, 119
UID, *see* user ID
uid_t data type, 57
uint16_t data type, 551
uint32_t data type, 551
UINT_MAX constant, 38
ulimit program, 51–52, 204
<ulimit.h> header, 30
ULLONG_MAX constant, 38
ULONG_MAX constant, 38
UltraSPARC, xxiii
umask function, 97–100, 204, 306, 425, 427
    definition of, 97
umask program, 98–99, 131
uname function, 171, 178, 306
    definition of, 171
uname program, 172, 178
unbuffered I/O, 8, 59–86
unbuffered I/O timing, standard I/O versus, 144
ungetc function, 141–142, 412
    definition of, 141
ungetwc function, 412
uninitialized data segment, 187
<unistd.h> header, 9, 29, 52, 60, 69, 103, 401,
    474, 721, 843
UNIX Architecture, 1–2
UNIX domain sockets, 594–601
    timing, 527
UNIX System implementations, 33
Unix-to-Unix Copy, *see* UUCP
UnixWare, 36, 309–310
unlink function, 107–114, 117, 131, 157, 306, 340,
    412, 456, 515, 592, 598–601, 857, 859, 878
    definition of, 109
un_lock function, 449, 725, 728, 845
unlockpt function, 682–685, 688, 690
    definition of, 682, 687, 690
Unrau, R., 159, 492, 888
unreliable signals, 301–303
unsetenv function, 194, 402
    definition of, 194

update program, 77
update_jobno function, 782, 795
uptime program, 568, 570, 572, 574–575, 577, 579,
    584
USER environment variable, 192, 264
user ID, 16, 237–241
    effective, 91–92, 94–95, 99, 103, 117, 130, 210,
        214, 235, 237–241, 257, 262, 264, 312, 354, 520,
        524, 530, 535, 542–543, 593, 600, 605, 771, 861,
        866
    real, 39, 42, 91–92, 95, 203, 210, 214–215,
        234–235, 237–241, 251, 257, 262, 264, 312,
        354, 541, 685, 867
USHRT_MAX constant, 38
usleep function, 411, 493, 875
/usr/lib/pt_chmod program, 685
UTC (Coordinated Universal Time), 20, 173,
    175–176
utimbuf structure, 116, 118
utime function, 116–119, 131, 306, 858
    definition of, 116
<utime.h> header, 29
utmp file, 170–171, 257, 287, 698–699, 866, 871
utmp structure, 171
<utmpx.h> header, 30
utsname structure, 171–172, 178
UUCP (Unix-to-Unix Copy), 172
uucp program, 473

va_end function, 847–851
va_list data type, 847–851
/var/account/acct file, 251
/var/account/pacct file, 251
/var/adm/pacct file, 251
<varargs.h> header, 151
variables
    automatic, 187, 197, 199, 201, 207
    global, 201
    register, 199
    static, 201
    volatile, 199, 201, 315, 332
/var/log/wtmp file, 171
/var/run/utmp file, 171
va_start function, 847–851
VDISCARD constant, 638
VDSUSP constant, 638
VEOF constant, 638–639, 664
VEOL constant, 638, 664
VEOL2 constant, 638
VERASE constant, 638
VERASE2 constant, 638

vfork function, 211, 216–218, 260, 864–865
vfprintf function, 151, 412
    definition of, 151
vfscanf function, 153
    definition of, 153
vfwprintf function, 412
vi program, 350, 457, 459, 632, 671–673, 882
VINTR constant, 638–639
vipw program, 163
VKILL constant, 638
VLNEXT constant, 638
VMIN constant, 663–665, 667
v-node, 71–72, 74, 126, 287, 602, 855, 887
vnode structure, 286–287
Vo, K. P., 125, 159, 887–888, 890
volatile variables, 199, 201, 315, 332
vprintf function, 151, 412, 854
    definition of, 151
VQUIT constant, 638
vread function, 487
VREPRINT constant, 638
vscanf function, 153
    definition of, 153
vsnprintf function, 151, 849, 851
    definition of, 151
vsprintf function, 151, 431
    definition of, 151
vsscanf function, 153
    definition of, 153
VSTART constant, 638
VSTATUS constant, 638
VSTOP constant, 638
VSUSP constant, 638
vsyslog function, 432
    definition of, 432
VT0 constant, 651
VT1 constant, 651
VTDLY constant, 637, 644, 649, 651
VTIME constant, 663–665, 667
VWERASE constant, 638
vwprintf function, 412
vwrite function, 487

wait function, 22, 213–214, 219–228, 231, 237,
        245, 249, 257, 259, 276, 293, 303–304,
        306–310, 326, 343, 345, 347, 411, 430, 459, 508,
        544, 878
    definition of, 220
Wait, J. W., xxviii
wait3 function, 227
    definition of, 227

wait4 function, 227
    definition of, 227
WAIT_CHILD function, 229, 337, 451, 493, 501, 539,
        846, 876
    definition of, 338, 502
waitid function, 226–227, 257, 411
    definition of, 226
WAIT_PARENT function, 229–230, 337, 451, 458,
        493, 501, 539, 846
    definition of, 338, 502
waitpid function, 11–13, 19, 219–227, 236, 242,
        246–249, 257, 259, 261, 270, 276, 291, 304, 306,
        345, 411, 458, 500, 507–508, 543–544, 573,
        877–878, 880
    definition of, 220
wall program, 685
wc program, 104
<wchar.h> header, 27, 134
wchar_t data type, 57
WCONTINUED constant, 224, 226
WCOREDUMP function, 221–222
wcrtomb function, 401
wcsrtombs function, 401
wcstombs function, 402
wctomb function, 402
<wctype.h> header, 27
Weeks, M. S., 188, 887
Weinberger, P. J., 71, 243, 709, 885, 890
Weinstock, C. B., 890
WERASE terminal character, 638, 642, 645–647,
        663
WEXITED constant, 226
WEXITSTATUS function, 221–222
who program, 171, 699
WIFCONTINUED function, 221
WIFEXITED function, 221–222
WIFSIGNALED function, 221–222
WIFSTOPPED function, 221–222, 224
Williams, T., 285, 890
Wilson, G. A., xxviii
window size
    pseudo terminal, 706
    terminal, 286, 297, 670–672, 691, 706–707
winsize structure, 286, 670–671, 691–692, 694,
        696, 707, 845, 882
Winterbottom, P., 211, 889
WNOHANG constant, 224, 226
WNOWAIT constant, 224, 226
W_OK constant, 96
Wolff, R., xxviii
Wolff, S., xxviii
WORD_BIT constant, 40

`<wordexp.h>` header, 29
working directory, 7, 13, 43, 49, 107, 125–126, 162,
    193, 215, 234, 291, 426
worm, Internet, 142
`wprintf` function, 412
Wright, G. R., xxviii
write
    delayed, 77
    gather, 483, 607
    synchronous, 61, 82–83
`write` function, 8–10, 20–21, 57, 59, 61, 65–66,
    68–69, 72, 74–75, 82–85, 117, 135–136, 145,
    155, 159, 212–213, 216, 229, 304, 306,
    317–318, 351, 354, 411, 434, 442–444, 451,
    454–458, 461–463, 468–469, 471, 475, 478,
    484–488, 491–493, 499–500, 502, 511–513,
    515–516, 521, 527, 543, 546, 548, 565, 569, 575,
    587, 603–604, 616–617, 629, 632, 718, 789,
    799, 855–856, 864, 868, 876–878
    definition of, 68
write mode, STREAMS, 468
`write` program, 685
`write_lock` function, 449, 453, 458, 781, 845
`writen` function, 485–486, 604, 697, 702, 772, 844
    definition of, 485–486
`writev` function, 40–42, 304, 411, 441, 483–485,
    493, 548, 566, 607, 617, 621, 718, 737, 739, 795,
    799
    definition of, 483
`writew_lock` function, 449, 451, 725, 735, 752,
    845
`wscanf` function, 412
`WSTOPPED` constant, 226
`WSTOPSIG` function, 221–222
`WTERMSIG` function, 221–222
`wtmp` file, 170–171, 287, 866
Wulf, W. A., 890
`WUNTRACED` constant, 224

`xargs` program, 234
`XCASE` constant, 651
Xenix, 33, 445, 685
`xinetd` program, 268
`X_OK` constant, 96
X/Open, xxii, 32, 890
X/Open Portability Guide, 32
    Issue 3, *see* XPG3
    Issue 4, *see* XPG4
`_XOPEN_CRYPT` constant, 32, 53
`_XOPEN_IOV_MAX` constant, 41
`_XOPEN_LEGACY` constant, 32, 53

`_XOPEN_NAME_MAX` constant, 41
`_XOPEN_PATH_MAX` constant, 41
`_XOPEN_REALTIME` constant, 32, 53
`_XOPEN_REALTIME_THREADS` constant, 32, 53
`_XOPEN_SOURCE` constant, 55
`_XOPEN_STREAMS` constant, 32
`_XOPEN_UNIX` constant, 29, 55
`_XOPEN_VERSION` constant, 53, 55
XPG3 (X/Open Portability Guide, Issue 3), xxvii,
    34, 890
XPG4 (X/Open Portability Guide, Issue 4), 32
XSI, 29–32, 52–55, 74, 88, 100, 102, 105, 121–122,
    125, 133, 150, 152, 156–158, 164, 167, 173,
    193–194, 202, 204, 221, 224, 226–227, 240,
    269, 271, 274, 291–292, 297, 304–305, 308,
    317, 325–326, 329, 391, 394, 401, 428,
    430–431, 445, 460, 474, 483, 487–489, 496,
    515, 523–525, 528, 533, 538, 540, 543–544,
    626, 634–635, 637, 645, 647, 649–651, 681,
    683, 686, 709–710, 858
XSI IPC, 518–522
`XTABS` constant, 650–651

Yigit, O., 710, 890

zombie, 219–220, 224, 260, 308, 326, 866